IB WORLD SCHOOLS
YEARBOOK 2022

Contents

INTERNATIONAL EDUCATOR CERTIFICATE (IEC) FOR INTERNATIONAL BACCALAUREATE QUALIFICATION

*IEC QUALIFIES FOR AN IB EDUCATOR CERTIFICATE IN TEACHING AND LEARNING WHICH MAKES YOU ELIGIBLE TO TEACH AMONGST THE 4,700 IB SCHOOLS WORLDWIDE

FEATURES

- Programme streams: Primary Years, Middle Years, and Diploma Programme

- Stream selection based on qualifications

- Ability to complete certification in 8 months

- Three intakes per year: January, June & September

- Four courses in total plus professional learning community (PLC) facilitated online

REGISTER TODAY!

uwindsor.ca/education/continuing/IEC • 519-253-3000 EXT.6734 • IB@uwindsor.ca

Message from Director General

IB World Schools share a common mission: education for a better world. If our students are to thrive, they must prepare to enter a dynamic and challenging world that requires transferable and adaptable skills.

If they are to compete, today's nations must build an entrepreneurial generation of disruptors, equipped to reinvent, reimagine and redefine not just the nature of work but entire industries.

In this unpredictable future, education is our greatest source of hope. By investing in our youth we equip them to become the thinkers, creators and engineers of tomorrow, ready to solve society's most pressing challenges and build a better, more sustainable world for all.

To do this, students need an education for life. Not for one career, but for many. Not for one culture, but for all. And, most importantly, for a world where a qualification is not the end state. It is the beginning.

The International Baccalaureate creates resilient, well-rounded young people who have the knowledge, skills and sense of purpose they need to thrive throughout their lives and contribute to making the world a better place.

Our curriculum is deliberately flexible, empowering students, teachers and schools to tailor an education that is appropriate to their culture, context, needs, interests and learning ability.

Through this local and global context, students connect their learning experiences to their real-world experiences, taking action to make a difference in their community, building practical problem-solving skills, critical thinking and a lifelong sense of curiosity.

The International Baccalaureate's internationally minded approach fosters empathy, open mindedness, diversity and cultural respect. This learning methodology moves past knowledge transfer to knowledge use, analysis and innovation.

With this solid academic foundation, the International Baccalaureate empowers students with transferable, future-ready skills and an internationally recognised qualification. It uncovers and develops the best in every child. And it prepares citizens of tomorrow, who are ready to step up as leaders and contribute to their world.

I hope that this Yearbook enables you to connect with the IB community and join us in building a better world through education.

Olli-Pekka Heinonen – IB Director General

OPENING MIND • SHAPING THE FUTURE

ACADEMIC EXCELLENCE

- Double Top **100***

  *QS World University Rankings 2022 & Times Higher Education World University Rankings 2022

- **5** subjects ranked in world's top 50#

  #QS World University Rankings by Subject 2021

GRADUATE EMPLOYABILITY

- World's top **20%** ^

  ^QS Graduate Employability Rankings 2020

- Guaranteed internship

Renewable Entry Scholarships up to *USD25,000 per annum*

Introduction, How to use this Yearbook

The International Baccalaureate (IB) offers high quality programmes of international education to a worldwide community of schools, aiming to develop internationally minded people who, recognizing their common humanity and shared guardianship of the plant, help to create a better, more peaceful world.

The IB works alongside state and privately funded schools around the world that share the commitment to international education, to deliver these programmes.

Schools that have achieved the high standards required for authorization to offer one or more of the IB programmes are known as 'IB World Schools'. As of November 2021 there were 1,176 schools with 1,316 programmes in candidate status (528 PYP, 447 MYP, 281 DP, 60 CP).

The IB World Schools Yearbook is the official guide to schools authorized to offer the Primary Years Programme, the Middle Years Programme, the Diploma Programme and the Career-related Programme. It tells you where the IB World Schools are situated and what they offer, and provides up-to-date information about IB programmes and the IB organization.

This is an ideal reference for school administration, parents and education ministries worldwide as it:

- provides a comprehensive reference of IB World Schools for quick and easy access
- raises the profile of IB World Schools within their local community and beyond
- provides comprehensive information about IB programmes and the IB.

How to use this yearbook

The Yearbook has been designed to be as easy as possible to use and has been divided into five sections.

1. **General information** about the IB and its programmes.
2. **Comprehensive information** about IB World Schools presented in alphabetical order by school name, colour coded according to IB geographical region. In this section, schools have been given the opportunity to highlight their best qualities by creating an enhanced profile for their school.
3. **Directory information** about every IB World School that offers one or more of the IB programmes as of November 2021. The directory is ordered by IB region and contains general and contact information about each school. Information about the three IB regions is also given in this section. (Those schools that have elected to purchase a profile in the Yearbook will appear in capital letters in the directory.)
4. **Appendices** containing information and lists relevant to the IB. These include addresses of IB offices, location of IB World Schools, Diploma Programme subjects offered (in 2022), IB Associations around the world, university acknowledgement of the Diploma Programme and Career-related Programme and universities offering IB scholarships.
5. **Index** of all schools listed geographically and alphabetically by name.

Are you looking for a specific IB World School?

If you know the name of the school but are unsure of its location, turn to the index on p. 673 where you will find an alphabetic listing of all IB World Schools.

Are you looking for an IB World School in a specific country?

Look first in the directory section; this will give you the basic information about all the schools in each region. More detailed information can be found in the profiles section for those schools marked with capitalized letters.

The IB website, ibo.org, also contains the most up-to-date information on IB World Schools. A school search option is available from every page on the site for people wanting to find an IB World School.

100%

**English Speaking Campus
American Degree
Tokyo**

Temple University, Japan Campus (TUJ) is a comprehensive overseas campus of Philadelphia's Temple University and located in the heart of Tokyo.

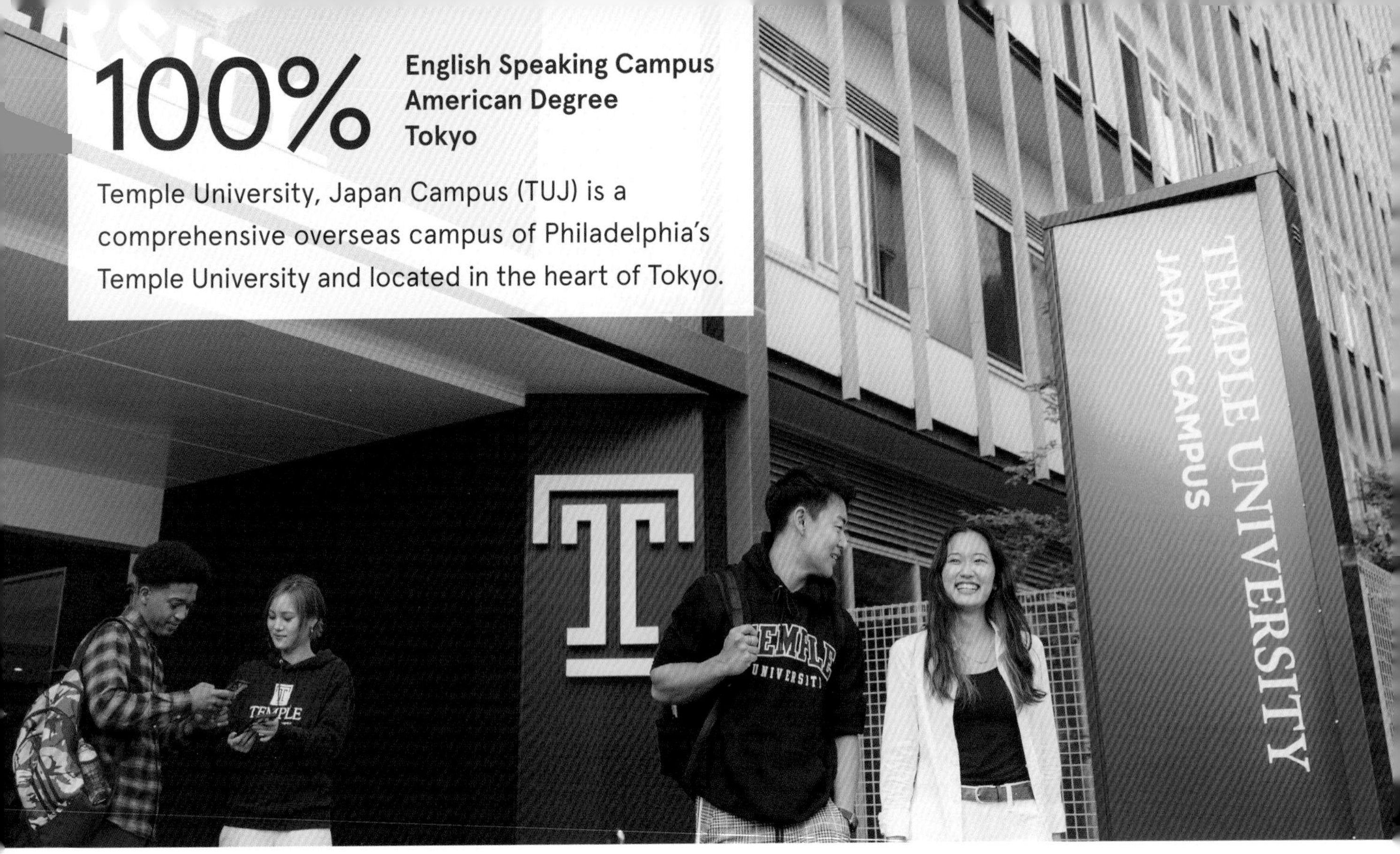

✎ Undergraduate Majors

International Business Studies / Japanese Language / Asian Studies / Communication Studies / International Affairs / Art / Psychological Studies / Economics / Political Science / General Studies

Computer Science (2+2 Program B.A./B.S., Minor, Fundamentals of Programming Certificate)

*Temple University Main Campus offers bachelor's degree programs in 173 areas.

International Campus

Students from around the world come to TUJ for its unique mix of academic rigor, central Tokyo location and Japanese cultural immersion. 57 nationalities are represented in the student body.

Career Preparation

With assistance from the Career Development Office, TUJ students have gone on to careers with some of the world's leading corporations, non-profits, and governments, or have started their own businesses.

Transfer credits based on IB subject and grade

Students who complete any IB courses may be awarded transfer credits based on the course subject and grade as determined by the Admissions Office.

Nationalities (Undergraduate)

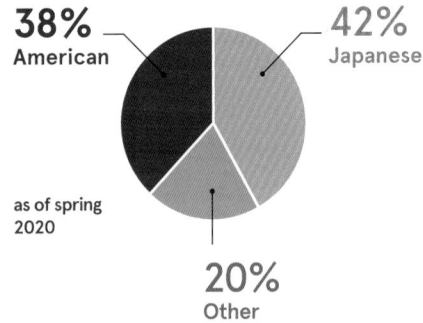

38%
American

42%
Japanese

as of spring 2020

20%
Other

Temple University, Japan Campus (TUJ)
Admissions Counseling Office

1-14-29 Taishido, Setagaya-ku, Tokyo 154-0004, Japan

ac@tuj.temple.edu | +81-3-5441-9800 | www.tuj.ac.jp

Temple University
Japan Campus

IB Mission Statement

The International Baccalaureate aims to develop inquiring, knowledgeable and caring young people who help to create a better and more peaceful world through intercultural understanding and respect.

To this end the organization works with schools, governments and international organizations to develop challenging programmes of international education and rigorous assessment.

These programmes encourage students across the world to become active, compassionate and lifelong learners who understand that other people, with their differences, can also be right.

Déclaration de mission de l'IB

Le Baccalauréat International (IB) a pour but de développer chez les jeunes la curiosité intellectuelle, les connaissances et la sensibilité nécessaires pour contribuer à bâtir un monde meilleur et plus paisible, dans un esprit d'entente mutuelle et de respect interculturel.

À cette fin, l'IB collabore avec des établissements scolaires, des gouvernements et des organisations internationales pour mettre au point des programmes d'éducation internationale stimulants et des méthodes d'évaluation rigoureuses.

Ces programmes encouragent les élèves de tout pays à apprendre activement tout au long de leur vie, à être empreints de compassion, et à comprendre que les autres, en étant différents, puissent aussi être dans le vrai.

Declaración de principios de IB

El Bachillerato Internacional tiene como meta formar jóvenes solidarios, informados y ávidos de conocimiento, capaces de contribuir a crear un mundo mejor y más pacífico, en el marco del entendimiento mutuo y el respeto intercultural.

En pos de este objetivo, la organización colabora con establecimientos escolares, gobiernos y organizaciones internacionales para crear y desarrollar programas de educación internacional exigentes y métodos de evaluación rigurosos.

Estos programas alientan a estudiantes del mundo entero a adoptar una actitud activa de aprendizaje durante toda su vida, a ser compasivos y a entender que otras personas, con sus diferencias, también pueden estar en lo cierto.

About the IB

Founded in 1968, the International Baccalaureate (IB) pioneered a movement of international education, and now offers four high quality, challenging educational programmes to students aged 3-19. The IB gives students distinct advantages by providing strong foundations, critical thinking skills, and a proficiency for solving complex problems, while encouraging diversity, curiosity, and a healthy appetite for learning and excellence. In a world where asking the right questions is as important as discovering answers, the IB champions critical thinking and flexibility in study by crossing disciplinary, cultural and national boundaries. Supported by world class educators and coordinators, the IB currently engages with more than 1.4 million students in over 5,300 schools across 158 countries. To find out more, please visit www.ibo.org.

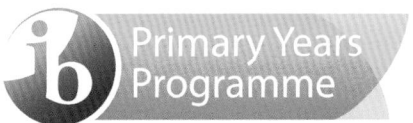

The **IB Primary Years Programme (PYP)**, for students aged 3 to 12, focuses on the development of the whole child as an inquirer, both in the classroom and in the world outside.

The **IB Diploma Programme (DP)**, for students aged 16 to 19, is an academically challenging and balanced programme of education with final examinations that prepares students for success at university and beyond.

The **IB Middle Years Programme (MYP)**, for students aged 11 to 16, provides a framework of academic challenge that encourages students to embrace and understand the connections between traditional subjects and the real world, and become critical and reflective thinkers.

The **IB Career-related Programme (CP)**, for students aged 16 to 19, incorporates the vision and educational principles of the IB programmes into a unique offering specifically designed for students who wish to engage in career-related learning.

IB programmes are available to students in a wide variety of schools and from a range of cultural, ethnic and socio-economic backgrounds. IB World Schools form a worldwide community in which there is no such thing as a "typical" school.

Figure 1: Types of IB World Schools (Information correct as of November 2021)

	Charter	Private	State	State subsidized	Total
Africa, Middle East	5	1041	324	64	1,434
Asia Pacific	2	936	157	14	1,109
Americas	129	806	1905	18	2,858
Total	**136**	**2,783**	**2,386**	**96**	**5,401**

Does not include European Platform schools. Includes MYP Partner Schools.

IB World Schools:
- share the mission and commitment of the IB to quality, international education
- play an active and supporting role in the worldwide community of IB World Schools
- share their knowledge and experience in the development of IB programmes
- are committed to the professional development of teachers

Funding for IB programmes comes from the fees paid by IB World Schools, with additional income from workshops and publication sales. Donors provide support for development projects that cannot be implemented from the organization's budget.

Figure 2: IB World Schools

Total number of IB World Schools: 5,363 in 158 countries (as of November 2021).

Breakdown by regions

Africa, Europe, Middle East	98 countries	1,434 Authorized schools
Asia Pacific	28 countries	1,109 Authorized schools
Americas	33 countries	2,858 Authorized schools
Total	**159 countries**	**5,401 Authorized schools**

Does not include European Platform schools. Includes MYP Partner Schools.

Breakdown by programmes

	PYP	MYP	DP	CP	Total
Africa, Europe, Middle East	514	413	1,139	103	2,169
Asia Pacific	650	289	696	25	1,660
Americas	879	846	1,652	176	3,553
Total	**2,043**	**1,548**	**3,487**	**304**	**7,382**

*As of November 2021

Does not include European Platform schools nor MYP Partner Schools.

As of November 2021, the four IB programmes are taught in 158 countries.

Figure 3: Growth of the four IB Programmes

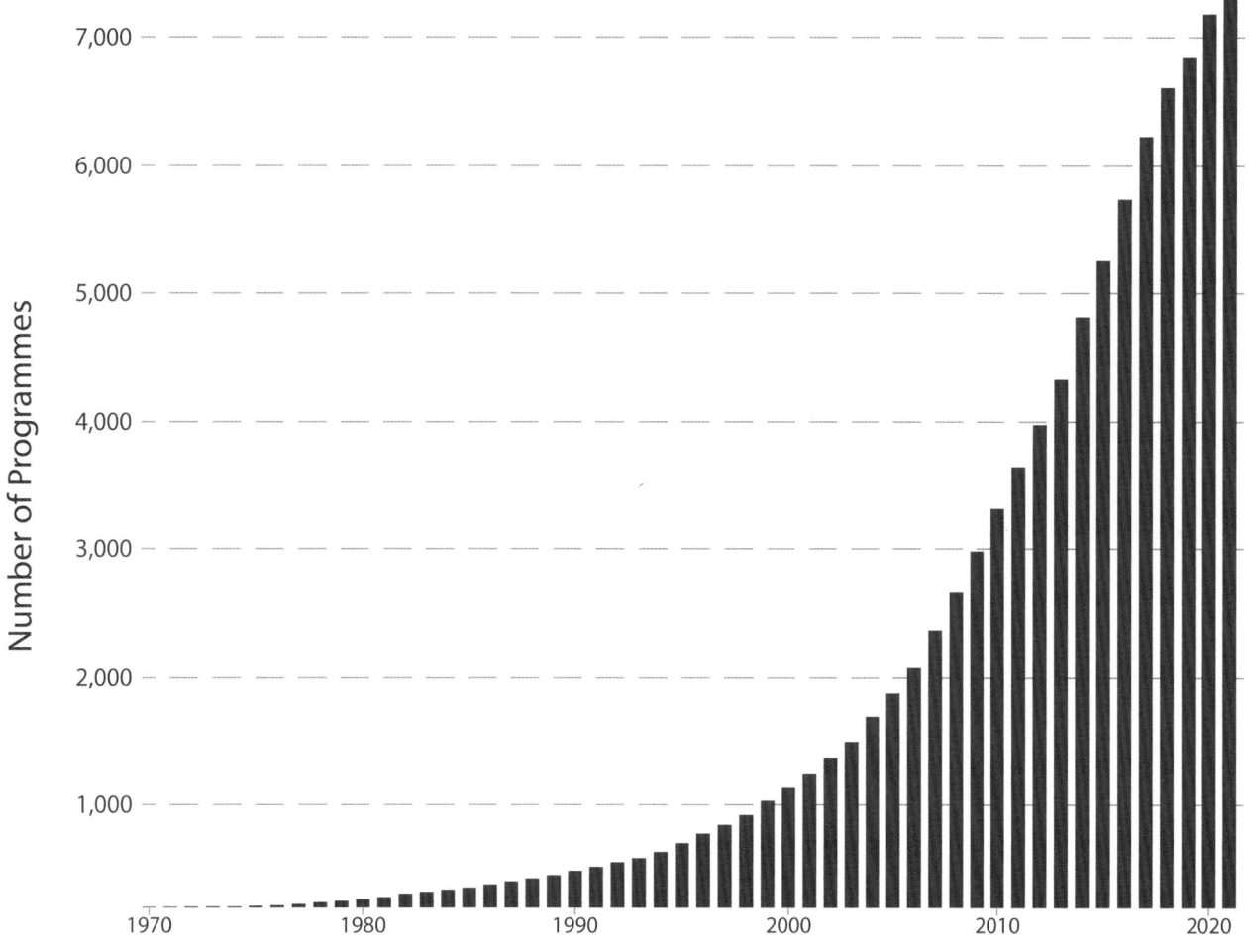

Does not include European Platform nor MYP Partner Schools

The IB Learner Profile

The aim of all IB programmes is to develop internationally minded people who, recognizing their common humanity and shared guardianship of the planet, help to create a better and more peaceful world

As IB learners we strive to be:

Inquirers	We nurture our curiosity, developing skills for inquiry and research. We know how to learn independently and with others. We learn with enthusiasm and sustain our love of learning throughout life.
Knowledgeable	We develop and use conceptual understanding, exploring knowledge across a range of disciplines. We engage with issues and ideas that have local and global significance.
Thinkers	We use critical and creative thinking skills to analyze and take responsible action on complex problems. We exercise initiative in making reasoned, ethical decisions.
Communicators	We express ourselves confidently and creatively in more than one language and in many ways. We collaborate effectively, listening carefully to the perspectives of other individuals and groups.
Principled	We act with integrity and honesty, with a strong sense of fairness and justice, and with respect for the dignity and rights of people everywhere. We take responsibility for our actions and their consequences.
Open-minded	We critically appreciate our own cultures and personal histories, as well as the values and traditions of others. We seek and evaluate a range of points of view, and we are willing to grow from the experience.
Caring	We show empathy, compassion and respect. We have a commitment to service, and we act to make a positive difference in the lives of others and in the world around us.
Risk-takers	We approach uncertainty with forethought and determination; we work independently and cooperatively to explore new ideas and innovative strategies. We are resourceful and resilient in the face of challenges and change.
Balanced	We understand the importance of balancing different aspects of our lives – intellectual, physical and emotional – to achieve well-being for ourselves and others. We recognize our interdependence with other people and with the world in which we live.
Reflective	We thoughtfully consider the world and own ideas and experience. We work to understand our strengths and weaknesses in order to support our learning and personal development.

EXPERIENCE THE DRURY DIFFERENCE

International Baccalaureate students excel at Drury University.

INTERNATIONAL BACCALAUREATE PROGRAMME STUDENTS HAVE A HEAD START AT DRURY BECAUSE:

› They appreciate a challenge
Much like the IB programme, Drury pushes students to look at real world problems through various lenses to discover dynamic and unique solutions.

› They receive Drury's top academic scholarship
Students pursuing the completion of either the IB Diploma Programme or IB Career-related Programme are automatically awarded the highest academic scholarship Drury offers.

› They earn college credit for their hard work
The time and effort spent by IB students is rewarded with college credit. Drury offers college credit for IB classes depending on qualifying test scores.

Apply today at **drury.edu/apply**.
Schedule a visit or take a virtual tour at **drury.eu/visit**.

/DruryUniversity   /DruryUniversityMO
@DruryUniversity   /DruryUniversity

Scan to read more about IB at Drury.

IB Programmes

What is an International Baccalaureate (IB) education?

An IB education is unique because of its rigorous academic and personal standards. IB programmes challenge students aged 3 to 19 to excel not only in their studies but also in their personal growth.

We aspire to help schools develop well-rounded students, who respond to challenges with optimism and an open mind, are confident in their own identities, make ethical decisions, join with others in celebrating our common humanity and apply what they learn in real-world, complex and unpredictable situations.

Through our high-quality programmes of international education, we aim to inspire a quest for learning throughout life that is marked by enthusiasm and empathy.

Our vision is to offer all students an IB education that:

- focuses on learners – our student-centred programmes promote healthy relationships, ethical responsibility, and personal challenge
- develops effective approaches to teaching and learning – our programmes help students to develop the attitudes and skills they need for both academic and personal success
- works within global contexts – our programmes increase understanding of languages and cultures and explore globally significant ideas and issues
- explores significant content – our programmes offer a curriculum that is broad and balanced, conceptual and connected.

Informed by values described in the IB Learner Profile, IB learners strive to become inquirers, knowledgeable, thinkers, communicators, principled, open-minded, caring, risk-takers, balanced, and reflective. These attributes represent a broad range of human capacities and responsibilities that go beyond intellectual development and academic success.

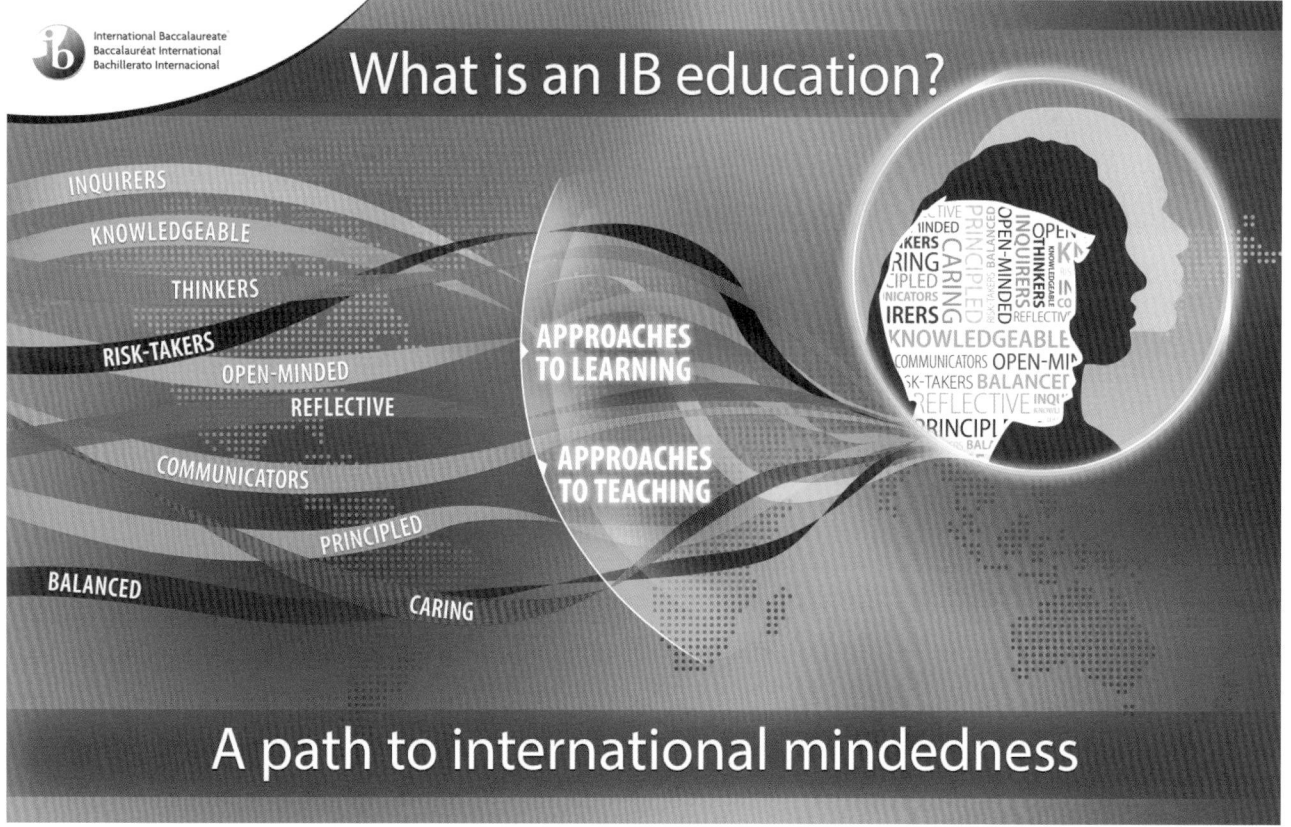

International Baccalaureate
Baccalauréat International
Bachillerato Internacional

What is an IB education?

INQUIRERS
KNOWLEDGEABLE
THINKERS
RISK-TAKERS
OPEN-MINDED
REFLECTIVE
COMMUNICATORS
PRINCIPLED
BALANCED
CARING

APPROACHES TO LEARNING

APPROACHES TO TEACHING

A path to international mindedness

What is the IB Primary Years Programme (PYP)?

A transformative and caring approach that builds a lifelong love of learning

The PYP, for children from 3-12 years, is the start to a lifelong love of learning. It is a caring and thoughtful approach that nurtures the 'whole' child and gives them ownership of their studies from the very beginning.

PYP teachers consider each child's unique abilities and interests, to develop inquiry-based learning environments that build universal skills for life, like thinking, researching and cultural understanding. Children explore across and beyond subject boundaries through transdisciplinary inquiries, investigating big – and small – questions about what it means to be human in today's world. But the most important thing children get from the programme is an inquiring mind, the ability to find things out for themselves and take action to benefit their local community.

Key features of the PYP curriculum framework

Informed by research into how children learn, how educators teach, and the principles and practices of effective assessment, the PYP places a powerful emphasis on conceptual, inquiry-based learning.

Transdisciplinary learning

The PYP is designed to support transdisciplinary learning because it mirrors the natural way children learn. Guiding learning experiences through transdisciplinary themes, across and beyond the boundaries of subjects, teachers build on what children know – and their areas of interest – to help them relate to the world around them.

Figure 4: IB Primary Years Programme model

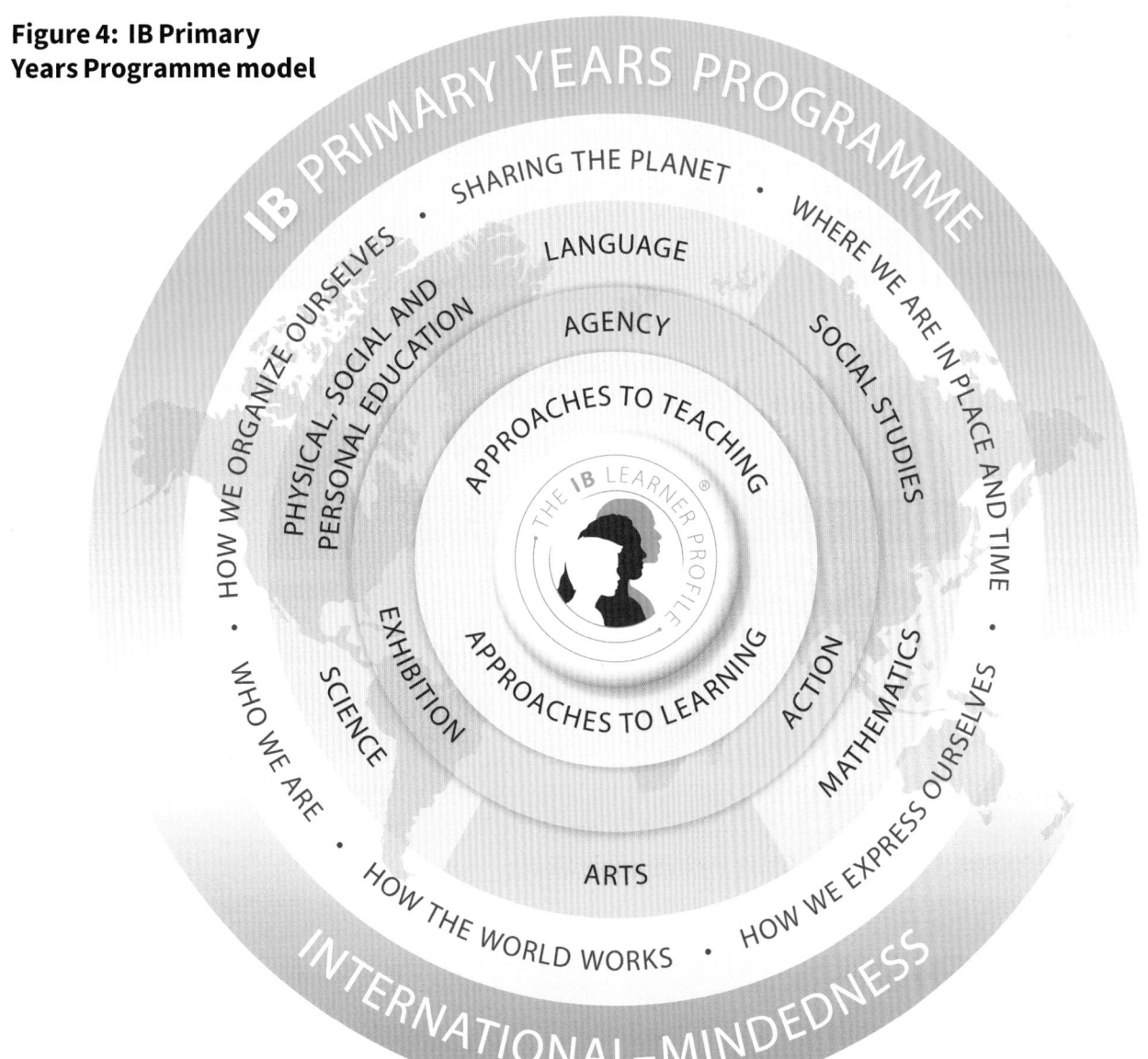

New times demand entrepreneurs

23 bachelor's programs

International community.
Taught in English.
Campuses in Barcelona, Geneva, Montreux, Munich and Online.

SCAN FOR
MORE INFORMATION

#StartHere

Transdisciplinary themes

- Who we are
- Where we are in place and time
- How we express ourselves
- How the world works
- How we organize ourselves
- Sharing the planet

Subject areas

- Arts
- Language
- Science
- Social studies
- Mathematics
- Personal, social and physical education

Agency

By encouraging agency (voice, choice and ownership), the PYP creates a culture where teachers can create relevant, authentic, challenging learning experiences and children develop a love of learning by finding things out for themselves.

Assessment

Assessment is ongoing in the PYP, deepening learning and providing opportunities for teachers to reflect on what their students know, what they understand and what they can do. Immediate, effective feedback and feed-forward helps children to self-monitor and adjust their learning experiences to gain confidence in their own abilities, increase well-being and build resilience.

The exhibition

In the PYP exhibition, children follow their passions to collaborate on an in-depth project, resulting in a community-wide celebration of their learning journey. Analysing, researching and proposing solutions to real world challenges and opportunities prepares them for success in the IB Middle Years Programme, or the next stage in their education.

PYP in the early years (3-6)

The PYP transdisciplinary framework is designed to provide authentic opportunities to strengthen key developmental skills and abilities in young children. Inquiring through play and exploration, young learners learn to self-regulate and build and test theories to make sense of the world around them.

What is the IB Middle Years Programme?

The IB Middle Years Programme (MYP) is designed for students aged 11 to 16. It provides a framework of learning that encourages students to become creative, critical and reflective thinkers. The MYP emphasizes intellectual challenge, encouraging students to make connections between their studies in traditional subjects and the real world. It fosters the development of skills for communication, intercultural understanding and global engagement – essential qualities for young people who are becoming global leaders.

The MYP is flexible enough to accommodate national or local curriculum requirements. It builds upon the knowledge, skills and attitudes developed in the IB Primary Years Programme (PYP) and prepares students to meet the academic challenges of the IB Diploma Programme (DP) and the IB Career-related Programme (CP).

The IB Middle Years Programme:

- addresses holistically students' intellectual, social, emotional and physical well-being
- provides students opportunities to develop the knowledge, attitudes and skills they need in order to manage complexity and take responsible action for the future
- ensures breadth and depth of understanding through study in eight subject groups and interdisciplinary learning.
- requires the study of at least two languages (language of instruction and additional language of choice) to support students in understanding their own cultures and those of others.
- empowers students to participate in service within the community.
- helps to prepare students for further education, the workplace and a lifetime of learning.

The MYP consists of eight subject groups: language acquisition, language and literature, individuals and societies, sciences, mathematics, arts, physical and health education, and design. Student study is supported by a minimum of 50 hours of instruction per subject group in each academic year. In years 4 and 5, students have the option to take courses from six of the eight subject groups, which provides greater flexibility, with optional MYP eAssessments at the end of year 5 for schools that wish for their students to have externally validated results.

Figure 5: IB Middle Years Programme model

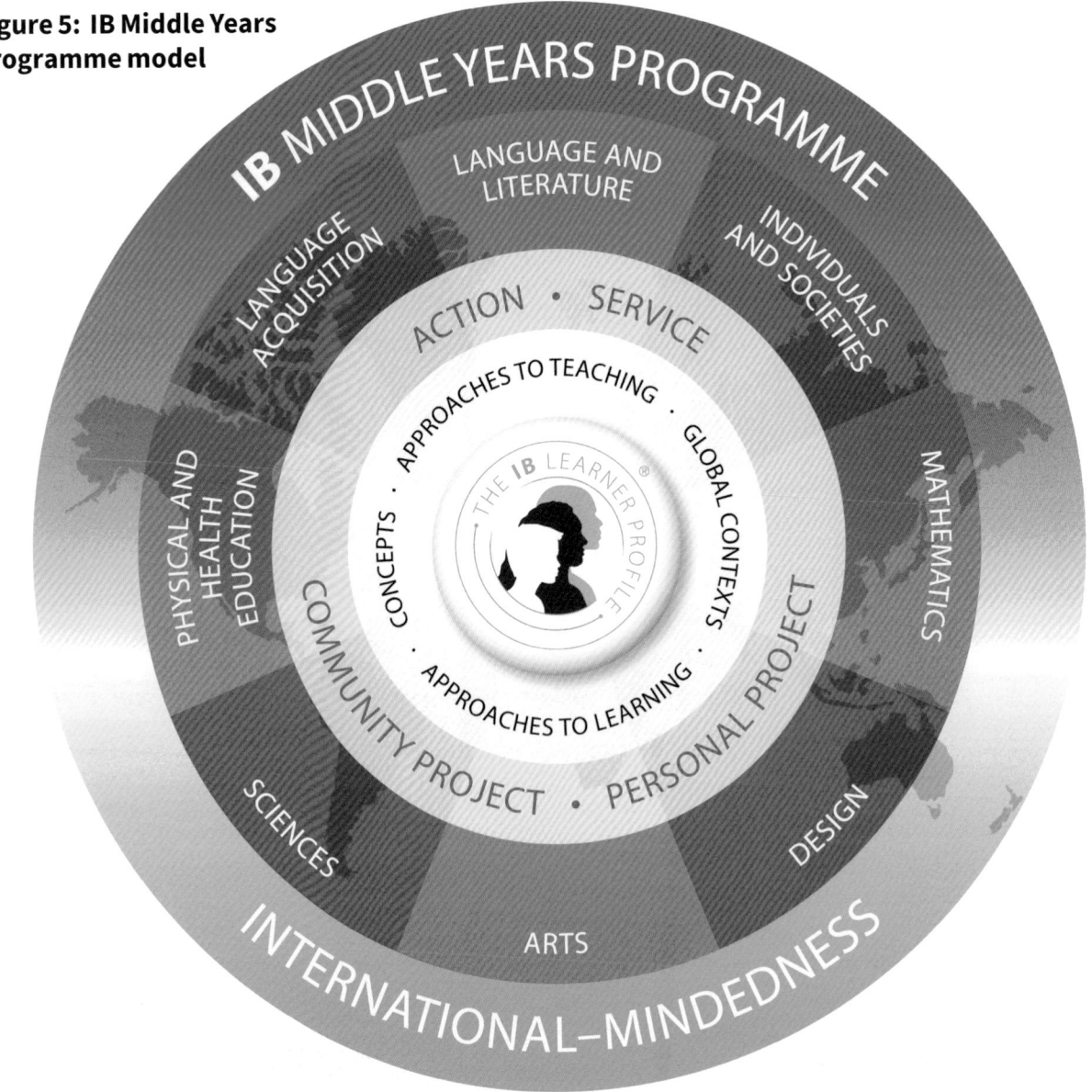

The MYP: a unique approach, relevant for a global society

The MYP aims to help students develop their personal understanding, their emerging sense of self and responsibility in their community. Using global contexts, MYP students explore human identity, global challenges and what it means to be internationally minded.

MYP teachers organize the curriculum with appropriate attention to:

- Teaching and learning in context
- Conceptual understanding
- Approaches to learning (ATL)
- Service as action
- Language and identity.

MYP projects

MYP projects provide students the opportunity to demonstrate what they have learned in the MYP. In schools that include MYP year 5, all students must complete the personal project. In programmes that include MYP years 4 or 5, schools may offer students the opportunity to do both the community project and the personal project. In schools that include MYP year 3 or 4, students must complete the community project.

- The community project encourages students to explore their rights and responsibilities to implement service as action in the community. Students may complete the community project individually or in small groups.
- Each student develops a personal project independently. Producing a truly personal and creative piece of work stands as a summative review of their ability to conduct independent work.

MYP assessment

The optional MYP eAssessment provides external evaluation for students in MYP year 5 (typically 15–16 years old) that leads to the internationally recognized IB MYP certificate and IB MYP course results.

MYP eAssessment represents a balanced, appropriately-challenging model that comprises examinations and coursework.

- Two-hour on-screen examinations in four subject groups (language and literature, sciences, mathematics, individuals and societies) and in interdisciplinary learning are individually marked by IB examiners.
- Portfolios of student work for four subject groups (language acquisition, physical and health education, arts, and design) are moderated by IB examiners to international standards.
- Long term personal project work is marked by school teachers and moderated by IB examiners to international standards.

These innovative assessments focus on conceptual understanding and the ability to apply knowledge in complex, unfamiliar situations. They offer robust and reliable assessment of student achievement in the MYP.

Registration for MYP eAssessment is highly flexible and can differ per candidate from a single subject to the full MYP certificate. IB World Schools can register their students for a variety of subjects, which provide the candidates with externally validated results. All candidates receive IB MYP course results; specific conditions apply for registration for the IB MYP certificate.

MYP eAssessments meet the General Conditions for Recognition established by England's Office of Qualifications and Examinations Regulation and is recognized by other national education systems as preparation for further study at the senior secondary level.

What is the IB Diploma Programme (DP)?

The DP gives students aged 16-19 a world-class preparation for higher education and life beyond. It's a comprehensive, challenging framework that allows students to flourish intellectually, physically, emotionally and ethically, helping them graduate with a unique, future-ready skillset.

To ensure both breadth and depth of knowledge and understanding, DP students must choose at least one subject from each of the six groups:

1. Studies in language and literature
2. Language acquisition
3. Individuals and societies
4. Sciences
5. Mathematics
6. The Arts

Students may choose either an arts subject from group 6 or a second subject from groups 1 to 5. In addition to disciplinary and interdisciplinary study, the DP features three core elements that broaden students' educational experience and challenge them to apply their knowledge and skills.

The DP core elements are:

- The **extended essay** improves students' approach to learning in higher education through an independent, self-directed 4,000-word piece of research.

- **Theory of knowledge (TOK)** enhances students and educators' critical thinking, deepening their understand of content and connections across disciplines by reflecting on the nature of knowledge and on how we know what we claim we know through this flagship seminar course.

- **Creativity, activity and service (CAS)** helps students develop an ethic of service, become more caring, open-minded and reflective, and develop more self-confident and maturity by embarking on a project in their community.

The DP prepares students for effective participation in a rapidly evolving and increasingly global society as they:

- develop the skills and a positive attitude towards learning that will prepare them for higher education

- study at least two languages and increase understanding of cultures, including their own

- make connections across traditional academic disciplines and explore the nature of knowledge through the programme's unique theory of knowledge course

Figure 6: IB Diploma Programme model

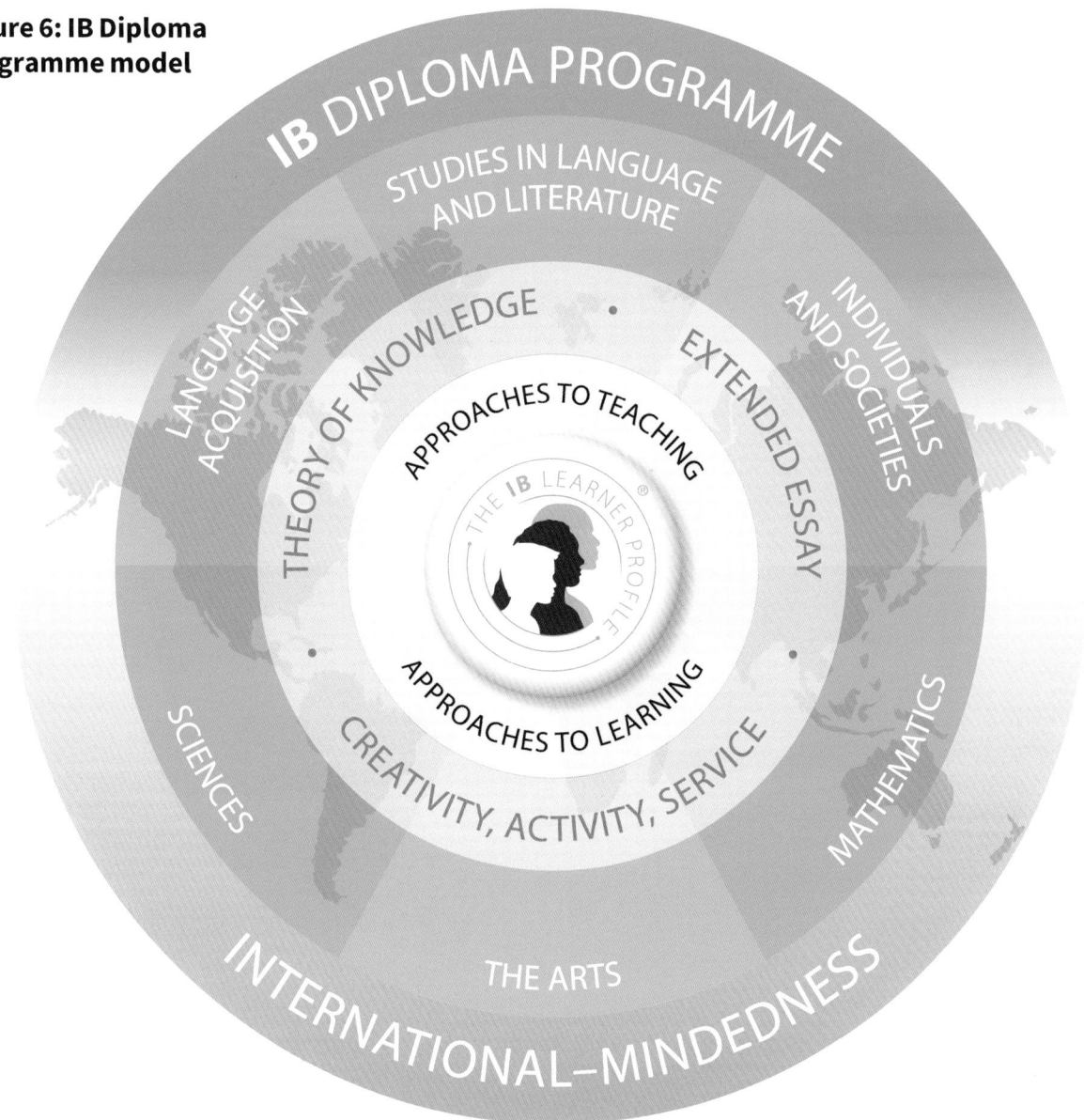

- undertake in-depth research into an area of interest through the lens of one or more academic disciplines in the extended essay
- enhance their personal and interpersonal development through creativity, activity and service

The DP is recognized and respected by the world's leading universities, and research suggests that higher rates of DP students go on to university and higher education study than non-IB students.

IB students apply to more than 3,300 higher education institutions each year, in close to 90 countries. The most popular of these institutions are ranked among the top universities in the world.

What is the IB Career-related Programme (CP)?

The IB Career-related Programme (CP) gives students aged 16-19 a head start in life, putting their skills, interests and ideas to the test with opportunities to delve into subjects not normally taught in the classroom and a chance to learn by doing. In turn, CP students graduate with the confidence, skills and experience needed to thrive in their future careers and higher education.

The CP's flexible educational framework allows schools to meet the needs, backgrounds and contexts of students. By engaging with a rigorous study programme that genuinely interests them, CP students gain transferable and lifelong skills in applied knowledge, critical thinking, communication and cross-cultural engagement.

The CP enables students to prepare for effective participation in an ever-changing world of work as they:

- consider new perspectives and other points of view
- engage in learning that makes a positive difference
- develop a combination of traditional academic skills and practical skills
- think critically and creatively in rapidly-changing and global workplaces
- communicate clearly and effectively
- work independently and in collaboration with others
- become self-confident, resilient and flexible.

Figure 7: IB Career-related Programme model

The CP framework allows students to specialize in, and focus on a career-related pathway. The CP provides a comprehensive educational framework that combines highly regarded and internationally recognized courses, from the IB Diploma Programme (DP), with a unique CP core and an approved career-related study.

The CP core

Personal and professional skills, designed for students to develop attitudes, skills and strategies to be applied to personal and professional situations and contexts now and in the future. It emphasizes skills development for the workplace, as these are transferable and can be applied in a range of situations.

Service learning is the development and application of knowledge and skills towards meeting an identified and authentic community need. Through service learning, students develop and apply personal and social skills in real life situations.

Language development is a central tenet of an IB education that ensures students have access and are exposed to a second language in order to increase their understanding of the wider world and enhance their skillsets within a highly competitive global workforce.

The **reflective project** is an in-depth body of work submitted towards the end of the programme. Students identify, analyze, critically discuss and evaluate an ethical dilemma associated with an issue from their career-related studies. The project can be submitted in different formats including an essay, web page or short film. This work encourages students to engage in personal inquiry, action, and reflection, and to develop strong research and communications skills.

Career-related study

Through personalized career-related studies, students are provided with practical, real-world approaches to learning, designed to prepare them for higher education, an internship or apprenticeship or even a job. It also provides the opportunities for students to learn about theories and concepts through application and practice while developing skills in authentic and meaningful contexts.

Career-related studies are offered and awarded by the school or an outside pathway provider. Popular studies at current CP schools include engineering, computer programming, business and finance, pre-med and health science, hospitality and tourism, and visual and performing arts.

For more information about the IB and its programmes, check out ibo.org

Your Destination

For International Baccalaureate® resources, visit Titlewave®, the largest online store for educators. Shop from our dedicated lists of complementary materials by programme, see readability measures, get free educator guides, read professional book reviews, and browse suggestions from librarians and teachers.

Textbooks and Supplemental Books
Shop Titlewave for books from top publishers, including Haese Mathematics, Pearson, Oxford University Press, and more. You'll also find book lists and recommendations aligned to programmes.

Exam Prep Materials
Help your students prepare with a Questionbank subscription or Exam and Markscheme Packs.

Posters and Brochures
Decorate your classroom or complement your curriculum with posters and educational brochures.

IB-Branded Merchandise
Browse our selection of sweatshirts, jackets, bags, school supplies, and more. You'll find lots of great gift ideas!

We also can support students and educators in these areas.

FREE Curation Service
Our team of licensed teachers and certified librarians can find resources aligned to your programme.

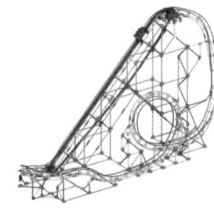

STE(A)M and Makerspace
Browse our STE(A)M and Makerspace products, hands-on resources, and a curated list of ideas for innovative learning.

Social and Emotional Learning
Explore resources to support the whole student, strengthen community, and develop empathy.

Diversity, Equity, and Inclusion
Expose students to the stories and voices of different cultures, abilities, backgrounds, locations, and identities around the world.

for All Things IB

Since 2015, Follett has been provider of all products and merchandise developed by the IB.

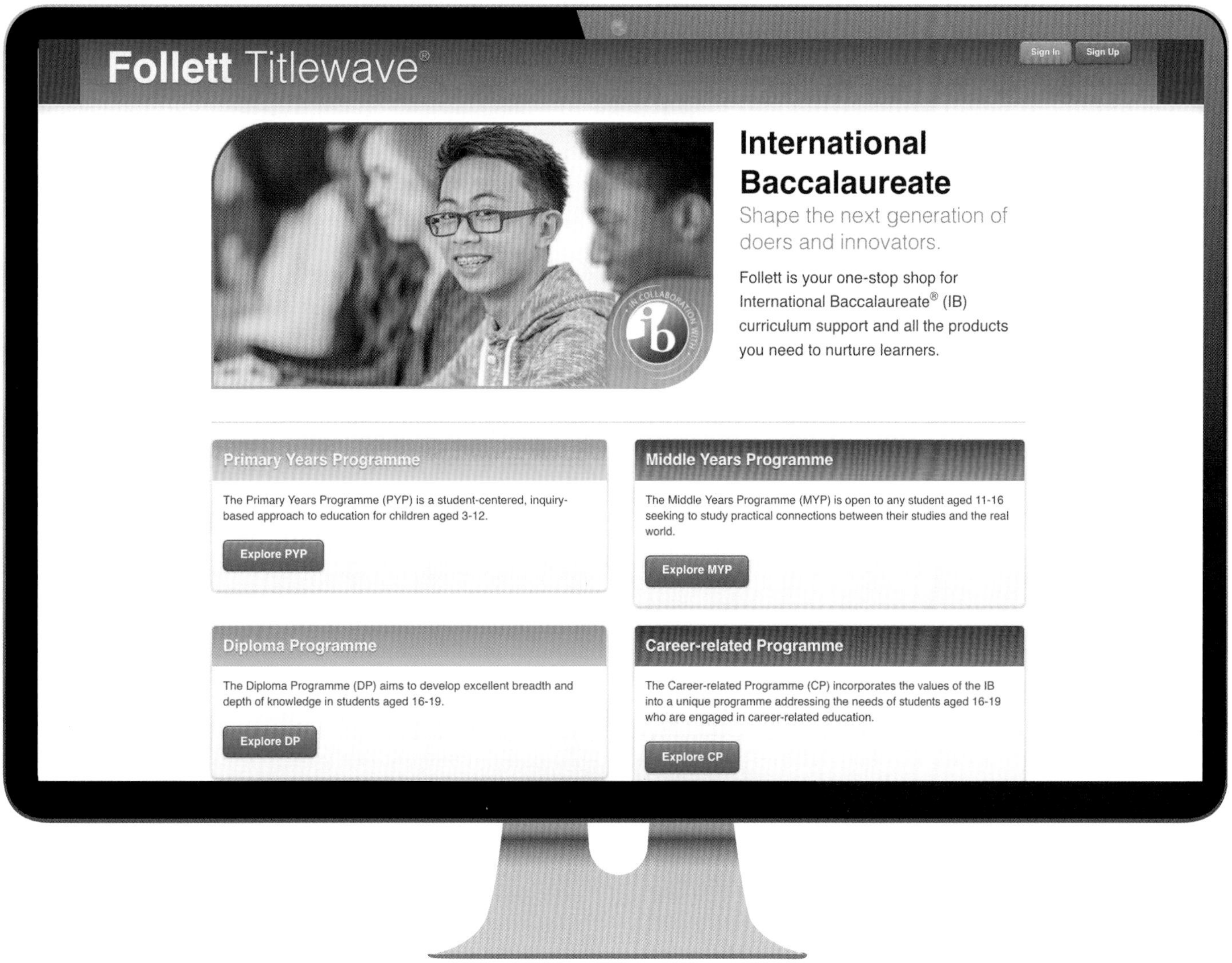

Follett Titlewave®

Sign In   Sign Up

International Baccalaureate

Shape the next generation of doers and innovators.

Follett is your one-stop shop for International Baccalaureate® (IB) curriculum support and all the products you need to nurture learners.

Primary Years Programme

The Primary Years Programme (PYP) is a student-centered, inquiry-based approach to education for children aged 3-12.

Explore PYP

Middle Years Programme

The Middle Years Programme (MYP) is open to any student aged 11-16 seeking to study practical connections between their studies and the real world.

Explore MYP

Diploma Programme

The Diploma Programme (DP) aims to develop excellent breadth and depth of knowledge in students aged 16-19.

Explore DP

Career-related Programme

The Career-related Programme (CP) incorporates the values of the IB into a unique programme addressing the needs of students aged 16-19 who are engaged in career-related education.

Explore CP

Visit **follettk12.link/iby21** to start shopping.

Don't have your free Titlewave account? See what you're missing at **follettk12.link/ibtw21**.

Earn a degree the world will recognise

At The University of Queensland we recognise the skills and qualities of IB students. We offer a range of opportunities to help you make the most of your time at university. From the day you commence, to graduation and beyond:

- Receive credits or exemptions for up to one semester, if eligible.
- Pursue multiple study interests through our dual programs.

- Continue your language or music learning through our concurrent diplomas.
- Expand your entrepreneurial mindset with UQ Ventures programs.
- Join a global network of more than 286,000 alumni spanning more than 170 countries.

future-students.uq.edu.au

47th
QS World
University
Rankings,

51st
ShanghaiRanking's
Academic Ranking
of World Universities

=54th
Times Higher
Education World
University Rankings,

More national
teaching awards than
any other Australian

IB Recognition

The IB works with the higher education community to support IB students in getting the recognition they have earned, as well as to examine and further develop our programmes to make sure we continue to offer the best preparation for university studies and life beyond. The IB prepares students to thrive in an ever-evolving world by nurturing the skills and attitudes they need to lead happy and successful lives. The programmes are designed to be innovative from the ground up, which means they're always ready to match the educational needs of today.

Through our programmes, students develop:
- social, leadership and self-efficacy skills.
- critical thinking and problem-solving skills students need to thrive in the future.
- reasoning, communication and collaboration skills essential for teamwork.
- fluency in a second language and global cultural awareness, giving them an edge in our increasingly connected world.

A number of online resources focusing on recognition of IB programmes are available on **www.ibo.org**. These include information about IB programmes, research and evidence into the effectiveness of IB programmes, support in policy development, and information on where and how the IB is recognized around the world. The purpose is to increase understanding of the IB's aims and the unique aspects of each of its programmes, their assessment and the way they prepare students for further education.

YOUR FUTURE STARTS HERE
DISCOVER THE WORLD OF BUSINESS & LOGISTICS

KLU
KÜHNE LOGISTICS UNIVERSITY

"The IB Diploma gave me opportunities around the globe, and I chose KLU in Hamburg, Germany. At this intercultural university, I was able to establish a network of classmates from around the world. KLU encouraged my development and supported me, building my confidence and allowing me to visualize my dream. After various experiences, I am now ready to transform from a student to an adult."

Minsang Eom
IB Diploma 2017
International American School of Warsaw
KLU Bachelor of Business Administration
Class of 2022

English
Language of instruction

Integrated Internship

Exchange semester

15 July 2022
Application Deadline

3 years/6 semesters
Bachelor of Science
Business Administration

1 year
Pathway program
(Studienkolleg)

Global Research, Professional Development and Government

IB research

Research plays a central role in the development, quality assurance and assessment of IB programmeoutcomes. The IB commissions research to leading research institutions and universities around the world.

The core of our work involves research on IB programmes. We conduct Outcomes research to investigate the impact of IB programmes on students, teachers and schools, and Curriculum research to inform the development and review of all programme curriculum and pedagogy. Policy research supports decision-making and policy development by providing cutting-edge research findings and practice recommendations on key educational issues.

We also conduct survey research, designing, distributing and analyzing surveys to support the IB's strategic decision-making, and quality assurance for IB products and services. The Assessment research department collects and analyses data to ensure assessments are well-grounded in current understanding of best practice. Lastly, we offer research resources, such as findings and figures for IB leaders, annotated bibliographies and Jeff Thompson Award studies.

For more information on IB Research, please visit **ibo. org/research.**

Professional development

Educators, school leaders and administrators are offered continuous support through plentiful IB professional development workshops and services. Development of a worldwide teaching and learning community committed to lifelong learning is an IB priority.

The IB is continuously seeking to ensure the accessibility of its professional development for all educators and that educators' professional learning needs are met. By offering four different delivery methods: face-to-face, online, virtual and a "blended" method combining remote and face-to-face learning, the IB aims to better accommodate the diverse learning and logistical needs of both educators and schools.

For more information, please visit ibo.org/pd.

The IB and governments

Engaging regional and national governments is at the centre of the IB's commitment to diversity and inclusivity. We are defined by our values and those include pedagogical leadership and international-mindedness. There is a growing awareness among governments that education systems have to work in an international society, not just a national one. We engage with many governments, either to create more IB World Schools or to influence national education systems. Across the world, the IB is working hand-in-hand with regional and national governments to ensure state access to IB programmes.

BACHELOR OF BUSINESS ADMINISTRATION

A renowned Business School

Established since 1971, IFM Business School is an accredited and innovative institution. IFM prepares people for successful business careers thanks to solid education expertise and outstanding business know-how. IFM provides inspiring learning opportunities for future leaders, who create value for their stakeholders, organisations and society.

The following bodies have recognised our excellence, innovative approach, cutting-edge curriculum and focus on career:

• Ranked #81 among the World's top business schools - Ceoworld Magazine 2021.
• Ranked in the top tier one for global MBA programs - CEO Magazine 2021.
• Among the top 1% of Business Schools holding triple accreditation.
• Awarded most Innovative Business School in Switzerland - Global Brands Magazine.
• Switzerland is ranked 3rd worldwide for university education - QS.

Kick-start your career

IFM's Bachelor degree prepares you for the challenges of the global business world. Our accredited programme focuses on your success and provides you with a practical business education so you can prepare for a brilliant career.

Our cutting-edge curriculum combines academic excellence, practical skills, new tools and technology to enhance students' employability. We do not simply teach business concepts, we prepare you to use what you learn at your future company. You will develop an entrepreneurial, innovative, digital and sustainable mindset. Thanks to our distinct real-business approach, you will become a confident professional, able to think differently, manage projects, lead a team, make decisions and face the challenges of a rapidly changing business landscape. Graduates will be ready for successful careers in various types and sizes of industry.

4 specialisations

• BBA in Management
• BBA in Finance
• BBA in International Business
• BBA in Entrepreneurship & Innovation

Program start dates
• March and October

Duration: 3 years

Language: English

Formats (2 possibilities)
• Traditional on-campus
• Hybrid (online & on-campus)

Location
• Geneva, Switzerland

Contacts
T. +41223222580 - info@ifm.ch

www.ifm.ch/english

IB Governance

IB Board of Governors

We are governed by a Board of Governors, whose members are appointed by the Board upon recommendation by the governance and organization committee. Membership comprises a diversity of gender, culture and geography with experience from both the business and academic worlds. Board members, with the exception of the Chair, are volunteers and receive no payment for their time or work on the Board.

Members as of November 2021

Chair

Dr Helen Drennen AM – Chief Executive Officer of Studio Schools of Australia, Queensland, Australia

Vice-chair

Dr Sijbolt Noorda, President of the Magna Charta Observatory, Bologna, Italy, and President of the Academic Cooperation Association, Brussels, Belgium

Members

Ms Sabine Chalmers, General counsel at BT Group Plc., London, United Kingdom

Mr Jean-Christophe Deberre, Former managing director of the Mission laïque française (Mlf) and the Office scolaire et universitaire international (OSUI), Paris, France

Ms Totty Ellwood Aris, Head of the Verdala International School, Malta

Ms Dianne Drew, Head of School, Dwight School, New York City, USA and Chair of IB Heads Council

Dr Peter Hoeben, Chair of IB Examining Board, The Hague, the Netherlands

Mr Steven Kim, Partner at Verdis Investment Management, Villanova, Pennsylvania, USA

Professor Ee Ling Low, Dean, Academic and Faculty Affairs, NIE, NTU, Singapore

Mr Cyrille NKontchou, Co-Founder and Managing Partner of Enko Capital, South Africa

Dr Coenraad Vrolijk, Regional CEO Africa at Allianz, Geneva, Switzerland

Chairs of the IB Board of Governors (formerly Council of Foundation)

1968–1981	John Goormaghtigh	Director of the European office of the Carnegie Endowment for International Peace, Belgium
1981–1984	Seydou Madani Sy	Rector of the University of Dakar, Senegal, and later minister for justice and special advisor to the president of Senegal.
1984–1990	Piet Gathier	Director General of secondary education, the Netherlands
1990–1996	Thomas Hagoort	International lawyer, USA
1996–1997	Bengt Thelin	Director General of education, Sweden
1997–2003	Greg Crafter	Former minister for education in South Australia, lawyer, Australia
2003–2009	Monique Seefried	Former Executive Director, Center for the Advancement and Study of International Education, USA
2009–2015	Carol Bellamy	Attorney, New York, USA
2015–2020	George Rupp	Former President of the International Rescue Committee, Connecticut, USA
2020–present	Helen Drennen AM	Chief Executive Officer of Studio Schools of Australia, Queensland, Australia

IB Directors General

Alec Peterson	1968-77
Gérard Renaud	1977-83
Roger Peel	1983-98
Derek Blackman	1998-1999
George Walker	1999-2006
Jeffrey Beard	2006-December 2013
Siva Kumari	2014-2021
Olli-Pekka Heinonen	2021-present

inspired®

A world leader in IB education

Inspired is a world leader in delivering the IB Diploma.

Available at over 20 schools in our global group, we share best practice throughout our IB schools and offer collaborative opportunities the world over.

Outstanding results year after year

Global opportunities for collaboration

Exchange programmes between Inspired schools for deeper enrichment

Europe

United Kingdom
- Fulham School, London

Switzerland
- International School Ticino
- St. George's International School, Montreux

Italy
- International School of Bergamo
- International School of Como
- International School of Milan
- International School of Modena
- International School of Monza
- International School of Siena
- St. Louis School, Milan

Portugal
- PaRK International School, Lisbon
- St. Peter's International School, Palmela

Spain
- King's College, The British School of Madrid
- Mirabal International School, Madrid
- Colegio San Patricio, Madrid
- International School San Patricio, Toledo
- Sotogrande International School, Cádiz

Belgium
- St. John's International School, Brussels

Asia-Pacific

Indonesia
- ACG School Jakarta

Vietnam
- Australian International School, Ho Chi Minh City
- European International School, Ho Chi Minh City

New Zealand
- ACG Parnell College

Americas

Peru
- Colegio Altair, Lima

Panama
- King's College, Panama

Costa Rica
- Blue Valley, San José

Visit our website today to learn more.

inspirededu.com

IB Certificates in Teaching and Learning

Two distinct certification opportunities in teaching and learning are offered by a network of universities in coordination with the IB. Educators can choose from nearly more than 50 highly ranked universities in locations all around the world.

1. Choose the **IB certificate in teaching and learning** to examine principles and practices associated with the Primary Years, Middle Years, Diploma Programme and Career-related programmes. These university courses of study help new and experienced educators develop themselves into reflective practitioners and teacher-researchers.

2. Pursue the **IB advanced certificate in teaching and learning research** to supplement IB experience with rigorous, systematic, investigative work in curriculum development, pedagogy and assessment.

The IB educator certificates can help you gain a rich learning experience, ongoing professional development and a career path leading to greater opportunities in the IB global community of schools. Your programme of study at an IB-recognized university will enable you to:

- improve the quality of your classroom teaching.
- demonstrate your deep understanding of student learning.
- enhance your competitive edge in the education job sector.
- interact with leading academics.
- demonstrate your commitment to continuous self-improvement and lifelong learning.
- establish a strong peer network for research and publishing consultation.
- gain access to IB community resources, including the IB's online Programme resource centre.

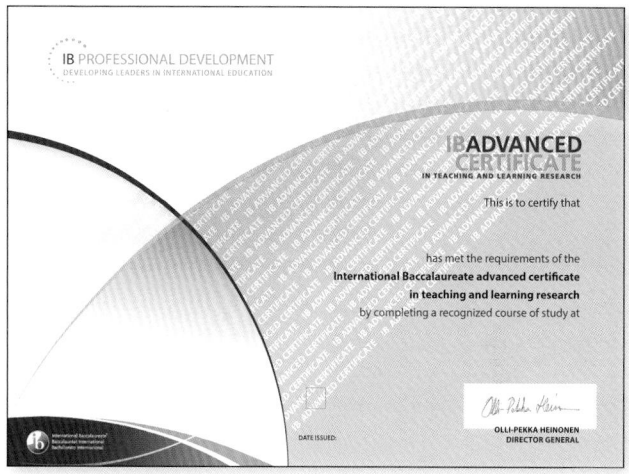

IB Certificates in Leadership

Certified IB leaders inspire and guide school communities as they implement and sustain IB programmes. IB certificates in leadership verify your understanding of principles and practices associated with leadership in an IB World School and in the IB community at large. Two distinct IB certificates in leadership development are offered by universities around the world.

1. The **IB certificate in leadership practice** is designed for aspiring educators and administrators who want to improve their leadership capabilities in an IB context. Through this programme, learn to refine your abilities to take on leadership responsibilities and to better understand your role in guiding a school through IB authorization and implementation

2. The **IB advanced certificate in leadership research** focuses on rigorous investigative work to give experienced leaders a more grounded understanding of IB leadership responsibilities and capabilities. Your training will include research within the context of IB leadership as well as deep reflection on your personal leadership practice.

Take the next step to becoming a certified IB educator or leader. Visit https://ibo.org/professional-development/about-our-workshops/professional-certificates/ for more information about the IB's partner universities, or contact pd.pathways@ibo.org.

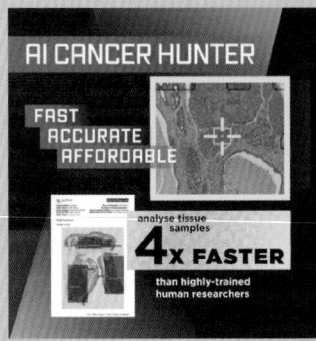

The IB Around the World

We currently work with IB World Schools in 158 countries. All our jurisdictions have not-for-profit or charitable status with headquarters in Geneva, Switzerland. Our four global centres are in Washington, USA, The Hague, Netherlands, Cardiff, UK, and Singapore. We employ approximately 700 IB staff worldwide.

Our IB staff and educators work closely with prospective and candidate schools as well as existing IB World Schools. They are also responsible for creating and sustaining relationships with governments, international and national agencies, universities and other educational institutions, foundations and concerned individuals. Through its strategic goals, we are also promoting wider educational access.

Core services we provide include:
For prospective schools
- introductory or orientation workshops
- consultation, advice, and materials on application and authorization
- training workshops
- authorization visits.

For IB World Schools
- professional development programmes for new and experienced IB teachers
- regional conferences
- support via webinar
- online access to resources and support via My IB
- periodic evaluations of schools' IB programmes
- ongoing support throughout a school's IB journey.

For universities
- information on the philosophy, structure and requirements of the IB Diploma and Career-related Programmes
- access to the content and requirements of the IB Diploma and IB Career-related Programme curriculums and assessment
- research to demonstrate the effectiveness of IB programmes
- advice on establishing an IB recognition policy.

For governments
- advice on how to integrate IB programmes into state educational systems
- consultation regarding recognition of the IB Diploma.

Figure 8: IB Global Centres

IB Global Centre, Washington DC

IB Global Centre, Cardiff
IB Global Centre, The Hague

IB Foundation Office, Geneva
IB Global Centre, Singapore

IB World Schools

This section is divided into the three IB regions. Here you will find editorial from each region, including facts and figures, enhanced profiles of selected schools and a full directory of all IB World Schools in the region.

Key		
IB Africa, Europe, Middle East	page 43	
IB Asia-Pacific	page 307	
IB Americas	page 491	

IB

AFRICA | EUROPE | MIDDLE EAST

(Founded 2004)

Head of School
Ms Janina Sparks

DP coordinator
Mr Lucio Pessia

Status Private

Boarding/day Day

Gender Coeducational

Language of instruction
English, German

Authorised IB programmes
DP

Age Range 2 – 18 years

Number of pupils enrolled
600

Fees
Preschool €3,360 – €4,560
Elementary School €8,040 –
€9,480
Secondary School €11,100 –
€16,800

Address
SÜDCAMPUS Bad Homburg
Am Weidenring 52-54
61352 Bad Homburg, Hesse |
GERMANY

TEL +49 61 72 984 141

Email
info@accadis-isb.com

Website
www.accadis-isb.com

Our mission

accadis ISB aims to develop confident, knowledgeable and caring young people prepared to create a better future. We aim to build within each child a sense of responsibility, a love for learning, self-discipline, and respect for others. Challenging programs, combined with inter-cultural understanding and respect, enable our students to reach their potential and become compassionate and lifelong learners.

Who we are

accadis ISB is situated in Bad Homburg, a leafy town in the Taunus mountains, just north of Frankfurt am Main. We are a non for profit, lively, friendly and expanding bilingual co-ed school which currently has approximately 600 students from 2 – 18 years of age, representing over 50 nationalities. Privately owned, it is part of a family business with links to the nearby accadis University of Applied Sciences. The school has a bilingual concept, teaching some subjects in English and some in German. accadis ISB is an official IB World School since January 2016. accadis ISB is also accredited by Cambridge Assessment International Education to teach the two year IGCSE course in Grades 9 and 10.

Our students

The school provides a supportive and challenging environment where students are encouraged to become responsible and independent learners. accadis ISB caters for a wide range of students, and is both a "local" school for families who live nearby and also an international school for students who come to us from all over the world.

Our school

accadis ISB was founded in 2004 and is situated on a state-of-the-art campus featuring its own sports hall with outdoor football pitch. Over the course of the last years, the school expanded into an adjacent building, adding an inviting library, two Art rooms, an IB Learning Suite reserved for students in Grades 11 and 12, a Drama room with stage equipment as well as further teaching rooms, providing more space for the growing Elementary and Secondary Schools. In 2022 – 2023 accadis ISB is opening a new building exclusively for Secondary School students, catering for the ever-increasing demand. It will feature more than 20 new classrooms, additional specialist spaces for Science, Art, Music and Drama as well as two libraries, a Cafeteria and an auditorium for up to 250 people.

The school focuses strongly on technology. The state-of-the-art learning environment includes Smartboards in each classroom, Google Chromebook laptops, school-wide high-speed Wi-Fi and a 3D printer.

ACORNS INTERNATIONAL SCHOOL
INSPIRING AND EMPOWERING

Head of School Ameena Lalani	**Age Range** 18 months – 18 years
PYP coordinator Rachelle Hale	**Number of pupils enrolled** 500
MYP coordinator Sam Weavers	**Fees** $2,358 – $8,850
DP coordinator Ken Kanyesigye	**Address** Plot 328, Kisota Road (Along) Northern Bypass, Kisaasi Roundabout Kampala | **UGANDA**
Status Private	
Boarding/day Day	**TEL** +256 393 202 665
Gender Coeducational	**Email** admissions@ais.ac.ug
Language of instruction English	**Website** www.ais.ac.ug
Authorised IB programmes PYP, MYP, DP	

Encapsulating the adage, 'A tree with strong roots laughs at storms', Acorns International School (AIS) bears fruits that stand the test of time.

Nestled between the verdant folds of Kampala, the capital city of Uganda, AIS is sprawled over a 5-acre state-of-the-art, purpose-built campus, that nurtures the balance between academics and extracurriculars.

Over two decades in the field of education, we have grown to represent more than 50 nationalities. The AIS team strives to inspire and empower every student to achieve their personal best and become inquiring, knowledgeable, pluralists and lifelong learners, who create a better and peaceful world, through intercultural understanding and respect.

Admissions are open throughout the academic year, subject to availability. We have a limit to the number of students per classroom, for uncompromised quality. This interface gives teachers an edge to assess each student's area of strength, and improvement. Teachers are supported in this process, with timely professional development sessions, to ensure growth and excellence. Through an open-door policy, we ensure that our main stakeholders, our parents, are full partners in the decision-making process and voice concerns not only of their children, but their own too.

The language of instruction is English, with French and Kiswahili as part of our dynamic curriculum. Through our engaging and rigorous, inquiry-based environment, students reach their full academic potential and become responsible, caring, multilingual, and culturally-literate global learners.

Our teaching team is not just diverse, they epitomize academic excellence and have a penchant for pastoral care.

AIS is non-sectarian and co-educational institution, founded on strong partnerships between parents, teachers and learners.

A visit to AIS allows your family to experience the school in a relaxed environment, meet with the administration, as well as visit homerooms, the science lab, performing arts rooms, libraries, swimming pool, auditorium, soccer fields and the basketball courts.

AIS is an authorised International Baccalaureate (IB) Continuum School, offering the Primary Years Programme (PYP), the Middle Years Programme (MYP) and the Diploma Programme (DP).

AIS is an inclusive school that accepts students in the Early Childhood Department (Crèche to Reception Class), Primary (Years 1 to 6), and Secondary (MYP1 – DP2).

It is always onwards and upwards for us, and we would love for you to join us!

Aiglon College

AIGLON
SWITZERLAND

Head of School
Mrs. Nicola Sparrow

Director of Learning
Mr. Tomas Duckling

DP coordinator
Mrs Laura Hamilton

Status Private

Boarding/day Mixed

Gender Coeducational

Language of instruction
English

Authorised IB programmes
DP

Age Range 9 – 18 years

Number of pupils enrolled 420

Fees
Day: CHF35,000 – CHF80,000
Boarding: CHF72,000 –
CHF120,000

Address
Avenue Centrale 61
1885 Chesières | **SWITZERLAND**

TEL +41 (0)24 496 6177

Email
admissions@aiglon.ch

Website
www.aiglon.ch

Education should be a way of life. School should be about the development of the whole person. When John Corlette founded Aiglon College in 1949, he had a unique vision: to combine the special character of mountain life with an innovative educational mission. Aiglon today guards this original vision and has grown into one of the world's most distinctive boarding schools.

Spirited, independent and a not-for-profit organisation, Aiglon's aim toward the balanced development of mind, body and spirit works to create a principle-driven environment where students and teachers alike are encouraged toward academic excellence, pursuit of physical challenge and the learning born through a deeply international culture.

Aiglon is an English-speaking school styled in the tradition of British education. Students follow the globally recognised IGCSE and International Baccalaureate (IB) programmes while simultaneously developing practical skills that integrate curriculum into all areas of life. The focused, individually tailored programme allows each student to access a unique course of study.

The school's professional University Advising team works closely with each student to help them understand and succeed in the university application process. Through these efforts, our students have access to the world's top universities. This tailored programme encourages, develops and ultimately matches every student with a university that can continue developing their education.

The character of Aiglon students is forged on the mountain. Aiglon is located just beyond the ski resort village of Villars-sur-Ollon in French-speaking Switzerland, at 1,258m. Making use of our safe, alpine environment we enjoy an open-style campus and are just 250m from the ski resort's main lift. Central to its educational philosophy, the uniquely crafted expedition programme utilises Aiglon's location in the Swiss Alps to engage students in activities designed to develop their sense of challenge and responsibility in a highly practical environment.

In winter, students ski twice per week as part of the physical education programme. Beyond winter, students participate in a wide range of competitive and noncompetitive activities from football and swimming to yoga.

All the teaching staff play a key role in pastoral care and learning support at Aiglon. From their roles as Houseparents, Assistant Houseparents or as tutors, teachers are available to students 24/7. In this community relationship, students and teachers are able to connect in unique ways that enable young people to grow and better understand their purpose and role at Aiglon.

Our unique combination of academic excellence and the spirit of living life on the mountain ensure that an Aiglon education provides your child with everything needed to succeed.

Al Hussan International School Khobar

ALHUSSAN EDUCATION

(Founded 1998)

School Head
Dr. Burhan Mazahreh

DP coordinator
Ms. Samar Deshmukh

Status Private

Boarding/day Day

Gender Coeducational

Language of instruction
English

Authorised IB programmes
DP

Age Range 3 – 18 years

Address
PO Box 297
Dammam
31411 | SAUDI ARABIA

TEL +966 13 858 7566
FAX +966 13 857 3874

Email
ahisk@alhussan.edu.sa

Website
international.alhussan.edu.sa

At Al Hussan We Excel

Al-Hussan International School (AHISK) is a private English language day school with 1,220 students, situated in three buildings in the city of Al-Khobar. The Pre-School-G2 campus currently houses students in Pre-K to Grade 2. The Girls' and Boys' Section campuses house Grades 3 to 12 respectively.

The school provides the environment and the experiences which promote the moral, social and intellectual development of all its pupils. Every child is cherished and receives support and encouragement within a strong, caring community.

The school offers a well-rounded education through its provision of different programmes of instruction for students from Pre-K to Grade 12. We acknowledge that every child is born with unique potential, and we seek to develop each child's creativity, expand their horizons and prepare them to be responsible global citizens and leaders. English is the language of instruction, with Arabic, French or Urdu offered as a second language and as a foreign language for non-native speakers. Islamic classes are offered to all students from KG to Grade 12. AHISK strives to continually improve the quality of education it provides. We are accredited by COGNIA and by Council of International schools(CIS). The Al Hussan curriculum is offered from KG to 12. High School Students are offered to sit for IGCSE or O Level exams in Grade 10 and to elect one of the two programs: British Program (A Level) or the IBDP in Grade 11 & 12. Courses on offer in the IB Diploma Programme are: English Literature, Arabic B, Arabic ab-initio, French B, French *ab-initio*, Business Management, Economics, Psychology, Biology, ITGS, Chemistry, Physics,

Computer Science, Math Analysis and Approaches (AA), Mathematics Applications and Interpretation (AI) and Visual Arts.

Our Vision
Leaders of Excellence in International Education

Our Mission
Al Hussan International School provides high quality education through a safe, stimulating, and multicultural environment to prepare leaders for a global society.

Our Beliefs
At AHISK, we believe:
1. all students can learn and realize their full potential.
2. a safe and stimulating environment promotes quality education.
3. in respecting cultural and individual differences.
4. all stakeholders share the responsibility for advancing our mission.
5. in preparing students to pursue further educational goals.
6. commitment to continuous improvement is imperative.

At AHISK we believe in preparing students to become well rounded young people, ready to meet the challenges in an ever-changing world. This is done through our challenging programs of study and with the help of an experienced and extensively trained team of teachers. Our student body is very active and striving to make a change in their community.

Our graduates are joining universities across the world, mostly in the Middle East, Far East, Canada, Europe and USA. We are proud of our AHISK family and we invite you to visit us and experience our loving and nurturing family ambiance.

AMADEUS International School Vienna

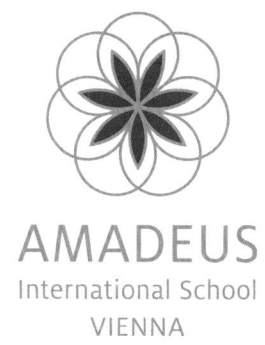

AMADEUS
International School
VIENNA

(Founded 2012)

Head of School Jeremy House

Head of Primary Maki Nishihara

Head of Secondary
Karsten Plöger

PYP coordinator
Melanie McGeever

MYP coordinator Yvan Wever

DP coordinator Alice Greenland

CP coordinator Ms Elke De Vries

Status Private

Boarding/day Mixed

Gender Coeducational

Language of instruction
English

Authorised IB programmes
PYP, MYP, DP, CP

Age Range 3 – 18 years

Number of pupils enrolled
300

Fees
Day: €13,235 – €29,820
Boarding: €46,640 – €52,110

Address
Bastiengasse 36-38
1180 Vienna | **AUSTRIA**

TEL +43 1 470 30 37 00

Email admissions@
amadeus-vienna.com

Website
www.amadeus-vienna.com

AMADEUS International School Vienna is a unique day and boarding IB World school with an integrated Music and Arts Academy. The AMADEUS education is one of Distinction with the mission of accompanying young people as they fulfil their highest potential.

AMADEUS is an International Baccalaureate school, offering PYP, MYP, DP, and CP for students ages 6-19. AMADEUS also offers an Early Years Kindergarten Programme for ages 3-6. The school engages students in inquiry-based learning that addresses real-life challenges and cultivates critical-thinking, problem-solving, and presentation skills. AMADEUS's community is distinguished by its internationalism representing over 50 different nationalities. To best teach the qualities of global citizenship, the school recruits educators from around the world. The school regularly outperforms the world average pass rates and diploma points and its alumni study in top universities around the globe.

Music and Arts plays a vital role in AMADEUS's learning approach which is emphasized in their dynamic co-curricular arts programme. This includes a variety of areas such as editorial design, music production, and musical theatre production. Students also have the opportunity to participate in the AMADEUS International Youth Orchestra, various forms of dance, drawing, painting, and more. Additionally, AMADEUS Music and Arts Academy offers

classes at Foundation, Advanced, and Professional levels to challenge and nurture artists at all stages of growth. The Academy helps artists thrive through intense study with distinguished instructors, practice, and performance opportunities. Finally, and uniquely, all students take part in the whole school choir.

Boarding at AMADEUS is possible for students in Grades 6-12. Our AMADEUS boarding provides students with a once in a lifetime educational experience. As the only international boarding school in Vienna, students from all around the world engage in an educational experience that is inclusive, happy, and respectful of different cultures. A strong sense of community cultivates a supportive and caring environment while promoting a healthy lifestyle that emphasizes nutritious food, physical exercise, social activities and overall wellbeing. Boarding students can look forward to a new fully renovated and exclusive boarding house which is scheduled to open in January 2022. If boarding houses had star ratings, this one would have five.

The location of the AMADEUS campus is just a short tram ride away from the city centre. Famous for its history, culture, and quality of life, Vienna is named 'the World's Most Liveable City' by The Economist. Home to numerous universities and nearly a dozen international schools, Vienna is Austria's hub of international education and learning.

American Creativity Academy

ACA
أكاديمية الابداع الأمريكية
American Creativity Academy

(Founded 1997)	**Authorised IB programmes** DP
Superintendent Sevag H. Kendirjian	**Age Range** 3 – 18 years
MHS Principals Dr. Lori Carpenter, Kadra Jama & Farhan Hashmi	**Number of pupils enrolled** 5500
	Address PO Box 1740, Hawally
DP coordinator Shaheed Carter	**32018 | KUWAIT**
Status Private	**HAWALLY CAMPUS** +965 2267 3333
	SALMIYA CAMPUS +965 2576 7900
Boarding/day Day	**Email** info@aca.edu.kw
Gender Segregated by campus	
Language of instruction English	**Website** www.aca.edu.kw

Mission and Beliefs

The American Creativity Academy is a private school that delivers a standards-based American curriculum within an environment in which Islamic values are respected and practiced. The school is dedicated to preparing students for university success.

Core Beliefs:

- Developing students' character with honesty, integrity and responsible behavior
- Partnership among parents, students and staff
- Students learn and thrive in a healthy, safe and caring environment
- Challenging students to think critically and creatively
- Developing the whole child intellectually, spiritually, socially and physically
- Preparing students to contribute constructively to a global society
- Effective communication
- Learning is a life-long process
- Inspiring excellence

Global Citizenship at ACA

Global Citizenship at ACA is the development of global citizens who have knowledge, skills and attitudes that make it possible to be actively involved in their local and international communities and systems that impact on their lives and the lives of others.

ACA offers a trans-disciplinary opportunity for students to expand their worldview and consider multiple perspectives. It's about both rights and responsibilities around global topics. Students engage with current issues to understand how they may interact in diverse social, economic, and political contexts that are not restricted by geographic boundaries.

American Curriculum

We have a vibrant, standards-based, American curriculum which is the result of years spent in horizontal and vertical alignment meetings, specialist group meetings, and cross-campus collaboration meetings. It is articulated, available to all staff on our Atlas platform, properly paced, and is the reference point from which our teachers derive instruction. It is used by all teachers for our K-12, non-IB subjects.

International Baccalaureate

ACA has been proudly offering the International Baccalaureate Diploma Program since 2008 for students in grades 11 and 12. The students go through a process of application, interviews, course selection based on their career goals, and discussions with parents. Students may opt for a full diploma or individual certificates. The process of preparing for the rigors of the IBDP high level courses starts as early as in grade 2 with students participating in the Enrichment Program (grades 2 to 8) and the Honors Program (grades 9 and 10). The Enrichment and Honors Programs use the same US standards-based curriculum as the mainstream classes; however, the standards of performance are set higher with more emphasis on critical thinking, logic, reasoning, research, writing, debate, and creativity. To participate in the Enrichment or Honors Programs, students must pass a series of assessments, teacher recommendations, interviews, and demonstrate the desire to be challenged.

IB DP Courses Offered at ACA

We offer a robust and diverse selection of IB courses that will

thoroughly prepare our children no matter where their post-secondary pursuits may take them.

Approaches to Teaching and Approaches to Learning

Our teachers are trained in IB's pedagogical strategies known as Approaches to Teaching and Learning, ATL. These strategies focus on inquiry, conceptual learning, developing local and global contexts, effective teamwork and collaboration, differentiation, and data-driven instruction.

Additionally, through ATL's learning strategies, our students are directly taught thinking, communication, social, self-management, and research skills. These skills aid them in the acquisition, personalization and ownership of their knowledge throughout life.

Every year, our IB team focuses on one Approach to Teaching and one Approach to Learning. We undergo a process of implementation, observation, feedback and reflection as part of our ATL Implementation cycle, which helps us to be reflective practitioners in our IB program.

Showcase School

We are a Microsoft Showcase School, defined by Microsoft as "an elite group of schools that exemplify the best of teaching and learning in the world today." Only a few institutions earn this designation, and we are proud to be one of them.

ACS Athens
American Community Schools

Empowering individuals to transform the world
as architects of their own learning

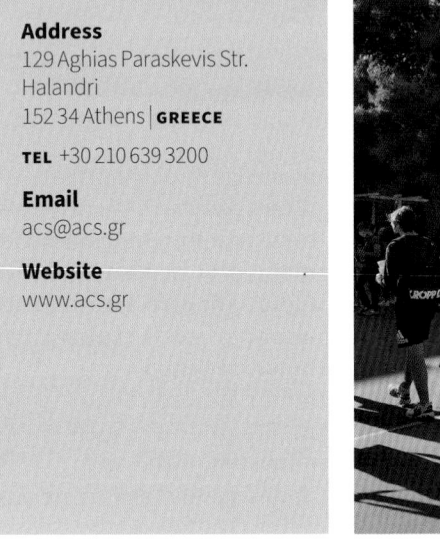

(Founded 1945)

President
Dr Peggy Pelonis

DP coordinator
Mark McGowan

Status Private

Boarding/day Day

Gender Coeducational

Language of instruction
English

Authorised IB programmes
DP

Age Range 3 – 18 years

Number of pupils enrolled
1100

Fees
€9,000 – €16,000

Address
129 Aghias Paraskevis Str.
Halandri
152 34 Athens | **GREECE**

TEL +30 210 639 3200

Email
acs@acs.gr

Website
www.acs.gr

ACS Athens has been an IB World School offering the IBDP since 1976. ACS Athens is the 66th school in the world to provide the IBDP and the first to introduce the program in Greece. Students from 60+ nationalities currently study at ACS Athens. The school is accredited by the Middle States Association of Colleges and Schools to offer an American High School Diploma, and it is the first and only one outside the US achieving the accreditation protocol of "Sustaining Excellence." ACS Athens is located at a suburb of Athens on a privately owned enclosed campus consisting of five main buildings. The campus features a 5-lane 25m swimming pool, a state-of-the-art theater, a green screen 4K TV studio suite with a podcast booth, a soccer field, an indoor gymnasium with a climbing wall, indoor and outdoor basketball and volleyball courts, and a fine arts suite.

Currently 66% of the upper class is enrolled in the IB Diploma programme and more than 89% of the remaining students have designed a program that combines IB and AP courses where they are enrolled in more than one IB or AP course. Full IBDP candidates at ACS Athens obtain a bilingual IB diploma, as well as an American High School Diploma when they complete the required courses successfully. ACS Athens has had a consistent average of 36 points, which is considerably higher than the average world score. Over 98% of ACS Athens graduates are admitted to top universities in the US, UK, Canada, the Netherlands, and elsewhere.

The extensive IB CAS program, including musical performances, participation in sports and service in hospitals, elderly care facilities, and refugee camps, broadens a student's education and perspectives and makes a student aware of real-life situations and concerns.

ACS Athens also embraces virtual learning, inaugurating its Virtual School in 2019-20, which offers mainstream and non-traditional high school accredited courses. Academic support through the Writing, Math and Research Studios assists and enhances the writing and mathematical skills of each student. Furthermore, a comprehensive program for college applications offered by our Student Affairs department facilitates admission to the finest institutions around the world. ACS Athens follows a best-fit university approach, ensuring students identify universities and colleges that will best suit them academically and personally.

The fundamental principles of ACS Athens' mission statement and its educational philosophy are in direct alignment with the philosophy and mission statement of the IBO. ACS Athens supports a student-centered environment and aims towards high academic achievement as well as active conscious citizenship; developing a community of inquirers who will make informed, intelligent and ethical decisions for improving life and living on the planet!

American International School of Kuwait

المدرسـة الأمريكـية الدولـية
American International School

(Founded 1991)

Superintendent Tobin Wait

Director Samera Al Rayes

PYP coordinator
Tanya Bradshaw

MYP coordinator
Teri Kwiatkowski

DP coordinator Amel Limam

Status Private

Boarding/day Day

Gender Coeducational

Language of instruction
English

Authorised IB programmes
PYP, MYP, DP

Age Range 4 – 18 years

Number of pupils enrolled
2324

Fees
Pre-K KD3,867
KG KD2,650 (KG 1) – KD2,871
(KG 2)
Grades 1-4 KD3,867
Grades 5-8 KD4,086
Grades 9-12 KD4,531

Address
PO Box 3267, Salmiya
22033 | KUWAIT

TEL +965 1 843 247

Email
superintendent@ais-kuwait.org

Website www.ais-kuwait.org

The American International School Kuwait (AIS) is a private independent day school serving students from pre-kindergarten through grade 12. AIS is an IB World School that is fully authorized for the Primary Years, Middle Years and Diploma Programmes. Our rigorous academic programme builds critical thinkers and inquirers in a nurturing educational environment.

The school has created intercultural learning by building bridges of understanding among diverse international students from around fifty countries across the world. This ethnic diversity builds resilient, empathetic, and competent leaders for the future.

The school has an outstanding extracurricular program that offers a wide variety of activities in sports, arts, music, and theatre. AIS students strive for balance and participate in a wide range of athletics and activities through our international activities conference, NESAC of which AIS is a full member. AIS also participates fully in KASAC, our local activities and athletics conference.

The well-designed learning space of our facilities and services contribute to the experience of students, educators, and community members. The school facility includes two gymnasia, several outdoor sports areas, music and theater spaces, strength training and aerobics rooms, as well as a 1200 seat auditorium. The walled campus includes over one hundred teaching spaces that surround two interior courts. Our Learning Commons offers a collaborative space for student inquiry, instructional coaching, and collaboration and houses a library with a large fiction, non-fiction, and Arabic collection.

Upon graduation, our students are extraordinarily well prepared for the academic requirements of university and they proudly enter many of the world's most respected and top-rated universities in the United States, Canada, and the United Kingdom.

American International School Vienna

(Founded 1959)	**Fees**
	Pre-Kindergarten €12,083
Director	Kindergarten-Grade 5 €18,868
Kathy Miner DEd	Grades 6-8 €20,936
	Grades 9-10 €21,776
DP coordinator	Grades 11-12 €22,099
Bridget Schroeder	
	Address
Status Private	Salmannsdorfer Strasse 47
	1190 Vienna | **AUSTRIA**
Boarding/day Day	
	TEL +43 1 401 32
Gender Coeducational	
Language of instruction	**Email**
English	info@ais.at
Authorised IB programmes	**Website**
DP	www.ais.at
Age Range 4 – 18 years	
Number of pupils enrolled	
800	

Set within the rich cultural context of Austria, the American International School Vienna is one of the top international schools in the country. Founded in 1959, AISV today serves around 800 students, representing over 60 countries, from Pre-Kindergarten through Grade 12 (International Baccalaureate (IB) or American diploma). AISV's core values — respect, aspire, and achieve — ensure that students develop intellectually and interculturally while internalizing the commitment and leadership necessary in today's globally-minded world.

AISV provides comprehensive opportunities for learners from around the world. Our students succeed academically, as well as in athletics, music, and visual arts. A variety of activities, including class trips to mountain ranges and service-oriented community projects, allow students to practice commitment, leadership, and meaningful self-reflection. We maintain a broad set of offerings to help us serve our students while staying true to our mission.

The tightly knit school community allows students to develop personal relationships with both highly qualified teachers and their peers. We maintain a culture of high expectations and close connection to the pulse of international education. Investments in the quality and skill of our staff are on-going, and recent enhancements to our facilities and technology assure our role as a vital partner and a leader in international education.

During the 2021-2022 school year, AISV celebrates 45 years as an IB World School. AISV has been an IB World School since 1977, just nine years after the IB Diploma Programme began. Since its inception at the school, the program has shown impressive growth. In 1977, its first year of the IB program, AISV had 10 IB Diploma candidates. Currently, AISV has 62 IB Diploma candidates. Perhaps most striking is the massive growth in the percentage of AISV seniors graduating with an IB Diploma: 18% in 1977 compared to a projected 89% in 2021-22. AISV was the 72nd IB school to be authorized, now out of over 5,500 schools worldwide. AISV is one of the most experienced IB schools in the region and the single most experienced IB school in Austria.

We welcome all to our community of innovative learners realizing their chosen futures with courage, curiosity, and joy. We make decisions based on the understanding that we are not only guiding children towards learning but building experiences and memories that will serve to inform futures not yet imagined.

American School of Milan

(Founded 1962)

Director
Wayne Rutherford

DP coordinator
Valeria Meroni

Status Private

Boarding/day Day

Gender Coeducational

Language of instruction
English

Authorised IB programmes
DP

Age Range 3 – 18 years

Number of pupils enrolled
840

Fees
Day: €10,800 – €20,300

Address
Via K. Marx, 14
20073 Noverasco di Opera (MI)
| **ITALY**

TEL +39 02 5300 0015

Email
admissions@asmilan.org

Website
www.asmilan.org

The American School of Milan (ASM) is an independent, co-educational college preparatory day school with a state-of-the-art campus located south of Milan. Founded in 1962, ASM has been educating international students from more than 50 countries for more than 50 years. ASM inspires students to discover their unique potential and to be curious learners, critical thinkers and global citizens who positively impact our world. ASM is accredited through the Middle States Association of Colleges and Schools and is an IB World School offering the Diploma Programme since 1983.

ASM offers a student-centered, American-style education that encourages children to develop their full potential, achieve personal excellence and become global citizens committed to lifelong learning. We embrace the IB learner profile along with our school values of respect, curiosity, integrity, courage and kindness. Technology is a key focus at ASM and an integral part of student learning. Our elementary school integrates ipads to prepare students for the 1:1 laptop program that begins in Grade 6. The school also offers 3D design, robotics, digital art and photography and film courses in our ultramodern film studio. There is wifi campus wide.

Set in 9 acres of green space, our modern campus boasts many state-of-the-art science laboratories, two full-sized American gymnasia, a tennis courts, a grass soccer field, and a 27,000 volume library complete with e-books, not to mention a 500-seat auditorium constructed in 2019.

Currently school enrollment is over 800 students and there are more than 100 full-time faculty employed. ASM teachers are talented, highly educated, experienced and, above all, inspiring leaders. The school encourages faculty continued learning through a substantial professional growth fund.

ASM was authorized to offer the International Baccalaureate Diploma in 1983. Students are also awarded the American School High School Diploma upon graduation. ASM student IB results have consistently surpassed world averages in terms of pass rate and average points.

AMERICAN
SCHOOL
OF PARIS

founded 1946

Head of School
Ms. Jane Thompson

DP coordinator
Alyssa Pierce

Status Private

Boarding/day Day

Gender Coeducational

Language of instruction
English

Authorised IB programmes
DP

Age Range 3 – 18 years

Number of pupils enrolled
800

Fees
K3 €19,000
K4 €25,590
K5–Grade 5 €30,400
Grades 6–8 €34,945
Grades 9–12 €35,150

Address
41 rue Pasteur
92210 Saint-Cloud | **FRANCE**

TEL +33 01 41 12 86 55

Email
admissions@asparis.fr

Website
www.asparis.org

The American School of Paris, established in 1946, is a coeducational, independent day school for students from ages 3–18. Home to a vibrant community of over 750 students representing over 65 countries, ASP students achieve their personal and academic best with innovative and internationally-recognized programs for learners of all ages.

ASP is accredited by the Council of International Schools and the Middle States Association of Colleges and Schools. Students learn an American curriculum (including IB and AP options) with a high priority on real-world, experience-based learning. While classes are delivered in English, all students in Grades K3–12 receive daily language instruction in French for beginners through Francophone students.

Students in Grades K3–1 participate in a play-based, Outdoor Learning program both on and off campus in the neighboring Parc de Saint-Cloud. All students use our dedicated science and technology spaces, with older children taking on independent projects in the Lower School Maker Space, and the Middle/Upper School Tech Shops, including application development, design, 3D printing, and coding projects.

Students flourish artistically at ASP, and can take advantage of a theater-style Performing Arts Center, a Black Box theater, and studio spaces for music recording, production, and film. ASP offers full band, orchestra, and choir options as both curricular and extra-curricular classes. After-school sports are offered from Grades K4–12, with an American varsity and junior varsity athletics program (part of the International School Sports Tournament consortium), available to students in Grades 9–12. From athletics and the arts to robotics and STEM, ASP students regularly compete at the international level.

The Upper School is the academic home of 350 students who are guided by a team of college counselors and academic advisors as they select from 30 IB courses, 12+ AP classes, and American high school courses. 90% of Upper School students participate in either the AP or IB program; 30% of students are candidates for the IB diploma each year, with over 40% of these students qualifying for the IB Bilingual Diploma.

In 2021, ASP students scored an average of 4 points higher on the IB exams than world averages, with 38% of ASP students scoring above 40 points. ASP students scored an average of .7 points higher on AP exams, and 87% earned above a 3 on their exams, with 34% of ASP students earning at least one 5 (perfect score). Students go on to attend prestigious universities across the USA, Canada, the UK, Europe, and Asia.

American School of The Hague

American School
of The Hague

(Founded 1953)

Director
J. Courtney Lowe , Ed.D.

DP coordinator
Mike Flaim

Status Private

Boarding/day Day

Gender Coeducational

Language of instruction
English

Authorised IB programmes
DP

Age Range 3 – 18 years

Number of pupils enrolled
1120

Fees
€14,695 – €22,960

Main Campus
Rijksstraatweg 200
2241 BX Wassenaar |
NETHERLANDS

ECC Campus
Deijlerweg 153, 2241 AE
Wassenaar | **NETHERLANDS**

Deylerhoeve Campus
175-177 Deijlerweg, 2241 AE
Wassenaar | **NETHERLANDS**

TEL +31 70 512 1060

Email admissions@ash.nl

Website www.ash.nl

ASH (est.1953) is one of the most established international schools in the Netherlands. ASH families hail from more than 70 countries on 6 continents, mirroring the diversity of cultures that make The Hague, known as the City of Peace and Justice, such a rich environment.

We are a private, not-for-profit institution that, at every level of organization, focuses on enhancing the student learning experience. It shows in the purpose-built ASH facilities, like our Early Childhood Center, a vibrant and joyous learning environment designed to harness inquiry and play.

From Pre-Kindergarten through High School graduation, we encourage ASH students to take control of their own learning. We know that our students will be working in jobs that may not even exist yet, so we aim to nurture confidence and agility in any stage of the learning journey here at ASH.

ASH is the only school in the Netherlands offering both AP and IB, creating a pathway to graduation based on their individual passions and talents. Our students consistently outperform global averages, and supported by our dedicated College Counseling Office, they find their ways into esteemed institutions of higher education across the globe. Our graduated Class of 2021 received offers from top colleges around the world.

Only at ASH, you will find a full-inclusion program of learning support, supporting every student with great intentionality to meet their emotional, social, physical, and academic needs.

American School of The Hague is accredited by the rigorous and independent New England Association of Schools and Colleges (NEASC).

What ASH students and faculty say:
"Being a critical thinker means to use your thinking process and be aware of the different aspects that make you think a certain way. And then apply that thinking process in a real-life situation, and ask yourself questions about what's happening in the world."
– Lucille, student

"I chose to take the IB curriculum because it offers me many opportunities, which is important to me. I know that I want to pursue a career in Technology, but if I change my mind, I believe the curriculum will help me recognize my talents."
– Vaibhav, student

"Our programs open up doors to universities around the world. Our role as counselors is to help students find the best fit and the best options for themselves. At ASH, this means in-depth course selection. We're here to guide students in making these decisions."
– Ms. Elizabeth, Counselor

Follow the ASH experience on @ AmericanSchoolOfTheHague to read more.

Anglo European School

(Founded 1973)	**Authorised IB programmes** DP, CP
Headteachers Mrs Jody Gee	**Age Range** 11 – 18 years
Director of Sixth Form Mr Stuart Newton	**Number of pupils enrolled** 1465
DP coordinator Mrs Susannah Porsz	**Address** Willow Green Ingatestone Essex **CM4 0DJ | UK**
CP coordinator Mr Ben Knights	
Status State	**TEL** 01277 354018
Boarding/day Day	**Email** admissions@aesessex.co.uk
Gender Coeducational	**Website** www.aesessex.co.uk
Language of instruction English	

The Anglo European School is a genuinely distinctive and unique comprehensive school committed, for almost 50 years, to achieving the highest academic success through its internationalist curriculum. The broad and balanced education, with its challenging additional experiences, produces open-minded and confident young people who are able to communicate effectively in a variety of languages and who have an appreciation and understanding of different cultures, religions and communities in modern Britain and beyond.

The Sixth Form is outstanding and has been awarded the highest Ofsted grades for over 20 years. In 1977 Anglo European School was the first UK state school to offer the International Baccalaureate Diploma and in 2010 became the first UK state school to offer the IB Career Programme. It also provides the opportunity to study A Levels, or A Levels with selected parts of the IB Diploma. All students have the opportunity to study a language ranging from introductory level, which assumes no prior knowledge, up to more advanced courses in the A Level and IB Diploma Routes. Eight languages are taught: Arabic, French, German, Italian, Japanese, Mandarin, Russian and Spanish. We believe that this gives an unrivalled opportunity for each student to combine qualifications in a way which best suits their

needs and makes them stand out in the global employment marketplace.

Situated in Ingatestone, with excellent rail and road connections, local children are joined by children from Essex, Suffolk, Hertfordshire, London and abroad who value its internationalist philosophy based on the mission of the International Baccalaureate. This diversity provides a rich education which prepares succeeding generations of students for the world they will live and work in, whatever their background or ability. It really is an education fit for the 21st Century.

A remarkable feature of the school is its visits and exchanges programme. Over 700 students every year take part in the exchange programmes and extended study visits in Europe, China and Japan. Sixth Form students also have the opportunity to undertake international work experience in Madrid, Frankfurt and Paris, visit the United Nations in Geneva and to do voluntary community work in Lesotho.

This is a caring, principled but purposeful school which is confident in its ambition and passionate about its mission. It is a school which is determined to ensure that an education with an international dimension is compatible with high academic success and outstanding personal development for all its students whatever their background or ability.

Asamiah International School

ASAMIAH
International
School

مــدرسة
السّـــامية
الـــدولية

(Founded 2010)

Principal
Ms. Janette Wakileh

PYP coordinator
Ms. Nour Maroun

MYP coordinator
Ms. Sima Barhoosh

DP coordinator
Ms. Yasmine Haddadin

Status Private

Boarding/day Day

Gender Coeducational

Language of instruction
English, Arabic

Authorised IB programmes
PYP, MYP, DP

Age Range 3 – 18 years

Number of pupils enrolled
725

Address
Khalda, Taqi al-Din al-Subki
Amman | **JORDAN**

TEL +962 6 5335 301

Email
info@ais.edu.jo

Website
www.ais.edu.jo

Asamiah International School (AIS) is an IB; co-educational, bilingual school offering KG children and Grades 1-5 IB PYP Curriculum, IB MYP for Grades 6-10 as well as the IB DP for grades 11 and 12. The school is easily accessible to parents and visitors with state-of-the-art facilities. We emulate comfortably and proudly alongside the best IB schools in the country; this is reflected on our students' outstanding characteristics and remarkable results. We are also proud of our alumni who receive prompt acceptance at the best universities worldwide.

AIS aims to develop inquiring, self-confident, independent, productive, respectful and caring lifelong learners who seek to make their societies a better place and who are willing to transfer their knowledge to community service and social development.

At AIS, we aim to provide every learner with the finest education possible through vibrant and engaging teaching approaches that are deeply stemmed from the IB pedagogy and practices. Our learners are thus enabled and challenged to become independent learners who acquire their personal knowledge through the five approaches to learning (ATL skills): Communication, social, thinking, self-management and research skills. Hence, our school is equipped with various facilities that help students enjoy and learn the necessary skills.

The after-school activities are designed to complement the school programs and provide students with an opportunity to acquire extra-curricular skills. They include a wide variety of choices such as athletics, basketball, football, mixed martial arts, photography, robotics, gaming, design, drama and dance classes, arts, individual & group music instrument lessons, languages in addition to our yearly enriching summer camps.

At AIS, we prepare children for the real world. We make our learners ready to meet the future with confidence and to contribute positively to their local and global society. Our educators work hard to ensure that the best possible quality of education is at the service of our dear learners.

AIS is authorized to offer the three IB Programmes; PYP, MYP and DP. These programmes support a smooth continuum of learning and have enriched our conceptual-based curricula and our teaching and learning approaches, making the learning process globally – oriented and linked to real life. We teach in compliance with the 21st century demands, and what is more essential is that we instill cultural diversity and international-mindedness in our students' mindset in order for them to learn how to embrace differences.

To put a closure to the IB journey, our DP students are encouraged to leave a tangible impact in their community by serving and taking actions to create novel solutions to apparent local conflicts through their DP/CAS projects which are set to align with the UN 17 sustainable development goals (SDGs) to benchmark a better society; a better world.

Ashcroft

Head of School Mr Douglas Mitchell	**Address** 100 West Hill London
DP coordinator Joseph Anson	**SW15 2UT | UK** **TEL** +44 (0)208 877 0357
Status State	**Email** joseph.anson@
Boarding/day Day	ashcroftacademy.org.uk
Gender Coeducational	**Website**
Language of instruction English	www.atacademy.org.uk

Authorised IB programmes
DP

Age Range 11 – 18 years

Number of pupils enrolled
1373

Ethos

The Sixth Form at Ashcroft Technology Academy is an exceptional place to learn. Students and staff have worked together to create a culture of aspiration and success. Our students enjoy their time at the Sixth Form and are given superb support and guidance, which combined with excellent teaching, enables our students to excel.

Academic

Students leave our sixth form articulate, confident, accomplished and ambitious young adults who understand the importance of rigour and high standards. Underpinning our proven track record of success is a team of highly motivated, hard working and qualified staff who have an unreserved belief in the ability and potential of young people to succeed. Our IB results are outstanding: in 2021 our average points score was 40.9 and the average grade per subject was 6.4. Each year, a number of students achieve over 40 points, allowing them to accept places at the very best universities such as Oxford, Cambridge, Imperial and Princeton.

Outside the Classroom

The extracurricular provision at the Academy is virtually unrivalled. Every member of staff at the Academy runs a club or society, providing our students with a wealth of enrichment opportunities. Advanced Collective Orchestra, Debating Society and Model UN have been particularly popular with IB students. Students attend a range of workshops, lectures and conferences both within and outside of school. The Academy offers a range of leadership opportunities, from House Captains to the Head Student Team. Furthermore, students who display a particular passion for a subject may also apply for our scholarship, receiving up to £500 to put towards an opportunity to develop in that field. Examples include pre-med courses or university summer schools.

Location and Facilities

Ashcroft Technology Academy has a superb location in South West London. Waterloo station is just 15 minutes away by train and we are located adjacent to the A3 and East Putney underground station. Facilities are exceptional; our purpose built Sixth Form Centre has a university style study area, classrooms designed for Sixth Formers and a Sixth Form exclusive annex to our main school library. Additional to our excellent existing resources, the Academy boast 10 state-of-the-art science laboratories, a sixth form Art Studio and two professional quality fitness suites.

Bavarian International School

(Founded 1991)

Head of School
Dr. Chrissie Sorenson

PYP coordinator
Nicola Moloney & Annette Austin

MYP coordinator Dr. Erin Foley

DP coordinator Loay Malek

CP coordinator Rob Clements

Status Private

Boarding/day Day

Gender Coeducational

Language of instruction English

Authorised IB programmes
PYP, MYP, DP, CP

Age Range 3 – 18 years

Number of pupils enrolled
1150

Fees Day: from €14,770

Haimhausen Campus
Hauptstrasse 1, 85778
Haimhausen, Bavaria | **GERMANY**

City Campus
Leopoldstrasse 208, 80804
Munich, Bavaria | **GERMANY**

TEL +49 (0)81 33 917 203

Email
admissions@bis-school.com

Website www.bis-school.com

Changemakers for a new tomorrow

The Bavarian International School (BIS) is a community of over 1,150 learners and 170 education leaders, working together to bring out the best in young people from over 60 nations, all within a caring and international environment. BIS students are supported to become global citizens with outstanding language and communication skills, an intercultural mindset, and a deep understanding of digital technology and modern collaboration.

BIS is an International Baccalaureate (IB) World School, spanning two campuses in Munich-Schwabing and Haimhausen, where talented, globally-focused educators care for students ages three to 18. BIS is a private, non-profit, all-day school which ranks among the best international schools in Germany and in Europe (IB Diploma score average at BIS in 2021: 37 points, world average score is 33). English is the language of instruction at both campuses, with 21 other languages offered.

A caring, international community

About 75% of BIS students come from international families, with the other 25% of students coming from local Munich families. One of the school's strengths is its connected, intercultural community which is continuously developing through a spirit of caring and inclusion.

"The children and young people are just happy at BIS. This positive spirit immediately inspires new families and every visitor," says Dr. Chrissie Sorenson, Head of School at BIS.

The caring culture at BIS is further defined by additional guidance for students at every turn: language and learning support, mentors, school counsellors, and university and career counsellors. Students are encouraged to develop themselves outside of the classroom as well, by taking part in one of 80 after school activities. These include drama, music, engineering, multimedia, athletics, as well as some signature programmes, such as the Model United Nations, the Duke of Edinburgh International Award, and the Eco School project.

Digital pioneers

Educational technology has been an integral component of the learning philosophy at BIS for nearly 20 years. Every child from grade 4 onwards is provided a BIS iPad, and every student from grade 7 onwards is provided with a BIS MacBook. The combination of digitally-savvy teachers, IT team and helpdesk team underlines BIS as a digital pioneer. In the context of the COVID-19 pandemic, the knowledge and technological advantage at BIS enabled the school to switch smoothly from in-person instruction to distance and hybrid teaching, without missing a day of lessons.

The school of the future – today

In 2021, BIS celebrated its 30th anniversary. The next chapter will include the funding and building of the new Creativity & Innovation Centre (CIC). Building on the foundation of its 30-year tradition, BIS is actively shaping the future of learning with plans for this new heart of the Haimhausen campus. This building will offer open, flexible and interdisciplinary learning spaces for around 750 students. The pedagogical design focus of the space will be "STEAM" (Science, Technology, Engineering, Arts, and Maths). The new 25 million euro innovation center underscores BIS's claim to be the school of the future – today.

(Founded 1972)	**Age Range** 2.5 – 18 years
School Director Pascale Hertay	**Number of pupils enrolled** 250
Finance & Administration Director Charlotte Van Brussel	**Fees** Please see website
Head of IB Programmes Andrew Mitchell	**Address** Avenue Franklin Roosevelt 21-23 Ixelles 1050 Brussels | **BELGIUM**
Status Private	
Boarding/day Day	**TEL** +32 2 648 43 11
Gender Coeducational	**Email** admissions@beps.com
Language of instruction English	**Website** www.beps.com
Authorised IB programmes MYP	

Established in 1972, BEPS International School is situated in beautiful buildings in the heart of one of Brussels' most desirable areas, close to the Bois de la Cambre and the University (ULB).

The school offers an inquiry-based learning approach through the International Early Years Curriculum, the International Primary Curriculum, the Middle Years Programme from the International Baccalaureate® (IB) and by implementing the IB Diploma Programme and the IB Career Related Programme.

The autumn of 2022 promises to be a turning point for BEPS International School. The Secondary School students will move into a new building, the newly acquired property adjoining the primary school. This will allow the growing BEPS Secondary School to join the Early Years & Primary School at the same location where the BEPS adventure started in 1972. The transformation of the new building will give BEPS the opportunity to design spaces for innovative, authentic, and engaging learning which matches the BEPS approach to learning in the Middle and High School.

With the growth of the Secondary school, BEPS will cater for children between 2.5 – 18 years old. The school aims to achieve its full capacity of 450 students in the coming years.

Children learning English and children with learning needs receive additional support. French is taught as a second language from the Early Years and the development of the children's Mother Tongue is encouraged. They benefit from PE and swimming, Music and ICT lessons all of which are taught by experienced specialist teachers.

A wide range of After school clubs are available as well as a Garderie and holiday clubs. A door-to-door bus service also runs for most areas in Brussels.

INSPIR✷TIONAL
Box Hill School

(Founded 1959)	**Fees**
Headmaster Cory Lowde	Day: £20,820
	Flexi Boarding: £25,470 – £27,570
DP coordinator Julian Baker	Weekly Boarding: £30,480
	Full Boarding: £37,545
Status Private	International Study Centre
	Boarding: £39,000
Boarding/day Mixed	
	Address
Gender Coeducational	London Road, Mickleham
Language of instruction	Dorking, Surrey
English	**RH5 6EA	UK**
Authorised IB programmes	**TEL** 01372 373382
DP	**Email**
Age Range 11 – 18 years	registrar@BoxHillSchool.com
Number of pupils enrolled 425	**Website** www.boxhillschool.com

Box Hill School is a co-educational day, flexi, weekly and full boarding school for girls and boys aged 11-18. We are a founding member of Round Square, a global network of schools that share a passion for learning through experience and character education, basing its educational philosophy on the teachings of educationalist Kurt Hahn. We follow this philosphy and its IDEALS of Internationalism, Democracy, Environmentalism, Adventure, Leadership and Service underpin our school ethos and values.

The school is located just 40 minutes from central London, in the heart of the beautiful Surrey Hills. Easily accessible and just 30 minutes from Heathrow Airport and 25 minutes from Gatwick Airport.

Academic – The Curriculum

Our focus is on achieving the best academic outcome for each student and ensuring each student fulfils their full potential. They are encouraged, nurtured and challenged in all that they do. It is important to us that we produce well-rounded, resilient and confident young people, who achieve academic success.

The school offers a dedicated Lower School for Years 7, 8 and 9 which follows the National Curriculum but broadens its scope to guarantee that courses are constructed to suit the abilities and interests of our students. In the Middle School we provide a wide range of GCSEs and (I)GCSEs and in the Sixth Form we offer our students the choice of the International Baccalaureate Diploma Programme (IBDP) or A Levels.

In our International Study Centre we offer overseas students the one year Pre-IB Diploma course (intensive) and a 2 week Summer Pre-School English course.

Co-Curricular

At Box Hill School, we provide our pupils with a wide range of co-curricular options to develop their interests and gain life skills.

All students participate in our activities programme, consisting of over 60 options, timetabled during the school day three afternoons a week. These range from team sports with weekly fixtures, through to high ropes, chess, debating clubs, robotics, Green Team and drama club.

The school is also actively involved in the Duke of Edinburgh's Award Scheme which runs in parallel to our programme of expeditions, all designed to encourage outdoor education.

As a Round Square school there are also opportunities for pupils to participate in global and regional conferences, exchange programmes and overseas community service projects.

Boarding

The Independent School's Inspectorate report, 2019 stated *"They (the students) enjoy school and thrive in the nurturing and supportive environment provided by the excellent pastoral care system and family atmosphere in boarding and day houses."*

Boarding life is structured around 6 boarding houses, where pupils are placed according to age and gender, with a mix of nationalities and cultures. They benefit from a diverse and varied activities programme, including weekly weekend trips all designed to develop interests, maximise the use of campus facilities and spend time with friends in a home-from-home environment.

Bradfield College

BRADFIELD COLLEGE

(Founded 1850)

Headmaster
Dr Christopher Stevens

DP coordinator
Colin Irvine

Status Private

Boarding/day Mixed

Gender Coeducational

Language of instruction
English

Authorised IB programmes
DP

Age Range 13 – 18 years

Number of pupils enrolled 820

Fees
Day: £32,280
Boarding: £40,350

Address
Bradfield
Berkshire
RG7 6AU | UK

TEL 0118 964 4516

Email admissions@
bradfieldcollege.org.uk

Website
www.bradfieldcollege.org.uk

Set in the village of Bradfield amidst unspoilt Berkshire countryside, Bradfield College enjoys a well-established reputation for being one of the country's leading co-educational, independent schools through its provision of academic excellence and a well-rounded education.

The College welcomes pupils from Britain and overseas and provides challenge and choice for all. We offer a personalised programme of study that is inspired by expert, passionate and engaging teaching and focuses on providing an education for life. We are acutely aware of the global community in which pupils will live and work when they leave the security and dynamism of Bradfield.

The Bradfield Sixth Form aims to provide an outstanding all-round education to prepare young people for success in a rapidly changing world. We care about the individual and pride ourselves in the warmth of a community in which young people feel happy and valued. We aim to foster an environment of high expectations in which all our students are encouraged to believe in themselves, to be inquisitive, to be resilient and to show ambition both within and beyond the classroom.

The IB Diploma Programme focuses on the education of the whole person whilst also seeking to provide an international perspective. This is very much in line with Bradfield's own education for life ethos and values. The IBDP emphasises the importance of Language, Science and Mathematics, as well as the Arts and Individuals and Societies. At the core of the curriculum model, Theory of Knowledge, Creativity, Activity and Service and Approaches to Teaching and Learning, both inside and outside of the classroom are all elements that Bradfield views as essential to an all-round education. We offer an unrivalled sports and co-curricular programme for all our pupils which ensures that every individual has the opportunity to develop valuable skills, wherever their interests lie. The need to complete the Extended Essay sits perfectly with Bradfield's drive towards creating independently-minded and curious young men and women by the end of the Sixth Form. In short, the IB Diploma and Bradfield fit perfectly together.

DP coordinator
Michael Harvey

Status Private

Boarding/day Day

Gender Coeducational

Language of instruction
English

Authorised IB programmes
DP

Address
Calle Salvia, Nº 48
28109 Alcobendas, Madrid |
SPAIN

TEL +34 91 650 43 00

Email
michael@colegiobrains.com

Website
www.colegiobrains.com

Brains International Schools is an educational project dedicated to teaching children how to develop their own physical and mental well-being and to become life-long learners. Four decades after its founding, Brains Schools has earned a reputation for being at the forefront of innovation in bilingual education and social-emotional learning. Living in today's complex and interconnected global village requires that educational methods develop the whole child and instill in each child a growth mindset to face the future with confidence and competence. Brains Schools has risen to this challenge.

Brains International School La Moraleja is located in the pleasant northern suburbs of Madrid, and well connected by the public bus and underground services. The school prides itself on its superb facilities for both educational and sporting excellence, whilst enjoying a modern and relaxed atmosphere within the school community.

Whilst the school is recognised as bilingual by the Spanish education curriculum, students on the Diploma programme are often from overseas and able to follow an entirely English curriculum, and with the option of Spanish B at both standard and high levels.

Students are able to specialise and diversify between subject groups, as subjects are offered at both SL and HL in either English or Spanish, and cover a large range of options in each subject group. We pride ourselves on innovation in education, and are constantly developing our programme to fit the needs of the student community. Recently we have added Self-taught Language A, Sports Exercise and Health Science, and Design and Technology to our list of options.

The success in the Diploma programme since first examinations in 2013 has set the path for a whole school IB community. Furthermore, Brains International school has developed programmes in La Moraleja for both PYP and MYP under the Spanish national curriculum, with full immersion of the programmes in their second years. We are also very proud of our Maria Lombillo site in the heart of Madrid, which received authorisation for the Diploma programme last year, opening a magnificent new wing entirely devoted to Diploma students (see Brains International School Maria Lombillo for more info).

Bromsgrove School

(Founded 1553)

Headmaster
Peter Clague

DP coordinator
Michael Thompson

Status Private

Boarding/day Mixed

Gender Coeducational

Language of instruction
English

Authorised IB programmes
DP

Age Range 13 – 18 years

Number of pupils enrolled
1300

Fees
Day: £17,940
Weekly Boarding: £26,610
Boarding: £40,155

Address
Worcester Road
Bromsgrove
Worcestershire
B61 7DU | UK

TEL +44 (0)1527 579679

Email
admissions@bromsgrove-school.co.uk

Website
www.bromsgrove-school.co.uk

FLAIR, DISCIPLINE, ACADEMIC RIGOUR

Set in 100 acres of beautiful parkland, Bromsgrove School caters for 1300 pupils with over 400 pupils in the hugely popular sixth form. Main intake is at ages 7, 11, 13 and 16, with international pupils joining at any of these stages.

Bromsgrove takes girls and boys between the ages of 7 and 18 in the hope of nurturing compassionate people who change the world for the better. International Baccalaureate and A level results place Bromsgrove in the first division. These impressive results combined with a massive sporting and extra-curricular programme means that at Bromsgrove breadth and quality are not mutually exclusive.

Life at Bromsgrove is dynamic. Great boarding schools offer pupils a home, not a place to sleep after work. People, not systems, must come first. The houses are different, as boarding houses in the best schools should be, but there are core values and structures shared by all. Houseparents are resident in the boarding houses with their own families. They are academic staff and are supported by a housemother. Bromsgrove boarders see family life going on around them. Each house has a dedicated tutor team, doing day and evening duties on a rota basis. Support, encouragement and trust are the watchwords.

A mix of over 50 different nationalities makes Bromsgrove vibrant. Bromsgrove School has an active International Students Department with full-time teachers who provide pastoral and academic support, specialising in the particular needs of the international pupils in the school. The department focuses lessons on the development of English language skills. International pupils are prepared for internationally recognised tests of English as an Additional Language. Bromsgrove results are outstanding: the IB Diploma average score was 40.2 in 2021.

Bromsgrove offers a unique weekend programme, covering a huge range of timetabled options from exclusively academic sessions to school trips. All staff work Saturday and the Sunday boarders' programme is extensive.

Admission for international students is by entrance test and, where possible, interview. Prospective students and their families are encouraged to visit. The Admissions Director has an extensive programme of international visits each year and will always try to meet prospective pupils in their own countries when she visits.

Bryanston School

BRYANSTON

(Founded 1928)

Acting Head
Richard Jones

DP coordinator
Jo Strange

CP coordinator
Rose Ings

Status Private

Boarding/day Mixed

Gender Coeducational

Language of instruction
English

Authorised IB programmes
DP, CP

Age Range 3 – 18 years

Number of pupils enrolled
806

Fees
Day: £33,525
Boarding: £40,890

Address
Blandford Forum
Dorset
DT11 0PX | UK

TEL 01258 484633

Email
admissions@bryanston.co.uk

Website
www.bryanston.co.uk

Bryanston is different from other independent schools. Inspired by 90 years of innovative practice, our approach to education and our distinctive culture nurtures purposeful, curious and well-rounded individuals.

At the heart of Bryanston's approach is our distinctive method of education, the Bryanston Method. It has been the keystone of the School's philosophy since our foundation in 1928, tailored to the needs and interests of each pupil. There is no Bryanston 'type' – we want our pupils to think for themselves.

Alongside high academic standards and expectations, we provide an emotionally and intellectually supportive environment, allowing pupils to develop independent, creative, and unbounded thinking. We encourage innovation and creativity in all areas of the curriculum, believing that imagination, perspective, and boldness are applicable in all subjects.

Pastoral care sits at the centre of everything we do and integrates with the academic through our one-to-one tutorial system. Each pupil is carefully matched to their tutor and the relationship lasts for the duration of their time at Bryanston. The tutor guides each pupil in becoming responsible for their own learning and discusses their wellbeing and progress at the weekly tutorial.

This ethos is reflected in the principles of the IB, making it a natural fit at Bryanston where we offer both the IB Diploma Programme and the IB Career-Related Diploma. In 2021, our seventh cohort of IB Diploma pupils achieved an average score of 38 points.

Entrance procedures for our IB courses require candidates to sit both an English and a maths test, have an interview with the Headmaster and meet Heads of Departments. Candidates unable to attend our Test and Interview Day can sit their papers at a suitable venue overseas and have a Skype interview with the Headmaster. Successful candidates are invited to an induction week in July to explore their chosen subjects before confirming their academic programme. This gives candidates the chance to familiarise themselves with the School, make friends and get to know their tutor. You can also attend an Information Afternoon, held in the autumn before you would be due to join us.

Outside the curriculum there is a fulfilling academic enrichment programme, as well as over 100 extra-curricular activities ranging from beekeeping and music production to eSports and filmmaking. As a full-time boarding school, weekends are an integral part of life at Bryanston, with the chance to participate in a range of sports fixtures, outdoor activities and rehearsals.

Casvi International American School

CEO of Casvi Group
Mr. Juan Luis Yagüe

PYP coordinator Ryan Posey

MYP coordinator
Laura Kelly McCutcheon

DP coordinator
Ana isabel Domínguez Sánchez

Status Private

Boarding/day Mixed

Gender Coeducational

Language of instruction
English, Spanish

Authorised IB programmes
PYP, MYP, DP

Age Range 3 – 18 years

Number of pupils enrolled
300

Fees
Nursery – Pre-K & Kindergarten
€550 – €609 per month
Grades 1-12 €738 – €879 per month
IB Diploma Program Supplement
€185 per month
Boarding School €1,324 per month

Address
C/ Gavilán, 2, Tres Cantos
28760 Madrid | **SPAIN**

TEL +34 91 804 02 12

Email info@casvitrescantos.es

Website
www.casvitrescantos.es

Casvi Schools Group was created in 1985, when Mr. Juan Yagiie Sevillano – who had spent 20 years working in education – founded the first Eurocolegio Casvi in Villaviciosa de Odón. From its beginnings with just one classroom per grade, it is grown into a large international private school with almost 1,300 students and 120 teachers.

Established in 2017, Casvi International American School is a private, international, American and co-ed school, located in the north of Madrid, and based on the American school system whose mission is to educate and create citizens of the world.

At Casvi International American School we are constantly adapting ourselves to society's new needs and requirements, and we educate our students for a successful personal and professional future. That is why we have a deep and ongoing commitment to innovation, both in terms of leveraging new technologies to help to learn and to introduce new teaching methods.

A fundamental pillar of our school is the implementation of the three International Baccalaureate (IB) study programmes at all teaching levels: the PYP (Primary Years Programme), MYP (Middle Years Programme), and DP (Diploma Programme). Casvi International American School is an authorized school for the three IB programmes mentioned above.

The International Baccalaureate methodology uses a skills-based, constructivist methodological framework designed to educate students to be inquirers, knowledgeable, thinkers, communicators, principled, open-minded, caring, risk-takers, balanced, and reflective.

In addition, international-mindedness, language acquisition and encouraging students' talents have been the foundation of this education system for more than three decades.

Young people from all over the world live and learn at Casvi International American Boarding School, where they develop deep friendships that last forever. Our main mission is to make our students grow personally and intellectually to achieve a real advantage in university, in the world of work, or in any real-life situation through the detection and development of talent, with an entrepreneurial spirit and an ethical commitment to our society.

Cultural exchange, recognition of diversity, acceptance and mutual respect make up our philosophy. Life at Casvi International American Boarding School is a life-changing experience. In our 250 sq. m. facilities, students not only find out about their interests, but also develop their talents.

Life in the residence offers a wide variety of fun and interesting activities. Being a resident student at Casvi International American Boarding School is fun and educational… it's like having a big family!

CATS Canterbury

(Founded 1952)

Principal
Severine Collins

DP coordinator
Nicola Robinson

Status Private

Boarding/day Mixed

Gender Coeducational

Language of instruction
English

Authorised IB programmes
DP

Age Range 14 – 21 years

Number of pupils enrolled 450

Fees
Day: £17,370 – £27,990
Boarding: £13,230 – £19,140

Address
68 New Dover Road
Canterbury
Kent
CT1 3LQ | UK

TEL +44 (0)1227866540

Email
registrar@catscanterbury.com
nrobinson@catscanterbury.com

Website
catsglobalschools.com/our-
schools/cats-canterbury

CATS Canterbury Our Mission: We encourage and enable all of our students to realise their potential, fostering independence and maturity in order to prepare them for their future as Global Citizens.

Why study at CATS Canterbury
You will be able to study alongside students from over 50 countries on the IBDP and on other courses (A-level, University Foundation, PRE and IGCSE programmes).

Who is the International Baccalaureate Diploma Programme for?
Students wishing to experience an inspiring education with classmates from around the world. This is a qualification that challenges, encourages and inspires students to become caring, critical thinkers; ready for university study and globally-focused careers.

What will you achieve?
You will:
- Be able to progress to an international university;
- Possess desirable study skills, such as critical thinking, independent research and real-world context;
- Gain life skills, such as independence, confidence, good communication and international mindedness – all essential for caniversity and your future career.

Key features of the IBDP:
- Study six subjects – Language and Literature, Language Acquisition, Individuals and Societies, Experimental Sciences, Mathematics and the Arts;

- The Theory of Knowledge asks you to reflect on the nature of knowledge and on how we know what we claim to know (epistemology). It is assessed through an oral presentation and a 1,600-word essay;
- An Extended Essay prepares you for the study skills required at university;
- Creativity, Activity, Service comprises Arts and other experiences that involve creative thinking; physical exertion contributing to a healthy lifestyle, which improves and complements your academic studies; and an unpaid and voluntary exchange that has a learning benefit;
- Additionally, throughout your course, you will be supported by career counselling via our Key Professions Programme and academic-skills workshops.

Our success rate
In 2021 our International Baccalaureate students received brilliant exam results. Their average total diploma score was 37 compared with 33 as the average global diploma score. Top-scoring students achieved 42 points, while only 5.8% of students globally achieved 42 or above in 2020.

We are especially proud that 94% of grades achieved were 5-7, which brings us to a 100% success rate on the Diploma Programme for the fifth consecutive year. The global pass rate for 2021 was 89%.

Charterhouse

CHARTERHOUSE

(Founded 1611)	**Number of pupils enrolled** 895
Head Dr Alex Peterken	**Fees** Day Boarding £11,406 per term Boarding £13,802 per term
DP coordinator Mr Peter Price	**Address** Godalming
Status Private	Surrey
Boarding/day Mixed	**GU7 2DX ǀ UK**
Gender Coeducational	**TEL** +44 (0)1483 291501
Language of instruction English	**Email** admissions@ charterhouse.org.uk
Authorised IB programmes DP	**Website** www.charterhouse.org.uk

Motto: *Deo Dante Dedi*

Founded in 1611, Charterhouse is one of the UK's leading independent boarding schools, providing a first class education for boys and girls aged 13 to 18.

Campus

The School is set within an inspiring 250-acre campus, conveniently located close to London and within 50 minutes of Heathrow and Gatwick airports.

With 17 grass sports pitches, 3 full-sized Astroturf pitches, an athletics stadium, a sports centre, 24 tennis courts and a 9-hole golf course, not to mention beautiful lawns and gardens, the campus is one of the best, if not the best, in the country. Combined with a 235-seat theatre and separate music performance and art display spaces, the School's setting encourages pupils to contribute, and provides a safe community in which to explore and grow.

Academic

A Charterhouse education is all about choice for the individual with the breadth of options available to each pupil at every stage helping it to stand out from the rest. The curriculum is firmly rooted in academic rigour, combining the best of ancient and modern. Intellectual curiosity is piqued by the academic clubs and societies that proliferate during the afternoons and evenings. Pupils can benefit from the dual offer available in the Sixth Form at Charterhouse, as it is one of the few schools to offer the breadth of the internationally-renowned IB Diploma Programme, with its focus on cross-curricular collaborative learning and the acquisition of intellectual independence. The university destinations of leavers reflect both their abilities and the quality of the education provided at the School: Oxbridge, Ivy League,

Russell Group and the top European institutions all feature in abundance this year.

Co-curricular Activities

Co-curricular activities are an essential element of a Charterhouse education. They combine opportunities for leadership development, creativity, exercise and team work. They are also great fun. With more than 80 different sports and activities, including music, drama and other creative opportunities, all pupils are encouraged to develop existing interests to exciting levels and to take up new ones. All pupils have the opportunity to enjoy themselves across a wide range of sports and creative arts, making use of the School's impressive facilities.

Boarding

The House is the centre of every pupil's life, and the Houses offer a strong sense of identity and community. House spirit is encouraged by competitions in a wide variety of activities, from art to waterpolo, and House colours can be awarded for cultural and sporting achievements, as well as upholding the School's values.

The Heads of Houses and their families live in the Houses, and are supported by a team of pastoral staff and tutors. Each tutor has a small number of pupils with whom he or she meets at least once a week to provide the help and encouragement that enables every pupil to make the most of life at the School.

It is fair to say that every pupil at Charterhouse feels that their House is the best!

Admissions

Around 110 pupils join the Sixth Form each year. Admission is by competitive examination and interview. Boys and

girls should submit an application form by October of the year before entry, and will be assessed at Charterhouse in early November. Offers of places are made on 1 December.

For further information please contact the Admissions Department: admissions@charterhouse.org.uk.

brains/
INTERNATIONAL SCHOOLS

Director
Ms Cristina Miralles

PYP coordinator
Daniel Prieto

DP coordinator
Linda Keys

Status Private

Boarding/day Day

Gender Coeducational

Language of instruction
English, Spanish

Authorised IB programmes
PYP, DP

Age Range 6 – 18 years

Address
Calle Maria Lombillo 5
28027 Madrid | SPAIN

TEL +34 91 742 10 60

Email
plopez@colegiobrains.com

Website
www.colegiobrains.com/en/
private-school/maria-lombillo

Brains International School, María Lombillo is situated in the Arturo Soria area of Madrid. Not only are classes equipped with the latest educational technology, but María Lombillo also offers a cutting-edge sustainable building which uses bioclimatic architecture to save energy and protect the environment. This building provides a unique opportunity for our DP students to experience how their classes, such as Environmental Sciences, connect to practical solutions in the professional fields of architecture, engineering and education. In their CAS experience, Brains En Verde, the students themselves raise awareness in our community about the importance of the environment and how humans can take action locally to make the world a better place. Combining the study of academic subjects with hands-on opportunities to solve global problems is what sets María Lombillo apart.

In our María Lombillo center, we offer a fully international Diploma Programme for both native Spaniards and those baccalaureate students hailing from around the globe. We pride ourselves on our diverse range of subject-language combinations delivered by a team of multi-lingual teaching staff from all over the world. Diploma students choose the subjects they wish to study from six subject areas in the official IB languages, Spanish and English. In this way,

students study a truly bilingual curriculum. This approach enables students to select courses at the level (Standard or High Level) that suits their individual academic aims. At Brains (María Lombillo), students find that they can design their own study programme to take advantage of their individual strengths and cultural backgrounds, while challenging themselves to grow into well-rounded knowers who are prepared for the rigors of university programmes.

Brains María Lombillo is pursuing authorization as an IB World School. Our two-year Diploma Programme for Baccalaureate students has been authorized and our first cohort of Diploma students started in September 2020. We are currently considered candidates to implement the Middle Years Programme (MYP) and the Primary Years Programme (PYP). The Middle Years Programme (MYP) is now in its second year of implementation with students in the first and second year of ESO fully immersed in the programme. Students are embracing inquiry and concept-based learning and are motivated by making real life connections to their learning. We have been working on implementing the PYP for the last 5 years. The teaching and learning community is actively involved in the different phases of programme development; teachers and administration; students and families.

Colegio San Patricio

(Founded 1958)

Headmaster
Mr. Borja Díaz

DP coordinator
James Smith

Status Private

Boarding/day Day

Gender Coeducational

Language of instruction
English, Spanish

Authorised IB programmes
DP

Number of pupils enrolled
850

Address
Calle Jazmin 148
El Soto de la Moraleja
28109 Alcobendas, Madrid |
SPAIN

TEL +34 916 50 06 02

Email
infosoto@colegiosanpatricio.es

Website
www.colegiosanpatriciomadrid.
com/en

Colegio San Patricio is a coeducational day school which provides Spanish education and IB Diploma Programme for children from 18 months to 18 years old.

Trusted generation after generation since 1958, our curriculum embeds and continually innovates with proven pedagogical methodologies, in order to offer a unique and comprehensive educational model. In our three campuses in Madrid we nurture every child's individual passions and talents in order to ensure that they flourish.

• CSP schools are consistently ranked in Top 10 of the El Mundo "100 Best schools in Spain" guide.
• Colegio San Patricio, has been ranked in the Top 5 among the best 50 schools in Spain according to Forbes Magazine.

San Patricio was founded in 1958. Since then, we have had the honour of educating generations of students.

Going to school at Colegio San Patricio means that you are part of more than just a school. You become part of the SanPa Family.

IB at Colegio San Patricio:

Our El Soto campus enjoys an unbeatable location in Soto de La Moraleja. Here, secondary cycles are taught after which students can choose between National Baccalaureate or International Baccalaureate. The school offers facilities specifically designed and built for children between the ages of 12 and 18 years and has a capacity for more than 800 students.

IB at San Patricio is more than simply a qualification, the IB Diploma provides a distinctive educational experience. It allows students to study a wide range of subjects throughout their final 2 years at school, while giving them the freedom to choose which subjects to study in greater depth.

IB students follow the Creativity, Activity, Service (CAS) programme, prepare an Extended Essay and take the Theory of Knowledge course.

2021 graduates enjoyed outstanding IB results, achieving a fantastic average grade of 36, the highest in the school's history.

Our school has achieved a 100% pass rate. 26% of our IB Diploma students have achieved more than 40 points, 34% have achieved more than 38 points and 46% above 36 points. The highest grade achieved so far was a very impressive 44.

Thanks to their outstanding results our students have been accepted by some of the best Universities in the world such as Imperial, Bath, UCL in the UK, and Georgetown and University of California in the USA.

Colegio Virgen de Europa

Head of School
Enrique Maestu

PYP coordinator
Sarah O'Halloran

MYP coordinator
Carmen Mosquera Mariño

DP coordinator
María Cruz Larrosa

Status Private

Boarding/day Day

Gender Coeducational

Language of instruction
English, Spanish

Authorised IB programmes
PYP, MYP, DP

Address
C/ Valle de Santa Ana No. 1
Las Lomas
28669 Boadilla del Monte, Madrid
| SPAIN

TEL +34 91 633 0155

Email mc_larrosa@
colegiovirgendeeuropa.edu.es

Website
www.cve.edu.es

Colegio Virgen de Europa was founded in 1968, we have celebrated our 50th anniversary as one of the leading schools in Madrid.

Since then, CVE has been committed with a fulfilling learning experience that involves culture and nature, developing critical thinking and creativity as pillars of a well-rounded education connected with the surrounding environment.

Our IB Diploma Programme relates to the school philosophy where the IB students can develop not only academic performance but also a holistic approach to the world we live in. Our students are eager to find answers by themselves connecting, extending, and challenging their inquiry and critical thinking profile.

Building knowledge is beyond our classrooms, CVE motivates young minds through school trips, art exhibitions, theater plays and interesting lectures with the aim to inspire our students to find their passions.

CVE physical education is a key element in our educational values since the early years, our school offers a variety of different sports, performing in our facilities, CVE counts with gym, running track, tennis and paddle courtyard surrounded by a quiet and peaceful environment in Madrid suburbs. In our IB Diploma, students carry out a Wellness & Mindfulness program as well.

CVE offers the IB Bilingual Diploma Programme through nine different itineraries that encompass subjects from Sciences to Environmental Systems, Social Studies, Design & Technology, and Visual Arts; led by passionate teachers who guide students through this meaningful learning process with full commitment to the IB mission.

Enhancing and motivating our IB students to be the best version of themselves in the path they have chosen and hence, leave trail.

Beau Soleil
Collège Alpin International

(Founded 1910)

Headmaster
Stuart White

DP coordinator
Helen Taylor-Cevey

Status Private

Boarding/day Boarding

Gender Coeducational

Language of instruction
English, French

Authorised IB programmes
DP

Age Range 11 – 18 years

Address
Route du Village 1
1884 Villars-sur-Ollon
SWITZERLAND

TEL +41 24 496 26 26

Email
info@beausoleil.ch

Website
www.beausoleil.ch

At Beau Soleil, we believe it's what you do that counts:
Our educational philosophy encourages students to become responsible and ambitious world citizens through the challenging and inspirational range of activities offered each day both inside and outside of the classroom setting.

Founded in 1910, we welcome students from more than 55 different nationalities, a melting pot of cultures that supports the IB philosophy of internationalism and global mindset. With educational pathways in both English and French, at IB level, our students are able to pursue their studies in either language or a combination of the two.

Outstanding academic results are ensured by our passionate teaching staff, who inspire and support students to achieve to their highest potential. With a teacher to student ratio of 1 to 4 we are able to offer a personalised approach to learning and a diverse range of educational experiences. Our dedicated college counsellor and mentoring programme supports our graduates to enter many of the world's leading universities.

Exciting experiences both inside and outside of the classroom – from extended curriculum days, to educational trips across the world, full-school challenges and our winter ski programme – help our students to develop a greater understanding and appreciation of the world around them and to develop skills including team work, collaboration and resilience.

The spectacular school campus, located in a beautiful and safe alpine village, gives access to an enviable lifestyle. Blending tradition with modernity, the campus offers facilities of the highest quality and inspiring views across the Swiss Alps.

A full boarding school with a capacity of 280 students, our boarders experience the ideal balance of warmth, care and discipline, encouraging in them a sense of independence. Our home from home boarding philosophy promotes the creation of lifelong friendships based on a common set of values: responsibility, respect, ambition and determination.

COLLÈGE CHAMPITTET
FONDÉ EN 1903

(Founded 1903)

Head of School
Philippe de Korodi

DP coordinator
David Newsam

Status Private

Boarding/day Mixed

Gender Coeducational

Language of instruction
English, French

Authorised IB programmes
DP

Age Range 3 – 18 years

Number of pupils enrolled
600

Fees
Day: CHF10,500 – CHF33,800
Boarding: CHF68,600 –
CHF92,600

Address
Chemin de Champittet 1
1009 Pully VD | **SWITZERLAND**

TEL +41 21 721 05 05

Email
admissions@champittet.ch

Website
www.champittet.ch

The Swiss heritage

Collège Champittet is a world-renowned Swiss School with a long tradition of being "open to the world".

Founded in 1903, the school is embedded in the cultural and academic fabric of the city of Lausanne. With internationally recognised curricula and a strong sense of values rooted in its Catholic heritage, the school nurtures and inspires its students to achieve their best.

Located at the shores of beautiful Lake Geneva, students have the option to live at school and enjoy the camaraderie and activities that come with it.

Academics

As a bilingual French-English school, it welcomes students of all nationalities and backgrounds from ages 3 to 18.

Pre-IB and IB classes are kept small guaranteeing its students individual attention and care to help every child achieve their best while developing a lifelong love of learning.

Student support includes a dedicated Dean, experienced tutors and homeroom teachers. In 2021, Collège Champittet achieved a 100% exam pass rate and an IB average score of 33.6 points.

Beyond the classroom

As part of the Nord Anglia Education family, the school supports learning beyond the classroom. All its students benefit from educational programmes designed in collaboration with world leading organisations such as Massachusetts Institute of Technology (MIT), The Juilliard School performing arts conservatory of New York, and UNICEF.

Students can also take part in sports tournaments against students from all over the world and engage in humanitarian missions in Madagascar, Cambodia and Thailand supported by the Collège Champittet Foundation.

COLLÈGE DU LÉMAN
International School · Geneva

(Founded 1960)

Director General
Mrs Pauline Nord

DP coordinator
Jana Krainova Samuda

CP coordinator
Sheena Tandy

Status Private

Boarding/day Mixed

Gender Coeducational

Language of instruction
English, French

Authorised IB programmes
DP, CP

Age Range 2 – 18 years

Fees
Day: CHF22,700 – CHF35,900
Boarding: CHF83,000 –
CHF94,400

Address
74, route de Sauverny
1290 Versoix GE | **SWITZERLAND**

TEL +41 22 775 56 56

Email
admissions@cdl.ch

Website
www.cdl.ch

We are an international day and boarding school located in Geneva, Switzerland. Our programmes offer taylor-made learning journeys and inspire students from Pre-school through to Grade 12 to be their best selves. We open doors for our students by creating a diverse and inclusive learning community that flourishes.

Our school sits on an 8-hectare landscaped campus nestled between the Jura mountains and Lake Geneva, 15 minutes away from the Geneva international airport. It offers comfortable residential facilities and recreational areas, providing students with a wide range of sport and leisure activities. In addition to our commitment to excellence in education, our philosophy also includes stimulating enthusiasm for lifelong learning and personal growth.

We have offered the IB Diploma Programme (DP) since 2005 and the IB Career-related Programme (CP) since 2016. Our 2021 Pass Rate for both programmes are an impressive 100%! The IB DP is very successful and attracts around half of our graduates every year. Our broad choice of subjects allows students to focus on their strengths and fulfil their interests. This, combined with a strong pastoral programme, which incorporates wellbeing as an essential part of students' education, and the professionalism and dedication of our teachers, contribute to consistently excellent exam results. For the IB CP we offer three career-related studies within the framework of Sustainable Business: Nature Conservation, Hospitality and Fashion. Each course is unique and has been developed in partnership with the Sustainable Management School in Gland. Students, in addition, study a minimum of 3 IB subjects. Our IB DP and IB CP graduates come from over 100 countries and our university advisory programme enables them to enroll in one of the universities of their choice, worldwide.

We belong to the Nord Anglia Family of schools, a worldwide group of elite schools, which offer students the highest standards in education and unique, international learning opportunities.

Collège Du Léman-Made for success, Made for you!

Deutsche Schule London

DEUTSCHE SCHULE LONDON

(Founded 1971)	**Address**
	Douglas House
Head of School	Petersham Road
Claudia Wolff-Lieser	Richmond
	Surrey
DP coordinator	**TW10 7AH | UK**
Edna Howard	
	TEL +44 (0)20 8940 2510
Status Private	
	Email
Boarding/day Day	info@dslondon.org.uk
Gender Coeducational	**Website**
	www.dslondon.org.uk
Language of instruction	
English, German	
Authorised IB programmes	
DP	
Age Range 3 – 18 years	

The DSL is part of a long-standing tradition of excellence in the worldwide network of more than 140 German Schools abroad and we currently welcome around 860 students from 30 nations at our school in Richmond.

We strive to empower our students, encouraging them to be open-minded, curious and committed learners as well as responsible members of our local community within an international context. We offer an appealing and challenging educational programme from Kindergarten to our dual programme in Years 11 and 12 with the International Abitur (DIA) and the IB Diploma.

This dual qualification (Abitur and IB DP) uniquely equips our students with bilingual (German and English) academic competencies, permitting them to meet the challenges of a university education and supporting them in becoming independent, global-minded citizens. In general, all students completing Year 10 at the DSL, or a comparable qualification with good academic results, are eligible to apply to the dual programme (Abitur and IB DP) at the DSL.

In combination with the Abitur subjects, IB students complete three higher level (HL) and three standard level (SL) courses as well as the core requirements (ToK, CAS, EE)

for a full IB Diploma. Students may choose between German and English as their IB Language A (HL and SL) and Spanish or French as IB Language B. Furthermore, we offer History, Economics, Geography, Psychology (SL), Biology, Chemistry, Physics, Mathematics Analysis & Approaches (SL) as well as Visual Arts (SL) and Music (SL). All Year 12 students at the DSL take their Abitur exams between February and April, ahead of their IB exams in the May session of the same year, which promotes thorough preparation for both examinations.

In addition to the full dual qualification (Abitur and IB Diploma), the DSL offers the category "course candidate" (CC), i.e. Abitur students may enrol in two or more individual IB courses and/or core elements, which allows them to study a subject of particular interest in more depth or to build a profile for their university application.

Quoting one of our 2019 alumni, *"The decision to go for the dual programme at the DSL is based on two things – an interest in a variety of subjects and a wish to challenge yourself. Additionally, the DSL isn't just a school, it is a community of students, parents and teachers that one feels connected to and welcome in at all times."*

Dwight School London

(Founded 1885)

Head
Mrs Alison Cobbin BA, Dip Ed, MBA

PYP coordinator
Srinanda Gupta

MYP coordinator
Karine Villatte

DP coordinator
William Bowry

Status Private

Boarding/day Day

Gender Coeducational

Language of instruction
English

Authorised IB programmes
PYP, MYP, DP

Age Range 3 – 18 years

Fees
Please see website

Address
6 Friern Barnet Lane
London
N11 3LX | UK

TEL 020 8920 0600

Email
admissions@dwightlondon.org

Website
www.dwightlondon.org

Join us at Dwight School London where we are dedicated to crafting a personalised journey for every student, which we call "igniting the spark of genius in every child."

A member of the world-renowned Dwight global family of schools, we share the same commitment to personalising education which began nearly 150 years ago when Dwight was founded in 1872 in New York.

Our students are encouraged to pursue their passions, believe in their own talents and celebrate and learn from the perspectives of others. They are also inspired to take intellectual risks through the academically rigorous International Baccalaureate curriculum – a pathway to top universities worldwide – nurturing creative critical thinkers empowered to help make our world a better place.

We invite you to visit us to see our school's warm, engaging environment and experience our spark of genius philosophy in action.

We are one of the UK's first IB World Schools to offer the full IB curriculum:

The Primary Years Programme (PYP) – ages 2 to 11

The Middle Years Programme (MYP) – ages 11 to 16

The Diploma Programme (DP) – ages 16 to 18

Through Dwight School London's personalised learning, EAL and mother tongue programmes, we enable all students to access the IB curriculum and become successful global citizens.

Through the academic breadth and depth of the IB, we nurture inquiring, knowledgeable and caring young people who help to create a better, more peaceful world through intercultural understanding and respect.

Our school rests on three pillars:

• Personalised learning: Customising an education for every student. We pride ourselves on getting to know each of our students and their families quite well. We shape the learning journey around how students best learn, where their skills lie, and what sparks their interest.

• Community: Encouraging students to contribute to their school and wider communities Through service learning, we foster every student's ability to make a positive difference to our school, among neighbours, and in the world beyond.

• Global vision: Educating global leaders. With students from around the world, Dwight is a culturally and socially rich and diverse school. We nurture learning within our own international community, the IB's larger global context and our network of Dwight Schools across continents.

To attend a virtual event then visit dwightlondon.org/yearbook

ÉCOLE
Jeannine Manuel
International understanding through a bilingual education

(Founded 1992)

Head of School
Constance Devaux

DP coordinator
Nicola French

Status Non-Profit Private

Boarding/day Mixed

Gender Coeducational

Language of instruction
French, English

Authorised IB programmes
DP

Age Range 3 – 18 years

Number of pupils enrolled 975

Fees
Day: €5,934
Boarding: €15,270 – €23,185
IB Classes €21,495

Address
418 bis rue Albert Bailly
Marcq-en-Baroeul
59700 | FRANCE

TEL +33 3 20 65 90 50

Email
admissions-lille@ejm.net

Website
www.ecolejeanninemanuel.org

École Jeannine Manuel Lille is a non-profit coeducational school founded in 1992 and welcomes students from nursery to 12th grade. As the sister campus of École Jeannine Manuel Paris, the school has the same educational project and mission: promoting international understanding through bilingual education. An associated UNESCO school, École Jeannine Manuel Lille is the only non-denominational independent school in Nord-Pas-de-Calais, with over 900 pupils representing 50 nationalities and every major cultural tradition. The school's academic excellence matches it diversity: École Jeannine Manuel Lille is regularly ranked among the best French high schools (ranked first for three consecutive years). The school is accredited by the French Ministry of Education, the International Baccalaureate Organization (IBO), the Council of International Schools (CIS), and the New England Association of Schools and Colleges (NEASC).

Ecole Jeannine Manuel Lille's campus extends over 8.5 acres. It includes a boarding house, a restaurant, and state-of-the-art sports facilities including a 1500 m2 gym with its own climbing wall, a 300m racing track, and two outdoor playing fields. The boarding house currently welcomes 120 pupils from 6th to 12th grade.

Each year, École Jeannine Manuel Lille welcomes non-French speaking students. These students integrate the school through the adaptation program, which provides intensive instruction in French, support in English as needed, help in understanding and adjusting to French culture, and differentiated coursework and assessment during their adaptation period. The lower and middle school follow the French national curriculum with several exceptions: English is taught every day and, in middle school, experimental sciences, history and geography are taught in English. The curriculum is enriched at all levels, not only with a more advanced English language and literature curriculum, but also, for example, with Chinese language instruction (compulsory in grades 3-4-5), an integrated science program in lower school, and independent research projects in middle school.

In upper school, tenth graders follow the French national curriculum, albeit taught 50% in French and 50% in English. In 11th grade, pupils choose between the French track (international option of the French baccalaureate (OIB)) and the International Baccalaureate Diploma Programme (IBDP). Approximately 25% of our pupils opt for the IBDP.

Admission

Although admission is competitive, the school makes every effort to reserve space for international applicants, including children of families who expect to remain in France for a limited period of time and wish to combine a cultural immersion in French education with the ability to re-enter their own school systems and excel.

International understanding through a bilingual education

(Founded 1954)

Principal
Jérôme Giovendo

DP coordinator
Sabine Hurley

Status Non-Profit Private

Boarding/day Day

Gender Coeducational

Language of instruction
English, French

Authorised IB programmes
DP

Age Range 4 – 18 years

Number of pupils enrolled
2400

Fees
Day: €7,100 – €7,449
IB Classes €24,795

Address
70 rue du Théâtre
Paris
75015 | FRANCE

TEL +33 1 44 37 00 80

Email
admissions@ejm.net

Website
www.ecolejeanninemanuel.org

École Jeannine Manuel is a non-profit pre-K-12 coeducational school founded in 1954 with the mission to promote international understanding through bilingual (French/English) education. An associated UNESCO school, École Jeannine Manuel welcomes pupils representing 80 nationalities and every major cultural tradition. The school's academic excellence matches its diversity: École Jeannine Manuel is regularly ranked among the best French high schools (state and independent) for its overall academic performance (ranked first for nine consecutive years). The school is accredited by the French Ministry of Education, the International Baccalaureate Organization (IBO), the Council of International Schools (CIS) and the New England Association of Schools and Colleges (NEASC).

Each year, the school welcomes more than 100 new non-French speaking pupils. These students integrate the school through our adaptation program, which provides intensive instruction in French, support in English as needed, help in understanding and adjusting to French culture, and differentiated coursework and assessment during their adaptation period.

The lower and middle school follow the French national curriculum with several exceptions: English is taught every day and, in middle school, experimental sciences, history and geography are taught in English. The curriculum is enriched at all levels, not only with a more advanced English language and literature curriculum, but also, for example, with Chinese language instruction (compulsory in grades 3-4-5), an integrated science program in lower school, and independent research projects in middle school.

In upper school, tenth graders follow the French national curriculum, albeit taught 50% in French and 50% in English. In 11th grade, pupils choose between the French track (international option of the French baccalaureate (OIB)) and the International Baccalaureate Diploma Programme (IBDP). Approximately 25% of our pupils opt for the IBDP.

Over the past three years, approximately 20% of our graduating class have gone to US colleges or universities, 48% chose the UK or Canada, 37% entered the French higher education system, and the balance pursued their education all over the world.

Admission:
Admission is competitive and applications typically exceed available spaces by a ratio of 7:1. The school nonetheless makes every effort to reserve space for international applicants, including children of families who expect to remain in France for a limited period of time and wish to combine a cultural immersion in French education with the ability to seamlessly re-enter the school system in their home country.

(Founded 1899)

Head of School
Mr David Johnson

DP coordinator
Ivor Gemmell

Status Private

Boarding/day Mixed

Gender Coeducational

Language of instruction
English, French

Authorised IB programmes
DP

Age Range 11 – 18 years

Number of pupils enrolled 320

Address
295 avenue Edmond Demolins
27130 Verneuil d'Avre et d'Iton |
FRANCE

TEL +33 (0) 232 6040 00

Email
ecoledesroches@
ecoledesroches.com

Website
www.ecoledesroches.com

Founded in 1899, École des Roches is an international coeducational day and boarding school located on a spacious wooded campus in the heart of the beautiful Normandy countryside. We welcome students aged 11 years to 18 years from 52 nationalities to our Middle and High school.

École des Roches offers several programmes: French curriculum, International curriculum with the IB Diploma Programme, French as a Foreign Language short stays or full academic year, and also summer and winter intensive language courses.

International Baccalaureate Diploma Programme

In response to the needs of its increasingly international community, École des Roches has been an IB World School since 2016, offering the International Baccalaureate Diploma Programme in English.

The school offers as well a special Pre-diploma year to prepare our students for the International Baccalaureate.

We also advise our students in their career choices and accompany them throughout the university admissions process.

In École des Roches, the IB Diploma Programme is characterised by:
• Its academic breadth, depth and rigour
• Small class sizes with individualized academic support
• The attention it gives to international awareness and the development of socially responsible citizens of the world.

In addition to preparing the students for the IB Diploma, all of our students are encouraged to take advantage of the school context, heritage and resources to improve in their French language proficiency, whether that be at a beginner, intermediate or advanced level.

Boarding Life

Our Boarding School consists of 7 residences called Maisons, which are large historic Normandy houses. Boys and girls are divided by age range in these single-sex boarding houses.

Foreign students are together with French-speaking students in pleasant and recently renovated rooms. From the start, the educational focus of École des Roches has been to offer educational, psychological and emotional support to our students in order to promote their intellectual and personal development. Extracurricular activities on offer range from horseback riding and golf to karting on the school's course located on campus.

Admissions

Students can apply to our school all year-round based on availability. Students must submit two years of school reports, a letter of recommendation, as well as a letter of motivation. For further information about admissions or to schedule a visit of the school, please contact us at ecoledesroches@ecoledesroches.com.

(Founded 1906)

General Director
Mr. Nicolas Catsicas

DP coordinator
Mr. Gaetan Franzini

Status Private

Boarding/day Mixed

Gender Coeducational

Language of instruction
French, English

Authorised IB programmes
DP

Age Range 3 – 18

Number of pupils enrolled
600

Fees
Day: CHF12,500 – CHF26,000
Weekly Boarding: CHF52,100 –
CHF60,400
Boarding: CHF65,000 –
CHF73,300

Address
Chemin de Rovéréaz 20
CP 161
1012 Lausanne **SWITZERLAND**

TEL +41 21 654 65 00

Email
info@ensr.ch

Website
www.ensr.ch

Ecole Nouvelle de la Suisse Romande (ENSR) / International Boarding School of Lausanne (IBSL)
Academic excellence since 1906
We offer

- Complete schooling from Kindergarten, including a Montessori section, through to High School in French and/or in English
- Bilingual French-English Programme from age 3 to 18 years
- Swiss Maturity in French
- International Baccalaureate Diploma programme in French, English or bilingual French-English
- All Cambridge, Goethe-Institut and Cervantes examinations
- Boarding facilities
- Camps (Ski, Easter, Summer, Windsurf, Fall)
- Holidays: day care for children aged from 3 to 7 years old

Languages
English is introduced at the age of 3 years old with French as the language of instruction until Grade 6 (11 y.o.). As of Grade 7 (12 y.o.), possibility to have English as the language of instruction or a bilingual French-English Programme.

German is introduced in Grade 4 (9 y.o.). Introduction classes to Spanish, Italian and Latin are proposed in the Middle School (10-14 y.o.). Other languages are offered in High School (14-19 y.o.).

French or English for beginners are provided for new students, beginners and those requiring further support.

Summer Camp
Our summer camp takes place from July to mid-August for children aged from 9 to 18 years old.

Mornings, 9 am to 12 pm: French and English classes (elementary, intermediate and intensive). Students are placed according to their language level in classes of 4 to 7 students.

Afternoons and weekends: sports, leisure, cultural activities and trips.

Multisports formula (only sports, no language classes).

Boarding School
Boarding facilities are offered for students as from Middle school, Grade 7, 12 years of age.

Our boarding school provides a friendly and warm atmosphere offering security, care and support.

Boarding is offered for either 5 or 7 days per week.

Ecole Oasis Internationale

ECOLE INTERNATIONALE

(Founded 1994)

Principal
Mrs. Esmat Lamei

PYP coordinator
Mrs. Imane Radwan

MYP coordinator
Mr. Omar El Sarky

DP coordinator
Fatma Hussein

CP coordinator
Fatma Hussein

Status Private

Boarding/day Day

Gender Coeducational

Language of instruction
French

Authorised IB programmes
PYP, MYP, DP, CP

Age Range 3 – 18 years

Number of pupils enrolled
1445

Address
Zahraa El Maadi
Quarter no 3 and no 7 Part A & B
Cairo | EGYPT

TEL +20 2 2516 2608

Email
admission@oasisdemaadi.com;
oasis.edu@oasisdemaadi.com

Website
www.oasisdemaadi.com

Being the first private trilingual school in Egypt and the first one certified to offer the four International Baccalaureate programmes in French, Oasis International School makes it a point to always put forward a quality education enabling students to thrive while developing their natural curiosity and open-mindedness.

Throughout our 32 years of educational service, we have achieved a high success rate having witnessed 13 graduations of exceptionally competent students that made their way to most prestigious universities in the United States of America, The United Kingdom, France, Egypt, and many others.

Oasis closely blends teaching pedagogy with technology. Thereby, the school implements advanced aspects of technology, such as the I-Pad One to One program to facilitate meaningful constructivist learning. Our job as educators is to be innovative with our teaching methods to make learning an enjoyable experience. The project has indeed supported student engagement and motivation through creative activities on campus, community service projects, and through *Adventure Learning*. In this context, students have the opportunity to participate in national as well as in international trips, in which they learn to put into practice their theoretical knowledge.

Under the headline and values of community service projects, patronage of a public school which the entire school community participates in. In fact, the *Egyptian International School-El Marag* is part of a national project and the result of an agreement between the Ministry of National Education, the International Baccalaureate Organization and *Oasis International School* for the first time in Egypt offered in a public school.

Our school has also improved teacher productivity while facilitating communication between both parties, thanks to the application of differential instruction and positive discipline. In addition, instructional methods and programs such as community learning have been implemented to further improve student engagement.

Last but not least, the school attributes its success mostly to the yearly extracurricular and academic activities that are being offered. A high percentage of its students participate every year in activities such as the *Model United Nations*, the *Francophonie Forum* and the *Model Arab League* in Egypt and abroad. In all of these activities, the IB Learner Profile that has been implemented over the years has made students better communicators and has helped them with their presentation and their negotiation skills. Emphasis is on both international mindedness and self-esteem. The future is looking good now that even some of our alumni have decided to join our staff after finishing their post-secondary education.

(Founded 1934)

Director CEO
Niki Holterman

Principal
Amy Ramsey

DP coordinator
Robert de Bruin

Status Private

Boarding/day Mixed

Gender Coeducational

Language of instruction
English

Authorised IB programmes
DP

Age Range 4 – 18 years

Number of pupils enrolled 85

Fees
Primary €8,500
Secondary Middle school
€19,700
Secondary High school €22,950
Boarding €23,200 (Flexible) –
€29,100 (Full)
Private room €43,400

Address
Kasteellaan 1
7731 PJ Ommen, Overijssel |
NETHERLANDS

TEL +31 52 9451452

Email
admission@eerdeibs.nl

Website
www.eerde.nl

Located on a tranquil tree lined historic country estate, we provide a top quality, rich cultural learning environment, with focus on health and wellbeing.

The learning experience at Eerde IBS is consciously small-scale to ensure individual attention for all students. Our approach will allow our students to discover their true potential and will empower them to develop personal leadership and life skills. We do so by inspiring academic excellence, stimulating inquiring minds and developing our students as active members in their community.

Our truly international and highly qualified staff at Eerde IBS helps each student to recognise their own style of learning and apply learning strategies to improve their study skills. Next to our International Baccalaureate, we also offer Foundation IB. This program is particularly well suited for students who wish to improve their English language before entering the IBDP.

We are also excited to announce we are in the process of gaining approval for the IBCP to be added to our curriculum in 2022-2023. It is a Career related program, part of the International Baccalaureate education and is specifically developed for students who wish to engage in career-related learning and can help them along the path to their chosen career.

When school is out on weekday afternoons, students can participate in a range of sporting, cultural and social activities and discover their unique talents and interests.

Eerde's partnership with the Rijksmuseum offers students an Enriching Educational Experience, benefiting from the ongoing partnership through workshops, internships, exclusive exhibits and exchanges. This experience is especially beneficial for the International Baccalaureate Visual Arts students.

Eerde IBS offers full and flexible boarding facilities. Homemade healthy meals are provided in the bistro, and homework and private study can be done in the castle library and study centre, supervised by subject teachers and our support team. Boarders share a double room and are looked after by our boarding parents, who are dedicated to creating a happy and safe home. They can join a variety of activities offered during the weekends. All members of our boarding community treat each other with respect, honesty and tolerance.

Our alumni go to universities all around the world, but also in The Netherlands because of the high-quality programmes and opportunities for international students they provide.

Please contact us through: admission@eerdeibs.nl or +31 529 451 452 or check us out at www.eerde.nl

ERMITAGE
INTERNATIONAL SCHOOL

(Founded 1941)

MYP coordinator
Christine Collie

DP coordinator
Wayne Hodgkinson

Status Private

Boarding/day Mixed

Gender Coeducational

Language of instruction
English, French

Authorised IB programmes
MYP, DP

Age Range 3 – 18 years

Number of pupils enrolled
1470

Fees
€19,645 – €40,990

Address
46 Avenue Eglé
78600 Maisons-Laffitte | **FRANCE**

TEL +33 139 62 81 75

Email
admissions@ermitage.fr

Website
www.ermitage.fr

Ermitage International School is a bilingual K-12 school located in the historic town of Maisons-Laffitte, just 20km west of Paris. With a student body of nearly 1470 students, representing over 70 nationalities, Ermitage offers student-centered learning, with a focus on bilingualism and leadership. Weekday and fulltime boarding is available in traditional French residences.

- IB Programs (IB MYP & IB DP), 230 students enrolled, offering English instruction, with French lessons from a beginner to native-level.
- French Bilingual Programs (French bac, OIB) 1240 students enrolled, instructed in French.

IB Middle Years Programme (MYP) 1-5
The MYP encourages students to be active learners, asking challenging questions, as well as developing a strong sense of identity, cultural understanding and communication skills. During the MYP, our team of experienced teachers accompany and guide students on their journey to becoming IB Learners. Emphasis is placed on individual growth and encouraging students to reflect upon their classroom projects and co-curricular initiatives. Teachers facilitate students' learning and help prepare them for the rigorous demands of the IB Diploma Programme.

IB Diploma Programme (DP) 1-2
Within the dynamic IB environment, students are encouraged to think critically and become independent learners, coming prepared to class, presenting the material and being coached by their teachers. Assignments are demanding, but by graduation the calibre of research, writing and project management skills will be exceptional. The balance between academic work and co-curricular activities allows students to tailor the programme according to their interests and develop an impressive university profile in the process.

Round Square
As a Global Member of the Round Square organization, Ermitage is connected to like minded schools, offering a variety of service-learning trips, global exchanges and leadership conferences. Students also discover their interests outside of the classroom through a daily co-curricular program with the opportunity to initiate projects, participate in leadership experiences, sports and more while connecting with local and global communities.

What sets us apart
- Student-centered approach with a balance of academics & character-developing projects
- Opportunities for student leadership via well-rounded daily co-curricular programs
- Teachers are approachable & serve as coaches, guiding students individually
- Students learn in engaging ways both inside & outside of the classroom
- Located in historic town 20km from Paris
- Weekday and full-time boarding is available in our traditional French residences

ES American School

(Founded 1999)

Head of School
Ms. Melanie Rose

PYP coordinator
Lauren Hopkins

Status Private

Boarding/day Day

Gender Coeducational

Language of instruction
English

Authorised IB programmes
PYP

Age Range 6 – 18 years

Number of pupils enrolled 97

Fees
Day: €10,636 – €16,000

Address
Autovia de Castelldefels C-31
Km 191
El Prat de Llobregat
08820 Barcelona, Catalonia |
SPAIN

TEL +34 93 479 1611

Email
info@es-school.com

Website
www.es-school.com

ES American School offers an independent, college preparatory American curriculum for 5 to 18 year olds (1st through 12th grades) located within the campus of the Emilio Sanchez Academy, Barcelona. Our Elementary is an authorized IB PYP school, offering the International Baccalaureate Primary Years Programme, a world-renowned curricular framework, where children learn to take ownership of their own learning, increasing confidence and self-motivation. In Middle School, the enrichment program supports students to have a broad range of learning experiences. The Advanced Placement (AP) program in High School offers students the opportunity to work at a more challenging level with the potential to earn university credit. Students who elect to take the Spanish program alongside the American curriculum are eligible to homologate their diploma.

With locations in Barcelona, Spain and Naples, Florida, USA, ES American School provides students with a truly international experience enabling them to excel both academically and athletically. All students receive individual attention, close academic guidance and personal counseling. The predominant language on campus is English.

Sports are an essential part of the curriculum and students benefit from the world-class tennis program and training facilities provided by Emilio Sanchez Academy. Our students have three distinct pathways with regards to sport: high-performance tennis (offered on-site), high-performance in other sports (offered off-site), including water polo, soccer, basketball, or horse riding OR our Physical Education Program for general fitness and well-being. ES American School, Barcelona is accredited by the Middle States Association of Colleges and Schools and is authorized by the Department of Education of the Catalan Government.

Eurocolegio Casvi Villaviciosa

Headteacher
Mr. Juan Luis Yagüe CEO of Casvi Group

PYP coordinator
Carolina García

MYP coordinator
Félix David Vozmediano León

DP coordinator
Jose Vicente Belizón Collado

Status Private

Boarding/day Day

Gender Coeducational

Language of instruction
Spanish

Authorised IB programmes
PYP, MYP, DP

Age Range 3 – 18 years

Number of pupils enrolled
1060

Fees
€133 – €722 per month

Address
Avenida de Castilla, 27
Villaviciosa de Odón
28670 Madrid | SPAIN

TEL +34 91 616 22 18

Email
casvi@casvi.es

Website
www.casvi.es

Eurocolegio Casvi International Private School is a private, co-educational school. Since 1985, its aim has always been to work with children and young people so that, when they finish their education with them, they are in an advantageous situation with respect to any citizen in the world.

The child who attends this school today, from Infant School to Baccalaureate, is within an IB methodology (International Baccalaureate). An active methodology, closer, real, effective, and adapted to the current times in which a globalized society dominates. Organized and synchronized from year to year, it promotes, from an early age, skills and attitudes that will help our pupils to face their future with guaranteed success.

Furthermore, at Casvi, the three International Baccalaureate programmes (PYP, MYP and DP) are fully implemented, and we are one of the few schools in Spain to offer a continuum of IB programmes. Thanks to this, at Eurocolegio Casvi they have the possibility of modelling the attributes of the IB profile from the age of 3.

In addition to all this, there is a clear commitment to internationality. These are the tools to achieve this:

Multilingualism. Pupils learn English from the first year of life; and Chinese and German from the 5th year of Primary School. This is done in small groups, by levels, and with native and bilingual teachers. Thanks to this methodology, practically all of our students complete the Diploma Programme with CAE and/or PROFICIENCY qualifications.

Language Exchanges. These are organized without any intermediary agency, through direct contact with schools all over the world. In the USA they last two months and our students from the age of 10 take part in them. Those in Germany last two weeks, and it is our PYP and PD students who enjoy this opportunity.

Presence of international students. The IB methodology, which seeks globalization in the educational field, invites many students from other countries to study at Casvi.

At Eurocolegio Casvi International Private School, the promotion of artistic skills is also very important. The aim is to detect the talents of the students, whatever their nature. Thus, the Schools of Art, Music and Theatre stand out.

As for the promotion of their sporting skills, they have swimming lessons as part of their school day and Sports Schools for Basketball, Football 7-a-side, Indoor Football, Rhythmic Gymnastics, Swimming and Synchronized Swimming.

Finally, with regard to New Technologies, the aim is to increase STEAM vocations and achieve the professional development of pupils. It also aims to promote their technological competence from the early years to their prior incorporation into the world of work. This is based on Robotics and the most cutting-edge programming languages used in the real world of work, which have been introduced in a pioneering way in their educational curriculum from the 1st year of Pre-school with the subject of Technology, Programming and Robotics.

Eyüboğlu Schools

(Founded 1970)

Head of School
Mr Cenk Eyüboğlu

PYP coordinator
Mevce Selek; Firuze Vanlıoğlu;
Meliz Katlav

MYP coordinator
Gülşah Çekiç;
Arzu Onat Konuşmaz

DP coordinator
Oğuz Günenç

Status Private

Boarding/day Day

Gender Coeducational

Language of instruction
Turkish, English

Authorised IB programmes
PYP, MYP, DP

Age Range 3 – 18 years

Number of pupils enrolled
2953

Fees
TL45,000 – TL84,250

Address
Esenevler Mah
Dr Rüstem Eyüboglu sok 3,
Ümraniye, 34762 Istanbul,
Marmara | **TURKEY**

TEL +90 216 522 12 12

Email
eyuboglu@eyuboglu.k12.tr

Website
www.eyuboglu.k12.tr

Founded in 1970 by Dr. Rüstem EYÜBOĞLU, Eyüboğlu Educational Institutions (EEI) are a group of private co-educational schools offering bilingual pre K-12 education.

Eyüboğlu Schools are comprised of six kindergartens, four elementary schools, three middle, one high school and one science and technology high school. All Eyüboglu Schools are accredited by CIS.

Eyüboğlu Schools have been an IB World School since September 1996, and are the first Turkish school authorized to offer all three IB programs; IB PYP, IB MYP, and IB DP in grades K-12. Eyüboğlu Schools are authorized in:

1996 IB Diploma Programme (Grades 11 – 12)
2002 IB Middle Years Programme (Grades 5 – 10)
2005 IB Primary Years Programme (Grades PreK – 4)

With this unique feature, the school's internationally recognized high standards of academic excellence enables Eyüboğlu graduates to further their studies both in the prestigious universities in Turkey and in the US, Canada, UK and Europe.

The school philosophy is based on academic excellence, internationalism, inter-culturalism, and social awareness. Students are encouraged to think critically, work collaboratively, and hence become innovative, lifelong learners. In addition to a heavy focus on IB qualifications, great importance is given to teaching foreign languages as stated in the school's mission to raise international-minded, bilingual students. We lead our students to English, German and Spanish proficiency exams such as Cambridge, IELTS, TOEFL, FIT and DELE.

The main campus is located on a 33,000 square meter (8 acre) campus on the Asian side of Istanbul.

There are excellent facilities such as four libraries containing 136,000 volumes. There are Biology, Physics, Chemistry and Virtual Reality labs. All the classrooms are all equipped with state-of-the-art technology. There is a fully equipped theatre hall, and one Astronomical Observatory that is equipped with a powerful telescope. There is a second Astronomical Observatory and a Planetarium at Kemerburgaz Campus.

There is also a wide variety of extracurricular activities in art, music, humanities, technology and drama. The current number of social clubs is over a hundred and they not only include traditional sports activities but also there are clubs for archery, golf, horse riding, fencing, folk dancing, modern dance and many more. These activities are carried out in a special sports and arts complex with a swimming pool, which also houses various arts studios and sports areas for handball, volleyball, athletics, basketball, golf, archery, ballet and folk-dancing.

Admission to Eyüboglu is offered on the basis of a school administered interview up to grade 3 and a written examination and interview for grade 3 and upwards. All students including Eyüboglu Middle School graduates are expected to meet the admission requirements to continue to Eyüboğlu High School in accordance with Turkish Ministry of Education regulations. Admitted students to high school are among the top scorers of national entrance exam takers.

FELIX-KLEIN-GYMNASIUM

Head of School
Michael Brüggemann

DP coordinator
Silke Neumann

Status State

Boarding/day Day

Gender Coeducational

Language of instruction
English

Authorised IB programmes
DP

Age Range 11 – 19 years

Address
Böttingerstrasse 17
37073 Göttingen, Lower Saxony |
GERMANY
TEL +49 551 400 2909

Email
fkgis@goettingen.de

Website
www.fkg-goettingen.de

mehle-hundertmark fotografie

At Felix-Klein-Gymnasium, we are committed to shaping the future through education – together, we strive to prepare young adults to be life-long learners in the world of the 21st century.

Founded in 1890, Felix-Klein-Gymnasium has a long history of academic excellence in the areas of experimental sciences and language education. The public, co-educational day school is situated in the beautiful southern city centre of Göttingen, the academic hub of Lower Saxony, surrounded by large prizewinning gardens that invite the school community to unwind.

On its two campuses, FKG offers educational programmes for Years 5-13 in German and English (CLIL), that award graduates the German Abitur. Since 2008, FKG has been accredited as an IB World School, which consolidated the school's excellent reputation as the leading provider of education in Göttingen. FKG is the only public school in Northern Germany to offer the IBDP in English separate from the German Abitur – this allows students to tailor their studies to their individual skills and interests and reflects the international-mindedness of the surroundings. Dedicated parents, international companies and academic institutions are our local partners, whom we value greatly.

The IBDP at FKG follows the recognition conditions by the German Conference of the Ministers of Education and Cultural Affairs – this guarantees access to all universities in Germany. FKG Diploma students consistently achieve results well above the world average and graduates go on to renowned tertiary education institutions in the area or all over the world.

The subject range is growing continuously and we have recently been able to broaden language options. Many graduates obtain a highly respected Bilingual Diploma, which represents their multi-facetted backgrounds and the cultural and linguistic diversity at FKG.

All IB teaching staff are long-term members of the school community. The team is highly committed to fostering our students' talents and help them maximize their potential. To achieve their individual educational objectives, our students are ready to take on responsibility for their own learning process and strive to develop their personalities, becoming considerate and open-minded members of the community. An academic counsellor guides them in this endeavor, and in Year 1, they have an older student companion at their side.

While the school is comparatively large, the classes in the IBDP offer a wonderful learning experience in small groups. Thus, extracurricular activities, joint projects, events and belonging to the big FKG family foster connections and friendships for life.

Felsted

(Founded 1564)

Headmaster
Mr Chris Townsend

DP coordinator
Karen Woodhouse

Status Private

Boarding/day Mixed

Gender Coeducational

Language of instruction
English

Authorised IB programmes
DP

Age Range 4 – 18 years

Fees
Senior Day £8,530 per term
Senior Full Boarder £13,055 per term
Prep Day £3,290 – £6,445 per term
Prep Full Boarder £8,875 per term

Address
Felsted
Great Dunmow
Essex
CM6 3LL | UK

TEL +44 (0)1371 822600

Email
intadmissions@felsted.org

Website
www.felsted.org

Shortlisted for Boarding School of the Year 2020, Prep School of the Year and Sport School of the Year 2019, by Times Education Supplement

A Felsted School education has become the popular choice for many families wanting a global education for their child. Families appreciate the school's focus on pupil wellbeing, small class sizes, dedicated teachers and modern boarding options. Based on a stunning village campus one hour north of London and south of Cambridge, Felsted places as much emphasis on each student's emotional development as on their academic progress. From the moment a child joins Felsted's supportive and close-knit community, they will be welcomed, nurtured and challenged. Highlights include:

- **Experienced IB Provision:** Felsted has a successful record of achieving at Diploma level, with an average score of 37 in 2021 and a 100% pass rate.
- **Top Results:** Across all subjects in 2021, 92% of results were a Level 5 or better and 70% a Level 6 or 7.
- **Leading University Entry:** Felsted IB students are offered places at some of the best universities around the world, in countries as diverse as Canada, the Netherlands, USA, Italy and of course the UK, with offers from Cambridge, Durham, Warwick, UCL, Bath, Exeter and City University, among others.
- **A Broad & Supportive Curriculum** with a full range of subject choices at GCSE, A Level and IB Diploma Levels. Superior provision for the very able, plus experienced

Learning and English Language support for those that need some extra help.
- **Extensive Co-curricular & Leadership Programme**, including fun and progressive Clubs & Societies, Model United Nations, Duke of Edinburgh and Combined Cadet Force Programmes.
- **Global Outlook:** As a member of the Round Square network of schools worldwide and with a diverse pupil body of over 30 nationalities, pupils get stuck into global debate, networking and exchanges. A highly acclaimed international summer school also delivers an outstanding global studies and English programme each year.
- **Professional Sporting & Creative Arts Pathways:** Professional partnerships with expert coaching, mentoring, facilities and performance opportunities and fixtures.
- **Superb Care Team**, including 24/7 medical team, wellbeing centre, tutors, matrons and house parents provide market leading mental health and wellbeing support. Part of the BSA Safe Schools Initiative.
- **Scholarships and awards**: in Academia, Music, Art, Sport, Design & Technology and Drama, worth up to 20% off the fees. Awards may be supplemented with a means-tested top-up bursary.

Find out more on felsted.org with a full range of Virtual Tours & Videos. On-site Open Morning Experiences also available.

Head of Pre Prep Di Steven	**Fees** Day: £18,420 – £21,567
Head of Prep Neill Lunnon	**Senior & Sixth Form**
Head of Senior & Sixth Form Chris Cockerill	1-3 Chesilton Road London **SW6 5AA** | **UK**
DP coordinator Chris Cockerill	**TEL** +44 20 8154 6751
Status Private	**Pre Prep** 47A Fulham High Street
Boarding/day Day	London **SW6 3JJ** | **UK**
Gender Coeducational	**TEL** +44 20 7371 9911
Language of instruction English	**Prep** 200 Greyhound Road London **W14 9SD** | **UK**
Authorised IB programmes DP	**TEL** +44 20 7386 2444
Age Range 4 – 18 years	**Email** admissions@fulham.school
Number of pupils enrolled 675	**Website** fulham.school

Independent and co-educational Fulham School provides a rich and diverse curriculum from Reception to Sixth Form.

At Fulham School we believe in co-education in its broadest sense: not just girls and boys learning together, but learners of all abilities understanding that they have much to offer each other, and teachers as keen to learn and evolve as their students. Good schools achieve consistently strong results. Great schools help each individual achieve their best outcomes.

Situated in the heart of Fulham, our locations are a wonderful place to learn, play and grow. Specialist teachers and support staff inspire our pupils to work to the limits of their potential to prepare them for the next steps in life while learning more about themselves and developing a broad range of interests.

Founded in 1996, Fulham School has grown from a single class to a school of over 700 pupils, while retaining the warmth and family atmosphere that we are well known for. In 2014 we were proud to join the global Inspired Group, which educates many students across an international network of over 70 schools on five continents. Being part of the group gives us a remarkable wealth of talent and experience on which to draw and exposes our pupils to global perspectives and the best in educational approaches across the world.

Combining the best of tradition with innovative skills and methods, and founded on the principles of co-education and a diverse ability range, at Fulham School, our goals are simple:

- To encourage the development of creative, problem-solving individuals who have tenacity, kindness, and secure self-worth.
- To provide the most distinctive, forward-thinking, and outward-looking co-educational environment, where diverse abilities are recognised, celebrated, and given fullest expression.

Fulham School supports the highest of academic high-flyers to achieve the scholarships and university places that will challenge them most alongside pupils whose chief passions and interests are expressed in practice and rehearsal rooms, on the sports field, or among friends. All pupils are encouraged to make contributions where their strengths lie and recognise the contributions of others.

جيـمـس مـودرن أكاديمـي
GEMS Modern Academy

(Founded 1986)	**Number of pupils enrolled** 217
Principal Mrs. Nargish Khambatta	**Fees** AED6,835 per month
DP coordinator Dr. Sunipa Guha Neogi	**Address** PO Box 53663 Nad al Sheeba 3,4
Status Private	Dubai | **UNITED ARAB EMIRATES**
Boarding/day Mixed	**TEL** +971 4 326 3339
Gender Coeducational	**Email** info_mhs@gemsedu.com
Language of instruction English	**Website** www.gemsmodernacademy- dubai.com
Authorised IB programmes PYP, DP	
Age Range 16 – 18 years	

Vision Statement: Inspiring children to be positive change-makers

In keeping with the vision of GEMS Education the founder and chairman, Mr. Sunny Varkey, GEMS Modern Academy (GMA) assures every student a world-class education that is wholesome and exciting. Spread over 120,000 square meters, this state-of-the-art institution is located in the heart of Dubai and has been making its mark on the local and global education scene for the last 35 years. The school is recognized and accredited by Ministry of Education, Dubai, UAE, the Council for Indian School Certificate Examinations (ICSE – New Delhi, India) and the International Baccalaureate to offer both the Primary Years Programme (since April 2021) and the Diploma Programme (since September 2014). Modern also received candidacy status for the Middle Years Programme in August 2021.

'Modern' as it is fondly called, lives up to its name as it strives ceaselessly to nurture 21st-century learners who will become active, sensitive and responsible world citizens. Our educational philosophy aims at making students independent and lifelong learners who will contribute positively to society. The faculty and management work passionately to keep the balance between modern educational demands and the wholesome traditional values that the institution embodies.

In addition to being rated as an 'Outstanding' school since 2011 by the Knowledge and Human Development Authority of Dubai, the school has also been awarded the coveted Hamdan Award for Distinguished Academic Excellence and School Administration. The highly qualified and committed faculty ensures that all pupils at Modern strive to reach their goals and prepares them to take their place in the world.

Modern's alumni regularly receive admission to Ivy League and other world renowned universities and the school boasts of a 100% placement record.

Modern offers the IB Diploma Programme to students of grades 11 and 12, with twenty seven individual subject options available. We are very pleased with the achievements of our six graduating batches since 2016. May 2021 batch achieved an average of 37 points with the topper securing a perfect score of 45 points each. This balance between strong academic performance and fantastic experiential outcomes from areas such as CAS is a hallmark of our growing Diploma Programme.

Modern also has a unique advantage that sets it apart from other IB schools – our bespoke "Bridge Programme". This consists of 14 modules designed and delivered by our teachers prior to students entering the Diploma Programme. The Bridge helps students develop a clear idea of the philosophy behind the Diploma Programme and the skills needed to be successful in it. This is accomplished through modules such as "Critical Thinking", "Global Citizenship", "Academic Honesty", "Cultural Diversity" and "Investigative Science" which are directly linked to key IB themes like approaches to teaching and learning, international mindedness, TOK and CAS. By proactively engaging students in these interactive modules, we aim to ensure that they hit the ground running in the Diploma Programme and aspire to be lifelong learners afterward.

Global Paradigm International School

GLOBAL PARADIGM
INTERNATIONAL
SCHOOL
Member of El Rabwa Network

Principal Sanaa Shoukri

DP coordinator Omnia Mostafa

Status Private

Boarding/day Day

Gender Coeducational

Language of instruction
English

Authorised IB programmes
DP

Address
First Settlement, Block K1,
Sector 8, New Cairo City,
Cairo **16834 | EGYPT**

TEL +20 222 461 809/10/12

Email info@gpschool-eg.com

Website www.gpschool-eg.com

EGYTPIAN CLOTHING
BANK VISIT

Global Paradigm International School is committed to preparing distinguished students from Pre-K to G12 to excel in a future of their choice. In Global Paradigm International School the love and lure for learning is nurtured and fostered in a way where the individual acquires confidence and competence. In an enriched diverse community of students, teachers and parents, we at GPIS value every individual as an independent thinker and decision maker.

Global Paradigm International School is a private international school owned by El Rabwa Company for Integrated Educational Services. The school follows the Common Core Learning Standards and Framework as well as the IB Diploma Curriculum. It is accredited by both the North Central Association Commission on Accreditation and School Improvement (NCA CASI) under the auspices of Cognia, and the Middle States Association Commissions on Elementary and Secondary Schools (MSA-CESS). GPIS has been an IB World School since March 2015 and offers the Diploma

Programme for 18 subjects at both the standard and high level.

The school occupies an area of about 8300 M2, housing 44 spacious classrooms providing the latest technology in teaching methods with smart boards operating in all classrooms. There are staff rooms, administrative offices, 3 Science Labs, 2 Computer labs, 2 music rooms, 3 art rooms, a 200-seat auditorium, a library, a cafeteria, a picnic area, a multi-purpose court, a, 2 soccer fields, A basketball field, a gymnasium, 3 playgrounds and a swimming pool. Playgrounds, sport court surfaces and out-door areas are covered with artificial shock-absorbent turf.

At GPIS we encourage respecting differences of others yet treasuring one's own traditions and values in order to present a responsible, self-content, and an assertive global citizen. The IB Learner Profile, CAS, International-mindedness and Approaches to Teaching and Learning are the lynchpins of learning at GPIS.

Godolphin and Latymer School

(Founded 1905)

Head Mistress
Dr Frances Ramsey

DP coordinator
Audrey Dubois

Status Private, Independent

Boarding/day Day

Gender Female

Language of instruction
English

Authorised IB programmes
DP

Number of pupils enrolled
800

Fees
Day: £23,085

Address
Iffley Road
Hammersmith
London
W6 0PG | UK

TEL +44 (0)20 8741 1936

Email office@
godolphinandlatymer.com

Website
www.godolphinandlatymer.com

Godolphin and Latymer School is an independent day school for girls aged between 11 and 18; it is located in Hammersmith, West London, and is easily accessible by public transport from the surrounding areas. Means-tested bursaries are available at 11+ and 16+ entry covering up to 100% of fees; music scholarships are offered at 11+ and art and music scholarships at 16+.

The school has an excellent academic record and students gain places on a huge range of competitive courses at the very best universities both in the UK and overseas. Godolphin is a research-informed school that places great emphasis on the quality of its teaching to provide a broad and well-rounded education. It embraces innovation and new opportunities to create learning environments which promote analytical skills, emotional intelligence, teamwork, adaptability, entrepreneurship, creative thinking and problem-solving. Students are encouraged to explore beyond the syllabus and to find passion in their study and to be brave in embracing new academic challenges. The academic and pastoral sides of school life operate very much in tandem and students

grow as independent and sophisticated thinkers and learners whilst being supported in their personal development as they learn key life skills.

The school prides itself on the amount of choice and opportunity it offers students. There is an exciting and ambitious curriculum with a wide range of subjects, and at Sixth Form it is one of the few schools in London that offers the choice of the A Level and the International Baccalaureate Diploma pathway. Beyond the classroom girls enjoy the most extensive extra-curricular programme and facilities to pursue their interests and talents, and there are many opportunities for students to take on leadership roles and positions of responsibility within the school community. There is a strong culture of community and voluntary service, caring for others and kindness which permeates the whole school. The school aims to develop students who will become the leading citizens of the future: young adults who are capable of thinking for themselves and who can demonstrate a critical awareness of the wider world, having a sense of their own worth whilst being appreciative of others.

Greenfield International School

(Founded 2007)

Principal Dr. Allan Weston

Vice Principal Andrew Mitchell

Head of Secondary Colin Gerrie

Head of Primary Graeme Naftel

PYP coordinator
Dr. Sanja Vicevic Ivanovic

MYP coordinator Chris Cooke

DP coordinator Sarah Atienza

CP coordinator Matt Christensen

Status Private

Boarding/day Day

Gender Coeducational

Language of instruction
English

Authorised IB programmes
PYP, MYP, DP, CP

Age Range 3 – 18 years

Number of pupils enrolled
1211

Fees
Pre-K: AED31,750
KG 1: AED36,750
KG 2: AED38,750
Grade 1 to 6: AED49,732
Grade 7 to 10: AED62,440
Grade 11 and 12: AED76,315

Address
Dubai Investments Park
Dubai | **UNITED ARAB EMIRATES**

TEL +971 (0)4 885 6600

Email admissions@gischool.ae

Website www.gischool.ae

Greenfield International School (GIS), a member of the highly regarded Taaleem group, opened its doors in 2007, and since then has promoted and inspired young minds from diverse backgrounds. We are fully authorised as an International Baccalaureate Continuum World School and offer the IB Curriculum from Pre-Kindergarten through to Grade 12. We were also one of the first schools in the Middle East that successfully piloted the IB's Career-related Programme. With our students coming from over 80 different countries, we are a truly international school, rich with cultural diversity. The spirit of internationalism is reflected in the philosophy of the school's curriculum, as well as extracurricular activities (ECA) we offer our students. This approach enriches our students' minds, their skills and talents through collaborative approaches to learning. Our holistic education allows students to not only achieve excellent academic results but also to thrive outside the classrooms by developing their talents and communication skills through extracurricular activities. As committed IB practitioners, our team are experienced international educators and the driving force behind the school's academic and pastoral success. Our classrooms are vibrant student-centred environments where inquiry-based approaches are balanced with direct teaching. Our teachers actively strive to encourage children's natural curiosity and a love of learning. They take great care to support each child's social and emotional growth. We also know how important it is to build strong parent-teacher relationships as we recognise what a pivotal role the teacher plays in the child's life. As a result, we encourage parents to be active participants in school life and we welcome them to be part of our many family events and class activities. As a mark of quality assurance, GIS is fully accredited by two of the world's most highly regarded accreditation bodies; the Council of International Schools (CIS) based in Europe and the New England Association of Schools and Colleges (NEASC), based in the USA. Along with the IB authorisation, the CIS and NEASC accreditation offer a guarantee of quality knowing that your school meets or exceeds international standards.

Gymnasium am Münsterplatz

 Erziehungsdepartement des Kantons Basel-Stadt
Gymnasium am Münsterplatz

Head of School
Dr. Eugen Krieger

DP coordinator
Dr. Manuel Pombo

Status State

Boarding/day Day

Gender Coeducational

Language of instruction
German, English

Authorised IB programmes
DP

Address
Münsterplatz 15
4051 Basel BS | **SWITZERLAND**

TEL +41 61 267 88 70

Email
gymnasium.muensterplatz@
bs.ch

Website
www.gmbasel.ch

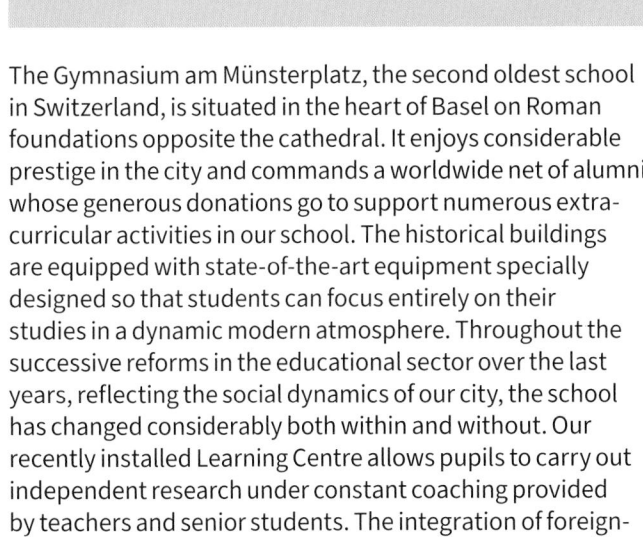

The Gymnasium am Münsterplatz, the second oldest school in Switzerland, is situated in the heart of Basel on Roman foundations opposite the cathedral. It enjoys considerable prestige in the city and commands a worldwide net of alumni whose generous donations go to support numerous extra-curricular activities in our school. The historical buildings are equipped with state-of-the-art equipment specially designed so that students can focus entirely on their studies in a dynamic modern atmosphere. Throughout the successive reforms in the educational sector over the last years, reflecting the social dynamics of our city, the school has changed considerably both within and without. Our recently installed Learning Centre allows pupils to carry out independent research under constant coaching provided by teachers and senior students. The integration of foreign-language-speaking pupils into Swiss society through the public school system is another of our major concerns.

The main objective of our Learning Support Centre is to provide individual didactic counselling, subject-specific backup courses, as well as various integrative measures for pupils with diverse educational biographies. It also aims to furnish individual, accompaniment and supervision for highly-talented pupils.

Apart from the modern foreign languages, French, English and Spanish, we also offer a choice of main elective subjects including; Latin, Greek, Spanish, English, and the combination Philosophy, Pedagogics, and Psychology. Of course, our Mathematics and Natural Science departments together with our Arts and Sports departments also furnish their necessary contribution to the education of our students.

The School has a rich and varied extra-curricular life. Every year, each of our 4th classes (11th grade) prepares and performs a drama project under the guidance of professional directors. We also have an annual Winter or Spring Ball. We have both a top-quality jazz band and a choir. Almost every year, one of our delegated teams to the National Session of the European Youth Parliament has been selected to represent Switzerland at the European Youth Parliament. We invite politicians and diplomats on a regular basis to discuss world affairs in our classrooms.

Apart from successfully preparing our students for third level education, the Gymnasium am Münsterplatz, in keeping with its humanistic tradition, places great importance on the development of individual personalities. We aim to address and promote our pupils as whole persons in their psychological, spiritual and physical integrity.

Outside our regular school programme, and our local interdisciplinary weeks, we also offer numerous activities away from Basel, such as study trips linked to the main elective subjects (Spain, Greece, Rome, UK, Vienna), annual skicamps, and concentrated study-weeks elsewhere in Switzerland.

As the first public school in Basel to be accredited in 2011, the GM has been offering the IB Diploma Programme as an ideal complement to the state gymnasium syllabus. Thanks to the great popularity of the IB Curriculum, our IB scores continue to improve every year and are well above world average, giving our students easier access to the world's leading universities.

Haganässkolan

Head of School
Mrs Elisabeth Roos-Jonsson

DP coordinator
Ms Karin Elisabet Ringblom

Status State

Boarding/day Day

Gender Coeducational

Language of instruction
English

Authorised IB programmes
DP

Age Range 16 – 19 years

Number of pupils enrolled
500

Address
Box 501
343 23 Älmhult, Kronoberg |
SWEDEN

TEL +46 476 552 22

Email
haganasskolan@almhult.se

Website
tinyurl.com/y6njaaw4

Welcome to a small school with a big heart and great results!
Should you begin your international journey in the Pre-Diploma or the Diploma Programme?
The Diploma Programme is the final 2 years of upper secondary education authorized by the International Baccalaureate Organisation. You are eligible to apply for the Diploma Programme if you have completed the equivalent of 10 years of compulsory school. The 2 years in the Diploma Programme, if completed successfully, will give you the basic requirements to apply to Universities in Sweden and around the world. The IBDP is literally an open door to your adventure on this globe!

Apply to the Pre-Diploma Programme if you have completed 9 years of compulsory schooling. In the Pre-Diploma Programme you will study the typical first year National Swedish upper secondary courses like English, Math, Biology, and Civics, for example. You will also get some orientation courses that allow you to narrow down your selection of subjects to take once you enter the Diploma Programme.

Why choose Haganässkolan for your IBDP adventure?
Haganässkolan is a small school with a big heart and great results. It is located in Älmhult which gives you the advantages of a small town with a unique international atmosphere. It is easy to live here and most things are close by. Due to our small class sizes and friendly teachers, students feel safe, happy, and supported; which affects their learning very positively. Haganässkolan also offers some special subjects that you might not find nearby, for example, if you have an interest in Global Politics, Business Management, Design Technology, or Visual Arts, then this may be the place for you!

Why not come and visit and see for yourself?
We would love to have you for a visit and get to meet you! If you are unable to visit, feel free to contact the Diploma Programme coordinator to discuss your interest and application at karin.ringblom@almhult.se

Haileybury

(Founded 1862)

The Master
Mr Martin Collier MA BA PGCE

DP coordinator
Kate Brazier

Status Private

Boarding/day Mixed

Gender Co-educational

Language of instruction
English

Authorised IB programmes
DP

Age Range 11 – 18 years

Number of pupils enrolled 915

Fees
Day: £18,240 – £27,435
Boarding: £23,610 – £37,215

Address
Haileybury
Hertford
Hertfordshire
SG13 7NU | UK

TEL +44 (0)1992 706353

Email
uk.admissions@haileybury.com

Website
www.haileybury.com

Founded in 1862, Haileybury is one of the UK's top independent co-educational boarding and day schools offering a well-rounded education to 11-18 year olds. The school is a short 20 miles north of London, nestled in over 500 acres of woodland, playing fields and superb facilities.

Academic

A key part of the school's philosophy is about empowering each child to follow their passion and build their self-confidence. Pupils are encouraged to be independent, creative and intellectually ambitious. The school offers a dedicated Lower School for Years 7 and 8, a wide range of GCSE and (I)GCSEs and the choice of the International Baccalaureate (IB) Diploma or A Level Course in Sixth Form. Haileybury is ranked Top 10 in The Times league table for co-ed independent schools which offer the IB.

We are creative and innovative in terms of our teaching and our curriculum. As such have partnered with Stanford University and the University of Oxford, to work as part of the global Stan-X study. This allows our pupils the opportunity to participate in this pioneering study of genetics, contributing to efforts to find cures for diseases such as pancreatic cancer and diabetes. We want our pupils to 'think the unthinkable and the not yet thought'.

Co-curricular

Haileybury offers an enormous range of co-curricular opportunities; pupils can choose from over 130 options. There is also a wide array of clubs and societies, broad enough to cater for the most eclectic individuals. From trekking in the Himalayas to debating global issues at its Model United Nations programme, to performing at the latest music or drama production. The school is among the Top 3 for 'Best for extra-curricular activities' according to the Good Schools Guide (2018).

Sport is central to Haileybury life and the school has an outstanding reputation for sport. The school is regularly selected as one of the top 100 secondary schools in the UK for its cricket provision by The Cricketer's Good School Guide.

Boarding

The Independent School's Inspectorate describes the quality of boarding at Haileybury as excellent. The houses lie at the heart of a Haileybury education and have done so for over 150 years. They are vibrant, happy, productive and homely communities where lifelong bonds are formed. The school believes that a caring environment is crucial to happiness and fulfilment. For those who board, Haileybury is like a home-from-home, warm and friendly where each and every child is supported to develop their confidence and to help them find their identity, embracing failings as much as successes in their personal journey of discovery.

Haut-Lac International Bilingual School

école internationale bilingue
international bilingual school

(Founded 1993)

Infant & Primary Head
Ms Lucy Sumner

Secondary Head
Ms Rossella Cosso

MYP coordinator
Julien Hernandez

DP coordinator Greg Wilson

CP coordinator Beatrice Gillet

Status Private

Boarding/day Mixed

Gender Coeducational

Language of instruction
English, French

Authorised IB programmes
MYP, DP, CP

Age Range 18 months – 18 years

Number of pupils enrolled
600

Fees
Day: CHF24,400 – CHF35,400
Boarding: CHF72,000 –
CHF88,000

Address
Ch. de Pangires 26
St-Légier-la Chiésaz
CH-1806 | SWITZERLAND

TEL +41 (0)21 555 50 00

Email admissions@haut-lac.ch

Website www.haut-lac.ch

Founded in 1993, Haut-Lac International Bilingual School is a day and boarding IB World School with 600 students. Its family-oriented directors, teachers and staff provide each of the children in their care with:

- personalised programmes & support enabling them achieve outstanding academic results, as seen by its 100% IBDP pass rate in 2020 and 2021
- truly bilingual, English or French pathways to top universities in Switzerland and worldwide
- opportunities to discover and get involved in different aspects of the school, the local and the international communities
- over 150 extra-curricular activities enabling them to make new friends, discover new passions and develop their talents
- exciting activities and events enabling families to get to know each other and feel at home at Haut-Lac
- family care, activities and trips for up to 30 boarders at a modern boutique boarding house, located a short walk away from its school campuses (haut-lac.ch/boarding/)

As a CIS-accredited school, it tailors the following programmes to each child's personal and learning needs to ensure they reach their goals and develop the transferable skills required for success.

- Infant & primary programme based on 21st century concepts, enabling students to develop and apply their knowledge and skills in real-world situations
- IB Middle Years Programme with or without Swiss modules enabling students to pursue the IBDP, the IBCP or a Swiss High School qualification
- English, French or Advanced Bilingual IB Diploma granting students access to universities worldwide
- IB Career-Related Programme with a focus in Sustainable Management, Art & Design or International Sport Management, enabling students to gain both the academic and professional skills needed for university and the work place
- IB Sport & Study programme accredited by the World Academy of Sport
  - flexible and/or extended IBMYP, IBDP and IBCP programmes enabling student-athletes to pursue both their academic and intense training programmes
  - offered in partnership with Ski Zenit as part of its Ski Racing Academy (haut-lac.ch/focus-areas/ski-racing-academy/)
- US High School Diploma enabling students to study in the US or Canada
  - double IBDP-USDP certification available

(Founded 2003)

Head of School
Abeya Fathy

PYP coordinator
Shymaa El Kotb

DP coordinator
Omneya Hamdy

Status Private

Boarding/day Day

Gender Coeducational

Language of instruction
English

Authorised IB programmes
PYP, DP

Number of pupils enrolled
1467

Fees
$12,628.50 *

Address
South of Police Academy
5th District
New Cairo | **EGYPT**

TEL +202 25373000/3333

Email admission@
hayahacademy.com

Website
www.hayahacademy.com

Hayah International Academy is committed to create and maintain an environment that fosters and enriches the personal and academic growth of each student. Hayah empowers students to live with purpose, honor their cultural identity, respect diversity, and serve humanity by positively impacting local and global communities.

Hayah International Academy is a distinguished entity founded on the belief that every child is creative, special, and capable of achieving outstanding results if provided with the proper support. Hayah provides a wide selection of educational programs and extra-curricular activities aiming to generate well rounded students and promoting social, academic and physical development.

The school campus is located over a land lot of 55,000 square meters with separate buildings for Early Childhood, Elementary and Middle/High school, all equipped to support various learning and extracurricular activities.

Our IB teachers are characterized by their educational excellence. They undergo on-going development to enhance their professional experience.

IB Diploma subjects offered at Hayah:
English Literature HL/SL – English Language and Literature HL/SL – English B HL – Arabic Language and Literature HL/SL – Arabic B HL – Arabic Ab-initio SL – French B HL/SL – French Ab-initio SL – Economics HL/SL – History HL/SL – Business and Management HL/SL – Psychology HL/SL – Information Technology in a Global Society ITGS HL/SL – Global Politics HL/SL. – Chemistry HL/SL – Physics HL/SL – Biology HL/SL – Environmental Systems and Societies SL – Mathematics Analysis & Approaches HL/SL – Mathematics Applications & Interpretations SL – Visual Arts HL/SL – Film HL/SL.

Class of 2021 students received outstanding results with the majority of the cohort scoring above the average scores. 42% of students scored 40 and above, and 51% of students scored 39 and above. For the very first time at Hayah, a student achieved the perfect score of 45. Four students scored 44 and three students scored 43. Six students scored 42, four students scored 41 and 12 scored 40.

Class of 2021 students have joined many top level universities both in Egypt and worldwide in countries such as: UK, UAE, USA, Canada, Switzerland and Netherlands.

*Fees are collected in EGP equivalent

H-FARM International School

(Founded 1995)

Head of School
Mr Mauro Bordignon

PYP coordinator
Rebecca Goswell

MYP coordinator
Alba Manso Perez

Status Private

Boarding/day Mixed

Gender Coeducational

Language of instruction
English, Italian

Authorised IB programmes
PYP, MYP

Age Range 3 – 18 years

Address
Via Olivetti 1
31056 Roncade (TV) | **ITALY**

TEL +39 0422 789503

Email
info.tv@h-is.com

Website
www.h-is.com/it/scuole/treviso

H-FARM International School, located just outside of Venice, Italy, empowers students to be internationally-minded citizens who are able to shape their own future in a rapidly changing global community. Through innovative learning environments and the development of relationships based on compassion and respect, we enable students to become confident, creative and collaborative.

We are a community of active lifelong learners. H-FARM International School serves a diverse and growing community of students and families. We offer a broad based education which uses English as the language of instruction and learning and which aims to promote international mindedness and global citizenship. The school is authorised by the IB to offer two programmes, the Primary Years Programme (Early Years Unit (EYU) and Elementary) and Middle Years Programme. The Early Years Unit (EYU) is also inspired by Reggio Children beliefs, values and practices. The International Baccalaureate (IB) Programmes provide a challenging, internationally focused and balanced educational experience across the Primary Years (PYP) and Middle Years (MYP) Programmes.

To provide the complete IB continuum, H-FARM joined with International School of Talents-Multicampus, using their combined knowledge and experience in nurturing talents, in order to provide both Italian and international students with unparalleled academic and life experiences. The International School of Talents – Multicampus provides the IB's Diploma Programme – an engaging curriculum entirely taught in English that prepares students to access the most prestigious universities and colleges in the world.

Our Campus, located just 10 minutes from Venice International Airport, boasts world class services for both boarding and day students. An unparalleled center for innovation in Europe, H-FARM students have access to a 240-bed boarding house, a sports complex with tennis & Padel courts, basketball and volleyball courts, a fully-equipped gymnasium, soccer fields, coffee shops and restaurants, innovative science and Virtual Reality laboratories.

Hochalpines Institut Ftan (HIF)

HOCHALPINES INSTITUT FTAN
SWISS INTERNATIONAL SCHOOL AND SPORTS ACADEMY

(Founded 1793)

Head of School
Stefanie Aichholz

DP coordinator
Peter Pasquill

Status Private

Boarding/day Mixed

Gender Coeducational

Language of instruction
English, German

Authorised IB programmes
DP

Age Range 12 – 19 years

Number of pupils enrolled 65

Fees
Boarding: CHF53,400 –
CHF57,000 Sports Academy
CHF2,250 – CHF5,050

Address
Chalchera 154
7551 Ftan GR | **SWITZERLAND**

TEL +41 81 861 22 11

Email
admissions@hif.ch

Website
www.hif.ch

HIF Swiss International School is an open-hearted campus community where young people from around the world can thrive in the sublime, health-giving environment of the Swiss Alps. It is a co-educational secondary school offering a range of educational programmes for students in school years/grades 7 to 12. It is accredited by the Canton of Graubünden to prepare and examine students for the Swiss Matura and by Cambridge Assessment as a centre for the International General Certificate of Secondary Education (IGCSE). HIF proudly holds IB World School status and offers the IB Diploma programme.

Our Vision

We are guided by the humanist traditions of Switzerland and the values of the great Swiss educators. True to their legacy, HIF fosters a student-centred school culture and caring relationships between educators and learners. This is manifested in high standards of teaching and learning, the discovery and development of individual talent and achievement within a motivating, supportive community.

Our Mission

At HIF we prepare our students to go out into the world with the knowledge, intellectual skills and emotional maturity to find fulfilment in their personal lives as well as in their academic and professional careers. The school aims to promote open-mindedness, critical thinking, self-directed research and teamwork through teaching and learning with a local, national and international outlook. We challenge our students to become global citizens with a sense of responsibility for our shared planet. We want them to understand that fairness, kindness and community spirit help to make the world a better place.

Your Home Away From Home

For our dedicated house parents at HIF nothing is more important than the happiness of their house and that depends on the health, happiness and safety of each child in their care. House parents are not just carers or activity organisers or supervisors. Although they are all of these, they are first and foremost educators. They work as a team in close cooperation with teachers, school leaders, sports coaches, medical staff and, of course, parents to provide the holistic education expressed in HIF's mission statement.

Sports Academy

Sport promotes health, well-being, resilience, self-discipline, and team spirit. What is more, sport is a source of joy, excitement and inspiration. With its team of expert coaches and high-profile training facilities, HIF enables students to combine competitive or leisure sports with an academic programme of their choice. Special support and mentoring programmes ensure the coordination of sport and academics.

(Founded 1980)	**Number of pupils enrolled** 900
Principal David Woods	**Fees** Boarding: £13,332 – £18,042
MYP coordinator Michelle Butler	**Address** Dunmow Road
DP coordinator Peter Bromfield	Bishops Stortford Hertfordshire
Status State	**CM23 5HX | UK**
Boarding/day Mixed	**TEL** 01279 658451
Gender Coeducational	**Email** admissions@hockerill.com
Language of instruction English	**Website** www.hockerill.com
Authorised IB programmes MYP, DP	
Age Range 11 – 18 years	

Situated on a leafy campus in Bishop's Stortford, 10 minutes from London Stansted Airport, Hockerill is a leading UK school which features in the Sunday Times Guide 2021, the Good Schools Guide and the Tatler Schools Guide. It is a strong, caring community of 900 boys and girls (400 boarders and 500 day students) aged between 11 and 18. All six boarding houses are located within the campus.

Student outcomes are exceptional with results and university destinations comparing favourably to those of top independent schools. 75% of those attending UK universities go on to Russell Group destinations, with 10% taking up an Oxbridge place in 2021. The Sunday Times placed Hockerill third of all comprehensives, based on academic achievement, in its 2021 guide to the best schools in the country.

The College offers a rigorous and broad curriculum and is proud to be one of the largest state schools offering the prestigious International Baccalaureate Middle Years and Diploma programmes with consistently outstanding results. Hockerill has a special focus on languages and music with both French/English and German/English bilingual sections.

The main intake years are at ages 11 and 16. The Lower College curriculum is based on the IB Middle Years programme offering a wide range of subjects with students taking their GCSEs before moving on.

The College has a strong extra-curricular provision which includes Sports, Music Ensembles and Choirs, BMX, CCF, Young Enterprise, Duke of Edinburgh, Debating, Model United Nations, Amnesty and Charity fundraising. There are some 100 clubs on offer.

The trips and exchanges programme runs throughout the College and encompasses destinations such as Uganda, India, Japan, China, Spain, France, Croatia, Belgium, Austria, Germany and Italy.

Many events take place during the year for students including formal dinners, concerts, Speech Day, International Boarders weekend (for students and their families). As part of the regular communication, there is a termly forum for boarding parents.

HOUT BAY
INTERNATIONAL SCHOOL
SOUTH AFRICA

(Founded 1999)

Head of School
Gavin Budd

PYP coordinator
Rhona Sehested-Larsen

MYP coordinator
Elani McDonald

DP coordinator
Winell Gous

Status Private

Boarding/day Day

Gender Coeducational

Language of instruction
English

Authorised IB programmes
PYP, MYP, DP

Age Range 2 – 18 years

Number of pupils enrolled
400

Fees
Day: R44,940 – R137,439

Address
61 Main Road, Hout Bay
Cape Town, **7806 | SOUTH AFRICA**

TEL +27 21 791 7900

Email
hbis@iesmail.com

Website www.
houtbayinternational.co.za

Introduction

Hout Bay International School is more than a school – it is a community of diverse individuals and families, a centre for academic excellence, for some a home away from home and yet more importantly a family for all those that are part of it. Few schools can boast that they belong to two international organisations spanning across almost every continent of the globe. The first being International Education Systems (IES), a family of international schools committed to quality educational experiences for all who attend and, second, the International Baccalaureate Organisation (IBO), renowned for its high quality and rigorous academic programme.

Our School is as diverse as the location in which it finds itself, our commitment to highlighting social injustice, the celebration of differences and the fostering of international mindedness goes beyond the classroom. Students are encouraged to 'think outside the box', 'have a voice' and engage on pertinent topics daily. From the Primary Years Programme (PYP), Middle Years Programme (MYP) through to the Diploma Programme (DP), students, staff and parents are part of a learning community that seeks to encourage awareness of the wider world. They have a sense of their own role as global citizens, who respect and value diversity, who have an understanding of how the world works and who take responsibility for their actions.

We are proudly South African, embodying an International mind-set, where the spirit of 'ubuntu' – the idea that humanity is bound together and expressed by caring for each other – can be seen and felt. The teachers genuinely care for their students and love practicing their craft. The students genuinely love learning and are encouraged to become life-long learners.

Facilities

Our campus is cradled between beautiful mountains on three sides with the sparkling Atlantic Ocean on the other; and houses the following facilities: 35 Classrooms (each equipped with Wi-Fi and Data Projectors). Two Fully Equipped Science/ Biology Laboratories, Robotics Lab, Black Box Drama Studio, Visual Art Studio, Design Studio, School Library, Music Studio, Creative Arts Outdoor Courtyard, Courtyards equipped with climbing walls and Sand pits, Canteen for daily lunches and snacks, Small hall, Stop and Drop / Pick Up Facilities, 2 Netball / Tennis Courts, 3 Cricket Nets, 2 Multi-purpose playing fields, Bio-Diversity Sanctuary, Sustainable Vegetable Garden. In 2019 our campus was enhanced with the completion of our brand new Early Years and Junior Primary building which also houses our newest addition, our Nursery Class.

Extra-Curricular Programme

Our students enjoy an extensive Extra-Curricular programme exposing them to various sports, creative arts, dance, martial arts, community service activities, all contributing to their 'Whole Child' educational experience and embracing the concept of CAS.

Admissions

We accept students year round, in all grade levels except the final year of the Diploma Programme which requires a two year commitment from the student. Application forms and previous school reports are required for entry.

Ibn Khuldoon National School

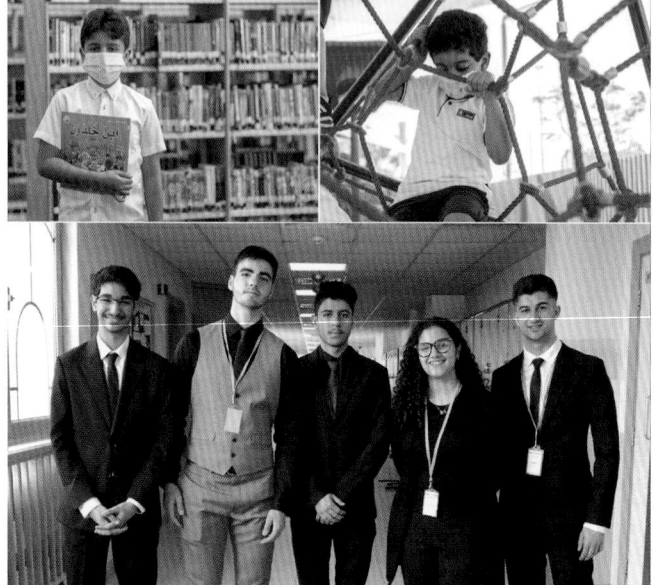

(Founded 1983)

President
Dr Kamal Abdel-Nour D.Ed

PYP coordinator
Rosy Johnson

DP coordinator
Gerda Marais

Status Private, Non-Profit

Boarding/day Day

Gender Coeducational

Language of instruction
English, Arabic

Authorised IB programmes
PYP, DP

Age Range 4 – 18 years

Number of pupils enrolled
1700

Address
Building 161, Road 4111
Area 841, P.O. Box 20511
Isa Town | **BAHRAIN**

TEL +973 17780661

Email
k.algosaibi@ikns.edu.bh

Website
www.ikns.edu.bh

Ibn Khuldoon National School (IKNS) is a non-profit self supporting coeducational institution that is dedicated to providing high quality education for local and expatriate students. The school offers a bilingual programme of study for students from Kindergarten to Grade 12. IKNS students can communicate in both Arabic and English with ease and lucidity from an early stage of their lives.

A diverse faculty, whether teaching in Arabic or English, provide a rich and supportive learning environment for students. The faculty is supported by a dedicated team of administrative and support staff.

At the top level of the school's governance stand the board of trustees, board of directors and specialist committees. Their members volunteer their expertise, time and effort to ensure that the school is always heading in a forward direction.

IKNS opened its doors to students in 1983. The first group of students walked up the graduation stage in 1992. Since then, the institution has graduated more than 2,200 young men and women, with a current student population of 1,700.

IKNS has been affiliated with the International Baccalaureate (IB) since 1990, as an IB Diploma Programme provider. The first group of students sat for the IB Diploma examinations in 1992. Since then, the IB Diploma has been a popular choice for motivated students at IKNS.

IKNS received its PYP authorization in July, 2020. It is also an MYP candidate school.

In addition to the IB Diploma, IKNS offers an American high school diploma. A large number of high school diploma students opt to study one or more DP courses. IKNS students go on to complete their tertiary education in different parts of the world including UK, USA, Canada and Arab countries, many gaining admission to prestigious institutions.

The school received its full accreditation from the Middle States Association of Colleges and Schools (MSA) in 1994, and it continues to be in good standing with the association. The Accredited status of the school affirms that it provides the level of quality in its educational programmes, services, activities and resources expected by its stakeholders. IKNS continues to be rated as an "Outstanding School" by the Education and Training Quality Authority (BQA).

international
bilingual
school munich
ibsm

(Founded 2010)

Head of School
Barbara Cox

PYP coordinator
Susanne Green

Status Private

Boarding/day Day

Gender Coeducational

Language of instruction
English, German

Authorised IB programmes
PYP

Age Range 6 – 10 years

Number of pupils enrolled 87

Address
Lerchenauerstrasse 197
80935 Munich, Bavaria | **GERMANY**

TEL +49 89 41 11 49 550

Email
admission@ibsm-school.eu

Website
www.ibsm-school.eu

Mission

At the International Bilingual School Munich, children are inspired to embrace their academic, cultural, physical, social and emotional learning potential in partnership with their peers, teachers and families within a stimulating and caring international and bilingual environment. The ibsm learning community supports students to become lifelong learners who strive to be active members of society shaping an internationally minded and peaceful world of tomorrow.

Our School

The ibsm is a small co-educational all-day school ranging from 1st–4th grade. The school is located in the heart of Munich, the capital of Bavaria, and includes a big variety of cultures in a small, family-like learning community. The ibsm has been a state-approved primary school since 2010 and a recognized IBO School since 2017. The four classes (1–4), normally accommodating up to 25 children, are based on a bilingual teaching concept. Each class is taught by an English-speaking and a German-speaking teacher. The teaching curriculum combines the PYP standards and the Bavarian state standards, providing students with a variety of options for secondary schools after their exhibition in 4th grade.

Our school community works closely together building and shaping our school and all the people within it. Our students take initiative and responsibility for their own learning and present their findings and abilities through creative and personalized approaches. Through the dedication and commitment of our staff, we create an intimate learning environment at ibsm with the focus on each child and their very individual development.

ICS CÔTE D'AZUR
INTERNATIONAL SCHOOL
Shaping the world

(Founded 2006)

Director
Ms Amanda Scott

PYP coordinator
Mrs Janet Goswell

Status Private

Boarding/day Day

Gender Coeducational

Language of instruction
English, French

Authorised IB programmes
PYP

Age Range 3 – 11 years

Number of pupils enrolled
130

Fees
Day: €10,070 – €13,470

Address
245 Route les Lucioles
06560 Valbonne | **FRANCE**

TEL +33 (0)4 93 64 32 84

Email
admissions@icscotedazur.com

Website
www.icscotedazur.com

ICS Côte d'Azur is a bilingual, co-educational, non-sectarian, IB World Primary School serving the international and local community in the Sophia Antipolis region. The school offers Early Years and Primary Years education from KG1 (age 3) to PY6 (age 11). ICS Côte d'Azur is a member of the Globeducate network.

Formerly known as EBICA, the school's multicultural learning community enjoys a modern and secure campus in Sophia Antipolis, Valbonne, southwest of Nice. Recognised as an IB World School since 2018, ICS Côte d'Azur welcomes students from around the world, offering an international education within the inquiry-based framework of the IB Primary Years Programme, whilst also integrating the national curricula for England and France.

The school attracts internationally-minded families with aspirations for their children to learn in French and English from the early years onwards. Within the multicultural community, students are immersed in both languages with equal measure, in an environment that promotes international understanding while fostering an appreciation of French culture.

ICS Côte d'Azur offers a language support programme for French as a foreign language (FFL) learners and English as a foreign language (EFL) learners. These support lessons for beginners assist acquisition in either language, bringing them the linguistic competencies required to access the curriculum and progress with confidence.

Through learner-centred teaching, ICS Côte d'Azur empowers students, as agents in their IB journey, to develop the self-knowledge and confidence to create their successes. In an environment that fosters cross-cultural understanding, students develop the attributes of the IB learner profile, which equips them with the essential skills to be successful in a diverse and connected world.

Sophia Antipolis is a rich area for science and technology, often referred to as the 'Silicon Valley' of Europe. To reflect its location, the school offers an innovative STEAM programme (Science, Technology, Maths, Art and Engineering), with a dedicated tinkering lab called 'The Hub', LEGO® Education kits, and Apple products in the classroom (the school is an Apple Distinguished School). The vision behind this cutting-edge STEAM initiative is for students to acquire the critical thinking, creativity and problem-solving skills that will be essential for the future.

ICSLONDON
INTERNATIONAL SCHOOL

Shaping the world

(Founded 1979)

Head of School
David Laird

PYP coordinator
James Kendall

MYP coordinator
Svetlana Klyuyeva

DP coordinator
Lucy Masters

Status Private

Boarding/day Day

Gender Coeducational

Language of instruction
English

Authorised IB programmes
PYP, MYP, DP

Age Range 3 – 19 years

Number of pupils enrolled 175

Fees
Day: £19,650 – £28,770

Address
7B Wyndham Place
London
W1H 1PN | UK

TEL +44 (0)20 729 88800

Email
admissions@ics.uk.net

Website
www.icschool.co.uk

ICS London is an independent day school in the heart of central London. We are one of only two IB World Schools in the city offering the full International Baccalaureate (IB) programme for learners aged 3 to 18 years.

Providing an inclusive and international community for early years, primary, secondary and high school students, our children and young people study on two close-by locations at our primary and secondary school sites in elegant Marylebone and Paddington.

With over 40 years' experience delivering globally-recognised education, today we serve our close-knit community of students and their families with the IB Primary Years Programme (PYP), the Middle Years Programme (MYP) and the Diploma Programme (DP). With instruction in English, we are a truly international school where diversity is celebrated with around 65+ different nationalities represented each year.

Quality is assessed, recognised and assured at ICS London through accreditation with the:

- IB World School: ICS London is authorised and accredited by the International Baccalaureate. This is subject to a strict accreditation process monitored by the IB which ensures our education provision is of the highest quality.
- Independent Schools Inspectorate: This is a government approved inspectorate for independent schools which ensures quality on behalf of the UK Department for Education (DfE).

ICS London also prides itself on offering a holistic and personalised learning experience:

- Class sizes: Between 6 and 18 students
- Teacher to student ratio: 1 to 5
- In Secondary School each student is assigned a mentor
- Individual study plans can be tailored to meet students' needs

As a rolling admissions policy is in place, students can join anytime throughout the year. Students can also easily transfer from other curriculums, such as the UK or US and join the IB programme at ICS London.

For further information please visit www.icschool.co.uk or call +44 (0)20 7298 8800.

Early Years & Primary School: 7B Wyndham Place, W1H 1PN
Middle Years and Diploma school: 21 Star Street, W2 1QB

ICSPARIS
INTERNATIONAL SCHOOL
Shaping the world

Director
Mrs. Angela Hollington

DP coordinator
Mr. Subhash Bhatia

Status Private

Boarding/day Day

Gender Coeducational

Language of instruction
English, French

Authorised IB programmes
DP

Age Range 3 – 18 years

Number of pupils enrolled
500

Fees
Day: €18,650 – €25,950

Address
23 rue de Cronstadt
75015 Paris | **FRANCE**

TEL +33 (0)1 56 56 60 70

Email
admissions@icsparis.fr

Website
www.icsparis.fr

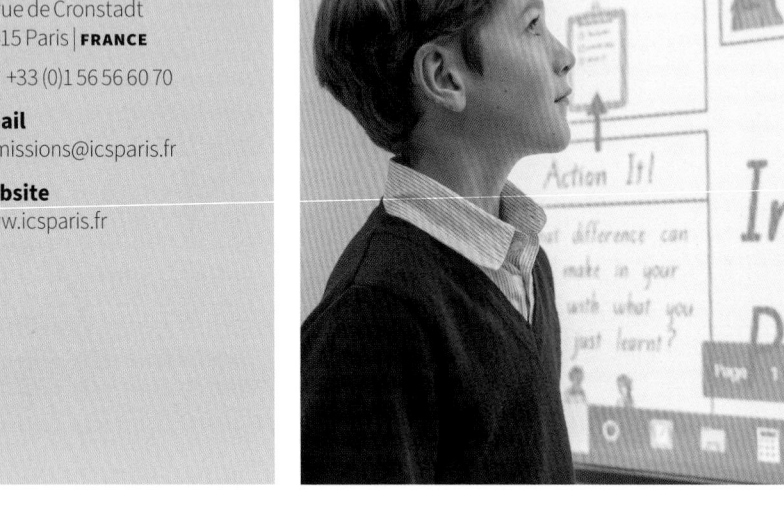

ICS Paris, (formerly EIB – The Victor Hugo School) is an international day school nestled in the heart of Paris. ICS Paris is offering world-class IB curricula.

We welcome students year-round from Nursery to Grade 12 who wish to follow their studies in an international, English speaking environment, obtaining the IB Diploma at the end of high school. Small class sizes at all levels (average 20) ensure that students remain at the centre of their learning.

Students in the Primary section follow a mix of the Cambridge International Curriculum and the International Primary Curriculum allowing them to develop their critical thinking skills and thirst for knowledge. ICS Paris is a candidate school for both the IB Middle Years (MYP) and Primary Years Programmes (PYP), and has been an IB Diploma Programme School for almost 20 years.

Our students may benefit from regular French-language lessons from Nursery to Grade 12. Welcoming students

from over 50 different nationalities, we are able to integrate children at all phases of their language learning. Beginner French lessons are available up to Grade 12, and we have additional English-language-support classes up to and including Grade 9.

Our students may also participate in a variety of activities on campus, including coding, music, theatre, and Model UN. As a member of Globeducate, a leading European educational group, our students have the opportunity for cultural exchange, travelling to other schools in Europe for academic, athletic and music competitions throughout the year.

Globeducate adds ICS Paris to its network of teachers around the world with which to share best practices and creative teaching resources.

For more information, visit our website at www.icsparis. fr or contact our admissions team directly at admissions@ icsparis.fr

Head of School
Victoria Hearn

DP coordinator
Bronwyn Wilson

CP coordinator
Leanne Gibbons

Status State

Boarding/day Day/Homestay

Gender Coeducational

Language of instruction
English

Authorised IB programmes
DP, CP

Age Range 11 – 19 years

Number of pupils enrolled
1311

Address
New Road
Impington
Cambridge
Cambridgeshire
CB24 9LX | UK

TEL 01223 200402

Email
international@ivc.tmet.org.uk

Website
www.impingtoninternational.
org.uk

A World Class IB education from Impington International College – your ticket to a world of opportunity
Why choose Impington International College?

1. **The quality of care is exceptional** – The tutor to student ratio is approximately 1 to 15, with a dedicated Student Manager for pastoral support and guidance. In lessons, the teacher to student ratio is, on average, 1 to 10.

2. **It delivers excellent outcomes** – The pass rate is 100% (international average: 80%) and the average International Baccalaureate (IB) point score is 35.

3. **Students go on to achieve great things** – In 2020, 90% of the students went on to study at university, with 25% offered Russell Group places (including Oxbridge). In addition to this, the remaining 10% of students were successful in their job applications and seamlessly moved into the world of work.

4. **Expert delivery of the International Baccalaureate** – for more than 30 years, Impington International College has offered the IB and was one of the first state schools in the UK to do so. The College is consistently rated 'Outstanding' by Ofsted.

5. **It is truly international** – around half of students attend Impington International College from overseas, creating a culturally diverse student cohort and unique opportunities for study and trips.

Impington International College offers the following programmes to students:

- IB Diploma Programme (DP)
- IB Career-related Programme (CP)
- The Performance School
- Sports Scholarship Programmes

Impington International College bases its teaching on the IB's mission statement and ethos, aiming to develop "inquiring, knowledgeable and caring young people who help to create a better and more peaceful world". Not only do students gain a valuable breadth of skills through either the DP or the CP but IB higher level subjects also provide the same depth of knowledge as A Levels, so students can go on to achieve excellence in whichever path they choose.

The driven cohort achieve outstanding results and have gone on to attend renowned higher education institutions around the world, including: University of Cambridge, University of Oxford, London School of Economics and Political Science, University College London, King's College London, Loughborough University, Leiden University, UCLA, The Place, Italia Conti, International University of Japan, and many more. Many students from the College's Performance School go on to join professional companies, with a number starring in the West End. Students from the sports scholarship programme often go on to study coaching and management at university, or play semi-professionally for local teams.

Institut Florimont

INSTITUT *florimont*

(Founded 1905)

Director General
Mr. Sean Power

DP coordinator
Noha Benani

Status Private

Boarding/day Day

Gender Coeducational

Language of instruction
English, French

Authorised IB programmes
DP

Age Range 3 – 18 years

Number of pupils enrolled
1625

Fees
Day: CHF15,800 – CHF26,300

Address
37 Avenue du Petit-Lancy
1213 Petit-Lancy GE |
SWITZERLAND

TEL +41 2287 90000

Email
admissions@florimont.ch

Website
www.florimont.ch

Institut Florimont is a co-educational day school offering children from 3 to 18 years of age a complete education from kindergarten to the three diplomas that will open the doors to higher education. As well as encouraging academic excellence, Florimont fosters the traditional values and beliefs that are important for life.

Since 1905, Florimont has been preparing students for the French Baccalaureate and, as of 1942, for the Swiss Maturité. Since September 2014 our range of final examinations includes the bilingual (French-English) International Baccalaureate. Therefore, Florimont offers children more opportunities and more choices, allowing them easier access to the world's best universities.

All sections of our school work together to ensure the continuity and coherence of the programme of study. Clear procedures are in place to ensure that new students joining us from other private or public schools are successfully integrated.

Close communication with parents, additional lessons and one-to-one tutoring are just some of the ways that Florimont supports students during their studies.

Our student body is made up of more than fifty nationalities making Florimont a rich multicultural and multilingual learning environment. The importance we attach to this is reflected in our language learning programme. In addition to English, emphasis is placed on German, Switzerland's predominant language, as well as on Chinese, Spanish and Italian. Other languages such as Russian and Arabic are individually tutored or taught to small groups. Bilingual classes in French and English are offered from the primary and throughout the school.

Priority is given to partnerships and exchanges with leading schools worldwide, as well as to many activities that can add value to a university application, such as the CAS programme.

Philosophy lessons are initiated in the primary years in preparation for a better appreciation of Theory of Knowledge in the IB Diploma Programme.

Our students are encouraged to be entrepreneurial, bold, adaptable and creative because we know that these qualities will not only strengthen their university applications but also prepare them to face the challenges of working life.

Find more information on www.florimont.ch

Institut
International
Lancy

(Founded 1903)

Head of School
Monique Roiné

Head of English Secondary
Marie Galmiche

DP coordinator
Tania McMahon

Status Private

Boarding/day Day

Gender Coeducational

Language of instruction
English, French

Authorised IB programmes
DP

Age Range 3 – 19 years

Number of pupils enrolled
1420

Fees
Day: CHF15,400 – CHF27,800

Address
24, avenue Eugène-Lance
Grand-Lancy
CH-1212 | SWITZERLAND

TEL +41 22 794 2620

Email
info@iil.ch

Website
www.iil.ch

The Institut International de Lancy was founded in 1903 (Pensionnat Marie-Thérèse). A private, co-educational school, IIL is a member of the Sisters of St. Joseph de Lyon European network of schools. IIL students, aged 3 to 19 years old, come from a wide variety of cultural and religious backgrounds and represent more than 90 countries. The school offers challenging and inspiring programmes with a strong emphasis on languages. Within a warm, nurturing and bilingual environment, IIL Early Years welcomes children from 3 to 6 years old in three learning paths: English, French and Bilingual (50/50).

An IB World School, IIL is certified to teach the International Baccalaureate Diploma Programme. The school is also a Cambridge University examination centre and is a member of the GESBF (Groupement des Ecoles Suisses qui préparent au Baccalauréat Français). The French Baccalaureate programme is taught under the aegis of the Académie de Grenoble.

Students in the French section follow the Education Nationale curriculum which leads to the Brevet des Collèges and French Baccalaureate diplomas and learn English from the age of 3.

The school prepares students for Cambridge and IELTS examinations, as well as for a number of certified examinations in other languages.

In the English section, students follow the National Curriculum for England, sit Cambridge IGCSE examinations, and prepare for the IB Diploma with multilingual exam options. They also prepare for University Admission tests. Children are taught French as a foreign language from the age of 4.

An Apple Distinguished School, IIL is a pioneer in incorporating information technology in education. In 2011, it became the first One-to-One iPad school in Switzerland, creating an individualised learning environment and a platform for clear information sharing between teachers, parents and students.

After-school supervision, as well as a wide variety of extra-curricular activities, are available for all age groups. IIL operates a regular school bus service. Students of all ages benefit from modern facilities including fully equipped sports halls.

INSTITUT
MONTANA – My Place to Grow®
ZUGERBERG

Director
Alexander Biner

DP coordinator
Emiliano Cori

Status Private

Boarding/day Mixed

Gender Coeducational

Language of instruction
English, German

Authorised IB programmes
DP

Age Range 6 – 19 years

Number of pupils enrolled
360

Address
Schönfels 5
6300 Zug ZG | **SWITZERLAND**

TEL +41 41 729 11 77

Email
admissions@montana-zug.ch

Website
www.montana-zug.ch

Institut Montana was founded in 1926 by Dr Max Husmann. His humanist vision continues to guide us to help every student find their own individual path and thrive.

Learning, Personal Growth, Community

Our combination of small class sizes and individual support fosters a family atmosphere that builds up enthusiasm for learning and motivation to excel. Our international school community is highly diverse yet also promotes typically Swiss values, such as a strong work ethic, respect for each other and dedication to achieving excellence. We are a fully accredited Swiss international boarding school. Since 1987 we have been an official IB World School.

A central location in a natural setting

Our 60 acres campus, at an altitude of 950m, offers seclusion and contact with nature while benefitting from its proximity to Switzerland's major cities Zug and Zürich and the rich opportunities they offer.

The Pursuit of Excellence

Students have the opportunity to choose the academic path that suits their interests and aspirations. We offer (grades 1-12) the best of Swiss and international educational programmes, carefully structured to ensure the highest standards of teaching and learning: Swiss Bilingual Elementary, Secondary and Senior High School, as well as International Cambridge CLSP, IGCSE, IB Diploma programmes.

Home at School

Life at Montana is unique: we breathe mountain air, drink our own spring water and eat fresh food that accommodates all dietary restrictions. Our daily routine promotes self-responsibility while maintaining a well-balanced, active lifestyle.

Summer Sessions

Our summer school is about combining learning with fun. Intensive classes in English and German dramatically improve the language level, while exciting afternoon workshops bring learning to life. Students from all over the world join us every year for a summer adventure filled with outdoor activities on the beautiful Zugerberg.

Empowering Students

We want our students to grow into confident adults who will make the most of their life. Our extracurricular activities encourage them to pursue their passion, whether that is athletic, intellectual or cultural. Our students participate in athletic competitions, Model United Nations conferences, entrepreneurship programmes, theatre productions and more. Our students are global citizens supporting charity projects within Switzerland and around the world.

Montana for Life

We are a vibrant community with strong connections that continue across years as across continents. From scientists to politicians and film directors, our alumni are a diverse group of passionate people who share the same background and values.

inter-community school zurich

EST. 1960

(Founded 1960)

Head of School
Mary-Lyn Campbell

Secondary Principal
James Penstone

Primary Principal
Nathaniel Atherton

PYP coordinator
Claire Febrey

MYP coordinator
Graham Gardner

DP coordinator
Ann Lautrette

Status Private

Boarding/day Day

Gender Coeducational

Language of instruction
English

Authorised IB programmes
PYP, MYP, DP

Age Range 18 months – 18 years

Number of pupils enrolled
840

Fees
Day: CHF12,220 – CHF36,950

Address
Strubenacher 3
8126 Zumikon | **SWITZERLAND**

TEL +41 44 919 8300

Email contact@icsz.ch

Website www.icsz.ch

School Description

The Inter-Community School Zurich (ICS) is the longest-established international school in the Zurich area. A private co-educational day school, established in 1960, we provide a world-class international education for students aged 18 months to 18 years.

Our language of instruction, in a multilingual context, is English. Our 'English as an Additional language' (EAL) programme supports students with limited English. All students learn German, the language of our host country.

Students undertake the full IB Diploma. As well as offering the full IB Diploma to all students, ICS champions excellence in Sports and Arts and offers students a broad range of exciting extra – curricular opportunities alongside the academic IB programme.

Learning Beyond the Classroom

ICS believes that learning beyond the classroom, as well as within, adds value to a rigorous educational experience. We offer collaborative and innovative extra-curricular activities to inspire and engage students.

Service Learning, both locally and internationally, is a key component of the ICS curriculum. Students are constantly encouraged to look beyond themselves. As a Round Square member school, ICS offers students opportunities to join Round Square Service initiatives.

Zurich, Switzerland

With vast natural and cultural resources, Switzerland is a perfect environment for "learning through doing". By deliberately structuring authentic learning experiences outside the classroom, we foster students' holistic development. Field trips are an integral part of learning at ICS, giving students the chance to apply their learning, broaden their horizons and develop leadership and independence.

Admissions

As an international school, we welcome students of all nationalities; we currently have students from 50+ countries here.

We welcome applications from prospective students throughout the year. Please contact us at contact@icsz.ch if you have any questions or if you would like to arrange a visit.

Location

We are conveniently located on a single campus, situated near the Zurich city centre and easily accessed by public transportation. We also offer a school bus service.

(Founded 1984)

General Director
Jean-Marc Gobbi

DP coordinator
Pablo Besozzi

Status Private

Boarding/day Mixed

Gender Coeducational

Language of instruction
English, French

Authorised IB programmes
DP

Age Range 2 – 18 years

Number of pupils enrolled
950

Fees
Day: €11,000 – €17,000
Boarding: €24,000 – €32,000

Address
500 Route de Bouc-Bel-Air
Domaine des Pins, Luynes
Aix en Provence
13080 | FRANCE

TEL +33 (0)4 4224 0340

Email
info@ibsofprovence.com

Website
www.ibsofprovence.com

The International Bilingual School of Provence, an independent coeducational school located near Aix-en-Provence in the south of France, owes its international character to the diversity of its student population. The school, established since 1984, has an annual enrolment of 800 students from more than 75 different countries in its day and boarding sections. In addition to the French students who make up 50% of the student population, IBS welcomes pupils from the five continents desiring to pursue their education in English, French or both.

A particularity of the school is that the international section is not dominated by any one nationality and new students are made to feel at home immediately. Committed to French-English bilingualism, the school offers both the International Baccalaureate Diploma Programme and the French Baccalaureate. The school also offers seven first languages to ensure that the student maintains his/her own language skills.

Philosophy

Small classrooms, qualified teachers, modern facilities in a tranquil, calm environment help ensure the success of each student. IBS of Provence recently invested in a new 7000m2 state-of-the-art campus which includes a sports complex, four new tennis courts (2 hard surface, 2 synthetic clay), football field, indoor gymnasium, 400+ seat auditorium for theatre performances and international conferences as well as a three-level academic building with fully equipped laboratories, art rooms, library, multi-media room and rooftop terrace.

The school also has a boarding section with 150 students residing in one of the five boarding houses which offer a home-like atmosphere in a beautiful Provençal setting. Involvement in various extracurricular activities is expected and enhances the development of each individual's character within the spirit of the school. Politeness, respect and consideration for others are important values at IBS. Students leave IBS, the majority for 1st choice university placements, as caring, responsible young citizens.

Summer school

During the spring and summer holidays, IBS offers intensive French as a Foreign Language and English immersion programmes. Over 400 students from all over the world join IBS every summer to develop their language skills while discovering the beauty of the Provence region. For more information about our summer program or group visits, please contact Ms. Lisa Ortola, Spring/Summer Camp Coordinator, by email at stages@ibsofprovence.com.

Admissions

We accept applications for admission to our school year-round based on availability. There is no formal entrance exam but students must submit two years' of school reports, a letter of recommendation from a teacher/Head of School as well as a letter of motivation. For more information about admissions or to schedule a tour of the school, please contact Ms Lena Junge at admissions@ibsofprovence.com.

International Kids Campus GmbH

international
kids campus
zweisprachiger
Kindergarten

(Founded 2007)

Head of School
Katharina Schmidt

PYP coordinator
Susanne Green

Status Private

Boarding/day Day

Gender Coeducational

Language of instruction
English, German

Authorised IB programmes
PYP

Age Range 2.5 – 6 years

Number of pupils enrolled 48

Address
Lerchenauerstrasse 197
80935 Munich, Bavaria | **GERMANY**

TEL +49 89 411 149 550

Email
info@theikc.com

Website
www.theikc.com

Our Mission
At the International Kids Campus, children are inspired to embrace their academic, cultural, physical, social and emotional learning potential in partnership with their peers, teachers and families within a stimulating and caring international and bilingual environment. The IKC learning community supports students to become lifelong learners who strive to be active members of society shaping an internationally minded and peaceful world of tomorrow.

Our Kindergarten
The International Kids Campus is a small private kindergarten in the Heart of Munich, the capital of Bavaria. We have two groups with mixed ages ranging from 2.5-6 years of age. The kindergarten is taught bilingually and integrates German and English throughout the entire day. Each group is taught by three full time teachers including at least one English and one German teacher.

The IKC is a private co-educational all-day school with flexible pick up times. Our day is structured with a variety of play, rest and learning phases. We always adapt the daily routine on a flexible basis to suit the needs of every child.

Our school community includes a wide range of different countries and cultures of the world, thriving from the relationships we build with the kids, parents and even extended family. We see ourselves as the first building block of shaping internationally minded and well-rounded little people that face the world with curiosity and confidence.

International School Basel

(Founded 1979)	**Boarding/day** Day
Director Bradley Roberts	**Gender** Coeducational
Senior School Principal Tico Oms	**Language of instruction** English
Middle School Principal Tara Waudby	**Authorised IB programmes** PYP, MYP, DP
Junior School Principal Michelle Phillips	**Age Range** 3 – 19 years
PYP coordinator Lyneth Magsalin	**Number of pupils enrolled** 1248
MYP coordinator Siân Thomas	**Address** Fleischbachstrasse 2 4153 Reinach | **SWITZERLAND**
DP coordinator Sean Coffey	**TEL** +41 61 715 33 33
Status Private	**Email** info@isbasel.ch
	Website www.isbasel.ch

Mission:

"We all want to learn more;
We all do it in different ways;
We all have fun learning;
We all help."
- ISB Student

ISB is a private, not-for-profit, co-educational day school established in 1979. Our students and teachers come from all corners of the world, creating a diverse and inclusive community. We live our Mission every day in every area of the school, as it reminds us to appreciate our learning differences, help each other out, and in our quest for excellence, find a way to make it fun and engaging.

Here at ISB, we firmly believe that true education neither ends nor begins in the classroom alone. As our students explore the world beyond the classroom, our well-qualified teachers and staff instil a skill set that will help them remain lifelong learners, no matter where they live and what they do in the world.

We live in a rapidly changing world, thus, education must lead that change. Investing in professional development at all levels to stay at the forefront of educational trends is our priority to prepare our students to embrace challenges and shape a better world.

Campuses

Our three campuses, located on the outskirts of the city of Basel on the edge of the Swiss countryside, provide students with world-class learning opportunities. An efficient public transport system and convenient pedestrian and bicycle paths ensure easy access to ISB campuses. Age-appropriate and supportive learning environments encourage students' potential and nurture their talents at all stages of intellectual, physical and emotional development, providing them with the means to grow and thrive.

Inclusion

We understand that all children learn differently and possess individual strengths and areas for growth. As stated in our Mission, "We all do it in different ways." ISB embraces diversity, not only in race or culture, but in the learning profiles of our students. ISB serves learners by aligning student needs with appropriate resources and support by qualified and experienced teachers and staff.

Academic Results

In 2021, 123 students took IB Diploma Programme exams and achieved an overall average of 37 points, well above the world average. 72% of students achieved 35 points or more, and 30% of students gained 40 points or more. In addition 5 students successfully completed IB Diploma Courses exams. ISB graduates have successfully transferred to top universities around the world.

(Founded 2009)

Head of School
Penny Garner

PYP coordinator
Rachel Bestow

MYP coordinator
Anne Vollmer

DP coordinator
Clare Lax

Status Private

Boarding/day Day

Gender Coeducational

Language of instruction
English

Authorised IB programmes
PYP, MYP, DP

Age Range 3 – 19 years

Number of pupils enrolled
150

Address
Via Benaco 34/B
Bedizzole
25080 Brescia | **ITALY**

TEL +39 030 2191182

WHATSAPP +39 3928970458

Email
info@isbrescia.com

Website
www.isbrescia.com

Teaching and learning at International School Brescia is about preparing our students in a global community to have the skills, the knowledge and the capacity to problem solve that will enable them to meet the challenges of the future. With a strong emphasis on developing the IB Learner Profile*, and by learning through inquiry, action and reflection our students acquire in-depth knowledge and become deep thinkers.

ISB is a co-educational private day school located close to Lake Garda in the province of Brescia, Italy. Founded in 2009 we are a fully authorised International Baccalaureate (IB) continuum school offering the Primary Years Programme (PYP), Middle Years Programme (MYP) and the Diploma Programme (DP).

ISB offer our students the best possible international education in a supportive and inclusive, caring environment. Principled IB learners are honest and fair and take responsibility for their own learning and actions and our students are guided to act with integrity.

Our open-minded and respectful culture encourages the whole school community to contribute to the teaching and learning in school and this collaboration and involvement makes our school a very welcoming and special place to learn.

Our student body is made up of around 18 nationalities and we cultivate a truly international outlook whilst fostering knowledge and experience of our host country, Italy. English is our language of instruction, and we provide support for those students joining us, who have limited knowledge, to be communicators.

In addition to delivering the IB subjects, our balanced curriculum provides many opportunities for extra-curricular experiences such as workshops, field trips, sporting exchanges and international travel. We support out of school interests and commitments and motivate our students to be active members of the community.

As ISB grows and develops we continue to reflect on our practices and to participate in the wider IB world community to produce a positive impact on student learning outcomes.

IB Learner Profile – International Baccalaureate Organisation 2006

INTERNATIONAL SCHOOL OF BELGIUM

(Founded 1979)

Head of School
Mr. Wayne Johnson

Head of Secondary
Ms. Karen Relf

DP coordinator
Ms Pauline Kimman

Status Private

Boarding/day Day

Gender Coeducational

Language of instruction
English

Authorised IB programmes
DP

Age Range 3 – 18 years

Number of pupils enrolled
200

Fees
Day: €9,220 – €19,600

Address
Kontichsesteenweg 40
2630 Aartselaar, Antwerp |
BELGIUM

TEL +32 3 271 0943

Email
info@isbedu.be

Website
www.isbedu.be/

Mission – *Dream. Achieve. Celebrate. Unite.*

Location

International School of Belgium (ISBe) is a private, fee paying, not for profit International School which is located in the small town of Aartselaar, about 10km south of the city of Antwerp. While the school has strong ties to the local Aartselaar community, our student population comes from Antwerp, Mechelen and Brussels.

Internationalism

Belgium is a multilingual country and as such, ISBe supports the importance of language learning through English as the main language of instruction and Dutch and French as foreign languages.

Demographics

As a small school from Preschool to Class 12, students experience a very personalised education. We are an international community with a diverse student population representing more than 20 countries. Our faculty is also very diverse and draws from countries all over the world.

Activities and Experiences

Students are afforded access to a range of opportunities to enhance their learning programme – sporting teams, drama & music productions, senior school CAS trip, art exhibitions, MUN conferences, educational excursions, leadership roles through student council and the House system, ski trip, community events, and an extensive co-curricular programme after school.

University Pathways

The IBDP provides the perfect passport for university entry worldwide. Commonly our students attend first choice universities in the UK, Belgium, The Netherlands and Asia. However, our alumni have attended universities in the USA and many other European countries.

We have a university and careers counsellor available to senior school students who advises them on and assists them with university choices, applications and processes. We also organise a variety of university fairs and talks each year to ensure that students are exposed to a range of options.

Heads of School
Mrs. Guia Ghidoli & Mrs. Chiara Traversi

Head of Primary
Roisin Cosgrove

Head of Secondary
Roberta Sana

PYP coordinator
Helen Bird

MYP coordinator
Roberta Sana

DP coordinator
Roberta Sana

Status Private

Boarding/day Day

Gender Coeducational

Language of instruction
English, Italian

Authorised IB programmes
PYP, MYP, DP

Age Range 2 – 18 years

Number of pupils enrolled
330

Address
Via Monte Gleno, 54
24125 Bergamo | **ITALY**

TEL +39 035 213776

Email
info@isbergamo.com

Website
www.isbergamo.com

Founded in 2011, the International School of Bergamo (ISBergamo) is part of the Inspired Education Group, a leading global schools group educating over 50,000 students across a network of more than 70 schools. Committed to delivering high quality educational programmes, ISB strives to develop the intellectual, personal, emotional and social skills needed to live, learn and work in a rapidly globalising world.

The school is authorised to offer the Primary Years, Middle Years and Diploma Programmes, providing an International Baccalaureate continuum education.

Joining ISBergamo offers a fantastic opportunity to enter a safe and nurturing environment, where the Italian culture is valued alongside the recognition and appreciation of a multicultural collective diversity. Technology plays an important role in the school and is embedded in the school curriculum through a blended approach where we feel it adds value to teaching and learning.

In our state-of-the-art campus, of around 15,000 sqm, students can benefit from specialised facilities, including a dedicated Early Years area, an Art & Design Lab, a school library, a cafeteria and an extensive outdoor area with a modern football pitch, a multipurpose sports facility, and fully equipped playgrounds.

Recent additions to the facility include a Secondary School wing with a specialised Science Laboratory, a Music, Drama & Dance studio, an Innovation Lab, and a newly expanded indoor gym.

The school is located in the Eastern part of Bergamo, in a green and quiet environment rich in sporting facilities; rugby fields, an indoor climbing wall and an athletics track can be found just at the end of the road.

Thanks to an efficient bus service, the school covers the city of Bergamo as well as a large number of the surrounding communities.

International School of Berne

(Founded 1961)	**Authorised IB programmes** PYP, MYP, DP
Director Denise Coates	**Age Range** 3 – 19 years
PYP Coordinator Richard Dowse	**Number of pupils enrolled** 276
Middle School Principal Kirsty DeWilde	**Fees** CHF13,220 – CHF36,035
Upper School Principal Brette Book	**Address** Allmendingenweg 9 3073 Gümligen
Status Private	Bern | **SWITZERLAND**
Boarding/day Day	**TEL** +41 (0)31 959 10 00
Gender Coeducational	**Email** admissions@isberne.ch
Language of instruction English	**Website** www.isberne.ch

The International School of Berne (ISBerne) is a multicultural community of 276 students, representing over 40 countries. We are located in the village of Muri-Gümligen, just 15 minutes from Berne, the capital city of Switzerland.

ISBerne is proud to be an IB World School, offering all three core IB Programmes. Additionally, ISBerne is accredited by the Council of International Schools (CIS) and the New England Association of Schools and Colleges (NEASC) and as such, offers a fully accredited US High School diploma, in addition to the IB Diploma. ISBerne also offers this US High School Diploma to successful graduates of its affiliate distance learning programme, ISBerne Online.

Admission to ISBerne is based upon two criteria; the potential of the applicant to benefit from the educational services provided and the capacity of the school to meet the educational needs of the applicant. ISBerne welcomes applications from students who have demonstrated academic and social skills, a sound character, reliability and an eagerness to learn. These traits, combined with an ISBerne education, will prepare students for the future, teach them cultural appreciation and enable them to work with others. Graduates from ISBerne are regularly accepted to top university around the world.

The ISBerne curriculum reflects a carefully considered balance between guided inquiry and the acquisition of essential skills. Students benefit from small class sizes, a highly qualified faculty, and numerous language programmes and are active in the local community through various field trips, sporting events and other experiences such as Outdoor Education Week and the Ski Fridays Programme. The curriculum is supported by an expansive extra-curricular After School Activities Programme as well as competitive sports teams which compete against teams across Switzerland in the Swiss Group of International Schools (SGIS) circuit.

As an IB World School, ISBerne takes its commitment to internationalism very seriously. The diversity of cultures that make up the school community requires an appreciation, acceptance and respect of oneself and others. ISBerne prides itself on developing positive and enriching relationships between teachers, students and parents. Through choices made, daily operations and the philosophy embraced, the school places the child at the center of all it does.

International School of Bucharest

(Founded 1996)

Director
Mr. Serdar Sakman

DP coordinator
Mr. Yusuf Suha Orhan

Status Private

Boarding/day Day

Gender Coeducational

Language of instruction
English

Authorised IB programmes
DP

Age Range 2 – 18 years

Number of pupils enrolled 710

Address
1R Gara Catelu Str., Sector 3
Bucharest 032991 | **ROMANIA**

TEL +40 21 3069530

Email
admissions@isb.ro

Website
www.isb.ro

2021 marks an important year in the history of ISB, as we celebrate our 25th year. Since 1996, the International School of Bucharest (ISB) has grown to become one of the most flourishing schools in Romania.

In Primary and Lower Secondary, ISB follows The National Curriculum for England and Wales, adapted to meet international best practices. We offer the Cambridge International General Certificate of Secondary Education (IGCSE) in Key Stage 4 and the International Baccalaureate Diploma Programme (IBDP) in the Sixth Form. The curriculum offers students from age of 2 to 18 a demanding and reflective education with an international perspective.

Our Mission is to provide each student with a broad, balanced education in a safe and supportive environment. We promote an enjoyment of learning, creativity and excellence, whilst working in close harmony with our diverse community. We enable students to reach their full potential and develop skills to become independent, respectful and caring adults who will be successful and contribute to global society.

We offer a wide variety of DP courses, all taught by specialist teachers, making use of an extensive range of facilities and up to date educational technology.

Our Sixth Form has a significant rate of acceptance from the top universities in the UK – Russell Group, the USA and the Netherlands. We expect our Sixth Form students to apply the core values of ISB in their future careers as independent and well-rounded individuals. IB DP enables them to discover their skills and interests, and encourage them to push their limits.

We take pride in our students' achievements, and teachers are committed to helping each individual succeed. This is at the heart of our community.

International School of Como

Head of School
Mr Gavin Williams

PYP coordinator
Rebecca Reider

MYP coordinator
Ben Thompson

DP coordinator
Natalie Ackers

Status Private

Boarding/day Day

Gender Coeducational

Language of instruction
English, Italian

Authorised IB programmes
PYP, MYP, DP

Age Range 2 – 18 years

Number of pupils enrolled 370

Address
Via Adda 25
22073 Fino Mornasco (CO) | **ITALY**

TEL +39 031 572289

Email
info@iscomo.com

Website
www.iscomo.com

Founded in 2002, the International School of Como (ISC) has grown to stand for excellence and has contributed to the expansion of international education in Northern Italy, as one of the almost 5,000 International Baccalaureate (IB) schools located worldwide. Today, ISC welcomes over 370 students from 2 to 18 years old of 46 nationalities and an international staff of more than 60 qualified teachers and assistants.

ISC is committed to providing children with the best educational experience possible. ISC offers the IB (International Baccalaureate) Primary Years, Middle Years and Diploma Programmes and aspires to create a community where learning is the central driving factor of a journey in which our students become ethical thinkers, creative problem-solvers, community-minded and individuals of action on the world stage.

Our state-of-the-art campus was designed and built specifically for our students and provides for every aspect of a vibrant, innovative and rigorous education. Over 10,000

square metres of internal and external spaces house our extremely large classrooms, a Robotics lab, two Art Studios, 3 fully-equipped Science Laboratories, A Drama Studio, a well-stocked Library, an indoor gym and outdoor multipurpose sports facility, cafeteria and playgrounds. Recent additions to the facility include an IBDP Study Centre and our 'CoLab', which is a shared work area / coffee bar.

With our efficient bus service we can cover a large number of the surrounding communities, and beyond, including: Como, Lecco, Varese, and Lugano (Switzerland).

At ISC we are driven by our Mission Statement which is: *"The International School of Como is a student-centered community of internationally-minded learners. We offer a balanced and challenging curriculum, in a safe and nurturing environment, where we respect and value the Italian culture and our collective diversity. We empower all students to be active, reflective and responsible lifelong learners who can achieve their full potential and contribute to an ever-changing world."*

International School of Islamabad

Superintendent
Ms Rose Puffer

Principal
Timothy Musgrove

Principal
Riffat Hassan

PYP coordinator
Mary Frances Penton

DP coordinator
Dora Flores

Status Private

Boarding/day Day

Gender Coeducational

Language of instruction
English

Authorised IB programmes
PYP, DP

Age Range 2 – 19 years

Number of pupils enrolled 270

Address
Sector H-9/1, Johar Road
P.O. Box 1124
Islamabad
44000 | PAKISTAN

TEL +92 51 443 4950

Email
school@isoi.edu.pk;
registrar@isoi.edu.pk

Website
www.isoi.edu.pk

The International School of Islamabad (ISOI) is a private, coeducational, college-preparatory day school. ISOI offers an inquiry-based curriculum to students of 38 nationalities. The school operates on the semester system and is accredited by Middle States Association of Colleges and Schools. ISOI is an IB World School, offering the International Baccalaureate Diploma (IBDP) in grades 11/12. ISOI is also an IB PYP school. ISOI was founded in 1965. The campus is located on 23+ acres on the outskirts of Islamabad, Pakistan. The campus includes Elementary School, Middle School and High School quads, a gym, an auditorium, an open-air theater, an IB art gallery, a physical education center, tennis courts, a climbing wall, a running track, playing fields, a swimming pool, two libraries and two technology centers. Students are admitted on the basis of previous academic records, standardized test scores, a writing sample and verification of the need for an international, English curriculum.

The school year runs from August to early June and is divided into two semesters. The first semester runs from August to December and the second semester runs from January to June. The school follows a two week, rotating block schedule.

Vision
The International School of Islamabad inspires open collaboration to create a student-centered, inquiry-based learning environment that cultivates enthusiastic and globally-minded individuals.

Mission
The International School of Islamabad ensures that each student strives for academic success, develops intellectual curiosity, and becomes a responsible global citizen.

International School of London

(Founded 1972)

Principal Mr Richard Parker

Primary Principal
Ms Kathryn Firebrace

Secondary Principal
Mr Paul Rose

PYP coordinator
Ms Iliana Gutierrez

MYP coordinator
Ms Hyun Jung Owen

DP coordinator
Paul Morris

Status Private

Boarding/day Day

Gender Coeducational

Language of instruction
English & Mother-tongue

Authorised IB programmes
PYP, MYP, DP

Age Range 3 – 18 years

Number of pupils enrolled
500

Fees
Day: £19,000 – £26,300

Address
139 Gunnersbury Avenue
London **W3 8LG | UK**

TEL +44 (0)20 8992 5823

Email mail@isllondon.org

Website www.isllondon.org

The International School of London (ISL) is an International Baccalaureate (IB) World School with embedded mother tongue language programmes and over 40 years' experience of delivering education excellence for ages 3-18. Our school has earned a global reputation as a leading International Baccalaureate (IB) school and is widely recognised as one of the UK's best and most experienced international schools.

We offer an exceptional world of learning for every student. Starting with a genuinely warm welcome to our multi-cultural environment from our award winning transitions team, we work with each child to devise an individual learning programme tailored to their unique needs and goals. Our strong focus on student wellbeing, in a supportive environment, is complemented in the classroom by dynamic teaching practises. It's this all-round approach that we believe leads to the academic and personal success that characterises ISL pupils.

We are a culturally diverse community. Students' cultural and linguistic identities are valued and nurtured through our international curriculum and mother tongue programme. Our school develops the attitudes, skills and understanding needed for active and responsible contributions to both local and global communities.

ISL has high academic standards, offering three IB programmes: the Primary Years, Middle Years and Diploma Programmes. These three align to the unique developmental needs of students from age three through to pre-university.

We are committed to intercultural and high-quality education taking learning beyond the walls of the classroom. We provide many opportunities in sports, service learning, and the arts which challenge our students to grow and develop. Our location in the city of London provides fantastic opportunities for innovative projects. The breadth and depth of our programmes ensure that our graduates are prepared for life at leading universities worldwide.

ISL has a family atmosphere, and we give a voice to all members of our community, with active parent groups and a committed student government. Students at ISL develop a keen sense of inter-cultural understanding which is something of great value in our globalised world. ISL actively celebrates this diversity throughout the year from class activities to whole school events.

International
School of London
Qatar

(Founded 2008)

Head of School Dr. Sean Areias

PYP coordinator
Danielle Robertson

MYP coordinator
Smita Shetty

DP coordinator
Jackie Isherwood

Status Private

Boarding/day Day

Gender Coeducational

Language of instruction
English

Authorised IB programmes
PYP, MYP, DP

Age Range 3 – 18 years

Number of pupils enrolled
1161

Fees
QR53,005 – QR75,655

Address
PO Box 18511
North Duhail
Doha | **QATAR**

TEL +974 4433 8600

Email
mail@islqatar.org

Website
www.islqatar.org

Founded in 2008, The International School of London (ISL) Qatar is an International Baccalaureate (IB) World School, authorized to offer the IB Primary Years, Middle Years and Diploma Programmes.

ISL Qatar has developed a strong presence both locally and internationally as a pioneering educational institution, that is continually exploring the process of learning and considering what constitutes effective learning. ISL Qatar has an outstanding reputation for high academic standards, prestigious International Baccalaureate (IB) programmes.

ISL Qatar is part of the International School of London Group, which has a tradition of over 40 years of outstanding educational achievement in the UK. The IB curriculum fulfils the School's vision of combining intellectual rigour and high academic standards with a strong emphasis on the ideals of international mindedness and responsible global citizenship.

ISL Qatar's unique and pioneering Mother Tongue programme is a particular highlight of the school, as we are the only school in Qatar to offer Mother Tongue Programmes in over 12 languages, with additional languages being developed each academic year. We are focused upon the students' cultural and linguistic identities as part of the learning experience, valuing their cultural identity as an integral part of being a member of the learning community. This facet of inclusion strives to maintain the home culture and language, fostering parental engagement and supporting the academic performance of our young learners.

ISL Qatar is a culturally diverse community which fosters a passion and enthusiasm for learning through outstanding educational practice from ages 3-18 from over 70 countries. The school's international staff represent 50 different nationalities. ISL Qatar develops the attitudes, skills and understanding needed for active and responsible contributions to both local and global communities.

Headmaster Mr. Darren Nicholas	**Age Range** 2 – 18 years (Boarding 14-18 years)
PYP coordinator Sara Lomas	**Number of pupils enrolled** 900
MYP coordinator Domenico Vetrisano	**Address** Via I Maggio, 20 20021 Baranzate (MI)	**ITALY**
DP coordinator Tony Burtenshaw	**TEL** +39 02 872581
Status Private	**Email** admissions@ism-ac.it
Boarding/day Mixed	**Website** www.internationalschoolofmilan.it
Gender Coeducational	
Language of instruction English	
Authorised IB programmes PYP, MYP, DP	

Welcome to the International School of Milan. Although we are the longest established international school here in the city, at our school you will find the strongest academic standards supported by the most progressive educational thinking that has served the international and Italian communities in Milan for over 60 years. We are confident that our ethos, focused on achievement and underpinned by opportunity for all, will enable your children to develop their confidence and be ready to embrace the challenges of the future.

The IB curriculum (which runs throughout all years) is a truly international one and is a perfect fit for the needs of all our students. Our PYP, MYP and IB Diploma programmes thoroughly prepare our students for further study all around the world, including at some of the world's leading universities. Our results are significantly above world averages with achievement in the Diploma for example at a particularly high level.

Our international, dedicated and skilled teaching body works well with our students in order to make them the success we know they can be. Their desire to challenge young minds is shaped by a growth mindset, ensuring that the focus is on every student achieving beyond what a school might 'normally expect'. In short, we believe your son or daughter can achieve more and be happier with us here at IS Milan.

We opened our brand new boarding house in September 2018 and can accommodate over 40 students. With the care and attention given by our staff, boarding at IS Milan provides a truly transformative international educational experience for 14 to 18-year-olds.

The International School of Milan is proud of its position in the city as the premier international IB school in terms of its curriculum and outlook and is renowned for its high educational standards and caring learning environment. We are also a diverse community with over 50 nationalities and a student body that is proud to belong to our school community and enthusiastic about the learning they take part in. We are certain that you will see the International School of Milan as a place where learning is genuinely celebrated and where each of our students are valued and challenged to succeed from the age of 2 up to 18.

Head of School
Mrs. Caroline Troughton

PYP coordinator
Michael Perry

MYP coordinator
Anna Chiara Forti

DP coordinator
Caroline Searle

Status Private

Boarding/day Day

Gender Coeducational

Language of instruction
English

Authorised IB programmes
PYP, MYP, DP

Age Range 3 – 18 years

Number of pupils enrolled
230

Address
Piazza Montessori, 1/A
41051 Montale Rangone (MO) |
ITALY

TEL +39 059 530649

Email
admissions@ismodena.it

Website www.
internationalschoolofmodena.it

Welcome to the International School of Modena. Inaugurated in 1998 as a joint venture with Tetra Pak, whose global research and development unit is located in Modena, ISM is a proud member of Inspired which is the fastest growing premium international schools' group operating on 5 continents and educating over 45,000 students globally. Our modern, purpose-built campus, surrounded by green open spaces, is located 12km outside of the city of Modena.

We are a truly international school representing approximately 30 different nationalities and offering the full continuum of International Baccalaureate (IB) education, with the Primary Years Programme (PYP) for children ages 3-11, Middle Years Programme (MYP) for ages 11-16 and the Diploma Programme (DP) for 16-18 years. ISM is one of only a handful of schools in Italy currently authorised to offer this programme which will thoroughly prepare your child for study all around the world, including at some of the world's leading universities.

Our innovative Early Years department features beautiful spaces and play structures specially designed to support the delivery of the IB PYP and Reggio-Inspired Early Years Curriculum.

The curriculum at ISM is carefully designed to reflect the ethos of the school and of the International Baccalaureate with a commitment to inquiry-based learning, encouraging every student to ask questions, to think for themselves and develop the skills to become confident, independent learners who will grow up to be balanced, caring and principled citizens. Our dedicated, international teaching body ensures that students achieve highly at the school. We believe in challenging young minds, ensuring that our focus is on every student achieving beyond expectations both inside and outside of the curriculum. Over the last three years we have achieved an average of 36 in the IB Diploma with a top score of 45 out of 45, allowing our students to access world class universities in numerous countries.

The International School of Modena is a small, friendly school, with just over 230 students at present but it is growing fast due to its popularity with both expat and local families. We are proud to be a premium international school offering high quality education in a caring environment with happy, contented students. We are certain that you will see that ISM is a place that celebrates learning and values each and every student, offering them a challenging, enjoyable education aimed at developing a range of skills required for future success.

(Founded 1984)

Head of School
Mr. Iain Sachev

PYP coordinator
Becky Taylor

MYP coordinator
Carman Natalie

DP coordinator
Gaëlle D'Inca

Status Private

Boarding/day Day

Gender Coeducational

Language of instruction
English, Italian

Authorised IB programmes
PYP, MYP, DP

Age Range 2.5 – 18 years

Number of pupils enrolled 275

Address
Via Solferino 23
20900 Monza (MB) | **ITALY**

TEL +39 039 9357701

Email
admin@ismonza.it

Website www.
internationalschoolofmonza.it

At ISMonza, a full International Baccalaureate (IB) continuum school authorised to offer the Primary Years Programme (PYP), Middle Years Programme (MYP) and Diploma Programme (DP), we endeavour to deliver the International Baccalaureate programmes in the purist of forms, with the school's core values and the IB's Learner Profile embodied in everything that we do. Both the school and the group to which it belongs, have an established record of success in the IB, from age 2 all the way through to admission to the world's leading universities at age 18.

Perhaps most of note is the sense of collaboration that exists amongst all members of the school community. This is most evident in the way in which our highly qualified mother-tongue teachers and inquisitive students work towards a common goal of academic success which is seamlessly balanced with an inherent commitment to active global citizenship at every level. Although all classrooms are fitted with smart TVs and students bring tablets or laptops to school, we use technology in a blended approach where we feel it adds value to teaching and learning and not merely to replace traditional methods (yes, we do use books and, yes, we do talk to one another).

All this takes place in our city-centre campus – a stylish and colourful factory conversion – which has been specifically designed to foster collaborative approaches to teaching and learning. Our science laboratories are fitted with state-of-the-art equipment and we also boast carefully designed on-site spaces which support the delivery of our Reggio-Inspired Early Years Curriculum, three beautiful libraries, as well as studios for visual arts, drama and music, supported by a brand new sports complex. That said, living in such a culturally rich part of the world, we take many opportunities to knock down our classroom walls and learn from opportunities in the local and not-so-local area.

International School of Nice

ISN NICE
INTERNATIONAL SCHOOL
Shaping the world

(Founded 1977)

Director
Mrs Mel Curtis

PYP coordinator
Ms Melissa Demiguel

DP coordinator
Mr Dominique Dubois

Status Private

Boarding/day Day

Gender Coeducational

Language of instruction
English

Authorised IB programmes
PYP, DP

Age Range 3 – 18 years

Number of pupils enrolled
405

Fees
Day: €12,524 – €19,700

Address
15 Avenue Claude Debussy
06200 Nice | **FRANCE**

TEL +33 (0)4 93 21 04 00

Email
admissions@isn-nice.com

Website
www.isn-nice.com

The International School of Nice is an accredited, co-educational, non-sectarian, IB World School, providing Anglophone education for the international community in the Cannes-Nice-Monte Carlo region. The school offers a complete international education from Young Explorers (age 3) to Grade 12 (age 18). ISN Nice is a member of the Globeducate network.

The Primary School follows the IB Primary Years Programme, a rich, inquiry-based approach to learning that focuses on the individual needs of every child. French is mandatory from age 5, and taught on a daily basis.

The Middle School operates as a self-contained unit with its own team of teachers. Skill development is common to all areas and particular attention is given to the student's personal development. An EAL programme parallels mainstream English in the Primary and Middle Schools.

The High School curriculum prepares students for the IGCSE exams and the IB Diploma. Students are guided and supported to reach their potential in a safe and caring environment. A team of highly-qualified and experienced teachers respond to students' diverse learning styles and challenges them through exciting and innovative practices. Over 95% of graduates go directly to college/university, primarily in the UK, France and North America.

The faculty represents over 30 nationalities, and the student body is truly a melting pot, representing over 40 nationalities, with students from Anglophone countries making up ca.20%. This enables cultural awareness and participation in a globalised world for all our students.

ISN offers a number of extra-curricular activities, including a variety of sports, field trips, and a student council. With other Globeducate schools, our students participate in Model United Nations, Academic Olympics, visual art competitions, and initiatives with the WWF, a Globeducate partner. The school occupies a purpose-built facility constructed in 1987 and is located five minutes from Nice International Airport.

ISN prepares its students to excel in the world of tomorrow in an inspiring, supporting and nourishing environment.

International School of Siena

Principal
Ms. Lianne Knibb

PYP coordinator
Brychan Gilbert

MYP coordinator
Letizia Rosati

DP coordinator
Joanne Walker

Status Private

Boarding/day Day

Gender Coeducational

Language of instruction
English, Italian

Authorised IB programmes
PYP, MYP, DP

Age Range 3 – 18 years

Number of pupils enrolled
200

Address
Via del Petriccio e Belriguardo,
49/1
53100 Siena | **ITALY**

TEL +39 0577 328103

Email
office@issiena.it

Website www.
internationalschoolofsiena.it

Founded in 2010, the International School of Siena has grown considerably in the past 11 years. We are the only IB through school in Tuscany, fully authorised for the Primary Years Programme (PYP), Middle Years Programme (MYP) and Diploma Programme (DP).

Learning at IS Siena is exciting and engaging, as students strive for excellence in a climate that is caring and responsive to individual needs and goals. Our global vision is coordinated by an outstanding team of educational leaders and implemented by our highly skilled and dedicated professional staff.

The school takes advantage of a purpose built building with 21st century technology where we enjoy a spacious, light, modern teaching spaces with a spacious indoor gym, Drama/Dance studio, 2 Libraries, Music and Art rooms and Science laboratories fitted out to the highest standards. Our Early Years spaces are specially designed to complement the Reggio Inspired teaching approach. Our Inspired approach to PYP Early Years also draws inspiration from the Reggio Approach.

Learning at the International School of Siena is an

international experience with students from around 25 nationalities. This leads to a perception of the world that merges understanding of our global context with the development of skills and attitudes that young people require to participate fully in the world of tomorrow, both as national and global citizens.

At the same time, we deeply appreciate the diversity of mother tongue languages in our school community and aim to utilise our diversity as well as supporting each student to appreciate our host country of Italy and become fully bilingual in English and Italian. We are so fortunate to be located in a beautiful area of Tuscany where we have access to a variety of cultural and educational resources in our local area which we strive to incorporate into the experience of the students, making connections between the classroom and the world around us.

We are a welcoming school community in which parents, students and staff work together to provide a stimulating programme, which engages each child in a concept-driven and inquiry-based environment.

International School of Ticino SA

Head of School
Mr. Andrew Ackers

PYP coordinator
Ms. Sarah Jane Lee

MYP coordinator
Mr. Graeme Wallbank

DP coordinator
Mr. Paul Highdale

Status Private

Boarding/day Day

Gender Coeducational

Language of instruction
English, Italian

Authorised IB programmes
PYP, MYP, DP

Age Range 3 – 18 years

Number of pupils enrolled
200

Address
Via Ponteggia, 23
Cadempino
6814 Lugano | **SWITZERLAND**

TEL +41 919710344

Email
frontoffice@isticino.com

Website
www.isticino.com

The International School of Ticino is a special and exciting place to be. We are the first and only accredited International Baccalaureate (IB), Primary Years Programme (PYP) and Middle Years Programme (MYP) school in Ticino, Switzerland and also offers the Diploma programme (DP).

At the International School of Ticino we place the student at the centre of all we do to facilitate them to become lifelong learners. We achieve this through our school culture, which is rooted in the IB Mission statement, which states: The International Baccalaureate aims to develop inquiring, knowledgeable and caring young people who help to create a better and more peaceful world through intercultural understanding and respect.

The school opened as a Kindergarten in 2014. It was established to offer the local and international residents of Ticino an IB education. As of 2017 the International school of Ticino joined the education group Inspired, who educate over 45000 students in 64 schools worldwide.

This grounding and combination with a leading education group has laid the foundations for the special community of learning which we see today in our new campus. The school now accommodates students from Kindergarten, 3 years old, to 18, offering the IB PYP, MYP and DP programme with our first graduation class in 2023.

The design and build of the new campus has drawn upon our foundations, the IB mission and the vision of the school; Inspiring the Extraordinary.

We accommodate our students in a facilitated student centred learning environment, where we equip all to develop in the international sector and in line with Ticino requirements, enabling your child to study at our school from the age of 3-18/19.

The International School of Ticino is a special and exciting place to be and we look forward to welcoming you to our community for a school visit, trial day and enrolment.

since 1963
INTERNATIONAL SCHOOL OF TURIN

(Founded 1963)

Head of School
Lara Pazzi

PYP coordinator
Magdalena Matysow

MYP coordinator
Francesca Parisi

DP coordinator
Clara Siviero

Status Private

Boarding/day Day

Gender Coeducational

Language of instruction
English

Authorised IB programmes
PYP, MYP, DP

Age Range 3 – 18 years

Fees
Nursery & Pre Kindergarten
€7,900
Kindergarten €9,800
IBPYP_Grade 1 to 5 €12,600
IBMYP_Grades 6 to 10 €15,500
IBDP_Grades 11 & 12 €17,900

Address
Strada Pecetto 34
10023 Chieri, Turin | **ITALY**

TEL +39 011 645 967

Email info@isturin.it

Website www.isturin.it

The International School of Turin is a private, non-profit organization school open to students from all over the world. Established in 1963 as the American School of Turin, it was refounded in 1974 as the American Cultural Association of Turin (ACAT) and in 2007 renamed as the International School of Turin (IST). Since its establishment, IST has been a point of reference for the international community as well as for local families wishing to raise their children to be ready for the challenges of today's global world.

Our mission is to "inspire lifelong learning and international mindedness, empowering each student to reach their full potential."

IST is an IB World School authorized to offer the IB full continuum of programs in English from Early Years to Grade 12: the Primary Years Programme (PYP), the Middle Years Programme (MYP) and the Diploma Programme (DP).

IST has also been accredited by CIS (Council of International Schools) and NEASC (New England Association of Schools and Colleges) since 1984.

The school's curriculum is international and leads to the completion of both the IST American High School Diploma and the IB Diploma, which is recognized by the Italian Ministry of Education as being legally equivalent to the Italian Maturità.

IST is the only international school in Piedmont to be granted Parità Scolastica (equivalency) by the Italian Ministry of Education for its Early Years and Primary sections.

As proof our school's commitment to sustainability, IST is also certified as a "Green School" by FEE – Foundation for Environmental Education. Our school garden and greenhouse provide endless teaching and learning opportunities for students of all grades to raise their awareness of this global issue.

IST is proud to be a non-selective school and as such we pride ourselves on a well-structured student support team to ensure all students equal opportunities to access the school curriculum and benefit from it. The English Language Learning is aimed at students whose level of English language knowledge requires further development to access regular class courses. The Learning Support team works with students who need additional support to help them develop skills and strategies that will enable them to work at their full potential.

IST's school counsellor is in charge of a school-wide advisory and counselling program and works alongside teachers to help students successfully develop their socio-emotional skills.

IST offers a university counselling service to guide students in their subject choices as well as supporting them with university applications and providing opportunities to learn more about the options available both locally and abroad.

Afterschool activities are an integral part of IST's academic offer and are aimed at promoting and supporting learning beyond the classroom. The IST Sports teams and the IST Orchestra are just two examples.

International School San Patricio Toledo

An **inspired** school

(Founded 2006)

Headmaster
Mr. Simon Hatton-Burke

PYP coordinator
Rebeca Albarrán Corroto

MYP coordinator
Pilar Molina

DP coordinator
Philip Brotherton

Status Private

Boarding/day Mixed

Gender Coeducational

Language of instruction
English, Spanish

Authorised IB programmes
PYP, MYP, DP

Number of pupils enrolled
550

Address
Juan de Vergara, 1
Urbanización La Legua
Toledo
45005 | SPAIN

TEL +34 925 280 363

Email
infotoledo@colegiosanpatricio.
es

Website
colegiosanpatriciotoledo.com/
en

International School San Patricio Toledo is a day and boarding School, offering the complete range of the International Baccalaureate (IBO continuum) from 1 to 18 years. PYP, MYP and DP, bilingual or English only.

Our School prides itself on its range of choice and opportunity be it the diverse subjects on offer at Diploma or the clubs and sporting facilities within our grounds.

Our very strong academic results can be seen once again in 2021 with our excellent 36 point average (our highest ever) and a superb 10% of our cohort achieving 40 points or more. Achieving such results give our students the necessary preparation for university life.

Uninterrupted excellence in extraordinary times, we have been tried and tested with our boarding school remaining open throughout and excellence in Hybrid Learning and In-class or Online: thus serving the needs of all our local and international students.

We are one of the first in Spain to be an official Google Education Reference School. We take great pride in the use of our technology to ensure maximum knowledge for our students and the world they live in.

Location:
Our school is located in an exclusive residential area of Toledo (1 hour from Madrid by car and 30 min by train). The grounds are large with over 30,000 square meters: our purpose built boarding school is within the school grounds, which facilitates the use of the premises at all times without the need for transfers or departures from the campus. This ensures that students live in a fully-equipped campus with maximum security and control.

Furthermore, our Boarding School has over 18 different nationalities providing students with a genuine international experience in the beautiful world heritage city of Toledo.

We offer a complete educational experience for students between 14 and 18 years of age and weekly boarding for students from 12 to 18 years old, allowing them to develop their communication and social skills.

All students have a designated boarding house tutor as well as an academic tutor who oversee the pastoral and academic wellbeing of each individual student. In addition we have a designated university counselor.

Foreign languages:
English, German, French, Chinese

Accommodation:
First class facilities. Rooms are designed to allow groups to be formed according to the personal characteristics and diversity of the students. We can therefore accommodate 2, 3, or 4 students per room on both male and female floors.

Weekends:
We take great pride in our programmed weekend activities for our boarding students allowing them to flourish and provide the necessary balance with their important academic studies.

(Founded 1980)	**Number of pupils enrolled** 160
Principal Júlia Ladeira Santos	**Fees** Day: €4,950 – €10,945
PYP coordinator Jenie Noite	**Address** Caminho dos Saltos 6
MYP coordinator Irene Wensley	9050-219 Funchal, Madeira | **PORTUGAL**
Status Private	**TEL** +351 291 773 218
Boarding/day Day	**Email** office@madeira.sharingschool.org
Gender Coeducational	
Language of instruction English	**Website** www.sharingschool.org
Authorised IB programmes PYP, MYP	
Age Range 3 – 16 years	

The International Sharing School is a highly respected school on the lovely island of Madeira, Portugal. The school offers the PYP and the MYP programmes, teaching students aged 3 to 16, currently representing 23 different nationalities and with teachers from 8 different countries, in an international, multilingual and multicultural environment.

With 40 years of experience in international education, International Sharing School offers both the PYP and MYP, thus being the only IB World School in Madeira offering both programmes.

We are dedicated to achieving enjoyment and excellence in education for all.

As we continue to follow our ethos statement – "The passion of learning, the pride of teaching" – International Sharing School aims to provide an excellent and continuous international educational experience, in order to develop enquiring knowledgeable and caring young people who help create a better and more peaceful world through intercultural understanding and respect.

International Sharing School offers a curriculum focused on personal and professional development, preparing students for an increasingly global, competitive, multicultural and multilingual world.

Students begin their school learning at 3 years of age in a bilingual environment, with educators who are English and Portuguese native speakers, so that by the age of 6 they enter PYP 1 with a sound billingual foundation. The language of instruction throughout the school is English and we offer daily lessons of the host country's language, Portuguese, for all students. In addition, the academic curriculum includes the teaching of German, Spanish, French, Mandarin and Russian. Students, therefore, are able to move to upper secondary and university education, having had the opportunity to learn, with a great degree of fluency, at least 5 of the 7 languages we offer.

We are very proud of our learning-journey and the traditions we have created. We are innovative and always strive to reflect the best of current practices and adapt to the demands of an ever-changing world.

Choosing a school is one of the most important decisions and has high significance as a long-term family investment. We offer a happy, enthusiastic and effective learning environment, combined with the expectation of challenging work experiences and high standards.

We encourage each and every student to fulfil their potential both academically and as a person in readiness for them to take their place successfully in the world of today and for the future.

(Founded 2006)

Principal
Júlia Ladeira Santos

PYP coordinator
Déspina Sarioglou

MYP coordinator
Viviana Serralha

DP coordinator
David Ferreira

Status Private

Boarding/day Day

Gender Coeducational

Language of instruction
English

Authorised IB programmes
PYP, MYP, DP

Age Range 1 – 18 years

Number of pupils enrolled
400

Fees
Day: €9,900 – €25,190

Address
Avenida Dr. Mário Soares 14
2740-119 Oeiras, Lisbon |
PORTUGAL

TEL +351 214 876 140

Email
office@taguspark.
sharingschool.org

Website
www.sharingschool.org

Founded 15 years ago, offering the Portuguese national curriculum, International Sharing School – Taguspark is installed in an award-winning building for its construction.

In 2018 the school was acquired by the Sharing Foundation who transformed it to become an international school, welcoming students from 4 months up to 18 years old (EYP, PYP, MYP, DP), with English as the language of instruction, having become an IB World School in 2020.

Located in Portugal's largest technology park, Taguspark, in Oeiras Valley, in Lisbon Metropolitan Area, International Sharing School– Taguspark intends to grow together with the entire technology park, with the construction of a new Campus, Country Club and Botanical Garden, with the design office www.RosanBosch.com and the architectural offices www.Openbook.pt and engineering www.Alphalink.pt as responsible for the project.

International Sharing School – Taguspark currently welcomes 400 students from 50 different nationalities and 85 highly qualified teachers and assistant teachers, all teaching and learning in a multilingual and multicultural environment.

In PYP and MYP, students have direct contact with 6 languages and 3 different alphabets, with students in DP focused on subjects in the areas in which they intend to continue their studies in higher education.

Our families can find in International Sharing School a warm, calm, personalized environment, integrated in green spaces and with easy access to the main circulation routes in Lisbon, Cascais and Sintra.

At International Sharing School, each student is unique, and fully integrated into the group, where teachers, motivated and rigorous, transmit to students much more than knowledge: they convey how to get to knowledge, through curiosity, research and sharing.

We educate responsible, creative, knowledgeable young people at International Sharing School – Taguspark, always respecting the environment that surrounds them, whether indoors or outdoors.

Integrated in Portugal's largest technology park, students at International Sharing School interact with the environment and with companies from Oeiras Valley, contacting realities that spike their curiosity and motivate them to push even further.

Learning Through Sharing

Head of School
Melike Ayhan Gül

PYP coordinator
Gamze Can

Status Private

Boarding/day Day

Gender Coeducational

Language of instruction
Turkish, English

Authorised IB programmes
PYP

Age Range 3 – 11 years

Number of pupils enrolled
625

Fees
TL43,250 (pre-school) – TL60,500 (primary school)

Address
Bagdat Cad. No. 238/1
Ciftehavuzlar, Kadiköy
34730 Istanbul, Marmara |
TURKEY

TEL +90 216 360 12 18

Email
baris.ilkokul@istek.k12.tr

Website
www.istek.k12.tr

The ISTEK Schools is comprised of several K-12 campuses. As an educational organization and a community that believes in life-long learning, the Foundation is committed to constant innovation and by providing scholarships the Foundation strives for equal opportunity education. Working in national and international contexts, aiming to make positive contributions to both the country and the world's future, and giving priority to scientific inquiry defines ISTEK as a foundation apart.

ISTEK Baris Schools' student body is mainly composed of Turkish students. About 5% come from bilingual/bicultural backgrounds. The Turkish National Curriculum is implemented under the PYP framework.

The school library is very active and has a central role in the lives of the school community. The classrooms that are equipped with modern technology, the field trips organized during the year and access to various databases develop students' research skills and lead them to become active inquirers.

With open mindedness as a goal, open communication is promoted by all the members of the school community. The Student Council is very active and participates in code of conduct related management decisions, regarding the suggestions and wishes of the students. Students are always encouraged to express their opinions and respect others' views. Their opinions are valued and they are provided with many opportunities to take action.

Learning together and learning from one another through cooperative learning and our reflective-thinking-oriented assessment system, support ongoing development of the students and play a pivotal role in leading them to become autonomous learners.

ISTEK Baris Schools as a community is committed to life long learning and responsible action that will help to create a better and more peaceful world.

Admission to ISTEK Baris Schools is offered on the basis of a school administered evaluation and according to the regulations of Turkish Ministry of Education.

Head of School
Yasemin Baysoy Gencten

PYP coordinator
Ayca Özkardes

Status Private

Boarding/day Day

Gender Coeducational

Language of instruction
English, Turkish

Authorised IB programmes
PYP

Age Range 3 – 11 years

Number of pupils enrolled
300

Address
Eski Edirne Asfalti No 512
Sultangazi
34110 Istanbul, Marmara |
TURKEY

TEL +90 212 594 26 11/12

Email
kasgarlimahmut@istek.org.tr

Website
www.istek.k12.tr/kasgarli-
mahmut-kampusu

Since its establishment by Mr. Bedrettin Dalan in 1985, ISTEK Foundation has been raising modern and entrepreneurial generations in line with Atatürk's principles and revolutions. Today, our foundation, which has a chain of education from Kindergarten to University, is prominent in the future of our country with 22 Kindergartens, 22 Primary Schools, 22 Middle Schools, 20 Anatolian High Schools, 14 Science High Schools and Yeditepe University.

ISTEK Kasgarli Mahmut Schools, started operating in the academic year of 1987 – 1988. Our school was named after one of our Turkish seniors, Kasgarli Mahmut, who was known as the first Turkish philologist. On our campus, students study from kindergarten to the last year of high school.

ISTEK Kasgarli Mahmut Campus is located in Sultangazi on a large area of 9360 square meters. Our school facilities include 320 seat conference hall, library, indoor sports complex, swimming pool, music and painting workshops, music recording studio, 4 science and computer laboratories, maker workshop, large dining hall, outdoor sports areas, activity halls, playgrounds and technologically equipped classrooms that allow our students to develop academic and social skills.

Our school, which was accepted to apply PYP with

Candidate School status in April 2016, received a Consultancy Visit by IB in April 2017. In February 2020, IB carried out a Verification Visit and both ISTEK Kasgarli Mahmut Kindergarten and ISTEK Kasgarli Mahmut Primary School were authorized to apply PYP in June 2020. Our school is now honoured with the status of IB World School.

We believe that learning different languages is the key to becoming a global citizen. For this reason, we offer our students an intensive English language education starting from the age of 4. Our students receive bilingual education in pre-school 5-6 age groups and in the first grade of the primary school. In the second grade they choose between German and Spanish languages and receive their second language education until they graduate.

We aim to create experiences that will make our students to be more sophisticated, organized, mature and socially responsible. In addition to our daily flow, our students also participate in different club activities in fields of science, arts and sports in line with their skills and interests. Supported by our enriched curriculum, our students successfully represent our school in national and international organizations.

ISTEK Kasgarli Mahmut Schools is committed to raising caring individuals who are ready to change the world.

Head of Primary School
Esra Türken

Head of Pre-School
Nihan Keles

PYP coordinator
Kevser Kilic

Status Private

Boarding/day Day

Gender Coeducational

Language of instruction
Turkish

Authorised IB programmes
PYP

Age Range 3 – 10 years

Address
Tarabya Bayiri Cad. No 60
Tarabya/Sariyer
34457 Istanbul, Marmara |
TURKEY

TEL +90 212 262 75 75

Email
kemalataturk@istek.k12.tr

Website
www.istek.k12.tr/kemal-ataturk-kampusu

Situated on the European side of Istanbul overlooking the Bosphorus, lies Istek Kemal Atatürk Schools, which educates students from pre-school to high school. Apart from the Preschool and Primary School National Education Curriculum, PYP was added with IB authorization in 2013.

Since 1985 Istek Kemal Atatürk Schools offers a safe environment with open and closed sport centers, a semi-olympic swimming pool, well equipped laboratories, and libraries rich in resources and modern educational technologies. One can also find a spacious dining area, art rooms, a bicycle training zone, and a 7400m garden!

We believe that every child is gifted in a unique way. We aim to discover those gifts by offering different programmes such as; chess, musical instruments, visual arts, swimming, gym, modern dance, drama and brain teasers.

Throughout the year we assess our students in order to provide the best support for those whose needs differ from their peers. Our educational program is continuously developing out of consideration for our children's age, level of development, needs and any international developments. The curriculum is enhanced by making changes that allows students to perform at their top cognitive capacity. We support them in reaching this capacity by activating their curiosity, asking them to research, explore and

solve problems. The IB Baccalaureate PYP Primary Years Programme helps students to experience learning and the process of knowledge. Taking into account each students individual differences, we have tutorials for students who need extra support. We believe that students should care about the issues facing their communities and environment, and it's our responsibility to create a community of well rounded, knowledgeable, internationally minded, and caring students.

English is taught intensively at our school. Our students are evaluated by internationally recognized tests such as Cambridge, Trinity, and GESE every year. From fourth grade on, we teach French and German intensively in an effort to broaden our students horizons and to show them that they are citizens of the world.

We aim to create experiences that will make our students well rounded, organized, mature and socially responsible. We open new clubs in areas where we see students show interest, in addition to the arts and sports lessons that they normally attend. Students are selected to take part in after school clubs aimed at advancing their knowledge of science, and their abilities in arts and sports. These students go on to represent our school in national and international competitions.

Jumeira Baccalaureate School

(Founded 2010)

Principal Richard Drew

Whole School IB Curriculum Leader David Bauzà-Capart

PYP coordinator Gregory Joiner

MYP coordinator Lisa Postlethwaite

DP & CP coordinator Michelle Andrews

Status Private

Boarding/day Day

Gender Coeducational

Language of instruction English

Authorised IB programmes PYP, MYP, DP, CP

Age Range 3 – 19 years

Number of pupils enrolled 1098

Fees
Pre-K to KG2: AED39,750 – AED48,500
Grade 1 to 5: AED52,500 – AED62,500
Grade 6 to 10: AED72,970
Grade 11 and 12: AED84,197

Address
53 B Street, off Al Wasl Road
Jumeira 1
Dubai | **UNITED ARAB EMIRATES**

TEL +971 (0)4 344 6931

Email admissions@jbschool.ae

Website www.jbschool.ae

Campus:

Founded in 2010, Jumeira Baccalaureate School (JBS) is part of Taaleem, the UAE's second largest education provider. The JBS campus sits on approximately eight acres of prime land in the heart of Dubai, with outstanding learning, sporting and performing arts facilities; including a FIFA sized grass field, 25m swimming pool and additional training pool, two large gymnasiums, two full-sized rooftop tennis courts, designated music and visual arts rooms, primary and secondary library and shared play areas for younger students.

Vision and Mission:

Our vision is to prepare all of our students for the innovation age by igniting their passions, purpose and curiosity through challenge and high expectations. Our students are responsible, confident and independent learners that embrace and celebrate diversity; they strive for excellence, whilst maintaining happiness and wellbeing.

Our mission is:

- To embrace and respect diversity
- To foster the wellbeing of all members of our community
- To create a culture in which learning can flourish
- To engage with high levels of challenge, enabling academic and personal success
- To support cognitive and social skill development using innovative, research-based practice to enhance learning for all
- To support the development of emotional intelligence, guided by the elements of the IB learner profile

- To promote environmental awareness, sustainability and entrepreneurship

Our Core values are:

- Wellbeing: promoting self-awareness; self-control; empathy; social skills; and personal responsibility.
- Innovation: promoting critical thinking; communication; collaboration; and creative problem-solving skills.
- High Expectations: promoting learner resilience; the capacity to reflect and act on constructive feedback; take pride in work; and a desire to excel.
- Inclusion: promoting a diverse learning community; building relationships with, and motivating, each learner, including students of determination, through differentiation.
- International Mindedness: promoting an attitude of respect to self and others.

Extended learning and Inclusion:

We aim to provide exceptional opportunities for each of our students in a supporting and challenging environment. We welcome all students to JBS. This could include students with special educational or learning needs, students with English as an additional Language (EAL), and those who are Gifted or Talented. Our dedicated Inclusion Team works on a graduated response to identify and remove barriers to learning. We pride ourselves on high academic standards, however we are more than this. Truly excellent education is about developing a passion for life-long learning and a capability for independent thinking.

KENT COLLEGE
CANTERBURY

(Founded 1885)

Head Mr Mark Turnbull

DP coordinator
Mr Graham Letley

Status Private

Boarding/day Mixed

Gender Coeducational

Language of instruction
English

Authorised IB programmes
DP

Age Range 0 – 18 years
(Boarding from 8)

Number of pupils enrolled
800

Fees
Day: £5,797 – £6,665 per term
Boarding: £8,967 – £12,339 per term

Address
Whitstable Road
Canterbury
Kent **CT2 9DT | UK**

TEL +44 (0)1227 763 231

Email
admissions@kentcollege.co.uk

Website www.kentcollege.com

Kent College Campus

The Senior School sits in 80 acres (32 hectares) of land with 26 acres of sports fields, grazing for the school farm and ancient woodland for walking and cross country running. Yet the centre of Canterbury, with its wide selection of shops, restaurants, theatres, cinemas and world-heritage site, within which sits Canterbury Cathedral, is just a short walk away.

The newly opened Great Hall, a state-of-the-art 600 seat versatile theatre for the performing arts, worship and concerts also hosts the annual Canterbury Festival, the largest Arts event in Kent. The Great Hall is an important step for Kent College in building a world-class campus, and it is used as a versatile and practical space for the school's highly regarded Drama and Music departments.

Curriculum

Kent College prides itself on offering personalised academic programmes, small class sizes and exceptionally well-qualified and experienced teaching staff. All students are provided with a laptop when they start at the school. Pupils achieve excellent academic results at GCSE, A Level, and in the International Baccalaureate (IB). An average point score of 37 in the IB consistently places Kent College in the top 10 IB schools in the UK. The school also offers a wide range of additional support for pupils, including access to a Learning Support Centre and specialist English language teaching for overseas students in the International Study Centre.

Kent College is very flexible when it comes to constructing the timetables for Diploma candidates and encourages applicants to identify courses and subjects they wish to study even if KC does not offer them as they are able to bespoke most options. Kent College offers outstanding levels of teaching and support for the IB Diploma with additional classes and tutoring available as standard to ensure the very best outcomes for individuals.

The academic life of the IB student is complemented with a rich and diverse extra curricular programme at KC. There are large numbers of clubs and societies for every interest and new ones established each year to meet the changing desires of our students. National representation in sport is common with equal standards in Music and Drama, there is simply something for everyone at KC.

Candidates for an IB Diploma scholarship (Year 12 only) must submit written work to the Deputy Head, Mr. Letley (deputyheadofseniorschool@kentcollege.co.uk). International students should contact Mr Letley directly about submitting their application. Written work – applicants must submit two reports: 1. (maximum 300 words) which should explain why you particularly want to study the IB. 2. (maximum 1,000 words) which should be an extended piece of writing based on an area of research that you have completed. This might be research based on reading or possibly some form of experiment/investigation. The assessment includes a short interview that will focus on the content of the two written reports.

Beyond the classroom

Kent College has a strong belief in "work hard, play hard"

and provides 60 different clubs and activities for students to participate in. They are actively encouraged to try something new every term. A cornucopia of clubs and societies are available from Archery to Zumba dancing. Students can try many different sports from basketball to rowing and fencing as well as joining the debating society, photography club or jewellry making. The school also runs an active Eco Warriors group and a woodland conservation team as well as the Duke of Edinburgh programme from Year 9 at Bronze, Silver and Gold award level.

Many students join the school's Farm Club and learn to care for animals at our working farm and show them at the Kent Show where they can also join the annual Young Farmers Camp. Horse Riding lessons are also available in the school's riding arena and our NESA team compete in events all over the country.

Pastoral Care

Kent College has a reputation for being a friendly and caring school, and our pastoral structure is designed to give all pupils the support they need from the start of their school career to the day they leave. Our mission is always pupil-centred and to focus on enabling every child to become the best they can be. The Heads of House lead their teams of Tutors and have overall responsibility for the academic and pastoral wellbeing of the pupils in their age groups. All of the Heads of House work in close co-operation with the Senior Teacher Pastoral and the Head of Student Personal Development and wellbeing as well as House Parents, and the Head to ensure that all students receive the care and

nurturing they need from the day they arrive to the time they leave Kent College. The school runs a Health and Wellbeing week and believes feelings of wellbeing are fundamental to the overall health of an individual, enabling them to successfully overcome difficulties and achieve their goals in life.

King Abdulaziz School

King Abdulaziz School

(Founded 2013)	**Number of pupils enrolled** 149
Principal Mohammad Vall	**Fees** Day: SR31,000 – SR35,000
PYP coordinator Raheela Akram	**Address** Ali Ibn Abi Taleb Road P.O. Box 43111 Medina **41561** | **SAUDI ARABIA**
MYP coordinator Mohammad Vall	
DP coordinator Mohammad Alhaj Baba	**TEL** +966 553 039 300/ +966 503 454 420
Status Private	**Email** mvall@kaism.org; rakram@kaism.org
Boarding/day Day	
Gender Male	**Website** www.kaism.org
Language of instruction English	
Authorised IB programmes PYP, MYP, DP	

King Abdulaziz School is proud to be the first IB World Continuum School in the city of Medina S.A. Our IB journey began in 2015 and subsequently became officially authorized to offer the Primary Years Programme by the International Baccalaureate (IB) in December 2017. Later on, KAS achieved the accreditation to offer the Middle Years Programme (MYP) in 2020 and the IB Diploma programme in 2021. With the authorization of the Diploma Programme, we are pleased and elated to be one of six IB schools in Saudi Arabia offering the continuum of IB programmes, the PYP, MYP and the DP.

Our Vision

KAS inspires the individual potential of all students to enable them to become principled, proficient, inquiring, and caring lifelong learners.

The School Mission Statement

Our Mission at King Abdulaziz School is to create international educational experiences that cultivate active and lifelong learners. KAS aims at to provide stimulating academic programmes supported by rigorous assessment, and implemented through inquiry, in a caring and nurturing learning environment. Learners are equipped with the skills they need to reach their full potential and become responsible global citizens. KAS prepares students to be open to other perspectives, values and traditions whilst recognising their own identity and taking pride in their cultural heritage.

Primary Years Programme at KAS

At KAS, we offer an inquiry-based, transdisciplinary curriculum framework that builds conceptual understanding and enables sound skill development. KAS offers transformative experiences for students, teachers, and the wider school community. We deliver effective outcomes by providing an education that is engaging, relevant, challenging, and significant. We focus on providing the best educational practices, having both local and global significance that help nurture our young children to adapt to the challenges in our rapidly changing world.

In line with IB learning, our PYP students are open to the perspectives, values and traditions of others, but whilst at the same time appreciating their own identities, and being proud of their cultural heritage. The school provides a supportive and challenging environment where students are encouraged to become responsible and independent learners.

Middle Years Programme at KAS

Learners start the MYP at a stage of development in their educational life. They transition from the nurturing; they received from the PYP in their foundational years, to maturing into creative independent thinkers who are then able to enter the DP. KAS provides a holistic and ideal learning environment for learners to flourish academically, socially and emotionally across through the IB's educational continuum, thereby equipping them to succeed in both a national and international context.

The MYP at KAS invites pupils to ask questions, try out ideas and be actively involved in their learning. The school-wide application of the Approaches to Learning Skills has

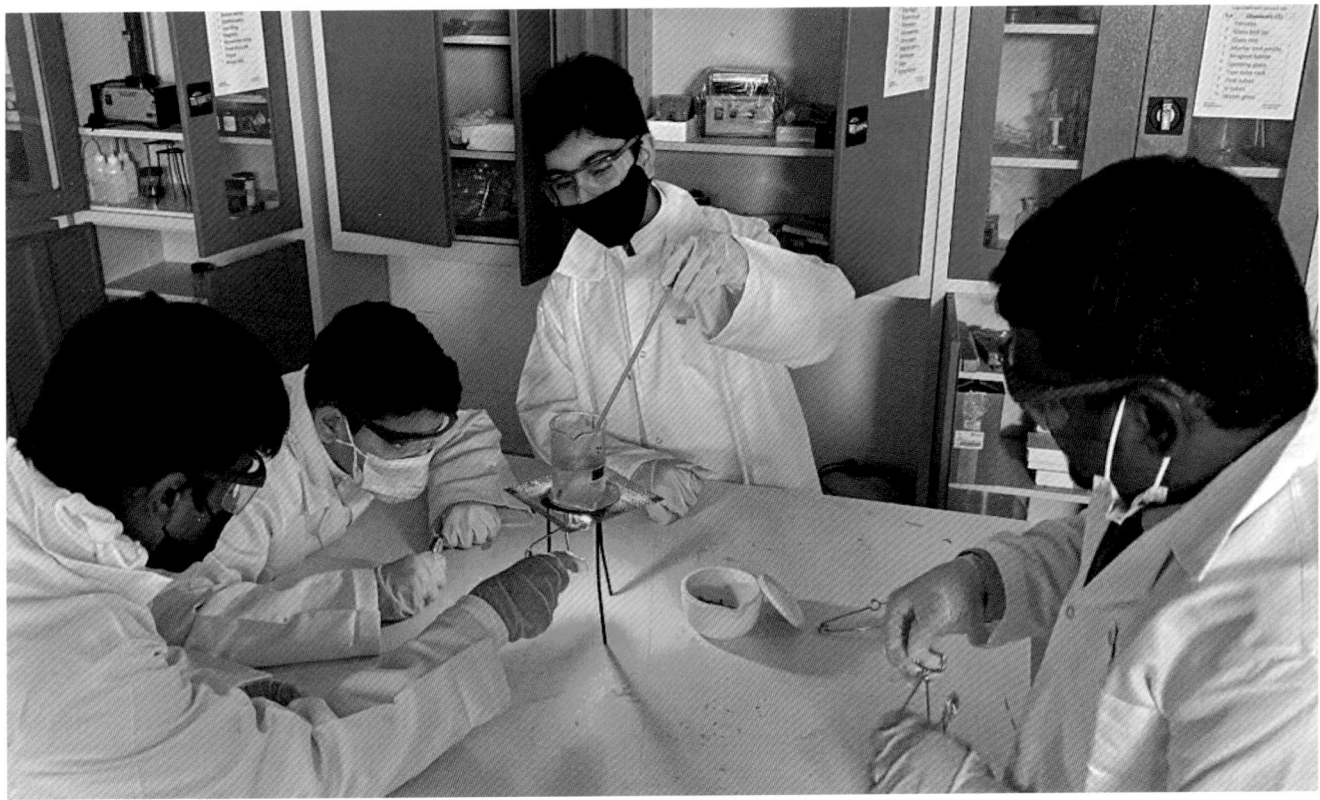

positively transformed the study habits of our MYP students by enabling them to confidently learn how to learn and develop into lifelong learners.

The Diploma Programme at KAS

The DP is a firm demonstration of our commitment to be an exemplary school with which shows our superb aspiration for quality and our value of robust education for our students. This quest for excellence is sought in collaboration with our students, teachers, parents and indeed the wider learning community. Learning and skills acquisition are a fundamental lifelong endeavors Thus, we firmly believe that the academic rigor of the Diploma, the conceptual approach to teaching and learning interactions supported by our versatile facilities, differentiated resources and experienced teachers will equip our students with the skills needed for university and beyond.

The experience that DP students gain from KAS will help to provide the foundation needed for success in higher education. Likewise, students will develop the much-needed capacity to deal with pertinent global issues, as the school aims to strengthen student learning by connecting their experiences to the real world.

We are thrilled to observe the enhanced intercultural awareness arising from the multilingual interactions during language acquisition lessons, that serve as a bridge to intercultural understanding and respect which demonstrate the beauty of the learner profile attributes in action, an aspect that what we all cherish in about our DP students at KAS.

Curricular and co-curricular Activities

King Abdulaziz School's academic enrichment initiatives are embedded in local and global programmes that are in line with the UN's sustainability goals. For example, peace and tolerance, celebrations of cultural and international events, e-learning, arts, sports, and student leadership programmes, all of which help to create a basis for real world and interactive experiential learning.

The Facilities

KAS strives to provide a wide array of facilities for both students and teachers in order to implement the IB programmes effectively. The facilities include a purpose-built campus, interactive classrooms, diverse libraries, digital computer labs, resourceful science laboratories, colorful art rooms, a multipurpose auditorium and health promoting cafeterias.

King Edward's
WITLEY

Head
Mrs Joanna Wright

DP coordinator
Andy Baynes

Status Private

Boarding/day Mixed

Gender Coeducational

Language of instruction
English

Authorised IB programmes
DP

Age Range 11 – 18 years

Number of pupils enrolled 424

Fees
Day: £21,585
Weekly Boarding: £33,225
Boarding: £34,995

Address
Petworth Road
Godalming
Surrey
GU8 5SG | UK

TEL 01428 686735

Email
admissions@kesw.org

Website
www.kesw.org

King Edward's Witley, a co-educational independent British boarding and day school for pupils aged 11-18, is situated in stunning 100-acre grounds in a designated Area of Outstanding Natural Beauty in Surrey. The School benefits from a convenient location with excellent road and rail links between London, the South Coast and Heathrow and Gatwick international airports.

Founded in 1553, King Edward's enjoys established links with the City. The School embraces its heritage and traditions with a modern outlook consistent with a world-class centre of excellence, with a commitment to the pastoral and education needs of the children it serves.

King Edward's is one of the UK's top co-educational day and boarding schools offering the International Baccalaureate Diploma Programme (IBDP), opening university opportunities in the UK and globally. In 2021 pupils achieved an average score of 35.9 points, well outstripping the worldwide average for IB students of 30 points out of a possible 45. 62% of individual subject grades were 7 or 6 – the equivalent to A Level A* and A, an outstanding achievement.

The School offers a Pre-Sixth one-year programme for overseas pupils as a stepping stone to the IB. Pre-Sixth gives students, aged 15-16, a taste of boarding life, an opportunity to improve their spoken and written English and enjoy cultural trips around the UK. For Pre-Sixth pupils looking to continue into King Edward's Sixth Form or return to education in their home country, they are able to take GCSE examinations in a range of subjects.

Living in Houses alongside pupils aged 11 – 18, our Pre-Sixth and Sixth Form pupils are fully integrated with their peers and build deep friendships. There are currently 424 boarding and day pupils from over 30 countries. 70% are English native speakers.

We will be unveiling our Upper Sixth Form House in 2022, which will become home to all Upper Sixth Form pupils, both boys and girls, in their final year at King Edward's. The new House will benefit from landscaped outdoor space, study and social areas and boarders will have their own study bedrooms with full en suite facilities. Our Upper Sixth Form House will provide the perfect stepping stone to university and independent living.

Academic and sporting facilities are extensive affording a broad curriculum and co-curricular programme. There are over 50 clubs & societies including many sporting opportunities; much music-making with over twenty ensembles and choirs; an array of art and DT workshops; extended drama and theatre experiences, trips and much more from the cerebral chess and debating to the challenging Duke of Edinburgh to the more mindful bee keeping.

KING WILLIAM'S COLLEGE

(Founded 1833)

Principal
Mr Joss Buchanan

DP coordinator
Alasdair Ulyett

Status Private

Boarding/day Mixed

Gender Coeducational

Language of instruction
English

Authorised IB programmes
DP

Age Range 11 – 18 years

Number of pupils enrolled
380

Fees
Day: £18,750 – £24,000
Boarding: £30,300 – £35,550

Address
Castletown
Isle of Man
IM9 1TP | UK

TEL +44 (0)1624 820110

Email
admissions@kwc.im

Website
www.kwc.im

We are a relatively small school, under 400 students. Approximately 20% of students board, with half of the boarders living on the Island and the rest from a wide variety of countries around the world. We are non-selective, but through the dedication of our staff, the structure of support for each individual and the work ethic of our students, we achieve excellent results. Our students go to top universities in the UK, Europe and the USA.

The Isle of Man is a beautiful environment in which to live. It is a safe haven with a very low crime rate, giving students the freedom to explore and take advantage of the fresh air, open countryside and beaches, away from the hustle and bustle and pollution of a busy city. The Island is easy to get to with air links from the major airports in the UK and Ireland.

We are one of a few schools where every student in the Sixth Form studies for the International Baccalaureate Diploma. The IB philosophy – particularly its emphasis on skills and its focus on internationalism – is central to our approach and we are one of the largest and most experienced IB schools in the British Isles.

Our pupils follow a broad curriculum of sporting activities, competing in the major sports against UK and Island schools. Every three years, the senior rugby and hockey teams embark on a world sports tour during the summer months. Golf, rock climbing and sailing are also on offer, along with a wide variety of other extracurricular activities.

Drama and Music thrive and pupils are given the opportunity to perform at many events and productions. There are workshops throughout the year and students are also encouraged to participate in competitions.

'An Island Education for a Global Future'

KING'S COLLEGE SCHOOL
WIMBLEDON

(Founded 1829)

Acting Head
Ms Jude Lowson MA

Acting DP coordinator
Paul Lloyd

Status Private

Boarding/day Day

Gender Male ages 7-18,
co-education sixth form

Language of instruction
English

Authorised IB programmes
DP

Number of pupils enrolled
1477

Fees
Please see website

Address
Southside
Wimbledon Common
London
SW19 4TT | UK

TEL 020 8255 5300

Email
admissions@kcs.org.uk

Website
www.kcs.org.uk

"An inclusive, friendly and friendly environment" (year 9 pupil 2021)

King's College School is an outstanding, independent day school for boys aged 7-18 and girls aged 16-18 located in one of the most attractive and peaceful parts of London, on the south side of Wimbledon Common.

King's has been rated the top boys' and co-educational independent school in London since 2017 by The Sunday Times Parent Power. Alastair McCall, editor of Parent Power, stated: *"KCS is the embodiment of everything you could want in a school"*. The Good Schools Guide Review (2020) reports: *"Intellectually exhilarating yet principled, this is selective education at its very best… a real golden ticket"*.

The curriculum is designed to offer a broad range of options and the quality of teaching is excellent. Lessons are fun, exhilarating, and purposeful, creating the best possible foundation for the future. We prepare sixth formers for both the IB and A Levels. In the last six years, almost 300 leavers have won places to study at Oxford or Cambridge.

The culture of King's is one of kindness, openness and support, and the wellbeing of pupils is paramount. Our pastoral system supports pupils' personal and social development, enabling them to excel in all areas of school life. It encompasses the day to day work of the tutor; the support and guidance of heads of house, the chaplain and heads of section; and the expertise of the head of mental health and wellbeing, school nurses and counsellors.

Our approach at all levels encourages pupils to look beyond academic excellence, as the vibrant success of our drama, music and games departments indicates. We are fully committed to the CCF, the DofE Award Scheme, community service and our partnerships with 30 local maintained schools. To enable so much to occur, Friday afternoons for year 9 and above are made over entirely to these, and other, activities.

King's prides itself on its combination of innovation and tradition. In 2010, the sixth form became co-educational and this has been an outstanding success; we admit around 50 girls each year. Since September 2016, King's has admitted boys aged 11 directly into the senior school which has increased access for a wider range of parental backgrounds.

In 2019, King's completed its ambitious masterplan for the renewal of the school site. Highlights included a new state-of-the-art music school and a new sports centre with a six-lane swimming pool.

Bursaries

King's has a long history of enabling bright young people from all backgrounds to access the school. We offer means-tested bursaries at 11+, 13+ and 16+ of up to 100% of tuition fees, as well as additional funding for extras such as school trips and uniform. Visit our Help With Fees page for further details.

King's College, The British School of Madrid

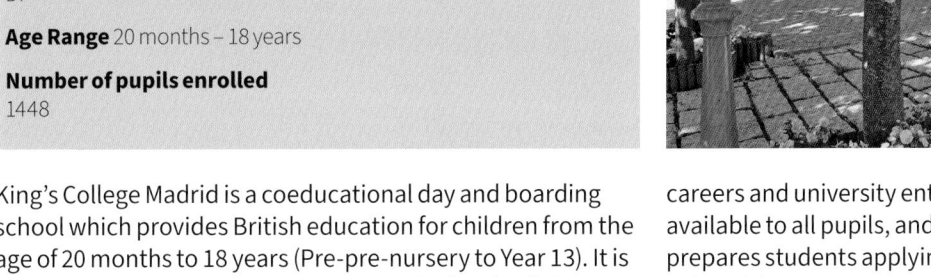

Soto de Viñuelas

(Founded 1969)

Head
Matthew Taylor

DP coordinator
Federica Menon

Status Private

Boarding/day Mixed

Gender Coeducational

Language of instruction
English

Authorised IB programmes
DP

Age Range 20 months – 18 years

Number of pupils enrolled
1448

Address
Paseo de los Andes 35
Soto de Viñuelas
28760 Madrid | SPAIN

TEL +34 918 034 800

Email
kc.admissions@
kingscollegeschools.org

Website
madrid-soto.
kingscollegeschools.org

King's College Madrid is a coeducational day and boarding school which provides British education for children from the age of 20 months to 18 years (Pre-pre-nursery to Year 13). It is located on an attractive 12-acre site in a leafy suburb, just 20 minutes' drive from Madrid and the main airport.

King's College is the only school in Madrid to offer both A Level & IB Diploma programmes of study in English. This allows students to choose their path of study depending on what type of learner they grow up to be enabling them to fulfil their future aspirations.

This freedom of choice, coupled with the highest quality of teaching and learning allows our students to excel across the curriculum:
- Academic Results are among the best in Europe
- Year 13 Graduates go on to study at some of the best universities in the world (Russell Group, Ivy League & Oxbridge)

Since it was founded in 1969, King's College has gained a reputation for high academic standards. An experienced careers and university entrance advisory department is available to all pupils, and the Oxbridge preparatory group prepares students applying to Oxford and Cambridge universities.

Our boarding house opened in September 2011 and offers some of the best boarding accommodation in Europe. Tenbury House is home to 60 pupils from all over the world. The new facilities offer a 'home from home' environment with shared and individual bedrooms all with en-suite bathrooms, underfloor heating and wireless internet. In addition, there is a dining room, a common room, a TV room, a study room, a kitchen that pupils can use to make light meals and a laundry. During the evenings and weekends, the students in Tenbury House have full use of these facilities and can also take advantage of many of the school's sports facilities.

King's College is the only school in Madrid accredited by the Department for Education in the UK as "Excellent" in every category that offers a British Curriculum from 20 months to 18 years.

Kristiansand International School

(Founded 2008)

Head of School
Mark Case

PYP coordinator
Jeremy Youell

MYP coordinator
Susan Heiseldal

Status Private

Boarding/day Day

Gender Coeducational

Language of instruction
English

Authorised IB programmes
PYP, MYP

Age Range 6 – 16 years

Number of pupils enrolled
194

Address
Kongsgård alle 20
4631 Kristiansand, Vest-Agder |
NORWAY

TEL +47 95826601

Email
post.international.school@
kristiansand.kommune.no

Website
www.kisschool.no

Kristiansand International School (KIS) opened in January 2008 with just five teachers and 15 students. The school was founded to serve the needs of the international business community in Kristiansand, as the flourishing businesses in and around Kristiansand attract engineers and professionals from around the world in sectors including the oil, chemical, renewable energy and education industries. In the years since the school opened, KIS has expanded and now offers an international education to 200 students from more than 30 countries, with 28 staff members representing 9 countries.

Academically, the school was authorised to offer both the Primary Years Programme (PYP) and the Middle Years Programme (MYP) in 2011 and offers an international education from 1st to 10th grade. All learning at the school follows the curricula and philosophy of the IB programmes, and we ensure that our curriculum meets or exceeds the expected learning outcomes of the Norwegian National Curriculum. The school aims to provide an engaging learning environment for our mixed body of students, with approaches to learning and teaching that focus on the development of international mindedness and fostering a passion for learning.

Throughout the school, there is a focus on understanding approaches to learning and helping students to build a deep knowledge of both the interconnected world that we live in and their own needs and preferences for creating understanding. The Service and Action programme runs through the school to create learners who appreciate the importance of giving back to the community and an abiding concern for the future of our world. With many students living outside their own culture, or having moved at vulnerable points in their lives, we have built a strong focus on student wellbeing, supported by the Random Acts of Kindness Programme studied in all grades.

Places at the school are prioritised for international families in line with the school's terms and conditions and admissions policy. The school was initially opened as a state or public school, but is now a private school under section 2:12 of Norway's Education Act. The school is owned by Stiftelsen (foundation) Kristiansand International School, but remains fee-free, thanks to generous support from both Kristiansand Kommune (Council) and various companies who sponsor the school's foundation.

La Côte International School Aubonne

LA CÔTE INTERNATIONAL SCHOOL
AUBONNE
A NORD ANGLIA EDUCATION SCHOOL

(Founded 2008)

Principal
Mr Andy Puttock

MYP coordinator
Emily Hardwicke

DP coordinator
Alexa Prior

Status Private

Boarding/day Day

Gender Coeducational

Language of instruction
English, French

Authorised IB programmes
MYP, DP

Age Range 2 – 18 years

Number of pupils enrolled 420

Fees
Day: CHF26,200 – CHF35,200

Address
Chemin de Clamogne 8
1170 Aubonne VD | **SWITZERLAND**

TEL +41 (0)22 823 26 26

Email
admissions@international-school.org

Website
www.international-school.org

La Côte International School is a private international school located in Aubonne, Switzerland. A co-educational day school, we offer our students unmatched international learning opportunities, combined with truly personalised academic support and the highest standards in education, motivating each and every student to achieve more than they ever thought possible.

Conveniently located between Lausanne and Geneva with a view of the Swiss Alps and Lac Léman, our modern campus features first-class facilities designed to inspire exceptional teaching and learning.

Our bespoke curriculum offers our students aged 2-18 the possibility of an English, French or bilingual route, following the Early Years Foundation Stage, a Primary curriculum incorporating aspects of the English National Curriculum and the International Primary Curriculum, and the IB MYP in Year 7-9, followed by the IGCSE and the IBDP in Secondary. Our broad choice of MYP and DP subjects allows students to focus on their strengths and fulfil their interests. In addition, we offer a preparatory Swiss Maturité programme.

As a member of Nord Anglia Education (NAE), the world's leading premium schools' organisation, we are proud to recruit the best internationally- and locally-trained teachers who are committed to nurturing and inspiring every child they care for. As dedicated and passionate professionals,

they strive to support our students not just to succeed, but to flourish, both academically and personally.

As a result, our students achieve outstanding academic results. With an average IBDP score of 36 points in the academic year 2020-21, our graduates have all been accepted to their top choice university, including MIT (Massachusetts Institute of Technology) and other top-ranking universities.

As a school that embraces over 37 nationalities, we recognise the value of supporting our children to flourish within their own culture and language, and, through outstanding education and international opportunities unmatched by other schools in the area, we nurture in them the values, attributes and skills needed to help them shape the future.

For instance, our Performing Arts programme is strengthened by our collaboration with The Juilliard School. Our collaboration with MIT takes a hands-on approach to teaching STEAM subjects. With UNICEF, we raise awareness of the UN Sustainable Development Goals and explore local solutions for global issues.

LCIS is led by Andy Puttock, formerly Global Education Director for NAE. With over 30 years of experience as an educator and leader, Mr. Puttock has been instrumental in driving NAE's strategy for building an outstanding education for their students worldwide.

Leighton Park School

LEIGHTON PARK
FOUNDED 1890

Head
Mr Matthew L S Judd BA, PGCE

DP coordinator
Mrs Helen Taylor

Status Private

Boarding/day Mixed

Gender Coeducational

Language of instruction
English

Authorised IB programmes
DP

Age Range 11 – 18 years

Number of pupils enrolled 525

Fees
£6,745 – £13,110 per term

Address
Shinfield Road
Reading
Berkshire
RG2 7ED | UK

TEL 0118 987 9600

Email
admissions@leightonpark.com

Website
www.leightonpark.com

Leighton Park exists to form young people of real character and confidence, with a determined desire to change the world, reflecting the school's Quaker values and forward-looking approach. We are a school that inspires Achievement with Values, Character and Community and academic excellence is the consequence of our approach.

Our vibrant learning community empowers each student to achieve excellent outcomes, through supporting their choices, nurturing individuality and encouraging talent in whatever direction it may lie. Ours is an education for succeeding in life, as well as in academic assessments. Set in 65 acres of beautiful parkland, our students have an enriching environment in which to learn, reflect and grow.

The success of our approach is demonstrated by UK Government 16-18 league tables, which place the school in the top 1% in England and best in Berkshire for the academic progress made by our Sixth Form students.

Leighton Park is particularly known for STEAM (Science, Technology, Engineering, Arts and Maths), with an emphasis on creative problem solving and interdisciplinary approaches. Music is another particular strength of the School with a state of the art Music and Media Centre providing students with exceptional facilities, including a Yamaha Live Lounge recording studio. Our Music department is accredited as a Flagship Yamaha Music Education Partner, the only school in Europe to hold this status.

With Quaker values held strongly at the centre of all that we do, our emphasis is on our students loving their learning, encouraging them to try a huge range of new experiences and developing their greatest talents. You will be struck on visiting us by the warmth of relationships that characterise the school, the wealth of opportunities for development of body and mind, and the sense of calm and space in which that development takes place.

Leysin American School in Switzerland

LEYSIN AMERICAN SCHOOL IN SWITZERLAND

(Founded 1960)

Head of School
Marc Ott

Dean of Academics
Sabina Lynch

DP coordinator
Ronan Lynch

Status Private

Boarding/day Boarding

Gender Coeducational

Language of instruction
English

Authorised IB programmes
DP

Age Range 12 – 18 years

Number of pupils enrolled
300

Fees
Boarding: CHF99,000

Address
3 Chemin de la Source
1854 Leysin VD | **SWITZERLAND**

TEL +41 24 493 4878

Email
admissions@las.ch

Website
www.las.ch

At Leysin American School, we develop innovative, compassionate, and responsible citizens of the world.

Our idyllic campus is tucked away in a beautiful mountain town. It provides the ideal environment for students, faculty, and staff to learn together in a safe, residential community in the Swiss Alps. Leysin, located in western Switzerland, represents the epitome of Swiss culture. Our striking, cozy hometown is an internationally-recognized ski destination with the hospitality, facilities, and lifestyle that appeal to students and global visitors alike. Leysin was also one of the host venues for the 2020 Youth Olympic Games.

We offer students an academically challenging setting with the goal of developing lifelong learners. Jointly accredited by NEASC and IBO, LAS provides a program for students at a variety of levels. IB Diploma students engage in deep, concentrated learning through engagement with the International Baccalaureate curriculum. The IB Diploma Programme has over 40 course offerings (SL/HL classes) available for students to select a program that best suits them and their future goals. In 2021, our overall average grade in the IB Diploma Programme was 34 points, which is above the world average. LAS had a 98% pass rate, which is ten percent above the world average. The top score was 44 points, and 8% of students scored more than 40 points. In total, 33% of students were awarded an IB Bilingual Diploma. LAS re-introduced AP subject exams in 2020, and the first cohort sat their AP exams in May 2021.

At LAS, we are committed to providing a stable, caring, supportive, family-like environment. We are a diverse, tight-knit community where staff members are always on hand to give students care and guidance as they navigate the responsibilities and challenges of young adulthood. We offer our students a balanced program of study, sports, recreation, and cultural travel to promote a well-rounded education. During the winter, students ski twice a week from our ski-in, ski-out campus.

At LAS, we seek out every chance to connect our students with impactful hands-on learning opportunities so they can see the practical applications of their studies at work in the real world. We augment traditional classes with programs and events that build on students' passions and address current global issues, helping our students develop fundamental skills in critical thinking, entrepreneurship, and teamwork.

We take pride not only in educating stellar students but also attracting the attention of strong universities. Our university advisors begin working with students in grade 9, building relationships that focus on character, gratitude, personal excellence, and relationships. We facilitate a dedicated weekly course to support them in their personal and academic goals once they leave LAS.

Luanda International School

School Director Dylan Hughes

Secondary Principal
Grant Rogers

Primary Principal Chris Boreham

PYP coordinator Julie Ranger

MYP coordinator
Catherine McCann

DP coordinator
Rene Bradford

Status Private, Non-Profit

Boarding/day Day

Gender Coeducational

Language of instruction
English

Authorised IB programmes
PYP, MYP, DP

Age Range 3 – 18

Number of pupils enrolled 416

Address
Via S6, Bairro de Talatona,
Município de Belas
Luanda | ANGOLA

TEL +244 932 337 056

Email lis@lisluanda.com

Website www.lisluanda.com

About

Luanda International School (LIS) is a vibrant school community in an exciting country. A curriculum based on inquiry and understanding, teachers intent on building safe and respectful relationships with their students, secure well-resourced premises and all within what could well be one of the world's greatest classrooms, Angola. The school was founded in 1996 with funding from six oil companies as an international, non-profit, independent school serving the expatriate and local community in Luanda, Angola. Enrollment from Pre K to Year 13 (grade 12) is approximately 416 students from 43 countries. We believe that happy children and a safe school community requires a strong sense of belonging and common purpose. Throughout the school there is a refreshing commitment to foster student engagement through hands-on inquiry, commitment to meaningful action and service and a dedication to value learning through the lens of inquiry and academic achievement as a result of grit and growth mindset. The common purpose that fosters this has now evolved through a future-focused Board, a relationship centered leadership team, a very hands-on Parent Teacher Association and a talented and committed teaching faculty. LIS also fully accredited with the New England Association of Schools and Colleges (NEASC) and the Council of International Schools (CIS).

Community & Mission

The LIS community is a diverse community of learners, committed to fostering compassionate, confident and socially responsible individuals who thrive in the world. Our teachers, students, and families come to Luanda from around the world. We have currently over 40+ nationalities represented in our community. Together in Luanda, we form a tight-knit community that cares deeply about relationships, respect, student voice, leadership, and growth.

Faculty

Our faculty members have a proven ability to empower, encourage and inspire learning that is concept based, inquiry-driven and focussed on the social, emotional and academic well being of children. Our team nurtures the social, emotional and cognitive well being of students, demonstrating care and compassion. We are a school prepared to search the globe for professional, internationally-minded teachers with a growth mindset and proven ability to build relationships and community.

Our Programme

Our school offers the three IB programmes throughout the age range and these programmes are currently the best available for ensuring a quality, rigorous academic curriculum in an international context. The IB programmes ensure that our students have the best chance for a smooth transition from one year to another, from one country to another and perhaps most critically, from school to college or university. We encourage students to become compassionate, life-long learners. This is developed throughout their learning with a focus on the attributes of the IB Learner Profile where learners strive to be inquirers, knowledgeable, thinkers, communicators, principled, open-minded, caring, risk-takers, balanced and reflective. International-mindedness is further developed through the learning of an additional language. As part of our school's core values, we respect the language of our host country, Portuguese, and aim

for all students to be able to function linguistically in the environment in which they live.

Creativity, Activity & Service (CAS)

Creativity, Activity and Service is at the core of our DP Programme and it is at the center of learning at LIS. Students engage in meaningful and authentic experiences that foster leadership, agency, perseverance, initiative, and the development of skills such as collaboration, problem solving and decision making. Our students have initiated and led highly successful projects that have made a strong impact on communities and the environment. The Association of International Schools in Africa awarded the school with two outstanding service project awards in 2019/2020 and 2020/2021. At LIS, our mission drives us – our DP students are addressing current and pressing issues such as the Covid-19 crisis which has affected thousands of people in Luanda, Angola. Masking Angola was born out of that need and they are currently collaborating with communities to deliver soaps, hand sanitizers and masks. Given their success, the Crescer Angola association is partnering with Masking Angola to expand the project to other provinces across the country. More projects like these ones are excellent examples of how at LIS, we are living our mission.

Co-Curricular Programme

Our co-curricular programme is designed to engage and extend our diverse community of learners in an enjoyable, safe and supportive environment. The programme enhances our sense of community through building sustainable and positive relationships within LIS, Angolan and global contexts. Student leadership is embraced in the programme to foster compassionate and socially responsible students who are confident to thrive in the world. The co-curricular programme encompasses four aspects at LIS: after school activities, the arts, sports and outdoor education. Each of these aspects is focused on developing student interest while providing further opportunities to be committed, challenged and excel, as students progress through the school.

Covid-19 Impact

On March 18, 2020, the LIS campus was temporarily closed and classes transitioned to online learning and teaching. In the days that followed, most expatriate families and teachers left Angola, so the decision was made to temporarily structure the school day around both synchronous and asynchronous learning. Thankfully, with a lot of hard work, the school campus was reopened in January 2021 to welcome students and staff back to where they belong – Luanda International School.

Lycée Franco-Britannique Ecole Internationale

(Founded 1989)

Head of School
Milijana Jovic

Administrator
Anna Milasin

PYP, MYP and DP coordinator
Nathaniel Akue Mackaya

Status Private

Boarding/day Day

Gender Coeducational

Language of instruction
French, English

Authorised IB programmes
PYP, MYP, DP

Age Range 3 – 18 years

Number of pupils enrolled
200

Address
Batterie IV
B.P. 159
Libreville | **GABON**

TEL +241 01 17 37 117

Email
ecolefrancobritannique@yahoo.
fr

Website
efblbv.org/ecole-franco-
britannique-lbv.php

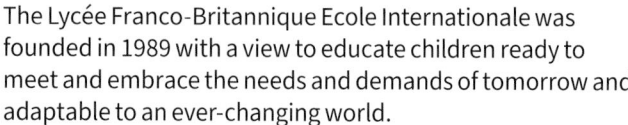

The Lycée Franco-Britannique Ecole Internationale was founded in 1989 with a view to educate children ready to meet and embrace the needs and demands of tomorrow and adaptable to an ever-changing world.

Our School was the first in Gabon to become a candidate school for the IB programmes as well as authorized to dispense the PYP and the MYP (both 2015). Pupils have the possibility to sit the Brevet des Collèges General (French exam) at the end of Middle School alongside the MYP Certificate.

At present, we are also authorized to offer the DP to ensure the continuum.

The core of our program is taught in French with a particular emphasis on foreign languages which occupy a key position within our School and are taught daily: English is offered from the age of 3 and Spanish from age 7 onwards. However this is not to the detriment of other subjects which all hold an equal importance within our taught curriculum.

Moreover, a plethora of nationalities are represented within our School. This multi-national spectrum nurtures a spirit of tolerance and respect for the values, beliefs and culture of every single pupil whilst encouraging cultural diversity and international awareness. Our philosophy has for aim to develop responsible and solidary citizens through the various activities undertaken during the Service and Action Programme.

Class size doesn't exceed 20 pupils per class which enables a personalised follow-up. In the afternoons, supervised study is offered to pupils with learning difficulties or to those with higher capabilities to deepen their knowledge. Students have the opportunity to partake in various extra-curricular activities (creative writing, film club, debating …) as well as swimming, athletics and team sports.

Throughout our 30 years of education, we take pride in seeing our pupils travel abroad to study in Europe and America. We believe that by offering a holistic education, which hones the abilities of each pupil so that they can fulfil their individual potential, we can reach our objective which is to endow them with the required skills to become active citizens of the world, driven by their will to change it for the better.

Head of School
Mireille Rabaté

DP coordinator
Maaike Kaandorp

Status Private, Independent

Boarding/day Day

Gender Coeducational

Language of instruction
English, French

Authorised IB programmes
DP

Age Range 3 – 18 years

Address
54 Forty Lane
London
HA9 9LY | UK

TEL +44 (0)203 824 4900

Email
admissions@lyceeinternational.
london

Website
www.lyceeinternational.london

Located on a leafy 5-acre campus in north London, Lycée International de Londres Winston Churchill is an independent, co-ed, non-selective, bilingual day school serving 850 students from ages 3 to 18 that aims to develop every child into a principled and forward-thinking world citizen.

Our students thrive in an international French-English environment underpinned by academic excellence and emotional support. They benefit from a unique bilingual immersion programme starting in Pre-Reception, as well as the choice of two tracks in Secondary school leading to the French baccalauréat or the English-language International Baccalaureate (IB Diploma).

Our belief is that each student deserves the best possible education according to his or her needs, with the goal of achieving excellence in both intellectual and social endeavours. Learning should be a fulfilling and exciting experience, and a school should stimulate curiosity, imagination, critical thinking, and open-mindedness. Lycée Churchill encourages individual and collective initiatives that allow children to think positively about themselves and to recognise and value their own abilities and those of others.

Unlike local schools taught in a single language that can tie students to a national curriculum and restrict their future options in other countries, Lycée Churchill opens worldwide educational avenues. The school is distinguished by remarkable diversity, with students from 45 countries and teachers and staff of 29 different nationalities. Our highly-qualified faculty collectively boast hundreds of years of teaching experience at all educational levels. More than 95% have advanced degrees, either Master's or PhDs.

We foster teamwork and a sense of solidarity within and outside the school, from collaboration and healthy competition in classrooms to volunteering and community engagement, both locally and globally. We believe that integrity is of paramount importance in building character, and we teach students to own their mistakes and learn from them, to embrace change, and to welcome life's inevitable challenges.

A member of the prestigious Council of International Schools, as well as the Independent Schools Association and AEFE, Lycée International de Londres Winston Churchill has been rated "Outstanding" by Ofsted for its Sixth Form Provision and for Wellbeing and Personal Development.

To book a private visit, write to our Admissions team or alternatively, visit the school's website and register to attend one of our next open days.

Application for a place should be made electronically through the school's website. Pre-registration for the following academic year opens in the autumn and the school accepts applications year round.

(Founded 1865)

Headmaster
Keith Metcalfe MA (Cantab)

DP coordinator
Jennifer Akehurst

Status Private, Independent

Boarding/day Mixed

Gender Coeducational

Language of instruction
English

Authorised IB programmes
DP

Age Range 13 – 18 years

Number of pupils enrolled
660

Fees
Boarder Sixth Form £13,384 per term
Day Pupil Sixth Form £9,028 per term
Pupils joining in Sixth Form:
Boarder £13,715 per term
Pupils joining in Sixth Form: Day
£9,028 per term

Address
College Road, Malvern
Worcestershire, **WR14 3DF | UK**

TEL +44 (0)1684 581515

Email admissions@
malverncollege.org.uk

Website
www.malverncollege.org.uk

The International Baccalaureate at Malvern College

The IB Diploma has been a highly successful part of the academic programme at Malvern since 1992 and it is a programme of study that is completely in tune with our holistic approach to education at the College.

Over the last five years, our IB graduates have averaged over 37 points, with over 30% of our pupils being awarded 40 points or more. With these results our pupils are consistently able to access the very best universities in the UK and across the world.

We offer a wide range of subjects, including Higher and Standard Level Maths in both Analysis and Approaches and Applications and Interpretation. We also offer both English Language and Literature and English Literature at both Higher and Standard Level.

We have recently introduced Psychology and Computer Science to our IB offering as well as School Supported Self Taught Language A, where pupils are able to study the literature of their native language with support from a school supervisor.

In all subject areas pupils are encouraged to develop communication skills, and the ability to think critically and reflectively, with the Theory of Knowledge course fundamental in developing the skills needed to enable pupils to test the validity of arguments and the strength of evidence.

At Malvern College we actively promote a set of well-tested, enduring human values which we call the Malvern Qualities. We believe that these values will enable our pupils to grow whilst they are with us and over time, equip our pupils for life's challenges, enabling them to adapt and succeed beyond Malvern.

Our pupil led Super-curriculum allows them to individualise their studies through a number of societies and these create the opportunities for intellectual stretch, further academic breadth and collaborative research. Our extensive Co-curricular programmes provide a significant range of opportunities for each pupil to engage in a range of sports, creative activities and service opportunities contributing to their Creativity, Activity and Service (CAS) component. Our holistic curriculum encourages and enables all pupils to develop the necessary skills, passions and ambitions, curiosity and personal qualities needed for building on their strengths, discovering new talents and becoming life-long learners.

Admissions

Please contact our Admissions team for details: admissions@ malverncollege.org.uk. Tel:+44 (0)1684 581515

MALVERN
COLLEGE EGYPT

Acting Headmaster and Head of Secondary School
Richard Moore

DP coordinator
Joseph Ford

Status Private

Boarding/day Day

Gender Coeducational

Language of instruction
English

Authorised IB programmes
DP

Age Range 2.6 – 18 years

Number of pupils enrolled 920

Fees
Day: 130,000 – 277,000

Address
B2-B3 South Ring Road
Investment Zone Kattameya
Cairo | **EGYPT**

TEL +202 26144400

Email
info@malverncollege.edu.eg

Website
malverncollege.edu.eg

Malvern College Egypt (MCE) opened in September 2016 with a first cohort of over 300 pupils. In 2020-21, we are proud to have over 850 pupils enrolled from Pre-Nursery to Year 13. The College was granted IBO authorization, in the 2018-19 academic year, to implement the IB Diploma Programme. The College also offers the International General Certificate of Secondary Education (IGCSE), and A-Levels.

As a renowned British school, in Egypt, the College is a member of the British Schools of the Middle East (BSME). Malvern College Egypt is a part of the family of Malvern College International (MCI) schools across the globe, including our mother school Malvern College UK, Malvern College Chengdu, Malvern College Hong Kong, and Malvern College Qingdao. We work closely with Malvern College UK, who regularly provide quality assurance visits to strengthen rapport and share educational best practice.

As MCE is a young school, we are fortunate to have over 150 years of experience in education from Malvern College UK. At the College, English is the primary language of instruction and our language of inclusion. We follow an enhanced form of the National Curriculum for England. The College academic staff all hold UK academic teaching qualifications and registration with the vast majority holding British citizenship. The College has outstanding local teachers of Arabic, social studies, and religion, maintaining the importance of the Egyptian culture. The College has outstanding facilities where a wide variety of co-curricular activities are provided. The College provides an inquiry-based, pupil-centered education, focusing on pupil character development as well as academic achievement. The College strives to develop the pupils in line with the Malvern Qualities of resilience, kindness, open-mindedness, self-awareness, independence, risk-taking, collaborative, curiosity, ambition, integrity, and humility.

Manaret Heliopolis
INTERNATIONAL SCHOOL

(Founded 1995)

Principal
Mr Michael Lethem

PYP coordinator
Radwa Mohamed

MYP coordinator
Sherwet Adel

Status Private

Boarding/day Day

Gender Coeducational

Language of instruction
English

Authorised IB programmes
PYP, MYP

Age Range 3 – 13 years

Number of pupils enrolled
600

Address
Hazem Salah Street, Ext. Mostafa
El Nahas
Nasr City
Cairo
11351 | EGYPT

TEL +20 224 71 33 32

Email
info@mhischool.net

Website
www.mhischool.net

Academics
We adopt a student-centred approach to learning, which means that we make our decisions based on what works best for learning and not what works best for teaching. We base our improvements on research-based methods to ensure best-practice at every level.

Vision
Our Vision is to be the inspiration for positive change for our whole community by offering an equal opportunity to all learners to choose to be the best they can be, and to empower them to use their voices to help improve the lives of others, both locally and in the wider world.

Mission
Our Mission is to always put our learners at the centre of our decisions as we build a safe, open-minded and engaging learning environment which is dedicated to academic excellence through best-practice and to student well-being through gender equality, differentiation, self-reflection, social awareness, civic responsibility, knowledge, and personal growth.

Our Beliefs
Students learn best in a community where academic disciplines are integrated, fostering an appreciation of how they interact and form a whole.

Our Approach
Our approach to the structure of each day is based on key concepts rather than time. In a traditional school the day is divided into minutes by subject with little if any connection. At our school connections are at the heart of each day – the more, the better.

Our Purpose and Success
Our purpose is to bring forth well-balanced members of society. And to succeed we provide a well-balanced curriculum and a solid academic foundation to prepare our students for success in life.

Mark Twain International School

(Founded 1995)

Head of School
Ms. Anca Macovei Vlasceanu

PYP coordinator
Ms. Orlandina Bulie

MYP coordinator
Ms. Floriana Florea

DP coordinator Ms. Olivia Fotescu

Status Private

Boarding/day Day

Gender Coeducational

Language of instruction
English, Romanian

Authorised IB programmes
PYP, MYP, DP

Age Range 2 – 19 years

Number of pupils enrolled
500

Fees
Preschool, starting at €5,000
Primary School, starting at €6,000
Middle School, starting at €6,500
High School, starting at €7,000

Junior Campus
25 Erou Iancu Nicolae Street
Voluntari, Ilfov **077190 | ROMANIA**

Secondary Campus
89-93 Erou Iancu Nicolae Street,
Voluntari, Ilfov **077190 | ROMANIA**

TEL +40 735 000 160

Email
contact@marktwainschool.ro

Website
www.marktwainschool.ro

Student-centred | Global-minded | High-performing

Celebrating its 26th anniversary in 2021, Mark Twain International School is proud to be one of the most experienced international schools in Romania. Challenging educational frontiers with its two divisions of study, Global Bilingual (English-Romanian) and International (English), the School has a strong portfolio of accreditations to support its mission: the full International Baccalaureate continuum (PYP, MYP & DP); the Cambridge International Education Assessment for Primary and Secondary; national recognition from the Ministry of Education via 4 accreditations covering the entire K-12 spectrum; the delivery of The Duke of Edinburgh's International Award in Romania; while also being a recognised Cambridge English Exam Preparation Centre.

At the core of the School's approach to quality FACE2FACE, HYBRID or ONLINE education is the IB continuum: a broad, conceptual, connected curriculum, empowering students, as early as the pre-primary stage up to graduation, to achieve intellectual and academic success, and to develop a wide range of human capacities and social responsibilities. Students are encouraged to be inquisitive, knowledgeable, communicative and brave life-long learners, and to become open-minded, caring, balanced, and principled global citizens of the 21st century. Critical thinking is promoted, as they strive to reflect upon and learn from their actions.

Annual pass rates for the International and National Baccalaureate are prevalently 100%, with graduates receiving offers to date from 136 of the world's top universities.

Healthy relationships, ethical responsibility and personal challenge are all promoted. Over 50 vibrant nationalities are represented in the student community, and as students increase their understanding of the world's cultures and languages (including their mother tongue), they explore globally significant ideas, become confident in their own identity, join with others to celebrate our common humanity, learn how they can make a change with their own voices.

The average teacher-student ratio is 1:6, and the annual teacher-turnover rate falls below 5%, thus facilitating optimal levels of consistency, care and attention to students' needs. The faculty is well-qualified, with most holding master and doctoral degrees, and being active participants in the Professional Development programmes offered in both national/international networks.

Operating in two green campuses near Baneasa Forest, Mark Twain International School welcomes its students to over 16,000 sq.m of verdant open spaces and 6,000 sq.m of modern buildings. The school offers 40+ extracurricular classes dedicated to arts, sports, and further academics, as well as student services: freshly-cooked meals, pastry bakery onsite, door-to-door school bus service, infirmary with on-campus doctor, well-being, counselling and mental health support, special home delivery of school resources/ care packs, parent support.

MARYMOUNT
INTERNATIONAL SCHOOL ROME

(Founded 1946)

Head of School
Ms. Sarah Gallagher

DP coordinator
Eleanor Moore

Status Private

Boarding/day Day

Gender Coeducational

Language of instruction
English

Authorised IB programmes
DP

Age Range 2 – 18 years

Number of pupils enrolled
850

Fees
€11,900 – €23,600

Address
Via di Villa Lauchli, 180
00191 Rome | **ITALY**

TEL +39 06 3629 1012

Email admissions@
marymountrome.com

Website
www.marymountrome.com

Marymount International School Rome is a private, Catholic, co-educational day school. The oldest international school in Italy, we are located on a 40-acre campus of protected parkland just 20 minutes north of the city center.

An English-language Early Childhood through 12th Grade School, our standards-based international curriculum is inclusive with an academic offering that is bespoke to the individual needs of every student. Enrichment opportunities are offered across all Grade Levels to encourage students to discover what they love doing and who they are as people in order to guide them towards the achievement of their full potential.

A wide range of extracurricular activities include Varsity athletics, S.T.E.A.M. classes, theatre, choir/band, and Model United Nations, in addition to visits to national and international sites of cultural importance. Marymount graduates obtain an accredited American High School Diploma and the majority of our students work towards the full IB Diploma with around 15% opting for individual IB course certificates.

Marymount has been an IB World School for over 35 years. The Diploma Programme (DP) has become an integral component of Marymount's academic program. School-wide curriculum alignment prepares students with the academic rigor necessary to fully engage with the Diploma. We offer over 30 subjects at this level, including 11 languages. Students also have the opportunity to choose among several Advanced Placement classes.

Marymount consistently obtains well above world average results. In 2021, for example, 100% of the School's DP candidates obtained the Diploma and the School's average score was 37 points. Marymount is a culturally and responsibly inclusive School, with an open admissions policy, and is therefore particularly proud of its students' results. The internationalism of the program is reflected in that over half of the students achieve the Bilingual Diploma.

The School's IB students go on to study in many of the world's top universities and colleges; in the UK this includes Cambridge, London School of Economics, Imperial College London, and King's College London, and Yale, New York University, Boston College, and Johns Hopkins in North America, in addition to Bocconi and more.

Classroom activities focus on conceptual understanding, authentic learning, and skills development. The School also has an ever-growing commitment to technology and Artificial Intelligence learning. All Marymount students work with personal Apple devices and the School is equipped with the latest technology, art and science labs, as well as a Forest School.

Marymount welcomes students from over 70 different nationalities and of all faiths to participate in its vibrant community life, where each student is valued and nurtured to achieve their full potential and develop a lifelong love of learning.

Marymount London

Headmistress
Mrs Margaret Giblin

MYP coordinator
Mark Gardner

DP coordinator
Nicholas Marcou

Status Private

Boarding/day Mixed

Gender Female

Language of instruction
English

Authorised IB programmes
MYP, DP

Number of pupils enrolled 260

Fees
Day: £26,510
Weekly Boarding: £42,980
Boarding: £44,880

Address
George Road
Kingston upon Thames
Surrey
KT2 7PE | UK

TEL +44 (0)20 8949 0571

Email admissions@
marymountlondon.com

Website
www.marymountlondon.com

Marymount London is an independent, day and boarding school for girls which nurtures the limitless potential of curious, motivated students (ages 11 to 18) of diverse faiths and backgrounds. Founded in 1955 through the charism of the Religious of the Sacred Heart of Mary (RSHM), the School proudly stands as the first all-girls' school in the United Kingdom to adopt the International Baccalaureate curriculum (IB MYP and Diploma), where girls are inspired to learn in a creative, collaborative, interdisciplinary, and exploratory environment.

Students are empowered to build their confidence, leadership skills, and sense of self on a seven acre garden campus conveniently located just twelve miles from Central London. The campus offers outstanding facilities, including a STEAM Hub, sports hall, dance studio, modern dining hall, and tennis courts. The School's challenging academic program is based on the International Baccalaureate curricula:

- The Middle Years Programme (MYP), offered in Grades 6 to 10, encourages students to draw meaningful connections between eight broad and varied subject groups. With a central focus on the development of conceptual understanding and effective approaches to learning (ATL) skills, the MYP is a student-centred, inquiry-based programme rooted in interdisciplinary learning.
- The International Baccalaureate Diploma Programme (DP) for Grades 11 and 12 builds on the strong foundation of the MYP, leading to independent research opportunities as well as exceptional university placement within the UK and around the world.
- Marymount's 2021 results are exceptional: 100% pass rate and an average of 38.22 points; the School provides a bespoke, student-centred college counselling programme which leads to successful placements in top universities in the UK and around the world.

Marymount's holistic approach to learning delivers a well-rounded education that encourages critical thinking, intercultural understanding, and participation in a wide array of interesting extracurricular offerings. Robust transport service from London/surrounding areas and boarding options (full, weekly, and flexi) are available.

Marymount offers year-round rolling admission as space allows. The admissions section of the website, featuring an online application portal, provides all of the information necessary to get started. Applicant families are encouraged to learn more about the School's strong tradition of excellence by exploring the website and making contact with the Admissions team by phone/email.

Mirabal International School

(Founded 1982)

Director
Ms Rosario de la Cruz López

MYP coordinator
Isabel Sargent Busquets

DP coordinator
Isabel Sargent Busquets

Status Private

Boarding/day Day

Gender Coeducational

Language of instruction
English, Spanish

Authorised IB programmes
MYP, DP

Age Range 0 – 18 years

Number of pupils enrolled
1957

Address
Calle Monte Almenara, s/n
28660 Boadilla del Monte, Madrid
| **SPAIN**

TEL +34 916 331 711

Email
mirabal@colegiomirabal.com

Website
www.colegiomirabal.com

Mirabal International School is a school of reference in Europe. Highly regarded by its' exceptional academic standards, Mirabal has historically achieved world top positions in the annual PISAreport for Schools, an educational evaluation promoted by the Organisation for Economic Co-operation and Development (OECD).

Founded in 1982 Mirabal International School is committed to the integral education of the students, promoting values such as independence, tolerance, responsibility (diligence, generosity, honour). Located in an outstanding natural setting in the north of Madrid, Mirabal offers excellent facilities at the service of an innovative educational project based on interactive and practical learning. The school occupies a total of 45,000 m2 and offers a wide range of sports and academic facilities, including tennis courts, athletics tracks, two swimming pools and several laboratories.

The constant training of teachers in active and innovative methodologies, the integration of iPads in the classroom and subjects such as robotics are some of the key tools used to bring students closer to the most advanced learning resources. Students learn to research, discriminate, contrast and select information from a very young age.

Students can choose to follow Spanish National Curriculum, the International Baccalaureate or a double-honors program. Its multilingual program is offered by native teachers and is especially designed to stimulate physical intellectual, social and artistic development.

Mirabal is a certified music school, where students can obtain an official Music Elementary Degree in the instrument of their choice. Emotional intelligence is a main focus of Mirabal's educational project. Cooperative learning, emotion management, motivation and education in values help students acquire skills such as creativity, leadership and initiative.

Modern Montessori School

(Founded 1985)

Principal
Randa Hasan

PYP coordinator
Rasha Hamzeh

MYP coordinator
Mariam Ellala

DP coordinator
Hoor Hawamdeh

Status Private

Boarding/day Day

Gender Coeducational

Language of instruction
English, Arabic

Authorised IB programmes
PYP, MYP, DP

Age Range 3 – 18 years

Number of pupils enrolled
1808

Address
PO Box 1941
Khilda
Amman
11821 | JORDAN

TEL +9626 5535190

Email
mms@montessori.edu.jo

Website
www.montessori.edu.jo

The Modern Montessori School (MMS) aims to provide a rich and stimulating environment where children can develop to their full potential. Understanding and appreciating the differences that make every student unique, each child is valued as an independent thinker and encouraged to make choices on his or her own.

Our system of personalised education encourages every student to develop his or her own talent, to respect the differences in others, and to be a respectable member of a community, thus achieving the finest possible holistic education. This aims to instil a pride in accomplishments, providing the students with the confidence needed to use their abilities to the fullest and enabling them to define and achieve success in college, career and, above all, in life.

To this end, the IB Diploma Programme at MMS is designed largely to cater for the needs of individuals, rather than for the collective needs of a group; our subject menu is varied and enjoys a degree of flexibility, which in turn allows students to choose the subjects that appeal to their different learning preferences and future university courses.

Furthermore, MMS has devised an extracurricular, three-level award scheme, which has the IB CAS perched atop its golden level. The Amin Hasan Award (AHA) provides students from grade 6-10 with the ability to participate in enjoyable yet beneficial and thought-provoking activities. This non-academic aspect of their education is extremely valuable in the overall development of the whole child, as it fosters a sense of compassion, teamwork, and mutual respect among students, in addition to promoting the principles of model citizenship and the importance of solidarity and togetherness among people, irrespective of their ethnic, religious, or gender differences. One of the many AHA activities was having students work together to meet the challenge of scaling Jordan's highest peak.

At MMS, we also believe in the inherent ability of each student to achieve distinction. This is why our LEAD Department (inclusive assessment) works hand-in-hand with administrators, programme coordinators, and teachers to cater for students who have special learning needs, through the application of an inclusion programme.

We also believe that cooperation between home and school is required to ensure the personal and intellectual development of each student. Consequently, we have designed an e-school portal where both parents and students are kept up-to-date with everything they need from report cards and academic calendars to forums and e-learning material.

As a PYP/MYP accredited school, the MMS prepares students through a devised preparation programme and curricula that will ultimately expose students to the IB continuum of international education.

The Modern Montessori School is accredited by the International Centre for Montessori Education (ICME), Cambridge and Edexcel International Examinations' syndicates and is an authorised IB World School. In addition, MMS has recently acquired membership from the Council of International Schools (CIS).

Moscow Economic School, Odintsovo Branch

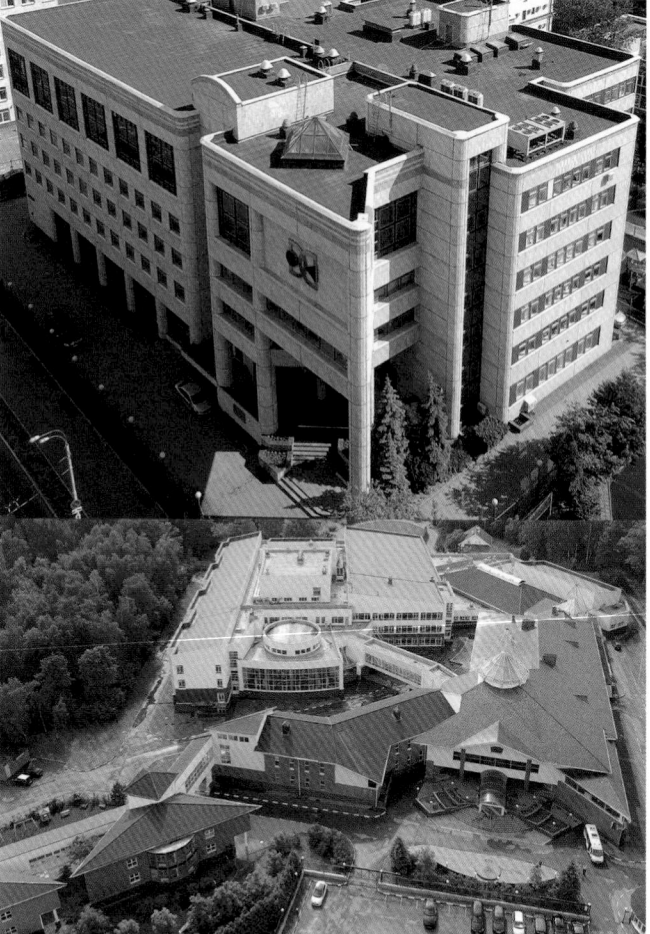

(Founded 1993)

Head of School Nataliya Kadzhaya

PYP coordinator
Larisa Zaitseva

MYP coordinator
Antonina Andrianova (Gaydash)

DP coordinator
Valeriya Rotershteyn

Status Private

Boarding/day Day

Gender Coeducational

Language of instruction
Russian, English

Authorised IB programmes
PYP, MYP, DP

Age Range 3 – 16 years

Number of pupils enrolled 620

Fees Day: US$17,500

Address
1-A, Zaitsevo Village
Odintsovo Region
Moscow Oblast
143020 | RUSSIAN FEDERATION

Presnya Campus
29 Zamorenova Street
Moscow
123022 | RUSSIAN FEDERATION

TEL +7 495 780 5230

Email mes@mes.ru

Website www.mes.ru

Moscow Economic School was registered on February 1, 1993, as a non-government educational institution.

MES is a secondary school with grades ranging from 1st through 11th. It also has a kindergarten and a pre-school department. The admission age ranges from 3 to 5 years.

There are two campuses. "Presnya" Campus is located in the center of Moscow. Odintsovo Branch is in the countryside, outside Moscow.

MES is a bilingual school with the languages of instruction being Russian and English. Other foreign languages include German, Spanish, French, Italian and Chinese, are introduced in the second grade.

Moscow Economic School is a member of the Council of International Schools (CIS), the European Council of International Schools (ECIS) and the Association for Advancement of International Education (AAIE).

Since 1996 the school has been following the International Baccalaureate programmes for primary (PYP), middle (MYP) and high (DP) schools (grades 1-11).

Since 2001 the school has been providing research opportunities for the Russian Academy of Education and for Moscow State Pedagogical University.

In 2013 the Council of International Schools (CIS) reaccredited MES.

Extra-curricular activities (art studios, clubs, etc.) are available. MES students actively take part in the "Moscow Giraffes" sport school and the children's "Camerton" school of music.

M-PESA Foundation Academy

(Founded 2016)

Executive Head of School
Alan Adlington-Corfield

BTEC Coordinator
Benjamin Kihika

MYP coordinator Julliet Kithinji

DP coordinator Jackline Otula

CP coordinator Jackline Otula

Status Private

Boarding/day Day

Gender Coeducational

Language of instruction
English

Authorised IB programmes
MYP, DP, CP

Age Range 13 – 18 years

Number of pupils enrolled 610

Address
P.O. Box 7954
01000 Thika | **KENYA**

TEL +254 703 200 000

Email info@
mpesafoundationacademy.
ac.ke

Website www.
mpesafoundationacademy.
ac.ke

The MPESA Foundation Academy is a state of the art, co-educational and residential High school offering the International Baccalaureate Career-Related Programme (IBCP), the International Baccalaureate Diploma Programme (IBDP), and the International Baccalaureate Middle Years Programme (IBMYP).

Driven by leadership, technology and innovation, the Academy serves talented but economically disadvantaged students with demonstrated leadership potential. M-PESA Foundation Academy offers a world class, well rounded learning environment to develop future leaders. The Academy places great emphasis on the holistic development of all our learners not just in academics but also in technology, sports, the arts, outdoor pursuits and community service. Learners are exposed to the latest technology as part of the day-to-day teaching. The school focuses on moulding future leaders and entrepreneurs by incorporating the core values of Curiosity, Leadership, Accountability, Innovation, Responsible Citizenship and Excellence (CLAIRE) as well as the IB Learner Profile attributes into every sphere of learning within the Academy.

Our Vision - To develop transformational leaders who strive for excellence and success for themselves, their communities and their world.

Our Mission - As a leadership development institution, we will deliver an innovative world class education through a holistic curriculum so that our learners are principled, reflective and open- minded. Through our programmes, we will nurture active, compassionate and successful lifelong learners.

MPESA FOUNDATION ACADEMY STUDENT LIFE

MPESA Foundation Academy residential life caters for students' life outside the teaching curriculum. The residential life compromises of staff members drawn from several departments which include: boarding life, clinic, counselling, leadership, sports, mentorship, child safeguarding and protection. The Head of Student Life works with all team members is ensuring that students develop holistically, their physical and psychological well-being is catered for, highly nutritious diet is provided to students and feel at home while they are in their residences. Residential life offers learners an opportunity to nurture their leadership skills and qualities. Students are attached to internal and external mentors who prepare them for life after school.

Child safeguarding and protection procedures have been put in place to protect learners from harm within and outside of the Academy.

TERTIARY PROGRAM

The Uongozi Centre offers a unique development program philosophically aligned to the IB curriculum, including a consistent approach to teaching and learning. The learning programme strives to create well informed, innovative lifelong learners and responsible global citizens who effectively contribute and understand issues shaping the world. Additionally, the Uongozi Centre supports the transition of the Academy's graduates into tertiary education institutions or employment alongside developing leadership and entrepreneurship skills.

Nord Anglia International School Dublin

NORD ANGLIA
INTERNATIONAL SCHOOL
DUBLIN

Principal
Paul Crute

PYP coordinator
Jack Odey

MYP coordinator
Andrew Bateson

DP coordinator
Joanna Cooper

Status Private

Boarding/day Day

Gender Coeducational

Language of instruction
English

Authorised IB programmes
PYP, MYP, DP

Age Range 3 – 18 years

Address
South County Business Park
Leopardstown
Dublin 18 | **IRELAND**

TEL +353 1 5442323

Email
admissions@naisdublin.com

Website
www.naisdublin.com

Nord Anglia International School Dublin (NAIS Dublin) is a member of Nord Anglia Education's global family of premium schools in Europe, South East Asia, North America and the Middle East. NAIS Dublin is Ireland's newest IB World School and is the only school in Ireland to unite an international curriculum with world-class learning opportunities and global experiences that enable students to achieve more than they ever thought possible.

Nord Anglia International School Dublin is fully credited to deliver the Primary Years Programme (PYP) from age 3 to 11, the Middle Years Programme (MYP) from age 11 to 16 and the Diploma Programme (DP) from age 16 to 18. NAIS Dublin is Ireland's first and only IB continuum school. These IB programmes teach students to think critically and interdependently, to inquire with care and logic, and to become confident and resilient. We have developed our curriculum in conjunction with the Massachusetts Institute of Technology and The Juilliard School of Performing Arts in New York.

True learning and innovation happens at the intersection of disciplines, so your child will be encouraged to tackle problems by calling on knowledge from several subjects. As a truly international school, our students collaborate and learn with over 70,000 of their peers in 32 countries every day through our Global Campus: whether that be physically in school, virtually online, or by travelling worldwide to other schools to participate in sporting events in the USA, cultural exchanges with China, adventure activities in Switzerland and philanthropic outreach experiences in Tanzania.

Our state-of-the-art campus has been designed for the future of learning and is centred around a custom designed building in Leopardstown, South County Dublin. Our facilities include a custom-built sports centre, dance studio, design and technology studios, performing arts spaces, auditorium, libraries and a parent café.

Parents choose a Nord Anglia Education because we offer academic, social and personal success for every student. Through opportunities to learn from the best, experiences beyond the ordinary, and the encouragement to achieve more than they ever thought possible, we help our students succeed anywhere through our unique global educational offer. We do this by investing in our people, our schools, and above all, our students. At Nord Anglia International School Dublin, your child will grow as a confident global citizen in an engaging environment, which will ensure that they will love learning for life.

Only schools authorized by the International Baccalaureate can offer any of its four academic programmes: the Primary Years Programme (PYP), the Middle Years Programme (MYP), the Diploma Programme or the Career-related Programme (CP).

Nord Anglia International School Rotterdam

NORD ANGLIA INTERNATIONAL SCHOOL ROTTERDAM

(Founded 1959)

Head of School
Alison Lipp

DP coordinator
Danielle Mashon

Status Private

Boarding/day Day

Gender Coeducational

Language of instruction
English

Authorised IB programmes
DP

Age Range 3 – 18 years

Number of pupils enrolled
250

Fees
Day: €15,200 – €19,700

Address
Verhulstlaan 21
3055 WJ Rotterdam, South
Holland | **NETHERLANDS**

TEL +31 10 4225351

Email
admissions@naisr.nl

Website
www.naisr.nl

Nord Anglia International School Rotterdam (NAISR) is a member of Nord Anglia Education's global family of premium schools. In addition to providing high quality international education for children from 3 to 18 years of age, NAISR is fully authorised to deliver the IB Diploma Programme (IBDP) for students in their final two years of school.

Students studying the IBDP develop life skills such as critical thinking, teamwork, research and time management, which sets them up for success at university and beyond. The programme aims to develop confident and enthusiastic learners who respond to challenges with optimism and an open mind.

Universities in the Netherlands and around the world understand the academic rigour of the IBDP and therefore hold the IB Diploma in high esteem. NAISR IBDP graduates are accepted into the best colleges and universities.

At NAISR, IB students have the opportunity to gain a bilingual IB Diploma. Bilingual students can study two language courses from the 'Studies in Language & Literature' subject group to be awarded with the prestigious 'IB Bilingual Diploma'. Alternatively, students who score highly in the 'Studies in Language & Literature' and in one other subject completed in a language other than English, will also receive the 'IB Bilingual Diploma'. This special qualification recognises a student's high level of multilingual skills and is well received on university applications.

NAISR is excited to open their brand new 'Nord Anglia IB Academy Rotterdam' – a space dedicated to their Years 12 and 13 students. This space provides students with a modern and purposeful space to study, collaborate, and relax. Students have easy access to the IB Coordinator and College Counsellor with a range of meeting spaces for students, staff and parents.

In recent years, NAISR students have achieved high academic outcomes, consistently scoring above the global average. In the 2019-20 school year, NAISR was awarded a top 3 place in the Netherlands based on its IBDP score, and in the 2020-21 school year NAISR's average IBDP score was 36.9.

If you have any questions, or you would like to learn more about the IB at NAISR, please don't hesitate to contact their friendly admissions team at admissions@naisr.nl or 010 422 5351.

North London
Collegiate School

Founded 1850

(Founded 1850)

Headmistress
Mrs Sarah Clark

DP coordinator
Mr Henry Linscott

Status Private

Boarding/day Day

Gender Female

Language of instruction
English

Authorised IB programmes
DP

Number of pupils enrolled
1080

Fees
Day: £5,956 – £7,049 per term

Address
Canons
Canons Drive
Edgware
Middlesex
HA8 7RJ | UK

TEL +44 (0)20 8952 0912

Email
office@nlcs.org.uk

Website
www.nlcs.org.uk

North London Collegiate School is internationally recognised as an outstanding school which provides an exceptional education. One of the oldest day schools for girls in England, we have maintained our position as an established force at the forefront of women's education, and our students consistently excel in every area. Our students leave us not just with outstanding qualifications, but also as articulate and independent young adults who possess the confidence, intellectual curiosity, and passion for learning and understanding that will endure for life.

Whilst ensuring academic excellence, equal attention is given to supporting the development of the whole person, inspiring confidence, individuality and self-esteem. Consequently, the school is a positive and energetic community where pupils are encouraged to take advantage of the opportunities open to them, with around 36 productions, 40 societies and 30 foreign trips offered each year.

International Outlook
NLCS has a highly international perspective that is unique amongst London day schools. We feel it is vital to prepare our students to become global citizens, by providing opportunities for them to be outward-looking, internationally minded and well informed about the world beyond school. Our growing family of sister schools in South Korea, Dubai and Singapore, with more branches planned

for the future, benefits pupils and staff through exchange opportunities and internships. The IB Diploma resonates with the values of NLCS, and its international dimension affords students the opportunity to be part of a programme which is offered in, and recognised by, almost every country in the world.

Academic Excellence
In 2020, we were ranked the No.1 school in the UK for the IB Diploma by The Sunday Times, and since offering the IB Diploma programme in 2004, we have had an exceptional record of success. In 2021, 31% of our students achieved a perfect score of 45, a result only achieved by about 0.4% of IB candidates worldwide. Our students consistently achieve an average score in excess of 41 points, making NLCS one of the top-performing IB schools in the world.

Looking to the future
Our IB students have received offers from a range of impressive institutions including Oxford, Cambridge, Harvard, Yale, Georgetown, Stanford and Princeton, as well as other leading universities such as Bristol, Edinburgh and the London colleges and medical schools.

The IB Diploma programme offered at NLCS ensures that students enjoy an exciting and academically stimulating Sixth Form experience, providing them with an excellent preparation for life at university and in the wider world beyond.

Oakham School

(Founded 1584)

Headmaster
Mr Henry Price MA (Oxon)

MYP coordinator
Dmitriy Ashton

DP coordinator
Carolyn Fear

Status Private

Boarding/day Mixed

Gender Coeducational

Language of instruction
English

Authorised IB programmes
MYP, DP

Age Range 10 – 18 years

Number of pupils enrolled
1040

Fees
Day: £18,450 – £22,830
Boarding: £28,200 – £37,800 Flexi
Boarding (2-5 nights) £22,185 –
£35,850

Address
Chapel Close
Oakham
Rutland
LE15 6DT | UK

TEL 01572 758758

Email
admissions@oakham.rutland.
sch.uk

Website
www.oakham.rutland.sch.uk

Oakham is well known and loved for being a friendly, unpretentious and highly successful school. Our uniquely structured student population – with 50:50 girls and boys, and 50% boarders and 50% day pupils – creates a genuinely inclusive and caring school community.

This year marks two major milestones in our history: 50 years of co-education and 20 years of offering the IB Diploma.

Academic

Our educational ethos reflects the IB's vision to nurture intellectually ambitious thinkers, giving our pupils the ability to learn effectively and independently at school and beyond. Our IB Diploma results far exceed the global average and our teachers are leading practitioners.

Having received accreditation as an IB MYP World School in summer 2021, we are equipping our pupils aged 11-14 with the knowledge, aptitudes and skills to thrive in the world of 2030 and beyond.

Pastoral Care

Our dedicated Houses for boarders and day pupils means that we can offer all pupils the benefits of our outstanding boarding provision in ways that suit modern family life. Led by a Housemaster or Housemistress, and supported by a team of Tutors, Prefects and a Matron, each of our 16 Houses provides our pupils with the care and support they need to develop intellectually, physically, emotionally and spiritually.

Our location

Pupils benefit from the School's location close to Rutland Water, in the heart of safe, rural England. Our beautifully green campus is just a few minutes' walk from Oakham's historic town centre and train station and Oakham's excellent road and rail links mean that London, Birmingham and Cambridge are all within easy reach. There is a direct train to Stansted Airport.

Co-curricular

We offer a spectacularly wide range of co-curricular opportunities. Hundreds of students take part in the Arts – there are five major drama productions every year, we teach over 500 individual music lessons each week, and our award-winning Art & Design Department is a hive of creative activity. Oakham has a national reputation for Sport, offering 30 different sports to students of all levels – from enthusiasts to elite athletes. Activities are also an integral part of life beyond the classroom, with students able to choose from over 125 activities to take part in each week, to discover and develop their interests and talents, and provide service to others. In addition to Duke of Edinburgh, CCF, and Voluntary Action, options range from dance to robotics, e-textiles to sailing.

PaRK INTERNATIONAL SCHOOL

Executive Head of School
Samantha Gonçalves

DP coordinator
Patricia Radoi

Status Private

Boarding/day Day

Gender Coeducational

Language of instruction
English

Authorised IB programmes
DP

Age Range 1 – 18 years

Number of pupils enrolled
1140

Fees
Day: €6,710 – €15,951 (excluding enrolment fee: €734-€4,725)

Address
Estrada de Alfragide 94
2610-015 Amadora, Lisbon |
PORTUGAL

TEL +351 215 807 000

Email
all@park-is.com;
admissions@park-is.com

Website
www.park-is.com

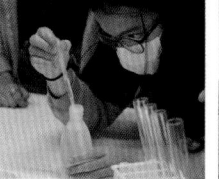

PaRK IS, an Inspired school, welcomes more than 2,000 students from 1 Year Old to Grade 12 across our four campuses in the Lisbon Area. An international school with Portuguese roots, PaRK IS offers the best education for both Portuguese and International families, welcoming students from over 50 nationalities. Our mission is to guide and inspire students to be successful and happy in their adult lives.

We are very proud to have our first cohort of IB students graduating in May 2022 in our Alfragide campus. With brand new, state-of-the-art facilities (opened in September 2020) in a 2,000sqm campus, PaRK IS Alfragide offers a demanding, dynamic, innovative and bespoke curriculum for each age group: a bilingual education from Early Learning until Grade 4, Cambridge (including the IGCSE) from Grade 5, and the internationally acclaimed IB Diploma Programme. Students receive a personalised and well-rounded education – besides the strong academic curriculum, our Well-Being department ensures that each student has their individual needs met. It is also responsible for the Social Skills programme, so important for our students' success and happiness. In addition, our student-centred college counselling programme offers each student the tools and support they need to follow the right university and career path for their unique profile.

We are always searching for the world's best practices in education and implementing the ones that best fit our students and their objectives. Technology is fully integrated into the curriculum, and we offer unique Arts and Drama classes, in addition to PaRK Music Academy, where students find a solid bridge between vocational and non-vocational music education. Furthermore, we provide our students with a wide range of sporting activities, including the exclusive Inspired Sports Programme, which offers individualised training for students from Grades 5 to 12. In this programme, students can dedicate themselves to the sport of their choice during school hours, getting the personalised coaching they need to excel both athletically and academically.

Inspired Education Group students have had the best IB Diploma results across the world – providing access to top universities in Europe and the US. As an Inspired School, PaRK IS gives its students access to world's best practices in education, outstanding arts and sports programmes, state of the art facilities, and Exchange Programmes.

With a PaRK IS education, students will be prepared for academic excellence, proficient in more than one language and equipped with key life skills to be successful in an ever-changing world.

Pierce – The American College of Greece

President
Dr. David G. Horner

DP coordinator
Dr. Emmanuel Vrontakis

Status Private, Non-Profit

Boarding/day Day

Gender Coeducational

Language of instruction
English, Greek

Authorised IB programmes
DP

Address
6 Gravias Street
Aghia Paraskevi
Athens
153 42 | GREECE

TEL +30 210 600 9800 (Ext:1060)

Email
pierceibsecretariats@acg.edu

Website www.pierce.gr

Founded in 1875, Pierce – The American College of Greece is a private, non-sectarian, non-profit institution accredited and regulated by the Greek Ministry of Education. Pierce has been offering the International Baccalaureate Diploma Programme (IBDP), since 2016.

The Pierce Mission

The mission of Pierce is to provide holistic education to form intellectually independent, morally responsible, socially engaged global citizens. *"Non ministrari sed ministrare"* ("Not to be served but to serve") defines our institutional character and our aspiration for our students.

Why Pierce-IB is unique

1. Small class sizes (5-15 students), which augment group work and learning, as well as facilitate interactive teaching and academic collaboration.

2. Pierce-IB DP students are supported with additional class sessions, enabling families to eliminate private tutoring and alleviate from additional expenses.

3. Supervised Study Sessions: since all Pierce-IB DP students follow the daily schedule of the mainstream program, with less number of courses (than those mandated by the Greek curriculum). Hence, each student will have – approximately – two 2-period sessions (per week) with no class. For these time slots our students have three options:

- To stay in class and prepare/read, for the next day or collaborate with their teachers/tutors.
- To use our Computer Lab and search for data, papers and information from the web, from digital libraries or from ManageBac (the online platform for teachers and students' communication).
- To go to Pierce library and search relevant bibliography or references, required for their Internal Assessments and/or Extended Essay.

4. Pierce-IB DP is supported by highly qualified and trained teachers, with extensive experience in the Diploma Programme and University education. The majority of teachers (55%) hold a PhD degree and all of them (100%) hold either an MSc or an MA degree. The IBO verification team was most impressed by the academic qualifications, the passion and the commitment of the school staff.

5. We take advantage of all divisions of The American College of Greece (Pierce, Deree, Alba), exchanging best teaching practices, undergraduate education experience and high-end facilities, such as:

- The ACG Art Gallery, which is a distinctive educational venue for students and faculty based on the academic program of Visual Arts. Each year we organize the annual VA exhibition, where our students' works are displayed.
- The ACG Simulated Trading Room is built to offer our students a real-world trading experience. This state-of-the-art trading room is expected to recreate a professional financial environment and is being supported by the latest trends in technology, including state-of-the-art hardware and software.
- The Fabrication Lab is a new technologies workshop which is equipped with 3D printers, a laser cutter, a 3D scanner, a vinyl cutter, a CNC machine, robotics kits and an electronics workbench for experimenting with creative electronics, such as sensors, microcontrollers, conductive ink, e-textiles, etc.

6. Pierce-IB DP is fully integrated with campus life and the regular high school program. Our students can take part in all activities the School has to offer, choosing from more than 50 Clubs, Pan-Hellenic or European contests and International Programs such as: Model United Nations, Harvard Model Congress Europe, University of Delaware Summer Program, Phillips Exeter Summer School.

Qatar Academy Al Khor

الخور **Al Khor**
أكاديمية قطر Qatar Academy

عـضـو فـي مـؤسـسـة قـطـر
Member of Qatar Foundation

Director
Ms. Lina F. Mouchantaf

PYP coordinator
Ms. Nadia Hussain

MYP coordinator
Mr. Martin McCurrach

DP coordinator
Mr. David Leadbetter

Status Private

Boarding/day Day

Gender Coeducational

Language of instruction
Arabic, English

Authorised IB programmes
PYP, MYP, DP

Age Range 3 – 18 years

Number of pupils enrolled
1243

Fees
Day: QR46,000 – QR75,000

Address
P.O.Box: 60774
Mowasalat Street
Al Khor | **QATAR**

TEL +974 44546775

Email
qaalkhor@qf.org.qa

Website
www.qak.edu.qa

Qatar Academy Al Khor (QAK) was established in 2008 to serve students who live in Al Khor and the different areas in the north of Qatar, extending our groundbreaking curriculum to a broader community. As a full IB World School that predominantly educates native Qatari students and long-time residents, QAK is especially dedicated to developing local human capital. QAK seamlessly blends its world-class international curriculum with Qatar's heritage and culture. In part, this is achieved by enabling students to thrive in a truly bilingual environment that develops rich language skills in English and Arabic concurrently, since the student base is predominantly Qatari.

QAK strives to empower students to be open-minded, inquiring and knowledgeable life-long learners who are able to adapt to an ever-changing world through intercultural understanding and respect.

At QAK, we envision our future leaders as courageous problem-solvers who will make a positive difference in the world.

Our mission at QAK is to create a safe yet dynamic learning environment that inspires innovation. QAK empowers learners to think critically as compassionate and principled global citizens grounded in Arab values while celebrating Qatari National heritage and culture.

Qatar Academy Al Wakra

Al Wakra الوكرة
Qatar Academy أكاديمية قطر

عـضـو فـي مـؤسـسـة قـطـر
Member of Qatar Foundation

(Founded 2011)

Director
Mrs. Bedriyah Itani

PYP coordinator
Mrs. Samira Jurdak

MYP coordinator
Ms. Molly Mosier

DP coordinator
Ms. Jaime Fontenot

Status Private

Boarding/day Day

Gender Coeducational

Language of instruction
Arabic, English

Authorised IB programmes
PYP, MYP, DP

Age Range 3 – 17 years

Number of pupils enrolled
1186

Fees
Day: QR50,000 – QR70,000

Address
P.O. Box: 2589
Al Farazdaq Street, street No.:
1034, Zone: 90
Doha | **QATAR**

TEL +974 44547418

Email
qataracademyal-wakra@qf.org.
qa

Website
www.qaw.edu.qa

Qatar Academy Al Wakra (QAW) is a premier private international school in Qatar, and a Member of Qatar Foundation, a world-class organization dedicated to building excellent educational institutions in Qatar and around the world.

Qatar Academy Al Wakra was established to serve the needs of the rapidly growing Al Wakra coastal community and surrounding areas in the southern region of Qatar. QAW serves over 1200 students from pre-school to Grade 12. QAW is an IB World School fully authorized for PYP, MYP and DP and accredited by the New England Association of Schools and Colleges and the Council of International Schools.

Through an educational model that enables learning in two languages, encourages innovation, and develops a strong code of ethics, QAW has been nurturing students to become leaders in their communities. The talented faculty at QAW go above and beyond to cultivate the spirit of discovery and creativity in students' learning experiences. QAW teachers and administrators are highly collaborative, energetic, and supportive team players who are passionate about working with children and making a difference.

The school moved into its new, state-of-the-art, purpose-built campus in September 2018. Facilities include sports and recreational spaces, swimming pools, a 450-seat theater, music and art studios, and well-equipped science, technology, engineering, art, mechanics, and food technology laboratories.

Learning at QAW is further enhanced through the variety of opportunities available through the vast network of Qatar Foundation, from experiential programs to athletics and community services that enable students to achieve their full potential in a nurturing and culturally grounded environment.

Qatar Academy Doha

أكاديمية قطر
Qatar Academy

عضو في مؤسسة قطر
Member of Qatar Foundation

(Founded 1996)

Director
Mr. Stephen Meek

Primary School Principal
Ms. Marie Green

Senior School Principal
Mr. Steven Thompson

PYP coordinator
Ms. Savannah Spillers

MYP coordinator
Ms. Roma Bhargava

DP coordinator
Ms. Zeina Jawad

Status Private

Boarding/day Day

Gender Coeducational

Language of instruction
Arabic, English

Authorised IB programmes
PYP, MYP, DP

Age Range 3 – 18 years

Number of pupils enrolled
1884

Address
P.O. Box: 1129
Luqta Street
Doha | **QATAR**

TEL +974 44542000

Email
qataracademy@qf.org.qa

Website
www.qataracademy.edu.qa

Vision: Empowering students to achieve high levels of academic growth and personal wellbeing and to be responsible citizens who are locally rooted and globally connected.

Qatar Academy Doha (QAD) is one of the Middle East's premier educational institutions; a leading private, non-profit international school established as the first learning organization in Qatar Foundation's landmark Education City. Founded in 1996, it marked an important step for a country on the cusp of transforming itself from a gas- and oil-producing economy to a knowledge-based society.

QAD was the first school in Qatar authorized to offer all three IB Programmes.

Over 1,800 students representing different nationalities experience an extensive academic and co-curricular program grounded in traditional values and steeped in the best practices in education.

Inquiry-based learning starts at the Primary School. Students, parents and faculty are encouraged to challenge themselves and their thinking through the framework of the PYP, and Units of Inquiry based on the IB transdisciplinary themes provide students with structure and direction in their learning. This learning environment extends beyond the classroom to involve the wider community, supporting real-world connections.

The MYP and DP are offered in the Senior School, with the Middle School serving to address the specific needs of the pre-adolescent age group from Grades 6-8.

QAD's strength lies in its comprehensive DP curriculum, and its rigorous and effective university preparation program.

Access to many community and service, athletic and academic after-school activities challenge students beyond the curriculum, and student e-portfolios and student-led conference structure ensure that focus is consistently on learning and growing, while acquiring the grades, necessary for success in the DP and beyond.

QAD teachers are recruited from a variety of academic and cultural settings. Through encouragement and a caring, innovative and creative approach to instruction, our faculty ensure that our students achieve their fullest potential in a learning environment designed to promote cultural understanding and respect.

Qatar Academy Msheireb

عضو في مؤسسة قطر
Member of Qatar Foundation

Director
Ms. Belinda Holland

PYP coordinator
Ms. Jennifer Magierowicz

Status Private

Boarding/day Day

Gender Coeducational

Language of instruction
English, Arabic

Authorised IB programmes
PYP

Age Range 3 – 10 years

Number of pupils enrolled
400

Fees
Day: QR46,033 – QR52,656

Address
Msheireb Downtown
Doha QATAR

TEL +974 44542116

Email
qamsheireb@qf.org.qa

Website
www.qam.qa

Established in 2014, Qatar Academy Msheireb (QAM), a member of Qatar Foundation, operating under Pre-University Education, is a state-of-the-art primary school authorized for the International Baccalaureate Primary Years Programme, and a member of the Council of International Schools.

QAM's mission is to create an effective learning environment to develop internationally minded and empathetic lifelong learners through a dual-language program emphasizing inquiry-based practices.

At QAM everything has a purpose, and learning is relevant to the 'real world' within a dual-language curriculum that is structured to be rigorous, stimulating and challenging. The Program of Inquiry centers around 'big ideas' and provides students with opportunities of learning about issues that

have local, national and global significance, and hence nurtures an understanding of human commonalities. The transdisciplinary nature of the themes ensures that learning transcends the confines of traditional subject areas, and facilitates student connections between life in school, life at home and life in the world.

QAM offers an inclusive education where students evolve as individuals who are self-motivated, creative and can think, question and reason logically, i.e. individuals who are independent, confident and capable of making decisions.

All students are encouraged to be curious about what they are learning, and differentiation allows them to demonstrate what they have learned by using a variety of mediums or tools at different levels that are appropriate to individual needs.

Qatar Academy Sidra

السدرة **Sidra**
أكاديمية قطر Qatar Academy

عـضـو فــي مـؤسـسـة قـطـر
Member of Qatar Foundation

Director
Dr. Carolyn Mason Parker

PYP coordinator
Mr. Barry Grogan

MYP coordinator
Ms. Susan Menand

DP coordinator
Mr. John Dugan

Status Private

Boarding/day Day

Gender Coeducational

Language of instruction
English

Authorised IB programmes
PYP, MYP, DP

Age Range 3 – 18 years

Number of pupils enrolled
680

Fees
Day: QR40,280 – QR74,556

Address
P.O. Box: 34077
Doha | **QATAR**

TEL +974 44542322

Email
qasidra@qf.org.qa

Website
www.qasidra.com.qa

Qatar Academy Sidra (QAS) is a rapidly growing school, currently serving over 620 students who represent approximately 40 nationalities. QAS was initially established to serve the needs of Qatar Foundation (QF) and Sidra Medicine employee families, and has since expanded to cater to the growing demand for QF schools.

QAS is a dynamic, kind and responsive learning community that challenges learners of today to inspire them to be the change-makers of tomorrow. QAS believes there is a leader in everyone. Students at QAS are empowered learners with strong skills and a sense of self for a life filled with opportunity. QAS graduates are compassionate responsible citizens who achieve their full academic and personal potential.

As an inclusive and multilingual community, QAS is committed to creating opportunities for every child so that every individual is personally and academically empowered with 'roots to grow and wings to fly'. The school values of respect, integrity and unity lead to a culture of kindness. This culture enables QAS to create a nurturing environment for each child's wellbeing, passion, and talents.

The school is currently located in the lively Education City campus and is in the process of designing a new maker-space inspired campus for the future.

QSI International School of Bratislava

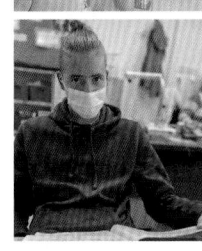

(Founded 1994)

Head of School
Mr. Daniel Blaho

DP coordinator
Mr. Jeff Varney

Status Private

Boarding/day Day

Gender Coeducational

Language of instruction
English

Authorised IB programmes
DP

Age Range 3 – 18 years

Number of pupils enrolled
288

Address
Záhradnicka 1006/2
Samorin 93101 | **SLOVAKIA**

TEL +421 903 704 436

Email
bratislava@qsi.org

Website
bratislava.qsi.org

QSI International School of Bratislava (QSIB) is a private, non-profit institution that opened in September of 1994. It offers a rigorous, high-quality American international education in the English language for children ages 3-18. The warm and welcoming community that is QSIB makes it an ideal setting for children to grow in ability with the finest faculty and educational opportunities in Bratislava. Students in the secondary earn stellar results in our International Baccalaureate (IB) and Advanced Placement (AP) Programs.

The brand-new state-of-the-art facility (opened in January 2018) is a large 2-story complex, which has 35 classrooms, a library (over 18,000 titles), two computer laboratories, a gymnasium, an atrium, several outdoor playgrounds, a full-court outdoor basketball court, an artificial grass mini-pitch for soccer, and several offices. QSI International School of Bratislava (QSIB) provides full security for its students, teachers, staff and visitors with guards, an advanced key card system and an elaborate security camera network. Partner facilities are found within the nearby Olympic training facility (www.x-bionicsphere.com/domov), including indoor and outdoor swimming pools, a fitness facility, dance/exercise rooms, track & field, a full soccer pitch, gymnastics hall, equestrian course, and a movie cinema. Free Shuttle Buses to/from the campus are available from six separate locations in and around Bratislava.

QSIB offers the IB Diploma Programme to students ages 16-19, during the final two years (Secondary III & IV). The QSI courses offered in Secondary I & II prepare students to take IB courses. Students may elect to enroll in the IB Diploma Programme as full diploma candidates or as course candidates. Enrollment of students is done through one-on-one counseling with the Director of Instruction and the IB Coordinator. Prerequisite skills are required for the program, but specific prerequisite courses are not typically required.

QSIB students enjoy a high success rate with 94% passing the rigorous diploma programme with an average score of 35.8 over the last 10 years.

SUBJECTS OFFERED:

GROUP 1 (Language A):
- English Language & Literature
- Slovak Literature

GROUP 2 (Language B):
- French B & French *Ab Initio*
- German B & German *Ab Initio*
- Spanish B & Spanish *Ab Initio*

GROUP 3 (Individuals & Society):
- Psychology
- Economics
- History

GROUP 4 (Science):
- Biology
- Chemistry
- Physics

GROUP 5 (Mathematics):
- Mathematics: Applications & Interpretations
- Mathematics: Analysis & Approaches

GROUP 6:
- Visual Arts

QSI Kyiv International School

KYIV INTERNATIONAL SCHOOL

(Founded 1982)

Head of School
Mr. Luke Woodruff

DP coordinator
Ms. Randi Assenova

Status Private

Boarding/day Day

Gender Coeducational

Language of instruction
English

Authorised IB programmes
DP

Age Range 3 – 18 years

Number of pupils enrolled 780

Address
3A Svyatoshinsky Provuluk
Kyiv 03115 | **UKRAINE**

TEL +38 (044) 452 27 92

Email
kyiv@qsi.org

Website
www.qsi.org/kyiv/

Kyiv International School is a private, nonprofit, day school, serving Preschool through Secondary IV. The school was founded in 1992 to provide a quality education in English for the children of expatriates living in Kyiv. Parents of its students are primarily employed by large corporations and governments. Kyiv International School is a member of Quality Schools International, a consortium of non-profit college-preparatory international schools with American-style curriculum. QSI has 37 schools in 31 countries. The world headquarters of QSI is in Ljubljana, Slovenia.

Mastery Learning Philosophy: Kyiv International School believes in personalized instruction within a positive learning environment leading to mastery of clearly defined objectives. The educational philosophy emphasizes cooperative and collaborative learning, reflection, innovation, and higher-order and critical thinking. Mastery learning prepares our students for the higher level thinking, reflection and self-motivation that is so fundamental for students engaged in the IB Diploma Programme.

International Baccalaureate Diploma Programme:
Kyiv International School has offered the International Baccalaureate Diploma Programme since 2004 and the program continues to grow and evolve through reflection and review. With more than twenty teachers involved with the IB curriculum and classes, there are varied opportunities for students enrolled in the program. Students are encouraged to enroll in the full diploma program, but also have the opportunity to enroll in classes for IB certificates.

IB Language Courses: KIS is proud to offer German, French, Spanish, Russian and Ukrainian which students can study as either a first or second language. We also encourage students to enroll in school-supported self-study of their native language. Students have recently received bilingual diplomas in Russian, French, Ukrainian, German, Italian and Korean.

Facilities and location: KIS is located just 10 km from the city center. The park like campus includes 95 classrooms (including fully equipped science laboratories to support Group 4 subjects), a learning center, 2 sensory rooms, 3 art rooms, 3 music rooms, a recording studio, 3 computer laboratories, 2 indoor gymnasiums, an indoor pool, fitness center, climbing wall, a cafeteria, a snack café, 2 playgrounds, a purpose built track, an artificial turf soccer field, an artificial turf soccer mini pitch, an outdoor basketball court, outdoor fitness area, other outdoor spaces, and a brand new auditorium with a seating capacity of 350.

QSI Tirana International School

(Founded 1991)

Director
Mr Jon Mudd

DP coordinator
Elizabeth Sloughter

Status Private

Boarding/day Day

Gender Coeducational

Language of instruction
English

Authorised IB programmes
DP

Age Range 2 – 18 years

Number of pupils enrolled 352

Address
Rruga Vilat Gjermane
Kutia Postare 1527
Tirana | **ALBANIA**

TEL +355 4 236 5239

Email
tirana@qsi.org

Website
tirana.qsi.org

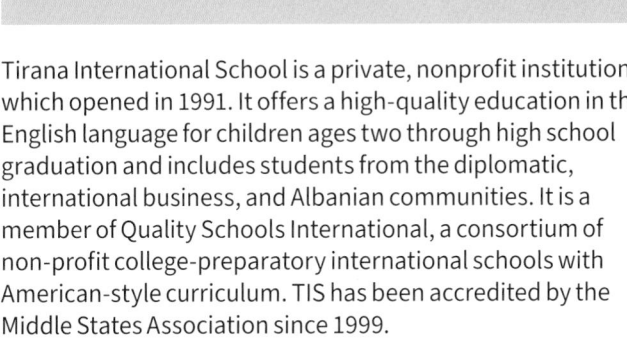

Tirana International School is a private, nonprofit institution which opened in 1991. It offers a high-quality education in the English language for children ages two through high school graduation and includes students from the diplomatic, international business, and Albanian communities. It is a member of Quality Schools International, a consortium of non-profit college-preparatory international schools with American-style curriculum. TIS has been accredited by the Middle States Association since 1999.

Students, Faculty & Staff

The school is growing and currently has over 300 students representing 31 nationalities. The school prides itself on hiring caring, qualified, and dedicated educators. Teachers at TIS are certified and experienced educators who bring a wealth of expertise, knowledge, and skills to their learning environments.

School Facilities and Location

The school facility is located on the south side of the city of Tirana, just outside the busy city. The campus occupies a beautiful, green 5.5-hectare site. The building was designed to accommodate growth in enrollment and to take advantage of the abundant Albanian sunshine, having lots of balconies and patios.

The sports complex boasts several playgrounds, a soccer field, a track, a tennis court, an indoor exercise room, a gymnasium, and a dance studio. The school building includes a full English-language elementary and secondary library, with additional resources to support Languages Other than English; multiple science laboratories; a technology lab; fully equipped music and art rooms; an indoor performance area;

a full-service cafeteria; and state-of-the-art, well-resourced and well-equipped classrooms. In addition, the school has many outdoor courtyards and respite areas for students to gather.

Academic Program & Philosophy

Tirana International School believes that every child can succeed and strives to offer a rigorous overall program – with equal emphasis on the acquisition of knowledge, skills, and success orientations – in an accepting, friendly, and supportive environment.

TIS follows QSI's mastery learning approach to teaching, in which students master specific objectives before moving on. This approach emphasizes success over mediocracy as well as rigor and critical thinking. The TIS curriculum well prepares students for the challenges of the IB DP.

IB Programme

The first IB cohort started in fall 2021 and is composed of five highly engaged students representing three different countries. Students are supported by a team of motivated, caring teachers, including the DP Coordinator, the Secondary Guidance Counselor, and the CAS Coordinator. The IB teachers are passionate about their subjects and collaborate with other QSI IB teachers as well as IB teachers worldwide.

IB Course Offerings

For the first cohort, TIS is offering English: Language and Literature, French B, Spanish B, Business Management, Biology, Chemistry, Mathematics: Analysis and Approaches, and Theatre. TIS is prepared to offer more courses as the program grows.

Raha International School

(Founded 2006)

Executive Principal
Iain Colledge

PYP coordinator
Vanessa Keenan

MYP coordinator
Vaughan Kitson

DP coordinator
Andrew Tomlinson

Status Private

Boarding/day Day

Gender Coeducational

Language of instruction
English

Authorised IB programmes
PYP, MYP, DP

Age Range 4 – 18 years

Number of pupils enrolled
2833

Fees
EY1: AED39,330
EY2: AED41,300
G1-G6: AED54,100
G7-G12: AED61,900

Gardens Campus
Khalifa City 'A', Al Raha Gardens
Abu Dhabi | **UNITED ARAB EMIRATES**

TEL +971 (0)2 556 1567

Khalifa City Campus
Khalifa City 'A', Sector 25, Cnr.
56th and Al Tashreef Street
Abu Dhabi | **UNITED ARAB EMIRATES**

TEL +971 (0)2 5505 271

Email admissions@ris.ae

Website www.ris.ae

At Raha International School, a member of the Taaleem family of schools, we believe that a successful education is all about inspired, imaginative teaching, centred on the learner as an individual. We nurture students not only to achieve academic success but also to become true global citizens. Raha is an International Baccalaureate World School catering for all grades from Early Years 1 to Grade 12. Our school community is made up of over 2,800 students from more than 80 nations who collectively speak over 45 mother tongues. We pride ourselves on being a big school but a small family.

Gardens Campus, situated on 14 acres of beautifully landscaped property in a bustling residential suburb, boasts an abundance of open spaces and play areas. We support our students and rigorous curriculum with state-of-the-art facilities that include; libraries, a purpose-built arts centre and auditorium, sports and training facilities, wellness areas, parent and visitors' café and more.

Just a 7-minute drive from Gardens sits Khalifa City Campus which opened in September 2020 and currently caters to our Early Years up to Grade 8 students and will be expanding to all grades in subsequent years. The Khalifa City Campus has been built to satisfy the exceptionally high demand for places at Raha, and the ever-increasing popularity of the International Baccalaureate curriculum. The new campus will eventually cater for up to 3,000 K-12 students.

Raha was the first school in Abu Dhabi to achieve accreditation in the full IB curriculum. The IB is internationally acclaimed and respected for its relevance in today's multicultural and increasingly global society. We are also the only K-12 school in Abu Dhabi to receive the highest rating of 'Outstanding' from the Abu Dhabi Department of Education and Knowledge for a second time, an amazing achievement for our staff and students.

Our programmes feature an inquiry approach that aligns student interest with what they learn, thereby enriching their natural curiosity and promoting a love of learning. Our team of internationally-experienced, skilled and passionate teachers model the attributes of the IB Learner Profile and encourage students to "respect themselves, others and the world around them". A strong sense of common purpose pervades our learning community. We believe that trust and strong parental participation are an integral part of a quality education and we see parents as our partners in their children's learning journey.

EXPANDING HORIZONS

(Founded 1844)

Head
Mr Jeremy Quartermain

DP coordinator
Bethan Jones

Status Private

Boarding/day Mixed

Gender Coeducational

Language of instruction
English

Authorised IB programmes
DP

Age Range 0 – 18 years

Number of pupils enrolled 821

Fees
Day: £8,865 – £14,430
Weekly Boarding: £15,285 –
£24,840
Boarding: £22,575 – £41,175

Address
Broadway
Fleetwood
Lancashire
FY7 8JW | UK

TEL +44 (0)1253 774201

Email
admissions@rossall.org.uk

Website
www.rossall.org.uk

Rossall has been described as a 'warm, inclusive and remarkably happy place to be'.

Set on an historic 160-acre campus, Rossall is one of the country's leading independent co-education boarding and day schools, where boys and girls aged 0-18 are nurtured in a safe, secure and supportive environment.

The School provides a broad curriculum with the senior school following the British National Curriculum culminating with GCSE/iGCSE examinations at the end of Year 11. In the Sixth Form, students choose from A Levels, IB Diplomas or BTEC in Sports.

In 2021, Rossall celebrated outstanding results. At A-Level 29% of grades awarded were the top mark of A*, firmly beating the national average of 19%. With 61% of pupils achieving A* or A grades. For IB Diplomas students had a 100% pass rate and average score of 35.

Year 11 students achieved excellent GCSE results. With 98% of results at grades 9-4 or A*-C including Maths and English and 55% at a grade of 7-9 or A*-A.

Rossall's enviable on-campus facilities include 45 acres of outdoor grassed sports pitches, floodlit all-weather surfaces, purpose built £4 million sports centre, heated indoor swimming pool, Fives courts, shooting range and multi use games-area.

Rossall runs an Elite Football Programme for boys and girls, in partnership with League One football club, Fleetwood Town, focusing on developing students by challenging them as athletes.

Rossall's Golf Academy is ranked number 1 by the ISGA, boasting an indoor golf studio, equipped with the latest video analysis equipment and GC2 launch monitor/simulator, as well as an indoor putting lab and swing room.

Through our International Piano Academy we have joined the All-Steinway Schools programme and our fleet of 21 Steinway pianos now includes 3 grand pianos and a Model D Concert Grand Piano.

The School is home to the Lawrence House Astronomy and Space Science Centre, the only centre of its kind in Britain, specialising in astronomy education.

A huge range of extracurricular activities are offered to all pupils throughout the school. Students can join everything from the world famous Chapel Choir to the oldest Combined Cadet Force in the country.

Admitting boarders as young as seven, Rossall's 'family structure' provides the framework for its exceptional standards of pastoral care. With regular investments in its 9 boarding houses, each house is a well equipped and comfortable home, modernised to the highest of standards.

Rossall School is a registered charity (No. 526685) that exists to provide education for children.

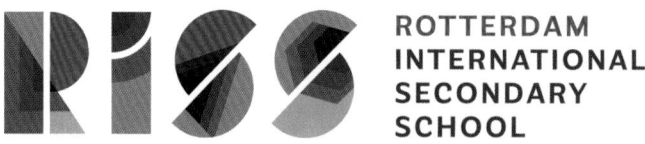

ROTTERDAM
INTERNATIONAL
SECONDARY
SCHOOL

(Founded 1988)

Principal
Ms Monicá Gilbert-Sáez

Deputy Principal
Ms Lani du Plessis

DP coordinator
Eva Noorduijn

Status State

Boarding/day Day

Gender Coeducational

Language of instruction
English

Authorised IB programmes
DP

Age Range 12 – 18 years

Number of pupils enrolled
380

Fees
Day: €8,000 (excluding extra
curricular activities and trips)

Address
Bentincklaan 294
3039 KK Rotterdam, South
Holland | **NETHERLANDS**

Senior Campus
Schimmelpenninckstraat 23,
3039KS, Rotterdam |
NETHERLANDS

TEL +31 (0)10 890 77 44

Email
admissions.riss@wolfert.nl

Website riss.wolfert.nl

Our Vision
Educating for self-awareness, curiosity and integrity in a
changing world.

Our Mission
Our mission is for every student to enjoy their youth.
We do this by providing innovative approaches to learning,
by encouraging achievement, by fostering international
mindedness with local and global engagement, by modelling
ethical behaviour and by acting respectfully and with
honesty.

Our Core Values
- Respect
- Responsibility
- Relationships
- Courage

RISS holds a unique position both within The Netherlands
and Rotterdam's Wolfert school group. We are a state
subsidised semi-private school and a provider of excellent
international education, as recognised by our recent CIS/
NEASC and IB re-accreditation and re-evaluation visits.

RISS serves the growing need Rotterdam has for quality
education serving foreign nationals and returning Dutch
citizens, one that is not based on exclusivity or privilege.

While many schools claim to be international simply
because of the curriculum they offer or the students they
serve, RISS offers a genuine and comprehensive coalition of
international teachers drawn from across the globe. What
unites us is the RISS school culture and our common belief
in an inclusive, culturally-diverse, student-centred, enquiry-
driven and concept-based education that not only prepares
young people for university and life beyond school, but also
ensures that they simply love their time being young.

RISS offers a caring community, dedicated to the broad
development of all students yet small enough to ensure that
all our young people are known and supported as individuals.
This is something backed up by our newly revamped pastoral
programme led by our tutors. English is our language of
instruction and students are also encouraged to study their
own language and sit their own language exams. And, of
course, Dutch is offered at all levels.

Our recent reaccreditation by both CIS and NEASC
underlines that we deliver the highest quality international
education and we offer external examinations both with
Cambridge Assessment (IGCSE) and the International
Baccalaureate Organisation (IBDP). Our students are well
placed to enter the many top higher education institutions
in The Netherlands and worldwide. We foster a culture of a
love for and enjoyment of learning and a joy in achievement.
This is inspired by high expectations from our leadership
team and all our staff with everyone collaborating to promote
collaboration, tolerance, diversity, belonging and a sense of
service.

(Founded 1865)

Head
Mrs Kate Reynolds

Head of Prep School
Ms Claire Lilley

DP coordinator
Ms Jude Taylor

Status Private

Boarding/day Mixed

Gender Female

Language of instruction
English

Authorised IB programmes
DP

Number of pupils enrolled
640

Fees
Day:
£4,865 per term
Weekly Boarding:
£9,674 per term
Boarding:
£10,762 per term

Address
Lansdown Road
Bath
Bath & North-East Somerset
BA1 5SZ | UK

TEL +44 (0)1225 313877

Email
admissions@rhsb.gdst.net

Website
www.royalhighbath.gdst.net

Royal High School Bath, GDST is a leading independent day and boarding school. Part of the GDST family, RHS provides outstanding, contemporary, education for girls aged 3-18. With a reputation as supportive and stimulating, our students realise new talents, fulfil their potential and go on to have bright futures. Our Steinway Music School and Art School highlight our commitment to our students' creativity.

Academic
Committed to high academic standards, Royal High School Bath offers a choice of A level or IB with a wide range of subjects delivered by specialist teachers. Staff are highly qualified and engage and inspire their students – with 16 years' experience of the Diploma Programme, the school's results are excellent, and consistently above the global average. In 2020 RHSB was recognised as a Top Global IB School and in 2021 students achieved an impressive average score of 40 points. Four students excelled with 45 points and another four achieved 44 points. Students go on to study at prestigious universities in the UK and overseas, including Oxford, Cambridge, Imperial and UCL.

Global perspective beyond the classroom
Students value the international-mindedness of the IB and enjoy a school exchange to Sweden. This gives experience of other young people from very different backgrounds and nationalities. Students choose from a wide range of CAS options including an expedition to Cambodia where they teach in a partner school. Model United Nations enables students to refine skills including public speaking, critical thinking and leadership.

Orientation
The school's expertise means the induction of students is quick and effective. A residential orientation experience helps students gain an understanding of the programme ahead, and provides the space to plan their final years at school.

Boarding
Our global community of boarders find their home from home in RHS. Girls aged 11-16 board in School House, our stunning neo-Gothic main building. Gloucester House is the Sixth Form boarding house and girls quickly settle into a caring and supportive community. House staff value students as individuals and the pastoral care and wellbeing of each girl is paramount.

Location
Situated in Bath, RHS has good transport links. Just 15 minutes from M4 motorway and with easy access to London, Bristol, Cardiff and Birmingham. Mainline rail links to London Paddington. Airports in Bristol, Southampton, Heathrow and Gatwick are easy to access and a shuttle to west London for weekly boarders can be arranged as required.

RYDE SCHOOL
WITH UPPER CHINE

(Founded 1921)

Headmaster
Mr Mark Waldron MA (Cantab)

DP coordinator
David Shapland

CP coordinator
David Shapland

Status Private, Independent

Boarding/day Mixed

Gender Coeducational

Language of instruction
English

Authorised IB programmes
DP, CP

Age Range 2 1/2 – 18 years

Number of pupils enrolled
800

Fees
Day: £7,935 – £14,190
Weekly Boarding: £27,420 –
£27,885
Boarding: £30,795 – £31,260

Address
Queen's Road
Ryde
Isle of Wight
PO33 3BE | UK

TEL 01983 562229

Email
admissions@rydeschool.net

Website
www.rydeschool.org.uk

The school has an excellent record of academic achievement throughout all age groups and was the first independent school in the UK to offer the IB Career-related Programme alongside the IB Diploma Programme and our A Level Plus Programme, through which pupils study for A Levels but also take advantage of the IB courses on offer and add them as enrichment options. We also offer a one year GCSE and Pre-Sixth Form course providing excellent preparation for entry into the Sixth Form.

Pupils leave to go on to study at Oxbridge, medical schools, other Russell Group Universities and Art, Music and Drama colleges. Pupils succeed academically and are well-mannered, characterful, happy and independent; a result of Ryde School's dynamic yet welcoming environment.

Our pupils benefit from an extensive range of excellent resources and extra-curricular activities. Sailing is on the curriculum in both the Junior and Senior Schools and has a strong focus throughout the School. In addition to the extensive academic, creative arts and sporting programmes, the location of our school enables us to offer a full extra-curricular programme including fencing, riding and water sports.

Situated in a beautiful, safe and idyllic island setting just off the South Coast of England, Ryde School with Upper Chine (known locally as Ryde School) is a thriving, prosperous independent day and boarding school for boys and girls aged 2.5 to 18, providing exceptional educational opportunities in a nurturing environment – helping them to be resourceful and resilient in the face of challenge and change.

Just ten minutes by Hovercraft from the mainland, the School and the boarding houses benefit from being near high-speed sea, rail and air links to regional, European and international destinations and the School is minutes from Cowes, the home of international sailing.

Constantly investing in the future of our pupils, we have recently updated the science labs and libraries, the Sixth Form Centre and added a parent and pupil coffee shop and two new boarding houses in the school grounds in Ryde. The aims of Ryde School as embedded in the School motto, 'Ut Prosim', have always been focused on service to others. Our pupils are encouraged towards self-knowledge, academic excellence and leadership in order to contribute positively in their careers and the wider world.

(Founded 1975)

Principal
Stephen Blackburn

PYP coordinator
Claire Webster

MYP coordinator
Simon Downing

DP coordinator
Maripaz Aguilera

Status Private

Boarding/day Day

Gender Coeducational

Language of instruction
English

Authorised IB programmes
PYP, MYP, DP

Age Range 3 – 18 years

Number of pupils enrolled
800

Fees
Day: €10,500 – €19,200

Address
Rua Maria Brown
Outeiro de Polima
2785-816 S Domingos de Rana,
Lisbon | **PORTUGAL**

TEL +351 21 444 0434

Email
school@dominics-int.org

Website
www.dominics-int.org

St. Dominic's International School, Portugal, is a highly respected and well-known international school. It was the first and is currently one of the few schools in Portugal authorised to offer three of the International Baccalaureate Programmes: Primary (PYP), Middle (MYP), and the Diploma, and is celebrating its 28th year as an IB World School.

Our commitment to the IB and its programmes is at the core of SDIS' educational philosophy of 'Nurturing and Educating International Minds'. The IB programmes encourage students to question perceived truths and beliefs and reflect on their place in, and contribution to, the society in which they live.

The principle of inquiry based learning ensures that students develop into independent learners, equipped to embrace both the challenges and opportunities they will face throughout their lives. Situated 15 kilometers from central Lisbon, in the district of Cascais, St. Dominic's is a private, non-selective, coeducational day school serving students aged 3 to 18 years in the international community, through the medium of English. We currently have 48 nationalities amongst our student population, making us a truly international school.

The school is housed in three one-storey buildings. In addition to 48 classrooms, it has a self-contained nursery and kindergarten for our youngest students, two gym halls, three art rooms, two libraries, five science and technology laboratories, two music rooms and a drama studio. Our ICT facilities include both dedicated ICT suites as well as portable devices. We have an excellent reputation for sport, and have facilities for football, basketball and volleyball on site; a wide range of other sports are played using outside facilities.

The junior school offers: English, Portuguese, mathematics, social studies, information technology, art, music, PE and social education through the curriculum of the PYP from nursery to grade 5. In the senior school, students in grades 6 to 10 study the MYP, and in grades 11 and 12 we prepare students for the full diploma or for diploma courses. Our students go on to study at prestigious universities and colleges around the World.

Classes begin in early September and run to the end of June with breaks for Christmas and Easter and shorter mid-term breaks. The teaching day is from 8:30am to 3:30pm, with a wide range of extra-curricular and co-curricular activities offered after school to support the holistic development of our students.

Sainte Victoire International School

(Founded 2011)

Head of School
Frederic Fabre

DP coordinator
Brad Edwards

Status Private

Boarding/day Mixed

Gender Coeducational

Language of instruction
English, French

Authorised IB programmes
DP

Age Range 5 – 18 years

Fees
Day: €9,900 – €17,200
Boarding: €21,200 – €30,100

Address
Domaine de Château l'Arc
Chemin de Maurel
13710 Fuveau | **FRANCE**

TEL +33 4 42 26 51 96

Email
contact@schoolsaintevictoire.com

Website
www.schoolsaintevictoire.com

SVIS – Sainte Victoire International School is an IB World School located near Aix-en-Provence in the south of France. The school offers both the International Baccalaureate Diploma Programme and the Cambridge IGCSE examinations. SVIS provides education for students aged 5 years to 18 years from over 40 nationalities in our Primary, Middle, and High School. From the Primary school level, teaching is bilingual, allowing students to achieve their academic potential in English and French. SVIS also offers mother-tongue classes for several additional languages.

SVIS provides an innovative and rigorous approach to teaching and learning, incorporating cross-disciplinary subjects as well as a wide range of learning opportunities that take place off-campus. These include an extensive range of local and international trips, an abundant offering of after school activities, and an ecology park. SVIS integrates sustainability goals and service-learning into the curriculum to develop students as global citizens.

The school is situated in the heart of an international 18-hole golf course, facing the Sainte Victoire mountain and offers students a healthy and peaceful school environment. SVIS is a family-friendly environment focusing on the whole child and provides opportunities for students to explore their passions in athletics and the arts. Class sizes are limited to 15 maximum allowing for individualised education programs.

School Facilities

The school facilities include an amphitheater, a library with computers, a theatre/art room, a science laboratory, an indoor gym and outstanding outdoor facilities: an 18-hole golf course, a football/rugby grass pitch, a tennis court, a basketball court and ecology park where students can grow fruit and vegetables.

Boarding Facilities

The boarding house is located 20 meters from the entrance to the school. This facility offers an exceptional living environment, where students enjoy a healthy pace of life, conducive to academic success. There is a maximum of 2 students per duplex. Each duplex is equipped with study rooms, a kitchen, 2 bathrooms, lounges, and a private terrace with outstanding views over the grounds.

Outstanding qualities of SVIS

- SVIS offers internationally renowned educational programs that are sought by leading universities.
- SVIS graduates have their first choice of leading universities.
- With more than 40 student nationalities, SVIS is a diverse and inclusive school.
- Each student receives individual support and guidance from teachers to achieve their maximum potential.
- The school provides students with opportunities to study a large variety of mother-tongue and foreign languages including English, Spanish, Russian, Chinese, Italian, German, Dutch, and Japanese.
- The school has an outstanding campus on an international 18-hole golf course in the south of France. The grounds are surrounded by pine forests.

Scarborough College

(Founded 1896)

Headmaster
Mr Guy Emmett

DP coordinator
Ms Katie Cooke

Status Private

Boarding/day Mixed

Gender Coeducational

Language of instruction
English

Authorised IB programmes
DP

Age Range 3 – 18 years

Number of pupils enrolled
484

Fees
Day: £14,121 – £15,741
Boarding: £24,528 – £32,277

Address
Filey Road
Scarborough
North Yorkshire
YO11 3BA | UK

TEL +44 (0)1723 360620

Email admin@
scarboroughcollege.co.uk

Website
www.scarboroughcollege.co.uk

In brief
Founded in 1896, Scarborough College is a leading independent school in the Northeast, nestled between the stunning North Sea coast and the North Yorkshire Moors. The College offers a forward-facing and holistic education to boys and girls aged three to 18 year old.

At Scarborough College, we believe that all pupils have hidden talents and through our challenging curriculum, we inspire children to find their love of learning and develop a 'can do' attitude that typefies Scardeburgians old and new, the world over.

Academic and Co-curricular
True to our founding principles of offering an outstanding education; we offer GCSEs, an exceptional range of co-curricular activities and an IB-only Sixth Form. Our nationally recognised Yorkshire Grit programme is a vital part of our curriculum, providing challenges beyond the classroom and an opportunity for pupils to become resilient, collaborative and compassionate individuals.

Sports play a central role in College life and children from as early as Year 3 are engaged in daily sports and games lessons. With hockey and rugby as representative sports, the College has two Centres of Excellence – cricket and golf – for boys and girls who are committed to train and perform at a higher level.

The SC Visual Arts department has been ranked among the top performing in the country and through our cooperation with the London Academy of Music and Dramatic Art, we have nearly a quarter of our pupils taking LAMDA examinations each year.

Boarding
Following recent investments, Scarborough College's boarding facilities rank among the very best in the country. In addition to a Junior Boys and a Junior Boys House, the College boasts a flagship co-ed Sixth Form house. While the boarding houses are comfortable and modern, including underfloor heating and bespoke modern furniture, the atmosphere within them is homely, caring and happy. Boarding the SC way is a blend of modern comforts, the foundation of lifelong friendships and warmth.

Schloss Krumbach International School GmbH

Schloss Krumbach International School

(Founded 2020)

Head of School
Dr. Oksana Volozhanina

Middle School Principal & CAS Coordinator
Mag. Teresa Schnabl

DP coordinator
Minka Peeters Weem

Status Private, Non-Profit

Boarding/day Boarding

Gender Coeducational

Language of instruction
English, German

Authorised IB programmes
DP

Age Range 12 – 19 years

Number of pupils enrolled 30

Fees
Half board €47,700 – €58,000
Full board €52,200 – €63,000

Address
Schloss 1
2851 Krumbach, Lower Austria |
AUSTRIA

TEL +43 6765 409630

Email
info@krumbach.school

Website
www.krumbach.school

A young school, in a historical setting. A small school, growing fast. We are SKIS, an eclectic community of world citizens. We all speak at least two languages and value our diversity.

Schloss Krumbach International School is a co-educational boarding school (Grades 7-12), located in a beautiful 13th century castle. An Austrian Hogwarts, or so they say.

SKIS already holds the following accolades:
• IB World School offering IB Diploma Programme
• Austria's only Cambridge International Education School offering Advanced Level (ALevel Diploma)
• Duke of Edinburgh (DoE) Award centre
• Applied to join the CIS (Council of International Schools)

Our Middle School students in Grades 7 to 9 follow the Austrian national curriculum and are taught in German and supported in English. Grade 10 transitions to English as a medium of instruction and prepares for Grades 11 and 12 (IBDP or A-level). During Grade 10, our Pre-Diploma Grade, the learning process is organized in a way that allows Grade 10 students to improve their language skills, accustom to the new studying environment, try and evaluate different subjects, and gain a final understanding of what they are going to take for the Diploma programme. SKIS Career Counselling Team helps students explore the potential college venues to facilitate their choice of the Diploma subjects.

SKIS at Glance:
• Premium education: offering IB world & A-Levels programmes, access to the most advanced studying equipment and innovative learning techniques
• Internationally renowned teachers with 30+ years of experience, PhD degrees and passion for pedagogics
• A truly unique setting: Austria's one and only one castle-based school
• A carefully designed bilingual system: studying in English and German throughout Grades 7-10 + additional language in Grades 10-12 (taught in English)
• Superb accommodation: study and reside in a magnificent campus-castle
• Healthy lifestyle: a 6-meals-a-day menu, carefully crafted in accordance with best nutritionist science practices and lots of sports
• Personalized family-alike atmosphere: small studying groups with no more than 16 students per each
• Student-focused approach: academic support centre, career orientation and university counselling
• An enriching boarding experience: culture trips around Europe and a wide range of extracurricular activities
• Lifelong learning habits: supervised homework time with professional teachers + mother tongue support
• Soft skills acquisition: a unique student leadership system and participation in global major forums
• A safe ecosystem: 24/7 security on campus, digital detox, COVID-19 extensive precautions

Hop on an incredible academic, social, and creative journey at our castle!

School of Young Politicians – 1306

Head of School
Dr. Elena Sporysheva

IB Continuum Coordinator
Mrs. Karina Salway PhD

PYP coordinator
Mr. Azat Mazkenov, MA

MYP coordinator
Ms. Asylkay Davydova, MA

DP coordinator
Mrs. Sholpan Mussina

Status State

Boarding/day Day

Gender Coeducational

Language of instruction
English, Russian

Authorised IB programmes
PYP, MYP, DP

Address
Michurinskiy avenue 15
Buildings 2-4
119192 Moscow | **RUSSIAN FEDERATION**

TEL +7 495 932 99 58

Email
1306@edu.mos.ru

Website
gymg1306.mskobr.ru

The School of Young Politicians (SYP), UNESCO Associated School, School 1306 is a Russian state school located in the Western administrative district of Moscow. Alongside offering the national curriculum it is one of the first state schools in Eastern Europe to realise the IB continuum programme as well as being selected this year by IBO as a pilot school for the IB Primary Years programme (PYP).

Great emphasis is placed on selecting teaching staff with all our teachers expected to have university qualifications as well as either IB experience and/or IB training certification. The School also provides the opportunity for further ongoing professional development. The staff includes teachers from Russia as well as from other countries with several members of staff having considerable international experience.

The student body, aged between 3-17, is comprised of children from 44 nationalities. This provides for an international environment that ensures cultural diversity and an ethos of tolerance as well as an open-mindedness beneficial to the educational process.

The School sees its mission as raising holistic life-long learners who care about the world around them. Therefore, we offer a wide range of subjects, including a variety of second acquisition languages (Arabic, Chinese, Japanese, French, German, Italian, Spanish), and a great choice of extra-curriculum activities such as chess, music (piano, flute, violin, etc), choir, ballroom and sport dancing, drama classes in English and Russian, robotechnics and many more. The School also offers some unique opportunities such as monthly meetings with distinguished people from various fields – writers, musicians, philosophers, sportsmen, entrepreneurs, among others. A Club of Young Politicians meets regularly, inviting well known public figures to discuss and debate issues of world politics, economics and international relationships.

The School is well equipped with libraries, science labs, a botanic garden, indoor and outdoor sport stadiums and other sports facilities, dance halls, choreography classrooms as well as a drama studio and fully equipped media centre, theatre and cinema halls.

In the arts field the School hosts an annual international arts festival that encourages and promotes theatre, dance and choral singing. A prestigious panel of judges and professional workshops and masterclasses offer students both a competitive and supportive experience.

The School plays a vital role in the life of the community. Children initiate and realise various projects addressing the needs of disadvantaged children, war veterans, victims of domestic abuse and others in need. As volunteers they support the work of several charity organisations, initiate fund-raising activities and other socially important campaigns.

This year is the 20th anniversary of the School and over that time it has been nominated for numerous awards and prizes. It offers a happy, productive environment for children to learn.

Principal
Dr. Mónica Prieto

MYP coordinator
Gareth Finn

DP coordinator
Gareth Finn

Status Private

Boarding/day Mixed

Gender Coeducational

Language of instruction
English

Authorised IB programmes
MYP, DP

Age Range 11 – 18 years

Address
Belvedere Hall
Windgates
Greystones, Co. Wicklow
A63 EY23 | IRELAND

TEL +35 31 287 41 75

Email
admissions-dublin@sek.ie

Website
sek.ie

Everything we do is based on supporting our students to become questioning and courageous individuals fit for the 21st century.

SEK International School Dublin is located in a stunning natural setting, where the landscape of the Irish countryside meets the Atlantic coast, between the cities of Bray and Greystones. The latter was named one of the best cities in the world to live as a family, and is only 30 km from Dublin. SEK-Dublin combines architectural tradition with cutting-edge technology, spanning over 250,000 m2 of grounds and boasting extensive green areas where our students can enjoy a diverse range of sports and outdoor activities, while enhancing their academic development.

SEK Dublin was the first school in Ireland authorised by the International Baccalaureate Organisation to teach the Middle Years Programme (11-16 years) and the Diploma Programme (16-18 years), taught fully in English with optional languages, including German, French, Irish and Spanish.

SEK-Dublin opened its doors in 1981. The success of the school is based on several factors including: a multicultural team of highly trained teachers; the effective use of learning technologies; an individualised programme to cover the educational needs of each student; small class sizes; and an outstanding programme guaranteed by SEK schools' standards of excellence. Aware that education does not only take place in the classroom, as well as day students, we offer residential options with carefully selected local host families or in our on-campus high quality residential facilities, and diverse extracurricular and cultural activities. These aspects combine to nurture the holistic personal and academic development of our students.

SEK Dublin has the infrastructure, digital devices and skilled staff to enable the delivery of distance or blended learning depending on changing external scenarios, to which we are able to respond in a flexible and agile manner.

SEK-Dublin has started the process of accreditation by the New England Association of Schools and Colleges (NEASC).

SEK International School Alborán

(Founded 1999)

Principal
Luis Carlos Jiménez Gámez

PYP coordinator
Elnara Israfilova

MYP coordinator
Sebastián Fuentes Valenzuela

DP coordinator
Estefania Sánchez

Status Private

Boarding/day Day

Gender Coeducational

Language of instruction
English, Spanish

Authorised IB programmes
PYP, MYP, DP

Age Range 4 months – 18 years

Number of pupils enrolled 756

Address
C/ Barlovento 141
Urb. Almerimar, El Ejido
04711 Almería, Andalusia | SPAIN

TEL +34 950 49 72 73

Email
sek-alboran@sek.es

Website
alboran.sek.es

Located on the seashore and adjacent to the Punta Entinas Natural Park, in Almería, SEK International School Alborán is regarded as a high quality international school in Andalusia. It is the only school in Almeria that offers three IB International Baccalaureate Programmes, from 3 to 18 years of age (Primary Years Programme Middle Years Programme – MYP and the Diploma Programme, either bilingually in English and Spanish or fully in English). These programmes are coordinated closely with the Spanish education system.

For the SEK Education Group, to which SEK-Alborán belongs, physical fitness and respecting one's health are an essential element of the learning process. SEK-Alborán has extensive recreational areas, and 28,000m2 of outdoor spaces, as well as extensive sports facilities and a heated indoor pool. Its classrooms are equipped with cutting-edge technology (makerspace, video recording and editing spaces, radio, 3D printer, robotic tables, TED ED Club). It is considered a model of educational innovation in Andalusia.

Social and emotional learning programmes are of particular importance in students' curricula to foster the social and personal awareness. In the Intelligent Classroom, each student progresses according to their potential, working in teams and having individual efforts rewarded. Teachers and tutors are afforded an open space for dialogue with students and parents both in-person and online. Students can take advantage of the Flipped Classroom to work on content and tackle issues from a broad perspective, solving doubts with their teachers, and learning by doing.

SEK Alborán has the infrastructure, digital devices and skilled staff to enable the delivery of distance or blended learning depending on changing external scenarios, to which we are able to respond in a flexible and agile manner.

SEK-Alborán offers a bilingual Spanish-English education that is incorporated progressively over all educational stages (50% of the subjects are taught in English). The school is the only Cambridge English School in Almeria that prepares students for the official exams, as well as Goethe Institut and Alliance Française exams.

SEK-Alborán has started the process of accreditation by the New England Association of Schools and Colleges (NEASC).

SEK International School Atlántico

Principal
Jacobo Olmedo

PYP coordinator
Sara Bouzada Sanmartin

MYP coordinator
Mónica Azpilicueta Amorín

DP coordinator
Yolanda Cenamor Montero

Status Private

Boarding/day Day

Gender Coeducational

Language of instruction
English, Spanish

Authorised IB programmes
PYP, MYP, DP

Age Range 4 months – 18 years

Number of pupils enrolled 750

Address
Rúa Illa de Arousa 4
Boavista. A Caeira, Poio
36005 Pontevedra, Galicia | **SPAIN**

TEL +34 98 687 22 77

Email
sek-atlantico@sek.es

Website
atlantico.sek.es

SEK International School Atlántico offers an outstanding international education to students, from 4 months to 18 years of age. SEK-Atlántico is the only school in Galicia authorised to teach three International Baccalaureate Organisation programmes (Primary Years, Middle Years and Diploma).

SEK International Schools are committed to offering each student a learning experience focused on personal development and learning, preparing them for success in later life. Situated close to Pontevedra and Vigo, between the sea and the mountains, SEK-Atlántico boasts modern well-designed school spaces and buildings.

Students are afforded a bilingual education and learn to live with other cultures from an early age. The school places great importance on students' oral and written expression, fostering fluency in different languages. Considered a leader in educational innovation in Galicia, SEK-Atlántico offers learning in Galician, Spanish, English and French from year 3 of Primary.

The SEK education model allows students to play a leading role in their education. They explore and discover for themselves, and build and organise their own knowledge and skills, with expert support from teachers.

SEK-Atlántico students learn in facilities designed for their physical, social and creative development. They include: makerspaces, a psychomotor skills classroom for younger students, laboratories, music and art rooms, a library, language classrooms, a learning lab and large indoor and outdoor sports and recreational areas.

SEK Atlántico has the infrastructure, digital devices and skilled staff to enable the delivery of distance or blended learning depending on changing external scenarios, to which we are able to respond in a flexible and agile manner.

From the second year of Primary to Baccalaureate, SEK-Atlántico students prepare for Cambridge University Examinations. In the Middle Years Programme and in Baccalaureate, students can also opt to take the Alliance Française Diplôme d'etude de langue française.

SEK-Atlántico has started the process of accreditation by the New England Association of Schools and Colleges (NEASC).

SEK International School Catalunya

(Founded 1995)

Principal
Roberto Prata

PYP coordinator
Concepció Muntada

MYP coordinator
Carmen Fernández

DP coordinator
Adrià Van Waart

Status Private

Boarding/day Mixed

Gender Coeducational

Language of instruction
English, Spanish, Catalan

Authorised IB programmes
PYP, MYP, DP

Age Range 4 months – 18 years

Number of pupils enrolled 975

Address
Av. del Tremolencs, 24
La Garriga
08530 Barcelona, Catalonia |
SPAIN

TEL +34 93 871 84 48

Email
sek-catalunya@sek.es

Website
catalunya.
sekinternationalschools.com

SEK International School Catalunya is located in a quiet and safe residential area spanning 100,000 m2, including a large expanse of Mediterranean forest. The school is in La Garriga, a picturesque town just 30 minutes from the centre of Barcelona, one of the most cosmopolitan cities in Europe.

SEK-Catalunya boasts modern facilities and innovative learning spaces and teaches the three International Baccalaureate Programmes. The Middle Years Programme is offered in Spanish and English and the Diploma Programme is offered entirely in English or in both languages. We lead international rankings thanks to our excellent results in IB Diploma exams.

SEK-Catalunya is accredited by the New England Association of Schools and Colleges (NEASC), which is a process of external globally recognised quality assurance. This allows our students to graduate with the American High School Diploma, recognized by US universities.

The school offers its Secondary School and Baccalaureate students the opportunity to take part in the prestigious Duke of Edinburgh's International Award. An all-round personal development scheme focused on the development and training of skills such as: leadership, autonomy, problem solving and teamwork.

We also offer international boarding, catering for students from Spain and abroad in modern, comfortable and functional facilities, designed for residents to live together, grow as individuals and develop their personal identity thanks to a multicultural environment and a rich offer of complementary activities.

SEK Catalunya has the infrastructure, digital devices and skilled staff to enable the delivery of distance or blended learning depending on changing external scenarios, to which we are able to respond in a flexible and agile manner.

(Founded 1977)

Principal
Cecilia Villavicencio

PYP coordinator
Marisa Iglesias Lorenzo

MYP coordinator
James Shaw

DP coordinator
Dinis Alves Costa

Status Private

Boarding/day Day

Gender Coeducational

Language of instruction
English, Spanish

Authorised IB programmes
PYP, MYP, DP

Age Range 4 months – 18 years

Number of pupils enrolled
1400

Address
Urb. Ciudalcampo, Paseo de las
Perdices, 2
San Sebastián de los Reyes
28707 Madrid | **SPAIN**

TEL +34 91 659 63 03

Email
sek-ciudalcampo@sek.es

Website
ciudalcampo.sek.es

SEK International Schools are committed to offering each student a learning experience focused on personal perfection, preparing for success in later life. SEK Schools are bilingual and pioneers in offering International Baccalaureate programmes, boasting an educational model that has made a tradition of innovation, placing them among the best schools in Spain since their foundation in 1892. SEK International School Ciudalcampo offers the IB Primary Years Programme, the IB Middle Years Programme, the IB Diploma Programme (in English and Spanish, or fully in English), and the Spanish Bachillerato LOMCE.

SEK-Ciudalcampo offers an innovative educational model based on early stimulation, immersion in English and the development of talent and creativity in a digital environment that favours the development of emotional intelligence.

SEK Ciudalcampo boasts over 20,000m2 of grounds and buildings and a large outdoor sports complex that exceeds 10,000m2.

Through an active learning approach, SEK-Ciudalcampo turns the classrooms into a flexible learning place for all students. The student becomes an active agent, building learning for themselves. The Design Thinking methodology helps students to develop skills such as cooperation, creativity and innovation.

The SEK Future Learning Model includes an integrated learning and teaching sequence that brings together key elements such as: clear pedagogical objectives, innovative teaching methods, new dimensions for the roles of teachers and students, motivating tasks and diversified and authentic assessment. The model also includes digitalization of learning when appropriate, and the central role of professional learning of the teaching staff.

SEK Ciudalcampo has the infrastructure, digital devices and skilled staff to enable the delivery of distance or blended learning depending on changing external scenarios, to which we are able to respond in a flexible and agile manner.

SEK-Ciudalcampo is accredited by the New England Association of Schools and Colleges (NEASC) and is the first Spanish school to be recognised as a global member of Round Square.

SEK International School El Castillo

(Founded 1972)

Head of School
Eloísa López

PYP coordinator
Fátima González

MYP coordinator
Elvira Chiquero

DP coordinator
Ana Karina Cisneros

Status Private

Boarding/day Mixed

Gender Coeducational

Language of instruction
English, Spanish

Authorised IB programmes
PYP, MYP, DP

Age Range 4 months – 18 years

Number of pupils enrolled
1210

Address
Urb. Villafranca del Castillo,
Castillo de Manzanares, s/n
Villanueva de la Cañada
28692 Madrid | **SPAIN**

TEL +34 91 815 08 92

Email
sek-castillo@sek.es

Website madrid.
sekinternationalschools.com

SEK International School El Castillo offers an innovative educational model based on early learning stimulus, talent development, creativity and emotional intelligence. We cater for students from over 50 different nationalities, living and learning in an environment of multicultural understanding, in a stunning natural setting in the north of Madrid.

The school has been authorised as an International Baccalaureate (IB) World School for over 40 years. We offer the IB Primary Years, Middle Years and Diploma programmes fully in English, or through an English-Spanish bilingual syllabus, with outstanding recent examination results. We boast first-rate sports facilities and offer international boarders an incomparable environment for the development of individualised, personal growth and personalised pastoral care, provided by specialised school staff, in a safe and secure environment.

In addition, as a sign of our commitment to talent development, we offer a high-performance sports programme, the SEK International Sports Academy, that allows athletes to combine their academic studies with the highest levels of sports training. Students on this programme can reside in the boarding house, allowing them to combine their academic enrichment with high performance sports programmes. We also offer to students the opportunity to take part in the prestigious Duke of Edinburgh International Award. We also provide Equestrian Studies as part of a middle level vocational programme of study. We are authorised by the Spanish Ministry of Education to deliver the Arts Baccaleaureate, both visual and musical performing strands.

SEK El Castillo has the infrastructure, digital environment and skilled staff to enable the delivery of distance or blended learning depending on changing external scenarios, to which we are able to respond in a flexible and agile manner.

SEK-El Castillo is accredited by the New England Association of Schools and Colleges (NEASC), which is a process of external globally recognised quality assurance. This accreditation allows us to award the American High School Diploma.

(Founded 2009)	**Authorised IB programmes**
	PYP, MYP, DP
Head of School	
Verónica Sánchez	**Age Range** 3 – 18 years
PYP coordinator	**Address**
Anthony Hamblin	Onaiza 65
	Doha | **QATAR**
MYP coordinator	
Imogen van der Vijl	**TEL** +974 4012 7633
DP coordinator	**Email**
Kim Derudder	info@sek.qa
Status Private	**Website**
	www.sek.qa
Boarding/day Day	
Gender Coeducational	
Language of instruction	
Arabic, English, Spanish	

SEK International School Qatar was founded in 2013 within the framework of the Outstanding Schools Programme of the Ministry of Education of Qatar. The school today caters for students from over 60 nationalities, with teachers from over 25 different countries. The school is an innovative coeducational, international and multilingual school in Qatar, with a cutting-edge learning campus located in the sophisticated West Bay district of Doha. English is the language of instruction, and the school also offers Spanish and Arabic courses for all students.

SEK-Qatar is an IB World School authorised to offer the IB Primary Years Programme (PYP), the Middle Years Programme (MYP) and the Diploma Programme (DP), from pre-school to grade 12. The IB offers high-quality and challenging educational programmes, with a reputation for their high academic standards. SEK-Qatar is also proud to be an accredited school by New England Association of Schools and Colleges (NEASC), one of the most prestigious international university and school accreditation agencies. It indicates that the school meets high standards of institutional quality through ongoing, independent, and objective process of peer-review.

SEK-Qatar has a unique educational model. We are committed to offering quality education that promotes individualisation, places emphasis on learning rather than teaching, and fosters activity and effort, freedom, interaction and teamwork and transformational learning. Technology, sports, artistic and social activities also play a major role in the SEK educational model.

SEK-Qatar has the infrastructure, digital devices and skilled staff to enable the delivery of online or blended learning depending on changing external scenarios, to which we are able to respond in a flexible and agile manner.

SEK International School Santa Isabel

Head of School
Jennifer Pro

PYP coordinator
William Ivey

Status Private

Boarding/day Day

Gender Coeducational

Language of instruction
English, Spanish

Authorised IB programmes
PYP

Age Range 3 – 12 years

Number of pupils enrolled 375

Address
Calle San Ildefonso, 18
28012 Madrid | SPAIN

TEL +34 91 527 90 94

Email
sek-santaisabel@sek.es

Website
santaisabel.sek.es

SEK International School Santa Isabel is one of ten schools comprising SEK International Schools. Located in the centre of Madrid, SEK-Santa Isabel is the only school in downtown Madrid authorised to offer the International Baccalaureate Primary Years Programme (PYP).

Set in the historical and cultural district, our learning goes far beyond the four walls of the classroom as we collaborate with our neighboring institutions.

Our flexible and innovative environments nurture collaboration and teamwork between students and teachers, and is equipped with all the resources necessary for learning.

Global citizenship and social innovation are integrated in our curriculum as students learn the skills and competencies necessary to solve problems of the future and create a better world, both locally and globally.

SEK-Santa Isabel teaches Early Childhood and Primary Education. The school is bilingual, with 65% of the learning and teaching in English. Our international student body represents 19 different nationalities. The teaching staff is native-English speaking or bilingual, with extensive experience and training in English-speaking countries.

In addition, the school also prepares its students to take external language examinations. The school has a spacious gym on the school grounds, as well as outdoor areas for sports such as swimming, tennis and padel tennis, football and basketball.

SEK Santa Isabel has the infrastructure, digital devices and skilled staff to enable the delivery of distance or blended learning depending on changing external scenarios, to which we are able to respond in a flexible and agile manner.

With our Future Learning Model, students learn the diverse skills necessary for the third millennium, through a hands-on and flexible learning environment that fosters critical thinking, global competencies and student-led learning.

Students at SEK Santa Isabel develop emotional and multiple intelligences, values, mindfulness, public speaking and communication skills, becoming technologically accomplished through STEM and makerspace.

One of our major objectives is to discover and nurture the talents of our students, through our Stellar Programme for high-achieving students, with the aim of enriching their personal development.

Sheikh Zayed International Academy

Sheikh Zayed International Academy - Islamabad

أكاديمية الشيخ زايد الدولية - إسلام أباد

(Founded 2003)

Principal
Wafaa Abdul Ghaffar

PYP coordinator
Nadeyah Adnan

MYP coordinator
Saadia Tariq

DP coordinator
Saima Sohail

Status Private

Boarding/day Mixed

Gender Coeducational

Language of instruction
English

Authorised IB programmes
PYP, MYP, DP

Age Range 2 – 18 years

Address
Street 8
Sector H-8/4
Islamabad | **PAKISTAN**

TEL +92 51 4939298

Email
info@szia.ae

Website
www.szia.ae

An IB World School

Sheikh Zayed International Academy is a renowned International Academic Institution for students of Nursery (EY1) to Grade 12 (DP2). Housed in 2003, on a spacious green area of six main buildings and two hostel boarding schools, the Academy is both a dynamic IB continuum school and a British curriculum institution as such. Offering both the IB and British curricula, SZIA stands as one of the most distinguished Academic institutions in Islamabad, Pakistan. The Academy is led by Mrs. Wafaa Abdul Ghaffar, an Academic Consultant and Educationalist, along with a five-member Board of Trustees from the Ministry of Presidential Affairs, the United Arab Emirates. Sheikh Zayed International Academy is a non- profit private co-educational international school of premium quality education and a state of the art campus that operates in Islamabad under the Embassy of the United Arab Emirates.

A Diverse and Welcoming Community

SZIA prides itself for true Internationalism reflected in a student body from twenty one various nationalities and a curriculum developed by its Academic Development Center, to cater for all students of different backgrounds, considering, at the same time, the difference in culture, societies and individual needs. Home to over 21 nationalities, different mother tongues and varied cultures and traditions, we manifest respect, tolerance, communication and genuine care for one another and prepare students of all backgrounds to excel in and contribute to a global world, to guarantee a successful future for each and ensure that each, in turn, be an active member of a better world.

Believing that each student is an intellectual, emotional, social and physical being with unique attributes and abilities, the caring and supportive, highly qualified faculty aims to help each individual student to excel to the utmost of his/her capabilities. Each teacher is an expert in ensuring that the years spent at SZIA are dynamic yet gentle, challenging yet reassuring, exciting yet reflective, and overall, follow a designed scope and sequences embodied in an annual strategic plan directed, in priority, to the student well-being in all sense.

Accreditation and Memberships:

Sheikh Zayed International Academy is the only IB World School in Islamabad which enjoys continuum accreditation of all three IB programs, namely, DP, MYP and PYP, and which offers simultaneously the IB, the British and the American curricula from Grades 9 to 12. SZIA is a member of the IB PAK Association, with an honor of having the Principal Mrs. Wafaa Abdul Ghaffar being the Chairperson of the IB Pakistan Association comprising nineteen IB schools in Pakistan. SZIA is also accredited by Cambridge and Pearson, Edexcel, British UK Boards of Examination and is affiliated with NESA, World Wildlife Fund, Kangourou Sans Frontieres-Pakistan, Drug free Pakistan foundation, Microsoft, Clean Green Punjab Index launched by CM Punjab.

Outstanding Academics:

SZIA's varied academic curricula offers a broad range of options including International Baccalaureate, Cambridge International Assessment Examinations and High School.

Trans-disciplinary and Interdisciplinary learning across disciplines is a hallmark of Sheikh Zayed International

Academy. It is ensured by carefully choosing experiences supported by reflection, critical analysis and synthesis. Experiences are structured to urge the learner to take initiative, make decisions and be accountable for results. Our learners are actively engaged in raising queries, researching and investigating with curiosity and enthusiasm, then reflecting on them with a final clear and academic presentation that is innovative, focused and goal-designated.

SZIA's comprehensive and challenging curricula prepares students to achieve academic excellence. Local and global service-learning opportunities are also an integral part of the curriculum and student life at SZIA. The student voice and agency provides a chance for the students to freely explore new passions, as well as dive deep into existing ones, leading to a journey of discovery and preparation for a life beyond SZIA.

University Placements:
Outstanding academic results and superb acceptance record of SZIA students at the best universities throughout the world speak volumes about the credibility and prestige of the Academy.

SZIA graduates have always secured acceptance at the most renowned universities worldwide: Harvard University and Carnegie Mellon University in the U.S.A. Oxford University and University of Edinburgh in the U.K. Queen's University in Canada, Melbourne University in Australia, American University of Sharjah, The United Arab Emirates and other international universities ranked highly for the fields of Avionics, Medicine, Engineering and Business among others.

A Vast array of Co-curricular Activities:
SZIA offers a broad range of co-curricular activities that ensure the growth of a student healthily from all perspectives. These activities include swimming, basketball, football, athlete games, Art, Music and so.. Our strong Community Service opportunities (to complete their Creativity, Activity and Service – CAS program) as well as the educational trips, all contribute to the healthy growth of balanced and caring individuals. As we believe that extra-curricular activities play a vital role in supporting the educational process; colorful activities, functions and ceremonies are held, where all students participate in both performance and presentation segments.

SZIA remains unparalleled in all aspects, with the main objective to promote international understanding through exposing students to ideas and concepts from different cultures and countries, by challenging them to understand and tackle real-world issues, and by connecting them with other students from all nationalities of the global world.

Sevenoaks School

(Founded 1432)

Head of School
Mr Jesse R Elzinga AB MSt FCCT

DP coordinator
Nigel Haworth

Status Private

Boarding/day Mixed

Gender Coeducational

Language of instruction
English

Authorised IB programmes
DP

Age Range 11 – 18 years

Number of pupils enrolled
1172

Fees
Day: £25,020 – £28,413
Boarding: £39,790 – £42,084

Address
High Street
Sevenoaks
Kent
TN13 1HU | UK

TEL +44 (0)1732 455133

Email
regist@sevenoaksschool.org

Website
www.sevenoaksschool.org

Sevenoaks is one of the leading schools in the UK, providing an outstanding modern education. All 450+ students in the sixth form study the IB Diploma Programme, which the school has taught since 1978. The leafy 100-acre campus is in the Kent countryside, just half an hour from Central London and Gatwick Airport. International students make up around 20 per cent of the student body and the school provides pupils with a balanced and intellectually stimulating education while promoting global understanding. Pastoral care is consistently excellent, enabling friendships between all members of a peer group to flourish. Sevenoaks is only one of a handful of schools to win *The Sunday Times Independent Secondary School of the Year* twice.

Curriculum

A wide range of subjects is offered at GCSE and IGCSE. In the sixth form all pupils study the IB Diploma Programme. Academic results are outstanding. In 2021, 30 students achieved the maximum 45 points in the IB Diploma, and the average score was 41.3 (around eight points above the world average). Virtually every student goes on to one of the world's best universities, with around 80 per cent taking places at leading UK universities, and 21 per cent accepting places at top US, Canadian, European and international universities.

A wide range of sport is offered, and pupils achieve honours in cross country, rugby, football, hockey, netball, cricket, athletics, sailing, shooting, swimming and tennis. There is

a strong emphasis on music, drama and art, with chamber music a particular strength. The school is proud of its strong tradition of community service and DofE Award participation.

Facilities

Facilities are first class. Recent developments include a striking, state-of-the-art boarding house, an award-winning performing arts centre, a Science & Technology Centre uniting the four core fields of science, and an innovative Sixth Form centre. There are seven boarding houses, including five single-sex houses (13-18), and two sixth form houses (16-18). A new girls' boarding house is being built and will open in 2023. The house will accommodate 60 girls in Year 9 and above.

Entrance

Year 7 (11+): entrance examination, school reference and interview.

Year 9 (13+): pre-assessment, entrance examination or Common Entrance or scholarship examination, plus school reference and interview.

Sixth form (16+): entrance examination, personal statement and interview.

Up to 50 scholarships are awarded annually at 11, 13 and 16, for academic excellence, music, sport, art and drama, and means-tested bursaries are available.

Sevenoaks School is a registered charity for purposes of education. Charity No. 1101358.

Sidcot
Live Adventurously

(Founded 1699)

Headmaster
Iain Kilpatrick BA MEd FRSA

DP coordinator Stefania Cauli

Status Private

Boarding/day Mixed

Gender Coeducational

Language of instruction
English

Authorised IB programmes
DP

Age Range 3 – 18 years

Number of pupils enrolled
603

Fees
Day: £2,900 – £6,510 per term
Boarding: £9,830 – £12,030 per term

Address
Oakridge Lane, Winscombe
Somerset, **BS25 1PD | UK**

TEL 01934 843102

Email
admissions@sidcot.org.uk

Website
www.sidcot.org.uk

Sidcot School is a lively and popular co-ed boarding and day school where students work hard and achieve excellent results. We encourage individuality, creativity, and challenge our students to think with greater depth to reach a better understanding of themselves and the world they live in. It is these characteristics which make the IB Diploma such a good fit for the School.

Boarding at Sidcot
Sidcot has a well-established international community with more than 30 different nationalities. The day and boarding students are extremely well integrated so that everyone benefits from the rich mixture of cultures and backgrounds. Within the boarding houses, international diversity is celebrated and shared. Sidcot is a Quaker school and welcomes students of all faiths and none with values based on Christian principles.

Convenient rural location
The School is close to Bristol and Bath and only two hours from London. Bristol International Airport is 20 minutes away by car. In this setting, students can enjoy the best of both rural and city life: a peaceful environment in which to concentrate on their studies, and access to the cities for educational opportunities and weekend activities.

Academic success
We set out to provide a creative and stretching education that inspires students to want to learn. We help them to develop the self-motivation that will enable them to take responsibility for their own learning. It is no surprise that these personal qualities go together with academic excellence. In 2021 the school achieved an IB Mean Score of 37.5 with one student achieving a world class score of 44 out of 45.

Outstanding facilities
As well as 160 acres of organic farmland, Sidcot has superb sporting grounds, a 25-metre indoor swimming pool, all-weather pitch, and an Equestrian Centre. Our Arts Centre bridges traditional genres with modern technology and includes studios for painting, sculpture and ceramics, textiles, photography, a digital media suite, a dedicated performance hall, practice rooms, recording studio and music technology suite and drama studio. We also have some more unusual facilities – for example, an allotment where students get involved in growing produce for the kitchens, a yurt village, bee hives to learn about beekeeping and even a well-equipped Observatory enabling students to explore the night sky.

Caring relationships
Quakers place a high value on equality – at Sidcot this is evident in the open and friendly relationships between staff and students, and between students of all ages and cultures. It is often remarked on that our students are extremely supportive of each other, making newcomers – students, teachers and visitors – quickly feel at home.

Special characteristics
- Outstanding reputation in sciences, maths and creative arts
- Centre for Peace and Global Studies
- Equestrian boarding school
- Year 11 Pathway – one-year GCSE course – integrated to give a truly UK boarding school experience and to prepare for the IB or A level programme to follow in the Sixth Form.

An **inspired** school

(Founded 1978)	**Age Range** 4 months – 18 years
Head of School Mr. James Kearney	**Number of pupils enrolled** 1027
PYP coordinator Andrea Bennett	**Fees** Please see our website
MYP coordinator Belén González	**Address** Avenida La Reserva SN
DP coordinator Hélène Caillet	Sotogrande Cádiz, **11310	SPAIN**
Status Private	**TEL** +34 956 795 902
Boarding/day Mixed	**Email**
Gender Coeducational	info@sis.gl
Language of instruction English	**Website** www.sis.ac
Authorised IB programmes PYP, MYP, DP	

Sotogrande International School (SIS) is a day and boarding school, that follows the IB programme from 3-18 years. Home to a passionate learning community who inspire and encourage learning and intercultural understanding, promoting education as a force for good in the world.

Academic results are consistently excellent, with both MYP and Diploma students achieving well above world average scores year after year. As a result of the impressive average point score of 35 in 2021, 11% of students achieved 40 points or more, with one student achieving the maximum 45 points being a boarding student.

With more than 1000 children from 50 countries, SIS is more than just a school, it's a place where individuals flourish. Throughout the IB programmes, internationally qualified teachers provide a challenging, nurturing and academically-rigorous education. SIS offers a bespoke Elite Sports Programme where students combine sports and education.

As an Apple Distinguished School, the use of technology is creatively embedded into the curriculum for all students from the age of 3, while the F1 in Schools programme and the Hyperbaric Challenge provide an exciting way for students to learn Science, Technology, Engineering and Maths (STEM) related subjects. Students are encouraged to think independently and critically, developing their unique interests, gifts and talents benefiting from opportunities to be the best they can be.

Sotogrande International Boarding House is a warm vibrant community, where the staff are dedicated to caring for, and getting the best out of each individual. The academic support received by students is reflected in IB Diploma exam results and University destinations of our boarding students.

Students are encouraged to take part in every aspect of boarding life helping them to grow into happy, motivated and morally committed citizens of the world.

St Andrew's College

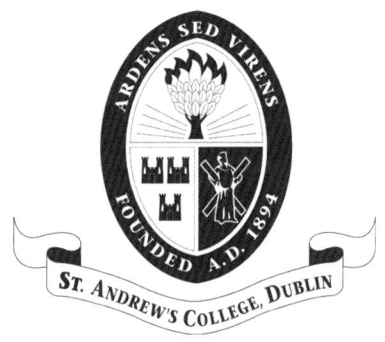

(Founded 1894)

Headmistress
Ms Louise Marshall

Head of IB
Julie Gillane

Status Private

Boarding/day Day

Gender Coeducational

Language of instruction
English

Authorised IB programmes
DP

Age Range 4 – 18 years

Number of pupils enrolled
1250

Address
Booterstown Avenue
Blackrock, County Dublin |
IRELAND

TEL +353 1 288 2785

Email
information@st-andrews.ie

Website
www.sac.ie

St Andrew's College was founded by the Presbyterian community of Dublin in 1894 to provide a broadly-based, liberal education. From its inception, the College attracted students from a variety of backgrounds and strove to unite them through a shared experience of working, learning and playing together. Over the years the College has evolved in many ways, and is now a flourishing, interdenominational, co-educational school of approximately 1,250 pupils and just over 100 teachers.

In 1985, St Andrew's College became the first school in Ireland to offer the International Baccalaureate. Over the last 28 years it has built up a well-deserved reputation for its excellent results and for its distinctive multicultural environment. The philosophy on which the College was founded and from which it draws its inspiration today is that a high-quality, rounded education is essential to the moral, social, spiritual, cultural and academic development and physical and mental well-being of the individual student. This philosophy is mirrored in the IB Learner Profile. The high quality of the education offered by the College and its commitment to continuous improvement are reflected in the fact that since 1984 St Andrew's has been fully accredited by the European Council of International Schools and the New England Association of Schools and Colleges.

The IB Diploma Programme combines academic rigour with a strong extracurricular dimension and various community service projects. The IB students at St Andrew's participate in a wide range of activities, representing their year on the Prefect Council, playing team sports such as hockey, rugby, tennis, basketball and badminton, taking part in activities such as the Model United Nations, being involved in environmental projects, assisting in the school library and local communities and helping various charities by fundraising and doing voluntary work. The IB Diploma Programme is the premier worldwide pre-university programme. Since 1985, St Andrew's IB students have been accepted into many universities throughout the world. In recent years these have included all the top Irish universities; MIT, Yale, Stanford, Berkeley and Columbia (USA), Cambridge, Durham, Bristol, Edinburgh and the LSE (UK), the Universities of Tokyo and Keio (Japan). These students universally acknowledge the extent to which their studies in the IB Diploma Programme has given them invaluable help in their university careers.

The IB student profile at St Andrew's College is a truly international one, with students coming from all continents. This ethnic and cultural diversity enriches the school community in many ways and provides a wealth of knowledge and experience which is of great benefit to other students in the school.

(Founded 1953)

Principal
Mr Andrew Rattue

Vice Principal Academic
Alastair Summers

Vice Principal Pastoral
Elena Hesse

DP coordinator
Darrel Ross

Status Private

Boarding/day Mixed

Gender Coeducational

Language of instruction
English

Authorised IB programmes
DP

Age Range 14 – 18 years

Number of pupils enrolled
280

Fees
Day: £20,480
Boarding: £42,626

Address
139 Banbury Road
Oxford
Oxfordshire
OX2 7AL | UK

TEL +44 (0)1865 552031

Email
admissions@stclares.ac.uk

Website
www.stclares.ac.uk

St Clare's Oxford is an independent, co-educational, day and boarding college located in elegant north Oxford and has been offering the International Baccalaureate Diploma for over 40 years, longer than any other school or college in England. It is also an IB World School. The college has a worldwide reputation for expertise in providing the IB Diploma and embraces internationalism and academic excellence as its core values.

Students from over 45 countries study at St Clare's, including a significant number of British students. The atmosphere is informal and friendly, with an equal emphasis on hard work and developing personal responsibility and mutual respect between staff and students.

St Clare's has an especially wide range of subjects on offer at higher and standard level and, in addition, can teach literature face-to-face in over 25 different languages, something that is not available in any other school in the UK. In recent years, 26 of our students have gained the maximum 45 points and obtained places at top ranking universities worldwide.

The college also offers a one year Pre-IB course which includes English and Maths iGCSEs, a two year Middle School Programme including 5 iGCSEs and a three week IB Introduction Course in the summer to prepare for the start of the diploma in September.

Students live in college houses close to the central campus, under the care of residential staff. St Clare's also welcomes students from the local area as day students.

There is an extensive programme of social, cultural and sporting activities and students are encouraged to take full advantage of the opportunities that Oxford provides.

St Clare's is most definitely different to any other college in Oxfordshire and rightly so. We have a different approach to studying, living and developing the students as young adults, creating knowledgeable, open-minded and inquiring minds.

St Edward's College, Malta

St Edward's College
Malta

(Founded 1929)

Headmaster
Mr Nollaig Mac an Bhaird

DP coordinator
Mr Jolen Galea

Status Private

Boarding/day Mixed

Gender Coeducational

Language of instruction
English

Authorised IB programmes
DP

Age Range 2 – 4 & 16-18 years

Fees
Day: €1,965 – €7,200
Boarding: €15,500 – €23,900

Address
Triq San Dwardu
Birgu (Vittoriosa)
BRG 9039 | MALTA

TEL +356 2788 1199

Email
admissions@stedwards.edu.mt

Website
www.stedwards.edu.mt

If you are looking for a top Sixth Form offering the IB Diploma programme, then look no further – St Edward's College in Birgu, Cottonera is only a few minutes from Malta's Capital, Valletta. St Edward's was established in 1929, basing itself on British Public School ideals, to fill the void left in the Maltese education system by the departure of the English Jesuits.

The College site originally served as a Military Hospital and has extensive grounds between the bastion walls and the old hospital buildings, which serve as ideal recreational areas. St Edward's College was authorised to offer the International Baccalaureate (IB) Diploma Programme (DP) commencing September 2009 and following successful years, applications for boarders and day students have been increasing.

Between the age of 16 and 18 we offer the 2-year International IB Diploma programme which is recognised by both local and international universities. The IB was designed to meet the needs of these students to ensure that they can effortlessly integrate into different International Schools when the need arises.

After carefully looking at the options available to Maltese students we reached a conclusion that the IB Diploma would also be their best option.

The International Baccalaureate® (IB) aims to do more than other curricula by developing inquiring, knowledgeable and caring young people who are motivated to succeed.

The College is an English speaking school so all the lessons are in conducted in English.

St Edward's offers a unique opportunity for parents seeking a boarding school also. We have five-day and seven-day options. Our boarding facilities are split over two floors where single and double rooms are available.

- The school operates on British boarding school principles with high academic standards
- The location and environment are superb with year round sunshine on a Mediterranean island
- Malta is within 3 hours of any European capital city by air
- The IB Diploma is recognised by all top universities
- Our fees offer some of the best value of any European boarding schools

Come and join our students on the IB Diploma Programme!

ST. EDWARD'S
OXFORD

(Founded 1863)

Warden
Alastair Chirnside

DP coordinator
Anna Fielding

Status Private

Boarding/day Mixed

Gender Coeducational

Language of instruction
English

Authorised IB programmes
DP

Age Range 13 – 18 years

Number of pupils enrolled
775

Fees
Day: £10,794 per term
Boarding: £13,489 per term

Address
Woodstock Road
Oxford
Oxfordshire
OX2 7NN | UK

TEL +44 (0)1865 319200

Email
registrar@stedwardsoxford.org

Website
www.stedwardsoxford.org

St Edward's

The number of pupils choosing to study the IB at St Edward's has increased significantly in recent years. We have an excellent balance in the Sixth Form between the IB and A Level, with equal numbers of candidates for both. The School sits on a vast 100-acre estate complete with landmark new university-style academic facilities, recently-completed Music School, professional-level North Wall Arts Centre and riverside boat house – yet it is only a five minute bus ride away from one of the most famous university cities in the world.

Oxford

Being so close to all the amenities and attractions of Oxford is of enormous benefit to our pupils. The city's rich architectural history and the University's global reputation for scholarship are an intoxicating combination. Venues such as the Ashmolean Museum, the Oxford Playhouse, The Museum of Modern Art and Blenheim Palace offer important learning opportunities – but also welcome distraction from the busy school day. In Oxford, pupils can attend talks and lectures by notable speakers at countless venues across the city. Pupils enjoy being part of this international cultural and intellectual community.

Sixth Form Achievements

In 2021, 94% of Higher Level grades were 7-5 and 66% were 7/6; the average points score was 36. Each year, a number of

pupils are awarded places at Oxford and Cambridge whilst the majority go on to top universities in Britain and overseas. Pupils are increasingly interested in studying outside the UK and we have considerable experience in this area. In recent years, pupils have gone on to study at US and Canadian universities including Harvard, Dartmouth, UCLA, McGill, Northeastern and NYU. Pupils have also been successful in their applications to universities in Hong Kong, Japan, Ireland and elsewhere in Europe.

Pastoral Care

The pastoral care system at St Edward's has long been regarded as one of the school's great strengths. Underpinned by a highly effective network of relationships, the system offers distinct but interwoven levels of care.

The School and the Admissions Process

St Edward's has around 775 pupils, 83% of whom board. The Sixth Form has around 330 pupils, some 25% of whom are from overseas (18% across the rest of the School), and the boy/girl split is 53%/47%. Entry to the Sixth Form is competitive with around 4 applicants per place. Academic and Music Scholarships are available along with further Awards in Sport, Art, Dance and Drama.

Find out more about school life on Teddies TV via the website.

ST GEORGE'S
BRITISH INTERNATIONAL SCHOOL **ROME**

(Founded 1958)

Principal
David Tongue

DP coordinator
Helen Andrew

Status Private

Boarding/day Day

Gender Coeducational

Language of instruction
English

Authorised IB programmes
DP

Age Range 3 – 18 years

Number of pupils enrolled
925

Fees
€11,100 – €21,900

Address
Via Cassia, km 16
La Storta
00123 Rome | **ITALY**

TEL +39 06 3086001

Email
admissions@stgeorge.school.it

Website
www.stgeorge.school.it

St George's is Rome's original and largest British international school, founded in 1958. Today it is home to 925 pupils from 92 different nationalities: a truly global community.

The school's main campus is a historic 14-acre site in the north of the city with extensive facilities: 7 fully-equipped science laboratories, two information technology classrooms, specialist music, art and design technology rooms, and multiple sports amenities, including two multi-purpose astro-turf pitches, an olympic- size running track, tennis, basketball and volleyball courts.

A proudly inclusive school, St George's welcomes new pupils throughout the year, subject to availability, and offers extensive learning support to pupils with additional educational needs, as well as EAL. Pupils follow the UK National Curriculum through to IGCSE. Thereafter, pupils progress to the IBDP, with over 30 separate DP courses offered. Teachers are almost exclusively UK-trained and mother-tongue English speakers.

Emphasis is on academic excellence, with exam results consistently amongst the best in the country and in Europe. The Class of 2021 achieved an average DP score of 37.2 points, and have accepted places at leading universities including Cambridge, UCL, King's College London and Warwick. For prospective families, virtual and in-person visits are available throughout the school year.

St Leonards School

St Leonards
St Andrews, Fife

AD VITAM

(Founded 1877)

Head Mr Simon Brian

PYP coordinator
Catherine Brannen

MYP coordinator
Kathryn McGregor

DP coordinator
Ben Seymour

CP coordinator
Ben Seymour

Status Private Independent

Boarding/day Mixed

Gender Coeducational

Language of instruction
English

Authorised IB programmes
PYP, MYP, DP, CP

Age Range 5 – 18 years

Number of pupils enrolled 575

Fees
Day: £9,840 – £15,939
Boarding: £24,342 – £37,920

Address
The Pends
St Andrews
Fife
KY16 9QJ | UK

TEL 01334 472126

Email
registrar@stleonards-fife.org

Website stleonards-fife.org

St Leonards is an independent, coeducational, boarding and day school situated in an historic campus at the heart of St Andrews. Less than an hour from Edinburgh airport, the seaside town is renowned as the home of golf and Scotland's first university. St Leonards was named Scotland's Independent School of the Year 2019 by The Sunday Times Good Schools Guide.

It is international and progressive in outlook, yet rooted in Scottish traditions. At present, there are pupils from 35 nationalities on the school roll; full, flexi and weekly boarding is offered from age ten. Over the past five years, St Leonards has invested £5 million in the refurbishment of its boarding houses, which are very much a 'home from home'. The renovated houses have stunning state-of-the-art kitchens and spacious, comfortable social areas. Many bedrooms have unrivalled views over the town's medieval cathedral ruins and the North Sea that lies beyond the school playing fields.

St Leonards was the first school to be accredited as an all-through IB school in Scotland, and is the only school in the UK to actively offer all four IB programmes. The youngest pupils follow the PYP, followed by the MYP and (I)GCSEs. In the Sixth Form, pupils choose between the CP and the DP.

The school fosters an imaginative choice of projects for CAS and Service Learning, as well as for the MYP Community Project. Recent examples include tree-planting and a sunrise swim in the North Sea for charity. To help pupils prepare for life after school, there is an annual higher education and careers fair featuring UK and international institutions, and a stimulating calendar of lectures delivered by guest speakers.

In 2021, the average points score was 35, with 82% of all Higher Level subjects graded 7, 6, or 5. This strong set of results led to 88% of leavers securing a place at their first choice university, including the Universities of Oxford, Edinburgh, and Glasgow.

Timetables are designed to establish a healthy balance of outstanding sporting and co-curricular programmes alongside excellent academic studies, with over 50 activities offered. The leading five-tier Golf Programme continues to go from strength to strength, as does the Duke of Edinburgh Award programme, and an exciting calendar of trips and activities ensures pupils leave St Leonards equipped with the skills required to succeed in today's ever-changing world. Truly an education 'Ad Vitam'.

Entry requirements

Tests and interviews are held throughout the year. For older pupils, entry is by CAT4 assessment, along with school reports and interviews. A Pre-IB programme is offered, usually for one year before a student starts Sixth Form.

ST. GEORGE'S INTERNATIONAL SCHOOL

LEVAVI OCULOS

SWITZERLAND

(Founded 1927)

Head of School
Dr. Ruth Norris

DP coordinator
Colin Travis

Status Private

Boarding/day Mixed

Gender Coeducational

Language of instruction
English

Authorised IB programmes
DP

Age Range 1.5 – 18 years

Number of pupils enrolled
400

Fees
Please enquire

Address
Chemin de St. Georges 19
CH-1815 Clarens/Montreux |
SWITZERLAND

TEL +41 21 964 3411

Email
admissions@stgeorges.ch

Website
www.stgeorges.ch

Founded in 1927, St. George's International School combines its well-structured, traditional ethos with academic excellence in an international environment. Enjoying a safe location, our whole school community fosters mutual respect and understanding whilst cultivating individual talents and potential.

As stated in our motto, 'Levavi Oculos', St. George's International School encourages students to lift their eyes and recognise positive qualities within themselves and others and to nurture a caring and dynamic attitude in today's demanding world.

The school's Learning Principles closely relate to the IB learner profile and students are challenged to become more curious, thoughtful, resilient, reflective, collaborative and balanced.

The school provides a 'Home away from Home' to approximately 80 boarders and over 300 day students from 60 different nationalities. Nestled between the Alps and Lake Geneva, the school includes tennis courts, football field, sports hall, play parks and opened landscaped grounds. During winter students ski and in the summer they make use of the lake, surrounding countryside and local sports facilities.

The curriculum contains the following subject groups:

Groups 1 & 2: Languages
Students usually select from English and French. Spanish, German, Chinese, Russian and other languages as part of the mother tongue Literature self-taught programme are also possible.

Group 3: Individuals and Societies
- Economics
- Geography
- History
- Environmental Systems and Societies
- Business Management

Group 4: Experimental Sciences
- Biology
- Chemistry
- Physics
- Sports, Exercise and Health Science
- Computer Science
- Environmental Systems and Societies

Group 5: Mathematics
St. George's offers Mathematics in higher and standard levels.
- Applications and Interpretations
- Analysis and Approaches

Group 6: The Arts (or elective subject)
Students can follow courses in either Visual Arts, Music, Dance or Theatre Studies.

Alternatively students may follow a second subject chosen from Groups 2, 3 or 4.

St. Gilgen International School

St. Gilgen International School

SALZBURG | AUSTRIA

(Founded 2008)

Head of School
Ms Martina Moetz

DP coordinator
John Patton

Status Private

Boarding/day Mixed

Gender Coeducational

Language of instruction
English

Authorised IB programmes
DP

Age Range 9 – 18 years

Number of pupils enrolled
220

Fees
Day: €25,900 – €39,600
Boarding: €53,200 – €59,800

Address
Ischlerstrasse 13
5340 St. Gilgen, Salzburg |
AUSTRIA

TEL +43 62 272 0259

Email
info@stgis.at

Website
www.stgis.at

An International educational experience in a breathtaking natural setting

English. German. Russian. Spanish... Just a few of the languages that float down our hallways at St. Gilgen International School (StGIS). Consisting of approximately 40 nationalities, our international student body with over 220 students is a diverse melting pot of talented students. Our school is nestled in the heart of a charming lake side village on the exquisite Wolfgangsee and surrounded by the Austrian alps. St. Gilgen is a stone's throw from the cultural hotspot of Salzburg and just a few hours from Vienna and Munich.

Our key promise is that every child has talent and we will develop it – so a main focus for us is making sure we provide the ideal environment for students. In order to ensure every student flourishes at StGIS, our philosophy of 'three pillars of excellence' applies to every child – excellence in education, care and activities. This means our highly qualified network of teachers, pastoral staff and nurses combine to ensure every student's unique talents are discovered, nurtured and developed.

With over 40 activities to choose from – the school treats the world as a classroom and ensures professional guidance is always at hand. For example, a state-approved mountain guide leads hiking expeditions and horse riding lessons are held in a first class stable. Students can also enjoy golf lessons and seasonal sports such as rowing, water skiing, canyoning, skiing, ice skating and climbing. StGIS also has a strong foundation in the Arts and all students have access to professional Art, Theatre, Dance and Music lessons.

A key focus of the school is to instill a love of learning in each student – and the curriculum and modern teaching methods are designed to fuel natural curiosity. Offering the coveted International Baccalaureate (IB) Diploma, StGIS students are equipped to go on to study at the world's best Universities. This is a place where teachers strive to build an energy of relentless curiosity in each classroom and empower young minds to stretch and fulfill their potential.

With school fees in line with the world's most prestigious educational institutions, StGIS is one of the best investments you can make in your child's future. After experiencing the unique school first-hand, it's absolutely clear that the reward is a magical education that lasts a lifetime.

We would be delighted to welcome you to show the very best of what Austrian education offers. Simply visit us at **www.stgis.at** and let the journey begin!

St. John's International School

ST JOHN'S
INTERNATIONAL SCHOOL
WATERLOO BELGIUM

(Founded 1964)

Head of School
Dr. David Brooke

PYP coordinator
Kathy Anderson

MYP coordinator
Maggie Adams

DP coordinator
Jennifer Bakalian

Status Private

Boarding/day Mixed

Gender Coeducational

Language of instruction
English

Authorised IB programmes
PYP, MYP, DP

Age Range 18 months – 18 years

Number of pupils enrolled
500

Fees
€7,000 – €37,600

Address
Drève Richelle 146
1410 Waterloo, Walloon Brabant
| BELGIUM

TEL +32 (0)2 352 06 10

Email
enquiries@stjohns.be

Website
www.stjohns.be

An Internationally trusted institution with an excellent reputation

Founded in 1964 in Waterloo, Belgium, St. John's International School has established itself as one of the leading international schools in Europe.

For more than 50 years, St. John's has been a trusted institution, serving the expatriate and local communities of the greater area with their promise of a soft landing for their new families and a welcoming community that will make them feel right at home.

Academic excellence and so much more

Being the only premium IB continuum school in the area, the school can count on more than 40 years of experience in teaching the International Baccalaureate, an invaluable asset in getting the most out of the IB experience.

Furthermore, it has built its reputation for excellence on a foundation of exceptional academics but realizes that there is so much more to personal growth than academics alone. That is why the school keeps investing in its unrivalled Visual and Performing Arts and Competitive Sports Programmes.

St. John's prides itself to be able to take the individual approach with small class sizes and outstanding pastoral care.

International in more than in name only

500 students between the ages of 2 1/2 and 18 years, representing 62 nationalities, find themselves in a truly cosmopolitan atmosphere while pursuing their curricular ambitions and extra-curricular interest.

Its students are instilled with the open-mindedness to think globally and take individual responsibility for life-long learning, service, and achievement.

Learning without limits

As an International Baccalaureate (IB) World School, offering the Primary Years Programme (PYP), the Middle Years Programme (MYP) and the Diploma Programme (DP), and the only school in the Brussels area to offer the Advanced Placement (AP) programme, St. John's is the perfect springboard to top universities all over the world.

Flexible options

And last but not least, their fully-flexible boarding options cater to the modern, mobile professional to accommodate every need.

St. Louis School

CARPE MAGNIFICENTIAM

Executive Principal High School Mr. Gerry Rafferty

Principal Colonna School Mrs. Kathleen Slocombe

Principal Caviglia School Mr. Jake Burnett

DP coordinator Hatty Rafferty

Status Private

Boarding/day Mixed

Gender Coeducational

Language of instruction English, Italian

Authorised IB programmes DP

Age Range 2 – 18 years (14-18 boarding)

Number of pupils enrolled 1500

Address SLS S.P.A., Via E. Caviglia, 1 20139 Milan | **ITALY**

St. Louis Colonna Via Marco Antonio Colonna, 24, 20149 Milan | **ITALY**

St. Louis High School Via Olmetto, 6, 20123 Milan | **ITALY**

TEL +39 02 55231235

Email info@stlouisschool.com

Website www.stlouisschool.com

Established in 1996, St. Louis is a leading co-educational Day & Boarding International School based in the Heart of Milan for 1500 students between the ages of 2 and 18.

Located across three sites, the south-east premises comprise of an Infant, Primary and Middle School, and the High School is located in a prime position, a stone throw from the Duomo. The Day & Boarding School, located in the Corso Sempione/Portello area, offers school opportunities for 2-14 year olds as well as full time boarding places for 14-18 year olds.

The St. Louis School's academic programme is rigorous and challenging. The Infant School programme is based on the British Early Years Foundation Stage (EYFS) Curriculum.

Primary and Middle School follow the British National Curriculum with an option for students 6 years and upwards to also follow the Italian curriculum.

The High School, which provides boarding facilities, comprises of IGCSE examinations for Years 10-11 and the International Baccalaureate Diploma (IB) for Years 12-13 with over 100 students each year studying this unique course.

The approach reinforces the importance of creative and critical thinking, with the school developing independent learners well equipped to succeed in the IB and beyond. St. Louis achieves outstanding academic scores within the IB diploma with the highest average attainment in Europe spanning the last 7 years (37 average).

The school opened its new High School in the centre of Milan (Palazzo Archinto) in September 2019. A magnificent historic building located in via Olmetto, will accommodate all senior school students from Years 10-13. Designed by architect Francesco Maria Richini in the 17th century and situated in the centre of Milan, the Palazzo provides the perfect learning environment for students of this age, blending state-of-the art educational facilities within historic surroundings.

St. Peter's International School

(Founded 1993)

Head of School
Mr. Alex Callow

DP coordinator
Mrs. Telma Luís Fresta

Status Private

Boarding/day Mixed

Gender Coeducational

Language of instruction
English, Portuguese

Authorised IB programmes
DP

Age Range 4 months – 18 years

Number of pupils enrolled
1458

Fees
€6,149 (Nursery) – €12,199 (IBDP)

Address
Quinta dos Barreleiros CCI 3952
Volta da Pedra
2950-201 Palmela, Setúbal |
PORTUGAL

TEL +351 21 233 6990

Email
geral@stpeters.pt

Website
www.st-peters-school.com

St. Peter's International school is a private school with over 27 years of experience. It provides a competitive, high-quality education from nursery to secondary school (from 4 months to 18 years old), ensuring students have access to the best opportunities and support to achieve their full academic and personal potential. St. Peter's mission is to build self-reliant, critical and creative students. As an authorised IB World School in Portugal, we offer the IB Diploma Programme in Grades 11 and 12.

St. Peter's International School provides a unique education model with a humanistic approach, adapted to each age group, where languages, sports, arts and technology are key. From Kindergarten to Junior School, we offer a personalised bilingual curriculum, and the option of the national Portuguese or the International curriculum (Cambridge Lower Secondary, IGCSE and IB Diploma Programme) from Grade 7 onwards. Academic excellence is guaranteed in both curricula: St. Peter's is a well-established school with proven outstanding academic results in both the national and the international exams, ensuring access to top tier universities in Portugal and abroad.

First-class extracurricular activities are available on-site for all ages, allowing students to pursue their interests. St. Peter's prepares students for academic, personal and professional success in an unpredictable future, developing vital soft skills which will help them overcome challenges and be successful in any career path they choose.

Located only 30 minutes from Lisbon's city centre, St. Peter's extensive 37,000 sqm campus has outstanding facilities for academics, arts and sports, including 3 football fields, 1 rugby pitch and 2 tennis courts, as well as specialised areas, with science and IT labs, art rooms, and a fully-equipped multimedia resource centre.

In addition, St. Peter's is home to the first boarding school in the area, an extension of our commitment to excellence: students have access to our top education and can develop life skills while nurturing life-long friendships. Now, families living abroad can guarantee their children have access to an international, individualised education in a safe environment and location. Being an on-campus boarding residence, surrounded by the mountains and the sea, students can benefit from an enriching range of extracurricular activities both during the week and the weekends.

Finally, as an Inspired Education Group school, St. Peter's offers unlimited opportunities to students, who have access to world's best practices in education, outstanding arts and sports programmes, state of the art facilities, and unique Exchange Programmes.

St. Stephen's School

(Founded 1964)	**Age Range** 14 – 19 years
Head of School Eric Mayer	**Number of pupils enrolled** 299
DP coordinator Nadia El-Taha	**Fees** Day: €25,650
Status Private	Boarding: €39,600
Boarding/day Mixed	**Address** Via Aventina 3
Gender Coeducational	00153 Rome | **ITALY**
Language of instruction English	**TEL** +39 06 575 0605
	Email
Authorised IB programmes DP	ststephens@sssrome.it
	Website www.sssrome.it

Why Choose St. Stephen's

St. Stephen's provides a demanding academic program taking full advantage of its location in the historic center of Rome. We offer a rigorous college preparatory curriculum, which is balanced by a diverse co-curricular program that fulfills the requirements for the full International Baccalaureate Diploma Programme and a US high school diploma.

The First IB School in Italy

In 1975, St. Stephen's was the first school in Italy to offer the International Baccalaureate Programme to students in grades 11 and 12. As a leading IB World School, our graduates have consistently ranked in the top percentile of IB exams, including perfect scores of 42 and the highest IB scores in the history of the School in recent years. Our average IB score is 35.

Building Futures Since 1964

St. Stephen's offers specialized career and university counseling services that aid students in the college or university search process, as well as potential academic and career choices. Our international student body applies to multiple education systems and matriculates to universities throughout the world whose admissions requirements vary widely.

A Focus on Internationalism and Global Citizenship

Our internationally-minded community aims to foster a keen sense of global citizenship in our students, who hail from more than fifty nations. We value the American roots of the School; we embrace Rome as our location, in both its historical and contemporary dimensions; and we are global in our outlook, both in terms of our active interest in histories, cultures, languages and belief systems from around the world, and in our awareness of the global impact of our actions. We welcome students, faculty, and staff from all backgrounds and believe that every one of us contributes in equal measure to the evolving cultural fusion that makes St. Stephen's special.

Rome Is Our Classroom

Our English language high school is surrounded by Western Civilization's most significant historic monuments, such as the Colosseum, the Roman Forum, and Circus Maximus – all within minutes of our campus. Teachers use the Eternal City as their classroom, and students gain first-hand knowledge of history, art, archaeology, classics, and cultural heritage. We provide a world-class education in an intellectually challenging environment that transforms young minds and prepares them to excel in high school and in their future endeavors.

World-Class Professionals Comprise Our Faculty

St. Stephen's employs award-winning authors, playwrights, researchers, archaeologists, art historians, accomplished musicians, scientists, and professionals in many sectors who have distinguished themselves in their respective fields. The real-life experience of our faculty enables them to share a high level of expertise with students. Ninety percent of our faculty have advanced degrees, and twenty percent have earned a PhD.

A Commitment to Discovering Rome and the World

A program unique to St. Stephen's is our dynamic faculty-led trips and experiential service-learning program. Trips take students to regions throughout Italy every fall, and to destinations throughout Europe and the Mediterranean Basin every spring. Paired with summer service-learning experiences in Rwanda, Senegal, and Sri Lanka, students benefit by gaining new insights and develop a global mindset balanced with compassion and consideration for others.

Signature Programs

Through the St. Stephen's Lyceum, students benefit from enriched classics courses and collaborations with prestigious institutions. Students may elect to take Classical Greek & Roman Studies in the IB Diploma Programme. Our classical studies courses build on the past and unite with the world of technology and globalization.

iLabs

Students enhance their technology skills in the iLab as they learn to design, program, build, and compete in robotics using EV3 Lego Mindstorm or Tetrix Java-based robots. Artists use Wacom tablets to design in 2D and digitally cut and assemble various products and models. Students explore 3D design via Google Sketchup, AutoDesk's Fusion 360 or Inventor programs, as well as Unity, widely used for creating animations and augmented and virtual reality. Students can learn to create and program a myriad of problem-solving devices using Arduino, and a variety of drones, photographic and video equipment, and small robots such as Sphero are available to explore and program. Students can explore virtual reality experiences and learn to make their own Virtual and Augmented Reality applications, and with Cozmo programmable robots, IBM Watson they construct chatbots and learn about creating and using Artificial Intelligence.

Molecular Genetics

St. Stephen's offers science students an advanced molecular genetics program. Developed in partnership with the European Molecular Biology Labs, Europe's flagship laboratory for Life Sciences, this collaboration allows students to develop inquiry-based lab skills and participate in university-level research with state-of-the-art equipment so they may expand and deepen their scientific literacy and competencies.

Five Core Values Anchor Our Community

A strong commitment to our core values of care, integrity, scholarship, independence, and creativity defines us and provides an essential foundation for building character. Students feel supported and free to achieve their personal best.

Abbey School Since 1120

(Founded 1120)

Rektor
P.Dr. Andri Tuor OSB

DP coordinator
Dr. Hansueli Flückiger

Status Private

Boarding/day Mixed

Gender Coeducational

Language of instruction
German, English

Authorised IB programmes
DP

Age Range 12 – 19 years

Number of pupils enrolled 120

Fees
Boarding: CHF41,000 –
CHF44,500
Weekend CHF6,000

Address
Benediktinerkloster 5
Engelberg
6390 | SWITZERLAND

TEL +41 41 639 61 00

Email
info@stiftsschule-engelberg.ch

Website
www.stiftsschule-engelberg.ch

Stiftsschule Engelberg is a Christian day and boarding school under the trusteeship of the Benedictine monastery of Engelberg, Switzerland. About 120 students attend the school, some 60 students are boarders. Stiftsschule Engelberg offers a coeducational college preparatory school (grades 7 to 12). All students graduate with both the Swiss high school diploma and the IB diploma. The dual qualification allows graduates to pursue their education without entrance examination at any Swiss university and facilitates admission to universities outside of Switzerland.

Engelberg is situated in Central Switzerland, near Lucerne. The town is a renowned mountain resort. Our students take advantage of the local facilities to participate in a variety of sports.

Stiftsschule Engelberg follows the Swiss curricula for bilingual college preparatory schools: All teaching from grade 7 to 9 is done in German, from grade 10 geography, biology and mathematics are taught in English. In grade 11 and 12 the teaching of these subjects follows IB curricula. Three languages, that is German, French and English, complete the number of the six IB subjects. Additional subjects are taught to meet the requirements of the Swiss high school diploma („Matura"). The dual qualification program provides a broad academic education to ensure that graduates are fully prepared to pursue their education at university in any subject of their choice, be it in Switzerland or abroad.

Besides mandatory education in sports, music and the arts our students have the opportunity to do a variety of sports, play musical instruments, join an orchestra and choir, or take part in plays.

Due to the bilingual character of the program applicants must have prior knowledge of German and must be willing to acquire proficiency in German during their stay at Stiftsschule Engelberg. Knowledge of English is expected to be appropriate to the grade applicants wish to enter. Applications are accepted throughout the year. Admission usually takes place at the beginning of the academic year in mid-August. For more information please contact the secretary's office at +41 41 639 61 00 or info@stiftsschule-engelberg.ch.

Stiftung Louisenlund

(Founded 1949)

Head of School
Dr Peter Rösner

DP coordinator
Damien Vassallo

Status Private

Boarding/day Mixed

Gender Coeducational

Language of instruction
English

Authorised IB programmes
DP

Number of pupils enrolled
440

Fees
€3,665

Address
Louisenlund 9
24357 Güby, Schleswig-Holstein
| **GERMANY**

TEL +49 (0)4354 999 0

Email
admission@louisenlund.de

Website
www.louisenlund.de/en

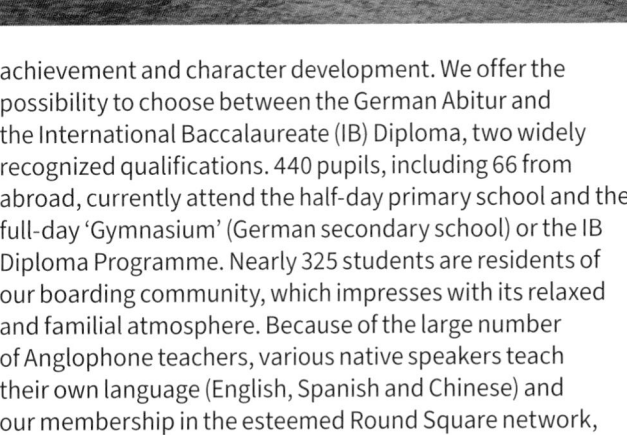

Preserving values, taking responsibility, shaping the future – Louisenlund, the only IB boarding school in Northern Germany, impresses with its beautiful surroundings, a thoroughly international character and education of the highest quality. Located on the Schlei, the school is committed to forming open-minded and responsible citizens.

Louisenlund seeks to develop personalities and promote talents. Practical, proactive and experiential learning enables students to actively acquire and develop knowledge and to achieve their individual educational objectives. Louisenlund's students are expected to become the principle players in their learning process and to be accountable for their own academic process. Nevertheless, each student is accompanied by a faculty mentor, who acts as an academic advisor and helps students maximize their potential. Committed to the IB Learner Profile, Louisenlund not only aims for the best possible academic achievement amongst our young learners; the sense of community, companionship and consideration for others, as well as the readiness to take on responsibility are of particular importance.

Since its founding in 1949, Stiftung Louisenlund stands for a top-class education, with high standards for academic achievement and character development. We offer the possibility to choose between the German Abitur and the International Baccalaureate (IB) Diploma, two widely recognized qualifications. 440 pupils, including 66 from abroad, currently attend the half-day primary school and the full-day 'Gymnasium' (German secondary school) or the IB Diploma Programme. Nearly 325 students are residents of our boarding community, which impresses with its relaxed and familial atmosphere. Because of the large number of Anglophone teachers, various native speakers teach their own language (English, Spanish and Chinese) and our membership in the esteemed Round Square network, Louisenlund enjoys a good reputation worldwide.

Another important feature is the exceptionally good relationship between students and staff, deriving from the small learning groups. Particular talents and weaknesses can be specifically fostered.

Besides the educational possibilities and the broad range of extracurricular activities, life at Louisenlund is a time to remember for other reasons: local and international projects, linguistic and cultural diversity on the campus, lifelong friendships and the exceptional team spirit of our community.

Stonyhurst College

STONYHURST

(Founded 1593)

Headmaster
Mr John Browne BA LLB MBA

DP coordinator
Mrs Deborah Kirkby BSc

CP coordinator
Emma Walker

Status Private

Boarding/day Mixed

Gender Coeducational

Language of instruction
English

Authorised IB programmes
DP, CP

Age Range 3 – 18 years

Number of pupils enrolled 801

Fees
Day: £21,750
Weekly Boarding: £31,500
Boarding: £36,600 – £39,300

Address
Stonyhurst
Clitheroe
Lancashire
BB7 9PZ | UK

TEL 01254 827073

Email
admissions@stonyhurst.ac.uk

Website
www.stonyhurst.ac.uk

Stonyhurst is the UK's leading co-educational Catholic boarding and day school for 3-18 year olds. Inspired by the beautiful Stonyhurst estate and the heritage of the world's oldest continuous Jesuit school, our students pursue academic excellence alongside spiritual and emotional growth and learn to embody their school motto: *"Quant je puis"*, meaning *"all that I can"*, in every activity. The IB mission reflects Stonyhurst's Jesuit mission and identity, in that both organisations seek to develop the whole person – intellectually, physically and emotionally.

Students come from the UK and around the world to experience an IB education at Stonyhurst. We offer an extremely full and enriching educational experience and our students flourish in a safe, happy, ordered environment and vibrant, close-knit community. Thoughtful, age-appropriate pastoral care encourages all students, whether day, weekly boarders or full boarders, to become increasingly self-reliant and considerate global citizens.

Since its introduction in 2013, we have found our IB offering has grown rapidly in popularity at Stonyhurst, and our year 12 IB intake now comprises around a quarter of total admissions into our sixth form. Our academic results for the IB Diploma bear testimony to the hard work and dedication of both highly qualified staff and motivated students. Our 2021 average points score in the Diploma was 37.8, a third of pupils achieved more than 40 points, placing them in the top 4% of candidates worldwide. Our IB students consistently perform above the world average and have gone onto prestigious universities in the UK and beyond, in a wide variety of challenging subjects, such as law, economics, medicine and engineering.

We also offer the IB Career-Related Programme with a sport or business career related pathway. With exceptional sports facilities, pupils who take on the IBCP sport related option can expect to study in one of the best environments in the country. This includes a brand new state of the art gym, an exciting outdoor pursuits programme, as well as the recent installation of LTA standard indoor tennis courts. Our global alumni network, as well as strong links with the local business community, can provide unique opportunities for our IBCP business students. Of course, these experiences are available for all students at Stonyhurst, and our students benefit from a huge range of co-curricular options, with over 100 clubs and societies running through the week.

An IB education at Stonyhurst provides an exceptional foundation for any young person, and we look forward to being a part of your future.

Tas Private Elementary School

İLKÖĞRETİM KURUMLARI
30. Yıl

(Founded 1991)

Head of School
Ms. Melek Tuzluca

PYP coordinator
Sena Bataklar

Status Private

Boarding/day Day

Gender Coeducational

Language of instruction
Turkish, English

Authorised IB programmes
PYP

Address
Cevizlik Mah. Hallac Hüseyin, Sk.
No. 11
Bakirköy
34142 Istanbul, Marmara |
TURKEY

TEL +90 212 543 60 00

Email
melektuzluca@taskolej.k12.tr

Website
www.taskolej.k12.tr

'Family is the cornerstone of our school.'

We believe that there is no such thing as an unsuccessful student. Our programme is based on this philosophy. We endeavour to develop not only the confidence and skills of our children, but to help them realize their maximum potential through balanced personal and interpersonal development. The positive environment is reinforced by the limited presence of externally imposed discipline – students are not punished, and bells are not rung. We focus on facilitating the knowledge, as well as the behaviour, attitudes and skills that will help our children become successful adults, whatever challenges they choose to undertake in the future.

We are committed to the responsibility and privilege of educating and nurturing inquirers and critical thinkers. Our goal is to become internationally recognised for our active participation in enriching the qualities of our countries'

human resource, and thereby improving the world we live in, and the cultural patrimony of future generations.

Towards this end we energetically pursue a course of study that holds the essential elements of the PYP (Action, Attitudes, Concepts, Knowledge and Skills) at its heart, and not only for our students. We embrace the continuing education of our parents as well by offering them a range of studies, and symposiums designed to stimulate and continue their personal development. We regularly reach out to our alumni and encourage them to maintain contact as role models and examples. Throughout the year our students participate in charity and fundraising events to support communities both locally and nationally.

The TAS School family; our parents, teachers, students, and support staff look forward to the challenges of the future. We embrace the diversity of our community and plan for our successes carefully and consciously.

· EST 1956 ·

Head of School
Christopher Nikoloff

DP coordinator
Kathy Anderson

Status Private

Boarding/day Mixed

Gender Coeducational

Language of instruction
English

Authorised IB programmes
DP

Age Range 3 – 19 years

Number of pupils enrolled 700

Fees
Day: CHF49,250
Boarding: CHF90,000

Address
Via Collina d'Oro 15
6926 Montagnola-Lugano |
SWITZERLAND

TEL +41 91 960 5151

Email
admissions@tasis.ch

Website
www.tasis.ch

Founded by M. Crist Fleming in 1956, TASIS is a day and boarding international school committed to creating global citizens through education, travel, and service.

The oldest American boarding school in Europe, TASIS welcomes approximately 700 students from 60 nations in grades Pre-Kindergarten (beginning at age three) through Postgraduate each year. About 250 students between ages 12-19 reside in dormitories on campus.

High School students can choose from individual Advanced Placement courses or pursue the International Baccalaureate (IB) Diploma, helping them receive offers from more than 400 universities in 20 different nations over the past five years. The School offers an extensive Fine Arts program that includes courses in Drama, Music, and the Visual Arts, enabling aspiring artists of any ilk to find their creative voice and nurture their talent.

Accredited by the European Council of International Schools (ECIS) and the New England Association of Schools and Colleges (NEASC), TASIS is proud to employ gifted, passionate educators who encourage intellectual curiosity. Nearly 80 percent of the High School faculty hold advanced degrees.

The campus includes more than 25 buildings dating from the 17th century Villa De Nobili to the state-of-the-art Campo Science Center. Perched on a hillside in sunny southern Switzerland with commanding views of snow-capped mountains, palm trees, and Lake Lugano, the School's enviable location makes possible an impressive Academic Travel program that brings students face-to-face with the rich cultural heritage of Europe and the spectacular natural beauty of the Alps and beyond.

The School's pioneering Global Service Program transforms lives by providing every High School student with a unique opportunity to connect across borders – whether geographic, economic, or social – through comprehensive experiences that build empathy and encourage personal responsibility. The Program awakens students to humanitarian needs, inspires them to build enduring relationships, and leads them toward a life of active service and committed service.

TASIS encourages physical fitness and healthy lifestyles. Varsity sports teams compete throughout Switzerland and Europe, and a variety of other fitness activities are offered to cater to all interests. Each year also brings many opportunities to ski and explore the breathtaking Alps. Students leave TASIS with a heightened appreciation for the outdoors and an understanding of what it takes to succeed in challenging environments.

Each summer, hundreds of students aged 4–18 journey to Lugano for the TASIS Summer Programs, which feature intensive academic courses, an unparalleled performing arts program, thrilling outdoor adventures, advanced sports training, and exciting cultural excursions around Europe.

Taunton School

TAUNTON SCHOOL

(Founded 1847)

Head of School
Mr. Lee Glaser

DP coordinator
Adrian Roberts

Status Private

Boarding/day Mixed

Gender Coeducational

Language of instruction
English

Authorised IB programmes
DP

Age Range 0 – 18 years

Number of pupils enrolled
1182

Fees
Day: £6,960 per term
Boarding: £11,920 – £12,960 per term

Address
Staplegrove Road
Taunton
Somerset
TA2 6AD | UK
TEL +44 (0)1823 703703

Email
enquiries@tauntonschool.co.uk

Website
www.tauntonschool.co.uk

"At Taunton School, the IB becomes your second family. Because the classes are so small and you spend so much time together, you become close with people from all over the world, and you gain an insight into different cultures and beliefs that A Levels just don't offer."

"After being offered the IB Scholarship at Taunton School, it has opened many doors and opportunities for me to prosper in a fantastic educational environment. Taunton School offered great facilities which supported and strengthened my studies in my subjects." **IB students at Taunton School**

At Taunton School, we have been offering the IB Diploma since becoming an IB World School in 2007. During that time over 300 students have obtained the diploma and its popularity continues to grow.

IB students do consistently well at Taunton School, achieving high scores equivalent to 5 A Levels and often obtaining places at their first-choice university, whether it's in the UK or overseas. Many students achieve top points and go onto study medicine at highly competitive universities.

In 2021, of all the 26 students who passed their Diploma, seven scored 40 or more points including one student achieving the maximum 45 points. The average points score per candidate of 36.4 was well in excess of the world average of 33 and was the highest achieved in the 14 years of running the IB Diploma at Taunton School.

Aside from lessons, everything else is done with the rest of the Sixth Form, such as sport, drama, music, social events, houses and tutor groups.

Adrian Roberts, IB Coordinator at Taunton School says: *"IB is going from strength to strength at Taunton School and our students consistently impress me with their willingness to aim high and extend themselves beyond the confines of a 'normal' Sixth Form curriculum."*

We are a leading independent school for boys and girls aged 0 to 18 years situated on a beautiful 56 acre campus in the picturesque county of Somerset, in South West England.

Our aim is to challenge, nurture and inspire young people to succeed in a global community.

We offer an IB Scholarship of up to 100% of fees. Contact us to find out more: www.tauntonschool.co.uk/scholarships-and-assisted-places/

The Abbey

(Founded 1887)

Head
Mr Will le Fleming

DP coordinator
Nicola McDonald

Status Private

Boarding/day Day

Gender Female

Language of instruction
English

Authorised IB programmes
DP

Number of pupils enrolled
1000

Fees
Day: £11,025 – £18,885

Address
Kendrick Road
Reading
Berkshire
RG1 5DZ | UK

TEL 0118 987 2256

Email
admissions@theabbey.co.uk

Website
www.theabbey.co.uk

Described as 'much more than a school', The Abbey is a place where academic excellence becomes a natural process of growth and curiosity at every stage of the journey, from the age of 3 to 18. We are a school that celebrates success in all its forms, and every girl is encouraged to explore her own unique strengths and discover her passions through a vast choice of opportunities – both inside and outside the classroom.

As an International Baccalaureate school, our internationally-minded ethos means that we collaborate across divides and strive to provide a real-world education that prepares students to step out into an uncertain world with confidence, empathy, and at ease with those from all cultures.

Our pioneering methods put the 'why' back at the heart of learning and our holistic approach places equal emphasis on academic achievement, intellectual agility and emotional wellbeing. The results of this more organic, relaxed approach to learning, speak for themselves. The Abbey is consistently one of the top performing schools academically – not only in the UK, but globally. In 2021, our students who studied the IB Programme, achieved an average of 40 points, compared to the global average of 30, placing the School firmly in the top tier of IB Schools in the World.

The Abbey's town centre location places us at the heart of a vibrant community, whilst our extensive coach network helps provide accessibility from locations across Oxfordshire and Berkshire for both Junior and Senior girls.

A range of scholarships are available, as well as financial assistance offered through means-tested bursaries. Above all, The Abbey is passionate about creating a learning experience that is joyful and meaningful. Our self-regulating culture helps us all to look after each other, and our inspiring teachers are dedicated to fostering a special relationship with each and every individual.

INTERNATIONAL SCHOOL · EST. 1985

(Founded 1985)

Headteacher
Clare Mooney

DP coordinator
Caroline Foster

Status Private

Boarding/day Day

Gender Coeducational

Language of instruction
English

Authorised IB programmes
DP

Age Range 2 – 19 years

Fees
Diploma Programme €12,000

Address
Camí de Son Ametler Vell, 250
07141 Marratxí,
Balearic Islands | **SPAIN**

Carrer d'Antoni Furió, 2
Ses Cases Noves,
Pont d'Inca, 07141 Marratxí,
Balearic Islands | **SPAIN**

TEL +34 971 605008

Email
info@theacademyschool.com

Website
www.theacademyschool.com

The Academy International School, established in 1985, has long been recognised as a centre of excellent academic achievement, where the whole school community shares the joy of learning. We are also proud to be the first International British School to bring the International Baccalaureate Diploma Programme to Mallorca.

In a beautiful setting in the Mallorcan countryside students enquire, discover, analyse and evaluate. They are creative, innovative and proud to be part of this school community. The Academy teaching team accompanies the students on a wonderful learning journey from our Nursery classrooms all the way through to IBDP.

Academy students are encouraged, supported and challenged. They are offered a broad and balanced curriculum, delivered by motivated and creative teachers, to ensure that learning is effective and promotes a lifelong passion for education. The Academy International School prepares students to compete in a rapidly changing international marketplace where academic content is important, but is no longer enough.

In today's evolving global society, inquiry, critical thinking, and international mindedness are essential skill sets that students must have to determine their success as a leader and in the workforce. The Academy International School offers students multiple ways to develop and demonstrate what they know and understand. Students complete collaborative projects, oral presentations, essay writing, inquiry-based experiments, and take part in discussion and debate that mirror what they will experience in the challenging fields they hope to enter after university.

The Academy students see how our school connects with the world at large through community projects and activities locally, nationally and internationally.

Our goal is to help students achieve their dreams.

(Founded 1970)

Head of Senior School
Mr. Christian Schmelz

Head of Junior School
Ms. Reeshma Charania

Head of Nursery School
Ms. Waseema Khawaja

PYP coordinator
Ms. Evelyn Awino

MYP coordinator
Mr. George Musili

DP coordinator
Mr. William Wanyonyi

Status Private

Boarding/day Day

Gender Coeducational

Language of instruction English

Authorised IB programmes
PYP, MYP, DP

Age Range 3 – 19 years

Number of pupils enrolled
1020

Address
1st Parklands Avenue,
off Limuru Road
PO Box 44424-00100
Nairobi | **KENYA**

TEL Junior: +254 0733 758 510,
Senior: +254 736 380 101

Email infos@akesk.org;
infoj@akesk.org

Website www.agakhanschools.
org/kenya/akan

Established in 1970, the Aga Khan Academy, Nairobi is a private, co-educational school located in the Parklands suburb of Nairobi, Kenya. The Nursery School is located on a separate campus on Kipande Road, at the bottom of Museum Hill in Nairobi.

Together, our schools have an enrolment of over 1,000 students and are authorised to offer the International Baccalaureate Primary Years Programme, Middle Years Programme and Diploma Programme.

School Overview
The Aga Khan Academy is one of few schools in Kenya offering International Baccalaureate Programmes, and is one of the two schools in Kenya authorized to offer the IB continuum – the Primary Years Programme (PYP), the Middle Years Programme (MYP) and the Diploma Programme (DP).

The Aga Khan Academy, in keeping with the IB philosophy, 'touches hearts as well as minds'. Our students not only learn to be knowledgeable, open-minded thinkers, inquirers, principled, risk takers, well-balanced, and caring but also to be leaders and stewards.

Mission statement
Enable many generations of students to acquire both the knowledge and the essential spiritual wisdom needed to balance that knowledge and enable their lives to attain the highest fulfilment.

Exam Results
The Aga Khan Academy provides an outstanding academic education and enables students to fulfil their potential. Although the Nursery School does not have a grading system, it typically holds an annual graduation and exhibition celebrating the completion of the Early Years PYP.

Relevant Curriculum
The IB curriculum enables students to learn using a transdisciplinary and an interdisciplinary approach and to develop critical thinking, creativity and international-mindedness – identified by leading educators globally as some of the necessary skills for the 21st Century learning.

Admission
Admission is based primarily on merit determined by a wide range of criteria, including academic strengths and overall potential.

Our curriculum combines academic excellence with athletics and visual performing arts programmes.

Examinations offered
MYP eAssessment, IB Diploma Programme (IB DP)

Facilities
ICT resource centres, film studio, music rooms, art rooms, science labs, well-resourced libraries, pool, wireless connectivity, data projectors in classrooms, a makerspace for the junior school and a well-resourced SEN and Guidance & Counselling room.

The British School of Brussels (BSB)

(Founded 1969)

Principal Melanie Warnes MA

Co-Heads of Post 16
Sue Munday & James Willis

DP coordinator James Willis

Status Private

Boarding/day Day

Gender Coeducational

Language of instruction
English, French (bilingual
programme for ages 4-14 years)

Authorised IB programmes
DP

Age Range 1 – 18 years

Number of pupils enrolled
1350

Fees
Day: €29,100 – €37,235

Address
Pater Dupierreuxlaan 1
3080 Tervuren | **BELGIUM**

TEL +32 (0)2 766 04 30

Email
admissions@britishschool.be

Website
www.britishschool.be

The British School of Brussels (BSB) was founded in 1969 and officially opened in 1970. It is located in a beautiful site of ten hectares, surrounded by woodlands and lakes near the Royal Museum of Central Africa in Tervuren (20 minutes' drive from central Brussels). The school is a co-educational, nonselective day school for children aged 1 to 18 years, with a 1,350 enrolment. There is also an Early Childhood Centre for children aged 1-3 years. There are 70 nationalities with 30% being British.

Students follow a British-based curriculum up to age 16 – (I) GCSE. This is adapted to the school's European context and international cohort and is followed by the choice of three internationally recognised pre-university examination courses from age 16-18: English GCE A level, The International Baccalaureate (IB) Diploma Programme (French/Dutch options) and BTEC Business, Hospitality, Sport and Applied Science. French and Dutch are taught from an early age and there is a bilingual French/English programme for students aged 4-14 years. German or Spanish language courses are additionally available from age 11.

The school has an Additional Educational Needs (AEN) department and extensive support is provided through the English as an Additional Language (EAL) programme. A specialist international careers team provides guidance and support to Post-16 students.

BSB's excellent facilities include a state-of-the-art design and technology workshop, food technology rooms, networked IT suites, drama studios, nine science laboratories, four art studios and a cafeteria. The sporting facilities of the school include world class amenities such as a multi-purpose sports hall, gymnasium, and fitness suite. In addition, the BSB is the only international school in Belgium to have its own competition standard swimming pool. The outdoor facilities include multiple sports pitches, tennis courts and the largest free-standing bouldering wall in any school in Europe.

Arts, music, and drama thrive at the school and a wide range of performances are held regularly in the 240-seat Brel theatre. The music department has a music technology suite, full-scale recording studio and a rehearsal studio. The BSB's academic results are amongst the highest of any international school in Europe and well above the worldwide average. In 2021 results at Post-16 for A level, BTEC and IB diploma were fabulous, translating into brilliant university places worldwide on a wide variety of competitive and exciting courses.

The school's IB Diploma students again produced some outstanding results with a 100% pass rate and a 40-point average. 92% of BSB students achieved the IB Diploma with a very impressive average of 37 points or higher. 35% of students achieved a score of 42pts or higher with three scoring the rare top grade of 45 pts. This places BSB as unequivocally the top performing IB school in Belgium and one of the top schools in the world.

At A Level, BSB students achieved a 100% pass rate, with 75% of grades between A*-B. 27% of students achieved an A* grade with two students achieving All A*s.

This year the school's results in the BTEC courses continue to be equally impressive with students once again gaining a 100% pass rate through this course. Half of BSB students' grades were achieved at Distinction* level which is the highest possible grade. 83% of grades were Distinction or Distinction* which is the equivalent of A/A* at A-level.

The British School of Milan (Sir James Henderson)

(Founded 1969)

Principal
Dr Chris Greenhalgh

DP coordinator
Miss Alba López Martín

Status Private, Not-For-Profit

Boarding/day Day

Gender Coeducational

Language of instruction
English

Authorised IB programmes
DP

Age Range 3 – 18 years

Number of pupils enrolled 720

Fees
€12,140 – €19,580

Address
Via Carlo Alberto Pisani Dossi, 16
20134 Milan | **ITALY**

TEL +39 02 210941

Email
info@bsm.school

Website
www.britishschoolmilan.com

The British School of Milan, founded in 1969, is the only school in Milan awarded the highest rating of excellent by UK Government Inspectors (ISI). It has been rated among the top 10 schools in Europe and in 2021, BSM achieved the highest IB results in Italy (39/45 Points – World Average 33 Points).

The BSM is a not-for-profit school which provides world-class education to 720 students aged 3 to 18 from over 40 different nationalities. The school values cultural diversity and offers a rich international experience while rigorously following the UK National Curriculum.

Academic results are outstanding and students progress to top universities around the globe. In the last few years they have gained places at Oxford, Cambridge, Yale, LSE, Imperial, University College London, The University of Edinburgh, Trinity College Dublin, Università Bocconi, University of British Colombia, Sciences-Po and many other leading universities.

There is a strong emphasis on co-curricular activities with over 100 options available. The school is particularly proud of its exceptional music, art and drama departments. In addition, BSM acts as the Italian centre for the UK-based ABRSM, the exam board of the Royal Schools of Music. The school nourishes a strong tradition of community service, with a scholarship and bursary fund recently inaugurated and its involvement in the International Duke of Edinburgh's Award Scheme.

The BSM is situated just outside the centre of Milan, close to the metro and on several bus routes. Linate airport and the popular Milano 2 residences are just minutes from the school.

Admission applications are accepted throughout the year.

The English School of Kyrenia

Head of School Hector MacDonald	**Number of pupils enrolled** 900
DP coordinator Ms Zelis Omer	
Status Private	**Fees** Day: £4,700 – £7,560
Boarding/day Day	**Address**
Gender Coeducational	Bilim Sokak, Bellapais Kyrenia, North Cyprus	**CYPRUS**
Language of instruction English	**TEL** +90 392 444 0375
Authorised IB programmes DP	**Email** info@englishschoolkyrenia.org
Age Range 2 – 18 years	**Website** www.englishschoolkyrenia.com

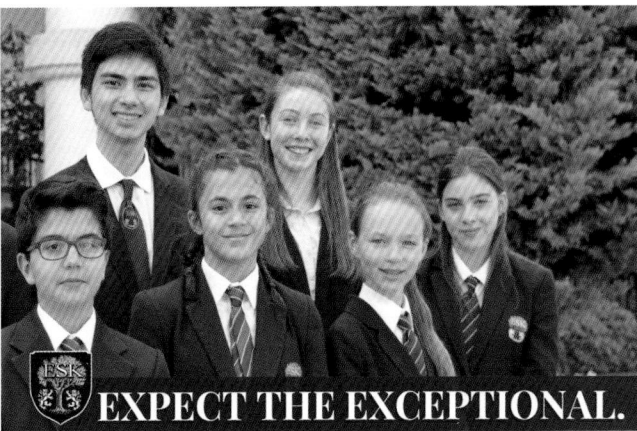

EXPECT THE EXCEPTIONAL.

The English School of Kyrenia (ESK) is a purpose-built modern IB World School offering exciting opportunities for academic excellence and personal development for boys and girls aged 2 to 18. An enviable and spacious learning environment, the campus is set in the inspiring surroundings of the Kyrenia foothills, overlooking the Mediterranean to the front and the Kyrenia mountains to the rear.

The Little Learners building is a welcoming, calming and nurturing environment for our Pre-Nursery students. Designed with soft, earth inspired tones, students thrive in the fundamental stage of their development along with support from our professional and qualified teachers. Our Nursery – Year 2 students are located in the eco-friendly Early Years building. The unique building aims to generate its own electricity requirements and seeks to provide all ESK students with a living example of green sustainability.

For the current 2020-2021 academic year, ESK has 900 students drawn from both international and local backgrounds. The sections of the school are Little Learners (Pre-Nursery), Early Years (Nursery – Year2), Primary (Year 1 – Year 6), and Secondary (Year 7 – Year 13). All classes are taught in English, with an addition of Turkish as a second language, and an option of Mandarin, Russian, French, or Spanish. The Early Years follow the UK's EYFS (Updated) curriculum and the Primary School follows the Cambridge International Primary Programme (CIPP).

In the Secondary School the widely respected IGCSE, A-Level and International Baccalaureate (IB) Diploma Programme give students the opportunity to develop an international perspective and attend the world's top universities. Over 88% of graduates attend University in the UK, and 10% in the EU or North America. Graduates have attended prestigious universities such as The University of Cambridge, Imperial College, UCL, LSE, University of Edinburgh, Parson's School of Design and Leiden University, to name a few.

Today's students are tomorrow's leaders and decision makers: we afford every opportunity for our boys and girls to reach their personal and academic potential whilst nurturing their curiosity and encouraging individuality and creative thought. IBDP Subjects available:

Group 1: English Language & Literature, Russian Language & Literature, Turkish Literature

Group 2: English B, Spanish ab initio, French

Group 3: Geography, History, Business and Management, Psychology, Economics

Group 4: Biology, Chemistry, Physics, Computer Science

Group 5: Mathematics Analysis and Approaches, Mathematics Interpretation and Application

Group 6: Visual Arts, Music, Theatre Arts or one other subject taken from groups 3-4 above

ÉCOLE
RUBAN VERT
International School of Gabon

(Founded 2013)

Head of School
Mr Jeff Shaw

Deputy Head
Mrs Marta Essinki

PYP coordinator
Eunah Njoroge

DP coordinator
Richard Welford

Status Private

Boarding/day Day

Gender Coeducational

Language of instruction
English, French

Authorised IB programmes
PYP, DP

Age Range 2 – 19 years

Address
Batterie IV
Libreville, Gabon
2144 | GABON

TEL +241 11 44 26 70

Email admissions@
ecolerubanvert.com

Website
www.ecolerubanvert.com

Welcome to École Ruban Vert – International School of Gabon.

Vision

To provide a legacy in education which promotes qualities of open-mindedness, tolerance and respect for others, which will provide a best practice model for the future of students from all nations in Gabon.

Mission

To become Africa's most enterprising school, focusing on sustainability and innovation to play a significant role in Gabon's and in Africa's education.

École Ruban Vert (ERV), offers a unique blend of bilingual, internationally focused education accredited by the Council of International Schools (CIS). ERV is an IB World School, offering Early Years, IBPYP, International GCSE, and the IBDP, with exceptional examination results.

Our students secure outstanding results in external examinations. The IBDP Pass Rate has been 100% for three years running, the pass rate for the Bilingual IBDP is also 100%, and in 2021 our highest scoring student achieved 42 points. Students have the opportunity to sit the EdEXCEL International GCSEs, where again the pass rate is 100%, and 2021 30% of students gained the highest grade, 9.

ERV students are recognised for their capacity to lead, innovate, serve, to respect resources and the environment, and for their commitment to making a significant impact on their school and their communities. Our world-class, green campus serves as the backdrop for an educational establishment that aims to facilitate radical thinking and achieve high standards of education. ERV is a forward thinking school whose aim is to enable students to learn to manage the future in a creative and sustainable way.

A programme of scholarships enables local Gabonese students accessibility to top-class education alongside children from diverse national and international backgrounds.

Our campus is a microscopic example of Gabon itself with every tree and shrub of Gabon planted within the campus. We believe it is one of the most beautiful in Africa with streams, bridges, green play areas and wildlife in abundance. Outstanding facilities include an auditorium, computer suites, gymnasium, library, music performance spaces, science labs and international sports stadium. We offer musical instrument tuition, Royal College of Music Examinations, yoga, ballet, the Duke of Edinburgh Award, and our Tennis Academy is the best in Libreville. ERV hosts the Moabi Festival, a celebration of local culture and the Gabon International Open Tennis Tournament.

THE INTERNATIONAL
SCHOOL OF MONACO

(Founded 1994)

Director
Mr. Stuart Bryan MA Hons, PGCE, ACE, NPQEL

DP coordinator
Hannah Gettel

CP coordinator
Tania Leyland

Status Private

Boarding/day Day

Gender Coeducational

Language of instruction
English, French

Authorised IB programmes
DP, CP

Age Range 3 – 18 years

Number of pupils enrolled 700

Fees
Day €21,500 – €27,900

Address
10-12 Quai Antoine Premier
Monte Carlo
98000 | MONACO

TEL +377 9325 6820

Email
admissions@ismonaco.com

Website
ismonaco.org

Founded in 1994, the International School of Monaco (ISM) is an independent, co-educational, not-for-profit day school, situated on Port Hercule in Monaco. ISM is the only fully accredited international private school in the Principality of Monaco and today caters to 700 pupils aged from 3-18, drawn from over fifty countries.

In August 2020 the school signed a historic partnership with King's College School, Wimbledon, as part of the school's aim to be among the best in Europe.

ISM's mission is to provide an outstanding education for students so that they are confident, independent, responsible and internationally-minded citizens that make a meaningful contribution to our fast-changing world.

The school's values emphasize integrity, caring, respect and learning, with clearly defined principles and expectations of its students.

ISM offers a distinctive bilingual education in English and French for classes Kindergarten to Year 6 and from Year 7, the Secondary School offers a broad and balanced programme taught in English, leading to Cambridge IGCSE and the IB Diploma qualifications. The school offers both the IBDP and, since September 2020, the IBCP. Languages are an important part of the curriculum with Spanish, Italian, Russian and German, in addition to French, on offer. Highly qualified teachers and support staff are recruited from around the world.

There is an extensive programme of enrichment including sports, Model United Nations, an annual Arts Festival, the Duke of Edinburgh International Award plus ABRSM and LAMDA music and drama qualifications. The school's unique location on the Cote d'Azur enables access to world-class museums and places of interest.

Outreach is an important element of school life: through giving projects, environmental associations and participation in charities from Monaco and France to Africa and Vietnam.

Pastoral care is a major priority for the school; an extensive PHSE programme is delivered by teachers who receive regular training in child protection and welfare, and a full-time Head of Wellbeing is supported by a wellbeing team including a school counsellor. Regular workshops are offered to parents.

ISM students are well-rounded, academically successful young people who are admitted to top universities in Europe, the UK and North America. ISM graduates are already pursuing exciting careers in many diverse fields.

The International School
of The Hague

(Founded 1983)	**Authorised IB programmes** MYP, DP, CP
Secondary Principal Richard Matthews	**Age Range** 4 – 18 years
Primary Principal Alan Lorenzini	**Number of pupils enrolled** 1500
MYP coordinator Maria Lamminaho	**Fees** Day: €8,000 – €10,000
DP coordinator Dr. Alma Trumic	**Address** Wijndaelerweg 11 2554 BZ The Hague, South Holland | **NETHERLANDS**
CP coordinator Dr. Alma Trumic	**TEL** +31 70 328 1450
Status State/Semi Private	
Boarding/day Day	**Email** admissions@ishthehague.nl
Gender Coeducational	**Website** www.ishthehague.nl
Language of instruction English	

We encourage students to pursue personal excellence by being curious, connected, and compassionate lifelong learners. Our vision is to shape a better future for all: inspiring students to become compassionate and proactive global citizens.

The International School of The Hague (ISH), with over 90 nationalities within the International City of Justice and Peace is well placed to provide a dynamic learning environment that is conducive to intercultural learning and global citizenship.

We offer a high quality international education, fostering academic success as well as encouraging sporting and creative abilities in a community based on honesty, fairness, open-mindedness and tolerance.

As a part of a Dutch school foundation, ISH benefits from the rich learning opportunities our host country offers. Dutch is taught to all students in the MYP to assist them in integrating in the Netherlands.

Our Primary School is the first in the world to have achieved accreditation at 'Mastering' Level from the International Primary Curriculum (IPC). Years 7-11 offer the International Baccalaureate Middle Years Programme (IB MYP), and Years 12-13 offer the International Baccalaureate Diploma Programme (IBDP) and Career-related Programme (IBCP).

The IBMYP provides the framework for the broad range of subjects that are offered in Years 7-11. Learning across the MYP eight subject groups is integrated through Approaches to Teaching and Learning, particularly focussing on concepts and inquiry, and through the global contexts. All students participate in our Service as Action Programme. Uniquely, our school's Pathfinder Programme allows MYP students to exercise more agency over their learning by co-constructing the curriculum with their teachers.

The IBDP aims to continue the education of critical and empathetic global citizens in six selected subjects and the mandatory components of Creativity, Activity and Service (CAS), Theory of Knowledge (TOK), and the Extended Essay, which prepares students for writing at university level.

The IBCP provides an opportunity for students who wish to focus their pre-university studies in Business. This rigorous and demanding programme provides an excellent route to university. Students study the BTEC Business course, plus a set of highly-relevant core IB activities that include Personal and Professional Skills, Service Learning, a Reflective Project and Language Development, as well as two IBDP diploma courses in subjects of their choosing.

Supporting our international community is key in all aspects of the school. Our EAL, Home Languages, Learning Support, and Wellbeing departments play important roles in meeting the individual needs of our students.

The KAUST School

THE KAUST SCHOOL

Director
Dr. Michelle Remington

Secondary Principal
David Tigchelaar

Elementary Principal
Jeff Woodcock

Kindergarten Principal
Tiffany Hill

PYP coordinator
Jon Davidson

MYP coordinator
Peter Powell

DP coordinator
Susan Rhodes

Status Private

Boarding/day Day

Gender Coeducational

Language of instruction
English

Authorised IB programmes
PYP, MYP, DP

Address
Safaa Gardens School,
Office 1132, 4700 KAUST
Thuwal
23955-6900 | SAUDI ARABIA

TEL +966 12 808 6803

Email
schools@kaust.edu.sa

Website
tks.kaust.edu.sa

INVESTIGATE SOLUTIONS

INSPIRE CREATIVITY

IGNITE CURIOSITY

The KAUST School (TKS) proudly serves a thriving multi-cultural University community, with an enrollment of approximately 1,700 students from more than 75 nations. As an International Baccalaureate World School authorized in three programs: Primary Years, Middle Years and the Diploma Programme, we share a common philosophy and a commitment to high quality, challenging international education for children from K1 through to Grade 12. TKS is accredited by the Council of International Schools (CIS) and the Middle States Association (MSA).

Our Resources
The school is uniquely located within the university campus of King Abdullah University of Science and Technology (KAUST), a destination of choice for world-class scientific and technological graduate education and research, north of Jeddah on the shores of the Red Sea.

The School is purpose built with a design that supports a balanced curriculum. The Gardens Campus which houses the Elementary and Secondary School, has technology equipped classrooms, science laboratories, a design and technology hub, two library media centers, two indoor gymnasiums, two performance theatres, outdoor basketball and tennis courts, an outdoor swimming pool and soccer pitch. The Kindergarten Campus is filled with natural light, color and materials that stimulate learning. The buildings include activity rooms, two libraries and several specialized rooms for Art, Music, Arabic and Islamic studies.

The School offers a state-of-the-art technology environment that incorporates a broad spectrum of educational solutions while maintaining a 1:1 Apple computing environment.

Our People
Our students are the children of KAUST academic and professional staff, TKS staff, graduate students and University partners.

TKS Staff consists of over 350 teachers, specialist support staff and administrators from across the globe, with over 70% having advanced degrees and the majority with previous international school experience.

The school maintains classroom ratios of one teacher to 15 students in early childhood; to 18 students in Elementary; and to 22 students in Secondary.

Our IB Diploma Curriculum
TKS offers a co-educational IB academic program in English. Targeted support is provided for students with instructional needs, including intensive English language support, as required. Arabic and French are offered as a first language to native speakers in secondary and Spanish, French and Arabic as an additional language (acquisition).

Co-curricular Activities
With the benefit of being located on a university campus and enclosed community, TKS utilizes all university and community facilities enriching the co-curricular programs.

Uptown International School

(Founded 2005)	**Age Range** 2 – 17 years
Principal Rob Commons	**Number of pupils enrolled** 1230
Vice Principal Pali Nahal	**Fees**
Acting Head of Secondary Sam Sweeney	Pre-KG: AED40,500 KG 1 to 2: AED46,500 – AED48,500
Head of Primary Jodie Eardley	Grade 1 to 5: AED57,500 Grade 6 to 10: AED67,500
PYP coordinator Geetha Ashok	Grade 11 & 12: AED72,500
MYP coordinator Hebatallah Gaber	**Address** Corner of Algeria Road & Tripoli Street, Mirdif, PO Box 78181
DP coordinator Adrian Duckett	Dubai | **UNITED ARAB EMIRATES**
Status Private	**TEL** +971 (0)4 2515001
Boarding/day Day	**ADMISSIONS MOBILE NUMBER**
Gender Coeducational	+971549903012
Language of instruction English	**Email** admissions@uptownschool.ae
Authorised IB programmes PYP, MYP, DP	**Website** www.uischool.ae

A member of Taaleem, Uptown International School, located in the heart of Mirdif since 2005, is a highly reputed and certified International Baccalaureate (IB) World School for the Primary Years Programme (PYP), the Middle Years Programme (MYP) and Diploma Programme (DP). Dedicated to nurturing the development in all aspects of education and personal growth. Our mission is to encourage curiosity and enthusiasm, creativity and independence, and compassion and communication through an exciting, rich and engaging learning experience.

Vision and Mission
A school for the whole of our international community, that delivers a World class education and achieves excellent student outcomes, by all measures, for all our students, in line with UAE National Agenda. Our Missions is to use education to make the world a better place to be, at the individual, community and global level.

KHDA Rating: "Very Good" with "Outstanding" features.

Our Facilities
Our facilities are spread over 14 acres of landscaped grounds and were designed to ensure that our students have the best environment to support their learning and development including a 25-metre swimming pool, a multi-purpose Sports Field, DT studios and more.

Our Teachers
Our teachers are highly qualified educators with vast experience in IB and education. All our teachers are trained IB practitioners, with many being IB workshop trainers and IB site visitors.

Student body
Co-educational, ages 2 to 17 years, over 80 different nationalities.

Extra-Curricular Activities
Our students have access to over 150 activities that fall under sports, arts, academic interests, and various enrichment programmes. Examples include: Model United Nations, TEDx Youth, Choir, Dance, Football, Gymnastics, Rugby, World Scholars Debate, Chess Club, French DELF, Emirates Literature Club, Lego Robotics and Coding and more.

Uptown International School (UIS) also offers a broad range of educational visits and excursions, which are a vital part of supporting our students' unit of inquiries. UIS is part of Taaleem, the United Arab Emirates' second largest school provider for early years, primary and secondary schools founded in 2005.

(Founded 1982)

Head of College
William Turner

DP coordinator
Roman Rudzinski

Status Private

Boarding/day Boarding

Gender Coeducational

Language of instruction
English

Authorised IB programmes
DP

Age Range 16 – 19 years

Number of pupils enrolled 168

Fees
Two-year Fee €23,000
(scholarships available)

Address
Località Duino 29
34011 Duino-Aurisina TS | **ITALY**

TEL +39 040 3739111

Email
uwcad@uwcad.it

Website
www.uwcad.it

UWC Adriatic is set in the seaside village of Duino, near Trieste, in an area strongly influenced by political and ethnic divisions during the two World Wars. By entering this arena of ethnic and historical complexity, UWC Adriatic has embraced an educational role of highly-charged political meaning and stepped into a world of extraordinary cultural diversity.

UWC Adriatic offers the IB Diploma standard courses, to which the College adds Arabic, several central European languages, Environmental Systems and Societies, and World Arts and Cultures. All students take Italian, though not necessarily as an IBDP exam subject. A particular emphasis is placed on the "service" component of its Creativity, Activity, Services (CAS) programme, with music playing a significant role thanks to the presence of the International Community Music Academy (ICMA).

UWC Adriatic is one of the oldest-standing UWCs and has collaborative relations with many associations that lead volunteering activities in a wide range of areas. UWC Adriatic also capitalises its seaside setting on Trieste's karst highlands nearby the Alps to offer its students a host of related outdoor activities: sailing, kayaking, climbing, hiking and cross-country skiing opportunities provide invigorating and highly enjoyable breaks from academic endeavors during students'

two years in Duino. The UWC educational model prioritises student initiative, so new student-led CAS activities are also encouraged.

Owing to the COVID-19 pandemic UWC Adriatic has re-thought its CAS programme and all aspects of College life to ensure the highest safety and hygiene standards for the protection of its students, staff and the local community while preserving the essence of UWC's added educational value.

The College has seven student residences, an academic building, a science laboratory and an art centre scattered around the village of Duino. Every residence is manned by one or more residence tutors. A fully equipped music centre is available, as well as sports facilities shared with local associations. Purnama House (a new residence currently being refurbished and used as a teacher residence), has formed part of the COVID-19 medical provisions since the 2020-21 academic year. The College also ensures that the medical staff are available 24 hours a day.

Admissions

Students can apply through their UWC national committee or through the UWC Global Selection Programme.

(Founded 1962)	**Fees**
Principal	Two-year fee £68,500
Naheed Bardai	(scholarships available)
DP coordinator	**Address**
Gabor Vincze	St Donat's Castle
Status Private	St Donat's
	Llantwit Major
Boarding/day Boarding	Vale of Glamorgan
	CF61 1WF | UK
Gender Coeducational	**TEL** +44 (0)1446 799000
Language of instruction	**Email**
English	admissions@atlanticcollege.org
Authorised IB programmes	**Website**
DP	www.atlanticcollege.org
Age Range 16 – 19 years	
Number of pupils enrolled	
350	

Changemaking students will lead the way in a post-Covid world

We're proud to be the founding college of the UWC – a global education movement that 'makes education a force for good to unite people, nations and cultures for peace and a sustainable future'.

In our magical campus – a 12th century castle by the sea in South Wales – we celebrate global diversity, with young people drawn together from around 90 different countries each year, from vastly differing political, religious, ethnic and socio-economic backgrounds, to engage with the possibility of social change through courageous action, personal example and selfless leadership. They enjoy playing their part in an exceptional movement, in our respectful and joyful community, and participating in a unique, transformational education.

The right time to join UWC Atlantic

The UWC movement has 18 global schools and colleges, guiding the promise, potential, energy and idealism of students towards empathy, responsibility and lifelong action. At UWC Atlantic, 16-19 year olds study the International Baccalaureate Diploma Programme, (co-created over 50 years ago here at the College), for two years. Whilst the IBDP remains inspirational, it needs to be reimagined, making it more relevant for the 21st century and providing students with new insights and perspectives, future-proofed skills, and the knowledge needed for success in a volatile, complex and ambiguous world. A UWC education is needed now, perhaps more than ever.

Students must develop the personal agency, courage and commitment to meet challenges, in a proactive, purposeful and impactful way. We've developed six pioneering changemaker units – Dialogue, Peace and Social Justice; Political Ecology; Taking a Stance: Oral Communication; Big Data: Decision-making for Social Change; Narratives for Social Change: and Ocean Systems and Coastal Management. This, along with the development of our signature seafront, enables students to develop a lifelong commitment to service (in line with our core Kurt Hahn ethos), alongside academics, activities and adventure.

An education at UWC Atlantic is transformational. Students come with a vision and graduate empowered to make a positive difference in the world.

There are two selection routes to a UWC college: through the UWC national committee in your country of residence or citizenship (for students who need scholarship funding and support). This is a fundamental UWC tenet, which ensures socio-economic diversity on all UWC campuses. You can also now apply through a new Global Selection Programme if you're a student who doesn't need funding and want to choose to come to UWC Atlantic.

UWC Maastricht

(Founded 2009)

Head of College
Lodewijk van Oord

MYP coordinator
Gökce Dagdeviren

DP coordinator
Sindhu Clark & Jack Borthwick

CP coordinator
Nathan Hunt

Status State

Boarding/day Mixed

Gender Coeducational

Language of instruction
English

Authorised IB programmes
MYP, DP, CP

Age Range 4 – 19 years

Number of pupils enrolled
900

Fees
Two-year fee: €68,000
(scholarships available)

Address
Discusworp 65
6225 XP Maastricht, Limburg |
NETHERLANDS

TEL +31 432 410 410

Email
admissions@uwcmaastricht.nl

Website
www.uwcmaastricht.nl

Introduction
In addition to the highly recognized International Baccalaureate curriculum, UWC Maastricht is a multicultural school that hosts students from more than 100 different nationalities. The school operates within the Dutch public educational system and is subsidized by the Dutch government. It is formed to serve both the needs of the Maastricht international community and the students chosen by UWC national committees all over the world.

Inside the Classroom
At age 4, children can start their education at UWC Maastricht. The Primary Curriculum (until 11 year) is composed of a variety of subjects, at various levels of English language proficiency. After primary school UWC Maastricht offers the IB-Middle Years Programme (11-16 year-olds) in which students are encouraged to become critical and reflective thinkers. For 16-19 year-olds, UWCM applies the IB Diploma Programme Curriculum (and the IB Career Programme as of September 2022). Alongside the IB standard courses, the school offers Dutch, Spanish, German, Italian, Arabic, World Arts and Cultures, Global Politics, Visual Arts, Film and Music.

Outside the Classroom
UWC Maastricht has designed a social impact programme including action-oriented courses, social entrepreneurship and community service projects. Students develop the skills and attitudes needed to be active participants in society, to identify problems and injustices wherever they exist. They design a local Project Week providing service to the Maastricht community, they organise and lead conferences and they learn to engage critically with the world around them. Because students come from all over the world and from many different backgrounds, there are always unique insights and always interesting discussions going on.

Campus and Facilities
UWCM campus is located in a very green and leafy part of Maastricht, close to the city centre. The site is surrounded by sports fields, a nature reserve and modern housing. CP and DP students live on residences across three buildings consisting of three floors, each comprised of six rooms. Every room hosts four students, of different nationalities, so it is a lively setting. Each floor has a common room, study room, laundry room and kitchenette and is supported by a Residence Mentor who lives in an apartment adjacent to the floors.

Admission
Day student applications for Primary and Secondary must meet the requirements of the Dutch Law on International Education. Residential IB Diploma Programme and Career Programme students are recruited through UWC's National Committee system (NC) or through the UWC Global Selection Programme. More info and applications via uwcmaasticht.nl.

(Founded 1993)

Founder, Director & Principal
Prof. Jerzy Waligóra

DP coordinator
Ewa Dudek

Status Private

Boarding/day Day

Gender Coeducational

Language of instruction
English

Authorised IB programmes
DP

Age Range 6 – 18 years

Number of pupils enrolled
830

Fees
Day: €2,700 – €5,500

Address
ul Karmelicka 45
31-128 Krakow | **POLAND**

TEL +48 12 632 93 13

Email
dyrektor@pack.edu.pl

Website
www.pack.edu.pl

PACK belongs to the group of most rapidly developing non-public schools in Krakow imparting holistic education to the students for over a period of 25 years.

The first school to open within the branches of Prywatne Akademickie Centrum Ksztalcenia (PACK) was VIII Prywatne Akademickie Liceum Ogólnoksztalcace, instituted in the year 1993. Afterwards, all the sister schools such as Friderick Chopin Private Academic Middle School (1999), Academos Private Primary School (2008), International Baccalaureate World School 006265 (2012), World Around Intercultural Middle School (2015), and World Around Intercultural Primary School (2015) began operating.

The vision of the Founder Director Principal Professor Jerzy Waligóra, is to ensure thorough intellectual and emotional growth. PACK aims toward academic excellence in order to educate and enable the youth leaders to be men and women of character who pursue their individual passions with the help of internationally recognized and innovative academic, and co-curricular programme. Thereby, becoming valued representatives of their local, national, and international communities.

For several years the school has taken the leading place in the All-Polish Secondary Schools League Tables compiled and published by "Perspektywy", "Rzeczpospolita" and "Gazeta Wyborcza". It has been ranked among the first five schools between the years 2015 to 2019 in the Malopolska region.

The academic programme benefits because of the teaching staff of the school, who are also academicians at Krakow universities, thus guaranteeing high standards of scholastic support.

The school offers the National Polish Curriculum for students of the primary and senior section. The International Baccalaureate Diploma Programme welcomes students from diverse nationalities.

Learning from life is an integral part of the curriculum. The school provides international, educational and cultural opportunities through community service projects, exchange programmes and international engagements. Each year students participate in the Exchange Programme with India, Nepal, the USA, Norway and Germany. They also collobrate and participate in International Summits, International Model United Nations Symposium and International Competetive Events. The School has also been accredited as UNESCO Associated School. The students participate in various global projects promoting peace and international understanding.

PACK's model of educational excellence and co-scholastic engagement enables and encourages its students to learn and discover and be mindful citizens of this millenium.

Villiers School

Headteacher
Jill A. Storey

DP coordinator
Shane Hanna

Status Private

Boarding/day Mixed

Gender Coeducational

Language of instruction
English

Authorised IB programmes
DP

Number of pupils enrolled
600

Fees
Day: €9,600 – €10,900
Boarding: €21,700 – €24,500

Address
North Circular Road
Limerick
V94 F983 | IRELAND

TEL +353 61 451447

Email
admissions@villiers-school.com

Website
www.villiers-school.com

In March 2017, Villiers School became only the second school in Ireland, and the only boarding school, to be authorised to offer the International Baccalaureate Diploma Programme (IBDP) as a senior cycle curriculum option, ideal for students with a global mindset. Villiers believes in a shared IB Schools philosophy: a commitment to high quality, challenging, international education for all its students. Academic excellence is a process of both formal and informal education, which traverses all programmes at Villiers School. It is intended that Villiers students will see education, in its' wider context, as a limitless and unending process to be enjoyed for a lifetime.

The DP at Villiers has grown from five students in the first cohort, the graduating class of 2020, to twenty students in our fourth cohort, the current DP Year 1 class. We are very proud to have a 100% DP graduation rate, and our average DP results are consistent with global IB average results.

Villiers School is fortunate to have growing numbers of students joining our DP class from a variety of cultures, backgrounds, and experiences, all of which adds to the intrinsic diversity that we value and foster within our school community. We currently have 18 nationalities represented within the DP in Villiers.

As we celebrate our 200th anniversary in 2021, management and staff at Villiers School embrace and maintain the traditional values of the school and balance them with modern, state of the art educational facilities, to develop an environment that engenders growth on an academic, cultural, and social level. Villiers offers both day and boarding options and we are home to approximately 150 boarders. The essence of Villiers is our inclusive family-based community. We are wholeheartedly committed to providing a safe, caring, welcoming and friendly atmosphere. Villiers is an environment where both individuality and community mindedness can flourish, and every student can achieve their full potential.

(Founded 2008)

Head of School
Marcella Margaria Bodo

DP coordinator
Deborah Gutowitz

Status Private

Boarding/day Day

Gender Coeducational

Language of instruction
English

Authorised IB programmes
DP

Age Range 3 – 19 years

Fees
Nursery School €5,000
Cambridge Primary €5,500
Cambridge Lower Secondary
€6,100
Cambridge IGCSE €10,100
IBDP €10,950

Address
Via delle Rosine 14
10123 Turin | **ITALY**

TEL +39 011 889870

Email
infovis@vittoriaweb.it

Website
www.vittoriaweb.it

Founded in 1975 as one of the first linguistic high schools in Italy, the Vittoria International School Torino offers bilingual education for children and young adults starting from elementary school and continuing through to the IB diploma. Located in the heart of Turin's city center, the school ensures a modern and innovative learning environment for students of all ages and nationalities.

Since the very beginning, we have leveraged the best of tradition and innovation both in the choice of educational pathways and teaching methods. Fully certified by the Italian Ministry of Education, the school offers bilingual primary and secondary programs in addition to traditional Italian and international, English-language high school programs.

We have been an authorized IB World School since 2008. We offer the IBDP grades 11 and 12. The Italian Government recognizes our DP as equivalent to the Italian Maturità Linguistico or Scientifico, depending on the track chosen by each candidate.

We have been a Cambridge Upper Secondary School IGCSE (grades 9 and 10) since 2010. We have welcomed students at all phases of their education beginning in the Primary years and Lower Secondary since September 2018.

Our curriculum is constantly growing and adapting to the individual needs of our students. The final scores and completion rates of our students are consistently above the international average. We provide professional, personalized career and university guidance, and many of our students go on to study at world-class universities around the globe. Our students are supported in their pursuit of excellence in extracurricular activities, and many have been rewarded nationally and internationally in sports and the arts.

A low student-teacher classroom ratio allows for individual attention as part of a socially and academically rich formative experience. Our door is always open to parents and students who have ideas to propose or concerns to express, and we use a centralized, password-protected system to keep parents and students updated on all school activities.

Our teachers are all university graduates; IB and Cambridge trained. They are passionate about their subjects and dedicated to their students.

A vibrant discussion of global issues begins in our classrooms and extends into CAS projects. Students experience world issues as they play out in our local community and abroad. We have an ongoing relationship important international organizations located in Turin.

1707
Warminster School

(Founded 1707)	**Age Range** 2 – 18 years
Headmaster Mr Matt Williams BA MA	**Number of pupils enrolled** 550
DP coordinator Simon Hall BSc Psychology PGCE	**Fees** Day: £5,740 per term Boarding: £11,770 per term
CP coordinator Simon Hall BSc Psychology PGCE	**Address** Church Street Warminster Wiltshire
Status Private	**BA12 8PJ	UK**
Boarding/day Mixed	**TEL** +44 (0)1985 210100
Gender Coeducational	**Email** admissions@ warminsterschool.org.uk
Language of instruction English	**Website** www.warminsterschool.org.uk
Authorised IB programmes DP, CP	

Warminster is a coeducational school of 550 students aged 2 to 18, located in the South-west of England. Founded in 1707, the school is a member of HMC and has been an authorized IB World School since December 2005.

Warminster School prides itself on its ability to combine a strong academic record and excellent facilities with a warm, friendly family ethos. A comprehensive pastoral care programme, centred around the role of the tutor, provides appropriate levels of support at all times.

Warminster School's students have consistently achieved excellent results, averaging 34 points in 2016, an average of 31 and a 100% pass rate in 2017, and an average of 30 in 2018. In 2019 the average was 29.9 and in 2020 the average was 30.3. 95% of our students go on to study at leading universities around the world, including Oxford and Cambridge, where the IB Diploma is particularly well received. Several individual candidates have secured exceptional IB results; the highest candidate points scored to date is an outstanding 44 points out of 45.

Warminster School welcomes students from over twenty-eight different countries into a community that celebrates its own diversity and encourages service to local, national and global societies. With a talented and enthusiastic staff and a diverse range of subjects and activities on offer, pupils are able to develop their potential to the full. The wide range of co-curricular activities include music, drama, a comprehensive range of sports and opportunities to go on challenging international visits.

Experienced resident house staff provide a supportive environment for boarding students in comfortable, well equipped boarding houses. Recreational activities and trips are arranged each weekend. For medical care there is a school nursing sister on duty every day.

Subjects offered vary according to student demand but typically include: English A and B, German A, 'self-taught languages', French B, Spanish B and Ab Initio, History, Geography, Economics, Psychology, Environmental Systems, Biology, Physics, Chemistry, Maths, Theatre, and Visual Arts. Additional online courses are available in Film, Business Management, Philosophy, French and Mandarin ab initio. As well as offering the Diploma Programme, from September 2017 Warminster School has offered the IB Career-Related Programme, combining Diploma Programme subjects with vocational qualifications (OCR Cambridge Technicals at level 3) in Business, Engineering and Sport.

(Founded 1963)

Head of College
Stephen Lowry

DP coordinator
Elizabeth Cummergen

Status Private

Boarding/day Mixed

Gender Coeducational

Language of instruction
English

Authorised IB programmes
DP

Age Range 11 – 20 years

Number of pupils enrolled
600

Fees
Two-year fee €38,000
(scholarships available)

Address
Waterford Park
Mbabane H100 | **ESWATINI**

TEL +268 24220867

Email
principal@waterford.sz

Website
www.waterford.sz

Introduction

Waterford Kamhlaba UWC of Southern Africa was founded in 1963 as a response to the separate and unequal educational systems in South Africa. When His Majesty King Sobhuza II visited the school, he gave it the name "Kamhlaba", which meant both "of the world" and also that we are "of the earth" and without distinctions such as race. Differently to all the other schools, the academic year at runs from January to November.

Inside the Classroom

Waterford offers the Waterford curriculum in the junior school, the University of Cambridge International General Certificate of Secondary Education (IGCSE) program in the middle school and the International Baccalaureate Diploma Programme in the senior school. For the IBDP, alongside standard courses SiSwati, French, Spanish, Anthropology, Psychology, Business Management, Music, Theatre are offered.

Outside the Classroom

Waterford is an ambassador of UWC's mission on the continent and having educated a large group of African changemakers since its inception. With the School having been the first multiracial school in Southern Africa; founded as a direct response to its system of apartheid, its history of embracing and celebrating diversity from across Africa and beyond is something deeply ingrained into Waterford Kamhlaba's nature and continues to be at the core of its values today. The School, through community service, has strong relations with local organizations such as the refugee camp and neighborhood care points (children welfare centres). A commitment to community service has been recognized as an essential part of the school's policy, organisation and life. A regular commitment to a service project is required of IBDP and Form 5 students, and projects usually vary from involvement at the local hospital to work for the disabled. UWC WK offers a wide variety of sporting- and recreational activities run by both staff and students (e.g. kayaking, art clubs, etc.).

Campus and Facilities

Ekukhuleni residence accommodates up to 80 Form 1, 2 and 3 students. Esiveni accommodates up to 110 Form 4 and 5 students. Emhlabeni and Elangeni accommodate, respectively, up to 130 and 68 IBDP students, in either single rooms or shared rooms; consisting of separate wings for males and females. Each day there is one male and one female residence tutor on duty in each residence.

Admissions

Students can apply through their UWC national committee or through the UWC Global Selection Programme.

Wellington College

WELLINGTON COLLEGE

(Founded 1853)	**Age Range** 13 – 18 years
Master Mr James Dahl	**Number of pupils enrolled** 1090
Director of IB Mr Richard Atherton	**Fees** Day: £31,140 – £35,760 Boarding: £42,630
DP coordinator Dr Robert Cromarty	
Status Private	**Address** Duke's Ride, Crowthorne Berkshire, **RG45 7PU | UK**
Boarding/day Mixed	
Gender Coeducational	**TEL** +44 (0)1344 444000
Language of instruction English	**Email** admissions@ wellingtoncollege.org.uk
Authorised IB programmes DP	**Website** www.wellingtoncollege.org.uk

Wellington College is a vibrant, inspiring and challenging all-round coeducational boarding and day school set in 400 acres of parkland, 40 minutes from Heathrow. At present there are 610 boys and 480 girls, of whom 230 are day pupils.

The College seeks to provide young people with the knowledge, skills and character to serve and help shape a better world by focusing on its key values of Kindness, Courage, Respect, Integrity and Responsibility, values which underpin every aspect of life at Wellington.

Its international reputation in sports, arts, service, wellbeing and leadership, and its genuine commitment to an education that extends far beyond the classroom ensures that students leave school equipped for the challenges and opportunities of tomorrow's world.

All learning at Wellington is supported by the Microsoft OneNote system, and our ongoing embrace of IT technology ensured that during lockdown periods of the pandemic all lessons and tutorials were delivered online (with recordings available for international students disadvantaged by different time zones). Currently 237 pupils take the IB Diploma in the Sixth Form. 80% are from England and the rest are from 40 different countries, which sets us apart from competitors who tend to have smaller programmes attracting only international pupils. In 2019, the last examined year, we had 95 Diploma students who obtained an average of 40.2 points, with 62% scoring 40 or more and nine students achieving the perfect score of 45. The virus-affected 2021 cohort achieved an average of 41.2, and 15 of the 89 went on to Oxbridge or Ivy League. Indeed, over 100 Wellingtonians have been offered places at Oxford or Cambridge over the past five years and on average 25 pupils move on to US universities each year, many to Ivy League institutions. The high academic expectations we have for our pupils are expressed through encouragement and support – nearly 40% of teachers have Masters or Doctorates and all are specialists.

Wellington College introduced the International Baccalaureate Diploma Programme in 2007. Its philosophy – of combining academic rigour with breadth and depth – is very much in sympathy with our own. We offer a wide range of subjects, at all levels, and we believe our support for the IB Core – the extended essay, theory of knowledge, and creativity, activity, service – is truly world class, combining as it does academic expertise with outstanding opportunities and resources. This is a school that actively promotes excellence without compromising the ideals embedded within the IB's learner profile.

Subjects offered in the IB Diploma Programme are all at both HL and SL unless stated:
Group 1: English literature, German literature, German language and literature, English literature and performance SL.
Group 2 Modern B (HL, SL and ab initio): German, Spanish, French, Mandarin.
Group 2 Modern B (HL and SL): Italian, Russian.
Group 2 Classical: Greek, Latin.
Group 3: business and management, economics, history, philosophy, psychology, geography, global politics, environmental systems and societies SL, art history SL.
Group 4: biology, chemistry, computer science, design technology, physics, sports, exercise and health science, environmental systems and societies SL, astronomy SL.
Group 5: analysis and approaches, applications and interpretation.
Group 6: music, visual arts, theatre arts.

(Founded 2007)	**Age Range** 3 – 19 years
Head of School Kathleen Battah	**Number of pupils enrolled** 758
PYP coordinator Nadine Daya	**Address** Al Mathaf, Main Street Near National Museum, PO Box 116-2134 Beirut | **LEBANON**
MYP coordinator Joanna Barrak	
DP coordinator Kathleen Saleh	**City Centre Campus (CCC)** Lamma Street, Ain El Roumaneh Area, PO Box 116-2134
Status Private	Beirut | **LEBANON**
Boarding/day Day	**TEL** +961 1 423 444
Gender Coeducational	**Email** info@wellspring.edu.lb
Language of instruction English	**Website** www.wellspring.edu.lb
Authorised IB programmes PYP, MYP, DP	

Wellspring Learning Community is the first IB Continuum World School in Lebanon and it is the realization of a belief that children of Lebanon deserve to study in a high quality learning environment that opens up space for developing their talents and intellectual potential, as well as their capacity for caring about the world around them. Wellspring is a non-sectarian community with no political affiliations. Depending on availability, enrolment is open throughout the year. We welcome inquiries and visits from interested families.

Authorization/Accreditations

Wellspring is authorized for the IB Diploma, Middle Years Programme, and Primary Years Programme, Council of International Schools (CIS), New England Association of Schools and Colleges(NEASC).

Vision and Mission

Wellspring is an inquiry-based learning environment where students are given every opportunity to realize their social, emotional and academic capacities. Teachers, students and parents work collaboratively in an atmosphere of mutual respect and trust by sharing a positive learning environment that builds on an ongoing process of self-assessment, evidence-based decision making, and continual improvement. Our students will become confident, resourceful, creative, caring, responsible and thinking citizens, prepared to use their education to contribute in meaningful ways to improve society; locally and internationally.

Teachers

Our 180 faculty members are highly qualified and experienced teachers; many are native English speakers. In addition to being IB trained, some teachers hold additional positions within the IB Educator Network (IBEN).

Students

Wellspring has a large international population, with 59 countries represented across our two campuses, in addition to our local students who come from diverse backgrounds within Lebanon.

Facilities

We are proud to offer two campuses in the vibrant heart of Beirut. Both environments are attractive, technologically advanced, and continuously upgraded to keep pace with the demands of the educational program. Facilities include music and art rooms, science labs, computer labs, cafeteria(CCC), libraries, play areas and sports spaces.

Windermere School

(Founded 1863)

Headmaster
Mr Thomas Hill

DP coordinator
Elizabeth Loughlin

CP coordinator
Theresa Murray

Status Private

Boarding/day Mixed

Gender Coeducational

Language of instruction
English

Authorised IB programmes
DP, CP

Age Range 3 – 18 years

Number of pupils enrolled
350

Fees
Day: £18,855
Weekly Boarding: £31,740
Boarding: £32,985

Address
Patterdale Road
Windermere
Cumbria
LA23 1NW | UK

TEL 015394 46164

Email
admissions@
windermereschool.co.uk

Website
www.windermereschool.co.uk

Nestled on a hillside within the Lake District National Park, a landscape that inspired writers such as Beatrix Potter and William Wordsworth, Windermere School enjoys one of the most picturesque views in the Lake District, and arguably, the best school view in the world.

Windermere is a leading independent day and boarding school for boys and girls aged 3 to 18. It is fully co-educational and consists of the Senior School (ages 11 to 18) and Junior School (ages 3 to 11). Windermere was named as the Sunday Times 'International Baccalaureate School of the Year 2017-2018'.

A non-selective school, Windermere offers four pathways through Sixth Form with the IB which are designed to challenge, extend, motivate and inspire students. You can be confident that the path you choose will equip you with the results needed for success beyond the school gates, with a future full of possibilities.

Transcending pure academics, our guided Round Square Service programme will hone key transferable life skills and the strong self-awareness needed for you to step out into the world with confidence. As part of this holistic training, students take on responsibilities to enrich both their experience as-well-as those of the wider school and local community while enhancing their employability portfolio. From organising house events, hosting clubs, adventurous expeditions, volunteering, and going on residential trips such as our annual trip to South Africa to support Thussanang Service project, there are a vast array of opportunities available.

The Sixth Form boarding house is designed to promote the successful transition between School and Higher Education. It is laid out in university style apartments with twin and single bedrooms, a bathroom, common room, and kitchen. There is also a large communal space for socialising in which numerous socials events are held throughout the year.

The Good Schools Guide describes Windermere as *"a school which revels in a hearty approach to everything from academia to friendships"*. In the latest inspection report by the Independent Schools' Inspectorate (February 2018), Windermere School received the highest grades for the quality of the education provided – recognised as 'Excellent' for both Academic and other achievements, and Personal Development.

WINS
WORLD INTERNATIONAL SCHOOL
TORINO

The Key to a Global Future

School Manager Ms Giulia Mazzocchi	**Language of instruction** English
PYP coordinator Ms Victoria Corkhill	**Authorised IB programmes** PYP, MYP, DP
MYP coordinator Ms Kristin Walter	**Address** Via Traves 28 10151 Torino | **ITALY**
DP coordinator Ms Barbara Battaglino	**TEL** +39 0111972111
Status Private	**Email** info@ worldinternationalschool.com
Boarding/day Mixed	**Website** worldinternationalschool.com
Gender Coeducational	

Who we are

World International School of Torino is an International Baccalaureate® World School for the PYP (Primary Years Programme), the MYP (Middle Years Programme) and the DP (Diploma Programme).

WINS was founded in 2017 by the Formiga Family, with their 60 years of experience in international education.

Teachers and students from all over the world, programs of excellence and integrated use of technology are joined by numerous creative, artistic and sporting activities.

Campus and facilities

Our 16,000 square meters Campus is equipped with a swimming pool, indoor and outdoor sports fields, libraries, music, science and art labs, spacious classrooms and a boarding house for students living far from Turin.

The high-quality internal canteen, a rich program of extra-curricular activities and the shuttle bus are only some of the services you can find at WINS, offered to ensure a welcoming, safe and comfortable environment for the students and their families.

Boarding House

Our Boarding House is the first one in Piedmont. It is designed for WINS students aged 13 and above who want to live an amazing international learning experience.

Our Community

Our community is made up of more than 60% international families and our teachers come from many different nations.

The truly multicultural context of our school and the high standards of its academic programs nurture the intellectual growth of our students, helping them become open-minded, principled, and inquiring citizens of the world.

Our values and mission

WINS core values are to be found in the daily commitment of teachers and each faculty member, who work together with families and students to ensure the proper differentiation and the fulfillment of students' potential.

Our mission is to create a safe and respectful learning environment to support children in the development of their individual talents by fostering critical thinking from an early age.

WINS Foundation

WINS Foundation pursues educational and cultural projects to lay the foundations for a better and sustainable society, made up of responsible, knowledgeable and international-minded citizens.

The Foundation has several courses of action: it provides money, goods or services to support people in need; it carries out projects in the fields of education, professional development and acts against educational poverty; it organizes cultural, artistic or recreational activities of social interest; it disseminates the culture of volunteering and organizes activities of educational guidance and prevention of early school leaving.

Accreditations

- AFEC: WINS is the first Athlete Friendly Education School in Italy, to support athletes in achieving their educational and athletic goals.
- CAMBRIDGE: WINS is a Cambridge English Exams Preparation Center and the only authorized Cambridge Assessment Admissions Testing Center within the Piedmont region.
- TRINITY: WINS is a registered Trinity College London® Examination Centre.
- KiVa: WINS implements the KiVa anti-bullying international program aimed at preventing bullying within the school.

XXI Century Integration International Secondary School

(Founded 1996)

Head of School Svetlana Kulichenko

PYP coordinator Kristina Moavad

MYP coordinator James Nevin

DP coordinator Nigiar Mekhtieva

Status Private

Boarding/day Day

Gender Coeducational

Language of instruction
English, Russian

Authorised IB programmes
PYP, MYP, DP

Age Range 5 – 18 years

Number of pupils enrolled 180

Fees
€8,700 – €18,000

Address
16 Marshala Katukova St.
Building 3, Moscow
123592 | RUSSIAN FEDERATION

TEL +7 495 750 3102

Email school@integration21.ru

Website www.integration21.ru

The XXI Century Integration School is an independent day school for girls and boys from Kindergarten to Grade 11. The school campus is located to the North-West of Moscow in Strogino, one of the green districts of the capital. The facilities are modern, well-equipped and easily accessible by public transport. XXI Century Integration is an internationally minded school that encourages cultural exchange and welcomes students from all over the world. The school has a proud tradition of excellence in education, sports and cultural pursuits.

XXI Century Integration has an inclusive school policy and all students are welcome. We offer the IB Primary Years Programme, the IB Middle Years Programme and the IB Diploma Programme and/or the National Programme. XXI Century Integration is comprised of a kindergarten for five and six-year olds, based on ideas such as respect, trust, compassion, rights and responsibilities; a primary school with an emphasis on numeracy and literacy and a senior school, where students choose from the National Programme, or the IB Diploma Programme or can do both. The Middle Years programme (MYP) at XXI Century Integration provides learners with a quality learning experience that is broad and challenging. The school places great emphasis on International-mindedness and students graduate from the MYP programme as knowledgeable, caring and independent young learners. During these exciting 5 years at XXI Century Integration, learners will have the opportunity to study a wide range of subjects from the 8 MYP subject group areas. XXI Century Integration prides itself on offering an English-Russian bilingual education, ensuring that the young learners understand the host-country language as well as be able to communicate fluently in English.

The IB Diploma Programme subjects on offer are Russian A: Literature, English A: Language and Literature, Languages B and *ab initio* (English, French, Italian, German, Chinese, Spanish), Business management, Economics, History, Environmental Systems and Societies, Biology, Chemistry, Physics, Computer Science, Mathematics: Analysis and Approaches, Visual Arts and Music.

XXI Century Integration's academic results are outstanding: 51% of the 2015-2020 IB Diploma students achieved a score of 38-42, the results of the 2021 IBDP students are 41-45. The school balances excellent academic results with a range of exciting co-curricular activities including sports, arts, music, drama and community service.

The most important attributes of school life are the school's five core values of relationships, courage, creative reflection, intellectual enquiry and engagement in life. It's values are aligned with the IB philosophy of developing inquiring, knowledgeable and caring people who create a better world through intercultural understanding. Students learn in an environment that nurtures important life skills, thus ensuring that students leave XXI Century Integration as well-rounded, self-reliant and confident individuals.

We participate in the IB Schools to Schools Projects in Russia and abroad. In July-August XXI Century Integration runs a summer school in a beautiful area of Croatia where students take part in fun activities that prepare them for future studies within all the IB Programmes.

XXI Century Integration also holds a signed agreement with the City University of Hong Kong (City U) to provide scholarship opportunities for highly talented students at our school, thereby allowing our students to pursue full-time undergraduate education at City U.

yago school

(Founded 2010)	**Address**
Chairman & Headmaster Ramón Resa	Avda. Antonio Mairena, 54 41950 Castilleja de la Cuesta, Seville, Andalusia | **SPAIN**
DP coordinator Blanca Domínguez	**TEL** +34 955 51 1234
Status Private	**Email** admissions@yagoschool.com
Boarding/day Day	**Website** www.yagoschool.com
Gender Coeducational	

Language of instruction
English, Spanish

Authorised IB programmes
DP

Age Range 0 – 18 years

Number of pupils enrolled
800

At Yago School, we are completely transforming the educational-learning system in the South of Spain so that our students from 0 to 18 years can successfully confront many of the educational challenges of the 21st century, by offering the Diploma Programme of International Baccalaureate, together with the Spanish educational system and by using the English and Spanish languages as a communicative instrument inside and outside the classroom, with Chinese and French as part of its dynamic curriculum. Our unique curriculum is also accredited by WASC (Western Association of Schools and Colleges).

Over a decade in the educational field, we have grown to represent more than 30 nationalities. The Yago team strives to inspire, nurture and empower every student to achieve their personal best and become enquiring, knowledgeable, lifelong learners who create a better world through intercultural understanding and respect.

Our purpose is for students to develop their abilities and potential to the maximum, to build knowledge through projects, broaden their interests and their own experience using integrative, innovative and cooperative methodologies in traditional and technological environments so that they can adapt to universities and successfully integrate into companies all over the world.

Yago School's principles have been built on five educational pillars: traditional values, bilingualism, sports, music and new technologies. Five bases that, combined with demanding academic training, provide our students with an extremely solid foundation promoting success in both their personal and professional lives. The use of technology is embedded in the curriculum for all students from the age of four. Music is performed at a wide range of events and students are prepared for examinations in theory, piano and singing with the Associated Board of the Royal Schools of Music. The outstanding sporting facilities, including sports pitches and a sports hall, provide many opportunities for students to compete in team and individual events.

The avant-garde architecture of its facilities, along with its privileged location in the "Aljarafe", just 15 minutes from the international airport and the high-speed AVE train station, all enhance the multitude of diverse and personalised opportunities and complementary experiences Yago School offers.

Admission: Admissions are open throughout the academic year, subject to availability. Every effort is made to reserve a space for international applicants. We currently arrange homestays for international students and, beginning in September 2023, we will offer a student residence for boarding which is under construction.

Directory of schools in the Africa, Europe and Middle East region

Key to symbols

● CP

● Diploma

● MYP

● PYP

$ Fee Paying School

B Boys' School

G Girls' School

C Coeducational School

● Boarding School

☀ Day School

ALBANIA

Albanian College Tirana

Rruga Dritan Hoxha 1, Tirana 1000
DP Coordinator Marcela Danisova
MYP Coordinator Callie Welstead
PYP Coordinator Fernando Ramirez
Languages English
T: +355 44 513 471
W: www.actirana.edu.al

International Learning Group School – ILG School

Veternik 1, 10000 Prishtina, Kosovo
MYP Coordinator Rebecca Bowery
PYP Coordinator Christy Dervishi
Languages English
T: +386 38 722 893
W: www.ilg-ks.org

QSI TIRANA INTERNATIONAL SCHOOL

Rruga Vilat Gjermane, Kutia Postare 1527, Tirana
DP Coordinator Elizabeth Sloughter
Languages English
T: +355 4 236 5239
E: tirana@qsi.org
W: tirana.qsi.org

See full details on page 181

World Academy of Tirana

Rruga e Rezervave, Lunder, Tirane
DP Coordinator Peter Thompson
MYP Coordinator Alena Namotu
PYP Coordinator Shikha Ahuja
Languages English
T: +355 69 6056 123
W: www.wat.al

ANDORRA

Agora International School Andorra

Poliesportiu de l'Aldosa, L'ALDOSA, La Massana, Principat d'Andorra
DP Coordinator Charmaine Lodge
Languages English, German, French, Chinese
T: +376 838 366
W: www.agorainternationalandorra.com

Centre de Formació Professional d'Aixovall

Ctra. d'Os de Civís, s/n, 600 Aixovall
CP Coordinator Mònica Sánchez
Languages Catalan, Valencian, Spanish

Escola Andorrana de batxillerat

C/ Tossalet i Vinyals, 45, AD500 La Margineda, Andorra la Vella
DP Coordinator Carles Vallverdú Berges
Languages Spanish, Catalan, Valencian
T: +376 723030
W: adbatx.educand.ad

ANGOLA

LUANDA INTERNATIONAL SCHOOL

Via S6, Bairro de Talatona, Município de Belas, Luanda
DP Coordinator Rene Bradford
MYP Coordinator Catherine McCann
PYP Coordinator Julie Ranger
Languages English
T: +244 932 337 056
E: lis@lisluanda.com
W: www.lisluanda.com

See full details on page 154

ARMENIA

Quantum College

Bagratuniats 23/2, Shengavit, Yerevan 0046
DP Coordinator Arpine Harutyunyan
Languages English
T: +374 10 422217
W: www.quantum.am

Shirakatsy Lyceum International Scientific-Educational Complex

35 Artem Mikoyan Street, Yerevan 0079
DP Coordinator Anna Stepanyan
MYP Coordinator Elina Shakaryan
PYP Coordinator Marina Sahakyan
Languages English, Armenian
T: +374 10 680 102
W: www.shirakatsy.am

UWC Dilijan

7 Getapnya Street, Dilijan 3903
DP Coordinator Sophie Duncker
Languages English
T: +44 (0)1446 799000
W: www.uwcdilijan.org

AUSTRIA

AMADEUS INTERNATIONAL SCHOOL VIENNA

Bastiengasse 36-38, 1180 Vienna
CP Coordinator Ms Elke De Vries
DP Coordinator Alice Greenland
MYP Coordinator Yvan Wever
PYP Coordinator Melanie McGeever
Languages English
T: +43 1 470 30 37 00
E: admissions@amadeus-vienna.com
W: www.amadeus-vienna.com

See full details on page 49

AMERICAN INTERNATIONAL SCHOOL VIENNA

Salmannsdorfer Strasse 47, 1190 Vienna
DP Coordinator Bridget Schroeder
Languages English
T: +43 1 401 32
E: info@ais.at
W: www.ais.at

See full details on page 54

Anton Bruckner International School (ABIS)

Bruckner Tower, Wildbergstrasse 18, 4040 Linz, Upper Austria
MYP Coordinator Paul Cartwright
PYP Coordinator Samantha Lyke
Languages English, German
T: +43 7327 11691
W: www.abis.school

BG/BRG Klosterneuburg

Buchberggasse 31, 3400 Klosterneuburg, Lower Austria
DP Coordinator Rebecca Kmentt
Languages English
T: +43 2243 32155
W: www.bgklosterneuburg.ac.at

Campus Wien West

Seuttergasse 29, 1130 Vienna
DP Coordinator Jutta Zopf-Klasek
Languages English
T: +43 680 5577 573
W: www.campus-wien-west.at

Danube International School Vienna

Josef-Gall Gasse 2, 1020 Vienna
DP Coordinator Rachel Pernet
MYP Coordinator Maura Lichtscheidl-Fegerl
PYP Coordinator Keitsa Brisson
Languages English
T: +43 1 7203110
W: www.danubeschool.com

GIBS Graz International Bilingual School

Georgigasse 85, 8020 Graz, Styria
DP Coordinator Ursula Schatz
Languages English
T: +43 316 771050
W: www.gibs.at

International Christian School of Vienna

Panethgasse 6a, (right by Wagramer Strasse), 1220 Vienna
DP Coordinator Adesola Adebesin
Languages English
T: +43 1 251122 0
W: www.icsv.at

International Highschool Herzogberg

Herzogbergstraße 230, 2380 Perchtoldsdorf, Lower Austria
DP Coordinator Veronika Weiss
Languages English, German
T: +43 6991 7750 055
W: www.am-herzogberg.com

International School Carinthia

Rosentaler Straße 15, 9220 Velden Am Worthersee, Carinthia
DP Coordinator Oliver Pope
MYP Coordinator Luke Ames
PYP Coordinator Scott French
Languages English, German
T: +43 4274 52471 10
W: www.isc.ac.at

International School Innsbruck

Angerzellgasse 14, 6020 Innsbruck, Tyrol
DP Coordinator Stephen Dea
Languages English
T: +43 512 58 70 64
W: agi.tsn.at

International School Kufstein Tirol

Andreas-Hofer-Straße 7, 6330 Kufstein, Tyrol
DP Coordinator Rick Lewis
Languages English
T: +43 5372 21990
W: www.isk-tirol.at

Linz International School Auhof (LISA)

Aubrunnerweg 4, 4040 Linz, Upper Austria
DP Coordinator Oliver Kim
Languages English
T: +43 732 245867- 23
W: www.europagym.at/lisa

AUSTRIA

Lower Austrian International School

Bimbo Binder-Promenade 7, 3100 St. Pölten, Lower Austria
DP Coordinator Michael Hofbauer
Languages English
T: +43 2742 73453
W: www.borglsp-stpoelten.ac.at

SALIS – Salzburg International School

Zaunergasse 3, 5020 Salzburg
DP Coordinator Holger Benz
Languages English, German
T: +43 662 439616 0
W: www.bgzaunergasse.at

SCHLOSS KRUMBACH INTERNATIONAL SCHOOL GMBH

Schloss 1, 2851 Krumbach, Lower Austria
DP Coordinator Minka Peeters Weem
Languages English, German
T: +43 6765 409630
E: info@krumbach.school
W: www.krumbach.school

See full details on page 190

ST. GILGEN INTERNATIONAL SCHOOL

Ischlerstrasse 13, 5340 St. Gilgen, Salzburg
DP Coordinator John Patton
Languages English
T: +43 62 272 0259
E: info@stgis.at
W: www.stgis.at

See full details on page 212

Vienna International School

Strasse der Menschenrechte 1, 1220 Vienna
DP Coordinator William Johnson
MYP Coordinator Joseph O'Rourke
PYP Coordinator Lea Pedlow
Languages English
T: +43 1 203 5595
W: www.vis.ac.at

AZERBAIJAN

Dunya School

9 Ajami Nakhchivani street, Baku AZ1130
DP Coordinator Rana Hasanova
PYP Coordinator Leila Mammadova
Languages English
T: +994 12 563 59 40/47/48
W: dunyaschool.az

Educational Complex No. 132-134

Istiglaliyyat 33A, Baku, Absheron AZ1001
DP Coordinator Francis Wilfrid Mang-Benza dit Manthota
Languages Azerbaijani
T: +994 (0)12 492 27 32
W: www.132-134.com

European Azerbaijan School

7 Basti Bagirova, Yasamal District, Baku City
DP Coordinator Qadir Mikayilov
MYP Coordinator Maria Elena Berardi
PYP Coordinator Benjamin Lind
Languages English
T: +994 12 539 89 35/36/37/38
W: www.eas.az

Idrak Lyceum

2 Samad Vurghun, Sumqayit 5001
DP Coordinator Nuriya Allahverdiyeva
Languages English
T: +994 18 655 59 73
W: idrak.edu.az

School-Lyceum N6

2 Sh Alakparova Str, Baku 1001
DP Coordinator Deepa Boodhoo
MYP Coordinator Elmir Manafov
PYP Coordinator Pinar Calis
Languages English
T: +99 412 492 2221

The International School of Azerbaijan, Baku

Yeni Yasamal, Stonepay, Royal Park, Baku AZ1070
DP Coordinator Gareth Hubbuck
MYP Coordinator Alejandro Franco
PYP Coordinator Brianne Eddy-Lee
Languages English
T: +994 12 404 01 12
W: www.tisa.az

BAHRAIN

Abdul Rahman Kanoo International School

P.O. Box 2512, Manama
DP Coordinator Kawthar Mustafa Ali Abbas Ali
Languages English, Arabic
T: +973 1787 5055
W: www.kanooschool.edu.bh

Al Rawabi School

Bldg 689, Road 3514, Block 435, Jeblat Hibshi, P.o.Box 18575, Manama, Jeblat Hibshi 435, 00973
DP Coordinator Fatema Radhi
Languages English
T: +973 17 595 252
W: alrawabi.edu.bh

Arabian Pearl Gulf (APG) School

PO Box 26299, Adliya, Manama
DP Coordinator John Labor
Languages English
T: +973 17 403 666
W: www.apgschool.com

Bahrain Bayan School

Building No. 230, Road 4112, Block 841, Isa Town
DP Coordinator Mervat Awamleh
Languages English
T: +973 7712 2244
W: www.bayanschool.edu.bh

Bahrain School

PO Box 934, Manama
DP Coordinator Constance McAninch
Languages English
T: +973 17727 828
W: www.dodea.edu/BahrainEHS

Britus International School

PO Box 18041, Building 208, Road 408, Block 704, Salmabad
DP Coordinator Sunny Vadlamudi
Languages English
T: +973 1759 8440
W: www.amais.edu.bh

Hawar International School

P.O. Box 38338, West Riffa
DP Coordinator Barbora Mastna
Languages English
T: +973 13 666 555
W: www.hawarschool.com

IBN KHULDOON NATIONAL SCHOOL

Building 161, Road 4111, Area 841, P.O. Box 20511, Isa Town
DP Coordinator Gerda Marais
PYP Coordinator Rosy Johnson
Languages English, Arabic
T: +973 17780661
E: k.algosaibi@ikns.edu.bh
W: www.ikns.edu.bh

See full details on page 106

Modern Knowledge Schools

PO Box 15826, Bldg 515, Manama
DP Coordinator Bindu Nair
Languages English
T: +973 17727838
W: www.mks.edu.bh

Naseem International School

PO Box 28503, Riffa
CP Coordinator Carlos Abou Mrad
DP Coordinator Fuad Prins
MYP Coordinator Ali AlShehab
PYP Coordinator Antoinette Pienaar
Languages English, Arabic
T: +973 17 782 000
W: www.nisbah.com

Riffa Views International School

PO Box 3050, Manama 934
DP Coordinator Victoria Johnson
Languages English
T: +973 1656 5000
W: www.rvis.edu.bh

Shaikha Hessa Girls' School

PO Box 37799, Riffa
DP Coordinator Maudhulika Jain
Languages English
T: +973 17 756 111
W: www.shgs.edu.bh

St Christopher's School

PO Box 32052, Isa Town
DP Coordinator Conal Smith
Languages English
T: +973 1760 5000
W: www.st-chris.net

BELGIUM

Antwerp International School

Veltwijcklaan 180, Ekeren, 2180 Antwerp
DP Coordinator Thierry Torres
MYP Coordinator Marianne Navarro
PYP Coordinator Wayne Quenneville
Languages English
T: +32 (0)3 543 93 00
W: www.ais-antwerp.be

BEPS INTERNATIONAL SCHOOL

Avenue Franklin Roosevelt 21-23, Ixelles, 1050 Brussels
MYP Coordinator Andrew Mitchell
Languages English
T: +32 2 648 43 11
E: admissions@beps.com
W: www.beps.com

See full details on page 62

Bogaerts International School

555 Rue Engeland, 1180 Brussels
DP Coordinator Colin Sinclair
MYP Coordinator Mark Trilling
PYP Coordinator Véronique Dehavay
Languages English, French
T: +32 2 230 03 39
W: www.bischool.com

IB AFRICA | EUROPE | MIDDLE EAST

Da Vinci International School
Verbondstraat 67, 2000 Antwerp
DP Coordinator Tijl Stynen
Languages English
T: +32 (0)3 216 1232
W: www.da-vinci.be

European School of Bruxelles-Argenteuil
Square d'Argenteuil 5, 1410 Waterloo, Brussels
DP Coordinator Soren Hansen
Languages English, French
T: +32 2357 06 70
W: www.europeanschool.be

International Montessori School
Kleinenbergstraat 97-99, 1932 St. Stevens-Woluwe, Flemish Brabant
DP Coordinator Charlotte Reilly-Davidson
MYP Coordinator Stéphanie Cnudde
Languages English, French
T: +32 2 767 63 60 / +32 2 721 21 11
W: www.international-montessori.org

INTERNATIONAL SCHOOL OF BELGIUM
Kontichsesteenweg 40, 2630 Aartselaar, Antwerp
DP Coordinator Ms Pauline Kimman
Languages English
T: +32 3 271 0943
E: info@isbedu.be
W: www.isbedu.be/
See full details on page 120

Montgomery International School – Brussels
Rue du Duc 133, 1200 Brussels
DP Coordinator Danielle Franzen Daoudy
MYP Coordinator Wendy Lapetite
PYP Coordinator Wendy Lapetite
Languages French, English
T: +32 2 733 63 23
W: www.ecole-montgomery.be

ST. JOHN'S INTERNATIONAL SCHOOL
Drève Richelle 146, 1410 Waterloo, Walloon Brabant
DP Coordinator Jennifer Bakalian
MYP Coordinator Maggie Adams
PYP Coordinator Kathy Anderson
Languages English
T: +32 (0)2 352 06 10
E: enquiries@stjohns.be
W: www.stjohns.be
See full details on page 213

THE BRITISH SCHOOL OF BRUSSELS (BSB)
Pater Dupierreuxlaan 1, 3080 Tervuren
DP Coordinator James Willis
Languages English, French (bilingual Programme For Ages 4-14 Years)
T: +32 (0)2 766 04 30
E: admissions@britishschool.be
W: www.britishschool.be
See full details on page 227

The Courtyard International School of Tervuren
Stationsstraat 49a, 3080 Tervuren
PYP Coordinator Stephanie Uceny
Languages English, French
W: www.thecourtyard.eu

The International School of Brussels (ISB)
Kattenberg 19, 1170 Brussels
CP Coordinator Stephanie Lacher
DP Coordinator Julie Deegan
Languages English
T: +32 2 661 4211
W: www.isb.be

BOSNIA & HERZEGOVINA

Druga Gimnazija Sarajevo
Sutjeska 1, Sarajevo 71000
DP Coordinator Dolores Hadzic
MYP Coordinator Elvira Kukuljac
Languages English
T: +387 33667438
W: www.2gimnazija.edu.ba

Gimnazija Banja Luka
Zmaj Jovina 13, Banja Luka 78000
DP Coordinator Dijana Jujic
Languages English
T: +387 51 213 259
W: www.gimnazijabanjaluka.org

Maarif Schools of Sarajevo
Ul. Hasiba Brankovica 2A, 71000 Sarajevo
DP Coordinator Ermin Dogan
Languages English, Bosnian
T: +387 33 257 260
W: www.maarifschools.edu.ba

UWC Mostar
Spanski trg 1, Mostar 88000
DP Coordinator Selma Sarancic
Languages English
T: +387 36 320 601
W: www.uwcmostar.ba

BOTSWANA

Enko Botho International School
Plot 60114, Block 7, near Botswana Qualifications Authority and HRDC, Gaborone
DP Coordinator Dorothy Tsalwa
Languages English
T: +267 363 54 19
W: enkoeducation.com/botho

Northside Primary School
PO Box 897, Plot 2786, Tshekedi Crescent Ext 9, Gaborone
PYP Coordinator Joanna Poweska Laverick
Languages English
T: +267 395 2440
W: www.northside.ac.bw

Westwood International School
Phase 4, Plot 22978, Mmankgwedi Road, Gaborone
DP Coordinator Mrs Karuna Datta-Bhatnagar
MYP Coordinator Anandhi Lakshminarayan
PYP Coordinator Nidhi Bhatnagar
Languages English
T: +267 390 6736
W: www.westwood.ac.bw

BULGARIA

American College Arcus
16 Dragoman Str., 5000 Veliko Tarnovo
DP Coordinator Kameliya Antonova
MYP Coordinator Albena Todorova
Languages English
T: +359 62 619959
W: www.ac-arcus.com

American College of Sofia
P.O. Box 873, 1000 Sofia
DP Coordinator Zornitsa Semkova
Languages English
T: +359 2 434 10 08
W: www.acs.bg

Anglo American School of Sofia
1 Siyanie St., 1137 Sofia
DP Coordinator Kalina Belivanova
Languages English
T: +359 2 923 88 10
W: www.aas-sofia.org

BRITANICA Park School
27 Momino Venche Street, Dragalevtsi Quarter, Sofia
DP Coordinator Antoaneta Kalenderova
Languages English, Bulgarian
T: +359 2 4887877
W: britanica-parkschool.bg

British International School Classic
7 Lady Strangford Street, 4000 Plovdiv
DP Coordinator Teodora Ivanovska
Languages English, Bulgarian
T: +359 886 902 295
W: www.classicschool.org

British School of Sofia
18, Radi Radev Street, Lozenets, 1700 Sofia
CP Coordinator Matthew Osborn
DP Coordinator Naomi van Wyngaarden
Languages English, Bulgarian
T: +359 886 510 510
W: www.bssofia.bg

Meridian 22 Private High School
Mladost 2 bl.227, 1799 Sofia
DP Coordinator Yoana Kalapish
Languages English
T: +359 2 8876 423; +359 2 8840 238
W: www.meridian22-edu.com

Private Primary School 'Progressive Education'-Sofia
107 Nishava Str., Sofia 1408
PYP Coordinator Nikol Istiliyanova
Languages English
T: +359 882 741 944

Uwekind International School
136 Voivodina Mogila Street, Knyajevo, 1619 Sofia
DP Coordinator Desislava Ilieva-Popova
MYP Coordinator Aglika Damaskova
Languages English
T: +359 2 8572000
W: www.uwekind.com

Zlatarski International School
49 Kliment Ohridski Boulevard, 1756 Sofia
DP Coordinator Raya Pancheva
Languages English
T: +359 2 876 67 67
W: www.zlatarskischool.org

BURKINA FASO

Enko Ouaga International School
Zogona, venant du Boulevard Charles de Gaulle, premier six-mètres après la mosquée de Zogona à gauche, Ouagadougou
DP Coordinator Fabrice Aguibou
Languages French, English
T: +226 25 36 01 77
W: enkoeducation.com/ouaga

International School of Ouagadougou

Ouagadougou 01 BP 1142
DP Coordinator Marie-Hélène Pichette
Languages English
T: +226 50 36 21 43
W: www.iso.bf

CAMEROON

Academic School of Excellence

Bastos, Yaoundé
DP Coordinator Jean-Victor Yogo
Languages English, French
T: +237 222 20 03 23
W: www.academicschool-ofexcellence.com

American School of Yaounde

BP 7475, Yaounde
DP Coordinator Bruce Doig
MYP Coordinator Jacob Akundo
PYP Coordinator Nadine Boribon
Languages English
T: +237 2223 0421
W: www.asoy.org

Enko Bonanjo International School

Rue 1.171, no. 414, in front of Camwater, Bonanjo, Douala
DP Coordinator Atumo Gerald ManiH Khurde
Languages English, French
T: +237 655 397 144
W: enkoeducation.com/bonanjo

Enko La Gaiete International School

P.O. Box 784728, Nouvelle Route Bastos (échangeur simplifié), Yaoundé 14853
DP Coordinator Veronica Agogho
Languages English
T: +237 653 23 56 52
W: enkoeducation.com/la-gaiete

COTE D'IVOIRE

Enko Riviera International School

Riviera Golf, Carrefour M'Pouto, Sol Beni, next to the Embassy of Lebanon, Abidjan
DP Coordinator Jimmy Goua
MYP Coordinator Rémi Pierre Joseph Goarin
Languages English, French
T: +225 22 54 10 98
W: enkoeducation.com/riviera

International Community School of Abidjan

Boulevard Arsène Usher Assouan, Riveria III, Abidjan
DP Coordinator Fatoumata Amany
Languages English
T: +225 22 47 11 52
W: www.icsabidjan.org

CROATIA

American International School of Zagreb

Damira Tomljanovica Gravrana 3, 10020 Zagreb
DP Coordinator Erin Henkels
Languages English
T: +385 1 7999 300
W: www.aisz.hr

Matija Gubec International School

Davorina Bazjanca 2, 10000 Zagreb
MYP Coordinator Linda Zelic
PYP Coordinator Zilha Redzebasic
Languages English
T: +385 1 364 9133
W: www.os-mgubec.hr

Prva Gimnazija Varazdin

Petra Preradovica 14, 42000 Varazdin
DP Coordinator Ksenija Kipke
Languages English
T: +385 42 302 122
W: www.gimnazija-varazdin.skole.hr

Prva rijecka hrvatska gimnazija

Frana Kurelca 1, 51000 Rijeka
DP Coordinator Amira Mahmutovic Redzic
Languages English, Croatian
T: +385 5 1339 115
W: www.prhg.hr

XV. Gimnazija

Jordanovac 8, 10000 Zagreb
DP Coordinator Zorana Franic
MYP Coordinator Darija Kos
Languages English
T: +385 1 230 2255
W: www.mioc.hr/wp

CUBA

International School of Havana

115 Calle 22 entre, Avenida 1ra y 3ra, Miramar, Havana
DP Coordinator Osmery Martínez
Languages English
T: +53 7214 0773
W: www.ishavana.org

CYPRUS

American International School in Cyprus

PO Box 23847, 11 Kassos Str, Nicosia 1686
DP Coordinator Kika Coles
Languages English
T: +357 22 316345
W: www.aisc.ac.cy

PASCAL Private English School – Larnaka

2, Polytechniou Street, Larnaka, 7103 Aradippou
DP Coordinator Despina Lioliou
Languages English
T: +357 22509300
W: www.pascal.ac.cy

PASCAL Private English School – Lefkosia

177, Kopegchagis Street, Lefkosia, 2306 Lakatamia
DP Coordinator Ariana Milutinovic
Languages English
T: +357 22509000
W: www.pascal.ac.cy

THE ENGLISH SCHOOL OF KYRENIA

Bilim Sokak, Bellapais, Kyrenia, North Cyprus
DP Coordinator Ms Zelis Omer
Languages English
T: +90 392 444 0375
E: info@englishschoolkyrenia.org
W: www.englishschoolkyrenia.com

See full details on page 229

CZECH REPUBLIC

1st International School of Ostrava

Gregorova 3, 702 00 Ostrava
GREGOROVA 3, 702 00 OSTRA
DP Coordinator Nitzan Hollander
Languages English
T: +420 723 332 653
W: www.is-ostrava.cz

Carlsbad International School

Slovenska 477/5, 360 01 Karlovy Vary
DP Coordinator Eniko Kiss
Languages English
T: +420 353 227 387
W: www.carlsbadschool.cz

Dino High School s.r.o.

Bellova 352, 109 00 Prague 10
DP Coordinator Stephan Starkweather
Languages Czech, English
T: +420 240 200 082
W: www.dinoskola.cz

Gymnasium Evolution

Jizni Mesto, Tererova 2135 / 17, 149 00 Prague 4
DP Coordinator Tomas Vavra
Languages English, Czech
T: +420 267 914 553
W: www.gevo.cz

Gymnazium a SOS Rokycany

Mládezníku 1115/II, 337 01 Rokycany
DP Coordinator Jan Zítek
Languages English, Czech
T: +420 371 725 363
W: www.gasos-ro.cz

Gymnázium Duhovka

Ortenovo námestí 34, Hole ovice, 170 00 Prague 7
DP Coordinator Keith Berry
Languages English, Czech
T: +420 241 404 217
W: www.duhovkagymnazium.cz

International School of Brno

Cejkovicka 10, 628 00 Brno-Vinohrady
DP Coordinator Dylan Vance
PYP Coordinator Jennifer Berry
Languages English
T: +420 544 212 313
W: www.isob.cz

International School of Prague

Nebusicka 700, 164 00 Prague 6
DP Coordinator Karen Ercolino
Languages English
T: +420 220 384 111
W: www.isp.cz

Open Gate School

Babice 5, 251 01 Rícany
DP Coordinator Rupert Marks
Languages English
T: +420 724 730 512
W: www.opengate.cz

Park Lane International School – Prague 1

Vald tejnská 151/6a, 118 01 Prague 1
DP Coordinator Jan Cihák
Languages Czech, English
T: +420 257 316 182
W: www.parklane-is.com

PORG International School – Ostrava

Rostislavova 7, 703 00 Ostrava
DP Coordinator Iain Benzie
Languages English
T: +420 597 071 020
W: www.porg.cz

PORG International School – Prague

Pod Krcskym lesem 1300/25, 142 00 Prague 4
DP Coordinator Jason Kucker
Languages English
T: +420 244 403 650
W: www.porg.cz

PRIGO Language and Humanities Grammar School

Mojmirovcu 1002/42, Mariánské Hory, 709 00 Ostrava
DP Coordinator Renata Zavodna
Languages English
W: www.jahu-prigo.cz

Riverside International School

Roztocka 9/43, Sedlec, 160 00 Prague 6
DP Coordinator Daniel Plummer
Languages English
T: +420 2 24315336
W: www.riversideschool.cz

The English College in Prague

Sokolovska 320, 190 00 Prague 9
DP Coordinator Stephen Hudson
Languages English
T: +420 2 8389 3113
W: www.englishcollege.cz

The Ostrava International School

Gregorova 2582/3, 702 00 Ostrava
DP Coordinator Paul Ahuja
MYP Coordinator Jiri Svoboda
PYP Coordinator Elina Prokharava
Languages English
T: +420 724 142 287
W: tois.world

The Prague British School – Kamyk Site

K Lesu 558/2, 142 00 Prague 4
CP Coordinator David Lawlor
DP Coordinator David Lawlor
Languages English
T: +420 226 096 200
W: www.nordangliaeducation.com/schools/prague/british-international

Ecole Internationale Bilingue Le Cartésien (EIBC)

34, 7ème Rue, Q. Industriel, Limete, Kinshasa
DP Coordinator Armand Ngolomingi Mudiandambu
Languages French, English
T: +243 812621704
W: www.lecartesien.cd

Jewels International School of Kinshasa

O.U.A., Commune of Ngaliema, Kinshasa
PYP Coordinator Sandip Munde
Languages English
T: +243 99 99 09 163
W: www.jewelsschool.cd

The American School of Kinshasa

Rte de Matadi, Ngaliema Kinshasa II, Kinshasha
DP Coordinator Garrett Austin
MYP Coordinator Kelley Marchant
PYP Coordinator Vitna Bailey
Languages English
T: +243 818846619
W: www.tasok.net

DENMARK

Aarhus Gymnasium

Halmstadgade 6, 8200 Aarhus N, Midtjylland
DP Coordinator Malene Sørensen
Languages English
T: +45 8937 3533
W: www.aarhusgym.dk

Aarhus International School

Dalgas Avenue 12, 8000 Aarhus, Midtjylland
MYP Coordinator Kathryn Templeman
PYP Coordinator Megan Behnke
Languages English
T: +45 2030 2079
W: www.aarhusacademy.dk

Birkerød Gymnasium, HF, IB & Boarding School

Søndervangen 56, 3460 Birkerød, Hovedstaden
DP Coordinator Christina Rye Tarp
Languages English
T: +45 4516 8220
W: www.birke-gym.dk

Copenhagen International School

Levantkaj 4-14, 2150 Copenhagen, Hovedstaden
DP Coordinator Mary Donnellan
MYP Coordinator Katie Ham
PYP Coordinator Rachel Curle
Languages English
T: +45 3946 3300
W: www.cis.dk

Esbjerg Gymnasium & HF

Spangsbjerg Møllevej 310, 6705 Esbjerg, Syddanmark
DP Coordinator Christina Jepsen
Languages English
T: +45 7514 1300
W: www.e-gym.dk

Esbjerg International School

Guldager Skolevej 4, 6710 Esbjerg, Syddanmark
MYP Coordinator Nicola Zulu
PYP Coordinator Grant Davis
Languages English, Danish
T: +45 7610 5399
W: www.esbjerginternationalschool.dk

EUC Syd

Hilmar Finsens Gade 8, 6400 Soenderborg, Syddanmark
DP Coordinator Mikkel Simonsen
Languages English
T: +45 7412 4242
W: www.eucsyd.dk

Grenaa Gymnasium

N. P. Josiassens vej 21, 8500 Grenaa, Midtjylland
DP Coordinator Eike Strandsby
Languages English
T: +45 8758 4050
W: www.grenaa-gym.dk

Hasseris Gymnasium

Hasserisvej 300, 9000 Aalborg, Nordjylland
DP Coordinator Karin Mølgaard Skals
Languages English
T: +45 9632 7110
W: www.hasseris-gym.dk

Herlufsholm Skole

Herlufsholm Allé 170, 4700 Naestved, Sjaelland
DP Coordinator Natascha Philip
Languages English
T: +45 5575 3500
W: www.herlufsholm.dk

Ikast-Brande Gymnasium

Bøgildvej 2, 7400 Ikast-Brande, Midtjylland
DP Coordinator Gitte Pilley
Languages English
T: +45 9715 3611
W: www.ikast-gym.dk

International School of Billund

Skolevej 24, 7190 Billund, Syddanmark
MYP Coordinator Tue Rabenhoej
PYP Coordinator Karen Serritslev
Languages English
T: +45 2632 7800
W: www.isbillund.com

International School of Hellerup

Rygårds Allé 131, 2900 Hellerup, Hovedstaden
DP Coordinator Antony Nesling
MYP Coordinator Abenaa Uttenthal
PYP Coordinator Joanna Christoffersen
Languages English
T: +45 7020 6368
W: www.ish.dk

Kolding Gymnasium, HF-Kursus

Skovvangen 10, 6000 Kolding, Syddanmark
DP Coordinator Mel Malone
Languages English
T: +45 7633 9600
W: www.kolding-gym.dk

Nörre Gymnasium

Mörkhöjvej 78, 2700 Bronshoj, Hovedstaden
DP Coordinator Jutta Rüdiger
Languages English
T: +45 4494 2722
W: www.norreg.dk

North Zealand International School

Christianshusvej 16, 2970 Hørsholm, Hovedstaden
DP Coordinator Karen Boettger
Languages English
T: +45 4557 2616
W: ngg.dk/international

Nyborg Gymnasium

Skolebakken 13, 5800 Nyborg, Syddanmark
DP Coordinator Ulrik Nørum
Languages English
T: +45 6531 0217

Denmark

Stenhus Gymnasium

Stenhusvej 20, 4300 Holbæk, Sjaelland
DP Coordinator Paul Bjergfelt
Languages English
T: +45 5943 6465
W: www.stenhus-gym.dk

Struer Statsgymnasium

Jyllandsgade 2, 7600 Struer, Midtjylland
DP Coordinator Morten Rødgaard Jensen
Languages English
T: +45 9785 4300
W: www.struer-gym.dk

Tietgen Handelsgymnasium

Elmelundsvej 10, 5200 Odense, Syddanmark
DP Coordinator Ruth Schaeffer
Languages English
T: +45 6545 2200
W: www.tietgen.dk

Viborg Katedralskole

Gl Skivevej 2, 8800 Viborg, Midtjylland
DP Coordinator Mads Henriksen
Languages English
T: +45 8662 0655
W: www.viborgkatedralskole.dk

EGYPT

AIA School

Plots 2 & 3 Section 1, Abis, Alexandria
DP Coordinator Christopher Thomas
Languages English, Arabic
T: +20 12 8621 5550
W: aia-alex.com

Al Rowad International School (IBCA)

Ring Road, Abis, Alexandria
DP Coordinator Karim Abo El-Ela
MYP Coordinator Karim Abo El-Ela
PYP Coordinator Mayssa Alam
Languages English
T: +20 3 955 6000
W: www.ibcaschool.com

American International School in Egypt – West Campus

Sheikh Zayed City, Entrance 2, Greens Compound, Giza 12588
DP Coordinator Hani Ramzy
Languages English
T: +20 2 3854 0600
W: www.aiswest.com

American International School in Egypt, Main Campus

PO Box 8090, Masaken, Nasr City, Cairo 11371
DP Coordinator Malak Issa
Languages English
T: +20 2 2618 8400
W: www.aisegypt.com

Bedayia International School

1st Urban Distrcit, El Banafseg Zone, New Cairo City, Cairo 11865
DP Coordinator Rania Aly
Languages English
W: www.bedayia.com

Cairo American College

PO Box 39, Maadi, Cairo 11431
DP Coordinator Niall Williams
Languages English
T: +20 2 2755 5555
W: www.cacegypt.org

Cairo English School

PO Box 8020, Masaken, Nasr City, Cairo 11371
DP Coordinator Heba Serry
Languages English
T: +20 22 249 0200
W: www.cesegypt.com

Deutsche Schule Beverly Hills Kairo

Beverly Hills, 16th District, Beverly Hills Rd, Giza, Cairo
DP Coordinator Shahira Yehia
Languages English
T: +20 38578070
W: www.bhs-egypt.com

Deutsche Schule Hurghada

Post Box 99, Hurghada, Red Sea
DP Coordinator Eckart Streb
Languages English
T: +20 100 4612747
W: deutsche-schule-hurghada.de

Dr Nermien Ismail Language School NIS

Tagamoa El-Awaal, End of Zakor Hussein, Cairo
DP Coordinator Soha Salem
Languages English
T: +20 114 5599992
W: www.nis-egypt.com

ECOLE OASIS INTERNATIONALE

Zahraa El Maadi, Quarter no 3 and no 7 Part A & B, Cairo
CP Coordinator Fatma Hussein
DP Coordinator Fatma Hussein
MYP Coordinator Mr. Omar El Sarky
PYP Coordinator Mrs. Imane Radwan
Languages French
T: +20 2 2516 2608
E: admission@oasisdemaadi.com; oasis.edu@oasisdemaadi.com
W: www.oasisdemaadi.com

See full details on page 84

Egyptian International School

13 district, Zayed, Giza
DP Coordinator Abd El Raouf Mohamed
MYP Coordinator Eman Hussein
PYP Coordinator Hala Seif
Languages English
T: +20 1128695389
W: www.eis-zayed.com

Elite International School

Behind El-Nozha airport, Abesten ring road, Alexandria
MYP Coordinator Alain Rodrigue
PYP Coordinator Alia Mostafa
Languages English, Arabic
T: +20 109 330 7078
W: www.onlineelite.net

Evolution International School

New Giza Campus, Km 22, Cairo/Alex desert Road, 6th October City, Giza 12588
DP Coordinator Farah Seif
Languages English
T: +20 1 0036 66223
W: www.eisng.lvng.net

GEMS Academy Alexandria

Kilo 13 Alexandria-Cairo Agricultural Road, Alexandria
PYP Coordinator Nadine Mouhasseb
Languages English, French
T: +2 03 5190 800
W: www.gaa.edu.eg

GLOBAL PARADIGM INTERNATIONAL SCHOOL

First Settlement, Block K1, Sector 8, New Cairo City, Cairo 16834
DP Coordinator Omnia Mostafa
Languages English
T: +20 222 461 809/10/12
E: info@gpschool-eg.com
W: www.gpschool-eg.com

See full details on page 94

Green Land – Pré Vert International Schools – GPIS-Egypt

405, Geziret Mohamed Road, Giza
DP Coordinator Mona Khalil
MYP Coordinator May Waly
PYP Coordinator Francoise Bencteux
Languages French, English, Arabic
T: +20 2 01002226053/50/54
W: gpis-egypt.org

HAYAH INTERNATIONAL ACADEMY

South of Police Academy, 5th District, New Cairo
DP Coordinator Omneya Hamdy
PYP Coordinator Shymaa El Kotb
Languages English
T: +202 25373000/3333
E: admission@hayahacademy.com
W: www.hayahacademy.com

See full details on page 101

International New Future School (Neue Deutsche Schule Alexandria)

El Prince Street, off Moustafa Kamel Street, Mandara Kebly, Alexandria
DP Coordinator Fatma Soliman
Languages English
T: +203 958 64 81
W: www.future-schools.com/DSA/English/index.aspx

International School of Elite Education

Road 90- Behind El Masraweya Compound, Cairo 11835
DP Coordinator Shaimaa AbdelHafez
Languages English
T: :+20 111 114 3225
W: www.eliteeducation-eg.com

Leaders International College

21 El Narges Service Area, 5th Settlement, New Cairo City, Cairo
DP Coordinator Menna Shawky
MYP Coordinator Menna Shawky
PYP Coordinator Ola Hakeem
Languages English
T: +20 127 292 4777
W: www.leadersintcollege.com

MALVERN COLLEGE EGYPT

B2-B3 South Ring Road, Investment Zone Kattameya, Cairo
DP Coordinator Joseph Ford
Languages English
T: +202 26144400
E: info@malverncollege.edu.eg
W: malverncollege.edu.eg

See full details on page 159

MANARET HELIOPOLIS INTERNATIONAL SCHOOL

Hazem Salah Street, Ext. Mostafa El Nahas, Nasr City, Cairo 11351
MYP Coordinator Sherwet Adel
PYP Coordinator Radwa Mohamed
Languages English
T: +20 224 71 33 32
E: info@mhischool.net
W: www.mhischool.net

See full details on page 160

Modern English School Cairo

South of Police Academy, PO Box 5, New Cairo City, Cairo 11835
DP Coordinator Brendan Rainford
Languages English
T: +202 2618 9600
W: www.mescairo.com

Narmer American College

20 El-Narguis Service Area, New Cairo City, Cairo 11477
DP Coordinator Salma Omar
Languages English
T: +202 29201200
W: www.nacegypt.com

Nefertari International School

Km 22 Cairo-Ismailia Desert Road, Nefertari Street, Cairo 11341
DP Coordinator Rania Allam
Languages English, Arabic
T: +20 1026604040
W: www.niscl.com

New Cairo British International School

Road 17, 1st Zone, 3rd Settlement, 5th District, New Cairo City, Cairo
DP Coordinator Susie Belal
PYP Coordinator Christina Seeley
Languages English
T: +20 2 2565 7115
W: www.ncbis.co.uk

New Vision International Schools

S1-14 Beverly Hills, Sheikh Zayed, Giza 12588
DP Coordinator Soha Nabil
MYP Coordinator Randa Gamal
PYP Coordinator Marwa Yassine
Languages Arabic, English
T: 0020 120 4265778
W: nviseg.com

Nile International College

New Cairo, Fifth Settlement, 5th District, (S5-1), Beside Qeba Mosque, Cairo 1121
MYP Coordinator Walaa Taha
PYP Coordinator Shaimaa Golshany
Languages English
T: +20 2 010 6883 6751
W: www.nic-edu.net

Notion International School

Metwaly el Sharawy street (Lebeny), Maryotyah, Giza
DP Coordinator Azza Fekry
MYP Coordinator Mariam Essam
PYP Coordinator Sofia Dourasse
Languages English
T: +20 1120004926
W: www.notion-edu.com

Princeton International School

New Cairo City, Cairo
DP Coordinator Iman Mounir
Languages English, French
T: +20 12 1221 1025

Rahn Schulen Kairo

Extension of Hassan Ma'moun Str., Zaher Buildings, Nasr City, Cairo 11371
DP Coordinator Marwa Afifi
Languages German
T: +20 10 27933321
W: www.rahn-schulen-kairo.org

The British International School, Cairo

PO Box 137, Gezira, Cairo
DP Coordinator Edward Baxter
Languages English
T: +202 3827 0444
W: www.bisc.edu.eg

The Egyptian International School in El Marag

Mogawra 2, Bloc G, Elmarag City, Maadi, Cairo 11435
DP Coordinator Ahmed Elwan
MYP Coordinator Ahmed Hossien
PYP Coordinator Maha Awaad
Languages English
T: +20 229700217
W: m-eis.com

Asmara International Community School (AICS)

Asmara
DP Coordinator Pheven Kahasay
Languages English
T: +291 1 161705
W: www.aicseritrea.com

Audentes School

Tondi str 84, 11316 Tallinn, Harju
DP Coordinator Anneliis Kõiv
Languages English
T: +372 699 6591
W: www.audentes.ee

International School of Estonia

Juhkentali 18, 10132 Tallinn, Harju
DP Coordinator Ashley Wallace
MYP Coordinator Kadri Tomson
PYP Coordinator Terje Äkke
Languages English
T: +372 666 4380
W: www.ise.edu.ee

International School of Tallinn

Keevise 2, 11415 Tallinn, Harju
MYP Coordinator Meena Gaikwad
PYP Coordinator Lisa Parker
Languages English, Estonian
T: +372 5066 080
W: ist.ee

Miina Härma Gümnaasium

Tõnissoni 3, 50409 Tartu
DP Coordinator Kirstin Karis
MYP Coordinator Sille Eero
PYP Coordinator Triinu Pihus
Languages English, Estonian
T: +372 736 1920
W: www.mhg.tartu.ee

Tallinn English College

10 Estonia Avenue, 10148 Tallinn, Harju
DP Coordinator Klemen Slabina
MYP Coordinator Luise Türkson
PYP Coordinator Marja Popov
Languages English
T: +372 6 46 13 06
W: www.tik.edu.ee

Tartu International School

J. Liivi 2d, 50409 Tartu
PYP Coordinator Maris Vohla
Languages English
T: +372 742 4241
W: www.istartu.ee

WATERFORD KAMHLABA UWC OF SOUTHERN AFRICA

Waterford Park, Mbabane H100
DP Coordinator Elizabeth Cummergen
Languages English
T: +268 24220867
E: principal@waterford.sz
W: www.waterford.sz

See full details on page 242

German Embassy School Addis Ababa

PO Box 1372, Addis Abeba
DP Coordinator Heba Hassan
Languages English
T: +251 11 553 4465
W: www.ds-addis.de

International Community School of Addis Ababa

Mauritania Road, Old Airport, Addis Ababa
DP Coordinator Deanna Milne
PYP Coordinator Kacey Molloy
Languages English
T: +251 11 317 1544
W: www.icsaddis.edu.et

Sandford International School

PO Box 30056 MA, Addis Ababa
DP Coordinator Colin Beet
Languages English
T: +251 111 233726
W: www.sandfordschool.org

Espoo International School

PL 3222, 02070 Espoo, Uusimaa
MYP Coordinator Darrell Germo
Languages English
T: +358 50 343 2460
W: www.espoo.fi/espoointernationalschool

Etelä-Tapiolan lukio

PL 3234, 02070 Espoo, Uusimaa
DP Coordinator David Crawford
Languages English
T: +358 9 816 39101
W: www.etela-tapiola.fi

Helsingin Suomalainen Yhteiskoulu

Isonnevantie 8, 00320 Helsinki, Uusimaa
DP Coordinator Minna Ankkuri
Languages English
T: +358 9 4774 1814
W: www.syk.fi

Imatran Yhteislukio upper-secondary school

Koulukatu 5, 55120 Imatra, South Karelia
DP Coordinator Marketta Kolehmainen
Languages English
T: +358 5 6815 820
W: www.imatranyhteislukio.fi

FINLAND

International School of Helsinki
Selkämerenkatu 11, 00180 Helsinki, Uusimaa
DP Coordinator Mark Kilmer
MYP Coordinator Minna Tammivuori-Piraux
PYP Coordinator Ben Bacon
Languages English
T: +358 9 686 6160
W: www.ishelsinki.fi

Joensuun Lyseon Lukio
Koskikatu 8, 80100 Joensuu, North Karelia
DP Coordinator Adam Lerch
Languages English
T: +358 13 267 7111
W: www.lyseo.jns.fi

Jyväskylän Lyseon Lukio
Yliopistonkatu 13, 40100 Jyväskylä, Central Finland
DP Coordinator Susanna Soininen
Languages English
T: +358 403414690

Kannaksen lukio
Kannaksenkatu 20, 15140 Lahti, Päijänne Tavastia
DP Coordinator Sami Sorvali
Languages English
T: +358 3 8144220
W: www.kannaksenlukio.fi

Kuopion Lyseon Lukio
Puijonkatu 18, 70110 Kuopio, North Savo
DP Coordinator Suvi Tirkkonen
Languages English
T: +358 17 184 563
W: www.koulut.kuopio.fi/lyseo/

Lyseonpuiston Lukio
IB section, Ruokasenkatu 18, 96100 Rovaniemi, Lapland
DP Coordinator Timo Lakkala
Languages English
T: +358 16 322 2540
W: www.lyska.net

Mattlidens Gymnasium
PB 3340, 02070 Esbo, Uusimaa
DP Coordinator Anna Martikainen
Languages English
T: +358 9 816 43050
W: www.mattliden.fi/gym

Oulu International School
Kasarmintie 4, 90130 Oulu, North Ostrobothnia
MYP Coordinator Marja Peedo
PYP Coordinator Heidi Tuomela
Languages English
T: +358 50 371 6977
W: ouka.fi/oulu/oulu-international-school/etusivu

Oulun Lyseon Lukio
Kajaaninkatu 3, 90100 Oulu, North Ostrobothnia
DP Coordinator Heli-Maarit Miihkinen
Languages English
T: +358 44 703 9451
W: www.lyseo.edu.ouka.fi

Oulun seudun ammattiopisto
Kiviharjuntie 6, 90220 Oulu, North Ostrobothnia
CP Coordinator Eeva Vehmas
Languages English, Finnish
W: www.osao.fi

Ressu Comprehensive School
PO BOX 3107, Kaupunki, 00099 Helsinki, Uusimaa
MYP Coordinator Petra Grönros
PYP Coordinator Anna Hart
Languages English, Finnish
T: +358 9 310 82102
W: www.ressuy.edu.hel.fi

Ressun Lukio
PO Box 3809, 00099 Helsinki, Uusimaa
DP Coordinator Karoliina Puumalainen
Languages English
T: +358 9 604 849
W: www.ressunlukio.fi

Tampereen Lyseon lukio
F E Sillanpään Katu 7, 33230 Tampere, Pirkanmaa
DP Coordinator Tuija Laurila
Languages English
T: +358 40 801 6717
W: lukiot.tampere.fi/lyseo

Tikkurilan Lukio
Valkoisenlahteentie 53, 01370 Vantaa, Uusimaa
DP Coordinator Maarit Berg
Languages English
T: +358 9 8392 5119
W: www.edu.vantaa.fi/tilu

Turun Normaalikoulu
Annikanpolku 9, 20610 Turku, Southwest Finland
DP Coordinator Marianna Vanhatalo
Languages English
T: +358 (0)29 450 1000
W: sites.utu.fi/tnk

Vasa Ovningsskola
Kirkkopuistikko 11-13, 65100 Vaasa, Ostrobothnia
DP Coordinator Henrik Lindgren
Languages English
T: +358 (0)6 324 7115
W: oldwww.abo.fi/vos/

AMERICAN SCHOOL OF PARIS
41 rue Pasteur, 92210 Saint-Cloud
DP Coordinator Alyssa Pierce
Languages English
T: +33 01 41 12 86 55
E: admissions@asparis.fr
W: www.asparis.org
See full details on page 56

Apex2100 Academy
Le Rosset, 73320 Tignes
CP Coordinator Jo Crowther
DP Coordinator Jo Crowther
Languages English, French
W: apex2100.org

Collège-Lycée Saint François-Xavier
3 rue Thiers, 56000 Vannes
DP Coordinator Chantal Thomas
Languages English, French
T: +33 (0)2 97 47 12 80
W: www.saint-francois-xavier.com

ECOLE DES ROCHES
295 avenue Edmond Demolins, 27130 Verneuil d'Avre et d'Iton
DP Coordinator Ivor Gemmell
Languages English, French
T: +33 (0) 232 6040 00
E: ecoledesroches@ecoledesroches.com
W: www.ecoledesroches.com
See full details on page 82

ÉCOLE JEANNINE MANUEL – LILLE
418 bis rue Albert Bailly, Marcq-en-Baroeul 59700
DP Coordinator Nicola French
Languages French, English
T: +33 3 20 65 90 50
E: admissions-lille@ejm.net
W: www.ecolejeanninemanuel.org
See full details on page 80

ÉCOLE JEANNINE MANUEL – PARIS
70 rue du Théâtre, Paris 75015
DP Coordinator Sabine Hurley
Languages English, French
T: +33 1 44 37 00 80
E: admissions@ejm.net
W: www.ecolejeanninemanuel.org
See full details on page 81

Ecole Privée Bilingue Internationale
Domaine de massane, 34670 Baillargues
DP Coordinator Alexandra David
MYP Coordinator Alexandra David
Languages English, French
T: +33 4677 07844
W: www.lycee-prive-international-montpellier.fr

ERMITAGE INTERNATIONAL SCHOOL
46 Avenue Eglé, 78600 Maisons-Laffitte
DP Coordinator Wayne Hodgkinson
MYP Coordinator Christine Collie
Languages English, French
T: +33 139 62 81 75
E: admissions@ermitage.fr
W: www.ermitage.fr
See full details on page 86

Hattemer
52 rue de Londres, 75008 Paris
DP Coordinator Mrs Deborah Garelik
Languages English, French
T: +33 1 43 87 59 14
W: www.hattemer.fr

ICS CÔTE D'AZUR
245 Route les Lucioles, 06560 Valbonne
PYP Coordinator Mrs Janet Goswell
Languages English, French
T: +33 (0)4 93 64 32 84
E: admissions@icscotedazur.com
W: www.icscotedazur.com
See full details on page 108

ICS PARIS
23 rue de Cronstadt, 75015 Paris
DP Coordinator Mr. Subhash Bhatia
Languages English, French
T: +33 (0)1 56 56 60 70
E: admissions@icsparis.fr
W: www.icsparis.fr
See full details on page 110

INTERNATIONAL BILINGUAL SCHOOL OF PROVENCE
500 Route de Bouc-Bel-Air, Domaine des Pins, Luynes, Aix en Provence 13080
DP Coordinator Pablo Besozzi
Languages English, French
T: +33 (0)4 4224 0340
E: info@ibsofprovence.com
W: www.ibsofprovence.com
See full details on page 116

258

International School of Lyon

80 Chemin du Grand Roule, 69110 Sainte Foy Lès Lyon
DP Coordinator Mark Ingrey
PYP Coordinator Alison Pattinson
Languages English
T: +33 (0) 478 866 190
W: www.islyon.org

INTERNATIONAL SCHOOL OF NICE

15 Avenue Claude Debussy, 06200 Nice
DP Coordinator Mr Dominique Dubois
PYP Coordinator Ms Melissa Demiguel
Languages English
T: +33 (0)4 93 21 04 00
E: admissions@isn-nice.com
W: www.isn-nice.com

See full details on page 131

International School of Paris

6 rue Beethoven, 75016 Paris
DP Coordinator Philip Anderson
MYP Coordinator Lucy Whitfield
PYP Coordinator Jenna Brooks
Languages English
T: +33 1 42 24 09 54
W: www.isparis.edu

International School of Toulouse

2 Allee De L'Herbaudiere, Route de Pibrac, 31770 Colomiers
DP Coordinator Gareth Hunt
PYP Coordinator Laura Maxwell
Languages English
T: +33 5 62 74 26 74
W: www.intst.eu

Le Gymnase Jean Sturm/ Lucie Berger

8 place des Etudiants, Alsace, 67000 Strasbourg
DP Coordinator Sindy Leveel
PYP Coordinator Johanna Dellantonio
Languages English
T: +33 3 88 15 77 10
W: www.jsturm.fr

Montessori International Bordeaux

47 Avenue de la Poterie, 33170 Gradignan
PYP Coordinator Rachael Bell
Languages English, French
T: +33 6 51 27 98 19
W: international-school33.fr

Notre Dame International High School

106, Grande-Rue, 78480 Verneuil-sur-Seine
DP Coordinator Emilie Champeix
Languages English, French
T: +33 9 70 40 79 22
W: www.ndihs.com

Ombrosa, Lycée Multilingue de Lyon

95 Quai Clemenceau, 69300 Caluire
DP Coordinator Sylvie Henderson
Languages English, French
T: +33 4 78 23 22 63
W: www.ombrosa.com

SAINTE VICTOIRE INTERNATIONAL SCHOOL

Domaine de Château l'Arc, Chemin de Maurel, 13710 Fuveau
DP Coordinator Brad Edwards
Languages English, French
T: +33 4 42 26 51 96
E: contact@schoolsaintevictoire.com
W: www.schoolsaintevictoire.com

See full details on page 188

Sem' de Walbourg

60 Grand Rue, 67360 Walbourg
DP Coordinator Noémie Celton
Languages English, French
W: www.sem-walbourg.eu

LYCÉE FRANCO-BRITANNIQUE ECOLE INTERNATIONALE

Batterie IV, B.P. 159, Libreville
DP Coordinator Nathaniel Akue Mackaya
MYP Coordinator Nathaniel Akue Mackaya
PYP Coordinator Nathaniel Akue Mackaya
Languages French, English
T: +241 01 17 37 117
E: ecolefrancobritannique@yahoo.fr
W: efblbv.org/ecole-franco-britannique-lbv.php

See full details on page 156

THE INTERNATIONAL SCHOOL OF GABON RUBAN VERT

Batterie IV, Libreville, Gabon 2144
DP Coordinator Richard Welford
PYP Coordinator Eunah Njoroge
Languages English, French
T: +241 11 44 26 70
E: admissions@ecolerubanvert.com
W: www.ecolerubanvert.com

See full details on page 230

European School

#2 I. Skhirtladze Str., Tbilisi 0177
DP Coordinator Ramaz Sartania
MYP Coordinator Oxana Akimova
PYP Coordinator Tinatini Gugushvili
Languages English
T: +995 32 239 59 64
W: europeanschool.ge/en/

New School, International School of Georgia

35 Tskneti Highway, 0179 Bagebi, Tbilisi
DP Coordinator Kety Tsurtsumia
MYP Coordinator Tamuna Dzidziguri
PYP Coordinator Deduna Iashsaghashvili
Languages English, Georgian
T: +995 32 223 1728
W: www.newschoolgeorgia.com

Newton Free School

Nutsubidze Plato I Micro-District, Bedia Street, Tbilisi 0183
DP Coordinator Tamari Berulava
Languages English
T: +995 570 705080
W: www.newton.edu.ge

ACCADIS INTERNATIONAL SCHOOL BAD HOMBURG

SÜDCAMPUS Bad Homburg, Am Weidenring 52-54, 61352 Bad Homburg, Hesse
DP Coordinator Mr Lucio Pessia
Languages English, German
T: +49 61 72 984 141
E: info@accadis-isb.com
W: www.accadis-isb.com

See full details on page 45

Aloisiuskolleg

Elisabethstraße 18, 53177 Bonn, North Rhine-Westphalia
DP Coordinator Uta Schäpers
Languages English, German
T: +49 228 82003 (101)
W: www.aloisiuskolleg.de

BAVARIAN INTERNATIONAL SCHOOL GAG (BIS) – CITY CAMPUS

Leopoldstrasse 208, 80804 Munich, Bavaria
PYP Coordinator Nicola Moloney
Languages English
T: +49 89 89655 203
W: www.bis-school.com

See full details on page 61

BAVARIAN INTERNATIONAL SCHOOL GAG (BIS) – HAIMHAUSEN CAMPUS

Hauptstrasse 1, 85778 Haimhausen, Bavaria
CP Coordinator Rob Clements
DP Coordinator Loay Malek
MYP Coordinator Dr. Erin Foley
PYP Coordinator Nicola Moloney & Annette Austin
Languages English
T: +49 (0)81 33 917 203
E: admissions@bis-school.com
W: www.bis-school.com

See full details on page 61

Berlin Brandenburg International School

Schopfheimer Allee 10, 14532 Kleinmachnow, Brandenburg
CP Coordinator Jane Barker
DP Coordinator Jane Barker
MYP Coordinator Daniel Stiles
PYP Coordinator Lisa Roy
Languages English
T: +49 33 203 8036 0
W: www.bbis.de

Berlin British School

Dickensweg 17-19, 14055 Berlin
DP Coordinator Gemma Ritchie
PYP Coordinator Joanne Wolff
Languages English
T: +49 (0)30 35109 180
W: www.berlinbritishschool.de

Berlin Cosmopolitan School

Rückerstrasse 9, 10119 Berlin
DP Coordinator Fatima Camara
PYP Coordinator Orlando Pola-Rivera
Languages English
T: +49 30 688 33 23 0
W: www.cosmopolitanschool.de

Berlin International School

Lentzeallee 8/14, 14195 Berlin
DP Coordinator Emma Jean Moffatt
PYP Coordinator Angeline Aow
Languages English
T: +49 (0) 30 8200 7790
W: www.berlin-international-school.de

Berlin Metropolitan School

Linienstrasse 122, 10115 Berlin
DP Coordinator Dorian Rosso
PYP Coordinator Justine Otte
Languages English, German
T: +49 30 8872 7390
W: www.metropolitanschool.com

Bertolt-Brecht-Gymnasium Dresden

Lortzingstrasse 01, 01307 Dresden, Saxony
DP Coordinator Laura Protextor
Languages English
T: +49 351 449040
W: www.bebe-dresden.de

Berufskolleg am Wasserturm

Herzogstrasse 4, Northrhine Westphalia, 46399 Bocholt, North Rhine-Westphalia
DP Coordinator Ellen Baumann
Languages English
T: +49 2871 2724300
W: www.bkamwasserturm.de

Bonn International School e.V.

Martin-Luther-King Strasse 14, 53175 Bonn, North Rhine-Westphalia
DP Coordinator Peter Owen
MYP Coordinator Cijith Jacob
PYP Coordinator Casey Ranson
Languages English
T: +49 228 30854 0
W: www.bonn-is.de

Dresden International School e.V

Annenstrasse 9, 01067 Dresden, Saxony
DP Coordinator Wendy Bassam-Coles
MYP Coordinator Flora Mather
PYP Coordinator Kimberly Aguirre
Languages English
T: +49 351 440070
W: www.dresden-is.de

Evangelisch Stiftisches Gymnasium Gütersloh

Feldstrasse 13, 33330 Gütersloh, North Rhine-Westphalia
DP Coordinator Marcus Kühle
Languages English
T: +49 5241 98050
W: www.esg-guetersloh.de

FELIX-KLEIN-GYMNASIUM

Böttingerstrasse 17, 37073 Göttingen, Lower Saxony
DP Coordinator Silke Neumann
Languages English
T: +49 551 400 2909
E: fkgis@goettingen.de
W: www.fkg-goettingen.de
See full details on page 90

Franconian International School

Marie-Curie-Strasse 2, 91052 Erlangen, Bavaria
DP Coordinator Ruth Greener
MYP Coordinator Matt Chambers
Languages English
T: +49 9131 940390
W: www.the-fis.de

Frankfurt International School

An der Waldlust 15, 61440 Oberursel, Hesse
CP Coordinator Ashley van der Meer
DP Coordinator Ashley van der Meer
PYP Coordinator Gioia Morasch
Languages English
T: +49 6171 2024 0
W: www.fis.edu

Frankfurt International School (Wiesbaden Campus)

Rudolf-Dietz-Strasse 14, Naurod, 65207 Wiesbaden, Hesse
PYP Coordinator Gioia Morasch
Languages English, German
T: +49 6127 99400
W: www.fis.edu

Friedrich-Ebert-Gymnasium

Ollenhauerstrasse 5, 53113 Bonn, North Rhine-Westphalia
DP Coordinator Gabriele Josten
Languages English
T: +49 228 777520
W: www.feg-bonn.de

Friedrich-Schiller-Gymnasium Marbach

Schulstrasse 34, 71672 Marbach am Neckar, Baden-Württemberg
DP Coordinator Andrea Saffert
Languages English, German
T: +49 7144 8458-0
W: www.fsg-marbach.de

Goethe-Gymnasium

Friedrich-Ebert-Anlage 22-24, 60325 Frankfurt, Hesse
DP Coordinator Hans-Dieter Bunger
Languages English
T: +49 69 2123 3525
W: www.gg-ffm.de

Goetheschule Essen

Ruschenstrasse 1, 45133 Essen, North Rhine-Westphalia
DP Coordinator Michael Franke
Languages English
T: +49 20 1 841170
W: www.goetheschule-essen.de

Gymnasium Birkenfeld

Brechkaul 12, 55765 Birkenfeld, Rhineland-Palatinate
DP Coordinator Dagmar Orlian
Languages English, German
T: +49 (0)6782 99940
W: www.gymnasium-birkenfeld-nahe.de

Gymnasium im Stift Neuzelle

Stiftsplatz 7, 15898 Neuzelle, Brandenburg
DP Coordinator Martin Jacob
Languages English, German
T: +49 341 3939 2810
W: rahn.education/en/freies-gymnasium-im-stift-neuzelle-.html

Gymnasium Paulinum

Am Stadtgraben 30, 48143 Münster, North Rhine-Westphalia
DP Coordinator Kirsten Brinkmann
Languages English
T: +49 251 510500-0
W: www.muenster.org/paulinum

Gymnasium Schloss Neuhaus

Im Schlosspark, 33104 Paderborn, North Rhine-Westphalia
DP Coordinator Denise Krämer
Languages English
T: +49 5254 992200
W: www.gymnasium-schloss-neuhaus.de

Hansa-Gymnasium, Hamburg-Bergedorf

Hermann-Distel-Strasse 25, 21029 Hamburg
DP Coordinator Vivien Dudek
Languages English
T: +49 (0)40 724 18 60
W: www.hansa-gymnasium.de

Heidelberg International School

Wieblinger Weg 7, 68782 Heidelberg, Baden-Württemberg
DP Coordinator Kevin Whitmore
MYP Coordinator Sarah Al-Benna
PYP Coordinator Erica Mingay
Languages English
T: +49 6221 75 90 600
W: www.hischool.de

Heidelberg Private School Centre (Heidelberger Privatschulcentrum)

Kurfürsten-Anlage 64-68, 69115 Heidelberg, Baden-Württemberg
DP Coordinator Constantin Metzger
PYP Coordinator Verena May
Languages English
T: +49 62 2170504 038
W: www.hpc-schulen.de

Helene-Lange-Gymnasium

Bogenstr 32, 20144 Hamburg
DP Coordinator Maike Fruehling
Languages English
T: +49 40 428 9810
W: www.hlg-hamburg.de

Helmholtz-Gymnasium Bonn

Helmholtzstr. 18, 53225 Bonn, North Rhine-Westphalia
DP Coordinator Brigitte Lauth
Languages English
T: +49 228 777250
W: www.helmholtz-bonn.de

Hermann-Böse-Gymnasium

Hermann-Böse-Straße 1-9, 28209 Bremen
DP Coordinator Till Stollmann
Languages English
T: +49 421 361 6272
W: www.hbg.schule.bremen.de

Hittorf-Gymnasium

Kemnastrasse 38, 45657 Recklinghausen, North Rhine-Westphalia
DP Coordinator Sandra Schmidt
Languages English, German
W: www.hittorf-gymnasium.de

IBSM – INTERNATIONAL BILINGUAL SCHOOL MUNICH GGMBH

Lerchenauerstrasse 197, 80935 Munich, Bavaria
PYP Coordinator Susanne Green
Languages English, German
T: +49 89 41 11 49 550
E: admission@ibsm-school.eu
W: www.ibsm-school.eu
See full details on page 107

INTERNATIONAL KIDS CAMPUS GMBH

Lerchenauerstrasse 197, 80935 Munich, Bavaria
PYP Coordinator Susanne Green
Languages English, German
T: +49 89 411149 550
E: info@theikc.com
W: www.theikc.com
See full details on page 117

International School Augsburg (ISA)

Wernher-von-Braun-Strasse 1a, 86368 Gersthofen, Bavaria
DP Coordinator Richard Tyler
PYP Coordinator Katharina Baumgartner
Languages English
T: +49 821 45 55 60 0
W: www.isa-augsburg.com

International School Braunschweig-Wolfsburg

Helmstedter Strasse 37, 38126 Braunschweig, Lower Saxony
DP Coordinator Nicholas Schulte
Languages English
T: +49 531 889210 0
W: www.cjd-braunschweig.de

International School Campus

Eggerstedter Weg 19, 25421 Pinneberg, Schleswig-Holstein
DP Coordinator Raquel Pena-Gutierrez
Languages English, German
T: +49 (0)41 01 80 503 00
W: www.isceducation.de

International School Hannover Region

Bruchmeisterallee 6, 30169 Hannover, Lower Saxony
DP Coordinator Naomi Resmer
MYP Coordinator Hanno Becker
PYP Coordinator Ashley Eames
Languages English
T: +49 511 270 416 50
W: www.is-hr.de

International School Mainfranken e.V.

Kalifornienstrasse 1, 97424 Schweinfurt, Bavaria
DP Coordinator Matthew Sullivan
PYP Coordinator Niko Lewman
Languages English
T: +49 9721 53861-80
W: www.the-ism.de

International School of Bremen

Badgasteiner Strasse 11, 28359 Bremen
DP Coordinator Aude Paulin
Languages English
T: +49 421 5157790
W: www.isbremen.de

International School of Düsseldorf e.V.

Niederrheinstrasse 336, 40489 Düsseldorf, North Rhine-Westphalia
DP Coordinator Clinton Olson
MYP Coordinator Laura Maly-Schmidt
PYP Coordinator Chris Coker
Languages English
T: +49 (0) 211-9406 6
W: www.isdedu.de

International School of Hamburg

Hemmingstedter Weg 130, 22609 Hamburg
CP Coordinator Michael Kent
DP Coordinator James Edward Dalton
MYP Coordinator Kathryn Freeburn
Languages English
T: +49 (0)40 8000 500
W: www.ishamburg.org

International School of Neustadt

Maximilianstrasse 43, 67433 Neustadt an der Weinstrasse, Rhineland-Pala+
DP Coordinator Jacques Marais
Languages English
T: +49 6321 8900 960
W: www.is-neustadt.de

International School of Stuttgart, Degerloch Campus

Sigmaringestrasse 257, 70597 Stuttgart, Baden-Württemberg
DP Coordinator Kristen Korczynski
MYP Coordinator Ellen Dutton
PYP Coordinator Nicola Ferger-Andrews
Languages English
T: +49 71 17696 000
W: www.issev.de

International School of Stuttgart, Sindelfingen Campus

Hallenserstrasse 2, 71065 Sindelfingen, Baden-Württemberg
MYP Coordinator Rebecca Jones-Buerk
Languages English
T: +49 70 316859 780
W: www.issev.de

International School of Ulm/Neu Ulm

Schwabenstraße 25, 89231 Neu-Ulm, Bavaria
DP Coordinator Richard Tomes
PYP Coordinator Charlotte Balsom
Languages English
T: +49 731 379 353-0
W: www.is-ulm.de

International School Ruhr

Moltkeplatz 1 + 61, 45138 Essen, North Rhine-Westphalia
DP Coordinator Joseph Ticar
PYP Coordinator Fiona Mayer
Languages English
T: +49 (0)201 479 104 09
W: www.is-ruhr.de

Internationale Friedensschule Koln

Neue Sandkaul 29, 50859 Cologne, North Rhine-Westphalia
DP Coordinator Edward Parker
PYP Coordinator Leonie Julien
Languages English, German
T: +49 221 310 6340
W: www.if-koeln.de

Internationales Gymnasium Geithain

Friedrich-Fröbel-Strasse 1, 04643 Geithain, Saxony
DP Coordinator Nabil Daaloul
Languages German
T: +49 34 34146 012
W: internationales-gymnasium-geithain.de

Internationales Gymnasium Reinsdorf

Mittlerer Schulweg 13, 08141 Reinsdorf, Saxony
DP Coordinator Heidi Schilling
Languages English, Spanish
T: +49 37 634082 300
W: www.saxony-international-school.de

ISF International School Frankfurt Rhein-Main

Strasse zur Internationalen Schule 33, 65931 Frankfurt, Hesse
DP Coordinator Dirk Lehmann
Languages English
T: +49 69 954319 710
W: www.isf.sabis.net

ISR International School on the Rhine – NRW

Konrad-Adenauer-Ring 2, 41464 Neuss, North Rhine-Westphalia
DP Coordinator Emil Cete
Languages English
T: +49 2131 40388-0, -11
W: www.isr-school.de

Leibniz Gymnasium Dortmund

Kreuzstrasse 163, 44137 Dortmund, North Rhine-Westphalia
DP Coordinator Martin Tiaden
Languages English
T: +49 231 912 3660
W: www.leibniz-gym.de

Leibniz Privatschule Elmshorn

Ramskamp 64B, 25337 Elmshorn, Schleswig-Holstein
DP Coordinator Dr. Stefan Wester
Languages English, German
T: +49 41 212610 40
W: www.leibniz-privatschule.de

Leipzig International School

Könneritzstrasse 47, 04229 Leipzig, Saxony
DP Coordinator Rebecca Hillyer
Languages English
T: +49 34 139377 500
W: www.lis.school

Leonardo Da Vinci Campus

Zu den Luchbergen 13, 14641 Nauen, Brandenburg
DP Coordinator Anne Pritzlaff
Languages English, Spanish
T: +49 33 217487 820
W: www.ldvc.de

Lessing-Gymnasium

Heerstr 7, 51143 Cologne, North Rhine-Westphalia
DP Coordinator Silke Flüßhöh
Languages English
T: +49 2203 99201 66
W: www.lessing-gymnasium.eu

Metropolitan International School (MIS Viernheim)

Walter-Gropius-Allee 3, 68519 Viernheim, Hesse
DP Coordinator Alastair Brandon
Languages English, German
T: +49 6204 7087 796
W: metroschool.de/en

Metropolitan School Frankfurt

Eschborner Landstrasse 134-142, 60489 Frankfurt, Hesse
DP Coordinator Katell Dodd
PYP Coordinator Natalie Murray
Languages English
T: +49 69 96 86 405-0
W: www.m-school.de

Munich International School e.V.

Schloss Buchhof, Percha, 82319 Starnberg, Bavaria
DP Coordinator Doris Herwig
MYP Coordinator Angela Brassington
PYP Coordinator Vicki Shaver
Languages English
T: +49 8151 366 0
W: www.mis-munich.de

Nelson Mandela State International School Berlin

Pfalzburgerstrasse 30, 10717 Berlin
DP Coordinator Charles Spiller
Languages English
T: +49 (0)30 902928 01
W: www.nelson-mandela-school.net

GERMANY

Nymphenburger Schulen

Sadelerstrasse 10, 80638 Munich, Bavaria
DP Coordinator Susanna Seibert
Languages English
T: +49 89 159 120
W: www.nymphenburger-schulen.de

Phorms Campus Munich

Maria-Theresia-Straße 35, 81675 Munich, Bavaria
DP Coordinator Marc Nevin
Languages English
T: +49 89 324 9337 00
W: www.muenchen.phorms.de

Sächsisches Landesgymnasium Sankt Afra zu Meissen

Freiheit 13, 01662 Meissen, Saxony
DP Coordinator Fabian Habsch
Languages German, English
T: +49 3521 456 0
W: www.sankt-afra.de

Schillerschule Hannover

Ebellstrasse 15, 30625 Hannover, Lower Saxony
DP Coordinator Bernd Flügge
Languages English
T: +49 511 16848777
W: www.schillerschule-hannover.de

Schule Schloss Salem

Schlossbezirk 1, 88682 Salem, Baden-Württemberg
DP Coordinator Constanze Schummer
Languages English, German
T: +49 7553 919 352
W: www.schule-schloss-salem.de

SIS Swiss International School Berlin

Heerstrasse 465, (school entrance at Reimerweg 11), 13593 Berlin
DP Coordinator Stephen Chae
Languages English
T: +49 30 36 43 98 20
W: www.swissinternationalschool.de/standorte/berlin

SIS Swiss International School Friedrichshafen

Fallenbrunnen 1, 88045 Friedrichshafen, Baden-Württemberg
DP Coordinator Marie Bertschinger
Languages English
T: +49 7541 954 37 0
W: www.swissinternationalschool.de/standorte/friedrichshafen

SIS Swiss International School Ingolstadt

Stinnesstrasse 1, 85057 Ingolstadt, Bavaria
DP Coordinator Juan Viacava
Languages English, German
T: +49 841 981 446 0
W: www.swissinternationalschool.de/standorte/ingolstadt

SIS Swiss International School Regensburg

Erzbischof-Buchberger-Allee 23, 93051 Regensburg, Bavaria
DP Coordinator Christine Scheid
Languages English, German
T: +49 941 9925 930 0
W: www.swissinternationalschool.de/standorte/regensburg

SIS Swiss International School Stuttgart-Fellbach

Schmidener Weg 7/1, 70736 Stuttgart-Fellbach, Baden-Württemberg
DP Coordinator Genea Pittman-Zupic
Languages English, German
T: +49 711 469 194 10
W: www.swissinternationalschool.de/standorte/stuttgart-fellbach

St Leonhard Gymnasium

Jesuitenstrasse 9, 52062 Aachen, North Rhine-Westphalia
DP Coordinator Sonja Rustemeyer
Languages English
T: +49 (0) 241 41 31 98 0
W: www.leoac.de

St. George's School Cologne

Husarenstrasse 20, 50997 Cologne, North Rhine-Westphalia
CP Coordinator Elizabeth Marshall
DP Coordinator Stephen Ryan
Languages English
T: +49 2233 808 870
W: www.stgeorgesschool.com

St. George's School Duisburg-Düsseldorf

Am Neuen Angerbach 90, 47259 Duisburg, North Rhine-Westphalia
CP Coordinator Eamonn Traynor
DP Coordinator Vincent Keat
Languages English
T: +49 203 456 860
W: www.stgeorgesschool.de/en/duisburg-dusseldorf

St. George's School Munich

Heidemannstrasse 182, 80939 Munich, Bavaria
CP Coordinator Matthew Jones
DP Coordinator Malcolm Fraser
Languages English, German
T: +49 89 72469 330
W: www.stgeorgesschool.com

Staedtisches Gymnasium Olpe

Seminarstrasse 1, 57462 Olpe, North Rhine-Westphalia
DP Coordinator Stephan Seidel
Languages English, German
T: +49 276196 500
W: www.gymnasium-olpe.de

State International School Seeheim-Jugenheim

Schuldorf Bergstrasse, Kooperative Gesamtschule, Sandstrasse, 64342 Seeheim-Jugenheim, Hesse
DP Coordinator Wolfgang Scheuerpflug
Languages English, German
T: +49 6257 9703 0
W: www.schuldorf.de

STIFTUNG LOUISENLUND

Louisenlund 9, 24357 Güby, Schleswig-Holstein
DP Coordinator Damien Vassallo
Languages English
T: +49 (0)4354 999 0
E: admission@louisenlund.de
W: www.louisenlund.de/en

See full details on page 219

See full details on page 219

Strothoff International School Rhein-Main Campus Dreieich

Frankfurterstrasse 160-166, 63303 Dreieich, Hesse
DP Coordinator Laura Hartel
MYP Coordinator Roser Amigó
PYP Coordinator Steve Snell
Languages English
T: +49 6103 8022 500
W: www.strothoff-international-school.de

Theodor-Heuss-Gymnasium

Freyastrasse 10, 67059 Ludwigshafen, Rhineland-Palatinate
DP Coordinator Martina Thiel
Languages English
T: +45 621 504 431 710
W: www.thg-lu.de

Thuringia International School – Weimar

Belvederer Allee 40, 99425 Weimar, Thuringia
DP Coordinator John Campbell
MYP Coordinator Aimee Tolentino
PYP Coordinator Alison Carl
Languages English
T: +49 (0)3643 776904
W: www.this-weimar.com

UWC Robert Bosch College

Kartäuserstrasse 119, 79104 Freiburg, Baden-Württemberg
DP Coordinator Carina Petruch
Languages English
T: +49 761 708 395 00
W: www.uwcrobertboschcollege.de

Werner-Heisenberg-Gymnasium

Werner-Heisenberg-Strasse 1, 51381 Leverkusen, North Rhine-Westphalia
DP Coordinator Beate Keil
Languages English
T: +49 2171 70670
W: www.whg-gp.de

GHANA

Al-Rayan International School

Boundry Road, East Legon, Accra
CP Coordinator Farah Abdul Wahab
DP Coordinator Dorinda Tham
MYP Coordinator David Oloo
PYP Coordinator Evon Mattouk
Languages English, French
T: +233 (0)541 897254
W: www.aris.edu.gh

Association International School

6 Patrice Lumumba Road, Airport Residential Area, Accra
DP Coordinator Stephen Owusu-Bempah
Languages English
T: +233 0302 777735
W: www.associationinternationalschool.org

Aves International Academy

VRA Road Community 25, Tema
DP Coordinator Julian Kitching
Languages English
T: +233 266 153097
W: www.avesacademy.com

Cornerstone International Academy

No.2. Harare Street, Off Mensah Wood Avenue, East Legon, Accra
PYP Coordinator William Gyamfi
Languages English, French
T: +233 265 055439
W: www.cia.edu.gh

Learning Skills International School

Adjiringanor, Near Buildaf Estates, Accra
PYP Coordinator Henrietta Love Commey
Languages English
T: +233 546 88 4146
W: lsis.edu.gh

Lincoln Community School
#126/21 Reindolf Road, Abelemkpe, Accra
DP Coordinator Michael Foxmann
MYP Coordinator Amber Rhinehart
PYP Coordinator Natalie Wilhelm
Languages English
T: +233 302 21 8100
W: www.lincoln.edu.gh

Morgan International Community School
PO Box SW 63, Gomoa-Manso, Swedru
DP Coordinator Anthony Abaidoo
Languages English
T: +233 205 560 199
W: www.mics.edu.gh

SOS-Hermann Gmeiner International College
Private Mail Bag, Community 6, Tema
DP Coordinator Ayeshat Addison
MYP Coordinator Jonathan Amengor
Languages English
T: +233 303 202907
W: www.soshgic.edu.gh

Tema International School
PO Box CO 864, Tema International Close, Tema
DP Coordinator Benjamin Darko
MYP Coordinator Yvonne Tagoe
PYP Coordinator Jacob Lumumba
Languages English
T: +233 24 9637 762; +233 30 3305134
W: www.tis.edu.gh

GREECE

AMERICAN COMMUNITY SCHOOLS OF ATHENS
129 Aghias Paraskevis Str., Halandri, 152 34 Athens
DP Coordinator Mark McGowan
Languages English
T: +30 210 639 3200
E: acs@acs.gr
W: www.acs.gr

See full details on page 52

Anatolia High School
PO Box 21021, 60 John Kennedy Avenue, 555 35 Pylea
DP Coordinator Anna Billi Petmeza
MYP Coordinator Elisavet Exidaveloni
Languages English (IBDP), Greek (MYP)
T: +30 2310 398 200
W: www.anatolia.edu.gr/highschool

Campion School Athens
PO Box 674 84, Pallini 153 02
DP Coordinator Kate Varey
Languages English
T: +30 210 607 1700
W: www.campion.edu.gr

Costeas-Geitonas School
Pallini – Attikis, Athens 15351
DP Coordinator Venia Papaspyrou
MYP Coordinator Jenny Matsota
PYP Coordinator Elpida Papa
Languages English
T: +30 210 6030 411
W: www.cgs.gr

Doukas School SA
151 Mesogion Street, 15125 Paradissos, Marousi, Athens 15125
DP Coordinator Nikolaos Sympouras
Languages English
T: +30 210 618 6000
W: www.doukas.gr

European Interactive School (DES)
Barakos Hill, Ribas 19400
PYP Coordinator Paraskevi Barmpoutsi
Languages English, Greek
T: +30 210 8974143
W: dimotiko.deschool.eu

Geitonas School
International Baccalaureate Diploma Programme, PO Box 74128, Sternizes, Koropi, Attiki 166 02
DP Coordinator Ilias Liakatas
Languages English
T: +30 210 9656200-10
W: www.geitonas-school.gr

HAEF, Athens College
15 Stephanou Delta Street, Psychico, Athens 154 52
MYP Coordinator Tania Gaitani
Languages English
T: +30 2106798100
W: www.athenscollege.edu.gr

HAEF, Psychico College
15 Stephanou Delta Street, Psychico, Athens 15452
DP Coordinator Antonios Apostolou
MYP Coordinator Panagiota Priovolou
Languages English
T: +30 2106798100
W: www.athenscollege.edu.gr

International School of Athens
PO Box 51051, Kifissia, Athens 14510
DP Coordinator Kalliope Pateras
MYP Coordinator Constantina Venieris
PYP Coordinator Athanasia Savvas
Languages English
T: +30 210 6233 888
W: www.isa.edu.gr

International School of Piraeus
66-70 Praxitelous street, Piraeus 18532
PYP Coordinator Antonia Daponti
Languages English
T: +30 210 417 5580
W: www.isp.edu.gr

Ionios School
PO Box 13622, Filothei 15202
DP Coordinator Stella Antonellou
Languages English
T: +30 210 6857130
W: www.ionios.gr

Lampiri Schools
Metamorphosis 155 and Ilissou, Moschato, Athens
DP Coordinator Neveen Zaki Shenouda
Languages English
T: +30 210 9480530
W: www.lampiri-schools.gr

Moraitis School
A Papanastasiou & Ag Dimitriou, Paleo Psychico, Athens 15452
DP Coordinator George Kartalis
Languages English
T: +30 210 679 5000
W: www.moraitis.edu.gr

PIERCE – THE AMERICAN COLLEGE OF GREECE
6 Gravias Street, Aghia Paraskevi, Athens 153 42
DP Coordinator Dr. Emmanuel Vrontakis
Languages English, Greek
T: +30 210 600 9800 (Ext:1060)
E: pierceibsecretariats@acg.edu
W: www.pierce.gr

See full details on page 173

Pinewood – American International School of Thessaloniki, Greece
14th km Thessalonikis – N. Moudanion, P.O. Box 60606, Thermi – Thessaloniki GR-57001
DP Coordinator Dimitrios Terzidis
Languages English
T: +30 2310 301 221
W: www.pinewood.gr

Platon School
Eleytheriou Venizelou Street, Glyka Nera, Attika 15354
DP Coordinator Miltiadis-Spyridon Kitsos
MYP Coordinator Maria Tsangari
PYP Coordinator Stelios Stilianidis
Languages English, German, Greek
T: +30 210 6611 793
W: www.platon.gr

St Catherine's British School
Leoforos Venizelou 77, Lykovrissi, Athens 141 23
DP Coordinator Anne Veronica Peters
Languages English
T: +30 210 2829 750
W: www.stcatherines.gr

HUNGARY

American International School of Budapest
Nagykovácsi út 12, Nagykovácsi 2094
DP Coordinator Raymond Lewis
Languages English
T: +36 26 556 000
W: www.aisb.hu

BME International Secondary School
Egry Jozsef utca 3-11, Budapest 1111
DP Coordinator Tibor Zahony .
Languages English
T: +36 12094983
W: www.bmegimnazium.hu

Budapest British International School
4 Zsolna utca, Budapest 1125
MYP Coordinator Martin Keon
Languages English
T: +36 70 425 5225
W: www.bbis.hu

International School of Budapest
Konkoly Thege M u 21, Budapest 1121
DP Coordinator Chadi Francois Nakhle
Languages English
T: +36 1 395 6543
W: www.isb.hu

Karinthy Frigyes Gimnázium
Thököly utca 7, Budapest 1183
DP Coordinator Attila Salamon
Languages English
T: +36 1 291 2072
W: www.karinthy.hu

HUNGARY

Korösi Csoma Sándor Két Tanítási Nyelvu Baptista Gimnázium

Szentendrei út 83, Budapest 1033
DP Coordinator Márta Korosi
Languages English
T: +36 1 250 17 44

SEK Budapest International School

Hüvösvölgyi út 131, Budapest 1021
DP Coordinator Emily LeBlanc
Languages English
T: +36 1 394 2968
W: budapest.iesedu.com

The British International School

Kiscelli Köz 17, Budapest 1037
DP Coordinator Ashley Phillipson
Languages English
T: +36 1 200 9971
W: www.bisb.hu

Tóth Árpád Gimnázium

Szombathi István utca 12., Debrecen 4024
DP Coordinator Ibolya Kovácsné Ilyés
Languages English
T: +36 52 411 225
W: www.tagdebr.sulinet.hu

ICELAND

Menntaskolinn vid Hamrahlid

Hamrahlí 10, Reykjavik 105
DP Coordinator Gu mundur Arnlaugsson
Languages English
T: +354 595 5200
W: www.mh.is

IRAN

German Embassy School Tehran (DBST)

Shariati, under the Sadr Bridge, Shahid Keshani St. (Mahale Darbdowom), Tehran
PYP Coordinator Mandana Rashidi
Languages English
T: +98 21 22 60 49 02
W: www.dbst.ir

Mehr-e-Taban International School

Ghasrodasht st, corner of Shahed st, Shiraz, Fars
DP Coordinator Fatima Farazinia
MYP Coordinator Fatima Farazinia
PYP Coordinator Fatima Farazinia
Languages English
T: +98 713 6359983
W: www.mehrschool.com

Shahid Mahdavi Educational Complex

Kouh-Daman, Mina, Zanbagh, Ejazi, Zafaranie St., Tehran 19888-7536
DP Coordinator Nasrin Barootchi
MYP Coordinator Hannaneh Hajiaghababa
PYP Coordinator Negar Nikkholgh
Languages English, Persian
T: +98 21 22435550 (EXT:190)
W: www.mahdavischool.org

Soodeh Educational Complex

End of Arabshahi Avenue, Ashrafi Isfahani Highway, Tehran 1461988511
MYP Coordinator Atefeh Khanjari
Languages English
T: +98 21 44 24 97 03
W: www.soodeh.com/?lang=en-US

Tehran International School

East Sarv Street, Kadj Sq Saadat Abad, Tehran 19816
DP Coordinator Nasrin Barootchi
Languages English
T: +98 21 2236 69757 / +98 21 2208 02401
W: www.tisschool.com

IRAQ

Da Vinci World School

Amed Street, Malta QR, Duhok, Kurdistan Region
DP Coordinator Zahra Khaled
MYP Coordinator Bassam Omar
PYP Coordinator Rewan Hussien
Languages English
T: +964 750 757 4333
W: www.leodv.com

Deutsche Schule Erbil

Postfach 67, Post Office Newroz, 100-Meter-Street, Erbil, Kurdistan
DP Coordinator Parthena Papadopoulou
Languages German
T: +964 770 3016 560
W: www.ds-e.org

Global United School

Iraq-Baghdad-Palestine Street, Residential Quarter 510-lane 16-building 20, Baghdad
PYP Coordinator Bassam Omar
Languages English
T: +964 782 714 9199
W: www.globalunitedschool.com

International College University School (ICUS) Baghdad

Zayouna, Baghdad
PYP Coordinator Dua Alqazaz
Languages English
T: +964 7828867431
W: icusbaghdad-ib.com

International Maarif Schools Erbil

P.O. Box No. 43/0383, Mardin District, 120m Street, Opposite to Toreq Village, Erbil
MYP Coordinator Thomas Hibbers
PYP Coordinator Inji shukur
Languages Arabic, English, Kurdish, Turkish
T: +964 (66) 264 49 17/18
W: maarifschools.edu.krd/

Mar Qardakh School

Mar Qardakh Street, P.O. Box 34, Erbil 1065
DP Coordinator Carolen Kossa
MYP Coordinator Madeleine Post
PYP Coordinator Yvette Salih
Languages English
T: +964 750 144 5031
W: www.marqardakh.com

IRELAND

International School of Dublin

Synge Street, Dublin D08 PW64
PYP Coordinator Nana Isa
Languages English, Spanish
T: +353 087 329 1417
W: www.internationalschooldublin.ie

NORD ANGLIA INTERNATIONAL SCHOOL DUBLIN

South County Business Park, Leopardstown, Dublin 18
DP Coordinator Joanna Cooper
MYP Coordinator Andrew Bateson
PYP Coordinator Jack Odey
Languages English
T: +353 1 5442323
E: admissions@naisdublin.com
W: www.naisdublin.com

See full details on page 168

SEK DUBLIN INTERNATIONAL SCHOOL

Belvedere Hall, Windgates, Greystones, Co. Wicklow A63 EY23
DP Coordinator Gareth Finn
MYP Coordinator Gareth Finn
Languages English
T: +35 31 287 41 75
E: admissions-dublin@sek.ie
W: sek.ie

See full details on page 192

ST ANDREW'S COLLEGE

Booterstown Avenue, Blackrock, County Dublin
DP Coordinator Julie Gillane
Languages English
T: +353 1 288 2785
E: information@st-andrews.ie
W: www.sac.ie

See full details on page 205

VILLIERS SCHOOL

North Circular Road, Limerick V94 F983
DP Coordinator Shane Hanna
Languages English
T: +353 61 451447
E: admissions@villiers-school.com
W: www.villiers-school.com

See full details on page 239

ISRAEL

Anglican International School Jerusalem

PO Box 191, 82 Rechov Haneviim, Jerusalem 91001
DP Coordinator Robin Press
MYP Coordinator Meira Yan
Languages English
T: +972 2 567 7200
W: www.aisj.co.il

Eastern Mediterranean International School

Hakfar Hayarok school, Ramat Hasharon 4870000
DP Coordinator Hannah Wenger
Languages English
T: +972 3 6730232
W: www.em-is.org

Givat Haviva International School

D.N. Menashe 37850
DP Coordinator Hannah Michelle
Languages English
T: +972542102636
W: www.gh-is.org

ITALY

Ambrit International School
Via F Tajani 50, 00149 Rome
MYP Coordinator Susan Kammerer
PYP Coordinator Kathryn Ramsay
Languages English
T: +39 06 5595 305/301
W: www.ambrit-rome.com
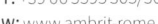

American Overseas School of Rome
Via Cassia 811, 00189 Rome
DP Coordinator Christopher Brown
Languages English
T: +39 06 334 381
W: www.aosr.org/admissions

AMERICAN SCHOOL OF MILAN
Via K. Marx, 14, 20073 Noverasco di Opera (MI)
DP Coordinator Valeria Meroni
Languages English
T: +39 02 5300 0015
E: admissions@asmilan.org
W: www.asmilan.org

See full details on page 55

Bilingual European School
Via Val Cismon 9, 20162 Milan
PYP Coordinator Aaron Downey
Languages English, Italian
T: +39 02 6611 7449
W: www.beschool.eu

Canadian School of Milan
Via M. Gioia 42, 20124 Milano
DP Coordinator Elena Cipullo
MYP Coordinator Elena Cipullo
Languages English
T: +39 02 67074775
W: www.canadianschool.it

Collegio San Carlo
Corso Magenta, 71, 20123 Milan
DP Coordinator Anne Hallihan
Languages English
T: +39 02 43 06 31
W: www.collegiosancarlo.it

Deledda International School
Corso Mentana 27, 16128 Genoa
DP Coordinator Elizabeth Coykendall Rice
MYP Coordinator Chiara Colucci
Languages English
T: +39 010 5536268
W: www.genoaschool.eu

Gonzaga International School
Via Piersanti Mattarella 38/42, 90141 Palermo
DP Coordinator Lorenzo Vantaggiato
MYP Coordinator Nina James
PYP Coordinator Emma Wagland
Languages English, Italian
T: +39 91 302093
W: www.gonzagaisp.it

H-FARM INTERNATIONAL SCHOOL
Via Olivetti 1, 31056 Roncade (TV)
MYP Coordinator Alba Manso Perez
PYP Coordinator Rebecca Goswell
Languages English, Italian
T: +39 0422 789503
E: info.tv@h-is.com
W: www.h-is.com/it/scuole/treviso

See full details on page 102

H-International School Vicenza
Borgo Santa Lucia, 51 Vicenza, 36100 Vicenza
DP Coordinator David Coppard
MYP Coordinator Carol Bailey
PYP Coordinator Stefania Pasquali
Languages English
T: +39 444 54 50 07
W: www.h-is.com/en/schools/vicenza

Institut Saint Dominique
Via Igino Lega 5, 00189 Rome
DP Coordinator Sonia Bouetté
Languages English, French
T: +39 06 303 10817
W: www.institutsaintdominique.it

INTERNATIONAL SCHOOL BRESCIA
Via Benaco 34/B, Bedizzole, 25080 Brescia
DP Coordinator Clare Lax
MYP Coordinator Anne Vollmer
PYP Coordinator Rachel Bestow
Languages English
T: +39 030 2191182
E: info@isbrescia.com
W: www.isbrescia.com

See full details on page 119

INTERNATIONAL SCHOOL OF BERGAMO
Via Monte Gleno, 54, 24125 Bergamo
DP Coordinator Roberta Sana
MYP Coordinator Roberta Sana
PYP Coordinator Helen Bird
Languages English, Italian
T: +39 035 213776
E: info@isbergamo.com
W: www.isbergamo.com

See full details on page 121

International School of Bologna
Via della Libertà 2, 40123 Bologna
DP Coordinator Ms. Nazanin Nikanjam
MYP Coordinator Ms. Helen Exler
PYP Coordinator Ms. Rachel Burgess
Languages English
T: +39 051 6449954
W: www.isbologna.com

INTERNATIONAL SCHOOL OF COMO
Via Adda 25, 22073 Fino Mornasco (CO)
DP Coordinator Natalie Ackers
MYP Coordinator Ben Thompson
PYP Coordinator Rebecca Reider
Languages English, Italian
T: +39 031 572289
E: info@iscomo.com
W: www.iscomo.com

See full details on page 124

International School of Florence
Via del Carota 23/25, Bagno a Ripoli, 50012 Florence
DP Coordinator Jason Blackstone
PYP Coordinator Nicky Shamash
Languages English, Italian
T: +39 055 6461 007
W: www.isfitaly.org

INTERNATIONAL SCHOOL OF MILAN
Via I Maggio, 20, 20021 Baranzate (MI)
DP Coordinator Tony Burtenshaw
MYP Coordinator Domenico Vetrisano
PYP Coordinator Sara Lomas
Languages English
T: +39 02 872581
E: admissions@ism-ac.it
W: www.internationalschoolofmilan.it

See full details on page 128

INTERNATIONAL SCHOOL OF MODENA
Piazza Montessori, 1/A, 41051 Montale Rangone (MO)
DP Coordinator Caroline Searle
MYP Coordinator Anna Chiara Forti
PYP Coordinator Michael Perry
Languages English
T: +39 059 530649
E: admissions@ismodena.it
W: www.internationalschoolofmodena.it

See full details on page 129

INTERNATIONAL SCHOOL OF MONZA
Via Solferino 23, 20900 Monza (MB)
DP Coordinator Gaëlle D'Inca
MYP Coordinator Carman Natalie
PYP Coordinator Becky Taylor
Languages English, Italian
T: +39 039 9357701
E: admin@ismonza.it
W: www.internationalschoolofmonza.it

See full details on page 130

INTERNATIONAL SCHOOL OF SIENA
Via del Petriccio e Belriguardo, 49/1, 53100 Siena
DP Coordinator Joanne Walker
MYP Coordinator Letizia Rosati
PYP Coordinator Brychan Gilbert
Languages English, Italian
T: +39 0577 328103
E: office@issiena.it
W: www.internationalschoolofsiena.it

See full details on page 132

International School of Talents – Multicampus (IST)
Via degli Alpini, 28/5, 31046 Oderzo, Treviso
DP Coordinator Monique Ottevanger
Languages English
T: +39 0422 789 503
W: internationalschooloftalentsmulticampus.com

INTERNATIONAL SCHOOL OF TURIN
Strada Pecetto 34, 10023 Chieri, Turin
DP Coordinator Clara Siviero
MYP Coordinator Francesca Parisi
PYP Coordinator Magdalena Matysow
Languages English
T: +39 011 645 967
E: info@isturin.it
W: www.isturin.it

See full details on page 134

International School of Verona
Aleardo Aleardi, Via Segantini 20, 37138 Verona
DP Coordinator Erik Johnstone
Languages English
T: +39 04557 8200
W: www.aleardi.it

Lonati Anglo American School
Via Bormioli 60, 25135 Brescia
PYP Coordinator Melania Ferrari
Languages English
T: +39 03 02 35 73 60
W: www.laaslonati.org

MARYMOUNT INTERNATIONAL SCHOOL ROME

Via di Villa Lauchli, 180, 00191 Rome
DP Coordinator Eleanor Moore
Languages English
T: +39 06 3629 1012
E: admissions@marymountrome.com
W: www.marymountrome.com

See full details on page 162

O.M.C. – Collegio Vescovile Pio X

Borgo Cavour 40, 31100 Treviso
DP Coordinator Moreno Caronello
Languages English
T: +39 0422 411725
W: www.fondazionecollegiopiox.org

Rome International School

Via Guglielmo Pecori Giraldi n.137, 00135 Rome
DP Coordinator Mrs Laela El Sheikh
PYP Coordinator Mrs Maïa Lawand
Languages English
T: +39 06 8448 2651
W: www.romeinternationalschool.it

Southlands International School

Via Teleclide 40, Casal Palocco, 00124 Rome
DP Coordinator Emmanuel Vaz
Languages English
T: +39 06 5053932
W: www.southlands.it

ST GEORGE'S BRITISH INTERNATIONAL SCHOOL, ROME

Via Cassia, km 16, La Storta, 00123 Rome
DP Coordinator Helen Andrew
Languages English
T: +39 06 3086001
E: admissions@stgeorge.school.it
W: www.stgeorge.school.it

See full details on page 209

ST. LOUIS SCHOOL

SLS S.P.A., Via E. Caviglia, 1, 20139 Milan
DP Coordinator Hatty Rafferty
Languages English, Italian
T: +39 02 55231235
E: info@stlouisschool.com
W: www.stlouisschool.com

See full details on page 214

ST. STEPHEN'S SCHOOL

Via Aventina 3, 00153 Rome
DP Coordinator Nadia El-Taha
Languages English
T: +39 06 575 0605
E: ststephens@sssrome.it
W: www.sssrome.it

See full details on page 216

THE BRITISH SCHOOL OF MILAN (SIR JAMES HENDERSON)

Via Carlo Alberto Pisani Dossi, 16, 20134 Milan
DP Coordinator Miss Alba López Martín
Languages English
T: +39 02 210941
E: info@bsm.school
W: www.britishschoolmilan.com

See full details on page 228

The English International School of Padua

Via Forcellini 168, 35128 Padova
DP Coordinator Debra Mackenzie
Languages English
T: +39 049 80 22 503
W: www.eisp.it

The International School in Genoa

Via Romana Della Castagna 11A, 16148 Genova
DP Coordinator Mrs. Elizabeth Rosser Boiardi
Languages English
T: +39 010 386528
W: www.isgenoa.it

UWC ADRIATIC

Località Duino 29, 34011 Duino-Aurisina TS
DP Coordinator Roman Rudzinski
Languages English
T: +39 040 3739111
E: uwcad@uwcad.it
W: www.uwcad.it

See full details on page 235

VITTORIA INTERNATIONAL SCHOOL

Via delle Rosine 14, 10123 Turin
DP Coordinator Deborah Gutowitz
Languages English
T: +39 011 889870
E: infovis@vittoriaweb.it
W: www.vittoriaweb.it

See full details on page 240

WORLD INTERNATIONAL SCHOOL OF TORINO

Via Traves 28, 10151 Torino
DP Coordinator Ms Barbara Battaglino
MYP Coordinator Ms Kristin Walter
PYP Coordinator Ms Victoria Corkhill
Languages English
T: +39 0111972111
E: info@worldinternationalschool.com
W: worldinternationalschool.com

See full details on page 246

JORDAN

Ahliyyah School for Girls

PO Box 2035, Jabal Amman, Amman 11181
CP Coordinator Eva Haddad
DP Coordinator Lana Zakarian
MYP Coordinator Abeer Sweiss
PYP Coordinator Rana Amarin
Languages English
T: +962 6 4649861
W: www.asg.edu.jo

Amman Academy

PO Box 840, Khalda 11821
DP Coordinator Zaid Kawar
MYP Coordinator Tania Masarwa
PYP Coordinator Yasmin Nasif
Languages English
T: +962 6 535 4118
W: www.ammanacademy.edu.jo

Amman Baccalaureate School

Al Hijaz Street, Dabouq, PO Box 441 Sweileh 11910, Amman
CP Coordinator Ms Gill Deesi
DP Coordinator Ms Jwan Kolaghassi
MYP Coordinator Ms Dina Katafago
PYP Coordinator Nermeen Abu Assaf
Languages English, Arabic
T: +962 6 5411191
W: www.abs.edu.jo

Amman Baptist School

P.O.Box 17033, Alrabieh – Abdallah Bin Rawaha St. 300 m off Mecca str+, Amman 11195
DP Coordinator Linda Kakish
Languages English, Arabic
T: +962 6 551 6907
W: www.baptist.edu.jo

Amman National School

PO Box 140565, Amman 11814
DP Coordinator Diana Dahleh
MYP Coordinator Samia Skafi
Languages English
T: +962 654 11067/8
W: www.ans.edu.jo

Aqaba International School

PO Box 529, 77110 Aqaba
DP Coordinator Aymen Azzam
Languages English, Arabic
T: +962 3 203 9933
W: www.aqabainternationalschool.com

ASAMIAH INTERNATIONAL SCHOOL

Khalda, Taqi al-Din al-Subki, Amman
DP Coordinator Ms. Yasmine Haddadin
MYP Coordinator Ms. Sima Barhoosh
PYP Coordinator Ms. Nour Maroun
Languages English, Arabic
T: +962 6 5335 301
E: info@ais.edu.jo
W: www.ais.edu.jo

See full details on page 59

British International Academy (BIA)

P.O.Box 829, Amman 11831
DP Coordinator Maram Theep
MYP Coordinator Zina Bata
PYP Coordinator Hanan Hamam
Languages English, Arabic
T: +962 6 5508200
W: www.bia.edu.jo

Cambridge High School

Al Rabia, Abdel Kareem Al Dabbas Street, PO Box 851771, Amman 11185
DP Coordinator Nancy Khair
MYP Coordinator Shireen Bakri
Languages English
T: +962 6 5512556
W: www.cambridge.edu.jo

Canadian International School – Amman

20 Al Mikyal Street, Deir Ghbar, Amman
DP Coordinator Ruba Al Jariri
MYP Coordinator Salaam Samara
PYP Coordinator Nadia Hindi
Languages English
T: +962 6 593 9370
W: www.cis.edu.jo

Collège De La Salle – Frères

P.O.Box 926126, Ar-Razi St., Jabal Al-Hussien, Amman 11110
DP Coordinator luma Alatrash
MYP Coordinator Maria Nemat
Languages English, Arabic
T: +962 6 5666428
W: www.lasallejordan.org

English Talents School

P.O.Box 18082, Amman 11195
DP Coordinator Norah Attari
MYP Coordinator Sawsan Rabi
Languages English
T: +962 65370201
W: www.englishtalentsschool.edu.jo

IBN Rushd National Academy
PO Box 940397, Amman 11194
DP Coordinator Ali Khalayleh
MYP Coordinator Fouad Majdalawi
PYP Coordinator Fouad Majdalawi
Languages English, Arabic
T: +962 6 5377601
W: www.ibnrushd.edu.jo

Islamic Educational College - Al Jubeiha
P.O Box 373, Amman 11941
DP Coordinator Abeer Al Azzeh
Languages English, Arabic
T: +962 6516 0121
W: www.islamic-ec.edu.jo

Jubilee School
P.O.Box: 830578, Amman 11183
DP Coordinator Yara Kajo
Languages English
T: +962 6 5238216
W: www.jubilee.edu.jo

Mashrek International School
PO Box 1412, Amman 11118
DP Coordinator Fadia Khoury
MYP Coordinator Ruba Daibes (Grades 9 & 10) Niveen Salem (Grades 7 & 8)
PYP Coordinator Reema Kassem (Primary) Reem Samara (KG)
Languages Arabic, English
T: +962 79 9577771
W: www.mashrek.edu.jo

Modern American School
P.O. Box 950553 – Sweifieh, Amman 11195
DP Coordinator Samah Hamad
Languages English, Arabic
T: +962 6 5862779
W: www.mas.edu.jo

MODERN MONTESSORI SCHOOL
PO Box 1941, Khilda, Amman 11821
DP Coordinator Hoor Hawamdeh
MYP Coordinator Mariam Ellala
PYP Coordinator Rasha Hamzeh
Languages English, Arabic
T: +9626 5535190
E: mms@montessori.edu.jo
W: www.montessori.edu.jo
See full details on page 165

National Orthodox School
P.O.Box: 941502, Amman 11194
DP Coordinator Alas Haddad
Languages Arabic, English
T: +962 6 5674418
W: www.oes.org.jo

The International Academy - Amman
PO Box 144255, King Hussein Parks, Sa'eed Khair Street, Amman 11814
DP Coordinator Justin Hayward
MYP Coordinator Rana Abu Laban
Languages English
T: +962 6550 2055
W: www.iaa.edu.jo

The Little Academy
PO Box 143771, Amman 11844
PYP Coordinator Rula Daher
Languages English
T: +962 65858282
W: www.tlacademy.edu.jo

KAZAKHSTAN

85 School-Lyceum
Kabanbai batyr Avenue 56/1, Astana 010017
MYP Coordinator Aliya Kozhabayeva
Languages Kazakh, Russian
T: +7 7172 336774
W: 85.astana-bilim.kz

Haileybury Astana
Panfilov Street, Bldg. 4, Nur-Sultan 010000
DP Coordinator Faye Fraser
Languages English
T: +7 (7172) 55 98 55 (122)
W: www.haileybury.kz

International College of Continuous Education Astana
2 Molodezhny Microdistrict, Astana 0100000 473000
MYP Coordinator Yelena Shebalina
PYP Coordinator Yelena Shebalina
Languages Russian, English
T: +7 7172 224590
W: www.mkno.kz

International College of Continuous Education, Almaty
69A Zheltoksan Street, Almaty 480004
MYP Coordinator Yekaterina Kunitsyna
PYP Coordinator Yekaterina Kunitsyna
Languages English, Russian
T: +7 3272 399736
W: www.icce-kazakhstan.kz

International School of Almaty
40b Satpayev Street, Almaty 050057
MYP Coordinator Madina Bekturova
PYP Coordinator Inna Klimenko
Languages Russian, English
T: +7 727 2744808 / +7 727 2748189
W: www.isoa.kz

International School of Nur-Sultan
Turkistan street, 32/1, Nur-Sultan city
DP Coordinator Miramgul Mashtakova
MYP Coordinator Roza Auyespayeva
PYP Coordinator Tlektes Tleulina
Languages English, Russian
T: +7 776 007 30 01
W: isa.nis.edu.kz

Kazakhstan International School
Al-Farabi Avenue 118/15, 050062 Almaty
DP Coordinator William Fox
MYP Coordinator Clare Gibbings
PYP Coordinator Shivani McAinsh
Languages English
T: +7 (727) 356 5000
W: www.kisnet.org

Miras International School, Almaty
190 Al-Farabi Avenue, Almaty
DP Coordinator Igor Guralnik
MYP Coordinator Aisulu Kurmanova
PYP Coordinator Elena Holina
Languages English, Kazakh, Russian
T: +7 727 227 6942
W: www.miras.kz

Miras International School, Astana
30 Ablai Khan Avenue, Astana 010009
DP Coordinator Anatoliy Kuznetsov
MYP Coordinator Vinaya Pandey
PYP Coordinator Oksana Makukhina
Languages English, Russian, Kazakh
T: +7 7172 369867
W: www.miras-astana.kz

Nazarbayev Intellectual School of Astana
35, Street 31, (crossing of Kabanbai Batyr and Turan Avenues), Astana 010000
DP Coordinator Azamat Mergenbayev
MYP Coordinator Gulden Issina
Languages English, Kazakh, Russian
T: +7 8 7172 558033
W: www.nisa.edu.kz

Specialized gymnasium 81 Astana English School
2 Omarov Street, Nur-Sultan 010000
MYP Coordinator Guldana Nessipbayeva
Languages English, Kazakh

KENYA

Aga Khan Academy Mombasa
PO Box 80100-90066, Mbuyuni Road, Kizingo, Mombasa
DP Coordinator Julius Menzah
MYP Coordinator Johnson Monari
PYP Coordinator Titus Makunyi
Languages English, Swahili
T: +254 (0)735 931 144
W: www.agakhanacademies.org/mombasa

Braeburn Garden Estate School
PO Box 16944, 00620 Mobil Plaza, Nairobi
CP Coordinator Mercy Gichuhi
DP Coordinator Rosie Bayerl
Languages English
T: +254 720 667 622
W: www.gardenestate.braeburn.com

International School of Kenya
End of Peponi Road/Kirawa Road, PO Box 14103, Nairobi 00800
DP Coordinator Linda Henderson
Languages English
T: +254 20 209 1308/9
W: www.isk.ac.ke

M-PESA FOUNDATION ACADEMY
P.O. Box 7954, 01000 Thika
CP Coordinator Jackline Otula
DP Coordinator Jackline Otula
MYP Coordinator Julliet Kithinji
Languages English
T: +254 703 200 000
E: info@mpesafoundationacademy.ac.ke
W: www.mpesafoundationacademy.ac.ke
See full details on page 167

Naisula School
P O Box 41, Nairobi-Namanga Road, 01100 Kajiado
DP Coordinator Maureen Mukanzi
Languages English, Swahili
T: +254 712245702
W: www.naisulaschool.ac.ke

St Mary's School
PO Box 40580, Rhapta Road, Nairobi 00100
DP Coordinator Paul Mungai
Languages English
T: +254 20 4444 569
W: www.stmarys.ac.ke

THE AGA KHAN ACADEMY, NAIROBI
1st Parklands Avenue, off Limuru Road, PO Box 44424-00100, Nairobi
DP Coordinator Mr. William Wanyonyi
MYP Coordinator Mr. George Musili
PYP Coordinator Ms. Evelyn Awino
Languages English
T: JUNIOR: +254 0733 758 510, SENIOR: +254 736 380 101
E: infos@akesk.org; infoj@akesk.org
W: www.agakhanschools.org/kenya/akan
See full details on page 226

The Aga Khan Nursery School, Nairobi
PO Box 14998, Nairobi 00800
PYP Coordinator Nellie Thuku
Languages English
T: +254 020 374 2114
W: www.agakhanschools.org/kenya/akan

KUWAIT

AMERICAN CREATIVITY ACADEMY
PO Box 1740, Hawally 32018
DP Coordinator Shaheed Carter
Languages English
T: +965 2267 3333
E: info@aca.edu.kw
W: www.aca.edu.kw
See full details on page 50

AMERICAN INTERNATIONAL SCHOOL OF KUWAIT
PO Box 3267, Salmiya 22033
DP Coordinator Amel Limam
MYP Coordinator Teri Kwiatkowski
PYP Coordinator Tanya Bradshaw
Languages English
T: +965 1 843 247
E: superintendent@ais-kuwait.org
W: www.ais-kuwait.org
See full details on page 53

Kuwait Bilingual School
PO Box 3125, Al Jahra City 01033
MYP Coordinator Fares Obeid
PYP Coordinator Alaa Alshemery
Languages English
T: +965 2458 1118; +965 1877 881
W: www.kuwaitbilingualschool.com

Little Land Nursery & Montessori Centre
House 7, Street 40, Block 4, Faiha, Kuwait City, Al Asimah
PYP Coordinator Joelle Filfili
Languages English, Arabic
T: +965 225 55433
W: www.littlelandkw.com

Reborn Kids Education Academy (RKEA)
Block 5, St. 507, Al-Siddiq
PYP Coordinator Kenneth Messenger
Languages English
T: +965 2208 6688
W: www.rebornkw.com

KYRGYZSTAN

ESCA Bishkek International School
67a Bronirovannaya Street, Chui Oblast, Bishkek 720044
DP Coordinator Makiko Inaba
MYP Coordinator Timothy Johnson
PYP Coordinator Alicia Grinsteinner
Languages English
T: +996 312 21 44 06
W: www.esca.kg

Oxford International School
Mira Avenue 153/1, Bishkek
DP Coordinator Oriana Guzman
Languages English, Russian
T: +996 700 55 11 55
W: www.oxford.kg

LATVIA

Exupery International School
Jauna iela 8, Pinki, Babites pagasts LV-2107
DP Coordinator Fleur Serriere
PYP Coordinator Kristina Potapova
Languages English
T: +371 26 62 23 33
W: exupery.lv

International School of Latvia
Meistaru 2, Pinki, Babites pag., Babites nov. LV-2107
DP Coordinator Rebekah Hommel
MYP Coordinator Joseph Szalay
PYP Coordinator Elizabeth Younk
Languages English
T: +371 6775 5146
W: www.isl.edu.lv

International School of Riga
Zvejnieku iela 12, Riga 1048
DP Coordinator Sarah McGinley
PYP Coordinator Ginta Karklina
Languages English
T: +371 6762 4622
W: www.isriga.lv

International School Premjers
1 Lomonosova Str., Bld. 7, Riga 1019
MYP Coordinator Agate Prakash
Languages English, Russian
T: +371 67218501
W: www.ispremjers.lv

Ogre Technical School
Aizupes, Tinuzi Parish, Ikskile District, Ogre 5001
CP Coordinator Ineta Grina
Languages English, Latvian
W: www.ovt.lv

Riga State Gymnasium No. 2
Kr. Valdemara str. 1, Riga 1010
DP Coordinator Inga Treimane
MYP Coordinator Ingrida Breidaka
Languages English
T: +371 67181225
W: www.r2vsk.edu.lv

Riga State Gymnasium No.1
Raina bulv 8, Riga 1050
DP Coordinator Liga Reitere
Languages Latvian (national Curriculum), English (ib Dp)
T: +371 67 228 607
W: www.r1g.edu.lv

LEBANON

Al-Hayat International School
Aramoun
MYP Coordinator Rana El Noamani
PYP Coordinator Dana Itani
Languages English
T: +961 5 806 306
W: www.his.edu.lb

American Community School at Beirut
PO Box 8129, Riad Solh, Beirut 11072260
DP Coordinator Nada Chatila
Languages English
T: +961 1 374 370
W: www.acs.edu.lb

Antonine International School
PO Box 55035, Ajaltoun, Dekwaneh
DP Coordinator Georgia Hachem Najem
Languages English
T: +961 9 230969
W: www.ais.edu.lb

Brummana High School
PO Box 36, Brummana BT
DP Coordinator George Rizkallah
Languages English
T: +961 4 960 430
W: www.bhs.edu.lb

Cadmous College
Tyre, Jwar Al Nakhel
DP Coordinator Ossama Salem
Languages English
T: +9617380391/2
W: www.cadmous.edu.lb

Collège Protestant Français Montana
Rue 4, Dik El Mehdi
DP Coordinator Anjel Lublubjian
Languages English, Arabic
T: +961 4 914 006
W: www.cpf.edu.lb

Eastwood College – Kafarshima
P.O. Box 46, Kafarshima
DP Coordinator Majida Harakeh
Languages English, Arabic
T: +961 5 431525
W: www.eastwoodcollege.com

Eastwood International School
Sami Solh St, Mansourieh El Metn
DP Coordinator Cendrella El Kettaneh
MYP Coordinator Denise Chammas
PYP Coordinator Hind Muzien
Languages English
T: +961 4 409307
W: eastwoodschools.com

German International School Beirut
PO Box 11-3888, Bliss Street, Ras Beirut, Beirut
DP Coordinator Petra Machlab
Languages English
T: +961 1 740523
W: www.dsb.edu.lb

Greenfield College
Al Mourouj Street – Bir Hassan, Beirut
DP Coordinator Nibal Hamdan
Languages English
T: +961 1 834 838
W: www.greenfieldcollege.com

Institut Moderne Du Liban
Rue 51 n.19 Metn nord, Fanar, Région Jaber 90593
DP Coordinator Gilbert Haroun
MYP Coordinator Rana Ghanem
Languages French
T: +961 1680160/1/2
W: www.instmod.edu.lb

International College Beirut

P.O. Box 113-5373, Hamra, Bliss Street, Beirut
DP Coordinator Rasha Daouk
PYP Coordinator Layal Tayara
Languages Arabic, English, French
T: +961 1 374980
W: www.ic.edu.lb

International College, Ain Aar

Bliss Street, PO Box 113-5373, Beirut
PYP Coordinator Alain Gholam
Languages Arabic, English, French
T: +96 149 28468
W: www.ic.edu.lb

LWIS Hazmieh

Hazmieh – 503A str., Near City Center, Beirut
PYP Coordinator Nada Hajj
Languages English, Arabic
T: +961 5 453 241
W: lwis-hazmieh.edu.lb

LWIS Keserwan-Adma International School

Mar Nohra, Fatqa, Keserwan
DP Coordinator Jacques El Khoury
Languages English
T: +961 9 740 226
W: www.lwis-ais.edu.lb

LWIS Universal School of Lebanon

Bterram Al-Koura
DP Coordinator Sassine Sarkis
Languages English, Arabic
T: +961 (6) 930 964
W: www.lwis-usl.edu.lb

LWIS-City International School

Hussein Beyhum Street, Zkak El-Blat, Down Town, Beirut
DP Coordinator Fuad El Haddad
Languages English, Arabic
T: +961 (1) 369 500
W: lwis-cis.edu.lb/lwis-international-school

Makassed Houssam Eddine Hariri High School

PO Box 67, Saida
DP Coordinator Mona Majzoub
PYP Coordinator Farah Darazi
Languages Arabic, English, French
T: +961 7 739898
W: www.mak-hhhs.edu.lb

Rafic Hariri High School – Saida

P.O.Box 384, Saidon
PYP Coordinator Samar Darazi
Languages English
T: +961 7 723 551
W: www.rhhs.edu.lb

Sagesse High School

Aïn Saadeh, Metn
DP Coordinator Lady Maalouf
Languages English
T: +961 1 872 145
W: www.sagessehs.edu.lb

WELLSPRING LEARNING COMMUNITY

Al Mathaf, Main Street, Near National Museum, PO Box 116-2134, Beirut
DP Coordinator Kathleen Saleh
MYP Coordinator Joanna Barrak
PYP Coordinator Nadine Daya
Languages English
T: +961 1 423 444
E: info@wellspring.edu.lb
W: www.wellspring.edu.lb
See full details on page 244

See full details on page 244

LESOTHO

Machabeng College, International School of Lesotho

PO Box 1570, Tona Kholo Rd, Maseru
DP Coordinator Motselisi Ismail
Languages English
T: +266 2231 3224
W: www.machcoll.co.ls

LITHUANIA

Alytus St. Benedict's Gymnasium

Topoliu g. 19A, 63331 Alytus
DP Coordinator Lina Butrimiene
MYP Coordinator Migle Stebulyte
Languages Lithuanian
T: +370 31 574 919
W: www.benediktogimnazija.lt

Erudito Licejus, Kaunas

J. Gruodzio g. 9, 44293 Kaunas
DP Coordinator Marta Bobiatynska
Languages English, Lithuanian
T: +370 65 788 820
W: erudito.lt

Erudito Licejus, Vilnius

Aludariu g. 3, 01113 Vilnius
DP Coordinator Marta Bobiatynska
Languages English, Lithuanian
T: +370 66 719 972
W: erudito.lt

Kaunas Jesuit High School

Rotuses a. 9, 44280 Kaunas
DP Coordinator Au rine erepkiene
Languages English
T: +370 8 37 28 05 25
W: www.kjg.lt

Kaunas Jonas Jablonskis Gymnasium

Au ros st. 3, 44173 Kaunas
DP Coordinator Jurate Zybartiene
MYP Coordinator Kristina Gimpelson
Languages English
T: +370 37 20 23 37
W: jablonskis.kaunas.lm.lt

Klaipeda Lyceum

Kretingos str. 44, 92317 Klaipeda
DP Coordinator Ramune Petrauskiene
Languages English, Lithuanian
T: +380 84 635 1286
W: www.klaipedoslicejus.lt

Klaipeda Universa Via International School

Baltikalnio street 11, Klaipeda
PYP Coordinator Kamile Kesyle
Languages English, Lithuanian
T: +370 8 46 38 34 65
W: www.universavia.lt

Siauliai Didzdvaris gymnasium

Vilniaus g 188, 76299 Siauliai
DP Coordinator Rima Tamosiuniene
Languages English
T: +370 41 431 424
W: www.dg.su.lt

Tauragës Versmës Gimnazija

J. Tumo-Vai ganto g. 10, 72261 Tauragë
DP Coordinator Ingrida Vaiciene
Languages English
T: +370 446 61922
W: www.versme.org

The American International School of Vilnius

Subaciaus 41, 11350 Vilnius
DP Coordinator Sofia Segedy
Languages English
T: +370 5 212 1031
W: www.aisv.lt

Vilniaus Karalienes Mortos mokykla

Luksines g. 29, 11332 Vilnius
DP Coordinator Laura Vizbariene
Languages English, Lithuanian
T: +370 63 007 474
W: www.karalienesmortosmokykla.lt

Vilnius International School

Turniskiu Str 21, Rusu Str 3, 01125 Vilnius
MYP Coordinator Deirdre Jennings
PYP Coordinator Kate Benson
Languages English
T: +370 5 276 1564
W: www.vischool.lt

Vilnius Lyceum

Sirvintu 82, 08216 Vilnius
DP Coordinator Vilija Balciunaité
Languages English
T: +370 5 2775836
W: www.licejus.lt

Vilnius Private Gymnasium

V. Grybo street 7, 10313 Vilnius
DP Coordinator Jelena Silova
Languages English, Lithuanian
T: +370 69 854 808
W: mokykla.lt

LUXEMBOURG

Athénée de Luxembourg

24 Bd Pierre Dupong, L-1430, Luxembourg
DP Coordinator Tommy Halsdorf
Languages English
T: +352 26 04 60
W: www.al.lu

Fräi-Ëffentlech Waldorfschoul Lëtzebuerg

45 rue de l'Avenir, Luxembourg 1147
DP Coordinator Michael Schulz
Languages French
T: +352 466932
W: www.waldorf.lu

International School of Luxembourg

36 Boulevard Pierre Dupong, 1430 Luxembourg
DP Coordinator Robert Sinclair
Languages English
T: +352 26 04 40
W: www.islux.lu

Lycée technique du Centre

106 avenue Pasteur, Luxembourg L-2309
DP Coordinator Mariette Kauthen
Languages French
T: +352 47 38 11 1
W: www.ltc.lu

OTR International School Luxembourg
7 Rue Val Ste Croix, 1371 Luxembourg
MYP Coordinator Silvia Cebrian Graullera
Languages English, French
T: +352 2609 45 42
W: otrschool.lu

MACEDONIA

IPS Macedonia
st. Dragisha Mishovic building 2, Detska gradinka Orce Nikolov, 1000 Skopje
PYP Coordinator Natasha Kanzurova-Manev
Languages English
T: +389 (0)2 3073 700
W: ips.mk

Josip Broz Tito – High School
Dimitrije Cupovski bb, 1000 Skopje
DP Coordinator Gordiana Gjorgova
Languages English
T: +389 2 3214 314
W: josipbroztito.edu.mk

NOVA International Schools
Praska 27, 1000 Skopje
DP Coordinator Eda Starova Tahir
Languages English
T: +389 2 3061 907
W: www.nova.edu.mk

OU Braka Miladinovci
Ul. Vladimir Komarov No.5, 1000 Skopje
MYP Coordinator Katerina Mirevska
PYP Coordinator Biljana Kirik
Languages English
T: +389 (02) 2 460 479
W: oubrakamiladinovci-aerodrom.edu.mk

MADAGASCAR

The American School of Antananarivo
Lotissement Le Park Alarobia, Antananarivo 101
DP Coordinator Kelly Elam
PYP Coordinator Kristen Vanollefen
Languages English
T: +261 20 22 420 39
W: www.asamadagascar.org

MALAWI

Bishop Mackenzie International School
PO Box 102, Lilongwe
DP Coordinator Jo Mcclenahan
MYP Coordinator Kathryn Leaper
PYP Coordinator Wayne Derrick
Languages English
T: +265 1 756 631
W: bmis.mw

MALI

Enko Bamako International School
Quartier du Fleuve, rue 310, porte 510, Ancien CompuMali, En face de l'industrie Boissons et G+, Bamako
DP Coordinator Mahamane Sidibe
Languages English, French
T: +223 63 21 24 26
W: enkoeducation.com/bamako

MALTA

ST EDWARD'S COLLEGE, MALTA
Triq San Dwardu, Birgu (Vittoriosa) BRG 9039
DP Coordinator Mr Jolen Galea
Languages English
T: +356 2788 1199
E: admissions@stedwards.edu.mt
W: www.stedwards.edu.mt
See full details on page 207

Verdala International School
Fort Pembroke, Pembroke PBK 1641
CP Coordinator Nicola Schembri
DP Coordinator Daphne Said
Languages English
T: +356 21375133
W: www.verdala.org

MAURITIUS

Clavis International Primary School
Montagne Ory, Moka
PYP Coordinator Nadine Koenig
Languages English
T: +230 433 4439/4337708
W: www.clavis.mu

International Preparatory School
Village Labourdonnais, Mapou 31803
PYP Coordinator Laura Nash
Languages English, French
T: +230 266 1973
W: www.ips.intnet.mu

Le Bocage International School (Progos)
Mount Ory, Moka 80803
CP Coordinator Namrata Gujadhur
DP Coordinator Yovna Mewasingh
MYP Coordinator Asha Joypaul
Languages English
T: +230 433 9900
W: www.lebocage.net

Northfields International High School
Labourdonnais Village, Mapou
DP Coordinator Rosemary Abbott
MYP Coordinator Harry Allen
Languages English
T: +230 266 9448/9
W: northfieldsinternational.school

Westcoast International Secondary School
Flic en Flac Road, Cascavelle
DP Coordinator Christina Appadoo
Languages English
T: +230 489 2034
W: westcoast-schools.com/home.html

MONACO

THE INTERNATIONAL SCHOOL OF MONACO
10-12 Quai Antoine Premier, Monte Carlo 98000
CP Coordinator Tania Leyland
DP Coordinator Hannah Gettel
Languages English, French
T: +377 9325 6820
E: admissions@ismonaco.com
W: ismonaco.org
See full details on page 231

MONTENEGRO

Adriatic College
13. Jula, Budva 85312
DP Coordinator Ekaterina Anokhina
Languages English
T: +382 69 324 101
W: www.adriaticcollege.com

KSI Montenegro
Seljanovo bb, Porto Montenegro, Tivat
DP Coordinator Lauren Streifer
MYP Coordinator Lauren Streifer
PYP Coordinator Marija Djukic
Languages English
T: +382 32 672 655
W: www.ksi-montenegro.com

MOROCCO

American Academy Casablanca
RN 3020 Ville Verte, Casa Green Town, Bouskoura 27182
DP Coordinator Wassif Benlarbi
Languages English, French
T: +212 529 039112
W: www.aac.ac.ma

American School of Marrakesh
Route de Ouarzazate, BP 6195, Marrakech
DP Coordinator Iveth Morillo
Languages English
T: +212 (0)24 32 98 60/61
W: www.asm.ma

Casablanca American School
Route de la Mecque, Lotissement Ougoug, Quartier Californie, Casablanca 20150
DP Coordinator Alina Zamfirescu
Languages English
T: +212 522 79 39 39
W: www.cas.ac.ma

Écoles Al Madina, Site Ain Sebaa
Km 9, route de Rabat, Hay Chabab, Ain sébàa, Casablanca 20250
MYP Coordinator Zhor Lerhmame
Languages French, Arabic
T: +212 0522 75 69 69
W: www.almadina.ma

Écoles Al Madina, Site Californie
Lotissement Bellevue 2, Rue 3 Californie, Casablanca
MYP Coordinator Kamar Guennoun
Languages French, Arabic
T: +212 522 5050 9 7/8/9
W: www.almadina.ma

Écoles Al Madina, Site Polo
52 Bd Nador, Casablanca 20420
MYP Coordinator Rajaa Boukhris
Languages French, Arabic
T: +21 20 22 210 505
W: www.almadina.ma

GDGSR – Khouribga
Bld 2 Mars, Khouribga
MYP Coordinator Salah Toufani
Languages Arabic, French
T: +212 (0)6 00 03 40 11
W: www.gdgsr.ma/site/khouribga

GDGSR – Youssoufia
Rue Allal Ben Abdellah, Youssoufia
MYP Coordinator Habiba Maanaoui
Languages Arabic, French
T: +212 (0)6 00 03 77 53
W: www.gdgsr.ma/site/youssoufia

George Washington Academy
Km 5.6 Rte d'Azemour, Dar Bouazza, Casablanca 20220
DP Coordinator Mason Grine
Languages English, French, Arabic
T: +212 522 953 000
W: www.gwa.ac.ma

Groupe scolaire Alkaraouiyine
350 Boulevard Sebta, Lotisement Anfa, Mohammedia 28000
MYP Coordinator Hanane Sbit
Languages Arabic, French
T: +212 23 30 13 57
W: www.alkaraouiyine.ma

Groupe Scolaire La Résidence
87-89 Avenue 2 mars, Casablanca
MYP Coordinator Soukaina Elidrissi Eljaid
Languages French
T: +212 522 809050/51
W: www.gsr.ac.ma

Institut Scolaire les Palmiers
76 Rue Abdelhamid Bnou Badis, Casablanca Ain sebâa 20250
PYP Coordinator Fatima Maroua
Languages Arabic, English, French
T: +212 522343757
W: www.institutscolairelespalmiers.com

Institution El Yakada
Lotisement Koutoubia, Route de Kenitra, Salé 11160
MYP Coordinator Mokhtar Saufi
Languages English
T: +212 (0)5 37 84 48 44
W: www.elyakada.com

International School of Morocco
3 Impasse Jules Gros, Quartier Oasis, Casablanca 20150
PYP Coordinator Meredith Achlim
Languages English
T: +212 0 552 993 987
W: www.ism-c.ma

Newton International School
Rue Ibn Khafaja, Anfa, Mohammedia 208000
MYP Coordinator Khalid Mouroudy
Languages French
T: +212 5 23 31 65 52
W: www.nischool.org

Planete Montessori International School
Lotissement Palm Tree Paradise No. 5, Mechouar Essaid, Marrakech
PYP Coordinator Soukaina Benkirane
Languages English, French
T: +212 6 23 86 14 29
W: www.planetemontessori.com

Rabat American School
c/o US Embassy, BP 120 Rabat
DP Coordinator Fabienne Gerard
Languages English
T: +212 537 75 85 90
W: www.ras.ma

MOZAMBIQUE

Aga Khan Academy Maputo
Av. Zimbabwe, 212 Matola, Maputo
DP Coordinator Morag Makey
MYP Coordinator Smita Gangola
PYP Coordinator Emma Wheatley
Languages English, Portuguese
T: +258 21 720963
W: www.agakhanacademies.org/maputo

American International School of Mozambique
Caixa Postal 2026, Maputo
DP Coordinator Sandeep Lyall
MYP Coordinator Michael BondClegg
PYP Coordinator Taryn BondClegg
Languages English
T: +258 21 49 1994
W: www.aism-moz.com

Enko Benga International School
Moatize, Tete
PYP Coordinator Christopher Fato
Languages English
T: +258 84 717 5447
W: www.enkoeducation.com/benga

Enko Riverside International School
Rua José Macamo 175, Polana, Maputo
DP Coordinator Rosa Maria Gadzicua
Languages English
T: +258 845 40 91 51
W: enkoeducation.com/riverside

NAMIBIA

Windhoek International School
P/Bag 16007, Scheppmann Street, Pioneerspark, Windhoek
DP Coordinator Rick Fitzpatrick
PYP Coordinator Avril van Zyl
Languages English
T: +264 61 241 783
W: www.wis.edu.na

NETHERLANDS

AMERICAN SCHOOL OF THE HAGUE
Rijksstraatweg 200, 2241 BX Wassenaar
DP Coordinator Mike Flaim
Languages English
T: +31 70 512 1060
E: admissions@ash.nl
W: www.ash.nl
See full details on page 57

Amity International School Amsterdam
Amsterdamseweg 204, 1182 HL Amsterdam, North Holland
PYP Coordinator Natalie Jensen
Languages English
T: +31 20 3454481
W: www.amityschool.nl

Amsterdam International Community School
Prinses Irenestraat 59, 1077 WV Amsterdam, North Holland
CP Coordinator Elizabeth Ann Young
DP Coordinator Elise McKenzie
MYP Coordinator Claudia Elena Casalino
PYP Coordinator Katina Rikkert
Languages English
T: +31 20 5771240
W: www.aics.espritscholen.nl

Amsterdam Liberal Arts & Sciences Academy (ALASCA)
Geertje Wielemaplein 1, 1095 MM Amsterdam, North Holland
DP Coordinator Ananda van der Pluijm
Languages English, Dutch
T: +31 20 2623240
W: alasca.espritscholen.nl

Basisschool Het Startpunt
Suze Robertsonstraat 103, 2526 WS The Hague, South Holland
PYP Coordinator Sophie De Graaf
Languages Dutch
T: +31 70 3803935
W: www.obshetstartpunt.nl

DENISE (De Nieuwe Internationale School van Esprit)
Piet Mondriaanstraat 140, 1061 TT Amsterdam, North Holland
DP Coordinator Amy Poon
Languages English
T: +31 20 4802700
W: denise.espritscholen.nl

EERDE INTERNATIONAL BOARDING SCHOOL NETHERLANDS
Kasteellaan 1, 7731 PJ Ommen, Overijssel
DP Coordinator Robert de Bruin
Languages English
T: +31 52 9451452
E: admission@eerdeibs.nl
W: www.eerde.nl
See full details on page 85

Gifted Minds International School
c/o Corporate Office, Landtong 18, 1186 GP Amstelveen, North Holland
PYP Coordinator Ramesh Mahalingam
Languages English
T: +31 23 888 8874
W: www.giftedmindsinternationalschool.com/gifted-minds-international-school/

International School Almere
Heliumweg 61, 1362 JA Almere Poort, Flevoland
DP Coordinator Simona Ghizdareanu
MYP Coordinator Sabrina Stremke
Languages English
T: +31 36 7600750
W: www.internationalschoolalmere.nl

International School Breda
Mozartlaan 27, 4837 EH Breda, North Brabant
DP Coordinator Mark Sherlock
MYP Coordinator Lilian Buuron
Languages English
T: +31 76 5601350
W: www.isbreda.nl

International School Delft
Jaffalaan 9, 2628 BX Delft
MYP Coordinator Evelyne Le Poole
PYP Coordinator Kayleigh Adams
Languages English
T: +31 15 2850038
W: www.internationalschooldelft.com

NETHERLANDS

International School Eindhoven

Oirschotsedijk 14b, 5651 GC Eindhoven, North Brabant
DP Coordinator David Bailly
MYP Coordinator Kris Pollard
Languages English
T: +31 40 2519437
W: www.isecampus.nl

International School Haarlem (ISH)

Oorkondelaan 65, 2033 MN Haarlem, North Holland
DP Coordinator Stavros Melachroinos
MYP Coordinator Hannah Mansbridge
Languages English
T: +31 23 2200001
W: www.internationalschoolhaarlem.nl

International School Hilversum 'Alberdingk Thijm'

Emmastraat 56, 1213 AL Hilversum, North Holland
DP Coordinator Nicola Isaac
MYP Coordinator Rachel Gorman
PYP Coordinator Anniek Bruijnzeels
Languages English
T: +31 35 6729931
W: www.ishilversum.nl

International School of Amsterdam

PO Box 920, Sportlaan 45, 1180 AX Amstelveen, North Holland
DP Coordinator Matt Lynch
MYP Coordinator Douglas Beam
PYP Coordinator Lisa Verkerk
Languages English
T: +31 20 347 1111
W: www.isa.nl

International School The Rijnlands Lyceum Oegstgeest

Apollolaan 1, BA 2341 Oegstgeest, South Holland
DP Coordinator Jonathan Symmons
MYP Coordinator Annelies Lynn Brabant
Languages English
T: +31 71 5193555
W: www.isrlo.nl

International School Twente

Tiemeister 20, 7541 WG Enschede, Overijssel
DP Coordinator Anke Kolkman
Languages English
T: +31 53 482 11 30
W: internationalschooltwente.nl

International School Utrecht

Van Bijnkershoeklaan 8, 3527 XL Utrecht
DP Coordinator Olivia Ayes
MYP Coordinator Liam Moody
PYP Coordinator Lindsey Dudgeon
Languages English
T: +31 30 8700400
W: www.isutrecht.nl

IPS Hilversum

Rembrandtlaan 30, BH 1213 Hilversum, North Holland
PYP Coordinator Stephanie Noda
Languages English
T: +31 35 6216053
W: www.ipsviolen.nl

Laar & Berg

Langsakker 4, 1251 GB Laren, North Holland
MYP Coordinator Eva Goossens
Languages English
T: +31 35 5395422
W: www.laarenberg.nl

Maartenscollege & International School Groningen

Hemmenlaan 2, 9751 NS Haren, Groningen
DP Coordinator Joke Jansma
MYP Coordinator Simone Hartholt
Languages English
T: +31 50 5340084
W: maartenscollege.nl

NORD ANGLIA INTERNATIONAL SCHOOL ROTTERDAM

Verhulstlaan 21, 3055 WJ Rotterdam, South Holland
DP Coordinator Danielle Mashon
Languages English
T: +31 10 4225351
E: admissions@naisr.nl
W: www.naisr.nl

See full details on page 169

Rivers International School Arnhem

Groningensingel 1245, 6835 HZ Arnhem, Gelderland
DP Coordinator Arthur van de Graaf
MYP Coordinator Micha Oosterhoff
Languages English
T: +31 26 3202840
W: www.arnheminternationalschool.nl

ROTTERDAM INTERNATIONAL SECONDARY SCHOOL

Bentincklaan 294, 3039 KK Rotterdam, South Holland
DP Coordinator Eva Noorduijn
Languages English
T: +31 (0)10 890 77 44
E: admissions.riss@wolfert.nl
W: riss.wolfert.nl

See full details on page 184

The British School in The Netherlands

Jan van Hooflaan 3, 2252 BG Voorschoten, South Holland
CP Coordinator Michelle Cooke
DP Coordinator Michelle Cooke
Languages English
T: +31 (0)70 315 4077
W: www.britishschool.nl

THE INTERNATIONAL SCHOOL OF THE HAGUE

Wijndaelerweg 11, 2554 BZ The Hague, South Holland
CP Coordinator Dr. Alma Trumic
DP Coordinator Dr. Alma Trumic
MYP Coordinator Maria Lamminaho
Languages English
T: +31 70 328 1450
E: admissions@ishthehague.nl
W: www.ishthehague.nl

See full details on page 232

UWC MAASTRICHT

Discusworp 65, 6225 XP Maastricht, Limburg
CP Coordinator Nathan Hunt
DP Coordinator Sindhu Clark & Jack Borthwick
MYP Coordinator Gökce Dagdeviren
Languages English
T: +31 432 410 410
E: admissions@uwcmaastricht.nl
W: www.uwcmaastricht.nl

See full details on page 237

Lycée Enoch Olinga

B.P. 366, Quartier Daresalam (face marché Daresalam), Niamey 8001
DP Coordinator Fumundjibo Kahila
Languages French
T: +227 94 54 60 75
W: www.lycee-enoch-olinga.org

American International School of Lagos

Behind 1004 Federal Estates, Lagos
DP Coordinator Scott Williams
Languages English
T: +234 11 77 64 535
W: www.aislagos.org

British Nigerian Academy

Drive 6, Prince and Princess, Duboyi District, P.M.B 5285, Wuse, Abuja
DP Coordinator Dawn Savage
Languages English
T: +234 8144084741
W: www.bna.edu.ng

Greensprings School, Lagos

P.O. Box 4801K Ikeja Headquarters, Ikeja, 32 Olatunde Ayoola Avenue, Anthony, Lagos
DP Coordinator Isaac Obashe
Languages English
T: +234 8776874
W: www.greenspringsschool.com

Ibadan International School

24 Jibowu Crescent, Iyaganku, Ibadan
PYP Coordinator Helen Chatburn-Ojehomon
Languages English
T: +234 2 291 8483
W: www.ibadaninternationalschool.com

The International School of IITA

PMB 5320, Ibadan, Oyo State
PYP Coordinator Edith Ekun
Languages English
T: +234 (0)700 800 4482 (EXT:2593)
W: iitaschool.com

Aalesund International School

Borgundvegen 418, 6015 Aalesund, Møre og Romsdal
MYP Coordinator Ana María Güelfo Borrajo
PYP Coordinator Ana Maria Güelfo Borrajo
Languages English
T: +47 908 69 948
W: www.aais.no

Arendal International School

Julius Smiths vei 40, 4817 His, Aust-Agder
MYP Coordinator Marius Larsen Strand
PYP Coordinator Antonia Fiksdalstrand
Languages English
T: +47 37 055 100
W: www.aischool.no

Arendal Videregående Skole

Postboks 325, 4803 Arendal, Aust-Agder
DP Coordinator Haldor Berge
Languages English
T: +47 37 00 02 00
W: www.arendal.vgs.no

Ås videregående skole

Postboks 10, 1430 Ås, Akershus
DP Coordinator Graham Ryan
Languages English
T: +47 64 97 57 00
W: www.aas.vgs.no

Asker International School

Johan Drengsruds Vei 60, 1383 Asker, Akershus
MYP Coordinator Brent Jane
PYP Coordinator Angela Hjelset-King
Languages English
T: +47 9089 0609
W: www.askeris.no

Bergen Cathedral School

Postboks 414 Marken, Kong Oscarsgate 36, 5832 Bergen, Hordaland
DP Coordinator Gillian Boniface
Languages English
T: +47 55 33 82 00
W: www.hordaland.no/bergenkatedralskole

Bjørnholt Skole

Slimeveien 17, 1277 Oslo
DP Coordinator Eirik Hardersen
Languages English
T: +47 23 46 35 00
W: bjornholt.osloskolen.no

Blindern Videregående Skole

Sognsveien 80, 0855 Oslo
DP Coordinator Emmanuelle Bjerkem
MYP Coordinator Aldo Alejandro Mercado Rivera
Languages English, Norwegian
T: +47 90 80 80 59
W: blindern.vgs.no

British International School of Stavanger

Gauselbakken 107, Gausel, 4032 Stavanger, Rogaland
CP Coordinator Victoria Reed
DP Coordinator Victoria Reed
MYP Coordinator Gina Ward
PYP Coordinator Nathalie Delgado
Languages English
T: +47 519 50 250
W: www.biss.no

Children's International School Fredrikstad

Torsnesveien 5-7, 1630 Gamle Fredrikstad, Østfold
MYP Coordinator Kylie Curteis
PYP Coordinator Alison Kronstad
Languages English
T: +47 690 02 500
W: cisschools.no/fredrikstad

Children's International School Moss

Moss Verk 1, 1534 Moss, Østfold
MYP Coordinator Pamela Castberg
PYP Coordinator Jennifer Thorvaldsen
Languages English
T: +47 400 01 128
W: cisschools.no/moss

Children's International School Sarpsborg

Tuneveien 20, 1710 Sarpsborg, Østfold
MYP Coordinator Anne Kari Rønsen
PYP Coordinator Lindsey Allan
Languages English, Norwegian
T: +47 400 02 607
W: cisschools.no/cis-sarpsborg

Elverum videregående skole

Postboks 246, 2402 Elverum, Hedmark
DP Coordinator Mikael Sjöholm
Languages English
T: +47 6243 1500
W: www.elverum.vgs.no

Fagerhaug International School

Post Office Box 4, 7510 Skatval, Trøndelag
MYP Coordinator Britt Geving
PYP Coordinator Cherise Kristoffersen
Languages English
T: +47 74 84 07 70
W: fagerhaugoppvekst.no/en/international-school

Frederik II videregående skole

PB 523, Merkurveien 2, 1612 Fredrikstad, Østfold
DP Coordinator Arvid Evjen Andersen
Languages English
T: +47 69 36 64 00
W: www.frederikii.vgs.no

Gjøvik videregående skole

PO Box 534, 2803 Gjøvik, Oppland
DP Coordinator Ada Bråthen Øye
Languages English
T: +47 61149400
W: www.gjovik.vgs.no

Gjøvikregionen International School

Studieveien 17, 2815 Gjøvik, Oppland
MYP Coordinator Samuel Rowe
PYP Coordinator Heidi Brenner
Languages English, Norwegian
T: +47 240 76 141
W: www.gjovikis.no

Haugesund International School

Halandvegen 175, 4260 Torvastad, Karmøy, Rogaland
MYP Coordinator Stacy Walter
PYP Coordinator Ryan Moore
Languages English, Norwegian
T: +47 40670871
W: www.hischool.no

International School of Bergen

Sandslihaugen 30, 5254 Bergen, Hordaland
MYP Coordinator Peter Ledger
PYP Coordinator Leanne Hagen
Languages English
T: +47 55 30 63 30
W: www.isob.no

International School of Stavanger

Treskeveien 3, 4043 Hafrsfjord, Rogaland
DP Coordinator Lynn Park
Languages English
T: +47 51 55 43 00
W: www.isstavanger.no

International School Telemark

Hovet Ring 7, 3931 Porsgrunn, Telemark
MYP Coordinator Julie Strøm
PYP Coordinator Tjandra Purnama
Languages English
T: +47 35291400
W: www.istelemark.no

Kirkenes Videregående Skole

Postboks 44, 9916 Hesseng, Finnmark
DP Coordinator Juha Törmikoski
Languages English
T: +47 78 96 18 00
W: www.kirkenes.vgs.no

Kongsberg International School

Dyrmyrgata 39-41, 3611 Kongsberg, Buskerud
MYP Coordinator Hilde Bakken
PYP Coordinator Sofie Jørstad
Languages English
T: +47 32 29 93 80
W: www.kischool.org

Kongsberg videregående skole

Postboks 424, 3604 Kongsberg, Buskerud
DP Coordinator Kelvin Peters
Languages English
T: +47 3286 7600
W: www.kongsberg.vgs.no

KRISTIANSAND INTERNATIONAL SCHOOL

Kongsgård alle 20, 4631 Kristiansand, Vest-Agder
MYP Coordinator Susan Heiseldal
PYP Coordinator Jeremy Youell
Languages English
T: +47 95826601
E: post.international.school@kristiansand.kommune.no
W: www.kisschool.no

See full details on page 150

Kristiansand Katedralskole Gimle

Postboks 1010, Lundsiden, 4687 Kristiansand, Vest-Agder
DP Coordinator Vibeke Lauritsen
Languages English
T: +47 38 70 50 00
W: www.kkg.vgs.no

Lillestrom Videregaende Skole

Postboks 333, Henrik Wergelands gt. 1, 2001 Lillestrom, Akershus
DP Coordinator Line Skaugset
Languages Norwegian, English
T: +47 63 89 06 00
W: www.lillestrom.vgs.no

Manglerud skole

Plogveien 22, 0681 Oslo
PYP Coordinator Hin Yan Gloria Suen
Languages English
T: +47 22 75 73 10
W: manglerud.osloskolen.no

Nesbru Videregående Skole

Halvard Torgersensvei 8, Postbox 38, 1378 Nesbru, Akershus
DP Coordinator Helen Elizabeth Laney-Mortensen
Languages English
T: +47 66 854 408
W: www.nesbru.vgs.no

Norlights International School

Skådalsveien 33, 0781 Oslo
MYP Coordinator Ismail Dikbas
PYP Coordinator Sakhi Kochar
Languages English
T: +47 40 07 35 50
W: nlis.noredu.no

NORWAY

Oslo International School

PO Box 53, 1318 Bekkestua, Akershus
DP Coordinator Susan Jensen
Languages English
T: +47 67 8182 90
W: www.os lointernationalschool.no

Porsgrunn videregående skole

Kjølnes ring 58, 3918 Porsgrunn, Telemark
DP Coordinator Margrethe Hauff
Languages English
T: +47 35 91 75 06
W: www.porsgrunn.vgs.no

Sandefjord Videregående Skole

Postboks 2006, 3202 Sandefjord, Vestfold
DP Coordinator Siân Stickler
Languages English
T: +47 33 488 690
W: www.svgs.vfk.no

Sandnes International School

Einartangen 2, 4309 Sandnes, Rogaland
PYP Coordinator Mary Kay Polly
Languages English
T: +47 512 01 575
W: www.sdis.no

Senja Vidaregåande Skole

Skoleveien 55, 9300 Finnsnes, Troms
DP Coordinator Vivian Jakobsen
Languages English
T: +47 77 85 08 00
W: www.finnfjordbotn.vgs.no

Skagerak International School

Framnesveien 7, 3222 Sandefjord, Vestfold
DP Coordinator Niklas Winander
MYP Coordinator Dylan Carter
PYP Coordinator Andrea Helgesen
Languages English
T: +47 33456500
W: www.skagerak.org

Spjelkavik videregående skole

Langhaugen 22, 6011 Alesund, Møre og Romsdal
DP Coordinator Camilla Moritz-Olsen
Languages English
T: +47 70178230
W: www.spjelkavik.vgs.no

St Olav Videregaende Skole

Jens Zetlitzgt. 33, 4008 Stavanger, Rogaland
DP Coordinator Fiona Andvik
Languages English
T: +47 51 84 99 00
W: www.st-olav.vgs.no

Tromsø International School

4 Breiviklia, 9019 Tromsø, Troms
MYP Coordinator Emil Sundal
PYP Coordinator Susanne Hebnes
Languages English
T: +47 99200780
W: www.trint.org

Trondheim International School

Festningsgata 2, 7014 Trondheim, Trøndelag
MYP Coordinator Virginia Neilsen
PYP Coordinator Hope Steen
Languages English, Norweigan
T: +47 7351 4800
W: www.this.no

Trondheim Katedralskole

Munkegaten 8, 7013 Trondheim, Trøndelag
DP Coordinator Elin Øksnes
Languages English
T: +47 73 19 55 00
W: www.trondheim-katedral.vgs.no

UWC Red Cross Nordic

Hauglandsvegen 304, 6968 Flekke, Sogn og Fjordane
DP Coordinator Natasha Lambert
Languages English
T: +47 5773 7000
W: uwcrcn.no

Vardafjell Videregående Skole

Spannaveien 25, 5532 Haugesund, Rogaland
DP Coordinator Gro Torill Nypan
Languages English
T: +47 5270 9910
W: www.vardafjell.vgs.no

OMAN

ABA – An IB World School

PO Box 372, Medinat Al Sultan Qaboos, Post Code 115, Muscat 115
DP Coordinator Guy Essex
MYP Coordinator Kym Brotherton
PYP Coordinator Bronwyn Matamu
Languages English
T: +968 24955800
W: www.abaoman.edu.om

Al Batinah International School

PO Box 193, Postal Code 321, Sohar
DP Coordinator Michael DeMaranville
MYP Coordinator Greg Perry
PYP Coordinator Maeve Doherty
Languages English
T: +968 26850001
W: www.abisoman.com

Al Sahwa Schools

PO Box 644, PC 116, Mina-Al-Fahal, Muscat
MYP Coordinator Abubaker Motala
PYP Coordinator Sandi Stone
Languages English, Arabic
T: + 968 2460 7620 / 7621 / 2469 3887

Alruwad International School

Al Salam Street, Opposite Al Khoudh Police Station, Seeb
DP Coordinator Vivek Gaur
MYP Coordinator Margaret Hawthorn
PYP Coordinator Izmat Dad
Languages English, Arabic
T: +968 2455 4711
W: ais.edu.om

MySchool Oman

Al Hail South, Al Seeb, Al Huda Street, Way # 2933, Building # 3344, Muscat
PYP Coordinator Parvaneh Bagheri Bahri
Languages English, Arabic
T: +968 24555171
W: www.myschool.edu.om

OURPLANET International School Muscat

Al-Inshirah Street, Building No. 205, Plot No. 95, Block No. 221, Muscat, 111
PYP Coordinator Ana Castro
Languages English
T: +968 2200 5642
W: www.ourplanet-muscat.com

The Sultan's School

PO Box 665, Seeb 121
DP Coordinator Charles Hearsum
Languages Arabic, English
T: +968 24536 777
W: www.sultansschool.org

PAKISTAN

Angels International College

Faisal Town, Near Faisal Valley, West Canal Road, Faisalabad, Punjab 38000
DP Coordinator Khawaja Haris Abbas
MYP Coordinator Muhammad Imran Shahid
PYP Coordinator Khawaja Musa Abbas
Languages English
T: +92 41 8850012
W: www.angelscollege.edu.pk

Beaconhouse College Campus Gulberg

3-C, Zafar Ali Road, Lahore 54000
DP Coordinator Asma Amanat
Languages English
T: +92 42 3588 6239
W: www.beaconhouse.edu.pk

Beaconhouse Newlands Islamabad

Hill View Road, Mohra Noor, Islamabad 44000
DP Coordinator Zubia Akbar
PYP Coordinator Sabahat Bokhari
Languages English
T: +92 51 261 3935/6/7
W: bni.beaconhouse.net

Beaconhouse Newlands Lahore

632/1 Street 10, Phase VI DHA, Lahore 54000
PYP Coordinator Urooj Shahab
Languages English
T: +92 (42) 111 111 020
W: www.beaconhousenewlands.net

Beaconhouse Newlands Multan

4A, Officers Colony, Khanewal Road, Multan, Punjab 60000
PYP Coordinator Iram Fayyaz
Languages English, Urdu
T: +92 61 111 111 020
W: bnm.newlands.net

Beaconhouse School System, Clifton Campus

Frere Town, 2/3 McNeil Road, Clifton, Karachi 75600
PYP Coordinator Tasneem Karbalai
Languages English
T: +92 21 35659190
W: www.beaconhouse.net/branch/clifton-campus-karachi

Beaconhouse School System, Defence Campus

207 A, Saba Avenue, Phase VIII, DHA, Karachi, Sindh 75500
DP Coordinator Ambreen Mustafa
Languages English
T: +92 2135847083 84
W: www.beaconhouse.net/branch/defence-campus-karachi

Beaconhouse School System, Margalla Campus

Pitras Bukhari Rd, H-8/4, Islamabad 44000
DP Coordinator Arham Kashif Sultan
Languages English
T: +92 3345501113
W: ib.beaconhouse.net

Beaconhouse School System, PECHS Campus

35P/1, Block 6 Extension, PECHS, Karachi 75100
DP Coordinator Ayesha Motan
Languages English
T: +92 21 34380045
W: www.beaconhouse.net/branch/beaconhouse-college-campus-pechs-bccp-karachi

Headstart School, Kuri Campus

Kuri Road, Off Park Rd, Near CDA/Park Enclave, Islamabad 44000
DP Coordinator Laraib Imdad
MYP Coordinator Sarah Munir
PYP Coordinator Mehak Temur
Languages English
T: +92 51 8435 473
W: www.headstart.edu.pk

Ilmesters Academy

B-31, PECHS, Block-6, Near Progressive Center, Karachi 75400
DP Coordinator Ms. Khadija Bilkhawala
MYP Coordinator Fizza Taimur
PYP Coordinator Ms. Neesha Feroz
Languages English, Urdu
T: +92 21 34524423
W: www.ilmesters.edu.pk

INTERNATIONAL SCHOOL OF ISLAMABAD

Sector H-9/1, Johar Road, P.O. Box 1124, Islamabad 44000
DP Coordinator Dora Flores
PYP Coordinator Mary Frances Penton
Languages English
T: +92 51 443 4950
E: school@isoi.edu.pk; registrar@isoi.edu.pk
W: www.isoi.edu.pk

See full details on page 125

Kingston College

1 Canal Road, Khaira, Lahore, Punjab
PYP Coordinator Hira Tanweer
Languages English
T: +92 42 3652 6047
W: www.kingstoncollege.net

Lahore Grammar School Defence (Phase 1)

136 – E, Phase 1 Defence Housing Authority (DHA), Lahore Cantt, Punjab, Lahore 54810
PYP Coordinator Saima Asim
Languages English
T: +92 (42) 358 94306
W: lgsdefence.webflow.io

Lahore Grammar School Defence (Phase V)

#483/4, Block G, Education City, Phase V, Defence Housing Authority (DHA), Lahore Cantt, Lahore, Punjab 54810
PYP Coordinator Irma Ahsan
Languages English
T: +92 42 37176005/6/7
W: lgsdefence.edu.pk/phase-v

Lahore Grammar School International

32/3, Sector J, DHA Phase VIII, Lahore 54972
DP Coordinator Sania Rasool
MYP Coordinator Fatima Sajjad
PYP Coordinator Fatima Khan
Languages English
T: +92 42 37175751
W: www.lgsinternational.edu.pk

Lahore Grammar School Islamabad

Plot # 86, Faiz Ahmad Faiz Road, Sector H-8/1, Islamabad 44000
PYP Coordinator Humarah Khalid
Languages English
T: +92 51 4922092
W: www.lgsdefence.edu.pk

Learning Alliance

32/1 J block, DHA Phase VIII, Lahore 54000
DP Coordinator Aurangzeb Akbar
MYP Coordinator Mehrunnisa Sammiullah
PYP Coordinator Sameen Ali
Languages English
T: +92 42 111 66 66 33
W: www.learningalliance.edu.pk

Roots International Schools Islamabad Pakistan

Campus # 66, Street 7, Wellington Campus H-8/4, Islamabad
DP Coordinator Syeda Sada Afaq
Languages English
T: +92 51 8439001-7
W: www.rootsinternational.edu.pk

Roots IVY International School – Chaklala Campus

Walayat Homes, Chakalala Scheme 3, Rawalpindi
PYP Coordinator Maimoona Malik
Languages English
T: +92 51 578 8380
W: www.rootsivyintschools.edu.pk

Roots Ivy International School – DHA Phase V Lahore

Plot #550/1, Sector G, DHA, Phase V (6,192.65 km), Lahore 54000
PYP Coordinator Manal Tahir
Languages English, Urdu
T: +92 302 6274309
W: www.rootsivyintschools.edu.pk

Roots IVY International School – Faisalabad Campus

Opposite Guttwala Park, Faisalabad
PYP Coordinator Rubya Azwar
Languages English
T: +92 321 8912555
W: www.rootsivyintschools.edu.pk

Roots Millennium Schools, One World Campus

Head Office, No.80, Street 1, Sector E-11/4, Islamabad 44000
MYP Coordinator Fomaz Aziz
Languages English
T: +92 51 111 111 193
W: www.millenniumschools.edu.pk

Sanjan Nagar Public Education Trust Higher Secondary School

117 A, Anum Street, Glaxo Town, Ferozepur Road, Lahore, Punjab
PYP Coordinator Danial Ishaq
Languages English
T: +92 42 35950676
W: www.snpet.org

Schole International Academy

273/1/1A, Adjacent Ilma University, Near Suzuki Showroom, Korangi Creek, Karachi, Sindh
PYP Coordinator Chandni Saigol Khan
Languages English, Urdu
T: +92 (21) 350 93330
W: www.scholeacademy.pk

SHEIKH ZAYED INTERNATIONAL ACADEMY

Street 8, Sector H-8/4, Islamabad
DP Coordinator Saima Sohail
MYP Coordinator Saadia Tariq
PYP Coordinator Nadeyah Adnan
Languages English
T: +92 51 4939298
E: info@szia.ae
W: www.szia.ae

See full details on page 200

SICAS DHA Phase VI

310/2F DHA, Phase 6, Lahore, Punjab 54770
PYP Coordinator Samrah Akram Bhatti
Languages English
T: +92 4237338361-3
W: www.sicas.edu.pk

The International School (TIS)

Executive, 51-C Old Clifton, Near Mohatta Palace, Karachi 75600
DP Coordinator Nayma Hasan
MYP Coordinator Akbar Muzna
PYP Coordinator Fehmeena Karim
Languages English
T: +92 21 35835805-6
W: www.tis.edu.pk

The Learning Tree

F-8, Khayaban-e-Saadi, Block 5, Clifton, Karachi, Sindh 75600
PYP Coordinator Afshan Bandeali
Languages English
T: +92 213 587 0001
W: tlt.edu.pk

TNS Beaconhouse Defence

483/3 Sector G, Phase 5, DHA, Lahore, Punjab
DP Coordinator Rashid Khalid
MYP Coordinator Hina Chaudhry
Languages English
T: +92 42 371 762 41 – 43
W: www.tns.edu.pk

TNS Beaconhouse Gulberg

1-H Jail Road, Gulberg II, Lahore, Punjab
MYP Coordinator Zoona Khan
Languages English, Urdu
T: +92 42 111 867 867
W: www.tns.edu.pk

PALESTINE

Ramallah Friends School (Lower School)

Ramallah
PYP Coordinator Sandy Ziadeh
Languages English
T: +970 2 295 6240
W: www.rfs.edu.ps

PALESTINE

Ramallah Friends School (Upper School)
P.O Box 66, Ramallah
DP Coordinator Luai Awwad
MYP Coordinator Mohammad Suleiman
Languages English
T: +970 2 295 2286
W: www.rfs.edu.ps

POLAND

2 Spoleczne Liceum Ogolnoksztalcace STO im. Pawla Jasienicy (2SLO)
ul. Nowowiejska 5, 00-643 Warsaw, Masovia
DP Coordinator Tomasz Mazur
Languages English
T: +48 22 825 11 99
W: www.2slo.pl

33 Liceum im M Kopernika
ul Bema 76, 01-225 Warsaw, Masovia
DP Coordinator Agnieszka White
MYP Coordinator Iwona Berse
Languages English
T: +48 22 632 75 70

Akademickie Dwujezyczne Liceum Oxford Secondary School
ul. Krakowska 30, 43-300 Bielsko-Biala, Silesia
DP Coordinator Agnieszka Strzelecka
Languages English
W: oxfordsecondary.pl

American School of Warsaw
Bielawa, ul Warszawska 202, 05-520 Konstancin-Jeziorna, Masovia
DP Coordinator Paul Lennon
MYP Coordinator Elizabeth Swanson
PYP Coordinator Charlotte Chestnut
Languages English
T: +48 22 702 8500
W: www.aswarsaw.org

ATUT Bilingual Primary School
ul. Raclawicka 101, 53-149 Wroclaw, Lower Silesia
MYP Coordinator Dorota Zielazna
Languages English
T: +48 71 782 26 25
W: www.dspatut.fem.org.pl

British International School of Cracow
ul.Smolensk 25, 31-108 Kraków, Lesser Poland
DP Coordinator Patrick Lagendijk
Languages English
T: +48 1229 264 78
W: www.bisc.krakow.pl

British International School of the University of Lodz
ul Matejki 34a, 90-237 Lodz
DP Coordinator Arkadiusz Glowacz
Languages English
T: +48 42 635 60 06
W: www.interschool.uni.lodz.pl

Da Vinci's International Schools
Pilotów 4c Street, 31-362 Kraków, Lesser Poland
DP Coordinator Joanna Grzybowska
Languages English
T: +48 608 322 388
W: is.edu.pl

I Liceum Ogolnoksztalcace Dwujezyczne im. E. Dembowskiego w Gliwicach
ul Zimnej Wody 8, 44-100 Gliwice, Silesia
DP Coordinator Anita Kwiatkowska
MYP Coordinator Joanna Korek
Languages English
T: +48 32 2314732
W: www.zso10.gliwice.pl

I Liceum Ogólnoksztalcace im St Staszica w Lublinie
Al Raclawickie 26, 20-043 Lublin
DP Coordinator Monika Trznadel
Languages English
T: +48 81 441 1460
W: www. 1lo.lublin.pl

I Liceum Ogólnoksztalcace im. A. Mickiewicza w Olsztynie
Mickiewicza 6, 10-551 Olsztyn, Warmia-Masuria
DP Coordinator Lukasz Jakubowski
Languages English, Polish
T: +48 (89) 527 5353
W: lo1.olsztyn.pl/mm

I Liceum Ogólnoksztalcace im. Leona Kruczkowskiego w Tychach
ul. Korczaka 6, 43-100 Tychy, Silesia
DP Coordinator Katarzyna Scislowicz
Languages English, Polish
T: +48 32 227 3634
W: kruczek.edu.pl

I Liceum Ogólnoksztalcace z Oddzialami Dwujezycznymi im. Ignacego Paderewskiego
ul. I.J. Paderewskiego 17, 58-301 Walbrzych, Lower Silesia
DP Coordinator Beata Urbaniak
MYP Coordinator Beata Urbaniak
Languages English, Polish
T: +48 74 842 36 83
W: www.1lo.walbrzych.pl

II Liceum Ogólnoksztalcace im Mieszka I
ul Henryka Poboznego 2, 70-507 Szczecin, West Pomerania
DP Coordinator Artur Strozynski
MYP Coordinator Monika Chorzepa
Languages English
T: +48 91 433 61 17
W: www.lo2.szczecin.pl

II Liceum Ogólnoksztalcace im Mikolaja Kopernika w Lesznie
Ul Boleslawa Prusa 33, 64-100 Leszno, Greater Poland
DP Coordinator Jolanta Perczak
Languages English
T: +486 5526 8485
W: www.IILO.leszno.eu

II Liceum Ogólnoksztalcace im Stefana Batorego
ul Mysliwiecka 6, 00-459 Warsaw, Masovia
DP Coordinator Joanna Szczesniak
Languages English
T: +48 22 628 2101
W: www.batory.edu.pl

II Liceum Ogólnoksztalcace im. Hetmana Jana Tarnowskiego
ul. Mickiewicza 16, 33-100 Tarnów, Lesser Poland
DP Coordinator Maria Trojanowska
MYP Coordinator Jowita Frac
Languages English
T: +48 14 655 8895
W: www.ii-lo.tarnow.pl

II Liceum Ogólnoksztalcace im. Romualda Traugutta w Czestochowie
Gmina Miasto Czestochowa, ul.Slaska 11/13, 42-217 Czestochowa, Silesia
DP Coordinator Tomasz Muskala
Languages English, Polish
T: +48 343612568
W: www.traugutt.net

II Liceum Ogólnoksztalcace im. Tadeusza Kosciuszki
ul. Szkolna 5, 62-800 Kalisz, Greater Poland
DP Coordinator Magdalena Grzegrzólka
Languages English
T: +48 6276 76657
W: www.2lo.kalisz.pl

II Liceum Ogólnoksztalcace in Bialystok
ul. Narewska 11, 15-840 Bialystok, Podlaskie
DP Coordinator Emilia Makarska
Languages English
T: +48 85 6511416
W: zso2bialystok.pl

II LO im Gen Zamoyskiej i H Modrzejewskiej
Matejki 8/10, 60-760 Poznan, Greater Poland
DP Coordinator Edyta Sobczak
Languages English
T: +48 61 866 2892
W: www.2lo.poznan.pl

III Liceum Ogolnoksztalcace im A. Mickiewicza w Katowicach
ul. Mickiewicza 11, 40-092 Katowice, Silesia
DP Coordinator Beata Zygadlewicz-Kocus
Languages English
T: +48 32 258 93 05
W: www.mickiewicz.katowice.pl

III Liceum Ogolnoksztalcace, Gdynia
Legionów 27, 81-405 Gdynia, Pomerania
DP Coordinator Zofia Krakowiak-Michlewicz
MYP Coordinator Marta Smalara-Lewandowska
Languages English, Polish
T: +48 58 622 1833
W: www.lo3.gdynia.pl

International American School
Ul Dembego 18, 02-796 Warsaw, Masovia
DP Coordinator Kenneth McBride
Languages English
T: +48 22 649 1442
W: www.ias.edu.pl

International European School Warsaw
ul. Wiertnicza 140, 02-952 Warsaw, Masovia
DP Coordinator Malcolm Bannerman
Languages English
T: +48 22 842 44 48
W: ies.waw.pl/en

International High School of Wroclaw
ul. Raclawicka 101, 53-149 Wroclaw, Lower Silesia
DP Coordinator Jillian Craig
MYP Coordinator Dorota Zielazna
Languages English
T: +48 71 782 26 26
W: www.highschool.fem.org.pl

International Primary School
52 Drukarska St, 53-312 Wroclaw, Lower Silesia
PYP Coordinator Hali Ray
Languages English
T: +48 503 188 843
W: www.ipschool.pl

International School of EKOLA
Ul Zielinskiego 56, 53-534 Wroclaw, Lower Silesia
DP Coordinator Adriana Kurowska-Mitas
Languages English
T: +48 71 3614 370
W: www.ekola.edu.pl

International School of Gdansk
ul. Sucha 29, 80-531 Gdansk, Pomerania
PYP Coordinator Malgorzata Macierzanka
Languages English, Polish
T: +48 58 342 31 00
W: www.isg.gfo.pl

International School of Krakow
ul Sw Floriana 57, Lusina, 30-698 Krakow, Lesser Poland
DP Coordinator Lou Panetta
Languages English
T: +48 12 270 1409
W: www.iskonline.org

International School of Poznan
Ul Taczanowskiego 18, 60-147 Poznan, Greater Poland
DP Coordinator Ewa Lysiak
PYP Coordinator Malgorzata Pyda
Languages English
T: +48 61 646 37 60
W: www.isop.pl

IS of Bydgoszcz
Ul. Galczynskiego 23, 85-322 Bydgoszcz, Kuyavia-Pomerania
DP Coordinator Malgorzata Kozielewicz
MYP Coordinator Marta Dereszynska
PYP Coordinator Anna Smigielska
Languages English
T: +48 523 411 424
W: www.isob.ukw.edu.pl

IV Liceum Ogolnoksztalcace im.Emilii Szczanieckiej
ul Pomorska 16, 91-416 Lódz
DP Coordinator Malgorzata Kudra
Languages English
T: +48 42 6336293
W: www.4liceum.pl

IX Liceum Ogólnoksztalcace im. Tadeusz Nowakowskiego
ul. Zofii Nalkowskiej 9, 85-060 Bydgoszcz, Kuyavia-Pomerania
DP Coordinator Monika Obrebska
Languages English
T: +48 52 361 0885
W: waszaedukacja.pl/ponadgimnazjalne/ix-liceum-bydgoszcz-938

IX Liceum Ogolnoksztalcace z Oddzialami Dwujezycznymi
ul. Orzeszkowej 8a, 35-006 Rzeszów, Subcarpathia
DP Coordinator Agata Stachowicz
Languages English, German
T: +48 17 748 2750
W: www.9lo.rzeszow.pl

Jam Saheba Digvijay Sinhji
UI Raszyñska 22, 02-026 Warsaw, Masovia
DP Coordinator Brian Williamson
Languages English
T: +48 22 822 25 15
W: www.bednarska.edu.pl

Kolegium Europejskie
ul. Metalowców 6, 31-537 Kraków, Lesser Poland
DP Coordinator Edyta Zajac
Languages English
T: +48 12 632 46 29
W: www.ke.edu.pl

Liceum im. Marii Konopnickiej w Suwalkach
ul. Mickiewicza 3, 16-400 Suwalki, Podlaskie
DP Coordinator Beata Szczecina
Languages English, Polish
T: +48 87 566 56 26
W: 1lo.suwalki.pl

Liceum Ogólnoksztalcace z Oddzialami Dwujezycznymi im. Wladyslawa Jagielly w Plocku
ul. 3 Maja 4, 09-402 Plock, Masovia
DP Coordinator Marcin Jaroszewski
Languages English
T: +48 24 364 5920
W: www.lwj.edu.pl

Liceum Ogólnoksztalcace z Oddzialami Dwujezycznymi w Boguchwale
ul. Suszyckich 11, 36-040 Boguchwala, Subcarpathia
DP Coordinator Zofia Machnicka
Languages English, Polish
T: +48 17 871 4421
W: www.liceum.boguchwala.pl

Monnet International School
ul. Abramowskiego 4, 02-659 Warsaw, Masovia
DP Coordinator Joanna Majorek
MYP Coordinator Angelika Maj
PYP Coordinator Aneta Borkowska
Languages English
T: +48 22 852 31 10
W: www.maturamiedzynarodowa.pl

Open Future International School
ul. Kwiecista 25, 30-389 Kraków, Lesser Poland
PYP Coordinator Karolina Teernstra
Languages English, Polish
T: +48 123 524 525
W: www.openfuture.edu.pl

Paderewski Private Grammar School
ul Symfoniczna 1, 20-853 Lublin
DP Coordinator Barbara Ostrowska
MYP Coordinator Magdalena Krzeminska
PYP Coordinator Katarzyna Kijek-Kubejko
Languages English
T: +48 81 740 7543
W: www.paderewski.lublin.pl

Private High School Gaudium et Studium
ul. st. Michala 50 M, 61-118 Poznan
DP Coordinator Joanna Borucka
Languages English, Polish
T: +48 60 892 1887
W: eduges.pl/HS/index_HS.php

Private Primary School 97
Abramowskiego Street 4, 02-659 Warsaw, Masovia
PYP Coordinator Aleksandra Fratczak
Languages English
T: +48 22 853 36 60
W: www.leonardo.edu.pl

Prywatne Liceum Ogolnoksztalcace im.M.Wankowicza
ul. Witosa 18, 40-832 Katowice, Silesia
DP Coordinator Justyna Proksza
Languages English
T: +48 32 254 9194
W: wankowicz.edu.pl

Publiczne Liceum Ogólnoksztalcace nr III z Oddzialami Dwujezycznymi
ul. Dubois 28, 45-070 Opole
DP Coordinator Anna Szymanska-Buscicchio
Languages English, Polish
T: +48 77 453 6406
W: www.lo3.opole.pl

Szczecin International School
ul Starzynskiego 3-4, 70-506 Szczecin, West Pomerania
DP Coordinator Diane Howlett
MYP Coordinator Kerstin Walter
PYP Coordinator Anna Piorkowska
Languages English
T: +48 91 4240 300
W: www.sis.info.pl

Szczecinska Szkola Witruwianska SVS
Wojska Polskiego, 164, 71-335 Szczecin, West Pomerania
PYP Coordinator Marta Ciesielska
Languages English, Polish
T: +48 512 868 176
W: svs.edu.pl

Thames British School (Meridian-IB DP)
31B Gladka Str., 02-172 Warsaw, Masovia
DP Coordinator Robert Hodgdon
Languages English
T: +48 510 161 597
W: www.meridian.edu.pl/high-school-grade-9-12

The British School Warsaw
Limanowskiego 15, 02-943 Warsaw, Masovia
DP Coordinator Neeraj Prabhu
Languages English
T: +48 22 842 32 81
W: www.thebritishschool.pl

The Canadian School of Warsaw
Kanadyjska Szkola Podstawowa, Ul. Belska 7, 02-638 Warsaw, Masovia
PYP Coordinator Irina Pawul
Languages English
T: +48 22 646 92 89
W: www.canadian-school.pl

The Nazareth Middle and High School in Warsaw
ul. Czerniakowska 137, 00-720 Warsaw, Masovia
DP Coordinator Marcin Jurkowski
Languages English, Polish
T: +48 22 841 3854/+48 601 644 102
W: www.nazaretanki.edu.pl

Towarzystwo Edukacyjne Vizja
Okopowa 59, 01-043 Warsaw, Masovia
DP Coordinator Malgorzata Byca
Languages English, Polish
T: +48 57 775 5001
W: okopowa.edu.pl/main-page

V Liceum Ogolnoksztalcace in Gem
Jakuba Jasinskiego, ul Grochowa 13, 53-523 Warsaw, Masovia
DP Coordinator Barbara Czuszkiewicz
Languages English
T: +48 71 361 92 66
W: lo5.wroc.pl

VI Liceum Ogólnoksztalcace im. Adama Mickiewicza w Krakowie

Waska 7, 31-057 Kraków, Lesser Poland
DP Coordinator Anna Moskala
Languages English
T: +48 12 430 6908
W: www.vilo.krakow.pl

VI Liceum Ogólnoksztalcace im J Slowackiego w Kielcach

ul Gagarina 5, 25-031 Kielce, Holy Cross Province
DP Coordinator Anna Pakula
Languages English
T: +48 41 361 55 56
W: slowacki.kielce.eu

VIII PRYWATNE AKADEMICKIE LICEUM OGÓLNOKSZTALCACE

ul Karmelicka 45, 31-128 Krakow
DP Coordinator Ewa Dudek
Languages English
T: +48 12 632 93 13
E: dyrektor@pack.edu.pl
W: www.pack.edu.pl

See full details on page 238

Warsaw Montessori High School

ul. Pytlasinskiego 13a, 00-777 Warsaw, Masovia
DP Coordinator Ewa Stawecka
Languages English, Polish
T: +48 787 095 835
W: highschool.wmf.edu.pl

Wroclaw International School

ul. Raclawicka 101, 53-149 Wroclaw, Lower Silesia
MYP Coordinator Jill Bieniek
PYP Coordinator Maria Hughes Potocka
Languages English
T: +48 71 782 26 24
W: www.wis.fem.org.pl

XXXV Liceum Ogólnoksztalcace z Oddzialami Dwujezycznymi im. Boleslawa Prusa

Zwyciezców 7/9, 03-936 Warsaw, Masovia
DP Coordinator Katarzyna Krajewska
Languages English, Polish
T: +48 22 617 74 13
W: www.prus.edu.pl

Zespól Szkól Ogólnoksztalcacych im. Pawla z Tarsu

ul Poezji 19, 04-994 Warsaw, Masovia
DP Coordinator Agnieszka Dziwota
Languages English
T: +48 22 789 14 02
W: www.kulszkola.pl

ZSO No.13 Gdansk

ul. Topolowa 7, 80-255 Gdansk, Pomerania
DP Coordinator Anna Orlowska
Languages English
T: +48 58 341 0671
W: zso13.edu.gdansk.pl/pl

PORTUGAL

Carlucci American International School of Lisbon

Rua Antonio dos Reis, 95, 2710-301 Linhó, Lisbon
DP Coordinator Ana Almeida
Languages English
T: +351 219 239 800
W: www.caislisbon.org

Colégio Atlântico

Av. da Ponte lt 356/A, Pinhal de Frades, 2840-167 Seixal, Lisbon
DP Coordinator Patricia Costa
Languages English, Portuguese
T: +351 212 247 828
W: www.colegioatlantico.pt

Colégio Mira Rio

Estrada de Telheiras 113, 1600-768 Lisbon
DP Coordinator Nelia Simões
Languages English, Portuguese
T: +351 213 030 480
W: www.colegiomirario.pt

Colegio Planalto

Rua Armindo Rodrigues 28, 1600-414 Lisbon
DP Coordinator António Nunes de Figueiredo
Languages English
T: +351 217 541 530
W: www.colegioplanalto.pt

Escola da APEL

Caminho dos Saltos 6 ou Rua do Til 69, 9050-219 Funchal, Madeira
DP Coordinator Graça Valerio
Languages English
T: +351 291 740 470
W: www.escola-apel.com

INTERNATIONAL SHARING SCHOOL – MADEIRA

Caminho dos Saltos 6, 9050-219 Funchal, Madeira
MYP Coordinator Irene Wensley
PYP Coordinator Jenie Noite
Languages English
T: +351 291 773 218
E: office@madeira.sharingschool.org
W: www.sharingschool.org

See full details on page 136

INTERNATIONAL SHARING SCHOOL – TAGUSPARK

Avenida Dr. Mário Soares 14, 2740-119 Oeiras, Lisbon
DP Coordinator David Ferreira
MYP Coordinator Viviana Serralha
PYP Coordinator Déspina Sarioglou
Languages English
T: +351 214 876 140
E: office@taguspark.sharingschool.org
W: www.sharingschool.org

See full details on page 137

Oeiras International School

Quinta Nossa Senhora da Conceicao, Rua Antero de Quental no 7, 2730-013 Barcarena, Oeiras, Lisbon
DP Coordinator Jan Van Hees
MYP Coordinator Carol Pratt
PYP Coordinator Jonathan Chambers
Languages English
T: +351 211 935 330
W: www.oeirasinternationalschool.com

Oporto British School

Rua da Cerca 338, Foz do Douro, 4150-201 Porto
DP Coordinator John Simpson
Languages English
T: +351 226 166 660
W: www.obs.edu.pt

PARK INTERNATIONAL SCHOOL

Estrada de Alfragide 94, 2610-015 Amadora, Lisbon
DP Coordinator Patricia Radoi
Languages English
T: +351 215 807 000
E: all@park-is.com; admissions@park-is.com
W: www.park-is.com

See full details on page 172

SAINT DOMINIC'S INTERNATIONAL SCHOOL, PORTUGAL

Rua Maria Brown, Outeiro de Polima, 2785-816 S Domingos de Rana, Lisbon
DP Coordinator Maripaz Aguilera
MYP Coordinator Simon Downing
PYP Coordinator Claire Webster
Languages English
T: +351 21 444 0434
E: school@dominics-int.org
W: www.dominics-int.org

See full details on page 187

St Julian's School

Quinta Nova, 2775-588 Carcavelos e Parede, Lisbon
DP Coordinator Noelle Lobato
Languages English
T: +351 214 585 300
W: www.stjulians.com

ST. PETER'S INTERNATIONAL SCHOOL

Quinta dos Barreleiros CCI 3952, Volta da Pedra, 2950-201 Palmela, Setúbal
DP Coordinator Mrs. Telma Luís Fresta
Languages English, Portuguese
T: +351 21 233 6990
E: geral@stpeters.pt
W: www.st-peters-school.com

See full details on page 215

QATAR

ACS Doha International School

PO Box 200568, Al Oyoun Street, Al Gharrafa, Doha
CP Coordinator Oliver Lemuel Chua
DP Coordinator Oliver Lemuel Chua
MYP Coordinator Holly Fairbrother
PYP Coordinator Rachel Wayne
Languages English
T: +974 4000 9797
W: www.acs-schools.com

American School of Doha

PO Box 22090, Doha
DP Coordinator Katrina Charles
Languages English
T: +974 4459 1500
W: www.asd.edu.qa

Arab International Academy

Al Sadd Area, Sports Roundabout, Doha 15810
DP Coordinator Nael Hamamra
MYP Coordinator Abdullah Azzam Khan
PYP Coordinator Rasha Hammoud
Languages Arabic, English
T: +974 40414999
W: www.aia.qa

Compass International School Doha, Madinat Khalifa

P.O. Box 22463, Al Baihaqi Street, Building 34, Zone 32, Street 926, Madinat Khalifa
DP Coordinator Ian Mchugh
Languages English, French
T: +974 4034 9888
W: www.nordangliaeducation.com/our-schools/doha/madinat-khalifa

Deutsche Internationale Schule Doha

Ibn Seena School Street No. 30, Doha
DP Coordinator Julia Karnebogen
Languages English, German
T: +974 4451 6836
W: www.ds-doha.de

Doha British School

PO Box 6142, Doha
DP Coordinator Nicholas Taylor
Languages English
T: +974 4019 8000
W: www.dohabritishschool.com

INTERNATIONAL SCHOOL OF LONDON (ISL) QATAR

PO Box 18511, North Duhail, Doha
DP Coordinator Jackie Isherwood
MYP Coordinator Smita Shetty
PYP Coordinator Danielle Robertson
Languages English
T: +974 4433 8600
E: mail@islqatar.org
W: www.islqatar.org

See full details on page 127

QATAR ACADEMY AL KHOR

P.O.Box: 60774, Mowasalat Street, Al Khor
DP Coordinator Mr. David Leadbetter
MYP Coordinator Mr. Martin McCurrach
PYP Coordinator Ms. Nadia Hussain
Languages Arabic, English
T: +974 44546775
E: qaalkhor@qf.org.qa
W: www.qak.edu.qa

See full details on page 174

QATAR ACADEMY AL WAKRA

P.O. Box: 2589, Al Farazdaq Street, street No.: 1034, Zone: 90, Doha
DP Coordinator Ms. Jaime Fontenot
MYP Coordinator Ms. Molly Mosier
PYP Coordinator Mrs. Samira Jurdak
Languages Arabic, English
T: +974 44547418
E: qataracademyal-wakra@qf.org.qa
W: www.qaw.edu.qa

See full details on page 175

QATAR ACADEMY DOHA

P.O. Box: 1129, Luqta Street, Doha
DP Coordinator Ms. Zeina Jawad
MYP Coordinator Ms. Roma Bhargava
PYP Coordinator Ms. Savannah Spillers
Languages Arabic, English
T: +974 44542000
E: qataracademy@qf.org.qa
W: www.qataracademy.edu.qa

See full details on page 176

QATAR ACADEMY MSHEIREB

Msheireb Downtown Doha
PYP Coordinator Ms. Jennifer Magierowicz
Languages English, Arabic
T: +974 44542116
E: qamsheireb@qf.org.qa
W: www.qam.qa

See full details on page 177

QATAR ACADEMY SIDRA

P.O. Box: 34077, Doha
DP Coordinator Mr. John Dugan
MYP Coordinator Ms. Susan Menand
PYP Coordinator Mr. Barry Grogan
Languages English
T: +974 44542322
E: qasidra@qf.org.qa
W: www.qasidra.com.qa

See full details on page 178

SEK INTERNATIONAL SCHOOL QATAR

Onaiza 65, Doha
DP Coordinator Kim Derudder
MYP Coordinator Imogen van der Vijl
PYP Coordinator Anthony Hamblin
Languages Arabic, English, Spanish
T: +974 4012 7633
E: info@sek.qa
W: www.sek.qa

See full details on page 198

Swiss International School Qatar

Al Hashimaya Street, Al Luqta, Doha
DP Coordinator Katherine Milton
MYP Coordinator Stephen Bradley
PYP Coordinator Yolandé Stander
Languages English
T: +974 40363131
W: www.sisq.qa

The Gulf English School

PO Box 2440, Doha
DP Coordinator Hannah Cashel
Languages English
T: +974 4457 8777
W: www.gulfenglishschool.com

American International School of Bucharest

Sos Pipera-Tunari 196, Voluntari, Jud Ilfov, 077190 Bucharest
DP Coordinator Aliza Robinson
MYP Coordinator Andrew Pontius
PYP Coordinator Courtney Hughes
Languages English
T: +40 (21) 204 4300
W: www.aisb.ro

Bucharest – Beirut International School

Sos.Vergului, nr.14, District 2, 022448 Bucharest
DP Coordinator Roxana Salajanu
Languages English
T: +40 (0)744 309 199
W: bbischool.ro

Genesis College

Straulesti Street, 89A District 1, Bucharest
MYP Coordinator Ioana Mindrut
PYP Coordinator Corina Huiu
Languages English, Romanian
T: +40 73 310 7914
W: genesis.ro

Hermann Oberth International German School

34E Pipera Blvd, Voluntari, Ilfov
DP Coordinator Adela Gavrilescu
Languages English, German
T: +4 021 231 20 45
W: www.scoala-germana.ro

INTERNATIONAL SCHOOL OF BUCHAREST

1R Gara Catelu Str., Sector 3, Bucharest 032991
DP Coordinator Mr. Yusuf Suha Orhan
Languages English
T: +40 21 3069530
E: admissions@isb.ro
W: www.isb.ro

See full details on page 123

Liceul Teoretic Scoala Europeana Bucuresti

33 Baiculesti st., 013913 Bucharest
DP Coordinator Ana-Maria Obezaru
Languages English
T: +40 21 3117 770
W: www.scoalaeuropeana.ro

Little London International Academy

Strada Erou Iancu Nicolae 65, Pipera, 077190 Voluntari, Ilfov
PYP Coordinator Costea Iuliana
Languages English
T: +40 721 689 762
W: www.lliacademy.ro

MARK TWAIN INTERNATIONAL SCHOOL

25 Erou Iancu Nicolae Street, Voluntari, Ilfov 077190
DP Coordinator Ms. Olivia Fotescu
MYP Coordinator Ms. Floriana Florea
PYP Coordinator Ms. Orlandina Bulie
Languages English, Romanian
T: +40 735 000 160
E: contact@marktwainschool.ro
W: www.marktwainschool.ro

See full details on page 161

Verita International School

Soldat Gheorghe Pripu Street 22A, 1st District, Bucharest
DP Coordinator Wendi Shumard
Languages English
T: +40 21 311 8811
W: www.veritaschool.ro

Alabuga International School

Nord Drive, Building 1, Yelabuga, Tatarstan 423600
PYP Coordinator Ksenia Mikhedekina
Languages English, Russian
T: +7 855 575 3405
W: alabugais.ru

Brookes Moscow

Lazorevyy Proezd, 7, Moscow 129323
DP Coordinator Daniella Spooner Lagos
MYP Coordinator Natasha Hale
PYP Coordinator Paul Ackers
Languages English
T: +7 (499) 110 70 01
W: moscow.brookes.org

Brookes Saint Petersburg

Tatarskiy Pereulok, 3-5, Saint Petersburg 197198
DP Coordinator Sajeena Mary Joseph
MYP Coordinator Jason Berkeley
PYP Coordinator Thomas Karisa
Languages English
T: +7 (812) 320 89 25
W: saintpetersburg.brookes.org

Colegio Rosalía de Castro No. 1558

Chukotsky Proyezd, 6, c/ Lenskaya 6, 28/1, 24, 19a, Moscow 129327
MYP Coordinator Irina Terekhova
Languages English
T: +7 495 472 47 30
W: colegio1558.ru

RUSSIAN FEDERATION

Deutsche Schule Sankt Petersburg

ul. Petrozavodskaya 12, Saint Petersburg 197110
DP Coordinator Bernd Juen
Languages English, German
T: +7 812 409 21 59
W: deutscheschule.ru

E. M. Primakov Gymnasium

Utrennyaya street, Razdory village, Odintsovo Region, Moscow Oblast 143082
DP Coordinator Nina Romashchenko
Languages English, Russian
T: +7 495 274 44 44
W: ogprim.ru

European Gymnasium

Sokolnichesky Val., d.28, Sokolniki, Moscow 107113
DP Coordinator Tagir Zainullin
MYP Coordinator Aleksandra Manukian
PYP Coordinator Maria Bogantseva
Languages English
T: +7 985 795 4273
W: www.eurogym.ru

Far Eastern Centre of Continuing Education (International Linguistic School)

44 Partizanskiy Av., Vladivostok 690990
DP Coordinator Natalia Tischenko
Languages English
T: +7 423 240 42 84
W: www.mlsh.ru

Gosudarstvennaya Stolichnaya Gymnasiya

94 Altyf'evskoye Shosse, Moscow 127349
PYP Coordinator Alla Zavidey
Languages English
T: +7 495 707 07 62
W: www.gsgschool.ru

International School in Novie Veshki

p. Veshki, residential complex Novie Veshki, Green Boulevard, VL.86, Mytishchi district, Moscow 141031
PYP Coordinator Elizabeth Rybakova
Languages English
T: +7 499 707 8899
W: school-novieveshki.ru

International School of Herzen University

Vosstania str., 8 "B", St. Petersburg
DP Coordinator Irina Tomashpolskaia
MYP Coordinator Irina Tomashpolskaia
Languages English, Russian
T: +7 812 275 7684
W: www.interschool.ru

International School of Kazan

5 Mavlyutova St., Kazan
DP Coordinator Chris Clover
MYP Coordinator Chris Clover
PYP Coordinator Alexandra Francesconi
Languages English, Russian
T: +7 843 204 12 82
W: www.iskazan.com

International School of Samara

ul. Kyibysheva, Building 32, Samara 443099
DP Coordinator Julia Tankeeva
PYP Coordinator Svetlana Tsareva
Languages English, French, Russian
T: +7 846 332 2880

Kaluga International School

Lunacharskogo 16, Kaluga
PYP Coordinator Jay Louie A. Torres
Languages English
T: +7 4843 400444
W: www.kischool.ru

Khoroshevskaya Shkola

45 Marshala Tukhachevskogo St., appt. 2, Moscow 123154
DP Coordinator Andrey Nozdrevatykh
Languages English, Russian
T: +7 (499) 401 02 71
W: horoshkola.ru/en

Kogalym Secondary School No. 8

11 Yantarnaya Street, Khanty-Mansiisk Autonomous Area, Yugra, Kogalym, Tyumen Region 628481
DP Coordinator Eskaeva Svetlana Ivanovna
Languages English
T: +7 34 66 72 71 13
W: www.school8-kogalym.narod.ru

Letovo School

35 Valovaya str., Moscow
DP Coordinator Pavle Milutinovic
MYP Coordinator Alexey Ivanovitch Mashkovtsev
Languages English, Russian
T: +7 8 800 100 51 15
W: letovo.ru/en/home

Linguistic School No. 1531

Godovikov Street 4, Moscow RU-129085
MYP Coordinator Svetlana Ushakova
Languages English
T: +7 495 287 25 71
W: gym1531sv.mskobr.ru

Lyceum 10 of Perm

22 Tehnicheskaya Street, Perm 614070
DP Coordinator Mikhail Novoselov
Languages English
T: +7 342 2819780
W: www.hselyceum.perm.ru

Medical Technical Lyceum

Polevaya str 74, Samara 443002
DP Coordinator Natalia Kabanova
Languages English
T: +7 846 237 0343

Moscow City University Comprehensive School

21A Khodynsky Blv., Moscow 125252
PYP Coordinator Elena Khristenko
Languages Russian
T: +7 499 762 6646
W: university-school.mskobr.ru

MOSCOW ECONOMIC SCHOOL, ODINTSOVO BRANCH

1-A, Zaitsevo Village, Odintsovo Region, Moscow Oblast 143020
DP Coordinator Valeriya Rotershteyn
MYP Coordinator Antonina Andrianova (Gaydash)
PYP Coordinator Larisa Zaitseva
Languages Russian, English
T: +7 495 780 5230
E: mes@mes.ru
W: www.mes.ru

See full details on page 166

MOSCOW ECONOMIC SCHOOL, PRESNYA CAMPUS

29 Zamorenova Street, Moscow 123022
DP Coordinator Alexander Galiguzov
MYP Coordinator Irina Nikitina
PYP Coordinator Tatyana Filatova
Languages English, Russian
T: +7 499 255 55 66
W: www.mes.ru

See full details on page 166

Moscow Gymnasium No. 1409

7, Khodynski blvd, Moscow 125252
MYP Coordinator Ada Kozaeva
Languages Russian
T: +7 499 740 5213

Moscow School No. 1231

Spasopeskovsky lane 6, building 7, Moscow 119002
DP Coordinator Irina Izmailova
PYP Coordinator Elena Alexandrova
Languages English, Russian
T: +7 499 241 43 81
W: sch1231.mskobr.ru

Moscow School No. 1296

Keramicheskiy proezd, Bld.55/3, Moscow 127591
PYP Coordinator Irina Rafalskaya
Languages English
T: +7 499 900 0852
W: cos1296.mskobr.ru

Moscow School No. 1329

Nikulinskaya street, 10, Moscow 119602
DP Coordinator Irina Gorkunova
Languages English
T: +7 495 651 33 97
W: sch1329.mskobr.ru

Moscow School No. 1527

17/5 Andropov prospect, Moscow 115407
MYP Coordinator Olga Shevchenko
Languages English
T: +7 49961 87005

Moscow School No. 1811

bul. Izmaylovsky, 52, Moscow 105077
PYP Coordinator Ekaterina Prokosheva
Languages English, Russian
T: +7 495 465 14 49
W: 1811.mskobr.ru

Moscow School No. 45

8 Grimau Str, Moscow 117036
DP Coordinator Marianna Rovneyko
MYP Coordinator Sofya Dobroshevskaya
PYP Coordinator Maria Andreichenko
Languages English
T: +7 499 126 33 82
W: www.ms45.edu.ru

Moscow State Budget School No. 1583

25, Smolnaya, Moscow 125493
MYP Coordinator Svetlana Dvoryantseva
Languages English
T: +7 499 458 02 57

Moscow State Lyceum No. 1575

6, Usievicha Street, Moscow 125319
MYP Coordinator Oksana Solosina
Languages English
T: +7499 151 89 24
W: lyc1575s.mskobr.ru

Moscow State Secondary General School No. 2086

5, Universitetsky prospect, Moscow 119296
MYP Coordinator Karina Alexandrova
PYP Coordinator Renald Lachashvili
Languages English, Russian
T: +7 910 450 11 70
W: the26.ru

Municipal Autonomous Educational Institute Multitype Lyceum 20

4, Novosondetski Avenue, Ulyanovsk 432072
DP Coordinator Natalia Shamsutdinova
MYP Coordinator Evgeniia Gennadievna Shulga
Languages English
T: +7 842 220 4550
W: education.simcat.ru/school20

President School

Ilyinsky Pod, 2, bld. 1 (in the village of ParkVille Zhukovka), Zhukovka village, Odintsovo district, Moscow Region 143082
DP Coordinator Natalia Vlasova
Languages English
T: +7 495 955 0000
W: school-president.ru

Private Lomonosov School Nizhny Novgorod

Gogol Street, 62, Nizhny Novgorod 603109
DP Coordinator Daria Klochkova
MYP Coordinator Dmitry Klochkov
PYP Coordinator Inna Klochkova
Languages Russian
T: +7 831 430 08 63
W: www.chastnayashkola.ru

Pushkin School No. 9 Perm

ul. Komsomolsky Prospect, 45, Perm 614039
MYP Coordinator Olga Fidan
Languages English
T: +7 342 212 80 71
W: www.school9.perm.ru

SBGEI of the Moscow City 'School No. 1411'

Severny boulevard, 1a, Moscow 127566
PYP Coordinator Alexandra Shumilova
Languages English, Russian
T: +7 (499) 204 43 11

School 1557 named after P. Kapitsa

Korp 529, Zelenograd, Moscow 124482
MYP Coordinator Marina Davydova
Languages English, Russian
T: +7 4997360846
W: lyczg1557.mskobr.ru

School No. 1560

7 Mnevniki street, building 5, Moscow 123308
MYP Coordinator Ekaterina Ilina
Languages English
T: +7 499 946 4196
W: 1560.mskobr.ru

School No. 1589, Moscow

Initsiativnaya street, house 1, Moscow 121357
DP Coordinator Elena Yurchenko
PYP Coordinator Tatiana Cherniavskaia
Languages English, Russian
T: +7 495 4442571
W: lycc1589.mskobr.ru

School No. 185 of the City of Moscow

Mikhalkovskaya Street, 3, Moscow 125008
PYP Coordinator Fatima Dokshukina
Languages English
W: sch185s.mskobr.ru/#

SCHOOL OF YOUNG POLITICIANS – 1306

Michurinskiy avenue 15, Buildings 2-4, 119192 Moscow
DP Coordinator Mrs. Sholpan Mussina
MYP Coordinator Ms. Asylkay Davydova, MA
PYP Coordinator Mr. Azat Mazkenov, MA
Languages English, Russian
T: +7 495 932 99 58
E: 1306@edu.mos.ru
W: gymg1306.mskobr.ru

See full details on page 191

Specialized English Language School No. 7

7450 Lunacharskiy Street, Perm 614000
PYP Coordinator Tatiana Zakirova
Languages English
T: +7 342 2360580
W: www.sc7.perm.ru

State Budget Educational Institution No. 1252 after Cervantes

Dubosekovskaya str.3, Moscow 125080
MYP Coordinator Liudmila Novikova
Languages English
T: +7 49915 80222

State Classical School No. 1272

17, 1st Kozhukhovsky pr., Moscow 115280
PYP Coordinator Irina Dobranskaya
Languages English
T: +7 495 710 36 39
W: sch1272.mskobr.ru

The Anglo-American School of Moscow

1 Beregovaya Street, Moscow 125367
DP Coordinator Sean Sonderman
PYP Coordinator Maureen Sackmaster Carpenter
Languages English
T: +7 (495) 231 44 88
W: www.aas.ru

The British International School, Moscow

Novoyasenevsky prospekt 19/5, Moscow 117593
DP Coordinator Jack Meadows
Languages English
T: +7 495 426 0311; +7 495 987 4486
W: www.bismoscow.com

The International Gymnasium of the Skolkovo Innovation Center

Skolkovo Innovation Center, Zvorykin Street 7, Moscow 143026
DP Coordinator Raisa Baragyan
MYP Coordinator Elena Andreeva
PYP Coordinator Maria Eliseeva
Languages English
T: +7 (495) 956 00 33
W: sk.ru/city/gymnasium

The Romanov School

3, Bolshoi Kondratievsky side-street, New Arbat street, 22, app. 118, Moscow 123056
DP Coordinator Svetlana Grunvald
Languages English
T: +7 916 115 61 50
W: 1240.ru

Vnukovo International School

Pervomaiskoe, Rogozinino Lugovaya Street 20b, Moscow 108808
DP Coordinator Tatiana Krasilnikova
Languages Russian
T: +7 (495) 431 70 70
W: vnukovo.school

XXI CENTURY INTEGRATION INTERNATIONAL SECONDARY SCHOOL

16 Marshala Katukova St., Building 3, Moscow 123592
DP Coordinator Nigiar Mekhtieva
MYP Coordinator James Nevin
PYP Coordinator Kristina Moavad
Languages English, Russian
T: +7 495 750 3102
E: school@integration21.ru
W: www.integration21.ru

See full details on page 247

Green Hills Academy

PO Box 6419, Nyarutarama, Kigali
DP Coordinator Mathias Ndinya
Languages English
T: +250 735 832 348
W: www.greenhillsacademy.rw

Advanced Learning Schools

PO Box 221985, Riyadh 11311
DP Coordinator Tania Maana
MYP Coordinator Maher Qanbaz
PYP Coordinator Haya Abdulrahim
Languages English
T: +966 1 207 0926
W: www.alsschools.com

Al Andalus Private Schools

Batarji Street, Azzahra Dist, Jeddah 21443
PYP Coordinator Ahmed Elkotby
Languages English, Arabic
T: +966 556 645 532
W: www.alandalus.edu.sa

Al Faris International School

Tawaan Area, Imam Saud Road, Khan Younes Street, Riyadh 9483
DP Coordinator Mrs. Farah Kiblawi
MYP Coordinator Mrs. Salwa Ghandour
PYP Coordinator Mrs. Rasha Ghraizi
Languages English
T: +966 011 454 9358
W: www.alfarisschool.com

AL HUSSAN INTERNATIONAL SCHOOL KHOBAR

PO Box 297, Dammam 31411
DP Coordinator Ms. Samar Deshmukh
Languages English
T: +966 13 858 7566
E: ahisk@alhussan.edu.sa
W: international.alhussan.edu.sa

See full details on page 48

Al-Bassam International School

Dammam
PYP Coordinator Rania Ezzeldeen
Languages English, Arabic
T: +966 013 843 4999
W: www.albassamis.com

American International School – Riyadh

PO Box 990, Riyadh 11421
DP Coordinator Liam Trimm
Languages English
T: +966 11 491 4270
W: www.aisr.org

Bright Minds International School

Pr. Sultan Street, Behind Haram Center, An Naim District, Jeddah
PYP Coordinator Alshaima Almarwai
Languages English, Arabic
T: +966 (0)12 654 2505
W: brightmindsschool.com

Deutsche Internationale Schule Jeddah

P.O. Box 7510, Jeddah 21472
DP Coordinator Tonia Whewell
Languages English
T: +966 12 691 3584
W: www.disj.de

Dhahran Ahliyya Schools

P.O.Box 39333, Dhahran 31942
MYP Coordinator Bilal El Bacha
PYP Coordinator Rola Abu-Sager
Languages English, Arabic
T: +966 138919222
W: www.das.sch.sa

Dhahran High School

PO Box 31677, Al-Khobar 31952
DP Coordinator Ewan Hunt
Languages English
T: +966 13 330 0555
W: dhs.isg.edu.sa

International Programs School

Prince Sultan Road, Qurtoba, Al Khobar 34236
DP Coordinator Gunseli Yuksel
PYP Coordinator Siham Dabouk
Languages English
T: +966 13 857 5603
W: www.ipsksa.com

International Schools Group (ISG) Jubail

PO Box 10059, Jubail 31961
DP Coordinator Sanjeev Jangra
Languages English
T: +966 13 341 7550
W: www.isg-jubail.org

Jeddah Knowledge International School

Al Salamah District, Mohammed Mosaud St. (Behind Iceland), PO Box 7180, 21462 Jeddah
DP Coordinator Natasha Awada
MYP Coordinator Sarah Bakkar
PYP Coordinator Amal Sinno
Languages English, Arabic
T: +966 2 691 7367
W: www.jks.edu.sa

KING ABDULAZIZ SCHOOL

Ali Ibn Abi Taleb Road, P.O. Box 43111, Medina 41561
DP Coordinator Mohammad Alhaj Baba
MYP Coordinator Mohammad Vall
PYP Coordinator Raheela Akram
Languages English
T: +966 553 039 300/+966 503 454 420
E: mvall@kaism.org; rakram@kaism.org
W: www.kaism.org

See full details on page 144

King Faisal Pre-School

PO Box 94558, Riyadh 11614
PYP Coordinator Randa Dahshe
Languages Arabic, English
T: +966 1 482 0802
W: www.kfs.sch.sa

King Faisal School

PO Box 94558, Riyadh 11614
DP Coordinator Yazan Mohammad
MYP Coordinator Mohammed Bahzat
PYP Coordinator Kalwant Rana
Languages English, Arabic
T: +966 1 482 0802
W: www.kfs.sch.sa

Les Écoles Internationales Al-Kawthar

PO Box 52280, Jeddah 21563
PYP Coordinator Hanene Karouch
Languages French
T: +966506561717; +966506359280
W: www.alkawthar.edu.sa

MADAC Schools

P.O.Box 444, Jabla bin Thour Street, Abu Kubir District, Medina
PYP Coordinator Sarah Mostafa
Languages English, Arabic
T: +966 555261230
W: madac.edu.sa

Qodrat Alajyal

Medina
PYP Coordinator Arwa AlQarni
Languages Arabic, French
W: qgs.edu.sa

Qurtubah Private Schools

Prince Sultan Street, North-West Al-Tareekh Square, Jeddah 21581
PYP Coordinator Ikrami Farraj
Languages Arabic
T: +966 551757472
W: qps.edu.sa

Radhwa International School Yanbu

P.B.No. 32006, Yanbu 41912
PYP Coordinator Osama Tosson
Languages English
W: www.radhwa.org

Rand International School

PO.box 9712, Dammam 31423
PYP Coordinator Sabana Mughal
Languages Arabic, English
T: +966 13 8504488
W: www.randschools.com

The British International School of Jeddah

PO Box 6453, Jeddah 21442
DP Coordinator Richard Young
Languages English
T: +966 1 2 699 0019
W: www.bisj.com

THE KAUST SCHOOL

Safaa Gardens School, Office 1132, 4700 KAUST, Thuwal 23955-6900
DP Coordinator Susan Rhodes
MYP Coordinator Peter Powell
PYP Coordinator Jon Davidson
Languages English
T: +966 12 808 6803
E: schools@kaust.edu.sa
W: tks.kaust.edu.sa

See full details on page 233

Yusr International School (YIS)

King Abdulaziz Rd, Opp Redsea Mall, An Nahdah, Jeddah 23614
PYP Coordinator Ahmed Abdelrazzaq
Languages English, Arabic
T: +966 55 506 3771
W: www.yusrschool.com

Cours Sainte Marie de Hann

Route Des Peres Maristes, BP 98, Dakar
DP Coordinator Honorine Tamba
Languages English, French
T: +221 33 832 08 29
W: www.mariste.sn

Enko Keur Gorgui International School

Cité Keur Gorgui, Mermoz-Sacré-Cœur, Dakar
DP Coordinator Siménou Titrikou
MYP Coordinator Elhadji Demba Wade Diop
Languages English, French
T: +221 33 821 30 64
W: enkoeducation.com/keur-gorgui

Enko Waca International School

BP 24340, Ouakam, Dakar
DP Coordinator Alanna Ross
Languages French
T: +221 33 820 49 29
W: enkoeducation.com/waca

International School of Dakar

BP 5136 Fann, Dakar
DP Coordinator Wendy Gifford
MYP Coordinator Denrol Carayol
PYP Coordinator Bradley Chumrau
Languages English
T: +221 33 860 2332
W: www.isdakar.org

Le Collège Bilingue de Dakar

Sacré Coeur 3, Cité Keur Gorgui No.53, Dakar 00221
DP Coordinator Souleymane DIAW
Languages English, French
T: +221 33 860 60 10
W: lecollegebilingue-dakar.net

Lycée Billes

Commune de Plan Jaxaay-Cité, Gendarmerie Rufisquel, Dakar
DP Coordinator Amadou Bamba Thiobane
Languages English, French
T: +221 77 413 73 55
W: lyceebilles.com

Crnjanski High School

Djordja Ognjanovica 2, 11030 Belgrade
DP Coordinator Gordana Medakovic
Languages English
T: +381 112 398 388
W: www.crnjanski.edu.rs

Deseta gimnazija 'Mihajlo Pupin'

Antifascist Struggles 1a, 11070 New Belgrade
DP Coordinator Mirjana Vlahovic
Languages English, Serbian
T: +381 113 114 142
W: xgimnazija.edu.rs

Gimnazija Svetozar Markovic
Ul. Branka Radicevica 1, 18000 Nis
DP Coordinator Ivana Babovic
Languages English
T: +381 18 254 396
W: gsm-nis.edu.rs

Gymnasium Jovan Jovanovic Zmaj
Zlatne grede 4, Novi Sad, Vojvodina
DP Coordinator Aleksandra Strahinic
Languages English, French
T: +381 21 529 977
W: jjzmaj.edu.rs/pocetna

International School
45 Sumatovacka Street, Belgrade
DP Coordinator Zorana Zivanovic
Languages English
T: +381 (0)11 4011 220
W: www.international-school.edu.rs

International School of Belgrade
Temisvarska 19, 11040 Belgrade
DP Coordinator Branka Sreckovic-Minic
MYP Coordinator Kristin Westby
PYP Coordinator Barbara Netzel
Languages English
T: +381 112 069 999
W: www.isb.rs

Ruder Bo kovic
Kneza Vi eslava 17, 11000 Belgrade
DP Coordinator Aleksandra Ivanovski
MYP Coordinator Jelena Pozni?
PYP Coordinator Katarina Milosevic
Languages English
T: +381 113 540 786
W: www.boskovic.edu.rs

SLOVAKIA

English International School of Bratislava
Kalinciakova 12, Bratislava 83101
DP Coordinator Bronislava Dvorecka
MYP Coordinator Lisa Kerwin
Languages English
T: +421 907 462 297
W: www.eisbratislava.com

QSI INTERNATIONAL SCHOOL OF BRATISLAVA
Záhradnicka 1006/2, Samorin 93101
DP Coordinator Mr. Jeff Varney
Languages English
T: +421 903 704 436
E: bratislava@qsi.org
W: bratislava.qsi.org
See full details on page 179

Spojená skola Novohradská
Novohradská 3, Bratislava 821 09
DP Coordinator Matej Gonda
MYP Coordinator Gabriela Markusová
PYP Coordinator Travis Seitsinger
Languages English
T: +421 25 557 6396
W: www.gjh.sk

Súkromná spojená skola
Starozagorská 8, 040 23 Ko ice
PYP Coordinator Vladimíra Klementová
Languages English, Slovak
W: www.schoolhuman.eu

The British International School, Bratislava
J. Vala tana Dolinského 1 (Pekníkova 6), Bratislava 841 02
DP Coordinator Monica Gautama
Languages English
T: +421 2 6930 7081
W: www.bis.sk

SLOVENIA

Danila Kumar Primary School
Godezeva 11, 1000 Ljubljana
MYP Coordinator Anja De man
PYP Coordinator Kristina Fürst
Languages English
T: +386 15 636 834
W: www.gimb.org

Gimnasija Kranj
Koroka Cesta 13, 4000 Kranj
DP Coordinator Nata a Kne
Languages English
T: +386 42 811 710
W: www.gimkr.si

Gimnazija Bezigrad
Periceva 4, 1000 Ljubljana
DP Coordinator Irena Cesnik
MYP Coordinator Katja Kvas
Languages English
T: +386 13 000 400
W: www.gimb.org

Gimnazija Novo Mesto
Seidlova cesta 9, 8000 Novo Mesto
DP Coordinator Polonca Centa
Languages English
T: +386 73 718 500
W: www.gimnm.org

II gimnazija Maribor
Trg Milosa Zidanska 1, 2000 Maribor
DP Coordinator Mateja Fosnaric
Languages English
T: +386 33 04 434
W: www.druga.si

Vector International Academy
Stula 23, 1000 Ljubljana
DP Coordinator Anda Eckman
Languages English, French
T: +386 40 862 445
W: vectoracademy.si

SOUTH AFRICA

American International School of Johannesburg
Midrand, Johannesburg
DP Coordinator Kelly Scotti
Languages English
T: +27 11 464 1505
W: www.aisj-jhb.com

Crawford International Bedfordview
7 Marais Road, Bedfordview, 2008 Johannesburg, Gauteng
PYP Coordinator Amy Venter
Languages English, Afrikaans
T: +27 87 350 4633
W: www.crawfordschools.co.za/bedfordview

Crawford International Fourways
16 Campbell Road, Craigavon, Fourways, Sandton, 2191 Johannesburg, Gauteng
PYP Coordinator Robyn Hardy
Languages English
T: +27 11 465 4418
W: www.crawfordschools.co.za/fourways

Crawford International La Lucia
79 Armstrong Avenue, La Lucia, 4001 Durban, KwaZulu-Natal
PYP Coordinator Angela Johnstone
Languages English, Afrikaans
T: +27 31 562 9444
W: www.crawfordschools.co.za/la-lucia

Crawford International Lonehill
17 Lonehill Boulevard, Lonehill, 2062 Johannesburg, Gauteng
PYP Coordinator Debbie Lynch
Languages English, Afrikaans
T: +27 11 467 0936/5
W: www.crawfordschools.co.za/lonehill

Crawford International North Coast
Watson Highway, 4399 Tongaat, KwaZulu-Natal
PYP Coordinator Sonia Jansen
Languages English, Afrikaans
T: +27 32 943 3240
W: www.crawfordschools.co.za/north-coast

Crawford International Pretoria
555 Sibelius Street, Lukasrand, 0181 Pretoria, Gauteng
PYP Coordinator Anthea Jordaan
Languages English, Afrikaans
T: +27 12 343 5903
W: www.crawfordschools.co.za/pretoria

Crawford International Ruimsig
Cnr Peter and Kuilstock Roads, Ruimsig, 1724 Roodepoort, Gauteng
PYP Coordinator Laurentia van Muylwyk
Languages English, Afrikaans
T: +27 11 958 0707
W: www.crawfordinternational.co.za/ruimsig

Crawford International Sandton
Crawford Estate Waterstone Drive (off Benmore Road), Benmore, Sandton, 2196 Johannesburg, Gauteng
PYP Coordinator Lucinda Pinto
Languages English, Zulu
T: +27 11 784 3447
W: www.crawfordschools.co.za/sandton

HOUT BAY INTERNATIONAL SCHOOL
61 Main Road, Hout Bay, Cape Town 7806
DP Coordinator Winell Gous
MYP Coordinator Elani McDonald
PYP Coordinator Rhona Sehested-Larsen
Languages English
T: +27 21 791 7900
E: hbis@iesmail.com
W: www.houtbayinternational.co.za
See full details on page 105

Mokopane Destiny Academy
c/o Geyser and Fourie, RET Centre, 0601 Mokopane, Limpopo
MYP Coordinator Chris van Zyl
PYP Coordinator Elaine van Rensburg
Languages English
T: +27 15 491 2049
W: destinyacademy.co.za

Redhill School
20 Summit Road, Morningside, Sandton, Johannesburg 2057
DP Coordinator Michele Marnitz
Languages English
T: +27 11 783 4707
W: www.redhill.co.za

SPAIN

SPAIN

Agora International School Barcelona

Carrer Puig de Mira, Sant Esteve Sesrovires, 08635 Barcelona, Catalonia
DP Coordinator Juan José Borrego
Languages English, Spanish, Catalan, French/german
T: +34 93 779 89 28
W: www.colegioagorabarcelona.com

Agora International School Madrid

Calle Duero, 35, Villaviciosa de Odón, 28670 Madrid
DP Coordinator Rachel Walker
Languages English, Spanish
T: +34 91 616 71 25
W: www.colegioagoramadrid.com

Agora Lledó International School

Camino Caminàs, 175, Castelló de la Plana, 12003 Castelló, Valencia
DP Coordinator Ester Escrig de Casas
Languages English, Spanish
T: +34 964 72 31 70
W: www.colegioagoralledo.com

Agora Portals International School

Carretera Vella Palma-Andratx, s/n, Portals Nous, 07181 Mallorca, Balearic Islands
DP Coordinator Rocio Baquero
Languages English, Spanish
T: +34 964 72 31 70
W: www.colegioagoraportals.com

Agora Sant Cugat International School

Carrer Ferrer i Guàrdia, s/n, Sant Cugat del Vallés, 08174 Barcelona, Catalonia
DP Coordinator Montse Martí Linares
MYP Coordinator Arnaldo Schapire Trapano
PYP Coordinator Mireia Cuxart
Languages English, Spanish, Catalan
T: +34 93 590 26 00
W: www.agorasantcugat.com

Aloha College

Urbanización el Angel, 29660 Marbella, Málaga, Andalusia
DP Coordinator Elaine Brigid Mc Girl
Languages English, Spanish
T: +34 95 281 41 33
W: www.aloha-college.com

American School of Barcelona

Calle Balmes 7, Esplugues de Llobregat, 08950 Barcelona, Catalonia
DP Coordinator Charmaine Monds
Languages English
T: +34 93 371 4016
W: www.asbarcelona.com

American School of Bilbao

Soparda Bidea 10, 48640 Berango, Biscay, Basque Country
DP Coordinator Mariana Curti
MYP Coordinator Nina Franco
PYP Coordinator Zeynep Dincer
Languages English
T: +34 94 668 0860
W: www.asob.es

American School of Madrid

Apartado 80, 28080 Madrid
DP Coordinator Martina Bree
Languages English
T: +34 91 740 19 00
W: www.asmadrid.org

American School of Valencia

Urbanización Los Monasterios, Apartado de Correos 9, 46530 Puzol, Valencia
DP Coordinator Josep Vicent Frechina
Languages English, Spanish, Valencia
T: +34 96 140 5412
W: www.asvalencia.org

Angel de la Guarda

Calle Andalucía 17-20, 03016 Alicante, Valencia
DP Coordinator Rosario Pérez Escoto
Languages English, Spanish
T: +34 9652 61899
W: www.angeldelaguarda.eu

Aquinas American School

Calle Transversal Cuatro, 4, Urbanización Monte Alina, Pozuelo de Alarcon, 28223 Madrid
DP Coordinator Ana Curbera
Languages English
T: +34 91 352 31 20
W: www.aquinas-american-school.es

Aula Escola Europea

Avinguda Mare de, Déu de Lorda, 34-36, 08034 Barcelona, Catalonia
DP Coordinator Cristina Buendia Fores
Languages Spanish
T: +34 93 203 03 54
W: www.aula-ee.com

Bell-Iloc Del Pla

Carrer de Can Pau Birol, 2, 17005 Girona, Catalonia
DP Coordinator Manel Juny Pastells
Languages Spanish
T: +34 972 232 111
W: www.bell-lloc.org/ca

Benjamin Franklin International School

Martorell i Pena 9, 08017 Barcelona, Catalonia
DP Coordinator Laura Blair
Languages English
T: +34 93 434 2380
W: www.bfischool.org

BRAINS INTERNATIONAL SCHOOL, LA MORALEJA

Calle Salvia, Nº 48, 28109 Alcobendas, Madrid
DP Coordinator Michael Harvey
Languages English
T: +34 91 650 43 00
E: michael@colegiobrains.com
W: www.colegiobrains.com

See full details on page 65

British College of Gava

Carrer de Josep Lluís Sert 32, 08850 Gavà, Barcelona, Catalonia
DP Coordinator Rachel Fenton
Languages English, Spanish
T: +34 932 777 899
W: www.britishcollegegava.com

C.E. Punta Galea

Urbanización Punta Galea Playa del Sardinero, 1, 28290 Las Rozas, Madrid
DP Coordinator Miguel Cardenal Grajera
Languages Spanish
T: +34 91 630 26 41
W: www.colegio-puntagalea.com

CASVI INTERNATIONAL AMERICAN SCHOOL

C/ Gavilán, 2, Tres Cantos, 28760 Madrid
DP Coordinator Ana isabel Domínguez Sánchez
MYP Coordinator Laura Kelly McCutcheon
PYP Coordinator Ryan Posey
Languages English, Spanish
T: +34 91 804 02 12
E: info@casvitrescantos.es
W: www.casvitrescantos.es

See full details on page 68

Centre Cultural I Esportiu Xaloc

Can Tries, 4-6, L'Hospitalet de Llobregat, 08902 Barcelona, Catalonia
DP Coordinator Martin Curiel
PYP Coordinator Francesc Xavier Dominguez Martín
Languages Spanish
T: +34 93 335 1600
W: www.xaloc.org

Centro de Estudios Ibn Gabirol Colegio Estrella Toledano

Paseo de Alcobendas 7 (La Moraleja), 28109 Alcobendas, Madrid
DP Coordinator Julio Fernando Zapata
Languages English
T: +34 916 50 12 29
W: www.colegiogabiroltoledano.com

Centro Educativo Agave

Camino de la Gloria no 17, 04230 Huercal de Almería, Almería, Andalusia
DP Coordinator Isabel Maria Fenoy Gázquez
Languages English
T: +34 9503 01026
W: www.colegioagave.com

Col·legi Sant Miquel dels Sants

Jaume I, 11, 08500 Vic, Barcelona, Catalonia
DP Coordinator Vanesa Ferrreres Vergés
Languages Catalan, Spanish
T: +34 93 886 12 44
W: www.santmiqueldelssants.cat

Colegio Adharaz

Urb. La Vina. C/ Garnacha 1, 41807 Espartinas, Seville, Andalusia
PYP Coordinator Ángela Muniáin
Languages English, Spanish
T: +34 955 713 820
W: attendis.com/colegios-sevilla/adharaz

Colegio Alameda de Osuna

Paseo de la Alameda de Osuna, 60, 28042 Madrid
DP Coordinator Arantza Carrillo Alonso
Languages English, Spanish
T: +34 91 742 70 11
W: www.colegio-alameda.com

Colegio Alauda

Cerillo 6, 14014 Córdoba, Andalusia
DP Coordinator Laura Paños Díaz
Languages English
T: +34 957 40 55 07
W: www.colegioalauda.org

Colegio Alegra

Calle de Sorolla 4, 28222 Majadahonda, Madrid
DP Coordinator Militza Hernandez
MYP Coordinator Beatriz Duro Aneiros
Languages English, Spanish
T: +34 916 39 79 03
W: www.alegrabritishschool.com

Colegio Altasierra

Urb. La Viña. C/ Garnacha 2., 41807 Espartinas, Seville, Andalusia
PYP Coordinator Jesús Hervías Gallardo
Languages English, Spanish
T: +34 954 614 760
W: attendis.com/colegios-sevilla/altasierra

Colegio Antamira

C/ Los Cuadros, 2, Miramadrid, 28860 Paracuellos de Jarama, Madrid
DP Coordinator Pedro Pablo Sacristán Sanz
Languages English, Spanish
T: +34 91 667 27 07
W: www.colegioantamira.com

Colegio Arcangel Rafael

Calle Maqueda no. 4, 28024 Madrid
DP Coordinator Pablo Osma Rodriguez
Languages English, Spanish
T: +34 91 711 93 00
W: www.colegio-arcangel.com

Colegio Arenas Atlántico

Paseo San Patricio, No 20, 35413 Trasmontaña, Las Palmas, Canary Islands
DP Coordinator David Arbelo Llorente
MYP Coordinator Encarnación Lorenzo de Armas
Languages Spanish
T: +34 928 629 140
W: www.colegioarenas.es

Colegio Arenas Internacional

Avenida del Mar 37, Lanzarote, 35509 Costa Teguise, Las Palmas, Canary Islands
DP Coordinator Jose Antonio Paz Botana
MYP Coordinator Brian Foster
PYP Coordinator Estela Medina
Languages Spanish
T: +34 928 590 835
W: www.colegioarenas.es

Colegio Arenas Sur

Las Margaritas s/n, 35290 San Agustín, Las Palmas, Canary Islands
DP Coordinator Patricia Bergström
Languages Spanish
T: +34 928 765 934
W: www.colegioarenassur.com

Colegio Atalaya

Calle Pico Alcazaba 24-28, Urbanización El Marqués, 29680 Estepona, Málaga
DP Coordinator Iraia Manterola Berrueta
Languages English, Spanish
T: +34 952 003 171
W: www.colegioatalaya.es

Colegio Base

Calle del Camino Ancho, 10, 28109 Alcobendas, Madrid
DP Coordinator Victor Acosta Ferreras
Languages Spanish
T: +34 9165 00313
W: www.colegiobase.com

COLEGIO BRAINS MARIA LOMBILLO

Calle Maria Lombillo 5, 28027 Madrid
DP Coordinator Linda Keys
PYP Coordinator Daniel Prieto
Languages English, Spanish
T: +34 91 742 10 60
E: plopez@colegiobrains.com
W: www.colegiobrains.com/en/private-school/maria-lombillo

See full details on page 72

Colegio Camarena Canet

C/ De la Rosa s/n, 46529 Canet d'en Berenguer, Valencia
MYP Coordinator Francisca Martinez Carbonell
PYP Coordinator Amparo Afortunado
Languages English, Spanish
T: +34 960 609 036
W: www.colegiocamarenacanet.es

Colegio Camarena Valterna

Calle Carlina s/n 46980, Valterna, Urb. Lloma Llarga, Paterna, Valencia
PYP Coordinator Ángela Meléndez Martín
Languages English, Spanish
T: +34 961 381 898
W: www.colegiovalterna.es

Colegio Cervantes

Avda. de la Fuensanta, 37, 14010 Córdoba, Andalusia
DP Coordinator Manuel Porras García
Languages English
T: +34 957 255150
W: www.maristascordoba.com

Colegio CEU Jesús María Alicante

Calle Deportista Alejandra Quereda 15, 03016 Alicante, Valencia
PYP Coordinator Pablo Jesús Díaz Tenza
Languages Catalan, Valencian, Spanish
T: +34 965 261 400
W: www.colegioceualicante.es

Colegio CEU San Pablo Montepríncipe

Avda. Montepríncipe, s/n, 28668 Boadilla del Monte, Madrid
DP Coordinator José Manuel Ruiz Vila
Languages English
T: +34 91 352 05 23
W: www.colegioceumonteprincipe.es

Colegio CEU San Pablo Sanchinarro

Niceto Alcalá Zamora, 43, 28050 Madrid
DP Coordinator Ruth Jiménez Balboa
Languages English
T: +34 91 392 34 40/41
W: www.colegioceusanchinarro.es

Colegio CEU San Pablo Valencia

Edificio Seminario Metropolitano, 46113 Moncada, Valencia
DP Coordinator Angel Luis Peris Suay
PYP Coordinator Francisco Haro Canet
Languages Spanish
T: +34 961 36 90 14
W: www.colegioceuvalencia.es

Colegio de San Francisco de Paula

C/ Santa Angela de la Cruz, 11, 41003 Seville, Andalusia
DP Coordinator German Delgado
MYP Coordinator Francis Banwell
PYP Coordinator Macarena Vázquez de Cruces
Languages Spanish, English
T: +34 95 422 4382
W: www.sfpaula.com

Colegio del Salvador

Padre Arrupe 13, 50009 Zaragoza, Aragon
DP Coordinator María Laguna MarinYaseli
Languages English, Spanish
T: +34 976 353 400
W: jesuitaszaragoza.es

Colegio Ecos

C/ Velázquez, 7. Urb. Elvira, La Mairena, Ojén, 29612 Marbella, Málaga, Andalusia
PYP Coordinator Telesforo Zabala Ordóñez
Languages English, Spanish
T: +34 952 831 027
W: attendis.com/colegios-marbella/ecos

Colegio El Romeral

Calle De Eolo 2, 29010 Málaga, Andalusia
PYP Coordinator Francisco Garcia Paine
Languages English, Spanish
T: +34 952 070 370
W: attendis.com/colegios-malaga/el-romeral

Colegio El Valle Alicante

Avda. Condomina 65, 03540 Alicante, Valencia
DP Coordinator Nuria Espinosa Juan
MYP Coordinator José Sánchez Segovia
PYP Coordinator Alberto Fernández de Aguilar
Languages English, Spanish
T: +34 965 155 619
W: www.colegioelvalle.com

Colegio El Valle II – Sanchinarro

Calle Ana De Austria, 60, 28050 Madrid
DP Coordinator Nuria Alvarez Herranz
Languages Spanish
T: +34 91 7188426
W: www.colegioelvalle.com

Colegio Heidelberg

Apartado de Correos 248, Barranco Seco 15, 35090 Las Palmas de Gran Canaria, Las Palmas, Can+
DP Coordinator Juan Antonio Domínguez Silva
MYP Coordinator Nacho Santa-María Megía
Languages Spanish
T: +34 928 350 462
W: www.colegioheidelberg.com

Colegio HH. Maristas Sagrado Corazón Alicante

Calle de la Isla de Corfú, 5, 03005 Alicante, Valencia
DP Coordinator Fernando Fuentes Guzmán
Languages Spanish
T: +34 965 130 941
W: www.maristasalicante.com

Colegio Internacional Ausiàs March

Urbanización Residencial Tancat de l'Alter s/n, 46220 Picassent, Valencia
DP Coordinator María Pérez Galván
Languages Spanish
T: +34 96 123 05 66
W: www.ausiasmarch.com

Colegio Internacional de Levante

Río Jalón 25 Urbanización Calicanto, 46370 Valencia
DP Coordinator Rubén Benet Santos
Languages Spanish
T: +34 961980650
W: www.colintlev.net

Colegio Internacional Meres

Carretera Meres, s/n, 33199 Meres, Asturias
DP Coordinator Maria Crespo Iglesias
MYP Coordinator Cristina Cuadrado Martínez
PYP Coordinator Carmen González Aller
Languages Spanish
T: +34 985 792 427
W: www.colegiomeres.com

Colegio Internacional SEK Eirís

C Castaño de Eiris, 1, 15009 A Coruña, Galicia
DP Coordinator Ana González
Languages English, Spanish
T: +34 981 28 44 00
W: www.eiris.edu.es

Colegio Internacional Torrequebrada

C/ Ronda del Golf Este, 7-11, Urbanización Torrequebrada, 29639 Benalmádena, Málaga, Andalusia
DP Coordinator Guillermo Chaves
MYP Coordinator Guillermo Chaves
PYP Coordinator Iciar Garcia
Languages English, Spanish
T: +34 952 57 60 65
W: www.colegiotorrequebrada.com

Colegio Las Chapas

Urb. Las Chapas s/n, 29604 Marbella, Málaga, Andalusia
PYP Coordinator Mercedes Cantera Cavestany
Languages English, Spanish
T: +34 952 831 616
W: attendis.com/colegios-marbella/las-chapas

Colegio Liceo Europeo

C/ Camino Sur 10, 28100 Alcobendas, Madrid
CP Coordinator Esther Arama Ibáñez
DP Coordinator Esther Arama Ibáñez
MYP Coordinator Rubén Moreno Ferreiro
PYP Coordinator Fatima Rodriguez Vicens
Languages English, Spanish
T: +34 91 650 00 00
W: www.liceo-europeo.es

Colegio Logos

Urbanización Molino de la Hoz c/, Sacre 2, 28232 Las Rozas, Madrid
DP Coordinator Héctor Martínez
Languages English
T: +34 91 630 34 94
W: www.colegiologos.com

Colegio Madrid

Avda. del Comandante Franco 8, 28016 Madrid
DP Coordinator Patricia Gamir Henderson
Languages Spanish
T: +34 910 572 501
W: www.madridcolegio.es

Colegio Manuel Peleteiro

Monte Redondo – Castiñeiriño, 15702 Santiago de Compostela, A Coruña, Galicia
DP Coordinator Rafael Gómez Montero
Languages Spanish
T: +34 98 1591475
W: www.peleteiro.com

Colegio Mater Salvatoris

Calle Valdesquí no. 4, 28023 Madrid
DP Coordinator Almudena Alonso
Languages Spanish
T: +34 91 307 1243
W: matersalvatoris.org

Colegio Montserrat

Av Vallvidrera, 68, 08017 Barcelona, Catalonia
DP Coordinator Juan Antonio Fernández-Arévalo
Languages English, Spanish
T: +34 932 038 800
W: www.cmontserrat.org

Colegio Nuestra Señora del Recuerdo

Plaza Duque de Pastrana 5, 28036 Madrid
DP Coordinator Paloma Guillem
Languages English
T: +34 91 3022640
W: www.recuerdo.net

Colegio Obradoiro

Rua Obradoiro 49, 15190 A Coruña, Galicia
DP Coordinator Fernando Vales Vázquez
MYP Coordinator Consuelo Gajino Cousillas
PYP Coordinator Jorge Muiños Guereca
Languages English, Spanish
T: +34 981 281 888
W: www.colegioobradoiro.es

Colegio Parque

Calle Piamonte, 19 Urbanización Parquelagos, La Navata, 28420 Galapagar, Madrid
DP Coordinator Raul Fernández Pascual
Languages English, Spanish
T: +34 918 590 630
W: www.colegioparque.com

Colegio Retamar

Madrid España, c/ Pajares 22, 28223 Madrid
DP Coordinator Juan Navalpotro
Languages Spanish
T: +34 91 714 10 22
W: www.retamar.com

Colegio San Cayetano

Av. Picasso 21, 07014 Palma De Mallorca, Balearic Islands
DP Coordinator Irene Pascual Sastre
Languages English, Spanish
T: +34 971 220 575
W: www.colegiosancayetano.com

Colegio San Cristóbal

Calle San Jorge del Maestrazgo, 2, 12003 Castellón de la Plana, Castellón, Valencia
DP Coordinator Ana Belen Baldayo
Languages English
T: +34 964 228 758
W: sancristobalsl.com

Colegio San Fernando

Avenida San Agustín, s/n, 33400 Avilés, Asturias
DP Coordinator María García Villa
MYP Coordinator Lucia Gonzalez
PYP Coordinator Adriana Álvarez
Languages English, Spanish
T: +34 985 565 745
W: www.sanfer.es

Colegio San Ignacio Jesuitas

Avenida Richard Grandío, S/N, 33193 Oviedo, Asturias
DP Coordinator Arnau Pla Novoa
Languages Spanish
T: +34 985 233 300
W: www.s-ignacio.com

Colegio San Jorge

Soc. Coop. Enseñanza la Alcayna. CIF: F30410328, Avda. Picos de Europa s/n, 30507 Molina de Segura, Murcia
DP Coordinator Mª Esther Pérez Esquerdo
Languages English, Spanish
T: +34 968 430 711
W: colegiosanjorge.es

Colegio San José Estepona

Avd. Litoral 22, 29680 Estepona, Málaga, Andalusia
DP Coordinator Miguel Angel Salazar Troya
Languages Spanish
T: +34 952 800 148
W: www.colegiosanjose.net

COLEGIO SAN PATRICIO

Calle Jazmin 148, El Soto de la Moraleja, 28109 Alcobendas, Madrid
DP Coordinator James Smith
Languages English, Spanish
T: +34 916 50 06 02
E: infosoto@colegiosanpatricio.es
W: www.colegiosanpatriciomadrid.com/en

See full details on page 73

Colegio Sierra Blanca

Avenida de Plutarco 34, 29010 Málaga, Andalusia
PYP Coordinator Carmen Martínez Torres
Languages English, Spanish
T: +34 952 070 650
W: attendis.com/colegios-malaga/sierra-blanca

Colegio Valdefuentes

Ana de Austria 6, Sanchinarro, 28050 Madrid
DP Coordinator Tomas Suarez Pizarro
Languages English, Spanish
T: +34 917 188 229
W: www.colegiovaldefuentes.es

COLEGIO VIRGEN DE EUROPA

C/ Valle de Santa Ana No. 1, Las Lomas, 28669 Boadilla del Monte, Madrid
DP Coordinator María Cruz Larrosa
MYP Coordinator Carmen Mosquera Mariño
PYP Coordinator Sarah O'Halloran
Languages English, Spanish
T: +34 91 633 0155
E: mc_larrosa@colegiovirgendeeuropa.edu.es
W: www.cve.edu.es

See full details on page 74

Colegios Ramón Y Cajal

C/ Arturo Soria, 206, 28043 Madrid
MYP Coordinator Patricia Martinez Obispo
PYP Coordinator Laura Pérez
Languages English
T: +34 91 413 56 31
W: www.colegiosramonycajal.es

Complejo Educativo Mas Camarena

C/ 1 Urbanización, Mas Camarena, 46117 Bétera, Valencia
DP Coordinator Louise Grint
MYP Coordinator John Henry Patton
PYP Coordinator Maite Navarro García
Languages Spanish
T: +34 961687535
W: www.colegios-sigloxxi.com

Cooperativa de Enseñanza San Cernin

Avda. Baranain 3, 31007 Pamplona, Navarre
DP Coordinator Arantxa Hernández
Languages English
T: +34 948176288
W: www.sancernin.es

El Plantío International School of Valencia

Calle 233 No36 Urb El Plantío, La Cañada, 46182 Paterna, Valencia
DP Coordinator Alicia Ocón Crespo
Languages English, Spanish
T: +34 96 132 14 10
W: plantiointernational.com

ES AMERICAN SCHOOL

Autovia de Castelldefels C-31 Km 191, El Prat de Llobregat, 08820 Barcelona, Catalonia
PYP Coordinator Lauren Hopkins
Languages English
T: +34 93 479 1611
E: info@es-school.com
W: www.es-school.com

See full details on page 87

Escola Internacional del Camp

Salvador Espiriu s/n, 43840 Salou, Tarragona, Catalonia
DP Coordinator Cristina Garcia Bardon
Languages English, Spanish
T: +34 977325620
W: www.escolainternacional.org

Escola Voramar

Passeig de García Fària, 08005 Barcelona, Catalonia
DP Coordinator Mirela Domitrovic
Languages English, Spanish
T: +34 932 251 324
W: www.voramon.cat

Escuela Ideo

Carretera de Colmenar a Alcobendas, Km. 0,500, 28049 Madrid
DP Coordinator Paloma Oñate Alguero
Languages English, Spanish
T: +34 917 523 343
W: www.escuelaideo.edu.es

Eurocolegio Casvi Boadilla

C/ Miguel Ángel Cantero Oliva, 13, Boadilla del Monte, Madrid
MYP Coordinator Francisco José Corchero Gómez
PYP Coordinator Álvaro Feijoo Pérez
Languages Spanish
T: +34 91 632 96 53
W: www.casviboadilla.es

EUROCOLEGIO CASVI VILLAVICIOSA

Avenida de Castilla, 27, Villaviciosa de Odón, 28670 Madrid
DP Coordinator Jose Vicente Belizón Collado
MYP Coordinator Félix David Vozmediano León
PYP Coordinator Carolina García
Languages Spanish
T: +34 91 616 22 18
E: casvi@casvi.es
W: www.casvi.es

See full details on page 88

Fundacion Privada Oak House School

Sant Pere Claver 12-18, 08017 Barcelona, Catalonia
DP Coordinator Elaine Sibley
Languages English
T: +34 932 524 020
W: www.oakhouseschool.com

Gredos San Diego (GSD) Buitrago

Avda. de Madrid 16, 28730 Buitrago del Lozoya, Madrid
DP Coordinator Luis Bartolomé Herrero
Languages Spanish
T: +34 91 868 02 00
W: www.gsdeducacion.com

Gredos San Diego (GSD) Las Rozas

C/ Clara Campoamor, 1, 28232 Las Rozas, Madrid
DP Coordinator Encarnación López Mateo
Languages English
T: +34 91 640 89 23
W: www.gsdeducacion.com

Green Valley School

Cami de la Vileta 210, Son Puig, 07011 Palma De Mallorca, Balearic Islands
DP Coordinator Carmelo Mancera
Languages English
T: +34 971 160 817
W: greenvalleyschool.es

GRESOL International-American School

Ctra. Sabadell a Matadepera, (BV-1248) km. 6, 08227 Terrassa, Barcelona, Catalonia
DP Coordinator Eduardo Torrecillas Sanchez
Languages English, Spanish
T: +34 937 870 158
W: www.gresolschool.com

Hamelin-Laie International School

Ronda 8 de Marc 178-180, 08390 Montgat, Barcelona, Catalonia
DP Coordinator Thom Gibbs
Languages English, Spanish
T: +34 93 5556717
W: www.hamelininternacionallaie.com

I.E.S. Alfonso X 'el Sabio'

Avda D Juan de Borbón 3, 30007 Murcia
DP Coordinator María Dolores Romero Carbonell
Languages Spanish
T: +34 968 232 040
W: www.iesalfonsox.com

I.E.S. Juan de la Cierva y Codorníu

C/San Antonio, 84, 30850 Totana, Murcia
DP Coordinator Vicente Sanz Duart
Languages Spanish
T: +34 968 42 19 19
W: www.murciaeduca.es/iesjuandelacierva/sitio

I.E.S. Maestro Matías Bravo

Avenida Mar Egeo S/N, Valdemoro, 28341 Madrid
DP Coordinator Anastasio Calvo de Miguel
Languages Spanish
T: +34 91 801 8044
W: www.educa.madrid.org/web/ies.maestromatiasbravo.valdemoro

IES Bachiller Sabuco

Albacete, Avenida de España 9, 02002 Albacete, Castilla-La Mancha
DP Coordinator María del Mar Buendía Navarro
Languages Spanish
T: +34 967 229 540
W: www.sabuco.com

IES Bilingüe Cervantes

Calle de Embajadores, 70, 28012 Madrid
DP Coordinator Luis Horrillo
Languages English, Spanish
W: external.educa2.madrid.org/web/centro.ies.cervantes.madrid

IES Cardenal López de Mendoza

Plaza Luis Martin Santos s/n, 09002 Burgos, Castile & León
DP Coordinator Antonio Becerro
MYP Coordinator Raul Ubierna Hortigüela
Languages Spanish
T: +34 947 257701
W: ieslopezdemendoza.centros.educa.jcyl.es

IES Carlos III de Toledo

Avenida de Francia 5, 45005 Toledo, Castilla-La Mancha
DP Coordinator Ángel Castelló Pola
Languages Spanish
T: +34 925 212 967

IES Castilla

Calle Alonso Velázquez s/n, 42003 Soria, Castile & León
DP Coordinator Ernesto Pastor Lebrero
Languages English
T: +34 975 221 283

IES Celia Vinas

C/ Javier Sanz 15, 04004 Almería, Andalusia
DP Coordinator Juan Diego Estrada Godoy
Languages Spanish
T: +34 950 156 151
W: iescelia.org/web

IES Diego de Guzmán y Quesada

Av. Manuel Siurot 11, 21004 Huelva, Andalusia
DP Coordinator Lorenzo Castilla Mora
Languages Spanish
T: +34 95 952 4835

IES Jorge Manrique

Avda. Republica Argentina s/n, 34002 Palencia, Castile & León
DP Coordinator Miguel Angel Arconada Melero
Languages Spanish
T: +34 979 720 384
W: www.iesjorgemanrique.com

SPAIN

IES Jorge Santayana
Calle Santo Tomás 6, 05003 Ávila, Castile & León
DP Coordinator Ana Rodríguez Pérez
Languages Spanish
T: +34 920 35 21 35
W: iesjorgesantayana.centros.educa.jcyl.es

IES José Saramago
Calle del Maestro 1, Majadahonda, 28220 Madrid
DP Coordinator Alicia Escalonilla González
Languages Spanish
T: +34 916 398 411
W: www.educa2.madrid.org/web/centro.ies.josesaramago.majadahonda

IES Los Castillos
Avd. de Los Castillos No. 5, 28925 Alcorcón, Madrid
DP Coordinator Juan Ignacio Cubero Pérez
Languages English, Spanish
T: +34 916 121 063
W: sites.google.com/iesloscastillos.com/iesloscastillos/inicio

IES Los Cerros
C/ Cronista Juan de la Torre 11, 23400 Úbeda, Jaén, Andalusia
DP Coordinator José Manuel Latorre Palacios
Languages English, Spanish
T: +34 953 779 990
W: loscerros.org

IES Lucas Mallada
C/Torre Mendoza No 2, 22005 Huesca, Aragon
DP Coordinator Laura Domingo Capella
Languages Spanish
T: +34 974 244 834
W: www.ieslucasmallada.com

IES Manacor
c/ Camí de Ses Tapareres, 32, 07500 Manacor, Balearic Islands
DP Coordinator Pilar Caldentey Gomila
Languages Spanish, Catalan, Valencian
T: +34 971 551 489
W: www.iesmanacor.cat

IES María Zambrano
C/ Cipriano Maldonado, 8 Torre del Mar, 29740 Málaga, Andalusia
DP Coordinator Lidia Acosta Gutierrez
Languages Spanish
T: +34 95 128 9559
W: www.iesmariazambrano.org

IES Marqués de Santillana
Avda España, 2, Torrelavega, 39300 Cantabria
DP Coordinator José Manuel Piñeiro Moratinos
Languages Spanish
T: +34 942 88 16 00
W: www.iesmarquesdesantillana.com

IES Martinez Montanes
C/Fernández de Ribera no. 17, 41005 Seville, Andalusia
DP Coordinator Jorge Mejías López
Languages Spanish
T: +34 955 623 877
W: iesmartinezm.es

IES Mateo Sagasta
Glorieta del Doctor Zubia s/n, 26003 Logroño, La Rioja
DP Coordinator Gloria Bernad Pérez
Languages Spanish
T: +34 941 256 500
W: iessagasta.edurioja.org

IES Medina Azahara
Av. Gran Vía Parque 2, 14005 Córdoba, Andalusia
DP Coordinator Francisco José Simón Torres
Languages Spanish
T: +34 957 73 46 15
W: www.iesmedinaazahara.es

IES Miguel Catalán
Paseo de Isabel La católica, 3, 50009 Zaragoza, Aragon
DP Coordinator Juan José Carracedo Doval
Languages Spanish
T: +34 976 402 004
W: www.ies-mcatalan.com

IES Navarro Villoslada
Arcadio Mª Larraona, 3, 31008 Pamplona, Navarre
DP Coordinator Gabriel María Rubio Navarro
Languages Spanish
T: +34 848 431 150
W: www.iesnavarrovilloslada.com

IES Padre Luis Coloma
Avda. Alcalde Álvaro Domecq, 10, Jerez de la Frontera, 11402 Cádiz, Andalusia
DP Coordinator Isabel Suárez Cachá
Languages Spanish
T: +34 671 565 351
W: www.iescoloma.es

IES Padre Manjón
Gonzalo Gallas s/n, 18003 Granada, Andalusia
DP Coordinator Paloma Soler Celdrán
Languages English, Spanish
T: +34 958 893 493
W: iespm.es

IES Pere Boïl
C/Ceramista Alfons Blat 20, 46940 Manises, Valencia
DP Coordinator Maria José Hellín Méndez
Languages Spanish
T: +34 961 20 62 25
W: www.pereboil.com

IES Príncipe Felipe
Calle de Finisterre No. 60, 28029 Madrid
DP Coordinator Rebeca González Barreiro
Languages Spanish
T: +34 913 14 63 12
W: iespf2014.villatic.org

IES Ramiro de Maeztu
C/ Serrano 127, 28006 Madrid
DP Coordinator Silvia Jiménez Hervás
Languages Spanish
T: +34 91 561 7842
W: www.educa.madrid.org/web/ies.ramirodemaeztu.madrid

IES Real Instituto de Jovellanos
Avenida de la Constitucion s/n, 33071 Gijon, Asturias
DP Coordinator Isabel Hompanera lanzos
Languages Spanish
T: +34 985 38 77 03
W: www.iesjovellanos.com

IES Rosa Chacel
Calle Huertas 68, Colmenar Viejo, 28770 Madrid
DP Coordinator Ignacio Valdés López
Languages Spanish
T: +34 91 846 48 01
W: ies.rosachacel.colmenarviejo.educa.madrid.org

IES Rosalia De Castro
San Clemente 3, Santiago de Compostela, 15705 A Coruña, Galicia
DP Coordinator Arantxa Fuentes
Languages Spanish
T: +34 981 569 650
W: www.iesrosalia.net

IES Santa Clara
c/ Santa Clara 13, 39001 Santander, Cantabria
DP Coordinator María Jesús Temprano Marañón
Languages Spanish
T: +34 942 216 550

Institut d'Educació Secundària Josep Lladonosa
Pla?a Maria Rúbies S/N, 25005 Lleida, Catalonia
DP Coordinator Jacint Llauradó
Languages Spanish
T: +34 97 3239531
W: www.insjoseplladonosa.cat

Institut D'Educacio Secundaria Son Pacs
Carretera de Soller 13, 07120 Palma De Mallorca, Balearic Islands
DP Coordinator Antonia Vidal Nicolau
Languages Catalan, Spanish, English
T: +34 97 1292050
W: www.iessonpacs.cat

Institut Dertosa
Av. Estadi, 14, 43500 Tortosa, Tarragona, Catalonia
DP Coordinator Núria Serra Benedicto
Languages Catalan, Valencian, Spanish
T: +34 977 501 310
W: agora.xtec.cat/insdertosa

Institut Forat del Vent
Pizarro, 35, Cerdanyola del Vallès, 08290 Barcelona, Catalonia
DP Coordinator Mavi Climent Savall
Languages Catalan, Valencian, Spanish
T: +34 936 911 200
W: agora.xtec.cat/iesforatdelvent

Institut Gabriel Ferrater i Soler
Carretera de Montblanc 5-9, 43206 Reus, Tarragona, Catalonia
DP Coordinator Beatriz Comella Dorda
Languages English
T: +34 977342010
W: institutgabrielferrater.wordpress.com

Institut Jaume Vicens Vives
Isabel la Católica, 17, 17004 Girona, Catalonia
DP Coordinator Farners Brugués
Languages Catalan, Spanish
T: +34 972 200 130
W: ins-jvicensvives.xtec.cat

IB AFRICA | EUROPE | MIDDLE EAST

Institut L'Alzina

Passatge Salvador Riera 2, 08027 Barcelona, Catalonia
DP Coordinator Cristina Sánchez-Guijaldo González
Languages Catalan, Spanish
T: +34 933 409 850
W: www.alzina.cat

Institut Moisès Broggi

Calle Sant Quintí 32-50, 08041 Barcelona, Catalonia
DP Coordinator Jaume Silvestre Llinares
Languages Spanish
T: +34 93 436 89 03
W: www.institutbroggi.org

Instituto de Educación Secundaria do Castro

C/Posada Curros 1, 36203 Vigo, Pontevedra, Galicia
DP Coordinator Angel Núñez Ramos
Languages Spanish
T: +34 986422974
W: centros.edu.xunta.es/iesdocastro

Instituto de Educación Secundaria Lancia

c. Egido Quintín, s/n, 24006 León, Castile & León
DP Coordinator Julio Fernandez Alcalde
Languages Spanish
T: +34 987259800
W: ieslancia.centros.educa.jcyl.es

Instituto Pedralbes

Av. Esplugues 36-42, 08034 Barcelona, Catalonia
DP Coordinator Marta Galindo Casas
Languages Spanish, Catalan
T: +34 932 033 332
W: www.institutpedralbes.cat

Internacional Aravaca

Calle Santa Bernardita 3, 28023 Madrid
PYP Coordinator Laura Oran
Languages English, Spanish
T: +34 913 571 256
W: internacionalaravaca.edu.es

International College Spain

C/Vereda Norte, 3, La Moraleja, 28109 Alcobendas, Madrid
DP Coordinator Jeroen Kuipers
MYP Coordinator Jennifer Barnett
PYP Coordinator Rosemary Cabedo
Languages English
T: +34 91 650 2398
W: www.icsmadrid.org

International School of Barcelona

Passeig Isaac Albeniz s/n, Vallpineda, 08870 Sitges, Barcelona, Catalonia
DP Coordinator Maria Kovac
Languages English
T: +34 93 894 20 40
W: educa4all.com

INTERNATIONAL SCHOOL SAN PATRICIO TOLEDO

Juan de Vergara, 1, Urbanización La Legua, Toledo 45005
DP Coordinator Philip Brotherton
MYP Coordinator Pilar Molina
PYP Coordinator Rebeca Albarrán Corroto
Languages English, Spanish
T: +34 925 280 363
E: infotoledo@colegiosanpatricio.es
W: colegiosanpatriciotoledo.com/en

See full details on page 135

Irabia-Izaga Colegio

Calle Cintruénigo, 31015 Pamplona, Navarre
DP Coordinator Daniel Doyle
Languages English, Spanish
T: +34 948 12 62 22
W: www.irabia-izaga.org

Jesuitinas Donostia, Nuestra Señora de Aranzazu

Paseo de Errondo 121, Aiete, 20009 Donostia-San Sebastian, Gipuzkoa, Basque Co+
DP Coordinator Miriam Sánchez Hernández
Languages English, Spanish
T: +34 943 212 307
W: www.jesuitinasdonostia.eus

KING'S COLLEGE, THE BRITISH SCHOOL OF MADRID

Paseo de los Andes 35, Soto de Viñuelas, 28760 Madrid
DP Coordinator Federica Menon
Languages English
T: +34 918 034 800
E: kc.admissions@kingscollegeschools.org
W: madrid-soto.kingscollegeschools.org

See full details on page 149

La Miranda the Global Quality School

Carrer del Canigó 15, 08960 Sant Just Desvern, Barcelona, Catalonia
DP Coordinator Aida Martín Valbuena
Languages English, Spanish
W: lamiranda.eu

La Salle Bonanova

Passeig de la Bonanova, 8, 08022 Barcelona, Catalonia
DP Coordinator Joan Ferretjans i Marco
Languages English
T: +34 93 254 09 50
W: www.bonanova.lasalle.cat

Laude El Altillo School

C/ Santiago de Chile, s/n, 11407 Jerez de la Frontera, Cádiz, Andalusia
DP Coordinator María Teresa Martos Martos
MYP Coordinator Manuel de la Rosa Marchante
Languages English, Spanish, French
T: +34 956 302 400
W: www.laudealtillo.com

Laude Newton College

Camino Viejo de Elche-Alicante Km, 3, Alicante, Valencia
DP Coordinator Francisco Beltrán Muñoz
MYP Coordinator Claudia Demartini
Languages Spanish, English
T: +34 96 545 14 28
W: www.laudenewtoncollege.com

Les Alzines

La Creu de Palau 2, 17003 Girona, Catalonia
DP Coordinator Roser Jorba Campo
Languages Spanish
T: +34 972 212162
W: www.institucio.org/lesalzines

Lestonnac L'Ensenyança

Carrer Arc de Sant Llorenç, 2, 43003 Tarragona, Catalonia
DP Coordinator Carmen García Valiente
Languages English
T: +34 977 23 25 19
W: lestonnac-tarragona.net

Liceo Sorolla c

Avda. Bularas 4, 28224 Pozuelo de Alarcón, Madrid
DP Coordinator José Manuel de los Ríos Beca
Languages English
T: +34 91 715 04 99
W: www.colegioliceosorolla.es

Lycée International Barcelona – Bon Soleil

Camí de la Pava, no. 15, Gavà, 08850 Barcelona, Catalonia
DP Coordinator Victor Solà Calzada
Languages English, French, Spanish
T: +34 93 633 13 58
W: www.bonsoleil.es

Maristes Sants Les Corts

C/Vallespir 160, 08014 Barcelona, Catalonia
DP Coordinator Isabel Mata Pérez
Languages Catalan, Valencian, Spanish
T: +34 934 908 625
W: www.slc.maristes.cat

MIRABAL INTERNATIONAL SCHOOL

Calle Monte Almenara, s/n, 28660 Boadilla del Monte, Madrid
DP Coordinator Isabel Sargent Busquets
MYP Coordinator Isabel Sargent Busquets
Languages English, Spanish
T: +34 916 331 711
E: mirabal@colegiomirabal.com
W: www.colegiomirabal.com

See full details on page 164

Princess Margaret School

Passeig de la Fond d'en Fargas 15-17, 8032 Barcelona, Catalonia
MYP Coordinator Renata Djuric
PYP Coordinator Marta García
Languages English, Spanish
T: +34 934 290 313
W: www.princessmargaret.org

Salesians Sant Àngel (Salesians de Sarrià)

Rafael Batlle nº 7, 08017 Barcelona, Catalonia
DP Coordinator Carlos Escriche Marco
Languages Spanish
T: +34 932031100
W: sarria.salesians.cat

SEK INTERNATIONAL SCHOOL ALBORÁN

C/ Barlovento 141, Urb. Almerimar, El Ejido, 04711 Almería, Andalusia
DP Coordinator Estefania Sánchez
MYP Coordinator Sebastián Fuentes Valenzuela
PYP Coordinator Elnara Israfilova
Languages English, Spanish
T: +34 950 49 72 73
E: sek-alboran@sek.es
W: alboran.sek.es

See full details on page 193

SEK INTERNATIONAL SCHOOL ATLÁNTICO

Rúa Illa de Arousa 4, Boavista. A Caeira, Poio, 36005 Pontevedra, Galicia
DP Coordinator Yolanda Cenamor Montero
MYP Coordinator Mónica Azpilicueta Amorín
PYP Coordinator Sara Bouzada Sanmartin
Languages English, Spanish
T: +34 98 687 22 77
E: sek-atlantico@sek.es
W: atlantico.sek.es

See full details on page 194

SEK INTERNATIONAL SCHOOL CATALUNYA

Av. del Tremolencs, 24, La Garriga, 08530 Barcelona, Catalonia
DP Coordinator Adrià Van Waart
MYP Coordinator Carmen Fernández
PYP Coordinator Concepció Muntada
Languages English, Spanish, Catalan
T: +34 93 871 84 48
E: sek-catalunya@sek.es
W: catalunya.sekinternationalschools.com

See full details on page 195

SEK INTERNATIONAL SCHOOL CIUDALCAMPO

Urb. Ciudalcampo, Paseo de las Perdices, 2, San Sebastián de los Reyes, 28707 Madrid
DP Coordinator Dinis Alves Costa
MYP Coordinator James Shaw
PYP Coordinator Marisa Iglesias Lorenzo
Languages English, Spanish
T: +34 91 659 63 03
E: sek-ciudalcampo@sek.es
W: ciudalcampo.sek.es

See full details on page 196

SEK INTERNATIONAL SCHOOL EL CASTILLO

Urb. Villafranca del Castillo, Castillo de Manzanares, s/n, Villanueva de la Cañada, 28692 Madrid
DP Coordinator Ana Karina Cisneros
MYP Coordinator Elvira Chiquero
PYP Coordinator Fátima González
Languages English, Spanish
T: +34 91 815 08 92
E: sek-castillo@sek.es
W: madrid.sekinternationalschools.com

See full details on page 197

SEK INTERNATIONAL SCHOOL SANTA ISABEL

Calle San Ildefonso, 18, 28012 Madrid
PYP Coordinator William Ivey
Languages English, Spanish
T: +34 91 527 90 94
E: sek-santaisabel@sek.es
W: santaisabel.sek.es

See full details on page 199

SOTOGRANDE INTERNATIONAL SCHOOL

Avenida La Reserva SN, Sotogrande, Cádiz, 11310
DP Coordinator Hélène Caillet
MYP Coordinator Belén González
PYP Coordinator Andrea Bennett
Languages English
T: +34 956 795 902
E: info@sis.gl
W: www.sis.ac

See full details on page 204

St Peter's School Barcelona

C/Eduard Toldrà, 18, 08034 Barcelona, Catalonia
DP Coordinator Xavier Salvado
MYP Coordinator Teresa Ferrer
PYP Coordinator Agustina Lacarte
Languages English, Spanish
T: +34 93 204 36 12
W: www.stpeters.es

St. George, The British School Madrid

Calle Padres Dominicos 1, 28050 Madrid
DP Coordinator Wyn Morgan
Languages English, Spanish
T: +34 916 508 440
W: stgeorgeinternational.es/madrid

St. George, The British school of Calalunya

Paseo de la Reina Elisenda de Montçada 18, 08034 Barcelona, Catalonia
DP Coordinator Danielle Best
Languages English, Spanish
T: +34 931 293 024
W: stgeorgeinternational.es/barcelona

Swans International Secondary School

C/Lago de los Cisnes, s/n, Urb. Sierra Blanca, 29602 Marbella, Málaga, Andalusia
DP Coordinator Jose Prieto
Languages English
T: +34 952 902 755
W: www.swansschoolinternational.es

THE ACADEMY INTERNATIONAL SCHOOL

Camí de Son Ametler Vell, 250, 07141 Marratxí, Balearic Islands
DP Coordinator Caroline Foster
Languages English
T: +34 971 605008
E: info@theacademyschool.com
W: www.theacademyschool.com

See full details on page 225

The British School of Aragon

Calle Valencia, KM 8,500, 50410 Cuarte de Huerva, Zaragoza
DP Coordinator Cristina Muñoz
Languages English, Spanish
T: +34 976 50 52 23
W: www.britanico-aragon.edu

YAGO SCHOOL

Avda. Antonio Mairena, 54, 41950 Castilleja de la Cuesta, Seville, Andalusia
DP Coordinator Blanca Domínguez
Languages English, Spanish
T: +34 955 51 1234
E: admissions@yagoschool.com
W: www.yagoschool.com

See full details on page 248

Zürich Schule Barcelona

73 Pearson Avenue, 08034 Barcelona, Catalonia
PYP Coordinator Alèxia Vallvé Marín
Languages German, Spanish
T: +34 932 037 606
W: www.zsbarcelona.com

Confluence International School of Khartoum

Building No.5, Gamhouria Avenue, Khartoum 11111
DP Coordinator Vishwas Kulkarni
MYP Coordinator Bhavna Kulkarni
PYP Coordinator Dominika Kawałek
Languages English, Arabic
T: +249 960099970
W: www.confluencesudan.org

Khartoum International Community School

PO Box 1840, Khartoum
DP Coordinator Linda Round
PYP Coordinator Darwin Balog-ang
Languages English
T: +249 183 215 000
W: www.kics.sd

Aranäsgymnasiet

Gymnasiegatan 44, 434 42 Kungsbacka, Halland
DP Coordinator Ruth Walton
Languages English
T: +46 300 83 40 00
W: www.aranasgymnasiet.kungsbacka.se

Åva Gymnasium

Box 1450, 183 14 Täby, Stockholm
DP Coordinator Jo-Anne Ahlmen
Languages English
T: +46 (0) 855 55 8000
W: www.taby.se/ava

Bladins International School of Malmö

Box 20093, Själlandstorget 1, 200 74 Malmö, Skåne
DP Coordinator Erik Ryberg
MYP Coordinator Valeria Fagiolani
PYP Coordinator Naomi Ridley
Languages English
T: +46 40 987970
W: bism.bladins.se

British International School of Stockholm

Östrka Valhallavagen 17, 182 68 Djursholm, Stockholm
DP Coordinator Melanie Stell
Languages English
T: +46 8 755 2375
W: www.bisstockholm.se

Carlforsska gymnasiet

Sångargatan 1, 722 19 Västerås, Västmanland
CP Coordinator Annelize Deuchar
DP Coordinator Tony Nicolas
Languages English
T: +4621390703
W: www.vasteras.se/carlforsska

Europaskolan in Södermalm

Gotlandsgatan 43, 116 65 Stockholm
MYP Coordinator Julian Bethell
PYP Coordinator Emelie Pettersson
Languages English, Swedish
T: +46 8 335054
W: www.europaskolan.nu

Europaskolan in Vasastan

Luntmakargatan 101, 113 51 Stockholm
MYP Coordinator Katarina Dybeck
PYP Coordinator Maria Angelidou
Languages Swedish
T: +46 8 335095
W: www.europaskolan.nu

HAGANÄSSKOLAN

Box 501, 343 23 Älmhult, Kronoberg
DP Coordinator Ms Karin Elisabet Ringblom
Languages English
T: +46 476 552 22
E: haganasskolan@almhult.se
W: tinyurl.com/y6njaaw4

See full details on page 98

Hvitfeldtska Gymnasiet

Rektorsgatan 2, 411 33 Göteborg, Västra Götaland
DP Coordinator James Du Priest
Languages English
T: +46 31 36 70 608
W: goteborg.se/hvitfeldtska

International High School of the Gothenburg Region
Molinsgatan 6, 411 33 Göteborg, Västra Götaland
DP Coordinator Shawanda Stockfelt
Languages English
T: +46 31 708 92 00
W: www.ihgr.se

International School of Helsingborg
Östra Vallgatan 9, 254 37 Helsingborg, Skåne
DP Coordinator Daniel Blair
MYP Coordinator Pernilla Rankin
PYP Coordinator Magdalena Simons
Languages English
T: +46 42 105 705
W: www.helsingborg.se/internationalschool

International School of Lund – Katedralskolan
Nygatan 21, 222 29 Lund, Skåne
MYP Coordinator Darrell Piper
PYP Coordinator Alison Kruckow
Languages English
T: +46 463 571 24

International School of the Gothenburg Region (ISGR)
Molinsgatan 6, 411 33 Göteborg, Västra Götaland
MYP Coordinator Alexei Gafan
PYP Coordinator Ellen Trelles
Languages English
T: +46 31 708 92 00
W: www.isgr.se

International School of the Stockholm Region
Bohusgatan 24-26, 116 67 Stockholm
DP Coordinator Martin Davidsson
MYP Coordinator Jenny Arvidsson
PYP Coordinator Justina Soewarso Sundström
Languages English
T: +46 8 508 426 50
W: internationalschoolofthestockholmregion.stockholm.se

Internationella Engelska Gymnasiet
Allhelgonagatan 4, 118 58 Stockholm
DP Coordinator Joseph Hemingway
Languages English
T: +46 8 562 28 700
W: www.engelskagymnasiet.se

IT-Gymnasiet i Skövde
Kylarvägen 1, 541 34 Skövde, Västra Götaland
DP Coordinator Ruth Morrisson Svensson
Languages English
T: +46 500 41 69 90
W: www.it-gymnasiet.se

Katedralskolan in Linköping
Platensgatan 20, 582 20 Linköping, Östergötland
DP Coordinator Jonathan Lowrey
Languages English
T: +46 132 07549
W: www.linkoping.se/katedral

Katedralskolan in Lund
St Södergatan 22, 222 23 Lund, Skåne
DP Coordinator Katarina Flennmark
Languages English
T: +46 4635 76 09
W: www.katte.se

Katedralskolan in Uppsala
Skolgatan 2, 753 12 Uppsala
DP Coordinator Therese Skytt
Languages English
T: +46 18 568100
W: www.katedral.se

Katedralskolan, Skara
Brunsbogatan 1, 532 88 Skara, Västra Götaland
DP Coordinator Annemarie Matsson
Languages English
T: +46 511 326 00
W: www.katedralskolan.nu

Lund International School
Warholmsväg 3, 224 65 Lund, Skåne
MYP Coordinator Lesley Pitman-Lundqvist
PYP Coordinator Jo Moore
Languages English
T: +46737087926
W: www.lundinternationalschool.com

Malmö Borgarskola
Box 17029, 200 10 Malmö, Skåne
CP Coordinator Andreas Lejon
DP Coordinator Anna Ellmark
Languages English
T: +46 4034 1000
W: www.malmoborgarskola.se

Malmö International School
Packhusgatan 2, 205 80 Malmö, Skåne
MYP Coordinator Patrick Kelly
PYP Coordinator Kristina Pettersson
Languages English, Spanish, German
T: +46 (0)733 23 70 37

Mora Gymnasium
Kristinebergsgatan 8-10, 792 32 Mora, Dalarna
DP Coordinator Marielle Hjort
Languages English, Swedish
T: +46 250 260 00
W: www.moragymnasium.se

Per Brahegymnasiet
Residensgatan, 553 16 Jönköping
DP Coordinator Allyson Neuberg
Languages English
T: +46 36 105 472
W: www.pb.edu.jonkoping.se

Rudbecksgymnasiet
Box 31160, 701 35 Örebro
DP Coordinator Anne-Sophie Skalin
Languages English
T: +46 19 21 65 69
W: www.ru.orebro.se

Sannarpsgymnasiet
Frennarpsvägen 1, 302 44 Halmstad, Halland
DP Coordinator Lotta Hydén
Languages English
T: +46 3513 7675
W: www.sannarpsgymnasiet.halmstad.se

Sigtunaskolan Humanistiska Läroverket
Box 508, 193 28 Sigtunase, Stockholm
CP Coordinator Christina Peters
DP Coordinator Adrian Feehan
MYP Coordinator Anna Johansson
Languages English, Swedish
T: +46 8 592 571 00
W: www.sshl.se

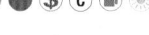

Söderportgymnasiet
Västra Boulevarden 53, 291 31 Kristianstad, Skåne
DP Coordinator Anna Cederlund
Languages English
T: +46 4413 6049
W: www.buf.kristianstad.se/soderport

St Eskils Gymnasium
Smedjegatan 3-5, 631 86 Eskilstuna, Södermanland
DP Coordinator Trevor Ayton
Languages English
T: +46 16 710 10 00
W: www.eskilstuna.se

Stockholm International School
Johannesgatan 18, 111 38 Stockholm
DP Coordinator Jarno Ampuja
MYP Coordinator Bradley Lister
Languages English
T: +46 (0)8 412 40 00
W: www.intsch.se

Sven Eriksonsgymnasiet
Sven Eriksonplatsen, 501 80 Borås, Västra Götaland
DP Coordinator Martin Idehall
Languages English
T: +46 33 35 80 48
W: boras.se/svenerikson

Täljegymnasiet
Erik Dahlbergs väg 1-3, 152 40 Södertälje, Stockholm
DP Coordinator Rose-Marie Fallgren
Languages English
T: +46 8 52301336
W: www.sodertalje.se

Teleborg Centrum Skola
Smedsvängen 72, 352 54 Växjö, Kronoberg
MYP Coordinator Erika Glawe
Languages English
T: +46 470 419 34
W: vaxjo.se/teleborgcentrum

The International School of Älmhult
Skolgatan 1, 343 23 Älmhult, Kronoberg
MYP Coordinator Ujjwala Bhatt
PYP Coordinator Harpreet Mehta
Languages English
T: +46 476 55188
W: www.almhult.se/english

Torsbergsgymnasiet
Läroverksgatan 36, 821 33 Bollnäs, Gävleborg
DP Coordinator Margaretta Eriksson
Languages English
T: + 46 278 254 91
W: www.torsbergsgymnasiet.se

Växjö Katedralskola
Samuel Ödmans Väg 1, 352 39 Växjö, Kronoberg
DP Coordinator Gilles Kennedy
Languages English
T: +46 470 41736
W: www.katedralskolan.se

SWITZERLAND

AIGLON COLLEGE
Avenue Centrale 61, 1885 Chesières
DP Coordinator Mrs Laura Hamilton
Languages English
T: +41 (0)24 496 6177
E: admissions@aiglon.ch
W: www.aiglon.ch
See full details on page 47

BKA International School
Gellertstrasse 25, 4052 Basel BS
PYP Coordinator Alexandara Schmid
Languages English, German
T: +41 61 311 76 62
W: www.bkabasel.ch

SWITZERLAND

COLLÈGE ALPIN BEAU SOLEIL

Route du Village 1, 1884 Villars-sur-Ollon
DP Coordinator Helen Taylor-Cevey
Languages English, French
T: +41 24 496 26 26
E: info@beausoleil.ch
W: www.beausoleil.ch

See full details on page 75

COLLÈGE CHAMPITTET, PULLY

Chemin de Champittet 1, 1009 Pully VD
DP Coordinator David Newsam
Languages English, French
T: +41 21 721 05 05
E: admissions@champittet.ch
W: www.champittet.ch

See full details on page 76

COLLÈGE DU LÉMAN

74, route de Sauverny, 1290 Versoix GE
CP Coordinator Sheena Tandy
DP Coordinator Jana Krainova Samuda
Languages English, French
T: +41 22 775 56 56
E: admissions@cdl.ch
W: www.cdl.ch

See full details on page 77

Collège et Lycée St-Charles

Route de Belfort 10, 2900 Porrentruy JU
DP Coordinator Nicole Pearce
Languages English
T: +41 32 466 11 57
W: www.saint-charles.ch

Ecole des Arches

Chemin de Mornex 2-4, PO Box 566, 1001 Lausanne VD
DP Coordinator Didier Curty
Languages French
T: +41 21 311 09 69
W: www.ecoledesarches.ch

Ecole Moser Genève

81 Chemin De-La-Montagne, 1224 Chêne-Bougeries GE
DP Coordinator Carine Marguet-Joly
Languages English, French
T: +41 (0)22 860 80 80
W: www.ecolemoser.ch/geneve

Ecole Moser Nyon

4-6 Avenue Reverdil, 1260 Nyon VD
DP Coordinator Richard Jones-Nerzic
Languages English, French
T: +41 (0)22 593 88 88
W: www.ecolemoser.ch/nyon

ECOLE NOUVELLE DE LA SUISSE ROMANDE – CHAILLY

Chemin de Rovéréaz 20, CP 161, 1012 Lausanne VD
DP Coordinator Mr. Gaetan Franzini
Languages French, English
T: +41 21 654 65 00
E: info@ensr.ch
W: www.ensr.ch

See full details on page 83

GYMNASIUM AM MÜNSTERPLATZ

Münsterplatz 15, 4051 Basel BS
DP Coordinator Dr. Manuel Pombo
Languages German, English
T: +41 61 267 88 70
E: gymnasium.muensterplatz@bs.ch
W: www.gmbasel.ch

See full details on page 97

Gymnasium Bäumlihof

Zu den drei Linden 80, 4058 Basel BS
DP Coordinator Isla Ward
Languages English, German
T: +41 61 606 33 11
W: www.gbbasel.ch

HAUT-LAC INTERNATIONAL BILINGUAL SCHOOL

Ch. de Pangires 26, St-Légier-la Chiésaz CH-1806
CP Coordinator Beatrice Gillet
DP Coordinator Greg Wilson
MYP Coordinator Julien Hernandez
Languages English, French
T: +41 (0)21 555 50 00
E: admissions@haut-lac.ch
W: www.haut-lac.ch

See full details on page 100

HOCHALPINES INSTITUT FTAN (HIF)

Chalchera 154, 7551 Ftan GR
DP Coordinator Peter Pasquill
Languages English, German
T: +41 81 861 22 11
E: admissions@hif.ch
W: www.hif.ch

See full details on page 103

Institut auf dem Rosenberg

Hohenweg 60, 9000 St Gallen SG
DP Coordinator Kevin Boyd
Languages English, German
T: +41 71 277 77 77
W: www.instrosenberg.ch

INSTITUT FLORIMONT

37 Avenue du Petit-Lancy, 1213 Petit-Lancy GE
DP Coordinator Noha Benani
Languages English, French
T: +41 2287 90000
E: admissions@florimont.ch
W: www.florimont.ch

See full details on page 112

INSTITUT INTERNATIONAL DE LANCY

24, avenue Eugène-Lance, Grand-Lancy CH-1212
DP Coordinator Tania McMahon
Languages English, French
T: +41 22 794 2620
E: info@iil.ch
W: www.iil.ch

See full details on page 113

Institut Le Rosey

Château du Rosey, 1180 Rolle VD
DP Coordinator Craig Foreman
Languages English, French
T: +41 21 822 5500
W: www.rosey.ch

INSTITUT MONTANA

Schönfels 5, 6300 Zug ZG
DP Coordinator Emiliano Cori
Languages English, German
T: +41 41 729 11 77
E: admissions@montana-zug.ch
W: www.montana-zug.ch

See full details on page 114

INTER-COMMUNITY SCHOOL ZURICH

Strubenacher 3, 8126 Zumikon
DP Coordinator Ann Lautrette
MYP Coordinator Graham Gardner
PYP Coordinator Claire Febrey
Languages English
T: +41 44 919 8300
E: contact@icsz.ch
W: www.icsz.ch

See full details on page 115

International School Altdorf

St. Josefsweg 15, 6460 Altdorf UR
DP Coordinator Nicoletta Scalabrin
Languages English
T: +41 41 874 0000
W: lisa.swiss

INTERNATIONAL SCHOOL BASEL

Fleischbachstrasse 2, 4153 Reinach
DP Coordinator Sean Coffey
MYP Coordinator Siân Thomas
PYP Coordinator Lyneth Magsalin
Languages English
T: +41 61 715 33 33
E: info@isbasel.ch
W: www.isbasel.ch

See full details on page 118

INTERNATIONAL SCHOOL OF BERNE

Allmendingenweg 9, 3073 Gümligen, Bern
DP Coordinator Brette Book
MYP Coordinator Kirsty DeWilde
PYP Coordinator Richard Dowse
Languages English
T: +41 (0)31 959 10 00
E: admissions@isberne.ch
W: www.isberne.ch

See full details on page 122

International School of Central Switzerland

Lorzenparkstrasse 8, 6330 Cham ZG
DP Coordinator Armando Caracheo
PYP Coordinator Armando Caracheo
Languages English
T: +41 41 781 44 44
W: iscs-zug.ch

International School of Geneva (Campus des Nations)

11 route des Morillons, 1218 Grand Saconnex GE
CP Coordinator Alexandra Juniper
DP Coordinator Alexandra Juniper
MYP Coordinator Robin Smith
PYP Coordinator Nikki Ross
Languages English, French
T: +41 22 770 4700
W: www.ecolint.ch/campus/campus-des-nations

International School of Geneva (La Châtaigneraie Campus)

2 chemin de la Ferme, 1297 Founex VD
DP Coordinator Michael Winter
PYP Coordinator Corine Van Den Wildenberg
Languages English
T: +41 22 960 9111
W: www.ecolint.ch/campus/la-chataigneraie

International School of Geneva (La Grande Boissière Campus)

62, route de Chêne, 1208 Geneva GE
DP Coordinator Conan de Wilde
Languages English, French
T: +41 22 787 2400
W: www.ecolint.ch/campus/la-grande-boissiere

International School of Lausanne

Chemin de la Grangette 2, 1052 Le Mont-sur-Lausanne VD
DP Coordinator Michael Humphrey
MYP Coordinator Darryl Anderson
PYP Coordinator Erin Threlfall
Languages English
T: +41 21 560 02 02
W: www.isl.ch

International School of Rheinfelden

Zürcherstrasse 9, Drei Könige, 4310 Rheinfelden AG
PYP Coordinator Bryan Murray
Languages German
T: +41 61 831 06 06
W: www.isrh.ch

International School of Schaffhausen

Mühlentalstrasse 280, 8200 Schaffhausen SH
DP Coordinator Silke Fox
MYP Coordinator Ebru Guever
PYP Coordinator Kaccey Mayer
Languages English
T: +41 52 624 1707
W: www.issh.ch

INTERNATIONAL SCHOOL OF TICINO SA

Via Ponteggia, 23, Cadempino, 6814 Lugano
DP Coordinator Mr. Paul Highdale
MYP Coordinator Mr. Graeme Wallbank
PYP Coordinator Ms. Sarah Jane Lee
Languages English, Italian
T: +41 919710344
E: frontoffice@isticino.com
W: www.isticino.com

See full details on page 133

International School of Zug & Luzern, Riverside Campus

Rothustrasse 4b, 6331 Hünenberg ZG
CP Coordinator Robert Sugden
DP Coordinator Zoe Badcock
MYP Coordinator Kelli Meeker
Languages English
T: +41 768 2950
W: www.iszl.ch

International School Rheintal

Aeulistrasse 10, 9470 Buchs SG
DP Coordinator Steven Bavaro
MYP Coordinator Oliver Beck
PYP Coordinator Nilde Pais
Languages English
T: +41 81 750 6300
W: www.isr.ch

International School Zurich North

Industriestrasse 50, 8304 Wallisellen ZH
PYP Coordinator Rebecca Nolan
Languages English
T: +41 44 830 7000
W: www.iszn.ch

Kantonsschule am Burggraben St. Gallen

Burggraben 21, 9000 St. Gallen SG
DP Coordinator Peter Litscher
Languages English, German
T: +41 712281414
W: ksbg.ch

Kantonsschule Wettingen

Klosterstrasse 11, 5430 Wettingen AG
DP Coordinator Heinz Anklin
Languages English
T: +41 (0)56 437 24 00
W: www.kanti-wettingen.ch

KV Zürich Die Wirtschaftsschule

Limmatstrasse 310, 8031 Zürich ZH
DP Coordinator Sara Bucher
Languages English, German
T: +41 44 444 66 00
W: www.kvz-schule.ch

LA CÔTE INTERNATIONAL SCHOOL AUBONNE

Chemin de Clamogne 8, 1170 Aubonne VD
DP Coordinator Alexa Prior
MYP Coordinator Emily Hardwicke
Languages English, French
T: +41 (0)22 823 26 26
E: admissions@international-school.org
W: www.international-school.org

See full details on page 151

La Garenne International School

Chemin des Chavasses 23, 1885 Chesières-Villars VD
DP Coordinator Adam Jozef
MYP Coordinator Aurelia McNicol
Languages English
T: +41 24 495 29 38
W: www.la-garenne.ch

Le Régent International School

Rue du Zier 4, CH-3963 Crans-Montana
DP Coordinator Jennifer Cogbill
Languages English, French
T: +41 (0)27 480 3201
W: regentschool.ch

Lemania College Lausanne

Chemin de Préville 3, 1003 Lausanne VD
DP Coordinator Giovanna Crisante
Languages English
T: +41 21 320 15 01
W: www.lemania.ch

LEYSIN AMERICAN SCHOOL IN SWITZERLAND

3 Chemin de la Source, 1854 Leysin VD
DP Coordinator Ronan Lynch
Languages English
T: +41 24 493 4878
E: admissions@las.ch
W: www.las.ch

See full details on page 153

Literargymnasium Rämibühl

Rämistrasse 56, 8001 Zürich ZH
DP Coordinator Annette Haueter
Languages English
T: +41 1 265 62 11
W: www.lgr.ch

Lyceum Alpinum Zuoz

Aguêl 185, 7524 Zuoz GR
CP Coordinator Erna Romeril
DP Coordinator Kieran Burgess
Languages English
T: +41 81 851 30 00
W: www.lyceum-alpinum.ch

Montreux International School

Avenue de Chillon 60, 1820 Montreux VD
CP Coordinator Zena Maria Lawton
Languages English
T: +41 79 596 29 06
W: montreuxis.ch

Mutuelle d'études secondaires

7 bis Boulevard Carl Vogt, 1205 Geneva GE
DP Coordinator Nathalie Rapaille
Languages French
T: +41 (0)22 741 00 01
W: www.ecolemes.ch

Neue Kantonsschule Aarau

Schanzmättelistrasse 32, 5000 Aarau AG
DP Coordinator Kathleen Noreisch
Languages English
T: +41 62 837 94 55
W: www.nksa.ch

Obersee Bilingual School

Eichenstrasse 4C, 8808 Pfaeffikon ZH
DP Coordinator Louise Hoyne-Butler
Languages English, German
T: +41 55 511 38 00
W: www.oberseebilingualschool.ch

Realgymnasium Rämibühl

Rämistrasse 56, 8001 Zürich ZH
DP Coordinator Philipp Wettstein
Languages English
T: +41 44 265 63 12
W: www.rgz.ch

Rudolf Steiner Schule Oberaargau

Ringstrasse 30, 4900 Langenthal BE
DP Coordinator Philip Pflugbeil
Languages English, German
T: +41 (0)62 922 69 05
W: www.rsso.ch

Scuola Rudolf Steiner ii Lugano Origlio

via ai Magi 4, 6945 Origlio TI
DP Coordinator Mosè Nodari
Languages English, Italian
T: +41 (0)91 966 29 62
W: scuolasteiner-lugano.ch

SIS Swiss International School Basel

Erlenstrasse 15, 4058 Basel BS
DP Coordinator James Brocklehurst
Languages English
T: +41 61 683 71 40
W: www.swissinternationalschool.ch/schulorte/basel

SIS Swiss International School Zürich

Seidenstrasse 2, 8304 Wallisellen ZH
DP Coordinator Christoph Neuenstein
Languages English
T: +41 44 388 99 44
W: www.swissinternationalschool.ch/schulorte/zuerich

SWITZERLAND

ST. GEORGE'S INTERNATIONAL SCHOOL, SWITZERLAND

Chemin de St. Georges 19, CH-1815 Clarens/Montreux
DP Coordinator Colin Travis
Languages English
T: +41 21 964 3411
E: admissions@stgeorges.ch
W: www.stgeorges.ch
See full details on page 211

STIFTSSCHULE ENGELBERG

Benediktinerkloster 5, Engelberg 6390
DP Coordinator Dr. Hansueli Flückiger
Languages German, English
T: +41 41 639 61 00
E: info@stiftsschule-engelberg.ch
W: www.stiftsschule-engelberg.ch
See full details on page 218

TASIS THE AMERICAN SCHOOL IN SWITZERLAND

Via Collina d'Oro 15, 6926 Montagnola-Lugano
DP Coordinator Kathy Anderson
Languages English
T: +41 91 960 5151
E: admissions@tasis.ch
W: www.tasis.ch
See full details on page 222

Zurich International School

Steinacherstr 140, 8820 Wädenswil ZH
DP Coordinator Sean Maley
Languages English
T: +41 58 750 2500
W: www.zis.ch

TANZANIA

Dar es Salaam International Academy

PO Box 23282, Dar es Salaam
DP Coordinator Linet Edison
MYP Coordinator Susan Ngoye
PYP Coordinator Saviona Furtado
Languages English
T: +255 22 2600 202
W: www.diatz.cc

International School of Tanganyika Ltd

United Nations Road, PO Box 2651, Dar es Salaam
DP Coordinator Jason Crook
MYP Coordinator Dharma Sears
PYP Coordinator Tina Fossgreen
Languages English
T: +255 22 2151817
W: www.istafrica.com

Iringa International School

PO Box 912, Lumumba Street, Gangilonga, Iringa
PYP Coordinator Kristeen Chachage
Languages English
T: +255 26 2702018
W: iis.ac.tz

The Aga Khan Mzizima Secondary School

P.O. Box 21563, Fire Road, Upanga, Dar es Salaam
DP Coordinator Simon Mutuku
PYP Coordinator Blandina Duwe
Languages English
T: +255 22 215 1253
W: www.agakhanschools.org/tanzania/akmss

UWC East Africa, Arusha Campus

PO Box 2691, Arusha
DP Coordinator Nathalie Vignard
MYP Coordinator Hamid Rezayi
PYP Coordinator Amanda Bowen
Languages English
T: +255 78 449 0133
W: www.uwcea.org

UWC East Africa, Moshi Campus

PO Box 733, Lema Road, Moshi
DP Coordinator Margaret Brunt
MYP Coordinator Farah Fawaz
PYP Coordinator Mboka Mwasongwe
Languages English
T: +255 27 2755004
W: www.uwcea.org

TOGO

Arc-en-Ciel International School

Nyekonakpoe, Lomé BP: 2985
DP Coordinator Taid Rahimi
MYP Coordinator Taid Rahimi
PYP Coordinator Taid Rahimi
Languages French, English
T: +228 2222 0329
W: www.arc-en-ciel.org

The British School of Lomé

Residence du Benin, Lomé 20050
DP Coordinator Paul Fairbrother
Languages English
T: +228 2226 46 06
W: www.bsl.tg

TUNISIA

American Cooperative School of Tunis

ACST BP150, Cite Taieb M' Hiri, Laouina 2045
DP Coordinator Lucie Lecocq Otsing
Languages English
T: +216 71 760 905
W: www.acst.net

École Canadienne de Tunis

Rue des Minéraux Charguia 1, Tunis 2035
DP Coordinator Mahmoud Nouaïri
MYP Coordinator Imen Ben aissa
PYP Coordinator Meriem Cammoun
Languages French
T: +216 71 206 035
W: www.ec-tunis.com

John Dewey School de Sousse

Sahloul, Sousse 4054
PYP Coordinator Asma Chebil
Languages Arabic, French
T: +216 73 823 401
W: www.johndewey-school.org

TURKEY

ABC Okullari

Yenibati Mahallesi 2398, Sok. No. 15, Batikent, Ankara, Central Anatolia
PYP Coordinator Sena Erhan
Languages English, Turkish
T: +90 312 256 12 22
W: en.karaca-algulhukuk.com

ABC Okullari Goksu Kampüsü

Göksu Mahallesi 93, Cadde No. 6/1A, Eryaman, Ankara, Central Anatolia
DP Coordinator Nalan Gürakar
PYP Coordinator Rabia Dasdandir
Languages English, Turkish
T: +90 312 444 2221
W: www.abc.k12.tr

Acibadem Schools – Acibadem Campus

Acibadem Mah. Cecen Sok. No:48 Ic Kapi No:1, Üsküdar, 34730 Istanbul, Marmara
PYP Coordinator Hande Özkeskin
Languages Turkish
T: +90 216 510 52 32
W: www.acibadem.k12.tr

Aka School

Radyum Sok No 21 Basin Sitesi, Bahcelievler, Istanbul, Marmara
DP Coordinator Nasstasha Stewart
Languages English
T: +90 212 557 27 72
W: www.akakoleji.k12.tr

ALKEV Schools

Alkent 2000 Mah. Mehmet Yesilgül Cd. No: 7, Büyükcekmece, 34535 Istanbul, Marmara
DP Coordinator Seda Cakir
Languages English, German
T: +90 212 886 88 40
W: www.alkev.k12.tr

American Collegiate Institute

Inonu Caddesi No. 476, Goztepe, 35290 Izmir, Aegean
DP Coordinator Mine Erim
Languages English
T: +90 232 285 34 01
W: www.aci.k12.tr

Ankara Türk Telekom Sosyal Bilimler Lisesi

Mutlukent Mah. 1919, Sokak No. 1 Ümitköy, Cankaya, 06810 Ankara, Central Anatolia
DP Coordinator Hülya Temizöz
Languages English
T: +90 312 236 63 77
W: asbl.meb.k12.tr

AREL Schools (Kindergarten/Primary/Middle/High)

Merkez Mah, Selahattin Pinar Sok, No:3 Yenibosna, Bahcelievler, 34197 Istanbul, Marmara
MYP Coordinator Burcu Geçici
PYP Coordinator Umut Brezina
Languages English, Turkish
T: +90 212 550 49 30
W: www.arel.k12.tr

Balikesir Aci College

Cayirhisar Mah. Yeni Izmir yolu Cad. 3B, 10185 Balikesir, Marmara
DP Coordinator Mertcan Kulavuz
Languages English, Turkish
T: +90 266 239 85 85
W: acikoleji.k12.tr

Besiktas Sakip Sabanci Anadolu Lisesi

Yildiz caddesi No 73, Besiktas, 34359 Istanbul, Marmara
DP Coordinator Murat Cetin
Languages English, Turkish
T: +90 212 227 46 10
W: sabancilisesi.meb.k12.tr

Beykoz Doga Campus

Fener Yolu Cad. No:6 Dereseki, Akbaba, Beykoz, 81650 Istanbul, Marmara
PYP Coordinator Nurcan Inan
Languages English
T: +90 216 320 52 00
W: www.dogaokullari.com/eng/schools/beykoz-doga-campus

IB AFRICA | EUROPE | MIDDLE EAST

Bilkent Erzurum Laboratory School

Prof. Dr. Ihsan Dogramaci Bulvari Cat Yolu, Palandöken, 25070 Erzurum, Eastern Anatolia
DP Coordinator Selin Sethi
Languages English
T: +90 442 342 61 74
W: bels.bilkent.edu.tr

Bilkent Laboratory & International School

East Campus, 06800 Ankara, Central Anatolia
DP Coordinator Feray Ozdemir Gur
PYP Coordinator Ayten Korkmaz
Languages English, Turkish
T: +90 312 290 53 61
W: www.blisankara.org

Bodrum Marmara Elementary School

Cumhuriyet Avenue No. 2, 48420 Bodrum, Aegean
PYP Coordinator Gul Pasali Yagci
Languages English, Turkish
T: +90 252 358 61 13
W: www.mek.k12.tr

Bodrum Marmara Private College

Cumhuriyet Avenue No. 2, 48420 Bodrum, Aegean
DP Coordinator Berrin Yurdakul
Languages English, Turkish
T: +90 252 358 61 13
W: www.mek.k12.tr

British International School Istanbul – Zekeriyaköy

Zekeriyaköy Mahallesi, Kilyos Caddesi No. 227/12, Sariyer, Istanbul, Marmara
DP Coordinator Seef Eddeen Marsden
Languages English
T: +90 212 202 70 27
W: www.bis.k12.tr

Cakir Schools

Orhaneli Yolu, Egitimciler Cd 15, Nilüfer, Bursa, Marmara
DP Coordinator Sencer Donmez
MYP Coordinator Selen Galiç
PYP Coordinator Gamze Sezer
Languages English, Turkish
T: +90 224 451 93 30
W: www.cakir.k12.tr

Çanakkale Özel ilkokulu

Izmir Yolu 12. Km Güzelyali, Güzelyali, 17100 Canakkale, Marmara
PYP Coordinator Pinar Usta
Languages English, Turkish
T: +90 286 232 86 86
W: www.canakkalekoleji.com

Deutsche Schule Izmir

Kuscular Cad. No. 82, Kuscular Köyü, Urla, 35430 Izmir, Aegean
DP Coordinator Filiz Ünal
Languages English
T: +90 232 234 75 07
W: www.ds-izmir.com

Egitmen Koleji

Istasyon Mah. Fevzi Çakmak Cad. No: 123, Tuzla, 34940 Istanbul, Marmara
PYP Coordinator Ahmet Kilic
Languages Turkish
T: +90 216 446 48 46
W: www.egitmen.k12.tr

Enka Schools – Adapazari Campus

Dagdibi Mahallesi, Enka Yolu Caddesi, No. 66/A, Adapazari, Marmara
MYP Coordinator Sunay Akyürek Türk
PYP Coordinator Zühal Ergül
Languages English
T: +90 264 323 37 74
W: www.enka.k12.tr/adapazari

Enka Schools – Istanbul Campus

Sadi Gülcelik Spor Sitesi, Istinye, 34460 Istanbul, Marmara
DP Coordinator Natalie Parker
MYP Coordinator Teni Karaman
PYP Coordinator Zeyneb Sengezer
Languages English, Turkish
T: +90 212 705 65 00
W: www.enka.k12.tr/istanbul

Ernst-Reuter-Schule

Tunus Cad 56, Kavaklidere, 06680 Ankara, Central Anatolia
DP Coordinator Suna Ahmad
Languages English
T: +90 312 426 63 82
W: www.ers-ankara.com

Eyüboglu Atasehir Primary School

2 Cadde 59 Ada Manolya 4, Bloklari yani No 6, Atasehir, 34758 Istanbul, Marmara
PYP Coordinator Firuze Vanlioglu
Languages Turkish, English
T: +90 216 522 12 22
W: www.eyuboglu.com

Eyüboglu Kemerburgaz Middle School

Mithatpasa Mah. Pirinccikoy Yolu, 34075 Istanbul, Marmara
MYP Coordinator Arzu Onat Konusmaz
Languages English, Turkish
T: +90 216 522 12 72
W: www.eyuboglu.com

Eyüboglu Kemerburgaz Preschool & Primary School

Mithatpasa Mah. Pirinccikoy Yolu, 34075 Istanbul, Marmara
PYP Coordinator Meliz Katlav
Languages English
T: +90 216 522 12 72
W: www.eyuboglu.com

EYÜBOGLU SCHOOLS

Esenevler Mah, Dr Rüstem Eyüboglu sok 3, Ümraniye, 34762 Istanbul, Marmara
DP Coordinator Oguz Günenç
MYP Coordinator Gülsah Çekiç; Arzu Onat Konusmaz
PYP Coordinator Mevce Selek; Firuze Vanlioglu; Meliz Katlav
Languages Turkish, English
T: +90 216 522 12 12
E: eyuboglu@eyuboglu.k12.tr
W: www.eyuboglu.k12.tr

See full details on page 89

Ezgililer Private Primary School

Kusculu Mah. 1728 Sok. No.6, Ilkadim, Samsun, Black Sea
PYP Coordinator Müge Öztürk
Languages English
T: +90 362 233 21 22
W: ezgililer.k12.tr

FMV Ayazaga Isik High School

Maslak Mah. Büyükdere Cad. No:106, Sisli, Sariyer, 34460 Istanbul, Marmara
DP Coordinator Melda Cemal
Languages English
T: +90 212 286 11 30
W: www.fmv.edu.tr

FMV Ayazaga Isik Primary & Middle School

Maslak Mah. Büyükdere Cad. No:106, Sisli, Sariyer, 34460 Istanbul, Marmara
PYP Coordinator Ozlem Mizrahi
Languages English, Turkish
T: +90 212 286 11 30
W: www.fmv.edu.tr

FMV Erenköy Isik High School

Sinan Ercan Cad. No:19, Erenköy, 34736 Istanbul, Marmara
DP Coordinator Sinem Özgöz
Languages English
T: +90 216 385 31 47
W: www.fmv.edu.tr

FMV Erenköy Isik Primary & Middle School

Sinan Ercan Cad. No:19, Erenköy, 34736 Istanbul, Marmara
PYP Coordinator Merve Ünal
Languages English, Turkish
T: +90 216 385 31 47
W: www.fmv.edu.tr

FMV Isik Primary & Middle School

Tesvikiye Cad. No:06, Nisantasi, 34365 Istanbul, Marmara
PYP Coordinator Omer Karabacak
Languages English, Turkish
T: +90 212 233 12 03
W: www.fmv.edu.tr

FMV Ispartakule Isik Primary & Middle School

Tahtakale Mah. Gaffar Okkan Cad. No: 5/7 Blok No: 1, Avcilar, 34325 Istanbul, Marmara
PYP Coordinator Gizem Dolu
Languages English, Turkish
T: +90 212 648 09 75
W: www.fmv.edu.tr

Gazi University Foundation Private High School

Ali Suavi Street, Eti Quarter No 15, Maltepe, 06570 Ankara, Central Anatolia
DP Coordinator Asya Geylan
Languages English
T: +90 312 232 28 12
W: www.kolej.gazi.edu.tr

Gaziantep Kolej Vakfi Cemil Alevli College

Guvenevler Mah., Hoca Ahmet Yesevi Caddesi, No. 2, Sehitkamil, 27060 Gaziantep, Southeastern Anatolia
DP Coordinator Ali Pamuk
Languages English
T: +90 342 321 01 00
W: www.gkv.k12.tr

Gökkusagi Koleji – Bahçelievler

Eski Londra Asfalti No: 15 Haznedar, Bahcelievler, 34180 Istanbul, Marmara
DP Coordinator Murat Kotan
Languages English, Turkish
T: +90 212 644 59 00
W: www.gokkusagi.k12.tr

Gökkusagi Koleji – Bahçesehir

Orhan Gazi Mah, 1654 sk. No. 40, Esenyurt, Istanbul, Marmara
PYP Coordinator Senem Dinç
Languages English, Turkish
T: +90 212 672 84 26
W: www.gokkusagi.k12.tr

Gökkusagi Koleji – Ümraniye

Inkilap Mh. Alemdag Cd. Üntel Sk. No. 30, Ümraniye, Istanbul, Marmara
PYP Coordinator Lale Tugba Oral
Languages English
T: +90 216 634 60 60
W: www.gokkusagi.k12.tr

TURKEY

Huseyin Avni Sozen Anatolian High School

Barbaros Mah. Mütevelli Cesme Cad. Sedef Sok., No 5/2 Kosuyolu, Üsküdar, Istanbul, Marmara

DP Coordinator Aysegul Sari

Languages English, Turkish

T: +90 216 651 65 81

W: hasal.meb.k12.tr

IDV Özel Bilkent High School

IDV Özel Bilkent Ilkokulu, Ortaokulu ve Lisesi Universiteler Mah 1600, Cad. No. 6, Dogu Kampus, 06800 Ankara, Central Anatolia

DP Coordinator Elif Günaydin

Languages English, Turkish

T: +90 312 290 89 39

W: www.obl.bilkent.edu.tr

IDV Özel Bilkent Middle School

IDV Özel Bilkent Ilkokulu, Ortaokulu ve Lisesi, Universiteler Mah 1600, Cad. No. 6, Dogu Kampus, 06800 Ankara, Central Anatolia

MYP Coordinator Linda Bruce-Ozdemir

PYP Coordinator Gülsen Çiçek Keskinsoy

Languages Turkish, English

T: +90 312 290 54 40

W: www.obi.bilkent.edu.tr

IELEV Private High School

Ensar Cad. No:4/3 Nisantepe Mah. B Blok, Çekmeköy, 34794 Istanbul, Marmara

DP Coordinator Mrs. Rüya Dogan

Languages English, German, Turkish

T: +90 216 304 30 92

W: www.ielev.k12.tr/tr/lise

Irmak School

Cemil Topuzlu Caddesi No. 100, Caddebostan P.K. 34728, Kadiköy, Istanbul, Marmara

PYP Coordinator Tuba Yoleri

Languages Turkish, English

T: +90 216 411 39 23

W: www.irmak.k12.tr

Isikkent Egitim Kampusu

6240/5 Sokak No. 3, Karacaoglan Mah., Yesilova, Bornova, 35070 Izmir, Aegean

DP Coordinator Lyudmyla Boysan

MYP Coordinator Lyudmyla Boysan

PYP Coordinator Evrim Yalcin Onder

Languages English, English

T: +90 232 462 71 00

W: www.isikkent.k12.tr

Istanbul International Community School

Karaagac Koyu Mahallesi, Kahraman Caddesi, 27/1, Buyukcekmece, 34500 Istanbul, Marmara

DP Coordinator Omer Kipmen

MYP Coordinator Heath Fontes

PYP Coordinator Evelyn Galan

Languages English

T: +90 212 857 82 64

W: www.iics.k12.tr

Istanbul Marmara Private College

Marmara Egitim Köyü, Maltepe, 34857 Istanbul, Marmara

DP Coordinator Guzide Pinar Cirpanli

PYP Coordinator Evren Turan

Languages Turkish, English

T: +90 216 626 10 00

W: www.mek.k12.tr

Istanbul Prof. Dr Mümtaz Turhan Sosyal Bilimler Lisesi

Fevzi Çakmak Cad. Fatih Mah., No. 2 Yenibosna, Bahçelievler, Istanbul, Marmara

DP Coordinator Özgen Yildirimtas

Languages English

T: +902 1255 161 46

W: www.isbl.k12.tr

ISTEK Acibadem Schools

Acibadem Mah. Bag Sok. No 6, Kadiköy, 34718 Istanbul, Marmara

DP Coordinator Gonca Tasar

PYP Coordinator Özlem Bogahan

Languages English

T: +90 216 325 30 75

W: www.istek.k12.tr/acibadem-kampusu

ISTEK Atanur Oguz Schools

Balmumcu Mah. Gazi Umurpasa Sk. No 26, Balmumcu, 34349 Istanbul, Marmara

DP Coordinator Pelin Etgu

PYP Coordinator Filiz Gunay

Languages English

T: +90 212 211 34 60

W: www.istek.k12.tr/atanur-oguz-kampusu

ISTEK BARIS SCHOOLS

Bagdat Cad. No. 238/1, Ciftehavuzlar, Kadiköy, 34730 Istanbul, Marmara

PYP Coordinator Gamze Can

Languages Turkish, English

T: +90 216 360 12 18

E: baris.ilkokul@istek.k12.tr

W: www.istek.k12.tr

See full details on page 138

ISTEK Belde Schools

Kuzguncuk Mah. Rasimaga Sok. No 7/4, Üsküdar, 34664 Istanbul, Marmara

PYP Coordinator Ebru Salman

Languages English

T: +90 216 495 96 23

W: www.istek.k12.tr/belde-kampusu

ISTEK Bilge Kagan Schools

Senlikköy Mah. Florya Cad. No 2 Florya, Bakirköy, 34153 Istanbul, Marmara

PYP Coordinator Süheyla Dincer

Languages English

T: +90 212 663 29 71

W: www.istek.k12.tr/bilge-kagan-kampusu

ISTEK KASGARLI MAHMUT SCHOOLS

Eski Edirne Asfalti No 512, Sultangazi, 34110 Istanbul, Marmara

PYP Coordinator Ayca Özkardes

Languages English, Turkish

T: +90 212 594 26 11/12

E: kasgarlimahmut@istek.org.tr

W: www.istek.k12.tr/kasgarli-mahmut-kampusu

See full details on page 139

ISTEK KEMAL ATATÜRK SCHOOLS (KINDERGARTEN & PRIMARY SCHOOL)

Tarabya Bayiri Cad. No 60, Tarabya/Sariyer, 34457 Istanbul, Marmara

PYP Coordinator Kevser Kilic

Languages Turkish

T: +90 212 262 75 75

E: kemalataturk@istek.k12.tr

W: www.istek.k12.tr/kemal-ataturk-kampusu

See full details on page 140

ISTEK Ulugbey Schools

Atalar Mah. Akgün Sok. No 23, Kartal, 34862 Istanbul, Marmara

PYP Coordinator Seray Kok

Languages English, Turkish

T: +90 216 488 13 08

W: www.istek.k12.tr/ulugbey-kampusu

ITÜ ETA Vakfi Doga Koleji

Barbaros Mah. Halk Cad. Kardelen Sok. N.:2 Incity C Blok, Atasehir, Istanbul, Marmara

DP Coordinator Mihrican Satis

Languages English

T: +90 216 4853580

W: www.dogakoleji.k12.tr

ITU Gelistirme Vakfi Özel Ekrem Elginkan Lisesi

ITU Ayazaga Kampusu, Maslak, 34469 Istanbul, Marmara

DP Coordinator Ahmet Bilaloglu

Languages English

T: +90 212 367 1300

W: www.itugvo.k12.tr/web/default.asp

Jale Tezer Educational Institutions

Jale Tezer Primary & Secondary Schools (Gazi Osman Pasa Campus), Bagcilar Mahallesi Acin Caddesi No:7, Cankaya, 06670 Ankara, Central Anatolia

DP Coordinator Nükte Engin

Languages English, Turkish

T: +90 312 447 49 49

W: www.jaletezer.k12.tr

Kartal Anadolu Imam Hatip Lisesi

Esentepe Mah. Pamuk Sk. No. 3, Kartal, 34870 Istanbul, Marmara

DP Coordinator Nalan Erdogan

Languages English

T: +90 216 387 15 44

W: kartalaihl.meb.k12.tr

Kirmizi Cizgi Schools

Fener Mah.1964 Sok. Yaliyar Si?t. No : 30/C-D, 07060 Antalya, Mediterranean

DP Coordinator Serpil Acikgöz

Languages English, Turkish

T: +90 242 242 99 98

W: www.kirmizicizgikoleji.com

Kocaeli Marmara Private College

Dumlupinar Mah. Sehit Turgut Cicek Cad. No. 47, 41250 Kartepe, Marmara

DP Coordinator Merve Gürel

Languages English, Turkish

T: +90 262 373 1313

W: en.mek.k12.tr

Kültür2000 College

Karaagac Mah., Sirtköy Bulvari No. 2, Büyükcekmece, 34500 Istanbul, Marmara

DP Coordinator Mrs. Nida Korkmaz

MYP Coordinator Handan Saat

Languages English, Turkish

T: +90 212 850 81 81

W: www.kultur.k12.tr

MEF International Schools, Istanbul – Ulus High

Ulus Mah. Leylak Sok. No. 22, Ulus, Besiktas, 34340 Istanbul, Marmara

DP Coordinator Seden Chouseinoglou

Languages English

T: +90 212 362 26 33 (EXT:1340)

W: www.mefis.k12.tr/istanbul

MEF International Schools, Istanbul – Ulus Primary

Ulus Mah. Leylak Sok. No. 22, Ulus, Besiktas, 34340 Istanbul, Marmara

PYP Coordinator Darren Richardson

Languages English

T: +90 212 362 26 33 (EXT:1340)

W: www.mefis.k12.tr/istanbul

Minecan Okullari

Karsli mah 82064 sok. No.
12-14, Cukurova, 010101 Adana,
Mediterranean
PYP Coordinator Aysin Gün
Languages English, Turkish
T: +90 322 233 30 45
W: minecan.com.tr

Muruvvet Evyap Schools

Maden District Bakir Street, No.
2A/2B/2C, Sariyer, 34450 Istanbul,
Marmara
PYP Coordinator Neslihan Sezer
Languages Turkish
T: +90 212 342 43 33
W: www.evyapokullari.k12.tr

Nesibe AYDIN Educational Institutions (Konya)

Beyhekim Mh. Darülhilafet Sk. No:1
Selcuklu, 42130 Konya, Central
Anatolia
PYP Coordinator Bengu Kesen
Languages Turkish
T: +90 332 320 85 11
W: www.nesibeaydin.k12.tr/konya

Nesibe Aydin Okullari

Haymana Yolu 5. Km, Karsiyaka
Mahallesi 577, Sokak No. 1, Gölbasi,
06830 Ankara, Central Anatolia
DP Coordinator Senol Recber
PYP Coordinator Ebru Hezen
Languages English
T: +90 312 498 25 25
W: www.nesibeaydin.k12.tr

Nilüfer Anadolu Imam Hatip Lisesi

Nilüfer Hatun Cad., Cumhuriyet, 16140
Nilüfer, Bursa, Marmara
DP Coordinator Saadet Dogan
MYP Coordinator Saadet Dogan
Languages English, Turkish
T: +90 224 453 10 22
W: niluferanadoluihl.meb.k12.tr/tema/
iletisim.php

NUN Middle & High School

Elmali Mahallesi, Beykoz Elmali Yolu
Sokak No. 5/1, Beykoz, Istanbul,
Marmara
DP Coordinator Fatin Bayraktar
MYP Coordinator Oguz Korkmaz
Languages English, Turkish
T: +90 216 686 16 86
W: www.nunokullari.com

NUN Primary School

Burhaniye Mahallesi Haci Resit
Pasa Sk. No. 18, Üsküdar, Istanbul,
Marmara
PYP Coordinator Ayse Akgünlü
Languages English
T: +90 216 686 16 86
W: www.nunokullari.com

Özel Antalya Toplum Koleji Anadolu Lisesi

Altinkale, Palmiye Cd. No 10/A, 07192
Dösemealti, Antalya, Mediterranean
DP Coordinator Paul Richardson
Languages English, Turkish
T: +90 242 443 30 80
W: www.antalyatoplumkoleji.com

Özel Ari Anadolu Lisesi

Ögretmenler cad. No. 16/ C 100, Yil
Cukurambar, Çankaya, 06530 Ankara,
Central Anatolia
DP Coordinator Bülent Inal
Languages English
T: +90 312 286 85 85
W: www.ariokullari.k12.tr

Özel Egeberk Anaokulu

Özlüce Mah. Hazal Sk. No:3 Nilüfer,
16010 Bursa, Marmara
PYP Coordinator Betul Basturk
Oznar
Languages English
T: +90 533 593 92 90
W: www.egeberkanaokulu.com

Özel Kariyer Ilkokulu

Turgut Özal Mh. 2212.Sk No:4,
Cakirlarciftligi/Batikent, 06370
Ankara, Central Anatolia
PYP Coordinator Pinar Demirel
Languages Turkish
T: +90 312 566 22 32
W: www.kariyerkoleji.com.tr

Private ALEV Schools

Kadirova Cad. 52/3, Ömerli Mah.
Cekmeköy, 34797 Istanbul, Marmara
DP Coordinator Burcu Isik Keser
Languages Turkish, German, English
T: +90 216 435 83 50
W: www.alev.k12.tr

Private Kocaeli Bahcesehir Anatolian High School

Fatih Mah, Demokrasi Cad No.8 B.K.3,
Köseköy, 41135 Kartepe, Marmara
DP Coordinator Orcun Baris
Languages English, Turkish
T: +90 262 373 69 69
W: kocaelianadolulisesi.bahcesehir.k12.
tr/en/

Private Sahin Schools

Prof. Dr. Sabahattin Zaim Bulvari
Karaman Yolu 4., Km Karakamis Mah.,
54100 Adapazari, Marmara
PYP Coordinator Hulya Caliskan
T: +90 264 777 17 00
W: www.sahinokullari.com

SEV American College

Nisantepe Mah. Kerem Sok. 76, No.
5-9, Cekmeköy, 34794 Istanbul,
Marmara
DP Coordinator Rachel Litwak
Languages English
T: +90 216 625 27 22
W: sevkoleji.k12.tr

Tarsus American School

Cengiz Topel Caddesi, Caminur
Mahallesi No. 66, Tarsus, 33440
Mersin, Mediterranean
DP Coordinator Dilek Yagucmen
Languages English
T: +90 324 241 81 81
W: www.tac.k12.tr

TAS PRIVATE ELEMENTARY SCHOOL

Cevizlik Mah. Hallac Hüseyin, Sk. No.
11, Bakirköy, 34142 Istanbul, Marmara
PYP Coordinator Sena Bataklar
Languages Turkish, English
T: +90 212 543 60 00
E: melektuzluca@taskolej.k12.tr
W: www.taskolej.k12.tr
See full details on page 221

TED Ankara College Foundation High School

Golbasi Taspinar Koyu Yumrubel,
Mevkii No. 310, 06830 Ankara, Central
Anatolia
DP Coordinator Serenay Tarhan
Guler
Languages English
T: +90 312 586 90 00
W: www.tedankara.k12.tr

TED Bursa College

21 Yüzyil Cad Mürsel, Köyü Mevkii,
Bademli, Bursa, Marmara
DP Coordinator Nuray Bayulgen
Languages English
T: +90 224 549 21 00
W: www.tedbursa.k12.tr

Terakki Foundation – Levent Campus

Ebulula Mardin Cad. Öztürk Sok No. 2,
Levent, 34335 Istanbul, Marmara
DP Coordinator Haluk Kocak
PYP Coordinator Hulya Salt Aygun
Languages English, Turkish
T: +90 212 351 00 60
W: www.terakki.org.tr

Terakki Foundation – Tepeoren High School

Medeniyet Blv. No. 55L, Tuzla, 34959
Istanbul, Marmara
DP Coordinator Yasar Kurun
Languages English, Turkish
T: +90 216 709 18 77
W: www.terakki.org.tr

Terakki Foundation – Tepeoren Kindergarten & Primary School

Medeniyet Blv. No. 55L, Tuzla, 34959
Istanbul, Marmara
PYP Coordinator Ebru Karakas
Duzyol
Languages English, Turkish
T: +90 216 709 18 77
W: www.terakki.org.tr

Tev Inanc Turkes High School For Gifted Students

Muallimköy Mah. 4126, Sok. No. 25/A,
41490 Gebze, Marmara
DP Coordinator Joshua Lisi
Languages English
T: +90 262 679 36 36
W: www.tevitol.k12.tr

The Koç School

Tepeören Mahallesi, Eski Ankara
Asfalti Caddesi No. 60, 34941 Istanbul,
Marmara
DP Coordinator Richard Fower
Languages Turkish, English
T: +90 216 585 62 00
W: www.kocschool.k12.tr

Uluslararasi Murat Hüdavendigar Anadolu Imam Hatip Lisesi

Hamitler, Sht. Saim Tuna Sk. No:6,
Osmangazi, 16150 Bursa, Marmara
DP Coordinator Nilay Gunay Yumsak
Languages English, Turkish
T: +90 224 242 22 28

Üsküdar American Academy

Vakif Sk., No. 1 Baglarbasi, Uskudar,
33664 Istanbul, Marmara
DP Coordinator David Simon
Cousens
Languages English
T: +90 216 333 11 00
W: www.uaa.k12.tr

Vefa High School

Kalenderhane Mah. Dede Efendi
Cad., No. 5 Sehzadebasi, Fatih, 34134
Istanbul, Marmara
DP Coordinator Evrim Gulec Akova
Languages English, Turkish
T: +90 212 527 38 72
W: vefalisesi.meb.k12.tr

Yeni Yol Schools

Yeniakcayir Mahallesi No. 551,
Tepebasi, Eskisehir, Central Anatolia
DP Coordinator Mustafa Yilmazer
PYP Coordinator Elvan Yildirim
Languages English, Turkish
T: +90 222 230 39 00
W: www.yeniyolokullari.com

YUCE Schools

Ozel YUCE Okullari, Zuhtu Tigrel Caddesi, Ismet Eker Sokak No 5, Oran, 06450 Ankara, Central Anatolia
DP Coordinator Tugce Soruklu
MYP Coordinator Ahu Unsal Batum
PYP Coordinator Sila Derici
Languages English, Turkish
T: +90 312 490 02 02
W: www.yuce.k12.tr

Yusuf Ziya Oner Fen Lisesi

Yesilbayir Mah. Mektep, Sok No. 5, Dösemealti, 07192 Antalya, Mediterranean
DP Coordinator Harun Akyol
Languages English, Turkish
T: +90 242 443 18 56
W: antalyafenlisesi.meb.k12.tr

Zafer Koleji

Eskisehir Yolu, Baglica Kavsagi No. 461, Cayyolu, 06790 Ankara, Central Anatolia
DP Coordinator Önder Sit
Languages English
T: +90 312 444 55 12
W: zaferkoleji.com.tr

UGANDA

ACORNS INTERNATIONAL SCHOOL (AIS)

Plot 328, Kisota Road, (Along) Northern Bypass, Kisaasi Roundabout, Kampala
DP Coordinator Ken Kanyesigye
MYP Coordinator Sam Weavers
PYP Coordinator Rachelle Hale
Languages English
T: +256 393 202 665
E: admissions@ais.ac.ug
W: www.ais.ac.ug

See full details on page 46

Aga Khan High School, Kampala

PO Box 6837, Kampala
DP Coordinator Alexander Kakungulu
Languages English
T: +256 414 308 245
W: www.agakhanschools.org

International School of Uganda

Plot 272/3 Lubowa Estate, Lubowa, Kampala
DP Coordinator Leigh Anne Toler
MYP Coordinator Craig Mcvicar
PYP Coordinator Sarah Ssengendo
Languages English
T: +256 757 754808
W: www.isu.ac.ug

Kampala International School Uganda (KISU)

P.O.Box 34249, Bukoto, Kampala
DP Coordinator Carine Jadot
Languages English
T: +256 752 711 882; +256 752 711 909
W: www.kisu.com

UK

ACS Cobham International School

Heywood, Portsmouth Road, Cobham, Surrey KT11 1BL
DP Coordinator Henrietta Knight
Languages English
T: +44 (0) 1932 867251
W: www.acs-schools.com

ACS Egham International School

Woodlee, London Road, Egham, Surrey TW20 0HS
CP Coordinator Stephanie Leahey
DP Coordinator Anne-Marie Robb
MYP Coordinator Marie MacPhee
PYP Coordinator Caroline MacLean
Languages English
T: +44 (0) 1784 430 800
W: www.acs-schools.com

ACS Hillingdon International School

Hillingdon Court, 108 Vine Lane, Hillingdon, Uxbridge, Middlesex UB10 0BE
CP Coordinator Sadie Lovell
DP Coordinator Dougal Fergusson
Languages English
T: +44 (0) 1895 259 771
W: www.acs-schools.com

ANGLO EUROPEAN SCHOOL

Willow Green, Ingatestone, Essex CM4 0DJ
CP Coordinator Mr Ben Knights
DP Coordinator Mrs Susannah Porsz
Languages English
T: 01277 354018
E: admissions@aesessex.co.uk
W: www.aesessex.co.uk

See full details on page 58

Ardingly College

College Road, Ardingly, Haywards Heath, West Sussex RH17 6SQ
DP Coordinator Marco Couch
Languages English
T: +44 (0)1444 893320
W: www.ardingly.com

ASHCROFT TECHNOLOGY ACADEMY

100 West Hill, London SW15 2UT
DP Coordinator Joseph Anson
Languages English
T: +44 (0)208 877 0357
E: joseph.anson@ashcroftacademy.org.uk
W: www.atacademy.org.uk

See full details on page 60

Aylesford School – Sports College

Teapot Lane, Aylesford, Kent ME20 7JU
CP Coordinator Ria Graham
Languages English
T: +44 (0)1622 717341
W: www.aylesford.kent.sch.uk

Bedford Girls' School

Cardington Road, Bedford, Bedfordshire MK42 0BX
DP Coordinator John Gardner
Languages English
T: 01234 361900
W: www.bedfordgirlsschool.co.uk

Bedford School

De Parys Avenue, Bedford, Bedfordshire MK40 2TU
DP Coordinator Mr Adrian Finch MA
Languages English
T: +44 (0)1234 362216
W: www.bedfordschool.org.uk

Bexley Grammar School

Danson Lane, Welling, Kent DA16 2BL
DP Coordinator Seth Auckland
Languages English
T: +44 (0)2083 048538
W: www.bexleygs.co.uk

BOX HILL SCHOOL

London Road, Mickleham, Dorking, Surrey RH5 6EA
DP Coordinator Julian Baker
Languages English
T: 01372 373382
E: registrar@BoxHillSchool.com
W: www.boxhillschool.com

See full details on page 63

BRADFIELD COLLEGE

Bradfield, Berkshire RG7 6AU
DP Coordinator Colin Irvine
Languages English
T: 0118 964 4516
E: admissions@bradfieldcollege.org.uk
W: www.bradfieldcollege.org.uk

See full details on page 64

Brentwood School

Middleton Hall Lane, Brentwood, Essex CM15 8EE
DP Coordinator Mrs Hollie Carter
Languages English
T: 01277 243243
W: www.brentwoodschool.co.uk

Bridgwater & Taunton College

Bath Road, Bridgwater, Somerset TA6 4PZ
DP Coordinator Rebecca Miller
Languages English
T: 01278 455464
W: www.bridgwater.ac.uk

Bristol Grammar School

University Road, Bristol BS8 1SR
DP Coordinator Ben Schober
Languages English
T: 0117 973 6006
W: www.bristolgrammarschool.co.uk

Broadgreen International School

Queens Drive, Liverpool, Merseyside L13 5UQ
CP Coordinator Claire McKendrick
DP Coordinator Claire McKendrick
Languages English
T: 0151 228 6800
W: www.broadgreeninternationalschool.com/

BROMSGROVE SCHOOL

Worcester Road, Bromsgrove, Worcestershire B61 7DU
DP Coordinator Michael Thompson
Languages English
T: +44 (0)1527 579679
E: admissions@bromsgrove-school.co.uk
W: www.bromsgrove-school.co.uk

See full details on page 66

BRYANSTON SCHOOL

Blandford Forum, Dorset DT11 0PX
CP Coordinator Rose Ings
DP Coordinator Jo Strange
Languages English
T: 01258 484633
E: admissions@bryanston.co.uk
W: www.bryanston.co.uk

See full details on page 67

Buckswood School

Broomham Hall, Rye Road, Guestling, Hastings, East Sussex TN35 4LT
DP Coordinator Carol Richards
Languages English
T: 01424 813 813
W: www.buckswood.co.uk

CATS CANTERBURY
68 New Dover Road, Canterbury, Kent
CT1 3LQ
DP Coordinator Nicola Robinson
Languages English
T: +44 (0)1227866540
E: registrar@catscanterbury.com
W: catsglobalschools.com/our-schools/
cats-canterbury
See full details on page 69

CHARTERHOUSE
Godalming, Surrey GU7 2DX
DP Coordinator Mr Peter Price
Languages English
T: +44 (0)1483 291501
E: admissions@charterhouse.org.uk
W: www.charterhouse.org.uk
See full details on page 70

Cheltenham Ladies' College
Bayshill Road, Cheltenham,
Gloucestershire GL50 3EP
DP Coordinator Becky Revell
Languages English
T: +44 (0)1242 520691
W: www.cheltladiescollege.org

Cherry Orchard Primary Academy
Cherry Orchard, Castle Hill, Ebbsfleet
Valley, Kent DA10 1AD
PYP Coordinator Sandra Foxwell
Languages English, Spanish
T: 01322 242 011
W: cherryorchardprimaryacademy.org.uk

Chester International School
Queen's Park Campus, Queen's Park
Road, Handbridge, Chester, Cheshire
CH4 7AE
CP Coordinator Abbey Peers
DP Coordinator Abbey Peers
MYP Coordinator Montanna Hull
Languages English
T: 01244 683935
W: www.christletoninternationalstudio.
co.uk

Christ's Hospital
Horsham, West Sussex RH13 0LJ
DP Coordinator Martin Stephens
Languages English
T: 01403 211293
W: www.christs-hospital.org.uk

Coopers School
Hawkewood Lane, Chislehurst, Kent
BR7 5PS
CP Coordinator Fran Lane
Languages English
T: +44 (0)20 8467 3263
W: coopersschool.com

Dallam School
Milnthorpe, Cumbria LA7 7DD
CP Coordinator Steven Henneberry
DP Coordinator Steven Henneberry
Languages English
T: +44 (0)15395 65165
W: www.dallamschool.co.uk

Dane Court Grammar School
Broadstairs Road, Broadstairs, Kent
CT10 2RT
CP Coordinator Melissa Linton
DP Coordinator Chris Pleasant
Languages English
T: +44 1843 864941
W: www.danecourt.kent.sch.uk

Dartford Grammar School
West Hill, Dartford, Kent DA1 2HW
DP Coordinator Michaela Kingham
MYP Coordinator Michaela Kingham
Languages English
T: 01322 223039
W: www.dartfordgrammarschool.org.uk

Dartford Primary Academy
York Road, Dartford, Kent DA1 1SQ
PYP Coordinator Declan Filsell
Languages English
T: 01322 224453
W: dartfordprimary.org.uk

DEUTSCHE SCHULE LONDON
Douglas House, Petersham Road,
Richmond, Surrey TW10 7AH
DP Coordinator Edna Howard
Languages English, German
T: +44 (0)20 8940 2510
E: info@dslondon.org.uk
W: www.dslondon.org.uk
See full details on page 78

Dover Christ Church Academy
Melbourne Avenue, Whitfield, Kent
CT16 2EG
CP Coordinator Victoria Wallis
Languages English
T: +44 (0)1304 820126
W: www.dccacademy.org.uk

DWIGHT SCHOOL LONDON
6 Friern Barnet Lane, London N11 3LX
DP Coordinator William Bowry
MYP Coordinator Karine Villatte
PYP Coordinator Srinanda Gupta
Languages English
T: 020 8920 0600
E: admissions@dwightlondon.org
W: www.dwightlondon.org
See full details on page 79

École Jeannine Manuel – London
43-45 Bedford Square, London WC1B
3DN
DP Coordinator Jeanne Gonnet
Languages English, French
T: 020 3829 5970
W: www.ecolejeanninemanuel.org.uk

EF Academy Oxford
Pullens Lane, Headington,
Oxfordshire OX3 0DT
DP Coordinator Dona Jones
Languages English
T: +41 (0) 43 430 41 00
W: www.efacademy.org

EIFA International School
36 Portland Place, London W1B 1LS
DP Coordinator Mark O'Brien
Languages English, French
T: +44 (0)20 7637 5351
W: www.eifaschool.com

Ellesmere College
Ellesmere, Shropshire SY12 9AB
DP Coordinator Dr Ian Tompkins
Languages English
T: 01691 622321
W: www.ellesmere.com

Eltham Hill School
Eltham Hill School, London SE9 5EE
CP Coordinator Rebecca Crean
Languages English
T: +44 (0)208 859 2843
W: elthamhill.com

Europa School UK
Thame Lane, Culham, Oxfordshire
OX14 3DZ
DP Coordinator Tanya Simpson
Languages English, French
T: +44 (0)1235 524060
W: europaschooluk.org

Exeter College
Hele Road, Exeter, Devon EX4 4JS
DP Coordinator Jan England
Languages English
T: 01392 400500
W: www.exe-coll.ac.uk

FELSTED SCHOOL
Felsted, Great Dunmow, Essex CM6 3LL
DP Coordinator Karen Woodhouse
Languages English
T: +44 (0)1371 822600
E: intadmissions@felsted.org
W: www.felsted.org
See full details on page 91

Fettes College
Carrington Road, Edinburgh EH4 1QX
DP Coordinator Mark Henry
Languages English
T: +44 (0)131 332 2281
W: www.fettes.com

FULHAM SCHOOL
1-3 Chesilton Road, London SW6 5AA
DP Coordinator Chris Cockerill
Languages English
T: 020 8154 6751
E: admissions@fulham.school
W: fulham.school
See full details on page 92

GODOLPHIN AND LATYMER SCHOOL
Iffley Road, Hammersmith, London
W6 0PG
DP Coordinator Audrey Dubois
Languages English
T: +44 (0)20 8741 1936
E: office@godolphinandlatymer.com
W: www.godolphinandlatymer.com
See full details on page 95

Gresham's Senior School
Cromer Road, Holt, Norfolk NR25 6EA
DP Coordinator Louise Futter
Languages English
T: 01263 714 614
W: www.greshams.com

Guernsey Grammar School and Sixth Form Centre
Les Varendes, St Andrews, Guernsey
GY8 6TD
CP Coordinator Paul Montague
DP Coordinator Paul Montague
Languages English
T: +44 (0)1481 256571
W: web.grammar.sch.gg

HAILEYBURY
Haileybury, Hertford, Hertfordshire
SG13 7NU
DP Coordinator Kate Brazier
Languages English
T: +44 (0)1992 706353
E: uk.admissions@haileybury.com
W: www.haileybury.com
See full details on page 99

Halcyon London International School
33 Seymour Place, London W1H 5AU
DP Coordinator Lori Fritz
MYP Coordinator Kerry Jenkins
Languages English
T: +44 (0)20 7258 1169
W: halcyonschool.com

Hartsdown Academy

George V Ave, Margate, Kent CT9 5RE
CP Coordinator Harvey Ovenden
Languages English
T: +44 (0)1843 227957
W: www.hartsdown.org

Hautlieu School

Wellington Road, St Saviour, Jersey
JE2 7TH
CP Coordinator Mandy Campbell
DP Coordinator Mandy Campbell
Languages English
T: +44 1534 736 242
W: www.hautlieu.net

Headington School Oxford

London Road, Oxford, Oxfordshire
OX3 7TD
DP Coordinator Mr James
Stephenson
Languages English
T: +44 (0)1865 759100
W: www.headington.org

HOCKERILL ANGLO-EUROPEAN COLLEGE

Dunmow Road, Bishops Stortford,
Hertfordshire CM23 5HX
DP Coordinator Peter Bromfield
MYP Coordinator Michelle Butler
Languages English
T: 01279 658451
E: admissions@hockerill.com
W: www.hockerill.com

See full details on page 104

Homewood School & Sixth Form Centre

Ashford Road, Tenterden, Kent TN30
6LT
CP Coordinator Claire Tyson
Languages English
T: 01580 764222
W: www.homewood-school.co.uk

Hugh Christie Technology College

White Cottage Road, Tonbridge, Kent
TN10 4PU
CP Coordinator Matt Goss
Languages English
T: 01732 353544
W: www.hughchristie.kent.sch.uk

ICS LONDON

7B Wyndham Place, London W1H 1PN
DP Coordinator Lucy Masters
MYP Coordinator Svetlana Klyuyeva
PYP Coordinator James Kendall
Languages English
T: +44 (0)20 729 88800
E: admissions@ics.uk.net
W: www.icschool.co.uk

See full details on page 109

IMPINGTON INTERNATIONAL COLLEGE

New Road, Impington, Cambridge,
Cambridgeshire CB24 9LX
CP Coordinator Leanne Gibbons
DP Coordinator Bronwyn Wilson
Languages English
T: 01223 200402
E: international@ivc.tmet.org.uk
W: www.impingtoninternational.org.uk

See full details on page 111

International School of Aberdeen

Pitfodels House, North Deeside Road,
Pitfodels, Cults, Aberdeen AB15 9PN
DP Coordinator Jennifer Grogan
Languages English
T: 01224 730300
W: www.isa.aberdeen.sch.uk

INTERNATIONAL SCHOOL OF LONDON (ISL)

139 Gunnersbury Avenue, London
W3 8LG
DP Coordinator Paul Morris
MYP Coordinator Ms Hyun Jung
Owen
PYP Coordinator Ms Iliana Gutierrez
Languages English & Mother-tongue
T: +44 (0)20 8992 5823
E: mail@isllondon.org
W: www.isllondon.org

See full details on page 126

KENT COLLEGE, CANTERBURY

Whitstable Road, Canterbury, Kent
CT2 9DT
DP Coordinator Mr Graham Letley
Languages English
T: +44 (0)1227 763 231
E: admissions@kentcollege.co.uk
W: www.kentcollege.com

See full details on page 142

King Edward's School

Edgbaston Park Road, Birmingham,
West Midlands B15 2UA
DP Coordinator Andrew Petrie
Languages English
T: 0121 472 1672
W: www.kes.org.uk

KING EDWARD'S WITLEY

Petworth Road, Godalming, Surrey
GU8 5SG
DP Coordinator Andy Baynes
Languages English
T: 01428 686735
E: admissions@kesw.org
W: www.kesw.org

See full details on page 146

King Ethelbert School

Can ter bury Road, Birch ing ton, Kent
CT7 9BL
CP Coordinator Rebecca Darch
Languages English
T: 01843 831999
W: www.kingethelbert.com

King Fahad Academy

Bromyard Avenue, Acton, London
W3 7HD
DP Coordinator Mohammed Baba
MYP Coordinator James Nevin
Languages English
T: 020 8743 0131
W: www.thekfa.org.uk

KING WILLIAM'S COLLEGE

Castletown, Isle of Man IM9 1TP
DP Coordinator Alasdair Ulyett
Languages English
T: +44 (0)1624 820110
E: admissions@kwc.im
W: www.kwc.im

See full details on page 147

KING'S COLLEGE SCHOOL

Southside, Wimbledon Common,
London SW19 4TT
DP Coordinator Paul Lloyd
Languages English
T: 020 8255 5300
E: admissions@kcs.org.uk
W: www.kcs.org.uk

See full details on page 148

Knole Academy

Bradbourne Vale Road, Sevenoaks,
Kent TN13 3LE
CP Coordinator Mrs Jane Elliott
Languages English
T: 01732 454608
W: www.knoleacademy.org

LaSWAP Sixth Form Consortium

Highgate Road, London NW5 1RL
CP Coordinator Ella Schlesinger
Languages English
T: +44 (0)20 7692 4157
W: laswap.camden.sch.uk

Leigh Academy Blackheath

Old Dover Road, Blackheath, London
SE3 8SY
MYP Coordinator Rocio Garcia
Languages English
T: +44 (0)20 8104 0888
W: leighacademyblackheath.org.uk

LEIGHTON PARK SCHOOL

Shinfield Road, Reading, Berkshire
RG2 7ED
DP Coordinator Mrs Helen Taylor
Languages English
T: 0118 987 9600
E: admissions@leightonpark.com
W: www.leightonpark.com

See full details on page 152

Lomond School

10 Stafford Street, Helensburgh, Argyll
& Bute G84 9JX
CP Coordinator Claire Chisholm
DP Coordinator Claire Chisholm
Languages English
T: +44 (0)1436 672476
W: www.lomondschool.com

Longfield Academy

Main Road, Longfield, Kent DA3 7PH
MYP Coordinator David O'Leary
Languages English
T: +44 (0)1474 700 700
W: longfieldacademy.org.uk

LYCÉE INTERNATIONAL DE LONDRES WINSTON CHURCHILL

54 Forty Lane, London HA9 9LY
DP Coordinator Maaike Kaandorp
Languages English, French
T: +44 (0)203 824 4900
E: admissions@lyceeinternational.london
W: www.lyceeinternational.london

See full details on page 157

MALVERN COLLEGE

College Road, Malvern, Worcestershire
WR14 3DF
DP Coordinator Jennifer Akehurst
Languages English
T: +44 (0)1684 581515
E: admissions@malverncollege.org.uk
W: www.malverncollege.org.uk

See full details on page 158

MARYMOUNT LONDON

George Road, Kingston upon Thames,
Surrey KT2 7PE
DP Coordinator Nicholas Marcou
MYP Coordinator Mark Gardner
Languages English
T: +44 (0)20 8949 0571
E: admissions@marymountlondon.com
W: www.marymountlondon.com

See full details on page 163

Mascalls Academy

Maidstone Road, Paddock Wood,
Tonbridge, Kent TN12 6LT
MYP Coordinator Sharon Mahon
Languages English
T: 01892 835366
W: mascallsacademy.org.uk

NORTH LONDON COLLEGIATE SCHOOL

Canons, Canons Drive, Edgware, Middlesex HA8 7RJ
DP Coordinator Mr Henry Linscott
Languages English
T: +44 (0)20 8952 0912
E: office@nlcs.org.uk
W: www.nlcs.org.uk
See full details on page 170

Northfleet School for Girls

Hall Road, Northfleet, Kent DA11 8AQ
CP Coordinator Alison Johnson
Languages English
T: +44 (0)1474 831 020
W: www.nsfg.org.uk

Northfleet Technology College

Colyer Road, Northfleet, Kent DA11 8BG
CP Coordinator Emma Campbell
Languages English
T: 01474 533802
W: ntc.kent.sch.uk

OAKHAM SCHOOL

Chapel Close, Oakham, Rutland LE15 6DT
DP Coordinator Carolyn Fear
MYP Coordinator Dmitriy Ashton
Languages English
T: 01572 758758
E: admissions@oakham.rutland.sch.uk
W: www.oakham.rutland.sch.uk
See full details on page 171

Oaks Primary Academy

Oak Tree Avenue, Maidstone, Kent ME15 9AX
PYP Coordinator Aoife Mehigan
Languages English
T: 01622 755960
W: oaksprimaryacademy.org.uk

Parkside Sixth

Parkside, Cambridge, Cambridgeshire CB1 1EH
CP Coordinator Rachel Biltcliffe
DP Coordinator Hannah Holt
Languages English
T: +44 (0)1223 712600
W: www.parksidesixth.org.uk

Plymouth College of Art

Tavistock Place, Plymouth, Devon PL4 8AT
CP Coordinator Michelle Lester
Languages English
T: +44 (0)1752 203434
W: www.plymouthart.ac.uk

ROSSALL SCHOOL

Broadway, Fleetwood, Lancashire FY7 8JW
DP Coordinator Bethan Jones
Languages English
T: +44 (0)1253 774201
E: admissions@rossall.org.uk
W: www.rossall.org.uk
See full details on page 183

ROYAL HIGH SCHOOL BATH, GDST

Lansdown Road, Bath, Bath & North-East Somerset BA1 5SZ
DP Coordinator Ms Jude Taylor
Languages English
T: +44 (0)1225 313877
E: admissions@rhsb.gdst.net
W: www.royalhighbath.gdst.net
See full details on page 185

Rugby School

Rugby, Warwickshire CV22 5EH
DP Coordinator Natalie Lockhart-Mann
Languages English
T: +44 (0)1788 556274
W: www.rugbyschool.net

RYDE SCHOOL WITH UPPER CHINE

Queen's Road, Ryde, Isle of Wight PO33 3BE
CP Coordinator David Shapland
DP Coordinator David Shapland
Languages English
T: 01983 562229
E: admissions@rydeschool.net
W: www.rydeschool.org.uk
See full details on page 186

SCARBOROUGH COLLEGE

Filey Road, Scarborough, North Yorkshire YO11 3BA
DP Coordinator Ms Katie Cooke
Languages English
T: +44 (0)1723 360620
E: admin@scarboroughcollege.co.uk
W: www.scarboroughcollege.co.uk
See full details on page 189

SEVENOAKS SCHOOL

High Street, Sevenoaks, Kent TN13 1HU
DP Coordinator Nigel Haworth
Languages English
T: +44 (0)1732 455133
E: regist@sevenoaksschool.org
W: www.sevenoaksschool.org
See full details on page 202

SIDCOT SCHOOL

Oakridge Lane, Winscombe, Somerset BS25 1PD
DP Coordinator Stefania Cauli
Languages English
T: 01934 843102
E: admissions@sidcot.org.uk
W: www.sidcot.org.uk
See full details on page 203

Southbank International School – Hampstead

16 Netherhall Gardens, London NW3 5TH
PYP Coordinator Flora Winter
Languages English
T: 020 7243 3803
W: www.southbank.org

Southbank International School – Kensington

36-38 Kensington Park Road, London W11 3BU
PYP Coordinator Charlotte Gregson
Languages English
T: +44 (0)20 7243 3803
W: www.southbank.org

Southbank International School – Westminster

63-65 Portland Place, London W1B 1QR
DP Coordinator Fabienne Fontaine
MYP Coordinator Angela Johnson
Languages English
T: 020 7243 3803
W: www.southbank.org

St Benedict's Catholic High School

Kinwarton Road, Alcester, Warwickshire B49 6PX
DP Coordinator Donna Munford
Languages English
T: +44 (0)1789 762888
W: www.st-benedicts.org

ST CLARE'S, OXFORD

139 Banbury Road, Oxford, Oxfordshire OX2 7AL
DP Coordinator Darrel Ross
Languages English
T: +44 (0)1865 552031
E: admissions@stclares.ac.uk
W: www.stclares.ac.uk
See full details on page 206

ST EDWARD'S, OXFORD

Woodstock Road, Oxford, Oxfordshire OX2 7NN
DP Coordinator Anna Fielding
Languages English
T: +44 (0)1865 319200
E: registrar@stedwardsoxford.org
W: www.stedwardsoxford.org
See full details on page 208

ST LEONARDS SCHOOL

The Pends, St Andrews, Fife KY16 9QJ
CP Coordinator Ben Seymour
DP Coordinator Ben Seymour
MYP Coordinator Kathryn McGregor
PYP Coordinator Catherine Brannen
Languages English
T: 01334 472126
E: registrar@stleonards-fife.org
W: stleonards-fife.org
See full details on page 210

St Simon Stock Catholic School

Oakwood Park, Maidstone, Kent ME16 0JP
CP Coordinator Andrew Williams
Languages English
T: 01622 754551
W: www.sssscs.co.uk

Stationers' Crown Woods Academy

145 Bexley Road, Eltham, London SE9 2PT
MYP Coordinator Joe Spark
Languages English
T: +44 (0)208 850 7678
W: scwa.org.uk

Stephen Perse Sixth Form

Bateman Street, Cambridge, Cambridgeshire CB2 1NA
DP Coordinator Jacqueline Paris
Languages English
T: 01223 454762
W: stephenperse.com/sixthform

STONYHURST COLLEGE

Stonyhurst, Clitheroe, Lancashire BB7 9PZ
CP Coordinator Emma Walker
DP Coordinator Mrs Deborah Kirkby BSc
Languages English
T: 01254 827073
E: admissions@stonyhurst.ac.uk
W: www.stonyhurst.ac.uk
See full details on page 220

Strood Academy

Carnation Road, Strood, Kent ME2 2SX
CP Coordinator Samira Nasim
MYP Coordinator Nicola Collison
Languages English
T: +44 (0)1634 717121
W: stroodacademy.org.uk

TASIS The American School in England

Coldharbour Lane, Thorpe, Surrey TW20 8TE
DP Coordinator Jessica Lee
Languages English
T: +44 (0)1932 582316
W: www.tasisengland.org

TAUNTON SCHOOL

Staplegrove Road, Taunton, Somerset TA2 6AD
DP Coordinator Adrian Roberts
Languages English
T: +44 (0)1823 703703
E: enquiries@tauntonschool.co.uk
W: www.tauntonschool.co.uk
See full details on page 223

Thamesview School

Thong Lane, Gravesend, Kent DA12 4LF
CP Coordinator Elizabeth Terry
Languages English
T: +44 (0)1474 566 552
W: www.thamesviewsch.co.uk

THE ABBEY SCHOOL

Kendrick Road, Reading, Berkshire RG1 5DZ
DP Coordinator Nicola McDonald
Languages English
T: 0118 987 2256
E: admissions@theabbey.co.uk
W: www.theabbey.co.uk
See full details on page 224

The Abbey School, Faversham

London Road, Faversham, Kent ME13 8RZ
CP Coordinator Nicci Jones
Languages English
T: +44 (0)1795 532633
W: www.abbeyschoolfaversham.co.uk

The Beaconsfield School

Wattleton Road, Beaconsfield, Buckinghamshire HP9 1SJ
CP Coordinator Fiona Palmer Garrett
Languages English
T: 01494 673450
W: www.beaconsfield.bucks.sch.uk

The Chalfonts Independent Grammar School

19 London Road, High Wycombe, Buckinghamshire HP11 1BJ
DP Coordinator Alexander Herriott
MYP Coordinator Bart Van Malssen
Languages English
T: +44 (0)1494 875502
W: www.thechalfontsgrammar.co.uk

The Ebbsfleet Academy

Southfleet Road, Ebbsfleet Garden City, Kent DA10 0BZ
CP Coordinator Jonathan Field
Languages English
T: +44 (0)1322 623100
W: theebbsfleetacademy.kent.sch.uk

The Halley Academy

Corelli Road, Blackheath, London SE3 8EP
CP Coordinator Will Burrows
MYP Coordinator Ernesto Godina
Languages English
T: +44 (0)208 856 2828
W: thehalleyacademy.org.uk

The Hundred of Hoo Academy

Main Road, Hoo St Werburgh, Rochester, Kent ME3 9HH
PYP Coordinator Jolene Baber
Languages English
T: 01634 251443
W: www.hundredofhooacademy.org.uk

The Leigh Academy

Green Street, Green Road, Dartford, Kent DA1 1QE
CP Coordinator Lee Forcella-Burton
MYP Coordinator Sarah McCabe Knowles
Languages English
T: +44 (0)1322 620400
W: leighacademy.org.uk

The Leigh UTC

The Bridge Development, Brunel Way, Dartford, Kent DA1 5TF
CP Coordinator Sophie Dickinson
MYP Coordinator Sophie Dickinson
Languages English
T: +44 (0)1322 626 600
W: theleighutc.org.uk

The Lenham School

Ham Lane, Lenham, Kent ME17 2LL
CP Coordinator Anna Burden
Languages English
T: 01622 858267
W: www.thelenham.viat.org.uk

The Malling School

Beech Road, East Malling, West Malling, Kent ME19 6DH
CP Coordinator Kelly Chimanga
DP Coordinator Kelly Chimanga
Languages English
T: +44 (0)1732 840995
W: www.themallingschool.kent.sch.uk

The Portsmouth Grammar School

High Street, Portsmouth, Hampshire PO1 2LN
DP Coordinator Simon Taylor
Languages English
T: +44 (0)23 9236 0036
W: www.pgs.org.uk

The Red Maids' Senior School

Westbury Road, Westbury-on-Trym, Bristol BS9 3AW
DP Coordinator Peter Brealey
Languages English
T: +44 (0)117 962 2641
W: www.redmaids.co.uk

The Rochester Grammar School

Maidstone Road, Rochester, Kent ME1 3BY
DP Coordinator Joanna Wadey
Languages English
T: +44 (0)1634 843049
W: www.rochestergrammar.medway.sch.uk

The Royal Harbour Academy

Newlands Lane, Ramsgate, Kent CT12 6RH
CP Coordinator Carla Spenner
Languages English
T: 01843 572500
W: www.rha.kent.sch.uk

The Sixth Form College, Colchester

North Hill, Colchester, Essex CO1 1SN
DP Coordinator Karen Burns
Languages English
T: 01206 500778
W: www.colchsfc.ac.uk

The Skinners' Kent Academy

Blackhurst Lane, Tunbridge Wells, Kent TN2 4PY
CP Coordinator David Holl
MYP Coordinator Katherine McCreadie
Languages English
T: +44 (0)1892 534377
W: www.twhs.kent.sch.uk

The Whitstable School

Bellevue Road, Whitstable, Kent CT5 1PX
CP Coordinator Luci Brown
Languages English
T: 01227 931300
W: www.thewhitstableschool.org.uk

Tonbridge Grammar School

Deakin Leas, Tonbridge, Kent TN9 2JR
DP Coordinator Darryl Barker
MYP Coordinator Caroline Ghali
Languages English
T: +44 (0)1732 365125
W: www.tgs.kent.sch.uk

Torquay Boys' Grammar School

Shiphay Manor Drive, Torquay, Devon TQ2 7EL
DP Coordinator James Hunt
Languages English
T: +44 1803 615 501
W: www.tbgs.co.uk

Towers School and Sixth Form Centre

Faversham Road, Ashford, Kent TN24 9ALE
CP Coordinator Victoria Reed
Languages English
T: +44 (0)1233 634171
W: www.towers.kent.sch.uk

Tree Tops Primary Academy

Brishing Lane, Maidstone, Kent ME15 9EZ
PYP Coordinator Stefan Bishop
Languages English
T: 01622 754888
W: treetopsprimaryacademy.org.uk

Truro and Penwith College

College Road, Truro, Cornwall TR1 3XX
DP Coordinator Angie Liversedge
Languages English
T: +44 (0) 1872 267000
W: www.truro-penwith.ac.uk

UWC ATLANTIC

St Donat's Castle, St Donat's, Llantwit Major, Vale of Glamorgan CF61 1WF
DP Coordinator Gabor Vincze
Languages English
T: +44 (0)1446 799000
E: admissions@atlanticcollege.org
W: www.atlanticcollege.org
See full details on page 236

Varndean College

Surrenden Road, Brighton, East Sussex BN1 6WQ
DP Coordinator Lee Finlay-Gray
Languages English
T: 01273 508011
W: www.varndean.ac.uk

WARMINSTER SCHOOL

Church Street, Warminster, Wiltshire BA12 8PJ
CP Coordinator Simon Hall BSc Psychology PGCE
DP Coordinator Simon Hall BSc Psychology PGCE
Languages English
T: +44 (0)1985 210100
E: admissions@warminsterschool.org.uk
W: www.warminsterschool.org.uk
See full details on page 241

WELLINGTON COLLEGE

Duke's Ride, Crowthorne, Berkshire
RG45 7PU
DP Coordinator Dr Robert Cromarty
Languages English
T: +44 (0)1344 444000
E: admissions@wellingtoncollege.org.uk
W: www.wellingtoncollege.org.uk
See full details on page 243

Westbourne School

Hickman Road, Penarth, Glamorgan
CF64 2AJ
DP Coordinator Lisa Phillips
Languages English
T: 029 2070 5705
W: www.westbourneschool.com

Westminster Academy

The Naim Dangoor Centre, 255
Harrow Road, London W2 5EZ
CP Coordinator Alex James
DP Coordinator Brian Brackrog
Languages English
T: +44 (0)20 7121 0600
W: www.westminsteracademy.biz

Whitgift School

Haling Park, South Croydon, Surrey
CR2 6YT
DP Coordinator Emma Mitchell
Languages English
T: +44 20 8633 9935
W: www.whitgift.co.uk

Wilmington Academy

Common Lane, Wilmington, Dartford,
Kent DA2 7DR
CP Coordinator Kathleen Sanders
MYP Coordinator Patrick Lonergan
Languages English
T: +44 (0)1322 272111
W: wilmingtonacademy.org.uk

WINDERMERE SCHOOL

Patterdale Road, Windermere,
Cumbria LA23 1NW
CP Coordinator Theresa Murray
DP Coordinator Elizabeth Loughlin
Languages English
T: 015394 46164
E: admissions@windermereschool.co.uk
W: www.windermereschool.co.uk
See full details on page 245

Worth School

Paddockhurst Road, Turners Hill,
Crawley, West Sussex RH10 4SD
DP Coordinator Bruna Gushurst-
Moore
Languages English
T: +44 (0)1342 710200
W: www.worthschool.co.uk

Wotton House International School

Wotton House, Horton Road,
Gloucester, Gloucestershire GL1 3PR
MYP Coordinator Daniel Sturdy
Languages English
T: +44 (0)1452 764248
W: www.wottonhouseschool.co.uk

Wrotham School

Borough Green Rd, Sevenoaks, Kent
TN15 7RD
CP Coordinator Samantha Williams
Languages English
T: +44 (0)1732 884207
W: www.wrothamschool.com

UKRAINE

Gymnasium A+

Berezneva Str. 14, 02160 Kyiv
DP Coordinator Olga Lytvynova
Languages English, Ukrainian
T: +38 44 363 14 03
W: gymnasiumplus.com.ua

Pechersk School International Kyiv

7a Victora Zabily, Kyiv 03039
DP Coordinator David Freeman
MYP Coordinator La Mor
PYP Coordinator Erika Olson
Languages English
T: +380 44 377 5292
W: www.psi.kiev.ua

QSI KYIV INTERNATIONAL SCHOOL

3A Svyatoshinsky Provuluk, Kyiv 03115
DP Coordinator Ms. Randi Assenova
Languages English
T: +38 (044) 452 27 92
E: kyiv@qsi.org
W: www.qsi.org/kyiv/
See full details on page 180

The British International School Ukraine (Pechersk Campus)

1 Dragomirova Street, Kiev 01103
DP Coordinator Paul Hodgson
Languages English
T: +38 (044) 596 18 28
W: britishschool.ua

UNITED ARAB EMIRATES

Abu Dhabi International (Pvt) School

Karamah Street, PO Box 25898, Abu
Dhabi
DP Coordinator Issam Kobrsi
Languages English
T: +971 2 443 4433
W: aisschools.com

Ajman Academy

Sheikh Ammar Road, Mowaihat 2,
Ajman
MYP Coordinator Deborah Vincent
PYP Coordinator Hala Sweilem
Languages English
T: +971 6 731 4444
W: www.ajmanacademy.com

Al Adab Iranian Private School for Boys

Behind Al Bustan Center, Al Nahda 1,
Qusais, Dubai
DP Coordinator Naghmeh Dadpanah
Languages English
T: +971 42633405
W: www.adabschool.org

Al Bateen Academy

PO Box 128484, Abu Dhabi
DP Coordinator Mahammed
Abdulahi
PYP Coordinator Ninetta Challita
Languages English
T: +971 2 813 2000
W: www.albateenacademy.sch.ae

Al Najah Private School

PO Box 284, Abu Dhabi
DP Coordinator Noel Debs
Languages English
T: +971 2 553 0935
W: alnajahschool.com

Ambassador International Academy

Al Khail Gate, Al Quoz, Plot No.
3653942, Dubai
PYP Coordinator Talia Lazarus
Languages English
T: +971 4 580 6999
W: aiadubai.com

American Community School, Abu Dhabi

PO Box 42114, Abu Dhabi
DP Coordinator Jonathan Diaz
Languages English
T: +971 2 681 5115
W: www.acs.sch.ae/acs

American International School in Abu Dhabi

PO Box 5992, Abu Dhabi
DP Coordinator Jodi Styre Yaseen
PYP Coordinator Meghan Dickie
Languages English
T: +971 2 4444 333
W: www.aisa.sch.ae

Australian International School

PO Box 43364, Sharjah
DP Coordinator Paul Lange
Languages English
T: +971 6 558 9967
W: www.ais.ae

Australian School of Abu Dhabi

Khalifa City B, PO Box 36044, Abu
Dhabi
DP Coordinator Mahmoud Dabet
MYP Coordinator Amal Elgamal
PYP Coordinator Ayan Abdullahi
Languages English
T: +971 2 5866980
W: australianschool.ae

Collegiate International School

50 Al Maydar Street, Umm Suqeim 2,
P.O. Box: 121306, Dubai
CP Coordinator Nishi Saran
DP Coordinator Purnima Sharma
Languages English
T: +971 4 427 1400
W: www.collegiate.sch.ae

Dar Al Marefa Private School

P.O.Box: 112602, Dubai 112602
DP Coordinator Sheugnet Carter
MYP Coordinator Adam Fitzgerald
PYP Coordinator Habiba Jaballah
Languages English
T: +971 42885782
W: www.daralmarefa.ae

Deira International School

PO Box 79043, Dubai
CP Coordinator Chantelle
Thomasson
DP Coordinator Brian Cleary
Languages English
T: +971 4 2325552
W: www.disdubai.ae

Dubai American Academy

PO Box 32762, Al Barsha, Dubai
DP Coordinator Katie Sheffield
Languages English
T: +971 4 347 9222
W: www.gemsaa-dubai.com

United Arab Emirates

Dubai International Academy, Al Barsha
P.O. Box: 118111, Al Barsha, Dubai
DP Coordinator Abigail Ferrari
MYP Coordinator Caterina Marras
PYP Coordinator Andrea Waller
Languages English
T: +971 4 524 4800
W: www.diabarsha.com

Dubai International Academy, Emirates Hills
P.O. Box: 118111, First Al Khail Street, Emirates Hills, Dubai
CP Coordinator Robert Bunyan
DP Coordinator Pam Parasram
MYP Coordinator Sean Kelly
PYP Coordinator Ruchika Sachdev
Languages English, Arabic
T: +971 4 368 4111
W: www.diadubai.com

Dunecrest American School
P.O. Box 624265, Wadi Al Safa 3 (next to Al Barari), Dubai
DP Coordinator Eric Barrett
Languages English
T: +971 4 508 7444
W: www.dunecrest.ae

Dwight School Dubai
Umm Sequim Street, Al Barsha South 2, Dubai
DP Coordinator Peter Atkins
MYP Coordinator Jaya Bhavnani
PYP Coordinator Katie Hendry
Languages English
T: +971 800 394448
W: www.dwightschooldubai.ae

Emirates International School – Jumeirah
PO Box 6446, Dubai
CP Coordinator Wissam Yehya
DP Coordinator Nausheen Arif
MYP Coordinator Sabina Pecoraro
PYP Coordinator Scott Kirkland
Languages English
T: +971 4 3489804
W: www.eischools.ae

Emirates International School – Meadows
PO Box 120118, Dubai
DP Coordinator Joanne Branicki-Tolchard
MYP Coordinator Sarah Robson
PYP Coordinator Natalie Bridges
Languages Arabic, English
T: +971 4 362 9009
W: www.eischools.ae

Emirates National School – Abu Dhabi City Campus
P.O. Box 44759, Abu Dhabi
DP Coordinator Lauren Brown
MYP Coordinator Rebecca Johnson
PYP Coordinator Deborah Anitelea
Languages English, Arabic
T: +971 2 642 5993
W: www.ens.sch.ae

Emirates National School – Al Ain City Campus
PO Box 69392, Al Ain
DP Coordinator Mohammad Al Adwan
MYP Coordinator Benjamin Smith
PYP Coordinator Dinaulu Neilako
Languages English, Arabic
T: +971 3 761 6888
W: www.ens.sch.ae

Emirates National School – Mohammed Bin Zayed Campus
PO Box 44321, Mussafah, Abu Dhabi
DP Coordinator Darine Darwiche
MYP Coordinator Nada Chreim
PYP Coordinator Peadar O Mahoney
Languages Arabic, English
T: +971 2 559 00 00
W: www.ens.sch.ae

Emirates National School – Ras Al Khaimah Campus
Ras Al-Khaimah
DP Coordinator George Heusner
MYP Coordinator Roxanne Power
PYP Coordinator Ugo Aimakhu
Languages English
T: +971 7 203 3333
W: www.ens.sch.ae

Emirates National School – Sharjah Campus
Al Rahmaniya, Sharjah
DP Coordinator Joseph Gleeson
MYP Coordinator Princess Lacewell
PYP Coordinator Jillane Strickland
Languages English
T: +971 6 599 0999
W: www.ens.sch.ae

Fairgreen International School
PO Box 392024, The Sustainable City, Dubai
CP Coordinator Catherine Williams
DP Coordinator Damayanti Rao
MYP Coordinator Anthony Copeland
PYP Coordinator David Gerber
Languages English
T: +971 4 875 4999
W: www.fairgreen.ae

GEMS American Academy – Abu Dhabi
PO Box 145161, Abu Dhabi
DP Coordinator Monica Martin
PYP Coordinator Tiffany Pulci
Languages English
T: +971 2 557 4880
W: www.gemsaa-abudhabi.com

GEMS International School – Al Khail
Al Khail Road, Dubai
CP Coordinator Mariona Coderch Lopez
DP Coordinator Adam Rooney
MYP Coordinator Sandy Trull
PYP Coordinator Mark Krabousanos
Languages English
T: +971 4 339 6200
W: www.gemsinternationalschool-alkhail.com

GEMS MODERN ACADEMY – DUBAI
PO Box 53663, Nad al Sheeba 3,4, Dubai
DP Coordinator Dr. Sunipa Guha Neogi
Languages English
T: +971 4 326 3339
E: info_mhs@gemsedu.com
W: www.gemsmodernacademy-dubai.com
See full details on page 93

GEMS Wellington Academy – Silicon Oasis
Dubai Silicon Oasis, Dubai
CP Coordinator Joel Nainie
DP Coordinator Joel Nainie
Languages English
T: +971 4 342 4040
W: www.gemswellingtonacademy-dso.com

GEMS Wellington International School
PO Box 37486, Al Sufouh 1, Sheikh Zayed Road, Dubai
CP Coordinator Beth Swinscoe
DP Coordinator Kavita Bedi
Languages English
T: +971 (4) 348 4999
W: www.wellingtoninternationalschool.com

GEMS World Academy – Abu Dhabi
Fatima Bint Mubarak Street, PO Box 110273, Abu Dhabi
PYP Coordinator Neil White
Languages English
T: +971 2 641 6333
W: www.gemsworldacademy-abudhabi.com

GEMS World Academy – Dubai
Al Khail Road, Al Barsha South, Dubai
CP Coordinator Chris Nitsche
DP Coordinator Chris Nitsche
MYP Coordinator James Sangster
PYP Coordinator Angela Roberts
Languages English
T: +971 4 373 6373
W: www.gemsworldacademy-dubai.com

German International School Sharjah
Al Abar, Sharjah
DP Coordinator Hana Hashi
Languages English
T: +971 6 5676014
W: www.dssharjah.org

GREENFIELD INTERNATIONAL SCHOOL
Dubai Investments Park, Dubai
CP Coordinator Matt Christensen
DP Coordinator Sarah Atienza
MYP Coordinator Chris Cooke
PYP Coordinator Dr. Sanja Vicevic Ivanovic
Languages English
T: +971 (0)4 885 6600
E: admissions@gischool.ae
W: www.gischool.ae
See full details on page 96

International Concept for Education (ICE Dubai)
Al meydan Rd, Nad al Sheba1, Near Meydan Hotel, Meydan, Dubai
PYP Coordinator Rémi Thomas
Languages English, French
T: +971 4 3377818
W: icedubai.org

JUMEIRA BACCALAUREATE SCHOOL
53 B Street, off Al Wasl Road, Jumeira 1, Dubai
CP Coordinator Michelle Andrews
DP Coordinator Michelle Andrews
MYP Coordinator Lisa Postlethwaite
PYP Coordinator Gregory Joiner
Languages English
T: +971 (0)4 344 6931
E: admissions@jbschool.ae
W: www.jbschool.ae
See full details on page 141

Jumeirah English Speaking School (JESS), Arabian Ranches
Main entrance of Arabian Ranches community, PO Box 24942, Dubai
DP Coordinator Kosta Lekanides
Languages English
T: +971 4 3619019
W: www.jess.sch.ae

Kent College Dubai
PO Box 334022, Dubai
DP Coordinator Clare Boyes
Languages English
T: +971 4 343 0987
W: www.kentcollege.ae

Nord Anglia International School, Dubai
off Hessa Street, Dubai
DP Coordinator Louise Brown
Languages English, French
T: +971 (0)4 2199 999
W: www.nasdubai.ae

North London Collegiate School Dubai
Nad Al Sheba, Mohammed Bin Rashid Al Maktoum City, Dubai
DP Coordinator Sara Noemi Gonzalez Saavedra
MYP Coordinator Stephanie Duarte
PYP Coordinator Michaela Carney
Languages Arabic, English
T: +971 (0)4 319 0888
W: www.nlcsdubai.ae

Raffles World Academy
Al Marcup Street, Umm Suqeim 3, P.O. Box 122900, Dubai
CP Coordinator Aine O'Donnell
DP Coordinator Stephen Pinto
MYP Coordinator Shagufta Abdul Qdoous
PYP Coordinator Yolanda Maccallum
Languages English
T: +971 4 4271351/2
W: www.rwadubai.com

RAHA INTERNATIONAL SCHOOL
Khalifa City 'A', Al Raha Gardens, Abu Dhabi
DP Coordinator Andrew Tomlinson
MYP Coordinator Vaughan Kitson
PYP Coordinator Vanessa Keenan
Languages English
T: +971 (0)2 556 1567
E: admissions@ris.ae
W: www.ris.ae
See full details on page 182

Ras Al Khaimah Academy
PO Box 975, Ras Al Khiamah
DP Coordinator Marc Groenewald
PYP Coordinator Jason Barton
Languages English
T: +971 7 236 2441
W: www.rakaonline.org

Repton School, Dubai
PO Box 300331, Nad Al Sheba 3, Dubai
CP Coordinator Hayley Hultum
DP Coordinator Zoe Cass
Languages English
T: +971 4 426 9300
W: www.reptondubai.org

Sunmarke School
District 5 (Behind Limitless Building on Al Khail Road), Jumeirah Village Triangle, Dubai
CP Coordinator Claire Young
DP Coordinator Thespina Newsome
Languages English
T: +971 4 423 8900
W: www.sunmarkedubai.com

Swiss International Scientific School in Dubai
Dubai Healthcare City, Phase 2, Al Jaddaf, PO Box 505002, Dubai
CP Coordinator Charles Cejka
DP Coordinator Urs Jungo
MYP Coordinator Carolyn Siklos
PYP Coordinator Shona Tait
Languages English, French, German
T: +971 4 375 0600
W: sisd.ae

The British International School, Abu Dhabi
PO Box 60968, Abu Dhabi
DP Coordinator Mrs. Victoria Collinson
Languages English
T: +971 2 510 0176
W: www.bisabudhabi.com

Towheed Iranian School for Boys
Al Qouz 1, Sheikh Zayed Rd, Dubai
DP Coordinator Fereshte Mohammadian Sefat
Languages English
T: +971 4 3389953
W: www.bi-st.com

Universal American School, Dubai
PO Box 79133, Al Rashidiya, Dubai
DP Coordinator Tracey Cummins
PYP Coordinator Nadia Fawzy
Languages English, Arabic
T: +971 4 232 5222
W: www.uasdubai.ae

UPTOWN INTERNATIONAL SCHOOL
Corner of Algeria Road & Tripoli Street, Mirdif, PO Box 78181, Dubai
DP Coordinator Adrian Duckett
MYP Coordinator Hebatallah Gaber
PYP Coordinator Geetha Ashok
Languages English
T: +971 (0)4 2515001
E: admissions@uptownschool.ae
W: www.uischool.ae
See full details on page 234

Victoria International School of Sharjah
PO Box 68600, Al Mamzar, Sharjah
DP Coordinator Sara Santrampurwala
Languages English
T: +971 6 577 1999
W: www.viss.ae/victoria-international-school

Oxbridge International School
Oymarik Street 10, Mirzo Ulug'bek District, Tashkent 100124
PYP Coordinator Khassiyat Saidiganiyeva
Languages English, Russian
W: oisuzbekistan.com

Tashkent International School
38 Sarikulskaya Street, Tashkent 100005
DP Coordinator Rana Mneimneh
MYP Coordinator Robert Tate
PYP Coordinator Robyn Ibrahim
Languages English
T: +998 71 291 9670
W: www.tashschool.org

American International School of Lusaka
PO Box 320176, Lusaka
DP Coordinator Monica Murphy
MYP Coordinator Ingrid Turner
PYP Coordinator Christine Kelly
Languages English
T: +260 211 260509
W: www.aislusaka.org

International School of Lusaka
PO Box 50121, Ridgeway, Lusaka
DP Coordinator Silvia Nithyanathan
PYP Coordinator Grace Kambeu
Languages English
T: +260 211 252291
W: islzambia.org

Pestalozzi Education Centre
Box 194 Postbag E835, Lusaka
DP Coordinator Kiran Pandey
Languages English
T: +260 978 950 599
W: enkoeducation.com/pestalozzi

Harare International School
66 Pendennis Road, Mount Pleasant, Harare
DP Coordinator Kate Reeler
MYP Coordinator Kasey Shiver
PYP Coordinator Vinu Kanda
Languages English
T: +263 4 870 514
W: www.harare-international-school.com

IB

ASIA-PACIFIC

Principal Shawn Hutchinson

Vice Principal
Richard Todd

PYP coordinator
Vanessa Ellison

DP coordinator
Richard Todd

Status Private

Boarding/day Day

Gender Coeducational

Language of instruction
English

Authorised IB programmes
PYP, DP

Age Range 3 – 17 years

Number of pupils enrolled
230

Fees
Day: IDR130,000,000 –
IDR310,500,000

Address
Jl Warung Jati Barat No.19, RW.5,
Jati Padang
Kec. Ps. Minggu, Kota Jakarta
Selatan, Daerah Khusus I
Jakarta, DKI
12540 | INDONESIA

TEL +62 21 2978 0200 / +62 816
297800

Email
acgjkt@acgedu.com

Website
jakarta.acgedu.com

ACG School Jakarta provides an educational pathway from Kindergarten to Year 13 and is regarded as an exceptional option for students seeking a dynamic international education in South Jakarta. We are a proud member of Inspired, a leading premium schools group with a network of more than 60 outstanding schools worldwide.

At ACG School Jakarta, our students enjoy the benefits of world-class teaching from specialist educators, and we are committed to ensuring every child is prepared for success. With proven quality and results in a values-driven, inclusive, and diverse environment, we concentrate on the needs of the individual, offering personalised programmes of study that reflect each student's ability and background.

Our globally recognised curricula deliver the best learning outcomes for our students:

- International Baccalaureate Primary Years Programme (IBPYP) and Diploma Programme (IBDP)
- Cambridge International Lower Secondary and IGCSE courses
- Kindergarten programme for students aged three years and up

With our international mindset and emphasis on academic achievement, we encourage students to become innovative problem solvers and advanced critical thinkers. We place a strong focus on inquiry, investigation and experiential discovery, allowing students to be at the forefront of their learning in creative, meaningful and authentic ways.

Additionally, our holistic learning approach and well-established pastoral care system actively supports every student socially, emotionally, and academically. This ensures they reach their full potential during their time with us and are well prepared for life beyond.

Accordingly, ACG School Jakarta students have performed extremely well on the global stage, with ACG graduates accepted to top universities around the world, including the prestigious University of Oxford, University of Cambridge and Stanford University in California.

Our dedication to developing the individual is also reflected in our co-curricular pursuits, featuring performing and fine arts, sporting and leadership opportunities. Combined with a range of cultural and service activities, this participation equips our students with invaluable life skills such as persistence, commitment, and teamwork, as they contribute to and acquire a wider sense of community.

ACG School Jakarta is uniquely permitted to enrol students who hold passports from Indonesia and other parts of the world. Our central location is ideal for families employed by embassies and multinational corporations. As a private, independent, co-educational school, ACG Jakarta has a non-selective admission policy, serving the needs of expatriate and local communities.

SINCE 1981

AISG

American International School of Guangzhou

(Founded 1981)

Head of School
Kevin Baker

PYP coordinator
Lydia Van Berkhout

DP coordinator
Matthew Wood

Status Private, Non-Profit

Boarding/day Day

Gender Coeducational

Language of instruction
English

Authorised IB programmes
PYP, DP

Age Range 3 – 18 years

Number of pupils enrolled
1000

Fees
Day: ¥175,000 – ¥247,300

Address
No 3 Yan Yu Street South
Ersha Island, Yuexiu District
Guangzhou, Guangdong
510105 | CHINA

TEL +86 20 8735 3392

Email
admissions@aisgz.org

Website
www.aisgz.org

The American International School of Guangzhou is an independent, non-profit, multicultural, and co-educational day school for foreign children from preschool to Grade 12. It is located in Guangzhou, China, with an Elementary School campus on ErSha Island, Yuexiu District and a Secondary School campus in Science Park, Huangpu District. Founded in 1981, AISG is the oldest and longest established non-profit international school in South China.

AISG is on the path to becoming an IB World Continuum School and seeks to add IB Middle Years Programme (MYP) to the already offered IB Primary Years Programme (PYP) and the IB Diploma Programme (IBDP). In addition, AISG has a standards-based curriculum; American Education Reaches Out (AERO), Common Core and Next Generation Science Standards (NGSS) are used throughout all phases to tailor a program most relevant to our unique context and learners.

AISG enrolls over 1,000 international students from preschool to Grade 12 and our student body demographics reflect our international environment with over 40 nationalities. Our students are guided by faculty who challenge them to achieve, nurtured in an environment where creativity and inquiry are celebrated, and supported by a community who understands the power of a growth mindset.

AISG is a caring community that employs experienced teachers who are passionate and bring their forward-thinking pedagogy along with an empathetic approach to enrich each child's learning. More than 78% of our 110 innovative faculty members have attained their master's degrees and more than 68% have over 11 years of experience in education.

Our campuses are designed with the future of learning in mind. Both campuses embrace world-class class learning environments, including open learning spaces to promote collaborative and transparent learning with a green building design and flexible spaces that can evolve with the pedagogical changes that lie ahead.

AISG boasts an extensive athletic program, giving our student athletes the opportunity to participate in a wide variety of sports against other schools both internationally and within China. In addition, AISG offers diverse options for its after-school activities program, ranging from academic, sports, arts, music, technology, and social, allowing students to enjoy a current passion or find a new one.

From our volunteer board members to our dedicated faculty, to our supportive parents, to our hard-working students, AISG has a sense of connection and community in working together to fulfill our mission of nurturing our future-ready individuals to aspire, achieve and contribute.

American School of Bombay

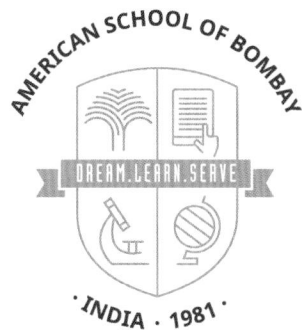

(Founded 1981)

Head of School (to July 2022)
Mr. Craig Johnson

Head of School (from July 2022)
Dr. Paul Richards

PYP coordinator Fay Martin

DP coordinator Tamara Pfantz

Status Private

Boarding/day Day

Gender Coeducational

Language of instruction
English

Authorised IB programmes
PYP, DP

Age Range 3 – 18 years

Number of pupils enrolled
550

Fees
Day: US$15,250 – US$34,020

Secondary School
SF 2, G-Block
Bandra Kurla Complex
Road, Bandra East, Mumbai,
Maharashtra **400051 | INDIA**

Elementary School
Commercial 2, Tower 4
Kohinoor City, Kirol Road,
Off LBS Marg, Kurla (W),
Mumbai, Maharashtra
400070 | INDIA

TEL SS: +91 22 6772 7272
ES: +91 22 6131 3600

Email inquiry@asbindia.org

Website www.asbindia.org

The American School of Bombay (ASB) celebrated 40 years of excellence in education in 2021, and continues to be a beacon of schooling internationally. We are 'what school should be', achieving this through modeling best practices and continually transforming how we teach and learn. During the COVID-19 pandemic, our remarkable educators utilized the strength of their established relationships with students – and with each other – to create a world-leading virtual learning platform. Through positively engaging students in new ways of learning, our educators created a deep sense of trust with our parents and families. Now back on campus, we are continually assessing and adapting our approach to ensure continuity of learning within a safe environment.

The focus of our educational philosophy is our students: they are at the center of their learning experience, they are empowered by dreams, and they are equipped with skills to become life-long learners. ASB's Mission is to inspire all of our students to continuous inquiry, empowering them with the skills, courage, optimism, and integrity to pursue their dreams and enhance the lives of others. Serving others, with a desire to make a positive impact in their world, underpins an ASB education.

With our home in India's vibrant cultural and financial capital, Mumbai, and a student population drawn from more than 50 countries, ASB is intentionally international. We identify the big issues affecting our students, and actively address diversity, equity, inclusion, and justice, both philosophically and through explicit teaching. We commit to open dialogue with our students, parents, and staff to better educate ourselves and each other and make a positive impact in our local and global community.

ASB is an accredited Middle States Association of Colleges and Schools (US) and IB World School, offering the Primary Years and Diploma Programs. Our graduates are awarded an American high school diploma and/or the IB Diploma. Our two campuses span over 200,000 square feet of purpose-built instructional spaces and state-of-the-art facilities, designed to deliver unique and individualized programs to our students.

Beyond the classroom, we are members of SAISA and ASIAC, offering opportunities for international inter-school collaboration and competition in sports and The Arts. Students also participate in Model United Nations and our Community and Social Responsibility (CSR) program is integrated across all grade levels, including a focused advisory program in our Middle & High Schools. ASB graduates are accepted at the world's finest colleges and universities, including MIT, Stanford, Johns Hopkins, Duke, University College London, Harvard, Princeton, University of Sydney, and University of Paris, and contribute personally and professionally across a diversity of fields.

AOBA-JAPAN INTERNATIONAL SCHOOL

Head of School Mr Ken Sell

PYP coordinator Karen Chen

MYP coordinator Chris Radnich

DP coordinator Kate Loke

Status Private

Boarding/day Day

Gender Coeducational

Language of instruction
English

Authorised IB programmes
PYP, MYP, DP

Age Range 2 – 18 years

Number of pupils enrolled
600

Hikarigaoka Campus
7-5-1 Hikarigaoka
Nerima-ku
Tokyo
179-0072 | JAPAN

TEL +81 3 4578 8832

Meguro Campus
2-11-5 Aobadai, Meguro-ku,
Tokyo
153-0042 | JAPAN

TEL +81 3 4520 2313

Email
enquiries@aobajapan.jp

Website
www.aobajapan.jp

Welcome
Our team is waiting to welcome you at our school either online or in person.

Mission Statement
A spirit of community shapes the Aoba experience. We are dedicated to developing global-minded, compassionate, collaborative learners inspired to learn, take risks, and lead positive change in the world.

Vision
Aoba will continue to be a leading international school. We provide our young people with a vigorous international education conducive to learning. Learners' needs and perspectives are supported and respected and their unique qualities valued and nurtured. Through a continued emphasis on educational excellence and innovation, each individual learner is provided with relevant resources and opportunities that will enable them to secure the best of what the future holds for them.

Our Philosophy
We believe that our young people are enabled to reach their full potential as international citizens who are dedicated to learning and who are inspired to succeed in an ever-changing world.

Our 5 Core Values
At Aoba we value the concepts of:
- Global Leadership
- Entrepreneurship and Innovation
- Effective Communication
- Wise Risk Taking
- Effective Problem Solving

Learning at Aoba
Aoba is one of the only full IB World Schools in the Tokyo area and features the typical characteristics expected of an IB school. Aoba has also been selected as the MEXT IB Consortium Chair in recognition of its expertise in IB curriculum and pedagogy.

What sets Aoba apart from other schools, however, is the innovative, progressive approaches to learning we employ from Kindergarten through Grade 12. Aoba consistently features authentic team-based inquiry in all three IB programmes at the school: PYP, MYP, and DP. We take a multi-age, transdisciplinary approach to the IB that really brings the programmes to life for our students.

Our students co-plan their learning with their teachers and are supported to truly take ownership of their learning whilst developing desirable marketplace skills and dispositions as described in our Core Values. Students move beyond simply solving problems for themselves or even solving them for others. We seek to develop students that can create the conditions to empower others to solve problems for themselves, a more sophisticated and powerful mode of, as we say in our Mission Statement, leading positive change in the world.

AUSTRALIAN INTERNATIONAL ACADEMY

Executive Principal
Ms Gafiah Dickinson

PYP coordinator
Ms Zawat Souki

MYP coordinator
Ms Naima Keddar

DP coordinator
Ms Berna Yusuf

Status Private

Boarding/day Day

Gender Coeducational

Language of instruction
English

Authorised IB programmes
PYP, MYP, DP

Age Range 5 – 18 years

Number of pupils enrolled
1700

Address
Melbourne Senior Campus
56 Bakers Road
North Coburg
VIC 3058 | AUSTRALIA

TEL +61 3 9350 4533

Email
aia@aia.vic.edu.au

Website
aia.vic.edu.au

Educating For The Future

The Australian International Academy of Education is dedicated to the provision of high-quality education for students from Foundation to Year 12. Australian International Academy is an International Baccalaureate school offering the (IB) programmes at all three campuses in Melbourne as well as the local Victorian Certificate of Education (VCE). The programmes allow AIA to enhance its local curriculum and to achieve its mission of developing productive Australian Muslim citizens who will help to create a better and more humane world through intercultural understanding and respect.

At the Australian International Academy of Education, we believe that each child is a unique individual. We promote intercultural understanding and a vision to inspire character and leadership. Our values are central to the students' learning experiences. The Academy offers a broad and a well-balanced curriculum with global perspectives to students in primary, secondary and post-secondary schooling. We encourage our students to constantly seek to broaden their horizons in a spirit of tolerance, compassion and co-operation with one another and with others outside the school.

Outstanding academic results are ensured by our passionate teaching staff, who inspire and support students to achieve to their highest potential. With small class sizes we are able to offer a personalised approach to learning and a diverse range of educational experiences, inside and outside the classroom. Our localised, interstate and overseas learning experiences allow students to develop a greater understanding and appreciation of the world around them.

The Academy also provides a wide range of co curricular activities that extend and complement the core curriculum, enrich student lives and develop their skills.

Our website includes further information on the IB Diploma at Australian International Academy including details of a range of subjects on offer.

An **inspired** school

Executive Principal
Ms Davina McCarthy

PYP coordinator Leanne Raeside

DP coordinator Gabriel Price

Status Private

Boarding/day Mixed

Gender Coeducational

Language of instruction
English

Authorised IB programmes
PYP, DP

Age Range 18 months – 18 years

Number of pupils enrolled
1200

Fees
Day: VND 248,000,000 – 699,000,000

**Thu Thiem Campus
(Kindergarten to Year 13)**
264 Mai Chi Tho Street
An Phu ward, Thu Duc City
Ho Chi Minh City | VIETNAM

**Thao Dien Campus
(Kindergarten to Year 6)**
36 Thao Dien Street,
Thao Dien Ward, Thu Duc City,
Ho Chi Minh City | VIETNAM

Xi Campus (Kindergarten)
190 Nguyen Van Huong Street,
Thao Dien Ward, Thu Duc City,
Ho Chi Minh City | VIETNAM

TEL +84 28 3742 4040

Email info@aisvietnam.com

Website www.aisvietnam.com

Leading to a bright future

At Australian International School (AIS), every action we take is designed to lead our students towards a bright future. Since our establishment in 2006, we have continued to achieve this aim by delivering high-quality international education. We are dedicated to creating an environment where we stimulate inquiry, creativity and innovation, to help our students embrace all opportunities that life brings them and to become global citizens.

Providing the IB curriculum

Understanding the significance of all that the IB curriculum offers, AIS has long identified its ability to foster both academic and personal success while challenging students to excel in their studies and their individual development. AIS was one of the first schools in Vietnam to become an authorised IB World School, and as such, we are now among the most experienced educators in the country to provide this curriculum.

Currently, AIS offers the IB Primary Years Programme (PYP) for both our Kindergarten and Primary School students and the IB Diploma Programme as part of its Senior School education. The University of Cambridge Secondary Programme with the International General Certificate of Secondary Education (IGCSE) is provided for our Lower Secondary School students.

For the IB Diploma, AIS has an extensive background in supporting and preparing students to study this acclaimed curriculum and develop real-world skills that extend beyond the classroom. Consequently, AIS graduates consistently obtain results above the world average, and students have gone on to gain places at leading universities around the globe, many with full or partial scholarships.

Exceptional education with modern facilities

Under the leadership and experience of AIS's Executive Principal, Ms Davina McCarthy, our team of enthusiastic, internationally-trained and qualified teachers are dedicated to challenging, inspiring, and supporting the individual needs of every student.

We support each child to reach their full academic potential, to nurture a love of arts, to become involved in and passionate about sport and to develop the resilience to overcome challenges. Our Australian values of fairness and a 'have a go' attitude, combined with a world-class curriculum, drive this ambition.

To aid our teaching staff, every classroom and learning environment is spacious, well-resourced, and technologically rich. Additionally, our students have access to an open garden style campus, swimming pools, a double gymnasium, an auditorium, soccer fields, a dedicated IB Centre, and much, much more.

BRANKSOME
HALL ASIA

(Founded 2012)

Principal
Dr. Cinde Lock

PYP coordinator
Ms. Jennifer Kesler

MYP coordinator
Dr. Paula Swartz

DP coordinator
Ms. Cheryl Osborne

Status Private

Boarding/day Mixed

Gender Female

Language of instruction
English

Authorised IB programmes
PYP, MYP, DP

Age Range 3 – 19 years

Address
234 Global edu-ro, Daejeong-eup
Seogwipo-si
Jeju-do
63644 | REPUBLIC OF KOREA

TEL +82 64 902 5000

FAX +82 64 902 5481

Email
admissions@branksome.asia

Website
www.branksome.asia

Founded in 2012, Branksome Hall Asia is an IB World School that offers the academically rigorous and challenging Diploma Programme, Middle Years Programme and the Primary Years Programme.

Branksome Hall Asia is the sister school of Branksome Hall, a 118-year-old independent girls' school in Canada, consistently ranked as one of the world's best boarding schools.

Co-educational Junior School (age 3-11) and a girls' school environment in Middle and Senior Schools (age 12-19), Branksome Hall Asia nurtures the development of global perspectives and leadership through academic rigor, physical activities, and service, which benefits all students as they discover their voice and their place as leaders locally, nationally and globally. Our distinctive educational journey actively pursues our mission, "To challenge and inspire students each day to love learning and to shape a better world." This educational journey promises to support each student to discover within themselves a strong voice, to take risks and step outside their comfort zones, and the power to lead lives of curiosity, empowerment, service to others, and personal fulfillment.

Our students grow as globally minded learners and leaders prepared for the challenges and opportunities they will meet in a rapidly changing interdependent world.

From JK Prep to Grade 12, our students share their learning and living in a state-of-the-art world-class facility that embodies and encourages our value for intellectual inquiry, collaboration, effective communication, and strength of character. Branksome Hall Asia vibrates with students' energy and warmth.

Experts in their field and dedicated to professional growth, our exceptional faculty fuels this energy via their commitment to the highest levels of learning, to ensure each student discovers their own pathway.

Branksome Hall Asia has an International Merit Scholarship program for non-Korean students to provide deserving future female leaders the chance to benefit from our IB World School program. Scholarships are given in recognition of a student's academic success, leadership commitments, co-curricular involvement, and other talents and achievements. More information is available through the school website.

(Founded 1923)

Principal
Mr Jonathan Walter BA, DipEd, MA

DP coordinator
Frédérique Petithory BA, PostGradCertEd, MA

Status Private

Boarding/day Day

Gender Coeducational

Language of instruction
English

Authorised IB programmes
DP

Age Range 3 – 18 years

Number of pupils enrolled
2671

Fees
Day (Local) $21,352 – $33,052
Day (International) $38,154 – $39,232

Address
349 Barkers Road
Kew
VIC 3101 | AUSTRALIA
TEL +61 3 9816 1222

Email
admissions@carey.com.au

Website
www.carey.com.au

In our complex and ever-changing world, it's clear that today's young people will be faced with a unique set of challenges in the future. To meet these challenges, fulfil their ambitions and contribute to the wider world, students must be equipped with capabilities that will enable them to thrive in a changing environment. At Carey Baptist Grammar School, we believe in adopting a broader expression of success and allowing students to leverage their strengths and follow their passions, whether they be academics, creators, innovators or athletes.

Founded in 1923, Carey is a Christian independent coeducational school offering 3-year-old Early Learning to Year 12. Carey is situated close to the Central Business District of Melbourne, within easy distance of public transport.

As one of Australia's leading schools, Carey maintains a gender balance, fostering the development of confidence, communication skills and self-esteem in all students. Carey works in partnership with families to develop wise, independent, motivated young people who are inspired and equipped to create positive change. The Senior School offers both IB and VCE and fosters a dynamic and stimulating environment. Our students achieve university entrance scores that place Carey amongst the top schools in Victoria.

The wellbeing of every student is at the heart of everything we do at Carey and our award-winning wellbeing program underpins all our activities, from the very beginning of each student's schooling. Through nurturing student wellbeing and supporting their individual interests, we foster an environment that supports them in achieving their best while also developing individuals with integrity, resilience and a social conscience.

Our IB educators are experts in their fields. With regular professional development and an active engagement with the IB Diploma Co-ordinator's network, we ensure that our program is always at the forefront of IB approaches to teaching and learning. We have a number of workshop leaders within the School. Our educators are committed, passionate and inspiring leaders and mentors for our IB students.

Carey's position as a globally-respected school enhances our students' engagement with the wider world and ensures that when they are applying for tertiary education, whether in Australia or abroad, their applications are looked upon with favour and esteem.

We welcome the cultural diversity that international students bring to our community.

For more information about our programs and purpose built facilities, visit www.carey.com.au or call our Admissions Manager on +61 3 9816 1242, or email admissions@carey.com.au

Chadwick International

Head of School
Frederick T. "Ted" Hill

PYP coordinator
Pamela Castillo (Lower Primary)
& Nancy Macharia (Upper Primary)

MYP coordinator
Emily Thomas

DP coordinator
Richard Kent

CP coordinator
Jason Reagin

Status Private

Boarding/day Day

Gender Coeducational

Language of instruction
English

Authorised IB programmes
PYP, MYP, DP, CP

Age Range 4 – 18 years

Number of pupils enrolled
1362

Address
45, Art center-daero 97 beon-gil
Yeonsu-gu, Incheon
22002 | REPUBLIC OF KOREA

TEL +82 32 250 5000

Email songdo-admissions@
chadwickschool.org

Website
www.chadwickinternational.org

Chadwick International is a PreK- G12 international school fully equipped with the state-of-the-art facility built in the Songdo International Business District, Incheon, Republic of Korea.

Chadwick International is the sister campus of Chadwick School, a K-12 school in the greater South Bay area of Los Angeles, which was founded by Margaret Lee Chadwick in 1935. The two campuses share the same mission that Chadwick Schools develop global citizens with keen minds, exemplary character, self-knowledge, and the ability to lead.

Chadwick International is an authorized four programme International Baccalaureate (IB) world school, offering PYP, MYP, DP and CP. Chadwick International emphasizes experiential and inquiry-based learning both in and outside the classroom including Outdoor Education and Service Learning programs. The Outdoor Education allows students to develop conflict-resolution abilities and leadership skills through various outdoor experiences. Meanwhile, Service Learning program teaches students how to interact with both their local and international communities and problem solve on a deeper level. These fundamental programs assist students in transferring valuable lessons learned in the classroom and develop them as contributing members and leaders of tomorrow.

Physical Education plays an integral part of the Chadwick curriculum as it focuses on the promotion of good personal health and a holistic lifestyle for our students. Its activity-based program emphasizes the skill development that improves the fitness and well-being of the individual student as well as healthy and safe lifestyles.

Chadwick International has rich and diverse Visual and Performing Arts programs. In these classes, students develop their knowledge, skills, creativity and ability to respond to artistic ideas. Also, students are exposed to a variety of theatrical mediums to express themselves and heighten their awareness of themselves in relation to the people and culture around them.

Chadwick International helps to achieve its educational mission through recruiting and supporting highly experienced, dedicated, and diverse faculty members from around the world. With the support of the faculty, Chadwick International is capable of a low teacher to student ratio of 1:8.

Chadwick International's superior educational facilities include an aquatic center with scuba diving capabilities, two gymnasiums, two performing arts indoor theaters, a television studio that allows production up to eight channels, a working garden, purpose-built science laboratories and three design/maker spaces. These facilities permit the students to cultivate their intellectual, artistic and physical abilities based on Chadwick International's experience-based curriculum.

Chadwick International is accredited by Western Association of Schools and Colleges (WASC) and Council of International Schools (CIS).

Chatsworth International School

(Founded 1995)

Head of School
Dr. Tyler Sherwood

PYP coordinator
Eleri Connor

MYP coordinator
Phavana Silva

DP coordinator
Iain Hudson

Status Private

Boarding/day Day

Gender Coeducational

Language of instruction
English

Authorised IB programmes
PYP, MYP, DP

Age Range 3 – 18 years

Number of pupils enrolled
600

Address
72 Bukit Tinggi Road
Singapore
289760 | SINGAPORE

TEL +65 6463 3201

Email
admissions.bt@chatsworth.
com.sg

Website
www.chatsworth.com.sg

Established in 1995, Chatsworth International School is a community-focussed and diverse K-12 international school in Singapore. As an IB World School, we are authorised to offer the Primary Years Programme (PYP), Middle Years Programme (MYP) and Diploma Programme (DP) of the International Baccalaureate. We pride ourselves on providing top quality international education at exceptional value, guided by our educational philosophy to inspire, educate and enlighten.

We offer the IB PYP for students from Kindergarten to Year 6 (ages 3 to 12). The final year of the PYP culminates in a Year 6 Exhibition, a powerful celebration and showcase of student learning and development. The MYP is offered to students from Years 7 to 11 (ages 12 to 15). The MYP emphasises intellectual challenge, encouraging students to make connections between their studies in traditional subjects and the real world, and sets students up for success in the IB Diploma Programme. In the High School, we offer the two-year IBDP in Years 12 and 13 (ages 16 to 18) and students who have successfully met our graduation requirements also earn our WASC-accredited Chatsworth High School Diploma.

As a non-selective school, we welcome students of all nationalities and abilities. From academics to arts to sports to service learning, our highly qualified and global teachers from over 20 nationalities strive to inspire and challenge the students to bring out their best selves. Our small class sizes allow students to gain an individualised education and ensure that they are heard and are recognised for their talents. All students are given equal opportunities to be fielded across sports teams and represent the school so long as they show a commitment.

Student well-being is at the heart of a Chatsworth education. Our established student services team provides a strong pastoral programme and offers the support that students need to thrive academically, personally and socially.

Chatsworth graduates have achieved excellent results in their IB Diploma and consistently scores well above the world average year-on-year. Our school average is 36 points for three consecutive years from 2019 to 2021. Chatsworth is one of the few international schools in Singapore to offer the full IBMYP eAssessment (includes seven subjects and a personal project) for our Year 11 students.

Loved for our close-knit community, the foundation of a Chatsworth education is more than academic success. The strong relationships that our teachers develop with their students and amongst the different key members of our community underpin the strength of our community. Our supportive Chatsworth Parent Group (CPG), where every parent is a member, contributes to our school culture and ensures families are engaged.

CRANBROOK
SCHOOL
EST. 1918

(Founded 1918)

Headmaster Nicholas Sampson

PYP coordinator
Genet Erickson Adam

MYP coordinator Kate Allen

DP coordinator
Nicholas Hanrahan

Status Private

Boarding/day Mixed

Gender Male (Mixed Pre-School)

Language of instruction
English

Authorised IB programmes
PYP, MYP, DP

Number of pupils enrolled
1500

Fees
Pre-School
AUS$8,073 – AUS$20,184
Junior School
AUS$26,064 – AUS$31,722
Senior School Day Boy
AUS$37,386 – AUS$38,862
Senior School Boarding
AUS$72,060 – AUS$73,536

Address
5 Victoria Road, Bellevue Hill
NSW 2023 | AUSTRALIA
TEL +61 2 9327 9000

Email
Enrol@cranbrook.nsw.edu.au

Website
www.cranbrook.nsw.edu.au

Located in the heart of Sydney, Cranbrook School is an IB Continuum School offering the Primary Years, Middle Years and IB Diploma Programmes. We are committed to developing knowledgeable, caring young people who respond to challenges with optimism and an open-mind, are confident in their own identities, make ethical decisions, join with others in celebrating our common humanity and are prepared to apply what they learn in real world, complex and unpredictable situations.

ACADEMIC EXCELLENCE: A LIFE-LONG LOVE OF LEARNING
Cranbrook School is committed to academic excellence, inspiring students to strive to achieve beyond their expectations and to broaden their horizons. Our dedicated teachers encourage young people to engage enthusiastically with intellectual challenges and develop a life-long love of learning.

THE ARTS: A WORLD CLASS PROGRAMME
We place great importance on cultural and artistic expression. Participation in these programmes aims to develop skills in leadership, performance, creativity and decision-making. Our vision is to provide a world class programme for a world class school: A programme which excites, inspires and encourages boys to dream, persevere and achieve.

SPORT: INCLUSIVENESS AND CHALLENGE
Our sports programme promotes inclusiveness, opportunity and competition. Students are driven to challenge themselves through the development of their skills, training and conditioning, with a strong focus on balancing the comradery of team success with the satisfaction of individual achievement.

CO-CURRICULAR: A HOLISTIC APPROACH TO EDUCATION
Reflecting the true ethos of the School, Cranbrook's co-curricular activities are broad, distinctive, holistic and well-rounded. Our students take part in a stimulating range of extra subjects over and above the set curriculum designed to widen each student's horizons, enable them to find their niche, and allow them to grow in confidence and achieve excellence in all that they do.

EXPERIENTIAL LEARNING: ESCAPING THE CONSTRAINTS OF CITY LIFE
All students also benefit from an enhanced focus on education within the natural environment as part of our 'Cranbrook in the Field' experience held at our experiential bush campus at Wolgan Valley and in the Australian Capital Territory. This unique educational experience gives us the opportunity to instil in our students the value of contemplation, camaraderie, reflection, conversation and wonder, free from the distraction of technology and city life.

BOARDING: A BRIDGE TO UNIVERSITY LIFE AND BEYOND
Ever since Cranbrook first opened its gates in 1918, our School has been a home away from home to boarding students, ensuring an academic environment and nurturing community where boys can learn and grow. Two Boarding Houses are home to 75 students from across Sydney, regional Australia and the world – all living, learning and growing together.

(Founded 1972)

Principal
Dr. Chan Kui Pui

DP coordinator
Mr. Paolo Yap

Status State

Boarding/day Day

Gender Coeducational

Language of instruction
Cantonese, English, Mandarin

Authorised IB programmes
DP

Age Range 12 – 18 years

Number of pupils enrolled 695

Fees
Secondary 4-6 HKDSE:
HK$3,000 (US$385)
IBDP Y1 and Y2:
HK$25,600 (US$3,290)

Address
1-3 Glee Path, Mei Foo Sun
Chuen, Kowloon
Hong Kong, SAR | **HONG KONG,
CHINA**

TEL +852 2741 5239

Email
gp@deliagroup.edu.hk

Website
www.deliagp.edu.hk

Delia Memorial School (Glee Path), a member of The Delia Group of Schools, is proud to offer the IB Diploma Programme as a curricular pathway for our students in the last two years of secondary school. Because of its academic rigor, balanced approach, and whole-person focus, the IBDP is an excellent option for our students who seek an internationally-recognized alternative to the local HKDSE curriculum and a thorough preparation for the demands of university education in Hong Kong and abroad.

As a school that affirms and celebrates our students' diverse backgrounds and multicultural identities, Glee Path is especially a committed believer in the IB mission. Our students, hailing mostly from South and Southeast Asia and studying side-by-side with local and overseas Chinese, learn together in a vibrant, academically rigorous, and English-speaking environment that promotes tolerance, empathy, and understanding.

To put into practice our educational belief in equity and equality, Glee Path makes the IBDP available to our students regardless of their financial circumstances. As such, our school offers the lowest tuition fees of any IB World School in Hong Kong, with full need-based scholarships also available to those who qualify. Even learning resources such as laptops, iPads, and course companions, are covered by financial aid as do our extracurricular activities and overseas study tours to places like Australia, Canada, Nepal, and Romania. These measures ensure that our students benefit not only from the equitable access to the IBDP but also from being fully included in the learning opportunities enjoyed by the Glee Path community.

As the only IB World School in Hong Kong's Mei Foo neighborhood, our school is easily accessible by public transportation options. So, why not drop by and pay us a visit? We would love to welcome you to Glee Path, where the journey towards excellence begins.

Dover Court International School Singapore

DOVER COURT INTERNATIONAL SCHOOL
A NORD ANGLIA EDUCATION SCHOOL

(Founded 1972)

Head of School
Mr. Richard Dyer

DP coordinator
Mr. Dominic O'Shea

Status Private

Boarding/day Day

Gender Coeducational

Language of instruction
English

Authorised IB programmes
DP

Age Range 3 – 18 years

Number of pupils enrolled
1800

Fees
S$22,470 – S$34,876

Address
301 Dover Road
Singapore
139644 | SINGAPORE

TEL +65 6775 7664

Email
admissions@dovercourt.edu.sg

Website
www.dovercourt.edu.sg

Founded in 1972, Dover Court International School is an international, multicultural and inclusive school community in the heart of Singapore. We are a community underpinned and guided by clear values, which resonate with the values of Singapore itself and with those upheld by global communities everywhere. We are unique in welcoming children of diverse strengths and talents and in providing an education which is aligned to each individual. We welcome students from 3 to 18 years old, from Nursery to Year 13, with our student body comprising of over 60 nationalities. As part of Nord Anglia Education we benefit from the unparalleled opportunities gained from being part of a larger network and we can draw on the experiences from other NAE schools. With over 70 schools worldwide.

We are highly ambitious for our students in all aspects of their academic and personal growth. Our students are energetic, articulate, motivated, confident, caring and they are eager to make their mark on the world. One of the great strengths of our British style international education is that such growth involves all aspects of students' moral, physical, emotional, aesthetic, social and academic development focused on each individual's personal best. Here at DCIS, this is achieved through superb teaching supported and complemented by Teaching Assistants and the guidance of Form Tutors and Progress Leaders.

At Dover Court International School, we have a fifty-year history of providing pathways to success for all students. We are unique in Singapore in welcoming students with diverse needs and talents and we deliver on our promises, with bespoke programmes that enable every student to thrive, to flourish and expand their potential. Education has never succeeded with a "one size fits all" approach but few schools manage to personalise education in the ways that Dover Court does: three pathways, many qualification routes, blended and customised to each individual.

Students from Nursery to Year 11 follow the English National curriculum, adapted for our international context, leading to the IGCSE qualifications. Sixth Form students, Years 12 and 13, complete either the IB Diploma Programme, IB Courses or the International BTEC in Business. Our 2021 Graduates achieved an average IBDP score of 36 points, three students achieved over 40 points with our highest score being 44 and with two students completing the bilingual diploma. Our graduates are now attending universities in Singapore, UK, USA, New Zealand, Canada, The Netherlands, Ireland and Australia.

DULWICH COLLEGE
| SINGAPORE |

(August 2014)

Headmaster
Mr. Nick Magnus

Head of Senior School
Ms. Melanie Ellis

DP coordinator
Ms. Lisa Nevers

Status Private

Boarding/day Day

Gender Coeducational

Language of instruction
English

Authorised IB programmes
DP

Age Range 2 – 18 years

Number of pupils enrolled
2700

Fees
Day: S$30,630 – S$47,730

Address
71 Bukit Batok West Avenue 8
Singapore
658966 | SINGAPORE

TEL +65 6890 1003

Email admissions.singapore@
dulwich.org

Website
singapore.dulwich.org

Heritage and Tradition

Dulwich College (Singapore) is an international school with a British independent school ethos and values, which draws upon 400 years of excellence and tradition from Dulwich College in London. Our traditions form part of our culture and are firmly embedded in all that we do. Additionally, our collaborations across the network of schools in Asia and London stimulate innovation and encourage an international outlook, which we believe fully prepares students for their futures. The result is a community where academic ability is nourished, creativity is valued, diversity is celebrated, and inspiration is paramount.

Our students go to some of the best universities and colleges in the world and we are proud of our individualised university counselling service and the network of schools which support this.

What is the Dulwich College (Singapore) IB Diploma Programme Difference?

- Embedded enrichment and leadership for all students
- Passionate, highly experienced IB Diploma Programme teachers who put students first
- Three-year (I)GCSE programme which ensures enriched activities and a focus on skills which enable students to be fully prepared for the IB Diploma Programme
- Part of a network of schools that truly supports students in terms of opportunities and shared knowledge
- Holistic programme where the arts and sport are a valued and integral part of each student's education
- Small cohort and class sizes which focus on student wellbeing
- Academically rigorous but holistic at the centre
- Personalised IB Diploma Programme application process
- Individualised university application process supported by the Dulwich College International network
- An IB Diploma Programme which focuses on feedback and metacognition, so students can independently plan and improve their own learning
- State-of-the-art facilities for IB students to collaborate, study independently and flourish, including a purpose built IB common room and quiet study areas
- A personalised pathway for every single student

DULWICH COLLEGE
| BEIJING |

北京德威英国国际学校

(Founded 2005)

Head of College
Mr Anthony Coles

DP coordinator
Mr Anthony Baldwin

Status Private

Boarding/day Day

Gender Coeducational

Language of instruction
English

Authorised IB programmes
DP

Age Range 3 – 18 years

Number of pupils enrolled
1577

Fees
Day: RMB212,000 – RMB320,000

Address
89 Capital Airport Road
Shunyi District
Beijing
101300 | CHINA

TEL +86 10 6454 9000

Email
admissions.beijing@dulwich.org

Website
beijing.dulwich.org

Our Heritage and Tradition

Dulwich College Beijing is an international school with British independent school ethos and values, which draws upon 400 years of excellence and tradition from Dulwich College, the founding College in London. Established in 2005, Dulwich College Beijing maintains strong ties with Dulwich College. We are proud to share a common heritage across the network of schools in Asia, and equally value the traditions, unique to our school, that we have created since we opened. Dulwich College Beijing was the winner of the Holistic Education and Science and Technology Awards at the British Schools Awards 2021.

Our diverse student body is represented by more than 1,570 students from age 3 to age 18, with over thirty different nationalities. We are extremely proud of our students who achieve excellent academic results while at the same time, engaging in sports, visual and performing arts, science and technology, community service, debating, leadership roles and anything else that they are passionate about. Our graduating classes have consistently achieved IB results and university placements that place the school among the world's best.

Our Curriculum

The primary teaching language is English, with a Dual Language approach in Mandarin and English in Early Years. Children up to age 5 follow the Early Years Foundation Stage, and from Year 1 to Year 9, they follow the National Curriculum of England and Wales, which is enhanced to meet the needs of our international student body.

In Year 10 they begin the IGCSE (International General Certificate of Secondary Education), a rigorous two-year course that requires students to take a broad range of subjects. It culminates in exams at the end of Year 11 and prepares students well for the two-year International Baccalaureate Diploma Programme (IBDP) starting in Year 12.

Extra-Curricular Activities

With 150 extra-curricular activities per term, our students can explore and expand their interests beyond academics. Our extra-curricular activities help develop social, leadership, organisational, creative, technical, speaking and listening skills, among others.

Consistent IB Results

We congratulate our Class of 2021 for their outstanding results and university matriculations:

- Average score of 39.4 points out of 45, significantly above the global average of 33 in 2021
- 100% full IBDP pass rate
- 53% of the students scored 40 points and above
- 9 students achieved full score of 45 points
- 11 students achieved a nearly perfect score of 44 points
- University matriculations include Oxbridge and Russell Group universities in the UK, Ivy League in the U.S., as well as top universities in Canada, Europe and Asia.

DULWICH COLLEGE

| SHANGHAI PUXI |

上海德威外籍人员子女学校（浦西）

(Founded 2016)

Head of College
David Ingram

DP coordinator
David Brown

Status Private

Boarding/day Day

Gender Coeducational

Language of instruction
English, Chinese

Authorised IB programmes
DP

Age Range 2 – 18 years

Address
2000 Qianpujing Road
Maqiao, Minhang District
Shanghai | **CHINA**

TEL +86 (21) 3329 9310

Email
admissions.shanghaipuxi@
dulwich.org

Website
shanghai-puxi.dulwich.org

Situated in the leafy and green west of Minhang district, Dulwich College Shanghai Puxi caters for families living in the west of Shanghai who are seeking the world-class holistic education that Dulwich College has become synonymous with. Drawing on 400 years of rich Dulwich heritage, at Dulwich College Shanghai Puxi our curriculum is academically rigorous, yet the education of the whole child is seen as critical. Our wellbeing programme and range of co-curricular opportunities available to all children encourages academic, physical, social and emotional growth. Our robust Mandarin programme ensures that all students, regardless of background, can thrive in the local culture and context. Committed to student leadership and service, our students uphold the College Values at all times: Aim High and Work Hard. Be Kind and Respectful. Make a Difference.

Our curriculum is based on the British National Curriculum and is appropriately enhanced to meet the needs of our international student body. In Years 10 and 11, our students complete the academically rigorous IGCSE, which then leads to the International Baccalaureate Diploma Programme in Years 12 and 13. At Dulwich College Shanghai Puxi, IB students must select three Higher Level and three Standard Level subjects. In combination with these subjects, students are required to fulfil the requirements of the Core components of TOK, EE and CAS to gain full certification in the IB Diploma Programme. All students will also undertake wellbeing lessons as part of their timetable.

Most of our Senior School students also complete the Duke of Edinburgh International Award throughout their time at the College. Although the Award is not compulsory, it fits in well with the CAS requirements of the IBDP and is an opportunity for students to gain an additional qualification. Participating in the Award is a personal challenge and not a competition against others; it pushes young people to their personal limits and recognises their achievements consistently. The Award encourages young people to design their own programme of activities, set their own goals and challenge themselves to achieve their aims.

Senior School at Dulwich College Shanghai Puxi is highly regarded not only for our academically rigorous programme and existing track record of strong results, but also for our broad, holistic provision. We place a strong emphasis on student leadership and wellbeing, enabling our students to Graduate Worldwise.

ELCHK Lutheran Academy

Principal
Patrick Hak Chung LAM

PYP coordinator
Julia ENG

MYP coordinator
Keith Henderson

DP coordinator
John Law

Status Private

Boarding/day Day

Gender Coeducational

Language of instruction
English, Cantonese, Mandarin

Authorised IB programmes
PYP, MYP, DP

Age Range 6 – 18 years

Number of pupils enrolled
1125

Fees
IBPYP HK$65,910 – HK$74,060
IBMYP HK$72,280
IBDP HK$90,130

Address
25 Lam Hau Tsuen Road
Yuen Long, New Territories |
HONG KONG

TEL +852 8208 2092

Email
info@luac.edu.hk

Website
www.luac.edu.hk

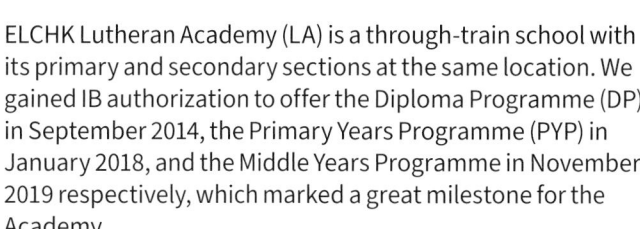

ELCHK Lutheran Academy (LA) is a through-train school with its primary and secondary sections at the same location. We gained IB authorization to offer the Diploma Programme (DP) in September 2014, the Primary Years Programme (PYP) in January 2018, and the Middle Years Programme in November 2019 respectively, which marked a great milestone for the Academy.

We offer a wide range of subjects for all the programmes. DP subjects comprise the 6 subject groups: Languages (Chinese, English, and French), Sciences (Physics, Chemistry, and Biology), Individuals and Societies (Economics, Business & Management, and History), Mathematics (Mathematics Analysis & Approaches, and Mathematics Application & Interpretation), and The Arts (Visual Arts and Music). MYP subjects encompass the 8 subject groups such as Languages (Chinese, English), Arts (Visual Arts, Drama, Music), and Design and so on.

The PYP, as the foundation of the curriculum, initiates students to develop ideas contributing to international mindedness. Embracing the Unit of Inquiry (UOI), students are encouraged to question and refine their understanding of individual wellbeing, learning communities, and the world from different perspectives.

Away from the hustle and bustle of city life in Hong Kong, we are dedicated to make a difference in students' lives. Creating a warm and friendly campus, students are nurtured to explore their potentials and develop their talents through diverse experiences.

By offering holistic and balanced Christian education, the professional teaching team with teachers from different cultural backgrounds is committed in nurturing students to strive for excellence and to become global leaders of tomorrow. To maximize the learning opportunities and provide adequate care to individual needs, LA adopts small-class teaching that our overall teacher-student ratio is around 1:8.

We encourage students to explore concepts in manifolds of forms to ensure their whole-person development. Students are exposed to learning from varieties of activities, including field trips, Co-curricular and Extra-Curricular activities. During the EOTC (Education Outside the Classroom) week, students visit places of diversified cultures around the world to experience the learning outside the classroom and broaden their horizons. After the tour, they showcase to share what they have acquired to their classmates, parents and teachers.

To support programme implementation, Information and Communication Technology (ICT) has been well integrated into education to equip students with ICT skills. With the "Apple One-to-One Program", each secondary student is equipped with a laptop for daily learning. Together with the whole school Wi-Fi coverage, the ICT-infused inquiry-based learning has been effectively and efficiently facilitated.

With the enthusiastic support from the LA community, the school is growing from strength to strength to provide high quality education for the future rising generation.

ABACUS INTERNATIONAL KINDERGARTEN

(Founded 2002)

Principal
Ms Frances Hurley

PYP coordinator
Ms Fiona Hall

Status ESF Educational Services Limited Kindergarten /Non-Profit

Boarding/day Day

Gender Coeducational

Language of instruction
English, Mandarin

Authorised IB programmes
PYP

Age Range 3 – 5 years

Number of pupils enrolled
190

Fees for 2021/22
English Stream HK$86,000
Bilingual Stream HK$100,000

Address
Mang Kung Uk Village
Clearwater Bay Road | HONG KONG

TEL +852 27195712

Email
kinder@abacus.edu.hk

Website
www.abacus.edu.hk

ESF Abacus International Kindergarten caters for children aged between three and five years of age and children attend school for three hours per day, five days per week. One class teacher and two educational assistants are responsible for each class of 24 children in our K1 and K2 classrooms. Abacus is authorised to deliver the International Baccalaureate Primary Years Programme (PYP), providing an inquiry-based and highly interactive programme. Children learn through play experiences and are encouraged to discover, experiment and reflect on their learning. Our aim at Abacus is to encourage children to become confident and independent learners. We encourage each child to reach their full potential whilst respecting themselves, others and the world around them.

Abacus offers Bilingual and English streams in both K1 and K2.

Bilingual

The Bilingual programme is jointly planned and delivered by an English and Chinese teacher working as a class team. Children receive instruction in both languages and all areas of the curriculum are delivered in both languages with the exception of English and Chinese languages. Children attending the bilingual class experience differentiated sessions in English language and Chinese language, to ensure their differing ability levels are catered for.

English

The programme is conducted in English with Chinese as an additional specialist language. The children are introduced to Chinese vocabulary and learn about Chinese customs and festivals through games, songs and stories.

BEACON HILL SCHOOL

(Founded 1967)

Principal
Ms Brenda Cook

PYP coordinator
Mr Andy Thompson

Status English Schools
Foundation School/Non-Profit

Boarding/day Day

Gender Coeducational

Language of instruction
English

Authorised IB programmes
PYP

Age Range 5 – 11 years

Number of pupils enrolled
540

Fees for 2021/22
Years 1 to 6 HK$115,800
Non-refundable capital levy:
HK$38,000 for each new Year 1
student

Address
23 Ede Road
Kowloon Tong | **HONG KONG**

TEL +852 2336 5221

Email
bhs@bhs.edu.hk

Website
www.beaconhill.edu.hk

Our Vision
To be a happy, diverse and inclusive community where everybody has confidence to aspire to be the best they can be, now and in the future.

Our Mission
- We create a safe, caring and supportive environment enabling purposeful challenge through a dynamic and rigorous curriculum
- We inspire and develop creativity and academic potential
- We encourage global and social responsibility
- We foster independence in thought and action

ESF Beacon Hill School is part of the English Schools Foundation (ESF), the largest provider of English-medium international education in Hong Kong.

Beacon Hill School was founded in 1967 and moved to its present location in 1968. It occupies a well-equipped seven storey building and has classroom space to accommodate a three form entry. There are a number of special purpose rooms that are state of the art. These include a fully equipped drama studio, music rooms, learning technologies room, art room and library.

Beacon Hill School staff is made up of dedicated professionals providing an all-round education of the very highest quality academically, creatively and socially, ensuring that each child has the opportunity to reach their potential. The students come to us from many countries and this international mix adds a great deal to the atmosphere and the richness of the school experience. An active Parent Teacher Association (PTA) and School Council support our school ensuring the school achieves its aims.

Beacon Hill School is an International Baccalaureate (IB) World School authorised to implement the Primary Years Programme (PYP). We have single-subject teachers for learning technology, PE, music and Chinese. We encourage the development of creativity amongst our students and place a strong emphasis on the arts. Our students at Beacon Hill use technology to support and enhance their learning. They will learn how to use design thinking to solve problems. This may involve more traditional tools with a construction project or coding, 3D printing and robotics. We are well resourced with 1:1 Chrome books from Years 3 to 6. We have a strong focus on language, both in the Chinese and English literacy provision. We are an inclusive school with 21 students with more moderate diverse educational needs. These students are catered for within the mainstream classes with additional learning support teachers and educational assistants. We offer a range of programmes to depending on the needs of the students, such as a Perceptual Motor Programme, Social Thinking, Friends for Life, B2 – Social/Emotional tracking system, Fine Motor and individualised sensory programmes. Our learning diversity provision is world leading.

BRADBURY SCHOOL

(Founded 1980)

Principal
Mrs Kate Gower

PYP coordinator
Ms Amanda Bremner

Status English Schools
Foundation School/Non-Profit

Boarding/day Day

Gender Coeducational

Language of instruction
English

Authorised IB programmes
PYP

Age Range 5 – 11 years

Number of pupils enrolled 720

Fees for 2021/22
Years 1 to 6 HK$115,800
Non-refundable capital levy:
HK$38,000 for each new Year 1
student

Address
43C Stubbs Road | **HONG KONG**

TEL +852 2574 8249

Email
enquiries@bradbury.edu.hk

Website
www.bradbury.edu.hk

ESF Bradbury School offers a safe, caring and fun environment in which all students thrive and are the best that they can be. The calibre of our staff and the positive, encouraging approach in our classrooms, provides children with an all-round education of the very highest quality, achieving outstanding results. With emphasis on student agency, we encourage our children to become independent thinkers who care about the world around them – through an active sustainability approach – and develop the skills required to become lifelong learners and leaders. We place a high importance on partnership with parents and see this as a cornerstone of how we operate on a daily basis. Our Parent Teacher Association (PTA) is active and hardworking, contributing much to the life of our school. We are governed by a knowledgeable and highly supportive School Council.

Bradbury School is an International Baccalaureate (IB) World School. We use the Primary Years Programme (PYP) as the basis of our instruction and to underpin our beliefs as expressed in our school vision – *Inspiring minds . Nurturing hearts . Enriching tomorrow*. At the same time, we place a high value on our students becoming emotionally literate in a 21st century learning environment, embracing an extended concept of the areas that new technologies offer us. Chinese is taught to all students, with levels of instruction adjusted according to ability and fluency.

Our school has excellent resources, offering a number of specialist subjects in dedicated spaces. We have a state of the art library, which is seen as the hub of inquiry throughout the school. In addition, we have a full gymnasium, school hall, music room, including soundproof studios, netball courts, a variety of large adventure playgrounds installed across various levels, undercover play areas, a large free form sandpit and art studio. Bradbury School has an extensive sports programme and offers amongst others: rugby, netball, cricket, soccer, swimming, basketball and running, as well as other activities such as judo and kickboxing. The school makes provision for 21 children with moderate learning difficulties through a Learning Support Programme and we believe in a full inclusion approach for all of our students.

ESF
英基 **CLEARWATER BAY**
SCHOOL

(Founded 1992)

Principal
Mr Michael Dewey

PYP coordinators
Ms Helen Read; Ms Chiara Holmes

Status English Schools Foundation School/Non-Profit

Boarding/day Day

Gender Coeducational

Language of instruction
English

Authorised IB programmes
PYP

Age Range 5 – 11 years

Number of pupils enrolled 720

Fees for 2021/22
Years 1 to 6 HK$115,800
Non-refundable capital levy:
HK$38,000 for each new Year 1 student

Address
DD229, Lot 235,
Clearwater Bay Road
New Territories | **HONG KONG**

TEL +852 2358 3221

Email
info@cwbs.edu.hk

Website
www.cwbs.edu.hk

ESF Clearwater Bay School is an International Baccalaureate (IB) World School serving the Sai Kung, Clearwater Bay and Tseung Kwan O communities in the Eastern New Territories of Hong Kong. We are accredited by both the Council of International Schools and the International Baccalaureate Organization and offer a world class international primary education to students in Years 1-6. There is strong demand for admissions and the school is currently at capacity with 720 students enrolled.

Our school values create a safe, welcoming learning environment that fosters care, respect and intercultural understanding. We value and celebrate the rich cultural diversity of students and families who come from more than 35 different nationalities and cultural backgrounds. Through the IB Primary Years Programme (PYP), we develop our students' creativity, confidence and willingness to achieve their personal best. High standards of academic achievement combined with a strong emphasis on the arts, physical education and sport provides students with a comprehensive, well-rounded curriculum. Specialist Chinese, physical education, music and library programmes are also taught. An extensive co-curricular programme provides opportunities for students to participate in a range of arts, sport and special interest activities.

We cater to the individual learning needs of students through a developmentally appropriate curriculum that is differentiated to extend students needing further challenge and to support students who experience difficulties. Specialist learning support, English as an additional language and counselling services are available.

We have skilled and passionate staff and an active parent community who work collaboratively to create a learning community that strives to provide every student with the best possible education.

DISCOVERY COLLEGE

(Founded 2007)

Principal Mr James Smith

PYP coordinator Ms Kate Agars

MYP coordinator
Ms Annette Garnett

DP coordinator Mr Brian McCann

CP coordinator Ms Emma Neuprez

Status A Private Independent School Of The English Schools Foundation

Boarding/day Day

Gender Coeducational

Language of instruction
English

Authorised IB programmes
PYP, MYP, DP, CP

Age Range 5 – 18 years

Number of pupils enrolled
1400

Fees for 2021/22
Years 1 to 6 HK$129,700
Years 7 to 11 HK$173,500
Years 12 to 13 HK$175,400
Non-refundable Building Levy:
HK$7,530 per student per year

Address
38 Siena Avenue, Discovery Bay,
Lantau Island | **HONG KONG**

TEL +852 3969 1000

Email office@dc.edu.hk

Website www.discovery.edu.hk

Grow. Discover. Dream. This vision statement, created by the College community when the school was founded in 2007, recognises ESF Discovery College's belief that students are to be independent, critical and creative thinkers, equipped with the skills, attitudes and values to contribute positively in this complex world in which we live. At Discovery College we believe that powerful learning and teaching occurs under a shared spirit of respect, which dignifies and prizes our diversity of experiences and perspectives, reaches into our traditions as well as into the future, excites a passion for ongoing inquiry and strives to help all learners reach for enduring excellence.

Discovery College was established by the English Schools Foundation to serve the needs of the local and expatriate communities in Hong Kong. It is a full Years 1 to 13 school offering the Primary Years Programme (PYP), Middle Years Programme (MYP), Diploma and Career-related programmes. Partial and full scholarships are available for exceptional secondary students.

The College strongly supports all subject areas with a robust academic curriculum, including the performing and creative arts, design and Information and Communication Technologies (ICT). Technology is embedded across the curriculum, supported by a number of digital literacy staff and a 1:1 laptop programme from Year 6 onwards.

The teaching staff represent more than 20 nationalities and are chosen from amongst the world's best. The student population comprises more than 45 nationalities and almost as many mother tongues.

The College uses English as the medium for teaching and learning. There is also a strong emphasis on the acquisition of Chinese (Putonghua) as a second language. The College focuses on international-mindedness throughout the community.

The College's facilities are second to none, with an award-winning design that incorporates an exceptional performing arts centre, gymnasium spaces, 25m rooftop heated swimming pool, library, science labs and design technology rooms.

(Founded 1959)

Principal
Mr Christopher Coyle

PYP coordinator
Ms Nia Sexton

Status English Schools
Foundation School/Non-Profit

Boarding/day Day

Gender Coeducational

Language of instruction
English

Authorised IB programmes
PYP

Age Range 5 – 11 years

Number of pupils enrolled
360

Fees for 2021/22
Years 1 to 6 HK$115,800
Non-refundable capital levy:
HK$38,000 for each new Year 1
student

Address
7 Hornsey Road
Mid Levels | **HONG KONG**

TEL +852 2522 1919

Email
enquiry@glenealy.edu.hk

Website
www.glenealy.edu.hk

ESF Glenealy School is a community-based school. We are proud of the positive relationships that we build with students, their families and the wider community. Being a two-form entry ESF primary school of 360 students, we are able to offer a personalised, inclusive and flexible approach to meeting the needs of our learners.

At Glenealy School, highly skilled teachers ensure an education that is transformational. We develop caring and curious global citizens who make a positive difference. We provide meaningful and relevant experiences where learners develop skills, knowledge, understanding and attitudes for success in life. Our safe, nurturing environment values learners' voice and choice, fostering positive relationships in which learners flourish.

At Glenealy School, our mission statement is to empower learners to flourish and make a positive difference. Our vision for every student is to be the best that they can be. At Glenealy School, we support and challenge students to ensure continual academic progress, personal growth and high standards.

As an International Baccalaureate (IB) World School we offer a significant, engaging and high quality international education for our students. Using the IB Primary Years Programme (PYP) as a framework, students learn through an inquiry approach where they are encouraged to explore concepts and ideas that are meaningful and relevant to their lives, now and in the future. Our modern, flexible learning spaces are integral to the learning process.

We help our students become confident, caring, curious, independent and resilient learners who are empowered to achieve their best in all aspects of life. The multitude of experiences offered through the arts, sport, the outdoors, learning Chinese language and culture, partaking in environmental action groups and opportunities for students to take on leadership roles within the school, offers the students many opportunities to find and follow their passions and interests.

When you join Glenealy School, you don't just join a school, you join a community of likeminded people who work in collaboration with the school so that every child can be the best that they can be.

HILLSIDE
INTERNATIONAL
KINDERGARTEN

(Founded 1999)

Head of School
Ms Audrey Tang

PYP coordinator
Ms Brenda Yuen

Status ESF Educational Services
Limited Kindergarten/Non-Profit

Boarding/day Day

Gender Coeducational

Language of instruction
English

Authorised IB programmes
PYP

Age Range 3 – 5 years

Number of pupils enrolled
366

Fees for 2021/22
HK$77,000

Address
43B Stubbs Road | **HONG KONG**

TEL +852 2540 0066

Email
admissions@hillside.edu.hk

Website
www.hillside.edu.hk

ESF Hillside International Kindergarten has eight classes, four in K1 and four in K2. Children start K1 in the year in which they are three years old. Children attend the kindergarten on a part time basis, five morning or five afternoon sessions per week, with sessions being three hours long. The school community is diverse with children and staff coming from a variety of ethnic groups, and we are able to draw on this cultural richness to enhance teaching and learning.

In January 2014 we were authorised as an International Baccalaureate (IB) World School, delivering the Primary Years Programme (PYP). Through their inquiry into four of the six PYP transdisciplinary themes each year, the children in both K1 and K2 develop knowledge and understanding, as well as skills and attitudes that they can use in Kindergarten and take with them into their future learning.

At ESF Hillside International Kindergarten, play is the primary mode of learning and the learning environment is set up to promote inquiry through a broad range of play opportunities that promote creativity, critical thinking, and communication. At Hillside International Kindergarten, the students develop their sense of self, and further develop the skills necessary to nurture positive friendships with other children. They become more aware of their place in the wider-world. Staff work with children on adult-initiated inquiries and to support those that are child-initiated.

The attributes of the learner profile have a significant place within our school and are acknowledged in the actions and achievements of both our children and staff.

ISLAND SCHOOL

(Founded 1967)

Principal Mr Stephen Loggie

MYP coordinator
Ms Andrea Walsh

DP coordinator Mr Matt Rappel

CP coordinator
Mr Roger Wilkinson

Status English Schools
Foundation School/Non-Profit

Boarding/day Day

Gender Coeducational

Language of instruction
English

Authorised IB programmes
MYP, DP, CP

Age Range 11 – 18 years

Number of pupils enrolled
1200

Fees for 2021/22
Years 7 to 11 HK$133,800
Years 12 to 13 HK$140,700
A one-off non-refundable capital
levy of HK$26,000 is required for
each new Year 7 student – and will
be reduced on a sliding scale for
students who join in later years.

Address
20 Borrett Road | **HONG KONG**

TEL +852 2524 7135

Email
school@online.island.edu.hk

Website www.island.edu.hk

At ESF Island School we do something different. Our focus is on igniting a passion for learning in every student. Teaching students facts and figures is no longer enough for them to succeed once they enter higher education and the workforce. We encourage students to problem solve, question and think creatively with new concepts and ideas. Students are encouraged to become resourceful, adaptable and confident learners.

Island School students come from all over the world, and central to our international heritage is the celebration and understanding of each others' cultures.

Students learn to care for each other, for the environment and for other people through our rich co-curricular programme and the family atmosphere of the House system.

Our academic record is excellent with students going on to many of the foremost universities and colleges in the world. In the senior years students can choose to study IB Diploma, IB Career-related and Business and Technology Education Council (BTEC) programmes. Island School prepares students for these qualifications with a broad-based middle school curriculum including International General Certificate of Secondary Education examinations (IGCSEs) and a wide range of exciting options in our unique futures curriculum. Our aim is to help students develop a passion for learning in arrange of areas, whether it be law or robotics and coding or music production.

Currently, Island School is going through a period of transition. The building at Borrett Road which has been Island School's home for 50 years is now being redeveloped. During this time the Island School community is using two temporary campuses in Sha Tin. The new campus will be opened in August 2022.

Temporary campuses:
Island School Sha Tin Wai (Years 7, 8, 12, 13):
Pok Hong Estate, Area 5A, Sha Tin, New Territories, Hong Kong
Island School Tai Wai (Years 9, 10, 11):
Sun Chui Estate, Sha Tin, New Territories, Hong Kong

ESF KENNEDY SCHOOL

(Founded 1961)

Interim Principal
Ms Mina Dunstan

PYP coordinator
Ms Yoon-Ah Lee

Status English Schools
Foundation School/Non-Profit

Boarding/day Day

Gender Coeducational

Language of instruction
English

Authorised IB programmes
PYP

Age Range 5 – 11 years

Number of pupils enrolled
900

Fees for 2021/22
Years 1 to 6 HK$115,800
Non-refundable capital levy:
HK$38,000 for each new Year 1
student

Address
19 Sha Wan Drive
Pokfulam | **HONG KONG**

TEL +852 2579 5600

Email
admissions@kennedy.edu.hk

Website
www.kennedy.edu.hk

ESF Kennedy School was established in 1961. The school occupies a pleasant location on the west of Hong Kong Island. It benefits from the use of the swimming and sporting facilities of the University of Hong Kong's Stanley Ho Sports Centre, which is adjacent to the school. Music, performing arts and physical education are strengths of the school. A strong interest in environmental and ecological issues is also a theme of the learning.

We offer a high-quality, modern, liberal education based on the International Baccalaureate Primary Years Programme (IB PYP) which is adapted to meet the needs of children living in Asia.

The school boasts a rich mix of nationalities and cultures among its 900 students. It received IB authorisation in December 2011 and had its tenth year evaluation visit in May 2020.

Occupying a pleasant location overlooking the South China Sea, the school has regular use of the adjacent Stanley Ho Sports Centre. All children receive regular swimming lessons in terms one and three. The school provides daily Chinese lessons for all students and also offers a very rich and varied extra-curricular programme.

KING GEORGE V SCHOOL

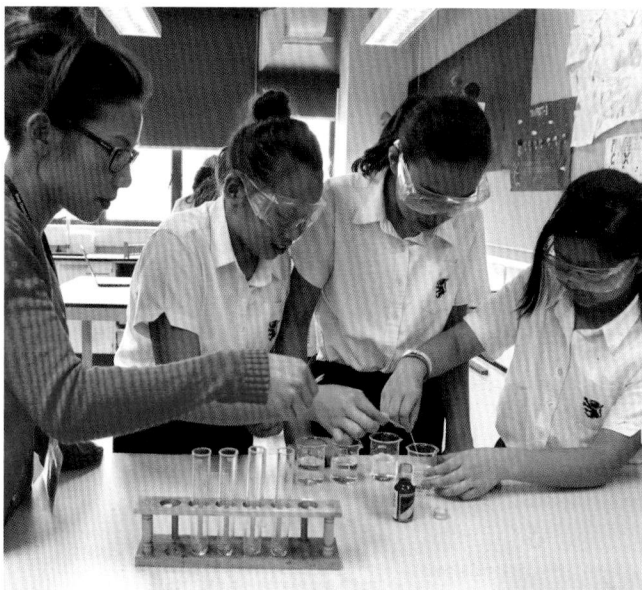

(Founded 1902)

Principal
Mr Mark Blackshaw

MYP coordinator
Mr Rowan Turner

DP coordinator
Mr Chris Wightman

Status English Schools
Foundation School/Non-Profit

Boarding/day Day

Gender Coeducational

Language of instruction
English

Authorised IB programmes
MYP, DP

Age Range 11 – 18 years

Number of pupils enrolled
1846

Fees for 2021/22
Years 7 to 11 HK$133,800
Years 12 to 13 HK$140,700
A one-off non-refundable capital
levy of HK$26,000 is required for
each new Year 7 student – and will
be reduced on a sliding scale for
students who join in later years.

Address
2 Tin Kwong Road
Homantin, Kowloon | **HONG KONG**

TEL +852 2711 3029

Email office@kgv.edu.hk

Website www.kgv.edu.hk

At ESF King George V School (KGV), our purpose is based on our belief that every student can 'be their own remarkable' as they achieve, improve and learn. Our vision is to create a 'school for one'; a place where each student feels that the school was created just for them. Through a lived experience, we want all to feel a deep sense of belonging, identity, and purpose.

We personalise learning so each and every person is supported and encouraged to achieve at a high level, and to develop holistically to be the best person they can be.

Our school thrives on a culture where a diversity of ideas, beliefs, and values are equally cherished, respected, and heard. We seek to continuously collaborate, innovate, and improve to make a difference in the communities we serve and lead.

The school is well known for its commitment to developing all aspects of student life and it has a fine tradition in academics, sport, music, drama, dance, community service, charity work and environmental sustainability. Our school has a very strong House system, which is run and inspired by our students and provides a wide range of learning opportunities and activities.

Our school promotes and celebrates our '*Honesty before Glory*' motto, which is underpinned by our three school values:

Honesty – Be truthful, fair, and authentic
Courage – Be vulnerable, brave, and resilient
Empathy – Be kind, understanding, and respectful

King George V School originated as the Kowloon British School in 1902, moving to its present site in 1936. The present name dates from 1948. Today it serves students from Kowloon and the New Territories. It occupies a large site of over ten acres and has its own AstroTurf sports field and all seasons swimming pool. There are two new buildings completed in 2013 (Performing Arts and a Science Block) on the school site and an extensive Learning Resource Centre (LRC).

Since 2017 our school has implemented the International Baccalaureate Middle Years Programme (IB MYP) in Years 7 to 9, after which the school delivers the International General Certificate of Secondary Education (IGCSE) in Years 10 and 11. Students then progress to study either the IB Diploma Programme or the more vocationally oriented Business and Technology Education Council (BTEC) applied learning programme.

KOWLOON JUNIOR SCHOOL

(Founded 1902)

Acting Principal
Dr Jamie Schmitz

PYP coordinator
Ms Dawn Doucette

Status English Schools
Foundation School/Non-Profit

Boarding/day Day

Gender Coeducational

Language of instruction
English

Authorised IB programmes
PYP

Age Range 5 – 11 years

Number of pupils enrolled
900

Fees for 2021/22
Years 1 to 6 HK$115,800
Non-refundable capital levy:
HK$38,000 for each new Year 1
student

Address
20 Perth Street
Homantin, Kowloon | **HONG KONG**

TEL +852 3765 8700

Email
office@kjs.edu.hk

Website
www.kjs.edu.hk

ESF Kowloon Junior School is a five-form entry school with 900 students. Our learning environments are designed to support our learners and help ignite their passions. Within our year group areas and dedicated Chinese area, the shared spaces ensure opportunities for true collaboration between students and teachers. Learning is further supported by access to a very spacious, light and airy library which houses a wide variety of books and resources. The dance studio, music suite, specialist creative arts area and multi-media room support students to express themselves in a wide variety of ways. Our gymnasium and diverse outdoor spaces, including an outdoor classroom designed by students, are used for a wide variety of sports, recreation and motivational learning experiences. The sustainable action by students of designing learning spaces at Kowloon Junior School includes further development of outdoor garden spaces to enhance student wellbeing. Our large hall and stage with professional light and sound, ensures our whole school community can enjoy a wide range of celebratory events.

The school's vision of 'Success for Every Child' permeates all levels of the school. Success at Kowloon Junior School is defined as Achieving, having Agency (the capacity to act intentionally, having voice, choice and ownership of learning), showing Respect (for self, others and the environment), taking advantage of Opportunities and having positive Wellbeing, we call these the AAROWs of Success at Kowloon Junior School!

Teachers and support staff take time to know their students, personalising learning goals to stretch learners and ensuring students are active participants in their learning process. Our Learning Enhancement Team provides excellent support for students with additional needs.

Kowloon Junior School works within the Primary Years Programme (PYP) framework which allows the school to incorporate the best educational practice from around the world and places a great deal of emphasis on developing international mindedness; positive learner attitudes; inquiry learning; creative, critical and collaborative thinking and learning through meaningful experiences. Our students enjoy stimulating learning within their homerooms together with the opportunity to learn with specialist teachers in music, dance, the arts, physical education and Chinese.

Students have an immense opportunity to pursue their passions through class unit of inquiry, specialist classes and the extensive co-curricular activities offered during the day, after school and on the weekends. Our students benefit from the ongoing working relationships that we have with ESF King George V School, our main feeder school. The close proximity of the schools ensures students have opportunities for support or extension whilst ensuring a smooth transition to the next phase of their education.

We warmly welcome visitors who would like to get a first hand experience of our school, Kowloon Junior School.

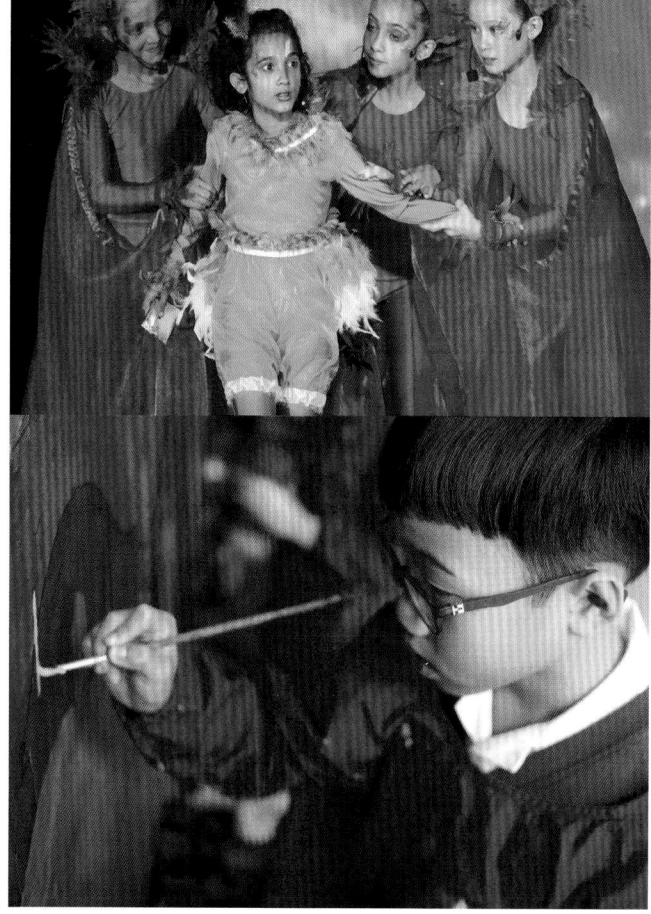

(Founded 1911)

Principal
Mr William (Bill) Garnett

PYP coordinator
Ms Chrissy Etchells-Bailey

Status English Schools
Foundation School/Non-Profit

Boarding/day Day

Gender Coeducational

Language of instruction
English

Authorised IB programmes
PYP

Age Range 4 – 11 years

Number of pupils enrolled
360

Fees for 2021/22
Years 1 to 6 HK$115,800
Non-refundable capital levy:
HK$38,000 for each new Year 1
student

Address
20 Plunkett's Road
The Peak | **HONG KONG**

TEL +852 2849 7211

Email
office@ps.edu.hk

Website
www.ps.edu.hk

ESF Peak School opened in 1911 and grew rapidly to serve the needs of the community in the area. We are a two-form entry school with 360 student places in Year 1 to Year 6. At Peak School, our mission is to become effective communicators, confident critical thinkers and enthusiastic life-long learners. In partnership with our community, we strive to have integrity and be socially responsible global citizens. The school prides itself on being a community school that respects and appreciates the contributions of everyone involved.

We offer the International Baccalaureate Primary Years Programme (IB PYP), which is based on an inquiry approach to learning. Our highly committed and skillful staff ensure that children experience the joy of learning through a curriculum that is relevant, significant, engaging and challenging. At Peak School, students are supported and encouraged to enhance their sense of wonder and creativity through exploration and experimentation, making mistakes and learning from them along the way. Students at Peak School have a lot of opportunity to exercise leadership skills and participate in a range of arts, environmental, and sporting activities.

The school is fortunate to be nestled within the lush hills of The Peak, where we are surrounded by nature and have easy access to trails. The school also boasts of a large playing field, a well-resourced library, and a cosy garden. Most of all, we are proud of the strong family atmosphere that the Peak School community has fostered for over a hundred years.

QUARRY BAY SCHOOL

(Founded 1926)

Interim Principal
Ms Sue Yee

PYP coordinator
Miss Ceri Hill

Status English Schools
Foundation School/Non-Profit

Boarding/day Day

Gender Coeducational

Language of instruction
English

Authorised IB programmes
PYP

Age Range 5 – 11 years

Number of pupils enrolled 720

Fees for 2021/22
Years 1 to 6 HK$115,800
Non-refundable capital levy:
HK$38,000 for each new Year 1
student

Address
6 Hau Yuen Path, Braemar Hill
North Point | **HONG KONG**

TEL +852 2566 4242

Email
office@qbs.edu.hk

Website
www.qbs.edu.hk

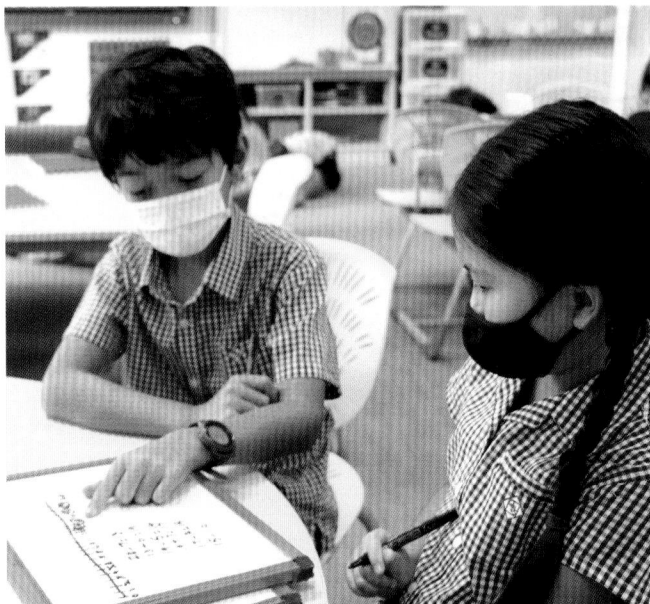

ESF Quarry Bay School opened over 80 years ago and was relocated to new, purpose-built premises at Braemar Hill, on the north eastern side of Hong Kong Island in 1985. In recent years, our school premises have benefitted from being refurbished and redesigned. This has resulted in the creation of an outstanding environment for teaching and learning. The school aims to encourage a love of learning by providing learning experiences both inside and outside the classroom that help to develop confident, enthusiastic and successful learners who are able to inquire about the world. We have 40 different nationalities represented in our school contributing to a rich and diverse learning environment. Quarry Bay School is an inclusive school where all students are included as part of the school community. We feel that all children have talents which can be developed and that all children can succeed. Our school provides equality of opportunity irrespective of race, gender, religion or disability for all children. We encourage our students to be active learners who work collaboratively and support one another.

Quarry Bay School prides itself on its high quality relationships; students and adults work collaboratively and support each other enabling all to reach their full potential. Children with a range of learning needs are effectively supported by the school's Individual Needs team. The school makes provision for children with moderate learning difficulties through the support of a specialist Learning Support teacher.

Quarry Bay School uses the International Baccalaureate's Primary Years Programme (PYP) as its curriculum framework. This transdisciplinary, concept-driven approach allows us to meet the challenges of educating in the 21st century by constructing a personalised programme that is engaging, relevant, challenging and significant for our diverse school population. Making use of collaborative planning in the development of teaching and learning engagements, teachers model lifelong learning and the attributes of the IB learner profile to the school community.

(Founded 2006)

Principal Dr Harry Brown

PYP coordinator
Mr Jason Doucette

MYP coordinator
Ms Brandy Stern

DP coordinator
Ms Jess Davey-Peel

CP coordinator Ms Wilma Shen

Status A Private Independent School Of The English Schools Foundation

Boarding/day Day

Gender Coeducational

Language of instruction
English

Authorised IB programmes
PYP, MYP, DP, CP

Age Range 5 – 18 years

Number of pupils enrolled
2100

Fees for 2021/22
Years 1 to 6 HK$124,000
Years 7 to 11 HK$166,000
Years 12 to 13 HK$167,900
Building Levy: HK$50,000 for each new Year 1 student

Address
5 Hang Ming Street, Ma On Shan, New Territories | **HONG KONG**

TEL +852 3556 3556

Email info@rchk.edu.hk

Website www.rchk.edu.hk

Exceed your expectations at RCHK!

ESF Renaissance College is an all-through International Baccalaureate (IB) school that creates global citizens that strive for excellence. We are a member of the English Schools Foundation (ESF); which is the largest provider of English medium international education in Hong Kong. Our vision is for every student to be the best that they can be, and our mission is to inspire creativity and nurture global citizens and leaders of the future. We do this by creating joyful learning environments led by a community of exceptional teachers who bring out the best in every child and by inspiring curious minds.

Renaissance College is a world-class co-educational independent IB World School offering all four of the IB programmes: Primary Years Programme (PYP), Middle Years Programme (MYP), Diploma Programme (DP) and Career-related Programme (CP). Students are educated from Year 1 to 13 on one site, guided and encouraged by a team of experienced international educators. Our student body comprises 40 nationalities with 20 languages represented. English is the medium of instruction with Chinese taught at every level. Technology is integrated college-wide throughout the curriculum and Creativity, Activity and Service (CAS) are integral to campus life. Students participate in a myriad of artistic, musical, sporting and service activities conducted on and off-campus.

Scholarships are offered to able and high-achieving secondary students, which include academic, music, visual arts, drama and sports. Scholarship criteria are based on demonstrated academic ability, artistic and creative aptitude, sporting prowess and a commitment to service and leadership. Financial aid is also offered to students and families in need. Contact admissions@rchk.edu.hk for more information!

(Founded 1982)

Principal Ms Carol Larkin

MYP coordinator Ms Janice Lee

DP coordinator Ms Kellie Fagan

CP coordinator
Mr Luke Smetherham

Status English Schools
Foundation School/Non-Profit

Boarding/day Day

Gender Coeducational

Language of instruction
English

Authorised IB programmes
MYP, DP, CP

Age Range 11 – 18 years

Number of pupils enrolled
1200

Fees for 2021/22
Years 7 to 11 HK$133,800
Years 12 to 13 HK$140,700
A one-off non-refundable capital
levy of HK$26,000 is required for
each new Year 7 student – and
will be reduced on a sliding scale

Address
3 Lai Wo Lane
Fo Tan, Sha Tin, New Territories
| **HONG KONG**

TEL +852 2699 1811

Email
info@shatincollege.edu.hk

Website
www.shatincollege.edu.hk

ESF Sha Tin College opened in September 1982 to meet the increasing demand for places from families in northern Kowloon and the New Territories. The school provides 1,250 places and has over 30 nationalities represented within the student body. Sha Tin College is committed to providing the best possible teaching and learning experiences for every individual through the medium of English. The education provided leads to a variety of internationally recognised examinations, granting students access to higher education and career opportunities worldwide.

Unique to Sha Tin College is a culture where we take responsibility for fulfilling our own potential and that of others for the good of humanity. Ample opportunities exist to challenge students to become mature, open-minded, caring, responsible and committed individuals with a passion for learning, creativity, sports and a sense of compassion.

With commanding views over the Sha Tin countryside, the College boasts a swimming pool and multipurpose sports hall, music rooms, drama studios, design and technology workshops, science labs and a food technology centre, senior school centre, climbing walls, and a counselling and wellbeing centre.

As part of quality assurance, Sha Tin College embraces review and accreditation processes with the International Baccalaureate (IB) five-year review; English Schools Foundation (ESF) internal review and ESF stakeholder surveys. These processes assist the school in its strategic developmental planning.

SHA TIN JUNIOR SCHOOL

(Founded 1988)

Principal
Mrs Rehana Shanks

PYP coordinator
Ms Trudy Mcmillin

Status English Schools Foundation School/Non-Profit

Boarding/day Day

Gender Coeducational

Language of instruction
English

Authorised IB programmes
PYP

Age Range 5 – 11 years

Number of pupils enrolled
900

Fees for 2021/22
Years 1 to 6 HK115,800
Non-refundable capital levy: HK$38,000 for each new Year 1 student

Address
3A Lai Wo Lane
Fo Tan, Sha Tin, New Territories |
HONG KONG

TEL +852 2692 2721

Email
info@sjs.esf.edu.hk

Website
www.sjs.edu.hk

ESF Sha Tin Junior School opened in 1988 and provides an English medium education for the children of families who reside in the New Territories of Hong Kong. We share a safe, secure and well-resourced site with our partner secondary school, Sha Tin College.

A recent school refurbishment programme has ensured the provision of new facilities and the upgrade of existing learning spaces for our 900 students. Facilities include well resourced Learning and Access Centres, a gymnasium, a performing arts studio, two music rooms, a Maker Space and a DARC (Design, Arts, Recording and Cooking) Room. Shared facilities (with ESF Sha Tin College) include an indoor swimming pool and a sports hall.

Our school vision – 'Learning for Life' – is underpinned by four core values. In order to aspire towards a life of learning, we encourage our students to focus on:

• Wellbeing
• Inclusivity
• Flexible minds
• Making a difference.

We offer a balanced programme ensuring learners have the opportunity to develop academically, mentally, socially and physically. Our programme is guided by the philosophy of Positive Education and is inquiry-based in outlook. Individual needs are catered for through an inclusive approach, implementing a range of teaching and learning approaches.

All stakeholders are encouraged to develop resilience, use a growth mindset and a 'can do' attitude. We empower learners to take meaningful action and realise the impact each and every one of us can have in reaching the 2030 Global Goals.

Sha Tin Junior School is fully authorised to offer the International Baccalaureate Primary Years Programme (IB PYP).

SOUTH ISLAND SCHOOL

(Founded 1977)	**Authorised IB programmes** MYP, DP, CP
Principal Mr Tom Vignoles	**Age Range** 11 – 18 years
MYP coordinator Mr Shaine Bushell	**Number of pupils enrolled** 1430
DP coordinator Ms Kelly Diaz	**Fees for 2021/22** Years 7 to 11 HK$133,800 Years 12 to 13 HK$140,700 Non-refundable capital levy: HK$26,000 for each new Year 7 student
CP coordinator Ms Nicola Bosson	
Status English Schools Foundation School/Non-Profit	**Address** 50 Nam Fung Road | **HONG KONG**
Boarding/day Day	**TEL** +852 2555 9313
Gender Coeducational	**Email** sis@sis.edu.hk
Language of instruction English	**Website** www.sis.edu.hk

ESF South Island School is a dynamic and innovative school, located in a green setting on the south side of Hong Kong Island. It caters for 1,430 students from a diversity of backgrounds and nationalities.

The school prides itself on its focus on student well-being, its personalised curriculum and its very high academic standards, developing students as global citizens and leaders of a sustainable future. South Island School fosters a student skill set which is creative and contemporary, and develops community responsibility under the banner 'Making a Difference'. The school makes excellent provision for children with moderate learning difficulties through a Learning Support Centre with 24 places. The school is authorised to offer International Baccalaureate Middle Years Programme (IB MYP), International General Certificate of Secondary Education (IGCSE), IB Diploma Programme (IBDP) and IB Career-related Programme (IBCP).

ESF Tsing Yi International Kindergarten

TSING YI INTERNATIONAL KINDERGARTEN

(Founded 1999)

Acting Head of School
Ms Suzannah Large

PYP coordinator
Ms Suzannah Large

Status ESF Educational Services Limited Kindergarten /Non-Profit

Boarding/day Day

Gender Coeducational

Language of instruction
English

Authorised IB programmes
PYP

Age Range 3 – 5 years

Number of pupils enrolled 352

Fees for 2021/22
HK$84,200

Address
Maritime Square,
33 Tsing King Road, Tsing Yi,
New Territories | **HONG KONG**

TEL +852 2436 3355

Email
kinder@tyk.edu.hk

Website
www.tyk.edu.hk

ESF Tsing Yi International Kindergarten has eight classes, four in K1 and four in K2. Children start K1 in the year in which they are three years old. Children attend the kindergarten on a part time basis, five morning or five afternoon sessions per week, with sessions being three hours long. The school community is diverse with children coming from 15 ethnic groups. The cultural richness within the school enhances the learning.

In July 2013 we were authorised as an International Baccalaureate (IB) World School, delivering the Primary Years Programme (PYP). Through their inquiry into four of the six PYP transdisciplinary themes each year, the children in both K1 and K2 develop knowledge and understanding, as well as skills and attitudes that they can use in kindergarten and take with them into their future learning.

At Tsing Yi International Kindergarten, play is the primary mode of learning and the learning environment is set up to promote inquiry through a broad range of play opportunities that promote creativity, critical thinking, and communication. At Tsing Yi International Kindergarten the students develop their sense of self, and further develop the skills necessary to nurture positive friendships with other children.

They become more aware of their place in the wider-world. Staff work with children on adult-initiated inquiries and to support those that are child-initiated. The attributes of the learner profile have a significant place within our school and are acknowledged in the actions and achievements of both our children and staff.

ESF Tung Chung International Kindergarten

ESF 英基 TUNG CHUNG
INTERNATIONAL KINDERGARTEN

(Founded 2016)

Principal
Ms Allison Banbury

PYP coordinator
Ms Cathy Boon

Status ESF Educational Services
Limited Kindergarten / Non-
Profit

Boarding/day Day

Gender Coeducational

Language of instruction
English

Authorised IB programmes
PYP

Age Range 3 – 5 years

Number of pupils enrolled 312

Fees for 2021/22
English Stream HK$86,000
Bilingual Stream HK$100,400

Address
1/F, Commercial Accommodation,
The Visionary,
1 Ying Hong Street,
Tung Chung, Lantau,
New Territories | **HONG KONG**

TEL +852 3742 3500

Email
admissions@tck.edu.hk

Website
www.tck.edu.hk

The custom-designed school for three to five year olds in Tung Chung opened in 2016, and offers both English and Bilingual Streams. It is structured into morning and afternoon three-hour sessions for both K1 and K2. The space is functional, adaptable and well-resourced to meet the dynamic needs of the three to five year olds who inhabit it. The spaces are not only carefully and intentionally planned, but are also places of beauty that support learning, stimulate imaginations, nurture children, families and staff – and truly inspire the wonderful memories of childhood. Both indoor and outdoor spaces, materials, technology and equipment intrigue, invite, and stimulate students to move, dance, role play, create art, develop language skills and investigate scientific principles.

The school reflects our aspiration for each of our children to flourish. Our goal is to nourish each child, individually, and meet their changing social and emotional needs every day. We strive to provide children with strong foundational skills for future academic success and also to equip them to participate as flexible, creative thinkers and engaged citizens in an increasingly complex and interdependent world.

WEST ISLAND
SCHOOL

(Founded 1991)

Principal Mr Christopher Sammons

MYP coordinator Ms Clare Haworth

DP coordinator
Mrs Helen Devine Costa

CP coordinator Ms Emily Buckland

Status English Schools
Foundation School/Non-Profit

Boarding/day Day

Gender Coeducational

Language of instruction
English

Authorised IB programmes
MYP, DP, CP

Age Range 11 – 18 years

Number of pupils enrolled
1220

Fees for 2021/22
Years 7 to 11 HK$133,800
Years 12 to 13 HK$140,700
A one-off non-refundable capital
levy of HK$26,000 is required for
each new Year 7 student – and will
be reduced on a sliding scale for
students who join in later years.

Address
250 Victoria Road
Pokfulam | **HONG KONG**

TEL +852 2819 1962

Email wis@wis.edu.hk

Website www.wis.edu.hk

ESF West Island School is a world class co-educational International Baccalaureate (IB) World School. The school motto 'Strength from Diversity' reflects that the school caters for students from over 40 countries in a modern building overlooking the University of Hong Kong and the vibrant shipping lanes of the South China Sea. The school has a strong focus on the value of international-mindedness and the importance of community.

It has a reputation for academic excellence balanced with compassion and service beyond the classroom. The vast majority of students graduate to a range of international universities with 90% achieving their first choice. In 2021, the average score of the IB diploma was 40 with 60% achieving 40 or more.

Students are encouraged to become 'responsible global citizens' as part of the mission of the school. Training for leadership roles within the school and beyond is a strength which the school believes heralds access to better choices beyond Year 13. Over 100 activities are offered termly and one week annually focuses exclusively on Creativity, Activity and Service (CAS) projects within Asia. Students meet individually with tutors regularly to discuss their academic progress and commitment to CAS.

The school has purpose built specialist rooms in all subjects and in particular: specialist science laboratories, a modern library, performance space for drama and dance, two gymnasiums, state of the art design technology workshops incorporating a graphics studio, textiles and food, three art studios, seven music studios and two music classrooms both with raised performance platforms, outdoor courts for a range of sports, a newly renovated 25-metre swimming pool and a large auditorium. The proximity to the University of Hong Kong playing fields provides further sport facilities. West Island School is a one-to-one laptop school with digital literacy as part of the curriculum.

Curriculum

West Island School is an authorised IB Diploma school offering Diploma Programme for 300 students at Post-16. Since 2018, West Island School offers the IB Career-related Programme (IBCP). International General Certificate of Secondary Education examinations (IGCSEs) and some Business and Technology Education Council (BTEC) courses are offered for Pre 16 students. West Island School is an authorised Middle Years Programme (MYP) school. As an IB World School, we share a common philosophy – a commitment to high-quality, challenging, international education – that we believe is important for our students.

WU KAI SHA INTERNATIONAL KINDERGARTEN

(Founded 2009)

Principal
Ms Frances Hurley

PYP coordinator
Ms Aylin Kip

Status ESF Educational Services Limited Kindergarten /Non-Profit

Boarding/day Day

Gender Coeducational

Language of instruction
English

Authorised IB programmes
PYP

Age Range 3 – 5 years

Number of pupils enrolled
343

Fees for 2021/22
HK$85,500

Address
599 Sai Sha Road
Ma On Shan,
Sha Tin | **HONG KONG**

TEL +852 2435 5291

Email
kinder@wksk.edu.hk

Website
www.wksk.edu.hk

ESF Wu Kai Sha International Kindergarten is located in Ma On Shan and opened in August 2009. We cater for children aged three to five years old and follow the International Baccalaureate Primary Years Programme (PYP). The school was authorised as an IB World School in July 2013.

In partnership with families we aim to develop confident, creative, knowledgeable children who respect all others and participate actively within the school community. Our inquiry-based curriculum encourages children to explore relevant concepts and ideas through child-centred play and exploration, real life experiences and focused learning and teaching activities, allowing them to develop a range of understanding, knowledge and skills in all areas of the curriculum.

We have a wonderful team of highly qualified and experienced teaching staff who are both nurturing and knowledgeable about early childhood education. Children work closely with their class teacher and educational assistants to develop a range of skills, knowledge and understanding. A range of groupings are used to enable all children to learn effectively. Learning is planned to cater for the needs of all children and is differentiated for individual children's skill levels.

We strive to provide an engaging and enriching environment that stimulates children's curiosity and supports independent learning. The school has large, bright spaces for learning and play and children spend their time in classrooms, shared areas and in the indoor and outdoor play areas. All classrooms have an excellent range of resources which includes a wealth of technology resources. We also have a dedicated, well stocked library from which children and families can borrow a range of books, story sacks and other resources.

EtonHouse®
International School • Suzhou
苏州伊顿外籍人员子女学校

(Founded 2003)

Head of School
Murray Fowler

PYP coordinator
Natasha D'Costa

MYP coordinator
Rodney Springer

DP coordinator
Rajesh Kripalani

Status Private

Boarding/day Day

Gender Coeducational

Language of instruction
English

Authorised IB programmes
PYP, MYP, DP

Age Range 2 – 18 years

Number of pupils enrolled
134

Address
102 Kefa Road
Suzhou Science & Technology Town
Suzhou, Jiangsu
215163 | CHINA

TEL +86 512 6825 5666

Email
enquiry-sz@etonhouse.com.cn

Website
www.suzhou.etonhouse.com

EtonHouse International School Suzhou is a small school with a big heart. With class sizes of between 10-20 students, only one class per age group and a student to teacher ratio of 6:1, at EtonHouse your child will be much more than a number. Every student can make a difference, no matter how gifted or otherwise.

EtonHouse International School Suzhou is part of the world-renowned EtonHouse International Education Group, with more than 100 schools throughout Asia,

We are a well-established IB World Continuum school for students from 6-18 years old. The PYP was accredited in 2008, MYP in 2011 and DP in 2016. Our Early Years Programme is based on the Regio Emilia approach and blends seamlessly with our Primary Years Programme.

We are an inclusive school that welcomes students of all abilities. EtonHouse believes that every student can succeed; any student who wishes to pursue the IB Diploma Programme is allowed and encouraged.

Our student population is highly multicultural. Despite being a small school, we have students from 22 nations, and no nationality represents more than 24% of the population.

Despite the small scale, EtonHouse International School Suzhou has all the facilities you would expect from a much larger school, with a heated swimming pool, all-weather sports field, gymnasium, well-stocked library, and assembly hall / theatre. The thoughtfully considered and aesthetically designed campus is set among the hills and trees west of downtown Suzhou, a learning environment which provides students with many opportunities for exploration, and provocations that support the rich inquiry-based learning programme offered at the campus.

European International School HCMC

EUROPEAN
International School
HO CHI MINH CITY

An **inspired** school

Head of School
Mr. John Veitch

PYP coordinator
Colin Attwood

MYP coordinator
Martin Grist

DP coordinator
Erin Tacey

Status Private

Boarding/day Day

Gender Coeducational

Language of instruction
English

Authorised IB programmes
PYP, MYP, DP

Age Range 2 – 18 years

Number of pupils enrolled
600

Fees
VND 229,600,000 – 632,000,000

Address
730 Le Van Mien Street
Thao Dien Ward, Thu Duc City
Ho Chi Minh City
70000 | VIETNAM

TEL +8428 7300 7257

Email
info@eishcmc.com

Website
www.eishcmc.com

With possibly the most convenient location in Thao Dien, the European International School Ho Chi Minh City (EIS) is the only boutique international school, set in lush garden surroundings, offering the International Baccalaureate (IB) continuum of studies for children aged 2-18.

Our vibrant, unified campus is a place where students, teachers and parents of all grade levels and different backgrounds interact freely with each other within a home-from-home, tranquil village atmosphere. EIS offers a truly diverse 'melting pot' of 40+ nationalities and global cultures, where students are encouraged to find their unique voice, to pursue languages, and to contribute to all aspects of school life.

EIS teachers, with over 13 years' average experience, are well-practiced in individualized learning methods. With a very low student-to-teacher ratio, particularly in the middle-high school sections of the school, students benefit directly from more frequent access to teachers.

Graduating IB Diploma students consistently achieve well-above the world averages, and have achieved acceptances into prestigious universities worldwide, often with significant merit-based scholarships.

EIS provides an outstanding world-class education for students, evidenced by our full accreditation status with the Council of International Schools (CIS).

Being a medium-sized school, we are large enough to offer a wide range of educational opportunities, while also being intimate enough to provide the unique personal attention and care that each child deserves.

Global Indian International School

(Founded 2002)

Principal
Melissa Maria

Academic Supervisor
Deepika Sodhi

Chairman and Co-Founder
Atul Temurnikar

PYP coordinator
Manju Nair

DP coordinator
Deepa Chandrasekaran

Status Private

Boarding/day Day

Gender Coeducational

Language of instruction
English

Authorised IB programmes
PYP, DP

Age Range 2 1/2 – 18 years

Number of pupils enrolled
2850

Address
27 Punggol Field Walk
Singapore
828649 | SINGAPORE
TEL +65 6914 7100

Website
singapore.globalindianschool.org

Global Indian International School (GIIS), operated by the Global Schools Foundation, is a frontrunner in international school education from Nursery to Grade 12, in Asia. The foundation manages a blossoming network of 22 campuses across 7 countries with a vision of becoming the global role model for teaching and learning through its award-winning holistic framework of 9 GEMS.

GIIS has two campuses in Singapore – East Coast Campus from Nursery to Grade 10 and SMART Campus, Punggol, from Nursery to Grade 12.

Our flagship campus, GIIS SMART Campus with a capacity of 3.5 K students is a school of the future. The campus offers cutting-edge facilities like digital classrooms, video conferencing, collaborative learning spaces, data analytics in sports and more than 40 skill-based studios, all of which add up to create an environment for students to effectively explore a world of ideas.

The school offers complete international curricula – IB Primary Years Programme (IB PYP), Cambridge Lower Secondary Programme, IGCSE and IB Diploma Programme (IB DP). Students begin their educational journey with a strong foundational framework like IB PYP, that sparks curiosity and makes them inquiry-driven. In middle-year grades, the Cambridge curriculum offers them analytical skills and a stronghold over diverse subjects, thus preparing them for the challenges of IBDP in Grades 11 and 12.

The IB DP at GIIS is a much sought after course with high achieving students, trained and qualified teachers and NextGen facilities at the SMART Campus. In the last 15 years, GIIS has produced 33 IB World Toppers (45/45 points) and 37 near-perfect scorers (44/45 points).

Close to 250 students graduate every year from the school. The school's unique performance-measuring metrics, called 7S, tracks and monitors each student's academic and all-round progress thus enabling teachers to roll-out a systematic improvement plan.

Our graduates are placed at prestigious universities across the world including the University of Cambridge, University of Oxford, University of California, Cornell University, Imperial College London, National University of Singapore, Nanyang Technological University, and many more.

An amalgamation of great factors including our international curricula, excellent teachers and infrastructure, and holistic education contribute towards making our students well-rounded individuals and global leaders of the 21st-century.

Promising Futures

School Director David Brazeau

PYP coordinator Monika Kala

MYP coordinator Dahlia Atabani

DP coordinator Rajeev Pargaien

Status Private

Boarding/day Mixed

Gender Coeducational

Language of instruction English

Authorised IB programmes PYP, MYP, DP

Age Range 2.5 – 18 years

Address
A-12, Sector 132
Noida Expressway, Uttar
Pradesh **201304 | INDIA**

TEL +91 9711 000626

Email info@genesisgs.edu.in

Website www.
genesisglobalschool.edu.in

Situated in Noida, a satellite city of Delhi, Genesis Global School is part of the National Capital Region (Delhi NCR). The School is spread over a 30-acre campus, with efficient connectivity via an Expressway. It is an hour's drive from Indira Gandhi International Airport, Delhi and around 25 minutes' drive from cosmopolitan South Delhi.

Genesis Global School has become a hub of national and international educational excellence, where every child is important and accepted for who they are. At GGS we ensure that our students have exposure to the best in current global practices, provide them with a truly holistic environment where modern facilities and high-quality teaching and learning practices allow our school ideals to be developed.

Our school ideals depicted in the School logo – the hexagon are: International mindedness; Educational Excellence; Integrity and Persistence; Resilience; Stewardship; Compassion and Care. These six pillars underpin our mission statement making them the guiding light of our practices.

Our Mission Statement is: "GGS graduates will be responsible global citizens empowered to contribute to society in various capacities by providing them the freedom to be, to act, to impress and to dream. GGS incorporates an inquiry–based curriculum and extensive co-curricular experiences, acknowledging the role of community voice and student agency."

A GGS education allows students to achieve their potential and take their place in the world. We continuously strive to develop and improve our curriculum to meet the needs of all learners in an ever-changing world both inside and outside the classroom.

As an IB World School, Cambridge accredited centre and a member of the Council of International Schools (CIS) GGS is also part of a community working collaboratively to shape international education. We are committed to incorporating

international and intercultural perspectives into our programmes so that students can move forward with the attitudes, knowledge and understanding that will provide them with a solid base wherever their studies or work may take them.

Junior School

The Junior School comprises of Grades Pre-Nursery to 5 and follows the IB Primary Years Curriculum (PYP). Project based and experiential learning opportunities allow our students to be encouraged and enable them to become independent critical thinkers who can take increasing responsibility for their learning. Our student to teacher ratio is 13:1 which enables every child to have the support they need. Students' progress is regularly assessed both formally and informally by staff to ensure every child reaches their potential.

Middle School

The Middle School (grades 6, 7, 8) follow the MYP framework of the IB curriculum. The skill-based, concept-based and context driven curriculum of the middle school enables our learners to be part of the teaching and learning process. The inquiry-based teaching approach ensures every child's voice is heard and every learner gets the best support to reach their highest potential.

Our curriculum is planned to consider student differences and is accessible to all. We give students the opportunity to find the area they are strongest in and to grow in it.

The teaching and learning approaches ensure that the learners explore and understand WHAT they are learning, HOW they are learning things and most importantly, WHY they are learning. The focus is not only on teaching academics but having students use their knowledge and skills in different known and unknown situations. By applying these skills they become lifelong learners, develop learner attributes such as being knowledgeable inquirers, who are

caring and open minded, who value everything and everyone who are ready to be global citizens and successful leaders.

Senior School

The Senior School has two phases: MYP 4-5 and DP year 1 and 2. In the senior school students are given the opportunity to specialise and explore subjects of their interest. Though academic rigour increases, students are still taught with a great focus on the development of their skills through an inquiry-based approach to teaching and learning. Complimenting the individualised teaching, our senior students also have the extensive guidance of the Support Department which is a combination of student counselling services, ESL support for international students, learning needs support and university counselling. This ensures that the students are provided with everything they need for a well-balanced life and studies to be successful learners both at and beyond their time at GGS.

Students in Residence

Our boarding houses are equipped with modern facilities providing "a home away from home". The School has air-conditioned residences for boys and girls, where they are given personal attention and care by experienced, professional House Parents.

Genesis Global School endeavours to nurture resilient, holistic, empathetic & lifelong learners in a multi-cultural environment, for a sustainable future.

Guangdong Shunde Desheng School

德勝學校（國際）

DESHENG SCHOOL (INTERNATIONAL)

(Founded 2011)

Head of School Ms. Chen Qingnian

DP coordinator Mr. Yu Yue

Status Private

Boarding/day Mixed

Gender Coeducational

Language of instruction English

Authorised IB programmes DP

Age Range 12 – 18 years

Number of pupils enrolled 300

Fees RMB120,000 – RMB170,000

Address Minxing Road, New District Daliang, Shunde, Guangdong **528300 | CHINA**

TEL +86 0757 22325121

Email admin.dsi@ desheng-school.com

Website www.desheng-school.com

A caring and innovative school that aims to transform students from good to great, Guangdong Shunde Desheng School has an illustrious history of achievements and has consistently ranked as a top school in Shunde, China based on its sterling academic results and student performance.

In 2011 under the visionary leadership of its Chairman, Mr. Chen Ji Ye, the school started the international education division to prepare students for an overseas education. The division is now known as Desheng School (International) (DSI).

DSI was accredited by the Cambridge Assessment International Education (CAIE) in 2014 to offer the Cambridge IGCSE and International A Levels. In 2015, the school was accredited by the International Baccalaureate Organisation to offer the International Baccalaureate Diploma Programme (IBDP).

DSI is proud to have:

- A Student-Centric Educational Philosophy
SCHOOL VISION
A global centre of excellence that promotes holistic education.
OUR MISSION
To nurture independent life-long learners who strive for excellence and serve with compassion.
SCHOOL CORE VALUES
R.I.S.E. – Respect. Integrity. Self-Discipline. Excellence.
DESIRED STUDENTS OUTCOMES
To be Scholars, Leaders, Global Citizens.
- A World Class Learning Environment
DSI is located in a newly built complex with state-of-the-art facilities. The environment is ideal for students to fully engage in academic and non-academic activities including the multi-media library, Artificial Intelligence laboratory, range of sports facilities and more facilities that meet the needs of teachers and students.

- Professional Educators
In DSI, our outstanding teaching staff includes experienced IB trained teachers, and are integral to the implementation of the curriculum. They are divided into the Pedagogical Team and the Student Development Team, who work together to lead, care and inspire, ensuring the overall wellbeing of students. The school is proud to have Dr. Hon Chiew Weng, former principal of Hwa Chong Institution, Singapore, as Education Director to enrich its management team.

- Holistic Education
DSI offers a wide range of subject options to cater to varying needs of students in line with the requirements of Cambridge IGCSE and IBDP.

From 2017 to 2021, five cohorts have graduated from DSI. 90% of the IBDP students have enrolled in top 50 universities in the world, including Oxford University, Imperial College London, University College London in the United Kingdom, New York University and University of California (various campuses) in the United States of America, University of Toronto in Canada, The Australian National University and University of Melbourne in Australia, and National University of Singapore and Nanyang Technological University in Singapore.

In terms of innovation, the school has a number of programmes that prepare them for the changing dynamics of the world. These comprise the Champions of Innovation, focusing on Artificial Intelligence, Cyber Safety, 3D Printing, and other cutting-edge information and communications technology. In the 1st International Artificial Intelligence Fair held in Beijing, Desheng School AI Challenge Team was awarded the Qomolangma Prize (The First Prize) for their project "Research on Nursing Home Caring System Based on

Deep Learning". This marked a milestone in DSI's history of developing the innovative potential of students.

DSI also puts emphasis on language development and critical thinking. In addition to compulsory Super Curriculum subjects such as Philosophy of Disciplines and Research Skills, we offer a wide variety of Co-Curricular Activities. Students gain national and international exposure through platforms such as the Model United Nation conferences, future problem solving programmes, as well as Experiential Programmes (Local/Overseas/University).

In terms of caring for the well-being of students, the House system, leadership education system, student care system and Career, Opportunities and Guidance team contribute to a dynamic culture on campus and inculcates a sense of camaraderie and excellence among DSI students.

With strong emphasis on both academic and student-centric activities, the school is well positioned to nurture its students to become Scholars, Leaders, and Global Citizens.
- Admission
For application enquiries, kindly contact the school directly.

Greenwood High International School

GREENWOOD HIGH
INTERNATIONAL SCHOOL

Head of School
Mr. Aloysius D'Mello

DP coordinator
Nishanth Nagavar

Status Private

Boarding/day Mixed

Gender Coeducational

Language of instruction
English

Authorised IB programmes
DP

Age Range 6 – 19 years

Address
No.8-14, Chickkawadayara Pura
Near Heggondahalli, Gunjur
Post, Varthur via
Bengaluru, Karnataka
560087 | INDIA

TEL +91 80 22010500

Email
admissions.intl@
greenwoodhigh.edu.in

Website
www.greenwoodhigh.edu.in

Greenwood High students pride themselves in being able to not only balance academics, sports and co-curricular activities, but excel in them. Greenwood High IB results far outshine the world average; this year (2019) two students achieved a perfect score of 45 in IBDP, in IGCSE results 78% students received a distinction and 20.2% students secured a merit. The school has produced India toppers in both IGCSE and ICSE. And yet, these very same industrious students immerse themselves in theatre and with support from their theatre, art and music teachers, and their talents blossomed into a musical 'Annie' that was compared to professional theatre productions. To encourage them further, the school has held various workshops including one from the prestigious Globe Education.

The school is an open art gallery, for its hallways and open spaces display artwork by the promising young artists. In sports too, the students are champions, for they have won various Basketball, Soccer and Badminton championships. The students are very socially aware, and the Model United Nations debates and forums begin from middle school itself, so that they grow into international minded global citizens.

Greenwood High students are extremely involved in social projects and have contributed to various causes. Our student designs include a six wheeled hand cart with steering, gears and brakes to help street vendors maneuver their hand carts over uneven, hilly terrains, and this has won her the

President's Award. Another student had developed a cell phone app 'Corner Shop' "aiming to give small time vendors a platform to boost their sales." One student developed an App for the blind to help them in purchasing groceries and was hailed by IBM while another launched an online debate forum at global level, which was funded by Google and Microsoft. One student has been awarded the Diana Legacy Award for setting up science laboratories in schools for the underprivileged.

The CAS students volunteer in hospitals, paint government run schools for the underprivileged, create breast cancer awareness, clean streets and recycle waste. They raise funds for education and health in rural areas. The CAS students also worked on a social project in Prague.

The students of Greenwood High aim high and reach higher. This year IBDP students have received acceptances in over 200 universities around the world, for many have been accepted in Ivy League colleges, with scholarships to a total of 7.1 million USD. Greenwood High already has students in the University of Pennsylvania, Columbia University, Cornell University, Brown University, Johns Hopkins, Georgia Tech, UCLA, Berkeley, Duke, Imperial College London, to name a few. Indeed, they all take the school motto 'Rooted in Knowledge' very seriously, and while spreading out their wings to soar high, remain rooted deeply in knowledge.

Hangzhou World Foreign Language School

杭 州 上 海 世 界 外 国 语 中 学
HANGZHOU WORLD FOREIGN LANGUAGE SCHOOL

(Founded 2018)

Head of School
Cen Xiaohua

DP coordinator
Wang Yanzhen

Status Private

Boarding/day Boarding

Gender Coeducational

Language of instruction
English, Chinese

Authorised IB programmes
DP

Age Range 13 – 18 years

Number of pupils enrolled 42

Fees
Boarding: RMB130,000

Address
66 Muge Road, Banshan Street
Gongshu District
Hangzhou, Zhejiang
310000 | CHINA

TEL +86 189 5814 3128

Email
hzsw_dp@wfl.sh.edu.cn

Website
hz.shwfl.edu.cn

Hangzhou World Foreign Language School (HZWFLS) is the second school established by Shanghai World Foreign Language Education Group (WFL Education) after the Shanghai branch to provide the complete IB curriculum in China. The school features three departments, namely, the Bilingual Junior Department, the Integrated Curriculum Junior Department and the International Senior Department of IBDP. To aim to cultivate "a young Chinese with a modern and global view", the school strives to explore and practice quality education to seek and develop the compassion, elegance, and forthright within the students. By Participation and Practice (P&P) in Cooperation and Creativity (C&C), the students' learner autonomy is augmented, potentials developed, abilities in collaboration fostered, and creativity nurtured.

The IBDP of HZWFLS was established in 2019 and was officially authorized by IBO in 2021 to become the first IBDP school in Hangzhou.

Located beside the Banshan National Forest Park, the school lies in the embrace of mountains and streams. With the soothing sceneries of nature, the campus is a perfect venue for students to pursue their academic success.

The school offers an IBDP course, which aims to develop inquiring, knowledgeable and caring young people who help to create a better and more peaceful world through intercultural understanding and respect.

The curriculum system consists of six subject groups, which together focus on the three core courses. Through approaches to teaching and learning, the courses train students to become independent thinkers, lifelong learners, well-grounded generalists, and participants in global contexts.

The course has no geographical restrictions and is recognized by all mainstream universities in the world. There is a wide range of universities to choose from, which can avoid the impact of changes in visa policies of various countries to the greatest extent.

All teaching faculty members of HZWFLS are certified by IBO, including established teachers with ample teaching experience as well as excellent Master's graduates commanding cutting-edge knowledge of their respective subjects. Currently, HZWFLS adopts small class teaching that our overall teacher-student ratio is around 1:2, the ratio will not exceed 1:5 in five years.

Hangzhou Greentown Yuhua School

Head of School
Zha Pinyang

MYP coordinator
Wang Xudong

Status Private

Boarding/day Mixed

Gender Coeducational

Language of instruction
Chinese, English

Authorised IB programmes
MYP

Address
No. 532 Wenyi West Road
Hangzhou, Zhejiang
310012 | CHINA

TEL +86 571 88477561

Email
greentownedu@163.com

Website
www.hzlcyhcz.cn

Hangzhou Greentown Yuhua School is a fully licensed, private school located at 532 Wenyi West Road, Hangzhou, China. Our mission is to cultivate global citizens with integrity, a rational spirit, cultural literacy and a strong sense of duty; to advocate for professionalism and a healthy lifestyle. We encourage our students to have global literacy, enable them to respect different cultures and beliefs and integrate into multicultural world. The Education Philosophy at Greentown Yuhua provides the students both academic and self-development educational streams, allowing for full cognitive and social development, meeting the requirements and needs of each individual student. Moreover, campus Life at Greentown Yuhua is devoted to improving the quality of student's life on campus. Activities include various student societies and clubs, such as tae kwon do, piano, painting, studios and foreign language courses. The school motto is "Being Benovelent and Tolerant while seeking the Truth". We are dedicated in providing a well-rounded educational experience for our students; both as individuals and as a collective.

Since its foundation in 1992, Greentown Yuhua School has been striving to achieve educational excellence by providing an all-round quality education that will serve the needs for the future development of local community. In previous years, the school was awarded "The National Outstanding Private School" by the Ministry of Education. Since 2000, Zhejiang Greentown Real Estate Group (a national Top 2 real estate company in year 2010) has invested more than 1 billion yuan RMB in the school. And the school now takes up an area

of 16.867 hectares, with the construction area about 70,000 square meters. The school is a modern institution with a beautifully landscaped environment and first-class facilities.

We provide Middle Years Programme for students from year 7 to year 9. In this program we are committed to cultivating learners to be inquirers, knowledgeable, thinkers, communicators, principled, open-minded, caring, risk-takers, balanced and reflective. In order to help students achieve these attributes, the school provides English language acquisition, Chinese language and literature, individuals and societies, mathematics, design, drama, music, and visual arts, science, physical and health education.

We encourage our students to become active, compassionate and lifelong learners who understand that other people, with their differences, can also be valuable. We participate in the construction of international courses based on the domestic compulsory curriculum to help students adapt to overseas study.

We have a faculty of 280 and 2400 students. All the teachers have the recognized qualifications and are conscientious in their work. They are dedicated to the well-being of each student and have a vacation to provide for the welfare, mentoring of individual students within the harmonious environment of their classes. We also have a beautiful campus, modern teaching facilities, technology and resources. The school has high-standard on-campus rooms for boarding students, along with spacious classrooms, specialized laboratories, a library, lecture halls, auditorium,

gymnasium, etc. We have a fully computerized management and monitoring system.

As the only world-wide affiliated boarding school in mainland China, a quality-oriented educationally advanced school in China, a grade-A model school in Zhejiang province, and one of "The most beautiful schools" in Hangzhou, nothing can stop us from constantly improving in warmth, safety, and dignity; both on campus and globally.

Head of School
Dr. Xu Xiangdong

DP coordinator
Frank Alfano

Status State

Boarding/day Mixed

Gender Coeducational

Language of instruction
English, Chinese

Authorised IB programmes
DP

Age Range 15 – 19 years

Address
No 42 Yin Gao Road
Bao Shan District
Shanghai
200439 | CHINA

TEL +86 21 65910979

Email
jdfzib@jdfzib.org

Website
www.jdfz.sh.cn

The High School Affiliated to Shanghai Jiao Tong University (known as JDFZ in Chinese Abbreviation) is one of Shanghai's most renowned and competitive public high schools, situated in northeastern Shanghai.

JDFZ established its International Curriculum Center in 2011 and got the IB authorization for the Diploma Programme in 2012. The first cohort of 65 students graduated in 2014, and the school has grown to nearly 350 students from the academic year of 2020-2021. In 2021 the International Curriculum Center marked its 10th anniversary.

Students are mainly from in and around Shanghai, and also from the neighbouring provinces across China. The vast majority of our students are boarders. Students undergo a foundation year at Grade 10 with CAIE IGCSE before being promoted into IBDP. The graduates have earned outstanding offers of admissions from the top Universities, mainly in the United States, Canada, and the UK, such as Yale, Chicago, Duke, Johns Hopkins, Northwestern, Cornell, Dartmouth, Toronto, McGill, Oxford and Cambridge.

JDFZ IB has an excellent result in its short history as an IB World School. Students achieved the final IBDP grades above the World average, nearly in every subject being offered at JDFZ. Continuous success comes from the hard work of the students and passionate teachers. Staff are dedicated, enthusiastic, and professional, hailing from both China and Overseas. It is an English medium school, and all lessons are in English except Group 1 Chinese A, and TOK in both Chinese and English.

One of the core elements of school ethos is the balance between love for one's mother country and the growth of an international outlook. This thread is woven into all subjects. The IB Learner Profile is the core in regular discussions, teaching, events, and activities. JDFZ also strives to utilize IB concepts to promote the educational reform of the national curriculum.

HKCA Po Leung Kuk School

Principal
Mr Perry Tkachuk

PYP coordinator
Ms Rose Hopewell-Fong

Status Private

Boarding/day Day

Gender Coeducational

Language of instruction
English, Putonghua

Authorised IB programmes
PYP

Age Range 3 – 12 years

Fees
Annual Tuition fee (Kindergarten)
HK$79,850
Annual Tuition fee (Primary)
HK$107,100

Address
62 Tin Hau Temple Road | **HONG KONG**

TEL +852 3465 8400

Email
info@plkis.edu.hk

Website
www.plkis.edu.hk

HKCA Po Leung Kuk School, established in 2017, is a non-profit school offering a high-quality education to local and non-local resident children aged 3-12. The school, located at 62 Tin Hau Temple Road, is a beautiful, small campus surrounded by trees and conveniently located to several means of public transport.

We believe your child will love learning at our school. We understand that children come to us with their own learning styles, strengths and challenges. We acknowledge and celebrate that children have unique values, knowledge and life experiences. By recognising each child as an individual, we can help them develop a love of learning within our strong culture of collaboration, mutual respect, support and problem-solving that involves the whole school community.

At HKCA Po Leung Kuk School, each child's personal learning journey includes support designed to build confidence and encourage lifelong learning. Individual interests, strengths and abilities are nurtured in an environment where children have voice, choice and ownership in their learning – a hallmark of the PYP programme. We are committed to offering an excellent education for children ages 3-12 that challenges them to reach their potential socially, emotionally, academically and physically while having fun along the way!

Our Vision:
Our students will become creative, critical thinkers who are internationally minded lifelong learners.

Our Mission:
- Provide a transdisciplinary, challenging learning environment in a happy, safe and caring school
- Develop our students' confidence and desire to inquire, in order to expand their knowledge, skills and understanding
- Nurture individual interests, strengths and abilities
- Foster an inclusive language atmosphere where English, Chinese and other mother-tongue languages are valued and respected.

HONG KONG ACADEMY

(Founded 2000)

Head of School Stephen Dare

Primary School Principal
Virginia Hunt

Secondary School Principal
Teresa Tung

PYP coordinator Carly Buntin

MYP coordinator Kristen Feren

DP coordinator Joanna Crimmins

Status Private

Boarding/day Day

Gender Coeducational

Language of instruction
English

Authorised IB programmes
PYP, MYP, DP

Age Range 3 – 18 years

Number of pupils enrolled
500

Fees
PreK1-PreK2 HK$149,800
K-G5 HK$197,700
G6-G8 HK$217,700
G9-G10 HK$226,800
G11-G12 HK$236,100

Address
33 Wai Man Road
Sai Kung | **HONG KONG**

TEL +852 2655 1111

Email
admissions@hkacademy.edu.hk

Website
www.hkacademy.edu.hk

At Hong Kong Academy, we value how children learn as well as what they learn. From Pre-K to Grade 12, we are committed to creating an engaging and supportive learning environment for every student. We value each child as an individual, and our small class sizes and exceptionally low student to teacher ratio ensure that we can provide the differentiated learning opportunities every student needs to flourish.

Our programmes are designed to challenge students to explore new perspectives, maximise opportunities for growth and develop a strong sense of their own identity. In addition to offering the International Baccalaureate Primary Years, Middle Years and Diploma programmes, all HKA graduates earn an HKA Diploma and the Global Citizen Diploma (GCD) Certificate. We also offer a comprehensive co-curricular programme, including after school activities, clubs, performing arts, sports and mother tongue classes, through which our students build on existing skills, explore new interests, compete, create and grow. As host of the International Schools Theatre Association, we are a regional hub for the performing arts with a variety of workshops, masterclasses and internships available.

Developing global citizens who recognise and respect the richness of human differences is a core component of our rigorous education. At every stage of their learning journeys, we provide students with a wealth of opportunities to initiate and participate in service to others, often working in collaboration with longstanding service partners. By learning about, through and from meaningful action, HKA students engage with both local and global communities with understanding, empathy and compassion, gaining an appreciation for diverse perspectives and experiences.

Our whole community is committed to providing a joyful and authentic learning environment for every child. HKA parents are highly engaged, contributing a wide range of backgrounds, expertise, skills and resources which enrich school life on a daily basis. And because we know that strong partnerships between home and school are beneficial to student wellbeing, HKA promotes a culture of thinking, trust and collaboration by hosting regular parent education events, social gatherings and community clubs throughout the year where everyone's voice is valued.

HKA graduates are able to effectively apply research, critical thinking and communication skills precisely, flexibly and intentionally across subject areas. The majority pursue post-secondary degrees at their first-choice universities and successfully secure employment in a wide variety of professions all over the world.

International School Bangkok

(Founded 1951)

Head of School
Dr. Andrew Davies

DP coordinator
Justyna McMillan

Status Private

Boarding/day Day

Gender Coeducational

Language of instruction
English

Authorised IB programmes
DP

Age Range 3 – 18 years

Number of pupils enrolled
1650

Fees
US$16,751 – US$30,441

Address
39/7 Soi Nichada Thani
Samakee Road, Pakkret
Nonthaburi
11120 | THAILAND

TEL +66 2 963 5800

Email
admissions@isb.ac.th

Website
www.isb.ac.th

International School Bangkok (ISB), widely recognized as one of the world's leading international schools, was the first to be established in Thailand. Opened on the grounds of the U.S. Embassy in 1951, ISB has proudly provided a high-quality international education to students from over a hundred nationalities and is the pioneer International Baccalaureate school in Thailand.

ISB is a learning-focused, US-accredited, IB authorized, independent Pre-K to Grade 12 school offering a challenging international curriculum to a multicultural and multilingual student body of over 1,650 students from 60 different nationalities. The school is a member of the Interscholastic Association of Southeast Asia Schools IASAS). Learning at ISB is informed by leading educational research and global best practice, incorporated into North American and International Baccalaureate Diploma frameworks.

ISB has long valued its globally-minded, inclusive and vibrant community and its strong culture of care. ISB is committed to encouraging students to follow their passions in academics, the arts, athletics, and many other areas both in and out of school. ISB maintains a constant focus on quality with respect to learning, faculty, leadership, professional development, and facilities.

ISB graduates attend colleges and universities around the world. ISB takes great pride in the accomplishments of thousands of alumni who are enriching our local and global communities.

Located in the safe and beautiful community of Nichada Thani, ISB's 15-hectare campus houses world-leading facilities purpose built to align with the multitude of subjects and activities on offer for students. These include state-of-the-art performance venues and studios, international standard sports facilities, fully-equipped science and design labs, innovative libraries and learning spaces, and cutting-edge technology integrated across the school.

Through outstanding teaching and learning, ISB inspires students to achieve their academic and personal potential; be passionate, reflective learners; become caring, global citizens, and lead active, healthy, balanced lives. ISB's vision is *to enrich communities through the intellectual, humanitarian and creative thoughts and actions of our learners.*

International School Ho Chi Minh City (ISHCMC)

International School HO CHI MINH CITY
Energized · Engaged · Empowered

Head of School
Ms. Kim Green

PYP coordinator
Ms. Ishbel How & Mr. Daniel Barker

MYP coordinator
Mr. Simon Scoones

DP coordinator
Ms. Laney Rweyemamu

Status Private

Boarding/day Day

Gender Coeducational

Language of instruction
English

Authorised IB programmes
PYP, MYP, DP

Age Range 2 – 18 years

Address
28 Vo Truong Toan St.
An Phu ward, Thu Duc City
Ho Chi Minh City | **VIETNAM**

Secondary Campus
1 Xuan Thuy Street, Thao Dien,
District 2, Ho Chi Minh City |
VIETNAM

TEL +84 28 3898 9100

Email
admissions@ishcmc.edu.vn

Website
www.ishcmc.com

As the most established International School in Ho Chi Minh City, ISHCMC represents a culturally diverse group of families and teachers from over 60 countries. The community is united in the common vision to create an inspiring world of education by building self-belief and empowering individuals to succeed. As a leader in the field of international education with a renowned reputation, ISHCMC is proud to deliver three International Baccalaureate Programmes in a unique way. Students construct understandings and knowledge of their world through personalized learning experiences and inquiries that develop a deep understanding of important concepts in global contexts.

Progressive in its view of education, ISHCMC is preparing students for their futures. Its educational approach is set within modern learning environments designed to develop both learning and social skills that have been identified as being important for the future. ISHCMC has built two outstanding campuses that encourage collaborative learning opportunities in state-of-the-art facilities, enhanced by technology, that encourages the development of the whole child whilst encouraging students to explore their passions and find their identity.

ISHCMC is renowned for its approach to the social and emotional wellbeing of its students. Its welcoming and supportive community has developed and embedded a deep-rooted Culture of Care within the school. ISHCMC provides a very safe learning environment in which students flourish whilst being supported by experienced, qualified, caring teachers, and a team of dedicated counselors and student support services. At ISHCMC we develop a love of learning in students that prepares them for the complex and unpredictable world beyond school.

JBCN
International School

Founder & Chairperson
Pinky Dalal

Managing Director Kunal Dalal

Principal Davi Sanchez Netto

PYP coordinator Manya Jain

DP coordinator Janos Öreg

Status Private

Boarding/day Day

Gender Coeducational

Language of instruction
English

Authorised IB programmes
PYP, DP

Age Range 3 – 18 years

Parel Campus 1
Yogi Mansion, CTS No. 244,
Dr Vinay Walimbe Road,
Off Dr. S.S. Rao Road,
Parel East Mumbai,
Maharashtra **400012 | INDIA**

Parel Campus 2
Yogi Tower, Dr. S.S. Rao Road,
Opp. Ashok Tower,
Behind ITC Hotel,
Parel East Mumbai,
Maharashtra **400012 | INDIA**

TEL +91 22 24114626

Email information.parel@
jbcnschool.edu.in

Website
www.jbcnschool.edu.in/parel/

JBCN International School, Parel

JBCN International School is a co-ed school located in Mumbai, India, offering a progressive education programme for learners from Kindergarten to Grade XII. Founded in 2009, JBCN now operates across four campuses in Mumbai. With over 4,000 learners and 450 faculty members across the campuses, JBCN International School's uniqueness shows itself through its innovative pedagogy, sustainable practices and developing future-ready skills through a dynamic curriculum delivered in the classroom each day.

The JBCN Philosophy: Why Educate, When You Can EduCreate

The EduCreative experience at JBCN International School, Parel comprises a gamut of challenging engagements and programmes, which along with a programme of academic excellence, facilitate the development of the "Mind-Body-Soul" of each learner.

PYP and International Baccalaureate Programme at JBCN

The JBCN International School, Parel, is authorised to offer the Primary Years Programme (PYP) and the International Baccalaureate Diploma Programme (IBDP). In addition to providing a well-designed curriculum through a variety of teaching-learning methodologies, learning at JBCN International Schools is further fortified through:

Global Affiliations: Learners engage with students, faculty and guest speakers worldwide. An Entrepreneurship Programme by Columbia Business School through Venture for all and certified courses in Design Thinking, Data Analytics, Persuasive Communication, Mindfulness, Robotics, Leadership

etc., add to the holistic development of JBCN learners.

iPROPEL: This unique programme comprises multiple skill-based programmes. Broadly classified as performing arts, research and reasoning, outreach, physical fitness, experiential learning and leadership skills, every programme component is age-appropriate and further augments the curriculum.

Events and Initiatives: Events such as intra-school MUN, theatre carnival, JBCN Radio, InsiprUs, the Innovators Convention and more, bring to the fore the skills the learners have acquired.

InspirUs is a multi-day event spanning a host of activities classified under four broad quadrants: Artistic, Athletic, Cerebral and Expressive, that aims to provide one of the largest ever platforms for the learners to showcase their passion and talents.

Innovators Convention celebrates the spirit of innovation and opens new arenas for the learners to explore, experiment and design solutions for real-life problems/needs.

Through a range of CAS activities such as fundraising, providing amenities and building homes in rural areas etc., learners bring about quantifiable changes in the world.

Career Counselling: An in-house Career Counselling Unit guides learners through subject, course and campus selection. They organise planned visits to universities in India and abroad, as well as opportunities for exchange programmes.

These are just a few of the highlights of the IB programme at JBCN International School.

Jerudong International School

(Founded 1997)

Principal
Nicholas Sheehan BSc.
Geography, PGCE

DP coordinator
Mr Alex Cook

Status Private

Boarding/day Mixed

Gender Coeducational

Language of instruction
English

Authorised IB programmes
DP

Age Range 2 – 18 years
(Boarding from 8 years)

Number of pupils enrolled
1672

Fees
Day: B$18,108 – B$26,952
Weekly Boarding: B$17,688 –
B$23,500
Boarding: B$23,688 – B$29,500

Address
Jalan Universiti
Kampong Tungku
Bandar Seri Begawan
BE2119 | BRUNEI DARUSSALAM

TEL +673 241 1000
(Ext: 1206/7100/1214)

Email office@jis.edu.bn

Website www.
jerudonginternationalschool.com

Jerudong International School (JIS) has offered the IB Diploma programme (IBDP) for over 10 years. It now has 100 students studying for the IBDP in a Pre-University faculty that also has a further 268 A Level students. This is a vibrant community where the student voice is actively nurtured.

Founded in 1997, JIS is located in South East Asia, in the small country of Brunei, on the island of Borneo. A direct flight from major international and regional hubs it is easy to access, making it an ideal school of choice for parents seeking an outstanding school in a safe, secure environment.

JIS is an IB World School; a British School Overseas (BSO), an international HMC School and recognised by the prestigious Good Schools Guide. A leading member of the Federation of British Schools in Asia (FOBISIA), Council of British International Schools (COBIS).

In January 2019, Jerudong International School, an IB World School, became the first international school in the world to achieve the highest rating in all nine areas inspected by the British Schools Overseas (BSO) inspectorate including Boarding.

The school is a thriving community with 1675 students from 55 countries (40% Bruneian), 3-18 years in age. 217 Boarders form a close community in bespoke accommodation, on campus. The School aims are: **Communication, Engagement, Integration, Leadership, Resilience and Thinking**. Students are encouraged to Challenge Yourself, Respect Others and Inspire Change.

The IB Diploma Programme at JIS
The 100 IBDP Students study in small classes (5-15 students)

with up to 21 subjects on offer across the six IB Group areas. Theory of Knowledge (TOK) is taught in lectures, small group discussions and supplemented by lunchtime lectures from outside speakers, staff and students. The IBDP programme at JIS is a student centred programme designed to enable students to be actively engaged in academic subjects but also thoroughly grounded in world events so they can really make a difference.

Outstanding IB Diploma Results
In 2021, JIS IB students' average score was 35.7. The World Average IB Score was 33; 65% of JIS students exceeded the world average. The highest score achieved by three students was 44 points. They are heading to University of Toronto, Canada, the National University of Singapore and KAIST (Korea Advanced Institute of Science and Technology). 33% of the JIS IB Diploma students achieved 38 points or more. These results are consistent and build upon the results of the past 10 years.

University Destinations
A specialist team of Higher Education advisors guide and prepare students for SATS, IELTS and University applications. 2021 and 2020 graduate destinations include UK – Durham University, University of Manchester, Sheffield University, University College London. USA – Columbia University, University of California – Berkeley. CANADA – University of Toronto, University of British Columbia. AUSTRALIA – Monash University, Melbourne. IB Diploma students also received a number of Scholarships.

Teaching Staff

JIS has almost 200 highly qualified teachers primarily from the UK but also a small number from Australia, New Zealand, South Africa. Our language teachers are native language speakers from China, France and Brunei. The IBDP is staffed by experienced academic teachers.

Pastoral Care

All students and teachers in the School are members of a House (a community of about 70 students) which plays a vital role in establishing and maintaining a strong school spirit and enabling leadership opportunities. The 16 Houses in Senior School, provide leadership, mentoring and teamwork opportunities. Weekly House sports competitions and other House Events including House Debates, House Music, JIS has Talent and Spelling Bees in addition to House social events are highlights.

The Campus

The 120 acre single campus is 'Outstanding'. A Raquet Sports facility was opened in January 2021 together with the expanded, refurbished library. The purpose-built, fully WiFi and networked school facility is located near the coast – a 15 minute drive from the airport. Students can use the Arts Centre (725 seat theatre, dance studio, black box theatre and rehearsal rooms), 27 science laboratories, extensive music faculty, art, design and technology and textile studios, libraries and traditional classrooms as well as the 2 swimming pools (50m and 25m), 3 large air-conditioned Sports Halls, outdoor netball/basketball and tennis courts and 3 soccer/rugby pitches. A well- equipped medical centre is on site to take care of students. An award winning Outdoor Discovery Centre – an eco-forestry initiative on tropical heathland on the campus is regularly used for activities and also as an Outdoor Classroom learning space.

Boarding facilities

The 'outstanding' Boarding facilities for students aged 8 years + are purpose designed and built for the community of boarders. 217 girls and boys presently enjoy separate Boarding Houses cared for by experienced staff, including a Junior House. The Boarding Housemaster or Housemistresses are all teachers in the School. Boarders can also use the school facilities. A programme of weekend activities is arranged for the boarders to fully embrace the wonderful environment of Brunei.

Co-curricular Programme

Creativity, Activity and Service (CAS) builds on an extensive co-curricular programme with over 300 activities including a mature International Award programme, Model United Nations (MUN), ECO JIS, Diving, Sports and Performing Arts programmes.

(Founded 1989)

Principal
Ms Anne Ford

PYP coordinator
Mrs Fiona Currey

Status Private, Independent

Boarding/day Day

Gender Coeducational

Language of instruction
English

Authorised IB programmes
PYP

Age Range 3 – 18

Number of pupils enrolled
1000

Fees
Please see website

Address
Centre Road
Camillo
WA 6111 | AUSTRALIA

TEL +61 (08) 9495 8100

Email
mail@jwacs.wa.edu.au

Website
www.jwacs.wa.edu.au

John Wollaston Anglican Community School is a co-educational day School serving families in Perth's south-east for Pre-Kindergarten to Year 12. We are inclusive and welcoming of families from all backgrounds and faiths; a school where every student finds their place in our safe and nurturing environment, where they are free to be and inspired to become.

We are a World School of the International Baccalaureate Primary Years Programme (IB PYP) with a strong academic and pastoral reputation. At John Wollaston, we focus on the development of the whole person, teaching students to be inquirers, knowledgeable thinkers and communicators who are motivated to think for themselves, be courageous and make a difference in the world.

We believe character development is as important as academic progress. Strong relationships underpin the whole school journey. Our students' lives are transformed through connection, creating a positive culture and opportunities to thrive. Our pastoral strategies are designed to embed social and emotional learning across all age groups.

Service Learning and Encounter experiences facilitate character development and personal growth. Students are challenged to be better people who are kind, resilient and confident in their abilities.

The IB PYP encourages students to think critically and creatively through an inquiry-led curriculum. This culminates with the Year 6 PYP Exhibition in which students interrogate a central idea to showcase the depth and breadth of their learning.

In the Secondary School students are exposed to Harvard Graduate School of Education's Project Zero, Cultures of Thinking. Cultures of Thinking focus on the development of both the individual and the group as effective learners and thinkers able to engage with and adapt to a changing world.

Senior Secondary students have the opportunity to follow a variety of pathways including ATAR/University or a Vocational Education and Training path. Students undertaking an ATAR pathway are offered a full complement of courses. The Vocational and Education and Training pathway offers Certificate courses and workplace learning experiences to prepare for the real world beyond school.

The School has differentiated programs for the gifted and those who require learning support. Co-curricular clubs and activities encompass academic, sport, artistic and cultural pursuits.

John Wollaston graduates leave with a strong foundation for life, valuing personal best and possessing integrity and compassion.

K.R. Mangalam Global School

K.R.MANGALAM GLOBAL SCHOOL
Greater Kailash , New Delhi -48
India

Principal
Ms Suman Sharma

PYP coordinator
Sandeep Kaur

Status Private

Boarding/day Day

Gender Coeducational

Language of instruction
English, Hindi

Authorised IB programmes
PYP

Address
N-Block, Nandi Vithi Road
Greater Kailash-1
New Delhi, Delhi
110048 | INDIA

TEL +91 97 1885 8181

Email
info@krmangalam.global

Website
krmangalam.global

KRM Global – Driven to Raise Progressive Lifelong Learners

Instilling the zeal of lifelong learning in kids is the first step in leading them towards greater accomplishments in life. After all, an individual with the eagerness and fervor to grow more by learning more and a keen desire to acquire knowledge is the one that's set up for grander success stories. On that note, let us take a closer look today at the KRM Global way of nurturing the present and brightening the future of the young minds of the nation.

The focus on creating an enriching learning environment

We believe that a learning environment should be such that it excites and inspires kids to come to school every single day, which is exactly what they find at the encouraging and positive atmosphere of K.R. Mangalam Global School. As a matter of fact, we are proud to have led the foundation of a booming space where ideas can be shared without hesitation, curiosity and creativity are lauded, and the learning is continuous and organic.

The diverse learning spaces to bring out the best among kids

When we speak of raising lifelong learners, we don't solely refer to creating academic achievers but rather imbibing the young individuals with diverse skillsets and fostering their varied interests. And, being the most prestigious International Baccalaureate School in Delhi, our wide-ranging learning spaces bear testimony to this fact. From well-equipped science laboratories, advanced robotics learning, keen attention to play areas, ardent focus on fine arts, to an expansive school library, we have left no stones unturned to bring out the best among our young budding geniuses.

Taking education beyond the boundaries of books and classrooms

We firmly believe that the zeal for learning is imbibed more effectively when real-world knowledge and practical learning is brought into the mix. Thus, in a bid to take education beyond books, we, at K.R. Mangalam Global School, organize various cultural and educational activities throughout the year. Through field trips, exhibitions, monthly workshops, book clubs, leadership camps, and more, we inculcate the love for learning in our young fledglings.

At K.R. Mangalam Global School GK-I, we strongly believe in encouraging children to walk on the path of relentless pursuit of knowledge, and our dedicated efforts in this direction have always translated into success stories for our students.

Head of School
Miss Jane Danvers

DP coordinator
Phillip Bird

Status Private

Boarding/day Mixed

Gender Female

Language of instruction
English

Authorised IB programmes
DP

Number of pupils enrolled
1000

Address
794 New South Head Road
Rose Bay
Sydney
NSW 2029 | AUSTRALIA
TEL +612 93886777

Email
enrolments@kambala.nsw.
edu.au

Website
www.kambala.nsw.edu.au

Authorised as an International Baccalaureate World School since 2010, Kambala is the first independent girls' school in Sydney's Eastern Suburbs to offer the IB. The Kambala girl, her care and academic development is at the heart of the School's Strategic Vision. With academic curiosity and a compassionate constitution, she is both self-aware and prepared to make a difference in the world. Kambala believes in raising women equipped to embrace and achieve their personal successes. This vision complements the aim of the IB Diploma Programme: to develop students who flourish physically, intellectually, emotionally and ethically.

Kambala's reputation as a leader of girls' education, enhanced by the exceptional results of its IB students, is a testament to the expertise of the staff and to the students' academic engagement and commitment. Kambala's academic success is complemented by its broad cultural extra curricular program and focus on charity that facilitates IB students' participation in the 'creativity, activity and service' components of the IB Diploma Programme. Kambala's large lawns and courtyard areas, grassy oval and tennis courts, are situated against the panoramic backdrop of iconic Sydney Harbour. Other facilities include flexible learning spaces, an indoor swimming pool and specialist learning areas for Music, Visual Arts, Science and various technological subjects.

Kambala's onsite boarding houses provide a nurturing and supportive communal family environment for 90 girls. Years 7 to 9 boarders occupy the beautiful heritage-listed Tivoli House, while Years 10 to 12 boarders enjoy the greater privacy, independence and social privileges of purpose-built Fernbank building. To assist boarders to structure their time in a positive way and to develop and maintain productive study habits, Kambala employs in-house tutors to work with girls on homework each evening. Technology enables parents who are not based in Sydney to have greater personal involvement with their daughter's learning, including three-way Skype sessions with the student and her teachers. The shared experience of boarding creates a strong network of friends and a feeling of community that lasts for life.

For further information contact Mrs Tracy Mulligan, Director of Enrolments, at +61 02 9388 6844 or email enrolments@kambala.nsw.edu.au.

Kardinia International College

Principal
Catherine Lockhart

PYP coordinator
Geoff Geddes

DP coordinator
Ainslie Howard

Status Private

Boarding/day Day

Gender Coeducational

Language of instruction
English

Authorised IB programmes
PYP, DP

Age Range 3 – 18 years

Address
29-31 Kardinia Drive
Bell Post Hill
Geelong
VIC 3215 | AUSTRALIA

TEL +61 3 5278 9999

Email
marketing@kardinia.vic.edu.au

Website
www.kardinia.vic.edu.au

For more than 20 years, Kardinia International College has focused on the ideal of international understanding. The College was established as a symbol of hope for the world by being a place of quality and exceptional personal development, where people from every corner of the earth feel welcome and at home.

One of our aims is educating our students to a profound sense of internationalism. Graduates of Kardinia live in a global village. An understanding and deep respect of all other cultures is an essential characteristic of leaders and productive citizens of the 21st Century.

The College is independent, coeducational and non-denominational, providing a caring environment for 1900 day and international students from Kindergarten-Year 12.

As an IB World school, we offer the Primary Years Programme (PYP) in Kindergarten-6, a vertical curriculum based on the guidelines of the Victorian Curriculum and Assessment Authority to students in Years 7-10 and both the International Baccalaureate Diploma Programme (IB) and the Victorian Certificate of Education (VCE) in Years 11 and 12.

In the Senior School, the vertical curriculum offers advantages as students progress at a rate appropriate to their ability. Able students can fast track subjects, while other students can allow extra time for consolidation. Some students complete the IB Diploma or VCE in five years, most in six. An extensive range of VCE and IB subjects are available.

The Senior School curriculum is further strengthened by our International Immersion Programs. Our Year 9 students can join our positive, life changing eight-week Chiang Mai program in Thailand. Students can also visit our sister schools; Gotemba Nishi High in Japan, Saint Alyre in France and Discovery College in Hong Kong.

Our world class facilities include; Katsumata Centre – our 1500 seat theatre and gymnasium, Goodfellow Aquatic Centre, a 25-metre indoor pool and cafe, School of Performing Arts, Learning Commons, Six ovals, six tennis courts, a 1560 seat outdoor Amphitheatre and much more. Our main, 22-hectare campus is in Geelong, our Year 5, 11-hectare farm campus in Lovely Banks and our 2.5-hectare campus in Chiang Mai, Thailand.

The emphasis at every year level at Kardinia International College is on academic rigour and we are renowned for the outstanding results our students achieve in Year 12 examinations every year. Integral to our success is that we encourage and expect positive student attitudes, understanding and actions towards each other, our community and the wider global environment.

KiiT
International School

Head of School Dr Mona Lisa Bal	**Fees** Day Boarders: INR526,000 Full Boarders: INR590,000
Principal Dr Sanjay Suar	**Address** KiiT Campus 9
DP coordinator Dr Arunananda Mukherjee	Patia Bhubaneswar, Odisha **751024	INDIA**
Status Private	**TEL** +91 674 2725805
Boarding/day Mixed	**Email**
Gender Coeducational	admission@kiitis.ac.in
Language of instruction English	**Website** www.kiitis.ac.in
Authorised IB programmes DP	
Age Range 3.5 – 18 years	
Number of pupils enrolled 1650	

KiiT International School is the first and the only school in the state of Orissa (India) which offers IBDP. The expansive lush green campus, near the International Airport, offers ample space and infrastructure for sporting, cultural, and leisure activities. Our school prides itself on modern boarding houses and fully equipped cafeteria that serves nutritious and delicious meals.

In a span of ten years, scores of our alumni have graduated from prestigious universities in the US, Canada, UK, Australia and India, and many more are pursuing various bachelor's programs in universities across the world.

Apart from strictly adhering to the IB's vision, the school in its mission ensures that a true passion for enquiry and life-long learning is fostered in our students, and that they also develop the necessary skills to be successful in a highly competitive and unpredictable world they are growing into. Our teachers are periodically trained and are totally committed to their profession, and they explore innovative ways to help learners widen their knowledge base and hone the skills required to meet the demands of future.

We also constantly strive to ensure that our students find pleasure in and are excited about the very process of learning as much as they are anxious about the end results.

The teachers and students are dedicated to our mission statement "Enriching Childhood with knowledge, insight, innovation and transformation."

The well-coordinated, collective efforts of our management, teaching and non-teaching faculty ensure that our students respect people of all cultures, languages and their ways of life and are also concerned about the well-being of other species of animals, and nature as a whole. They are groomed and transformed into true global citizens.

KiiT International School has evolved rapidly to become one of the most reputed schools in Odisha. The Education World Indian Schools ranking of 2017 placed KiiT International School among the top-10 residential schools in India, and No. 1 in Odisha.

The school has a well-stocked ever expanding physical and digital library and well-trained librarians who work closely with our IBDP students. Our labs are state-of-the art and are regularly modernized. As we are growing rapidly, we have started the construction of a separate modern facility exclusively for IBDP, PYP and MYP programs with a view to developing a full-fledged IB World school in a couple of years.

Kingston International School

Kingston International School
京斯敦國際學校

(Founded 1996)

Head of School
Ms. Eliza Wong Ting Fong

PYP coordinator
Ms. Kellie Berry (Primary);
Ms. Michelle Chu (Early Years)

Status Private

Boarding/day Day

Gender Coeducational

Language of instruction
English, Mandarin

Authorised IB programmes
PYP

Age Range 1 – 11 years

Number of pupils enrolled 420

Fees HK$59,400 – HK$159,000

Kingston International School (Lower Primary Campus)
113 Waterloo Road
Kowloon Tong | **HONG KONG**

Kingston International School (Upper Primary Campus)
105 Waterloo Road,
Kowloon Tong | **HONG KONG**

Kingston Children's Centre and Kingston International Kindergarten
12-14 Cumberland Road,
Kowloon Tong | **HONG KONG**

TEL +852 2337 9031

Email enquiry@kingston.edu.hk

Website www.kingston.edu.hk

Kingston's mission is to provide a challenging and stimulating environment that nurtures the balanced development of students who, in their own unique way, grow into active and responsible world citizens. Kingston Children's Centre was established in 1996 and quickly grew into a highly successful bilingual Kindergarten using English and Mandarin Chinese as the medium of instruction. With popular demand from our parent community, our Primary School opened in September 2001 as a pathway for our students to continue their education in a bilingual setting and with the Kingston philosophy. The International Baccalaureate Primary Years Programme was introduced at the same time. In 2004, Kingston was the first school in Hong Kong to gain IBPYP authorisation. Since 2010, Kingston has been able to offer our students a through-train to the IBDP through our partnership with ICHK Secondary School.

Our school is spread over three cozy campuses, located very near each other in Kowloon Tong, Hong Kong. Members of the community who take the opportunity to walk the halls and visit the classrooms of Kingston often comment on the fluidity with which our students switch between the two living languages of our school, Mandarin and English. Collaborative teaching practices ensure an ideal environment for native fluency in both of our languages of instruction.

The Kingston community feels like an extended family in which multicultural collaboration has resulted in an excellent, rigorous, bilingual program. We value inclusive learning, which is reinforced by our approach of keeping class numbers low and teacher numbers high. All of our teachers are fully qualified native speakers of their taught languages and come from all over the globe, bringing with them a wide variety of experiences.

For over 25 years, Kingston has successfully provided a bilingual education for learners whose families wanted an international education for their child without foregoing the opportunity for their child to become a bilingual communicator who is confident in using both English and Mandarin. At Kingston we remain committed to the transdisciplinary approach to education, to innovation and to a lifelong learning journey.

International School

(Founded 1998)

Head of School
Paul Johnson

PYP coordinator
Tania Mansfield

MYP coordinator
Alison Ya-Wen Yang

DP coordinator
Daniel Trump

Status Private

Boarding/day Day

Gender Coeducational

Language of instruction
English

Authorised IB programmes
PYP, MYP, DP

Age Range 3 – 19 years

Number of pupils enrolled 750

Fees
Baht363,000 – Baht765,000

Address
999/123-124 Pracha Utit Road
Samsennok, Huay Kwang
Bangkok
10310 | THAILAND

TEL +66 (0)2 2743444

Email
admissions@kis.ac.th

Website
www.kis.ac.th

KIS International School continues its vision of Inspiring Individuals!

We believe quality learning takes place through personalized and authentic teaching where students are inspired to develop the tools to become life-long learners, successful leaders, and responsible global citizens. KIS is the only school in Bangkok to offer all 4 IB programs, and our students don't just gain knowledge, they learn critical thinking and problem-solving skills that serve them well throughout their lives.

Beginning in August 2022, KIS will offer the International Baccalaureate® (IB) Career-related Programme (CP), making it the only school in the Bangkok area to offer all four IB programmes. The IBCP is for Grade 11 and 12 students to engage in career specific learning while gaining transferable skills and cross-cultural engagement. The innovative programme is increasingly valued by universities as it leads to practical apprenticeship and increased employment opportunities.

KIS students consistently demonstrate high academic success with an average IB score of 37 points, well above the global average of 33 points. Over 1/3 of our graduating class received a score of 40 or above.

With an excellent student to teacher ratio of 1 teacher for every 8 students, learners are guided by dynamic, highly-qualified IB trained educators from all around the world.

KIS offers a challenging and well-rounded programme of sports, arts, and community service. Activities include arts and crafts, technology and robotics, games, dance, competitive sports, non-competitive sports, leadership programmes, Model United Nations, and entrepreneurial activities. The school also supports a robust language curriculum with an average of 10-20 different languages taught at KIS at any given time.

Our lush campus is situated in a gated housing estate near the city centre, providing a spacious learning environment away from the noise and pollution while being easily accessible from both central Bangkok and the suburbs. In addition to well-equipped science labs, state-of-the-art-design workshops, art and drama studios, libraries, and an auditorium, the sporting facilities are also impressive, with grass sports fields, indoor air-conditioned courts, and three swimming pools.

A vibrant community atmosphere is one of the school's great strengths. Students and parents quickly feel at home and develop a sense of pride in their school.

We invite you to see why our community stands apart. KIS provides all students, from the youngest children entering a classroom for the first time, to graduates heading off to the best universities, with the tools they need to be inspiring individuals.

Head of School
Bethany Riseley

PYP coordinators
Alan Noye & Andrew Comley

Status State

Boarding/day Day

Gender Coeducational

Language of instruction
English

Authorised IB programmes
PYP

Age Range 3 – 12 years

Number of pupils enrolled
1600

Address
130 Tenterfield Drive
Burnside Heights
VIC 3023 | AUSTRALIA
TEL +61 3 8358 0600

Email
kororoit.creek.ps@
education.vic.gov.au

Website
www.kororoitcreekps.vic.edu.au

Kororoit Creek Primary School is a fully authorized PYP school, catering for 3-12-year olds. The school is in Public-Private Partnership, maintained and operated through a connection of government and private sector companies. Established in a high growth area, the school has grown from 260 students in 2011 to over 1600 in 2020. We pride ourselves on being a true representation of our community, with over 50 languages and cultural backgrounds.

The school implements the PYP framework underpinned by the Victorian Curriculum, a transdisciplinary curriculum outlining the key outcomes and expectations of the Victorian Government. The curriculum supports us to unpack the Essential Elements using explicit Scope and Sequence documents, ensuring all students are working within their Zone of Proximal Development.

Being a PYP school, we have a major focus on documented curriculum, assessment and shared pedagogical approaches. We also have a major emphasis on evidence-based school improvement strategies. These strategies include the moderation of common student assessment tasks, data collection and analysis as well as evaluation of student learning growth over time. Timely and effective feedback to its community of learners underpins every student's personal learning goals. Teacher professional practice activities are rigorous and differentiated.

With a whole school approach to health, wellbeing, inclusion and engagement, KCPS supports strong community values that underpin its safe and orderly learning environment. These contribute directly to the school's positive standing and high reputation within the immediate and broader area.

Kristin
EARLY LEARNING - SENIOR SCHOOL
FUTURE READY

(Founded 1973)

Headmaster
Mr Mark Wilson

PYP coordinator
Mr Rob Hutton

MYP coordinator
Mr John Osborne

DP coordinator
Mrs Debbie Dwyer

Status Private

Boarding/day Day

Gender Coeducational

Language of instruction
English

Authorised IB programmes
PYP, MYP, DP

Age Range 6 months – 18 years

Number of pupils enrolled
1750

Address
360 Albany Highway
Albany,
Auckland 0632 | **NEW ZEALAND**

TEL +64 9 415 9566

Email
admissions@kristin.school.nz

Website
www.kristin.school.nz

Kristin School is an independent, modern, co-educational International Baccalaureate (IB) World School located in Albany, Auckland with approximately 1750 students aged from six months to 18 years old. Established in 1973, Kristin is non-denominational and welcomes students from all cultures and backgrounds, attracting students from over 40 different nationalities.

Based in New Zealand's most dynamic city, all of Kristin's learning environments share the same 50-acre, park-like campus: Little Doves Early Learning Centre, Kristin Kindergarten, Kristin Junior School (for 5-10 year olds), Kristin Middle School (for 10-15 year olds) and Kristin Senior School (for 15-18 year olds).

Kristin was the first IB World School in New Zealand offering the IB Diploma Programme since 1986, and the first school to offer the IB Primary Years Programme, IB Middle Years Programme and IB Diploma Programme (DP) catering for students from Year 0-13. Consistently, over 20% of our DP students have been awarded 40+ points out of the potential 45. Our students also receive a high quota of scholarships to Oxbridge, Ivy League and top universities in Asia Pacific.

Our small class sizes are critical in providing personalised learning opportunities, and a balanced education at Kristin goes beyond providing a positive school culture. We ensure students are taught skills that will enhance their wellbeing, help them cope with life's challenges, strengthen their relationships with others and enable them to pursue a happy, healthy and prosperous life.

In summary, Kristin offers a:
• Modern, multicultural, co-educational, non-denominational environment with solid, aspirational values
• Proud record of high academic results and scholarships being awarded locally and internationally
• High level of teaching expertise, with many teachers internationally trained and experienced
• Focus on student wellbeing and developing future-ready citizens
• Choice between national NCEA or IB Diploma Programme curriculum options for senior students
• Nationally acclaimed performing arts and outdoor education programmes
• Vast range of community service and leadership opportunities
• 29 different popular and niche sporting codes
• Experiential Learning through a wide array of trips and exchanges with over 15 partner schools overseas
• 50-acre, park-like campus and extensive facilities: two theatres, art, dance and drama studios, a green room/media suite, ski lodge, huge library, numerous sports fields, gyms and courts, technology workshops and more!
• Dedicated bus service travelling 20 routes across Auckland

For all admission enquiries, please visit kristin.school.nz or call our Admissions Manager on +64 9415 9566 ext 2324. We look forward to sharing more information with you to help show why Kristin School is the right choice for your child.

Léman International School Chengdu

LÉMAN CHENGDU
INTERNATIONAL SCHOOL

A NORD ANGLIA EDUCATION SCHOOL

Principal
Tom Ferguson

MYP coordinator
Jarrett Brown

DP coordinator
Thomas Ainsworth

Status Private

Boarding/day Day

Gender Coeducational

Language of instruction
English

Authorised IB programmes
MYP, DP

Age Range 2 – 18 years

Number of pupils enrolled 450

Fees
Day: RMB135,000 – RMB245,000

Address
No.1080 Da'an Road,
Zheng Xing County
Tianfu New Area
Chengdu, Sichuan
610218 | CHINA

TEL +86 28 6703 8650

Email
admissions@lis-chengdu.com

Website
www.lis-chengdu.com

Léman International School Chengdu (LIS) welcomes students from Pre-nursery to Year 13 on its 50 acre campus.

The Primary School uses the English National Curriculum for Maths, English, Computing and PSHE. This is integrated with the International Primary Curriculum (IPC), currently used in over 1000 schools in 65 countries, to give a truly international educational experience throughout the Primary years. The Secondary School, from Years 7 to 11, is based upon the International Baccalaureate Middle Years Programme, with Year 12 and 13 following the International Baccalaureate Diploma Programmme. LIS offers foreign languages including Mandarin and French. Korean is also offered to its native speakers.

LIS has world class facilities on an extensive campus, including fully equipped modern classrooms, science laboratories, an art studio, music studios, I.T. rooms, maker spaces, gymnasium, 25 meter indoor swimming pool and further outdoor sports facilities, including two full size football pitches; this allows us to offer an extensive extra-curricular activity program as well as comprehensive sports and arts programs.

We are proud that 3 out of 4 of our graduates have chosen, and been admitted to, the world's top universities (according to the QS World University Rankings 2020). Our graduates attend the very best universities in the world, including Oxford, Tsinghua, UCL, LSE, UBC and NYU. We have graduates attending top Art & Design Institutes, including University of Arts London, the School of Visual Arts, and the Fashion Institute of Technology.

LIS is accredited by the Council of International Schools (CIS) and the New England Association of Schools and Colleges (NEASC).

LIS is part of the global Nord Anglia Education family and this gives us a unique link to collaborate with schools and pursue opportunities worldwide. This includes the world leader of performing arts education, The Juilliard School, and the world's top university, MIT, as well as our collaboration with UNICEF, whereby students have their social consciousness raised so they care more deeply about the world and the people in it. Our unique online and classroom collaboration platform, Global Campus, connects more than 68,100 Nord Anglia students, and the Nord Anglia University platform enables the very best professional development for our staff.

(Founded 1992)

Principal
Arnett Edwards

DP coordinator
Beta Chau

Status State

Boarding/day Boarding

Gender Coeducational

Language of instruction
English

Authorised IB programmes
DP

Age Range 16 – 19 years

Number of pupils enrolled
256

Fees
Local Hong Kong students
HK$300,000
Overseas students HK$396,000

Address
10 Lok Wo Sha Lane,
Sai Sha Road
Ma On Shan,
Sha Tin | HONG KONG,

TEL +852 2640 0441

Email
office@lpcuwc.edu.hk

Website
www.lpcuwc.edu.hk

Li Po Chun United World College of Hong Kong (LPCUWC) is one of 18 colleges that share the value and philosophy of the UWC movement and the mission of UWC.

Sharing a firm commitment to diversity, LPCUWC is a boarding school that goes beyond being "international." It is a vibrant community interwoven by more than 250 students from over 90 different nationalities, cultures, and various socio-economic backgrounds supported by scholarships. Living on a fully residential campus, students get to learn from and with friends of different backgrounds in their shared living experiences.

Students are exposed to a strong presence of many traditions and cultures. Everyone gets a chance to immerse themselves in the cultures of other regions of the world and showcase their own at cultural evenings. Students from abroad also have the opportunity to explore Chinese culture in depth, with Mandarin as a subject and Dragon and Lion Dance as *Quan Cai* (whole person development) activities. Students are given the chance to develop a deeper understanding of China and Asia through China Week and Project Week service trips to Mainland China, East, and Southeast Asia.

Like many other UWCs with scenic campuses, LPCUWC is a tight-knit community in a quiet location in Ma On Shan close to nature. However, we are also just a stone's throw away from the heart of Hong Kong, a dynamic coastal cosmopolitan at the crossroads of cultural, political and historical contexts. With an eclectic selection of Quan-Cai activities that bridges citizenship on and off campus, service in the school and local community forms an integral part of education at LPCUWC. Beyond Ma On Shan, there is also a plethora of natural terrains and urban neighborhoods for students to explore. At LPCUWC, the city becomes our campus.

Linden Hall High School

Head of School
Ms. Asuka Tsuzuki

DP coordinator
Ms. Karen Hunter

Status Private

Boarding/day Mixed

Gender Coeducational

Language of instruction
English, Japanese

Authorised IB programmes
DP

Age Range 12 – 18 years

Number of pupils enrolled 86

Fees
¥1,518,000

Address
3-10-1 Futsukaichikita
Chikushino, Fukuoka, Kyushu
818-0056 | JAPAN

TEL +81 92 929 4558

Email
hunter@lindenhall.ed.jp

Website
www.lindenhall.ed.jp

Located approximately 30 minutes from the centre of Fukuoka city, Linden Hall High School's goal is to nurture individuals who will play an active role in a rapidly globalizing, dynamic world. Our mission statement, "Develop the individual, instill them with confidence, and send them out into the world" reflects this. In 2013, we became the first Article 1 school (a school recognized as meeting the requirements of the Japanese National Curriculum, guaranteeing that IB graduates are awarded a Japanese High School Diploma as well as the IB Diploma) in Kyushu certified as an International Baccalaureate World School.

In this fast-changing global society, with all its challenges, the need to cultivate open-minded global citizens, who can utilise English fluently in various intercultural settings, is increasingly apparent. We have therefore adopted an English immersion approach, in which the majority of classes, other than Japanese Language classes, are conducted in English. Through interacting with teachers and students from around the world, students naturally acquire both English language skills and respect for diversity. Our classroom methods encourage students to engage actively in their learning and discover the joy of unravelling the world's mysteries. Until high school, students progress through a common curriculum before electing, in Year 10, to pursue either the

International Baccalaureate Diploma Programme (IBDP) or the Think and Inquire (TI) Course (for students wishing to continue the National Curriculum).

We also provide numerous opportunities for students to study abroad and participate in international exchange and volunteer programmes. In 2018, we became a member of Round Square, an association of approximately 200 private schools from over 50 countries. Founded in 1966 to develop the next generation of international leaders, member schools participate in international exchanges, conferences and various other activities.

The school building is an airy structure, built to make the most of natural light. It is fully air-conditioned with learning facilities such as IT, Art, and Music rooms, a Science laboratory and Wi-Fi in every classroom. The Library houses 12,000 books, one-third of which are in English, and provides access to paid online resources. Next to the school is the cafeteria, where chefs and registered dieticians serve Japan's first year-round organic school meals. The surroundings feature lush greenery and the classrooms offer a panoramic view, including the 60,000m² English Garden – an ideal place to relax and observe nature. Our dormitories, one for boys and one for girls, are within walking distance.

(Founded 1969)

Principal
Nicolas L'Hotellier

DP coordinator
Marcel Hennes

Status Private

Boarding/day Day

Gender Coeducational

Language of instruction
English

Authorised IB programmes
DP

Age Range 3 – 18 years

Number of pupils enrolled
1089

Fees
For families AUS$21,000 –
AUS$26,251
For companies AUS$42,000

Address
758 Anzac Parade
Maroubra, Sydney
NSW 2035 | AUSTRALIA

TEL +61 2 9344 8692

Email
ib@condorcet.com.au

Website
www.condorcet.com.au

Where better to study the IB diploma than at the International French School of Sydney? Located between Sydney's famous beaches and the central business district, the Lycée Condorcet is an international school with a welcoming and friendly campus. Here, for the past 50 years students of all nationalities from ages 3-18 study the rigorous French curriculum, renowned for its excellent academic standard. Since 2005, the Lycée Condorcet also offers the IB Diploma Programme in Year 11 and 12, attracting ambitious students from diverse backgrounds with one common goal; to become informed, inquiring and active global citizens.

While other Lycée Condorcet pupils study at a native French and English level, IB students are not required to have any prior French language knowledge as the program is taught in English. Therefore, students will learn French at their own pace with classes ranging from introductory to native level. In fact, students benefit from the opportunity to obtain the prestigious bilingual IB diploma in French and English.

Importantly, although situated in Australia, the school operates on the northern hemisphere calendar – the school year begins in August and final IB diploma examinations are held in May. We offer a two-month IB and French Preparatory program in May-June in which students will be able to get a taste of different IB subjects to help them choose which ones they would like to study when the program begins in August.

Although the Lycée Condorcet student body consists of approximately 1100 students representing over 50 different nationalities, the school consciously limits the IB class sizes in order to facilitate individualised learning. Through the promotion of French and Australian cultures, we aim to develop inquiring, knowledgeable and caring young people while working to promote international and intercultural understanding and respect.

The Lycée Condorcet belongs to the global network of French Schools Abroad, the AEFE, an active network in which students interact regularly through projects, sports competitions, cultural events and more. Students are able to not only transfer seamlessly from one school within the network to another, but also to meet and build friendships with children from all over the world, making friends for life.

Visit our website to embark on your IB journey!

MALVERN
COLLEGE HONG KONG
香港墨爾文國際學校

Headmaster
Dr Robin A. Lister

Head of Senior
Wayne Maher

Head of Prep
Maria Gebrial

Status Private

Boarding/day Day

Gender Coeducational

Language of instruction
English

Authorised IB programmes
PYP, MYP, DP

Age Range 5 – 18 years

Number of pupils enrolled
900

Fees
Primary HK$173,670
Secondary HK$197,550
Please see website for 2022/23

Address
3 Fo Chun Road
Pak Shek Kok | **HONG KONG**

TEL +852 3898 4688

Email admissions@
malverncollege.org.hk

Website
www.malverncollege.org.hk

World-class education through the Five Centres of Excellence

Malvern College Hong Kong (MCHK) is an IB World School offering the PYP, MYP and DP curriculum to its culturally diverse pupil body. Following its successful launch in August 2018, primary and secondary classes now operate from Prep 1 (Year 1) to Lower Sixth (Year 12). The first cohort of Sixth Form pupils have commenced their Diploma Programme studies in August 2021 and will graduate in May 2023.

MCHK is located in Pak Shek Kok, New Territories, just adjacent to the Hong Kong Science Park. Its state-of-the-art campus facilities feature a 450-seat auditorium ("Big School"), an open-plan library, a dining hall ("Grub"), visual and performing arts studios, a ceramics studio, science laboratories, design workshops and maker spaces, a food technology room, a multi-purpose indoor sports hall and 6-lane 25m indoor heated swimming pool (both with viewing galleries), a primary sports hall with climbing wall and an outdoor sports pitch, located on the school's roof top.

Small class sizes give teachers the chance to engage personally and differentiate according to aptitude, skill set and need within lessons. Dedicated tutor-time and a genuine concern for the individual, built around an active house system, are additional key features. The school is strongly committed to holistic education and offers an extensive co-curricular activities programme for pupils to build on their existing talents and to explore new activities. Lower primary classes attend regular outdoor education sessions at the school's Forest-Beach School learning site.

MCHK is member of a growing network of Malvern schools across the globe including the UK, Egypt, Qingdao, Chengdu, Hong Kong and, most recently, Switzerland. Although each Malvern school has its own unique identity, they all share the same DNA and ethos built around the "Five Centres of Excellence", namely: British-style Pastoral Care, Enhanced Learning, Entrepreneurial Education, Outdoor and Environmental Education and a Global Network.

Malvern seeks to develop independent, forward-thinking individuals who demonstrate strength of character, leadership and responsibility. By providing a caring, supportive and ambitious learning environment, the school enables its pupils to maximise their academic potential, develop their talents and to flourish as individuals. The aim is for Malvern pupils to become truly open-minded, global citizens capable of building consensus, respect and an ability to collaborate with those from backgrounds different to their own.

MERCEDES COLLEGE

(Founded 1954)

Principal
Mr Andrew Balkwill

PYP coordinator
Mr Simon Munn

MYP coordinator
Mr Stuart Wuttke

DP coordinator
Mr Marc Whitehead

Status Private

Boarding/day Day

Gender Coeducational

Language of instruction
English

Authorised IB programmes
PYP, MYP, DP

Age Range 5 – 18 years

Fees
Day: AUS$12,095 – AUS$18,200

Address
540 Fullarton Road
Springfield
SA 5062 | AUSTRALIA

TEL +61 8 8372 3200

Email
mercedes@mercedes.catholic.
edu.au

Website
www.mercedes.catholic.edu.au

Mercedes College understands the importance of nurturing and inspiring students to become lifelong learners to meet the demands of the 21st century.

The co-educational Catholic school incorporates the globally renowned International Baccalaureate (IB) framework with the Australian curriculum to provide students with a world class education.

Set in a single location at the base of the Adelaide Foothills, and as one of few South Australian schools to offer the IB from Reception to Year 12, Mercedes presents a wealth of opportunities to nurture and challenge students, and enables continuity of learning at the same campus across their entire schooling.

"In such a rapidly evolving world, there is no way to be sure what today's young people will face in their future academic, employment and spiritual journeys, but we can provide them with the skills to meet the challenges and adapt to whatever lies ahead," said Principal Andrew Balkwill.

The College is proud of its history of academic excellence and is also committed to supporting students beyond the classroom. A range of pastoral care programmes are designed to help develop the whole person and enable students to flourish.

Mercedes College is a learning community in the Mercy tradition, committed to being people who are responsible, compassionate and loyal, show integrity and mutual respect, and have a strong sense of justice.

"It is one thing to declare good intentions and another to live them each day," said Principal Andrew Balkwill. "We invite you to visit our school and experience the sense of welcome and belonging that is a fundamental part of our culture."

For information about enrolment opportunities please visit www.mercedes.catholic.edu.au.

Merici College

(Founded 1959)

Principal
Anna Masters

MYP coordinator
Natalie Fairfax

DP coordinator
Natalie Fairfax

Status Private

Boarding/day Day

Gender Female

Language of instruction
English

Authorised IB programmes
MYP, DP

Age Range 11 – 18 years

Number of pupils enrolled 780

Fees
Day: AUS$8,400 – AUS$10,729

Address
Wise Street
Braddon
ACT 2612 | AUSTRALIA

TEL +61 2 6243 4100

Email
reception@merici.act.edu.au

Website
www.merici.act.edu.au

Mission

Merici College empowers women to love life, have hope, be faithful and build futures more wondrous than they dare to dream.

Vision

Merici College endeavours to be a vibrant, faithful learning community that fosters excellence, and takes positive action to build a shared global future.

Merici College is a Year 7-12 Catholic girls' college, situated in Braddon in the heart of Canberra. We are very proud to be the oldest established Catholic girls' secondary school in Canberra.

Merici is a vibrant community committed to preparing confident and competent young women well equipped to contribute to the world beyond high school. We create innovative learning environments that meet the needs of individual students and inspire them to strive for the highest levels of personal achievement. We challenge our students to take risks within and beyond the classroom to achieve individual academic excellence.

Merici College is a welcoming community, where authentic relationships are nurtured, and dignity and integrity are affirmed. We seek to foster a life-long love of learning within our students, where each young woman is given the opportunity to grow spiritually and intellectually to make a positive contribution to society. Families also enrich Merici from diverse Christian and other faith traditions.

Academic

We teach the Australian Curriculum in the Junior Years (Years 7-10) delivered through the Middle Years Framework. At the senior level, students choose to study either the IB DP, or our local curriculum. We offer a range of opportunities for gifted and talented students, including differentiated teaching, acceleration, enrichment, and support for students with specific learning needs.

Cocurricular

We believe it's vital that every Merici Girl gets the chance to explore their passion, be creative and try something new. Our co-curricular and enrichment opportunities have something to suit everyone, from our Sustainability at Merici (SAM) group to Art Club and a vast array of sporting teams, including a robust set of Netball teams.

Vertical House System

One of the strengths of our college is the strong House System and excellent pastoral care provided. The six Pastoral Care (PC) Groups in each House are vertically streamed, and students remain in the same PC group throughout their six years at Merici. This encourages positive relationships and a sense of belonging and continuity for students and their families. It also provides leadership opportunities for older students who support and mentor the younger ones.

MLC
SCHOOL

(Founded 1886)

Principal
Lisa Moloney

DP coordinator
Chris Barnes

Status Private

Boarding/day Day

Gender Female

Language of instruction
English

Authorised IB programmes
DP

Number of pupils enrolled
1297

Fees
AU$13,000 – AU$33,000

Address
Rowley Street
Burwood
Sydney
NSW 2134 | AUSTRALIA
TEL +61 2 9747 1266
FAX +61 2 9745 3254

Email
enrol@mlcsyd.nsw.edu.au

Website
www.mlcsyd.nsw.edu.au

MLC School is an independent, non-selective Uniting Church school for girls from Pre-Kindergarten to Year 12 in the Inner West of Sydney. From Pre-Kindergarten through to their time as Senior School students, MLC School girls dare to be more. In 2020, MLC School was the highest ranked IB School in Australia.

Led by a highly professional staff under the guidance of Principal Lisa Moloney, girls are challenged and encouraged to question traditional perceptions and roles of women and are instilled with the skills and confidence to take their place in an ever-changing society. MLC School prepares girls for a life of learning by motivating them to pursue excellence, demonstrate integrity, celebrate diversity, embrace world citizenship and live with humility. A wide selection of subject choices, as well as an extensive co-curricular program aims to empower girls to be self-reliant and play an active role in their futures.

The award-winning Senior Centre, opened in 2019, takes classroom practice to a new level and is reflective of modern workplaces. The aim is to equip girls with the skills to be successful in a collaborative, team environment and to be comfortable in open-planned, flexible spaces designed for impromptu group work sessions.

Year 7 to Year 10 are pivotal years at MLC School where girls experience Immersive Learning journeys that broaden each year. The experiences, that may take place locally, regionally, or abroad, aim to broaden horizons, encourage resilience and foster a growth mindset to underpin success in their senior years of schooling. Each immersive learning experience is unique in its design, but they all have some common threads that link the experiences together. Academically, each girl takes responsibility for her own path in the final years, and this is a crucial stage in her journey towards becoming an independent, fearless and empowered young woman.

Girls can choose between the Higher School Certificate (HSC) or the International Baccalaureate (IB) Diploma Programme, with nearly 40 per cent of students choosing to study the IB. In 2020, the School was named No 1 IB School in Australia and a Top 50 Global IB School.

Over 52 MLC School girls have achieved the perfect IB Diploma score of 45, since the programme was introduced in 2002, and all girls consistently score well.

Visit the campus, meet the girls and professional teaching staff, and experience the benefits of joining the MLC School community.

Nahar International School

Nahar International School
AIM:INFINITY

Head of School
Mrs. Vandana Arora

DP coordinator
Resham Puri

Status Private

Boarding/day Day

Gender Coeducational

Language of instruction
English, Hindi

Authorised IB programmes
DP

Number of pupils enrolled
1200

Address
Nahar's Amrit Shakti, Chandivali
Farm Road
Off Saki Vihar Road, Andheri East
Mumbai, Maharashtra
400072 | INDIA

TEL +91 (0)22 6838 5500

Email
info@nahar-is.ac.in

Website
www.nahar-is.ac.in

Nahar International School (NIS) is a young school that uses its fresh perspective in dynamic and innovative ways. It aims at creating globally adept world citizens and leaders for the future. Students are encouraged to be participators in academics, sports, and performing arts through programs that are rigorous but not rigid.

The school campus is an eight-story structure, located in an elegant neighborhood within the busy city of Mumbai. It is equipped to offer education at international standards, providing SmartBoards and electronic methods of knowledge dissemination, fitted-out with well-thought infrastructures such as modern workshops, German-design science labs, iMac computer studios, a vast digitized library, spacious conference rooms, a multi-purpose auditorium with a performance platform, and a large turf-based playground.

NIS inculcates a holistic and learning-centric way of life. It aims to endow students with the right attitude, attributes, skills, and social traits to care for themselves, their immediate society, and the community at large.

The NIS philosophy highlights nine attributes – Reverence, Responsibility, Empathy, Courage, Fairness, Perseverance, Resilience, Collaboration, and Initiative-taking. Being closely aligned to the IB learner profile, these values combine beautifully with traditional Indian values to instill in the entire NIS team an optimistic and constructive approach to making the world a better place and being responsible global citizens.

At NIS, CAS is a 'way of life'. Students across all age groups are active participants in CAS. Through our various Club Activities (Film Making, Photography, Carpentry, Cookery, Dance, Lawn Tennis, Archery, Football, Basketball, etc.)

We offer our students numerous opportunities to engage themselves creatively, athletically, and socially.

Service, being an integral part of NIS, students are encouraged to actively engage themselves in service-related projects. Such projects have included working with organizations such as Bookwallah (an NGO that helps set up libraries at orphanages). Our Students extended their services at multiple levels: firstly, raising awareness about the NGO, then running a book collection campaign, and finally organising a fundraiser to generate funds for the organisation's work. Students regularly volunteer at a nearby municipal school where they teach younger students every week, and design teaching aids for the faculty. Through the school's tie-up with Rotaract, students are offered a larger platform to discuss social issues and serve the community, leading to improved social interaction.

Another important manner in which the IBDP school year engages DP students creatively, through CAS, is the DP Dramatic Production. It immerses the students in a 3 – 4 weeks engagement with theatre – understanding the nuances of acting, dialogue-delivery, use of stage space, costume creation and assembly, prop creation, use of sound and light, and backstage coordination. During this process, the students become actors, learn to manage materials, space and time, work collaboratively, watch plays in a similar vein to the genre they're performing, and overall, grow as individuals who have learned to don multiple creative hats.

Newington College

(Founded 1863)	**Number of pupils enrolled**
Headmaster Mr Michael Parker	2067
PYP coordinator Benjamin Barrington-Higgs	**Fees** Boarding: AUS$28,332 (inc GST)Tuition: AUS$20,196 – AUS$35,271
DP coordinator Ms Cheryl Priest	
Status Independent	**Address** 200 Stanmore Road, Stanmore **NSW 2048	AUSTRALIA**
Boarding/day Mixed	
Gender Male	**TEL** +61 2 9568 9333
Language of instruction English	**Email** admissions@ newington.nsw.edu.au
Authorised IB programmes PYP, DP	**Website** www.newington.nsw.edu.au

In the hub of Sydney, Australia

Newington College is an International Baccalaureate World School in inner Sydney. It includes a Primary Years Programme (PYP) satellite prep school in Lindfield, on Sydney's upper north shore, and a boarding house for secondary school students on the main campus in Stanmore, in the inner west. The College attracts students from greater Sydney, regional areas and the Asia Pacific.

Its location in the heart of an expanding, coastal international city gives boys of all ages the opportunity to access a range of learning and cultural resources. Surrounded by universities, theatres, libraries and museums, Newington College regularly engages with experts from nearby centres of learning.

The College has 25 acres of gardens and playing fields that create an oasis of learning within a busy city. Newington is only 10 minutes from Sydney International Airport and Central Station and five minutes from the University of Sydney.

A liberal tradition of innovation

Newington College was founded in 1863 with a liberal policy of inclusion that declared it 'open to the sons of all'. Its fathers realised the need for a quality educational establishment to develop boys of promise into men of substance.

Newington College's approach, with its focus on critical and creative thinking, makes it a remarkable place to educate your son.

A diverse and inclusive community

Newington College is committed to providing a holistic education for boys.

Its families value the broad perspectives and liberal outlook of the College community. They embrace the opportunity for their sons to believe that others can be different – and also be

right, a belief espoused by the IB. Every day, boys at there are encouraged to approach their education with rigour and a mind open to diverse views and perspectives.

Newington College strives to create young men of integrity who are courageous, open-minded, creative and curious; whose views are formed through truly critical thinking and who value both independence and teamwork.

Academic Rigour in Learning and Teaching

In the primary years, Lindfield Preparatory School offers the PYP. Newington College's senior school is the only Greater Public School in Sydney that offers a choice between the state-wide Higher School Certificate examination and the IB Diploma Programme. The IB Diploma at Newington College is a popular option for many boys and the results achieved by the College are outstanding.

Newington is committed to providing an internationally respected education with access to the best teachers, facilities and opportunities. Students are encouraged to take a global perspective and to immerse themselves in their own particular areas of interest and passion.

The College is equipped with the latest technology infrastructure and subject specific, industry level facilities including a modern technology centre, 200-seat drama theatre, light-filled library, lecture theatre and super-labs.

Well-being and character

At Newington College, teachers share their passion for their area of expertise and build strong relationships with their students. They tailor their teaching to suit the learning styles of each student.

The College is committed to ensuring that every person feels respected and valued in the school community. The

The boys are expected to build a sense of social responsibility and justice and are encouraged to test out their ideas and to seize every opportunity available to them.

Co-curricular Engagement

Newington College is committed to providing all boys with the chance to experiment and thrive through participating in a varied range of co-curricular activities and tours in Australia and abroad. These opportunities are a large part of what distinguishes the College. Boys combine academic life with sports, arts, outdoor education and hands-on learning activities. They are supported and encouraged in the journey to discovering their unique passions and interests.

Community in Partnership

An exceptional sense of community is part of the Newington College culture, which emphasises service to others and the development of strong and lasting relationships. This involves not only teachers and students but parents, families and Old Boys. The College strives for every member of the Newington community to feel welcome, connected and appreciated.

Results

In 2020, Newington College students achieved a median IB score of 38/45 (97.3 ATAR equivalent). This is well above the global average score of 29.8/45. Its top performing IB student achieved a perfect 45/45. Of the 46 students who completed the IB Programme in 2020, 31 achieved an equivalent ATAR over 95. Underpinning these results were some exceptional individual performances across all subjects.

boys admire their teachers and coaches for their genuine interest in each student's well-being, passions, goals and setbacks.

Spirituality, Values and Ethics

As a Uniting Church school, Christian values are a strong part of the way that the College has built its community. This includes welcoming students and families of all faiths and cultural backgrounds.

Nexus International School (Singapore)

(Founded 2007)

Principal
Judy Cooper

PYP coordinator
Paul Rimmer

DP coordinator
Vicky Holdcroft

Status Private

Boarding/day Day

Gender Coeducational

Language of instruction
English

Authorised IB programmes
PYP, DP

Age Range 3 – 18 years

Number of pupils enrolled
1050

Fees
Day: S$21,800 – S$40,760

Address
1 Aljunied Walk
Singapore
387293 | SINGAPORE

TEL +65 6536 6566

Email
enquiries@nexus.edu.sg

Website
www.nexus.edu.sg

Nexus International School (Singapore) is an international school with children from over 50 different nationalities, catering from ages 3 to 18. International Baccalaureate (PYP, MYP* and Diploma) and the UK IGCSE curricula are offered, ensuring the easiest transition from home country to Singapore and to the next adventure.

At Nexus, every child is taught based on their personal motivations, understanding and talents. We empower children to learn by encouraging them to be independent and teaching them to be critical thinkers. Outcomes in our core subjects of English, Mathematics and Science measure well above the international average and our ongoing assessments allow us to track every child's performance. Our child-centred philosophy is echoed by every teacher, in every class and in every extra-curricular activity.

We strive to ensure that your child has a world-class education; internationally recognised and accredited by the most respected awarding bodies. We believe in providing a strong community where parents, teachers and children collaborate in learning-focused relationships, built upon an open-door policy that encourages regular communication between parents and teachers.

The focus at Nexus is on developing the whole learner. Nexus was purposefully designed and built with innovative learning environments at the centre of the decision-making process to support and enhance the learning process. By giving learners the opportunity to choose their own learning style and surroundings, it allows them to develop self-efficacy. As an Apple Distinguished School, we pride ourselves on innovative approaches to tap into children's natural motivation to learn.

We also believe that learning entrepreneurship skills benefits learners from all backgrounds, inspiring out-of-the-box thinking and innovation. If learners bring ideas forward, we try to support them to make things happen.

Our results back this up. In 2021, the average IB grade was 37 points, up from 34 in 2020 and 32 in 2019 and 44% of diplomas were bilingual. At IGCSE in 2021, 38% of all entries were A/A* grade and 93% pass rate for A* to C, an increase from 33% and 85% respectively in 2020.

Nexus International School (Singapore) is a candidate school for the IB MYP. This programme will continue for each subsequent academic year, MYP Year 8 in 2022/23 and MYP Year 9 in 2023/2024. Until then, learners will continue the English National Curriculum.

WITH BOARDING

(Founded 2008)

Principal
Mr David Griffiths

DP coordinator
Ms Amanda O'Hara

Status Private

Boarding/day Mixed

Gender Coeducational

Language of instruction
English

Authorised IB programmes
DP

Age Range 3 – 18 years

Address
No 1 Jalan Diplomatik 3/6
Presint 15
62050 Putrajaya | **MALAYSIA**

TEL +60 3 8889 3868

Email
admissions@nexus.edu.my

Website
www.nexus.edu.my

Nexus International School is the Top IBDP School in Malaysia, ranked top 2% in the World and Top 50 in Asia

Nexus International Malaysia is extremely proud to be ranked as Top 2% Global IB Schools in the World and Top 50 in Asia according to Education Advisers Ltd (see IB-Schools.com), cementing its position as the Top IBDP School in Malaysia. The International Baccalaureate Diploma Programme (IBDP) is the World's fastest growing curriculum with more than 5400 schools having adopted it to date.

Founded in 2008, Nexus International Schools offers the IBDP as a pre-university qualification for senior learners. This follows the International Early Years and International Primary Curriculum in the Primary school as well as the Middle School and IGCSE curriculum in lower secondary. The delivery of the curriculum and the philosophy of the school – The Nexus Way, offers seamless transition in style, structure and approach to the IB Diploma Programme.

Achieving Excellence, The Nexus Way

With IB scores that consistently surpass worldwide averages, Nexus has also enabled learners to achieve a perfect 45 points in the past three consecutive years. A Perfect Score in IBDP examinations is an extraordinary achievement with a very small percentage of learners (typically fewer than 1% per year) achieving this feat worldwide. Khoo Qi Xuan, Ahmad Matin Moors, Caryn Chan and Ju Eun Bae are all Nexus learners who have scored 45 points since 2019.

Growing from Strength to Strength with a New IB Learning Hub

With growth and expansion of the IB Programme at Nexus, the school has built a new and exciting IB Learning Hub for its learners. With the growth and expansion of the IB Programme at Nexus, the school has invested and built a new and exciting IB Learning Hub for its learners. This fantastic, learner-focussed space has dedicated quiet study areas as well as areas for group discussion and collaboration. With a desire to look after the wellbeing of the learners during the challenges and rigour of the IBDP, there are also dedicated spaces for relaxation and recreation. The IB teaching team is able to support the learners using dedicated spaces for individual meetings and higher education consultations.

Book a Physical Tour or Virtual Consultation

Contact our Admissions team at admissions@nexus.edu.my / +603-8889 3868 for more information.

NIST INTERNATIONAL SCHOOL

(Founded 1992)

Head of School
Dr James Dalziel

PYP coordinator
Bryony Maxted-Miller

MYP coordinator
Jacqueline Arce

DP coordinator
Robin Wilensky

Status Private

Boarding/day Day

Gender Coeducational

Language of instruction
English

Authorised IB programmes
PYP, MYP, DP

Age Range 3 – 18 years

Number of pupils enrolled
1700

Fees
THB541,800 – THB975,900

Address
36 Sukhumvit Soi 15
Wattana
Bangkok
10110 | THAILAND

TEL +66 2 017 5888

Email
admissions@nist.ac.th

Website
www.nist.ac.th

As the first and only full, not-for-profit IB World School in Bangkok, NIST International School offers a world-class education to students from the early years to high school levels. Established in 1992 with the guidance and support of the United Nations, the school now welcomes over 1,600 students representing more than 60 nationalities. NIST is governed by the parent-elected NIST International School Foundation and was the first school in Thailand to receive triple accreditation through the Council of International Schools (CIS), New England Association of Schools and Colleges (NEASC) and Office for National Education Standards and Quality Assessment (ONESQA).

Recognized worldwide for its progressive approach and international scope, the IB framework provides students with critical 21st century skills that align to the demands of the modern workplace. Through the IB and its own unique programmes, NIST aims to inspire, empower and enrich lives. The academic structure encourages students to explore, take risks and make connections across disciplines. Student-driven service learning plays a central role, as they learn to understand and empathize with others, and take an active role in solving local, national and global issues. NIST also

partners with other top schools around the globe to offer the Global Citizen Diploma, an optional qualification that allows graduates to showcase strengths in leadership, service and community engagement.

In addition to its rigorous academics, NIST offers an expansive World Languages Programme and over 300 extra-curricular activity options. As one of the founding members of the Southeast Asia Student Activity Conference (SEASAC), the NIST Falcons compete against their peers from other top schools in Southeast Asia, as well as students around the globe. NIST has also committed itself to excellence and innovation in the use of technology. Students benefit from personal MacBook Air computers, iPads, a completely wireless campus, SMART Boards, the FrontRow classroom amplification system, and LCD-equipped classrooms.

NIST represents the future of learning through its stellar academic achievements and expansive resources. More importantly, the school has been successful in fostering reflective, principled learners with a passion for making a difference in the lives of others. With its graduates attending the best universities around the globe and going on to become community leaders, NIST has become recognized as one of the world's leading international schools.

NORD ANGLIA
INTERNATIONAL SCHOOL
SHANGHAI, PUDONG

(Founded 2002)

Principal
Lesley-Ann Wallace

DP coordinator
Emma Hughes

Status Private

Boarding/day Day

Gender Coeducational

Language of instruction
English

Authorised IB programmes
DP

Age Range 2 – 18 years

Fees
RMB117,370 – RMB333,680

Address
2888 Junmin Road
Pudong New District
Shanghai
201315 | CHINA

TEL +86 (0)21 5812 7455

Email
admissions@naispudong.com

Website
naispudong.com

Established in 2002, Nord Anglia International School Shanghai, Pudong (NAIS Pudong) is an excellent international school focusing on high achievement for every child and success across all subject areas. The school offers the very best of the British education system in China for children aged 2 to 18 years.

NAIS Pudong provides students with a highly academic environment, and a warm, welcoming and diverse international community. Its rigorous, contemporary and globally focused curriculum challenges and excites children from their early years through to the International Baccalaureate Diploma Programme (IBDP).

To complement classroom teaching, NAIS Pudong offers a broad co-curricular programme that encourages students to take risks, nurture their passions and serve others. Globally respected curricula are enhanced by innovative collaborations with world leading organisations such as The

Juilliard School, Massachusetts Institute of Technology (MIT) and UNICEF to ensure that every student develops the skills and mindset needed to thrive in an ever-changing world. Its Global Campus connects the Nord Anglia Education family of 69 schools, giving NAIS Pudong students access to a variety of exceptional learning opportunities worldwide.

NAIS Pudong wholeheartedly embraces the educational philosophy and pedagogical principles that underpin all IB programmes. This approach has resulted in the establishment of an optimal learning environment whereby its students are able to achieve outstanding academic results.

At NAIS Pudong, we nurture every student to achieve academic success, enabling entry into the world's leading universities.

You want your child to excel, so do we.

NORD ANGLIA INTERNATIONAL SCHOOL HONG KONG

(Founded 2014)

Principal Mr Kenny Duncan

DP coordinator Sarah Alexander

Status Private

Boarding/day Day

Gender Coeducational

Language of instruction English

Authorised IB programmes DP

Age Range 3 – 18 years

Fees
Pre-school HK$81,000 –
HK$170,000
Primary HK$170,000
Secondary (Year 7 – 11)
HK$190,190
Secondary (Year 12 – 13)
HK$192,010

Primary Campus
11 On Tin Street, Lam Tin,
Kowloon | **HONG KONG**

Secondary Campus
19 Yuet Wah Street, Kwun Tong,
Kowloon | **HONG KONG**

Early Years Campus
285 Hong Kin Road,
Tui Min Hoi, Sai Kung, N.T.,
Kowloon | **HONG KONG**

Early Years Campus
Redhill Plaza, Tai Tam,
Hong Kong Island | **HONG KONG**

TEL +852 3958 1428

Email admissions@nais.hk

Website www.nais.hk

Nord Anglia International School (NAIS) is part of Nord Anglia Education's (NAE) global family of international schools. A through-train school known for its warm and friendly global community, made up of over 40 nationalities, NAIS nurtures every child to develop a love of learning, enabling them to achieve more than they ever thought possible.

NAE's Global Campus helps students explore the world, learn new skills and set their sights higher, developing a truly international perspective through outstanding online, in-school and worldwide experiences.

NAIS educates children for the future, enhancing its curricula through collaborations with the world's best organisations including MIT and Juilliard. Through opportunities to learn from the best, experiences beyond the ordinary, and the encouragement to achieve more than what they thought possible, NAIS helps students succeed anywhere through a unique global educational offer.

NAIS follows the frameworks of EYFS, IGCSE and IBDP. With a focus on individualised learning, the school's rigorous curricula ensure that students have a creative and challenging learning experience.

(Founded 2011)

Principal
Ms Lynne Oldfield

DP coordinator
Ms Justine Oliver

Status Private

Boarding/day Mixed

Gender Coeducational

Language of instruction
English

Authorised IB programmes
DP

Age Range 4 – 18 years

Number of pupils enrolled
1486

Fees
Day: 17,220,000 – 24,138,750
Boarding: 15,411,000 – 15,786,000

Address
33, Global edu-ro 145beon-gil
Daejeong-eup
Seogwipo-si, Jeju-do
63644 | REPUBLIC OF KOREA

TEL +82 64 793 8001

Email
admissions@nlcsjeju.kr

Website
www.nlcsjeju.co.kr

North London Collegiate School Jeju, is internationally recognised as a school which provides an exceptional education. Our students consistently excel in every area. They leave us with outstanding qualifications, but also become articulate and independent young people who possess the confidence, intellectual curiosity, and passion for learning and understanding that will endure for life.

In tandem with our mission to develop academic excellence, we are also dedicated to supporting the development of the whole person. Our programme is designed to inspire confidence, individuality and develop self-esteem. Modelled on our mother school in London, we are a positive and energetic community where both boarders and day students are encouraged to take advantage of the exceptional range of opportunities open to them; academic, sporting and cultural.

International Outlook
NLCS students are internationally minded and well informed about the world beyond school. The IB Diploma resonates with the values of NLCS, and its international dimension affords students the opportunity to be part of a programme which is recognised throughout the world.

Academic Excellence
We have offered the IB programme since 2011 and have had a consistent record of success. 115 Diploma candidates in the Class of 2021 achieved an average of 39 points, with 58 achieving 40 points or higher, including a maximum 45. 82% of entries were awarded 7/6.

Looking to the future
The Class of 2021 showed another outstanding performance. This is the second consecutive year that NLCS Jeju IBDP candidates passed the Diploma with an average score of 39 points and now they begin their studies at many of the world's top universities. Offers and acceptances include places at Cambridge, Imperial, King's, UCL and LSE in the UK as well as Cornell, Stanford, Chicago, UC Berkeley, Duke and Carnegie Mellon in the US. Other destinations around the world are Australia, Canada, Hong Kong, Japan, Singapore and South Korea. The IB Diploma programme offered at NLCS Jeju ensures that students enjoy an exciting and academically stimulating Sixth Form experience, providing them with an excellent preparation for life at university and in the wider world beyond.

NPS

(Founded 2008)	**Number of pupils enrolled**
	1750
Head of School	
Dr Matthew Sullivan B.A., D.Phil. (Oxford)	**Fees**
	Day: S$15,000 – S$30,000
DP coordinator	
Sushmita Chatterjee	**Address**
	10-12 Chai Chee Lane
Status Private	Singapore
	**469021	SINGAPORE**
Boarding/day Day	
	TEL +65 62942400
Gender Coeducational	
	Email
Language of instruction	headofschool@npsis.edu.sg
English	
	Website
Authorised IB programmes	www.npsinternational.edu.sg
DP	
Age Range 3 – 18 years	

NPS Singapore rank 13th in the world Global Top IB Schools. Our graduating class of IB students have achieved impressive IB results in 2021 with an average score of 41.6. 70% of our students have scored 40 points or more with 13 students scoring a perfect 45 points. We are very pleased with the broad-based performance of the cohort!

National Public School (NPS) group of educational institutions headquartered in Bangalore, India, has an enviable track record of academic excellence spread over six decades, nurturing 15,000 children each year in over 10 campuses. NPS International School is housed in a large, well-equipped six-acre campus at Chai Chee Lane, near Bedok, in the East of Singapore.

In operation since 2008, the School, a day school, welcomes students to its child-centred environment, offering Montessori, Nursery, Kindergarten and Grades I to XII and the IBDP and IGCSE programmes. Student teacher ratio is a healthy 1:11 and the IBDP subjects have an average class size of 16-18. The key difference between NPS and many other groups of schools is that its founding governors are educationists with vast experience in a wide range of educational contexts.

That richness of experience brings a maturity of systems and vision has been recognised, valued and endorsed by parents.

Join NPSI – an International School located in the East of Singapore as we strive to foster academic excellence and a sense of wellbeing in our carefully curated positive learning environment. We encourage your child to blossom into an active learner, and a compassionate and critical thinker. Be a part of us and enjoy the impactful educational experience!

Our Vision

Inspiring young minds and empowering them to have a positive impact on the world.

Our Mission

- Providing a child-centred, holistic and value-based learning experience.
- Encouraging creativity, innovation, confidence and critical thinking in a safe and nurturing environment.
- Fostering leadership, empathy and engagement in humanitarian and environmental service.

ONE WORLD
INTERNATIONAL
SCHOOL

Head of School
Michelle Dickinson

PYP coordinator
Rashmi Tourani

DP coordinator
Thomas Croft

Status Private

Boarding/day Day

Gender Coeducational

Language of instruction
English

Authorised IB programmes
PYP, DP

Age Range 3 – 18 years

Number of pupils enrolled
1450

Fees
Day: S$17,970 – S$20,661

Address
21 Jurong West Street 81
Singapore
649075 | SINGAPORE

TEL +65 69146700

Email
admissions@owis.org

Website
www.owis.org

A Thoughtfully-priced Education, A Lifelong Impact
One World International School offers a rigorous, developmentally-appropriate IB education at a thoughtfully priced fee structure, which is almost half the cost of other premium IB schools in Singapore. Our IB curriculum combines a personalised approach with international standards, focusing on nurturing the natural love of learning within every child. Research has repeatedly demonstrated that for children to thrive academically, they must be engaged and enthused about their learning. At OWIS, our carefully designed curriculum incorporates hands-on learning experiences within a supportive environment to prepare students to become the leaders of tomorrow.

A truly international learning environment
OWIS brings together students from over seventy nationalities with a diverse staff. Children have the opportunity to learn and discover in an international environment that prepares them for our global society. As part of our programme, we are committed to providing all students with opportunities to learn other languages with a particular focus on Mandarin across the whole school.

A holistic learning environment
Students at OWIS have access to a future-ready curriculum that not only sets them on the path of academic excellence, but also emphasises the importance of holistic development. Children are nurtured within and outside the classroom environment with rich and varied opportunities to learn sports, perform on stage and work with hands-on projects that stimulate their love of learning.

At OWIS, we understand the importance of personalised learning with each child being given individualised attention and feedback. Our classes, therefore, are capped at 24 students to maintain a small and inclusive environment and ensure that each child receives the attention they need to thrive academically, emotionally and socially. The deep relationships that our teachers develop with their students help to create a welcoming, safe environment for every child to succeed.

Access to the latest in technology and education
Society has rapidly become dominated by digital technology and students today need to be given appropriate opportunities to embrace these technologies. At OWIS, we believe that students should have access to this technology under the guidance of their teachers who carefully consider how and when to incorporate it into the teaching and learning. Our focus is to enhance every child's creativity, communication skills and technical skills. The OWIS values of being "One with the World" provide a balanced, rigorous educational experience that nurtures lifelong learners, unique thinkers and future leaders.

深圳东方英文书院
Shenzhen Oriental English College

(Founded 1994)

Head of School
Mr Weiquan Shen

PYP coordinator
Ling Luo (Caroline)

DP coordinator
Kongjing Wang

Status Private

Boarding/day Boarding

Gender Coeducational

Language of instruction
Chinese, English

Authorised IB programmes
PYP, DP

Age Range 6 – 18 years

Fees
RMB60,000 – RMB130,000

Address
No 10 Xuezi Road
Education Town, Bao'an
Shenzhen, Guangdong
518128 | CHINA

TEL +86 755 2751 2624
FAX +86 755 2751 2866

Email
principal@oecis.cn

Website
www.szoec.com.cn

History and development

OEC International School (OECIS) is funded by Daming Group and is a division of Shenzhen Oriental English College founded in 1994. OECIS is a co-educational school with students enrolled from primary school to high school. Our school is a set of primary school, secondary school, Hong Kong and Taiwan schools and an IB International School in one of the fulltime, full-boarding private schools.

OECIS has been an authorized IB World School since 2004, delivering an IB structured curriculum for over 15 years. OEC covers an area of 150,000 square meters (about 37 acres). With more than 120 classroooms, about 5000 students and staff and advanced facilities, the campus provides for collaborative spaces and areas for group and individual teaching and learning. Located in the Baoan Education District, only a five-minute drive from the Shenzhen International Airport, it is situated at the foot of the Phoenix Mountain and surrounded by picturesque natural scenery. Shenzhen City, also known as the first Special Economic Zone in China is easily accessible from Guangzhou and Hong Kong.

Curricula

A well-acclaimed international IB programme is offered to meet our students' diverse educational needs. In addition, we also offer intensive English training courses to help students prepare for both their English instruction in class and the various language requirements set by universities. The ratio of student-faculty is 6:1, which ensures each student receives enough attention and guidance. Our students have achieved remarkable results and continue to excel in all areas.

Classrooms

All classrooms have a comprehensive range of resources which includes a wealth of technology resources. Each classroom is equipped with interactive white boards and are used to present classes. We also have a dedicated, well stocked library from which children and families can borrow a range of books, story sacks and other resources.

Technology

By integrating technology and computers in the classroom students are learning faster and expressing themselves creatively more than ever before. With WeChat Work (School information system) students, parents and teachers enjoy an open classroom environment, bringing parents closer to the classroom. Empowering students through innovation in the classroom is the goal, here at OECIS!

QSI International School of Chengdu

QSI | QSI INTERNATIONAL SCHOOL OF CHENGDU

(Founded 2002)

Director
Dr. Clare McDermott

Secondary Director of Instruction
Mr. Robert G. Mullins

Elementary Director of Instruction
Ms. Hafida Becker

DP coordinator
Mr. David Becker

Status Private

Boarding/day Day

Gender Coeducational

Language of instruction
English

Authorised IB programmes
DP

Age Range 3 – 18 years

Number of pupils enrolled
350

Address
American Garden
188 South 3rd Ring Road
Chengdu, Sichuan
610041 | CHINA

TEL +86 28 8511 3853

Email
chengdu@qsi.org

Website
chengdu.qsi.org

Mission
QSI International School of Chengdu promotes the success for every child through quality instruction and character development in a caring, challenging, multicultural environment.

Academic Program
QSI has a strong belief that all students can succeed. The learned outcomes needed at mastery level are clearly defined; students have more than one chance to be successful in demonstrating mastery.

In addition to academics, our Success Orientations are a vital part of the entire school experience. Personal habits, the ability to interact successfully with others, responsibility, trustworthiness, kindness, and other factors in this realm areas important as the knowledge one learns and the competencies one gains. The QSI Success Orientations compliment the IB Learner Profile.

IB Program
The IB program at QSI Chengdu is our most rigorous college preparatory program offered and take an inclusive approach with all students and do not restrict access to IB courses. We encourage students to challenge themselves and have a 100% pass rate on all IB exams.

Faculty & Staff
We are a family of leaders and learners at QSI Chengdu. Our faculty and staff come from across the world, which reflects our student diversity. Our staff come prepared with qualifications and training in best practices to ensure they have the skills to facilitate higher level learning and social-emotional development of all students.

Accreditation
QSI International School of Chengdu has been accredited by the Middle States Association since 2008.

QSI International School of Haiphong

(Founded 2005)	**Address**
DP coordinator	Lot CC2, Me Linh Village
Clarissa Sammons	Anh Dung Ward, Duong Kinh District
Status Private	Haiphong | **VIETNAM**
Boarding/day Day	**TEL** +84 31 381 4258
Gender Coeducational	**Email**
Language of instruction	haiphong@qsi.org
English	**Website**
Authorised IB programmes	haiphong.qsi.org
DP	
Age Range 2 – 18 years	

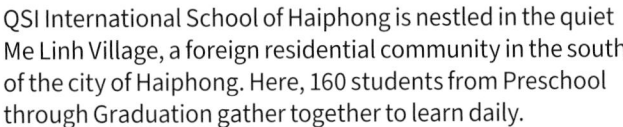

QSI International School of Haiphong is nestled in the quiet Me Linh Village, a foreign residential community in the south of the city of Haiphong. Here, 160 students from Preschool through Graduation gather together to learn daily.

The school, in operation since 2004, has recently moved to its current campus where it offers two new purpose-built buildings that includes a full English Elementary library, a Secondary library & learning center, two science laboratories, a music exploration wing, an indoor performance area, full-service cafeteria, well-equipped early childhood center, and state-of-the-art, well-resourced and well-equipped classrooms. The school has access to a full-length swimming pool, tennis courts, a turfed soccer field, and an outdoor court for basketball, volleyball, and badminton.

QSI International School of Haiphong is accredited through the Middle States Association of Colleges and Schools (MSA), an accrediting body from the United States. Last year, the school was also invited to join the International Baccalaureate Organization.

The school offers students both the opportunity to take the full DP or certificate courses. As a brand new member of the IBO with a small first year cohort, we current offer Language & Lit, Physics, Mathematics, Theatre, Chinese ab initio, and History. As we grow our program, we are looking to add Chemistry, other languages, and allow students to work towards a dual-language diploma in Vietnamese & English.

QSI INTERNATIONAL SCHOOL OF SHENZHEN

(Founded 2000)

Director
John Shirley

Secondary Director of Instruction
Erin Burnett

DP coordinator
Sandra Jung

Status Private

Boarding/day Day

Gender Coeducational

Language of instruction
English

Authorised IB programmes
DP

Age Range 2 – 18 years

Number of pupils enrolled
1000

Address
5th Floor, Bitao Building, 8 Tai Zi Road
Shekou
Shenzhen, Guangdong
518067 | CHINA

TEL +86 755 2667 6031

Email
shenzhen@qsi.org

Website
shenzhen.qsi.org

QSI International School of Shenzhen is a private, nonprofit preschool through Secondary IV co-ed, college-preparatory, day school. It was founded in 2001 to provide a quality education in English for the children of expatriates in Shenzhen. The school is part of Quality Schools International, a consortium of nonprofit international college-preparatory schools with American style curriculum. It is fully accredited by the Middle States Association of Colleges and Schools (MSA) and is a member of the East Asian Council of Overseas Schools (EARCOS) and the Association of China and Mongolia International Schools (ACAMIS).

QSI International School of Shenzhen believes in a personalized approach to instruction leading to mastery of clearly defined objectives within a positive and enjoyable learning environment. It offers a challenging academic curriculum for students age 2 through Secondary IV and utilizes the Mastery Learning model of instruction. This model results in students learning more information compared to traditional school methods in which students receive a percentage grade and then move on. As a Mastery Learning school, we care about our students mastering 100% of their course content because we believe that any gaps in learning, if left unchecked, turn into deficits, difficulties, and frustrations in learning in the future. Therefore, QSI teachers work with students until all course content is mastered and allow students to use time as a resource, instead of a limiting factor, in their classroom.

Success for All is the motto of Quality Schools International. Research indicates that successful people have developed personal orientations that lead to success, and these character traits are at least as important as the knowledge one learns and the competencies one gains through classroom instruction. The Success Orientations are actively encouraged and taught in virtually all areas of the QSI school curriculum with the view of making them a vital part of one's life pattern. QSI promotes trustworthiness, responsibility, aesthetic appreciation, concern for others, kindness and politeness, independent endeavor, and group interaction as character traits that are necessary for personal success beyond the classroom.

QSI International School of Shenzhen is proud to participate in the IB Diploma Programme and continues to offer one of the top IB programs in the area. With scores consistently higher than the world average, our graduates are well-prepared for success at university, and joined with QSI's holistic approach to education our graduates are also prepared for success in life.

Queensland Academy
for Science Mathematics
and Technology

(Founded 2007)

Principal
Ms Kathryn Kayrooz

MYP coordinator
Sandra Davey

DP coordinator
Rebecca Skarshewski

Status State

Boarding/day Day

Gender Coeducational

Language of instruction
English

Authorised IB programmes
MYP, DP

Age Range 11 – 18 years

Number of pupils enrolled
1255

Fees
DP AUS$3,900 approx.
MYP AUS$2,000 approx.

Address
78 Bywong Street
Toowong
QLD 4066 | AUSTRALIA

TEL +61 7 3377 9333

Email
admin@qasmt.eq.edu.au

Website
qasmt.eq.edu.au

Queensland Academy for Science Mathematics and Technology (QASMT) is located in Brisbane's inner west, and is a Queensland state school for highly capable students in Years 7 to 12. QASMT inspires high achieving students through exclusively offering the International Baccalaureate Middle Years Programme (IB MYP) and Diploma Programme (IB DP).

In conjunction with the University of Queensland and other leading universities, QASMT offers an enriched program to enhance the development of students with an interest and ability in the STEM fields of Science, Mathematics and Technology.

QASMT students achieve outstanding academic results and have a proven record in attaining offers to some of the world's most prestigious universities. In 2018, 2019 and 2020, QASMT was named Queensland's Top Performing School (www.bettereducation.com.au/Results/QCE_ATAR.aspx), and has the largest cohort graduating with an IB Diploma in Australia. The QASMT average IB score for 2020 was 35.31, with over 93% of graduates exceeding the world average Diploma score (29.59). In comparison with other Australian curricula, this means that 31.1% of the graduating cohort received the highest attainable QSR/ATAR 99+ or OP1 equivalent, versus 2.7% (Queensland average).

Underpinning our academic success is an outstanding pastoral care system which ensures every student feels a part of the QASMT 'family'. Student welfare is implemented through our bespoke positive education program and House structure, which ensures every student is known by a significant adult, their House Dean. We believe in the importance of guiding students to become responsible and caring individuals, who are sensitive, open-minded and respectful of all cultures. QASMT aims to develop tomorrow's leaders; individuals who are internationally minded world citizens.

We develop students' abilities to research, investigate and reflect on local and global matters. The relationship between the students and teachers is based on intellectual challenge and interdependent inquiry.

Our campus and facilities are world standard. Our state-of-the-art STEM and Languages Precincts opened in 2020, and provide dynamic use and enhancement of our learning environments. A central hub of the Academy, our Research Centre, provides innovative learning spaces, such as the Robotics and Digital laboratories and 3D printing Makerspace, quiet individual study nooks and collaborative learning areas with up to date e-resources.

Students enjoy the benefits of working in wireless learning spaces with computer network access from all work and recreation areas. In addition, we have virtual classrooms, an observatory, and extensive recreational and sporting facilities. Students also enjoy the contemporary university style lecture theatre and large auditorium, plus well equipped music and art rooms.

For more information, please visit our Virtual Academy Tour at: qasmt.eq.edu.au/enrolments/virtual-tour

QUEENWOOD

Per aspera ad astra

(Founded 1925)

Principal
Ms Elizabeth Stone

DP coordinator
Jennifer Brown

Status Private

Boarding/day Day

Gender Female

Language of instruction
English

Authorised IB programmes
DP

Number of pupils enrolled
900

Address
Locked bag 1
Mosman
NSW 2088 | AUSTRALIA

TEL +61 2 89687777

Email
q@queenwood.nsw.edu.au

Website
www.queenwood.nsw.edu.au

A rigorous academic curriculum within a balanced program of activities has been the hallmark of a Queenwood education for over 90 years.

Within a strong learning community, we create space for our girls to engage with big ideas and connect with a diverse range of people and communities. At Queenwood, our commitment is to a liberal education – an education which, at its core, develops rigorous thinking and the practice of inquiry.

Our Programs

We are an independent Kindergarten to Year 12 non-selective day school for girls that provides a well-balanced curriculum catering to individual differences. We seek to develop in our students the knowledge, skills and habits which will be the foundation for a lifelong awakening to the complexity of the world. As girls move through the school there are increasing opportunities and expectations for independence. Our curriculum, pastoral care structures and extra-curricular programs create a safe but challenging framework within which girls learn to manage their work, their time, their relationships and responsibilities – skills which are essential to a happy and productive life.

International Baccalaureate

We offer dual IB and HSC pathways for Years 11 and 12 students, and each girl has the opportunity to choose the pattern of study which best suits her individual interests. Our IB results demonstrate the commitment to academic rigour offered at Queenwood, with 56% of students completing our last IB Program placing in the Top 5% of the state with their overall mark. This has enabled our alumnae to attend Universities within Australia, as well as in the United Kingdom and the United States of America, including Oxford, Cambridge, Harvard and Brown Universities. Our commitment to the life of the mind reaches far beyond the examination syllabus, and we recognise the school years as an essential grounding in developing an intelligent and sensitive awareness of the world.

Our Values

Truth, Courage and Service underpin a Queenwood education. Growing in wisdom with a strong sense of identity and self-knowledge aid students in seeking a deep understanding of the truths of the world. That sense of purpose, the willingness to engage with challenge and the desire to make a contribution remain at the heart of Queenwood's mission. By thinking and acting independently, our girls are keen to courageously engage with contemporary social and political issues, thereby deepening their knowledge of themselves and gaining deeper and more nuanced perspectives on the world. We encourage our students at every level to contribute in thought, word and deed: responding to the vulnerable and marginalised with respect and compassion; speaking out with courage; and taking action in their service.

Ravenswood

(Founded 1901)

Principal
Mrs Anne Johnstone

PYP coordinator
Anne Gruenewald

DP coordinator
Monique Connor

Status Private

Boarding/day Mixed

Gender Female

Language of instruction
English

Authorised IB programmes
PYP, DP

Address
10 Henry Street
Gordon
NSW 2072 | AUSTRALIA

TEL +612 9498 9898

Email
admin@ravenswood.nsw.edu.au

Website
www.ravenswood.nsw.edu.au

Since its foundation in 1901, Ravenswood has embraced a strong tradition of academic excellence with an emphasis on wholistic education. As a proudly non-selective school from Pre-Kindergarten to Year 12, we are committed to being at the forefront of education and wellbeing for girls, aiming to ignite the potential of every student – inspiring her passion and purpose to lead her most meaningful life.

Ravenswood is a Uniting Church school, governed by a Christian ethos and our guiding principles of Excellence, Respect, Courage, Optimism and Compassion. Our motto is semper ad meliora – Always towards better things.

Ravenswood offers the International Baccalaureate Diploma Programme (IBDP) to students in Years 11 to 12. We are also one of few schools in Australia to offer the International Baccalaureate Bilingual Diploma. The International Baccalaureate Primary Years Programme (IBPYP) is provided from Pre-Kindergarten to Year 6.

Ravenswood's IBDP cohort grows each year and the School's results are always excellent. Our students have achieved perfect scores of 45 for the last four years running. Two perfect scores were achieved in 2020, while almost a quarter of our students achieved a score of 40 or above.

As one of the first Visible Wellbeing Schools in NSW, Ravenswood has embedded evidence-based positive education strategies into the curriculum, recognising that learning and well-being are inextricably linked.

For the last three years, we have been recognised by The Educator as one of Australia's most innovative schools and named 'a school to watch' in the areas of Science,

Technology, Engineering and Mathematics (STEM) and positive education. In 2021, we were named a Best Wellbeing Program Awardee in the Australian Education Awards.

Ravenswood prizes its reputation as a warm and connected community, where every student feels known and cared for. As the Vice-Chair of the International Positive Education Network and the Chair of the Positive Education Schools Association, Principal Anne Johnstone is an internationally recognised leader and sought-after speaker in the area of youth wellbeing.

Ravenswood girls have access to more than 100 diverse co-curricular choices designed to extend their development beyond the classroom, including; gymnastics, snow sports, dance and music to name a few. Our girls also enjoy co-educational opportunities in partnership with our brother school, Knox Grammar School, including army cadets, careers, musical performances and service activities.

Ravenswood girls enjoy the benefits of award-winning world-class facilities including the Mabel Fidler Building, state-of-the-art Learning Resources Centre and SciTech Centre. The Centenary Centre features a Performing Arts Auditorium, Music Centre, open exhibition space and dance studios. The indoor sports and recreation centre includes a strength and conditioning facility and 25-metre heated indoor swimming pool and diving apparatus.

Our beautiful new Senior Learning Centre is a forward thinking 21st century learning space designed to provide both flexible academic spaces and relaxation areas for our Years 11-12 students.

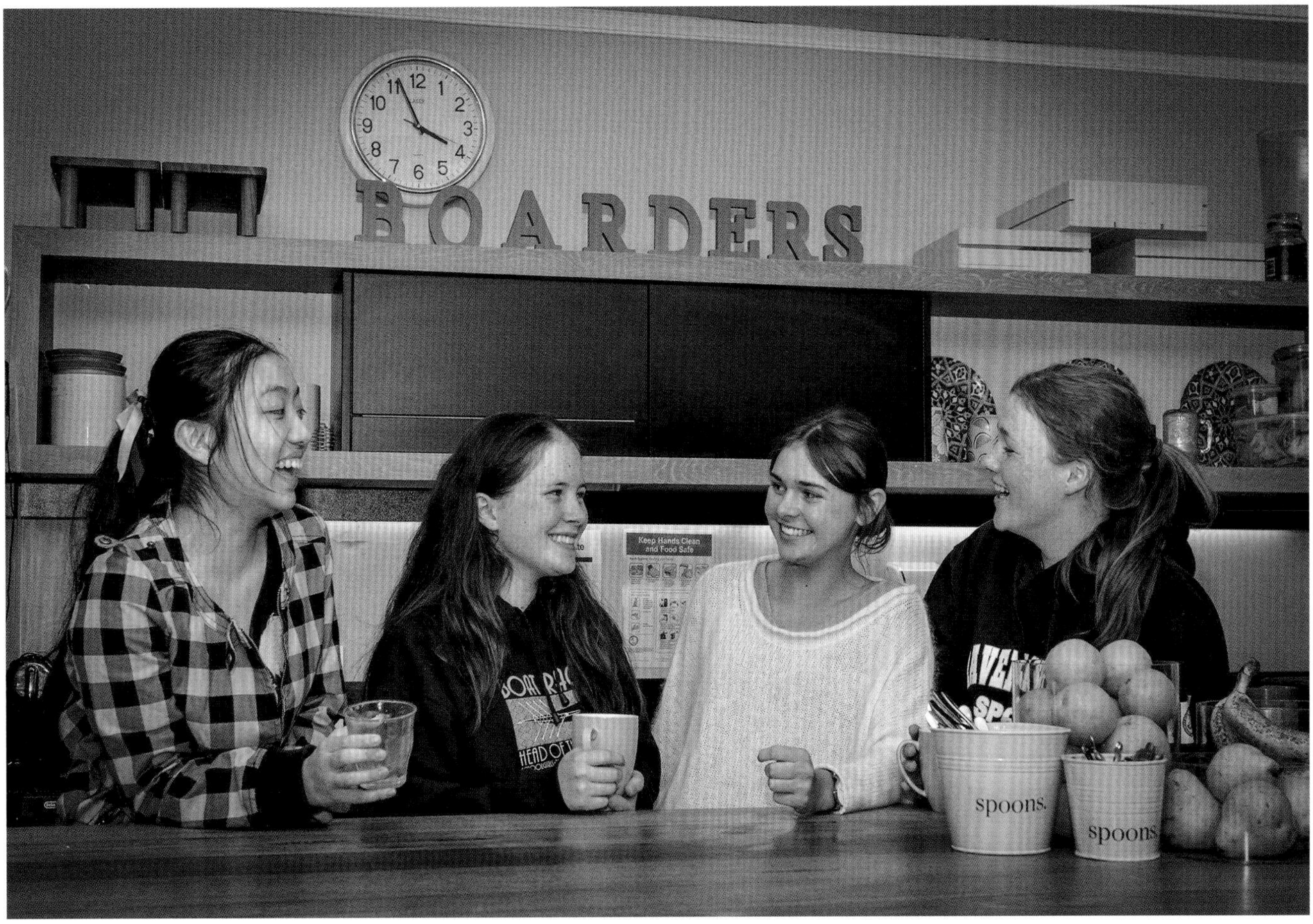

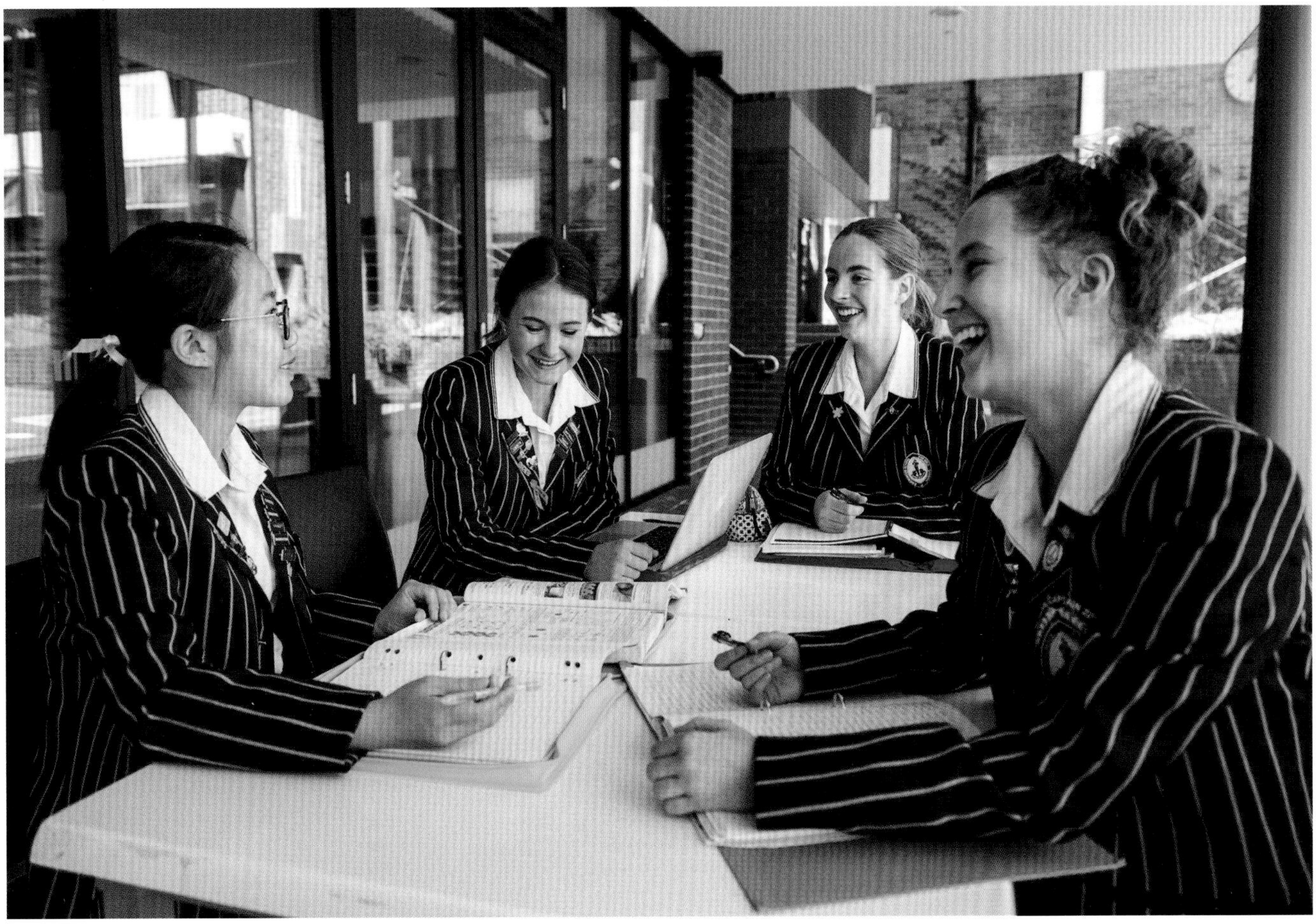

Rangitoto College

Principal
Patrick Gale

DP coordinator
Catherine Brandt

Status State

Boarding/day Day

Gender Coeducational

Language of instruction
English

Authorised IB programmes
DP

Address
564 East Coast Road
Mairangi Bay
Auckland 0753 | **NEW ZEALAND**

TEL +64 9 477 0150

Email
info@rangitoto.school.nz

Website
www.rangitoto.school.nz

This world-class institution is the largest school in New Zealand with over 3000 students, and is perhaps the most internationally acclaimed New Zealand school. Rangitoto's success is the result of expert teaching in a wide range of academic subjects and extensive extra-curricular opportunities including music, dance, drama and over 40 different sports. The facilities, passionate staff and culture of excellence inspire students to become the best they can be.

Rangitoto has a focus on diversity and has around 50 different nationalities in the school. Our IB students have been accepted into some of the world's best universities, including Cambridge and Oxford in the UK, and Princeton in the USA.

Rangitoto College is located on the beautiful, safe North Shore of Auckland, New Zealand. The school is close to beaches, parks, shops and cinemas, and is about 25 minutes from downtown.

Rangitoto College has some of the best facilities in the Southern Hemisphere including: modern classrooms, a library and information centre featuring senior study and reading rooms, computer access for all students, an auditorium, an Olympic standard all weather hockey turf, three gymnasiums and a weights room, an all-weather athletics track, five sports fields. A purpose built Science block with laboratories for Physics, Chemistry, Biology and Electronics. An English block featuring television and film studios and drama rooms, a music block with practice and performance space. A new dance studio with sprung floor, and a large modern swimming pool and sports institute on the school boundary.

Rangitoto College has been hosting international students for over 15 years and we have developed excellent systems to help students adapt to life in a new country. First language support is available for Korean, Chinese and Spanish speaking students.

A dedicated team of non-teaching and teaching staff, the IB Diploma co-ordinator and a Deputy Principal takes care of our IB students, meeting with them regularly to check they are doing well academically and personally.

LET YOUR LIGHT SHINE

(Founded 1884)

Principal
Mr Stephen Webber

DP coordinator
Darren Taylor

Status Private

Boarding/day Day

Gender Coeducational

Language of instruction
English

Authorised IB programmes
DP

Age Range 3 – 19 years

Address
272 Military Road
Cremorne
NSW 2090 | AUSTRALIA

TEL +61 2 9908 6479

Email
dtaylor@redlands.nsw.edu.au
registrar@redlands.nsw.edu.au

Website
www.redlands.nsw.edu.au

Redlands is a leading Australian independent school that offers a contemporary real world education, fostering academic excellence and confidence for life.

We have offered the International Baccalaureate Diploma Programme for Years 11-12 since 1988, longer than any other school in New South Wales. The 30-year association with the IB has helped the school build its reputation as a leading provider of a well-rounded global education.

Redlands provides an extensive range of opportunities – academic, sports, creative, outdoor education, service – for students to learn, to achieve and to develop their unique skills and talents.

The rich and balanced education program is aimed at developing well-rounded, confident and compassionate young adults who are prepared for life after school, ready to meet challenges and embrace opportunities and change in the 21st century.

Our students work together within an inclusive, real world, coeducational environment, complemented by a comprehensive leadership and service programme, to develop the knowledge, capability and confidence to let their light shine – at school and beyond.

At Redlands students receive an outstanding academic education as a result of the school's individual approach, committed teachers and world-class learning programmes and resources.

In embarking on the IB Diploma Programme at Redlands, students will commit themselves to:

- a two-year journey of discovery and self-awareness;
- an experience that will be ultimately both rewarding and empowering; and
- an outcome that will enable a smooth transition between school and university.

As a non-selective school, students who come from over 30 different countries have the opportunity to study for the IB Diploma Programme if they so wish. Careful guidance is undertaken in considering course structure and styles of learning to assist students in making the right choice for them. Each year approximately 50% of Redlands students select the IB.

Redlands IB Results

- In recent years, eleven Redlands students have achieved the perfect IB score – 45/45, putting them in the top 0.2% of IB Diploma Programme students worldwide.
- In 2020, 43% of candidates achieved an IB score of 37+, equating to an ATAR of 95 and above.
- Over the past ten years, a number of candidates were awarded rare bilingual diplomas – in French, German, Italian, Chinese, Japanese, Korean, Dutch, Danish, Swedish and Spanish.

At Redlands, all components of the IB Diploma Programme are delivered by a strong team of IB teachers, including moderators in their subject areas, IB trained workshop leaders and experienced teachers.

For more information about Redlands please contact the Registrar or visit our website: www.redlands.nsw.edu.au.

Regents International School Pattaya

REGENTS INTERNATIONAL SCHOOL
PATTAYA
A NORD ANGLIA EDUCATION SCHOOL

(Founded 1994)

Principal
Mrs. Sarah Osborne-James

DP coordinator
Sara Morrow

Status Private

Boarding/day Mixed

Gender Coeducational

Language of instruction
English

Authorised IB programmes
DP

Age Range 2 – 18 years

Number of pupils enrolled
800

Fees
From THB316,350

Address
33/3 Moo 1, Pong
Banglamung
Chonburi
20150 | THAILAND

TEL +66 (0)93 135 7736

Email admissions@
regents-pattaya.co.th

Website
www.nordangliaeducation.com/
our-schools/pattaya

Be Ambitious Be Regents

About Our School

Regents International School Pattaya is like no other school in Thailand. As part of the global family of 76 premium Nord Anglia schools located around the world, we provide unique learning opportunities far beyond the ordinary. We are an exciting, vibrant and inclusive school which has something to offer to every child and every family in our dynamic and diverse community.

We have approximately 800 students aged from 2 to 18, spread evenly across our Early Primary, Primary and Secondary schools, including around 50 boarding students. As both a day and boarding school we encourage our students to be ambitious in their learning and believe there is no limit to what your child can achieve. We are the most successful school on the Eastern Seaboard with a long-established reputation over the past 27 years. Our students are successful because our approach encourages children to think for themselves, how to question, how to learn – skills that will last them for a lifetime.

Regents is the leading school on the Eastern Seaboard for good reason. We have joined forces with the world famous Juilliard School of Performing Arts in New York, and we also collaborate with the prestigious Massachusetts Institute of Technology (MIT). As well as being part of the Nord Anglia family of schools, who provide an outstanding education to over 68,000 students around the world, we are also proud to be a Round Square school, offering unique opportunities for our students to take part in many exciting global projects.

Boarding

We provide a safe, friendly and active boarding community with the emphasis on continued learning. We provide opportunities to collaborate, study independently, have fun, be active and have a sense of adventure. Our boarders develop into confident, independent, resilient and caring individuals who will make the world a better place. The outstanding range of learning opportunities and new environments to discover in Thailand and in South East Asia, make the boarding experience here so much richer and better value-for-money when compared with boarding schools in the UK, Western Europe and North America.

We Invite You to Experience It For Yourself

Choosing the right community and learning environment for your child is a major decision. We hope you agree that Regents is not only a fabulous school but also the right school for you and we look forward to welcoming you into our family.

RITSUMEIKAN

(Founded 1994)

Head of School
Dr. Joseph Hicks

DP coordinator
Dr. Marcelo Schwarz

Status Private

Boarding/day Mixed

Gender Coeducational

Language of instruction
English, Japanese (IBDP in English)

Authorised IB programmes
DP

Age Range 12 – 17 years

Number of pupils enrolled
1702

Fees
IB course: ¥1,910,000
IP course: ¥1,190,000

Address
33-1 Hachikenyadani
Hirono-cho
Uji, Kyoto, Kansai
611-0031 | JAPAN

TEL +81 774 41 3000

Email
ib-info@ujc.ritsumei.ac.jp

Website
www.ujc.ritsumei.ac.jp/ujc_e/

About

Ritsumeikan Uji Junior and Senior High School is located in scenic Uji City, within a short distance of Kyoto and Osaka. The school is mixed boarding and day, coeducational, and offers an integrated six-year curriculum. Ritsumeikan Uji High School was established in 1994 as an affiliated school of Ritsumeikan University, one of the largest and most prestigious universities in Japan. The school was rebuilt in its current location in 2002 and established a junior high school in 2003.

IP

Beginning in April 2021, the IP Course has been designed to provide Japanese returnees and foreign students with an authentic Japanese educational environment, while engaging in a rigorous core of academic subjects taught in English by experienced International Baccalaureate teachers. IPC homerooms are managed by Japanese and English speaking IB staff, where students can enjoy learning a variety of Japanese cultural traditions as well as core IB curricular elements such as the Approaches to Learning. On completion, students will have an intimate understanding of life in Japan, as well as the knowledge, skills and maturity to find success in our senior high school IB Course.

IB

Since our authorisation in 2009, Ritsumeikan Uji's English language IB Course has endeavoured to provide the highest levels of guidance and support for the academic and personal growth of our multicultural student body. Indeed, our course structure guarantees students the chance to graduate with

a bilingual International Baccalaureate diploma, as well as the Japanese high school certificate. Our IB Course prides itself on small class sizes, individualised care, and an inclusive learning community, guided by a team of experienced and committed staff. With their cultural fluency and world class educational backgrounds, our graduates go on to study at top Japanese institutions as well as prestigious schools overseas including Duke University, Imperial College London, the National University of Singapore and many others.

C Building

The Ritsumeikan Uji IB Course recently moved into the new, specially designed C Building on the Uji campus. The new building houses two fully equipped laboratories, an art studio, collaborative and private study spaces, and a large common lounge area. C Building integrates harmoniously with neighbouring parkland to provide students with a peaceful environment for reflection and focused study.

Events

Our community calendar is full of events, including the annual culture and sports days, as well as supervised trips to destinations across Japan and internationally. These shared experiences strengthen our community and enable IBDP students to broaden their world view.

Boarding

High school students are welcome to stay in our dormitory throughout their three years of study. The dormitory provides meals, wireless internet, is a short bus ride to campus and an easy walk to the city centre.

(Founded 2014)

Head of College
Ms Christine Lucas

PYP coordinator
Caryn Johnson

Status Private

Boarding/day Day

Gender Coeducational

Language of instruction
English

Authorised IB programmes
PYP

Age Range 3 – 18 years

Number of pupils enrolled
673

Fees
Day: AUS$4,477 – AUS$7,968
(Tuition only)

Address
Gate 6, 500 Soldiers Road
Clyde North
VIC 3978 | AUSTRALIA

TEL +61 3 9703 9777

Email
admin@rivercrest.vic.edu.au

Website
www.rivercrest.vic.edu.au

Imagine a campus uniquely and specifically designed for the conceptual age. Imagine a curriculum that is grounded in 21st century thinking, while still encompassing a strong Christian world view.

Welcome to Rivercrest Christian College.

Rivercrest is where technology is fully integrated into the framework of the curriculum; where the learning promotes critical and creative thinking; where the learning spaces are tailor-designed to facilitate such learning and the graduates will be life-long learners, equipped to play their role in the local and global community.

At Rivercrest, students are encouraged to see themselves as global citizens. In addition to acquiring knowledge, they are encouraged to recognise the contribution and responsibility they have to engender greater harmony among the people of the world; to be respectful, compassionate, creative and critical thinkers, who, although prepared to challenge prevailing ideas, are also sensitive and reflective.

Students are encouraged to communicate effectively and work collaboratively with others. Throughout their years at Rivercrest they will be challenged to become citizens of the world who epitomise Christ's commission to love and serve others.

Our Primary Campus caters for students from 3 years-of-age (in our Early Learning Centre) to Year 5. Our growing Middle Years Campus offers classes from Year 6. Additional year levels will open every calendar, reaching Year 12 in 2025.

In offering the International Baccalaureate programme at Rivercrest, we provide a world-leading framework for learning that prepares students for the future with confidence.

Rivercrest Christian College is part of the Crest Educational precinct, including Hillcrest Christian College, Ayr Hill Equestrian Centre and our Environmental Reserve, all on a leafy 138 acre property.

Ruamrudee International School

(Founded 1957)

Head of School Dr. James O'Malley

DP coordinator Ms. Nicole Sabet

Status Private, Non-Profit

Boarding/day Mixed

Gender Coeducational

Language of instruction
English

Authorised IB programmes
DP

Age Range 3 – 18 years

Number of pupils enrolled
900

Fees
US$16,310 – US$24,330

Address
6 Ramkhamhaeng 184
Minburi, Bangkok
10510 | THAILAND

TEL +66 (0)2 791 8900

Email admissions@rism.ac.th

Website www.rism.ac.th

Ruamrudee International School (RIS), founded in 1957 by Catholic Redemptorist Fathers, is one of the first international schools in Southeast Asia to be accredited by the Western Association of Schools and Colleges (WASC). An IB World School since 1998, RIS offers a rigorous and extremely successful International Baccalaureate Diploma Programme (38 courses) and is one of the region's only schools to simultaneously offer the Advanced Placement program (13 courses).

RIS features a diverse group of experienced teachers who are passionate, supportive, and experts in their fields; 72% of whom hold master's degrees or higher. From Pre-K 3 through Grade 12, students benefit from small class sizes; relevant and innovative electives; modern languages; a vibrant performing and visual arts program; and a comprehensive extended day program with creative enrichment opportunities.

Located in the Minburi district of Bangkok along the city outskirts, RIS is less than half an hour from Suvarnabhumi International Airport and is surrounded by a thriving local community. Campus highlights include 21st-century learning spaces, a culinary arts center, recording studio, industrial design studio, a makerspace/robotics lab, and a contemporary boarding residence with a warm, familial feel. The school's lush 29-acre campus and facilities also support one of the largest athletic programs of any international school in Southeast Asia.

In the last few years, RIS IB Diploma students have scored an average of 35, far above world averages, with 2021 culminating in a five-year high of 37 for the year's graduates. After graduation, RIS students go on to attend the most prestigious universities in the world, and a close-knit alumni community can be found working as government leaders, diplomats, and researchers; in all branches of medicine; as startup entrepreneurs; in the entertainment and film industries; as professional athletes; and in the fields of AI and design technologies.

At RIS, the community is deeply involved in student-led, service learning-based extracurricular clubs, activities, and committees or in organizing events in support of charities and causes. The IB Theory of Knowledge (TOK) and Creativity, Action, Service (CAS) elements at RIS count as a required Values credit, and by the end of a two-year commitment, CAS students will have assessed authentic needs within the community and collaborated with friends and organizations, developing new skills and connections along the way. These CAS experiences are compiled into an annual school publication, written by the students themselves, aptly titled *Reflections*.

In 2019, RIS expanded its opportunities for students with the opening of the Ratchapruek campus in Bangkok's Nonthaburi district and more recently the RIS Early Years campus on Prayasuren Road in 2020. In 2022, RIS will launch yet another campus in Phuket, Thailand, as well as celebrate 65 years in education. For more than six decades, the school has offered a deeply ingrained culture of self-reflection and self-improvement, which has resulted in students and alumni who are creative, compassionate, critical thinkers. Their shared commitment to leading happy, healthy lives while helping others to do the same is why the RIS community continues to forge positive, lasting legacies for the world.

SAINT KENTIGERN

(Founded 1953)

Principal
Russell Brooke

DP coordinator
Suzie Tornquist

Status Private, Independent

Boarding/day Mixed

Gender Coeducational

Language of instruction
English

Authorised IB programmes
DP

Age Range 11 – 18 years

Number of pupils enrolled
2250

Address
130 Pakuranga Road
Pakuranga, Auckland
1021 | NEW ZEALAND

TEL +64 9 577 0749

Email
skc_admissions@
saintkentigern.com

Website
www.saintkentigern.com

Welcome to Saint Kentigern College

As strong today as the day the College opened in 1953, the Mission of Saint Kentigern is to provide an education that 'Inspires students to strive for excellence in all areas of life for the glory of God and the service of others'.

Saint Kentigern College delivers a world class education for boys and girls from ages 11 to 18 years old in Auckland, New Zealand. The College is located on a leafy 100-acre campus bordering the beautiful Tamaki Estuary in Pakuranga, Auckland.

Curriculum

Academic success is expected of every student at Saint Kentigern and we challenge our young men and women to excel. An unparalleled range of subjects is taught in modern, specialist facilities. In the final two years of school, the International Baccalaureate Diploma programme is taught by talented educators, who are highly qualified and passionate in their areas of expertise. They are committed to creating an environment that encourages, motivates, and challenges every student to realise their personal potential.

Co-Curricular Activities

Our sports facilities and coaches are among New Zealand's best and we enjoy success in regional and national competitions. We are also deeply committed to the performing arts. Our Drama and Dance students learn in dedicated spaces and perform in a purpose-built performance venue. In addition, our separate Music Centre provides superb, soundproofed facilities for our choral and instrumental enthusiasts.

Boarding

Bruce House, with separate houses for boys and girls, is the place our boarders call home. Boarders are involved in every facet of College life and develop lasting friendships and a strong sense of school spirit. Students from as far afield as Germany, Russia, China, Korea, Thailand and the Pacific Islands come to Saint Kentigern to enjoy the many benefits of studying in New Zealand and to enjoy Saint Kentigern's unique learning environment.

Student Wellbeing

Our students receive the best pastoral care. A dedicated team of teachers and personal care specialists monitor the students' progress socially, academically, and emotionally, ensuring they thrive at school.

Enrolment Enquiries Welcome

We look forward to introducing you to 'A World of Opportunity for Boys and Girls' at Saint Kentigern College in clean, green Auckland, New Zealand.

If you would like more information please contact us by email: skc_admissions@saintkentigern.com or phone us: 0064 9 577 0703.

Sanjay Ghodawat International School

Head of School
Mrs. Sasmita Mohanty

Chairman
Mr. Sanjay D. Ghodawat

DP coordinator
Dr. Bonila Sinha

Status Private

Boarding/day Mixed

Gender Coeducational

Language of instruction
English

Authorised IB programmes
DP

Address
Gat No. 555
Kolhapur – Sangli Highway
Atigre, Maharashtra | **INDIA**

TEL +91 231 2689700

Email
principal@sgischool.in

Website
www.sgischool.in

Education should prepare students today to cope with global challenges. An international curriculum like the IB helps students broaden their horizon of perspective and be more accommodating. The Sanjay Ghodawat International School which has many firsts to its credit is the first school to offer International Baccalaureate (IB) in the Pune to Bengaluru belt. SGIS has carved a niche as the abode of quality education. SGIS is the sole institution to provide world class education through IB Curriculum in the Southern Maharashtra as well as North Karnataka region.

Nestled in the idyllic and serene locale away from the hustle and bustle of city life, SGIS offers the ideal high seat of learning. The state of the art infrastructure complements the needs of the 21st century learner. The attributes of the IB learner profile are emphasized at SGIS to provide all round education which nurture young people to make changes in the country they live in. Our core values, leadership, discipline, academic excellence and global citizenship, illuminate our way, as we guide our students to become independent and productive humans.

We offer residential facilities with comfortable and cozy pastoral care. The hightech classrooms, top notch psychology and science laboratories, world class sports facilities make SGIS the perfect destination for global education. We offer variety of indoor and outdoor sports including horse riding, swimming, archery, rifle shooting, badminton, table tennis, lawn tennis etc. While Multi- Gym is the biggest attraction, the magnanimous stadium can host international sporting events like Cricket, Football, Volley Ball. SGIS takes utmost care about the health and wellness. The balanced nutritious food is the icing on the cake. All these facilities are provided at very affordable fees with the sole intention of extending global curriculum to the beloved students.

Scottish High International School

(Founded 2005)	**Age Range** 3 – 17 years
Head of School Ms Sudha Goyal	**Fees** On request
PYP coordinator Ms Seema Bhati	
DP coordinator Ms Sudha Goyal	**Address** G-Block, Sector 57 Sushant Lok-II Gurugram, Haryana **122011	INDIA**
Status Private	
Boarding/day Mixed	
Gender Coeducational	**TEL** +91 124 4112781-90
Language of instruction English	**Email** schooldirector@ scottishigh.com
Authorised IB programmes PYP, DP	**Website** www.scottishhigh.com

With its distinguished slogan 'Building Personalities, Not Just People', the Scottish High International School, Gurugram, India, stands distinct amidst many. Enterprisingly productive with IB since 2008 (13 Years), Scottish High, the IB World School is going strong with its cosmopolitan vision. Building World Citizens since its inception, it is the institution where the idea of internationalism and inclusiveness has become the way of life.

Housing more than 1600 IB students under one roof, Scottish High International School is a diverse mix of students from across the country and the globe. Looking over the diversity and the infrastructural provisions, one can say that the idea of developing world citizens is rightly justified at Scottish High as the school proudly strives to provide 'one of the best in the world' facilities to the students to foster a consistent and competent climate of international mindedness.

With EOMS ISO 21001:2018 Certification, for Educational Organisation Management System, Scottish High sustains and maintains its proud heritage of quality teaching & learning, occupational health & safety and safe environmental practices through the combined effort of the dedicated students, staff and parents. It is also the first school in India to be associated with this standard to maintain high-quality education.

Curriculum/Examinations offered

Scottish High International School offers:
- IB Primary Years Programme for Nursery to Grade V
- CAIE Secondary I and IGCSE for Grades VI to X
- IB Diploma Programme for Grades XI & XII
- The National Curriculum (ICSE) for Grades VI to X and ISC for Grades XI & XII

Apart from the academic curriculum, Scottish High:

- Has an authorized NCC (National Cadet Corps) wing for boys and girls
- Partners with The Global Education Leadership Foundation (TGELF), which trains young students to cultivate leadership qualities
- Is an authorized centre by CAIE to run the professional development qualifications for teachers
- Is a partner with TAISI, The Association of International Schools of India
- Is associated with Special Olympics, Bharat
- Collaborates with the Govt. of India for research in Autism
- Is an Institutional member of 'The British Council Library', 'The American Center Library', 'The Alliance Francaise De Delhi', 'DELNET' (Developing Library Network)

Facilities:
Structural

- CCTV Secured & Fully Wi-Fi enabled Campus
- A fleet of Air-Conditioned Buses with GPS & CCTV
- 1000 seating air-conditioned dining hall
- 1100 seating air-conditioned auditorium
- Modern medical infirmary with resident doctor and nurses. Fully-equipped with AED, ECG machine, Nebulisers, Inhalers, Ambo Bags, Oxygen Cylinders, and Dental Chair/ availability of Emergency Medicines at all times
- Day Care facility handled with professionals
- AV rooms with a seating capacity of 100 people
- IT centre with cutting-edge facilities
- Maximum 25 children in one classroom
- Exclusive 1:12 teacher-student ratio
- Autism research centre

- More than 300 Admin Professionals & Academic staff along with 250 housekeeping, security, drivers & conductors
- Extended Day Boarding–8:00 am to 4 pm.

Scholastic

- Maths, Science, Social Science, Language, Home Science, IT labs
- Language labs & state-of-the-art activity rooms
- Atal STEM Lab
- CLUBS- Zumba, Photography, Robotics, Astronomy, Bridge Environment
- Special Olympics, MUN, Heritage, Quilling etc.
- State-of-the-art 'Innovation Lab' with hi-tech servers and computers
- Classrooms equipped with audio-visual and computer facilities
- Open shelf library and research centre
- Resource centre for Research & International Curriculum

- Authorized NCC (National Cadet Corps) wing for boys and girls
- Integrated Department for children with special needs
- Spanish, German and French language in addition to English, Hindi & Sanskrit

Sports & Physical Education

- Archery, Gymnastics, Cricket, Soccer, Scuba Diving, Tennis mentored by International level coaches
- Half Olympic size swimming pool/ Splash Pool for toddlers
- Highly equipped Indoor Golf Academy with simulators for professional training
- Splash pool with misty sprays for the toddlers
- Badminton, chess, yoga & judo
- Table tennis & Basket Ball
- Skating, Horse-riding Bridge & Taekwondo
- Athletic track and playing field

Admissions open for the next academic year around August/ September of the previous year

SCOTS COLLEGE

Learning. For Life

EST. 1916

(Founded 1916)

Headmaster Mr Graeme Yule

Senior School Principal
Mr Christian Zachariassen

Middle School Principal
Mr Matt Allen

Junior School Principal
Mr Richard Kirk

PYP coordinator Rosie Roland

MYP coordinator
Ms Kate Bondett

DP coordinator
Mr Mike McKnight

Status Private

Boarding/day Mixed

Gender Coeducational

Language of instruction
English

Authorised IB programmes
PYP, MYP, DP

Age Range 5 – 18 years

Number of pupils enrolled
960

Address
PO Box 15064, Strathmore,
Wellington **6243 | NEW ZEALAND**

TEL +64 4 388 0850

Email enrolments@
scotscollege.school.nz

Website
www.scotscollege.school.nz

Scots College was founded in 1916 and has a proud history for providing a world-class education. It is the only co-educational independent school in New Zealand's capital city, Wellington. Scots rigorous academic curriculum is supported by a diverse range of sporting, cultural, service and leadership opportunities, enabling each student to reach their potential in all aspects of their lives.

The College is comprised of three schools; Junior, Middle and Senior. It is an authorized IB World School and the IB programmes are an integral part of the school's ethos and curriculum design, developing students prepared to learn for life. The school House system provides another dimension to student life with a Dean and Tutor overseeing the pastoral care of each student.

Scots Junior School (Years 1-6) provides a safe and caring environment where students can experience the joys and challenges of learning as they build strong foundations for their future years. The Junior School proudly delivers the IB Primary Years Programme (PYP).

Scots Middle School (Years 7-10) provides a positive and supportive learning environment. Students take specialist classes, specifically in science, arts, technology and languages, and are provided opportunities outside the classroom with weekly sporting programmes, service initiatives and an EOTC programme. The Middle School delivers the IB Middle Years Programme (MYP).

Scots Senior School (Years 11-13) prepares students to succeed now and in their futures with the knowledge and soft skills required for a rapidly evolving work place. Year 11 students undertake a programme that provides a depth and breadth of learning and teaching with a dual pathway offered in Years 12 and 13 of the IBDP or NCEA qualifications.

Scots College is proudly an internationally minded school with a diverse community which welcomes students from around the globe. An active international services team work closely with the international student community. Language options offered in the curriculum include English, Chinese, French, Spanish and Te Reo Maori.

Outside of the classroom Scots is a leader among schools for the quality of its extra-curricular programme. Students are encouraged to try new activities, learn new skills and develop as teams and individuals. Students are encouraged to join a team and or cultural activity with so many on offer. In addition, there are a number of specialist academies for high performance athletes including football (soccer), rugby, netball and cricket. The College has a proven track record of assisting top athletes with pathways to US universities.

Scots College is located in Wellington, a harbour city at the heart of government, home to international embassies and renowned for its vibrant city culture and cosmopolitan population of 180,000 centrally, and 450,000 within the region. The Scots College campus is located in the suburb of Strathmore, a ten minute drive to the central city. Scots College's boarding house provides accommodation and care for over 100 students in a supportive and family orientated environment.

Sendai Ikuei Gakuen

Head of School
Takehiko Katoh

MYP coordinator
Bryan Stevens

DP coordinator
Anthony Sweeney

Status Private

Boarding/day Mixed

Gender Coeducational

Language of instruction
English, Japanese

Authorised IB programmes
MYP, DP

Age Range 12 – 18 years

Number of pupils enrolled
3150

Fees
Tuition ¥700,000
Dormitory ¥1,100,000 plus
tuition

Address
2-4-1 Miyagino
Miyagino-ku
Sendai, Miyagi, Tohoku
983-0045 | JAPAN

TEL +81 22 256 4141

Email
t.sweeney@sendaiikuei.jp

Website
sendaiikuei-english.jp

Sendai Ikuei Gakuen High School is located in the coastal area of north-east Japan, 90-minutes from Tokyo by bullet train. Sendai is the capital city of Miyagi and a home to over 1 million people. It is a thriving metropolis boasting vibrant festivals, local specialty cuisine and a hub for the Arts.

Sendai Ikuei Gakuen offers the MYP and DP in a unique dual language environment. It is committed to equipping students with the knowledge and skills needed for the 21st century. Though it is impossible to predict what today's students will face in the 21st century, it is possible to give them the skills to succeed in an uncertain future. Through offering the IB programmes at Sendai Ikuei Gakuen, we aim to:
- Be sincere and confident global communicators.
- Be responsible in our learning.
- Be innovative in addressing local and international issues in our community.

In order to enable students to achieve their post-high school goals, at either Japanese or International universities, Sendai Ikuei Gakuen offers a comprehensive IB course in two streams – the regular IB Diploma Programme (with all subjects except language B conducted in English) and the Dual Language Diploma Programme: in which students can take up to four subjects in Japanese.

There is a growing number of international students studying at Sendai Ikuei Gakuen from a variety of backgrounds including China, Korea, Indonesia, Thailand, Uganda, and Kazakhstan – many of whom aspire to enter Japanese universities. The IB programmes at Sendai Ikuei Gakuen provide these students with the opportunities to further their horizons in the future by strengthening both their English and Japanese language skills to an academic level. Students can board at the school dormitory close to the Tagajo campus.

Sendai Ikuei Gakuen IB students experience a unique bilingual (English and Japanese) education in an international environment. Opportunities to study abroad, participate in local field trips and cultural activities, interact in Japanese and English with teachers and students from a variety of countries, study in state-of-the art facilities, engage in school-based Model United Nations camps, and CAS workshops, while experiencing the uniqueness and richness of Japanese culture.

Headmaster
Prof. Kenji Tamura

DP coordinator
Regina Ver-Santos

Status State

Boarding/day Day

Gender Coeducational

Language of instruction
English, Japanese

Authorised IB programmes
DP

Age Range 15 – 18 years

Number of pupils enrolled
480

Fees
¥800,000

Address
1-24-1 Chiyoda
Sakado, Saitama, Kanto
350-0214 | JAPAN
TEL +81 49 281 1541

Website
www.sakado-s.tsukuba.ac.jp

Senior High School at Sakado, University of Tsukuba (UTSS) is Japan's first "Integrated Course" high school, actively promoting reforms in education and research. In line with the school's mission to provide diverse learning opportunities to students, UTSS is now an IB World School offering the dual-language Diploma Programme in Japanese and English.

UTSS is an affiliated Article One high school of the University of Tsukuba. The school campus is located at Sakado, Saitama, approximately an hour from the center of Tokyo, with access through the Tobu Tojo line.

Students in the IBDP course of UTSS complete a three-year programme, beginning Year 1 with pre-DP and foundational courses, followed by Years 2 and 3 covering the 6 groups in the IBDP. The high school currently offers the following subjects under the IBDP:

Subjects in Japanese
  • Japanese A: Language and Literature (HL)
  • History (HL)
  • Biology (SL)
  • Mathematics AI (SL)

Subjects in English
  • English B (HL)
  • Economics (SL)
  • Theatre (SL)

The core subjects, Creativity, Activity and Service (CAS), Extended Essay (EE) and Theory of Knowledge (TOK) are delivered and supervised in Japanese, however, students have the option to write their EE in English.

The dual-language program requires the students to work in the context of Japanese and English. The curriculum practices and develops reading, speaking, listening and writing skills in both languages, with emphasis on the use of higher order thinking skills.

Students use Japanese and English as a means to understand and express critical and analytical ideas, thus, they are expected to have a solid grasp of both languages.

Even before becoming an IB World School, UTSS has consistently exercised experiential learning through fieldwork, school camps, research, clubs, volunteer work and international student exchange. These activities provide diverse platforms to enrich their learning experiences, and complement the core subjects of the IBDP.

The teachers and staff of UTSS recognize that each student is an individual with unique capabilities and intelligences. The curriculum is designed to encourage and support students in choosing career paths where they will thrive. UTSS graduates are empowered to meet the challenges of a changing world – both local and international.

CELEBRATING 40 YEARS OF THE BRITISH SCHOOL,
40 YEARS OF IBDP & THE 110TH ANNIVERSARY OF SFS

(Founded 1912)

Head of School Mr. Colm Flanagan

Elementary School Principal
Damian Prest

Middle School Principal
Justin Smith

High School Principal
Dr. Nancy Le Nezet

PYP coordinator
Michael Lucchesi

MYP coordinator Chris Horan

DP coordinator Piotr Kocyk

Status Private, Non-Profit

Boarding/day Day

Gender Coeducational

Language of instruction
English

Authorised IB programmes
PYP, MYP, DP

Age Range 2 – 18 years

Number of pupils enrolled
1500

Address
39 Yeonhui-ro 22-gil
Seodaemun-gu
Seoul 03723 | **REPUBLIC OF KOREA**

TEL +82 2 330 3100

Email
admissions@seoulforeign.org

Website
www.seoulforeign.org

Seoul Foreign School Inspiring Excellence, Building Character – since 1912

Seoul Foreign School is the longest established international school in Korea and one of the first 10 international schools in the world. Founded in 1912, it offers a community of teaching and learning excellence, coming together to educate children at all ages and stages. Seoul Foreign School inspires a passion for learning, pursues academic and creative excellence and is dedicated to the service of others.

An unrivalled legacy is combined with state-of-the-art facilities on our 25 acre campus in central Seoul. With a current population of over 1450 students from more than 50 countries and with many diverse backgrounds, our students are able to learn and grow as truly global citizens.

Four sections, Elementary School, Middle School, High School and the British School, are situated together on a world class campus benefitting from individual space but aligned with one purpose and ethos. Academic, physical and spiritual needs are served across the facilities. Students have the opportunity to participate in various activities – within the school day and in extracurricular time – including many competitive sports, arts, sciences and holistic interests.

Seoul Foreign School is an IB continuum school – a Pre-K to Grade 12 IB World School and additionally Foundation to Year 9 British School. The IB Primary Years Programme and IB Middle Years Programme are offered along with the English National Curriculum and both lead into the IB Diploma Programme. Based on its history of 40 years of IB Diploma Programme, SFS High School provides students an outstanding flexibility allowing 160 combinations of subjects, including unique course offerings in Seoul such as Design & Technology.

Teachers are rigorously selected and their passion, inspiration and academic excellence ensure that students go on to attend prestigious universities and colleges and succeed in all walks of life. Seoul Foreign School is a Christian school for all. Students enjoy an education surrounded by rich heritage in preparation for a future as global contributors.

HONGQIAO-PUDONG

(Founded 1996)

Director of Schools
Daniel Eschtruth

PYP coordinator Vincent Lehane

MYP coordinator Tetsuo Ishii

DP coordinator Scott Simmons

Status Private

Boarding/day Day

Gender Coeducational

Language of instruction
English

Authorised IB programmes
PYP, MYP, DP

Age Range 2 – 18

Number of pupils enrolled
1550

Fees
Day: RMB122,000 – RMB277,500

Hongqiao Campus
1161 Hongqiao Road, Shanghai
200051 | CHINA

TEL +86 21 6261 4338

Hongqiao ECE Campus
2212 Hongqiao Road, Shanghai
200336 | CHINA

TEL +86 21 6295 1222

Pudong Campus
198 Hengqiao Road, Zhoupu,
Pudong, Shanghai **201315 | CHINA**

TEL +86 21 5812 9888

Email
admissions@scis-china.org

Website www.scis-china.org

Established in 1996 as one of Shanghai's first international schools, Shanghai Community International School (SCIS) is a non-profit educational day school, governed by a self-perpetuating board of directors and overseen by the International Schools Foundation.

With over twenty years of rich tradition, SCIS offers a truly unique international experience. The SCIS community is unparalleled, consisting of a diverse mix of outstanding teachers, students, and parents representing over sixty nationalities and thirty-five languages, across six continents. SCIS leverages this unique community to provide a personalized approach to holistic education, ensuring all students have the opportunity to be successful.

SCIS is one of the first international schools in Shanghai to become fully authorized as an International Baccalaureate (IB) Continuum World School, a world class academic program aimed at rigorous critical thinking and global citizenship. This accreditation extends across all SCIS Campuses, including Hongqiao and Pudong, providing a seamless program for students aged 2-18, and comprised of the Primary Years Programme (PYP), Middle Years Programme (MYP), and Diploma Programme (DP).

Primary Years Programme (PYP) prepares students to become active, caring, lifelong learners who demonstrate respect for themselves and others and have the capacity to participate in the world around them. It focuses on the development of the whole child as an inquirer, both within and beyond the classroom. (Age 2-10)

Middle Years Programme (MYP) is a challenging framework that encourages students to make practical connections between their studies and the real world. The MYP is a five-year programme, which can be implemented in a partnership between schools. Students who complete the MYP are well-prepared to undertake the IB Diploma Programme (DP). (Age 11-15)

Diploma Programme (DP) is designed as an academically challenging and balanced program of education with final examinations that prepares students for success at university and life beyond. (Age 16-17)

上海協和双語学校

SHANGHAI UNITED INTERNATIONAL SCHOOL

(Founded 2003)

Principal
Mr David Walsh

PYP coordinator
Jayanthi Nayak

DP coordinator
Ben Griffiths

Status Private

Boarding/day Day

Gender Coeducational

Language of instruction
English

Authorised IB programmes
PYP, DP

Number of pupils enrolled
1985

Gubei Campus
248 Hong Song Road (E), Gubei
Minhang District
Shanghai
201103 | CHINA

Hongqiao Campus
999 Hong Quan Road
Minhang District
Shanghai
201103 | CHINA

TEL +8621 51753030

Email
annie.yan@suis.com.cn

Website
www.suis.com.cn

Shanghai United International School was founded in 2003 and was authorized as an IB World School in 2010.

Situated in Shanghai it caters for more than 2,300 students on two campus,Hongqiao and Gubei. Hongqiao Campus offers IB PYP, Gubei Secondary Campus offers Key Stage 3, IGCSE and IBDP.

Students are drawn from more than 40 nationalities, represented across the schools. Close links with nearby Chinese primary and secondary schools allow for rich academic and cultural exchanges leading to the enhancement of the school's signature 'East meets West' characteristic.

At the end of Grade 5, students are bilingual, proficient in both Chinese and English and able to comfortably access the curriculum of their secondary school. Some students use three languages with ease.

Augmenting the academic work of the school is a wide-ranging programme of extracurricular activities catering for the cerebral, the athletic, the artistic and the social aspects of life – hugely supported and enjoyed by the students. The aim of the school is to produce students who are prepared to live life to the full and to contribute to making the world a better place for all.

School facilities include an extensive games field, a 400 seat auditorium, an indoor heated swimming pool, a very large gymnasium and a cultural centre for the benefit of the students (and community at weekends). The range of laboratories and specialist teaching rooms necessary to support the IB programmes are also available.

Staff are recruited from many countries, with the USA, Canada, the UK and Australia being particularly well represented. This staff teaches alongside highly qualified and talented local Chinese teachers to provide a practical cross-cultural pedagogical framework in which students thrive. A comprehensive programme of staff professional development, both locally and internationally, is in place to enhance IB skills and to develop further the expertise of all staff.

Living in Shanghai at the beginning of the 21st century is an extraordinary opportunity for students to be part of a rapidly developing social and economic milieux, with all the benefits and opportunities this possesses. Shanghai United International School is ideally positioned to work with students to maximize their learning in preparation for being truly global citizens.

Introducing Tomorrow's Innovators, Today

Shekou International School

(Founded 1988)

Head of School
Greg Smith

PYP coordinator
Alice Cheung

DP coordinator
Craig Ortner

Status Private

Boarding/day Day

Gender Coeducational

Language of instruction
English

Authorised IB programmes
PYP, DP

Age Range 2 – 18 years

Number of pupils enrolled
1000

Address
Jingshan Villas, Nanhai
Boulevard
Shekou, Nanshan
Shenzhen, Guangdong | CHINA

TEL +86 755 2669 3669

Email
admissions@sis.org.cn

Website
www.sis-shekou.org

Shekou International School (SIS) is a two-campus, private, co-educational, not-for-profit school located in Shenzhen, China. For over 30 years, SIS has long been at the forefront of international education for expatriate children in the region. SIS is an IB World School offering the Primary Years Programme (PYP) and the IB Diploma Programme (IBDP), and is fully accredited by the Western Association of Schools and Colleges (WASC). We are a member of the East Asian Council of Overseas Schools (EARCOS), the Association for the Advancement of International Education (AAIE), and a founding member of All-China and Mongolia International School (ACAMIS) organization.

SIS currently enrolls over 1000 international students from Nursery through Grade 12 (ages 2-18). Our student body represents more than 40 different countries, including the US, Canada, South Korea, Hong Kong, India, France, and Germany. We currently employ over 250 world-class licensed faculty and staff members hailing from over 20 different countries. Our faculty and staff are masters of their craft, inspiring our students to become lifelong learners.

SIS provides a well-balanced, rigorous education that challenges students across all disciplines. At SIS, we use the best global practices in our curriculum. Our curriculum and programs develop students' knowledge, self-awareness, and self-confidence, allowing them to become the best representatives of the school as they enter universities and achieve success in a wide array of contexts. The language of instruction is English for all classes except for proficiency level Mandarin and French courses.

Service-learning is an essential part of the educational experience at SIS. Engaging students in community service projects is a way of encouraging our students to be principled, caring, and open-minded. Learning outside the classroom and helping others promotes empathy and understanding that supports students' ability to impact global and local communities.

Our co-curricular program engages students in opportunities to develop and extend themselves outside the classroom. Students are encouraged to participate in a wide variety of sporting events, after school activities, clubs, and service. We believe these play an essential role in the broader holistic program offered by our school.

A partnership between educators, parents, and students, all working together to create a caring, supportive, and engaged community is the foundation of life here at SIS. Together, we provide a vibrant learning environment that extends beyond the classroom. Our Parent Support Association (PSA) are an integral part of our community that enhances and promotes school spirit.

At SIS, our Mission is to provide a rigorous education in a caring community and inspires our students to become principled, innovative contributors in a transforming world.

SHIV NADAR SCHOOL
Education for Life

Director Principal
Ms. Monica Sagar

DP coordinator
Sriparna Chakrabarti

Status Private

Boarding/day Day

Gender Coeducational

Language of instruction
English

Authorised IB programmes
DP

Fees
Day: £6,755

Address
DLF City, Phase -1 Block -E
Pahari Road
Gurugram, Haryana | **INDIA**

TEL +91 124 4549200

Email
admissions.gurgaon@sns.edu.in

Website
shivnadarschool.edu.in/gurgaon

Shiv Nadar School is an initiative of the Shiv Nadar Foundation and made its foray into urban K12 private education in 2012 to deliver educational excellence and nurture ethical, respectful, happy and purposeful citizens of society. At Shiv Nadar School, the term "school" has a different meaning. The school for us is a Sensitive(S) and Child-centric(C) environment fostering Critical enquiry, which is like a 'Home(H)' away from home and where the children develop a love for Life-long learning(L) through Observation(O) and experience, to become Outstanding(O) human beings. Our motto is Education for Life for students who are agents of change, who are strong and resilient yet flexible in the changing fortunes of time.

The School is progressive in its approach, follows an experiential pedagogy and integrates technology into its educational practices giving considerable curricular emphasis on IT, Sports and Arts. Learning at our schools is never linear; instead, students are immersed in the multidimensional and the experiential. They are encouraged towards value-led pursuits so that they comprehend their role in the larger context of community and the world. We integrate an experiential pedagogy and extensive use of technology into our educational practices. Our faculty is challenged and empowered to engage students in processes that help them develop initiative, risk-taking, self-esteem, self-discipline, cooperation, and the self-motivation necessary to be successful human beings. They learn how to think, not what to think – and we believe that's the best way to be prepared for life in the 21st century.

Our core values of integrity and loyalty, commitment to excellence, openness and transparency, life-long learning, respect and compassion and a sense of responsibility and purpose, define everything that we do. We offer IBDP to grades XI & XII, IGCSE to grades IX & X as a choice; and CBSE from grades Nursery - Grade XII.

ST ANDREW'S CATHEDRAL SCHOOL

(Founded 1885)

Head of School
Dr Julie McGonigle

MYP coordinator
Kathleen Layhe

DP coordinator
Sharon Munro

Status Private

Boarding/day Day

Gender Coeducational

Language of instruction
English

Authorised IB programmes
MYP, DP

Age Range 5 – 18 years

Number of pupils enrolled
1440

Fees
Day: AUS$20,588 – AUS$36,304

Address
Sydney Square
Sydney
NSW 2000 | AUSTRALIA

TEL +61 2 9286 9500

FAX +61 2 9286 9550

Email
enrolments@sacs.nsw.edu.au

Website
www.sacs.nsw.edu.au

St Andrew's Cathedral School (SACS) is a dynamic, independent school located in the centre of Sydney's CBD. With modern facilities and innovative learning environments, our urban location presents innumerable opportunities for students to engage beyond the classroom; at city museums, concert halls, theatres, national institutions and galleries.

Our central city location enables students to travel with their parents to work, or easily reach the school by train, car or bus.

Our Academic Programme

SACS caters for all learners, encouraging each to develop a lifelong love of learning. The overwhelming majority of students pursue university education following graduation – with increasing numbers going overseas to study.

SACS offers two credentials for the final years of school (Years 11 – 12): the Higher School Certificate (HSC) from the NSW Board of Studies, Teaching and Educational Standards, and the International Baccalaureate Diploma Programme (DP). Typically, around 70 per cent of our Diploma students receive ATAR (Australian Tertiary Admissions Rank) conversion scores above 90, that is, in the top 10 per cent of the state of New South Wales. As a fully comprehensive school, St Andrew's differentiates teaching practices to accommodate students with a broad range of interests and abilities. Our performance in public Australian examinations suggests an atmosphere of highly accomplished learning and teaching.

At SACS, every student is nurtured, encouraged and valued. A growing number of international students enrol every year and a diverse community of students are drawn from all over Sydney and beyond.

Extracurricular Activities

Our comprehensive student wellbeing programs encourage a passion for learning and a culture of participation across sport, music, outdoor education and the performing arts. There are more than 20 music and drama ensembles at the school, along with an impressive variety of sporting opportunities and a comprehensive outdoor education program, based at the school's rural Southern Highlands property.

Please take a virtual tour here: www.sacs.nsw.edu.au/virtual-tour

For further information, contact us by telephone on +61 2 9286 9579 or +61 2 9286 9664 or email the Enrolments Department at enrolments@sacs.nsw.edu.au.

St Andrews International School Bangkok

ST ANDREWS INTERNATIONAL SCHOOL
BANGKOK
A NORD ANGLIA EDUCATION SCHOOL

(Founded 1997)

Head of School
Mr. Paul Schofield

DP coordinator
Mr. William Taylor

Status Private

Boarding/day Day

Gender Coeducational

Language of instruction
English

Authorised IB programmes
DP

Age Range 2 – 18 years

Number of pupils enrolled
2000

Fees
Day: THB331,000 – THB702,000

Address
1020 Sukhumvit Road
Phra Khanong, Khlong Toei
Bangkok
10110 | THAILAND

High School
1020 Sukhumvit Road, Phra
Khanong, Khlong Toei, Bangkok
10110 | THAILAND

TEL +662 056 9555

Email
officehs@standrews.ac.th

Website
www.standrews.ac.th

St Andrews International School Bangkok was founded in 1997 on an attractive, conveniently located site, with excellent facilities and good access to local transportation. Today we are a school of more than 2,000 students representing some 50 nationalities ranging from Nursery (2 years) to Year 13 (18 years). In August 2017 we opened an additional campus at a nearby prime city centre location which delivers state of the art purpose-built learning facilities to our High School.

Our school provides a high quality, professional, well-resourced learning environment where each child's talents and abilities are recognised and nurtured, and their needs supported. Our teachers are professional and caring, selected for their awareness of the needs of a broad range of children who may come from different social, cultural, religious and educational backgrounds. They are capable educators who take care with their preparation of the curriculum, use a variety of strategies for its delivery and pay close attention to the progression of each individual.

We are an inclusive school that welcomes students of all abilities. To ensure that all our children have an equality of opportunity, we have a professional Learning Support Department. This team works with class teachers to identify and support children in their learning across the school, whether they need extra help with their studies or have been identified as gifted and talented.

The curriculum draws on the best UK practices, adapted to reflect the international context of the school. Students take IGCSE examinations at the end of Year 11 and then follow the Senior Studies Programme in Years 12 and 13. Our school offers the International Baccalaureate Diploma Programme, alongside an alternative school-based curriculum, both of which lead to graduation and provide the opportunity to apply to prestigious universities all around the world. As part of Nord Anglia Education, the world's leading premium schools organisation, we collaborate with the preeminent performing arts conservatory, The Juilliard School, and one of the world's leading universities, the Massachusetts Institute of Technology (MIT), to bring truly inspiring learning experiences to all of our students.

With high quality teaching, excellent facilities and small class sizes, St Andrews International School Bangkok offers students the opportunity to fulfil their academic potential in a stimulating, caring and nurturing environment. We are fully accredited by CfBT Education Trust and Thailand's Office for National Education Standards and Quality Assessment (ONESQA), the first school in Thailand to receive this joint accreditation award.

St Margaret's College
Balanced foundations, bright futures.

(Founded 1910)

Executive Principal
Mrs Diana Patchett

International Dean
Ms Deanne Gath

DP coordinator
Ms Beth Rowse

Status Private, Independent

Boarding/day Mixed

Gender Female

Language of instruction
English

Authorised IB programmes
DP

Number of pupils enrolled
830

Fees
International from NZ$45,684.15 excluding boarding

Address
12 Winchester Street
Merivale
Christchurch
8014 | NEW ZEALAND

TEL +64 3 379 2000

Email
enrol@stmargarets.school.nz

Website
www.stmargarets.school.nz

St Margaret's College is one of New Zealand's leading girls' school with a proud 110-year history of academic, sporting and cultural excellence. An education at St Margaret's College offers a dual academic pathway to leading universities around the world through the International Baccalaureate as well as NCEA, the only girls' school in New Zealand's South Island to do so. Students regularly top both the New Zealand IB and NCEA rankings, opening opportunities at leading international and New Zealand universities.

St Margaret's College values the cultural diversity that students from around the world bring to the school community as they learn to live and lead in a global society. St Margaret's College has played host to thousands of forward-thinking young women and educators over the last century. It leads the way in providing a world-class education in a teaching and learning environment tailored to suit girls while celebrating the traditions of its founding values.

All students are offered a breadth of opportunities where they can shine, unencumbered by gender stereotypes. While academic results are consistently outstanding, it is the variety of curriculum offerings and opportunities available that ensure the interests and learning styles of every girl are catered for. Our international students are completely integrated into school life and, where appropriate, receive additional support in specific areas of the curriculum. Girls come to St Margaret's from many different countries and are actively encouraged to experience and participate in the rich sporting, cultural and social life of the school, Christchurch and Canterbury while studying for the International Baccalaureate Diploma.

The school enjoys the most modern school campus in Christchurch, providing a future-proofed learning environment, including our leading Centre for Innovation and STEM programmes, that attracts high quality teachers and provides students with a safe and inspirational space to learn.

St Margaret's College values the cultural and global dimension students from around the world bring and provides a warm, caring home-away-from-home in its three boarding houses. The boarding houses are arranged in year groups, tailored to the specific needs of each developmental stage, and provide the opportunity of a first-class education while building strong friendships and learning lifelong values.

St Margaret's College is a family that values each girl for the gifts and talents she brings, that provides a safe place for her to take on new challenges and empowers her to live and lead.

St. Joseph's Institution International

ST. JOSEPH'S INSTITUTION INTERNATIONAL

(Founded 2007)

High School Principal
Mrs Roisin Paul

Elementary School Principal
Ms Catherine Nicol

DP coordinator Guy Bromley

Status Private

Boarding/day Mixed

Gender Coeducational

Language of instruction
English

Authorised IB programmes
DP

Age Range 4 – 18 years

Number of pupils enrolled
2000

Fees
From S$32,978

Address
490 Thomson Road
298191 | SINGAPORE

TEL +65 6353 9383

Email admissions.hs@
sji-international.com.sg

Website
www.sji-international.com.sg

Established in 2007, St. Joseph's Institution International offers a holistic, values-driven and international educational experience to a diverse student body of 40 nationalities rooted in the context of Singapore.

As a school with a Lasallian Catholic foundation, our community welcomes students, teachers, parents, friends and supporters of all faiths and cultural backgrounds. Our mission is to enable students to learn how to learn and learn how to live, empowering them to become people of integrity and people for others. Our core Lasallian values are central to everything that we do: spirituality, mutual respect, internationalism, leadership, experiences and service.

Today, we celebrate a community of 2,000 students across two schools on one campus. The Elementary School offers the International Primary Curriculum for pre-school Prep 1 – 2 (ages 4 turning 5 – 6) and Grade 1 – 6 (ages 7 – 12), while the High School offers the IGCSE followed by the IB Diploma Programme in Grades 7 – 12 (ages 12 – 18).

The IB Diploma Programme
The attributes of the IB Learner profile underpin much of the teaching and learning throughout SJI International with a desire to develop curious, independent and confident learners. The most important principle within the school's educational philosophy is that of active learning. Crucially, active learning is about students doing. This involves a wide range of activities within the programme which will vary according to the subject: research, role plays, simulations, thinking exercises, decision-making exercises, debates, presentations and so on. These provide a stimulating educational environment and one that is intellectually challenging for the students.

Values, education and character-building are achieved through a range of challenging activities in sports, adventure and creativity, with a special emphasis on service, featuring weekly service activities and overseas projects that help students connect with and serve the local and global community.

We are justifiably proud of the outstanding achievements of our IB Diploma students. Many of our graduates have continued their studies at many of the top universities around the world. But outstanding academic results are only part of what we strive for. Our students leave SJI International ready for lifelong learning.

Stonehill International School

STONEHILL
INTERNATIONAL SCHOOL

An Embassy Group Education Initiative

(Founded 2008)

Head of School
Dr. Brian D. Brumsickle

Primary School Principal
Karen Crooke

Secondary School Principal
Joe Lumsden

PYP coordinator Zita Joyce

MYP coordinator Jitendra Pandey

DP coordinator Manpreet Kaur

Status Private

Boarding/day Mixed

Gender Coeducational

Language of instruction
English

Authorised IB programmes
PYP, MYP, DP

Age Range 3 – 18 years

Number of pupils enrolled
550

Address
Near the International Airport,
No.259/333/334/335
Tarahunise Post, Jala Hobli
Bengaluru, Karnataka
562157 | INDIA

TEL +91 70 2666 6911

Email admissions@stonehill.in

Website www.stonehill.in

Founded in 2008, Stonehill International School is one of the most widely reputed international schools in Bangalore, India. We are an IB school and are accredited by the Council of International Schools (CIS), and the New England Association of Schools and Colleges (NEASC). Stonehill is also a member of the Australian Boarding Schools Association (ABSA).

The expansive 34-acre lush green campus, near the International Airport, offers ample space and infrastructure for sporting, cultural, and leisure activities. Besides state-of-the art classrooms, the world-class facilities include a 25-meter temperature-controlled pool, synthetic turf football field, tennis and volleyball courts, an Arts Centre, a STEM block, and a multipurpose sports hall. Stonehill also prides itself on modern boarding houses and a fully equipped cafeteria that serves nutritious and healthy meals.

As a world class educational institution, Stonehill is a dynamic, inclusive, and friendly day and boarding school. Our students and faculty comprise 35 different nationalities. We are dedicated to our mission statement – *"To provide stimulating, engaging academics integrated with enhanced opportunities for technological innovation, sports, and the arts."*

University Placement Programme

Our Career and College Counselling Department works with students from Grade 9 onwards to identify their aptitude, understand their interests, and guide them towards colleges that will help them meet their academic and personal goals.

Stonehill graduates have been accepted to some of the most prestigious universities across the globe including, Stanford University, University of Cambridge, Dartmouth College, London School of Economics (LSE), New York University (NYU), University of California, Los Angeles (UCLA), Sarah Lawrence College, University of Southern California (USC), Massachusetts Institute of Technology (MIT) Boston, University of British Columbia (UBC), LaSalle School of Arts, City University of Hong Kong, and many more.

English as an additional language (EAL)

Stonehill offers support to non-native English-speaking students. Individual programmes are developed to enable English language acquisition in students. To aid faster learning, EAL students are included in regular classes, as often as possible.

Sports

Through our sports programme, importance is given to not just students' health and fitness, but also to developing skills, learning to work in teams and building leadership and personal growth. Stonehill students also compete regularly with teams from other schools in Bangalore, India, and Asia. Our students have made us proud by demonstrating commitment, great attitude and the spirit of teamwork. Swimming, tennis, equestrian sports, basketball, football, volleyball, and cricket are just a few of our sports offerings.

Arts

Stonehill prides itself on a committed Arts department with a special focus on Visual Art, Drama, and Music. Stonehill uses the creative arts to promote attitudes such as empathy

and appreciation, and skills such as analysis, that help see the uniqueness of each person as well as explore the commonalities that connect each other.

We have a dedicated Arts Centre, that has purpose built spaces for music, visual art, and drama. We also offer private music lessons for instruments such as piano, guitar, drums, violin and cello along with numerous opportunities to perform at concerts, assemblies and other gatherings.

Technology

At Stonehill, we have a 1:1 policy for devices and our students use a wide variety of tools to communicate, collaborate, research, and create.

In the Primary School, the digital citizenship programme teaches students to be safe and responsible in the online world. They use an all in one digital platform for planning, assessments, portfolios, projects, and reports, which they can independently navigate. Learning is supported through the Makerspace where digitally enhanced Lego and robotics work alongside the traditional elements of design, sewing, and construction.

Technology in the Secondary School is seamlessly integrated into all subjects. Additionally, Product Design, Digital Design, Design Technology, and Computer Science are offered as subjects.

Boarding

Stonehill offers weekly and full time boarding options to students. The residential programme at Stonehill is for students from Grade 6 onwards, and is designed to extend learning the IB way through academics, extracurricular activities, and the social aspects of boarding. It offers students a home away from home, with spacious and comfortable living areas, and access to a host of extracurricular activities. The small number of boarders provides a warm atmosphere and creates a sense of community.

The boarding houses at Stonehill feature twin and quad sharing rooms, a common lounge, and a study room. The houses are supported by a cafeteria, a fitness centre, and a 24-hour medical centre. Experienced House Parents, tutors, and service staff take care of children and their individual needs.

Suzhou Singapore International School

Suzhou Singapore International School
苏州新加坡外籍人员子女学校

(Founded 1996)

Head of School Samer Khouri

PYP coordinator
Katriona Hoskins

MYP coordinator Peter Coats

DP coordinator
Laurence Mueller

Status Private

Boarding/day Day

Gender Coeducational

Language of instruction
English

Authorised IB programmes
PYP, MYP, DP

Age Range 2 – 18 years

Number of pupils enrolled
1000

Address
208 Zhong Nan Street
Suzhou Industrial Park
Jiangsu **215021** | **CHINA**

TEL +86 512 6258 0388

Email information@
mail.ssis-suzhou.net

Website www.
suzhousinternationalschool.com

Suzhou Singapore International School (SSIS) was founded in 1996 in the Suzhou Singapore Industry Park. It is a fully authorized IB World School as well as the oldest and largest international school in Suzhou, China. Since its establishment, SSIS has grown from 20 students in a few rooms into a school of a 14-hectare campus with 1000+ students from 45 different nationalities.

SSIS offers a challenging curriculum to cultivate global citizens and life-long learners. Everyday students are challenged to actively participate in their education. This produces students that consistently perform well above world averages, and is why SSIS is one of the best schools in China.

Values and Mission
SSIS provides an excellent international education to the children of expatriate families. Faculty and staff are committed to creating a learning environment that encourages and enables students to be self-motivated, lifelong learners. SSIS educate students to become global citizens that value other cultures and are responsible, meaningful participants in the international community.

Curriculum and Activities
SSIS offers three IB programs including PYP, MYP and DP from preschool to Grade 12 along with a German curriculum in the elementary school. A strong partnership between students, faculty and parents, enables SSIS to maintain a rigorous and challenging education. SSIS offer a wide range of academic, cultural and recreational programs ensuring to deliver the highest quality international education possible. SSIS offers more than 100+ activities, whether it is the visual arts program, showcased by a week-long celebration of the Arts;

SSIS Book Week, celebrating global literacy or the much-anticipated International Family Day, there is something for everyone. SSIS students also have the opportunity to compete against other peer schools in academics, arts and sports, through its memberships with ACAMIS, SISAC, EARCOS and CISSA.

Accreditations and Affiliations
SSIS is accredited by external agencies including IB (International Baccalaureate Organization), CIS (International Association of Schools) and NEASC (New England Association of Schools). SSIS is also a member of the Association of China and Mongolia International Schools (ACAMIS) and the East Asia Regional Council Schools (EARCOS).

Faculty and Staff
SSIS attracts the highest caliber of teachers with masters degrees and doctorates. Faculty is comprised of over 150 dedicated professionals from over 20 countries, each bringing their own unique perspective on teaching and learning.

Campus
Spread across a spacious 14 hectometer campus, the building boasts integrated technology and air purification systems throughout all classrooms and common areas. Art and Performance facilities include 600-seat theater, black box theater, orchestra room, 3 dance studios, individual music practice spaces and art carrels. Recreational facilities include 3 playgrounds, 2 gymnasiums, a new soccer pitch, 400M running track, 25M swimming pool and tennis courts. The Science and Design facilities include fully equipped science, food technology and hard materials labs. The Learning Technology Center includes 500+ ipads, charging stations, green room, podcast facilities and Lego robotics room.

Taipei Kuei Shan School

Head of School Dr. Peter Tsai

PYP coordinator Elizabeth Hu

MYP coordinator Caleb Lin

DP coordinator Robert Chung

Status Private

Boarding/day Day

Gender Coeducational

Language of instruction Chinese, English

Authorised IB programmes PYP, MYP, DP

Age Range 4 – 18 years

Number of pupils enrolled 700

Address
200 Mingde Road
Taipei
11280 | TAIWAN

TEL +886 2 2821 2009

Email
info@kss.tp.edu.tw

Website
www.kshs.tp.edu.tw

Taipei Kuei Shan School is an International Baccalaureate World School offering three programmes – PYP, MYP, and DP. It is fully accredited by the Taipei City Government Department of Education and a member of the Association of Christian Schools International.

Kuei Shan was established in 1963 as a K-9 school, founded by Professor Hsiong Hui-Ying as a research project to improve Taiwan Education. Many decades ago, education in Taiwan was a "one-size-fits-all" approach. To allow a holistic development of learners, Professor Hsiong built Kuei Shan as a small school environment with smaller class size to promote active learning, both academically and socially. She practiced the use of unit teaching and theme-based learning to engage students in hands-on and collaborative learning activities. Upon the success of this long-term research, the school continues its commitment to educational research and excellence.

In 2015, the high school program was added, and Kuei Shan's first DP cohort graduated in 2017. As a small private school, we provide a lively campus community for more than 700 students from Pre-Kindergarten to Grade 12 by blending educational excellence and an international perspective with Christian values. About 80% of our student body are Taiwan nationals and 20% are from 13 other countries.

Our Mission

Taipei Kuei Shan School is a Christ-centered community where students have opportunities to know God, follow Him and strive to live uprightly in a way He would approve. Our mission is to educate the whole person and develop life-long learners who are equipped to become knowledgeable and critical thinkers, effective communicators, responsible and engaged world citizens, virtuous servant-leaders, and enthusiastic stewards to serve one another, their community, Taiwan, and the world.

Activities and Service

- The school supports students to participate in a Taiwan team sports program which includes basketball, volleyball, soccer, softball, swimming, track & field, and cross-country.
- Students have opportunities to participate in band, string ensemble, choir, worship band, and drama.
- Students have opportunities to conduct a wide range of outreach and community service for underprivileged children and people in need.
- Students participate in student government, scouts, model UN, and Global Issues Network.

Academic Achievement

Our five cohorts (2017-2021) earned Diploma mean grade and average total points above worldwide average. Students are currently attending four-year universities in various regions – Asia, Australia, Canada, Europe, the U.K., and the U.S.

At Kuei Shan, we celebrate our distinctive place in PreK-12 education – where teaching, learning and faith guide the mind in understanding the complex diversity of God's creation and prepare the whole person for service and leadership.

Our students strive to be:
Scholars
Effective communicators
Reflective thinkers
Virtuous servant-leaders
Enthusiastic stewards

TANGLIN TRUST

SCHOOL

EST. 1925

(Founded 1925)

CEO Mr Craig Considine BA MA

DP coordinator Joseph Loader

Status Private

Boarding/day Day

Gender Coeducational

Language of instruction
English

Authorised IB programmes
DP

Age Range 3 – 18 years

Number of pupils enrolled
2800

Fees
Nursery to Reception
S$28,794 – S$35,295
Year 1 to Year 6
S$35,850 – S$37,575
Year 7 to Year 13
S$43,095 – S$46,965

Address
95 Portsdown Road
139299 | SINGAPORE

TEL +65 67780771

Email
admissions@tts.edu.sg

Website
www.tts.edu.sg

Established in 1925, Tanglin Trust School is the oldest British international school in South East Asia. Tanglin provides the English National Curriculum with an international perspective to children from 3 to 18 years in Singapore.

Tanglin is a vibrant co-educational school of 2,800 students representing over 50 nationalities and provides a unique learning environment for children from Nursery right through to Sixth Form. As a not-for-profit school, tuition fees are devoted to the provision of an outstanding education.

As the only school in Singapore to offer A Levels or the IB Diploma in Sixth Form, all of Tanglin's Sixth Formers study a programme that is tailored both to the subjects they are passionate about and to the style of learning that most suits them, ensuring they thrive and flourish.

Tanglin has an excellent academic reputation. Students' examination results consistently surpass Singapore and global averages, with around 95% of graduates typically receiving their first or second choice university, which are among the best in the world.

Tanglin is inspected every year within the British Schools Overseas (BSO) framework, recognised by Ofsted. All three schools have been awarded 'Outstanding', the highest possible grade in their latest inspections (2017, 2018 and 2019).

Drawing on professional and dynamic staff, Tanglin aims to nurture students to achieve their intellectual, spiritual, cultural, social and physical goals. We strive to make every individual feel valued, happy and successful. Responsibility, enthusiasm and participation are actively encouraged, and

integrity is prized. Working together in a safe, caring yet stimulating environment, we set high expectations whilst offering strong support, resulting in a community of lifelong learners who can contribute with confidence to our world.

Tanglin encourages both broad participation and the achievement of excellence in the arts, sport, outdoor education and co-curricular activities.

Over 140 teams compete in 17 different sports each year, both in Singapore and the wider region. Exceptional sporting facilities enable students to participate in a wide range of competitive and non-competitive events. We look forward to the opening of our new world class facilities, which include a 50m pool, gymnastics centre, climbing wall, physiotherapy clinic and sport science centre.

Tanglin has a thriving and energetic Arts programme which plays an important part in school life. Students develop their skills in art, design, drama, music, and film-making, facilitating creative, social and intellectual development. Nearly 25% of students participate in a Music co-curricular activity. Throughout the year, there are many opportunities for students to participate in high-quality ensembles, recitals, performances and exhibitions.

Tanglin students are also encouraged to contribute actively to the local community, support service projects and participate in a wide variety of extra-curricular pursuits that stimulate and broaden student experience. These include 80 outdoor education trips, the International Duke of Edinburgh (DofE) Award, and the Creativity, Activity, Service (CAS) programme.

THE FRIENDS' SCHOOL

(Founded 1887)

Principal
Nelson File

PYP coordinator
Wendy Crow

DP coordinator
Sarah Walker

Status Private

Boarding/day Mixed

Gender Coeducational

Language of instruction
English

Authorised IB programmes
PYP, DP

Age Range 4 – 18 years

Number of pupils enrolled
1250

Fees
AUS$10,940 – AUS$21,120
(includes GST)

Address
23 Commercial Road
North Hobart
TAS 7002 | AUSTRALIA

TEL +61 3 6210 2200

Email
enquiries@friends.tas.edu.au

Website
www.friends.tas.edu.au

Situated in the heart of Hobart in Tasmania, The Friends' School is an independent, coeducational day and boarding school that caters for students from Early Learning to Year 12.

A strong sense of community at the School provides a rich and stimulating environment for students. The School's philosophy aims to develop the whole person and for students to show a willingness to contribute to something greater than the individual. We offer a diverse range of co-curricular activities including sports, student-led committees, social functions and service opportunities. Our hope is that our students will leave the School with a broad understanding of and empathy for the Quaker testimonies of Simplicity, Peace, Integrity, Community, Equality and Stewardship.

Who We Are

Guided by Quaker values, The Friends' School thrives on an intrinsic spirit of warmth and friendliness, and its strong community atmosphere reflects the intentions of the founding Quakers whose original vision for the School in 1887 was an education for spiritual and intellectual growth.

We are proud of our consistently high academic results, varied curriculum and co-curricular opportunities, but we are prouder still of our students and all that they go on to achieve.

Our Location

The Friends' School is hidden in the picturesque city of Hobart in the heart of Tasmania, which has a worldwide reputation as a clean, safe and beautiful capital city, making it the perfect study destination.

Tasmania offers spectacular, unique mountain and coastal scenery, with extensive national parks and World Heritage Areas protecting the island's wilderness. Our enriching Outdoor Education program takes full advantage of our beautiful and diverse landscapes.

Our Learning Experience

Students of The Friends' School are offered high levels of flexibility and support so that they may pursue individual interests and passions. We encourage students to challenge themselves academically while exploring the many opportunities available to them through the school.

Students entering into Year 11 have three academic pathways available to them: The Tasmanian Certificate of Education (TCE), the International Baccalaureate Diploma Programme (IBDP) or varied Vocational Education and Training (VET) programs that they can complete alongside their TCE.

The Quaker Difference

The School celebrates the academic success of our students, while still valuing the individual strengths and abilities of each child in our care.

The commitment to connecting with the good in each person and nurturing their 'inner light' is a central aspect of what makes a Friends' education so special. The Quaker commitment to equality is also core to The Friends' School and is demonstrated in the respectful relationships that develop between students and other members of the Friends' community.

The International School of Kuala Lumpur (ISKL)

THE INTERNATIONAL SCHOOL OF KUALA LUMPUR

(Founded 1965)

Head of School
Mr Rami Madani , MA, BSc

DP coordinator
Ms Ebony Manning, MA, BA

Status Private

Boarding/day Day

Gender Coeducational

Language of instruction
English

Authorised IB programmes
DP

Age Range 3 – 18 years

Number of pupils enrolled
1500

Fees
Day: RM52,730 – RM106,695

Address
2, Lorong Kelab Polo Di Raja
Ampang Hilir
55000 Kuala Lumpur | **MALAYSIA**

TEL +60 3 4813 5000

Email
admissions@iskl.edu.my

Website
www.iskl.edu.my

The International School of Kuala Lumpur (ISKL) believes that its success today is based on how well it prepares its 1,500 students for their future. Offering a diverse academic and co-curricular program, ISKL challenges each student to 'Be All You Are' and supports learners in exploring and developing the passions, skills, and competencies they need to be future-ready, not only for university and their career but for life itself.

The school is located on a 26-acre, state-of-the-art campus in the heart of Kuala Lumpur and is home to students representing more than 65 nationalities. Students benefit from its robust international curriculum that combines leading North American educational frameworks with global best practices.

ISKL is a fully inclusive school and offers the International Baccalaureate Diploma Programme (IBDP) on a non-selective basis. Established in 1965 and authorized to run the IBDP in 1989, ISKL is Malaysia's longest-running IB World School. With IBDP results that are consistently above the world average, ISKL's 30-year pass rate of 97% is a testament to the strength of its program and expert international educators. In 2021, 36.8% of ISKL students scored 40 or more points, and 18.8% earned a Bilingual Diploma. Multilingual students can take IB Language and Literature courses in English, Chinese, Japanese, Korean, and Spanish.

ISKL offers transdisciplinary pathways designed to enable every learner to choose a curriculum best suited to their needs. High School options include PRAXIS 2030 (Grade 9-10) and ISKL's Pursuits Program combining individual IB, Advanced Placement, and High School courses for students who want to create their own program of study and take a deep dive into an area of interest. The flexibility of ISKL's academic program enables students to take advantage of higher education opportunities worldwide, as typified by the graduating Class of 2021, who received more than 280 acceptances and offers from over 130 universities in 12 countries spanning four continents.

ISKL is accredited internationally through the Council of International Schools and in the United States through the Western Association of Schools and Colleges. ISKL has a strong focus on service and sustainability and is a member of the Eco-Schools organization and the Green Schools Alliance. ISKL was the recipient of the 2021 International School Award in the Well-being Initiative category and Malaysia's Eco-Schools Green Award 2011-2021.

Find out more about ISKL at www.iskl.edu.my and follow us on social media.

The International School of Penang (Uplands)

(Founded 1955)

Acting Principal
Emily Vallance

PYP coordinator
Maggie Dawson

DP coordinator
Gregory Verdon

Status Private

Boarding/day Mixed

Gender Coeducational

Language of instruction
English

Authorised IB programmes
PYP, DP

Age Range 4 – 18 years

Number of pupils enrolled
650

Fees
Day: RM20,000 – RM55,880
Boarding: RM47,790 – RM50,260

Address
Jalan Sungai Satu
Batu Feringgi
11100 Penang | **MALAYSIA**

TEL +604 8819 777

Email
info@uplands.org

Website
www.uplands.org

The International School of Penang (Uplands) is a non-profit, co-educational Reception to Primary and Secondary School with boarding facilities, open to children aged 4 to 18 years old. It is one of the leading international schools in Malaysia, offering the IB PYP, IB Diploma and IGCSE qualifications.

Since being established in 1955 at the top of Penang Hill we are now established in a modern campus in Batu Feringgi. During our rich history, Uplands has strived to embody a caring community; a school where both international and Malaysian students are happy to learn in with our motto of Respect for Self. Respect for Others.

Students receive a wealth of quality education from an international teaching faculty as well as a range of sporting and extracurricular activities cultivating our values of respect, integrity, inquiry, diversity, collaboration, resilience and balance. Year upon year Uplands students have attained academic results that are consistently higher than global averages, with some achieving perfect scores in the IB Diploma pre-university course and receiving prestigious university scholarships.

Uplands is an IB World School, who are also recognised by the Malaysian Ministry of Education and permitted to admit both foreign and local students. Continuing its long history of excellence in education, Uplands received accreditation by The Council of International Schools (CIS), a global organisation committed to ensuring high-quality international education. Uplands is also accredited by The International Baccalaureate Organisation (IBO) and a

member of:
- The Federation of British International Schools in Asia (FOBISIA);
- The Association of International Malaysian Schools (AIMS);
- The Boarding Schools' Association (BSA).

The School is approved to offer external examinations by The International Baccalaureate Organisation (IBO), Cambridge International Examinations (CIE) and Edexcel International Examinations.

Languages offered at the school are English, Bahasa Malaysia, Mandarin, Spanish, French and German. School facilities include air-conditioned and well-resourced classrooms, 25 metre swimming pool, sports field, library, refectory, playground, basketball court, badminton court, IT resource centre, science laboratories, multi-purpose hall, audio/visual room, art rooms, music rooms, drama rooms, design technology workshops and world class boarding facilities. The campus is fully networked with wired and wireless access.

Student support services are also on deck including university guidance counsellors, learning support and school counsellors. Students are able to engage in a wide variety of extracurricular activities using our excellent campus facilities. The International School of Penang (Uplands) is proud to provide an environment for personal and academic challenge, helping our students to achieve, thrive and develop.

The Kilmore International School

(Founded 1990)

Principal
Peter Cooper

DP coordinator
Deanna Krilis

Status Private

Boarding/day Mixed

Gender Coeducational

Language of instruction
English

Authorised IB programmes
DP

Age Range 8 – 18 years

Number of pupils enrolled
400

Fees
Domestic AUS$10,270 –
AUS$15,780
International AUS$32,575

Address
40 White Street
Kilmore
VIC 3764 | AUSTRALIA

TEL +61 3 5782 2211

Email
enquiries@kilmore.vic.edu.au

Website
www.kilmore.vic.edu.au

The Kilmore International School seeks to form young women and men who have a true understanding of themselves, their values, and their view of the world. Our students choose to embrace an ever-changing world with confidence, engage others with a positive, loving attitude, and are prepared to act when needed.

A good school cares for the individual, practices diversity, offers experiences for growth, is grounded in community, values the learning process, has teachers that are respectful and respected, and, importantly, places the needs of the child at the centre of its decision making. A great school, such as The Kilmore International School, has these characteristics embedded in its culture and daily practice.

Such an ambitious environment takes commitment and teamwork, and our students are joined in their journey by highly qualified, experienced and inspirational teachers, teachers who understand that a child will not care about how much they know, until they know how much they care.

The heart of a Kilmore International School education is expressed in our motto, Excellentia Academica Persequenda, the pursuit of academic excellence. Our graduates attend leading universities throughout the world, taking with them a joy of learning and a willingness to make a positive difference to the lives of others.

Boarders experience a family atmosphere where girls and boys from Melbourne, country Victoria and from around the world become part of a close-knit international learning community.

The rural township of Kilmore is recognised as Victoria's oldest inland town, settled in 1837. Melbourne, Australia's most cosmopolitan city, is nearby and is reached by train in less than an hour.

By offering a challenging and supportive environment with a wide range of co-curricular activities, every student has the opportunity to be recognised for their character and achievements. With encouragement and guidance, students are expected to take on positions of responsibility and to harness their talents.

There are many opportunities to perform at assemblies and exhibitions. Plays and concerts are held regularly, while camps bring the curriculum alive through experiential learning and challenge students through activities such as rock climbing, skiing, horse riding and canoeing.

The Kilmore International School…world ready, future ready.

The Overseas School of Colombo

(Founded 1957)

Head of School
Dr. Michelle Kleiss

PYP coordinator
Samantha Wood

MYP coordinator Jacob Eagle

DP coordinator William Duncan

Status Private

Boarding/day Day

Gender Coeducational

Language of instruction
English

Authorised IB programmes
PYP, MYP, DP

Age Range 3 – 18 years

Address
PO Box 9, Pelawatte
Battaramulla, **10120 | SRI LANKA**

TEL +94 11 2784 920-2

Email admissions@osc.lk

Website www.osc.lk

The Overseas School of Colombo (OSC) was established in 1957 and is the only IB World School in Sri Lanka. It is Sri Lanka's oldest internationally accredited educational institution – fully accredited by the Middle States Association (MSA) and the Council of International Schools (CIS) – and is authorised by the IB to offer the Primary Years Programme, Middle Years Programme, and the Diploma Programme.

Home to a vibrant student community of over 40 nationalities, OSC is an international family that stays true to its motto – 'Unity in Diversity' by fostering intercultural awareness, understanding, and collaboration. With an excellent teacher to student ratio of 1 : 6, learners are guided by exceptional educators from around the world to whom teaching is more a passion than a profession. Our consistent 100% pass rate is a testament to our ethos of continually pushing ourselves to improve, highlighting that there is no limit to what our students can achieve.

OSC is driven by its mission to develop the whole person as a responsible learner, striving for personal excellence within a culturally diverse environment. It strives to be a model of excellence in education and puts a great deal of commitment, passion, and energy into its arts, athletics, design, after-school and co-curricular programmes – thereby holistically nurturing and empowering its community of learners to achieve global success.

OSC is committed to learning that goes beyond the academic life of students and encompasses academic, social, physical and community interests that shape individuals who embrace lifelong learning, with attitudes and values that transcend barriers of race, class, religion, and gender.

OSC's lush green self-contained campus is equipped with air-conditioned classrooms, 2 libraries, 3 design labs, 4 newly renovated state-of-the-art science labs, specialist rooms for art, drama and music, IT labs, Counselling offices, a 400-seat auditorium, black-box studio theatre, covered primary school playground, cafeteria, and a coffee shop.

Sports facilities include a spacious grass football field, a 25-meter swimming pool, a professional level outdoor basketball court, a gymnasium with a rock-climbing wall, basketball, badminton and volleyball courts, a movement room and cardio/weight room. Additionally, OSC effectively integrates the latest technologies and teaching methods to leverage and enhance student learning and foster creativity, collaboration, and communication within and beyond the classroom.

The Overseas School of Colombo is steadfast in its support of personalised excellence and remains holistic and inclusive while demonstrating a strong ethos towards service and experiential learning.

Tokyo Metropolitan Kokusai High School

Head of School Tamako Yonemura	**Number of pupils enrolled** 720
DP coordinator Kazumasa Aoki	**Fees** Annual Fees: ¥118,800 (US$1,130)
Status State	**Address**
Boarding/day Day	2-19-59 Komaba, Meguro-ku, Tokyo **153-0041** | **JAPAN**
Gender Coeducational	**TEL** +81 3 3468 6811
Language of instruction English	**Email** ibdp1@ kokusai-h.metro.tokyo.jp
Authorised IB programmes DP	**Website** www.kokusai-h.metro.tokyo.jp
Age Range 15 – 18 years	

Tokyo Metropolitan Kokusai High School is a coeducational public high school that was established in 1989 and is maintained by the Tokyo Metropolitan Government. Located in a leafy suburb not far from the cosmopolitan west side of Tokyo, the school's motto is "Your Wings to the World" and its aim is to provide education to nurture well-balanced students with an international mindedness.

In May 2015, Tokyo Metropolitan Kokusai High School was authorised as an International Baccalaureate World School offering the Diploma Programme, the first of which to be offered in a Japanese public high school.

Kokusai High School conducts the IBDP in English with the aim of cultivating internationally-minded students who will study overseas after graduation. The Kokusai IBDP strives to nurture future global leaders, and based on this philosophy, the ideal Kokusai IB students should demonstrate the following attributes.
A Kokusai High School IBDP student should:
1. Demonstrate a clear goal to enter the IBDP, a desire to contribute to a global society, and the willingness to gain entrance into universities overseas.
2. Approach learning with a self-starter mentality by showing a strong sense of inquiry and a willingness to use their own initiative, while having the courage to handle difficult challenges.
3. Exemplify a well-rounded character, being cooperative and considerate of others, and also have the willingness to positively accept and understand different perspectives and opinions.
4. Be motivated to broaden their perspectives, and be able to maintain a healthy mental and physical mindset and actively participate in extracurricular activities.

5. Demonstrate strong academic performances across all subjects, and have a high level of English proficiency.

Kokusai High School offers entrance examinations twice per year; the April enrollment session (held in January) and the September enrollment session (held in July). The April session is for students who will finish Year 9 school education by the end of March, and the September session is for those who will finish Year 9 school education between April and August. The maximum number of successful applicants in 2020 was 25. The ratio of Japanese students to International students for each enrollment session is announced by the Tokyo Metropolitan Board of Education. The assessment methods used in the entrance examinations are the English Language Skills Test, the Mathematics Academic Performance Test, the Essay, the Individual Interview, and the Certificate of Academic Record.

Kokusai High School offers a three-year programme; Year 1 (Grade 10) is the Foundation Year, Year 2 (Grade 11) and Year 3 (Grade 12) are the IBDP. Students also graduate with a Japanese High School Diploma. The subjects we offer are listed below:
Studies in Language and Literature
Year 1: Comprehensive English, English for Academic Purposes, Contemporary Japanese Language, Language Culture.
Year 2 and 3: IB Diploma English A SL and HL (Language and Literature); Japanese A SL and HL (Literature).
Language Acquisition
Year 1: Comprehensive English, English for Academic Purposes, Contemporary Japanese Language, Language Culture.
Year 2 and 3: IB Diploma English B SL and HL; Japanese B SL and HL.

Individuals and Societies
Year 1: Public, Geography for Cultural Understanding, Modern and Contemporary History.
Year 2 and 3: IB Diploma History SL and HL, Economics HL, Geography HL.

Science
Year 1: Basic Physics, Basic Chemistry, Basic Biology.
Year 2 and 3: IB Diploma Physics SL and HL, Chemistry HL, Biology SL and HL.

Mathematics
Year 1: Mathematics I
Year 2 and 3: IB Diploma Mathematics: analysis and approaches SL and HL, IB Diploma Mathematics: applications and interpretation HL.

Other subjects
Year 1: Physical Education, Health, Art and Design, Basic Home Economics.
Year 2 and 3: Physical Education, Health, Homeroom Activity, International Relations, Information Study by Scientific Approach, Theory of Knowledge (TOK), Creativity, Activity, Service (CAS).

Creativity, Activity, Service (CAS)
Throughout their DP years, IB students explore their interests and personal development by participating in a wide range of CAS experiences such as sports, arts and music. Former IB students' passion led to many volunteer activities both locally and internationally, including in Tokyo, Hiroshima, Kenya, Senegal and Ghana. Students engaged actively in volunteer groups such as "Child Doctor Japan", "Green Bird", "Earth Day Tokyo 2019" and "Teens Fiesta in Meguro". While doing these experiences for CAS, students also won various awards such as the 2018 and 2019 World Scholar's Cup.

Some universities where students have been accepted
UK: University College London, Imperial College London, University of Edinburgh, King's College London, University of Manchester, SOAS. USA: Princeton University, Purdue University, Georgia Institute of Technology, University of California Los Angeles, Williams College. Canada: University of Toronto, University of British Columbia, McGill University. Australia: Australian National University, University of Melbourne, University of Sydney. Germany: Technical University of Munich, Jacobs University. Netherlands: Leiden University, University of Groningen. Hong Kong: University of Hong Kong, Hong Kong University of Science and Technology.

(Founded 2015)

Head of College
Pelham Philip Lindfield Roberts

DP coordinator
Christopher Hodachok

Status Private

Boarding/day Boarding

Gender Coeducational

Language of instruction
English

Authorised IB programmes
DP

Age Range 15 – 19 years

Number of pupils enrolled
580

Fees
Two-year fee ¥720,000
(scholarships available)

Address
No. 88 Kunchenghuxi Road
Changshu, Jiangsu
215500 | CHINA

TEL +86 512 5298 2602

Email
info.admissions@uwcchina.org

Website
www.uwcchina.org

Introduction

UWC Changshu China was founded in 2015 as the first UWC in the mainland of China for students in grades 10, 11 and 12. The college emphasizes a connection to its location and offers education focused on Chinese language and culture, innovation, youth leadership and environmental activism.

Learning at UWC Changshu China

The College defines learning as an iterative process in which we engage and inquire, reflect on the experience considering diverse perspectives, and intentionally apply what we learn to better ourselves, our communities, and the world. UWC Changshu China offers a Foundation Programme for grade 10 and the IB Diploma Programme for grades 11 and 12 with an emphasis on experiential learning to develop critical thinking skills and self-management skills, as well as focusing on community engagement, physical activities, service to others and creative pursuits. The Yunshan Academy on campus houses the Centre for Design and Innovation to support innovation and design thinking, as well as the Centre for Chinese Programmes to further learners' understanding of the essence of Chinese culture and language.

Outside the classroom

Students at UWC Changshu China engage in a wide range of cultural, sporting and social activities. The name of its Creativity, Activity, Service (CAS) programme is Zhi Xing, which means 'learning by doing' as well as 'putting knowledge into action'. The extra-curricular Zhi Xing programme allows students to connect to the UWC mission and values through selecting to participate in one or more of its nine service streams, which are physical education; ecology and biodiversity; media and communication; design, innovation and engineering; outdoor activities; peace and justice; the arts; education and research; and culture, diversity and identity.

Campus and facilities

The 24-acre campus is built on an island on the northwest side of Kuncheng Lake. In architectural design, the campus is reminiscent of a southern Chinese waterside village, where connections between all parts are seamless and unobstructed. The campus is comprised of cutting-edge technologies to enhance its sustainability. With an abundance of open spaces, modern facilities include a multi-function performing art space, STEM hub, wellbeing centre, swimming pool, athletics track and sporting facilities, residential houses for students and faculty, a dining hall and a library.

Admission

IBDP applicants apply through their UWC national committee or the UWC Global Selection Programme. Foundation Programme applicants need to contact the school directly.

(Founded 1997)	**Number of pupils enrolled** 240
Head of College Dr. Dale Taylor	**Fees** Two-year fee $61,000 (scholarships available)
Deputy Head of College Charlotte Blessing	**Address** Village Khubavali, PO Paud
DP coordinator Ainhoa Orensanz	Taluka Mulshi Pune, Maharashtra **412108 | INDIA**
Status Private	**TEL** +91 97644 4275154
Boarding/day Boarding	**Email**
Gender Coeducational	info@muwci.net
Language of instruction English	**Website** uwcmahindracollege.org
Authorised IB programmes DP	
Age Range 15 – 19 years	

Introduction

UWC Mahindra is a vibrant college with a rich tradition of curricular innovation and community engagement. Programs such as the IB's World Studies Extended Essay were conceived and piloted here. The College also runs a bridge program and the Akshara Foundation, both of which enhance the positive local impact of the College and provide students with numerous opportunities for project-based and service learning.

Inside the Classroom

UWC Mahindra College offers the International Baccalaureate Diploma Programme curriculum. Alongside standard courses, the College offers Art, Theatre, Film, Psychology, Global Politics. Additionally, students also benefit from the MUWCI Core – a specially designed curriculum for the College that encompasses the areas of Political Education, Social and Emotional Education, Host Studies and Ecological and Outdoor Education. UWC Mahindra also offers the Project Based Certificate to interested students, wherein they can utilize the second year to conceive and execute an impact-driven project.

Outside the Classroom

UWC Mahindra College offers an immense variety of co-curricular activities through its Creativity, Activity, Service program, referred to as "Triveni" program, which facilitates project-based learning. Students can choose from a rich diversity of Service Learning opportunities on and off campus spanning areas like menstrual health, organic farming, mental health and rural public education. Students are also active participants in decision-making processes that affect campus life, such as envisioning and executing resource management initiatives on campus. Students benefit from the cultural diversity of the surrounding valley and India at large and have immersive experiences in other parts of the country through Experiential Learning Weeks. MUWCI also conducts short programs which bring together students from around the world to learn about issues such as sustainability and globalization.

Campus and Facilities

Students live together in five residential clusters known as "wadas", each of which forms a more intimate community. The campus also offers many informal locations for gathering and hiking, and several areas are well known among students for their gorgeous vistas of the valley during sunset. Academic facilities include a science lab, a library, an art space overlooking the valley, specialized facilities for theatre and music practice and a large sporting ground along with a makerspace tinkering lab for STEAM projects.

Admissions

Students can apply through their UWC national committee or through the UWC Global Selection Programme.

The School With A Difference

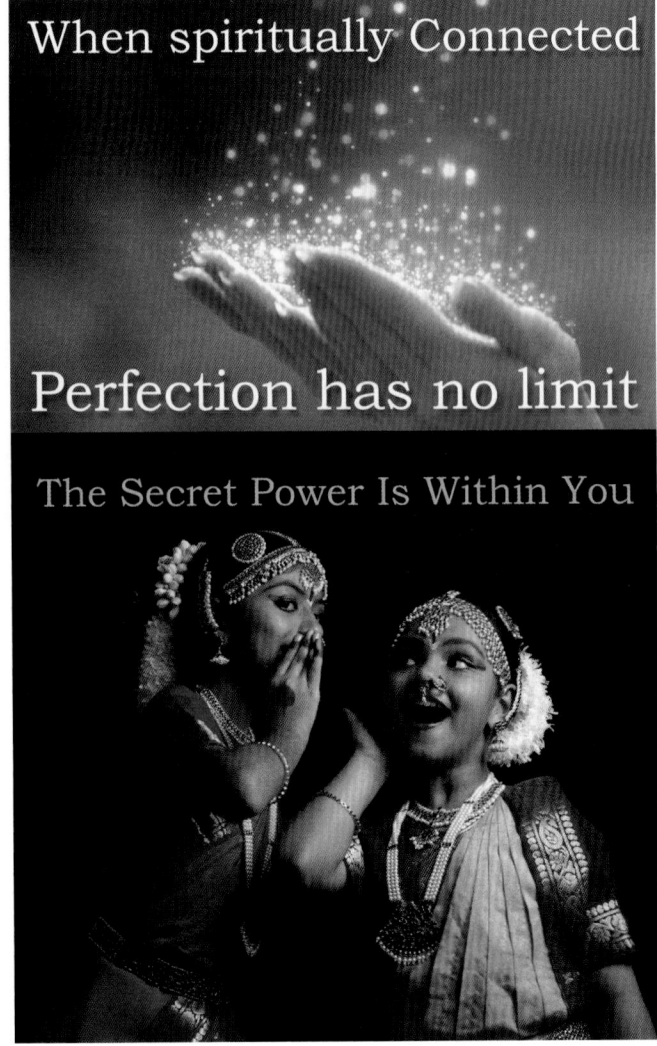

When spiritually Connected

Perfection has no limit

The Secret Power Is Within You

(Founded 6th January 1997)	**Language of instruction** English
Founder President Robbin Ghosh	**Authorised IB programmes** PYP, MYP, DP
Vice President & Principal Saarada Ghosh	**Age Range** 6 weeks – 19 years
Director Sports Romen Ghosh	**Number of pupils enrolled** 906
DP & MYP Head Jaya Kalsy	
PYP Head Ira Ghosh	**Fees** Tuition Fee US$4,326 average
EYP Head Desiree Dhami	**Address** Kharadi
PYP & EYP coordinator Pritisha Ahir	Pune, Maharashtra **411014 | INDIA**
MYP & DP coordinator Vishwajeet Kumar	**TEL** +91 20-67116300/1/2
Status Private	**Email** robbinghosh@ victoriouskidsseducares.org
Boarding/day Day	**Website** www. victoriouskidsseducares.org
Gender Coeducational	www.vkidss.org

Every Child Matters
We Teach, We Touch Lives and We Make Dreams Come True.

Victorious Kidss Educares (VKIDSS) pervades the world of education with latest of the world's research-based Teaching and Learning pedagogy of IB, coupled with India's rich heritage of Vedanta. We are aware that 'The secret power of concepts, with the highest performance, of inquiry-based intelligent teaching and learning, with smart application of memory, is inherent in every child. Discovering that secret power from within the child, is parenting and making it happen in real life is schooling.' This principle underlying philosophy, brings up an enjoyable practice, a gratifying journey with simple understanding. It is carefully guided to make it a mental process – with all participating parents, teachers, and students. It develops an attitude of mindful consciousness of 'Learning to Love to Learn'.

Achievements:
- Despite the Academic Year (2020-2021) being entirely virtual, our DP student joined the World Topper Rank – scoring a perfect 45/45 and topping amongst 5 to 6 Lakh students in the world. All other students securing first division.
- In the Academic Year 2019-2020, MYP and DP results were 100 percent, with the highest score being 56/56 – World Topper – in MYP and 44/45 in DP.
- In their 2019 MYP Evaluation Report, the IB Evaluation Team has requested the school, to share the standards and practices, and apply to present the concepts at a global IB conference.
- VKIDSS Hackathon Team – champions of the International CAS Virtual Hackathon, INALA Mental Health Foundation, South Africa, (24 October 2021).
- Ms. Rida Merchant (MYP4) – Selected to represent VKIDSS at Harvard MUN 2022.
- Ms. Rishita Patil (MYP 1) – Winner of Under 12 Tennis Series, All India Tennis Association (AITA) 2021.
- Ms. Siya Siddharth Shah, (MYP 1) – Gold Medalist in Shotokon Karate Championship.
- Ms. Tanishka Shah (MYP V World Topper – 2020) – Chosen as The Chief Executive Officer (CEO), 'SaafSaans' (Environmental NGO).

The pedagogy of Teaching and Learning of IB coupled with the wisdom of Vedanta, guides the children to discover what their potentials are. The students are guided to that education by which character is formed, strength of mind is increased.

We work with the insight, 'Every child has greater potential for intelligence at birth than Leonardo Da Vinci, Isaac Newton, or Albert Einstein ever had'. We believe that every

One **Lion** Can **Transform** The World Not **Millions Of Sheep**

child is born with a special ability, and the brain of every child has infinite potential. As school management core team, we work with an alertness that 'our children are no longer the people, as we were in the school'.

We make special efforts to ensure the Teachers at VKIDSS are kind, caring and loving and professionally trained and are experienced, as per IB guidelines.
VKIDSS thoughtfully offers the following:

- VKIDSS pioneered and was ready for remote classes long before the pandemic with well-equipped classrooms and striving to upgrade to the latest of educational technologies.
- All round sporting facilities with basketball, volleyball, handball, football, cricket, badminton, tennis, table tennis, swimming, skating, mallakhamba, gymnastics, yoga, trike cycles and athletics.
- TED-Ed program for MYP students.
- Vedic Mathematics, Robotics, Abacus and Design Technology.
- Visual Art, Performing Art, 3D Digital Arts Lab and Pottery Studio.

- Diversified Exposure in Performing Arts (Indian Classical, Western, Dance – Bharatanatyam, Hip Hop, Freestyle)
- Careers Fair – 100 Plus National and International Universities visiting on campus.
- Career Counseling, Placements, Internships & Scholarships in top Universities for DP Students. Understanding the platform for psychometric tests.
- Concentration Techniques – Pranayama, Yogic breathing exercises.
- Model UN Programme from Primary Years to ensure our students learn the art of communication and negotiation.

Through establishment of a harmonious ambience, giving freedom to explore and learn through challenges and inquiry, we have been successful in nurturing this power of awareness of proving the 'truth' within one's life. With this conscious understanding and concept – we discover, 'Success for Every Child'.

The students of VKIDSS march on the path of truth, purity, patience, and perseverance and become the torchbearers of IB learner profile.

Vientiane International School

VIENTIANE INTERNATIONAL SCHOOL

(Founded 1991)

Head of School
Elsa H. Donohue

PYP coordinator
Olwen Millgate

MYP coordinator
Elizabeth England

DP coordinator
Elizabeth England

Status Private

Boarding/day Day

Gender Coeducational

Language of instruction
English

Authorised IB programmes
PYP, MYP, DP

Age Range 4 – 18 years

Number of pupils enrolled 455

Fees
Day: US$10,500 – US$24,140

Address
PO Box 3180, Phonesavanh Road
Saphanthong Tai Village,
Sisattanak District
Vientiane | **LAOS**

TEL +856 21 31 8100

Email contact@vislao.com

Website www.vislao.com

Mission – We challenge, inspire, and empower our learners to develop their unique potential in our changing world.
Vision – We will lead the way toward a sustainable future.
Values – We value Balance, Respect, Resilience, Innovation, and Courage.
VIS Definition of Learning – We learn when we build and apply new understandings and skills in a variety of contexts.

VIS is an independent, non-profit school offering an international-standard curriculum. We are the only school in Laos accredited by the Western Association of Schools and Colleges (WASC) and the Council of International Schools (CIS). We are also the only IB World School in the country, delivering the IB Continuum Program (PYP, MYP, DP). Over the years, VIS has demonstrated consistent improvement in the IB results. Our 2021 Class IB Diploma Average Score was 36.4, above the world average of 33.

The diverse student body of 455 learners draws from 42 nationalities. Most families represent the non-government and diplomatic sectors; international and local businesses are also represented. Our unique VIS Mother Tongue program supports the development and maintenance of 9 different languages. We also offer an English Language Acquisition (ELA) program. In 2021, 40% of our IB Diploma graduates were awarded bilingual diplomas, well above the world average of 27%.

At VIS, we strive to develop empathy, cultural understanding, and global awareness through meaningful interactions with the Lao community. As a Mekong River International Schools Association (MRISA) member, our students participate in sporting and cultural exchanges with schools in neighboring countries.

Our current campus facilities include two swimming pools, two soccer pitches, two basketball courts, ample playground spaces, a collaborative library, a Makerspace, and a "BlackBox" Theater. In December 2020, we started improving and expanding our facilities through the Campus Gateway Project. The VIS facilities will enable novel spaces that expand the learning opportunities of our students and community by offering:

- A new multipurpose Performing Arts Center with a capacity of 350+ pax. Retractable seats make space versatile for events and community gatherings;
- An indoor Gymnasium with 2 full-size basketball courts integrated into our sports hub (pool and soccer field);
- A modern administration building with community areas.

Years of strategic planning have set the ground for building new facilities without impacting our operations, budget, or school fees. These campus improvements will help us fulfill our school's mission and vision: developing our learners' unique potential while leading the way toward a sustainable future.

Western Australian
International School System

(Founded 2010)

School Principal
Dr. Rung Tran

DP coordinator
Bao Tran

Status Private

Boarding/day Day

Gender Coeducational

Language of instruction
English

Authorised IB programmes
DP

Age Range 2 – 18 years

Number of pupils enrolled
2500

Address
43 Nguyen Thong Street
Ward 7, District 3
Ho Chi Minh City | **VIETNAM**

TEL +84 28 7109 5077

Email
schooloffice@wass.edu.vn

Website
www.wass.edu.vn/en

The Western Australian International School System (WASS) provides education from Kindergarten through to Senior Secondary School, and is currently offering various international curriculums for all students. We are proud to be one of the only two schools in Vietnam licensed by the Western Australian Department of Education and to be recognized as an Australian Oversea School in Vietnam.

We are also one of the only 13 international schools in Vietnam allowed to teach the International Baccalaureate Diploma Programme, one of the only 2 schools in Vietnam allowed to offer the West Australian Certificate of Education program (WACE) and the Western Australian Program (WAP) in teaching.

The school is accredited by the Vietnamese Ministry of Education and Training, the International Baccalaureate Organization (IBO), and School Curriculum and Standards Authority (SCSA). These two pathway programs (IBDP and WACE) at WASS will provide our students with the choice and opportunity to follow their dreams by selecting the most suitable higher-level education course for their future. In 2021, Western Australian School System officially launched the Advanced Placement (AP) program which is accredited by the College Board.

WASS educates students in a multicultural, open-minded,

loving and friendly environment. We are always aiming for sustainable development, not only equipping students with knowledge but also the ability to think critically and form social skills so that they are confident and well – prepared to step into the future challenging world. For the past 10 years, WASS has become the home of hundreds of students from over 10 different countries around the world. With English as the primary language of instruction, standardised academic programs and enthusiastic support, our students have gained the skills to integrate into the dynamic and global world.

WASS has five modern, state-of-the-art, campuses in excellent city centre locations in Ho Chi Minh City, Southern Vietnam. The facilities are carefully designed to help inspire students towards their qualifications, goals and future adventures in life. It is WASS's mission to educate talented young people and build a high quality, world-class and global education – helping students open the gate to the world and achieve success in the future. From the enthusiasm and belief of "A world-class education with the world in your class", WASS is committed to providing the younger generation with a modern, dynamic and educational environment that energizes the students with the confidence to perform spectacular jumps to reach their dreams.

Western International School of Shanghai (WISS)

Headteacher
Dr. Greg Brunton

PYP coordinator
Lisa Kane & Inga Bela

MYP coordinator
Amanda Narkiewicz

DP coordinator
Edwige Singleton

CP coordinator
Stewart Paterson

Status Private

Boarding/day Day

Gender Coeducational

Language of instruction
English

Authorised IB programmes
PYP, MYP, DP, CP

Age Range 2 1/2 – 17+ years

Number of pupils enrolled 631

Fees
Day: CNY 170,500 – 275,600

Address
555 Lian Min Road
Xujing Town, Qing Pu District
Shanghai
201702 | CHINA

TEL +86 21 6976 6388

Email
admissions@wiss.cn

Website
www.wiss.cn

The Western International School of Sahnghai (WISS) challenges and empowers students through an unparalleled IB education and this year, WISS celebrates 15 years of excellence in education. Offering all four IB Programmes – the Primary Years Programme (IBPYP), the Middle Years Programme (IBMYP), the Diploma Programme (IBDP), and the Career-related Programme (IBCP) – WISS broadens the minds of the children in our care through innovative, high-quality, inquiry-based learning and teaching, with individualized student pathways.

Their unrivaled IBCP creates a highly personalized curriculum that gives Grade 11 – 12 students the unique opportunity to take university-level classes in Aeronautics, Art & Design, Business & Sustainability, and Sports while still in high school.

Continually striving for high standards of professional performance in international education WISS holds WASC Accreditation and was recently granted membership in the Council of International Schools (CIS), which is the first step towards obtaining CIS Accreditation. Located on the western side of Shanghai, close to many popular housing compounds in the expatriate community, WISS has one of the largest international school campuses in Shanghai. The modern campus features open plan, bright classrooms equipped with ceiling air purification units, a well-resourced library, state of the art science and technology labs, spacious art studios, sleek film and music studios, and theatre spaces including a black box classroom and the innovative Orsini Theatre. Sports facilities include an impressive Astroturf football fields, basketball courts, a large gymnasium equipped with a rock-climbing wall, and two swimming pools. Their robust after school activity program includes many distinguished programs and world-class academies such as the ISTA Performing Arts Academy, the Stoke City FC Football Academy, GAIL, the Duke of Edinburgh's International Award, and MUN. Additionally, Early Years and Primary students enjoy one afternoon per week of activities during the school day.

Students from over 40 different countries create an exciting blend of cultures that forms a vibrant learning community eager to promote new perspectives and explore challenging aspects of the world around us. WISS offers a truly international learning environment, while still fostering an appreciation and respect for our host country through well-developed Mandarin language and literature classes and by being actively engaged in the local community.

Woodstock School

(Founded 1854)

Head of School
Dr. Craig Cook

MYP coordinator
Imtiaz Rai

DP coordinator
Mousumi Basu

Status Private

Boarding/day Boarding

Gender Coeducational

Language of instruction
English

Authorised IB programmes
MYP, DP

Age Range 11 – 18 years

Number of pupils enrolled 435

Fees
Grades 6-8 US$22,500
Grades 9-10 US$23,250
Grades 11-12 US$25,000

Address
Mussoorie, Uttarakhand
248179 | INDIA

TEL +91 135 263 9000

Email
admissions@woodstock.ac.in

Website
www.woodstock.ac.in

Fostering Global Citizenship Since 1854

Woodstock School is Asia's original international boarding school, and has been bringing together a diverse range of cultures and identities from around the world for more than 165 years. Situated in protected forest in the Indian Himalayas, Woodstock provides an unforgettable educational experience.

A Woodstock education combines the very best features of high academic challenge with a unique approach to enrichment and personal development. Everything is designed to develop the whole person, to help each student to become visionary, articulate and ethical – equipped to achieve their full potential in leadership and in life.

Discovering students' passion in life

Woodstock offers the MYP and DP curriculums, with 29 courses offered at DP level. Students also graduate with a US High School Diploma, and go on to universities around the world, with the majority continuing their studies in North America and Europe. Students participate in more than 100 enrichment activities, from MUN to Rock Climbing, and hiking and exploring the great outdoors which are iconic features of school life. Woodstock has a long-held reputation for excellence in music and performing arts. Wherever a child's passion may lie, the school helps it to grow and develop.

Cutting-edge facilities in the Indian Himalayas

Woodstock's campus combines heritage buildings with cutting-edge facilities, all surrounded by the school's 300-acre woodland campus. Over recent years, the school's classrooms and communal areas completely transformed into contemporary, collaborative learning spaces. The newly renovated science block houses state of the art laboratories and STEAM facilities. The Centre for Imagination is Woodstock's dedicated interdisciplinary space, where students find the space and support to pursue projects they are passionate about. The Hanifl Centre for Outdoor Education and Environmental Studies is Woodstock's dedicated hub for outdoor leadership and experiential learning, and India's leading facility of its kind.

Four separate residential dorms for younger and older boys and girls provide a homey atmosphere, and a safe space to relax, play and explore the natural environment. Woodstock's world-class gymnasium, swimming pool and sporting facilities enable students to enjoy and excel at sports. Woodstock's Health Centre has a dedicated team of healthcare professionals and modern facilities including discrete Covid-19 isolation wards, should the need arise.

Admissions

Woodstock welcomes applications from highly motivated students from diverse backgrounds who are looking for a transformative education. For those who demonstrate merit and financial need, Woodstock offers a comprehensive programme of financial aid that is unmatched in India.

Yew Chung International School of Hong Kong

Yew Chung International School of Hong Kong
香港耀中國際學校
YCIS

(Founded 1932)

Principals (Secondary School)
Sam Sze and Elizabeth Trustrum

DP coordinator
Alan Ramm

Status Private

Boarding/day Day

Gender Coeducational

Language of instruction
English, Mandarin

Authorised IB programmes
DP

Age Range 6 months – 18 years

Address (Admissions)
3 To Fuk Road
Kowloon | **HONG KONG**

TEL +852 2338 7106

Email
admissions@ycef.com

Website
www.ycis-hk.com

Founded in 1932 in Hong Kong, Yew Chung has been providing bilingual education in a multicultural environment for 90 years. With profound experience in international education, Yew Chung International School (YCIS) provides educations commence in Early Childhood, extend through Primary and Secondary education, culminating in the International General Certificate of Secondary Education (IGCSE) and International Baccalaureate (IB) Diploma Programme.

Global Education in YCIS

YCIS offers the unique richness and diversity of both Eastern and Western cultures that equip children to be bilingual, global-minded, competitive, appreciative and caring global citizens. Students are nurtured in a multicultural environment with a fully rounded and balanced education which transforms them into global thinking individuals.

Integrating East and West

YCIS combines the best of Eastern and Western cultures by promoting fluency in two major world languages, creating a truly bilingual learning environment, providing courses of study in Eastern and Western philosophy.

Co-Principals and Co-Teaching Models

Two Co-Principals, one Western and one Chinese, serve as partners in the operations and administration of the school. In addition, two fully-qualified teachers, one Western and one Chinese, together plan lessons and conduct classes in the Early Childhood Education and Primary School, and providing excellent role models who respect and value one another's culture.

YCIS Education Programme

YCIS's international curriculum is based on the framework and learning criteria from the National Curriculum for England (NCE). The research based curriculum allows high standards and ease of transition for international students.

Highlight of YCIS Global Education

- A Bilingual focus within a multicultural environment will give your child the global mindset and intercultural competence they need for the 21st Century.
- Unique Co-Teaching and Co-Principals models help students to learn two cultures and give equal emphasis to both English and Chinese.
- The Learning Communities or flexible learning spaces encourage active learning, connections across the curriculum, and the development of learning disposition which meet the future needs of the students.
- YCIS integrates Character Formation programmes into our curriculum, focusing on developing positive values.
- YCIS raises globally competent and compassionate leaders with a servant's heart and uphold moral and spiritual values based on Christian faith, affirming the worth and dignity of each individual, to act towards a better world.
- Strong music programme enhances children's reasoning skills, develops memory span, concentration and coordination.
- Our unique violin programme for students in Years 1-3 not only help children build confidence and presentation skills, they also develop extremely strong instrumental skills and a lifelong appreciation for music.
- YCIS maintains 100% university placement with students admitted to top universities in Hong Kong and overseas.

Today YCIS has expanded beyond Hong Kong, and is now established in Shanghai, Beijing, Chongqing and Qingdao in China and Silicon Valley in the United States, with a total student enrolment of exceeding 6,000.

Age of Students

Early Childhood Education 6 months – 5 years
Primary School (Year 1 – 6) 5 – 11 years
Secondary School (Year 7 – 9) 11 – 14 years
IGCSE (Year 10 – 11) 14 – 16 years
IB Diploma (Year 12 – 13) 16 – 19 years

International Recognition

YCIS – Secondary is authorised by the International Baccalaureate Organization (IBO) as an IB World School and is an approved authorised Cambridge International Examination (CIE) Centre. YCIS – Secondary has received accreditations from Council of International Schools (CIS).

Highlights of YCIS Hong Kong's IBDP 2021 results

• 100% pass rate
• 2 students achieved a perfect score of 45
• 5 students achieved the near-perfect score of 44
• 31 students achieved a score of 40 points or higher (39% of the cohort)
• 75% of students received the Bilingual Diploma
• An overall average score of 37.6

The excellent results of 2021 led each of our students to receive three or more offers from the first choice, top ranking and reputable universities across the world, including five offers from the Faculty of Medicine in Hong Kong and two entrances to the prestigious Tsinghua University. Offers at a glance:
China: Tsinghua University
Hong Kong: The University of Hong Kong, The Chinese University of Hong Kong
UK: Imperial College London, University of St Andrews, University College London, Durham University
USA: Columbia University, New York University, UC – Berkeley, UC - Los Angeles, Boston University
Australia: University of Sydney, The University of Melbourne, Monash University
Canada: University of British Columbia, University of Toronto, McGill University
   And many more...

Directory of schools in the Asia-Pacific region

Key to symbols

- ● CP
- ● Diploma
- ● MYP
- ● PYP
- Ⓢ Fee Paying School
- Ⓑ Boys' School
- Ⓖ Girls' School
- Ⓒ Coeducational School
- ◕ Boarding School
- ☀ Day School

Aberfoyle Park High School
36A Taylors Road, East Aberfoyle Park SA 5159
DP Coordinator Ryan Brown
Languages English
T: +61 8 8270 4455
W: intra.aphs.sa.edu.au

Al Zahra College
3-5 Wollongong Road, Arncliffe NSW 2205
DP Coordinator Kothar Elrida
MYP Coordinator Lisa Russell
PYP Coordinator Michelle Ryan
Languages English
T: +061(002)9599-0161
W: www.azc.nsw.edu.au

Alamanda K-9 College
PO Box 6606, Point Cook VIC 3030
PYP Coordinator Carmen Sacco
Languages English
T: +61 3 8376 5200
W: alamandacollege.vic.edu.au

Albert Park College
83 Danks Street, Albert Park, Melbourne VIC 3206
DP Coordinator Jessica Langdon
Languages English
T: +61 3 8695 9000
W: www.albertparkcollege.vic.edu.au

Anglican Church Grammar School
Oaklands Parade, East Brisbane QLD 4169
DP Coordinator Catherine Prosser
PYP Coordinator Scott Warfield
Languages English
T: +61 7 3896 2200
W: www.churchie.com.au

Annesley Junior School
28 Rose Terrace, Wayville SA 5034
PYP Coordinator David Taylor
Languages English
T: +61 8 8422 2288
W: www.annesley.sa.edu.au

Aspendale Gardens Primary School
96 Kearney Drive, Aspendale Gardens VIC 3195
PYP Coordinator Kelly Cornelius
Languages English
T: +61 (03) 9587 0877
W: www.agps.vic.edu.au

Aspendale Primary School
23 Laura Street, Aspendale, Melbourne VIC 3195
PYP Coordinator Helenor Regester
Languages English
T: +61 (0)3 9580 3255
W: www.aspendale.vic.edu.au

Auburn South Primary School
419 Tooronga Road, East Hawthorn, Melbourne VIC 3123
PYP Coordinator Sharron Bailey
Languages English
T: +61 3 9882 2140
W: www.auburnsthps.vic.edu.au

AUSTRALIAN INTERNATIONAL ACADEMY
Melbourne Senior Campus, 56 Bakers Road, North Coburg VIC 3058
DP Coordinator Ms Berna Yusuf
MYP Coordinator Ms Naima Keddar
PYP Coordinator Ms Zawat Souki
Languages English
T: +61 3 9350 4533
E: aia@aia.vic.edu.au
W: aia.vic.edu.au

See full details on page 313

Australian International Academy – Caroline Springs Campus
183-191 Caroline Springs Boulevard, Caroline Springs, Melbourne VIC 3023
PYP Coordinator Zawat Souki
Languages English
T: +61 3 8372 5446
W: cs.aiahome.net

Australian International Academy – Kellyville Campus
57-69 Samantha Riley Drive, Kellyville, Sydney NSW 2155
DP Coordinator Paul Apostolou
MYP Coordinator Lubna Sayed
PYP Coordinator Oznur Aydemir
Languages English
T: +61 02 8801 3100
W: kellyville.aia.nsw.edu.au

Australian International Academy – Sydney Campus
420 Liverpool Road, Strathfield, Sydney NSW 2135
DP Coordinator Simran Khan
MYP Coordinator Bedrieh Kheir
PYP Coordinator Maryam Atalla
Languages English
T: +61 2 9642 0104
W: strathfield.aia.nsw.edu.au

Ballarat Grammar
201 Forest Street, Wendouree VIC 3355
PYP Coordinator Maria Cahir
Languages English
T: +61 3 5338 0700
W: www.bgs.vic.edu.au

Balwyn North Primary School
Buchanan Avenue, Balwyn North VIC 3104
PYP Coordinator Nicole McLean
Languages English
T: +61 (0)3 9859 4258
W: balwynnorthps.vic.edu.au

Barker College
91 Pacific Highway, Hornsby NSW 2077
PYP Coordinator Lisa Bonazza
Languages English
T: +61 2 8438 7999
W: www.barker.college

Bayswater South Primary School
Enfield Drive, Bayswater VIC 3153
PYP Coordinator Karyn Georgios
Languages English
T: +61 3 9729 2862
W: www.baysouthps.vic.edu.au

Beaumaris North Primary School
Wood Street, Beaumaris, Melbourne VIC 3193
PYP Coordinator Debbie Murnane
Languages English
T: +61 3 9589 5449
W: www.beaumarisnorthps.vic.edu.au

Belair Primary School
45-83 Main Road, Belair SA 5052
PYP Coordinator Natalie Holmes
Languages English
T: +61 8 8370 3733
W: www.belairps.sa.edu.au

Benowa State High School
PO Box 5733, Gold Coast Mail Centre, Benowa QLD 9726
DP Coordinator Adrian Hays
Languages English
T: +61 (07) 5582 7333
W: www.benowashs.eq.edu.au

Benton Junior College
261 Racecourse Road, Mornington VIC 3931
PYP Coordinator Jodie Brasher
Languages English
T: +61 3 5973 9100
W: www.benton.vic.edu.au

Berwick Primary School
37 Fairholme Boulevard, Berwick VIC 3806
PYP Coordinator Gillian Hartman
Languages English
T: +61 03 97071026
W: www.berwickprimary.vic.edu.au

Blackwood High School
4 Seymour Street, Eden Hills SA 5050
MYP Coordinator Lachlan McFarlane
Languages English
T: +61 8 8278 0900
W: www.bhs.sa.edu.au

Blackwood Primary School
4 Seymour Street, Eden Hills SA 5050
PYP Coordinator Natalie Campbell
Languages English
T: +61 8 82785355
W: www.blackwoodps.sa.edu.au

Brighton Primary School
59 Wilson Street, Brighton, Melbourne VIC 3186
PYP Coordinator Joel Snowden
Languages English
T: +61 39592 0177
W: www.brighton.vic.edu.au

Brighton Secondary College
120 Marriage Road, Brighton East VIC 3187
DP Coordinator Katherine Perry
Languages English
T: +61 3 9592 7488
W: brightonsc.vic.edu.au

Burwood Heights Primary School & Kindergarten
Cnr Hawthorn & Mahoneys Roads, East Burwood VIC 3151
PYP Coordinator Clare Matthews
Languages English
T: +61 3 9803 8311
W: www.burwoodhps.vic.edu.au

Cairns State High School
PO Box 5643, Cairns QLD 4870
DP Coordinator Stefanie Biancotti
Languages English
T: +61 7 4050 3033
W: www.cairnsshs.eq.edu.au

Calamvale Community College
11 Hamish Street, Calamvale QLD 4116
DP Coordinator Melissa Ellis
PYP Coordinator Mark Smith
Languages English
T: +61 (0)7 3712 6333
W: calamvalecc.eq.edu.au

Canberra Girls Grammar School
Melbourne Avenue, Deakin ACT 2600
DP Coordinator Sarah Trotter
PYP Coordinator Alex Galland
Languages English
T: +61 2 6202 6400
W: www.cggs.act.edu.au

Canberra Grammar School
40 Monaro Crescent, Red Hill,
Canberra ACT 2603
DP Coordinator Graham Maltby
PYP Coordinator Sarah Dunn
Languages English
T: + 61 2 6260 9700
W: www.cgs.act.edu.au

CAREY BAPTIST GRAMMAR SCHOOL
349 Barkers Road, Kew VIC 3101
DP Coordinator Frédérique Petithory BA, PostGradCertEd, MA
Languages English
T: +61 3 9816 1222
E: admissions@carey.com.au
W: www.carey.com.au
See full details on page 316

Caulfield Grammar School – Caulfield Campus
PO Box 610, 217 Glen Eira Road East, St Kilda VIC 3185
PYP Coordinator Jacinta Crimmins
Languages English
T: +61 3 9524 6300
w: www.caulfieldgs.vic.edu.au

Caulfield Grammar School – Wheelers Hill Campus
74-82 Jells Road, Wheelers Hill VIC 3150
MYP Coordinator Peter Muir
PYP Coordinator Jonathan Twigg
Languages English
T: +61 3 8562 5300
W: www.caulfieldgs.vic.edu.au

Caulfield South Primary School
Bundeera Road, Caulfield South, Melbourne VIC 3162
PYP Coordinator Andrew McKibbin
Languages English
T: +61 3 957 83718
W: www.caulfieldsthps.vic.edu.au

Cleveland District State High School
Russell Street, Cleveland QLD 4163
DP Coordinator Laura Ewan
Languages English
T: +61 (0)7 3824 9222
W: clevelanddistrictshs.eq.edu.au

Coatesville Primary School
21 Mackie Road, East Bentleigh VIC 3165
PYP Coordinator Matthew Cameron
Languages English
T: +61 03 9570 1652
W: www.coatesps.vic.edu.au

Concordia College
24 Winchester St, Highgate SA 5063
DP Coordinator Joanne Wegener
MYP Coordinator Emily Johnson
PYP Coordinator Rachel Muldoon
Languages English
T: +61 8 8272 0444
W: www.concordia.sa.edu.au

Cornish College
65 Riverend Rd, Bangholme VIC 3175
PYP Coordinator Alexandra Parrington
Languages English
T: +61 3 9781 9000
W: www.cornishcollege.vic.edu.au

Coromandel Valley Primary School
339 Main Road, Coromandel Valley SA 5051
MYP Coordinator Liz Pelling
PYP Coordinator Kate ODriscoll
Languages English
T: +61 8 8278 3693
W: www.coromandps.sa.edu.au

CRANBROOK SCHOOL
5 Victoria Road, Bellevue Hill NSW 2023
DP Coordinator Nicholas Hanrahan
MYP Coordinator Kate Allen
PYP Coordinator Genet Erickson Adam
Languages English
T: +61 2 9327 9000
E: Enrol@cranbrook.nsw.edu.au
W: www.cranbrook.nsw.edu.au
See full details on page 319

Creek Street Christian College
91 Creek Street, Bendigo VIC 3550
DP Coordinator Marie Boulanger
Languages English
T: +61 3 5442 1722
W: www.creekstreet.vic.edu.au

Dingley Primary School
111-115 Centre Dandenong Road, Dingley Village VIC 3172
PYP Coordinator Lauren Thomas
Languages English
T: +61 3 9551 3555
W: www.dingleyps.vic.edu.au

Elonera Montessori School
21 Mount Ousley Road, Wollongong NSW 2519
DP Coordinator Carlos Hubbard
Languages English
T: +61 2 4225 1000
W: www.eloneramontessori.com.au

Encounter Lutheran College
64 Adelaide Road, Victor Harbor SA 5211
MYP Coordinator Adam Pfeiffer
PYP Coordinator Alicia Puiatti
Languages English
T: +61 8 8552 8880
W: www.encounter.sa.edu.au

Essendon North Primary School
112 Keilor Road, North Essendon VIC 3041
PYP Coordinator Alice Mckenzie
T: +61 (03) 9379 3979
W: www.enps.vic.edu.au

Fintona Girls' School
79 Balwyn Road, Balwyn VIC 3103
PYP Coordinator Cara Mearns
Languages English
T: +61 3 9830 1388
W: www.fintona.vic.edu.au

Firbank Grammar Junior School – Brighton Campus
51 Outer Crescent, Brighton, Melbourne VIC 3186
PYP Coordinator Michelle Worth
Languages English
T: +61 3 9591 5141
W: www.firbank.vic.edu.au

Firbank Grammar Junior School – Sandringham Campus
45 Royal Avenue, Sandringham VIC 3191
PYP Coordinator Karen Chandler
Languages English
T: +61 3 9533 5711
W: www.firbank.vic.edu.au

Footscray Primary School
PO Box 6019, West Footscray VIC 3012
PYP Coordinator Janine Bell
Languages English
T: +61 3 9687 1910
W: www.footscrayps.vic.edu.au

Forrest Primary School
Hobart Avenue, Forrest, Canberra ACT 2603
PYP Coordinator Jemma O'Brien
T: +61 2 6205 5644
W: www.forrestps.act.edu.au

Geelong Grammar School
50 Biddlecombe Avenue, Corio VIC 3214
DP Coordinator Trudy Purcell
PYP Coordinator Trudy Purcell
Languages English
T: +61 3 5273 9200
W: www.ggs.vic.edu.au

German International School Sydney
33 Myoora Road, Terrey Hills NSW 2084
DP Coordinator Mrs Annie Thomson
Languages English, German
T: +61 2 9485 1900
W: www.germanschoolsydney.com

Glenferrie Primary School
78-98 Manningtree Road, Hawthorn VIC 3122
PYP Coordinator Alexander Murray
Languages English, Italian
T: +61 3 9818 4338
W: www.glenferrieps.vic.edu.au

Glenroy West Primary School
P.O. Box 547, York Street, Glenroy VIC 3046
PYP Coordinator Lisa Brandecker
Languages English
T: +61 (0)3 9306 8955
W: www.glenroywestps.vic.edu.au

Glenunga International High School
L'Estrange Street, Glenunga SA 5064
DP Coordinator Corin Bone
Languages English
T: +61 88 379 5629
W: www.gihs.sa.edu.au

Gold Creek School
74 Kelleway Avenue, Nicholls, Canberra ACT 2913
MYP Coordinator Ingrid Little
PYP Coordinator Kirrally Talbot
Languages English
T: +61 (02) 6205 2955
W: www.goldcreek.act.edu.au

Golden Grove Lutheran Primary School
Corner of Richardson Drive and Sunnybrook Drive, Wynn Vale SA 5127
PYP Coordinator Jayne Zadow
Languages English
T: +61 8 8282 6000
W: www.goldengrove.sa.edu.au

Good News Lutheran College
580 Tarneit Road, Tarneit VIC 3029
PYP Coordinator Jessica Clark
Languages English
T: +61 3 8742 9000
W: www.goodnews.vic.edu.au

Good Shepherd Lutheran College – Howard Springs Campus

Corner of Whitewood Road & Kundook Place, Howard Springs NT 0835

MYP Coordinator Kathryn Cummins
PYP Coordinator Elizabeth Walker
Languages English
T: +61 8 89830300
W: www.goodshepherd.nt.edu.au

Good Shepherd Lutheran College – St Andrew Leanyer Campus

95 Leanyer Drive, Leanyer NT 0812
PYP Coordinator Rebecca Fletcher
Languages English
T: +61 8 8983 0300
W: www.goodshepherd.nt.edu.au

Good Shepherd Lutheran School – Angaston

7 Neldner Avenue, Angaston SA 5353
PYP Coordinator Fiona McDonald
Languages English
T: +61 8 8564 2396
W: www.goodshepherd.sa.edu.au

Grace Christian College

20 Kinchington Road, Leneva, Mellboune VIC 3691
DP Coordinator Joel Robotham
Languages English
T: +61 02 6056 2299
W: gcc.vic.edu.au

Heany Park Primary School

Buckingham Drive, Rowville VIC 3178
PYP Coordinator Kym Ryan
Languages English
T: +61 (0)3 9764 5533
W: www.heanyparkps.vic.edu.au

Helena College

PO Box 52, Glenn Forrest WA 6071
MYP Coordinator Peter Coombs
PYP Coordinator April Ledger
Languages English
T: +61 89 298 9100
W: www.helenacollege.wa.edu.au

Highton Primary School

PO Box 6093, Highton VIC 3216
PYP Coordinator Tracy Thornton
Languages English
T: +61 3 5243 1494
W: www.hightonps.vic.edu.au

Hills International College

105-111 Johanna Street, Jimboomba QLD 4280
PYP Coordinator Stuart Ablitt
Languages English
T: +61 7 5546 0667
W: www.hills.qld.edu.au

Holy Trinity Primary School

18-20 Theodore Street, Curtin ACT 2605
PYP Coordinator Ms Katie Smith
Languages English
T: +61 26281 4811
W: www.holytrinity.act.edu.au

Hunter Valley Grammar School

42 Norfolk Street, Ashtonfield NSW 2323
CP Coordinator Pauliene O'Grady
MYP Coordinator Pauliene O'Grady
PYP Coordinator Madeleine Smith
Languages English
T: +61 2 4934 2444
W: www.hvgs.nsw.edu.au

IES College

495 Boundary Street, Spring Hill QLD 4004
DP Coordinator Cassandra Magar
Languages English
T: +61 7 3832 7699
W: iescollege.com

Immanuel College

32 Morphett Road, Novar Gardens SA 5040
MYP Coordinator Jolanta Stephens
Languages English
T: +61 08 8294 3588
W: www.immanuel.sa.edu.au

Immanuel Gawler

11 Lyndoch Road, Gawler East SA 5118
PYP Coordinator Andrew Boesch
Languages English
T: +61 8 8522 5740
W: www.ilsg.sa.edu.au

Immanuel Primary School

Saratoga Drive, Novar Gardens SA 5040
PYP Coordinator Katherine Baird
Languages English
T: +61 8 8294 8422
W: www.immanuelps.sa.edu.au

Indooroopilly State High School

PO Box 61, Ward Street, Indooroopilly, Brisbane QLD 4068
DP Coordinator Peter Day
Languages English
T: +61 7 3327 8333
W: www.indurooshs.eq.edu.au

International School of Western Australia

193 St Brigids Terrace, Doubleview, Perth WA 6018
DP Coordinator Mini Balachandran
MYP Coordinator Paul Turner
PYP Coordinator Fleur Churton
Languages English
T: +61 8 9285 1144
W: www.iswa.wa.edu.au

Islamic College of Melbourne (ICOM)

83 Wootten Road, Tarneit VIC 3029
DP Coordinator Maha Elsayegh
Languages English
T: +61 3 8742 1739
W: icom.vic.edu.au

Ivanhoe Grammar School

PO Box 91, The Ridgeway, Ivanhoe VIC 3079
DP Coordinator Nicholas Mercer
Languages English
T: +61 3 9490 3501
W: www.ivanhoe.vic.au

John Paul College

John Paul Drive, Daisy Hill QLD 4127
PYP Coordinator Rebecca McAlister-Visic
Languages English
T: +61 7 3826 3333
W: www.jpc.qld.edu.au

JOHN WOLLASTON ANGLICAN COMMUNITY SCHOOL

Centre Road, Camillo WA 6111
PYP Coordinator Mrs Fiona Currey
Languages English
T: +61 (08) 9495 8100
E: mail@jwacs.wa.edu.au
W: www.jwacs.wa.edu.au

See full details on page 366

KAMBALA

794 New South Head Road, Rose Bay, Sydney NSW 2029
DP Coordinator Phillip Bird
Languages English
T: +612 93886777
E: enrolments@kambala.nsw.edu.au
W: www.kambala.nsw.edu.au

See full details on page 368

KARDINIA INTERNATIONAL COLLEGE

29-31 Kardinia Drive, Bell Post Hill, Geelong VIC 3215
DP Coordinator Ainslie Howard
PYP Coordinator Geoff Geddes
Languages English
T: +61 3 5278 9999
E: marketing@kardinia.vic.edu.au
W: www.kardinia.vic.edu.au

See full details on page 369

Kew Primary School

Peel Street, Kew, Melbourne VIC 3101
PYP Coordinator Alex Darlington
Languages English, French
T: +61 3 9853 8325
W: www.kewps.vic.edu.au

Kingston Heath Primary School

25 Farm Road, Cheltenham VIC 3192
PYP Coordinator Annaka Wheatley
Languages English
T: +61 3 9584 5805
W: www.khps.vic.edu.au

Kingsville Primary School

58 Bishop Street, Yarraville VIC 3013
PYP Coordinator Jeff McDonald
Languages English
T: +61 03 9315 8569
W: www.kingsvilleps.vic.edu.au

Kingswood College

355 Station Street, Box Hill, Melbourne VIC 3128
PYP Coordinator Heather Westwood
Languages English
T: +61 3 9896 1700
W: www.kingswoodcollege.vic.edu.au

KOROROIT CREEK PRIMARY SCHOOL

130 Tenterfield Drive, Burnside Heights VIC 3023
PYP Coordinator Alan Noye & Andrew Comley
Languages English
T: +61 3 8358 0600
E: kororoit.creek.ps@education.vic.gov.au
W: www.kororoitcreekps.vic.edu.au

See full details on page 373

Kunyung Primary School

50 Kunyung Road, Mt Eliza VIC 3930
PYP Coordinator Melanie Woodland
Languages English
T: +61 (3) 9787 6102
W: www.kunyung.vic.edu.au/

Launceston Church Grammar School

10 Lyttleton Street, East Launceston TAS 7250
PYP Coordinator Claire Calvert
Languages English
T: +61 3 6336 5900
W: www.lcgs.tas.edu.au

Lauriston Girls' School

38 Huntingtower Road, Armadale VIC 3143
DP Coordinator Sandra Mccowan
Languages English
T: +61 3 9864 7555
W: www.lauriston.vic.edu.au

AUSTRALIA

Le Fevre High School

90 Hart Street, Semaphore South, Adelaide SA 5019
MYP Coordinator Sarah Craddock
Languages English
T: +61 8 8449 7004
W: www.lefevrehs.sa.edu.au

Linden Park Primary School

14 Hay Road, Linden Park, Adelaide SA 5065
PYP Coordinator Nicole Scrivener
Languages English
T: +61 (0)8 8379 2171
W: www.lindenpkr7.sa.edu.au

Lloyd Street School

Lloyd Street, East Malvern VIC 3145
PYP Coordinator Roshni Amaria
Languages English
T: +61 3 9571 0261
W: www.lloydstps.vic.edu.au

LYCÉE CONDORCET – THE INTERNATIONAL FRENCH SCHOOL OF SYDNEY

758 Anzac Parade, Maroubra, Sydney NSW 2035
DP Coordinator Marcel Hennes
Languages English
T: +61 2 9344 8692
E: ib@condorcet.com.au
W: www.condorcet.com.au

See full details on page 378

Macclesfield Primary School

405 Macclesfield Road, Macclesfield VIC 3782
PYP Coordinator Andrea Goodey
Languages English
T: +61 3 5968 4734
W: www.macclesfieldps.vic.edu.au

Mansfield Steiner School

91 Highett Street, Mansfield VIC 3722
DP Coordinator Sue Plumb
Languages English
T: +61 3 57791445
W: mansfieldsteiner.vic.edu.au

Mater Christi College

28 Bayview Road, Belgrave, Melbourne VIC 3160
MYP Coordinator Collette Bond
Languages English
T: +61 3 9754 6611
W: www.materchristi.edu.au

McKinnon Primary School

253 Tucker Road, Ormond VIC 3204
PYP Coordinator Chris Barker
Languages English
T: +61 3 9578 1851
W: mckinnon-primary.vic.edu.au

Melba Copland Secondary School

Copland Drive, Melba ACT 2615
DP Coordinator Gai Britt
MYP Coordinator Lee Pietrukowski
Languages English
T: +61 2 6142 0333
W: www.mcss.act.edu.au

Melbourne Montessori School

741 Hawthorn Road, Brighton East VIC 3187
DP Coordinator Casper Buisman
Languages English
T: +61 3 9131 5200
W: melbournemontessori.vic.edu.au

Mentone Girls' Grammar School

11 Mentone Parade, Mentone VIC 3194
PYP Coordinator Donnah Ellen Ciempka
Languages English
T: +61 3 9581 1200
W: www.mentonegirls.vic.edu.au

MERCEDES COLLEGE

540 Fullarton Road, Springfield SA 5062
DP Coordinator Mr Marc Whitehead
MYP Coordinator Mr Stuart Wuttke
PYP Coordinator Mr Simon Munn
Languages English
T: +61 8 8372 3200
E: mercedes@mercedes.catholic.edu.au
W: www.mercedes.catholic.edu.au

See full details on page 380

MERICI COLLEGE

Wise Street, Braddon ACT 2612
DP Coordinator Natalie Fairfax
MYP Coordinator Natalie Fairfax
Languages English
T: +61 2 6243 4100
E: reception@merici.act.edu.au
W: www.merici.act.edu.au

See full details on page 381

Methodist Ladies' College

207 Barkers Road, Kew VIC 3101
DP Coordinator James Prowse
Languages English
T: +61 3 9274 6316
W: www.mlc.vic.edu.au

Mildura West Primary School

Ninth Street, Mildura VIC 3500
PYP Coordinator Luke Jeffers
Languages English, Chinese
T: +61 3 50231336
W: mildurawestps.vic.edu.au

Miles Franklin Primary School

Alderman Street, Evatt, Canberra ACT 2617
PYP Coordinator Sylvia Headon
Languages English
T: +61 2 6205 7533
W: www.mfps.act.edu.au

Milgate Primary School

96 Landscape Drive, East Doncaster, Melbourne VIC 3109
PYP Coordinator Sarah Brown
Languages English, Mandarin
T: +61 3 9842 7744
W: www.milgateps.vic.edu.au

MLC SCHOOL

Rowley Street, Burwood, Sydney NSW 2134
DP Coordinator Chris Barnes
Languages English
T: +61 2 9747 1266
E: enrol@mlcsyd.nsw.edu.au
W: www.mlcsyd.nsw.edu.au

See full details on page 382

Monte Sant' Angelo Mercy College

PO Box 1064, 128 Miller Street, North Sydney NSW 2059
DP Coordinator Kim Vandervelde
MYP Coordinator Jennifer Symington
Languages English
T: +61 2 9409 6200
W: www.monte.nsw.edu.au

Moreton Bay Boys' College

302 Manly Road, Manly West QLD 4179
PYP Coordinator Larissa Guy
Languages English
T: +61 07 3906 9444
W: www.mbbc.qld.edu.au

Moreton Bay College

450 Wondall Rd, Manly West QLD 4179
PYP Coordinator Nicole Bowers
Languages English
T: +61 7 3390 8555
W: www.mbc.qld.edu.au

Mornington Primary School

Vale Street, Mornington VIC 3931
PYP Coordinator Tahlia Anver
Languages English
T: +61 3 5975 2561
W: www.morningtonps.vic.edu.au

Mount Eliza North Primary School

Moseley Drive, PO Box 219, Mount Eliza VIC 3930
PYP Coordinator Peita Cooper
Languages English
T: +61 3 9787 6611
W: www.menps.vic.edu.au

Mount Eliza Secondary College

Canadian Bay Road, Mount Eliza VIC 3930
MYP Coordinator Danielle Vaughan
Languages English, Indonesian
T: +61 3 9787 6288
W: www.mesc.vic.edu.au

Mount Macedon Primary School

641 Mount Macedon Rd, Mount Macedon VIC 3441
PYP Coordinator Simon Dohler
Languages English
T: +61 3 5426 1446

Mount Scopus Memorial College

245 Burwood Highway, Burwood VIC 3125
MYP Coordinator Matthew Dufty
PYP Coordinator Edna Sackson
Languages English, Hebrew
T: +61 3 9834 0000
W: www.scopus.vic.edu.au

Mount View Primary School

Shepherd Road, Glen Waverley VIC 3150
PYP Coordinator Cheryl Reynolds
Languages English
T: +61 3 9560 0471
W: www.mountviewps.vic.edu.au

Mountain Creek State High School

Lady Musgrave Drive, Mountain Creek QLD 4557
DP Coordinator Adam Duus
Languages English
T: +61 (0)7 5457 8333
W: mountaincreekshs.eq.edu.au

Murrumbeena Primary School

Hobart Road, Murrumbeena VIC 3163
PYP Coordinator Angela Houghton
Languages English
T: +61 3 9568 1300
W: www.murrumbeenaps.vic.edu.au

Narrabundah College

Jerrabomberra Avenue, Narrabundah ACT 2604
DP Coordinator Christine Ward
Languages English
T: +61 2 6142 3200
W: www.narrabundahc.act.edu.au

Navigator College

PO Box 3199, Port Lincoln SA 5606
MYP Coordinator Sarah Smith
PYP Coordinator Nola Kennedy Williams
Languages English
T: +61 8 86825099
W: www.navigator.sa.edu.au

NEWINGTON COLLEGE – LINDFIELD

26 Northcote Road, Lindfield, New South Wales NSW 2070
PYP Coordinator Benjamin Barrington-Higgs
Languages English
T: +61 2 9416 4280
W: www.newington.nsw.edu.au

See full details on page 384

NEWINGTON COLLEGE – STANMORE

200 Stanmore Road, Stanmore NSW 2048
DP Coordinator Ms Cheryl Priest
Languages English
T: +61 2 9568 9333
E: admissions@newington.nsw.edu.au
W: www.newington.nsw.edu.au

See full details on page 384

North Ainslie Primary School

122 Majura Avenue, Ainslie, Canberra ACT 2602
PYP Coordinator Rikkie Klootwijk
Languages English
T: +61 02 62056533
W: www.nthainslieps.act.edu.au

Oakleigh Grammar

77-81 Willesden Road, Oakleigh VIC 3166
MYP Coordinator Melisa Fitzgerald
Languages English
T: +61 3 9569 6128
W: www.oakleighgrammar.vic.edu.au

Our Lady of the Nativity

29 Fawkner Street, Aberfeldie VIC 3040
PYP Coordinator Catherine Simone
Languages English
T: +61 3 9337 4204
W: www.olnaberfeldie.catholic.edu.au

Our Saviour Lutheran School

28 Taylors Road West, Aberfoyle Park SA 5159
PYP Coordinator Amanda McDonald
Languages English
T: +61 8 8270 5488
W: osls.sa.edu.au

Pedare Christian College

2-30 Surrey Farm Drive, Golden Grove SA 5125
MYP Coordinator Hayley Mayer
PYP Coordinator Laura Logan
Languages English
T: +61 8 8280 1700
W: www.pedarecc.sa.edu.au

Pembroke School

342 The Parade, Kensington Park SA 5068
DP Coordinator Gabi Walldorf-Davis
PYP Coordinator Belinda Reitstatter
Languages English
T: +61 8 8366 6200
W: www.pembroke.sa.edu.au

Presbyterian Ladies' College – Perth

14 McNeil Street, Peppermint Grove, Perth WA 6011
DP Coordinator Rebecca Garbenis
PYP Coordinator Jennifer Rickwood, Paul O'Brien
Languages English
T: +61 8 9424 6444
W: www.plc.wa.edu.au

Presbyterian Ladies' College Melbourne

141 Burwood Highway, Burwood VIC 3125
DP Coordinator Peter Francis
Languages English
T: +61 3 9808 5811
W: www.plc.vic.edu.au

Preshil – The Margaret Lyttle Memorial School

395 Barkers Road, Kew, Melbourne VIC 3101
DP Coordinator Karoline Kuti
MYP Coordinator Natalie Kunst
PYP Coordinator Cressida Batterham-Wilson
Languages English
T: +613 9817 6135
W: www.preshil.vic.edu.au

Prince Alfred College

PO Box 571, Kent Town SA 5071
DP Coordinator Martin Luke McKinnon
PYP Coordinator Lisa Foster
Languages English
T: +61 8 8334 1200
W: www.pac.edu.au

Queensland Academies Creative Industries Campus

61-73 Musk Avenue, Kelvin Grove QLD 4059
CP Coordinator Michael Zornig
DP Coordinator Karen Casey
Languages English
T: +61 7 3552 9333
W: qaci.eq.edu.au

Queensland Academies Health Sciences Campus

102 Edmund Rice Drive, Southport QLD 4215
DP Coordinator Alan Craig-Ward
Languages English
T: +61 7 5510 1100
W: qahs.eq.edu.au

QUEENSLAND ACADEMY FOR SCIENCE MATHEMATICS AND TECHNOLOGY (QASMT)

78 Bywong Street, Toowong QLD 4066
DP Coordinator Rebecca Skarshewski
MYP Coordinator Sandra Davey
Languages English
T: +61 7 3377 9333
E: admin@qasmt.eq.edu.au
W: qasmt.eq.edu.au

See full details on page 398

QUEENWOOD

Locked bag 1, Mosman NSW 2088
DP Coordinator Jennifer Brown
Languages English
T: +61 2 89687777
E: q@queenwood.nsw.edu.au
W: www.queenwood.nsw.edu.au

See full details on page 399

Radford College

College Street, Bruce, Canberra ACT 2617
DP Coordinator Nick Moss
PYP Coordinator Nick Martin
Languages English
T: +61 2 6162 5332
W: www.radford.act.edu.au

RAVENSWOOD

10 Henry Street, Gordon NSW 2072
DP Coordinator Monique Connor
PYP Coordinator Anne Gruenewald
Languages English
T: +612 9498 9898
E: admin@ravenswood.nsw.edu.au
W: www.ravenswood.nsw.edu.au

See full details on page 400

Red Hill School

PO Box 22, Red Hill ACT 2603
PYP Coordinator Emma Campbell
Languages English
T: +61 2 6205 7144
W: www.redhillps.act.edu.au

Redeemer Lutheran School, Nuriootpa

Box 397, Nuriootpa SA 5355
PYP Coordinator Petrea Booth
Languages English
T: +61 885 621655
W: www.redeemer.sa.edu.au

REDLANDS

272 Military Road, Cremorne NSW 2090
DP Coordinator Darren Taylor
Languages English
T: +61 2 9908 6479
E: dtaylor@redlands.nsw.edu.au
W: www.redlands.nsw.edu.au

See full details on page 403

RIVERCREST CHRISTIAN COLLEGE

Gate 6, 500 Soldiers Road, Clyde North VIC 3978
PYP Coordinator Caryn Johnson
Languages English
T: +61 3 9703 9777
E: admin@rivercrest.vic.edu.au
W: www.rivercrest.vic.edu.au

See full details on page 406

Rochedale State School

694 Rochedale Road, Rochedale, Brisbane QLD 4123
PYP Coordinator Paul Kelly
Languages English
T: +61 733408333
W: www.rochedalss.eq.edu.au

Roma Mitchell Secondary College

Briens Road, Gepps Cross SA 5094
DP Coordinator Lorraine Securo
MYP Coordinator Lorraine Securo
Languages English
T: +61 (0)8 8161 4600
W: rmsc.sa.edu.au

Rose Park Primary School

54 Alexandra Avenue, Rose Park, Adelaide SA 5067
PYP Coordinator Rebecca Weber
Languages English
T: +618 8331 7521
W: www.roseparkps.sa.edu.au

Roseville College

Locked Bag 34, 27 Bancroft Avenue, Roseville NSW 2069
PYP Coordinator Jane Sloane
Languages English
T: +61 2 9884 1100
W: www.roseville.nsw.edu.au

Sacred Heart College Geelong

Retreat Road, Newtown VIC 3220
MYP Coordinator Bridget Dunstan
Languages English
T: +61 3 52214211
W: www.shcgeelong.catholic.edu.au

Santa Maria College

50 Separation Street, Northcote, Melbourne VIC 3070
MYP Coordinator Bradley Denny
Languages English
T: +61 3 9488 1600
W: www.santamaria.vic.edu.au

Santa Sabina College

90 The Boulevarde, Strathfield, Sydney NSW 2135
DP Coordinator Julie Harris
PYP Coordinator Karen Campbell
Languages English
T: +61 2 9745 7000
W: www.ssc.nsw.edu.au

Scotch College
76 Shenton Road, Swanbourne, Perth WA 6010
DP Coordinator Brendan Zani
MYP Coordinator Cara Fugill
PYP Coordinator Warwick Norman
Languages English
T: +61 8 9383 6800
W: www.scotch.wa.edu.au

Seabrook Primary School
83-105 Point Cook Road, Seabrook VIC 3028
PYP Coordinator Rima El Souki
Languages English
T: +61 3 9395 1758
W: www.seabrook.vic.edu.au

Seaford North Primary School
81 Hallifax Street, Seaford VIC 3198
PYP Coordinator Chloe Gannon
Languages English
T: +61 3 9786 5674
W: seaford-northps.vic.edu.au

Seymour College
546 Portrush Road, Glen Osmond, Adelaide SA 5064
DP Coordinator Natalie Paelchen
PYP Coordinator Vanessa Browning
Languages English
T: +61 8 8303 9000
W: seymour.sa.edu.au

Somerset College
Somerset Drive, Mudgeeraba QLD 4213
DP Coordinator Michele Sauer
MYP Coordinator Allison Foster
PYP Coordinator Brenda Millican
Languages English
T: +61 (0)7 5559 7100
W: www.somerset.qld.edu.au

Sophia Mundi Steiner School
St. Mary's Abbotsford Convent, 1 St Heller's Street, Abbotsford, Melbourne VIC 3067
DP Coordinator Helen Ashley Falzarano Dufty
Languages English
T: +61 3 9419 9229
W: www.sophiamundi.vic.edu.au

Southern Christian College
150 Redwood Road, Kingston, Tasmania TAS 7050
DP Coordinator Veronica Schuth
MYP Coordinator Luke Headley
PYP Coordinator Melanie Curé
Languages English
T: +613 6229 5744
W: www.scc.tas.edu.au

ST ANDREW'S CATHEDRAL SCHOOL
Sydney Square, Sydney NSW 2000
DP Coordinator Sharon Munro
MYP Coordinator Kathleen Layhe
Languages English
T: +61 2 9286 9500
E: enrolments@sacs.nsw.edu.au
W: www.sacs.nsw.edu.au
See full details on page 420

St Andrews Lutheran College
PO Box 2142, Burleigh BC QLD 4220
PYP Coordinator Jacqueline Faulkner
Languages English
T: +61 7 5568 5900
W: www.standrewslutheran.qld.edu.au

St Andrew's School
22 Smith Street, Walkerville SA 5081
PYP Coordinator Heather Wood
Languages English
T: +61 8 81685537
W: www.standrews.sa.edu.au

St John's Anglican College
College Avenue, Forest Lake QLD 4078
PYP Coordinator Martin Brownlow
Languages English
T: +61 (0)7 3372 0111
W: stjohnsanglicancollege.com.au

St John's Lutheran School, Eudunda, Inc.
8 Ward Street, Eudunda SA 5374
PYP Coordinator Mandy Verco
Languages English
T: +61 8 8581 1282
W: www.stjohns-eudunda.sa.edu.au

St Leonard's College
163 South Road, Brighton East, Melbourne VIC 3187
DP Coordinator Craig Rodgers
PYP Coordinator Chris Stickman
Languages English
T: +61 3 9909 9300
W: www.stleonards.vic.edu.au

St Margaret's School
27-47 Gloucester Avenue, Berwick, Melbourne VIC 3806
PYP Coordinator Melissa Graham
Languages English
T: +61 3 9703 8111
W: www.stmargarets.vic.edu.au

St Mary Star of the Sea College
15 Harbour St, Wollongong NSW 2500
MYP Coordinator Katrina Wall
Languages English
T: +61 (0)2 4228 6011
W: www.stmarys.nsw.edu.au

St Michael's Lutheran School
6 Balhannah Rd, Hahndorf SA 5250
PYP Coordinator Darlene Hall
Languages English
T: +61 8 8388 7228
W: www.stmichaels.sa.edu.au

St Paul's Grammar School
Locked Bag 8016, Penrith NSW 2751
DP Coordinator Antony Mayrhofer
MYP Coordinator Mary Robyn
PYP Coordinator Corinne Day
Languages English
T: +61 2 4777 4888
W: www.stpauls.nsw.edu.au

St Peter's Anglican Primary School
Howe Street, Campbelltown NSW 2560
PYP Coordinator Melinda Richardson
Languages English
T: +61 (2) 4627 2990
W: www.stpeters.nsw.edu.au

St Peter's College
Hackney Road, Hackney, Adelaide SA 5069
DP Coordinator Paul Hadfield
Languages English
T: +61 8 8404 0400
W: www.stpeters.sa.edu.au

St Peter's Girls' School
Stonyfell Road, Stonyfell SA 5066
DP Coordinator Carolyn Victoria Farr
PYP Coordinator Helen Smith
Languages English
T: +61 88 334 2200
W: www.stpetersgirls.sa.edu.au

St Peters Lutheran College
66 Harts Road, Indooroopilly QLD 4068
DP Coordinator Roslynne Midgley
PYP Coordinator Simone Mitchell
Languages English
T: +61 7 3377 6222
W: www.stpeters.qld.edu.au

St Peters Lutheran School
71 Cumming Street, Blackwood SA 5051
PYP Coordinator Nicolle Jakube
Languages English
T: +61 8 8278 0800
W: www.stpeterslutheran.sa.edu.au

St Peter's Woodlands Grammar School
39 Partridge Street, Glenelg, Adelaide SA 5045
PYP Coordinator Lisa Harris
Languages English
T: +61 (8) 8295 4317
W: www.spw.sa.edu.au

Stradbroke School
73 Koonga Avenue, Rostrevor SA 5073
MYP Coordinator Sarah Button
PYP Coordinator Sarah Button
Languages English
T: +61 8 8337 2861
W: www.stradsch.sa.edu.au

Suzanne Cory High School
225 Hoppers Lane, Werribee VIC 3030
DP Coordinator Jasmine Byrne
Languages English
T: +61 3 8734 2800
W: www.suzannecoryhs.vic.edu.au

Tara Anglican School for Girls
Masons Drive, North Parramatta, Sydney NSW 2151
MYP Coordinator Cassandra Winfield
PYP Coordinator Wendy Abernethy
Languages English
T: +61 2 9630 6655
W: www.tara.nsw.edu.au

Telopea Park School / Lycée Franco-Australien de Canberra
New South Wales Crescent, Barton ACT 2600
MYP Coordinator Michele McLoughlin
Languages English
T: +61 2 6142 3388
W: www.telopea.act.edu.au

The Armidale School
Locked Bag 3003, 87 Douglas Street, Armidale NSW 2350
MYP Coordinator Rachael Harrison
PYP Coordinator Veronica Waters
Languages English
T: +61 2 6776 5800
W: www.as.edu.au

THE FRIENDS' SCHOOL
23 Commercial Road, North Hobart TAS 7002
DP Coordinator Sarah Walker
PYP Coordinator Wendy Crow
Languages English
T: +61 3 6210 2200
E: enquiries@friends.tas.edu.au
W: www.friends.tas.edu.au
See full details on page 429

The Illawarra Grammar School
10-12 Western Ave, Wollongong NSW 2500
PYP Coordinator Mrs Karen Wallace
Languages English
T: +61 2 4220 0200
W: www.tigs.nsw.edu.au

THE KILMORE INTERNATIONAL SCHOOL
40 White Street, Kilmore VIC 3764
DP Coordinator Deanna Krilis
Languages English
T: +61 3 5782 2211
E: enquiries@kilmore.vic.edu.au
W: www.kilmore.vic.edu.au
See full details on page 432

The King's School
PO Box 1, Parramatta NSW 2124
PYP Coordinator Shannon O'Dwyer
Languages English
T: +612 9683 8555
W: www.kings.edu.au

The King's School, Tudor House
6480 Illawarra Highway, Moss Vale NSW 2577
PYP Coordinator Caitlin Hayman
Languages English
T: +61 2 4868 0000
W: www.tudorhouse.nsw.edu.au

The Mac.Robertson Girls' High School
350-370 Kings Way, Melbourne VIC 3004
DP Coordinator Shungo Sawaki
Languages English
T: +61 3 9864 7700
W: www.macrob.vic.edu.au

The Montessori School
PO Box 194, Landsdale WA 6065
DP Coordinator Katharina Stillitano
Languages English
T: +61 89 409 9151
W: www.themontessorischool.wa.edu.au

The Norwood Morialta High School
Morialta Road West, Rostrevor SA 5073
MYP Coordinator Leisa Westerhof
Languages English
T: +61 8 83650455
W: www.nmhs.sa.edu.au

The Riverina Anglican College
127 Farrer Road, Wagga Wagga NSW 2650
DP Coordinator Patricia Humble
Languages English
T: +61 (0)2 6933 1811
W: www.trac.nsw.edu.au

The Scots School Albury
393 Perry Street, Albury NSW 2640
PYP Coordinator Georgie Parker
Languages English
T: +61 (0)2 6022 0000
W: www.scotsalbury.nsw.edu.au

Tintern Grammar
90 Alexandra Road, PO Box 26, Ringwood East VIC 3135
DP Coordinator Nola Joy Brotchie
Languages English
T: +61 3 9845 7777
W: www.tintern.vic.edu.au

Toorak College
PO Box 150, Mount Eliza VIC 3930
PYP Coordinator Philippa Morgan
Languages English
T: +61 3 9788 7200
W: www.toorakcollege.vic.edu.au

Townsville Grammar School
45 Paxton Street, North Ward QLD 4810
DP Coordinator Emma Crassini
Languages English
T: +61 7 4722 4900
W: www.tgs.qld.edu.au

Treetops Montessori School
PO Box 59, Darlington WA 6076
CP Coordinator Sharon Crossman
DP Coordinator Sharon Crossman
Languages English
T: +61 8 9299 6725
W: www.treetops.wa.edu.au

Trinity Grammar School Preparatory School
115-125 The Boulevarde, Strathfield NSW 2135
PYP Coordinator Kirsti Hitz-Morton
Languages English
T: +61 2 8732 4600
W: www.trinity.nsw.edu.au

Trinity Grammar School, Kew
40 Charles Street, Kew VIC 3101
PYP Coordinator Jonathan Knight
Languages English
T: +61 3 9854 3600
W: www.trinity.vic.edu.au

Trinity Grammar School, Sydney
119 Prospect Road, Summer Hill NSW 2130
DP Coordinator Andrew Scott
PYP Coordinator Merilyn Ormes
Languages English
T: +61 2 9581 6000
W: www.trinity.nsw.edu.au

Trinity Lutheran College
PO Box 322, Ashmore City QLD 4214
PYP Coordinator Melissa O'Shea
Languages English
T: +61 7 5556 8200
W: www.tlc.qld.edu.au

Trinity Lutheran College
920 Fifteenth Street, Mildura VIC 3500
PYP Coordinator Joanne Botha
Languages English
T: +61 3 5023 7013
W: www.tlc.vic.edu.au

Unley High School
Kitchener Street, Netherby SA 5062
DP Coordinator Christina Tedesco
Languages English
T: +61 8 8394 5400
W: uhs.sa.edu.au

Urquhart Park Primary School
49 Inkerman Street, Newington, Ballarat VIC 3350
PYP Coordinator Hollie Searl
Languages English
T: +61 3 5330 5400
W: urquhartps.vic.edu.au

Waikerie Lutheran Primary School
16 McCutcheon Street, Waikerie SA 5330
PYP Coordinator Michelle Burns
Languages English
T: +61 8 8541 2344
W: www.wlps.sa.edu.au

Wales Street Primary School
Wales Street, Thornbury VIC 3071
PYP Coordinator Luisa Kalenjuk
Languages English
T: +61 (03) 9484 394
W: www.walesstps.vic.edu.au

Walford Anglican School for Girls
316 Unley Road, Hyde Park SA 5061
DP Coordinator Mayra Franco
MYP Coordinator Jessica London
PYP Coordinator Annabel Howard
Languages English
T: +61 8 8272 6555
W: www.walford.asn.au

Wenona School
176 Walker Street, North Sydney NSW 2060
PYP Coordinator Carlie Plummer
Languages English
T: +61 2 9409 4400
W: www.wenona.nsw.edu.au

Werribee Secondary College
PO Box 314, Werribee VIC 3030
DP Coordinator Angela Callea
Languages English
T: +61 3 9741 1822
W: www.werribeesc.vic.edu.au

Wesley College Melbourne – Elsternwick Campus
5 Gladstone Parade, Elsternwick VIC 3185
MYP Coordinator Kate Watts
PYP Coordinator Halley Welsh
Languages English
T: +61 3 8102 6808
W: www.wesleycollege.net

Wesley College Melbourne – Glen Waverley Campus
620 High Street Road, Glen Waverley VIC 3150
MYP Coordinator James Carroll
PYP Coordinator Kathy Saville
Languages English
T: +61 3 8102 6508
W: www.wesleycollege.net

Wesley College Melbourne – St Kilda Road Campus
577 St Kilda Road, Melbourne VIC 3004
DP Coordinator Anne-Louise Szujda
MYP Coordinator Linda Pizzarello
PYP Coordinator Sarah Ho
Languages English
T: +613 8102 6508
W: www.wesleycollege.edu.au

Westbourne College Sydney
Harris Street, Ultimo, Sydney NSW 2007
DP Coordinator Elicia Mendonca
Languages English
T: +61 2 8088 0719
W: www.westbournecollege.com.au

Woodcroft College
Bains Road, Morphett Vale SA 5162
DP Coordinator Richard Pope
MYP Coordinator Elyse O'Malley
PYP Coordinator Karen McCulloch
Languages English
T: +61 8 8322 2333
W: www.woodcroft.sa.edu.au

Xavier College, Kostka Hall Campus
47 South Road, Brighton, Melbourne VIC 3186
PYP Coordinator Elena Serraglio
Languages English
T: +61 3 9519 0600
W: www.xavier.vic.edu.au

Abdul Kadir Molla International School
16/8 Baghdi (Dhaka-Sylhet Highway), Narsingdi Sadar, Narsingdi 1600, Dhaka
PYP Coordinator Asnaha Farheen
Languages English, Bengali
W: www.akmis.net

IB ASIA-PACIFIC

AUSTRALIA

American International School, Dhaka

PO Box 6106, Gulshan, 1212 Dhaka
DP Coordinator Kaitlyn Leach
PYP Coordinator Nancy Snyder
Languages English
T: +880 2 984 2452
W: www.aisdhaka.org

American Standard International School

Plot 20B, Road No. 79/82, Gulshan, 1212 Dhaka
DP Coordinator Ahmed Anwar Hasan
Languages English
W: www.asisbd.com

Australian International School, Dhaka

Joarshahara, Khilkhet, 1229 Dhaka
DP Coordinator Stephen Patrick
MYP Coordinator Rijwana Ameen Chowdhury
PYP Coordinator Taslima Khatoon
Languages English
T: +880 17 11567236
W: www.ausisdhaka.net

Crans-Montana International School

1492, C D A Avenue, East Nasirabad, Panchlaish, Chittagong
PYP Coordinator Jalal Uddin
Languages English, Bengali
T: +880 3 165 7126
W: cmisbd.org

International School Dhaka (ISD)

Plot 80, Block E, Bashundhara R/A, (Opposite Apollo Hospitals Dhaka), 1229 Dhaka
DP Coordinator Dixon Kibengo
MYP Coordinator Nilanthi Das
PYP Coordinator Lynette (Lyn) Weke-Kyalo
Languages English
T: +880 2 843 1101
W: www.isdbd.org

Pledge Harbor International School

Singer Dighi, Maona, Gazipur 1741, Dhaka
CP Coordinator Sujata Chowdhury
DP Coordinator Sujata Chowdhury
MYP Coordinator Rajani Roy
PYP Coordinator Babita Sidhu
Languages English
T: +880 961 443 3444
W: pledgeharbor.org

The Aga Khan School, Dhaka

Road 9, Sector 4, Uttara Model Town, 1230 Dhaka
DP Coordinator Usha Kasana
PYP Coordinator Tanjina Hossain
Languages English
T: +880 2 589 54042
W: www.agakhanschools.org/Bangladesh/AKSD/Index

BRUNEI DARUSSALAM

International School Brunei

Jalan Utama Salambigar, Kampong Sungai Hanching, Berakas 'B' BC2115
DP Coordinator Mrs. Jane Snell
Languages English
T: +673 233 0608
W: www.isb.edu.bn

JERUDONG INTERNATIONAL SCHOOL

Jalan Universiti, Kampong Tungku, Bandar Seri Begawan BE2119
DP Coordinator Mr Alex Cook
Languages English
T: +673 241 1000 (EXT: 1206/7100/1214)
E: office@jis.edu.bn
W: www.jerudonginternationalschool.com

See full details on page 364

CAMBODIA

Australian International School Phnom Penh

76 Angkor Boulevard, Sangkat Toul Sangke, Khan Russey Keo, Phnom Penh
CP Coordinator Jacob Evans
DP Coordinator Charles Campbell
MYP Coordinator Bradley Kremer
PYP Coordinator Wanita Woithe
Languages English, Khmer
T: +855 (0)92 111 136
W: www.aispp.edu.kh

Canadian International School of Phnom Penh

Koh Pich (Diamond Island), Elite Town Street, Phnom Penh
DP Coordinator Anthony George
Languages English, French
T: +855 23 900 399
W: www.cisp.edu.kh

HOPE International School – Phnom Penh Campus

PO Box 2521, Phnom Penh 3 12000
DP Coordinator Jane Lim
Languages English
T: +855 12 550 522
W: www.hope.edu.kh

International School of Phnom Penh

PO Box 138, Hun Neang Boulevard, Phnom Penh
DP Coordinator Angelique Hiscox
MYP Coordinator Matthew Clouter
PYP Coordinator Rachel Garthe
Languages English
T: +855 23 425 088
W: www.ispp.edu.kh

Northbridge International School Cambodia

PO Box 2042, Phnom Penh 3
DP Coordinator Kohulan Jeganathan
MYP Coordinator Gillian Presland
PYP Coordinator Angela Botero
Languages English
T: +855 23 900 749
W: www.nisc.edu.kh

The Giving Tree School

761 Preah Monivong Blvd, Phnom Penh
PYP Coordinator Anya Weil
Languages English, French
T: +855 17 997 112
W: www.thegivingtreeschool.edu.kh

CHINA

Alcanta International College

14 Guang Sheng Road, Nansha District, Guangzhou City, Guangdong 511458
DP Coordinator David (Jiacun) Dai
Languages English, Mandarin
T: +86 20 8618 3999/3666
W: aicib.org

AMERICAN INTERNATIONAL SCHOOL OF GUANGZHOU

No 3 Yan Yu Street South, Ersha Island, Yuexiu District, Guangzhou, Guangdong 510105
DP Coordinator Matthew Wood
PYP Coordinator Lydia Van Berkhout
Languages English
T: +86 20 8735 3392
E: admissions@aisgz.org
W: www.aisgz.org

See full details on page 310

Bade Intercultural Academy, Chengdu

168 Zhongli Road, Banzhuyuan Town, Xindu District, Chengdu, Sichuan
MYP Coordinator Patrick Meersman
PYP Coordinator Brian Hoblit
Languages English, Chinese
T: +86 130 7600 8225
W: bademeiji.com

Baowei Kindergarten

No.4 Baiyun Road, Xicheng District, Beijing 100045
PYP Coordinator Maezel Feranil
Languages Chinese, English
T: +86 13716522908
W: www.kidspower.cn

Bashu Secondary School

No. 51 Bei Qu Road, Yuzhong District, Chongqing 400013
DP Coordinator Yun Liang
Languages English, Chinese
T: +86 23 6300 2371
W: www.bashu.com.cn

Beanstalk International Bilingual School BIBS – Chengdu Campus

No. 351 Honghe Street, Longquanyi district, Chengdu, Sichuan
DP Coordinator Matthew Jelley
PYP Coordinator Ting Long
Languages English, Chinese
T: +86 28 8481 0088
W: www.bibs.com.cn

Beanstalk International Bilingual School BIBS – Kunming Campus

No. 986 Yongzheng Street, Chenggong District, Kunming, Yunnan
DP Coordinator Aaron Russo
PYP Coordinator Louie Desloge
Languages English, Chinese
T: +86871 6747 8668
W: www.bibs.com.cn

Beanstalk International Bilingual School BIBS – Shunyi Campus

No. 15 Liyuan Jie, TianZhu County, Shunyi District, Beijing 100000
DP Coordinator Ling Ruan
MYP Coordinator Xue Liu
PYP Coordinator Ginna Daza
Languages English
T: +86 10 6456 0618
W: www.bibs.com.cn

Beanstalk International Bilingual School BIBS – Upper East Side Campus

No.6 North East 4th Ring Rd, Chaoyang District, Beijing 100016
PYP Coordinator Adrian Gaunt
Languages English
T: +86 10 5130 7951
W: www.bibs.com.cn

Beijing 101 Middle School

11 Summer Palace Road, Haidian District, Beijing
DP Coordinator Eli Walker
Languages English, Chinese
T: +86 10 5163 3264
W: www.beijing101.com

Beijing BISS International School

No 17, Area 4, An Zhen Xi Li, Chaoyang District, Beijing 100029
DP Coordinator Valentina Trpkoska
MYP Coordinator Vicky Guo
PYP Coordinator Michael Bancroft
Languages English
T: +86 10 64 433151
W: www.biss.com.cn

Beijing Chaoyang KaiWen Academy

No.46 Baoquansan Street, Chaoyang District, Beijing
DP Coordinator John Whitehead
Languages English, Chinese
T: +86 108 302 8199
W: cy.kaiwenacademy.cn

Beijing City International School

77 Baiziwan Nan Er Road, Chaoyang District, Beijing 100022
DP Coordinator David Nguyen
MYP Coordinator Cornel Marais
PYP Coordinator Chantelle Parsons
Languages English
T: +86 10 8771 7171
W: www.bcis.cn

Beijing Haidian International School

No.368-2 Hanhe Road, Haidian District, Beijing 100195
DP Coordinator David Eriksen
Languages English
T: +86 10 8843 8003
W: www.bjhdis.com

Beijing Huijia Kindergarten, Beiou Campus

No.80 Maliandao Road, Xicheng District, Beijing 100085
PYP Coordinator Kelly Min Li
Languages Chinese, English
T: +86 10 63354580
W: www.hjkids.com

Beijing Huijia Kindergarten, Changhewan Campus

No.59 Gaoliangqiao Xiejie Road, Changhewan Community, Haidian District, Beijing 100044
PYP Coordinator Lina Tang
Languages Chinese, English
T: +86 10 82149978
W: www.hjkids.com

Beijing Huijia Kindergarten, Shijixin Campus

No. 3 Landianchang West Road, Haidian District, Beijing 100097
PYP Coordinator Gao Jinling
Languages Chinese, English
T: +86 10 88874145
W: www.hjkids.com

Beijing Huijia Kindergarten, Wanquan Campus

No. 35 Bagou South Road, Wanquan Xinxin Jiayuan Building 14, Haidian District, Beijing 100089
PYP Coordinator Shidan Xu
Languages Chinese
T: +86 10 8255 1751
W: www.hjkids.com

Beijing Huijia Kindergarten, Xibahe Dongli Campus

No.103 Xibahe Dongli, Chaoyang District, Beijing 100028
PYP Coordinator Melissa Peng
Languages Chinese
T: +86 (10) 64655212
W: www.hjkids.com

Beijing Huijia Private School

157 Changhuai Road, Changping District, Beijing 102200
DP Coordinator Yao Chen
MYP Coordinator Jingyu Li
PYP Coordinator Catherine Ma
Languages Chinese, English
T: +86 (10) 608 49399
W: www.huijia.edu.cn

Beijing International Bilingual Academy

Monet Garden, No 5 Yumin Road, Houshayu, Shunyi, Beijing 101300
DP Coordinator Matt Lawson
MYP Coordinator John Michael Cuepo
Languages English
T: +86 10 80410390
W: www.bibachina.org

Beijing National Day School

No. 66 Yuquan Road, Haidan District, Beijing 100039
DP Coordinator Jhony Arias Vivas
Languages English
T: +86 (10) 88625495
W: www.bndsedu.com

Beijing No 55 High School

12# Xin Zhong Jie Street, Dong Cheng District, Beijing 100027
DP Coordinator Ying Ying Wu
MYP Coordinator Tian Jieping
Languages English, Chinese
T: +86 10 64162247

Beijing No. 80 High School

WangjingBeiluJia 16, Chaoyang District, Beijing 100102
DP Coordinator Xiaojun Li
Languages English
T: +86 10 5804 7300

Beijing Royal Foreign Language School

No. 11, Wangfu Street, Changping District, Beijing 102209
MYP Coordinator Yue Wang
PYP Coordinator Jordan Sprentz
Languages Chinese, English
T: +86 10 81 785 511
W: www.brs.edu.cn

Beijing Royal Kindergarten

No. 11, Wangfu Street, Changping District, Beijing 102209
PYP Coordinator Ling Deng
Languages English, Chinese
W: www.brs.edu.cn

Beijing Royal School

No. 11, Wangfu Street, Changping District, Beijing 102209
DP Coordinator Dan Yan
Languages English, Chinese
T: +86 10 81 785 511
W: www.brs.edu.cn

Beijing World Youth Academy

18 Hua Jia Di Bei Li, Chao Yang District, Beijing 100102
DP Coordinator Richard Ambler
MYP Coordinator Juan Xia
Languages English
T: +86 10 6470 6336
W: www.ibwya.net

Boston International School

9 Jinghui West Road, New District, Wuxi, Jiangsu 214000
DP Coordinator Matthew Kirk
MYP Coordinator Laura Ward
PYP Coordinator Jerica Claassen
Languages English
T: +86 400 032 8000
W: www.bostonis.org

Bright Academy

Building 39#, ShiFoYing XiLi, Chaoyang District, Beijing 100025
PYP Coordinator Tracie Chen
Languages English, Chinese

British School of Beijing, Shunyi

South Side, No. 9 An Hua Street, Shunyi District, Beijing 101318
DP Coordinator Sarah Donnelly
Languages English
T: +8610 8047 3558
W: www.bsbshunyi.com

Bubble Kingdom International Kindergarten

No. 431, Linjiang Avenue, Zhujiang New Town, Tianhe District, Guangzhou, Guangdong 510620
PYP Coordinator Lingbo Sun
Languages English, Chinese
T: +86 20 6622 2520
W: www.bkik-kingold.com

Canada British Columbia International Schools – Hefei

5th Floor, International Department, Hefei No.1 High School, 2356 Xizang Road, Binhu New District, Hefei, Anhui
DP Coordinator Grant Van Wyk
Languages English, Chinese
T: +86 199 5605 8176
W: www.cbcschools.ca/hefei

Canadian Foreign Language School-Cambridgeshire

Inside Agile Cambridgeshire, Nancun Town, Panyu District, Guangzhou, Guangdong 511442
PYP Coordinator Ting Yi
Languages English, Chinese
T: +86 186 2078 9095
W: en.cls-c.com

Canadian International School Kunshan

1799 Zuchongzhi Road, Kunshan, Jiangsu 215347
DP Coordinator Kristie Newton
PYP Coordinator Ruby Fan
Languages English
T: +86 400-828-0084
W: www.ciskunshan.org

Canadian International School of Beijing

38 Liangmaqiao Lu, Chaoyang District, Beijing 100125
DP Coordinator Anjali Tyagi
MYP Coordinator Paul Steffan
PYP Coordinator Ashley Heath
Languages English
T: +86 10 64657788
W: www.cisb.com.cn

Canadian International School of Beijing – Jianguomen DRC Campus

No.1 Xiushui Street, Chaoyang District, Beijing 100600
PYP Coordinator Penny Liu
Languages Chinese, English
T: +86 10 85315312
W: www.cisb.com.cn/drc

CHINA

Canadian International School of Hefei

Fuxing Rd., High-Tech Zone, Hefei, Anhui 230088
DP Coordinator Ryan Walsh
MYP Coordinator Sean Miller
PYP Coordinator Christian Lee
Languages English
T: +86 551 6267 6776
W: www.cish.com.cn

Canadian International School of Shenyang

No.301 Hui Shan Road, Hunnan District, Shenyang, Liaoning 110167
DP Coordinator Patricia Larrondo
MYP Coordinator Ryan Steinberg
PYP Coordinator Alfonso Maldonado Ortiz
Languages English, Chinese
T: +86 24 66675379
W: www.cisshenyang.com.cn

Changchun American International School

2899 Dong Nan Hu Road, Changchun, Jilin 130033
DP Coordinator Santo Kurniawan
MYP Coordinator Barbara Dilthey
PYP Coordinator Michael Rylance
Languages English
T: +86 431 8458 1234
W: www.caischina.org

Changjun High School International Department

No. 328 Chazishan Road, Yuelu District, Changsha, Hunan 410023
DP Coordinator Peng Peng
Languages Chinese, English
T: +86 (0)731 85287942
W: changjunap.xhd.cn

Changping Huijia Kindergarten of Beijing

Building No.25, Zone 1, Yunqu Garden, Huilongguan Cultural Community, Changping District, Beijing 102208
PYP Coordinator Wanni Zhao
Languages Chinese, English
T: +86 10 81715252
W: www.hjkids.com

Changsha Huijia Kindergarten, Jujiangyuan Campus

Jintai Road, Xiangjiangshijicheng Community, Kaifu District, Changsha, Hunan 410000
PYP Coordinator Kiki Xie
Languages English, Chinese
T: +86 (0)731 85798618
W: www.hjkids.com

Changsha Huijia Kindergarten, Yongjiangyuan Campus

Jiangwan Road, Kaifu District, Changsha, Hunan 415000
PYP Coordinator Xiaojuan Jin
Languages Chinese, English
T: +86 731 85185289
W: www.hjkids.com

Changsha WES Academy

8 Dongyi Road, Xingsha, Changsha National Economic & Technical Development Zone, Changsha, Hunan 410100
DP Coordinator Yujing Wu
PYP Coordinator David Jones
Languages English
T: +86 731 82758900
W: www.wes-cwa.org

Changwai Bilingual School

No.66 Hengshan Road, Changzhou, Jiangsu 213022
DP Coordinator Ruby Huang
MYP Coordinator Yuefang Han
PYP Coordinator Yun Ding
Languages English, Chinese
T: +86 519 86921160
W: www.cztis.com

Chengdu Meishi International School

1340 Middle Section of Tianfu Avenue, Chengdu, Sichuan 610042
DP Coordinator Lorry Luo
MYP Coordinator Linda Guo
PYP Coordinator Timothy Riva
Languages English, Chinese
T: +86 028 8533 0653
W: www.meishischool.com

Chengdu Shude High School

No.398, Bairihong West Road, Jinjiang District, Chengdu, Sichuan 610000
DP Coordinator Amy Jingyu Li
Languages English
T: +86 28 86119628/98
W: www.sdgj.com

Chenshan School

QiYunXiDaDao, XiuNing District, Huangshan, Anhui 245400
DP Coordinator Amee Loftis
Languages English, Chinese
T: +86 559 7511878
W: www.chenshanschool.com

China World Academy Changshu

No.8 Yijia Road, Changshu, Jiangsu 215500
DP Coordinator Hu Yetao
Languages English, Chinese
T: +86 185 0152 9096
W: www.cwacs.cn

Citic Lake Bilingual International School

Citic Lake Community, Lishui Town, Nanhai District, Foshan, Guangdong
DP Coordinator Snober Sohail
PYP Coordinator Shailani Borges
Languages English
T: +86 (0)757 81008639
W: www.cbis-gd.com

Cogdel Cranleigh School, Changsha

117 Lixin Street, Changsha Economy and Technology Zone, Changsha, Hunan
DP Coordinator Mengjiao Tang
Languages English, Chinese
T: +86 731 8406 1777
W: www.cogdel.com

Country Garden Silver Beach School

Country Garden Silver Beach, Renshan Town, Huidong County, Huizhou, Guangdong 516347
DP Coordinator Miaomiao Song
PYP Coordinator Falin Zhang
Languages English, Chinese
T: +86 139 2910 2096
W: sbs.gd.cn

Daystar Academy

No. 2, Shunbai Road, Chaoyang District, Beijing
MYP Coordinator Jon Howarth
PYP Coordinator Yvonne Featherer
Languages English
T: +86 (0)10 64337366
W: daystarchina.cn

Dehong Shanghai

1935 Shuguang Road, Maqiao, Minhang District, Shanghai 201111
DP Coordinator Rebecca Curtin
Languages English, Chinese
T: +86 21 3329 9480
W: shanghai.dehong.cn

Dongguan Hanlin Experimental School

Chuangye Road No.5, Wanjiang District, Dongguan, Guangdong 523000
PYP Coordinator Ashley Yao Shujun
Languages Chinese
T: +86 769 22783301

DULWICH COLLEGE BEIJING

89 Capital Airport Road, Shunyi District, Beijing 101300
DP Coordinator Mr Anthony Baldwin
Languages English
T: +86 10 6454 9000
E: admissions.beijing@dulwich.org
W: beijing.dulwich.org

See full details on page 323

Dulwich College Shanghai Pudong

266 Lan An Road, Shanghai 201206
DP Coordinator Anthony Gillett
Languages English, Chinese
T: +8621 3896 1200
W: shanghai-pudong.dulwich.org

DULWICH COLLEGE SHANGHAI PUXI

2000 Qianpujing Road, Maqiao, Minhang District, Shanghai
DP Coordinator David Brown
Languages English, Chinese
T: +86 (21) 3329 9310
E: admissions.shanghaipuxi@dulwich.org
W: shanghai-puxi.dulwich.org

See full details on page 324

Dulwich College Suzhou

360 Gang Tian Road, Suzhou Industrial Park, Suzhou, Jiangsu 215021
DP Coordinator Aidan Jones
Languages English
T: +86 512 6295 9500
W: suzhou.dulwich.org

ECNU Affiliated Bilingual

569 Anchi Road, Jiading District, Shanghai 201805
DP Coordinator Ru Wang
Languages English
T: +86 400 920 6698
W: ecnuas.com

ECNU Affiliated Bilingual Kindergarten

221 Rong Ze Road, Shanghai 201805
PYP Coordinator Iuliia Shmatkova
Languages English, Chinese
T: +86 13 5246 94182
W: www.ecnuak.com

Escola Kao Yip

Avenida Xian Xing Hai, NAPE, Macau SAR
DP Coordinator Darren Lam
MYP Coordinator Ka Wai Leong
PYP Coordinator Liyuan Liu
Languages English, Chinese
T: +853 2875 0013
W: wp.kaoyip.edu.mo/secib

EtonHouse International School Times Residence, Chengdu

180 Zhiquan Section, East Avenue, Times Residence, Chengdu, Sichuan 610061
PYP Coordinator Elaine Wang
Languages English
T: +86 28 8477 7977
W: chengdu.etonhouse.com.cn/timesresidence

EtonHouse International School, Dongguan

19 Guangchang North Road, Gaobu, Dongguan, Guangdong 523270
PYP Coordinator Josanne Bally
Languages English
T: +86 769 8878 5333
W: www.etonhouse-dg.com

EtonHouse International School, Foshan

32 Fufeng Square, 1st Foping No.4 Road, Guicheng, Nanhai, Foshan, Guangdong
PYP Coordinator Robert Daws
Languages English, Chinese
T: +86 757 6668 8333
W: www.foshan.etonhouse.com.cn

EtonHouse International School, Nanjing

10 South Qing'ao Rd, Jianye District, Nanjing, Jiangsu 210019
PYP Coordinator Amber Li
Languages English
T: +86 25 8669 6778
W: nanjing.etonhouse.com.cn

EtonHouse International School, Riverside

AddressSouth Pudong Road 1570, Pudong, Shanghai
PYP Coordinator Melody Ying
Languages English, Chinese
T: +86 21 5068 9695
W: sh.etonhouse.com.cn

ETONHOUSE INTERNATIONAL SCHOOL, SUZHOU

102 Kefa Road, Suzhou Science & Technology Town, Suzhou, Jiangsu 215163
DP Coordinator Rajesh Kripalani
MYP Coordinator Rodney Springer
PYP Coordinator Natasha D'Costa
Languages English
T: +86 512 6825 5666
E: enquiry-sz@etonhouse.com.cn
W: www.suzhou.etonhouse.com

See full details on page 347

EtonHouse International School, Wuxi

Regent International Garden, Junction of Taishan Road & Xixing Road, Wuxi New District, Jiangsu 214028
PYP Coordinator Juliana Sali
Languages English
T: +86 510 85225333
W: wuxi.etonhouse.com.cn

Fudan International School

No 324 Guoquan Road, Yangpu District, Shanghai 200433
DP Coordinator Moqian Zhang
Languages English
T: +86 (0) 21 65640560
W: www.fdis.net.cn

Fuzhou International Preschool @ 1 Park Avenue

1 Park Avenue, Jinju Road 826, Jinshan District, Fuzhou, Fujian 350000
PYP Coordinator Junnan Zhang
Languages English, Chinese
T: +86 0591 83505222
W: www.srgedu.com/school/1/

Golden Apple International Preschool and Kindergarten

6 Chuangrui Street, Hi-tech District, Chengdu, Sichuan 610041
PYP Coordinator Xuemei Zhong
Languages English, Chinese
T: +86 28 8523 7403
W: www.61bb.com

Golden Apple Jincheng No 1 Secondary School

No. 99 Xianglong 3rd Street, High-tech Zone, Chengdu, Sichuan
DP Coordinator Zoe Yi
Languages English, Chinese
T: +86 28 6010 9299
W: intl.jpgzx.com

Golden Apple Tianfu International Preschool and Kindergarten

Shengxing East Rd.,Jiannan Street North, Hi-tech District, Chengdu, Sichuan 610041
PYP Coordinator Yao Chen
Languages English
T: +86 28 8517 1648

Guangdong Country Garden School

Beijiao Town, Shunde District, Foshan City, Guangdong
DP Coordinator Lizhu (Rita) Zhao
MYP Coordinator Zequn Deng
PYP Coordinator Josie Jiuhong Wang
Languages Chinese, English
T: +86 757 2667 7888
W: bgy.gd.cn

GUANGDONG SHUNDE DESHENG SCHOOL

Minxing Road, New District, Daliang, Shunde, Guangdong 528300
DP Coordinator Mr. Yu Yue
Languages English
T: +86 0757 22325121
E: admin.dsi@desheng-school.com
W: www.desheng-school.com

See full details on page 352

Guangzhou Foreign Language School

No. 102, Fenghuang Avenue, Nansha District, Guangzhou, Guangdong 511455
DP Coordinator Sherry She
Languages Chinese, English
T: +86 (0)20 22908716
W: chgzfls.com

Guangzhou Huamei International School

No. 23 Huamei Road, Tianhe District, Guangzhou, Guangdong 510520
PYP Coordinator Yichun Huang
Languages English, Chinese
T: +86 20 8721 0178
W: en.hm163.com

Guangzhou International Kindergarten Huangpu ZWIE

No. 438 Fengle South Road, Huangpu District, Guangzhou, Guangdong 510700
PYP Coordinator Jin Wan
Languages Chinese
T: +86 20 6298 6871
W: yey.czwie.com

Guangzhou International Middle School Huangpu ZWIE

No. 438 Fengle South Road, Huangpu District, Guangzhou, Guangdong 510700
MYP Coordinator Xiaoming Zhang
Languages English, Chinese
T: +86 40 0780 2003
W: zx.czwie.com

Guangzhou International Primary School Baiyun ZWIE

No. 998 Tonghe Road, Baiyun District, Guangzhou City, Guangdong 510515
PYP Coordinator Hannah Palmer
Languages English, Chinese
T: +86 20 3724 8716
W: wx.czwie.com

Guangzhou International Primary School Huangpu ZWIE

No. 188 Huangpu East Road, Huangpu District, Guangzhou, Guangdong 510700
PYP Coordinator Qin Hu
Languages English, Chinese
T: +86 40 0780 2003
W: sx.czwie.com

Guangzhou Nanfang International School

No.1 Yu Cui Yuan North, Yinglong Road, Longdong, Tianhe District, Guangzhou, Guangdong
DP Coordinator Lihong Yang
MYP Coordinator Yanyan Jin
PYP Coordinator Lisa Ding
Languages English
T: +86 20 8708 5090
W: www.gnischina.com

Guiyang Huaxi Country Garden International School

Country Garden Community, Mengguan Town, Huaxi District, Guiyang, Guizhou 550026
PYP Coordinator Huitao Yu
Languages English, Chinese
T: +86 (0)851 83651885

Hailiang Foreign Language School

No. 199 West 3rd Ring Road, Taozhu Street, Zhuji, Zhejiang
DP Coordinator Tingting Wang
Languages English, Chinese
T: +86 575 8900 3608
W: www.hailiangeducation.com

Hangzhou Binjiang Wickham Kindergarten

No.525 Weiye Road, Binjiang District, Hangzhou, Zhejiang 31500
PYP Coordinator Jasmine Jiang Xijiao
Languages English, Chinese

Hangzhou Future Sci-Tech City Wickham Kindergarten

No. 968-8, Gaojiao, Road, Yuhang District, Hangzhou, Zhejiang 311100
PYP Coordinator Qian Liu
Languages English, Chinese
T: +86 571 88665991

Hangzhou Greentown Yuhua Qinqin School

2 Zhujia Road, Yuhang District, Hangzhou, Zhejiang 311112
PYP Coordinator Jing Liu
Languages English, Chinese

IB ASIA-PACIFIC

CHINA

HANGZHOU GREENTOWN YUHUA SCHOOL

No. 532 Wenyi West Road, Hangzhou, Zhejiang 310012
MYP Coordinator Wang Xudong
Languages Chinese, English
T: +86 571 88477561
E: greentownedu@163.com
W: www.hzlcyhcz.cn

See full details on page 356

Hangzhou International School

78 Dongxin Street, Bin Jiang District, Hangzhou, Zhejiang 310053
DP Coordinator Jessamine Koenig
MYP Coordinator Patricia Long
PYP Coordinator Cilla Giannopoulos
Languages English
T: +86 571 8669 0045
W: www.his-china.org

Hangzhou Shanghai World Foreign Language School

167 Li Shui Road, Hangzhou, Zhejiang 310015
PYP Coordinator Frederic (Eric) Thiart
Languages English
T: +86 571 8998 1588

Hangzhou Victoria Kindergarten (Landscape Bay)

Hongyi Road, Xiaoshan District, Hangzhou, Zhejiang
PYP Coordinator Hu Yue
Languages English, Chinese
T: +86 571 83515277
W: victoriachina.com

Hangzhou Wesley School (Binjiang)

426 Wentao Road, Binjiang, Hangzhou, Zhejiang 310000
PYP Coordinator Bradford Evans
Languages English, Chinese
T: +86 133 7253 9991
W: www.wesleyschool.cn

Hangzhou Wesley School (Gongshu)

269 Gongfa Road, Gongshu District, Hangzhou, Zhejiang 311231
PYP Coordinator Wen Zhang
Languages English, Chinese
T: +86 (0)571 88828880
W: www.wesleyschool.cn

Hangzhou Wickham International School

533 Jingchang Road, Yuhang District, Hangzhou, Zhejiang
PYP Coordinator Shuhan Zhou
Languages Chinese
T: +86 0571 88665901
W: www.wickham.com.cn

HANGZHOU WORLD FOREIGN LANGUAGE SCHOOL

66 Muge Road, Banshan Street, Gongshu District, Hangzhou, Zhejiang 310000
DP Coordinator Wang Yanzhen
Languages English, Chinese
T: +86 189 5814 3128
E: hzsw_dp@wfl.sh.edu.cn
W: hz.shwfl.edu.cn

See full details on page 355

Hangzhou Yuhang Xixi Huadongyuan Kindergarten

NO.161 Gaojiao road Xianlin Street, Yuhang District, Hangzhou, Zhejiang 310000
PYP Coordinator Xixi Miao
Languages Chinese

Hefei Run'an Boarding School

292 Fanhua West Road, Economic & Technology Development Zone, Hefei, Anhui 230601
MYP Coordinator Zichang Sun
PYP Coordinator Sue Yang
Languages Chinese, English
T: +86 551 6982 1861
W: runanid.com

Hefei Xinhua Academy

No.7888 Changjiang West Road, Hefei, Anhui 230088
PYP Coordinator Vanessa Pfoehler
Languages English, Chinese
T: +86 551 6558 6888
W: en.xhacademy.com

Henan Jianye Little Harvard Bilingual School

No.31, East Section of Weisi Road, Jinshui District, Zhengzhou, Henan
PYP Coordinator Ian Gu Bo
Languages English, Chinese
T: +86 371 8655 0161
W: www.xiaohafo.cn

Hengyang Royal Kindergarten

No. 8 Changfeng Avenue, Huaxin, Hengyang, Hunan
PYP Coordinator Andrew Lacey
Languages English, Chinese
T: +86 73 4841 7888
W: www.englandroyal.com.cn

High School Affiliated To Nanjing Normal University

37 Chahaer Road, Nanjing, Jiangsu 210003
DP Coordinator Gong Yan
Languages English
T: +86 258 3469000
W: www.nsfz.net

HIGH SCHOOL AFFILIATED TO SHANGHAI JIAO TONG UNIVERSITY

No 42 Yin Gao Road, Bao Shan District, Shanghai 200439
DP Coordinator Frank Alfano
Languages English, Chinese
T: +86 21 65910979
E: jdfzib@jdfzib.org
W: www.jdfz.sh.cn

See full details on page 358

High School Attached to Northeast Normal University

No 377 Boxue Road, Jingyue District, Changchun, Jilin 130117
DP Coordinator Mashome Ramotubei
Languages Chinese, English
T: +86 431 85608927

Hong Qiao International School

218 South Yi Li Road, Shanghai 201103
PYP Coordinator Scott Aylwin
Languages English
T: +86 21 62682074
W: www.hqis.org

Huaer Zizhu Lemania College Shanghai

A9, No. 155 Tan Jiatang Road, Min Hang District, Shanghai 200241
DP Coordinator Yi Yan
Languages English, Chinese
W: www.hzl-sh.cn

Huanan Country Garden International Kindergarten

Huanan Country Garden, Nancun Town, Panyu District, Guangzhou, Guangdong 511442
PYP Coordinator Fang Wang
Languages English, Chinese
W: hbyey.brightscholar.com

Hübschmann Zhan International School

No. 2-1 Hun He Shi Street, Economic & Technological Development Area, Shenyang, Liaoning 110027
DP Coordinator Christopher J. Dawe
Languages English, German
T: +86 24 3120 0049
W: en.huz-school.com

Innova Early Years Center, Yizhuang Campus

Floor 1, Building B, Zhaolin Plaza, Yizhuang, Beijing 100026
PYP Coordinator Lara Ronalds
Languages English, Chinese

International School of Beijing-Shunyi

No 10 An Hua Street, Shunyi District, Beijing 101318
DP Coordinator Belinda McRoberts
Languages English
T: +86 10 8149 2345 EXT 1001
W: www.isb.bj.edu.cn

International School of Dongguan

#11 Jin Feng Nan Road, Dongguan, Guangdong 523000
DP Coordinator Alissa Gouw
Languages English
T: +86 769 2882 5882
W: www.i-s-d.org

International School of Nanshan Shenzhen

11 Longyuan Road, Taoyuan Sub-District, Nanshan District, Shenzhen 518052
DP Coordinator Sean Carroll
MYP Coordinator Ernie Boyd
PYP Coordinator Blessy Monica & Jennifer Nicklas
Languages English
T: +86 755 2666 1000
W: www.isnsz.com

International School of Tianjin

Weishan Road, Shuanggang, Jinnan District, Tianjin 300350
DP Coordinator Darryl Davies
MYP Coordinator Jess Chaudhry
PYP Coordinator Jane Lobsey
Languages English
T: +86 22 2859 2001
W: www.istianjin.org

ISA International School of Guangzhou

Block C2-2 Redtory, No.128 Siheng Road, Yuan Village, Tianhe District, Guangzhou, Guangdong 510655
MYP Coordinator Michael Urquhart
PYP Coordinator Joshua Jacob
Languages English
T: +86 20 3703 9193
W: www.isagz.org

ISA Science City International School

66 Yushu South Road, Science City, Huangpu District, Guangzhou, Guangdong
DP Coordinator David Edwards
Languages English, Chinese
T: +86 20 3736 2580
W: www.isagzsc.com

IB ASIA-PACIFIC

IVY Kindergarten of Tongzhou District, Beijing

Hebin Road No.1, Yongshun Town, Tongzhou District, Beijing 101100
PYP Coordinator Alex Ibrahim
Languages English, Chinese
T: +86 10 8969 6628
W: www.cqtkid.com

Jianye Xie He Cheng Bang Kindergarten

Minhang Road, Zhongzhou Avenue, Zhengzhou, Henan 450003
PYP Coordinator Hongyan Li
Languages English, Chinese

Jiaxiang International High School

No. 6, Chenhui North Road, Jinjiang District, Chengdu, Sichuan
DP Coordinator Tracy (Minjie) Wang
Languages English
T: +86 (0)28 69919908
W: www.cdjxihs.com

Jurong Country Garden School

No.2 Oiuzhi Road, Jurong Economic Development Zone, Zhengjiang City, Jiangsu 212400
DP Coordinator Cuicui Jia
MYP Coordinator Huang Fangfang
PYP Coordinator Daisy Xiaomin Xu
Languages English
T: +86 511 8078 0326
W: www.jrbgy.net

Kang Chiao International School (East China Campus)

No.500, Xihuan Rd., Huaqiao Economic Development Zone, Kunshan City, Jiangsu 215332
DP Coordinator Francis Abdurahman
MYP Coordinator Robert Staples
Languages English, Chinese
T: +86 512 3686 9833
W: en.kcisec.com

Keystone Academy

11 Anfu Street, Houshayu, Hou Sha Yu Town, Shunyi District, Beijing 101318
DP Coordinator Nicholas Daniel
MYP Coordinator Hongwei Gao
Languages English, Chinese
T: +86 10 8049 6008
W: www.keystoneacademy.cn

Kunming World Youth Academy

Building 2, No.3 High School Dianchixingcheng Campus, Chenggong District, Kunming, Yunnan 650500
DP Coordinator Kyle Gray
Languages English, Chinese
T: +86 871 6745 1511
W: www.kwya.top

Lanzhou Country Garden School

Qingbaishi Street, Chengguan District, Lanzhou, Gansu 730000
DP Coordinator Xiaofan Zhang
PYP Coordinator Zheng Da
Languages English, Chinese
T: +86 931 8790000

LÉMAN INTERNATIONAL SCHOOL CHENGDU

No.1080 Da'an Road, Zheng Xing County, Tianfu New Area, Chengdu, Sichuan 610218
DP Coordinator Thomas Ainsworth
MYP Coordinator Jarrett Brown
Languages English
T: +86 28 6703 8650
E: admissions@lis-chengdu.com
W: www.lis-chengdu.com
See full details on page 375

Manila Xiamen International School

No 735 Long Hu Shan Lu, Zeng Cuo An, Si Ming District, Xiamen, Fujian 361005
DP Coordinator Eve Denise Coronel
MYP Coordinator Raymond Ceferino III Meris
Languages English
T: +86 592 2516373
W: www.mxis.org

MOK Kindergarten

Huatang Golf Villa comprehensive Business Building, Yanjiao, Sanhe, Langfang, Hebei 065201
PYP Coordinator Lili Xie
Languages English, Chinese
W: www.mok2012.com

Morgan Henry Bilingual Kindergarten

567 Jinfeng Road, Huacao Town, Minhang District, Shanghai 201107
PYP Coordinator David graham
Languages English, Chinese
T: +86 21 6091 3366
W: www.shmhkids.com

Nanchang International School

1122 Phoenix Centre Road, Hong Gu Tan District, Nanchang, Jiangxi 330038
PYP Coordinator Luis Hernandez Quintero
Languages English
T: +86 791 83855352
W: www.wes-ncis.org

Nanjing Eternal Sea Kindergarten

No. 8 Huitong Road, Qixia District, Nanjing, Jiangsu 210000
PYP Coordinator Malena Jin
Languages English
T: +852 25 5870 6268
W: www.eternalsea.cn

Nanjing Foreign Language School

No. 35-4 North Taiping Road, Nanjing City, Jiangsu 210018
DP Coordinator Amit Roy
Languages English
T: +86 25 8328 2300
W: www.nfls.com.cn

Nanjing International School

No. 8 Xueheng Road, Nanjing, Jiangsu 210023
DP Coordinator Ruairi Cunningham
MYP Coordinator Mrs. Ruth Clarke
PYP Coordinator Mr. Adam Dodge
Languages English
T: +86 25 85899111
W: www.nischina.org

Nantong Stalford International School

No. 46 Hongxing Road, NETDA, Nantong, Jiangsu 226015
DP Coordinator Xian Neng How
Languages English, Chinese
T: +86 4008 4008 63
W: www.ntsis.com

Nanwai King's College School

188 Qingyuan Road, Jingkai District, Wuxi, Jiangsu
DP Coordinator Chaminda Marasinghe
Languages English, Chinese
T: +86 0510 6851 6972
W: www.nkcswx.cn

New Oriental Academy

101 Manbai Road, Machikou Town, Changping District, Beijing 102206
DP Coordinator George Mitov
MYP Coordinator George Mitov
Languages English, Chinese
T: +86 40 0688 1000
W: noa.xdf.cn

New Oriental Stars Kindergarten

Room 506, 5th Floor, Building F, Phoenix Plaza, No. A5, Shuguangxili, Chaoyang District, Beijing 100028
PYP Coordinator Jana Zhou
Languages English
T: +86 40 0066 5030
W: www.babybrightfuture.cn

Ningbo Huamao International School

No 2 Yinxian dadao (Middle), Ningbo, Zhejiang 31519
DP Coordinator Shameek Gosh
MYP Coordinator Keola Johnson
PYP Coordinator Reinette Roberts
Languages English, Chinese
T: +86 574 8821 1160
W: www.nbhis.com

Ningbo Huijia Kindergarten, Tingxiangyuan Campus

Tingxiangyuan of Century City, Hangzhouwan New District, Ningbo, Zhejiang 315336
PYP Coordinator Ying Wu
Languages English, Chinese
T: +86 (0)574 58975889
W: www.hjkids.com

Ningbo Xiaoshi High School

178 Baiyang Street, Ningbo, Zhejiang 315012
DP Coordinator Jacob Miles
Languages English
T: +86 574 8715 9613

Nord Anglia Chinese International School, Shanghai

1399 Jinhui Road, Minhang, Shanghai 201107
DP Coordinator David Jefferson-Gleed
Languages Chinese, English
T: +86 (021) 2403 8800
W: www.nordangliaeducation.com/our-schools/nacis/shanghai

NORD ANGLIA INTERNATIONAL SCHOOL SHANGHAI, PUDONG

2888 Junmin Road, Pudong New District, Shanghai 201315
DP Coordinator Emma Hughes
Languages English
T: +86 (0)21 5812 7455
E: admissions@naispudong.com
W: naispudong.com
See full details on page 389

Nord Anglia School Beijing, Fangshan

No. 236 Beiliuzhuang Village, Qinglonghu Town, Fangshan District, Beijing
DP Coordinator David Anthony Burgin
Languages English, Chinese
T: +86 10 8865 8000
W: fangshan.nacis.cn

CHINA

Nord Anglia School Foshan

No. 55 Dongxi Avenue, West Bank, Xiqiao Town, Nanhai District, Foshan, Guangdong
DP Coordinator Judith Donohue
Languages English
T: +86 757 8121 7688
W: foshan.nacis.cn

Nord Anglia School Jiaxing

No. 353 Qingze Road, Economic Development Zone, Jiaxing, Zhejiang 314000
DP Coordinator Scott Sloan
Languages English, Chinese
T: +86 189 6734 1988
W: www.nasjiaxing.cn

Nord Anglia School Nantong

No. 99, Jiangcheng Road, Sutong Park, Nantong, Jiangsu 226000
DP Coordinator Hiranmoy Gupta
Languages English, Chinese
T: +86 513 8918 3800
W: nantong.nacis.cn

Nord Anglia School Ningbo, Fenghua

No. 88 Wenbo Road, Xiaowangmiao Street, Fenghua District, Ningbo, Zhejiang 315500
DP Coordinator Jami Wimberly
Languages English, Chinese
T: +86 574 8720 3280
W: www.nordangliaeducation.com/schools/asia/china/ningbo

Northeast Yucai School

No.41 Shiji Road, Hunnan New District, Shenyang, Liaoning 110179
DP Coordinator Xun Sun
PYP Coordinator Tianliang Chen
Languages Chinese
T: +86 24 23783945
W: www.neyc.cn

Oriental Cambridge International School (Shenyang/Benxi Campus)

No 23, Mulan Road, Xihu District, Benxi, Liaoning 117000
DP Coordinator Bo Song
Languages English, Chinese
W: www.oceg.com/en/node/international/690.html

ORIENTAL ENGLISH COLLEGE, SHENZHEN

No 10 Xuezi Road, Education Town, Bao'an, Shenzhen, Guangdong 518128
DP Coordinator Kongjing Wang
PYP Coordinator Ling Luo (Caroline)
Languages Chinese, English
T: +86 755 2751 2624
E: principal@oecis.cn
W: www.szoec.com.cn

See full details on page 394

Oujing International Kindergarten

Beicun Road, Yiwu, Zhejiang 322000
PYP Coordinator Rochelle Boshoff
Languages English
T: +86 159 8561 7777
W: www.oujinginternational.com

Overseas Chinese Academy Suzhou

208 Zhong Nan Street, Suzhou Industrial Park, Jiangsu 215021
DP Coordinator Anthony Bernardo
PYP Coordinator Jeremiah Chua
Languages Chinese, English
T: +86 (512) 65001600
W: ocac-suzhou.com/zh

Oxstand International School, Shenzhen

No.2040, BuXin Road, Luohu District, Shenzhen, Guangdong
DP Coordinator Swati Nigam
Languages English
T: +86 755 2580 5707
W: www.oxstand.net

Peking University Experimental School (Jiaxing)

No.2339, Huayuan Road, Jiaxing, Zhejiang
DP Coordinator Han Li
PYP Coordinator Graham Wood
Languages English, Chinese
T: +86 573 8280 8280
W: www.pkujx.cn

Phoenix City International Kindergarten

No. 1 Yaxi Road, Phoenix City, Yongnin Street, Zengcheng District, Guangzhou, Guangdong 511340
PYP Coordinator Rita Fu
Languages English, Chinese
T: +86 20 3298 8186

Phoenix City International School

Xintang Town, Zengcheng City, Guangzhou, Guangdong 511340
MYP Coordinator Yue Zhang
PYP Coordinator Yangyi Chen
Languages Chinese, English
T: +86 20 6228 6902
W: www.pcis.com.cn

Qingdao Academy

No 111 Huazhong Road, Gaoxin District, Qingdao, Shandong 266111
DP Coordinator Andie Tong Wang
Languages English, Chinese
T: +86 532 5875 3788
W: www.qdzx.net

Qingdao Amerasia International School

68 Shandongtou Lu, Qingdao, Shandong 266061
DP Coordinator Giovanni Romeo
MYP Coordinator Kevin Wheeler
PYP Coordinator Kirsten Loza
Languages English
T: +86 532 8388 9900
W: qingdaoamerasia.org

QSI INTERNATIONAL SCHOOL OF CHENGDU

American Garden, 188 South 3rd Ring Road, Chengdu, Sichuan 610041
DP Coordinator Mr. David Becker
Languages English
T: +86 28 8511 3853
E: chengdu@qsi.org
W: chengdu.qsi.org

See full details on page 395

QSI INTERNATIONAL SCHOOL OF SHENZHEN

5th Floor, Bitao Building, 8 Tai Zi Road, Shekou, Shenzhen, Guangdong 518067
DP Coordinator Sandra Jung
Languages English
T: +86 755 2667 6031
E: shenzhen@qsi.org
W: shenzhen.qsi.org

See full details on page 397

Sanya Foreign Language School Kindergarten

No. 84,Hedong Road, Jiyang District, Sanya, Hainan
PYP Coordinator Sander Langerak
Languages English, Chinese
T: +86 898 8869 1631
W: www.sls-sanya.com/en/?page_id=928

Sanya Overseas Chinese School – Nanxin Campus

Shang Bao Po Road, Lizhi District, Sanya, Hainan
DP Coordinator Xiaoyan Yao
Languages English, Chinese
T: +86 89 8886 9023
W: www.sanyaocs.cn

School of the Nations

Rua de Minho, Taipa, Macau SAR
DP Coordinator William Leong
Languages English
T: +853 2870 1759
W: www.schoolofthenations.com

Seven Star Kindergarten Xiamen

No. 146 Qixing West Road, Siming District, Xiamen, Fujian
PYP Coordinator Joan Hong
Languages English, Chinese
T: +86 59 2766 6678
W: xmsevenstar.com

Shandong Zibo Shiyan High School

No.11 Zhangzhou Rd, Zibo, Shandong
DP Coordinator Hui Sun
Languages English, Chinese
T: +86 533 2851216
W: www.zsis.cn

Shanghai American School (Pudong Campus)

Shanghai Links Executive Community, 1600 Lingbai Road, Sanjiagang, Pudong, Shanghai 201201
DP Coordinator Philip Hayes
Languages English
T: +86 21 6221 1445 (Ext:2000)
W: www.saschina.org/admission

Shanghai American School (Puxi Campus)

26 Jinfeng Road, Huacao Town, Minhang District, Shanghai 201107
DP Coordinator Jonathan Smith
Languages English
T: +86 21 6221 1445
W: www.saschina.org

Shanghai Baoshan Happykids Kindergarten

No. 218, Lane 2488, Wenchuan Road, Baoshan District, Shanghai
PYP Coordinator Danli Luo
Languages English, Chinese
T: +86 21 5678 7887
W: www.happy-bs.com

SHANGHAI COMMUNITY INTERNATIONAL SCHOOL – HONGQIAO CAMPUS

1161 Hongqiao Road, Shanghai 200051
DP Coordinator Scott Simmons
MYP Coordinator Tetsuo Ishii
PYP Coordinator Vincent Lehane
Languages English
T: +86 21 6261 4338
E: admissions@scis-china.org
W: www.scis-china.org

See full details on page 416

SHANGHAI COMMUNITY INTERNATIONAL SCHOOL – PUDONG CAMPUS

800 Xiuyan Road, Kangqiao, Pudong, Shanghai 201315
DP Coordinator Jill Sculerati
MYP Coordinator Naomi Shanks
PYP Coordinator Heather Knight
Languages English
T: +86 21 5812 9888
W: www.scischina.org

See full details on page 416

462

Shanghai Foreign Language School

Zhong Shan Bei Yi Road No. 295, Shanghai 200083
DP Coordinator Jia Zhang
Languages English, Chinese
T: +86 (0)2165 423105
W: www.sfls.cn

Shanghai High School

400 Shangzhong Road, Xuhui, Shanghai 200231
DP Coordinator Hao Jiang
Languages English
T: +86 21 64765516
W: www.shsid.org

Shanghai Hongwen School

No 318 Chuanda Road, Pudong, Shanghai
DP Coordinator Charlotte Stonehouse
Languages English, Chinese
T: +86 189 1784 6368
W: www.hongwenschool.com.cn/En

Shanghai Jin Cai High School

2788 Mid-Yanggao Road, Pudong New Area, Shanghai 200135
DP Coordinator Angela Ying Zhang
MYP Coordinator Angela Ying Zhang
Languages Chinese, English
T: +86 21 6854 1158
W: www.jincai.sh.cn

Shanghai Liaoyuan Bilingual School

No. 150, Pingyang Road, Minhang District, Shanghai 201102
DP Coordinator Prachi Gupta
MYP Coordinator Kevin Fields
PYP Coordinator Sally Li
Languages English, Chinese
T: +86 21 6480 6128
W: www.liaoyuanedu.org

Shanghai Pinghe School

261 Huang Yang Road, Pudong, Shanghai
DP Coordinator Jing Xu
Languages English
T: +86 21 5031 0791
W: www.shphschool.com

Shanghai Pudong New Area Private Xuelexing Kindergarten

HongYa Road, Pudong District, Shanghai 201210
PYP Coordinator Qian Qian Li
Languages English, Chinese
T: +86 21 6070 2628

Shanghai Qibao Dwight High School

Physical Campus, 3233 Hongxin Road, Minhang District, Shanghai 201101
DP Coordinator Wendy Lin
Languages English
T: +86 21 6461 0367
W: www.qibaodwight.org

Shanghai Qingpu World Foreign Language Kindergarten

639 Panwen Road, Qingpu, Shanghai 201702
PYP Coordinator Chen Yi
Languages English, Chinese
T: +86 21 3988 6958
W: qpwflk.wfl-ischool.cn

Shanghai Shangde Experimental School

No 1688 Xiu Yan Road, Pudong New District, Shanghai 201315
DP Coordinator Ting Feng
MYP Coordinator Honglin Xu
PYP Coordinator Lina Li
Languages English
T: +86 21 6818 0001 OR +86 21 6818 0191
W: www.shangdejy.com

Shanghai Shixi High School

404 Yuyuan Rd, Jing'an District, Shanghai 200040
DP Coordinator Lily Hua Su
Languages English
T: +86 21 62521018
W: www.shixi.edu.sh.cn

Shanghai Singapore International School

301 Zhujian Road, Minhang District, Shanghai 201106
CP Coordinator Adam Crossley
DP Coordinator Adam Crossley
Languages English
T: +86 21 62219288
W: www.ssis.asia

SHANGHAI UNITED INTERNATIONAL SCHOOL

248 Hong Song Road (E), Gubei, Minhang District, Shanghai 201103
DP Coordinator Ben Griffiths
PYP Coordinator Jayanthi Nayak
Languages English
T: +8621 51753030
E: annie.yan@suis.com.cn
W: www.suis.com.cn

See full details on page 417

Shanghai Victoria Kindergarten (Gumei)

No. 300 Gu Mei Road, Xuhui, Shanghai
PYP Coordinator Simon Francis Marginson
Languages English
T: +86 (021) 6401 1084
W: gm.victoria.sh.cn

Shanghai Victoria Kindergarten (Pudong)

No. 38, Lane 39, Yin Xiao Road, Pudong, Shanghai
PYP Coordinator Selina Fang
Languages English
T: +86 (021) 5045 9084
W: pd.victoria.sh.cn

Shanghai Victoria Kindergarten (Xinzhuang)

No. 15, Lane 155, Bao Cheng Road, Xinzhuang, Shanghai
PYP Coordinator Jerry Wong
Languages Chinese, English
T: +86 (021) 5415 2228
W: xz.victoria.sh.cn

Shanghai Victoria Kindergarten (Xuhui)

No. 1, Lane 71, Huating Road, Xuhui, Shanghai
PYP Coordinator Aron Simmons
Languages Chinese, English
T: +86 (021) 5403 6901
W: xh.victoria.sh.cn

Shanghai Weiyu High School

No 1 Weiyu Road, Xuhui District, Shanghai 200231
DP Coordinator Li Chen
Languages English
T: +86 21 64966996 #8008
W: www.weiyu.sh.cn

Shanghai World Foreign Language Middle School

380 Pu Bei Road, Xu Hui District, Shanghai 200233
DP Coordinator Hector Jiachun Chen
MYP Coordinator Ye Wang
Languages Chinese, English
T: +8621 6436 3556
W: www.wflms.cn

Shanghai World Foreign Language Primary School

No 380 Pubei Road, Xu Hui District, Shanghai 200233
PYP Coordinator Halina Werchiwski
Languages English, Chinese
T: +86 21 5419 2245
W: www.wflps.com

SHEKOU INTERNATIONAL SCHOOL

Jingshan Villas, Nanhai Boulevard, Shekou, Nanshan, Shenzhen, Guangdong
DP Coordinator Craig Ortner
PYP Coordinator Alice Cheung
Languages English
T: +86 755 2669 3669
E: admissions@sis.org.cn
W: www.sis-shekou.org

See full details on page 418

Shen Wai International School

29 Baishi 3rd Road, Nanshan District, Shenzhen, Guangdong 518053
DP Coordinator Lindsay O'Sullivan
MYP Coordinator Vera Wu
PYP Coordinator Tiffany (Shasha) Xia
Languages English
T: +86 755 8654 1200
W: www.swis.cn

Shenwai Longgang International School (SLIS)

Huancheng East Rd, Longgang District, Shenzhen, Guangdong
MYP Coordinator Richard Greaves
PYP Coordinator Eda Erica Go
Languages English, Chinese
T: +86 755 28910303
W: www.slis.net.cn

Shenzhen Longgang Bantian Walton International Kindergarten

No.7-99 Yayuan Road, Bantian Street, Longgang District, Shenzhen, Guangdong 518000
PYP Coordinator Chen Xiuhong
Languages English, Chinese

Shenzhen Senior High School

Chuntian Road, Futian District, Shenzhen, Guangdong 518040
DP Coordinator Suzhen Wen
Languages English, Chinese
T: +86 755 8394 8654
W: www.cn-school.com

Shenzhen Shiyan Public School

No. 8 Yucai Rd, Shiyan Street, Baoan District, Shenzhen, Guangdong 518108
DP Coordinator Fangfang Kong
Languages English, Chinese
T: +86 755 2776 6766
W: sygx.baoan.edu.cn

SNU-K International Department

Yidu Road Longchengyihao, Chengdu, Sichuan 610101
PYP Coordinator Jian Kang
Languages Chinese, English
T: +86 18428393839

Songjiang District Xuelexing Qingcheng Kindergarten

Lane 2501, Guyang Road (N), Songjiang District, Shanghai
PYP Coordinator Na Wei
Languages English, Chinese

CHINA

Soochow Foreign Language School

No. 188, Yucheng Road, Xiangcheng District, Suzhou, Jiangsu
DP Coordinator Kaiqiu Jin
PYP Coordinator Lan Zhang
Languages English, Chinese
T: +86 512 8918 0556
W: www.cscfls.com

Springboard International Bilingual School

Gucheng Village, 15 Huosha Road, Houshayu Town, Shunyi District, Beijing 101318
DP Coordinator Andrew Peacock
Languages English, Chinese

Suzhou Industrial Park Foreign Language School

No.89, Suzhou Industrial Park, Suzhou, Jiangsu 215021
DP Coordinator Echo Zuo
Languages English
T: +86 512 6289 7710
W: www.sipfls.com

Suzhou Innovation Academy

100 Xiangcheng Ave, Xiangcheng District, Suzhou, Jiangsu
DP Coordinator Cheng Rui Eric Liu
Languages English
T: +86 (0)512 65490211
W: rhodes-ib.com

Suzhou Science and Technology Town Foreign Language School

No. 180 Jia Ling Jiang Road, Suzhou New District, Suzhou, Jiangsu 215163
PYP Coordinator Vanessa Pfoehler
Languages English, Chinese
T: +86 512 69370111

SUZHOU SINGAPORE INTERNATIONAL SCHOOL

208 Zhong Nan Street, Suzhou Industrial Park, Jiangsu 215021
DP Coordinator Laurence Mueller
MYP Coordinator Peter Coats
PYP Coordinator Katriona Hoskins
Languages English
T: +86 512 6258 0388
E: information@mail.ssis-suzhou.net
W: www.suzhouinternationalschool.com

See full details on page 426

Suzhou Victoria Kindergarten

Bayside Garden, Phase 3, No.1 Linglong Street, Suzhou, Jiangsu 215027
PYP Coordinator Sian Eatwell
Languages Chinese, English
T: +86 512 8081 1610
W: www.victoriasuzhou.com

Taicang Walton Foreign Language School

No. 200 Middle Suzhou Road, Taicang, Jiangsu 215400
DP Coordinator Beibei Li
PYP Coordinator Zhaonian Liu
Languages English, Chinese
T: +86 (0)512 33062226
W: en.chiwayedu.com

The Affiliated Foreign Language School of SCNU

No. 2, Science Avenue, Science City, Huangpu District, Guangzhou, Guangdong 510633
MYP Coordinator Lisa May Loveless
PYP Coordinator Robbie Faninghan
Languages English, Chinese
T: +86 20 3205 1890
W: www.scnufl.com

The British International School Shanghai, Puxi

111 Jinguang Road, Huacao Town, Minhang District, Puxi, Shanghai 201107
DP Coordinator Katherine Rose
Languages English
T: +86 (0)21 62217542
W: www.bisspuxi.com

The Garden International School

Agile Cambridgeshire, Panyu District, Guangzhou, Guangdong 511400
PYP Coordinator Feifei Wu
Languages English
T: +86 (0)20 3482 3833
W: www.tgisgz.com

The High School Affiliated to Renmin University of China

No. 37 Zhongguancun Street, Haidian District, Beijing 100080
DP Coordinator Yujie Bai
Languages English
T: +86 10 62513962
W: www.rdfz.cn/en

The International School of Macao

Macau University of Science and Technology (Block K), Avenida Wai Long, Taipa, Macau SAR
DP Coordinator Jody Hubert
Languages English
T: +853 2853 3700
W: www.tis.edu.mo

The Kindergarten of Hefei Run'an Boarding School

No. 268 Cui Wei Road, Economic and Technogical Development Zone, Hefei, Anhui 230601
PYP Coordinator Su Yang
Languages English
T: +86 (0)551 63821888
W: www.hfrayey.com

The MacDuffie School

No. 799, North Hui Feng Road, Fengxian Area, Shanghai 201403
DP Coordinator David Scoggins
Languages English
T: +86 21 400 600 2260
W: www.macduffie.cn/en

The Second Experimental Kindergarten of Jinhua

No.136 Shuanglong South Street, Wucheng District, Jinhua, Zhejiang
PYP Coordinator Lena Wang
Languages English, Chinese
T: +86 579 8916 9590
W: www.tsekjh.com

Tianjin Experimental High School

No 1 Pingshan Road, Hexi District, Tianjin 300074
DP Coordinator Lu Gan
MYP Coordinator Simon Zhang
Languages English, Chinese
T: +86 22 2335 4658
W: www.tjsyzx.cn

Times College

18 Shennong Road, Qixia District, Nanjing, Jiangsu
DP Coordinator Walter Nagles
MYP Coordinator Gerard Langan
PYP Coordinator Yi Yang
Languages English, Chinese
T: +86 25 85539090
W: www.timescollege.com

Tungwah Wenzel International School

No. 17 Keyuan Road, Songshan Lake High-Tech Industrial Zone, Dongguan, Guangdong
DP Coordinator Sebastien Gaillard
Languages English
T: +86 769 2289 0858
W: dgtwis.com

ULink College of Shanghai

No.559,Laiting South Road, Jiuting, Songjiang District, Shanghai 201615
DP Coordinator Miranda Lin
Languages English
T: +86 (0)21 67663819
W: en.ulink.cn/shanghai

Utahloy International School Guangzhou (UISG)

800 Sha Tai Bei Road, Bai Yun District, Guangzhou, Guangdong 510515
DP Coordinator Paul Johnson
MYP Coordinator Shwetangna Chakrabarty
PYP Coordinator Noah Beaumont
Languages English
T: +8620 8720 2019
W: www.utahloy.com

Utahloy International School Zengcheng (UISZ)

San Jiang Town, Zeng Cheng City, Guangdong 511325
DP Coordinator Andrea Bozzetti
MYP Coordinator Stuart Simpson
PYP Coordinator Jennifer Verontaye
Languages English
T: +86 20 8291 3201
W: www.utahloy.com

UWC CHANGSHU CHINA

No. 88 Kunchenghuxi Road, Changshu, Jiangsu 215500
DP Coordinator Christopher Hodachok
Languages English
T: +86 512 5298 2602
E: info.admissions@uwcchina.org
W: www.uwcchina.org

See full details on page 436

Vanke School Pudong

No 1700-2-4 Kangqiao Road, Pudong, Shanghai
DP Coordinator Haitao Zhang
Languages English, Chinese
T: +86 21 3463 3623
W: vsp.dtd-edu.cn

Victoria Kindergarten Shenzhen (Arcadia Court)

No.1008, Haitian Road, Futian Central District, Shenzhen, Guangdong
PYP Coordinator Vicky Zou
Languages English
T: +86 755 8302 8229
W: www.victoria-sz.com

Victoria Kindergarten Shenzhen (Futian)

No. 19, Xinzhou Er Jie, Fuqiang Road, Futian Central District, Shenzhen, Guangdong
PYP Coordinator Jane Liu
Languages Chinese, English
T: +86 755 8296 1010
W: www.victoria-sz.com

Victoria Kindergarten Shenzhen (Le Parc)

No. 3011, Fuzhong 1st Road, Futian Central District, Shenzhen, Guangdong
PYP Coordinator Lynn Zhang
Languages Chinese, English
T: +86 755 8328 2004
W: www.victoria-sz.com

Wahaha International School

5 Yaojiang Road, Shangcheng District, Hangzhou, Zhejiang 310008
PYP Coordinator Daniel Mannering
Languages English, Chinese
T: +86 571 8780 1933
W: www.wischina.org

IB ASIA-PACIFIC

Wellington College International Shanghai
No.1500 Yao Long Road, Pudong, Shanghai 200124
DP Coordinator Martin OBrien
Languages English
T: +86 21 5185 3866
W: www.wellingtoncollege.cn/shanghai

Western Academy Of Beijing
PO Box 8547, 10 Lai Guang Ying Dong Lu, Chao Yang District, Beijing 100102
DP Coordinator Scott Lindner
MYP Coordinator Stephen Taylor
PYP Coordinator Jonathan Mueller
Languages English
T: +86 10 5986 5588
W: www.wab.edu

WESTERN INTERNATIONAL SCHOOL OF SHANGHAI (WISS)
555 Lian Min Road, Xujing Town, Qing Pu District, Shanghai 201702
CP Coordinator Stewart Paterson
DP Coordinator Edwige Singleton
MYP Coordinator Amanda Narkiewicz
PYP Coordinator Lisa Kane & Inga Bela
Languages English
T: +86 21 6976 6388
E: admissions@wiss.cn
W: www.wiss.cn
See full details on page 442

WHBC of Wuhan Foreign Languages School
7th Floor Administration Building, 48 Wan Song Yuan Road, Wuhan, Hubei 430022
DP Coordinator Daniel Hwang
MYP Coordinator Yi Zhang
PYP Coordinator Taylor Bartlett
Languages English
T: +86 27 8555 7389
W: www.whbc2000.com/english

Wuhan Australian International School
No.322 Luoshi Road, Hongshan District, Wuhan, Hubei
PYP Coordinator Xiaoling Xia
Languages Chinese
T: +86 27 8710 5088
W: www.waisedu.com

Wuxi Foreign Language School
1 Xifeng Road, Taihuxincheng, Wuxi, Jiangsu 214131
PYP Coordinator Yixin Chen
Languages Chinese
W: www.wxfls.net/section/154

Wuxi No 1 High School
98, Yun He Donglu, Wuxi, Jiangsu 214031
DP Coordinator David Brandau
Languages English, Chinese
T: +86 51082809787
W: www.wxyzedu.net

Wuxi United International School
No. 8, Wenjing Road, Xishan District, Xidong New Town, Wuxi, Jiangsu 214104
DP Coordinator Vinod Pokhrel
Languages English
T: +86 510 8853 7700
W: wuxi.suis.com.cn

Xiamen International School
262 Xing Bei San Lu, Xinglin, Jimei District, Xiamen, Fujian 361022
DP Coordinator James Sutcliffe
MYP Coordinator Ralph Emmerink
PYP Coordinator Mary Collins
Languages English
T: +86 592 625 6581
W: www.xischina.com

Xi'an Hanova International School
188 Yudou Road, Yanta District, Xian, Shaanxi 710077
DP Coordinator Sharon Zhangyu Zhu
MYP Coordinator Rui (Amy) Hou
PYP Coordinator Lu (Grace) Bi
Languages English
T: +86 29 88693780
W: www.his-xian.com

Xi'an Liangjiatan International School (XLIS)
International Community, Xi'an, Shaanxi 710100
DP Coordinator Jaimala Quinlan
MYP Coordinator Daun Yorke
PYP Coordinator Maria Theresa Zialcita
Languages English
T: +86 29 85915100-8000
W: xalis.com

Xiaomiao Kindergarten (Luoxiu Campus)
1977 Luoxiu Road, Minghang District, Shanghai 201104
PYP Coordinator Alisa Zhang
Languages English, Chinese
T: +86 21 5481 6417
W: en.ys-edu.com.cn

Xiaomiao Kindergarten (Xinsong Campus)
No.47, Lane 499, Xinli Road, Minhang District, Shanghai
PYP Coordinator Pei Ji
Languages English, Chinese
T: +86 21 6492 0495
W: en.ys-edu.com.cn

Yew Chung International School of Beijing
Honglingjin Park, 5 Houbalizhuang, Chaoyang District, Beijing 100025
DP Coordinator Jonathan Mellen
Languages English
T: +86 10 8585 1836
W: www.ycis-bj.com

Yew Chung International School of Chongqing
No 2 Huxia Street, Yuan Yang Town, New Northern Zone, Chongqing 401122
DP Coordinator Kirsten Chapman
Languages English, Chinese
T: +86 23 8879 1600
W: www.ycef.com

Yew Chung International School of Qingdao
72 Tai Hang Shan Lu, Qingdao West Coast New Area, Huangdao, Shandong 266555
DP Coordinator Kyle Polizotto
Languages English
T: +86 532 8699 5551
W: www.ycis-qd.com

Yew Chung International School of Shanghai – Century Park Campus
1433 Dong Xui Road, Pudong, Shanghai 200127
DP Coordinator Matthew Grady
Languages English
T: +86 21 2226 7666
W: www.ycis-sh.com

Yew Chung International School of Shanghai – Hongqiao Campus
11 Shui Cheng Road, Puxi, Shanghai 200336
DP Coordinator David Potter
Languages English, Chinese (mandarin)
T: +86 21 2226 7666
W: www.ycis-sh.com

YK Pao School
1800, Lane 900, North Sanxin Road, Songjiang District, Shanghai 201602
DP Coordinator Helen Lambie-Jones
Languages English
T: +86 21 61671999
W: www.ykpaoschool.cn

Zhangjiagang Foreign Language School
256 Ji Yang Dong Lu, Zhangjiagang, Jiangsu 215600
DP Coordinator Cathy Zhang
Languages English
T: +86 512 5828 5972
W: www.zjgfls.com

Zhengzhou Middle School
2# Yinghua Street, Hi – Tech Development Zone, Zhengzhou, Henan 450001
MYP Coordinator Judy Zhu
Languages Chinese
T: +86 371 67996825
W: www.zzms.com

Zhongshan Academy
No.9, Area 4, Tiantongyuan, Changping District, Beijing
PYP Coordinator Maria Shatalova
Languages English, Chinese
T: +86 10 8482 9307
W: www.oceg.com/zsa

Zhuhai International School
Qi ' Ao Island, Tang Jia Wan, Zhuhai, Guangdong 519080
DP Coordinator Anthony kietzmann
MYP Coordinator Mike Piotrowski
PYP Coordinator Daniel Spears
Languages English
T: +86 756 331 5580
W: www.zischina.com

DOMINICAN REPUBLIC

Instituto Leonardo Da Vinci
Carretera Don Pedro Km 1, Esq. Calle El Guano, Santiago de los Caballeros
DP Coordinator Freddy Núnez Ureña
Languages English, Spanish
T: +1 809 734 1535
W: www.leonardo-da-vinci.edu.do

EAST TIMOR

Dili International School
14 Rue Avenue de Portugal, Pantai Kelapa, Dili
MYP Coordinator Cheryl Stephens
PYP Coordinator Jordan Harries
Languages English
T: +670 77316065
W: www.distimor.org

FIJI

International School Nadi

Box 9686 Nadi Airport, Nadi
DP Coordinator Bethan Paterson
MYP Coordinator Shabha Begum
PYP Coordinator Belinda Lalor
Languages English
T: +679 6702 060
W: www.isn.school.fj

International School Suva

Lot 59, Siga Road, Laucala Beach Estate, Suva
DP Coordinator Yiyuan Chen
PYP Coordinator Rosi Uluiviti
Languages English
T: +679 339 3300
W: www.international.school.fj

GUAM

St John's School

911 Marine Drive, Tumon Bay 96913
DP Coordinator Ellen Petra
Languages English
T: +1 (671) 646 8080
W: www.stjohnsguam.com

HONG KONG, CHINA

American School Hong Kong

6 Ma Chung Road, Tai Po, New Territories, Hong Kong, SAR
DP Coordinator Anthony Brewer
Languages English
W: www.ashk.edu.hk

Australian International School Hong Kong

3A Norfolk Road, Kowloon Tong, Hong Kong, SAR
DP Coordinator Peter Phillips
Languages English
T: +852 2304 6078
W: www.aishk.edu.hk

Canadian International School of Hong Kong

36 Nam Long Shan Road, Aberdeen, Hong Kong, SAR
DP Coordinator Brian Hull
MYP Coordinator Julie Cook
PYP Coordinator Stephen Brown
Languages English
T: +852 2525 7088
W: www.cdnis.edu.hk

Carmel School

460 Shau Kei Wan Road, Shau Kei Wan, Hong Kong, SAR
DP Coordinator Nick Webber
MYP Coordinator Janice Town
PYP Coordinator Jeffrey-Dean Cain
Languages English
T: +852 3665 5388
W: www.carmel.edu.hk

Causeway Bay Victoria International Kindergarten

32 Hing Fat Street, Causeway Bay, Hong Kong, SAR
PYP Coordinator Charlotte Chong
Languages English, Chinese
T: +852 2578 9998
W: www.cbvictoria.edu.hk

Chinese International School

1 Hau Yuen Path, Braemar Hill, Hong Kong, SAR
DP Coordinator Janelle Codrington
MYP Coordinator Francis Murphy
Languages English, Mandarin
T: +852 2 510 7288
W: www.cis.edu.hk

Christian Alliance International School

33 King Lam Street, Lai Chi Kok, Kowloon, Hong Kong, SAR
DP Coordinator Benjamin Myers
Languages English, Chinese
T: +852 3699 3899
W: www.caisbv.edu.hk

Creative Primary School

2A Oxford Street, Kowloon Tong, Kowloon, Hong Kong, SAR
PYP Coordinator Bonnie Cheng Mei Wah
Languages Chinese, Englisg
T: +852 2336 0266
W: www.creativeprisch.edu.hk

Creative Secondary School

3 Pung Loi Road, Tseung Kwan O, Sai Kung, NT, Hong Kong, SAR
DP Coordinator Maria Cristina Guevara
MYP Coordinator Nazerke Mukazhanova
Languages English, Chinese
T: +852 2336 0233
W: www.css.edu.hk

DELIA MEMORIAL SCHOOL (GLEE PATH)

1-3 Glee Path, Mei Foo Sun Chuen, Kowloon, Hong Kong, SAR
DP Coordinator Mr. Paolo Yap
Languages Cantonese, English, Mandarin
T: +852 2741 5239
E: gp@deliagroup.edu.hk
W: www.deliagp.edu.hk

See full details on page 320

Diocesan Boys' School

131 Argyle Street, Mong Kok, Kowloon, Hong Kong, SAR
DP Coordinator Charles Kar Lun Wu
Languages English
T: +852 2711 5911
W: www.dbs.edu.hk

ELCHK LUTHERAN ACADEMY

25 Lam Hau Tsuen Road, Yuen Long, New Territories, Hong Kong, SAR
DP Coordinator John Law
MYP Coordinator Keith Henderson
PYP Coordinator Julia ENG
Languages English, Cantonese, Mandarin
T: +852 8208 2092
E: info@luac.edu.hk
W: www.luac.edu.hk

See full details on page 325

ESF ABACUS INTERNATIONAL KINDERGARTEN

Mang Kung Uk Village, Clearwater Bay Road, Hong Kong SAR
PYP Coordinator Ms Fiona Hall
Languages English, Mandarin
T: +852 27195712
E: kinder@abacus.edu.hk
W: www.abacus.edu.hk

See full details on page 326

ESF BEACON HILL SCHOOL

23 Ede Road, Kowloon Tong, Hong Kong SAR
PYP Coordinator Mr Andy Thompson
Languages English
T: +852 2336 5221
E: bhs@bhs.edu.hk
W: www.beaconhill.edu.hk

See full details on page 327

ESF BRADBURY SCHOOL

43C Stubbs Road, Hong Kong SAR
PYP Coordinator Ms Amanda Bremner
Languages English
T: +852 2574 8249
E: enquiries@bradbury.edu.hk
W: www.bradbury.edu.hk

See full details on page 328

ESF CLEARWATER BAY SCHOOL

DD229, Lot 235, Clearwater Bay Road, New Territories, Hong Kong SAR
PYP Coordinator Ms Helen Read; Ms Chiara Holmes
Languages English
T: +852 2358 3221
E: info@cwbs.edu.hk
W: www.cwbs.edu.hk

See full details on page 329

ESF DISCOVERY COLLEGE

38 Siena Avenue, Discovery Bay, Lantau Island, Hong Kong SAR
CP Coordinator Ms Emma Neuprez
DP Coordinator Mr Brian McCann
MYP Coordinator Ms Annette Garnett
PYP Coordinator Ms Kate Agars
Languages English
T: +852 3969 1000
E: office@dc.edu.hk
W: www.discovery.edu.hk

See full details on page 330

ESF GLENEALY SCHOOL

7 Hornsey Road, Mid Levels, Hong Kong SAR
PYP Coordinator Ms Nia Sexton
Languages English
T: +852 2522 1919
E: enquiry@glenealy.edu.hk
W: www.glenealy.edu.hk

See full details on page 331

ESF HILLSIDE INTERNATIONAL KINDERGARTEN

43B Stubbs Road, Hong Kong SAR
PYP Coordinator: Ms Brenda Yuen
Languages English
T: +852 2540 0066
E: admissions@hillside.edu.hk
W: www.hillside.edu.hk

See full details on page 332

ESF ISLAND SCHOOL

20 Borrett Road, Hong Kong SAR
CP Coordinator Mr Roger Wilkinson
DP Coordinator Mr Matt Rappel
MYP Coordinator Ms Andrea Walsh
Languages English
T: +852 2524 7135
E: school@online.island.edu.hk
W: www.island.edu.hk

See full details on page 333

ESF KENNEDY SCHOOL

19 Sha Wan Drive, Pokfulam, Hong Kong SAR
PYP Coordinator Ms Yoon-Ah Lee
Languages English
T: +852 2579 5600
E: admissions@kennedy.edu.hk
W: www.kennedy.edu.hk

See full details on page 334

ESF KING GEORGE V SCHOOL

2 Tin Kwong Road, Homantin, Kowloon, Hong Kong SAR
DP Coordinator Mr Chris Wightman
MYP Coordinator Mr Rowan Turner
Languages English
T: +852 2711 3029
E: office@kgv.edu.hk
W: www.kgv.edu.hk

See full details on page 335

ESF KOWLOON JUNIOR SCHOOL

20 Perth Street, Homantin, Kowloon, Hong Kong SAR
PYP Coordinator Ms Dawn Doucette
Languages English
T: +852 3765 8700
E: office@kjs.edu.hk
W: www.kjs.edu.hk

See full details on page 336

ESF PEAK SCHOOL

20 Plunkett's Road, The Peak, Hong Kong SAR
PYP Coordinator Ms Chrissy Etchells-Bailey
Languages English
T: +852 2849 7211
E: office@ps.edu.hk
W: www.ps.edu.hk

See full details on page 337

ESF QUARRY BAY SCHOOL

6 Hau Yuen Path, Braemar Hill, North Point, Hong Kong SAR
PYP Coordinator Miss Ceri Hill
Languages English
T: +852 2566 4242
E: office@qbs.edu.hk
W: www.qbs.edu.hk

See full details on page 338

ESF RENAISSANCE COLLEGE

5 Hang Ming Street, Ma On Shan, New Territories, Hong Kong SAR
CP Coordinator Ms Wilma Shen
DP Coordinator Ms Jess Davey-Peel
MYP Coordinator Ms Brandy Stern
PYP Coordinator Mr Jason Doucette
Languages English
T: +852 3556 3556
E: info@rchk.edu.hk
W: www.rchk.edu.hk

See full details on page 339

ESF SHA TIN COLLEGE

3 Lai Wo Lane, Fo Tan, Sha Tin, New Territories, Hong Kong SAR
CP Coordinator Mr Luke Smetherham
DP Coordinator Ms Kellie Fagan
MYP Coordinator Ms Janice Lee
Languages English
T: +852 2699 1811
E: info@shatincollege.edu.hk
W: www.shatincollege.edu.hk

See full details on page 340

ESF SHA TIN JUNIOR SCHOOL

3A Lai Wo Lane, Fo Tan, Sha Tin, New Territories, Hong Kong SAR
PYP Coordinator Ms Trudy Mcmillin
Languages English
T: +852 2692 2721
E: info@sjs.esf.edu.hk
W: www.sjs.edu.hk

See full details on page 341

ESF SOUTH ISLAND SCHOOL

50 Nam Fung Road, Hong Kong SAR
CP Coordinator Ms Nicola Bosson
DP Coordinator Ms Kelly Diaz
MYP Coordinator Mr Shaine Bushell
Languages English
T: +852 2555 9313
E: sis@sis.edu.hk
W: www.sis.edu.hk

See full details on page 342

ESF TSING YI INTERNATIONAL KINDERGARTEN

Maritime Square, 33 Tsing King Road, Tsing Yi, New Territories, Hong Kong SAR
PYP Coordinator Ms Suzannah Large
Languages English
T: +852 2436 3355
E: kinder@tyk.edu.hk
W: www.tyk.edu.hk

See full details on page 343

ESF TUNG CHUNG INTERNATIONAL KINDERGARTEN

1/F, Commercial Accommodation, The Visionary, 1 Ying Hong Street, Tung Chung, Lantau, New Territories, Hong Kong SAR
PYP Coordinator Ms Cathy Boon
Languages English
T: +852 3742 3500
E: admissions@tck.edu.hk
W: www.tck.edu.hk

See full details on page 344

ESF WEST ISLAND SCHOOL

250 Victoria Road, Pokfulam, Hong Kong SAR
CP Coordinator Ms Emily Buckland
DP Coordinator Mrs Helen Devine Costa
MYP Coordinator Ms Clare Haworth
Languages English
T: +852 2819 1962
E: wis@wis.edu.hk
W: www.wis.edu.hk

See full details on page 345

ESF WU KAI SHA INTERNATIONAL KINDERGARTEN

599 Sai Sha Road, Ma On Shan, Sha Tin, Hong Kong SAR
PYP Coordinator Ms Aylin Kip
Languages English
T: +852 2435 5291
E: kinder@wksk.edu.hk
W: www.wksk.edu.hk

See full details on page 346

French International School

165 Blue Pool Road, Happy Valley, Hong Kong, SAR
DP Coordinator Pauline Hall
Languages English
T: +852 25776217
W: www.fis.edu.hk

G. T. (Ellen Yeung) College

10, Ling Kong Street, Tiu Keng Leng, Tseung Kwan O, Hong Kong, SAR
DP Coordinator Vincent Tam
Languages English, Chinese
T: +852 2535 6867
W: www.gtcollege.edu.hk

Galilee International School

G/F & 1/F, Peace Garden, 2 Peace Avenue, Ho Man Tin, Kowloon, Hong Kong, SAR
PYP Coordinator Mr Arthur Kenji Noguchi
Languages English, Mandarin, Cantonese
T: +852 2390 3000
W: www.gis.edu.hk

German Swiss International School

11 Guildford Road, The Peak, Hong Kong, SAR
DP Coordinator Sean Wray
Languages English
T: +852 2849 6216
W: www.gsis.edu.hk

Han Academy

G/F – 2/F, 33-35 Wong Chuk Hang Road, Aberdeen, Hong Kong, SAR
DP Coordinator Vahagn Vardanyan
Languages English, Chinese
T: +852 3998 6300
W: www.hanacademy.edu.hk

HKCA PO LEUNG KUK SCHOOL

62 Tin Hau Temple Road, Hong Kong, SAR
PYP Coordinator Ms Rose Hopewell-Fong
Languages English, Putonghua
T: +852 3465 8400
E: info@plkis.edu.hk
W: www.plkis.edu.hk

See full details on page 359

HONG KONG ACADEMY

33 Wai Man Road, Sai Kung, Hong Kong, SAR
DP Coordinator Joanna Crimmins
MYP Coordinator Kristen Feren
PYP Coordinator Carly Buntin
Languages English
T: +852 2655 1111
E: admissions@hkacademy.edu.hk
W: www.hkacademy.edu.hk

See full details on page 360

International College Hong Kong

60 Sha Tau Kok Road, Shek Chung Au, Sha Tau Kok, New Territories, Hong Kong, SAR
DP Coordinator Flora Lai
Languages English
T: +852 2655 9018
W: www.ichk.edu.hk

International College Hong Kong – Hong Lok Yuen

20th Street, Hong Lok Yuen, Tai Po, New Territories, Hong Kong, SAR
PYP Coordinator Charlotte Beard
Languages English
T: +852 26586935
W: www.ichk.edu.hk

Japanese International School

4663 Tai Po Road, Tai Po, New Territories, Hong Kong, SAR
PYP Coordinator Catherine Wan
Languages English
T: +852 2834 3531
W: www.jis.edu.hk

Kiangsu-Chekiang College, International Section

20 Braemar Hill Road, North Point, Hong Kong, SAR
DP Coordinator Calvin Tse
Languages English
T: +852 2570 1281
W: www.kcis.edu.hk

Kingston International Kindergarten

12-14 Cumberland Road, Kowloon Tong, Hong Kong, SAR
PYP Coordinator Michelle Chu
Languages English
T: +852 2337 9049
W: www.kingston.edu.hk

IB ASIA-PACIFIC

KINGSTON INTERNATIONAL SCHOOL

113 Waterloo Road, Kowloon Tong, Hong Kong, SAR

PYP Coordinator Ms. Kellie Berry (Primary); Ms. Michelle Chu (Early Years)

Languages English, Mandarin

T: +852 2337 9031

E: enquiry@kingston.edu.hk

W: www.kingston.edu.hk

See full details on page 371

Kornhill Victoria International Kindergarten

2/F., 18 Hong On Street, Kornhill, Quarry Bay, Hong Kong, SAR

PYP Coordinator Ms Vincci Wong

Languages English, Cantonese, Putonghua

T: +852 2885 1888

W: www.victoria.edu.hk

LI PO CHUN UNITED WORLD COLLEGE OF HONG KONG

10 Lok Wo Sha Lane, Sai Sha Road, Ma On Shan, Sha Tin, Hong Kong, SAR

DP Coordinator Beta Chau

Languages English

T: +852 2640 0441

E: office@lpcuwc.edu.hk

W: www.lpcuwc.edu.hk

See full details on page 376

Logos Academy

1 Kan Hok Lane, Tseung Kwan, Hong Kong, SAR

DP Coordinator Patricia Yeung

Languages English

T: +852-23372123

W: www.logosacademy.edu.hk

MALVERN COLLEGE HONG KONG

3 Fo Chun Road, Pak Shek Kok, Hong Kong, SAR

DP Coordinator Lianne Yu

MYP Coordinator Katrina Englart

PYP Coordinator Benedicte Benoit

Languages English

T: +852 3898 4688

E: admissions@malverncollege.org.hk

W: www.malverncollege.org.hk

See full details on page 379

NORD ANGLIA INTERNATIONAL SCHOOL, HONG KONG

11 On Tin Street, Lam Tin, Kowloon, Hong Kong, SAR

DP Coordinator Sarah Alexander

Languages English

T: +852 3958 1428

E: admissions@nais.hk

W: www.nais.hk

See full details on page 390

Parkview International Pre-school

Tower 18 Parkview, 88 Tai Tam Reservoir Road, Hong Kong, SAR

PYP Coordinator Joshua Hunter

Languages English

T: +852 2812 6023

W: www.pips.edu.hk

Parkview International Pre-School (Kowloon)

Podium Level, Kowloon Station, 1 Austin Road West, Kowloon, Hong Kong, SAR

PYP Coordinator Lin Chan

Languages English

T: +852 2812 6801

W: www.pips.edu.hk

Po Leung Kuk Choi Kai Yau School

6 Caldecott Road, Piper's Hill, Kowloon, Hong Kong, SAR

DP Coordinator James Kuan

Languages English

T: +852 2148 2052

W: www.cky.edu.hk

Po Leung Kuk Ngan Po Ling College

26 Sung On Street, Tokwawan, Kowloon, Hong Kong, SAR

DP Coordinator Yiu Iu

Languages English

T: +852 2462 3932

W: www.npl.edu.hk

Singapore International School (Hong Kong) – Secondary Section

2 Police School Road, Wong Chuk Hang, Hong Kong, SAR

DP Coordinator Alvin Soon

Languages English, Putonghua

T: +852 2919 6966

W: www.singapore.edu.hk

St. Paul's Co-educational College

33 MacDonnell Road, Central, Hong Kong, SAR

DP Coordinator Christopher Koay

Languages English

T: +852 2523 1187

W: www.spcc.edu.hk

St. Stephen's College

22 Tung Tau Wan Road, Stanley, Hong Kong, SAR

DP Coordinator Derek Barham

Languages English

T: +852 2813 0360

W: www.ssc.edu.hk

Stamford American School Hong Kong

25 Man Fuk Road, Ho Man Tin, Kowloon, Hong Kong, SAR

DP Coordinator Michael Galligan

Languages English

T: +852 3467 4500

W: www.sais.edu.hk

The Independent Schools Foundation Academy

1 Kong Sin Wan Road, Pokfulam, Hong Kong, SAR

DP Coordinator Kevin Hoye

MYP Coordinator Alan Johns

Languages English, Chinese

T: +852 2202 2000

W: www.isf.edu.hk

Think International School

117 Boundary Street, Kowloon Tong, Hong Kong, SAR

PYP Coordinator Rebecca Tupling

Languages English

T: +852 2338 3949

W: www.think.edu.hk

Victoria (Belcher) International Kindergarten

Portion of Level 3 (Kindergarten Area), The Westwood, 8 Belchers Street, Hong Kong, SAR

PYP Coordinator Sharon Lui

Languages English, Chinese

T: +852 2542 7001

W: www.victoria.edu.hk

Victoria (Harbour Green) International Kindergarten

8 Sham Mong Road, G/F., Harbour Green, Kowloon, Hong Kong SAR

PYP Coordinator Kit Cheng

Languages English

T: +852 2885 1928

W: www.victoria.edu.hk

Victoria (Homantin) International Nursery

1/F., Carmel-on-the-Hill, 9 Carmel Village Street, Homantin, Kowloon, Hong Kong, SAR

PYP Coordinator Cheng Kar Wai Flora

Languages English

T: +852 2762 9130

W: www.victoria.edu.hk

Victoria (South Horizons) International Kindergarten

Podium Level 2, Phase 2, South Horizons, Ap Lei Chau, Hong Kong, SAR

PYP Coordinator Sau Kei Wendy Lam

Languages Cantonese, English, Mandarin

T: +852 2580 8633

W: www.victoria.edu.hk

Victoria Kindergarten

G/F., 2-8 Hong On Street, Kornhill, Hong Kong, SAR

PYP Coordinator Kathy SIU

Languages English

T: +852 2885 3331

W: www.victoria.edu.hk

Victoria Nursery

Ko Fung Court, Harbour Heights, 5 Fook Yum Road, North Point, Hong Kong, SAR

PYP Coordinator Claudia Wong Tsz Kwan

Languages Cantonese, English, Mandarin

T: +852 2571 7888

W: www.victoria.edu.hk

Victoria Shanghai Academy (VSA)

19 Shum Wan Road, Aberdeen, Hong Kong, SAR

DP Coordinator Chloe Pollack

MYP Coordinator Jennifer Whitehair

PYP Coordinator Yu Sze (Carol) Ng

Languages English, Putonghua

T: +852 3402 1000

W: www.vsa.edu.hk

YEW CHUNG INTERNATIONAL SCHOOL OF HONG KONG

3 To Fuk Road, Kowloon, Hong Kong, SAR

DP Coordinator Alan Ramm

Languages English, Mandarin

T: +852 2338 7106

E: admissions@ycef.com

W: www.ycis-hk.com

See full details on page 444

INDIA

Aditya Birla World Academy

Vastushilp Annexe, Gamadia Colony, J D Road, Tardeo, Mumbai, Maharashtra 400034

DP Coordinator Shalini John

Languages English

T: +91 22 2352 8400

W: www.adityabirlaworldacademy.com

Aga Khan Academy Hyderabad

Survey No 1/1 Hardware Park, Maheshwaram Mandal, Rangareddy District, Hyderabad, Telangana 501510

DP Coordinator Sudipta Roy

MYP Coordinator Meenakshi Joshi

PYP Coordinator Abhimanyu Das Gupta

Languages English

T: +91 40 66291313

W: www.agakhanacademies.org/ hyderabad

Ahmedabad International School

Opp Rajpath Row Houses, Behind Kiran Motors, Judges Bungalow Road, Bodakdev, Ahmedabad 380015
DP Coordinator Deepti Shah
PYP Coordinator Jemily Kulkarni
Languages English
T: +91 79 2687 2459
W: www.aischool.net

Ajmera Global School

Yogi Nagar, Eksar Road, Borivali West, Mumbai, Maharashtra 400092
PYP Coordinator Pushpalata Ajit
Languages English
T: +91 22 32401053
W: www.ajmeraglobalschool.com

Akal Academy Baru Sahib

Via Rajgarh, Teh. Pachhad, Distt. Sirmore, Himachal Pradesh 173101
PYP Coordinator P.D Mani
Languages English
T: +91 9816400538
W: www.akalacademybarusahib.com

Akshar Árbol International School – ECR Campus

Bethel Nagar, North 9th Street, Injambakkam, Chennai, Tamil Nadu 600115
PYP Coordinator Latha Muthukrishnan
Languages English
T: +91 94449 73275
W: www.aksharbol.edu.in

Akshar Árbol International School – West Mambalam

The Secondary Space (Grade 6 – 12), 16, Umapathy Street, West Mambalam, Chennai, Tamil Nadu 600033
DP Coordinator Nandini N
PYP Coordinator Prabha Dixit
Languages English
T: +91 44248 33275
W: www.aksharbol.edu.in

aLphabet School

178 St. Mary's Road, Alwarpet, Chennai, Tamil Nadu 600018
MYP Coordinator Suparna Banerjee
PYP Coordinator Minu Simon
Languages English
T: +91 44 4211 2025
W: www.alphabet.school

American Embassy School

Chandragupta Marg, Chanakyapuri, New Delhi, Delhi 110021
DP Coordinator Teresa Hjellming
Languages English
T: +91 11 2688 8854
W: aes.ac.in

American International School – Chennai

100 Feet Road, Taramani, Chennai 600113
DP Coordinator Chris Galaty
Languages English
T: +91 44 2254 9000
W: www.aisch.org

AMERICAN SCHOOL OF BOMBAY

SF 2, G-Block, Bandra Kurla Complex Road, Bandra East, Mumbai, Maharashtra 400051
DP Coordinator Tamara Pfantz
PYP Coordinator Fay Martin
Languages English
T: SS: +91 22 6772 7272 ES: +91 22 6131 3600
E: inquiry@asbindia.org
W: www.asbindia.org

See full details on page 311

Amity Global School, Gurgaon

Main Sector Road 4, Sector 46, Gurgaon, Harayana 122002
DP Coordinator Ved Prakash
PYP Coordinator Chandrei Choudhury
Languages English
T: +91 84 4848 1410
W: www.amityglobalschool.com/gurgaon

Amity Global School, Noida

A Block, C Block, Sector 44, Noida, Uttar Pradesh 201301
PYP Coordinator Vishakha Jain
Languages English
T: +91 12 0243 2959
W: amityglobalschool.com/noida

Apeejay School International, South Delhi

Sheikh Sarai-Phase I, Panchsheel Park, New Delhi, Delhi 110017
DP Coordinator Neha Sharma
MYP Coordinator Pragati Agnihotri
PYP Coordinator Shalini Fate
Languages English
T: +91 11 26016935
W: intl.apeejay.edu

Ascend International School

5 'F' Block, Opp. Govt. Colony, Bandra Kurla Complex (Bandra E), Mumbai, Maharashtra 400051
DP Coordinator Angie Tarun
MYP Coordinator Varsha Agarwal Rodewald
PYP Coordinator Jonathan Martin
Languages English
T: +91 22 7122 2000
W: www.ascendinternational.org

Bangalore International School

Geddalahalli, Hennur Bagalur Road, Kothanur Post, Bengaluru, Karnataka 560077
DP Coordinator Deepak Babu
Languages English
T: +91 80 2846 5060/2844 5852
W: www.bangaloreinternationalschool.org

BD Somani International School

625 GD Somani Marg, Cuffe Parade, Mumbai, Maharashtra 400005
DP Coordinator Rupesh Solgaonkar
Languages English
T: +91 22 2216 1355
W: www.bdsomaniinternationalschool.com

Billabong High International School (Thane)

Road no. 27, Shreenagar, Wagle Estate, Thane West, Thane, Maharashtra 400604
DP Coordinator Vaishali Phatak
Languages English, Hindi
T: +91 84960 60000
W: www.billabongthane.com

BLiSS Edify International School, Pune

38 Phase 1, Rajiv Gandhi Infotech Park, Hinjawadi, Pune, Maharashtra 411057
MYP Coordinator Sheeza A.K.
Languages English
T: +91 77 4185 0000
W: blissedify.org

Bloomingdale International School

Municipal Employee Colony, Main Road, Vijayawada, Andhra Pradesh 520010
MYP Coordinator Lavanya Balaji
PYP Coordinator Harsimran Kapany
Languages English
T: +91 7799787827
W: bloomingdale.edu.in

Bodhi International School

Shikargarh Enclave, Near Mini Market, Jodhpur, Rajasthan 342015
PYP Coordinator Shikha Srivastava
Languages English
T: +91 291 2970100-1
W: www.bodhijodhpur.com

Bombay International School

Gilbert Building, 2nd Cross Lane, Babulnath, Mumbai, Maharashtra 400007
DP Coordinator Disha Sengupta
PYP Coordinator Nita Luthria Row
Languages English
T: +91 22 2364 8206
W: bis.edu.in

Bunts Sangha's S.M. Shetty International School & Jr. College

Hiranandani Gardens, Powai, Mumbai, Maharashtra 400076
DP Coordinator Snehal Bhortake
Languages English
T: +91 22 61327346
W: smshettyinstitute.org

Calcutta International School

724 Anandapur, E M Bypass, Kolkata, West Bengal 700107
DP Coordinator Tina Servaia
Languages English
T: +91 33 2443 2054
W: www.calcuttais.edu.in

Caledonian International School

Near Power Gym, Saili Road, Pathankot, Punjab 145001
MYP Coordinator Shagun Gupta
Languages English
T: +91 98880 00189
W: www.caledonian.in

Calorx Olive International School

Besides Ahmedabad Dental College, Near Arjun Farm, Ranchodpura – Bhadaj Road, Ahmedabad, Gujarat 380058
DP Coordinator Ankur Upadhyay
MYP Coordinator Swini Bagga
PYP Coordinator Sujata Paul
Languages English, French, Hindi
T: +91 90 9993 3804
W: www.cois.edu.in

Cambridge International School

Choti Baradari, Phase II, Jalandhar, Punjab 144001
DP Coordinator Rashmi Saini
PYP Coordinator Meenu Huria
Languages English
T: +91 181 462 3955
W: www.cambridgejalandhar.in

Canadian International School

Survey No 4 & 20, Manchenahalli, Yelahanka, Bengaluru, Karnataka 560064
DP Coordinator Aditi Bhattacharya
Languages English
T: +91 80 4249 4444
W: www.cisb.org.in

INDIA

Canary The School

1-110/3/B,Gautami Valley Near
Substation Road, Madinaguda,
Miyapur, Hyderabad, Telangana
500049
PYP Coordinator Madhavi Dutt
Languages English
W: www.canaryschool.in

Candor International School

Koppa-harapanhalli Road, Hullahalli,
Off, Bannerghatta Main Rd, near
Electronic City, Bengaluru, Karnataka
560105
DP Coordinator Gourab Das Sharma
PYP Coordinator Ms. Kiran Singh
Languages English
T: +91 77 6029 9992
W: candorschool.edu.in

Chatrabhuj Narsee School

Valley of Flower, Next to Gundecha
Premiere Tower, off. Western Express
Highway, Kandivali East, Mumbai,
Maharashtra 400101
DP Coordinator Aditi Chakrabarti
Languages English
T: +91 22 2886 6677
W: cns.ac.in

Chennai Public School

TH Road, SH 50, Thirumazhisai,
Chennai, Tamil Nadu 600124
DP Coordinator Jayu Ganesh
Languages English
T: +91 44 2654 4477
W: www.chennaipublicschool.com

Chinmaya International Residential School

Nallur Vayal Post, Siruvani Road,
Coimbatore, Tamil Nadu 641114
DP Coordinator Ganesh Eswaran
Languages English
T: +91 422 261 3300/3303
W: www.cirschool.org

Chinmaya International Vidyalaya

P-125, Warangade, Maan, Taluka and
Dist: Palghar, Boisar, Maharashtra
401501
PYP Coordinator Haritha
Raghunandanan
Languages English, Hindi
T: +91 73 7848 9121
W: chinmayainternationalvidyalaya.com

CHIREC International

1-55/12C, CHIREC Avenue, Kothaguda,
Kondapur, Hyderabad, Telangana
500084
DP Coordinator Sony Sharma
Languages English
T: 91 40 44760999
W: www.chirec.ac.in

Choithram International

Choithram Hospital Campus, 5 Manik
Bagh Road, Indore, Madhya Pradesh
452014
DP Coordinator Amit Puranik
MYP Coordinator Kamayani Sharma
PYP Coordinator Meenal Gavlani
Languages English
T: +91 731 2360345/6
W: www.choithraminternational.com

Christ Church School

Clare Road, Byculla, Mumbai,
Maharashtra 400008
DP Coordinator Avila Luke
Languages English
T: +91 22 2309 9892
W: www.christchurchschoolmumbai.org

Christ Junior College

29 Hosur Road, Suddagunte Palya,
Bengaluru, Karnataka 560029
DP Coordinator Sheela Chacko
Languages English
T: +91 80 40129292
W: www.christjuniorcollege.in

Christ Junior College – Residential

Mysore Road, Kanmanike,
Kumbalgodu, Bengaluru, Karnataka
560074
DP Coordinator Nancy Mariyan
Languages English
T: +91 80 28437915
W: www.cjcib.in

CP Goenka International School – Juhu

Plot No 44, Gulmohar Cross Road No
1, JVPD, Vile Parle (West), Mumbai,
Maharashtra 400049
DP Coordinator Neha Pandit
Languages English
T: +91 93 2259 1709
W: www.cpgoenkajuhu.com

Crossroads International School

11-12 Modern Complex, Devendra
Dham Ki Gali, Opposite Celebration
Mall, Udaipur, Rajasthan 313001
PYP Coordinator Shikha Rathore
Languages English, Hindi
T: +91 29 4298 0215
W: crossroadsschool.in

D Y Patil International College

DY Patil Knowledge City, Charholi(BK),
Via. Lohegaon, Pune, Maharashtra
412105
DP Coordinator Shylaja Salwan
Languages English
T: +91 20 30612700/752/753
W: www.dypispune.in

D Y Patil International School, Nerul

Dr D Y Patil Vidhyanagar, Sector 7,
Nerul, Navi Mumbai, Maharashtra
400706
DP Coordinator Shan Liz Sanju
Languages English
T: +91 22 47700840
W: www.dypisnerul.in

D Y Patil International School, Worli

Opp MIG Colony A, Worli, Mumbai,
Maharashtra 400025
DP Coordinator Huzefa Kagalwala
PYP Coordinator Sakina Gadiwala
Languages English
T: +91-22 69047999
W: www.dypisworli.com

Delhi Public School Ghaziabad

Site #3, Industrial Area, Meerut Road,
Ghaziabad, Uttar Pradesh 201002
DP Coordinator Gopalraj
Rangaswamy
PYP Coordinator Monalisa Sunit
Kumar
Languages English
T: +91 120 2712236
W: www.dpsghaziabad.com

Dhirubhai Ambani International School

Bandra-Kurla Complex, Bandra (East),
Mumbai, Maharashtra 400098
DP Coordinator Soma Basu
Languages English
T: +91 22 40617000
W: www.da-is.org

Don Bosco International School

Nathalal Parekh Marg, Matunga (E),
Mumbai, Maharashtra 400019
DP Coordinator Aarti Malik
PYP Coordinator Gladys Gonsalves
Languages English
T: +91 22 2412 7474
W: dbis.in

DPS International, Gurgaon

HS-01, Block W, South City II,
Gurgaon, Haryana 122001
DP Coordinator Jyotika Singh
MYP Coordinator Ekta Singh
PYP Coordinator Arpita Saxena
Languages English
T: +91 8377000164
W: www.dpsiedge.edu.in

Dr Pillai Global Academy

Plot No 1, RSC 48, Gorai – II, Borivali
(W), Mumbai, Maharashtra 400092
DP Coordinator Roshni Rajan
Languages English
T: +91 22 2868 4467/87
W: www.drpillaiglobalacademy.ac.in

Dr Pillai Global Academy, New Panvel

Sector-7, Khanda Colony, New Panvel,
Navi Mumbai, Maharashtra 410206
DP Coordinator Mousumee Mishra
Languages English
T: +91 22 2748 1737
W: dpgapanvel.ac.in

DRS International School

Survey No. 523 Opp.Apparel Park,
Gundla Pochampally, Medchal
Mandal, Telangana, Hyderabad
500100
DP Coordinator Pushyami
Chennupati
PYP Coordinator Harsha Gandhi
Languages English, French, Spanish,
Hindi
T: +91 40 237 92123/4/5
W: www.drsinternational.com

DSB International School

Urmi Estate 95, Ganpatrao Kadam
Marg, Opposite Peninsula Business
Park, Mumbai, Maharashtra 400013
DP Coordinator Angharad Davies
Languages English, German
T: +91 73 0459 7529
W: www.dsbindia.com

Eastern Public School

Ward 1, Abbas Nagar, Bhopal, Madhya
Pradesh 462036
DP Coordinator Fraz Ahmed
PYP Coordinator Syeda Humera
Riyaz
Languages English
T: +91 755 2805695
W: www.e-p-s.in

Ebenezer International School Bangalore

Singena Aghara, Via Huskur Road,
Near APMC Fruit Yard, Electronic City
Phase-I, Bengaluru, Karnataka 560099
DP Coordinator Abhinav Awasthi
PYP Coordinator Jyoti Andrew
Languages English
T: +91 80 67612222
W: www.eisbangalore.edu.in

Ecole Mondiale World School

Gulmohar Cross Road No. 9, J.V.P.D.
Scheme, Juhu, Mumbai, Maharashtra
400049
DP Coordinator Ms. Vidya Bhaskar
MYP Coordinator Rachel Satralkar
PYP Coordinator Shilpa Dholakia
Languages English
T: +91 22 26237265/66
W: www.ecolemondiale.org

Edubridge International School

Wadilal A. Patel Marg, Grant Road (East), Mumbai, Maharashtra 400007
DP Coordinator Tracy Waller
MYP Coordinator Radha Trivady
PYP Coordinator Disha Kerkar
Languages English
T: +91 22 238 999 11
W: www.edubridgeschool.org

Ela Green School

No.1 Karambur Village, Chengalpattu Taluk, Kandchipuram District, Urapakkam, Maraimalai Nagar, Chennai, Tamil Nadu 603209
PYP Coordinator Suhaina Sultan
Languages English
T: +91 89 3995 8989
W: elagreenschool.org

Elpro International School

Elpro compound, Entrance from Shridhar Nagar road, Pimpri-Chinchwad Link Road, Pune, Maharashtra 411033
DP Coordinator Shefali Tewary
Languages English
T: +91 20 6733 3500
W: www.elproschools.edu.in

Excelsior American School

Sector 43 behind Dell Building, C-2 Block, Sushant Lok, Phase 1, Gurugram, Haryana 122001
DP Coordinator Ruchi Gambhir
Languages English
T: +91 1 124 4049342
W: www.excelsioreducation.org

Fazlani L'Académie Globale

Shiv das Chapsi Marg, Opp. Wallace Flour Mills, Mazagaon, Mumbai, Maharashtra 400009
PYP Coordinator Kinjal Shah
Languages English
T: +91 222 373 2730
W: www.flag.org.in

FirstSteps School

Opp. Blind Girls Hostel, Sector 26, Chandigarh, Punjab 160019
PYP Coordinator Rachanjit Kaur
T: +91 172 2793992
W: firststepsschool.org

Focus High School

Behind Salar Jung Museum, 22-8-321 Darushifa, Hyderabad, Telangana 500024
PYP Coordinator Sheherbanoo Fathi
Languages English
T: +91 40 2440 4060
W: www.focushighschool.org

Fountainhead School

Opp Ambetha Water Tank, Kunkni, Rander-Dandi Road, Surat, Gujarat 395005
DP Coordinator Bhargavi Bergi
MYP Coordinator Chinki Chhapia
PYP Coordinator Nandini Aswani
Languages English
T: +91 800 0130 031
W: www.fountainheadschools.org

G D Goenka World School

GD Goenka Education City, Sohna-Gurgaon Road, Sohna, Haryana 122103
DP Coordinator Dr Manisha Mehta
PYP Coordinator Poonam Singh
Languages English
T: +91 124 3315900
W: gdgws.gdgoenka.com

G Global School

29A, Rajagoundampalayam 2nd Street, Pallipalayam Road, Tiruchengodu, Tamil Nadu 637211
PYP Coordinator Sathyavarthini Gunasekaran
Languages English, Tamil
T: +91 42 8825 0999
W: www.gglobalschool.com

Garodia International Centre for Learning

153, Garodia Nagar, Ghatkopar East, Mumbai, Maharashtra 400077
DP Coordinator Elza Eldo Maliyil
Languages English
T: +91 22 25061133/3157
W: www.gicl.edu.in

Gateway International School

TOD Ashram, Jabakadal Street, Padur, Kazhipattur Post, Kelambakkam, Chennai, Tamil Nadu 603103
DP Coordinator P. Letishia Arputhamani Ebenezer
MYP Coordinator Dharakeswari G
PYP Coordinator Susan Pramod
Languages English
T: + 91 860 811 7700
W: gatewayschools.edu.in

GEMS Modern Academy – Kochi

Plot B1-4, Smart City Kochi, Opp. Infopark Phase II, Brahmapuram, Kochi, Kerala 682303
PYP Coordinator Remi Rajan
Languages English
T: +91 48 4258 7800
W: www.gemsmodernacademy-kochi.in

GENESIS GLOBAL SCHOOL

A-12, Sector 132, Noida Expressway, Uttar Pradesh 201304
DP Coordinator Rajeev Pargaien
MYP Coordinator Dahlia Atabani
PYP Coordinator Monika Kala
Languages English
T: +91 9711 000626
E: info@genesisgs.edu.in
W: www.genesisglobalschool.edu.in

See full details on page 350

GJR International School

1/1 & 1/2 Chinnappanahalli, Bangalore, Karnataka 560037
PYP Coordinator Neelam Ravi
Languages English
T: +91 96 0648 9500
W: gjrinternationalschool.edu.in

Glendale International School

Plot A, Road No. 20, HMDA Layout, Tellapur, Hyderabad, Telangana 502032
PYP Coordinator Ms Neerja M.
Languages English
T: +91 90 3000 1128
W: www.glendale.edu.in/glendale-international-school/ib-pyp-tellapur

Goldcrest International

Sector 29, Plot No: 59, Near Rajiv Gandhi Park, Navi Mumbai, Maharashtra 400703
DP Coordinator Usha Karan Rana
Languages English
T: +91 22 2789 2261
W: www.goldcresthigh.com

Good Shepherd International School

Good Shepherd Knowledge Village, M Palada PO, Ootacamund, Tamil Nadu 643 004
DP Coordinator Suresh Thangarajan
Languages English
T: +91 423 2550371
W: www.gsis.ac.in

GPS Brookes Kochi

P.O, Thiruvaniyoor, Thiruvankulam – Chottanikkara Rd, Kochi, Kerala 682308
DP Coordinator Anuradha Varma
Languages English
T: +91 484 271 3745
W: gpsbrookeskochi.org

Grassroots Global School

7/4, Lynwood Avenue, Mahalingpuram, Chennai, Tamil Nadu 600034
PYP Coordinator Sharanya Anil Bajaj
Languages English, Tamil
T: +91 44 2825 5969
W: www.grassrootsschool.in

GREENWOOD HIGH INTERNATIONAL SCHOOL

No.8-14, Chickkawadayara Pura, Near Heggondahalli, Gunjur Post, Varthur via, Bengaluru, Karnataka 560087
DP Coordinator Nishanth Nagavar
Languages English
T: +91 80 22010500
E: admissions.intl@greenwoodhigh.edu.in
W: www.greenwoodhigh.edu.in

See full details on page 354

Harvest International School

Carmalaram post silk farm, Kodathi village, Off sarjapur road, near Kodathi village, Bangalore, Karnataka 560035
PYP Coordinator Jayalakshmy Nambiar
Languages English, Hindi
T: +91 80 6733 1884
W: www.harvestinternationalschool.in

Heritage Xperiential Learning School, Gurgaon

Sector 62, Gurgaon, Haryana 122011
DP Coordinator Poonam Dahiya
Languages English
T: +91 124 2855124
W: www.ths.ac.in

HFS International Powai

Richmond Street, Hiranandani Gardens, Powai, Mumbai, Maharashtra 400076
DP Coordinator Jagruti Joshi
Languages English
T: +91 22 2576 3001
W: www.hfsinternationalpowai.com

Hill Spring International School

C Wing, NSS Educational Complex, MP Mill Compound, Tardeo, Mumbai, Maharashtra 400034
DP Coordinator Prashant Gohil
PYP Coordinator Nisha Vahi
Languages English
T: +91 22 2355 6201
W: www.nsseducation.org

HUS International School

5/63 Old Mahabalipuram Ro, Egattur Village, Padur PO, Kelambakkam, Chennai, Tamil Nadu 600130
DP Coordinator Tejinder Kaur
MYP Coordinator Tejinder Kaur
PYP Coordinator Rajarajeswari Thulasiram
Languages English
T: +91 9500 118651
W: www.hus.edu.in

India International School

Kshipra Path, Opp VT Road,
Mansarovar, Jaipur, Rajasthan 302020
DP Coordinator Mukta Khandelwal
Languages English
T: +91 141 2786401
W: www.icfia.org

Indus International School (Bangalore)

Billapura Cross, Sarjapur, Bengaluru,
Karnataka 562125
DP Coordinator Lakshmi Chetan
MYP Coordinator Nidhi Beriwal
PYP Coordinator Rachel Philip
Languages English
T: +91 80 2289 5900
W: www.indusschool.com

Indus International School, Hyderabad

Survey No 424 & 425, Kondakal
Village, Near Mokila (M), Shankarpally,
Hyderabad, Telangana 501203
DP Coordinator Karthik Mangu
MYP Coordinator Swetha Kothapalli
PYP Coordinator Sushmita Mohanty
Languages English
T: +91 8417 302100
W: www.indusschoolhyd.com

Indus International School, Pune

576 Bhukum, Near Manas Resort, Tal
Mulshi, Pune, Maharashtra 411042
DP Coordinator Namita Bansal
MYP Coordinator Karn Ragade
PYP Coordinator Puja Grover
Languages English
T: +91 80 2289 5900
W: www.indusschoolpune.com

International School of Hyderabad

c/o ICRISAT, Patancheru, Hyderabad,
Telangana 502324
DP Coordinator Vandana Gupta
Languages English
T: +91 4030713865
W: www.ishyd.org

International Village School Chennai

33A, Clasic Farms Road,
Sholinganallur, Chennai, Tamil Nadu
600119
PYP Coordinator Dasha Narendra
Singh
Languages English
T: +91 44 4860 3757
W: internationalvillage.org

Jain International Residential School

Jakkasandra Post, Kanakpura Road,
Ramanagara District, Bengaluru,
Karnataka 562112
DP Coordinator Kalai Rajan. N
Languages English
T: +91 80 2757 7750
W: www.jirs.ac.in

Jamnabai Narsee International School

Narsee Monjee Bhavan, N.S. Road
No.7, J.V.P.D Scheme, Vile Parle (West),
Mumbai, Maharashtra 400049
DP Coordinator Rini Ghosh
MYP Coordinator Sonal Chabria
PYP Coordinator Purti Singh
Languages English
T: +91 (0)22 26187575/ 7676
W: www.jns.ac.in

Jayshree Periwal International School

Mahapura, SEZ Road, Ajmer Road,
Jaipur, Rajasthan 302026
DP Coordinator Manisha Razdan
PYP Coordinator Juhi Trivedi
Languages English
T: +91 97827 44444/44445
W: www.jpischool.com

JBCN INTERNATIONAL SCHOOL – OSHIWARA

Survey No. 41, CTS No. 1, Off Andheri
Link Road, Behind Tarapore Towers,
Mhada Colony, Oshiwara, Andher+,
Mumbai, Maharashtra 400058
DP Coordinator Ana Dominguez
PYP Coordinator Sharana Saxena
Languages English
T: +91 22 ?26302441
W: www.jbcnschool.edu.in/oshiwara
See full details on page 363

JBCN INTERNATIONAL SCHOOL – PAREL

Yogi Mansion, CTS No. 244, Dr Vinay
Walimbe Road, Off Dr S.S. Rao Marg,
Parel East, Mumbai, Maharashtra
400012
DP Coordinator Janos Öreg
PYP Coordinator Manya Jain
Languages English
T: +91 22 24114626
E: information.parel@jbcnschool.edu.in
W: www.jbcnschool.edu.in
See full details on page 363

JG International School

JG Campus of Excellence, JG Campus
Road, Ahmedabad, Gujarat 380061
DP Coordinator Kavita Sharma
Languages English
T: +91 79 65411315
W: www.jgcampusindia.com

Johnson Grammar School ICSE&IBDP

Street No 3, Kakatiya Nagar,
Habsiguda, Hyderabad, Andhra
Pradesh 500007
DP Coordinator Bindu C G
Languages English
T: +91 81064 72685
W: www.johnsonibdp.org

K.R. MANGALAM GLOBAL SCHOOL

N-Block, Nandi Vithi Road, Greater
Kailash-1, New Delhi, Delhi 110048
PYP Coordinator Sandeep Kaur
Languages English, Hindi
T: +91 97 1885 8181
E: info@krmangalam.global
W: krmangalam.global
See full details on page 367

K.R. Mangalam Global School, Gurugram

D-23, South City 1, Near Patio Club,
Gurugram, Haryana 122001
PYP Coordinator Neha Nagarsheth
Languages English, Hindi
T: +91 87 5004 5132
W: krmglobalgurgaon.com

Kai Early Years

66/2, 2nd Main Road, Nallurhalli,
Whitefield, Bangalore, Karnataka
560066
PYP Coordinator Sharayu Thampi
Languages English, Hindi
T: +91 97 4048 0123
W: kaiearlyyears.com

KC High

12/4, Arunachalam Road,
Kotturupuram, Chennai, Tamil Nadu
600085
DP Coordinator Meera Sampath
Languages English
T: +91 (44) 2447 3551
W: www.kchigh.com

KIIT INTERNATIONAL SCHOOL

KiiT Campus 9, Patia, Bhubaneswar,
Odisha 751024
DP Coordinator Dr Arunananda
Mukherjee
Languages English
T: +91 674 2725805
E: admission@kiitis.ac.in
W: www.kiitis.ac.in
See full details on page 370

Kodaikanal International School

PO Box 25, Seven Roads Junction,
Kodaikanal, Tamil Nadu 624101
DP Coordinator Alex Kurian
MYP Coordinator Graham Lambert
PYP Coordinator Pearlin Joseph
Languages English
T: +91 4542 247500
W: www.kis.in

Kohinoor American School

Old Mumbai – Pune Highway, Near
to The Dukes Retreat, Khandala,
Maharashtra 410301
DP Coordinator Ms. Anuradha Paul
MYP Coordinator Ms. Monica Drego
Languages English
T: +91 9324323003
W: www.kohinooramericanschool.ac.in

Lady Andal Venkatasubba Rao Matriculation School

Shenstone Park, No.7 Harrington
Road, Chennai, Tamil Nadu 600031
PYP Coordinator Michelle Teresa
Noronha
Languages English
T: +91 44 2836 3404
W: www.ladyandalschool.com

Lalaji Memorial Omega International School

79, Omega School Road (Pallavaram
Road), Kolapakkam, Kovur Post,
Chennai, Tamil Nadu 600128
DP Coordinator Satish Srividhya
Languages English
T: +91 44 66241127
W: www.omegaschools.org

Lancers International School

DLF Phase V, Sector 53, Gurgaon,
Haryana 122001
DP Coordinator Arpit Sharma
MYP Coordinator Lilit Harutyunyan
PYP Coordinator Annabelle
Villamarin
Languages English
T: +91 124 4171900
W: www.lancersinternationalschool.in

Legacy School, Bangalore

6/1 A, 6/2 Byrathi Village, Bidarahalli
Hobli, East Taluk, Bengaluru,
Karnataka 560077
DP Coordinator Anthony Gonsalves
Languages English
T: +91 70222 92405
W: lsb.edu.in

M Ct M Chidambaram Chettyar International School

179, Luz Church Road, Mylapore,
Chennai, Tamil Nadu 600004
DP Coordinator Sangita Varma
Languages English
T: +91 44 2467 0120
W: www.mctmib.org

IB ASIA-PACIFIC

Mahatma Gandhi International School

Sheth Motilal Hirabhai Bhavan, Opp. Induben Khakhrawala, Mithakali, Navrangpura, Ahmedabad, Gujarat 380006
CP Coordinator Meenakshi Ganeriwala
DP Coordinator Ravinder Kaur
MYP Coordinator Minoo Joshi
Languages English, Hindi
T: +91 79 2 646 3888
W: www.mgis.in

Mahindra International School

P26, Rajeev Gandhi Infotech park, Phase 1, Hinjewadi, Pune, Maharashtra 411057
DP Coordinator Vijeta Sinha
MYP Coordinator Jose Campillo Campillo
PYP Coordinator Carla Swinehart
Languages English
T: +91 2042954444
W: misp.org

Mainadevi Bajaj International School

Plot No: 23-A, 24-28 Swami Vivekanand Road, Malad (West), Mumbai, Maharashtra 400064
DP Coordinator Husien Burhani Dohadwalla
Languages English
T: +91 22 28733807
W: www.mbis.org.in

Manchester International School

SF 29/3A, Hudco Colony, Vellakinar, Coimbatore, Tamil Nadu 641029
DP Coordinator Ashok Kumar
MYP Coordinator Kaivalya Mohan Menon
PYP Coordinator Vishnu Carthica Guru Subbaian
Languages English
T: +91 422 655 5551
W: www.manchesters.in

Meridian School, Banjara Hills

#8-2-541, Road No.7, Banjara Hills, Hyderabad, Telangana 500034
PYP Coordinator Sailaja Koduri
Languages English, Hindi
T: +91 80 9691 8857
W: meridianschool.in/banjarahills

Meridian School, Madhapur

#11/4 & 11/5, Opp: Hitech City, Kukatpally Bypass Road, Khanamet Village, Sherlingampally Mandal, Hyderabad, Telangana 500081
PYP Coordinator Jyothi Malhotra
Languages English, Hindi
T: +91 99 4804 3440
W: www.meridianschool.in/madhapur

Modern High School for Girls

78, Syed Amir Ali Avenue, Kolkata, West Bengal 700019
DP Coordinator Mrs Sheta Saha
Languages English
T: +913322875326
W: www.mhsforgirls.edu.in

Modern School

Sector E, Aliganj, Lucknow, Uttar Pradesh 226024
PYP Coordinator Manisha Rathore
Languages English, Hindi
T: +91 955 493 3337
W: modernschool.org

Mody School

Mody Institute of Education & Research, Lakshmangarh, Rajasthan 332311
DP Coordinator Chagan Samour
Languages English
T: +91 91 16637196
W: www.modyschool.ac.in

Mount Litera School International

GN Block, Behind Asian Heart Hospital, Near UTI Building, Bandra Kurla Complex, Bandra- East, Mumbai, Maharashtra 400051
DP Coordinator Suzanne Patel
MYP Coordinator Saolee Roy
PYP Coordinator Bushra Khan
Languages English
T: +91 22 6229 6000
W: www.mlsi.in

Mussoorie International School

Srinagar Estate, Polo Ground, Mussoorie, Uttarakhand 248179
DP Coordinator Ponny Chacko
Languages English
T: +91 135 2630250
W: www.misindia.net

NAHAR INTERNATIONAL SCHOOL

Nahar's Amrit Shakti, Chandivali Farm Road, Off Saki Vihar Road, Andheri East, Mumbai, Maharashtra 400072
DP Coordinator Resham Puri
Languages English, Hindi
T: +91 (0)22 6838 5500
E: info@nahar-is.ac.in
W: www.nahar-is.ac.in

See full details on page 383

Navrachana International School

Vasna Bhayali Road, Bhayali, Vadodara, Gujarat 391410
DP Coordinator Jyoti Nagar
MYP Coordinator Srilakshmi Devi
PYP Coordinator Viraaj Jhaveri
Languages English
T: +91 265 225 3851/2/3/4
W: www.navrachana.ac.in

Neerja Modi School

Shipra Path, Near Building Technology Park, Mansarovar, Jaipur, Rajasthan 302020
DP Coordinator Sarita Nathawat
Languages English
T: +91 141 2785 484
W: www.nmsindia.org

Neev Academy – North Campus

No. 14, Park Road, Tasker Town, Bengaluru, Karnataka 560001
PYP Coordinator Kalpita Jain
Languages English
T: +91 80 41144285
W: www.neevacademy.org

Neev Academy – Yemalur Campus

No. 16, Yemalur-Kempapura Main Road, Opp. Sai Garden Apartments, Yemalur, Bengaluru, Karnataka 560037
DP Coordinator Colin Leslie Kelman
MYP Coordinator Vineet Singh
PYP Coordinator Soumya Anil Venkatram
Languages English
T: +91 80 71101700
W: www.neevacademy.org

NES International School Dombivli

Sankara Nagar, Kalyan-Shil Road Opp. DNS Bank, Sonarpada, Dombivli (E), Thane, Mumbai, Maharashtra 421203
PYP Coordinator Jyoti Hoskoti
Languages English, Hindi
T: +91 84 22994436
W: www.nesisd.org

NES International School Mumbai

Malabar Hill Road, Vasant Garden, Mulund(W), Mumbai, Maharashtra 400082
DP Coordinator Ramaswamy Varadarajan
MYP Coordinator Cimmy Ajithkumar
PYP Coordinator Rakhi Vishwakarma
Languages English
T: +91 22 25911478
W: www.nesinternational.org

NEXT School

Park Road, Off Devi Dayal Road, Mulund W, Mumbai, Maharashtra 400080
DP Coordinator Amar Dixit
MYP Coordinator Nikhil Bangera
PYP Coordinator Pragna Kolar
Languages English
T: +91 22 25600036
W: www.nextschool.org

Niraj International School

Kandlakoya, 5 km from Dhola-ri-Dhani, Hyderabad, Telangana 132133
PYP Coordinator Jayashree Arraguntla
Languages English
T: +91 84 18200476
W: www.nirajinternationalschool.com

Oakridge International School, Bachupally

Survey No 166/6, Bowrampet Village, Near Bachupally, Hyderabad, Telangana 500043
DP Coordinator Saikrishna Pammi
PYP Coordinator Deepa Devarakonda
Languages English
T: +91 720 764 8111
W: www.oakridge.in/bachupally

Oakridge International School, Bengaluru

Varthur Road, Near Dommassandra Circle, Sarjapur Hobli, Bengaluru, Karnataka 562125
DP Coordinator Ajay Kumar
MYP Coordinator Richa Mehrotra
PYP Coordinator Bindu Thomas
Languages English
T: +91 0802 254 3600
W: www.oakridge.in/bengaluru

Oakridge International School, Gachibowli

Khajaguda, Nanakramguda Road, Cyberabad, Hyderabad, Telangana 500008
DP Coordinator Deepalatha Subramanian
MYP Coordinator Savitri Potluri
PYP Coordinator Vasundhara Achanta
Languages English
T: +91 7207 648 111
W: www.oakridge.in/gachibowli

Oakridge International School, Mohali

Next to Thunderzone Amusement Park, Mohali, Punjab 140307
PYP Coordinator Meera Chhabria
Languages English
T: +91 752 701 3370
W: www.oakridge.in/mohali

Oakridge International School, Visakhapatnam

NH 5 Road, Behind HP Petrol Bunk, Maharajpeta Junction, Tagarapuvalasa, Visakhapatnam, Andhra Pradesh 531162
DP Coordinator Pallavi Joshi
Languages English
T: +91 773 081 6999
W: www.oakridge.in/contact

Oberoi International School

Oberoi Garden City, Off Western Express Highway, Goregaon (E), Mumbai, Maharashtra 400063
DP Coordinator Rucha Bhayani
MYP Coordinator Manju Upadhyaya
PYP Coordinator Neha Minda
Languages English
T: +91 22 4236 3131
W: www.oberoi-is.org

Oberoi International School – JVLR Campus

Jogeshwari Vikroli Link Road, Jogeshwari East, Mumbai, Maharashtra 400060
DP Coordinator Anjali Bhardwaj
MYP Coordinator Barbara Batchelor
PYP Coordinator Archana Gera
Languages English
W: oberoi-is.org/jvlr-campus

Pathways School (Gurgaon NCR South)

Baliawas, Off Gurgaon Faridabad Road, Gurgaon, Haryana 122003
DP Coordinator Megha Oberoi
MYP Coordinator Varsha Sinha
PYP Coordinator Shefali Lakhina
Languages English
T: +91 124 487 2000
W: www.pathways.in/gurgaon

Pathways School Noida

Sector 100, Noida NCR East, New Delhi, Delhi 110062
DP Coordinator Samuel Osmond
MYP Coordinator Anshu Sharma
PYP Coordinator Vandana Parashar
Languages English
T: +91 120 461 7000
W: www.pathways.in/noida

Pathways World School

Aravali Retreat, Off Gurgaon Sohna Road, Gurgaon, Haryana 122102
DP Coordinator Ila Pandey
MYP Coordinator Monika Bajaj
PYP Coordinator Monica Bhimwal
Languages English
T: +91 124 451 3000
W: www.pathways.in

Podar International School

Ramee Emerald Building, Near Shamrao Vithal Bank, S.V.Road, Khar (West), Mumbai, Maharashtra 400052
DP Coordinator Hema Rajan
PYP Coordinator Saachi Setpal
Languages English
T: +91 22 2648 7321
W: www.podarinternationalschool.com

Podar O.R.T International School, Worli

PODAR-ORT School Building, 68, Worli Hill Estate, Worli, Mumbai, Maharashtra 400018
DP Coordinator Sreelaxmi Murthy Madhusudan
MYP Coordinator Sanjeevani Chindarkar
PYP Coordinator Shreya Mahindra
Languages English
T: +91 7506112200
W: www.podareducation.org/school/worli

Prometheus School

I-7, Jaypee Wishtown, Sector 131, Noida, Uttar Pradesh 201304
DP Coordinator Jyoti Deveshwar
MYP Coordinator Pallavi Sharma
PYP Coordinator Ketaki Kapoor
Languages English, Hindi
T: +91 99 9987 6583
W: prometheusschool.com

Rasbihari International School

Vrindavan, Nashik-Ozar Road, Nashik, Maharashtra 422003
PYP Coordinator Shilpa Ahire
Languages English
T: +91 253 230 4622
W: www.rasbihari.org

RBK International Academy

Opp. Indian Oil Nagar, Near Shankara Colony, Ghatkopar-Mankhurd Link Road, Mumbai, Maharashtra 400088
DP Coordinator Prashant Kamble
MYP Coordinator Shreya Mudaliar
PYP Coordinator Mona Chaudhary
Languages English
T: +91 7400091646/7/8/9
W: www.rbkia.org

Redbridge International Academy

#114, S Bingipura Village, Hulimangala Post, Begur-Koppa Road, Bangalore, Karnataka 560105
DP Coordinator Karen Kunder
Languages English
T: +91 9620863456
W: www.rbia.in

Rockwell International School

Sy No.160(p), Gandipet Main Rd, Kokapet, Hyderabad, Telangana 500075
DP Coordinator Shruti Sareen
Languages English
T: +91 9618662201
W: rockwellinternationalschool.com

Rungta International School

Near Nandan Van, Veer Savarkar Nagar, Raipur, Chhattisgarh 492099
DP Coordinator Madhuri Paleti
MYP Coordinator Gagandeep Dhillon
PYP Coordinator Keathi Sharma
Languages English
T: +91 98261 45333
W: www.rungtainternational.org

Ryan Global School

Yamuna Nagar, Lokhandwala, Andheri (west), Mumbai, Maharashtra 400058
PYP Coordinator Bhavi Furia
Languages English
T: +91 22 2632 0203/05
W: www.ryanglobalschools.com

Sangam School of Excellence

N.H. 79, Atun, Bhilwara By Pass, Chittorgarh Highway, Bhilwara, Rajasthan 311001
DP Coordinator Shruti Modi
Languages English
T: +91 1482 249 700
W: www.sangamschoolbhilwara.com

SANJAY GHODAWAT INTERNATIONAL SCHOOL

Gat No. 555, Kolhapur – Sangli Highway, Atigre, Maharashtra
DP Coordinator Dr. Bonila Sinha
Languages English
T: +91 231 2689700
E: principal@sgischool.in
W: www.sgischool.in

See full details on page 409

Sanskar School

117-121, Vishwamitra Marg, Hanuman Nagar Ext., Sirsi Road, Jaipur, Rajasthan 302012
DP Coordinator Manisha Chandra
PYP Coordinator Smita Benuskar
Languages English
T: +91 0141 2246189
W: www.sanskarjaipur.com

Sarala Birla Academy

Bannerghatta PO, Jigni Road, Bengaluru, Karnataka 560083
DP Coordinator Manoj Jaiswal
Languages English
T: +91 80 41348200/03
W: www.saralabirlaacademy.com

SCOTTISH HIGH INTERNATIONAL SCHOOL

G-Block, Sector 57, Sushant Lok-II, Gurugram, Haryana 122011
DP Coordinator Ms Sudha Goyal
PYP Coordinator Ms Seema Bhati
Languages English
T: +91 124 4112781-90
E: schooldirector@scottishigh.com
W: www.scottishigh.com

See full details on page 410

Seedling International Academy

Sector-4, Park Lane, Jawahar Nagar, Jaipur, Rajasthan 302004
DP Coordinator Shruti Kukar
Languages English
T: +91 141 2653377
W: www.seedlingschools.com

Shantiniketan International School

35-25, GKColony, Ramakrishnapuram, Secunderabad, Telangana 500056
PYP Coordinator Madhavi Mutyala
Languages English
T: +91 73311 95555
W: snis.org.in

Sharanya Narayani International School

#232/1, Thoranahalli, Byranahalli post, Near Hoskote, Bengaluru, Karnataka 563130
DP Coordinator Thavamani Thangarathinam
PYP Coordinator Kapil Mehrotra
Languages English
T: +91 80 46629500
W: snis.edu.in

SHIV NADAR SCHOOL GURUGRAM

DLF City, Phase -1 Block -E, Pahari Road, Gurugram, Haryana
DP Coordinator Sriparna Chakrabarti
Languages English
T: +91 124 4549200
E: admissions.gurgaon@sns.edu.in
W: shivnadarschool.edu.in/gurgaon

See full details on page 419

Shiv Nadar School Noida

Plot No -SS -1, Expressway Sector 168, Noida, Uttar Pradesh 201305
DP Coordinator S. R. Radhakrishnan
Languages English
T: +91 8130200199
W: shivnadarschool.edu.in

Silver Oaks International School, Bangalore

Sy No:188/3 & 188/4, Sarjapur Road, Dommasandra village, Bengaluru, Karnataka 562125
DP Coordinator Remya Ramachandran
MYP Coordinator Radha Rani Mishra
PYP Coordinator Chithra Muralidhar
Languages English
T: +91 97394 75900
W: www.silveroaks.co.in/bangalore

Silver Oaks International School, Hyderabad

Miyapur-Dindigal Road, Bachupally, Hyderabad, Telangana 500090
PYP Coordinator Sangeeta Pratti
Languages English
T: +91 40 23047777
W: www.silveroaks.co.in/hyderabad

Silver Oaks International School, Visakhapatnam

Adj Gitam Medical College, Yendada Road, Rushikonda, Visakhapatnam, Andhra Pradesh 530045
PYP Coordinator Kousalya Bozza
Languages English, Telugu
W: www.silveroaks.co.in/visakhapatnam

Singapore International School, Mumbai

On National Highway No. 8, Post Mira Road, Dahisar, Mumbai, Maharashtra 401104
DP Coordinator Shirley Pereira
PYP Coordinator Peter Keslake
Languages English
T: +91 222 828 5200
W: www.sisindia.net

Smt. Sulochanadevi Singhania School

Pokharan Road No.1, J K Gram, Thane (West), Maharashtra 400606
DP Coordinator Sangeeta Kapur
Languages English
T: +91 22 4036 8410/1
W: www.singhaniaschool.org

Sreenidhi International School

Near Appa Junction, Moinabad, Hyderabad, Telangana 500075
DP Coordinator Sreedevi V
MYP Coordinator Tonderai Mutasa
PYP Coordinator Mary Vinodhini
Languages English
T: +91 9912244409
W: www.sis.edu.in

SRV International School

Marappan Thottam, 4/3 Gandhi Salai, Pattanam Road, Rasipuram, Namakkal, Tamil Nadu 637408
PYP Coordinator Fathima Sabeena
Languages English
T: +91 96 5562 4458
W: www.srvisglobal.org

Step by Step School

Plot A 10, Sector 132 Taj Expressway, Noida, Uttar Pradesh 201303
DP Coordinator Urmi Debroy
Languages English
T: +91 12 0508 7300
W: www.sbs-school.org

STONEHILL INTERNATIONAL SCHOOL

Near the International Airport, No.259/333/334/335, Tarahunise Post, Jala Hobli, Bengaluru, Karnataka 562157
DP Coordinator Manpreet Kaur
MYP Coordinator Jitendra Pandey
PYP Coordinator Zita Joyce
Languages English
T: +91 70 2666 6911
E: admissions@stonehill.in
W: www.stonehill.in

See full details on page 424

Strawberry Fields High School

Sector 26, Chandigarh, Punjab 160019
DP Coordinator Smita Satyarthi
T: +91 172 279 5903/5904
W: www.strawberryfieldshighschool.com

Suncity School

Suncity Township, Sector 54, Gurgaon, Haryana 122002
DP Coordinator Vivek Mandal
Languages English
T: +91 (0)124 4845300 (Ext:302)
W: www.suncityschool.in

Sunshine Worldwide Secondary School

20/1-B, Bainguinim, Off NH-748 By-pass Kadamba Road, Old Goa. Goa 403402
PYP Coordinator Ashalatha Ravishankar
Languages English, Hindi
T: +91 98 5032 3818
W: www.sunshineworldwideschool.com

SVKM JV Parekh International School

CNM School Campus, Dadabhai Road, Off. S.V. Road, Vile Parle (West), Mumbai, Maharashtra 400056
DP Coordinator Shoma Bhattacharya
Languages English
T: +91 22 4233 3030
W: www.jvparekhintnl.ac.in

Symbiosis International School

Symbiosis Viman nagar Campus, Off. New AirPort road, Viman Nagar, Pune, Maharashtra 411014
DP Coordinator M. Madan Mohan
PYP Coordinator Preethy Sunil
Languages English
T: +91 20 2655 7300
W: www.symbiosisinternationalschool.net

TCIS

Survey no. 215/3, Varthur Sharjapur, Whitefield Main Road, Bangalore, Karnataka
PYP Coordinator Anita Varghese
Languages English, Hindi
T: +91 78 9902 5222
W: tciswhitefield.in

The British School

Dr Jose P Rizal Marg, Chanakyapuri, New Delhi, Delhi 110021
DP Coordinator Monisha Singh
Languages English
T: +91 11 4066 4166
W: www.british-school.org

The Cathedral & John Connon School

6 Purshottamdas Thakurdas Marg, Mumbai, Maharashtra 400001
DP Coordinator Latha Balaji
Languages English
T: +91 22 2200 1282
W: www.cathedral-school.com

The Cathedral Vidya School, Lonavala

Village Shilatne, Taluk Maval, Post Office Karla, Pune, Lonavala, Maharashtra 410405
DP Coordinator Lucy Massey
Languages English
T: +91 2114 282693
W: cathedral-lonavala.org

The Doon School

Mall Road, Dehradun, Uttarakhand 248001
DP Coordinator Mohammad Istemdad Ali
Languages English
T: +91-135 2526 400
W: www.doonschool.com

The DPSG International (Delhi Public School Ghaziabad International)

P.O. Dasna, Hindon Nagar, Dasna, Kallu Garhi, Ghaziabad, Uttar Pradesh 201303
PYP Coordinator Malavika Yadav
Languages English
T: +91 858 795 1424
W: www.thedpsgint.in

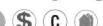

The Galaxy School

SNK Main Building, University Road, Rajkot, Gujarat 360005
DP Coordinator Chirag Jhala
Languages English
T: +91 281 2588391/2588392
W: www.tges.org

The Gaudium School

Survey No. 148, Nanakramguda Village, Serilingampally, Nanakramguda, Hyderabad, Telangana 500008
DP Coordinator Varsha Dillikar
PYP Coordinator Trishna Sharma
Languages English, Hindi
T: +91 73370 00200
W: www.thegaudium.com

The Heritage School, Kolkata

994 Maduraha, Chowbaga Road, Anandpur, PO East Kolkata Township, Kolkata, West Bengal 700107
DP Coordinator Seema Sapru
Languages English
T: +91 33 2443 0448
W: www.theheritageschool.org

The International School Bangalore

Whitefield-Sarjapur Road, Near Dommasandra Circle, Bengaluru, Karnataka 562125
DP Coordinator Vijayalakshmi Jayakumar
Languages English
T: +91 80 6723 5900
W: tisb.org

The Shri Ram School

Moulsari Avenue DLF Phase-3, Gurgaon, Haryana 122002
DP Coordinator Anjali Sharma
Languages English
W: www.tsrs.org

The Universal School

Plot No. 17, Near Lion's Garden, Tilak Road, Ghatkopar (E), Mumbai, Maharashtra 400077
DP Coordinator Lakshmi Thevar
Languages English, Hindi
T: +91 773 8146 123
W: ghatkopar.universalschool.edu.in

The White School International

HiLITE Knowledge Village, Parammal, Perumanna, Kozhikode, Kerala 673019
DP Coordinator Selvakumari Sankaranarayanan
MYP Coordinator Varaprasad Adidala
PYP Coordinator Venicia Reneesh
Languages English, Malayalam
T: +91 95260 777 78
W: www.thewhiteschool.in

TIPS Chennai

No. 50/51, First Main Road, Perungudi Industrial Estate, Perungudi, Chennai, Tamil Nadu 600069
DP Coordinator Ramya Kumaraswamy
PYP Coordinator Agnes Joseph
Languages English
T: +91 44 7118 8011
W: tipschennai.com

INDIA

TIPS Coimbatore

193 Sathy Road, S.S.Kulam P.O., Coimbatore, Tamil Nadu 641107
DP Coordinator Ibson T. Arimbur
PYP Coordinator Sita Subramaniam
Languages English
T: +91 42 2236 6666
W: www.tipsglobal.org

TIPS Erode

Chennimalai Road, Senapathipalayam, Goundachi palayam post, Erode, Tamil Nadu 638112
PYP Coordinator Nadia Patel
Languages English
T: +91 967745 8888
W: theindianpublicschool.org/location-erode

TIPS Kochi

Edachira, Thengode(Post), Kakkanad, Kochi, Kerala 682030
PYP Coordinator Mridula Vinod
Languages English
T: +91 44 4485 4850
W: www.tipsglobal.org/tips_kochi.php

TIPS Salem

No 2, Mangayarkarasi Street, Off Advitha Ashram Road, Fairlands, Salem, Tamil Nadu 636016
PYP Coordinator Renu Koshti
Languages English, Tamil
T: +91 92 8258 8888
W: theindianpublicschool.org/location-salem

Treamis

Hulimangala Post, near Electronics City, Bengaluru, Karnataka 560105
PYP Coordinator Nisha Rajesh
Languages English, Kannada
T: +91 99723 99046
W: www.treamis.org

Trio World Academy

3/5 Kodigehalli Main Road, Sahakar Nagar, Bengaluru, Karnataka 560092
DP Coordinator Moinudin Sha
PYP Coordinator Chitra R
Languages English
T: +91 80 40611222
W: trioworldschool.com

Trivandrum International School

Edackode, PO Korani, Trivandrum, Kerala 695104
DP Coordinator Rachel Jacob
PYP Coordinator Sanjay Prabhakaran
Languages English
T: +91 471 2619051
W: www.trins.org

UWC MAHINDRA COLLEGE

Village Khubavali, PO Paud, Taluka Mulshi, Pune, Maharashtra 412108
DP Coordinator Ainhoa Orensanz
Languages English
T: +91 97644 42751 54
E: info@muwci.net
W: uwcmahindracollege.org
See full details on page 437

VICTORIOUS KIDSS EDUCARES

Survey No. 53, 54 & 58, Hissa No. 2/1A, Off. Shreeram Society, Nagar Road, Kharadi, Pune, Maharashtra 411014
DP Coordinator Vishwajeet Kumar
MYP Coordinator Vishwajeet Kumar
PYP Coordinator Pritisha Ahir
Languages English
T: +91 20-67116300/1/2
E: robbinghosh@victoriouskidsseducares.org
W: www.victoriouskidsseducares.org
See full details on page 438

Vidsan Charterhouse

Delhi NCR, Sector 93, Faridabad, Haryana 121002
DP Coordinator Ipsa Mohanty
Languages English
T: +91 9999116900/01
W: vidsancharterhouse.com

Vidya Global School

Vidya Knowledge Park, Baghpat Road, Meerut, Uttar Pradesh 250002
PYP Coordinator Tandra Sharma
Languages English
T: +91 121 2439188/89/92
W: vidyaglobalschool.com

Vishwashanti Gurukul

Rajbaug, off Pune-Solapur Highway, Loni, Pune, Maharashtra 412201
DP Coordinator Evelynn Sheen Singh
MYP Coordinator Rohit Jain
PYP Coordinator Ashwini Patwardhan
Languages English
T: +91 20 39210000
W: www.mitgurukul.com

VIVA The School

Beside VVIT college campus, NAMBUR village, Pedakakani Mandal, Nambur, Guntur, Andhra Pradesh 522508
PYP Coordinator Madhavi Ayinada
Languages English, Telugu
T: +91 73 3114 2336
W: www.viva.school

Wockhardt Global School

Dr Habil Khorakiwala Education and Health Foundation, E-1/NP-1, SEZ, Five Star Industrial Estate, MIDC, Shen+, Aurangabad, Maharashtra 431154
DP Coordinator Nirmalendu Tripathy
MYP Coordinator Mandar Gurjar
PYP Coordinator Hetal Ahivasi
Languages English
T: +91 240 6662888
W: wockhardtschools.com

WOODSTOCK SCHOOL

Mussoorie, Uttarakhand 248179
DP Coordinator Mousumi Basu
MYP Coordinator Imtiaz Rai
Languages English
T: +91 135 263 9000
E: admissions@woodstock.ac.in
W: www.woodstock.ac.in
See full details on page 443

INDONESIA

ACG SCHOOL JAKARTA

Jl Warung Jati Barat No.19, RW.5, Jati Padang, Kec. Ps. Minggu, Kota Jakarta Selatan, Daerah Khusus I, Jakarta, DKI 12540
DP Coordinator Richard Todd
PYP Coordinator Vanessa Ellison
Languages English
T: +62 21 2978 0200 / +62 816 297800
E: acgjkt@acgedu.com
W: jakarta.acgedu.com
See full details on page 309

ACS Jakarta

Jl Bantar Jati, Kelurahan Setu, Jakarta Timur, DKI 13880
DP Coordinator Jigs Tadeo
Languages English
T: +62 21 8459 7175
W: www.acsjakarta.sch.id

Al Firdaus

Jl. Dr. Soepomo No 6A, Surakarta, Jateng 57131
MYP Coordinator Riana Oktavia
PYP Coordinator Aris Suwastini Ariyanti
Languages English, Indonesian
W: alfirdausina.net

Al Jabr Islamic School

Jl Bango II No 38, Pondok Labu, Jakarta, DKI 12450
CP Coordinator Dina Anggraini
MYP Coordinator Novia Rozet
PYP Coordinator Ryandika Anindra
Languages English
T: +62 21 75913675
W: aljabrislamicschool.sch.id

Australian Independent School (AIS) Indonesia

Jalan Imam Bonjol No.458a, Pemecutan, Denpasar Barat, Denpasar, Bali 80119
DP Coordinator Thomas Allan
Languages English
T: +62 361 845 20000
W: www.ais-indonesia.com

Australian Independent School, Jakarta – Pejaten Campus

Jl. Pejaten Barat No. 69, Pejaten Barat, Pasar Minggu, Jakarta Selatan, DKI 12510
DP Coordinator Kieran Pascoe
Languages English
T: +62 21 7884 8285
W: www.ais-indonesia.com

Bali Island School

Jalan Danau Buyan IV No. 15, Sanur, Denpasar, Bali 80228
DP Coordinator Klaus Weber
MYP Coordinator Mary MacDonald
PYP Coordinator Nadia Demolder
Languages English
T: +62 361 288 770
W: www.baliinternationalschool.com

Bandung Independent School

Jl. Surya Sumantri No. 61, Bandung, Jabar 40164
DP Coordinator Elizabeth Russell
PYP Coordinator Katherine Stone
Languages English
T: +62 22 201 4995
W: www.bisedu.or.id

Beacon Academy

Jalan Pegangsaan Dua. No 66, Kelapa Gading, Jakarta Utara, DKI 14250
DP Coordinator Suprio Bhowmick
PYP Coordinator Khona Bhattacharjee
Languages English
T: +62 21 460 3480
W: www.beaconacademy.net

Binus School Simprug

Jl Sultan Iskandar, Muda Kav G-8, Simprug, Jakarta Selatan, DKI 12220
DP Coordinator Erdolfo L Lardizabal
MYP Coordinator Jyoti Gupta
PYP Coordinator Richel Langit-Dursin
Languages English
T: +62 21 724 3663
W: www.binus-school.net

IB ASIA-PACIFIC

British School Jakarta

Bintaro Jaya Sector IX, Jl. Raya Jombang, Ciledug, Pondok Aren, Tangerang, Banten 15227
CP Coordinator Daniel Harbridge
DP Coordinator Jane Kilpatrick
MYP Coordinator Katie Sharp
Languages English
T: +62 21 745 1670
W: www.bis.or.id

BTB School (Sekolah Bina Tunas Bangsa)

Jl. Pluit Tumur Blok MM, Jakarta Utara, DKI 14450
DP Coordinator Christine Macaraig
Languages English
T: +62 21 30031300
W: www.btbschool.org

Canggu Community School

Jalan Subak Sari, Banjar Tegal Gundul, Canggu, Bali 80361
DP Coordinator Dan Horwood
Languages English
T: +62 361 8446391
W: www.ccsbali.com

Cita Hati Christian Senior School – East Campus

JL Kejawan Putih Barat 28-30, Pakuwon City, Surabaya, Jatim 60112
DP Coordinator Syanne Helly
Languages English
T: +62 31 591 5773
W: www.bchati.sch.id

Cita Hati Christian Senior School – West Campus

Jl. Bukit Golf L2 No. 1, Citraland, Surabaya, Jatim 60211
DP Coordinator Sarwanti Purwandari
Languages English
T: +62 31 7404959
W: www.bchati.sch.id/citahati

Gandhi Memorial Intercontinental School, Jakarta

Jl HBR Motik Block-6D Kav-1 Kemayoran, Jakarta Pusat DKI 14410
CP Coordinator Dr. Manish Kumar Semwal
DP Coordinator Ms Rowena R. J. Macaraig
MYP Coordinator Ms Hanspal Gurpreet Kaur
PYP Coordinator Ms Rachna Johar
Languages English
T: +62 21 65865671
W: www.gandhijkt.org

Global Jaya School

Emerald Boulevard, Bintaro Jaya Sektor IX, Pondok Aren, Tangerang, Banten 15224
DP Coordinator Ram Pandey
MYP Coordinator Dannandyatti Priambodo
PYP Coordinator Anindya Hartono
Languages English
T: +62 21 745 7562
W: www.globaljaya.com

GMIS – Bali

Jl Tukad Yeh Penet No 8A Renon, Denpasar, Bali 80235
CP Coordinator Emil Macaraig
DP Coordinator Emil Macaraig
MYP Coordinator Brij Bhoomi Singh
PYP Coordinator Sonia Ganguly
Languages English
T: +62 361 239744
W: www.gandhibali.org

IPEKA Integrated Christian School

Komplek Taman Meruya Ilir, Jalan Batu Mulia Blok K, RT.11/RW.7, Meruya Utara, Kembangan, RT.11/RW.7, Meruya Utara, Kem+, Jakarta Barat, DKI 11620
DP Coordinator Anika Browne-Jones
Languages English, Indonesian
T: +62 21 58905890
W: www.iics.sch.id

Jakarta Intercultural School

Jalan Terogong Raya No. 33, Cilandak, Jakarta Selatan, DKI 12430
DP Coordinator Darren Seath
Languages English
T: +62 21 769 2555
W: www.jisedu.or.id

Jakarta Multicultural School

Jl. Pisangan Raya No. 99 (Taman Wisata Situ Gintung), Cirendeu, Ciputat Timur, Banten 15419
DP Coordinator Corey Allison
Languages English
T: +62 21 744 4864
W: jms.sch.id

Madania

Telaga Kahuripan, Parung, Bogor, Jabar 16330
PYP Coordinator Nida Nidiana
Languages English
T: +62 251 602777
W: www.madania.sch.id

Medan Independent School

Jl. Jamin Ginting Km. 10 / Jl. Tali Air No.5, Medan, North Sumatra 20141
DP Coordinator Karl Sloane
MYP Coordinator Gregory McGuire
PYP Coordinator Elizabeth Acomb
Languages English
T: +62 61 836 1816
W: www.mismedan.org

Mentari Intercultural School Bintaro

Jalan Perigi Baru No.7A, Tangerang, Pd. Aren, Tangerang Selatan, Banten 15228
DP Coordinator Alquin Alva
Languages English
T: +62 21 745 8418
W: mis.sch.id/w/mis-bintaro.html

Mentari Intercultural School Jakarta

Jl. H. Jian No.2, RT.4/RW.3, North Cipete, Kby. Baru, Jakarta Selatan, DKI 12150
DP Coordinator Maria Reylene Tiburcio
MYP Coordinator Matthew Roberge
PYP Coordinator Patricia Manning
Languages English
T: 21 727 94 870
W: mis.sch.id/w/mis-jakarta.html

Mt Zaagkam School

Tembagapura Raya Street No. 605, Tembagapura, Papua 99967
PYP Coordinator Raquel Acedo Rubio
Languages English
T: +62 901 408 767
W: www.mzs.sch.id

Mutiara Harapan Islamic School

Jl. Pondok Kacang Raya No. 2, Pondok Kacang Timur, Pondok Aren, Tangerang, Banten 15426
PYP Coordinator Anjali Tewari
Languages English
T: +62 (0)21 74860451
W: mutiaraharapan.sch.id

North Jakarta Intercultural School

PO Box 6759/JKUKP, Jalan Raya Kelapa Nias, Kelapa Gading Permai, Jakarta Utara, DKI 14250
DP Coordinator Warren Wessels
MYP Coordinator Hendriadi Hendriadi
PYP Coordinator Ezra Alexander
Languages English, Indonesian
T: +62 21 4586 5222; +62 21 36 700 770
W: www.njis.org

Sampoerna Academy, Jakarta Campus

L'Avenue Campus, Jln. Raya Pasar Minggu, Kav. 16 Pancoran, Jakarta 12780
DP Coordinator Devendar Singh Rawat
Languages English, Indonesian
T: +62 (0)21 5022 22 34
W: www.sampoernaacademy.sch.id

Sampoerna Academy, Medan Campus

Jln. Jamin Ginting, Kompleks Citra Garden, Medan
DP Coordinator Sharad Detha
Languages English, Indonesian
T: +62 (0)61 821 27 15
W: www.sampoernaacademy.sch.id/en/medan-campus

SDK BPK Penabur Banda

Jl Bahureksa No 26, Bandung, Jabar 40115
PYP Coordinator Puteri Pamela
Languages English
T: +62 22 4210787
W: www.pissecondary.penabur.sch.id

Sekolah Bogor Raya

Perumahan Danau Bogor Raya, Bogor, Jabar 16143
DP Coordinator Aditya Rao
PYP Coordinator Diana Karitas
Languages English
T: +62 251 837 8873
W: www.sekolahbogorraya.com

Sekolah Buin Batu

Jl Kayu Besi No 400, Townsite PTAMNT, Buin Batu, West Sumbawa, NTB
PYP Coordinator Arief Budiman
Languages English
T: +62372 635318 Ext:48443
W: www.sekolahbuinbatu.org

Sekolah Cikal Amri-Setu

Jl. Setu Raya No. 3, Cipayung, Jakarta Timur, DKI
DP Coordinator Anggi Swardhani
MYP Coordinator Mimin Sri Wahyuni
Languages English
T: +62 811 1156 599
W: www.cikal.co.id

Sekolah Cikal Cilandak

Jl. Letjen. TB. Simatupang Kav. 18, Cilandak, Jakarta Timur, DKI
PYP Coordinator Marsaria Primadonna
Languages English
T: +62 21 7590 2580
W: www.cikal.co.id

INDONESIA

Sekolah Cikal Surabaya

Jl. Raya Lontar No. 103, Kelurahan Lontar, Kecamatan Sambikerep, Surabaya, Jatim
PYP Coordinator Cholifah Yuniati
Languages English
T: +62 815 1550 1010
W: www.cikal.co.id

Sekolah Ciputra, Surabaya

Puri Widya Kencana, Citraland, Surabaya, Jatim 60213
DP Coordinator Simon Bradshaw
MYP Coordinator Jay Kalsey
PYP Coordinator Diana Sumadianti
Languages English
T: +62 31 741 5018
W: www.sekolahciputra.sch.id

Sekolah Global Indo-Asia

Jalan Raya Batam Centre Kav SGIA, Batam Centre, Batam Island, Kepri
DP Coordinator Amit Badola
PYP Coordinator Peggy Ratulangi
Languages English
T: +62 778 467333
W: www.sgiaedu.org

Sekolah Mutiara Nusantara

Jl. Sersan Bajuri – Setiabudi, Km 1.5, RT 3 RW 1, Bandung, Jabar 40559
DP Coordinator Sean Broussard
Languages English
T: +62 22 201 7773
W: www.mnis.sch.id

Sekolah Paradisa Cendekia

Jalan Pulo, Leuwinanggung, Kalimanggis, Cibubur, DKI
PYP Coordinator Agusman Armansyah
Languages English, Indonesian
T: +62 21 28671700
W: www.spc.sch.id

Sekolah Pelita Harapan, Kemang Village

Jl. Pangeran Antasari 36, Kemang Village, Jakarta Selatan, DKI 12150
DP Coordinator Joseph Chong
Languages English
T: +62 21 290 56 789
W: kemangvillage.sph.edu

Sekolah Pelita Harapan, Lippo Cikarang

Jl. Dago Permai No.1 Komp. Dago Villas, Lippo Cikarang, Bekasi, Jabar 17550
DP Coordinator Sofia Sinaga
Languages English
T: +62 21 897 2786 87
W: lippocikarang.sph.edu

Sekolah Pelita Harapan, Lippo Village

2500 Boulevard Palem Raya, Lippo Village, Tangerang, Banten 15810
DP Coordinator Ezmieralda Kallista
MYP Coordinator Esther McIntyre
PYP Coordinator Ratna Setyowati Putri
Languages English
T: +62 21 546 0234
W: www.sph.edu

Sekolah Pelita Harapan, Sentul City

Jl. Babakan Madang, Sentul City, Bogor, Jabar 16810
DP Coordinator Elisabeth Pristiwi
MYP Coordinator Lisajanti Widjaja
PYP Coordinator Fany Oktavia
Languages English
T: +62 21 8796 0234
W: sentulcity.sph.edu

Sekolah Pilar Indonesia

Jl Dewa 9, Ciangsana, Kawasan Cibubur, Bogor, Jabar 16968
PYP Coordinator Martini Sayuti
Languages English
T: +62 21 84936222
W: www.sekolah-pilar-indonesia.sch.id

Sekolah Tunas Bangsa

Jalan Arteri Supadio, (Achmad Yani II) Km 2, Pontianak, Kalbar 78391
PYP Coordinator Ronald Sahat Tua Simbolon
Languages English
T: +62 561 725555
W: www.tunasbangsa.sch.id

Sekolah Victory Plus

Jl Kemang Pratama Raya, AN 2-3 Kemang Pratama, Bekasi, Jabar 17116
DP Coordinator Justin Skea
MYP Coordinator Agnes Budiastuti
PYP Coordinator Early Hapsari
Languages English
T: +62 21 8240 3878
W: svp.sch.id

Sinarmas World Academy

Jl TM Pahlawan Seribu, CBD Lot XV, BSD City, Tangerang, Banten 15322
DP Coordinator Flora Tate
MYP Coordinator Alexander Nenes
Languages English
T: +62 21 5316 1400
W: www.swa-jkt.com

Singapore Intercultural School Bona Vista

Jl. Bona Vista Raya, Lebak Bulus, Jakarta Selatan, DKI 12440
DP Coordinator Andi Elisa
Languages English
T: +62 21 759 14414
W: www.sisschools.org/sisbv

Singapore School, Pantai Indah Kapuk

Jl. Mandara Indah 4, Pantai Indah Kapuk, Jakarta Utara, DKI 14460
DP Coordinator Callie Shyong
T: +62 21 588 3835
W: www.sis-pik.com

SIS Kelapa Gading

Jl. Pegangsaan Dua No.83, Kelapa Gading, Jakarta Utara, DKI 14250
DP Coordinator Alfredo Iii Garcia
Languages English
T: +62 21 460 8888
W: www.sis-kg.com

SIS Medan

Royal Sumatra Complex, Jl. Letjen Jamin Ginting Km. 8,5, Medan, Sumut
DP Coordinator Raja Shekhar Reddy Malapati
Languages English
T: +62 61 836 2880
W: www.sis-medan.com

SMA Pradita Dirgantara

Jl. Cendrawasih No.4. Adi Sumarmo Airport Complex, Surakarta, Jateng 57375
DP Coordinator Oscar Carascalao
Languages English
T: +62 71 7467 569
W: sma.praditadirgantara.sch.id

Stamford School, Bandung

Allegro Altura Complex, Jalan Citra Green, Dago, Bandung, Jabar 40142
DP Coordinator Jaya Gopalakrishnan
Languages English, Indonesian
T: +62 22 251 5255
W: stamford.sch.id

Stella Maris School

Sektor 8A, Vatican Cluster, Gading Serpong, Tangerang, Banten 15310
DP Coordinator Arsenia Lotivo
Languages English
T: +62 21 54 212 999
W: www.stellamaris.co.id

Surabaya Intercultural School

Citra Raya, Lakarsantri, Tromol Pos 2/ SBDK, Surabaya, Jatim 60225
PYP Coordinator Rajani Nair
Languages English
T: +62 31 741 4300
W: sis.sch.id

Tunas Muda School Kedoya

Jl Angsana Raya D8/2, Taman Kedoya Baru, Jakarta Barat, DKI 11520
PYP Coordinator Meilianny Jap
Languages English
T: +62 21 581 8766
W: www.sekolahtunasmuda.com

Tunas Muda School Meruya

Jl. Meruya Utara No. 71, Kembangan, Jakarta Barat, DKI 11620
DP Coordinator Hendra Rusli
MYP Coordinator Arniel Defita
PYP Coordinator Maria Imaculata Addelin
Languages English, Bahasa Indonesia
T: +62 (0)21 587 0329
W: www.tunasmuda.sch.id

Tzu Chi School, Pantai Indah Kapuk

Jl. Pantai Indah Kapuk Boulevard, Tzu Chi Centre, Kelurahan Kamal Muara, Kecamatan Penjaringan, Jakarta Utara, DKI 14470
DP Coordinator Kate Siaron
MYP Coordinator Patrick O Sullivan
Languages English
T: +62 21 5055 6668
W: tzuchi.sch.id

Yogyakarta Independent School

Jl. Tegal Mlati No. 1, Jombor Lor, Sinduadi, Mlati, Sleman, Yogyakarta, DIY 55284
DP Coordinator Elia Ekanindita
MYP Coordinator Kencana Candra
PYP Coordinator Veronika Swanti
Languages English
T: +62 274 530 5147
W: www.yis-edu.org

YPJ School Kuala Kencana

Jalan Irian Jaya Barat No.1, Kuala Kencana, Timika, Papua 99910
PYP Coordinator Vini Quamilla
Languages English
W: ypj.sch.id

YPJ School Tembagapura

Jalan Raya Tembagapura No. 605, PO Box 14, Tembagapura, Papua 99910
PYP Coordinator Easter Lusiana
Languages Indonesian
W: ypj.sch.id

Abroad International School – Okayama

Yanagimachi 1-10-9, Kitaku, Okayama, Chugoku 700-0904
PYP Coordinator Hasan Kose
Languages English, Japanese
T: +81 86 221 0144
W: abroadschools.jp/okayama

IB ASIA-PACIFIC

Abroad International School – Osaka

Being Yotsubashi Bldg 6F, 1-3-2 Kitahorie, Nishi-ku, Osaka, Kansai 550-0014
PYP Coordinator Stacy O'Sullivan
Languages English
T: +81 (0)6 6535 0500
W: osaka.abroadschools.jp

AICJ Junior & Senior High School

2-33-16 Gion, Asaminami-ku, Hiroshima, Chugoku 731-0138
DP Coordinator Andrew Brown
Languages English
T: +81 82 832 5037
W: www.aicj.ed.jp

AIE International High School

1-48 Hama, Awaji, Hyogo, Kansai 656-2304
DP Coordinator Naoko Watanabe
Languages English
T: +81 799 74 0020
W: www.aie.ed.jp

Angel Kindergarten

80-6 Ojiri Shimonagakubo, Nagaizumi, Shizuoka, Chubu 411-0934
PYP Coordinator Simon Lund
Languages English, Japanese
T: +81 55 987 5323
W: www.angel-kindergarten.com

Aoba-Japan Bilingual Preschool – Mitaka Campus

4-15-41 Shimorenjaku, Mitaka, Tokyo, Kanto 181-0013
PYP Coordinator Kana Inoue
Languages English, Japanese
T: +81 42 229 8977
W: aoba-bilingual.jp/mitaka

Aoba-Japan Bilingual Preschool – Waseda Campus

1-14-8 Takadano-baba, Shinjuku-ku, Tokyo, Kanto 169-0075
PYP Coordinator Sho Katsumoto
Languages English, Japanese
T: +81 3 6385 2818
W: aoba-bilingual.jp/waseda

AOBA-JAPAN INTERNATIONAL SCHOOL

7-5-1 Hikarigaoka, Nerima-ku, Tokyo 179-0072
DP Coordinator Kate Loke
MYP Coordinator Chris Radnich
PYP Coordinator Karen Chen
Languages English
T: +81 3 4578 8832
E: enquiries@aobajapan.jp
W: www.aobajapan.jp
See full details on page 312

Aoba-Japan International School JCQ Bilingual Preschool

Harumi Triton West 2f, 1-8-2 Harumi, Chuo-Ku, Tokyo, Kanto 104-0053
PYP Coordinator Jeremy Guckert
Languages English, Japanese
T: +81 3 6228 1811
W: www.jcq.jp

Asahijuku Secondary School

2590 Mitsushitori, Kita-ku, Okayama, Chugoku 709-2136
DP Coordinator Yukihiro Maruyama
MYP Coordinator Yukihiro Maruyama
Languages English, Japanese
T: +81 86 726 0111
W: m-asahijuku.ed.jp

Canadian Academy

4-1 Koyo-Cho Naka, Higashinada-ku, Kobe, Hyogo, Kansai 658-0032
DP Coordinator Greg River
MYP Coordinator Sarah Tudge
PYP Coordinator Trevor Rehel
Languages English
T: +81 78 857 0100
W: www.canacad.ac.jp

Canadian International School Tokyo

5-8-20 Kitashinagawa, Shinagawa-ku, Tokyo, Kanto 141-0001
PYP Coordinator Peter Cassidy
Languages English
T: +81 3 5793 1392
W: www.cisjapan.net

Chiyoda Jogakuen Senior High School

Chiyoda-ku, Tokyo, Kanto 102-0081
DP Coordinator Ryo Sakamoto
Languages English, Japanese
T: +81 3 3263 6551
W: www.chiyoda-j.ac.jp

Deutsche Schule Kobe International (DSKI)

3-2-8 Koyochonaka, Higashinada-ku, Kobe, Hyogo, Kansai 658-0032
PYP Coordinator Benjamin Huber
Languages English
T: +81 78 857 9777
W: www.dskobe.org

Doshisha International Academy Elementary School

7-31-1 Kizugawa-dai, Kizugawa, Kyoto, Kansai 619-0225
PYP Coordinator Aki Rojas
Languages English
T: +81 774 71 0810
W: www.dia.doshisha.ac.jp/?page_id=5

Doshisha International School, Kyoto

7-31-1 Kizugawa-dai, Kizugawa, Kyoto, Kansai 619-0225
DP Coordinator Vijay Thapliyal
PYP Coordinator John Wishart
Languages English
T: +81 774 71 0810
W: www.diskyoto.com

Eisugakkan School

980-1, Hikino-cho, Fukuyama, Hiroshima, Chugoku 721-8502
DP Coordinator Nerissa Momo
PYP Coordinator Takafumi Namba
Languages English
T: +81 84 941 4115
W: www.eisu-ejs.ac.jp

Enishi International School

2-12-32 Kikui Nishi Ward, Nagoya, Aichi 451-0044
MYP Coordinator Mahmut Kaya
PYP Coordinator Mark Jones
Languages English, Japanese
T: +81(0)52 581 0700
W: www.enishi.ac.jp

Fukuoka Daiichi High School

22-1 Tamagawa cho, Minami-ku, Fukuoka, Kyushu 815-0037
DP Coordinator Taiyo Rious
Languages English, Japanese
T: +81 9 2541 0165
W: f.f-parama.ed.jp

Fukuoka International School

3-18-50 Momochi, Sawara-ku, Fukuoka, Kyushu 814-0006
DP Coordinator Christian Chiarenza
MYP Coordinator Ken Forde
PYP Coordinator Michelle Jasinska
Languages English
T: +81 92 841 7601
W: www.fis.ed.jp

Global Indian International School (GIIS) Higashi Kasai Campus

9-3-6 Higashikasai, Edogawa-Ku, Tokyo, Kanto 134-0084
DP Coordinator Madhu Khanna
PYP Coordinator Carole Saunders
Languages English, Japanese
T: +81 35 676 5081
W: tokyo.globalindianschool.org

Gunma Kokusai Academy

1361-4 Uchigashima-cho, Ota, Gunma, Kanto 373-0813
DP Coordinator James Taylor
Languages English
T: +81 276 47 7711
W: www.gka.jp

Hiroshima Global Academy

3137-2 Okushi, Osakikamijima-cho, Toyota-gun, Hiroshima, Chugoku 725-0303
DP Coordinator Sean Richards
MYP Coordinator Yoshihiro Furuichi
Languages English, Japanese
T: +81 84 667 5581
W: higa-s.jp

Hiroshima International School

3-49-1 Kurakake, Asakita-Ku, Hiroshima, Chugoku 739-1743
DP Coordinator Alexandra Omukova
MYP Coordinator Marybeth Kamibeppu
PYP Coordinator Marisa Villarreal
Languages English
T: +81 82 843 4111
W: www.hiroshima-is.ac.jp

Horizon Japan International School

1-24 Onocho, Kanagawa-ku, Yokohama, Kanagawa, Kanto 221-0055
DP Coordinator Synthia Titley Cardona
MYP Coordinator Barbara Bilgre
PYP Coordinator Shailja Jhamb Datt
Languages English
T: +81 45 624 8717
W: www.horizon.ac.jp

Hosei University Kokusai High School

1-13-1 KIshiya, Tsurumi-ku, Yokohama, Kanagawa, Kanto 230-0078
DP Coordinator Andrew Gibbs
Languages English
T: +81 45 571 4482
W: hosei.ac.jp/general/jyoshi

Ikeda Junior High School Attached to Osaka Kyoiku University

1 Chome-5-1, Midorigaoka, Ikeda, Osaka, Kansai 563-0026
MYP Coordinator Atsuko Torii
Languages English, Japanese
T: +81 72 761 8690
W: www.ikeda-j.oku.ed.jp

Ikuei Nishi Jr. & Sr. High School

637-1 4 chome Mimatsu, Nara 631-0074
MYP Coordinator Isamu Yoshizawa
Languages English, Japanese
T: +81 74 247 0688
W: www.ikuei.ed.jp/ikunishi

IB ASIA-PACIFIC

JAPAN

India International School in Japan

1-20-20, Ojima, Koto-Ku -135-0004, Tokyo, Kanto 136-0072
DP Coordinator Suresh Bhakta Shrestha
Languages English
T: +81 03 3635 7850
W: www.iisjapan.com

International School of Nagano

1-2-2 Minami-Matsumoto, Matsumoto, Nagano, Chubu 390-0832
PYP Coordinator Shizuka Tateiwa
Languages English
T: +81 26 387 5971
W: isnedu.org

K. International School Tokyo

1-5-15 Shirakawa, Koto-ku, Tokyo, Kanto 135-0021
DP Coordinator Hiro Komaki
MYP Coordinator Robert White
PYP Coordinator Oliver Sullivan
Languages English
T: +81 3 3642 9993
W: www.kist.ed.jp

Kaichi Nihonbashi Gakuen

7-6 Nihonbashi Bakurocho 2-chome, Chuo-ku, Tokyo, Kanto 103-8384
DP Coordinator Kenji Kondo
MYP Coordinator Jonathan Anzai
Languages English, Japanese
T: +81 3 3662 2507
W: www.kng.ed.jp

Kaichi-Nozomi Elementary School

3400 Tutudo Aza Suwa, Tsukubamirai, Ibaraki, Kanto 300-2435
PYP Coordinator Shingo Noguchi
Languages English, Japanese
T: +81 0297 38 6000
W: www.kaichigakuen.ed.jp/nozomi

Kanagawa Prefectural Yokohama Senior High School of International Studies

1-731 Mutsukawa, Minami-ku, Yokohama, Kanagawa 232-0066
DP Coordinator Mitsuhiro Kimura
Languages English, Japanese
T: +81 45 721 1434
W: yokohamakokusai-h.pen-kanagawa.ed.jp

Kansai International Academy

4-1-31 Shinzaike-Minamimachi, Nada-ku, Kobe, Hyogo, Kansai 657-0864
DP Coordinator Yoko Homma
PYP Coordinator Yoko Morisaki
Languages English, Japanese
T: +81 78 882 6680
W: www.kis-g.jp

Katoh Gakuen Gyoshu Junior & Senior High School

1361-1 Nakamiyo Okanomiya, Numazu, Shizuoka, Chubu 410-0011
DP Coordinator Craig Sutton
MYP Coordinator Gay-Ann Bagotchay
Languages English, Japanese
T: +81 55 924 3322
W: www.katoh-net.ac.jp/gyoshuhs

Kids Tairiku Yokohama Nakagawa

1-19-23 Nakagawa, Tsuzuki-Ku, Yokohama, Kanagawa, Kanto 224-0001
PYP Coordinator Yukiko Gemma
Languages English, Japanese
T: +81 45 914 3770
W: www.kidstairiku.jp/school/nakagawa

Kochi Kokusai Junior and Senior High School

2-5-70 Kamobe, Kochi, Shikoku 780-8052
DP Coordinator Ukyo Ishimaru
MYP Coordinator Miki Igei
Languages English, Japanese
T: +81 88 844 1221
W: www.kochinet.ed.jp/kokusai-jh

Kofu Nishi High School

Shimoiida 4-1-1, Kofu, Yamanashi, Chubu 400-0064
DP Coordinator Yasuko Nozaki
Languages English, Japanese
T: +81 (0)55 228 5161
W: www.nishi.kai.ed.jp

Korea International School

2-13-35 Toyokawa, Ibaraki, Osaka, Kansai 567-0057
DP Coordinator Sea Jin Cho
Languages English
T: +81 72 643 4200
W: www.kiskorea.ed.jp

Kumamoto International School

2-18-8 Nishibaru, Higashi-ku, Kumamoto, Kyushu 861-8029
PYP Coordinator Matthew Ohm
Languages English, Japanese
T: +81 96 285 3938
W: kumamotointer.jp

Kyoto International School

252 Shinhigashidoin-cho, Sakyo-ku, Kyoto, Kansai 606-8355
PYP Coordinator Sharyn Skrtic
Languages English
T: +81 75 451 1022
W: www.kyotointernationalschool.org

LINDEN HALL HIGH SCHOOL

3-10-1 Futsukaichikita, Chikushino, Fukuoka, Kyushu 818-0056
DP Coordinator Ms. Karen Hunter
Languages English, Japanese
T: +81 92 929 4558
E: hunter@lindenhall.ed.jp
W: www.lindenhall.ed.jp

See full details on page 377
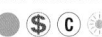

Machida Kobato Kindergarten/ Gakkouhoujin Kanzou Gakuen

2904 Hon-Machida, Machida, Tokyo, Kanto 194-0032
PYP Coordinator Toshiko Ishikawa
Languages Japanese
T: +81 42 723 1494
W: www.m-kobato.ed.jp

Marist Brothers International School

1-2-1 Chimori-Cho, Suma-Ku, Kobe, Hyogo, Kansai 654-0072
DP Coordinator David Lynch
Languages English
T: +81 78 732 6266
W: www.marist.ac.jp

Matsumoto Kokusai High School

3-6-25 Muraimachi minami, Matsumoto, Nagano, Chubu 399-0036
DP Coordinator Sjaak Mintjens
Languages English, Japanese
T: +81 263 88 0033
W: m-kokusai.ac.jp

Meikei High School

1-1 Inarimae, Tsukuba, Ibaraki, Kanto 305-8502
DP Coordinator Hideaki Matsuzaki
Languages English, Japanese
T: +81 29 851 6611
W: www.meikei.ac.jp

Miura Gakuen High School

3-80 Kinugasa-sakae, Yokosuka, Kanagawa 238-0031
DP Coordinator Kosaku Tanaka
Languages English, Japanese
T: +81 46 852 0284
W: miura.ed.jp

Miyagi Prefectural Sendai Nika Junior and Senior High School

1 Chome-4-1 Renbo, Wakabayashi Ward, Sendai, Miyagi, Tohoku 984-0052
DP Coordinator Osamu Jinushi
Languages English, Japanese
T: +81 22 296 8101
W: nika.myswan.ed.jp

Mizuho School

3-2-25, Shakujiidai, Nerima-ku, Tokyo, Kanto 177-0045
PYP Coordinator Kiyohiko Motohashi
Languages English
T: +81 3 5372 1525
W: www.mizuho-edu.co.jp

Nagoya International Junior and Senior High School

1-16, Hiroji-Honmachi, Showa-Ku, Nagoya, Aichi, Chubu 466-0841
DP Coordinator Christopher Yap
Languages English
T: +81 52 858 2200
W: www.nihs.ed.jp

Nagoya International School

2686 Minamihara, Nakashidami, Moriyama-ku, Nagoya, Aichi, Chubu 463-0002
DP Coordinator Ian Radcliffe
MYP Coordinator Peter Goodman
PYP Coordinator Nina Radcliffe
Languages English
T: +81 52 736 2025
W: www.nisjapan.net

Okayama University of Science High School

Daiomachi No. 1, Kita-ku, Okayama, Chugoku 700-0005
DP Coordinator Akemi Morioka
Languages English, Japanese
T: +81 (0)86 256 8511
W: okayama.ridaifu.net

Okinawa International School

143 Tamagusuku Fusato, Nanjo City, Okinawa, Kyushu 901-0611
DP Coordinator Shogo Okuma
MYP Coordinator Yugo Nakamura
PYP Coordinator Sayuri Tatetsu
Languages English, Japanese
T: +81 (0)98 948 7711
W: www.ois-edu.com

Omiya Elementary School

654-1 Birafu, Kami, Kochi, Shikoku 781-4212
PYP Coordinator Yosei Momota
Languages English, Japanese
T: +81 88 759 2136
W: www.fureai-cloud.jp/omiya-e

Osaka City Suito Kokusai Junior and Senior High School

3-7-13 Minami- Konaka, Suminoe-ku, Osaka, Kansai 559-0033
DP Coordinator Goro Sato
Languages English, Japanese
T: +81 67 662 9600
W: osaka-city-ib.jp

Osaka International School of Kwansei Gakuin

4-4-16 Onohara-nishi, Minoh, Osaka, Kansai 562-0032
DP Coordinator Stephen Frater
MYP Coordinator Stephanie Ruth Alcantara
PYP Coordinator Ingela Summerton
Languages English
T: +81 72 727 5050
W: www.senri.ed.jp

Osaka Jogakuin Senior High School

2-26-54 Tamatsukuri, Chuo-ku, Osaka, Kansai 540-0004
DP Coordinator Nobumasa Kagimura
Languages English, Japanese
T: +81 6 6761 4113
W: www.osaka-jogakuin.ed.jp

Osaka YMCA International School

6-7-34 Nakatsu, Kita-ku, Osaka, Kansai 531-0071
DP Coordinator Jamie Riddalls
MYP Coordinator Monique Palmer
PYP Coordinator Brendan O'Leary
Languages English
T: +81 6 6345 1661
W: www.oyis.org

RITSUMEIKAN UJI JUNIOR AND SENIOR HIGH SCHOOL

33-1 Hachikenyadani, Hirono-cho, Uji, Kyoto, Kansai 611-0031
DP Coordinator Dr. Marcelo Schwarz
Languages English, Japanese (ibdp In English)
T: +81 774 41 3000
E: ib_info@ujc.ritsumei.ac.jp
W: www.ujc.ritsumei.ac.jp/ujc_e/

See full details on page 405

Sai Sishya International School

6-18-2 Higashi Kasai, Edogawa Ku, Tokyo, Kanto 134-0084
PYP Coordinator Rebecca Yarita
Languages English, Japanese
T: +81 70 1393 5515
W: saisishya.jp

Saint Maur International School

83 Yamate-cho, Naka-ku, Yokohama, Kanagawa, Kanto 231-8654
DP Coordinator Oliver Alexander
Languages English
T: +81 45 641 5751
W: www.stmaur.ac.jp

Saitama Municipal Omiya International Secondary School

4 Chome-96 Mihashi, Omiya Ward, Saitama, Kanto 330-0856
MYP Coordinator Bradley Semans
Languages English, Japanese
T: +81 48 622 8200
W: www.city-saitama.ed.jp/ohmiyakokusai-h

Sapporo Kaisei Secondary School

1-1 Kita 22 Higashi 21 Higashiku, Sapporo, Hokkaido 065-8558
DP Coordinator Ken Kuroi
MYP Coordinator Thomas Belshaw
Languages English
T: +81 11 788 6987
W: www.kaisei-s.sapporo-c.ed.jp

Seisen International School

1-12-15 Yoga, Setagaya-ku, Tokyo, Kanto 158-0097
DP Coordinator Dean Bevan
MYP Coordinator Eric Usher
PYP Coordinator Serrin Smyth
Languages English
T: +81 3 3704 2661
W: www.seisen.com

SENDAI IKUEI GAKUEN

2-4-1 Miyagino, Miyagino-ku, Sendai, Miyagi, Tohoku 983-0045
DP Coordinator Anthony Sweeney
MYP Coordinator Bryan Stevens
Languages English, Japanese
T: +81 22 256 4141
E: t.sweeney@sendaiikuei.jp
W: sendaiikuei-english.jp

See full details on page 413

SENIOR HIGH SCHOOL AT SAKADO, UNIVERSITY OF TSUKUBA

1-24-1 Chiyoda, Sakado, Saitama, Kanto 350-0214
DP Coordinator Regina Ver-Santos
Languages English, Japanese
T: +81 49 281 1541
W: www.sakado-s.tsukuba.ac.jp

See full details on page 414

Shiga Prefectural Torahime High School

2410 Miyabe-cho, Nagahama, Shiga, Kansai 529-0012
DP Coordinator Mariko Tomioka
Languages English, Japanese
T: +81 (0)749 73 3055
W: www.torahime-h.shiga-ec.ed.jp

Shinagawa International School

4-8-8 Higashishinagawa, Shinagawa, Tokyo, Kanto 140-0002
PYP Coordinator Thomas Broadbent
Languages English
T: +81 3 6433 1531
W: sistokyo.jp

Shizuoka Salesio School

3 Chome-2-1 Nakanogo, Shimizu Ward, Shizuoka, Chubu 424-8624
PYP Coordinator Taku Harada
Languages English, Japanese
T: +81 54 345 2296
W: www.ssalesio.ac.jp

Shogaku Gakuen Educational Foundation

747 Kokuba, Naha, Okinawa, Kyushu 902-0075
DP Coordinator Noriko Bousckri
Languages English
T: +81 98 832 1767
W: www.okisho.ed.jp/en

Shohei Junior and Senior High School

851 Shimono, Sugito, Saitama, Kanto 345-0044
DP Coordinator Kohei Maeda
MYP Coordinator Wakako Totsune
Languages English
T: +81 48 034 3381
W: www.shohei.sugito.saitama.jp/contents/jhs

Shukoh Middle School

Sendai Ikuei Gakuen, 241 Miyagino, Miyagino-ku, Sendai, Miyagi, Tohoku 985-0853
MYP Coordinator Kerry Winter
Languages English, Japanese
T: +81 22 256 4141
W: www.sendaiikuei.ed.jp/shukoh

St. Joseph's Primary School

11-1 HigashiTerao-Kitadai, Tsurumi-ku, Yokohama, Kanagawa, Kanto 230-0016
PYP Coordinator Mami Saito
Languages English, Japanese
T: +81 45 581 8808
W: www.st-joseph.ac.jp/primary

St. Mary's International School

1-6-19 Seta, Setagaya Ku, Tokyo, Kanto 158-8668
DP Coordinator Christopher Tihor
Languages English
T: +81 3 3709 3411
W: www.smis.ac.jp

Summerhill International School

2-13-8 Moto-Azabu, Minato-ku, Tokyo, Kanto 106-0046
PYP Coordinator Hana Fujishiro
Languages English, Japanese
T: +81 3 3453 0811
W: www.summerhill.jp

Sunnyside International School

Iwai 4-10-25, Gifu, Chubu 501-3101
PYP Coordinator Clare Barnfather
Languages English, Japanese
T: +81 58 241 1000
W: www.sunnyside-international.jp

Tamagawa Academy K-12 & University

6-1-1 Tamagawa Gakuen, Machida, Tokyo, Kanto 194-8610
DP Coordinator Angela Rasmussen
MYP Coordinator Aidan Leach
Languages English
T: +81 42 739 8111
W: www.tamagawa.jp/en

Tohoku International School

7-101-1 Yakata, Izumi-ku, Sendai, Miyagi, Tohoku 981-3214
DP Coordinator Jordan Nogaki
PYP Coordinator Hiroko Yoshida
Languages English
T: +81 22 348 2468
W: www.tisweb.net

Tokai Gakuen High School

2-901 Nakahira Tenpaku-ku, Nagoya, Aichi, Chubu 468-0014
DP Coordinator Trevor Wilson
Languages English, Japanese
T: +81 52 801 6222
W: tokaigakuen.ed.jp

Tokyo Gakugei University International Secondary School

5-22-1 Higashi-Oizumi, Nerima-ku, Tokyo, Kanto 178-0063
DP Coordinator Maki Komatsu
MYP Coordinator Masumi Kobayashi
Languages English, Japanese
T: +81 3 5905 1326
W: www.iss.oizumi.u-gakugei.ac.jp

IB ASIA-PACIFIC

Tokyo International School

3-4-22 Mita, Minato-Ku, Tokyo, Kanto 108-0073
MYP Coordinator Catherine Dick
PYP Coordinator Kim Engasser
Languages English
T: +81 3 5484 1160
W: www.tokyois.com

TOKYO METROPOLITAN KOKUSAI HIGH SCHOOL

2-19-59 Komaba, Meguro-ku, Tokyo 153-0041
DP Coordinator Kazumasa Aoki
Languages English
T: +81 3 3468 6811
E: ibdp1@kokusai-h.metro.tokyo.jp
W: www.kokusai-h.metro.tokyo.jp

See full details on page 434

Tsukuba International School

Kamigo 7846-1, Tsukuba, Ibaraki, Kanto 300-2645
DP Coordinator Peter Congreve
MYP Coordinator Vincent Jan Africa
PYP Coordinator Ian Woollard
Languages English
T: +81 29 886 5447
W: www.tis.ac.jp

UPBEAT International School – Atsuta Campus

2-3-18, Hachiban, Atasuta, Nagoya, Aichi, Chubu
PYP Coordinator Astrid Manosalva
Languages English, Japanese
T: +81 (0)52 661 3155
W: www.upbeatjapan.com

UWC ISAK Japan

5827-136 Nagakura, Karuizawa-machi, Kitasaku-gun, Nagano, Chubu 389-0111
DP Coordinator Yaling Chien
Languages English
T: +81 26 746 8623
W: uwcisak.jp

Wakakusa Kindergarten

3-15-4 Yoshida, Nagano, Chubu 381-0043
PYP Coordinator Misato Nicoll
Languages English, Japanese
T: +81 26 241 4151
W: wakakusa-kg.net

Willowbrook International School

2-14-28 Moto-azabu, Minato-ku, Tokyo, Kanto 106-0046
PYP Coordinator Louise Boddy
Languages English
T: +81 3 3449 9030
W: www.willowbrookschool.com

Yamanashi Gakuin School

13-3-1, Sakaori, Kofu, Yamanashi, Chubu 400-0805
DP Coordinator Priw-Prae Litticharoenporn
PYP Coordinator Hidetoshi Horikawa
Languages English
T: +81 55 224 1200
W: www.ygk.ed.jp

Yamata Kindergarten

351-1 Higashiyamatacho, Tsuzuki Ward, Yokohama, Kanagawa, Kanto 224-0024
PYP Coordinator Manami Nishiyama
Languages Japanese
T: +81 45 592 4850
W: www.yamata-youchien.com

Yokohama International School

258 Yamate-cho, Naka-ku, Yokohama, Kanagawa, Kanto 231-0862
DP Coordinator Giles Pinto
MYP Coordinator Medeha Zahid
PYP Coordinator Jocelyn Hartley
Languages English
T: +81 45 622 0084
W: www.yis.ac.jp

Yoyogi International School

5-67-5 Yoyogi, Shibuya-ku, Tokyo, Kanto 151-0053
PYP Coordinator Mike Mural
Languages English
T: +81 3 5478 6714
W: www.yoyogiinternationalschool.com

LAOS

VIENTIANE INTERNATIONAL SCHOOL

PO Box 3180, Phonesavanh Road, Saphanthong Tai Village, Sisattanak District, Vientiane
DP Coordinator Elizabeth England
MYP Coordinator Elizabeth England
PYP Coordinator Olwen Millgate
Languages English
T: +856 21 31 8100
E: contact@vislao.com
W: www.vislao.com

See full details on page 440

MALAYSIA

Cempaka International School

No 19, Jalan Setiabakti 1, Damansara Heights, Kuala Lumpur
DP Coordinator Nik Zakiah Nik Kar
Languages English
T: +60 3 2094 0623
W: www.cempaka.edu.my

EtonHouse Malaysia International School

No. 9 Persiaran Stonor, 50450 Kuala Lumpur
PYP Coordinator Tarra Tanauan
Languages English
T: +60 3 2141 3301/02
W: etonhouse.edu.my

Fairview International School

Lot 4178, Jalan 1/27D, Section 6, Wangsa Maju, 53300 Kuala Lumpur
DP Coordinator Dr. Evan Hui See Chin
MYP Coordinator Dr. Evan Hui See Chin
PYP Coordinator Ms. Elaine Wong
Languages English, Mandarin
T: +60 3 4142 0888
W: www.fairview.edu.my

Fairview International School Ipoh

Hala Lapangan Suria Medan Lapangan, Suria, 31350 Ipoh, Perak
MYP Coordinator Vigneswary V
PYP Coordinator Poh Yi Kan
Languages English
W: www.fairview.edu.my

Fairview International School Johor

Kompleks Mutiara Johor Land, Jalan Bukit Mutiara, Bandar Dato' Onn, 88100 Johor Bahru, Johor
MYP Coordinator Ariel Schatenstein
PYP Coordinator Diya Upadhaya
Languages English
T: +60 7 358 5385
W: www.fairview.edu.my

Fairview International School Penang

Tingkat Bukit Jambul 1, 11900 Bayan Lepas, Penang
MYP Coordinator Eswari Subramaniam
PYP Coordinator Samantha Leong
Languages English
T: +60 4 640 6633
W: www.fairview.edu.my

Fairview International School Subang

2A, Jalan TP 2, Sime UEP Industrial Park, 47600 Subang Jaya, Selangor
MYP Coordinator Cynthia Patricia Nicholas
PYP Coordinator Munira Izbakieva
Languages English
T: +60 3 8023 7777
W: www.fairview.edu.my

IGB International School

Jalan Sierramas Utama, Sungai Buloh, Kuala Lumpur, Selangor 47000
CP Coordinator Magnus Drechsler
DP Coordinator Magnus Drechsler
MYP Coordinator Lennan MacDonald
PYP Coordinator Aga Chojnacka
Languages English
T: +60 3 6145 4688
W: www.igbis.edu.my

Kolej MARA Banting

Bukit Changgang, 42700 Banting, Selangor
DP Coordinator Rosmaria Abdullah
Languages English
T: +60 3 3149 1318
W: www.kmb.edu.my

Kolej Tunku Kurshiah

Kompleks Pendidikan Nilai, Bandar Enstek, 71760 Seremban, Negeri Sembilan
DP Coordinator Hafitah Baharuddin
MYP Coordinator Ahmad Bidin
Languages English
T: +60 6 7979800
W: www.tkc.edu.my

Malay College Kuala Kangsar

Jalan Tun Abdul Razak, 33000 Kuala Kangsar, Perak
DP Coordinator Norsafaliza Ibrahim
MYP Coordinator Azlinda Muda
Languages English
T: +60 5 7761400
W: www.mckk.edu.my

Marlborough College Malaysia

Jalan Marlborough, 79200 Iskandar Puteri, Johor
DP Coordinator Mr Kenton Tomlinson
Languages English
T: +60 7 560 2200
W: www.marlboroughcollege.my

Mont'Kiara International School

22 Jalan Kiara, Mont'Kiara, 50480 Kuala Lumpur
DP Coordinator Claudia Fidalgo
MYP Coordinator Benjamin Nicholson
PYP Coordinator Sarah Herbert
Languages English
T: +60 3 2093 8604
W: www.mkis.edu.my

MRSM Balik Pulau (Mara Junior Science College)

Jalan Pondok Upeh, Kampung Shee Tan, 11000 Balik Pulau, Penang
MYP Coordinator Haseena Kader
Languages English
T: +60 4 8669499
W: bpulau.mrsm.edu.my

MRSM Tun Dr Ismail, Pontian

Jalan Benut Jelutong, 82100 Pontian, Johor
MYP Coordinator Amalina Zakaria
Languages English
T: +60 7 6933744
W: mrsmpontian.edu.my

MRSM Tun Mohammad Fuad Stephens Sandakan

Education Hub, Batu 10, Jalan Sungai Batang, 90000 Sandakan, Sabah
MYP Coordinator Farah Ab Aziz
Languages English
T: +60 8 9225609
W: tmfs.mrsm.edu.my/cms

NEXUS INTERNATIONAL SCHOOL MALAYSIA

No 1 Jalan Diplomatik 3/6, Presint 15, 62050 Putrajaya
DP Coordinator Amanda O'Hara
Languages English
T: +60 3 8889 3868
E: principal@nexus.edu.my
W: www.nexus.edu.my

See full details on page 387

Raffles American School

Raffles K12 Sdn Bhd, Jalan Raffles, 79050 Iskandar Puteri, Johor
DP Coordinator William Hope-Ross
Languages English
T: +60 7 509 8750
W: www.raffles-american-school.edu.my

Repton International School Malaysia

No. 8, Jalan Purnama, Bandar Seri Alam, 81750 Johor Bahru, Johor
DP Coordinator Joan Malabuyoc
Languages English
T: +60 7 888 999
W: www.repton.edu.my

Sekolah Menengah Kebangsaan Dato' Sheikh Ahmad

Jalan Besar Arau, 02600 Arau, Perlis
MYP Coordinator Shaharom Bakar
Languages English
T: +60 4 9861239
W: www.smkdsaperlis.edu.my

Sekolah Menengah Kebangsaan Sultanah Bahiyah

Lebuhraya Sultanah Bahiyah, 05350 Alor Star, Kedah
MYP Coordinator Noor Afiza Salleh
Languages English
T: +60 4 7331531
W: www.smksultanahbahiyah.edu.my

SMK Pantai, W.P Labuan

Jalan Pohon Batu, 87027 Labuan
MYP Coordinator Maureen Imang Jau
Languages English
T: +60 8 7410863
W: www.smkpantaiwpl.webs.com

SMK Putrajaya Presint 9(2)

Jalan P9A, Presint 9, Wilayah Persekutuan, 62250 Putrajaya
MYP Coordinator Syafini Ismail
Languages English
T: +60 3 8881 1207
W: www.smkpp92.com

SMK Seri Tualang

28000 Temerloh, Pahang
MYP Coordinator Nur Amalina Mazlan
Languages English
T: +60 9 290 1061
W: www.smkseritualang.com

SMK Sungai Tapang

KM 13, Jalan Penrissen, 93250 Kuching, Sarawak
MYP Coordinator Angelina Suzie Anak Rinyod
Languages English
T: +60 8 2612851
W: www.smksungaitapang.edu.my

SMKA Sheikh Abdul Malek

20400 Kuala Terengganu
MYP Coordinator Huzzaimah Basir
Languages English
T: +60 96235155
W: www.shams.edu.my

SMS Tengku Muhammad Faris Petra

Taman Orkid, Kota Bharu, 16100 Pengkalan Chepa
MYP Coordinator Roziah Mohd Ali
T: +60 9 773 8277
W: www.smstmfp.edu.my

Sri KDU International School

No. 3, Jalan Teknologi 2/1, Kota Damansara, 47810 Daerah Petaling, Selangor
DP Coordinator Phillip Weatherup
Languages English
T: +60 3 6145 3888
W: www.srikdu.edu.my

St. Joseph's Institution International School Malaysia (Tropicana PJ Campus)

No. 1, Jalan PJU 3/13, 47410 Petaling Jaya, Selangor
DP Coordinator Maureen Fitzgerald
Languages English
T: +60 3 8605 3605
W: www.sji-international.edu.my

Stella Maris Medan Damansara

7, Lorong Setiabistari 2, Bukit Damansara, 50490 Kuala Lumpur
DP Coordinator Madhu Singh
Languages English
T: +60 3 20830025
W: stellamaris.edu.my/home

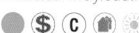

Sunway International School, Bandar Sunway

No. 3, Jalan Universiti, Bandar Sunway, 47500 Selangor
DP Coordinator Mark Milberg
T: +60 3 7491 8070
W: sis.sunway.edu.my

Sunway International School, Sunway Iskandar

Jalan Persiaran Medini 3, Sunway Iskandar, 79250 Johor
CP Coordinator Kenneth Tuttle Wilhelm
DP Coordinator Kenneth Tuttle Wilhelm
Languages English
T: +60 7 533 8070
W: sis.sunway.edu.my

THE INTERNATIONAL SCHOOL OF KUALA LUMPUR (ISKL)

2, Lorong Kelab Polo Di Raja, Ampang Hilir, 55000 Kuala Lumpur
DP Coordinator Ms Ebony Manning, MA, BA
Languages English
T: +60 3 4813 5000
E: admissions@iskl.edu.my
W: www.iskl.edu.my

See full details on page 430

THE INTERNATIONAL SCHOOL OF PENANG (UPLANDS)

Jalan Sungai Satu, Batu Feringgi, 11100 Penang
DP Coordinator Gregory Verdon
PYP Coordinator Maggie Dawson
Languages English
T: +604 8819 777
E: info@uplands.org
W: www.uplands.org

See full details on page 431

UCSI International School

1 Persiaran UCSI International School, 71010 Port Dickson, Negeri Sembalan
DP Coordinator Zaina Shihabi
MYP Coordinator Peter Vinoj
PYP Coordinator Peter Vinoj
Languages English
T: +60 6653 6888
W: www.uis.edu.my

International School of Ulaanbaatar

PO Box 36/10, Khan-Uul District 15th Horoo, 4 Seasons Garden, Ulaanbaatar-36 17032
DP Coordinator Torie Leinbach
MYP Coordinator Jonathan Armitage
PYP Coordinator Jeanne Peloquin
Languages English
T: +976 70160010
W: www.isumongolia.edu.mn

Shine Ue School

UNESCO St 12, Sukhbaatar District, Ulaanbaatar 14220
DP Coordinator Khandjav Terbish
Languages English
T: +976 7012 8044
W: shineue.edu.mn

The English School of Mongolia

Bayanzurkh District, 1 Khoroo, Ulaanbaatar 13380
DP Coordinator Michael Depear
Languages English
T: +976 70 15 40 15
W: esm.edu.mn

Bahan International Science Academy

No.25, Po Sein Road, Bahan Township, Yangon
DP Coordinator Mirzobedil Jamolzoda
Languages English
T: +95 1 548452
W: www.bfi-edu.com

The International School Yangon

20 Shwe Taungyar Street, Bahan Township, Yangon 11181
DP Coordinator Steven Powers
Languages English
T: +95 1 512793/94/95
W: www.isyedu.org

MYANMAR

Yangon American International School

No. 2A, Yangon-Insein Road, Building (2), No. 9 Ward, Hlaing Township, Yangon
PYP Coordinator Emily Samaniego Morris
Languages English, Burmese
T: +95 997 701 2100
W: yangonamerican.edu.mm

Yangon International School

No. 117 Thumingalar Housing, Thingangyun Township, Yangon
DP Coordinator Mou Maiti
Languages English
T: +95 1 578171
W: www.yismyanmar.com

NEPAL

Genius School Lalitpur

Ringroad, Mahalaxmisthan, Lalitpur
PYP Coordinator Prakash Laxmi Joshi
Languages English
T: +977 1 5170746
W: www.geniusschool.edu.np

Premier International School

Khumaltar Height, Satdobato, Lalitpur
MYP Coordinator Pravina Thapa
PYP Coordinator Pravina Thapa
Languages English, Nepali
T: +977 1 552 8032
W: www.premier.edu.np

Ullens School

Khumaltar-5, Lalipur, Post Box Number 8975, EPC 1477, Kathmandu
DP Coordinator Raisa Pandey
Languages English
T: +977 1 5230824
W: www.ullens.edu.np

NEW ZEALAND

ACG Senior College

66 Lorne Street, Auckland 1141
DP Coordinator Alex Marshall
Languages English
T: +64 9 3074 474
W: www.acgedu.com/nz/senior

Ashburton Borough School

Winter St, Ashburton 7700
PYP Coordinator Dewdene Percy
T: +64 3 307 8529
W: ashborough.school.nz

Auckland International College

37 Heaphy Street, Blockhouse Bay, Auckland 0600
DP Coordinator Maureen Forsyth
Languages English
T: +64 9 309 4480
W: www.aic.ac.nz

Auckland Normal Intermediate School

Poronui Street, Mt Eden, Auckland 1024
PYP Coordinator Shane Devery
Languages English
T: +64 96 301109
W: ani.school.nz

Bay of Islands International Academy

935 Purerua Road, Kerikeri, Northland 0294
PYP Coordinator Jennifer Grant
Languages English
T: +64 9 407 9749
W: www.boi.ac.nz

Berkley Normal Middle School

26 Berkley Avenue, Hamilton, Waikato 3216
PYP Coordinator Beth Germaine
Languages English
T: +64 7856 6537
W: www.berkley.school.nz

Bucklands Beach Intermediate School

247 Bucklands Beach Road, Bucklands Beach, Auckland 2012
PYP Coordinator Brett Nugent
Languages English
T: +64 9 534 2896
W: www.bbi.school.nz

Diocesan School for Girls

Clyde Street, Epsom, Auckland 1051
DP Coordinator Susan Marriott
PYP Coordinator Nicole Lewis
Languages English
T: +64 9 520 0221
W: www.diocesan.school.nz

Glendowie College

21 Crossfield Road, Glendowie, Auckland 1071
MYP Coordinator Sharon Hewetson
Languages English
T: +64 9 575 9128
W: www.gdc.school.nz

Glendowie Primary School

217 Riddell Road, Glendowie, Auckland 1071
PYP Coordinator Christine Matos
Languages English
T: +64 9 575 7374
W: www.glendowieprimary.school.nz

John McGlashan College

2 Pilkington Street, Maori Hill, Dunedin 9010
DP Coordinator Brendan Porter
Languages English
T: +64 3 4676620
W: www.mcglashan.school.nz

KRISTIN SCHOOL

360 Albany Highway, Albany, Auckland 0632
DP Coordinator Mrs Debbie Dwyer
MYP Coordinator Mr John Osborne
PYP Coordinator Mr Rob Hutton
Languages English
T: +64 9 415 9566
E: admissions@kristin.school.nz
W: www.kristin.school.nz

See full details on page 374

Milford School

34 Shakespeare Road, Milford, Auckland 0620
PYP Coordinator Sara Baker
Languages English
T: +64 9 489 7216
W: www.milford.school.nz

Mt Pleasant Primary School

82 Major Hornbrook Road, Mt Pleasant, Christchurch 8081
PYP Coordinator Maria Arneil
Languages English
T: +64 03 384 3994
W: www.mtpleasant.school.nz

Queen Margaret College

53 Hobson Street, PO Box 12274, Thorndon, Wellington 6011
DP Coordinator Holly Payne
MYP Coordinator Camille Le Prou
PYP Coordinator Jan Treeby
Languages English
T: +64 4 473 7160
W: www.qmc.school.nz

RANGITOTO COLLEGE

564 East Coast Road, Mairangi Bay, Auckland 0753
DP Coordinator Catherine Brandt
Languages English
T: +64 9 477 0150
E: info@rangitoto.school.nz
W: www.rangitoto.school.nz

See full details on page 402

SAINT KENTIGERN COLLEGE

130 Pakuranga Road, Pakuranga, Auckland 1021
DP Coordinator Suzie Tornquist
Languages English
T: +64 9 577 0749
E: skc_admissions@saintkentigern.com
W: www.saintkentigern.com

See full details on page 408

SCOTS COLLEGE

PO Box 15064, Strathmore, Wellington 6243
DP Coordinator Mr Mike McKnight
MYP Coordinator Ms Kate Bondett
PYP Coordinator Rosie Roland
Languages English
T: +64 4 388 0850
E: enrolments@scotscollege.school.nz
W: www.scotscollege.school.nz

See full details on page 412

Selwyn House School

PO Box 25049, 122 Merivale Lane, Christchurch 8014
PYP Coordinator Gregory Pearce
Languages English
T: +64 3 3557299
W: www.selwynhouse.school.nz

St Cuthbert's College

122 Market Road, Epsom, Auckland 1051
DP Coordinator Buino Vink
Languages English
T: +64 9 520 4159
W: www.stcuthberts.school.nz

ST MARGARET'S COLLEGE

12 Winchester Street, Merivale, Christchurch 8014
DP Coordinator Ms Beth Rowse
Languages English
T: +64 3 379 2000
E: enrol@stmargarets.school.nz
W: www.stmargarets.school.nz

See full details on page 422

St Mark's Church School

13 Dufferin Street, PO Box 7445, Wellington 6021
PYP Coordinator Angelee Jarrett
Languages English
T: +64 4 385 9489
W: www.st-marks.school.nz

St Peter's School, Cambridge

1716 Hamilton Road, Private Bag 884, Cambridge 3450
DP Coordinator Toni Foley
Languages English
T: +64 7 827 9899
W: www.stpeters.school.nz

IB ASIA-PACIFIC

Takapuna Grammar School

PO Box 33-1096, Takapuna, Auckland 0740
DP Coordinator Jack Chapman
Languages English
T: +64 94894167
W: www.takapuna.school.nz

Takapuna Normal Intermediate School

54B Taharoto Road, Takapuna, Auckland 1309
PYP Coordinator Alex Reynolds
Languages English
T: +64 9 489 3940
W: www.tnis.school.nz

Te Hihi School

767 Linwood Rd, Karaka, Auckland
PYP Coordinator Charlotte Stoppard
Languages English
T: +64 9 292 7706
W: www.tehihi.school.nz

Waiheke Primary School

26 Seaview Road, Waiheke Island, Ostend 1971
PYP Coordinator Kate Ernst
Languages English
T: +64 9 372 2006
W: www.waiheke.school.nz

Port Moresby International School

PO Box 276, Boroko
DP Coordinator Ronan Moore
Languages English
T: +675 325 6690
W: ieapng.net

Brent International School – Baguio

Brent Road, Baguio City 2600
DP Coordinator Paul Engler
Languages English
T: +63 74 442 2260
W: www.brentbaguio.edu.ph

Brent International School – Manila

Brentville Subdivision, Mamplasan, Biñan, Laguna 4024
DP Coordinator Maria Cristina Pozon
Languages English
T: +63 2 6001 0300/9
W: www.brent.edu.ph

Brent International School Subic

Building 6601 Binictican Drive, Subic Bay Freeport Zone, Zambales, Subic 2222
DP Coordinator Sheila Marie Griarte
Languages English
T: +63 47 252 6871/72
W: www.brentsubic.edu.ph

British School Manila

36th Street, University Park, Bonifacio Global City, Taguig City, Makati, Metro Manila 1634
DP Coordinator Mathilde Mouquet
Languages English
T: +63 2 8860 4800
W: www.britishschoolmanila.org

Cebu International School

PO Box 735, Pit-os, Talamban, Cebu City 6000
DP Coordinator Emily Cornet
MYP Coordinator Jonathan Denton
PYP Coordinator Maureen Juanson
Languages English
T: +63 32 401 1900/1/2/3
W: www.cis.edu.ph

Chiang Kai Shek College

1274 Padre Algue Street, Tondo, Manila
DP Coordinator Jon Aldrin Antonio
Languages English, Pilipino
T: +63 2 252 6161
W: www.cksc.edu.ph

Chinese International School Manila

Upper McKinley Road, McKinley Hill, Fort Bonifacio, Taguig City 1634
DP Coordinator Pierre Jasper Bacolod
Languages English
T: +63 (2) 815 2476
W: www.cismanila.org

Domuschola International School

Dormitory 1, Philsports Complex, Molave Street, Ugong, Pasig City
DP Coordinator Mark Angilo Alceso
PYP Coordinator Ginalyn Delizo
Languages English, Filipino
T: +63 2 6359743
W: www.dis.edu.ph

German European School Manila

75 Swaziland Street, Better Living Subdivision, Paranaque City 1711
CP Coordinator Santanu Bhowmik
DP Coordinator Santanu Bhowmik
PYP Coordinator Viola Buck
Languages English
T: +63 2 776 1000
W: www.gesm.org

Hope Christian High School

1242 Benavidez Street, Tondo, Manila, Metro Manila 1008
PYP Coordinator Jan Laurice Ong
Languages English, Chinese
T: +63 2 5310 8071
W: www.hchs.edu.ph

Immaculate Conception Academy

10 Grant St., Greenhills, San Juan, Metro Manila
DP Coordinator Paula Mae Mendoza
Languages English, Tagalog
T: +63 (02) 723 7041
W: www.icagh.edu.ph

International School Manila

University Parkway, Fort Bonifacio Global City, Taguig City 1634
DP Coordinator Andrea Thompson
Languages English
T: +63 2 840 8400
W: www.ismanila.org

Keys School Manila

951 Luna Mencias St., corner Araullo St., Mandaluyong City 1550
DP Coordinator Sandra Teresita Adriano
Languages English
T: +63 9175823909
w: www.ksm.ph

Noblesse International School

Circumferential Roas, Friendship Highway, Barangay CutCut, Angeles City, Pampanga 2009
DP Coordinator Vladimir Sousek Medrano
PYP Coordinator James McKone
Languages English
T: +63 (45) 459 9000
W: www.nis.com.ph

Saint Jude Catholic School

327 Ycaza Street, San Miguel, Manila 1005
DP Coordinator Genalyn Alfonso
Languages English
T: +63 (2) 735 6386
W: www.sjcs.edu.ph

Singapore School Cebu

Zuellig Avenue, North Reclamation Area, Mandaue City, Cebu 6014
DP Coordinator Barbara Magallona
Languages Chinese, English
T: +63 (32) 2365 772
W: www.singaporeschoolcebu.com

Singapore School Manila

Lots 1 & 40, Block 2 East Street, East District, Asena City, Paranaque
DP Coordinator Denise Villegas
Languages English
T: +63 27 500 4672
W: www.singaporeschoolmanila.com.ph

Southville International School & Colleges

1281 Tropical Avenue Corner, Luxembourg Street, BF Homes International, Las Pinas City 1740
DP Coordinator Armie Ababa
Languages English
T: +63 28 825 0766
W: www.southville.edu.ph

The Beacon Academy

Cecilia Araneta Parkway, Biñan, Laguna 4024
DP Coordinator Iris Morga
MYP Coordinator Roy Aldrin Villegas
Languages English
T: +632 425 1326
W: www.beaconacademy.ph

The Beacon School

PCPD Building, 2332 Chino Roces Avenue Extension, Taguig City 1630
MYP Coordinator Erica Gancayco
PYP Coordinator DJ Leonardia
Languages English
T: +632 840 5040 LOC 105
W: www.beaconschool.ph

Victory Christian International School

339 Robinson Circle, Capt. Henry Javier Drive, Oranbo, Pasig City 1600
DP Coordinator Joanne Miranda
Languages English
T: +63 28 671 8505
W: www.vcis.edu.ph

Xavier School

64 Xavier Street, Greenhills West, San Juan City, Metro Manila 1500
DP Coordinator Michael Ryan Bulosan
Languages English
T: +63 2 8 723 0481
W: www.xs.edu.ph

BRANKSOME HALL ASIA

234 Global edu-ro, Daejeong-eup, Seogwipo-si, Jeju-do 63644
DP Coordinator Ms. Cheryl Osborne
MYP Coordinator Dr. Paula Swartz
PYP Coordinator Ms. Jennifer Kesler
Languages English
T: +82 64 902 5000
E: admissions@branksome.asia
W: www.branksome.asia

See full details on page 315

IB ASIA-PACIFIC

British International Academy

24, Deokpo 3-gil, Geoje 53213
DP Coordinator Angela Walker
MYP Coordinator Tara Dhital
PYP Coordinator Tara Dhital
Languages English
T: +82 055 688 5154
W: www.biakorea.org

CHADWICK INTERNATIONAL

45, Art center-daero 97 beon-gil, Yeonsu-gu, Incheon 22002
CP Coordinator Jason Reagin
DP Coordinator Richard Kent
MYP Coordinator Emily Thomas
PYP Coordinator Pamela Castillo (Lower Primary) & Nancy Macharia (Upper Primary)
Languages English
T: +82 32 250 5000
E: songdo-admissions@chadwickschool.org
W: www.chadwickinternational.org
See full details on page 317

Chung Nam Samsung Academy

77 Samseong-ro, Tangjeong-myeon, Asan-si, Chungcheongnam-do
DP Coordinator Nikki Birdsall
Languages English, Korean
T: +82 41 339 3000
W: www.cnsa.hs.kr/hpwEng

Daegu Samyoung Elementary School

Naegok-ro 63, Sasu-dong Buk-gu, Daegu
PYP Coordinator Won Ho Cho
Languages English, Korean
T: +82 53 233 4950
W: www.ensamyoung.com

Dulwich College Seoul

6 Sinbanpo-ro 15-gil, Seocho-gu, Seoul 06504
DP Coordinator Rebecca Gardner
Languages English
T: +82 23 015 8505
W: seoul.dulwich.org

Dwight School Seoul

21 World Cup Buk-ro 62-gil, Mapo-gu, Seoul 03919
DP Coordinator Samuel Peyton
MYP Coordinator Cameron Forbes
PYP Coordinator Beth Overby
Languages English
T: +82 2 6920 8600
W: www.dwight.or.kr

Gyeonggi Academy of Foreign Languages

30, Gosan-ro 105 Beon-gil, Uiwang-si, Gyeonggi-do 16075
DP Coordinator Robin Ibbotson
Languages English
T: +82 (0)31 361 0500
W: www.gafl.hs.kr

Gyeonggi Suwon International School

451 YeongTong-Ro, YeongTong-Gu, Suwon City, Gyeonggi-Do 16706
DP Coordinator Hoin Kim
MYP Coordinator Nishtha Daniel
PYP Coordinator Jabbie Rosario
Languages English
T: +82 31 695 2800
W: www.gsis.sc.kr

Gyeongnam International Foreign School

49-22, Jodong-gil, Sanam-myeon, Sacheon-si, Gyeongnam 52533
DP Coordinator Samuel Kuntz
PYP Coordinator Timothy Balaz
Languages English
T: +82 (0)55 853 5125
W: www.gifs.or.kr

International School of Busan

50 Gijang-daero, Gijang-eup, Gijang-gun, Busan 46081
DP Coordinator Merriss Shenstone
MYP Coordinator Jennifer Montague
PYP Coordinator Michelle Roland
Languages English
T: +82 51 742 3332
W: www.bifskorea.org

Korea Foreign School

7-16, Nambusunhwan-ro 364-gil, Seocho-gu, Seoul 06739
MYP Coordinator Hanna Jang
PYP Coordinator Steven Taylor
Languages English
T: +82 2 571 2917/18
W: koreaforeign.org

Kyungpook National University Elementary School

2150 Dalgubeol-daero, Jung-gu, Daegu, North Gyeongsang 41959
PYP Coordinator Yun sung Choe
Languages English, Korean
T: +82 53 232 5804
W: www.ksadae.es.kr/index.do

Kyungpook National University High School

2178 Dalgubeol-daero, Jung-gu, Daegu, North Gyeongsang 41950
DP Coordinator Unah Lyu
Languages English, Korean
T: +82 53 231 9410
W: www.knu.hs.kr/index.do

Kyungpook National University Middle School

2178 Dalgubeol-daero, Jung-gu, Daegu, North Gyeongsang 41950
MYP Coordinator Eunyoung Kim
Languages English, Korean
T: +82 53 232 8234
W: ivy.knu.ac.kr/index.do

Namsan International Kindergarten

8-6, Dasan-ro 8-gil,, Jung-Gu, Seoul 04597
PYP Coordinator Cathy Brown
Languages English
T: +82 2 2232 2451
W: www.nikseoul.org

NORTH LONDON COLLEGIATE SCHOOL JEJU

33, Global edu-ro 145beon-gil, Daejeong-eup, Seogwipo-si, Jeju-do 63644
DP Coordinator Ms Justine Oliver
Languages English
T: +82 64 793 8001
E: admissions@nlcsjeju.kr
W: www.nlcsjeju.co.kr
See full details on page 391

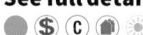

Posan High School

556-13 Biseul-ro, Hyeonpung-eup, Dalseong-gun, Daegu, North Gyeongsang 43005
DP Coordinator Sangwook Park
Languages English, Korean
T: +82 53 231 5300
W: www.posan.hs.kr/index.do

Pyoseon High School

22-15 Pyoseonjungang-ro, Pyoseon-myeon, Seogwipo-si, Jeju-do 63629
DP Coordinator JaeYoung Lee
Languages Korean
T: +82 64 786 5560
W: jjps.jje.hs.kr

SEOUL FOREIGN SCHOOL

39 Yeonhui-ro 22-gil, Seodaemun-gu, Seoul 03723
DP Coordinator Piotr Kocyk
MYP Coordinator Chris Horan
PYP Coordinator Michael Lucchesi
Languages English
T: +82 2 330 3100
E: admissions@seoulforeign.org
W: www.seoulforeign.org
See full details on page 415

Taegu Foreign Language High School

21 Seonwon-ro 11-gil, (1675 Sindang-dong), Dalseo-gu, Daegu, North Gyeongsang 42603
DP Coordinator Soojin Baek
Languages English, Korean
T: +82 53 231 7777
W: www.taegu-fh.hs.kr/index.do

Taejon Christian International School

77 Yongsan 2 Ro, Yuseong Gu, Daejeon 305-500
DP Coordinator Andy Hay
MYP Coordinator Jonathan Hayhoe
PYP Coordinator Jodi Deuth
Languages English
T: +82 42 620 9000
W: www.tcis.or.kr

ACS (International), Singapore

61 Jalan Hitam Manis, Singapore 278475
DP Coordinator Carol Ling
Languages English
T: +658 6472 1477
W: www.acsinternational.com.sg

Anglo-Chinese School (Independent)

121 Dover Road, Singapore 139650
DP Coordinator Siew Hwa Chock
Languages English
T: +65 6773 1633
W: www.acs.sch.edu.sg/acs_indep

Ascensia International School

Blk 106A Henderson Crescent, #01-01 Henderson Area Office, Singapore 151106
PYP Coordinator Wai Kong Wong
Languages English
T: +65 6466 5505
W: www.aais.edu.sg

Australian International School, Singapore

1 Lorong Chuan 556818
DP Coordinator Adriaan Van Wijk
PYP Coordinator Kerryl Howarth
Languages English
T: +65 6653 7906
W: www.ais.com.sg

Barker Road Methodist Church Kindergarten

70 Barker Road, Singapore 309936
PYP Coordinator Linda Tay
Languages English, Chinese
T: +65 6255 8430
W: www.brmck.edu.sg

Canadian International School, Lakeside Campus

7 Jurong West Street 41, Singapore 659414
DP Coordinator Elsa Baptista
MYP Coordinator Victor De Melo
PYP Coordinator Simone Lieschke
Languages English
T: +65 6743 8088
W: www.cis.edu.sg

Canadian International School, Tanjong Katong Campus

371 Tanjong Katong Road, Singapore 437128
PYP Coordinator Na Gao
Languages English
T: +65 6345 1573
W: www.cis.edu.sg

CHATSWORTH INTERNATIONAL SCHOOL

72 Bukit Tinggi Road, Singapore 289760
DP Coordinator Iain Hudson
MYP Coordinator Phavana Silva
PYP Coordinator Eleri Connor
Languages English
T: +65 6463 3201
E: admissions.bt@chatsworth.com.sg
W: www.chatsworth.com.sg

See full details on page 318

DOVER COURT INTERNATIONAL SCHOOL SINGAPORE

301 Dover Road, Singapore 139644
DP Coordinator Mr. Dominic O'Shea
Languages English
T: +65 6775 7664
E: admissions@dovercourt.edu.sg
W: www.dovercourt.edu.sg

See full details on page 321

DULWICH COLLEGE (SINGAPORE)

71 Bukit Batok West Avenue 8, Singapore 658966
DP Coordinator Ms. Lisa Nevers
Languages English
T: +65 6890 1003
E: admissions.singapore@dulwich.org
W: singapore.dulwich.org

See full details on page 322

EtonHouse International School, Broadrick

51 Broadrick Road, Singapore 439501
PYP Coordinator Mr Peter Dart
Languages English
T: +65 6346 6922
W: www.etonhouse.edu.sg/school/broadrick

EtonHouse International School, Mountbatten 718

718 Mountbatten Road, Singapore 437738
PYP Coordinator Neha Kaprani
Languages English
T: +65 6846 3322
W: www.etonhouse.edu.sg/school/mountbatten718

EtonHouse International School, Newton

39 Newton Road, Singapore 307966
PYP Coordinator Asmita Sharma
Languages English
T: +65 6352 3322
W: www.etonhouse.edu.sg/school/newton

EtonHouse International School, Orchard

10 Tanglin Road, Singapore 247908
DP Coordinator Sylvie Edwards
PYP Coordinator Greg Hattle
Languages English, Spanish
T: +65 6513 1155
W: www.etonhouse.edu.sg/school/orchard

Etonhouse International School, Thomson

8 Thomson Lane, (5 mins from Newton/Novena & 10 mins from Orchard), Singapore 297743
PYP Coordinator Mike Carrigan
Languages English, Mandarin
T: +65 6252 3322
W: www.etonhouse.edu.sg/school/thomson

GESS International School

2 Dairy Farm Lane, Singapore 677621
DP Coordinator Joanna Fitts
MYP Coordinator Rebecca Scrivener
PYP Coordinator Kristyn Holland
Languages English, German
T: +65 6461 0881
W: www.gess.sg

Global Indian International School (GIIS) East Coast Campus

82 Cheviot Hill, Singapore 459663
PYP Coordinator Odaia Ranido
Languages English
T: +65 6914 7100
W: singapore.globalindianschool.org

GLOBAL INDIAN INTERNATIONAL SCHOOL (GIIS) SMART CAMPUS

27 Punggol Field Walk, Singapore 828649
DP Coordinator Deepa Chandrasekaran
PYP Coordinator Manju Nair
Languages English
T: +65 6914 7100
W: singapore.globalindianschool.org
See full details on page 349

Hillside World Academy

11 Hillside Drive 548926
DP Coordinator Xiaoxia Huang
MYP Coordinator Josephine Fong
PYP Coordinator Winnie Tan
Languages English, Chinese
T: +65 6254 0200
W: www.hwa.edu.sg

Hwa Chong International School

663 Bukit Timah Road, Singapore 269783
DP Coordinator Archana Vijaykumar Kusurkar
Languages English
T: +65 6464 7077
W: www.hcis.edu.sg

ISS International School

21 Preston Road 109355
DP Coordinator Mr Christopher Garden
MYP Coordinator Dr Dharshini Jeremiah
PYP Coordinator Ms Ariana Rehu
Languages English
T: +65 6475 4188
W: www.iss.edu.sg

Madrasah Aljunied Al-Islamiah

30 Victoria Lane, Singapore 198424
DP Coordinator Khalidah Abdullah
Languages English, Malay
T: +65 6391 5970/1
W: www.aljunied.edu.sg

NEXUS INTERNATIONAL SCHOOL (SINGAPORE)

1 Aljunied Walk, Singapore 387293
DP Coordinator Vicky Holdcroft
PYP Coordinator Paul Rimmer
Languages English
T: +65 6536 6566
E: enquiries@nexus.edu.sg
W: www.nexus.edu.sg

See full details on page 386

North London Collegiate School Singapore

130 Depot Road, Singapore 109708
DP Coordinator Emma Graham
Languages English
T: +65 6989 3000
W: nlcssingapore.sg

NPS INTERNATIONAL SCHOOL

10-12 Chai Chee Lane, Singapore 469021
DP Coordinator Sushmita Chatterjee
Languages English
T: +65 62942400
E: headofschool@npsis.edu.sg
W: www.npsinternational.edu.sg

See full details on page 392

Odyssey The Global Preschool – Fourth Avenue

20 Fourth Avenue 268669
PYP Coordinator Melise Wang
Languages English, Chinese
T: +65 6781 8800
W: www.theodyssey.sg

Odyssey The Global Preschool – Wilkinson

101 Wilkinson Road 436559
PYP Coordinator Alice Alagan
Languages English, Chinese
T: +65 6781 8800
W: www.theodyssey.sg

ONE WORLD INTERNATIONAL SCHOOL

21 Jurong West Street 81, Singapore 649075
DP Coordinator Thomas Croft
PYP Coordinator Rashmi Tourani
Languages English
T: +65 69146700
E: admissions@owis.org
W: www.owis.org

See full details on page 393

Overseas Family School

25F Paterson Road, Singapore 238515
DP Coordinator Phil Riordan
MYP Coordinator Nathalie Buckland-Brough
Languages English
T: +65 6 738 0211
W: www.ofs.edu.sg

School of the Arts, Singapore

1 Zubir Said Drive, Administration Office #05-01, Singapore 227968
CP Coordinator Cheryl Lim
DP Coordinator Ronald Lim
Languages English
T: +65 63389663
W: www.sota.edu.sg

Singapore Sports School

1 Champions Way, Woodlands 737913
DP Coordinator Han Yong Lim
Languages English
T: +65 6766 0100
W: www.sportsschool.edu.sg

St Francis Methodist School

492 Upper Bukit Timah Road 678095
DP Coordinator Choon Lee Chong
Languages English
T: +65 6760 0889
W: www.sfms.edu.sg

St. Joseph's Institution

21 Bishan Street 14, Singapore 579781
DP Coordinator Woh Un Tang
Languages English
T: +65 62500022
W: www.sji.edu.sg

SINGAPORE

ST. JOSEPH'S INSTITUTION INTERNATIONAL

490 Thomson Road, Singapore 298191
DP Coordinator Guy Bromley
Languages English
T: +65 6353 9383
E: admissions.hs@sji-international.com.sg
W: www.sji-international.com.sg
See full details on page 423

Stamford American International School

1 Woodleigh Lane 357684
DP Coordinator Amit Khanna
MYP Coordinator Rhonda Weins & Natalie Martin
PYP Coordinator Michael Hughes
Languages English
T: +65 6653 7907
W: www.sais.edu.sg

TANGLIN TRUST SCHOOL, SINGAPORE

95 Portsdown Road 139299
DP Coordinator Joseph Loader
Languages English
T: +65 67780771
E: admissions@tts.edu.sg
W: www.tts.edu.sg
See full details on page 428

The Little Skool-House International (By-the-Vista)

170 Ghim Moh Road, Ulu Pandan Community Club, #03-01, Singapore 279621
PYP Coordinator Nurazura Binte Mohamed Amran
Languages English
T: +65 6468 3725
W: www.littleskoolhouse.com

UWC South East Asia, Dover Campus

1207 Dover Road 139654
DP Coordinator Jensen Hjorth
Languages English
T: +65 6775 5344
W: www.uwcsea.edu.sg

UWC South East Asia, East Campus

1 Tampines Street 73 528704
DP Coordinator Gemma Elford Dawson
Languages English
T: +65 63055344
W: www.uwcsea.edu.sg

XCL World Academy

2 Yishun Street 42, Singapore 768039
CP Coordinator Michael Fletcher
DP Coordinator Michael Fletcher
MYP Coordinator Kylie Begg
PYP Coordinator Tylene Desfosses
Languages English
T: +65 6871 8835
W: www.xwa.edu.sg

SOLOMON ISLANDS

Woodford International School

Prince Philip Highway, P.O. Box R44, Kukum, Honiara
PYP Coordinator Vivienne Wallace
Languages English
T: +677 30186
W: www.wis.edu.sb

SRI LANKA

THE OVERSEAS SCHOOL OF COLOMBO

PO Box 9, Pelawatte, Battaramulla 10120
DP Coordinator William Duncan
MYP Coordinator Jacob Eagle
PYP Coordinator Samantha Wood
Languages English
T: +94 11 2784 920-2
E: admissions@osc.lk
W: www.osc.lk
See full details on page 433

TAIWAN

Dah Yung Kao Mei Preschool

No. 267 Cuihua Road, Gushan District, Kaohsiung City 80449
PYP Coordinator Ching I Yang
Languages English, Chinese
T: +886 7 533 6746

Dayuan International Senior High School

No. 8, Section 2, Dacheng Road, Dayuan District, Taoyuan City 337
DP Coordinator Chingyu Tsai
Languages English, Chinese
T: +886 3 381 3001
W: www.dysh.tyc.edu.tw

I-Shou International School

No 6, Sec 1, Xuecheng Rd., Dashu Dist., Kaohsiung City 84048
DP Coordinator Dan William Powell
MYP Coordinator William Tolley
PYP Coordinator Yu-Ya Kung
Languages English, Chinese
T: +886 7 657 7115
W: www.iis.kh.edu.tw

Kang Chiao International School (Taipei Campus)

No. 800, Huacheng Road, Xindian District, New Taipei City 23153
DP Coordinator Steven Bates
MYP Coordinator Joseph Sun
Languages Chinese, English
T: +886 2 8665 2070
W: www.kcis.com.tw

Kaohsiung American School

889 Cueihua Road, Zuoying District, Kaohsiung City 81354
DP Coordinator Sara Brodhead
MYP Coordinator Sara Brodhead
Languages English
T: +886 7 586 3300
W: www.kas.tw

Mingdao High School

497, Sec. 1, Zhongshan Rd., Wuri Dist., Taichung City 41401
DP Coordinator Alexandra Lopez
MYP Coordinator Feon Chau
Languages English
T: +886 4 23372101
W: mdhs-id.online

Starlight International Kindergarten

No.569, Sec. 7, Fengyuan Blvd., Shengang District, Taichung 42945
PYP Coordinator Eric Chang
Languages English, Chinese

Starlight International Kindergarten – Hui Wen Campus

No. 8, Sec. 1, Huilai Road, Nantun District, Taichung
PYP Coordinator Yung-I Fu
Languages English, Chinese
T: +886 4 2251 4007

Taipei American School

800 Chung Shan North Road, Sec 6, Taipei
DP Coordinator Warren Emanuel
Languages English
T: +886 22 873 9900
W: www.tas.edu.tw

Taipei European School

Swire European Campus, 31 Jian Ye Road, Yang Ming Shan, Shihlin, Taipei 11193
DP Coordinator Ian Stewart
Languages English
T: +886 2 8145 9007
W: www.taipeieuropeanschool.com

TAIPEI KUEI SHAN SCHOOL

200 Mingde Road, Taipei 11280
DP Coordinator Robert Chung
MYP Coordinator Caleb Lin
PYP Coordinator Elizabeth Hu
Languages Chinese, English
T: +886 2 2821 2009
E: info@kss.tp.edu.tw
W: www.kshs.tp.edu.tw
See full details on page 427

Taipei Municipal Xisong High School

No.7 Lane 325 Jian Kang Road, Taipei
DP Coordinator Hyeseong Ahn
Languages English, Chinese
T: +886 2 25286618
W: www.hssh.tp.edu.tw

Victoria Academy

1110 Jhen-Nan Rd., Douliu, Yun-Lin 640
DP Coordinator Nerissa Puntawe
Languages Chinese, English
T: +886 5 5378899 (Ext:22)
W: www.victoria.ylc.edu.tw

THAILAND

American Pacific International School

158/1 Moo 3, Hangdong-Samoeng Road, Banpong, Hangdong, Chiang Mai 50230
DP Coordinator Brian Beck
MYP Coordinator John Salgado
PYP Coordinator Erika Vargas
Languages English
T: +66 53 365 303/5
W: www.apis.ac.th

Ascot International School

80/82 Ramkhamhaeng Soi 118, Sapansung, Bangkok 10240
DP Coordinator Mark Allen
PYP Coordinator Karel Linden
Languages English
T: +66 2 373 4400
W: www.ascot.ac.th

Bangkok Patana School

643 La Salle Road, Sukhumvit 105, Bangkok 10260
DP Coordinator Susan Brosnahan
Languages English
T: +66 2 785 2200
W: www.patana.ac.th

British International School, Phuket

59 Moo 2, Thepkrasattri Road, T. Koh Kaew, A. Muang, Phuket 83000
DP Coordinator Jason Perkins
Languages English
T: +66 (0) 76 335 555
W: www.bisphuket.ac.th

Canadian International School of Thailand

1001 Charan Sanitwong 46, Bangyeekhan, Bang Phlat, Bangkok 10700
MYP Coordinator Cade Sommerville
PYP Coordinator Rhonda Anderson
Languages English, Thai
T: +66 02 886 9464
W: www.canadianschool.com

Concordian International School

918 Moo 8, Bangna-Trad Highway Km 7, Bangkaew, Bangplee Samutprakarn 10540
DP Coordinator Markus Mattila
MYP Coordinator Rachel Samson
PYP Coordinator Ariel Wang
Languages English
T: +66 2 706 9000
W: www.concordian.ac.th

D-PREP International School

38, 38/1-3, 39, Moo 6, Bangna Trad Rd., Km. 8, Bang Kaeo, Bang Phli District, Samut Prakan 1054
PYP Coordinator Maricar Dorego
Languages English, Thai
T: +66 95 879 4944
W: www.dprep.ac.th

Garden International School (Rayong Campus)

188/24 Moo 4, Pala-Ban Chang Road, Tambol Pala, Ban Chang, Rayong 21130
DP Coordinator Lauren Hucknall
Languages English
T: +66 3803 0808
W: www.gardenrayong.com

Hua Hin International School

549 Moo 7, Hin Lek Fai, Hua Hin, Prachuap Khiri Khan 77110
DP Coordinator David Coulson
Languages English, Thai
T: +66 32 900 632
W: www.huahinschool.com

INTERNATIONAL SCHOOL BANGKOK

39/7 Soi Nichada Thani, Samakee Road, Pakkret, Nonthaburi 11120
DP Coordinator Justyna McMillan
Languages English
T: +66 2 963 5800
E: admissions@isb.ac.th
W: www.isb.ac.th

See full details on page 361

International School Eastern Seaboard

282 Moo 5 T. Bowin, SriRacha, Chonburi 20230
DP Coordinator Richard Kennedy
Languages English
T: +66 38 372 591
W: www.ise.ac.th

KIS INTERNATIONAL SCHOOL

999/123-124 Pracha Utit Road, Samsennok, Huay Kwang, Bangkok 10310
DP Coordinator Daniel Trump
MYP Coordinator Alison Ya-Wen Yang
PYP Coordinator Tania Mansfield
Languages English
T: +66 (0)2 2743444
E: admissions@kis.ac.th
W: www.kis.ac.th

See full details on page 372

Magic Years International School

22/122, Moo 3, Soi Prasoet Islam, Bang Talat, Pakkret, Nonthaburri 11120
PYP Coordinator Tahireh Thampi
Languages English
T: +66 2156 6222
W: www.magicyears.ac.th

NIST INTERNATIONAL SCHOOL

36 Sukhumvit Soi 15, Wattana, Bangkok 10110
DP Coordinator Robin Wilensky
MYP Coordinator Jacqueline Arce
PYP Coordinator Bryony Maxted-Miller
Languages English
T: +66 2 017 5888
E: admissions@nist.ac.th
W: www.nist.ac.th

See full details on page 388

Pan-Asia International School

100 Moo 3, Charaemprakiat, Rama 9 St, Soi 67, Kwang Dokmai Prawet District, Bangkok 10250
DP Coordinator Amani Naiem Ahmad Saleh
MYP Coordinator Robert Swartz
Languages English
T: +66 2 726 6273-4
W: www.pais.ac.th

Panyaden International School

218 Moo 2, T.Namprae, A.Hang Dong, Chiang Mai 50230
DP Coordinator Charles Tetreault
Languages English
T: +66 80 078 5115
W: www.panyaden.ac.th

Prem Tinsulanonda International School

234 Moo 3, Huay Sai, Mae Rim, Chiang Mai 50180
CP Coordinator Lisa Murphy
DP Coordinator Joe Holroyd
MYP Coordinator Sarah Porter
PYP Coordinator Mary Ann Van De Weerd
Languages English
T: +66 53 301 500
W: www.ptis.ac.th

REGENTS INTERNATIONAL SCHOOL PATTAYA

33/3 Moo 1, Pong, Banglamung, Chonburi 20150
DP Coordinator Sara Morrow
Languages English
T: +66 (0)93 135 7736
E: admissions@regents-pattaya.co.th
W: www.nordangliaeducation.com/our-schools/pattaya

See full details on page 404

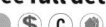

RUAMRUDEE INTERNATIONAL SCHOOL

6 Ramkhamhaeng 184, Minburi, Bangkok 10510
DP Coordinator Ms. Nicole Sabet
Languages English
T: +66 (0)2 791 8900
E: admissions@rism.ac.th
W: www.rism.ac.th

See full details on page 407

Satit Bilingual School of Rangsit University

52/347 Muang Ake, Phahonyothin Road., Lak Hok, Mueang, Pathum Thani 12000
PYP Coordinator Babita Seth
Languages English
T: +66 2 792 7500 4
W: bkk.sbs.ac.th

Singapore International School of Bangkok

Pracha Utit Campus, 498/11 Soi Ramkhamhaeng 39 (Tepleela 1), Wangthonglang, Bangkok 10310
DP Coordinator Jason Tee Hong Wei
Languages English, Chinese, Thai
T: +66 2 158 9191
W: www.sisb.ac.th

ST ANDREWS INTERNATIONAL SCHOOL BANGKOK

1020 Sukhumvit Road, Phra Khanong, Khlong Toei, Bangkok 10110
DP Coordinator Mr. William Taylor
Languages English
T: +662 056 9555
E: officehs@standrews.ac.th
W: www.standrews.ac.th

See full details on page 421

St Andrews International School, Green Valley Campus

Moo 7, Ban Chang-Makham Koo Road, Ban Chang, Rayong 21130
DP Coordinator Andrew Emery
PYP Coordinator Faye Wood
Languages English
T: +66 38 030611
W: www.standrewsgreenvalley.com

St Andrews International School, Sukhumvit Campus

7 Sukhumvit 107 Road, Bangna, Bangkok 10260
CP Coordinator Thea Wilson
DP Coordinator Thea Wilson
PYP Coordinator Charlotte Brown
Languages English
T: +66 (0)2393 3883
W: www.standrewssukhumvit.com

The Regent's School, Bangkok

601/99 Pracha-Uthit Road, Wangthonglang, Bangkok 10310
DP Coordinator Alan Perkins
Languages English
T: +66 (0)2 957 5777
W: www.regents.ac.th

Udon Thani International School (UDIS)

222/2 Moo. 2 Mittrapab Road, Tumbonkudsra, Aumpearmuang, Udon Thani 41000
PYP Coordinator Emaretta Hines
Languages English
T: +66 (0)42 110 379
W: www.udoninternationalschool.com

UWC Thailand International School

115/15 Moo 7 Thepkasattri Road, Thepkasattri, Thalang, Phuket 83110
DP Coordinator Katharine Feather
MYP Coordinator Remke Langendonck
PYP Coordinator Jen Friske
Languages English
T: +66 76 336 076
W: uwcthailand.ac.th

Wells International School – Bang Na Campus

10 Srinakarin Soi 62, Nong Bon, Prawet, Bangkok 10250
PYP Coordinator Sunee Steyn
Languages English, Thai
T: +66 02 746 6060 1
W: www.wells-school.com

IB ASIA-PACIFIC

Wells International School – On Nut Campus

2209 Sukhumvit Road, Bangchak, Prakanong, Bangkok 10260
DP Coordinator Katherine Caouette
Languages English
T: +66 097 920 8511
W: www.wells-school.com

VIETNAM

American International School of Vietnam

220 Nguyen Van Tao, Nha Be District, Ho Chi Minh City
DP Coordinator Chandra McGowan
PYP Coordinator Karin Tellis
Languages English
T: +84 28378 00808
W: www.ais.edu.vn

AUSTRALIAN INTERNATIONAL SCHOOL (AIS)

264 Mai Chi Tho Street, An Phu ward, Thu Duc City, Ho Chi Minh City
DP Coordinator Gabriel Price
PYP Coordinator Leanne Raeside
Languages English
T: +84 28 3742 4040
E: info@aisvietnam.com
W: www.aisvietnam.com

See full details on page 314

British International School, Hanoi

Hoa Lan Road, Vinhomes Riverside, Long Bien District, Hanoi 100000
DP Coordinator Gemma Archer
Languages English
T: +84 24 3946 0435
W: www.bishanoi.com

British International School, Ho Chi Minh City

246 Nguyen Van Huong Street, Thao Dien, Thu Duc City, Ho Chi Minh City
DP Coordinator Daphnee Deleporte
Languages English
T: +84 (0)28 3744 2335
W: www.bisvietnam.com

Canadian International School – Vietnam

No. 86, Road 23, Phu My Hung, Tan Phu Ward, District 7, Binh Chanh District, Ho Chi Minh City
DP Coordinator Nur Karadayi
Languages English
T: +84 94 295 8557
W: www.cis.edu.vn

EUROPEAN INTERNATIONAL SCHOOL HCMC

730 Le Van Mien Street, Thao Dien Ward, Thu Duc City, Ho Chi Minh City 70000
DP Coordinator Erin Tacey
MYP Coordinator Martin Grist
PYP Coordinator Colin Attwood
Languages English
T: +8428 7300 7257
E: info@eishcmc.com
W: www.eishcmc.com

See full details on page 348

Hanoi International School

48 Lieu Giai Street, Ba Dinh District, Hanoi
DP Coordinator Heather Anne Neill
MYP Coordinator Jeffrey Joseph Araula
PYP Coordinator Lara Johnston
Languages English
T: +84 4 3832 8140
W: www.hisvietnam.com

International German School HCMC

12 Vo Truong Toan, An Phu Ward, District 2, Ho Chi Minh City
DP Coordinator Franziska Barnickel
Languages English, German
T: +84 (0)28 37 44 63 44
W: igs-hcmc.org

INTERNATIONAL SCHOOL HO CHI MINH CITY (ISHCMC)

28 Vo Truong Toan St., An Phu ward, Thu Duc City, Ho Chi Minh City
DP Coordinator Ms. Laney Rweyemamu
MYP Coordinator Mr. Simon Scoones
PYP Coordinator Ms. Ishbel How & Mr. Daniel Barker
Languages English
T: +84 28 3898 9100
E: admissions@ishcmc.edu.vn
W: www.ishcmc.com

See full details on page 362

International School of Vietnam

No. 6-7 Nguyen Cong Thai Street, Dai Kim Urban area, Hoang Mai, Hanoi
DP Coordinator Gita Gemuts
PYP Coordinator Jason Barton
Languages English
T: +84 (0)435 409 183
W: www.isvietnam.edu.vn

International Schools of North America

Street 20, Him Lam Residential Area, Binh Chanh District, Ho Chi Minh City
DP Coordinator Lauralynn Stefureak
MYP Coordinator Patric Elder
Languages English
T: +84 28 730 197 99
W: sna.edu.vn

QSI INTERNATIONAL SCHOOL OF HAIPHONG

Lot CC2, Me Linh Village, Anh Dung Ward, Duong Kinh District, Haiphong
DP Coordinator Clarissa Sammons
Languages English
T: +84 31 381 4258
E: haiphong@qsi.org
W: haiphong.qsi.org

See full details on page 396

Renaissance International School Saigon

74 Nguyen Thi Thap Street, Binh Thuan Ward, District 7, Ho Chi Minh City
DP Coordinator Richard Fluit
Languages English
T: +84 283 7733 171
W: www.renaissance.edu.vn

Saigon South International School

78 Nguyen Duc Canh, Tan Phong Ward, District 7, Ho Chi Minh City 70000
DP Coordinator Cassandra Armstrong
Languages English
T: +84 28 5413 0901
W: www.ssis.edu.vn

United Nations International School of Hanoi

G9 Ciputra, Tay Ho, Hanoi
DP Coordinator Elliott Cannell
MYP Coordinator Daniel Cooper
PYP Coordinator Kay Strenio Anagnost
Languages English
T: +84 24 7300 4500
W: www.unishanoi.org

Vietnam-Finland International School

01, D1 Street, Tan Phong Ward, District 7, Ho Chi Minh City
DP Coordinator Catherine Symes-Matheus
Languages English, Vietnamese
T: +84 28 37 755 110
W: vfis.tdtu.edu.vn

International Schools of North America

WESTERN AUSTRALIAN PRIMARY AND HIGH SCHOOL

43 Nguyen Thong Street, Ward 7, District 3, Ho Chi Minh City
DP Coordinator Bao Tran
Languages English
T: +84 28 7109 5077
E: schooloffice@wass.edu.vn
W: www.wass.edu.vn/en

See full details on page 441

IB
AMERICAS

Atlanta International School

(Founded 1984)

Head of School
Kevin Glass

PYP coordinator
Leonie Ley-Mitchell

MYP coordinator
Carmen Samanes

DP coordinator
Adam Lapish

Status Private, Non-Profit

Boarding/day Day

Gender Coeducational

Language of instruction
English, Chinese, French,
German, Spanish

Authorised IB programmes
PYP, MYP, DP

Age Range 3 – 18 years

Number of pupils enrolled
1319

Address
2890 North Fulton Drive
Atlanta
GA 30305 | USA

TEL +1 404 841 3840

Email
admission@aischool.org

Website
www.aischool.org

Atlanta International School. Developing Courageous Leaders Who Shape Their World For The Better

Founded over thirty years ago by people who wanted a different sort of school in Atlanta, Atlanta International School offers a comprehensive and challenging International Baccalaureate (IB) curriculum from 3K to Grade 12, enhanced with a world-class language acquisition program.

At Atlanta International School (AIS) students are focused on developing the skills to creatively collaborate on the challenges of the future and are equipped to become changemakers.

Offering an authentic, nurturing, learning community, AIS values curiosity, empathy and a passion to create a world with environmental, economic and social well-being for everyone.

Faculty from around the world are focused on genuinely getting to know, value and nurture each and every student, and his or her unique skills and strengths. The result is a spirit of community and a celebration of the diversity of perspectives that come from students, families, faculty and staff representing 90 nationalities and over 65 languages.

A full immersion preschool program for children ages three and four is offered in German, French, Chinese and Spanish. From 5K through Grade 5, the inquiry-based IB curriculum is taught in two languages. All faculty are mother tongue speakers of the language they teach.

Students not only learn at least one other language, they learn through language, developing so much more than linguistic proficiency. At AIS students are taught to develop 'intercultural competence', the ability to easily navigate and flow between and among different nationalities and complex cultural situations – and to do so with tremendous empathy, diplomacy and tact.

Students entering Secondary School have varied language backgrounds and a wide range of options to develop their language proficiency, from beginner to taking both Language & Literature and Humanities courses at an advanced level, many choosing to pursue dual language IB Diplomas.

The curriculum is complemented by an extensive range of age-appropriate activities to enhance students' learning experiences beyond the classroom.

The athletics department is home to more than 40 teams pursuing 12 different sports. Theatrical and musical talent is showcased via regular performances alongside frequent art exhibitions.

In Secondary School, in addition to internships that students complete as part of a STEM or STEAM Diploma Endorsement, students participate in many other activities including service projects, Model United Nations, Mock Trial, the AIS Space Program, Robotics and educational international trips.

Parents, alumni, faculty, staff and students actively participate in the growth and sustainability of the school, with community firmly at the centre of all activities. The result is a pioneering and courageous spirit built upon local impact and global reach.

(Founded 1995)

Principal
Natasha Malachowski K.

PYP coordinator
Sandra Nicoli

MYP coordinator
Paloma Krüger

DP coordinator
Yolanda Meneses

Status Private

Boarding/day Day

Gender Coeducational

Language of instruction
Spanish, English

Authorised IB programmes
PYP, MYP, DP

Age Range 2 – 18

Number of pupils enrolled
900

Fees
Day: S/ 15,400 – 35,970

Address
Av. La Arboleda 385
Urb. Sirius, La Molina
Lima 15024 | **PERU**

TEL +51 13 650298

Email
admision@altair.pe

Website
www.altair.edu.pe

Colegio Altair is a private institution founded in 1995, whose purpose is to provide a co-educational, bilingual, modern, and holistic education. Altair is a member of Inspired, a leading global group of premium schools, with over 70 schools across five continents. A definitive statement of excellence in private education; Inspired is an independent school group designed to inspire students, to achieve their maximum potential in a nurturing, progressive academic environment.

At Colegio Altair we seek to meet our students' intellectual, physical, emotional, and social needs with a high-quality and personalized education. Our student community is enriched by multicultural families, which significantly influences our students' formation. Around 12% of the families are from different nationalities.

Our Academic Programme combines the Peruvian Ministry of Education requirements with the guidelines of the three levels of the International Baccalaureate: Primary Years Programme, Middle Years Programme, and Diploma Programme. The curriculum is holistic and balanced with various art courses, including Performing & Visual Arts, Drawing, and Music. A Talent program is offered from grades 3 to 6.

Colegio Altair offers a wide range of afterschool activities. These include sports such as basketball, football, volleyball; cultural activities such as MUN and debate; and musical activities such as choir, big band, wooden, metal and string instruments among others. MUN and Debate are very popular after school activities and curricular subjects from Grades 6 to 11. The primary skill developed with these two programs is the ability to speak in public effectively. They also promote a high level of analysis, synthesis, supporting arguments, investigation, negotiation and teamwork.

Colegio Altair has an Accreditation Programme that accounts for credits earned based on high school students' participation in social, sports, and/or cultural activities. It aims to encourage our students' involvement in those activities that support soft skills development, allowing them to develop a comprehensive profile. Students develop awareness and social responsibility through their participation in our community. Learning by experience, they become aware of the importance of social work to create constant and sustainable development. Students go to different communities to work with and for them during school hours and work on an action plan that is executed proactively.

Colegio Altair has a personalized Counselling Programme for students from grades 9 to 11 and Diploma. Students are encouraged and closely oriented to reflect upon their skills, interests, and preferences to identify what national and international universities offer regarding the careers that match their profile.

Colegio del Valle S.A.(Blue Valley School)

An **inspired** school

(Founded 1989)

General Director
Kathryn Scanlan

DP coordinator
Patricia Prats

Status Private

Boarding/day Day

Gender Coeducational

Language of instruction
English, Spanish

Authorised IB programmes
DP

Age Range 3 – 18 years

Number of pupils enrolled
857

Address
From Multiplaza, 1.2 Km.
northwest
right hand side of the road,
Guachipelín, Escazú
San José | **COSTA RICA**

TEL +50 6 2215 2204

Email
admissions@bluevalley.ed.cr

Website
www.bluevalley.ed.cr

School, Community and Students

Founded in 1989, BVS is a private, co-educational, bilingual Pre-K to 12th grade school which offers a challenging integrated curriculum of Costa Rican and International curricula. Student Nationalities: 67.2% are Costa Rican and 32.8% are international. While English is the language of instruction for the majority of the curriculum, Spanish is the social language and our students switch effortlessly between the two.

In 2018, Blue Valley joined INSPIRED, a leading global premium schools group educating over 48,000 students across an international network of over 62 schools on 5 continents. All the Inspired schools are individually developed and designed in response to their environment and location, delivering an excellent education to their respective communities.

Vision

Become the school of choice for parents who expect and appreciate an excellent bilingual, holistic education for their children.

Mission

To offer cutting-edge academic preparation and ensure that our students become individuals guided by a strong moral compass. A proper balance between the Humanities and the Sciences will support our academic goals, guided by the principle of a sound mind in a sound body. Blue Valley School models and teaches students to become architects of their destiny, wise decision makers, prudent risk takers, and active participants in local and global communities, safeguarding individual and collective rights and responsibilities inherent to a free society.

Colegio El Camino

EL CAMINO

VIRTUS ET HONOR

(Founded 1983)

Head of School
Mr. Heath Sparrow M.A., M.Sc.

PYP coordinator
Ginger Fell

DP coordinator
Isaac Pérez

Status Private

Boarding/day Day

Gender Coeducational

Language of instruction
English, Spanish

Authorised IB programmes
PYP, DP

Age Range 3 – 18 years

Fees
Kindergarten MEX$67,600
Elementary MEX$91,250
Middle School MEX$101,300
High School MEX$111,850

Address
Callejon del Jornongo #210
Colonia El Pedregal
Cabo San Lucas, B.C.S.
C.P. 23453 | MÉXICO

TEL +52 624 143 2100 (Ext:112)

Email
info@elcamino.edu.mx

Website
www.elcamino.edu.mx

Colegio El Camino is a Private K-12, non sectarian, nonprofit organization governed by a permanent board of governors made up by members of the three founding families and other invited members of the community.

Our mission at Camino is "to develop honorable, inquiring and caring life-long learners with intercultural understanding and respect for others who, through creativity and rigorous curriculum, become passionate leaders and participants in a global community."

El Camino has a current student population of 420 students. The majority of students are Mexican nationals but the school is represented by 23 nationalities that include Americans, Canadians, Australians, Israelis, Japanese, French, Swiss, Germans, Venezuelans, Brazilians, Peruvians and other Latin nationalities.

The increased diversity is a result of our international accreditation with both Cognia and the International Baccalaureate Organization.

We are 1 of 41 Cognia accredited schools in Mexico demonstrating our commitment and adherence to the high standards of quality required by their organization based out of the United States.

We are honored to be 1 of the 120 IB World Schools in Mexico. We offer both the Diploma and Primary Years Programmes and are currently in the process of the feasibility study for the Middle Years Programme. We are registered with the Mexican Ministry of Education in all sections.

Camino is celebrating 36 years in offering the vanguard global education in Los Cabos to students from all nationalities, religions, cultures and socio economic standing. Our school provides students with a safe and caring learning environment supported by trained and certified staff from multiple nationalities.

In addition to our bilingual curriculum we offer many support services including certified and licensed psychologists, a mentoring program, career and college counseling, afternoon academic academies, afternoon sports program, the Camino Language Acquisition Support Program (CLASP), para-academic workshops and the IB Diploma CAS (Creativity, Activity, Service) program.

Founding Principal/Head of School
Dr Laurie B. Midgette

PYP coordinator
Sara Pena

Status State

Boarding/day Day

Gender Coeducational

Language of instruction
English, Spanish

Authorised IB programmes
PYP

Age Range 5 – 10 years

Number of pupils enrolled
280

Address
1400 Linden Blvd
Brooklyn
NY 11212 | USA

TEL +1 718 683 3300

Email
caacs@caa-ny.org

Website
www.culturalartsacademy.org

Cultural Arts Academy Charter School offers a dynamic elementary education of both the mind and heart, focusing on developing the whole child. Our mission is to provide a college preparatory education, with exemplary cultural arts proficiency, to young leaders who will profoundly impact the human condition.

Established over ten years ago, CAACS boasts two global recognitions; The prestigious Franklin Covey Lighthouse School designation, attained in 2017, and authorization as an International Baccalaureate (IB) World School, attained in 2019. Through these two designations, CAACS operates one synergistic learning model, rooting in student-lead learning and leadership.

Our goal is to fully prepare our scholars for college, career, and citizenship, starting with instilling the foundational principles of open-mindedness, problem-solving, strong character, and intrinsic motivation. Establishing 21st century skills through project-based learning across all grade levels equips our scholars with the necessary tools for success.

At the core of our school, of course, is culture and the arts. All scholars, from Kindergarten through 5th grade, receive extensive education through the arts, including Dance, Drama, Music, and the Visual Arts. Learning through multiple forms of expression provides our scholars with a deep appreciation and passion for the arts across time periods and cultures, as well as an ownership of self-expression.

True evidence of student learning, mastery, and success comes not only from their research-backed presentations, artistic performances, and creative projects, but through their ability to identify problems within the world around them and construct reasonable and effective solutions. Recently, the strength of their character is seen in the resiliency they exhibit amongst all the changes happening within their school and home life, given the nature of the state of the world. CAACS is proud of the self-motivation and agency our scholars exercise during these times of remote learning.

DWIGHT SCHOOL

Igniting the spark of genius in every child

PERSONALIZED LEARNING · COMMUNITY · GLOBAL VISION

(Founded 1872)

Chancellor
Stephen H. Spahn

Vice Chancellor
Blake Spahn

Head of School
Chris Beddows

PYP coordinator
Brittany Dallal

MYP coordinator
Beth Billard

DP coordinator
Liz Hutton

Status Private

Boarding/day Day

Gender Coeducational

Language of instruction
English

Authorised IB programmes
PYP, MYP, DP

Age Range 2 – 18 years

Number of pupils enrolled 921

Fees
Day: US$53,550

Address
291 Central Park West
New York, NY 10024 | USA

TEL +1 212 724 6360

Email
admissions@dwight.edu

Website
www.dwight.edu

Founded in 1872, Dwight School is an internationally renowned college preparatory school with a rich tradition of academic excellence and igniting the "spark of genius" in every child. Dwight's world-class education rests on three pillars: personalized learning, community, and global vision. The School's diverse faculty and student body represent over 40 countries, deepening the internationally minded, innovative learning environment.

A leader in global education, Dwight is the first school in the Americas to offer the comprehensive International Baccalaureate (IB) curriculum for students from preschool through grade 12. It was also the first school in New York City to offer the PYP. The rigorous IB is recognized as the "gold standard" in pre-university preparation. Through the IB, Dwight is educating students to become caring, open-minded and critical-thinking global leaders. Foreign language instruction is extensive and begins in preschool.

Through Spark Tank, Dwight's unique incubator designed to nurture innovation, entrepreneurship, and leadership skills beyond the classroom, K-12 students develop their own ideas for new businesses, non-profits, and products.

Dwight School in New York is the flagship campus of a global network, which includes schools in London, Seoul, Shanghai and Dubai. Dwight Global Online School – a campus in the cloud – extends a world-class Dwight education everywhere. Dwight Schools educate students around the world, who benefit from a wide range of exciting cross-campus academic, leadership, and creative collaborations.

Dwight School has a comprehensive college guidance program beginning early in grade 9. Graduates attend the finest colleges and universities in the world, including Harvard, Yale, Princeton, MIT, Stanford, Oxford, St. Andrew's and the University of Edinburgh, among many others. Upon graduation, they join an extensive global network of alumni leaders – all dedicated to making our world a better place.

Dwight is accredited by the Council of International Schools, the International Baccalaureate, the Middle States Association of Colleges and Secondary Schools, and the World Academy of Sport. Financial aid is granted on the basis of need.

Edgewood High School

Principal
Roni Maddox Ed.D

MYP coordinator
Manny Co

DP coordinator
Veronica Perez

CP coordinator
Veronica Perez

Status State

Boarding/day Day

Gender Coeducational

Language of instruction
English

Authorised IB programmes
MYP, DP, CP

Age Range 14 – 18 years

Number of pupils enrolled
846

Address
1625 W Durness
West Covina
CA 91790 | USA

TEL +1 626 939 4600

Email
vperez@wcusd.org

Website
edgewoodib.wcusd.org

Edgewood High School is a public high school located in the city of West Covina, 19 miles east of Los Angeles. Edgewood is an International Baccalaureate World School authorized to offer the Middle Years Programme, Diploma Programme, and Career-related Programme. Edgewood is a school of choice serving a diverse population of 846 students. Edgewood recently reopened as a high school in 2010 with our first graduation class in May of 2014. In addition to being an IB World School since 2011, Edgewood has been accredited by the Western Association of Schools and Colleges.

Edgewood offers a smaller learning community focused on preparing creative, inquiring, and caring students prepared for college and career. This can be seen in our Mission Statement, *"Edgewood, an IB World School, is committed to building a globally aware community of lifelong learners who achieve high academic standards. Edgewood provides a diverse, challenging curriculum that is student-centered and develops inquisitive, knowledgeable, and empathetic students who actively engage in and contribute to their family, community, and the world around them."*

Edgewood offers a variety of courses to meet our diverse student needs. The curriculum includes: honors courses in 9th and 10th grade, both standard level and higher level IB courses, a world language program, a fine arts department offering visual arts, music, and drama, a health and physical education program, career and technical education pathways in athletic training, game design, public safety, and video production, and support services for special education and English learner students. Students at Edgewood learn in state of the art facilities including a brand new Event Center. The Event Center features a 350-seat auditorium and freestanding seats, and houses the IB Career Programme courses in Game Design and Video Production.

Students at Edgewood are also provided personal and social development opportunities created by participation in extracurricular activities such as ASB, clubs, yearbook, dances, study trips, performances, cheer and athletics. Edgewood offers CIF sports in cross country, baseball, softball, tennis, basketball, volleyball, water polo, soccer, wrestling, track and swim. The completion of the new Edgewood Sports Complex features an Olympic-size swimming pool, updated locker rooms, two digital scoreboards capable of video playback, a high-quality sound system, and updated basketball courts.

Edgewood Middle School

Principal
Roni Maddox Ed.D

MYP coordinator
Manny Co

Status State

Boarding/day Day

Gender Coeducational

Language of instruction
English

Authorised IB programmes
MYP

Age Range 11 – 14 years

Number of pupils enrolled
534

Address
1625 W. Durness St.
West Covina
CA 91790 | USA

TEL +1 626 939 4600

Email
mco@wcusd.org
rmaddox@wcusd.org

Website
edgewoodib.wcusd.org

Edgewood, an IB World School, is committed to building a globally-aware community of lifelong learners who achieve high academic standards.

Edgewood provides a diverse, challenging curriculum that is student-centered and develops inquisitive, knowledgeable, and empathetic students who actively engage in and contribute to their family, community, and the world around them.

Edgewood Middle School is a public school located in the city of West Covina, 19 miles east of Los Angeles. Edgewood Middle School is an International Baccalaureate World School authorized to offer the IB Middle Years Programme. Edgewood is a school of choice serving a diverse population of 534 students in grades 6-8. Edgewood received the IB Middle Years Programme authorization in December 2018. Edgewood provides a smaller learning community focused on preparing creative, inquiring, and caring students ready to make connections between subjects studied and the real world as well as develop critical and reflective thinking skills.

EMS offers a variety of courses to meet our diverse student needs. The curriculum includes: honors courses in 7th and 8th grade, a world language program offering both Mandarin and Spanish, a fine arts department offering visual arts, music, and drama, a health and physical education program, ROP Dance, yearbook, and services for special education and English learner students.

Edgewood Middle School offers outstanding student support through committed, compassionate teachers that provide multi-tiered systems of interventions and enrichment opportunities. Edgewood students are holistically taught in diverse learning environments that prepare students for a global workplace. Partnerships with community, local agencies, and organizations provide opportunities for students to participate in activities for service. Students at Edgewood get to learn in our state of the art new facilities including a brand new Event Center. The Event Center features a 350-seat auditorium and freestanding seats, and houses the IB Career Programme courses in Game Design and Video Production. The new Edgewood Sports Complex features an Olympic-size swimming pool, updated locker rooms, two digital scoreboards capable of video playback, a high-quality sound system, and updated basketball courts. Students at EMS are provided personal and social development opportunities created by participation in extracurricular activities such as WEB, clubs, dances, performances, cheer and athletics. Edgewood offers sports in track and field, flag football, softball, basketball, volleyball, and soccer.

EF ACADEMY

International
Boarding Schools

Head of School
Dr. Vladimir D. Kuskovski

DP coordinator
Amy Park

Status Private

Boarding/day Mixed

Gender Coeducational

Language of instruction
English

Authorised IB programmes
DP

Age Range 14 – 19 years

Number of pupils enrolled
500

Fees
US$62,250 (US$20,750 per term)

Address
582 Columbus Avenue
Thornwood
NY 10594 | USA

TEL +1 914 495 6056

Email
academy.admissions@ef.com

Website
www.efacademy.org

EF Academy International Boarding Schools prepares students for a global future with an exceptional high school education in the US or UK. We empower every student to succeed through our renowned curriculum, quality one-to-one guidance and experiential learning opportunities. Our students, representing 75 nationalities, live the IB ethos of intercultural understanding and respect every single day and benefit from learning in a diverse environment that emphasizes multilingualism and cultural exchange.

The School
Our IB World School is located approximately 45 minutes from Manhattan. EF Academy's secure campus offers 100 acres of landscaped grounds, running trails and playing fields in the quiet suburban town of Thornwood. Our facilities include a premier STEM center, spacious classrooms, a fully-equipped gym and renovated sports facilities, comfortable on-campus residences and a Health Center.

Academics
Instruction and guidance at EF Academy New York is highly personal. Students follow the US High School Diploma from Grade 9, which prepares them for the opportunity to enroll in the full IB Diploma Programme or take individual IB Courses in Grade 11. All students who successfully complete the IB Diploma at EF Academy New York are also awarded a nationally recognized New York State High School Diploma.

Support and Guidance
Each student at EF Academy New York is assigned a Pathway Manager who helps them select the right courses, monitors their academic progress and supports their social and emotional wellbeing. In addition to receiving one-on-one support from teachers, students also work together with university advisors who help them research and apply to the universities that best suit their goals and interests.

University Placements
EF Academy New York graduates have been accepted to universities such as Harvard University, Yale University, the University of Oxford, schools in the University of California network and other international universities ranked highly for fields including business, medicine and engineering among others. Some of our artistically talented students have been accepted to Rhode Island School of Design and Parsons School of Design.

Student Life
With over 120 co-curricular clubs and activities on offer, students are provided with a wealth of special-interest clubs, varsity sports and community service opportunities to complete their Creativity, Activity and Service (CAS) program. Our school's activities coordinators also arrange teacher-led excursions so students can extend their learning beyond the classroom and take advantage of the impressive museums, historical sights and other advantages that being a student in New York has to offer.

ESCOLA
AMERICANA
DO RIO
DE JANEIRO

(Founded 1937)

Headmaster Dr. Nigel J. Winnard

Gávea Campus Principals
Ms. Doreen Garrigan (Lower) &
Dr. Howard De Leeuw (Upper)

Barra Campus Principals
Ms. Kirstin White (Lower) &
Mr. Scott Little (Upper)

DP coordinator
Ms. Flavia DiLuccio
(Gávea Campus) &
Ms. Deborah Dale (Barra Campus)

Status Private

Boarding/day Day

Gender Coeducational

Language of instruction
English

Authorised IB programmes
DP

Age Range 3 – 18 years

Number of pupils enrolled
1200

Gávea Address
Estrada da Gávea 132
Gávea, Rio de Janeiro
RJ 22451-263 | BRAZIL

TEL +55 21 2125 9000

Email
admissions.gavea@earj.com.br

Barra Campus
Rua Colbert Coelho 155,
Barra da Tijuca,Rio de Janeiro
RJ 22793-313 | BRAZIL

TEL +55 21 3747 2000

Email
admissions.barra@earj.com.br

Website www.earj.com.br

Escola Americana do Rio de Janeiro is one of Latin America's most respected international teaching institutions. Established in 1937, and an IB World School since 1982, EARJ is a non-profit school, providing an American international education to the expatriate and Brazilian communities of Rio de Janeiro. It blends a rigorous academic program with rich co-curricular opportunities.

EARJ occupies two campuses in different parts of the city, each offering programs from Preschool to the IB Diploma. EARJ is distinctive in that its 1,200 students can work towards graduating with three Diplomas concurrently: the IB Diploma, the US High School Diploma, and the Brazilian Diploma. Every year, EARJ graduates are accepted to the world's leading universities, and we pride ourselves on each student finding the institution that is best for them. Whilst a few graduates remain to study in Brazil, the vast majority head abroad to the USA, Canada and Europe for university.

EARJ is proud to offer a holistic education that, through the philosophy and practices of the IB, inspires creativity, critical thinking, collaboration, communication, and the confidence to lead and excel in an ever-changing global community. The institution has a long tradition with the IB, being the second school in Brazil to implement the DP Programme.

Currently, EARJ is on the journey towards becoming an IB World Continuum School, and has developed a comprehensive two-year roadmap for the implementation of the Primary and Middle Years Programmes (PYP and MYP). During the Candidate Phase, faculty, students and parents are being trained in programme standards and practices in the form of professional development and specific workshops. The coming years EARJ will extend its belief in and commitment to the IB Programme Standards and Practices with the adoption of the PYP by 2023 and MYP by 2024.

EARJ is a diverse international community of learners. Across our two campuses, our student body comprises 70% Brazilian and 30% International students, with our faculty demographic reflecting that same balance. The past three years have seen tremendous growth in our enrollment, with further growth expected in the coming years. Our community is spread far and wide, via our Panther Alumni network, who keeps us connected to our past as we work towards an even brighter future.

Escola Americana do Rio de Janeiro gladly accepts applications for entry in all grade levels throughout the year. For any further information please visit our website at www. earj.com.br and follow us on social media (@earj.official).

Foxcroft Academy

Head of School
Mr Arnold Shorey

DP coordinator
Donna Newhouse

Status Private

Boarding/day Mixed

Gender Coeducational

Language of instruction
English

Authorised IB programmes
DP

Age Range 14 – 18 years

Number of pupils enrolled 420

Address
975 West Main Street
Dover-Foxcroft
ME 04426 | USA

TEL +1 207 564 8351

Email
admissions@foxcroftacademy.org

Website
www.foxcroftacademy.org

Foxcroft Academy, home of the Ponies, is an independent high school founded in 1823 on the principle that knowledge is power. Foxcroft Academy is committed to providing students from central Maine and beyond a rigorous college and career preparatory academic curriculum designed to produce informed and active global citizens. Foxcroft Academy will furnish all students with the underlying skills needed for post-secondary success while embracing its safe community and natural environment.

198 years since its founding, Foxcroft Academy exists as one of only nine remaining (from an original 122) private academies that serve the public trust as part of its mission.

Today Foxcroft Academy is proud to have an enrollment of more than 400 day and boarding students from 16 Maine communities and over 20 different nations. Students at Foxcroft Academy can choose from more than 150 different course offerings, including college prep, AP, IB, and more. This extensive curriculum represents the core liberal arts requirements, college preparatory courses, advanced placement courses, vocational/technical courses, and an alternative education program. We offer over 20 interscholastic varsity sports and have dozens of clubs and organizations for students to work with and belong to. Learn more about Foxcroft Academy at www.foxcroftacademy.org. Together, we will ride on.

(Founded 1980)

Head of School
Mr. Francis Gianni

DP coordinator
Jaimeson Lynch

Status Private

Boarding/day Day

Gender Coeducational

Language of instruction
English, French

Authorised IB programmes
DP

Age Range 3 – 18 years

Number of pupils enrolled
725

Fees
Tuition, per year US$29,000 –
US$37,540

Address
320 East Boston Post Road
Mamaroneck
NY 10543 | USA

TEL +1 914 250 0000

Email
admissions@fasny.org

Website
www.fasny.org

The French-American School of New York (FASNY) is an international and bilingual independent coeducational day school providing an international education to approximately 725 students in Nursery through Grade 12. FASNY develops globally literate, multicultural lifelong learners through a unique program that integrates French, American, and international curricula.

A unique location

FASNY is located in Westchester County, New York, 20 miles north of Manhattan (35 minutes from Grand Central Station by rail) and 9 miles south of Greenwich, Connecticut. Most families choose to enjoy the space and quiet that this peaceful yet active area has to offer with a convenient commute to Manhattan.

Stellar academics

FASNY is the only school in the New York metropolitan area to be accredited by the International Baccalaureate Organisation and by the French Ministry of Education (AEFE). We are also accredited by the New York State Association of Independent Schools. Our students enjoy the unique privilege of graduating with either the IBDP or the French Baccalaureate (with or without the International Option) and a New York State High School Diploma.

The school offers a bilingual immersion program in Nursery through Kindergarten, bringing children of all cultural and linguistic backgrounds to academic fluency in French and English. In grades 1 through 8, students have the option to continue with the French-American Track or a new International Track. New in 2020, FASNY offers a predominantly English speaking curriculum for students in grades 1 through 8. With little to no french required, students study roughly 70% of their subjects in English, with the remaining 30% in French, at the individual level and pace of each child's language skills. This lower and middle school International Track naturally leads students to our current 9-12 international curriculum, creating a cohesive 1-12 learning environment.

Each year FASNY sends students to top colleges and universities. Our acceptance list includes: Columbia, Harvard, MIT, Princeton, Stanford, and Yale in the United States, and Cambridge, Imperial College, LSE, Oxford, and UCL in the United Kingdom. Many students also choose to study in Canada, France, and other fine European institutions.

A vast array of co-curricular activities

Our strong STEM, Arts, Music, and Athletics programs along with our many clubs ensure a well-rounded education and encourage leadership. Strong Community Service, educational trips, and a large choice of clubs all contribute to the development of balanced and caring individuals.

A diverse and welcoming community

Our community of teachers and students represents over 50 nationalities, and the fabric of our school is one of tolerance, acceptance, and appreciation of our diversity. We mix French and American school-life traditions, creating a warm and engaging experience for our students.

GEORGE SCHOOL

(Founded 1893)

Head of School
Sam Houser

DP coordinator
Kim McGlynn

Status Private

Boarding/day Mixed

Gender Coeducational

Language of instruction
English

Authorised IB programmes
DP

Age Range 13 – 19 years

Address
1690 Newtown Langhorne Rd
Newtown
PA 18940-2414 | USA

TEL +1 215 579 6500

Email
admission@georgeschool.org

Website
www.georgeschool.org

Founded in 1893, George School is a Quaker, co-ed boarding and day school for students in grades 9 to 12 located in Newtown, PA. The school is close to major cities on a picturesque, expansive 240-acre campus of open lawns and beautiful woods. Students arrive from nearly fifty countries and more than twenty states.

George School is an experienced leader in education, offering the International Baccalaureate (IB) Diploma Programme for more than thirty-five years and boasting a diploma success rate of 95 percent over the past ten years. In addition to the IB diploma, George School offers nearly 20 Advanced Placement (AP) courses.

Experiential learning across disciplines is a hallmark of a George School education. Students gain practical experience in subjects such as film, artificial intelligence, robotics, human geography, stagecraft, and more. Local and global service-learning opportunities are also an integral part of the curriculum and student life at George School. The chance to freely explore new passions, as well as dive deep into existing ones, makes for a journey of discovery and preparation for life beyond George School.

Understanding that knowledge and character go hand in hand is at the foundation of the George School community. Graduates enter the world confident and capable leaders rooted in self-awareness, self sufficiency, and the ability to listen deeply to others while letting their lives speak. They attend the most selective colleges and universities worldwide.

Greengates School

(Founded 1951)

General Director
Clarisa Desouches Ph.D.

Headmaster
Rupert Cox

Head of the Secondary School
Christopher Woodall

DP coordinator
David Grant

Status Private

Boarding/day Day

Gender Coeducational

Language of instruction
English

Authorised IB programmes
DP

Age Range 3 – 18 years

Number of pupils enrolled
1100

Fees
Please contact the school

Address
Av. Circunvalación Pte. 102
Balcones de San Mateo
Naucalpan, Estado de México
C.P. 53200 | MÉXICO

TEL +52 55 5373 0088

Email
kuroda@greengates.edu.mx

Website
www.greengates.edu.mx

Greengates School, Mexico has been held in high esteem for 70 years. Its British style international education caters to 1100 students, aged 3-18. The student body is largely made up from the diplomatic and business communities of Mexico City.

International-mindedness and cultural diversity are experienced daily with the participation of over 50 nationalities in our community.

The mission statement of Greengates School holds as true as ever today as it did when it was written in 1951. We encourage our students to develop character and self-discipline, while fostering respect and reflection in a challenging learning environment that honours individual differences. In Greengates we act with integrity and seek to motivate our students to become socially responsible citizens while achieving academic excellence.

As a British international school English is the language of instruction, from the age of six all students also study Spanish. Support in both languages is given as required. Furthermore, French is taught in the Secondary School and can be further studied at the levels of the IGCSE and the IB Diploma. Added to this, Korean and Japanese are also available as study options in the school's delivery of the diploma.

Graduates from Greengates attend some of the most prestigious universities in the world. Of the 2021 cohort 23% are attending universities in the USA, with acceptances to institutions like Stanford University, University of California

San Diego, University of California Berkeley, Boston University and many others. Additionally, another 13% of the year group are studying in Canadian top universities like the University of Toronto, University of British Columbia and McGill University. Offers were also received from Imperial College London, University of Edinburgh, University College London, and many other institutions in the UK. We also have students attending prestigious universities around the globe like Waseda University in Japan, Yonsei University in Korea, Erasmus University Rotterdam and University of Amsterdam in the Netherlands among others. Our students also cumulatively received scholarship offers totalling over $0.65M USD.

The teaching body in Greengates is comprised of almost 140 teachers from a wide variety of backgrounds. Alongside the many British teachers, highly qualified and experienced educators come from across the world. Teachers bring a variety of different skills and modern methods to the classroom and these approaches to teaching are central to the students' success.

The Primary School is fully accredited in the International Early Years Curriculum (IEYC) as well as in the International Primary Curriculum (IPC); with recognition given to the school's mastering in its practice of the curriculums. The Secondary School prepares students for the International General Certificate of Education (IGCSE). The IGCSE two-year course is studied prior to embarking on the IB Diploma Programme. The Secondary School has been authorised to

offer the IB Diploma Programme since 1986. In each of the last five years the pass rate has been 98-100%, with overall point scores being consistently well above the world average.

The Greengates campus covers an area of 20,000 square metres, with purpose-built facilities including two libraries, nine sciences laboratories, six computer media centres, four art studios, a theatre, an auditorium, a large gymnasium, basketball courts, an indoor swimming pool, an organic learning garden used by all students, a cafeteria, an adventure playground designed by the famous architect Javier Senosiain and an all-weather field.

Enrolment is open throughout the year, depending on availability. We always welcome enquiries and visits from prospective families.

(Founded 1934)

Head of School
Mr. David Perry

DP coordinator
Kurt Supplee

Status Private

Boarding/day Day

Gender Coeducational

Language of instruction
English, Spanish

Authorised IB programmes
DP

Age Range 3 – 18 years

Number of pupils enrolled
1600

Address
Av. El Rodeo 14200
Lo Barnechea
Santiago | CHILE

TEL +56 2 2339 8100

Email
admissions@nido.cl

Website
www.nido.cl

Nido de Aguilas was founded in 1934 as a private, co-educational, non-sectarian, non-profit day school rooted in the best traditions of Chilean and North American education. Today, Nido has over 1600 students from 50 countries and offers a comprehensive liberal arts, college preparatory educational program from Early Years (age three) through Grade 12. Nido serves the international business and diplomatic community of Santiago, as well as local students seeking an English-language, U.S.-style education.

Nido has offered the IB Diploma since 1982, and today, over 50% of our Grade 11 and 12 students enroll in the full IB Diploma Programme. Their IB Diploma scores are above the worldwide average, and our IB Coordinator ensures that students complete all required courses and register for all necessary external examinations. IB Diploma candidates are examined internally at Nido and externally by the IB Organization to award IB Diploma results.

Students must apply for acceptance into the full IB Diploma Programme at the beginning of the second semester of Grade 10, before the course registration process the following year.

Admission to the program is based on a student's academic record, including having a record of academic honesty. Students transferring from IB programs with good standing in those programs may continue in the IB program at Nido. In the case of English language learners, they must meet English language proficiency requirements to participate in the full IB diploma.

IB courses are open to non-Diploma students. All Nido HS students are exposed to the IB curriculum during their academic career, as many upper-level courses are taught at the IB level. It is possible to earn the IB Diploma simultaneously as the Nido/US diploma and the Chilean National Plan Diploma.

Nido's high school faculty includes 30 IB teachers recruited from the best schools in the world. Collectively, they have an average IB teaching experience of over ten years, and all attend official workshops in their subject group. In addition, Nido has a robust mentoring program for teachers new to the IB.

International School of Boston

(Founded 1962)

Head of School
Mr. Richard Ulffers

Secondary School Director
Mr. Philippe Caron-Audet

DP coordinator
Mr. John Bray

Status Private

Boarding/day Day

Gender Coeducational

Language of instruction
English, French, Spanish

Authorised IB programmes
DP

Age Range 2 – 18 years

Number of pupils enrolled
550

Fees
Day: US$27,825 – US$39,165

Address
45 Matignon Road
Cambridge
MA 02140 | USA

TEL +1 617 499 1451

Email
admissions@isbos.org

Website
www.isbos.org

The International School of Boston (ISB) is an independent, non-profit, age 2 – grade 12 multilingual school located in Cambridge, MA. This world-class accredited academic institution places the development of the bilingual brain at the heart of its mission. Offering a rich experience with rigorous programs and featuring a wide range of both local and international students and faculty, ISB prepares its students for a lifetime of learning and service.

Long known for its excellence in bilingual French and English education, ISB has now added another world language, Spanish, for our students to explore and master starting in Grade 2. Our youngest students, in Pre-K through Grade 1, are also expanding their knowledge of Spanish and Chinese in our Éveil aux langues program, which helps them to start awakening to and exploring these languages. This gives our Elementary students the opportunity to become trilingual, while our Secondary students have the option to study Spanish at the novice or fluent level within the English-based International Baccalaureate curriculum.

Whether students join us in Maternelle, Lower, Middle or Upper School, ISB graduates stand apart from other day schools' graduates, because their knowledge of the world is enhanced by learning across the disciplines in multiple languages and by connecting with diverse classmates from more than 40 countries. All ISB students graduate with an American high school diploma, having chosen between two internationally renowned diplomas, the French or the International Baccalaureate. Thus they have the opportunity to thrive at leading universities in the United States, France, and around the world.

One of the many beneficial programs offered to Upper School students at ISB is the "Agora Monde" platform that allows them to connect with 60,000+ students and alumni from Lycées in the AEFE (agency for French education abroad) network around the world. They also have the opportunity to study for up to a trimester at a partner school abroad. Our younger students take advantage of all that the Greater Boston area has to offer in terms of culture, arts, and history through experiential learning programs. ISB also has a very strong athletic program that includes its Blue Terriers Varsity Interscholastic soccer, basketball, volleyball and fencing teams.

Accreditations & Memberships
ISB is accredited by the Council of International Schools (CIS), the French Ministry of National Education, the International Baccalaureate Organization (IBO), and the New England Association of Schools and Colleges (NEASC).

ISB is a member of the Agence pour l'enseignement français à l'étranger (AEFE), the Association of French Schools in North America (AFSA), the Association of Independent Schools in New England (AISNE), the National Association of Independent Schools (NAIS), and the Mission laïque française (MLF).

We invite you to contact the ISB Admissions Office at admissions@isbos.org.

International School of Los Angeles

International School Los Angeles **Lycée International**

(Founded 1978)

Head of School
Mr Michael Maniska

DP coordinator
Donald Buer

Status Private

Boarding/day Day

Gender Coeducational

Language of instruction
English, French

Authorised IB programmes
DP

Age Range 3 – 18 years

Number of pupils enrolled
1040

Fees
Day: $19,495 – $24,900

Address
1105 W. Riverside Drive
Burbank
CA 91506 | USA

TEL +1 626 695 5159

Email
admissions@lilaschool.com

Website
www.internationalschool.la

The International School of Los Angeles is an independent, international, preschool through 12th grade school committed to bilingual education and academic excellence in a nurturing environment. Students study a common bilingual program from preschool through 8th grade, after which they choose one of two rigorous programs that culminates in the International Baccalaureate® Diploma (taught in English) or the French baccalauréat (taught in French). Thanks in part to its long commitment to academic excellence and small class sizes, the International School of Los Angeles is now recognized as one of the most academically challenging private high schools in the United States.

The School has offered the IB Diploma Programme for more than 20 years. Possessing such a robust bilingual background, many of its students pursue the prestigious Bilingual Diploma, demonstrating their proficiency by completing the requirements in both English and French at Literature level. This highly sought-after credential has become another mark of distinction for the International School of Los Angeles' IB students.

In the 2019-2020 school year, the School extended its international track to the beginning of 9th grade, thereby realigning its entry points to reflect the US educational model, further internationalizing its curriculum, and providing students an additional year of preparation ahead of the IB Diploma Programme. Students entering the international track in 9th grade are not required to demonstrate proficiency in French but should display an openness to learning another language.

With multiple Los Angeles-area campuses (Burbank, Los Feliz, Pasadena, and West Valley), and more than 1,000 students, the International School of Los Angeles holds accreditation from the French Ministry of Education, the Western Association of Schools and Colleges (WASC), the California Association of Independent Schools (CAIS), and the International Baccalaureate® (IB). The School is also a member of the National Association of Independent Schools (NAIS) and the National Honor Society (NHS) networks.

The International School of Los Angeles is committed to the values of respect, excellence, and diversity, and to preparing students of all backgrounds to excel in and contribute to a global world. Since 1978, the School has been instilling the love of learning in all its students through small classes and low student-to-teacher ratios. With over 65 nationalities and 40 spoken languages represented on the campuses, students study and live in a diverse global community every day.

ISLANDS INTERNATIONAL SCHOOL

Principal
Prof. Estela María Irrera de Pallaro

DP coordinator
Clotilde Alleva

Status Private

Boarding/day Day

Gender Coeducational

Language of instruction
Spanish, English, Italian, Portuguese

Authorised IB programmes
DP

Age Range 2 – 18 years

Address
Amenábar St. 1840
1428 Ciudad de Buenos Aires |
ARGENTINA

TEL +54 11 4787 2294

Website
www.intschools.org/school/
islands

Working together with Southern International School and Northern International School.

In 1981 Mrs. Estela María Irrera de Pallaro and her husband Andrés Pallaro founded a kindergarten in a lovely house situated in O'Higgins St. in Belgrano, which was later to become Islands International School. Some years later, as a result of hard work, clear objectives and true commitment, a primary school was opened in a spacious building situated in Virrey del Pino and Arcos St. In 1988, a secondary school was opened with a curriculum based on the latest, most prestigious syllabi in Argentina and the whole world. The new building situated in Amenábar St. offered our students appropriate facilities and modern equipment to meet the highest educational standards.

From the beginning, our aim has been to present our students with a demanding curriculum while emphasizing the values of hard work, effort and commitment. The outstanding achievements of our alumni both in college and later on in their jobs are irrefutable proof of our success.

In 1990 Islands embraced a new challenge by joining the International Baccalaureate Organization, a well known association of schools seeded in Geneva, Switzerland whose main objective is to foster the students' skills so that they can perform successfully in an increasingly demanding academic world and expanding job market. Furthermore, it is essential that our students should acquire full command of the languages taught at our school: Spanish, English and Italian.

By getting an IB diploma our students can also get the "Maturità Linguistica o Scientifica", which is a diploma issued by the Government of Italy at the end of secondary school and which grants students admission to European Universities.

Our school emphasizes the values of respect and hard work as the main tools, which will enable our students to achieve success. Islands International School provides students with quality education, which comprises the latest technological breakthroughs and the practice of human and social values.

KEHOE-FRANCE
—NORTHSHORE—
GOD · COUNTRY · DISCIPLINE

Head of School
Brad Humphreys

PYP coordinator
Brandy Calato

Status Private

Boarding/day Day

Gender Coeducational

Language of instruction
English

Authorised IB programmes
PYP

Age Range 8 weeks – 13 years

Address
25 Patricia Drive
Covington
LA 70433 | USA

TEL +1 985 892 4415

Email
kfninfo@kf-ns.com

Website
www.kf-ns.com

Kehoe-France Northshore is an independent, non-denominational, coeducational school open to students from 8 weeks old through 7th grade, which includes early childhood, preschool, elementary and middle school.

At Kehoe-France, importance is placed on developing social skills and building character among our students. Our purpose is to develop the child intellectually, spiritually, emotionally and socially. It is in a child's formative years that a love for learning develops, and Kehoe-France offers the opportunity to embrace and enjoy that adventure. We are a family-oriented community committed to academic excellence. Through the close cooperation of parents, faculty and administration, we foster a nurturing environment, developing the individual potential and ability of each child. We encourage enthusiasm for learning, confidence in pursuing school tasks independently and respect for others while working cooperatively. These tools are what help prepare the Kehoe-France student for high school, college and life beyond.

Accreditation
Kehoe-France Northshore is an International Baccalaureate World School, authorized to offer the Primary Years Programme (PYP), and a candidate for the Middle Years Programme (MYP). KFN is also approved by the BESE and the Louisiana Department of Education/US Department of Education, NIPSA (National Independent Private School Association) and Cognia (formerly SACS, Southern Association of Colleges and Schools).

Campus Facilities
Now in our 26th year in St. Tammany Parish, Kehoe-France maintains a serene and wholesome environment that draws many families from the surrounding area in which to raise and educate their children. Uniquely, Kehoe-France Northshore is a privately owned school that was founded and continues to operate without the aid of fund-raising drives and only on the tuition and fees of the students.

King's College, The British School of Panama

King's College
The British School of Panama

(Founded 2012)

Headteacher
Mr. Nigel Fossey

DP coordinator
Laura Guisasola

Status Private

Boarding/day Day

Gender Coeducational

Language of instruction
English, Spanish

Authorised IB programmes
DP

Age Range 3 – 18 years

Address
Edificio 518
Calle al Hospital
Clayton | **PANAMA**

TEL +507 282 3300

Email
kcp.admissions@kingsgroup.org

Website
www.panama.
kingscollegeschools.org

King's College Panama is proud to be leading the way in British education in Panama. As the only British school in Panama, we are a unique community that can offer families the opportunity to be a part of a world-class school with 50 years of tradition and part of a premium group of 70 schools around the world. Our values and traditions support our mission to provide a transformative learning experience for every student in our care; a learning experience that cultivates innate talents develops interests and encourages curiosity and a love of learning.

We have chosen to embark on the High Performance Learning (HPL) Award in 2021. This best represents our belief that every child can attain high performance and succeed. At King's College Panama, we don't "teach to the middle" but ensure that every child achieves their full potential, regardless of their starting point. It is therefore not surprising that our academic results are outstanding, and have exceeded those of many selective UK independent schools. All King's College Panama graduates have gained entry to their first choice universities around the world.

King's College is a fully accredited British school and is a member of both AoBSO (Association of British Schools Overseas) and the LAHC (Latin Americas Heads Conference). The school attained a grade of "outstanding" during its last UK inspection. We are also a Duke of Edinburgh International Award Centre and have close links with local charities and NGOs.

The school is well-placed to take advantage of our location to offer students opportunities for field study in the surrounding tropical rainforest. We also offer a rich and varied extra-curricular programme. As an Inspired school we integrate the "Three Pillars" of Sport, The Arts and Academic Excellence. We are very proud of our student's involvement in dance, drama and public speaking and have a very well established and active student council.

From August 2021, King's College Panama also offers the IB Diploma Programme. Since its conception in 1968, this highly reputed course of study has promoted international-mindedness as well as intellectual rigour and academic flexibility.

The programme offers breadth of study through the range of subjects studied, the unifying nature of the Theory of Knowledge programme and the holistic nature of the Creativity, Action and Service programme. Depth of study is provided through the study of three subjects at the Higher Level and the Extended Essay.

Successful completion of the IB Diploma has proved to be a valuable asset when applying to universities in the UK and worldwide. The critical thinking required for the Diploma Course gives students a significant advantage at university.

2022 is a very important year in the life of our world class school. Not only do we celebrate our tenth anniversary here in Panama City, but we are also moving to a new, state-of-the-art purpose built campus here in Clayton. We would be delighted to meet you and show you around. Please do not hesitate to contact us.

La Scuola d'Italia Guglielmo Marconi

LA SCUOLA D'ITALIA
GUGLIELMO MARCONI

www.lascuoladitalia.org

(Founded 1977)

Interim Head of School
Michael Prater

DP coordinator
Dr. Beatrice Paladini

Status Private

Boarding/day Day

Gender Coeducational

Language of instruction
English, Italian

Authorised IB programmes
DP

Age Range 2 – 18 years

Number of pupils enrolled
125

Fees
Preschool US$26,000
Elementary US$29,000
Middle & High School US$34,000

Address
12 East 96th Street
New York
NY 10128 | USA

TEL +1 212 369 3290

Email
admissions@lascuoladitalia.org

Website
www.lascuoladitalia.org

La Scuola d'Italia is a multicultural, multilingual institution located in the heart of Manhattan. At La Scuola, students pursue Italian and U.S. rigorous curricula simultaneously, supported by a nurturing international community comprised by people from all over the world who recognize the value of an internationally minded, multilingual, and academically challenging education.

In addition to being recognized by the Italian Ministry of Education, La Scuola is chartered by the Regents of the University of the State of New York and accredited by the New York State Association of Independent Schools (NYSAIS). As a further confirmation of the quality of its educational offering, La Scuola was officially authorized to offer the International Baccalaureate Diploma Programme to its 11th and 12th grade students in May 2018.

As a result, La Scuola students enjoy the unique possibility of graduating with a high school diploma that is fully recognized by every university institution in Europe and the United States. Thanks to their International Baccalaureate Diploma Programme affiliation, our students now benefit from even greater opportunities to truly stand-out on the global stage.

La Scuola is committed to the harmonious integration of different disciplines, cultures, and languages into its carefully designed K-12 curriculum. An exceptionally dedicated and highly qualified faculty refines the curriculum regularly in a low teacher-student ratio environment.

La Scuola strives to prepare students for the academic, professional, social, cultural, and ethical challenges deriving from a globalized world. The education we offer aims to: a) develop in students the specific skills and knowledge required to excel in higher education and beyond within the domains of mathematics, science, modern and classical languages, history, philosophy, the arts and business management; b) foster in students a deeper understanding of their future role as thoughtful, respectful, caring and principled human beings in an ever-expanding world community.

Head of School
Valentina Imbeni Ph.D.

Director of Admissions
Nichole Leon

PYP coordinator Leticia Dias

MYP coordinator
Douglas Lowney

Status Private, Non-Profit

Boarding/day Day

Gender Coeducational

Language of instruction
English, Italian and Spanish

Authorised IB programmes
PYP, MYP

Age Range 2 – 14 years

Number of pupils enrolled 321

Fees
Preschool Half Day (AM),
5-day-schedule US$29,850
Preschool Full Day,
5-day-schedule US$37,325
(Full day is until 5:30 PM)
Elementary (K-5) US$36,750
Middle (6-8) US$38,850 All lunch
fees are included in tuition fees

Preschool Campus
728 20th Street, San Francisco
CA 94107 | USA

K-8 Campus:
3250 18th Street, San Francisco
CA 94110 | USA

TEL +1 415 551 0000

Email admissions@lascuolasf.org

Website www.lascuolasf.org

Open to the World

The world has changed and it's time for education to catch up. That's why, every day, it's the students at La Scuola who ask the provocative questions… they lead – and embrace – their own ability to learn across languages, cultures and subject areas. Because when children are open to the world and protagonists in their own education, there's no limit to their ability to learn, find beauty in life, and discover extraordinary answers.

At La Scuola International School – the only Reggio Emilia inspired, International Baccalaureate-PYP and Italian language immersion school in the world – our mission is to inspire brave learners to shape the future.

We offer an inquiry based, immersive Italian language curriculum for Preschool-8th grade students. With Inquiry as the leading tool of our education, students foster critical and creative thinking skills, confidence, collaboration, and empathy.

La Scuola is also recognized as an Italian Accredited School abroad by the Ministry of Education in Italy. In our diverse and multicultural and multilingual school, students grow in a community that balances academic rigor with creativity and real-life tools like cultural awareness and global citizenship.

Nothing Without Joy!

Niente Senza Gioia!

¡Nada Sin Alegría!

Lincoln Park High School

(Founded 1899)

Principal
Dr. Eric Steinmiller

MYP coordinator
Theresa McCormick

DP coordinator
Mary Enda Tookey

CP coordinator
James Conzen

Status State

Boarding/day Day

Gender Coeducational

Language of instruction
English

Authorised IB programmes
MYP, DP, CP

Age Range 13 – 19 years

Number of pupils enrolled
2055

Address
2001 North Orchard Street
Chicago
IL 60614 | USA

TEL +1 773 534 8149

Email
lpibprogram@aol.com

Website
www.lincolnparkhs.org

Lincoln Park High School, founded in 1899, is a Chicago public high school that offers very successful IB Diploma, MYP & CP Programmes within the context of a college preparatory school for students of all ability levels. Students living in our attendance area or anywhere within the Chicago city limits can make application to Lincoln Park's Magnet Programs, which include the IB Diploma Programme, the IBCP (Performance Music, ROTC, Sports/Exercise, Theatre, and Visual & Digital Arts), an Advanced College Prep (Honors/Double Honors/AP) Program, and a Performing/Fine Arts Program with concentrations available in drama, band, strings or visual arts. After admission, any student may elect music or visual arts. Special consideration for admission is extended to students from other IB schools and to international students from the business and diplomatic communities.

Fluent/bilingual French students can participate in a special program (EFAC) that can include preparation for DELF or the French Baccalaureate in addition to college prep, AP, and/or IB classes. All students with special needs are supported in their IB and college preparatory classes by a full special services program.

Newsweek magazine has ranked Lincoln Park as one of the top 100 high schools in the US and for the last seven years US News & World Report awarded the school gold and silver medal rankings.

Its staff places high value on rigor, mutual respect and creativity, while encouraging students in both their academic and extracurricular activities to develop their talents and interests to the full. Personal excellence, a willingness to challenge oneself, inventiveness, and a can-do spirit are at the core of Lincoln Park's culture.

Students come from over 80 countries and speak more than 60 different languages at home. A significant number of students in the IB Diploma Programme were born in other countries, are first-generation in this country, or the children of internationals. Within this diverse urban context students acquire insight into others and the leadership skills needed in a global society.

A wide variety of extracurricular activities (50) and interscholastic sports opportunities (currently 26) are available for all students. IB students are active in sports, drama, music, art, school clubs, and local organizations. Many do community service beyond the CAS requirement and are active in their individual churches, synagogues, and mosques. In addition to their work in their classes, all Lincoln Park students participate in a number of academic competitions in writing, history, experimental science, literature, social issues, world languages, and the fine and performing arts; many have gone on to the national and international levels of these competitions. Every year, the boys' and girls' athletic teams win division and sectional championships. The music program regularly earns superior ratings in competitions and is currently ranked among the top music programs in the state of Illinois.

Since 1984 approximately 80% of the IB students have gained the IB diploma on completion of the IB Diploma Programme. Lincoln Park enjoys an outstanding record of university acceptances both in the US and internationally.

Head of School
Franco Marchese

DP coordinator
Abeera Atique

Status Private

Boarding/day Mixed

Gender Coeducational

Language of instruction
English, Spanish

Authorised IB programmes
DP

Age Range 13 – 18 years

Number of pupils enrolled
150

Fees
Day: CAD$33,000
International Boarders:
CAD$49,000 all inclusive

Address
365 Richmond Street
London, ON
N6A 3C2 | CANADA

TEL +1 519 433 3388

Email
admissions@lia-edu.ca

Website
www.lia-edu.ca

London International Academy (LIA) is a Private Canadian Secondary Day & Boarding School, and International Baccalaureate (IB) Authorized World School, located in the beautiful 'Forest City' of London, Ontario, Canada. LIA is the only private secondary boarding school in the city of London to offer the IB Diploma Programme (Gr. 11 & 12). The goal is to prepare all students for post-secondary education and life after high school to ensure a successful Canadian integration academically, socially, and culturally.

LIA's IB cohort student average in 2021 was 38, and the highest grade achieved in 2021 by a LIA student was 43. The IB students have a 100% subject pass rate, and 100% graduation rate. LIA is also known for their highly academic and hands on STEM program and is recognized for being amongst the top competitors in mathematics, robotics, and science competitions across Canada. The school provides both boarding and homestay options. The boarding facility offers 24/7 supervision and meals provided by several local restaurants offering a variety of international cuisine. Its main campus, located in the heart of the city of London (Ontario), is a vibrant hub for activities and student innovation. The school offers small class sizes, Ontario Certified Teaching (OCT) qualified educators, individualized assistance with university applications, and a variety of extracurricular and student-led initiatives. LIA looks to educate young, bright minds while providing opportunities that allow students to stand out amongst the crowd.

Lyceum Kennedy

French American School

(Founded 1964)

Head of School
Pierre-Ludovic Perrot

DP coordinator
Dr. Vera Pohland

Status Private

Boarding/day Day

Gender Coeducational

Language of instruction
French, English

Authorised IB programmes
DP

Age Range 3 – 18 years

Number of pupils enrolled
300

Address
225 East 43rd Street
New York
NY 10017 | USA

TEL +1 212 681 1877

Email
lkadmissions@LyceumKennedy.
org

Website
www.LyceumKennedy.org

Founded in 1964, Lyceum Kennedy French American School serves the needs of French and English speaking families living in New York City and the metropolitan region. Fifty years later, the school is worldly recognized, offering a nurturing yet rigorous bilingual education to its students.

The school operates two campus locations – in the heart of Manhattan, just two blocks from Grand Central Terminal. The International Baccalaureate Diploma Programme (IBDP) is offered at the school's 815 Second Avenue campus location.

Currently, Lyceum Kennedy welcomes 300 students from more than 40 nationalities, ages 3 through 18 years old and provides a family-oriented school environment. Our teacher/student ratio in the upper school allows us to work with each student as an individual in order to instill a love of learning and to ensure academic success.

IBDP Mission
Lyceum Kennedy's mission is to provide its students with a unique bilingual and bicultural education based on the principles of self-expression and differentiated pedagogy. Committed to the IB Programme Lyceum Kennedy fulfills high educational standards through challenging programs of international education and rigorous assessment.

Core Values
At Lyceum Kennedy, we emphasize multiculturalism, bilingual education, transdisciplinary academic inquiry and critical thinking. We aim to develop inquiring, knowledgeable and caring people who help to create a better and more peaceful world through intercultural understanding and respect. The IB Programme encourages students to become active, compassionate and lifelong learners who understand that other people, with their differences, can also be right.

Curriculum and IB
In September 2014, Lyceum Kennedy became an authorized IB school for the Diploma Programme. We offer 11th and 12th graders a unique, bilingual French and English IB DP, with Spanish and German as additional foreign languages. This program is ideal for all students seeking an exceptional education that prepares them to become responsible citizens of the world and the leaders of tomorrow. In addition, students follow the New York State Board of Regents program and are encouraged to take Advanced Placement (AP) exams.

Additional language support is provided to help students strengthen their second language so that they can participate in all English and French programs with native speakers. We also provide a wide range of after-school enrichment classes which allows students to fully develop further in their intellectual, creative and physical activities.

Madison Campus Monterrey

(Founded 1978)

Head of School
Lic. Esthela Diaz de May

PYP coordinator
Ricardo Domínguez Gámez

MYP coordinator
Perla Priscila Vargas Andrade

Status Private

Boarding/day Day

Gender Coeducational

Language of instruction
English, Spanish

Authorised IB programmes
PYP, MYP

Age Range 2 – 15 years

Fees
PYP Programme US$4,900
MYP Programme US$5,800

Address
Marsella #3055
Col. Alta Vista
Monterrey, Nuevo León
C.P. 64840 | MÉXICO

TEL +52 81 8359 06276

Email
contacto@colegiosmadison.
edu.mx

Website
madisonmonterrey.edu.mx

Madison schools have been nurturing minds and creating successful learning experiences for more than 40 years in our community. We have been fulfilling internationally certified academic standards through collaborative work, positive attitudes and core values. These are highly regarded in our schools.

Madison Campus Monterrey was the first school founded in the Madison Group of Schools, which are located in different Mexican states: Nuevo León, Coahuila, Yucatán, and Chihuahua.

Monterrey is a modern and industrial city, known as one of the three most industrious and important cities in Mexico.

Monterrey has at least four well-known universities with important international exchange programs and several smaller ones.

Madison Campus Monterrey became bilingual in 1994. Since then, it has had a strong emphasis on the English language.

The school has programs that nurture its students' development:

- "Ruta de Independencia" School Trip: 5th-grade students spent five days travelling throughout different places in Mexico where the Independence Movement took place. This program enriches what they had learned in their classes, so they can live, themselves, a real learning experience.
- United Nations Model: Academic simulation of the United Nations that aims to educate participants about civics, effective communication, globalization, and multilateral diplomacy.
- Youth Leader Explorer exhibition: organized by one of the most important high schools in Mexico where students develop different scientific skills.
- French Immersion Program: a week program held in Quebec, Canada.
- International trips: Every year we offer a complete Educational Travel Program to reinforce our main objective, that is to educate citizens of the world.

In 1999 the school decided to become part of the IB and began working towards its authorization. The school achieved authorization to offer the International Baccalaureate Primary Years Programme (PYP) in 2003 and the International Baccalaureate Middle Years Programme (MYP) in 2007.

We have had students from Russia, Argentina, Venezuela, Canada, Nicaragua, Colombia, United States, Philippines, Lebanon, Poland, Switzerland, Germany, Spain, India, and Japan.

One of Madison Group of Schools' greatest strengths is an International Teachers Program that enhances our students' abilities to interact with foreign cultures and learn from them.

For the last fifteen years, we have had instructors from Canada, China, Costa Rica, Croatia, Cuba, England, Ireland, Lebanon, Scotland, Poland, and the United States, teaching at our schools. Students and graduates from our school are well appreciated by the community and by the high schools they attend. Our well-articulated, inquisitive, mature and responsible graduates and students have already made a difference here in Mexico.

Madison Campus Monterrey is a certified school by SEP, an active member of FEP as well as IBAMEX.

Madison International School

(Founded 2007)

Head of School
Samanta Galvan

PYP coordinator
Rolando De La Torre

MYP coordinator
Eduardo Vargas

Status Private

Boarding/day Day

Gender Coeducational

Language of instruction
English, Spanish

Authorised IB programmes
PYP, MYP

Age Range 1 – 15 years

Number of pupils enrolled
837

Fees
PYP US$8,000
MYP US$8,500

Address
Camino Real #100
Col. El Uro
Monterrey, Nuevo León
C.P. 64986 | MÉXICO

TEL +52 81 8218 7909

Email
admisiones@mis.edu.mx

Website
www.mis.edu.mx

We belong to the Madison Group of Schools, which has more than 40 years of educational experience.

On a national level, we have campuses in the cities of Chihuahua and Mérida*. Locally, we have the Madison International School (MIS), Instituto Anglo Británico, and Madison Monterrey.

Our particular campus opened its doors in 2007 in the south of Monterrey, in the area of El Uro, and we offer Nursery, Kindergarten, Primary and Secondary levels of schooling.

MIS is located in Monterrey, an industrial and modern city in Northeastern Mexico. The city is anchor to the third-largest metropolitan area in Mexico. Its economic, cultural and social influence makes it one of Mexico's most developed cities with the highest per capita income in the nation.

MIS provides a first-class education for students and gives children a head start in the modern world by taking their English skills to a higher level. Madison's superb bilingual program teaches children English beginning in their most formative years.

Madison International School uses the constructivist educational method and is also based on inquiry, reflexion, and active participation of our students.

As part of our international profile we encourage our students to participate in different programmes that nurture their development, such as:

- Destination Imagination: engage participants in project-based challenges that are designed to build confidence and develop extraordinary creativity, critical thinking, communication, and teamwork skills.
- Model United Nations: academic simulation of this international organization, which aims to educate participants about effective communication, globalization and multilateral diplomacy.

Madison International School proudly boasts some of the best student facilities in Monterrey such as computer and science labs, video and conference halls, library, cafeteria, music and art rooms, and substantial sports fields that are all staffed by teachers committed to creating a fun and interesting learning environment for the children. The school offers extracurricular classes ranging from guitar, piano, robotics, to sports teams. Madison's dedication to students' safety and wellbeing is the most important element, which is why we provide excellent security features that will give every parent and child peace of mind.

We encourage diversity and internationalism and therefore we welcome students, teachers and families from any religion, race, and nationality.

MARYLAND
INTERNATIONAL SCHOOL

(Founded 2017)

Head of School
Rebekah Ghosh

PYP coordinator
Rebekah Ghosh

MYP coordinator
Nikki Tanner

DP coordinator
Nikki Tanner

Status Private

Boarding/day Day

Gender Coeducational

Language of instruction
English

Authorised IB programmes
PYP, MYP, DP

Age Range 6 – 18 years

Number of pupils enrolled
200

Fees
Domestic Students: US$12,850 –
US$19,250
International Students:
US$24,450 – US$32,000

Address
6135 Old Washington Road
Elkridge
MD 21075 | USA

TEL +1 410 220 3792

Email info@
marylandinternationalschool.org

Website www.
marylandinternationalschool.org

The future belongs to the curious. The ones who are not afraid to try something, explore it, poke at it, question it and turn it inside out.

About

Maryland International School (MDIS) is an independent, private school in Howard County, Maryland, conveniently located in the Baltimore-Washington metropolitan area. MDIS is the first school in the state of Maryland, and the second in the mid-Atlantic region, to offer three International Baccalaureate (IB) programs: Primary Years Programme (PYP), Middle Years Programme (MYP), and Diploma Programme (DP).

Our beautiful 9 acre campus serves students from grades 1-12. Our mission and vision is to provide an academically rigorous and supportive college-preparatory education with an interdisciplinary and applied focus on the Science, Technology, Engineering, and Mathematics (STEM) disciplines in order to prepare students to become creative problem solvers, effective communicators, and tomorrow's leaders who think ethically, independently, and globally.

IB & STEM

Our curriculum integrates the International Baccalaureate curriculum with STEM specific programs and pathways. Our STEM-integrated curriculum was developed taking into account the principles of Universal Design for Learning (UDL), technology standards, disciplinary literacy standards, Next Generation Science Standards (NGSS), and transdisciplinary core content lessons. Our curriculum is designed to promote critical thinking, collaboration, and innovation in order to develop the academic, emotional and social skills that

students will need to live and work in a globalized world. Our after school STEM programs include, but are not limited to: Robotics Club, Science Olympiad, FIRST Lego League, Coding Club, and a Drone Club.

Signature Programs & Events

MDIS highlights the IB philosophy of building international-mindedness through our Global Ambassadors Program (GAP), Mother Language Day, and Celebration of Nations. GAP, our study abroad immersion program with a service-learning component builds leadership beyond the classroom. It includes an international student program bringing students together from around the world to study at MDIS. We celebrate the cultures, languages, and traditions of countries around the world with our Celebration of Nations and our Mother Language day. These events showcase the diversity of our students by giving them a day to share their experiences, teach their language and to build connections through the use of the 10 learner profiles.

Admissions

Our admissions process operates on a rolling basis and so we welcome student applications year-round. When considering an applicant, we recognize that every child is unique. We evaluate a student's overall academic and developmental readiness and whether they will thrive in, and benefit from, the academic challenges of our curriculum. For additional information, please reach out by phone or email to learn more about the MDIS admission process.

MERCYHURST
Preparatory School

A Sponsored Ministry of the Sisters of Mercy

(Founded 1926)

Principal Tom Rinke

President
Joseph J. Haas

DP coordinator
Paul Cancilla

Status Private

Boarding/day Mixed

Gender Coeducational

Language of instruction
English

Authorised IB programmes
DP

Age Range 13 – 18 years

Number of pupils enrolled 425

Address
538 East Grandview Boulevard
Erie **PA 16504 | USA**

TEL +1 814 824 2323

Email
aorlando@mpslakers.com

Website www.mpslakers.com

Mission

Mercyhurst Preparatory School (MPS) is a four year coeducational Catholic secondary school founded by the Sisters of Mercy to prepare students from all religious and ethnic backgrounds for a successful, productive, and compassionate life in an ever-changing and interdependent world. A Mercyhurst Prep education is based upon the teachings of Jesus Christ, the Mercy charism, and a modeling of Judeo Christian values. We strive for excellence in academic and co-curricular programs, promote service to our local and global communities, and foster the dedication and active support of the students, parents, faculty, staff, and alumni of the Mercyhurst community.

Community

Mercyhurst Prep is located on the beautiful shores of Lake Erie in the USA where students experience seasonal change and access to numerous outdoor activities in this safe community of 200,000. Erie, Pennsylvania has easy access to major US cities – Cleveland, Buffalo, and Pittsburgh – as well as Toronto, Canada.

Curriculum

As a college preparatory school, the curriculum is rigorous. 98% of graduates matriculate to post-secondary institutions. The school offers a wide range of courses at the college prep, honors, and International Baccalaureate (IB) levels. Implemented in 1985, the International Baccalaureate program is geared towards knowledgeable and caring students who are motivated to succeed in a well-rounded interdisciplinary curriculum, which leads to IB certificates or the IB diploma.

Students take eight courses in each of the school's three terms. Our block schedule classes are ninety minutes long.

We encourage every student to study at least one IB course.

STEAM (Science, Technology, Engineering, Arts, and Math in the Classroom)

One-to-one iPad deployment provides a tremendous blending of cutting-edge classroom technology with best educational practice. MPS faculty receives extensive ongoing training in the use of iPads. Faculty and students are supported by a full-time technology expert and coach. iPad integration occurs across the curriculum.

Creative Arts

The school offers 54 courses in the performing and visual arts taught by a faculty of active award-winning artists. Students exhibit and perform year-round in the school's nationally recognized musical theatre, dance, and choral groups.

Collaboration with Mercyhurst University

Academically advanced students may begin college course work or pursue a subject in greater depth at Mercyhurst University. Some students may complete freshman year of college and senior year of high school simultaneously. The two schools are adjoined by a walkway, making each easily accessible to the other.

Athletics, Activities, and Clubs

A wide variety of extracurricular programs meets the interests of our students and helps them develop time management skills, hone their ability to prioritize, assume responsibility for learning and social events, and compete in ventures that highlight their talents. Athletic teams include football, soccer, tennis, golf, volleyball, basketball, swimming, softball, cheerleading, baseball, rowing, cross country, and track. MPS teams regularly win district, regional, and state titles with a program philosophy that emphasizes dedication, teamwork, and good sportsmanship.

Boarding Opportunities

While 95% of the students are day students, the school also serves international students from countries such as China, Vietnam, Taiwan, India, Brazil, Canada, Mexico, and Russia. Partnerships with Pennsylvania International Academy (PIA) and Christian Boarding provide dormitory housing for international and American students who board full-time as well as weekdays. Visit mpslakers.com/boarding for more information.

A small sampling of colleges attended by Mercyhurst Prep grads includes:

- Boston University
- Brandeis University
- Carnegie Mellon University
- Case Western University
- Dartmouth University
- New York University
- Penn State University
- Rochester Institute of Technology
- Rutgers University
- Swarthmore College
- University of Notre Dame
- Wake Forest University
- Villanova University

Faculty

60% of our faculty/administration hold postgraduate degrees. The student to faculty ratio is 11:1. Besides in-depth expertise in their specific fields, our faculty embody the Mercy charism, an attribute that makes them unique and exceedingly qualified to work with teens. Many teachers travel extensively during breaks and summer vacation, bringing an international mindset to instruction.

Admissions Policy

Mercyhurst Prep admits students of any race, creed, color, or national origin without discrimination. When any student applies for admission, every effort is made to determine whether the school offers an educational program which will allow that student to develop intellectually, socially, spiritually, emotionally, and physically.

Future Ready and Engaging

The Bill and Audrey Hirt DREAM Lab and Room 201 serve as learning environments where the infusion of new digital tools and technology can enhance the learning process. Teachers utilize proven and emerging teaching strategies while students learn fundamental concepts like communication, collaboration, critical thinking, and creativity.

Examples of our technology include: 9 Touchscreens, 2 Video Walls, 40 Lenovo Intel Laptops, 16 Makerbot 3D Printers, 3 Workstations with Touchscreens, Drones, 3 Oculus Rift Immersive Virtual Reality Systems, 12 zSpace Combined Virtual Reality and Augmented Reality Systems, 12 Oculus Quest 2, 5 DJI Robomaster S-1, 15 Sphero Bolts, 10 Lego Mindstorm Expansion Kits, 8 Lego Spike Expansion Kits, 24 Lenovo Laptops, 15 Raspberry Pi 4 Desktop Kits, 6 HP Omen Gaming Computers.

Performing Arts Center (PAC)

Our newly renovated PAC boasts a cutting-edge flying system, acoustics, lighting, and climate control. These improvements will help prepare our students for the creative endeavors of a 21st century actor, dancer, vocalist, musician, lighting designer and technician.

METROPOLITAN SCHOOL OF PANAMA

A NORD ANGLIA EDUCATION SCHOOL

(Founded 2011)

Headteacher
Mr. Daniel McKee

PYP coordinator
Ms. Shelley Love

MYP coordinator
Mr. Ryan Manary

DP coordinator
Mr. Ryan Skinner

Status Private

Boarding/day Day

Gender Coeducational

Language of instruction
English

Authorised IB programmes
PYP, MYP, DP

Age Range 3 – 18 years

Number of pupils enrolled 755

Fees
Day: $10,149 – $20,169

Address
Green Valley,
Panama Norte
Panama City | **PANAMA**

TEL +507 317 1130

Email admissions@
themetropolitanschool.com

Website www.
themetropolitanschool.com

The Metropolitan School of Panama (MET), is an International Baccalaureate (IB) World School for students aged 3-18, and the only IB continuum school in Panama authorized to offer the PYP, MYP and DP programmes in Panama.

Celebrating 10 years of world-class academics, the MET offers Preschool through 12th grade programs, with more than 775 students hailing from 45 nationalities.

Our school is committed to each child reaching their personal level of excellence through a balanced academic program that nurtures their self-esteem and potential and engages them in the world around them.

The MET is proud to form part of Nord Anglia Education, the world's leading premium schools organization, uniting with 75 other outstanding schools in 31 countries worldwide. NAE's global family of schools share a common philosophy that there is no limit to what its students can achieve. Our students benefit from collaborations with world renowned institutions through our Juilliard-Nord Anglia Performing Arts Programme, preparing them for the world's stage. Our MIT STEAM curriculum which focuses on transferable skills in an evolving world. Our global scale enables us to recruit and retain the best teachers in the world, offering a quality education in Panama.

New Campus. New Opportunities.
The MET opened a new 5 hectare campus in 2020 offering unparalleled educational facilities, not just in Panama but in Central America.

MET students discover a world beyond the traditional classroom with modern learning spaces designed for collaborative learning; including 7 fully-equipped science labs, a STEAM lab, black box theater, FIFA sized soccer field, a 25 meter pool and specialized areas for design, technology and music.

We are a school committed to the education of the future and are proud to offer a 1-to-1 technology program for all students, implementing Apple technology throughout the school.

Our goal is to educate your child for the future, enhancing learning through collaborations with the world's best organizations. We Individually tailor our approach to your child enabling them to achieve outstanding academic results while developing the skills and mind-set to thrive in a changing world.

The MET's excellent results and acceptances at the world's leading universities are a testament to our excellent execution of the IB Program and our dedicated, experienced and highly qualified teachers. The 2021 MET class achieved an excellent 96% IB pass rate, significantly higher than the international average of 89%. Our highest IB score was 43 points. MET graduates attend some of the most prestigious colleges and universities worldwide. This year, our 2021 graduating class has received scholarship offers totalling over $3M USD.

Come and learn about the Metropolitan School of Panama. You want the best for your child. So do we. You won't find an international school in Panama better equipped to prepare your child for a successful future.

Enrolment is open throughout the year and we always welcome enquiries and visits from prospective families. To explore the MET difference please contact: admissions@themetropolitanschool.com

MEADOWRIDGE SCHOOL

(Founded 1985)

Head of School
Mr. Scott Banack

Deputy Head of School
Mr. Terry Donaldson

PYP coordinator
Mrs. Heather Nicholson

MYP coordinator
Mr. Scott Rinn

DP coordinator
Ms. Kristal Bereza

Status Private

Boarding/day Day

Gender Coeducational

Language of instruction
English

Authorised IB programmes
PYP, MYP, DP

Age Range 4 – 18 years

Number of pupils enrolled 670

Fees
Domestic Fees C$25,925
International Fees C$35,925

Address
12224 240th Street
Maple Ridge BC
V4R 1N1 | CANADA

TEL +1 604 467 4444

Email
admissions@meadowridge.
bc.ca

Website
www.meadowridge.bc.ca

Meadowridge School exists as a point of departure for parents and students who seek more meaning from education; an unfettered education that has a greater impact on the whole individual and more relevance to the realities of the world.

Our school is an International Baccalaureate (IB) Continuum World School, accredited through multiple organizations. We celebrate teaching and learning through the most balanced, demanding, and international curriculum, and have built a culture which enables it: a community of families who believe that children learn best in a culture of conscious care, academic challenge, clear and high expectations, constant communication, intercultural understanding, collaboration with families, creative teaching, and open and inviting facilities. At Meadowridge, we live what we teach and model what we believe – and we do it together with our families.

Meadowridge is a school which values academic achievement, but one which also insists our children live well, live balanced lives, and flourish within a community. Students learn through inquiry, experience, and exploration, and they learn about themselves, our communities, and our world. Meadowridge develops young adults who, as leaders, understand that the way to excellence involves understanding and working with and for others, and who have developed the skills, knowledge, and dispositions to be able to engage with complex issues in intercultural settings, with a foundation of fairness and just treatment of all.

Our school, from classroom to natural woodland, is the setting for this program. Just 45 minutes east of Vancouver, British Columbia, Meadowridge is located in beautiful Maple Ridge on a unique, pastoral 27-acre campus complete with gardens, greenhouses, a discovery forest, and stream for students across the continuum to engage and explore. Our 150,000+ square foot facility includes state-of-the-art science labs, a theatre, a design lab, an international-sized soccer pitch, and a nine-classroom high school complex.

Through our outstanding teaching, programs, and facilities, Meadowridge develops the confidence in students to not only meet the future, but also to create it. To discover more about Meadowridge visit us online at meadowridge. bc.ca/discover.

Mott Hall Science and Technology Academy

Principal
Dr. Patrick Awosogba

Assistant Principals
Ms. Marcia Thomas & Mr. Stany Leblanc

MYP coordinator
Mr. Thomas Moore

Status State

Boarding/day Day

Gender Coeducational

Language of instruction
English, Spanish

Authorised IB programmes
MYP

Age Range 11 – 14 years

Number of pupils enrolled
402

Address
250 East 164th Street
Bronx, New York
NY 10456 | USA

TEL +1 718 293 4017

Email
MHSTAIB@motthallsta.org

Website
www.motthallsta.org

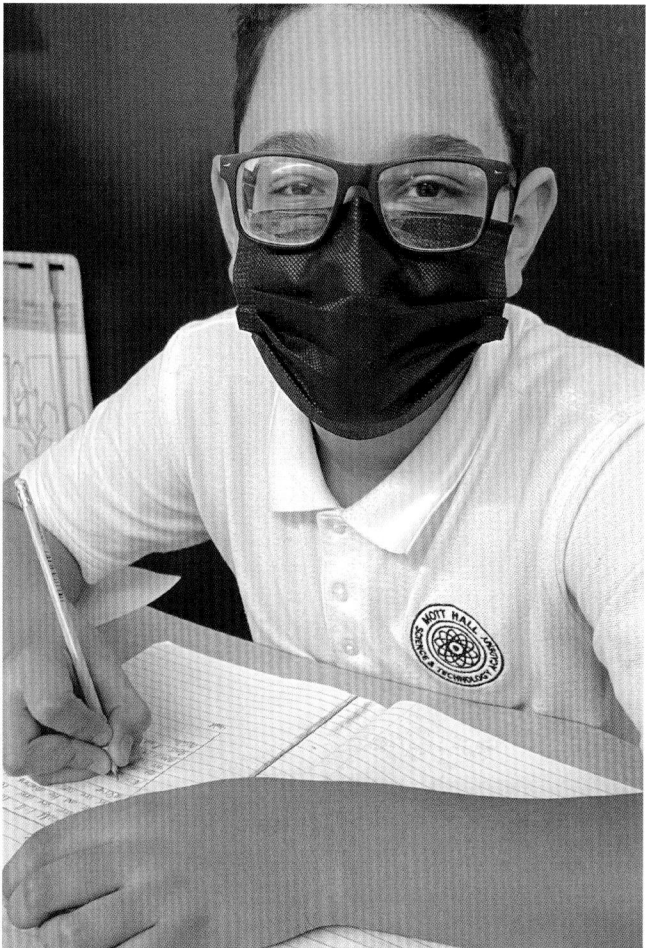

Mott Hall Science and Technology Academy is a rigorous math, science, and technology focused middle school. We offer families the opportunity for their children to meet the highest academic expectations and standards, to make smooth transitions to selective high schools, to compete successfully for admission to top public and private colleges and to succeed as a global citizen. Our school culture is characterized by a shared vision for academic excellence, the healthy personal growth of all students, and a commitment to our strong belief that all students can and will succeed in their endeavors.

At Mott Hall, students, faculty, and staff members have a shared vision of the individual's ability to achieve personal success each day as preparation to become active members of our global society. The journey our students embark on when they enter our doors is marked by continuous support and guidance academically, emotionally, and physically, to ensure the holistic development of our young people. Students enter a community that embraces them while challenging them.

Instruction in our school is rooted in collaboration and inquiry, which leads to deeper individual understanding of content and application of this content to real life. During this time of blended and distance learning, our curriculum remains driven by conceptual learning, using digital activities and personalized differentiation to meet the needs of our students. We aim to provide an equitable education that allows each student to discover and utilize their full potential, while finding joy in learning.

Along with strong support in our classrooms, we create a safe learning environment for our students, nurturing and supporting them as they grow. Students are equipped with tools to overcome obstacles they may face and to help them become understanding and respectful of different identities and cultures. To do so, we focus on our school's core values: respect, responsibility, integrity, compassion, and fairness, along with the International Baccalaureate learner profile traits. With these tools, our students become life long learners ready to actively participate in the world.

In 2014, our school became the first New York City public middle school to be certified as an International Baccalaureate Middle Years programme. In addition, we have been a certified Advancement Via Individual Determination (AVID) model school since 2013. After over a decade of service to our students and families, we look forward to our continued growth as a community.

Mulgrave, The International School of Vancouver

(Founded 1993)	**Age Range** 3 – 18 years
Head of School John Wray	**Number of pupils enrolled** 1025
PYP coordinator Janet Hicks & Shanaz Ramji	**Fees** Day: CND$25,000
MYP coordinator Mike Olynyk	**Address** 2330 Cypress Bowl Lane West Vancouver BC
DP coordinator Aziz Batada	**V7S 3H9	CANADA**
Status Private	**TEL** +1 604 922 3223
Boarding/day Day	**Email** admissions@mulgrave.com
Gender Coeducational	**Website** www.mulgrave.com
Language of instruction English	
Authorised IB programmes PYP, MYP, DP	

Mulgrave, The International School of Vancouver is a multicultural, gender-inclusive International Baccalaureate World School (pre-school to Grade 12). Nestled on the slopes of Cypress Mountain, overlooking the Pacific Ocean and downtown Vancouver, our stunning campus provides students and faculty custom-built spaces where they can inspire each other as they are all inspired by the views. Our diverse community is united in its commitment to develop the interpersonal and intercultural skills, attitudes, and values that will allow our students to thrive and be happy no matter where in the world they find themselves. Our graduates go on to post-secondary institutions across the globe; this year, they have accepted offers spanning from UBC and McGill in Canada, to UPenn and USC in the United States, and to UCL in and Hong Kong University abroad.

Our Mission: Inspiring Excellence in Education and Life

Through the continuous pursuit of personal best, Mulgrave strives to equip lifelong learners to thrive in a culturally diverse and interdependent world. Our goal is for students to embrace, with passion and confidence, their responsibility to make a difference by serving their communities, both locally and in the world at large.

Our Culture: A warm, vibrant, supportive community

Developing a strong aptitude for learning, service, and leadership is inherent to our school's ethos, as is a strong culture of caring and support. Mulgrave is highly valued for our positive community spirit, enriched by the diversity of

families from more than 42 countries, and its vibrant learning atmosphere. Experienced teachers from around the world provide a comprehensive, appropriately challenging, and personalised IB curriculum to an equally ambitious and capable student body.

Our Strategic Plan 2021-2024: Weaving Our Future, Common Threads

Over this three year period, it is our intention, while being true to our school's guiding statements, to build on our success from our previous strategic plan and to ensure that we continue to provide an outstanding future-oriented education for the students in our care. We will engage student agency and technology to continue to support increased personalisation of learning, curriculum and support. We will focus on student health and wellbeing with more emphasis on social and emotional learning and the use of outdoor education experiences. And we will focus on students' skill development with special emphasis on creativity, global citizenship, and social entrepreneurship.

Accreditations

Mulgrave is proud to be an accredited member of the Council of International Schools (CIS), the Independent Schools Association of British Columbia (ISABC), and Canadian Accredited Independent Schools (CAIS), and is also authorised by the International Baccalaureate Organization as an IB Continuum School.

Navajo Preparatory School

Navajo Preparatory School, Inc.
Yideeską́ą́góó Naat'áanii
Leaders Now and Into the Future

(Founded 1991)

Head of School
Shawna Becenti

DP coordinator
Donna Fernandez

Status State

Boarding/day Mixed

Gender Coeducational

Language of instruction
English

Authorised IB programmes
DP

Age Range 13 – 18 years

Number of pupils enrolled 265

Fees
Day: US$1,000 (Native American)
– US$3,000 (Non-Native
American)

Address
1220 West Apache Street
Farmington
NM 87401 | USA

TEL +1 505 326 6571

Email
sbecenti@navajoprep.com

Website
www.navajoprep.com

Navajo Preparatory School's mission reflects the integral values of the International Baccalaureate Programme:

- To develop inquisitive, compassionate life-long learners and leaders through a challenging curriculum of international education and assessment.
- To promote a strong foundation of Navajo Philosophy and holistic world view that fosters intercultural understanding and respect in a global society.
- The mission is reflected in the IB Learner Profile and the School's motto:

"Yideeskaago Naat'aanii – Leaders Now and Into the Future"

Navajo Preparatory School is an IB World School authorized to offer the Diploma Programme. We uniquely serve Native American and non-Native American students, offering a rigorous college-preparatory curriculum. We develop the whole person, in a balanced educational experience of international-mindedness and Navajo Philosophy of learning.

Our school is located in the enchanting Four Corners area on 82 acres offering a small school learning environment.

It steeps students in a deep appreciation of the Navajo language, culture and history.

We employ the Navajo philosophy of learning Nitsáhákees (East-White) – Thinking, Nahat'á (South-Blue) – Planning, Iiná (West-Yellow) – Action, Sihasin (North-Black) – Reflection to guide our educational curriculum and Navajo Prep mindset.

Students have opportunities to engage in STEM activities, writing and reading enjoyment, and leadership development. Armed with this impressive, balanced education, students graduate with the skills to succeed in college and an understanding of the world around them.

Students participate in numerous Gifted & Talented programs, Student Senate, clubs, and interscholastic sports such as football, volleyball, basketball, baseball, softball, golf, cross country and track. Students also have opportunities for community service.

Over 95% of our graduates are accepted into college. Our school is a Mac environment, students are provided with a Mac Airbook for school use. Campus has 5 modern and comfortable residential halls.

(Founded 1821)

Head of School Joe Williams

DP coordinator
Jennifer McMahon

Status Private

Boarding/day Mixed

Gender Coeducational

Language of instruction
English

Authorised IB programmes
DP

Age Range 14 – 19 years

Number of pupils enrolled
340

Fees
Day: US$37,200
Boarding: US$64,700

Address
70 Main Street
New Hampton
NH 03256 | USA

TEL +1 603 677 3401

Email
admission@newhampton.org

Website
www.newhampton.org

Lifelong Learners and Active Global Citizens

New Hampton School is an independent, coeducational, college preparatory school for boarding and day students, grades 9 through 12 and postgraduate. Nestled in the foothills of New Hampshire's White Mountains and in the heart of the beautiful Lakes Region, yet just 90 minutes from Boston, Massachusetts, the 350-acre campus features six contemporary classroom buildings. On-campus housing includes 13 dormitories, varying in size, each with resident dorm parents/family and complementary dorm life programming activities throughout the year.

Sharing the whole world

Our school's mission is to cultivate lifelong learners who will serve as active global citizens. Core values focused on respect and responsibility provide an essential foundation, while our inclusive community immerses students in an on-campus network of diverse cultures and a worldwide network of alumni, families, and travel opportunities. By allowing classroom conversations to represent more points of view, expertise from outside sources, and intellectual links to coursework, we ensure students are introduced to a full range of insights. Ours is a conscious curriculum, built on an interconnected understanding of the world.

The student body includes representation from 28 states and 30 different countries. Twenty-five percent of students are international. New Hampton routinely sends students to top colleges and universities including Dartmouth College, University of Michigan, Princeton University, Cornell University, Williams College, Syracuse University, UCLA, and University of Chicago.

Empowering Technology

New Hampton School features a 1:1 iPad Program and is considered a leader in technology integration. Our school is an Apple Distinguished School since 2012; this distinguishing recognition is only given to those schools embracing a vision of "continuous innovation." Students are assured of vital connectivity, file sharing, video conferencing, organizational tools, interactive course materials and tests, and all of the latest innovations via Apple.

Enlivened Learning

Our school is proud of programmatic variety including our strong athletic program, art offerings including Animation by the Walt Disney Family Museum, student leadership opportunities, clubs and activities. International Baccalaureate classes begin in eleventh grade and can be taken as part of the full Diploma Programme or as certificate courses. The IB philosophy pervades the curriculum, and ninth and tenth graders are prepared to embrace its challenges. Equally prominent is the school's commitment to the delivery of durable skills using relevant content with emphasis on experiential education, Habits of Mind, and career partnerships. The average class size is 11 and the breadth of academic offerings ranges from university rigor to support, from the IB Diploma Programme, honors courses, and independent study to tutorials and International Support classes that accommodate individual methods and pace of learning.

Weekend activities on and off campus include dances, dinner trips, shopping, hikes, concerts, day trips to Boston, and student-designed outings. The school's dining hall has been recognized for its outstanding cuisine.

NORTH BROWARD PREPARATORY SCHOOL
A NORD ANGLIA EDUCATION SCHOOL

Head of School
Bruce Fawcett

DP coordinator
Tamara Wolpowitz

Status Private

Boarding/day Mixed

Gender Coeducational

Language of instruction
English

Authorised IB programmes
DP

Age Range 3 – 18 years

Address
7600 Lyons Road
Coconut Creek
FL 33073 | USA

TEL +1 954 247 0179

Email
admissions@nbps.org

Website
www.nbps.org

Come Explore the Extraordinary Learning Environment at North Broward Preparatory School

Located in Sunny South Florida, North Broward Preparatory School is an extraordinary community of learners. Our teachers and leadership team think beyond traditional education to transform learning and provide an academically challenging environment including the International Baccalaureate Diploma Program, often referred to as the gold standard of learning.

The International Baccalaureate Diploma Programme is a balanced program of education that prepares students for success at university and life beyond. It is designed to address the intellectual, social, emotional and physical wellbeing of students. At the heart of the IB program is a focus on developing students who are inquirers, thinkers, knowledgeable, communicators, principled, open-minded, caring, risk-takers, balanced and reflective.

At North Broward Preparatory School we believe in developing these qualities, not only in the students but also in our faculty members. Our teachers strive to support the personal needs of each student and create a customized learning environment that ensures their success.

Through our boarding and five-day residential programs, North Broward Preparatory School serves as a home away for students from 25 countries, including the U.S. that we welcome to our International Village. Boarding students are surrounded by a nurturing environment with caring, dedicated professionals available 24-hours a day. Our Residential Life team ensures that students are given the resources they need to thrive both academically and socially.

As part of Nord Anglia Education, the world's leading educational organization, the student learning experience is enhanced through collaborations with Juilliard, MIT and UNICEF. We encourage you to schedule a tour to learn more about how we can customize the learning experience for your child, ignite their curiosity and ensure that your child loves coming to school. To schedule a tour, call 954-247-0179 or go to www.nbps.org/admissions.

NORTHERN
INTERNATIONAL
SCHOOL

Principal
Prof. Estela María Irrera de Pallaro

DP coordinator
Marisa Zárate

Status Private

Boarding/day Day

Gender Coeducational

Language of instruction
Spanish, English, Italian, Portuguese

Authorised IB programmes
DP

Age Range 2 – 18 years

Address
Ruote 8 Km 61.5.
1633. Pilar, Buenos Aires |
ARGENTINA

TEL +54 2322 49 1208

Website
www.intschools.org/school/northern

Together with Islands International School and Southern International School.

Northern International School opened its doors in 1997 in a site of 8 hectares in Pilar.

Its founder, Prof. Estela María Irrera de Pallaro, has as an aim to offer a demanding educational quality for families looking for a better lifestyle for their children. With the benefits that contact with nature offers, Northern International School develops all its regular activities in a bright and cheerful environment.

The International Baccalaureate, of which we have been members since 1997, is key in this institution; that is why teachers and heads are trained regularly.

The school has all the facilities needed to comply with this modern and demanding programme: science and IT labs, a library for research, a multi-purpose hall as well as comfortable and bright classrooms.

Our three schools have fully equipped laboratories for the experimental sciences; they are an essential facility for classes in Physics, Chemistry and Biology. Our laboratory provisions are not only for demonstration classes but also for students to become personally acquainted with different research techniques and apply them in practice in experiments ranging from the simple to the more complex.

Our students learn to handle laboratory materials safely and efficiently and make full use of them in different pieces of research.

At primary level, research projects include: photosynthesis, animal nutrition, the ill effects of tobacco, analysis of animal movements, electrical resistance, the structure of materials, magnetism, the human body, heat energy, ecosystems, soil, water, cells, life process in vegetables and diet in humans.

At secondary level, research projects include: coefficients of contact, genetics, physical and chemical properties of hydrocarbons, evolutionary theory, population growth, biodiversity, pollution of the environment, ecosystems, and health and human physiology.

Year after year, our students take part in different events and competitions, among these Physics and Biology Olympiads, science fairs organized by ESSARP (English Speaking Scholastic Association of the River Plate), local representative of the University of Cambridge, and Mathematics Olympiads organized by OMA (Argentine Mathematics Olympiads). In recent years the schools have taken part in the worldwide NASA projects and one of our schools has on three occasions won the regional competition and taken part in the world finals in Houston in the United States.

NORTHLANDS

SINCE 1920

(Founded 1920)

Head of School Lucila Minvielle PhD

PYP coordinator
Maria Ines Martinez Beccar Varela
& Natalia Torlaschi

DP coordinator Alicia Olea

Status Private

Boarding/day Day

Gender Coeducational

Language of instruction
English, Spanish

Authorised IB programmes
PYP, DP

Age Range 2 – 18 years

Number of pupils enrolled
1828

Olivos site
Roma 1248, Olivos
Buenos Aires | ARGENTINA

TEL +54 11 4711 8400

Email admissionsolivos@
northlands.edu.ar

Nordelta site
Av de los Colegios 680, Nordelta,
Buenos Aires | ARGENTINA

TEL +54 11 4871 2668/9

Email admissionsnordelta@
northlands.edu.ar

Website www.northlands.edu.ar

NORTHLANDS is a coeducational, bilingual IB World School that, through caring and innovative teaching, educates young people to the full extent of their individual potential. It is a school that values its Anglo-Argentine roots, while respecting all cultures, religions and nationalities. It offers an all-encompassing friendly environment reflected in its motto: Friendship & Service.

We aim to strengthen our position as leaders in education and innovation by focusing on our students' wellbeing and helping them discover their individual learning paths. We are expanding project based learning, Design and Technology and Education for Sustainable Development, instilling a culture of healthy lifestyle choices. We keep developing our campuses to meet the needs of our highly demanding programmes, and continue to develop a closely knit community influenced by the diversity of our families. We appreciate the richness of diversity and promote international mindedness as we currently have 11% of international families in Olivos and 19% in Nordelta.

Kindergarten Education
An all-embracing curriculum that works on physical, social, emotional, intellectual, ethical and aesthetic aspects through teaching and learning strategies focused on encouraging curiosity and the desire to know in children.

Primary Education
Our integral curriculum is based on inquiry and research as the ideal vehicles for learning. We provide a caring and stimulating environment where children enjoy doing their work and develop positive academic and interpersonal attitudes, self-confidence and self-discipline.

Secondary Education
During this phase students develop critical thinking skills, creativity and autonomy. Individual talents and personal interests are nurtured so that students can make satisfactory career choices at the end of their school life.

While we constantly pursue academic excellence, NORTHLANDS embraces many different programmes where students can develop a variety of skills. We consider Physical Education as an integral part of education as the well being of our students is accomplished through physical, mental and emotional balance. The Visual & Performing Arts Programme stimulates children to find alternative ways to express themselves. As students mature, they have the opportunity to explore visual arts, music and drama through a variety of techniques, instruments and cultures. Our Design & Technology Programme seeks to build a culture of innovation through the implementation of different techno-educational abilities such as construction, designing, programming and robotics, where students apply them to the real world by investigating digital solutions. Finally, our Personal & Social Education Programme is a central part of the comprehensive education that NORTHLANDS aims for its students. We help develop the values of integrity based on high moral standards enabling our children to freely choose what is right.

Orangewood Elementary

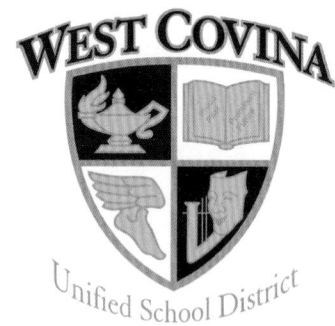

Principal
Ms. Janet Shirley

PYP coordinator
Mrs. Candice Hernandez

Status State

Boarding/day Day

Gender Coeducational

Language of instruction
English, Spanish, Mandarin

Authorised IB programmes
PYP

Age Range 4 – 11 years

Number of pupils enrolled
600

Address
1440 S. Orange Avenue
West Covina
CA 91790 | USA

TEL +1 626 939 4820

Website
orangewood.wcusd.org

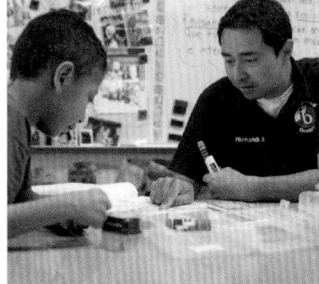

Reflecting Southern California's rich, multicultural heritage, Orangewood Elementary is a diverse TK-grade 5 learning community located in the San Gabriel Valley. Recognizing the power of the IB programmes, West Covina Unified School District established the International World Schools of West Covina, a TK-grade 12 continuum. In July 2017, Orangewood Elementary earned World School authorization, taking its place as the starting point for that continuum.

Students who read, write, think and communicate in two languages are best prepared for college, career, and the global economy. Dual immersion not only provides students with the advantage of bi-literacy, it cultivates cognitive flexibility and international mindedness. At Orangewood, families have the choice of enrolling their child in a Spanish or Mandarin dual immersion pathway. Students who continue their language studies in WCUSD will be eligible to earn the California Seal of Biliteracy with their high school diploma.

As part of Orangewood's commitment to providing a well-rounded curriculum, we incorporate technology and the arts. To enhance learning through 21st century skills, we introduce the use of 1:1 tech devices beginning with iPads in kindergarten and Chromebooks in grade 2. Coding and robotics are studied by all Orangewood students, serving as an early bridge to our district Career Technical Education pathway. Additionally, weekly dance lessons allow all students to explore, study and perform throughout elementary school.

Ultimately, the strength of Orangewood Elementary lies in our wholehearted approach to creating a principled, caring community that honors the uniqueness of each child. In 2021, Orangewood's commitment to kindness earned the distinction of being named a Capturing Kids'sHearts National Showcase School for the fourth consecutive year. The enthusiastic involvement of our families and the promotion of student action are evident in our grade level "IB Scholar Spotlights" and the numerous collaborative projects undertaken in our Learning Garden and the broader community.

Mission Statement:

"Orangewood Elementary is dedicated to developing globally-minded problem solvers. We enhance learning by inspiring students to inquire through transdisciplinary units, while empowering them to take action using the attributes of the Learner Profile."

Parkland Secondary School

Head of School
Kal Russell

DP coordinator
Erin Stinson

Status State

Boarding/day Day

Gender Coeducational

Language of instruction
English

Authorised IB programmes
DP

Number of pupils enrolled
500

Fees
Day: CND$250 deposit + $150 per IB course to a maximum of $500 CAN per year

Address
10640 McDonald Park Road
Sidney BC
V8L 5S7 | CANADA

TEL +1 250 655 2700

Email
krussell@saanichschools.ca

Website
parkland.sd63.bc.ca

Parkland Secondary School is located on the northern tip of the Saanich peninsula on beautiful Vancouver Island in British Columbia, Canada. We are within kilometers of the Victoria International Airport and the Schwartz Bay Ferry Terminal making for easy access to students and visitors. Parkland Secondary is mere steps from the Pacific Ocean creating fantastic opportunities for students in our Outdoor Education programs and our Sailing Academy. The school's catchment area includes Sidney, North Saanich and the Indigenous communities of Tseycum, Pauquachin and Tsawout. Every year Parkland hosts a number of International students from around the world-attracted to our school and community for the beautiful location and the myriad of programs offered for students.

Parkland Secondary is proud of its innovative, inspiring and inclusive learning environment on which it's built a solid reputation for unique programs. Parkland has a diverse selection of courses offerings including its renowned Marine Academy complementing the region's rich coastal geography. Students can also choose from courses in Trades, Technology, Visual and Performing Arts, and Athletics including a Hockey Academy and Canada's only Judo Academy.

The addition of the International Baccalaureate Diploma Programme makes Parkland the only English speaking public school on Vancouver Island to offer the IB Diploma Programme for students in their final two years of high school. The IB Diploma Programme prepares students for participation in a rapidly evolving and increasingly global society as they develop intellectually, emotionally, physically and ethically while acquiring skills that will prepare them for further education and life in the 21st century.

Students and families interested in finding out more about Parkland Secondary and the IB Diploma Programme can visit the Parkland website parkland.sd63.bc.ca/ and the Parkland IB website www.parklandib.ca/. If you are an international student you can visit the Saanich International Student Program website studyinsaanich.ca/. To find out more information about Parkland Secondary School and our IB Diploma Programme you are also welcome to contact Kal Russell, the principal, at krussell@saanichschools.ca or Erin Stinson, the IB Diploma Programme Coordinator, at estinson@saanichschools.ca.

PRIDE SCHOOLS

Superintendent
Dr. Brenda McDonald

IHS Principal
Brian Via

PRIDE Prep Principal
Crystal Oliver

MYP coordinator
Nicky Jones

DP coordinator
Nicky Jones

Status State

Boarding/day Day

Gender Coeducational

Language of instruction
English, Spanish

Authorised IB programmes
MYP, DP

Age Range 11 – 18 years

Number of pupils enrolled 698

Address
811 E Sprague Ave
Spokane
WA 99202 | USA

TEL +1 509 309 7680

Email
info@prideschools.org

Website
www.prideschools.org

PRIDE Schools is a public charter school district for PRIDE Prep Middle School and Innovation High School located in eastern Washington in downtown Spokane. Both schools are International Baccalaureate world schools authorized to offer the Middle Years Program and the Diploma Program. These are choice schools that serve a diverse population of students from all over the city and outlying rural towns.

PRIDE Schools offer students the opportunity to develop their skills through an inquiry-based curriculum with a focus on creating relevant projects that benefit both the student and our community. We regularly work with local businesses and colleges to give our students a holistic education that encompasses life both in and outside the school building. We encourage our students to follow their curiosity and discover new passions. *"The mission of PRIDE Schools is to honor the diversity and capacity of people through innovative education design. Our students are inspired to create, innovate, and challenge the status quo in a world that demands better designed systems, new solutions, and increased communication."* We fully believe that if students have a say in their education, then the students will invest more of their time in creating unique and innovative solutions and projects to better our community.

RIDLEY COLLEGE
SINCE 1889

(Founded 1889)

Headmaster
Mr. J. Edward Kidd

PYP coordinator
Marcie Lewis

MYP coordinator
Paul O'Rourke

DP coordinator
Saralyn Covent

Status Private

Boarding/day Mixed

Gender Coeducational

Language of instruction
English

Authorised IB programmes
PYP, MYP, DP

Age Range 4 – 18 years

Number of pupils enrolled 711

Fees
Day: CAD$20,500 – CAD$35,950
Domestic Boarders: CAD$63,950
International Boarders:
CAD$72,250

Address
PO Box 3013
2 Ridley Road
St Catharines ON
L2R 7C3 | CANADA

TEL +1 905 684 1889

Email
admissions@ridleycollege.com

Website
www.ridleycollege.com

Canada's leader in positive education, Ridley College is focused on educating the whole child and provides students with the tools that will help them lead flourishing lives. The coeducational boarding school was established in 1889 and is one of Canada's oldest and most prestigious, located on a beautiful 90-acre campus in St. Catharines, Ontario. Campus is an hour's drive from Toronto, ten minutes from Niagara Falls, and easily accessible from the Toronto Pearson and Buffalo Niagara International Airports. With nearly 380 boarders, Ridley has the largest CAIS boarding programme in Ontario. Students range from JK through Grade 12 and come from more than 60 countries worldwide.

"World Prep" is what you'll find here: a forward-looking, rigorous programme that prepares students for university and a promising future. Ridley is one of only three International Baccalaureate (IB) continuum boarding schools in North America, offering the Primary Years Programme, Middle Years Programme and Diploma Programme. In addition to the IB Programme, Ridley offers the Ontario Secondary School Diploma and a wide range of summer programmes, including the EAL credit course. Graduates are equipped with the knowledge and skills for success, going on to study at some of the top colleges and universities in Canada, the U.S. and beyond.

And in addition to its impressive academics, students experience a diverse co-curricular programme comprised of arts, athletics, leadership development, and community service. For more than 132 years, Ridley College has held true to its motto, *Terar Dum Prosim*, which translates to "May I be consumed in service." Students have plenty of opportunities year-round to give back to their communities and to explore new interests, cultivate passions and reach their potential in a challenging and supportive environment.

One of the school's defining features is its traditional House system, which integrates both boarding and day students into 10 boarding houses on campus, each of which has its own distinctive identity and sense of community. By incorporating local day students into its boarding programme, Ridley provides each member the opportunity to learn more about global cultures – all while enjoying a uniquely Canadian experience.

Santiago College

(Founded 1880)

Director
Ms Lorna Prado Scott

PYP coordinator
Mónika Naranjo

MYP coordinator
Angel Girano

DP coordinator
Renato Hamel

Status Private

Boarding/day Day

Gender Coeducational

Language of instruction
Spanish, English

Authorised IB programmes
PYP, MYP, DP

Age Range 3 years 9 months –
18 years

Number of pupils enrolled
1970

Address
Av. Camino Los Trapenses 4007
Lo Barnechea
Santiago | **CHILE**

TEL +56 2 27338800

Email
master@scollege.cl

Website
www.scollege.cl/index.php/es/

Santiago College is a bilingual, independent, co-educational day school, founded as a non-sectarian institution in 1880 with support from the US Methodist Church.

The educational programme at Santiago College meets the requirements of the Chilean Ministry of Education and is authorized to offer three of the IB Programmes: PYP, MYP and DP. Santiago College is accredited by CIS and NEASC.

Students normally enter Santiago College at PK level and stay until they graduate from 12th Grade. Students applying for admission to PK must be four years old by December 31st of the year prior to school entry. Santiago College accepts students without regard to gender, colour, creed, or ethnic, nationality or social origin. The selection process includes an interview with prospective students and their parents. Although most students are Chilean, a considerable number of students come from other countries and priority admission is given to overseas applicants. Approximately 90% of the graduating class enters Chilean universities and the remainder pursues studies in the USA or Europe.

The school operates a 180-day minimum calendar starting in early March and ending in mid-December. PK and kindergarten children have a half-day schedule. All other grades have a full school day beginning at 7:55am and ending between 3:30 and 5:10 pm. The school campus of 11 hectares is located in Lo Barnechea, 30 minutes drive from the city centre. Facilities include a library of 40,000 volumes, 98 classrooms, AV rooms, an auditorium, gymnasium, swimming pool, playing fields, science and computing labs, music and art studios and one cafeteria. All classrooms are equipped with interactive projectors, and numerous devices are available for student use at all grade levels, to support the integration of technology into learning.

Somersfield Academy

SOMERSFIELD ACADEMY
Montessori & International Baccalaureate Programmes

(Founded 1991)

Head of School
Mr. Peter T. Howe

MYP coordinator
Summer Wood Brice Pursell

DP coordinator
Kate Ross

Status Private

Boarding/day Day

Gender Coeducational

Language of instruction
English

Authorised IB programmes
MYP, DP

Age Range 3 – 18 years

Number of pupils enrolled 529

Address
107 Middle Road
Devonshire
DV 06 | BERMUDA

TEL +1 441 236 9797

Email
admissions@somersfield.bm

Website
www.somersfield.bm

Somersfield is a co-educational day school serving children from age 3 to 18. Students in the Children's House and Lower Primary Divisions follow the Montessori programme. The Upper Primary Division is designed for students aged 9 through 11. Secondary Division students aged 11-18 follow the International Baccalaureate Programmes: the 5 year Middle Years Programme (MYP) followed by the 2 year Diploma Programme (DP). The school received formal authorisation in 2005 from the IB in Geneva, Switzerland to conduct the MYP and became the first school in Bermuda to offer this programme. DP authorisation was awarded in 2019 and the school opened its new purpose-built DP building to our students in Sept 2019.

The five-year MYP offers students a rigorous, comprehensive and well-rounded academic preparation for moving on to the final two years, (grades 11 and 12) with the internationally-regarded IB Diploma Programme.

College Preparation

The IB Diploma Programme is an academically challenging and balanced programme of education with rigorous coursework and final examinations that prepare students, aged 16-19, for success at university and in life beyond. The DP aims to encourage students to be knowledgeable, inquiring, caring, open-minded and to develop intercultural understanding and the attitude necessary to appreciate a range of viewpoints. In addition to their DP courses, students wishing to attend a US University are supported with SAT preparation classes in English and Math.

Mission

Somersfield Academy will provide a unique educational experience for all its students based firmly on the ideals of The Somersfield Promise, the explicit beliefs of the Core Values Statement and our commitment to Diversity.

Our Promise

To stimulate intellectual curiosity and accomplishment; to instill compassion and respect; and always to honour the daring dreams and hidden talents of the individual.

Our Core Values

We are a learning community
We practice peace
We inspire intellectual curiosity
We foster independence and responsibility
We embrace a sense of joy and wonder
We honour the strength and courage to stand for truth
We instill respect for self and others.

Vision

Our school aims to prepare students to be global citizens, independent, life-long learners and to acquire the problem-solving skills and knowledge necessary for educational success. Teachers encourage self-expression and creative thinking as well as respect for and understanding of different philosophies and cultures in accordance with the school's learner profile.

SOUTHERN INTERNATIONAL SCHOOL

Principal
Prof. Estela María Irrera de Pallaro

DP coordinator
Paula Cantero

Status Private

Boarding/day Day

Gender Coeducational

Language of instruction
Spanish, English, Italian, Portuguese

Authorised IB programmes
DP

Age Range 2 – 18 years

Address
Freeway Buenos Aires – La Plata Km 34.
1884 Hudson, Buenos Aires |
ARGENTINA

TEL +54 11 4215 3636

Website
www.intschools.org/school/southern

Working together with Islands International School and Northern International School.

A community committed to education

In 1999 Mrs. Estela María Irrera de Pallaro, backed up and encouraged by her experience in founding and developing a comprehensive educational project, creates a new school with the aim of improving the institution objectives in a place where families can not only find peace and privacy but also a space in contact with nature.

The school mission is to teach students to interact and adapt to a complex social environment in which they need numerous tools to be able to succeed, accompanied by a teaching staff permanently trained. For this purpose, with a history of more than three decades, the school provides a demanding education that not only abides by academic aspects but expects to educate upright people as well.

Southern International School develops the students'

capacities through different activities so that they can interact with full independence and freedom in today's society.

International Baccalaureate Programme

International Schools want their students to complete their studies hand in hand with this organization. Born in Geneva, Switzerland, these programmes, which demand a strong commitment from teachers and heads, are worldwide recognized by their excellent quality.

To belong to or to be a member of this organization implies meeting certain requirements such as having fully equipped experimental sciences laboratories, where the students acquire and handle different research techniques in order to apply them in class in a practical manner, which will help them achieve a better understanding of all kinds of topics, easy or complex.

Southpointe
ACADEMY

(Founded 2000)

Head of School
Gordon MacIntyre

PYP coordinator
Smita Karam

MYP coordinator
Christine Yang

Status Private

Boarding/day Day

Gender Coeducational

Language of instruction
English

Authorised IB programmes
PYP, MYP

Fees
Kindergarten – Grade 12
CND$18,900 – CND$21,500
International CND$37,370

Address
1900 56th Street
Tsawwassen BC
V4L 2B1 | CANADA

TEL +1 604 948 8826

Email
admissions@southpointe.ca

Website
www.southpointe.ca

Established in 2000, Southpointe is an independent university preparatory school for Grades K-12 that is characterized by passionate teaching, open-mindedness and a warm community atmosphere. In the classroom, our teachers provide the inspiration and support that enable students to learn, lead and succeed.

Southpointe is an authorized International Baccalaureate World School. We offer the IB Primary Years Programme (PYP) and Middle Years Programme (MYP).

IB World Schools share a common philosophy – a commitment to high-quality, challenging, international education – that we believe is important for our students. The IB provides a framework of learning that encourages students to become creative, critical and reflective thinkers. Students are intellectually challenged and encouraged to make connections between their studies and the global world.

Our senior students are offered the College Board's Advanced Placement (AP) Capstone Programme in Grades 11-12. By focusing on critical thinking, collaborative problem solving, and research skills, the AP Capstone Programme prepares students for college and beyond.

Our History

Since its inception in the year 2000, Southpointe Academy has sought to cultivate a safe and positive learning environment which prepares its students for the rigours of post-secondary education. Attracted to the promise of a university-preparatory education in South Delta, the school welcomed nearly one hundred students to temporary premises in September 2000.

With the intention of expanding to Grade Twelve within four years, the school enrolled students ranging from Pre-Kindergarten to Grade Eight during its inaugural session. Owing to firm support from its founding families, faculty and staff, the school was able to realize this goal. In 2005, Southpointe bid farewell to its first graduating class.

Following an extended search, the school secured a site to house a permanent facility. A tireless and generous parent community banded together to secure the capital necessary to fund and develop a new, state-of-the-art facility. In January 2012, Southpointe welcomed over five hundred students back for the Winter Term into its brand-new 68,000 square foot facility.

In 2019, Southpointe added another 8,200 square foot addition to its top floor. The project included a new 270-seat, multipurpose dining hall along with cutting-edge drama, art and fitness studios.

Southpointe Academy has always sought to expand the boundaries of what is possible, enhancing its curriculum and extra-curricular opportunities for students. The Project Discover outdoor education programme develops self-reliance, decision-making, leadership and respect for our natural environment.

Today, Southpointe Academy remains committed to its founding mandate as a university preparatory school. Since 2005, its graduates have graced the halls of some of the most renowned and prestigious post-secondary institutions in Canada, the United States and the United Kingdom.

ST. FRANCIS COLLEGE

(Founded 2003)

College Principal
Mrs Shirley Hazell

Head of Early Years & Primary
Carolina Giannetto

Head of Secondary
Andrés Suárez

PYP coordinator Emily Hays

MYP coordinator
Thomas Holesgrove

DP coordinator
Gloria Malagón

Status Private

Boarding/day Day

Gender Coeducational

Language of instruction
English, Portuguese

Authorised IB programmes
PYP, MYP, DP

Age Range 3 – 18 years

Number of pupils enrolled
850

Fees
Day: US$21,000 – US$29,000

Address
Rua Joaquim Antunes 678
Pinheiros, São Paulo
SP 05415-001 | BRAZIL

TEL +55 11 3728 8053

Email office@stfrancis.com.br

Website www.stfrancis.com.br

St. Francis College is an international school which strives for excellence providing a warm and friendly community committed to the IB Philosophy. We offer a challenging educational programme with rigorous assessment through inquiry-based instruction.

We empower pupils to be passionate lifelong learners, achieve academic and personal excellence and be committed to impact the world positively.

Curriculum

The international curriculum offered is taught in English. The formal curriculum is guided by the Brazilian and British National Curriculum and the IB Programmes. A broad approach of concept-based learning encompasses the humanities, arts, sciences, mathematics, and information technology. An important element in the curriculum are the Portuguese language subjects, which include Brazilian literature, Portuguese language as well as the history and geography of Brazil. The College provides pupils with academic challenge and key life skills in a flexible and transdisciplinary programme. We are a continuum school and offer three of the IB Programmes. Throughout the primary school we offer the IB PYP, in the secondary school we offer the IB MYP and the IB DP in the last two years.

IGCSE exams are taken in the main subjects in MYP 5. Pupils will conclude their secondary education having obtained their Brazilian and IB diploma.

A wide range of physical activities and sports is offered to students as well as outstanding programmes in visual arts, drama and music, from Early Years throughout Secondary Years. Once our students graduate from St. Francis College they go on to both Brazilian and international universities and continue to excel academically, personally and professionally.

Extracurricular activities

Extracurricular activities offered include football, basketball, volleyball, dance, skateboarding, martial arts, cooking, drama, music, arts, and MUN (Model United Nations).

World-class school

We are a world-class school, members of the IBO, LAHC, College Board, BAIBS and we are a SAT and Cambridge Assessment Centre.

St. Paul's School

St. Paul's School

MANIBUS POTENTIA STUDIUM ANIMIS

(Founded 1926)

Head Teacher
Mr Titus Edge

DP coordinator
Ana Carolina Belmonte

Status Private

Boarding/day Day

Gender Coeducational

Language of instruction
English

Authorised IB programmes
DP

Age Range 3 – 18 years

Address
Rua Juquiá 166
Jardim Paulistano
São Paulo
SP 01440-903 | BRAZIL

TEL +55 11 3087 3399

Email
head@stpauls.br

Website
www.stpauls.br

St. Paul's School was the first British School to be established in São Paulo (Brazil) and continues to offer an Anglo-Brazilian curriculum, embracing the best of both cultures. As an all-through (ages 3-18) co-educational school, offering the IGCSE and IB courses to pupils, we are affiliated to a global network of top UK Schools through our membership of HMC (Headmaster's Conference) and COBIS (Council of British International Schools). Almost 100 years old, we draw on our proud heritage as the first British school in Latin America to be recognised as a British School Overseas (BSO) by the UK government. Yet, we look forward with creativity and confidence.

At St. Paul's we always strive to be our better selves. We have the courage of our convictions, essential values, freedom to imagine and create. This is achieved through our high quality British and Brazilian holistic education which drives the personal and academic development of pupils, within a framework of a caring, inclusive and united community.

It is our aim to discover the passion and talents of every pupil, and create the right environment to develop these. The school prides itself on an excellent enrichment programme ranging from MUN to Duke of Edinburgh, from knitting classes to a robotics programme, from mathematical Olympiads to outstanding drama and music. We have been awarded as a Microsoft Showcase School and an Apple Distinguished School in recognition for our excellence in transforming and enhancing our physical and online learning environment to deliver more personalised education to our pupils.

The school is a positive agent of change, helping its pupils to be caring individuals ready to inspire and mobilise those around them to impact the world for the best. Our commitment to broad educational experiences opens many opportunities for pupils who go on to leading universities in the United Kingdom, America and Brazil.

We believe in helping our pupils achieve their full intellectual, emotional, social, physical, artistic, creative and spiritual potential. An innovative, structured curriculum, combined with excellent teaching, state of the art facilities, and the best in pastoral care, equip pupils to flourish.

STRATFORD HALL
IB WORLD SCHOOL

(Founded 2000)

Head of School
Dean Croy

Junior School Principal
Dr. Michael Palmer

Senior School Principal
Meg Chamberlin

PYP coordinator
Amanda Lempriere

MYP coordinator
Mark Pulfer

DP coordinator
Dr. Benedict Hung

Status Private

Boarding/day Day

Gender Coeducational

Language of instruction
English

Authorised IB programmes
PYP, MYP, DP

Age Range 5 – 18 years

Number of pupils enrolled
540

Fees
Annual Tuition:
CAD$23,370 – CAD$27,300

Address
3000 Commercial Drive
Vancouver BC **V5N 4E2 | CANADA**

TEL +1 604 436 0608

Email info@stratfordhall.ca

Website www.stratfordhall.ca

Stratford Hall is an independent, co-educational, nondenominational, university preparatory day school with a student population of 540 ranging from Kindergarten to Grade 12. Our location in a vibrant, urban setting in East Vancouver, British Columbia reflects our diverse community of students. Through the continuum of International Baccalaureate (IB) programmes, the Primary Years Programme (Kindergarten – Grade 5), Middle Years Programme (Grade 6 – 10) and Diploma Programme (Grade 11 & 12) the School provides a level of individual challenge and academic rigour beyond the norm. Equally important is our commitment to the IB Learner Profile as a guide fostering international-mindedness in students and adults alike.

At Stratford Hall, your child will be given the opportunity to learn and to thrive; to discover their unique strengths, and to explore the diverse opportunities our rapidly changing world offers. Under the care and guidance of Stratford Hall staff, they will grow and mature, while equipping themselves with intellectual tools, strength of character, and a global perspective.

Stratford Hall is a not-for-profit school operating under the authority of the Ministry of Education of British Columbia.

Our Mission

Stratford Hall educates students to the highest global standards through the programmes of the International Baccalaureate. Excellence and confidence are developed through a challenging academic curriculum with further emphasis on creativity, activity and service. We foster a strong pluralistic community built on integrity and respect.

Our Vision

Stratford Hall strives to be a global leader in the International Baccalaureate community. Our students will gain a deep understanding of the world around them, and they will act on their connections to the outside community. They will excel to the best of their abilities, and graduates will be equipped to achieve their chosen goals. This is accomplished by acquiring and retaining the best teachers, and by a commitment to a balanced and enriched curriculum. The success of Stratford Hall is deeply rooted in the establishment of a supportive, knowledgeable and committed community.

Stratford Hall is proud to be an accredited member of the Independent Schools Association of British Columbia (ISABC), Canadian Accredited Independent Schools (CAIS), National Association of Independent Schools (NAIS), and is authorized by the International Baccalaureate Organization as an IB Continuum School.

Tf**S** | CANADA'S INTERNATIONAL SCHOOL | L'ÉCOLE INTERNATIONALE DU CANADA

(Founded 1962)	**Age Range** 2 – 18 years
Head of School Norman Gaudet	**Number of pupils enrolled** 1500
PYP coordinator Zein Odeh	**Fees** Day: CAD$21,530 – CAD$36,620
MYP coordinator Leslie Miller	**Address** 306 Lawrence Avenue East Toronto ON **M4N 1T7	CANADA**
DP coordinator Dr. Jennifer Elliott	1293 Meredith Avenue, Mississauga, ON **L5E 2E6**
Status Private	
Boarding/day Day	**TEL** +1 416 484 6533
Gender Coeducational	**Email** admissions@tfs.ca
Language of instruction French, English	**Website** www.tfs.ca
Authorised IB programmes PYP, MYP, DP	

Individuals who reflect,
ENTHUSIASTIC INQUIRER
citizens
EXPERIMENTAL ARTIST
who act.

Bilingual and co-educational since 1962, TFS is renowned as Canada's leading bilingual International Baccalaureate (IB) school, providing an internationally focused education with high academic standards to 1,485 students. Teaching the curricula of France and Ontario through the framework established by the IB programs, we offer our students an education that is rich in academic excellence, diversity and opportunity.

Authorized to offer the PYP, MYP and IB Diploma, TFS is an IB World School and the only full continuum bilingual IB school in Canada.

We welcome boys and girls from age two to university entrance. No prior knowledge of French is required for entry up to and including Grade 7. Thanks to our Introductory Program, we successfully integrate students with no background in French. While 90% of TFS students have little or no knowledge of French when they enrol, they graduate fully bilingual with an international outlook that sets them on a path to a bright future.

TFS' mission is to develop multilingual, critical thinkers who celebrate difference, transcend borders and strive for the betterment of humankind.

Our educators come from around the world to teach at either our Toronto or West Campus in Mississauga, and provide a caring and supportive learning environment that encourages students of diverse backgrounds to become individuals who reflect, and citizens who act.

We demonstrate our commitment to the development of the whole child through stimulating academic and co-curricular programs that include recreational and competitive sports, music, visual and dramatic arts.

In addition to being authorized by the IB, TFS is accredited by the Ministry of Education of Ontario, the French Ministry of Education, and Canadian Accredited Independent Schools (CAIS). TFS is also a member of the Conference of Independent Schools of Ontario (CIS), the Council of International Schools, and Agence pour l'enseignement français à l'étranger (AEFE).

Please visit us at www.tfs.ca.

The Baldwin School of Puerto Rico

(Founded 1968)

Head of School
Mr. Greg MacGilpin

PYP coordinator
Mrs. Sarah Loinaz

MYP coordinator
Mrs. Cristina Castillo

DP coordinator
Mrs. Laura Maristany

Status Private

Boarding/day Day

Gender Coeducational

Language of instruction
English

Authorised IB programmes
PYP, MYP, DP

Age Range 3 – 18 years

Number of pupils enrolled 820

Fees
US$9,646 – US$14,995

Address
PO Box 1827
Bayamón 00960-1827 | **PUERTO RICO**

TEL +1 787 720 2421

Email
admission@baldwin-school.org

Website
www.baldwin-school.org

The Baldwin School of Puerto Rico, located in the greater San Juan metropolitan area, is the premier independent, PPK-12, college preparatory English language day school in Puerto Rico. It is the first school on the Caribbean island to offer the Primary, Middle and Diploma levels of the International Baccalaureate (IB) program. "What is most congruent with our mission and the IB, is how both are focused on the type of environment that optimizes student learning," says Head of School, Mr. Greg MacGilpin. "We grow with the IB as it challenges us to reflect and act iteratively because of the diversity of our learners' experiences."

At Baldwin School, technology is broadly integrated in the classroom. Students use a range of platforms, applications and web-based software; to research, organize and create content. A fully modern, wireless digital mainframe allows students to leverage the world's resources and conceive original content. Touchscreen technology supports literacy and numeracy across all grades. Interior and exterior laboratories combine hands-on and digital learning. "We were fortunate and deliberate in the transition to online platforms during our pandemic response. Our students and adults have innovated in both, grand and simple ways to share learning," says Mr. MacGilpin.

Baldwin offers a beautiful and spacious twenty-three acre campus, which is also a Certified Wildlife Habitat. Its location means that students can take part in a range of outdoor activities. Spectacular facilities include a swimming pool, tennis courts, field house, outdoor courts, soccer field, and a rainforest biological field station. Indoor facilities include science and computer labs, a performing arts center, a recording studio, multiple art studios, a dance studio, and music rooms.

Baldwin's student body very much reflects Puerto Rico's diverse population. Students participate in dozens of co-curricular activities. Athletes compete at mini, youth, junior varsity, and varsity levels. Math, Science and Model United Nations teams also compete at the national level. Campus life includes opportunities to participate in many clubs and organizations, most of which serve the broader community through both service and donations. All of Baldwin's graduates go on to study at university, mostly abroad, including the United States' most prestigious colleges and universities.

Baldwin School is committed to the belief that every child can flourish if they are given the right combination of time, opportunity, and support.

![THE BILTMORE SCHOOL logo]

THE
BILTMORE
SCHOOL

Established 1926

(Founded 1926)

Principal
Gina C. Duarte-Romero M.Ed.

Assistant Principal
Ana V. Seoane

PYP coordinator
Isbel Salgueiro

Status Private

Boarding/day Day

Gender Coeducational

Language of instruction
English

Authorised IB programmes
PYP

Age Range 1 – 14 years

Number of pupils enrolled
200

Fees
US$9,800 – US$20,800

Address
1600 S. Red Road
Miami
FL 33155 | USA

TEL +1 305 266 4666

Email
info@biltmoreschool.com

Website
www.biltmoreschool.com

Originally founded in Coral Gables in 1926, The Biltmore School is one of the oldest schools in Miami Dade County. Our school enjoys a tradition of educational excellence that has provided guidance to children for the past 90 years.

Our Principal, Gina Romero and our Biltmore Staff members are actively involved in the "Project Zero" research initiative, sponsored by Harvard University that promotes creative thinking, encourages children to be self-reliant, and empowers them to think "outside the box" through a challenging curriculum that incorporates instruction that maximizes the multiple intelligences, individual learning styles and modalities. Through participation in ongoing professional development workshops in partnership with Florida International University, our staff actively explores "Visible Thinking" strategies that promote the highest levels of abstract and critical thinking in children of all ages.

During the 2007-2008 school year our school was awarded accreditation by AISF (Association of Independent Schools of Florida), SACS (Southern Association of Colleges and Schools) and CASI (Council on Accreditation and School Improvement).

The Biltmore School has also been an IB World School since March 2012 and offers the IB Primary Years Programme and is currently a candidate school for the IB Middle Years Programme.

The Biltmore School believes that students are capable and knowledgeable agents of their learning. We feel that it is the responsibility of the educator to be both the partner and guide in the growth and development of the child. It is through much research and collaboration that our school has embraced and synthesized diverse educational views and practices to best benefit our students.

The Biltmore School offers a comprehensive program for students from age one through eighth grade.

**THE BRITISH
COLLEGE
OF BRAZIL**

A NORD ANGLIA EDUCATION SCHOOL

Principal
Mr. Nick West

DP coordinator
Mr. Timothy Jones

Status Private

Boarding/day Day

Gender Coeducational

Language of instruction
English

Authorised IB programmes
DP

Address
Rua Álvares de Azevedo, 50
Chácara Flora
São Paulo
SP 04671-040 | BRAZIL

TEL +55 11 5547 3030

Email
info@britishcollegebrazil.org

Website
www.britishcollegebrazil.org

The British College of Brazil (BCB), a Nord Anglia Education school, is São Paulo's school of choice for expatriate families looking to provide their children with an international education. We offer engaging learning environments to students in Early Years, Primary and Secondary in a warm and supportive atmosphere where they can thrive. Our schools and the one-of-a-kind opportunities we create inside and outside the classroom enrich learning, instill life-long memories and a deep sense of achievement. We welcome your family to become a valued member of our community.

At the British College of Brazil we teach the English National Curriculum adapted to an international environment, the IGCSE in Year 10 and 11 followed by the IB Diploma Programme. Throughout our core curricula and programs we help your child to develop a global mindset and nurture essential skills such as creativity, collaboration and resilience. We want every student to become lifelong learners, to try something new and, above all, to be ambitious.

We are part of the Nord Anglia Education family of 76 international schools, boarding schools and private schools located in 31 countries around the world. Together we are able to enrich your child's learning experience with opportunities beyond the ordinary. From online debates and challenges, to expeditions to the savannah of Tanzania or participating in our Performing Arts Festival in Miami, Nord Anglia's Global Campus connects our students around the world to learn together every day.

Additionally, our collaborations with world leading institutions such as The Julliard School, The Massachusetts Institute of Technology (MIT), and UNICEF enhance the curriculum and offer exceptional professional development for teachers. This approach results in high academic outcomes, and equips students with the skills that are essential to thrive in the 21st century.

We believe that there is no limit to what our students, our people, and our communities can achieve. We encourage your child to set their sights higher by fostering a global perspective together with our school's personalized approach to learning – helping every child to succeed, thrive and love learning.

The British School, Rio de Janeiro

The British School Rio de Janeiro

A caring community, striving for excellence, where every individual matters.

(Founded 1924)

Directors
John Nixon MBE, Carlos Lima & Sonia Salgado

DP coordinator
Guy Smith & Leah Wilks

Status Private

Boarding/day Day

Gender Coeducational

Language of instruction
English

Authorised IB programmes
DP

Age Range 2 – 18 years

Number of pupils enrolled
2200

Fees
Day: R70,000 approx

Address
Rua Real Grandeza 99
Botafogo, Rio de Janeiro
RJ 22281-030 | BRAZIL

TEL +55 21 2539 2717

Email
edu@britishschool.g12.br

Website
www.britishschool.g12.br

Founded in 1924, we are a non-profit, independent and coeducational day school offering a complete and coherent curriculum for students of all nationalities from ages 2-18. Our school aims to give students a broad, balanced and relevant educational experience. The educational philosophy and practice are primarily British in nature with international and Brazilian elements incorporated. Programmes of study are: Early Years Foundation Stage (EYFS) and International Primary Curriculum (IPC) for 2 to 11 year olds; Key Stage 3 (Middle Years) of the UK National Curriculum for 11 to 14 year olds; Cambridge IGCSE for 14 to 16 year olds; and the International Baccalaureate (IB) Diploma for 16 to 18 year olds. Over 80% of our students are Brazilian and the remainder are from over 30 different countries, with British and other European students being the biggest proportion.

English is the main language of instruction with Portuguese, French and Spanish also being taught. We are an IB World School accredited by the Council of International Schools (CIS). The director is a member of the Latin American Heads Conference (LAHC). There are 2200 students located on three sites. The Zona Sul Unit is split into two Sites: Botafogo Site (primary school) and Urca Site (secondary school). The Barra Unit caters for students from age 2 (Pre-Nursery) to age 18.

Classes are small and school environment is pleasant, well-resourced and stimulating, with a strong focus on health, safety and security. Performing arts, sports, Model United Nations, Duke of Edinburgh's Award Scheme and work experience provide a wide range of co-curricular opportunities. There are numerous local day visits, national or international residential trips for most year groups. Our teachers are well-qualified (some 30% being recruited from overseas) and supported by a robust and effective programme of continuing professional development.

Our school provides a caring and friendly, yet demanding, learning environment and makes every effort to ensure that each individual has the opportunity to develop their particular abilities and talents to the full. Emphasis on academic achievement is also balanced by our concern to meet our students' physical, emotional and social needs. We place a high value on good social behaviour and ethical standards, with respect for the individual and the environment.

We want our students to be happy in school and we hope that their school experience will be fondly and warmly remembered for life. We believe that this can be achieved through high expectations; clear guidelines and limits; constant encouragement; and addressing individual needs.

Extracurricular Activities
Football, capoeira, volleyball, basketball, ballet, artistic gymnastics, judo, choir, music (instruments and singing), cooking, drama and arts are available.

Facilities
Air-conditioned classrooms, interactive Whiteboards, computers, laptops, tablets, science and computer & technology & robotics labs, libraries, gymnasiums and open spaces for sports and games, playgrounds with a variety of toys, auditoriums for Drama classes, presentations and art exhibitions, sickbays (first-aid – nurses), and dining halls.

The Newman School

(Founded 1945)

Head of School
Michael Schafer

MYP coordinator
Elizabeth Esposito

DP coordinator
Andrew Nagy

Status Private

Boarding/day Mixed

Gender Coeducational

Language of instruction
English

Authorised IB programmes
MYP, DP

Age Range 11 – 18 years

Number of pupils enrolled 240

Fees
Domestic tuition: US$28,000
International tuition: US$39,000
+ Boardings

Address
247 Marlborough Street
Boston
MA 02116 | USA

TEL +1 617 267 4530

Email
admissions@newmanboston.
org

Website
www.newmanboston.org

The Newman School's motto, "Heart Speaks to Heart", is woven through all areas of school life. Relationships are at the core of who we are. Students develop through inquisitive academic exploration and apply critical and creative thinking skills to resolve complex problems and contribute to our community.

Founded in 1945, located on Marlborough Street, in the heart of Boston's extraordinary Back Bay neighborhood. Newman serves students from grades 7-12 who come from the city of Boston, surrounding towns and 22 countries.

Our small community nestled in a larger city environment offers students a chance to be both known and independent. We are committed to providing an IB global education, recognized by universities around the world for it's depth and rigor. Our extraordinary faculty have deep international and independent school experience. Students are engaged in individualized learning with support and challenge.

Newman students participate in activities, the arts and sports at school and throughout Boston, pursuing their passions in the "education city". Sports offered include crew, sailing, soccer, cross country, basketball, volleyball, and tennis.

Extracurricular clubs and enrichment activities include: AMC Math, Model United Nations, Mock Trial, robotics, computer science, NASA, environmental, chess, musical performance, Junior Achievement, film & media, art, and a broad range of service opportunities. Partnerships with the Boston Public Library, Greater Boston YMCA, Community Rowing Club and Community Boating enrich our students' experience.

Our unique boarding program around the corner from the school, gives students a full boarding experience, providing a cozy home in the heart of the city. Students are surrounded by art, innovation, culture, and recreation. Our location is a short walk to the Boston Public Library, Symphony Hall, the Boston Ballet, the Museum of Fine Arts, and the many colleges and universities – including Harvard, Boston College, Northeastern University, Boston University, and MIT – for which Boston is world-renowned.

The Village School

THE VILLAGE SCHOOL

A NORD ANGLIA EDUCATION SCHOOL

(Founded 1966)

Head of School
Mr. Bill Delbrugge

DP coordinator
Kerri Peters

Status Private

Boarding/day Mixed

Gender Coeducational

Language of instruction
English

Authorised IB programmes
DP

Age Range 2 – 18 years

Number of pupils enrolled
1400

Fees
Day: US$22,075 – US$30,700
Boarding: US$52,680 – US$72,680

Address
13051 Whittington Drive
Houston
TX 77077 | USA

TEL +1 281 496 7900

Email
admissions@thevillageschool.com

Website
www.thevillageschool.com

One World. One Village.

The Village School, a pre-k through 12th grade private day and boarding school in Houston, delivers a global perspective, exceptional learning experiences, and access to world-class teachers. Voted the #1 most diverse private school in Houston, Village is home to a collaborative, supportive and global community. Recognized for our excellence in STEAM education, world-class internships and differentiated programs, we offer a rigorous but nurturing individualized environment. The Village School provides a rich selection of academic, arts, and athletics to help our students prepare for future success at the best colleges and universities around the world.

Exceptional Learning Experiences

At Village, we offer a unique and enriched approach inclusive of entrepreneurship, internships, and experiential learning, along with collaborations with world-leading institutions. Our visionary teachers inspire your child to excel and foster a thirst for knowledge. This unique approach to teaching and learning enables our students to gain a better grasp of concepts, think more creatively, and allows for greater reflection on experiences.

Three Diploma Options

Village is proud to offer three rigorous diploma options: the International Baccalaureate Diploma Program, the Entrepreneurship Diploma, and The Village School U.S. Diploma.

Cultivating a Global Perspective

The Village School student body represents over 80 different countries across almost every continent, offering our students the opportunity to interact with and learn from students across the globe. This culturally rich environment helps cultivate a global perspective and awareness and provides access to people from other ethnicities, cultures, schools of thought, and viewpoints.

Preparing for the Future

We offer our students access to experienced college advisors who know the ins and outs of the application process and university requirements for schools both nationally and abroad. Our advisors have a proven trackrecord for helping Village students gain acceptance into the top colleges and universities. In addition, our recent graduating class earned an impressive total of $12.2M in scholarships towards higher education institutions around the world.

Premier Collaborations

Village students benefit from our collaborations with esteemed institutions such as the Massachusetts Institute of Technology (MIT), The Juilliard School, and UNICEF.

Visit Village!

Schedule a tour or take a virtual tour online at www.thevillageschool.com. Find out more information by emailing admissions@thevillageschool.com or calling (281) 496-7900.

(Founded 1966)

Principal
Prof. María Elena Abreu

Academic Vice Principal
Prof. María Angélica Villota

Pedagogical Leader of IB Programs
Prof. Miranda Di Silvestri

MYP coordinator
Prof. Gianna De Sena

DP coordinator
Prof. Yajaira Graterol

Status Private

Boarding/day Day

Gender Coeducational

Language of instruction
Spanish, English

Authorised IB programmes
MYP, DP

Age Range 4 – 18 years

Number of pupils enrolled 520

Address
Calle C, Urb. Colinas de Valle Arriba
Caracas 1080 | **VENEZUELA**

TEL +58 212 9757077

Email
academiawashington@aw.edu.ve

Website
www.washington.academy

About us
Washington Academy is a private, bilingual (English/Spanish), K-12, co-ed school located in Caracas, Venezuela and registered in the Venezuelan School System, offering an integral high school diploma. Founded in 1966 by American educators, the school is non-profit and has an enrollment of Venezuelan children and other nationalities. Our classrooms are of no more than 20 students, and we have science laboratories, a library, two computer labs, two art rooms and outdoor sports facilities.

Curriculum and extracurricular activities
Washington Academy's curriculum follows the Venezuelan official program as well as an intensive English language program. Based on our holistic model of education, students are required to demonstrate to the school community their learning through specific projects designed for each grade, such as Science Fair and Math Fair among others. Our school offers the IB MYP and DP, and self-evaluates its performance through American standardized tests. Following the IB philosophy, we have recently included French and Japanese classes, clubs such as Debate & Persuasion, Logic & Math, Theater, Chess, and an Internship Program.

International minded education has always been present; our Washington Academy Model of United Nations started 16 years ago and we also participate in the International Moot Court and The Masters competition. This academic year, the school has adjusted all its activities to a hybrid learning modality complying with the requirements of our biosecurity protocols derived from the Covid 19 pandemic.

Mission
W.A. promotes the integral education of students by emphasizing intellectual, personal, emotional, and social development through our educational model in conjunction with IB programs.

Our motto states: "Washington Academy gives students the tools to cope with life."

Vision & Values
W.A. aims for excellence, "La excelencia hecha colegio", from a holistic standpoint, taking into consideration academic training, a conscientious practice of Washington Spirit, and support among our professional learning community.

W.A. acts with integrity, honesty, responsibility, respect for others' rights and awareness of their own; being an agent of social integration, promoting healthy mind and body, with a broad worldview and a vast cultural background.

Westlake Middle School

Principal
Anthony Mungioli

MYP coordinator
TBD

Status State

Boarding/day Day

Gender Coeducational

Language of instruction
English

Authorised IB programmes
MYP

Age Range 10 – 14 years

Number of pupils enrolled 438

Address
825 West Lake Drive
Thornwood
NY 10594 | USA

TEL +1 914 769 8540

Email
amungioli@mtplcsd.org

Website
wms.mtplcsd.org

Westlake Middle School (WMS) is a public school located in the leafy suburbs of Westchester County in New York. The school is housed on a large green campus with ample outdoor athletic fields and indoor facilities. Served well by public transportation, it is approximately 45 minutes by train to the heart of New York City. The school offers The IB Middle Years Programme years 1-3, USA grades 6-8. At Westlake, all students engage in the full MYP Programme of eight subjects. Westlake Middle School is recognized as a middle school of excellence and is ranked by Niche as an 'A' school. WMS supports the whole child and our mission is to engage and develop independent, inquisitive, tenacious and open-minded students who think critically, perform innovatively and act ethically in our local and global community.

All students at Westlake have the opportunity to study the core subjects as well as the arts, design, physical education and health. Languages are offered in Spanish and Italian at all grade levels. WMS has a full inclusion program where students who require special education supports are given the necessary structures for them to thrive within the framework of the IB program. In MYP Year 3, students have the opportunity to take high school level classes in

Algebra and Living Environment. The Community Project is the culminating experience for all year 3 students allowing them to connect to a personal passion or a community organization. They can grow themselves as caring, thoughtful human beings. Students also participate in advisory sessions where their social and emotional learning and well-being is supported. The school has full-time school counselors, a school psychologist and a school social worker to support students and families.

Extracurriculars are offered and open to all students. All Fours on Paws, Engineering Club, Environmental Club, Art Club, Student Council and Yearbook Club are just a few examples. Students also participate in national competitions such as Science Olympiad, Math League and the Robotics Competition Team, often bringing home medals of achievement. Competitive sports include track, lacrosse, football, cheerleading, baseball, volleyball, soccer, basketball, cross country and softball.

The community of Westlake Middle School is part of the Town of Mount Pleasant. There is a vibrant 'Westlake Wildcat' spirit surrounding the school and families move to our sought-after area for a safe and stable place to live and grow.

Westlake Academy

(Founded 2003)

Executive Director
Dr. Mechelle Bryson

Primary Principal Rod Harding

Middle Years Principal
Kaylene Rudd

Diploma Years Principal
Dr. James Owen

PYP coordinator
Alison Schneider

MYP coordinator Terri Watson

DP coordinator Dr. James Owen

Status State Charter

Boarding/day Day

Gender Coeducational

Language of instruction
English

Authorised IB programmes
PYP, MYP, DP

Age Range 5 – 18 years

Number of pupils enrolled 879

Address
2600 J.T. Ottinger Road
Westlake **TX 76262 | USA**

TEL +1 817 4905757

Email info@westlakeacademy.org

Website
www.westlakeacademy.org

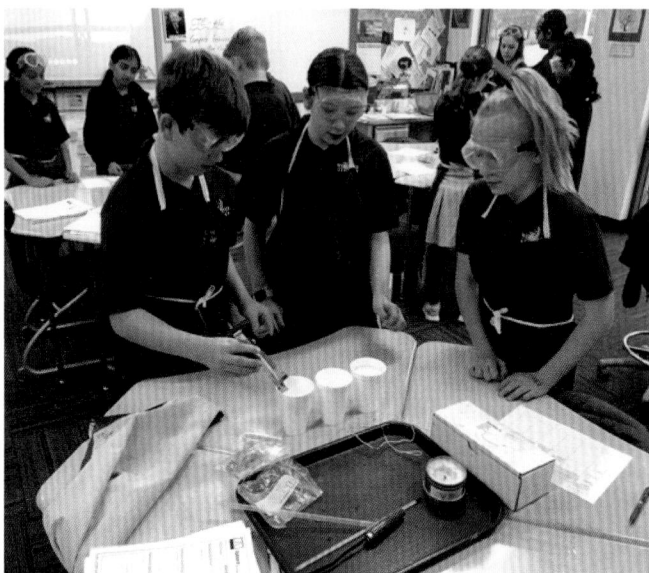

Who we are
Founded in 2003 with a mission to achieve academic excellence and develop life-long learners who become well-balanced, responsible global citizens, Westlake Academy is the first and only municipally-owned charter school in the State of Texas, USA. Celebrating 19 years of excellence, and having just graduated its twelfth class, the Academy is nationally ranked and was awarded a top score (98%) for the fourth year in a row from the state education agency. These achievements are a direct reflection of the power of an IB World Education.

IB World School
Westlake Academy was the fifth public school in the US offering three IB programmes (PYP,MYP,DP) on a single campus. The IB curriculum and the school's smaller class sizes are enhanced by a breath-taking outdoor campus of innovatively designed stone-clad buildings clustered among 23 acres of verdant pastures and the crown of oak-adorned hills. Imagine how this helps create a premier, knowledge-based community that is truly unique.

College Preparation
Westlake Academy is an open enrollment college preparatory charter school, where great care and consideration is given to the mission and vision by the town leaders, citizens, and educational staff dedicated to academic excellence and personal achievement. The Town of Westlake is proud that results focus on high student achievement while offering IB for all, strong parent and community connections, financial stewardship and sustainability, student engagement in extracurricular activities and service, and effective educators and staff.

Mission
Westlake Academy is an IB World School whose mission is to provide students with an internationally minded education of the highest quality to become well-balanced and respectful life-long learners.

Vision
Westlake Academy inspires college bound students to achieve their highest individual potential in a nurturing environment that fosters the traits found in the IB learner profile.

Values
Maximizing Personal Development, Academic Excellence, Respect for Self and Others, Personal Responsibility, Compassion and Understanding, Global Citizenship.

International Mindedness
Providing an internationally minded education of the highest quality means students will become globally well-balanced. This is not an alternative to cultural and national identity, but an essential component of life in the 21st century. Successful interaction requires our students to clearly communicate, solve problems and create new possibilities in a global context, connecting individuals from around the world.

Extracurricular Activities
Westlake Academy believes student clubs, honor societies and after-school activities allow young citizens to further their academic foundation while developing essential interpersonal skills. After school clubs are student driven

under the guidance of our faculty. IB learner profile traits are reinforced outside the classroom via athletics, music, art, foreign language, theatre, technology and specialty niches including math, coding, and science.

Global Citizenship and Collaboration

As internationally-minded educators, Westlake Academy creates authentic global collaboration experiences that prepare our students to meet the demands of the 21st century marketplace while encouraging them to think globally and act locally:

Costa Rica and Argentina: Student and teacher exchange programs offered with a school in Costa Rica and in Argentina.

International Student Leadership Symposium (ISLS): Students in grade 10 can apply to be a delegate at the ISLS with 8 other schools across the globe including Germany, China, Oman, South Africa to name a few.

Global Service: Extended service opportunities with Students Shoulder to Shoulder include destinations such as Tibet, Peru, Kenya and more.

Leadership: Our teachers and administration host the annual Westlake Academy International Mindedness Educator Symposium with 7 countries represented and over 50 participants.

Youth Ambassadors Program: We partner with neighboring cities Southlake and Fort Worth offering worldwide student travel opportunities.

Class Trips: Students are given experiential travel opportunities beginning in third grade.

Technology: Teachers and students engage in collaborative learning in a 1:1 iPad environment.

YingHua International School

YING HUA
INTERNATIONAL SCHOOL
English-Chinese Immersion School of Princeton

Excellence • Diversity • Integrity • Compassion

Interim Head of School
Dr. Kevin Merges

PYP coordinator
WenLin Su

Status Private

Boarding/day Day

Gender Coeducational

Language of instruction
English, Chinese

Authorised IB programmes
PYP

Age Range 18 months – 13 years

Number of pupils enrolled 118

Fees
Day: US$11,000 – US$24,000

Address
25 Laurel Avenue
Kingston
NJ 08528-0088 | USA

TEL +1 609 375 8015

Email
admissions@yhis.org

Website
yhis.org

Nestled in the outskirts of Princeton, New Jersey, YingHua International School (YHIS) is the only not-for-profit, independent school in the greater Princeton area that offers English-Chinese dual language education with an internationally-focused, inquiry-based curriculum. YHIS is also the only school in the Eastern United States that offers the IB Primary Years Programme with whole-school Chinese immersion.

YingHua International School (YHIS) was founded in 2007 with a mission to enable academic excellence and prepare students for compassionate, effective, and ethical global citizenship through English and Chinese language acquisition and instilling a passion for lifelong learning. A hidden gem in Central New Jersey, YHIS accomplishes its mission by combining total Chinese Immersion with IB inquiry-based learning.

Through this unique approach, YHIS enables ethnically diverse students from as young as 18 months old through 8th grade, to develop the skills and mindset needed to become leaders in an increasingly global world. Through exposure at an early age to a language-immersive environment combined with IB inquiry-based learning, YHIS students gain deeply rooted cognitive benefits that stay with them well into adulthood.

At YHIS this approach is further characterized by small, nurturing, and inclusive classes led by passionate, dedicated teachers. The results are students who consistently outperform their suburban and private school peers on the local and national stage and in standardized testing. While many parents are initially drawn to YHIS for Chinese immersion, they often stay because of its ability to foster independence and self-reliance while instilling critical thinking skills and academic excellence in students.

Much of YHIS' success can be attributed to its core values of Excellence, Diversity, Integrity and Compassion. Excellence is striving for and being the best that we can be. It means high standards of teaching, learning, and all that we do. It includes well-rounded development in addition to intellectual curiosity and rigor. It requires teamwork, community service and leadership. Diversity is embracing difference and building on the best of all worlds. It embraces equity among cultures and peoples, and suggests respect for the natural world including its animal and plant inhabitants. Integrity is excellence of character and Compassion is caring for diverse others: both integrity and compassion are essential for guiding how we relate to and treat one another and are critical cornerstones for what YHIS stands for.

YHIS welcomes all into its warm and nurturing community!

Directory of schools in the Americas region

Key to symbols

- ⬤ CP
- ⬤ Diploma
- ⬤ MYP
- ⬤ PYP
- Ⓢ Fee Paying School
- Ⓑ Boys' School
- Ⓖ Girls' School
- Ⓒ Coeducational School
- ⬤ Boarding School
- ☀ Day School

ANGUILLA

Omololu International School
P.O Box 703, The Valley BWI, AI2640
PYP Coordinator Lorraine Thompson
Languages English
T: +1 264 497 5430
W: www.omoloschool.org

ANTIGUA

Island Academy International School
Oliver's Estate, PO Box W1884, St John's
DP Coordinator Mckala Fleming
Languages English
T: +1 268 460 1094
W: www.islandacademy.com

ARGENTINA

Asociación Cultural Pestalozzi
R Freire 1882, 1428 Ciudad de Buenos Aires
DP Coordinator Mariel Santarelli
Languages Spanish
T: +54 11 4555 3688
W: www.pestalozzi.edu.ar

Asociación Escuelas Lincoln
Andres Ferreyra 4073, 1637 La Lucila, Buenos Aires
DP Coordinator Sarah Fang
Languages English
T: +54 11 4851 1700
W: www.lincoln.edu.ar

Austin Eco Bilingual School (Austin EBS) Argentina
Porto 463, Campana, Buenos Aires
DP Coordinator Jessica Gino
Languages Spanish, English
T: +54 3489 462203/4
W: www.austin-ebs.com.ar

Colegio 4 DE 9 Nicolás Avellaneda
El Salvador 5228, 1414 Ciudad de Buenos Aires
DP Coordinator Veronica Converti
Languages English
T: +54 11 4771 4022
W: colegio4de9.wixsite.com/nicolasavellaneda

Colegio Alemán Córdoba
Recta Martinoli 6230 (Esq. Neper), 5021 Argüello, Córdoba
DP Coordinator Silvina Martinez
Languages Spanish
T: +54 35 4342 0834
W: www.colegioalemancba.edu.ar

Colegio De La Salle
Ayacucho 665, 1025 Ciudad de Buenos Aires
DP Coordinator Laura Simonotto
Languages Spanish
T: +54 011 4374 6449
W: www.lasalleba.edu.ar

Colegio de Todos Los Santos
Thames 798, Villa Adelina, 1607 San Isidro, Buenos Aires
DP Coordinator Pedro Pablo Koller
Languages English, Spanish
T: +54 114 766 3878
W: www.tls.edu.ar

Colegio Lincoln
Olleros 2283, Belgrano, Ciudad de Buenos Aires
DP Coordinator Andrea García
Languages Spanish, English
T: +54 11 4772 0108
W: www.lincoln.esc.edu.ar

Colegio Mark Twain
José Roque Funes 1525, 5009 Córdoba
DP Coordinator Pablo Esteban Cedro
Languages Spanish
T: +543 514 830 664
W: www.marktwaincba.com.ar

Colegio Montessori de Luján
Mitre 1247, Lujan, Buenos Aires
DP Coordinator Estefanía Fusco
Languages English, Spanish
T: +51 23 2343 3981
W: colegio-montessori.com.ar

Colegio Palermo Chico
Thames 2037/41, 1425 Ciudad de Buenos Aires
DP Coordinator Nora Cavuto
Languages Spanish
T: +54 114 774 3975
W: www.colegiopalermochico.edu.ar

Colegio San Ignacio
Guardias Nacionales 1400, 5806 Río Cuarto, Córdoba
DP Coordinator Horacio Toledo Carranza
Languages English, Spanish
T: +54 (358) 464 8484/0802
W: www.colegiosanignacio.edu.ar

Colegio San Jorge
Godoy Cruz, Pedro J Godoy 1191, 5547 Mendoza
DP Coordinator Patricia Arias
Languages Spanish
T: +54 2 614 287 247
W: colegiosanjorge.com.ar

Colegio San Marcos
Nivel Secundario, Jorge Miles 153, 1842 Monte Grande, Buenos Aires
DP Coordinator Gustavo Junco
Languages Spanish
T: +54 11 4296 3138
W: www.stmarks.com.ar

Colegio San Patricio
Moreno y Las Higueritas, 4107 Yerba Buena, Tucumán
DP Coordinator Mauro Juliano
Languages Spanish
T: +54 381 4250 708
W: www.sanpatriciotucuman.edu.ar

Colegio San Patricio de Luján
Acceso Oeste 2145, Lujan, Buenos Aires
DP Coordinator Maria Belen Mastellone
Languages Spanish
T: +54 23 2343 7998
W: www.sanpatriciodelujan.com

Colegio Santa María
Coronel Suárez 453, 4400 Salta
DP Coordinator Florencia Rovaletti
Languages Spanish
T: +54 387 421 3127
W: www.colegiosantamariasalta.com

Colegio Tarbut
Rosales 3019, 1636 Olivos, Buenos Aires
DP Coordinator Andrea Lichtensztein
Languages Spanish
T: +54 11 4794 3444
W: www.tarbut.edu.ar

Deutsche Schule Temperley
Av. Fernández 27, 1834 Temperley, Buenos Aires
DP Coordinator Cecilia Quarleri
Languages English, Spanish
T: +54 114244 2832
W: www.temperleyschule.edu.ar

Dover High School
San Martín y Ruta 26, 1623 Maschwitz, Buenos Aires
DP Coordinator Rodrigo Negro
Languages English, Spanish
T: +54 93488 441106
W: www.dover.edu.ar

Escuela Goethe Rosario
España 440, 2000 Rosario, Santa Fe
DP Coordinator Eduardo Palandri
Languages Spanish
T: +54 34 1426 3024
W: goetherosario.org

Escuela Municipal Paula Albarracin de Sarmiento
Juan Bautista Alberdi 1227, Olivos, Buenos Aires
DP Coordinator Romina Biga
Languages Spanish
T: +54 11 4513 9873
W: escuelas.mvl.edu.ar/empas

Escuela Normal Superior en Lenguas Vivas
Av. Córdoba 1951, 1120 Ciudad de Buenos Aires
DP Coordinator Fernando Grisi
Languages English
W: www.ens1caba.edu.ar

Escuela Normal Superior en LV 'Sofia Broquen de Spangenberg'
Juncal 3251, 1425 Ciudad de Buenos Aires
DP Coordinator Ursula Schroder
Languages Spanish
T: +54 114 807 2967/2966

Escuela Tecnica 32 DE 14 - Gral. Jose de San Martin
Teodoro Garcia 3899, 1427 Ciudad de Buenos Aires
DP Coordinator Marisa Casares
Languages Spanish
T: +54 11 4551 9121
W: escuelatecnica32.com.ar

Escuela Técnica N°24 D.E. 17- Defensa de Buenos Aires
Ricardo Gutierrez 3246, 1417 Ciudad de Buenos Aires
DP Coordinator Marcelo Saporito
Languages Spanish
T: +54 11 45019251
W: www.et24debsas.blogspot.com.ar

Escuela Técnica N°28 D.E. 10 República Francesa
Cuba 2410, 1428 Ciudad de Buenos Aires
DP Coordinator Daniel Vena
Languages English
T: +54 11 47816881/31
W: www.et28.net

Escuela Técnica N°29 D.E. 6 - Reconquista de Buenos Aires
Av. Boedo 760, 1218 Ciudad de Buenos Aires
DP Coordinator Dario Balbuena
Languages Spanish
W: www.tecnica29.org

ARGENTINA

Escuela Técnica Nº 9 D.E. 7 Ingeniero Luis A. Huergo
Martín de Gainza 1060, 1405 Ciudad de Buenos Aires
DP Coordinator Luciano Cocciro
Languages Spanish
T: +54 11 4582 6690
W: www.et9huergo.edu.ar

Holy Trinity College
Gascón 544, 7600 Mar del Plata, Buenos Aires
DP Coordinator Valeria Tommasi de Ruival
Languages English, Spanish
T: +54 223 486 3471
W: www.trinity.esc.edu.ar

Instituto Ballester
Calle 69 N° 5140 (ex San Martín 444), 1653 Villa Ballester, Buenos Aires
DP Coordinator Sergio García
Languages Spanish
T: +54 11 4768 0760
W: iballester.edu.ar

Instituto Santa Brígida
Av Gaona 2068, 1416 Ciudad de Buenos Aires
DP Coordinator Gladys Lesmi Dallas
Languages Spanish
T: +54 1 145 811 268
W: www.santabrigida.esc.edu.ar

Instituto Wolfsohn
2972, AEB, Amenábar, 1429 Ciudad de Buenos Aires
DP Coordinator Florencia Bacci
Languages English, Spanish
T: +54 11 4545 6020
W: wolfsohn.edu.ar

ISLANDS INTERNATIONAL SCHOOL
Amenábar St. 1840, 1428 Ciudad de Buenos Aires
DP Coordinator Clotilde Alleva
Languages Spanish, English, Italian, Portuguese
T: +54 11 4787 2294
W: www.intschools.org/school/islands
See full details on page 511

NORTHERN INTERNATIONAL SCHOOL
Ruote 8 Km 61.5., 1633. Pilar, Buenos Aires
DP Coordinator Marisa Zárate
Languages Spanish, English, Italian, Portuguese
T: +54 2322 49 1208
W: www.intschools.org/school/northern
See full details on page 532

NORTHLANDS SCHOOL
Olivos Site: Roma 1248, Olivos, Buenos Aires
DP Coordinator Alicia Olea
PYP Coordinator Maria Ines Martinez Beccar Varela & Natalia Torlaschi
Languages English, Spanish
T: +54 11 4711 8400
E: admissionsolivos@northlands.edu.ar
W: www.northlands.edu.ar
See full details on page 533

Northlands School Nordelta
Nordelta site: Av de los Colegios 590, Nordelta, Buenos Aires B1670NNN
DP Coordinator Alicia Olea
PYP Coordinator Natalia Torlaschi
Languages English
T: +54 11 4871 2668/9
W: www.northlands.edu.ar

Orange Day School
Av. San Martín 1651/7, 1657 Ramos Mejia, Buenos Aires
DP Coordinator María Penén Ramirez
Languages English, Spanish
T: +54 11 4464 7014
W: www.orangeschool.com.ar

Poplars School
Estrada 335, 9400 Río Gallegos, Santa Cruz
DP Coordinator Milena Navarro
Languages English, Spanish
T: +54 29 6642 5703
W: poplarsschool.edu.ar

Saint Mary of the Hills School
Xul Solar 6650, 1646 San Fernando, Buenos Aires
DP Coordinator Gastón Arana
Languages Spanish
T: +54 11 4714 0330
W: www.stmary.edu.ar

Saint Mary of the Hills School Sede Pilar
Ruta 25 y Caamaño, 1644 Pilar, Buenos Aires
DP Coordinator Mariana Xanthopoulos
Languages Spanish
T: +54 2304 458181
W: www.stmary.edu.ar

Saint Patrick College
Av. Maipú 3187, Corrientes
DP Coordinator Lucila Abate
Languages English, Spanish
W: www.saintpatrick.edu.ar

SOUTHERN INTERNATIONAL SCHOOL
Freeway Buenos Aires - La Plata Km 34., 1884 Hudson, Buenos Aires
DP Coordinator Paula Cantero
Languages Spanish, English, Italian, Portuguese
T: +54 11 4215 3636
W: www.intschools.org/school/southern
See full details on page 540

St George's College
Guido 800, 1878 Quilmes, Buenos Aires
DP Coordinator María Soledad Texidó
PYP Coordinator Mabel Orlando
Languages English, Spanish
T: +54 (11) 4350 7900
W: www.stgeorges.edu.ar/quilmes

St George's College North
Mosconi 3500 y Don Bosco s/n, 1613 Los Polvorines, Buenos Aires
DP Coordinator Noelia Zago
PYP Coordinator Enzo Speranza
Languages English, Spanish
T: +54 (11) 4663 2494
W: www.stgeorges.edu.ar/north

St Mary's International College
Martin Garcia 1435/1236/1501, 1804 Ezeiza, Buenos Aires
DP Coordinator Gloria María Morchio
Languages English, Spanish
T: +54 11 5075 0370
W: www.stmarys.edu.ar

St Matthew's College - Sede Fundadora
Moldes 1469, 1426 Ciudad de Buenos Aires
DP Coordinator Patricia Capecce
Languages Spanish, English
T: +54 11 4783 1110
W: www.smc.edu.ar

St Matthew's College - Sede Norte
Caamano 493, 1631 Pilar, Buenos Aires
DP Coordinator Graciela Mouzo
Languages Spanish
T: +54 230 4693600
W: www.smcn.edu.ar

St Xavier's College
José Antonio Cabrera 5901, 1414 Ciudad de Buenos Aires
DP Coordinator José Luis Goñi
Languages English
T: +54 114 777 5011/14
W: www.colegiosanjavier.com.ar

St. Andrew's Scots School
Roque Saenz Peña 601, 1636 Olivos, Buenos Aires
DP Coordinator Analia Heidenreich
Languages English
T: +54 11 4846 6500
W: www1.sanandres.esc.edu.ar

St. Catherine's Moorlands - Belgrano
Carbajal 3250, 1426 Ciudad de Buenos Aires
DP Coordinator Sofia Hughes
MYP Coordinator Mariela Buracco
Languages English, Spanish
T: +54 11 4552 4353
W: www.scms.edu.ar/es/belgrano

St. Catherine's Moorlands - Tortuguitas
Ruta Panamericana Km 38 Ramal Pilar, 1667 Tortuguitas, Buenos Aires
MYP Coordinator Alejandro Elia
Languages English
T: +54 348 463 9001/2
W: www.scms.edu.ar/es/tortuguitas

St. Francis School
Av. Benavidez 1326, 1621 Benavidez, Buenos Aires
DP Coordinator Silvina Massa
Languages English
T: +54 11 2078 4200
W: www.saintfrancis.edu.ar

St. John's School - Beccar
España 348/370, 1643 Beccar, Buenos Aires
DP Coordinator Martín Russi
PYP Coordinator María Julieta Romero Vagni
Languages Spanish
T: +54 11 4513 4400
W: www.stjohns.edu.ar

St. John's School - Pilar
Panamericana Km. 48.800, 1629 Pilar, Buenos Aires
DP Coordinator Luciano Cappuccio
PYP Coordinator Lucila Romeo
Languages English, Spanish
T: +54 (0) 2304 667 667
W: www.stjohns.edu.ar

Sunrise School
Chacra 116 Colonia Lucinda, 8324 Cipolletti, Río Negro
DP Coordinator Juan Manuel Ginez
Languages Spanish
T: +54 299 4786590
W: www.sunriseschoolpatagonia.com

Villa Devoto School
Pedro Morán 4441, 1419 Ciudad de Buenos Aires
DP Coordinator Roberto Mancuso
Languages English
T: +54 114 501 9419
W: vds.edu.ar

Washington School
Avenida Federico Lacroze 2012, 1426 Ciudad de Buenos Aires
DP Coordinator Sonia Pino
PYP Coordinator Verónica Sartoni
Languages Spanish
T: +54 11 4772 8131
W: www.washingtonschool.edu.ar

Woodville School
Av. Los Pioneros km 2,900, 8400 San Carlos de Bariloche, Río Negro
DP Coordinator Andrew Schwartz
Languages Spanish, English
T: +54 2944 44 11 33
W: www.woodville.org

BAHAMAS

Lucaya International School
Chesapeake Drive, Freeport
DP Coordinator Kerry Gray
PYP Coordinator Erin Cordes
Languages English
T: +1 242 373 4004
W: www.lisbahamas.com

Lyford Cay International School
Lyford Cay Drive, PO Box N-7776, Nassau NB
CP Coordinator Timothy Connolly
DP Coordinator Michèle (Scullion) Mindorff
MYP Coordinator Harry Almond
PYP Coordinator Katina Seymour
Languages English
T: +1 242 362 4774
W: www.lcis.bs

St Andrew's International School
PO Box EE 17340, Yamacraw Hill Road, Nassau, NP
DP Coordinator Ashish Bowen
PYP Coordinator Vashni Carey
Languages English
T: +1 242 677 7800
W: www.standrewsbahamas.com

BARBADOS

The Codrington School
St John BB 20008
DP Coordinator Darryl Brown
MYP Coordinator Nicola Leedham
PYP Coordinator Susanne Fischer
Languages English
T: +1 246 423 2570
W: www.codrington.edu.bb

BERMUDA

Bermuda High School
19 Richmond Road, Pembroke HM08
DP Coordinator Sarah Wheddon
Languages English
T: +441 295 6153
W: www.bhs.bm

SOMERSFIELD ACADEMY
107 Middle Road, Devonshire DV 06
DP Coordinator Kate Ross
MYP Coordinator Summer Wood Brice Pursell
Languages English
T: +1 441 236 9797
E: admissions@somersfield.bm
W: www.somersfield.bm
See full details on page 539

Warwick Academy
117 Middle Road, Warwick PG01
CP Coordinator Sara Jackson
DP Coordinator Sara Jackson
Languages English
T: +1 441 236 1917/239 9452
W: www.warwick.bm

BOLIVIA

American International School of Bolivia
Casilla 5309, Cochabamba
DP Coordinator Ximena Aguilera
Languages English
T: +591 4 428 8577
W: www.aisb.edu.bo

Colegio Alemán Santa Cruz
Casilla 624, Av San Martin s/n, Santa Cruz
DP Coordinator Alexandra Kempff
Languages Spanish
T: +591 3 3326820
W: ds-santacruz.bo

Saint Andrew's School
Casilla 1679, Av Las Retamas s/n La Florida, La Paz
DP Coordinator Eduardo Blanco
PYP Coordinator Mónica Villarreal
Languages English, Spanish
T: +591 22 79 24 84
W: www.saintandrews.edu.bo

BRAZIL

ABA Global School
Av. Rosa e Silva, 1510, Aflitos, Recife, Pernambuco PE 52050-245
PYP Coordinator Maria do Rozario Botelho
Languages English
T: +55 81 3427 8800
W: www.estudenaaba.com

American School of Brasilia
SGAS 605, Conjunto E, Lotes 34/37, Brasília DF 70200-650
DP Coordinator Maria Sieve
Languages English
T: +55 61 3442 9700
W: www.eabdf.br

American School of Campinas - Escola Americana de Campinas
Rua Cajamar, #35, Campinas, São Paulo SP 13090-860
DP Coordinator Erika Bonet
Languages English
T: +55 19 21021006
W: www.eac.com.br

Associação Educacional Luterana Bom Jesus / IELUSC
Rua Princesa Isabel, 438, Joinville, Santa Catarina SC 89201-270
DP Coordinator Marcelli Mazzei Ramalho
Languages English
T: +55 47 3026 8000
W: www.ielusc.br

Beacon School
Rua Berlioz 245, Alto de Pinheiros, São Paulo SP 05467-000
DP Coordinator Karine Vairo
PYP Coordinator Maiara Terra
Languages English, Portuguese
T: +55 11 3021 0262
W: www.beaconschool.com.br

Centro Internacional de Educacao Integrada
Estrada do Pontal 2093, Recreio dos Bandeirantes, Rio de Janeiro RJ 22790-877
DP Coordinator Pedro Fernandes
PYP Coordinator Vanessa Vianna
Languages English
T: +55 21 2490 1673
W: www.ciei.g12.br

Chapel School – The American International School of Brazil
Rua Vigário João de Pontes, 537, Chácara Flora, São Paulo SP 04748-000
DP Coordinator Donald Campbell
Languages English
T: +55 11 2101 7400
W: www.chapelschool.com

Colégio 7 de Setembro
R. Henriqueta Galeno, 1011, Dionísio Torres, Fortaleza, Ceará CE 60135-420
DP Coordinator Janaina Façanha
Languages English, Portuguese
T: +55 85 4006 7777
W: www.c7s.com.br

Colégio Miguel de Cervantes
Avenida Jorge João Saad, 905, São Paulo, Morumbí SP 05618-001
DP Coordinator Katia Pupo
Languages Portuguese, Spanish, English
T: +55 11 3779 1800
W: cmc.com.br

Colegio Positivo Internacional
Professor Pedro Viriato de Souza St 5300, Curitiba, Paraná PR 81280-330
DP Coordinator Juliana Lazari
MYP Coordinator Maria Fernanda Caneparo
PYP Coordinator Michelline Ramos
Languages Portuguese, English
T: +55 (41) 3335 3535
W: www.colegiopositivo.com.br

Colegio Sao Luis
Av. Dr. Dante Pazzanese, 295, Vila Mariana, São Paulo SP 04012-180
DP Coordinator Andrea Rodrigues
Languages English, Portuguese
W: www.saoluis.org

Colégio Soka do Brasil
Avenida Cursino, 362, Saúde SP 04132-000
DP Coordinator Tania Sakuma
Languages English, Portuguese
T: +55 11 5060 3300
W: www.colegiosoka.org.br

Colégio Suíço-Brasileiro de Curitiba
Rua Wanda dos Santos Mallmann, 537, Jardim Pinhais, Pinhais, Paraná PR 83323-400
DP Coordinator Carlos Machado
Languages English
T: +55 41 3525 9100
W: www.chpr.com.br

IB AMERICAS

BRAZIL

Coree International School

R. Gothard Kaesemodel 961, Anita Garibaldi, Joinville, Santa Catarina SC 89203-522
DP Coordinator Rebeca Alonso Saeta
PYP Coordinator Dorota Szczepanska Oliveira
Languages English
T: +55 47 3121 6700
W: coree.org.br/home-coree/international-school

Escola Americana de Belo Horizonte

Av. Professor Mario Werneck, 3002, Bairro Buritis, Belo Horizonte, Minas Gerais MG 30575-180
MYP Coordinator Leonardo Botaro
PYP Coordinator Judy Imamudeen
Languages English, Portuguese
T: +55 31 3378 6700
W: www.eabh.com.br

ESCOLA AMERICANA DO RIO DE JANEIRO - BARRA DA TIJUCA

Rua Colbert Coelho 155, Barra da Tijuca, Rio de Janeiro RJ 22793-313
DP Coordinator Deborah Dale Fontes
Languages English
T: +55 21 3747 2000
W: www.earj.com.br
See full details on page 502

ESCOLA AMERICANA DO RIO DE JANEIRO - GÁVEA

Estrada da Gávea 132, Gávea, Rio de Janeiro RJ 22451-263
DP Coordinator Ms. Flavia DiLuccio (Gávea Campus) & Ms. Deborah Dale (Barra Campus)
Languages English
T: +55 21 2125 9000
E: admissions.gavea@earj.com.br
W: www.earj.com.br
See full details on page 502

Escola Beit Yaacov

Av Marques de Sao Vicente no 1748, Barra Funda, São Paulo SP 01139-002
DP Coordinator Raphael Silva
PYP Coordinator Alexandra Cunha
Languages English, Hebrew, Portuguese
T: +55 11 3611 0600
W: www.beityaacov.com.br

Escola Bilíngue Pueri Domus - Aclimação Campus

Rua Muniz de Sousa 1051, Aclimação, São Paulo SP 01534-020
DP Coordinator Cintia Etsuko Yamashita
Languages English, Portuguese
T: +55 11 3478 7701
W: www.pueridomus.com.br

Escola Bilíngue Pueri Domus - Itaim Campus

Rua Itacema 214, Itaim Bibi, São Paulo SP 04530-050
DP Coordinator Ricardo Lourenco
Languages English, Portuguese
T: +55 11 3078 6999
W: www.pueridomus.com.br

Escola Bilíngue Pueri Domus - Perdizes Campus

Rua Ministro Godói 1697, Perdizes, São Paulo SP 05015-001
DP Coordinator John Whittlesea
Languages English, Portuguese
T: +55 11 3803 4240
W: www.pueridomus.com.br

Escola Bilíngue Pueri Domus - Verbo Divino Campus

Rua Verbo Divino 993-A, Chacara Sto. Antonio, São Paulo SP 04719-001
DP Coordinator Ms Cindy Obi
Languages English, Portuguese
T: +55 11 3512 2222
W: www.pueridomus.com.br

Escola Castanheiras

Alameda Castanheiras, 250, Res. Tres (Tambore), Santana de Parnaíba, São Paulo SP 06543-510
DP Coordinator Airton Pretini Junior
Languages English
T: +55 114 152 4600
W: www.escolacastanheiras.com.br

Escola Eleva - Botafogo

Rua General Severiano, 159, Botafogo, Rio de Janeiro RJ 22290-040
DP Coordinator Dulce Simas
Languages English, Portuguese
T: +55 21 4042 2492
W: escolaeleva.com.br

Escola Internacional de Alphaville

Av. Copacabana, 624, Cond. Empresarial 18 do Forte, Alphaville, Barueri SP 06472-001
PYP Coordinator Roberta Deliberato
Languages English
T: +55 11 4134 6066
W: www.escolainternacional.com.br

Escola Internacional UniSociesc Blumenau

Rua Pandiá Calógeras 272, Jardim Blumenau, Blumenau, Santa Catarina SC 89010-350
DP Coordinator Abdul Lima
PYP Coordinator Juliane Chicatto
Languages English, Portuguese
T: +55 47 2111 2966
W: www.eiublumenau.com.br

Escola Internacional UniSociesc Florianopolis

Rua Salvatina Feliciana dos Santos, 525, Florianópolis, Santa Catarina SC 88034-600
DP Coordinator Leonardo Gomes Oliveira
PYP Coordinator Pedro Henrique Coimbra
Languages English, Portuguese
T: +55 47 2111 2966
W: unisociesc.com.br/unidades/florianopolis-campus-ilh

Escola Lourenco Castanho

Rua Fiandeiras 77, Vila Olímpia, São Paulo SP 04545-000
DP Coordinator Maria Cecília R. Palma T. Pastorelli
Languages English, Portuguese
T: +55 11 3047 0099
W: www.lourencocastanho.com.br

Escola Nova

Rua Major Rubens Vaz, 392, Gávea, Rio de Janeiro RJ 22470-070
DP Coordinator Gustavo Paiva
Languages English, Portuguese
T: +55 21 3875 9899
W: www.escolanova.com.br

Escola Suíço-Brasileira (ESB) by SIS Swiss International School

Rua Corréa de Araújo 81, Barra da Tijuca, Rio de Janeiro RJ 22611-060
DP Coordinator Maurício Da Silva Drumond Costa
MYP Coordinator Soraia Dale-Harris
PYP Coordinator Aline Costa
Languages English
T: +55 21 33 89 20 89
W: www.swissinternationalschool.com.br

Escola Suíço-Brasileira de São Paulo

Rua Visconde de Porto Seguro 391, Alto da Boa Vista, São Paulo SP 04642-000
DP Coordinator Andreas Panse
Languages English
T: +55 11 5682 2140
W: www.esbsp.com.br

GIS SP - The International School of São Paulo

Alameda dos Jurupis 485, Moema, São Paulo SP 04088-000
PYP Coordinator Jaqueline Weber
Languages English, Portuguese
T: +55 11 3900 8931
W: www.issaopaulo.com.br

Graded - The American School of São Paulo

Av. José Galante, 425, São Paulo SP 05642-000
DP Coordinator Justin Morris
Languages English
T: +55 11 3747 4800
W: www.graded.br

Gurilândia International School

Av. Cardeal Da Silva 1433, Federacao, Salvador, Bahia BA 40231-250
PYP Coordinator Denise Lima De Araújo Rocha
Languages English, Portuguese
T: +55 71 3336 6595
W: www.gurilandia.com.br

International School of Curitiba

Ave. Eugenio Bertolli, 3900, Sta. Felicidade, Curitiba, Paraná PR 82410-530
DP Coordinator Lukas Gohl
Languages English
T: +55 41 3525 7400
W: www.iscbrazil.com

Land School

Av. Cardeal da Silva, No. 136, Federacao, Salvador, Bahia BA 40231-250
MYP Coordinator Alexandre Kanegae
Languages English, Portuguese
T: +55 71 3021 2550
W: www.landschool.com.br

Pan American School of Bahia

Av Ibirapitanga, Loteamento Patamares, s/n, Salvador, Bahia BH 41680-060
DP Coordinator Roberta Rodrigues
PYP Coordinator Sam Whitney
Languages English
T: +55 71 3368 8400
W: www.escolapanamericana.com

Pan American School of Porto Alegre

Av. João Obino 110, Petrópolis, Porto Alegre, Rio Grande do Sul RS 90470-150
MYP Coordinator Bruno Britto
PYP Coordinator Elizabeth Hines
Languages English, Portuguese
T: +55 513 334 5866
W: www.panamerican.com.br

Red House International School

Rua Engenheiro Edgar Egidio de Souza 444, Pacaembu SP 01233-020
PYP Coordinator Henrique Oliveira
Languages English
T: +55 11 2309 7999
W: www.redhouseschool.com.br

Saint Nicholas School

Av Eusébio Matoso 333, Pinheiros, São Paulo SP 05423-180
DP Coordinator Saulo Vianna
PYP Coordinator Stephen Eagles
Languages English
T: + 55 11 3465 9666
W: www.stnicholas.com.br

SIS Swiss International School Brasília

SGA/SUL, Quadra 905, cj B, Brasília DF 70390-050
MYP Coordinator Mikke Marttinen
PYP Coordinator Hayley Waghorn
Languages English
T: +55 61 34 43 41 45
W: www.swissinternationalschool.com.br/school-locations/brasilia

Sphere International School

Av Anchieta, 908 - Jardim Nova Europa, Sao José dos Campos, São Paulo SP 12242-280
MYP Coordinator Sandra Araujo
PYP Coordinator Melissa Therriault Zaramella
Languages English, Portuguese
T: +55 12 3322 1255
W: www.escolaesfera.com.br

St Nicholas School - Alphaville Campus

Av. Honório Álvares Penteado, 5463, Tamboré, Santana de Parnaíba SP 06543-320
MYP Coordinator Gudrun Ingimundardottir
PYP Coordinator Jennifer Fletcher
Languages English, Portuguese
T: +55 11 3465 9658
W: stnicholas.com.br

ST. FRANCIS COLLEGE, BRAZIL

Rua Joaquim Antunes 678, Pinheiros, São Paulo SP 05415-001
DP Coordinator Gloria Malagón
MYP Coordinator Thomas Holesgrove
PYP Coordinator Emily Hays
Languages English, Portuguese
T: +55 11 3728 8053
E: office@stfrancis.com.br
W: www.stfrancis.com.br
See full details on page 542

ST. PAUL'S SCHOOL

Rua Juquiá 166, Jardim Paulistano, São Paulo SP 01440-903
DP Coordinator Ana Carolina Belmonte
Languages English
T: +55 11 3087 3399
E: head@stpauls.br
W: www.stpauls.br
See full details on page 543

THE BRITISH COLLEGE OF BRAZIL

Rua Álvares de Azevedo, 50, Chácara Flora, São Paulo SP 04671-040
DP Coordinator Mr. Timothy Jones
Languages English
T: +55 11 5547 3030
E: info@britishcollegebrazil.org
W: www.britishcollegebrazil.org
See full details on page 548

THE BRITISH SCHOOL, RIO DE JANEIRO

Rua Real Grandeza 99, Botafogo, Rio de Janeiro RJ 22281-030
DP Coordinator Guy Smith & Leah Wilks
Languages English
T: +55 21 2539 2717
E: edu@britishschool.g12.br
W: www.britishschool.g12.br
See full details on page 549

The British School, Rio de Janeiro - Barra Site

Rua Mario Autuori, 100, Barra da Tijuca RJ 22793
DP Coordinator Leah Wilks
Languages English
T: +55 21 3329 2854
W: www.britishschool.g12.br

Valley International School

Av. Osvaldo Reis, 2000 Praia Brava, Itajai, Santa Catarina SC 88306-600
PYP Coordinator Virginia Nichele
Languages English, Portuguese
T: +55 47 3349 0969
W: valleyschool.com.br

BRITISH VIRGIN ISLANDS

Cedar International School

Waterfront Drive, Kingston
DP Coordinator Thibaud Guenegou
MYP Coordinator Catherine Armstrong
PYP Coordinator Lesley Bayles
Languages English
T: +1 284 494 5262
W: cedar.vg

CANADA

Alberta

Annunciation

9325-165 Street, Edmonton AB T5R 2S5
PYP Coordinator Ashley Jennings
Languages English
T: +1 780 484 4319
W: www.ecsd.net/8001

Archbishop Macdonald

14219-109 Avenue, Edmonton AB T5N 1H5
DP Coordinator Jennifer Vandendooren
MYP Coordinator Helen Grijo
Languages English
T: +1 780 451 1470
W: www.ecsd.net/8403

Bellerose Composite High School

49 Giroux Road, St Albert AB T8N 6N4
DP Coordinator Clayton Wowk
Languages English
T: +1 780 460 8490

Bishop David Motiuk Elementary/Junior High School

855 Lewis Greens Drive NW, Edmonton AB T5T 4B2
MYP Coordinator Lyndsy Panizzon
PYP Coordinator Andrea Olivieri
Languages English, French
T: +1 780 409 2603
W: www.ecsd.net/1967

Bishop O'Byrne High School

Suite 500, 333 Shawville Blvd SE, Calgary AB T2Y 4H3
DP Coordinator Brendan Bulger
Languages English
T: +1 403 500 2103
W: www.cssd.ab.ca/schools/bishopobyrne

Calgary French and International School

700-77th Street SW, Calgary AB T3H 5R1
DP Coordinator Christian Legault
Languages English, French
T: +1 403 240 1500
W: www.cfis.com

Coronation School

10925-139 Street, Edmonton AB T5M 1P8
PYP Coordinator Rachel Mcouat
Languages English
T: +1 780 455 2008
W: coronation.epsb.ca

Glenora School

13520-102 Avenue, Edmonton AB T5N 0N7
MYP Coordinator Laura Johnson
Languages English
T: +1 780 452 4740

Grande Prairie Composite High School

11202 - 104 Street, Grande Prairie AB T8V 2Z1
DP Coordinator Lee Brentnell
Languages English
T: +1 780 532 7721
W: www.gppsd.ab.ca/school/gpcomposite

Harry Ainlay High School

4350 111 Street NW, Edmonton AB T6J 1E8
DP Coordinator Dean Zuberbuhler
Languages English
T: +1 780 413 2700
W: harryainlay.epsb.ca

Henry Wise Wood High School

910 - 75th Avenue SW, Calgary AB T2V 0S6
DP Coordinator Scott Garen
Languages English
T: +1 403 253 2261
W: school.cbe.ab.ca/school/henrywisewood

Holy Trinity High School

7007-28th Avenue, Edmonton AB T6K 4A5
DP Coordinator Richard Downing
MYP Coordinator Kathryn Wojcicki
Languages English
T: +1 780 462 5777
W: www.holytrinity.ecsd.net

John G Diefenbaker High School

6620 - 4th Street NW, Calgary AB T2K 1C2
DP Coordinator Glenn Finockio
Languages English
T: +1 403 274 2240
W: school.cbe.ab.ca/school/johngdiefenbaker

Lester B Pearson High School

3020 52nd Street NE, Calgary AB T1Y 5P4
CP Coordinator Tammy Lock
DP Coordinator Pawanbir Minhas
Languages English
T: +1 403 244 2278
W: www.schools.cbe.ab.ca

Lillian Osborne High School

2019 Leger Road NW, Edmonton AB T6R 0R9
DP Coordinator Jane Taylor
Languages English
T: +1 780 970 5249
W: lillianosborne.epsb.ca

Lindsay Thurber Comprehensive High School

4204-58th Street, Red Deer AB T4N 2L6
DP Coordinator David Smith
Languages English
T: +1 403 347 1171
W: lindsaythurber.rdpsd.ab.ca

Louis St Laurent

11230-43 Avenue, Edmonton AB T6J 0X3
DP Coordinator Nicole Schatz
MYP Coordinator Jocelyn Johnston
Languages English
T: +1 780 435 3964
W: www.louisstlaurent.ecsd.net

M.E. LaZerte School

6804 144 Ave, Edmonton AB T5C 3C7
DP Coordinator Jennifer Hewko
Languages English
T: +1 780 408 9800
W: www.melazerte.com

McNally High School

8440-105 Avenue, Edmonton AB T6A 1B6
DP Coordinator Omneya Khamis
Languages English
T: +1 780 469 0442
W: mcnally.epsb.ca

Millarville Community School

130 Millarville Rd, Millarville AB T0L 1K0
PYP Coordinator Karla Davis
Languages English
T: +1 403 938 7832
W: millarville.fsd38.ab.ca

Old Scona Academic High School

10523-84th Avenue, Edmonton AB T6E 2H5
DP Coordinator Jeff Karas
Languages English
T: +1 780 433 0627
W: oldscona.epsb.ca

Prairie Waters Elementary School

201 Invermere Drive, Chestermere AB T1X 1M6
PYP Coordinator Breanna Baxter
Languages English
T: +1 403 285 6969
W: prairiewaters.rockyview.ab.ca

Ross Sheppard High School

13546-111th Avenue, Edmonton AB T5M 2P2
DP Coordinator Jennifer Gross
Languages English
T: +1 780 448 5000
W: shep.epsb.ca

Salisbury Composite High School

#20 Festival Way, Sherwood Park AB T8A 4Y1
DP Coordinator Michelle Wyman
Languages English
T: +1 780 467 8816
W: www.salcomp.ca

Sir Winston Churchill High School, Calgary

5220 Northland Drive NW, Calgary AB T2L 2J6
DP Coordinator Arlene Lee
Languages English
T: +1 403 289 9241
W: school.cbe.ab.ca/school/sirwinstonchurchill

St Albert Catholic High School

33 Malmo Drive, St Albert AB T8N 1L5
DP Coordinator Damon Clayton
Languages English
T: +1 780 459 7781
W: www.sachs.gsacrd.ab.ca

St Clement Catholic Elementary/Junior High School

7620 Mill Woods Road South, Edmonton AB T6K 2P7
MYP Coordinator Rosanne Boutin
PYP Coordinator Meaghan Jenny
Languages English
T: +1 780 462 3806
W: www.stclement.ecsd.net

St. Boniface Catholic Elementary School

11810-40 Avenue, Edmonton AB T6J 0R9
PYP Coordinator John Edwards
Languages English
T: +1 780 434 0294
W: www.stboniface.ecsd.net

St. Edmund IB World School

11712-130 Avenue, Edmonton AB T5E 0V2
MYP Coordinator Laura Manucci
PYP Coordinator Laura Manucci
Languages English
T: +1 780 453 1596
W: www.ecsd.net/8215

St. Mary's High School

111-18th Avenue SW, Calgary Catholic, Calgary AB T2S 0B8
DP Coordinator Cathy Harradence
Languages English
T: +1 403 500 2024
W: www.cssd.ab.ca/schools/stmarys

Strathcona-Tweedsmuir School

RR 2, Okotoks AB T1S 1A2
DP Coordinator Chris Ruskay
MYP Coordinator Gabe Kemp
PYP Coordinator Shannon Taggart
Languages English
T: +1 403 938 4431
W: www.sts.ab.ca

Victoria School of the Arts

10210 - 108 Avenue, Edmonton AB T5H 1A8
CP Coordinator Joanne Lowry
DP Coordinator Joanne Lowry
MYP Coordinator Wendy Plum
PYP Coordinator Wendy Plum
Languages English
T: +1 780 426 3010
W: www.victoria-school.ca

Western Canada High School

641 17 Avenue S.W., Calgary AB T2S 0B5
DP Coordinator Susan Rivers
Languages English
T: +1 403 228 5363
W: school.cbe.ab.ca/school/westerncanada

Westglen School

10950-127 Street, Edmonton AB T5M 0S7
MYP Coordinator Laura Johnson
Languages English
T: +1 780 454 3449
W: westglen.epsb.ca

Westminster School

13712-102 Avenue, Edmonton AB T5N 0W4
MYP Coordinator Laura Johnson
Languages English
T: +1 780 452 4343

Winston Churchill High School

1605-15th Avenue North, Lethbridge AB T1H 1W4
DP Coordinator Morgan Day
Languages English
T: +1 403 328 4723
W: wchs.lethsd.ab.ca

British Columbia

Abbotsford Middle School

33231 Bevan Avenue, Abbotsford BC V2S 0A9
MYP Coordinator Laura Inglis
Languages English
T: +1 604 859 7125
W: abbymiddle.abbyschools.ca

Abbotsford Senior Secondary School

33355 Bevan Avenue, Abbotsford BC V2S 0E7
DP Coordinator Michael Keeley
Languages English
T: +1 604 853 3367
W: abbysenior.sd34.bc.ca

Alexander Academy

200-688 West Hastings Street, Vancouver BC V6B 1P1
DP Coordinator Spencer Todd
Languages English, French
T: +1 604 687 8832
W: www.alexanderacademy.ca

Aspengrove School

7660 Clark Drive, Nanaimo BC V0R 2H0
DP Coordinator Robert Ohly
MYP Coordinator Carrie Turunen
PYP Coordinator Susan Riordan
Languages English
T: +1 250 390 2201
W: www.aspengroveschool.ca

Britannia Secondary School

1001 Cotton Drive, Vancouver BC V5L 3T4
DP Coordinator Hubert Wong
Languages English
T: +1 604 713 8266
W: britannia.vsb.bc.ca

Brockton School

3467 Duval Road, North Vancouver BC V7J 3E8
CP Coordinator Noble Kelly
DP Coordinator Svetlana Catia
MYP Coordinator Lindsay Foster
PYP Coordinator Christina Miller
Languages English
T: +1 604 929 9201
W: www.brocktonschool.com

Brookes Westshore

1939 Sooke Road, Victoria BC V9B 1W2
DP Coordinator Rui Li
MYP Coordinator Melanie Moroz
Languages English
W: westshore.brookes.org

Capilano Elementary School

1230 West 20th Street, North Vancouver BC V7P 2B9
PYP Coordinator Arash Kaboli
Languages English
T: +1 604 903 3370
W: www.sd44.ca/school/capilano/Pages/default.aspx

Carson Graham Secondary School
2145 Jones Avenue, North Vancouver BC V7M 2W7
DP Coordinator Liz Thornhill
MYP Coordinator Cora Pross
Languages English
T: +1 604 903 3555
W: carsongraham.ca

Cypress Park Primary School
4355 Marine Drive, West Vancouver BC V7V 1P2
PYP Coordinator Bea Sedgwick
Languages English
T: +1 604 981 1330
W: westvancouverschools.ca/cypresspark-primary

École Andre-Piolat
380 West Kings Road, North Vancouver BC V7L 2L9
DP Coordinator Trâm Tran
MYP Coordinator Trâm Tran
Languages English
T: +1 604 980 6040
W: andrepiolat.csf.bc.ca

Ecole Cedardale Elementary
595 Burley Drive, West Vancouver BC V7T 1Z3
PYP Coordinator Kristina Hayes
Languages English
T: +1 604 981 1390
W: westvancouverschools.ca/ecole-cedardale-elementary

École des Pionniers Port Coquitlam
1618 Patricia Ave, Port Coquitlam BC V3B 4A8
DP Coordinator Richard Hoole
MYP Coordinator Karine De Serres
Languages French
T: +1 604 552 7915
W: pionniers.csf.bc.ca

École Gabrielle-Roy
6887, 132 Rue, Surrey BC V3W 4L9
DP Coordinator Jean-Philippe Schall
Languages French, English
T: +1 604 599 6688
W: gabrielleroy.csf.bc.ca

École Jules-Verne
5445 rue Baillie, Vancouver BC V5Z 3M6
DP Coordinator Pierre-Luc Davidson
Languages French
T: +1 604 731 8378
W: julesverne.csf.bc.ca

École Victor-Brodeur
637 Head Street, Victoria BC V9A 5S9
DP Coordinator Joelle Briant
Languages French
T: +1 250 220 6010
W: brodeur.csf.bc.ca

Elsie Roy Elementary School
150 Drake Street, Vancouver BC V6Z 2X1
MYP Coordinator Melissa Martin
Languages English
T: +1 604 7135890

English Bluff Elementary
402 English Bluff Road, Delta BC V4M 2N2
PYP Coordinator Jessica Elkin
Languages English
T: +1 604 943 0201
W: eb.deltasd.bc.ca

Fraser Valley School
19533 64th Avenue, Surrey BC V3S 4J3
PYP Coordinator Natalie Morris
Languages English
T: +1 604 427 2282
W: fraservalleyschool.ca

Garibaldi Secondary School
24789 Dewdney Trunk Road, Maple Ridge BC V4R 1X2
DP Coordinator Kyle Ludeman
Languages English
T: +1 604 463 6287
W: gss.sd42.ca

Glenlyon Norfolk School
801 Bank Street, Victoria BC V8S 4A8
DP Coordinator Mme. Angela Girard
MYP Coordinator Mrs. Gina Simpson
PYP Coordinator Mrs. Leanne Giommi
Languages English
T: +1 250 370 6801
W: www.mygns.ca

Hugh Boyd Secondary School
9200 No. 1 Road, Richmond BC V7E 6L5
MYP Coordinator Eva Tong
Languages English
T: +1 604 668 6615
W: boyd.sd38.bc.ca

Island Pacific School
671 Carter Road, Box 128, Bowen Island BC V0N 1G0
MYP Coordinator Amanda Szabo
Languages English
T: +1 604 947 9311
W: www.islandpacific.org

Johnston Heights Secondary School
15350-99 Avenue, Surrey BC V3R 0R9
DP Coordinator Emily Hayler
MYP Coordinator Jennifer Macdonald
Languages English
T: +1 604 581 5500
W: www.surreyschools.ca

King George Secondary School
1755 Barclay Street, Vancouver BC V6G 1K6
MYP Coordinator Erin Stacey
Languages English
T: +1 604 713 8999
W: kinggeorge.vsb.bc.ca

Lord Roberts Elementary School
1100 Bidwell Street, Vancouver BC V6G 2K4
MYP Coordinator Kay Shetty
Languages English
T: +1 604 713 5055
W: lordroberts.vsb.bc.ca

Lowell High School
750 Hamilton Street, Suite 210, Vancouver BC V6B 2R5
DP Coordinator Sean Murray
Languages English, Chinese
T: +1 604 336 0456
W: www.lowellhighschool.ca

MEADOWRIDGE SCHOOL
12224 240th Street, Maple Ridge BC V4R 1N1
DP Coordinator Ms. Kristal Bereza
MYP Coordinator Mr. Scott Rinn
PYP Coordinator Mrs. Heather Nicholson
Languages English
T: +1 604 467 4444
E: admissions@meadowridge.bc.ca
W: www.meadowridge.bc.ca
See full details on page 526

Mountain Secondary School
7755-202 A Street, Langley BC V2Y 1W4
DP Coordinator Tina Costopoulos
Languages English
T: +1 604 888 3033
W: www.msssd35.bc.ca

MULGRAVE, THE INTERNATIONAL SCHOOL OF VANCOUVER
2330 Cypress Bowl Lane, West Vancouver BC V7S 3H9
DP Coordinator Aziz Batada
MYP Coordinator Mike Olynyk
PYP Coordinator Janet Hicks & Shanaz Ramji
Languages English
T: +1 604 922 3223
E: admissions@mulgrave.com
W: www.mulgrave.com
See full details on page 528

New Westminster Secondary School
835 Eighth Street, New Westminster BC V3M 3S9
DP Coordinator James Janz
Languages English
T: +1 604 517 6220
W: nwss.ca

NorKam Senior Secondary School
730 12th Street, Kamloops BC V2B 3C1
DP Coordinator Murray Williams
Languages English
T: +1 250 376 1272
W: nkss.sd73.bc.ca

Pacific Academy
10238 168th Street, Surrey BC V4N 1Z4
DP Coordinator David Rosborough
Languages English
T: +1 604 581 5353
W: www.pacificacademy.net

PARKLAND SECONDARY SCHOOL
10640 McDonald Park Road, Sidney BC V8L 5S7
DP Coordinator Erin Stinson
Languages English
T: +1 250 655 2700
E: krussell@saanichschools.ca
W: parkland.sd63.bc.ca
See full details on page 535

Pearson College UWC
650 Pearson College Drive, Victoria BC V9C 4H7
DP Coordinator Sherry Crowther
Languages English
T: +1 250 391 2411
W: www.pearsoncollege.ca

Port Moody Secondary School
300 Albert Street, Port Moody BC V3H 2M5
DP Coordinator Sean Lenihan
Languages English
T: +1 604 939 6656
W: www.sd43.bc.ca/secondary/portmoody

Princess Margaret Secondary High School

120 Green Avenue W., Penticton, BC V2A 3T1
MYP Coordinator Marcus Krieger
Languages English, French
T: +1 250 770 7620
W: www.sd67.bc.ca/school/princessmargaretsecondary

Queen Mary Community School

230 West Keith Road, North Vancouver BC V7M 1L8
PYP Coordinator Jen Aragon
Languages English
T: +1 604 903 3720
W: www.queenmary.ca

Richmond Secondary School

7171 Minoru Boulevard, Richmond BC V6Y 1Z3
DP Coordinator David Miller
Languages English
T: +1 604 668 6400
W: rhs.sd38.bc.ca

Rockridge Secondary School

5350 Headland Drive, West Vancouver BC V7W 3H2
MYP Coordinator Stephanie Langlois
Languages English
T: +1 604 981 1300
W: westvancouverschools.ca/rockridge-secondary

Seaquam Secondary School

11584 Lyon Road, Delta BC V4E 2K4
DP Coordinator Dhana Matthews
Languages English
T: +1 604 591 6166
W: se.deltasd.bc.ca

Semiahmoo Secondary School

1785 - 148th Street, Surrey BC V4A 4M6
DP Coordinator Karine Guezalova
Languages English
T: +1 604 536 6174
W: www.surreyschools.ca/schools/semi

SenPokChin School

1156 SenPokChin Blvd, Oliver BC V0H 1T8
PYP Coordinator Ms. Julie Shaw
Languages English, Nsyilxcen
T: +1 250 498 2019
W: www.senpokchin.ca

Sir Winston Churchill Secondary School, Vancouver

7055 Heather Street, Vancouver BC V6P 3P7
DP Coordinator Karen Puzio
Languages English
T: +1 604 713 8189
W: churchill.vsb.bc.ca

Southlands Elementary School

5351 Camosun Street, Vancouver BC V6N 2C4
PYP Coordinator Joanna Wood
Languages English
T: +1 604 713 5414
W: www.vsb.bc.ca/schools/southlands

SOUTHPOINTE ACADEMY

1900 56th Street, Tsawwassen BC V4L 2B1
MYP Coordinator Christine Yang
PYP Coordinator Smita Karam
Languages English
T: +1 604 948 8826
E: admissions@southpointe.ca
W: www.southpointe.ca

See full details on page 541

Southridge School

2656 160th Street, Surrey BC V3S 0B7
MYP Coordinator Alison Ito
PYP Coordinator Jo-Ann Murchie
Languages English
T: +1 604 535 5056
W: www.southridge.bc.ca

St. John's Academy Shawnigan Lake

2371 Shawnigan Lake Road, Shawnigan Lake BC V0R 2W5
MYP Coordinator Bradley Myrholm
Languages English
T: +1 250 220 4888
W: stjohnsacademy.ca/shawniganlake

St. John's School

2215 West 10th Avenue, Vancouver BC V6K 2J1
DP Coordinator Christine Miklitz
MYP Coordinator Stephanie Brook
PYP Coordinator Leslie Morden
Languages English
T: +1 604 732 4434
W: www.stjohns.bc.ca

STRATFORD HALL

3000 Commercial Drive, Vancouver BC V5N 4E2
DP Coordinator Dr. Benedict Hung
MYP Coordinator Mark Pulfer
PYP Coordinator Amanda Lempriere
Languages English
T: +1 604 436 0608
E: info@stratfordhall.ca
W: www.stratfordhall.ca

See full details on page 544

Unisus Junior School

7808 Pierre Dr, Summerland BC V0H 1Z2
PYP Coordinator Tara Avenia
Languages English, Spanish
T: +1 250 404 3232
W: www.unisus.ca

Unisus School

7808 Pierre Dr, Summerland BC V0H 1Z2
DP Coordinator Tara Avenia
Languages English
T: +1 250 404 3232
W: www.unisus.ca

West Bay School

3175 Thompson Place, West Vancouver BC V7V 3E3
PYP Coordinator Morikke Espenhain
Languages English
T: +1 604 981 1260
W: westvancouverschools.ca/westbay-elementary

West Vancouver Secondary School

1750 Mathers Avenue, West Vancouver BC V7V 2G7
DP Coordinator Joanne Pohn
Languages English
T: +1 604 981 1100
W: www.sd45.bc.ca

White Rock Christian Academy

2265 -152nd Street, Surrey BC V4A 4P1
DP Coordinator Jeff Weichel
MYP Coordinator Natalie Poirier
PYP Coordinator Emily Berry
Languages English
T: +1 604 531 9186
W: www.wrca.ca

Manitoba

Balmoral Hall School

630 Westminster Ave, Winnipeg MB R3C 3S1
PYP Coordinator Cathy Doerksen
Languages English
T: +1 204 784 1600
W: www.balmoralhall.com

Collège Louis-Riel

585 rue Saint-Jean-Baptiste, Winnipeg MB R2H 2Y2
DP Coordinator Benoît Pellerin
Languages French
T: +1 204 237 8927
W: www.louis-riel.mb.ca

Collège Sturgeon Heights Collegiate

2665 Ness Ave, Winnipeg MB R3J 1A5
DP Coordinator Jennifer Peters
Languages English
T: +1 204 888 0684
W: www.sjasd.ca/school/sturgeonheights

Kelvin High School

155 Kingsway, Winnipeg MB R3M 0G3
DP Coordinator Melani Decelles
Languages English
T: +1 204 474 1492
W: www.winnipegsd.ca/schools/kelvin

Miles MacDonell Collegiate

757 Roch Street, Winnipeg MB R2K 2R1
DP Coordinator Laura McMaster
Languages English
T: +1 204 667 1103
W: www.retsd.mb.ca/school/miles

River Heights School

1350 Grosvenor Ave., Winnipeg MB R3M 0P2
MYP Coordinator Amanda Tetrault
Languages English, French
T: +1 204 488 7090
W: www.winnipegsd.ca/riverheights

Westwood Collegiate

360 Rouge Road, Winnipeg MB R3K 1K3
DP Coordinator Art Penning
Languages English
T: +1 204 888 7650
W: www.sjasd.ca/school/westwood

New Brunswick

Ecole Mathieu-Martin

511 rue Champlain, Dieppe, Nouveau-Brunswick NB E1A 1P2
DP Coordinator Daniel Bourgeois
Languages French
T: +1 506 856 2791

École Sainte-Anne

715 rue Priestman, Fredericton NB E3B 5W7
DP Coordinator Michelle Foreman
Languages English
T: +1 506 453 3991
W: esa.nbed.nb.ca

Rothesay Netherwood School

40 College Hill Road, Rothesay NB E2E 5H1
DP Coordinator Tammy Earle
Languages English
T: +1 506 847 8224
W: www.rns.cc

St John High School
170-200 Prince William Street, #8, Saint John NB E2L 2B7
DP Coordinator Tracy Lutz
Languages English
T: +1 506 658 5358
W: www.sjhigh.ca

Newfoundland and Labrador

Holy Heart of Mary High School
55 Bonaventure Avenue, St. John's NL A1C 3Z3
DP Coordinator Michelle O'Connell
Languages English
T: +1 709 754 1600
W: www.holyheart.ca

Lakecrest Independent School
58 Patrick Street, St. John's NL A1E 2S7
PYP Coordinator Lisa Dove Major
Languages English
T: +1 709 738 1212
W: www.lakecrest.ca

Nova Scotia

Charles P. Allen High School
200 Innovation Dr., Bedford NS B4B 0G4
DP Coordinator Christopher Hall
Languages English
T: +1 902 832 8964
W: cpa.hrce.ca

Citadel High School
1855 Trollope Street, Halifax NS B3H 0A4
DP Coordinator Heather Michael
Languages English
T: +1 902 491 4444
W: www.qeh.ednet.ns.ca

Cobequid Educational Centre
34 Lorne Street, Truro NS B2N 3K3
DP Coordinator Taunya Pynn Crowe
Languages English
T: +1 902 896 5700
W: cec.ccrsb.ca

Cole Harbour District High School
2 Chameau Cresent, Dartmouth NS B2W 4X4
DP Coordinator Michael Jean
Languages English
T: +1 902 464 5220
w: chd.hrce.ca

Dr. John Hugh Gillis Regional High School
105 Braemore Avenue, Antigonish NS B2G 1L3
DP Coordinator Lindsay MacInnis
Languages English
T: +1 902 863 1620
W: drjhg.srce.ca

École du Carrefour
201A Avenue du Portage, Dartmouth NS B2X 3T4
DP Coordinator Richard Bernier
Languages French
T: +1 902 433 7000
W: carrefour.ednet.ns.ca

Halifax Grammar School
945 Tower Road, Halifax NS B3H 2Y2
DP Coordinator Laura Brock
Languages English
T: +1 902 423 9312
W: www.hgs.ns.ca

Halifax West High School
283 Thomas Raddall Drive, Halifax NS B3S 1R1
DP Coordinator Joanne Des Roches
Languages English
T: +1 902 457 8900
W: www.hwhs.ednet.ns.ca

Horton High School
75 Greenwich Road S, Greenwich NS B4P 2R2
DP Coordinator Jason Fuller
Languages English
T: +1 902 542 6060
W: hortonhighschool.ca

King's-Edgehill School
11 King's-Edgehill Lane, Windsor NS B0N 2T0
DP Coordinator Derek Bouwman
Languages English
T: +1 902 798 2278
W: www.kes.ns.ca

Northumberland Regional High School
104 Alma Road, Westville NS B0K 2A0
DP Coordinator Christina Cameron
Languages English
T: +1 902 396 2750
W: nrhs.ccrsb.ca

Park View Education Centre
1485 King Street, Bridgewater NS B4V 1C4
DP Coordinator Charlotte Brooks
Languages English
T: +1 902 541 8200
W: www.pvec.ednet.ns.ca

Prince Andrew High School
31 Woodlawn Road, Dartmouth NS B2W 2R7
DP Coordinator Tracy Giffin
Languages English
T: +1 902 435 8452
W: www.pahs.ednet.ns.ca

Sydney Academy
49 Terrace Street, Sydney NS B1P 2L4
DP Coordinator Heather Urquhart
Languages English
T: +1 902 562 5464
W: sites.google.com/gnspes.ca/sydneyacademy

Yarmouth Consolidated Memorial High School
146 Forest Street, Yarmouth NS B5A 0B3
DP Coordinator Colleen Daley
Languages English
T: +1 902 749 2810
W: www.ycmhs.com

Ontario

Académie de la Capitale
1010 Morrison Dr Suite 200, Ottawa ON K2H 8K7
PYP Coordinator Shannon Neill
Languages English, French
T: +1 613 721 3872
W: www.acadecap.org

Académie Ste Cécile International School
925 Cousineau Road, Windsor ON N9G 1V8
DP Coordinator Laurie Bruce
MYP Coordinator Loranda Burton
Languages English, French
T: +1 519 969 1291
W: www.stececile.ca

Alexander Mackenzie High School
300 Major Mackenzie Dr. W., Richmond Hill ON L4C 3S3
DP Coordinator Keith Auyeung
Languages English
T: +1 905 884 0554
W: www.yrdsb.ca/schools/alexandermackenzie.hs

Ancaster High School
374 Jerseyville Road West, Ancaster ON L9G 3K8
DP Coordinator Del Taylor
Languages English
T: +1 905 648 4468
W: www.hwdsb.on.ca/ancasterhigh

Ashbury College
362 Mariposa Avenue, Ottawa ON K1M OT3
DP Coordinator Shannon Howlett
Languages English
T: +1 613 749 5954
W: www.ashbury.ca

Assumption College Catholic High School
1100 Huron Church Road, Windsor ON N9C 2K7
DP Coordinator Brianne Trudell
MYP Coordinator Michelle Baggio
Languages English
T: +1 519 256 7801 EXT:278
W: sites.google.com/a/catholicboard.ca/acs-website

Bayview Secondary School
10077 Bayview Avenue, Richmond Hill ON L4C 2L4
DP Coordinator Lara Joffe
Languages English
T: +1 905 884 4453
W: www.yrdsb.ca/schools/bayview.ss

Bishop Macdonell Catholic High School
200 Clair Road West, Guelph ON N1L 1G1
DP Coordinator Amanda Belluz
Languages English
T: +1 519 822 8502
W: www.wellingtoncdsb.ca/school/bishopmacdonell/Pages/default.aspx

Branksome Hall
10 Elm Avenue, Toronto ON M4W 1N4
DP Coordinator Leslie Miller
MYP Coordinator Owen Williams
PYP Coordinator Andrea Mills
Languages English
T: +1 416 920 9741
W: www.branksome.on.ca

Bristol Road Middle School
210 Bristol Rd E, Mississauga ON L4Z 3V5
MYP Coordinator Sarah Rowsell
Languages English
T: +1 905 755 9809

Bronte College
88 Bronte College Court, 1444 Dundas Cres, Mississauga ON L5C 1E9
DP Coordinator Wynn Looi
Languages English
T: +1 905 270 7788
W: www.brontecollege.ca

Cameron Heights Collegiate Institute

301 Charles St. E., Kitchener ON N2G 2P8
DP Coordinator Julie Clancy
Languages English
T: +1 519 578 8330
W: chc.wrdsb.ca

Cardinal Carter Catholic High School

210 Bloomington Rd. W., Aurora ON L4G 0P9
DP Coordinator Kevin DeFreitas
Languages English
T: +1 905 727 2455
W: www.ycdsb.ca/cch

Cardinal Carter Catholic Secondary School

120 Ellison Ave., Leamington ON N8H 5C7
DP Coordinator Elisa Houston
MYP Coordinator Ruth Paesano
Languages English, French
T: +1 519 322 2804
W: sites.google.com/site/cougarscardinalcarter

Catholic Central High School

450 Dundas Street, London ON N6B 3K3
CP Coordinator Carla Mascherin Walton
DP Coordinator Carla Mascherin Walton
Languages English
T: +1 519 675 4431
W: www.ldcsb.on.ca

Chippewa Secondary School

539 Chippewa St. West, North Bay ON P1B 4R4
DP Coordinator Kim Larivee
Languages English
T: +1 705 475 2341
W: www.nearnorthschools.ca/chippewa

Cobourg Collegiate Institute

335 King Street East, Cobourg ON K9A 1M2
DP Coordinator Bruce LePage
Languages English
T: +1 905 372 2271
W: cci.kprdsb.ca

Collège Catholique Franco-Ouest

411 promenade Seyton, Nepean ON K2H 8X1
DP Coordinator Kim Brisebois
MYP Coordinator Christine Leduc
Languages French
T: +1 613 820 2920
W: franco-ouest.ecolecatholique.ca

Collège catholique Mer Bleue

6401 chemin Renaud, Orléans ON K1W 0H8
CP Coordinator Kim Brisebois
DP Coordinator Valérie Labelle
MYP Coordinator Marie-Pier Parisien
Languages French
T: +1 613 744 4022
W: mer-bleue.ecolecatholique.ca

Colonel By Secondary School

2381 Ogilvie Road, Ottawa ON K1J 7N4
DP Coordinator Lewis Harthun
Languages English
T: +1 613 745 9411
W: www.colonelby.com

Craig Kielburger Secondary School

1151 Ferguson Dr., Milton ON L9T 7V8
DP Coordinator Jude Miranda
Languages English, French
T: +1 905 878 0575
W: cks.hdsb.ca

Dr. G.W. Williams Secondary School

39 Dunning Ave., Aurora ON L4G 1A2
DP Coordinator Nicole Gordner
Languages English
T: +1 905 727 3131
W: drgwwilliams.ss.yrdsb.ca

Eastside Secondary School

275 Farley Avenue, Belleville ON K8N 4M2
DP Coordinator Mary Reuvekamp
Languages English
T: +1 613 962 8668
W: ess.hpedsb.on.ca

École élémentaire catholique Au Coeur d'Ottawa

88 rue Main, Ottawa ON K1S 1C2
PYP Coordinator Isabelle Gauthier-Cossette
Languages English, French
T: +1 613 216 0017
W: aucoeurdottawa.ecolecatholique.ca

École élémentaire catholique Corpus Christi

362, avenue Hillside, Oshawa ON L1J 6L7
PYP Coordinator Epiphane Dohou
Languages English
T: +1 905 728 0491
W: cc.cscmonavenir.ca

École élémentaire catholique Jean-Paul II

1001 avenue Hutchison, Whitby ON L1N 2A3
PYP Coordinator Caroline Rivest
Languages French
T: +1 905 665 5393
W: jpii.cscmonavenir.ca

École élémentaire publique L'Odyssée

1770, promenade Grey Nuns, Orléans ON K1C 1C3
PYP Coordinator Jacinthe Chapdelaine
Languages French
T: +1 613 834 2097
W: www.odyssee.cepeo.on.ca/Ecole

École élémentaire publique Michaëlle-Jean

11 chemin Claridge, Ottawa ON K2J 5A3
PYP Coordinator Sandra Sauvé
Languages English
T: +1 613 823 2288
W: www.michaelle-jean.cepeo.on.ca

École élémentaire publique Rose des Vents

1650, 2e Rue Est, Cornwall ON K6H 2C3
PYP Coordinator Samantha Sabourin
Languages French
T: +1 613 932 4183
W: www.rose-des-vents.cepeo.on.ca

École publique Renaissance

301 Shirley St, Timmins ON P4R 1N5
DP Coordinator Chantal Goold
MYP Coordinator Chantal Goold
Languages English, French
T: +1 705 264 7474

École secondaire catholique l'Essor

13605, St Gregory's Road, Windsor ON N8N 3E4
DP Coordinator Jason Defoe
Languages French
T: +1 519 735 4115
W: vibe.cscprovidence.ca/lessor

École secondaire catholique Monseigneur-de-Charbonnel

110, avenue Drewry, Toronto ON M2M 1C8
DP Coordinator Florence Kulnieks
Languages French
T: +1 416 393 5537
W: esmdc.cscmonavenir.ca

École secondaire catholique Père-Philippe-Lamarche

2850 Eglinton Ave E., Scarborough ON M1J 2C8
DP Coordinator Johanne Joly
Languages English, French
T: +1 416 986 6414
W: esppl.cscmonavenir.ca

École secondaire catholique Père-René-de-Galinée

450, chemin Maple Grove, Cambridge ON N3H 4R7
MYP Coordinator Danica Lalich
Languages French
T: +1 519 650 9444
W: esprdg.cscmonavenir.ca

École secondaire catholique Renaissance

700, chemin Bloomington, Aurora ON L4G 0E1
DP Coordinator Zinta Anna Amolins
MYP Coordinator Helene Robert
Languages French
T: +1 905 727 4631
W: esr.cscmonavenir.ca

École secondaire catholique Saint Frère André

330, avenue Lansdowne, Toronto ON M6H 3Y1
DP Coordinator Dumitru Trinca-Costica
Languages French
T: +1 416 393 5324
W: essfa.cscmonavenir.ca

École secondaire catholique Saint-Charles-Garnier

4101, rue Baldwin Sud, Whitby ON L1R 2W6
MYP Coordinator Eric McLean
Languages French
T: +1 905 655 5635
W: esscg.cscmonavenir.ca

École secondaire catholique Sainte-Famille

1780, boulevard Meadowvale, Mississauga ON L5N 7K8
CP Coordinator Christine Guindy
DP Coordinator Emmanuel Sincennes
MYP Coordinator Henriette Tebit Nwabang
Languages French
T: +1 905 814 0318
W: essf.cscmonavenir.ca

École secondaire catholique Sainte-Trinité

2600, Grand Oak Trail, Oakville ON L6M 0R4
DP Coordinator Emmanuel Denou
MYP Coordinator Michael Lefebvre
Languages French
T: +1 905 339 0812
W: esst.cscmonavenir.ca

École secondaire Gaétan-Gervais

1075, McCraney Street East, Oakville ON L6H 1H9
DP Coordinator Emmanuelle Ritson
Languages English, French
T: +1 289 529 0065
W: gaetangervais.csviamonde.ca

École secondaire Hanmer

4800, Ave Notre-Dame, Hanmer ON P3P 1X5
DP Coordinator Michelle Jobin-Quenville
Languages French
T: +1 705 969 4402
W: esh.cspgno.ca

École secondaire Jeunes sans frontières

7585 promenade Financial, Brampton ON L6Y 5P4
DP Coordinator Beatrice Khemiss
Languages French
T: +1 905 450 1106
W: csviamonde.ca/ecoles/jeunessansfrontieres

École secondaire publique Gisèle-Lalonde

500 Boulevard Millenium, Orléans ON K4A 4X3
DP Coordinator Caroline Joly
MYP Coordinator Francine Foisy
Languages English, French
T: +1 613 833 0018
W: www.gisele-lalonde.cepeo.on.ca

École secondaire publique L'Héritage

1111 chemin Montréal, Cornwall ON K6H 1E1
DP Coordinator Jasmine Bernier
MYP Coordinator Laurie Crawford
Languages English
T: +1 613 933 3318

École secondaire publique Le Sommet

894, boul. Cécile, Hawkesbury ON K6A 3R5
DP Coordinator Chantal Lalonde
MYP Coordinator Chantal Lalonde
Languages French
T: +1 613 632 6059
W: lesommet.cepeo.on.ca

École Secondaire Publique Mille-Îles

72 Gilmour Avenue, Kingston ON K7M 9G6
DP Coordinator Stephanie Mailhot
MYP Coordinator Michèle Guitard
Languages French
T: +1 613 547 2556
W: www.mille-iles.cepeo.on.ca

École secondaire publique Odyssée

480, avenue Norman, North Bay ON P1B 0A8
DP Coordinator Ashli Lewis
MYP Coordinator Ashli Lewis
Languages French
T: +1 705 474 5500

École Secondaire Publique Omer-Deslauriers

159 Chesterton Dr, Nepean ON K2E 7E6
DP Coordinator Sophie Tchu-Ut-Gnon
MYP Coordinator Tej Kouraichi
Languages French
T: +1 613 820 0992
W: omer-deslauriers.cepeo.on.ca

École secondaire Toronto Ouest

330, Avenue Lansdowne, Toronto ON M6H 3Y1
DP Coordinator Amy Morris
Languages French
T: +1 416 532 6592
W: ecolesecondairetorontoouest.csviamonde.ca

Elmwood School

261 Buena Vista Road, Ottawa ON K1M 0V9
DP Coordinator Jason Levesque
MYP Coordinator Alyson Bartlett
PYP Coordinator Kate Meadowcroft
Languages English
T: +1 613 749 6761
W: www.elmwood.ca

Erindale Secondary School

2021 Dundas Street West, Mississauga ON L5K 1R2
DP Coordinator Carolyn LaRoche
Languages English
T: +1 905 828 7206
W: schools.peelschools.org/sec/erindale

Father Michael McGivney Catholic Academy

5300 Fourteenth Avenue, Markham ON L3S 3K8
DP Coordinator Christine Gomes
Languages English
T: +1 905 472 4961
W: fmmh.ycdsb.ca

Georgetown District High School

70 Guelph Street, Georgetown ON L7G 3Z5
DP Coordinator Kyle Stewart
Languages English
T: +1 905 877 6966
W: geo.hdsb.ca

Glenforest Secondary School

3575 Fieldgate Drive, Mississauga ON L4X 2J6
DP Coordinator Daphne Habib
MYP Coordinator Diana Wang-Martin
Languages English
T: +1 905 625 7731
W: schools.peelschools.org/sec/glenforest

Glenview Park Secondary School

55 McKay Street, Cambridge ON N1R 4G6
DP Coordinator Colleen Caplin
Languages English
T: +1 519 621 9510
W: gps.wrdsb.on.ca

Harold M. Brathwaite Secondary School

415 Great Lakes Drive, Brampton ON L6R 2Z4
DP Coordinator Colin Parker
Languages English
T: +1 905 793 2155
W: www.hmbss.com

Holy Cross Catholic Academy

7501 Martin Grove Road, Woodbridge ON L4L 9E4
DP Coordinator Dina Monaco
Languages English
T: +1 905 851 6699
W: hocr.ycdsb.ca

I E Weldon Secondary School

24 Weldon Road, Lindsay ON K9V 4R6
DP Coordinator Erin Matthew
Languages English
T: +1 705 324 3585
W: www.tldsb.on.ca/schools/iewss

Kenner CVI & Intermediate School

633 Monaghan Road South, Peterborough ON K9J 5J2
DP Coordinator Peter Mullins
Languages English
T: +1 705 743 2181
W: www.kenner.kprdsb.ca

Khalsa Community School

69 Maitland Street, Brampton ON L6S 3B5
MYP Coordinator Kiran Bedi
Languages English
T: +1 905 791 1750
W: khalsacommunityschool.com

Khalsa School Malton

7280 Airport Rd., Mississauga ON L4T 2H3
MYP Coordinator Neha Paul
Languages English
T: +1 905 671 2010
W: www.khalsaschoolmalton.com

King Heights Academy

28 Roytec Road, Woodbridge ON L4L 8E4
PYP Coordinator Kirti Pankaj
Languages English
T: +1 905 652 1234
W: kingheightsacademy.com

Kingston Collegiate & Vocational Institute

235 Frontenac Street, Kingston ON K7L 3S7
DP Coordinator Adam Watson
Languages English
T: +1 613 544 4811

Korah Collegiate and Vocational School

636 Goulais Avenue, Sault Ste Marie ON P6C 5A7
DP Coordinator Kathryn Johnstone
Languages English
T: +1 705 945 7180
W: www.korahcvs.com

La Citadelle International Academy of Arts & Science

36 Scarsdale Road, North York, Toronto ON M3B 2R7
MYP Coordinator Denise Voinica
Languages English, French
T: +1 416 385 9685
W: www.lacitadelleacademy.com

Le Collège Français

100 rue Carlton, Toronto ON M5B 1M3
DP Coordinator Odin Cabrera
MYP Coordinator Christina Campisi
Languages French
T: +1 416 393 0175

Leamington District Secondary School

80 Oak St. W., Leamington ON N8H 2B3
DP Coordinator Lisa Jeffery
Languages English, French
T: +1 519 326 6191
W: www.publicboard.ca/school/ldss

Lo-Ellen Park Secondary School

275 Loach's Road, Sudbury ON P3E 2P8

DP Coordinator Julie Wuorinen
Languages English
T: +1 705 522 2320

LONDON INTERNATIONAL ACADEMY

365 Richmond Street, London, ON N6A 3C2

DP Coordinator Abeera Atique
Languages English, Spanish
T: +1 519 433 3388
E: admissions@lia-edu.ca
W: www.lia-edu.ca

See full details on page 517

Lynn-Rose Heights Private School

7215 Millcreek Drive, Mississauga ON L5N 3R3

DP Coordinator Lisa Little
MYP Coordinator Roselle Aranha
PYP Coordinator Heidi Corley
Languages English
T: +1 905 567 3553
W: www.lynnroseheights.com

MacLachlan College

337 Trafalgar Road, Oakville ON L6J 3H3

PYP Coordinator Ashleigh Woodward
Languages English
T: +1 905 844 0372
W: www.maclachlan.ca

Maple High School

50 Springside Rd., Maple ON L6A 2W5

DP Coordinator Giovanna Pace
Languages English
T: +1 905 417 9444
W: maple.hs.yrdsb.ca

Merivale High School

1755 Merivale Road, Nepean ON K2G 1E2

DP Coordinator Lewis Harthun
Languages English, French
T: +1 613 224 1807
W: merivalehs.ocdsb.ca

Michael Power - St Joseph High School

105 Eringate Drive, Toronto ON M9C 3Z7

DP Coordinator Claudia Grilo
Languages English
T: +1 416 393 5529

Milliken Mills High School

7522 Kennedy Rd, Unionville ON L3R 9S5

DP Coordinator Natalie White
Languages English
T: +1 905 477 0072
W: www.yrdsb.ca/schools/millikenmills.hs

Monarch Park Collegiate

1 Hanson Street, Toronto ON M4J 1G6

DP Coordinator Jacqueline Allen
Languages English
T: +1 416 393 0190
W: www.monarchparkcollegiate.ca

Nicholson Catholic College

301 Church Street, Belleville ON K8N 3C7

DP Coordinator Justin Walsh
Languages English
T: +1 613 967 0404
W: www.nccschool.org

NOIC Academy

50 Featherstone Avenue, Markham ON L3S 2H4

DP Coordinator Risha Chattopadhyay
Languages English
T: +1 905 472 2002
W: noic.ca

Notre Dame Secondary School

2 Notre Dame Avenue, Brampton ON L6Z 4L5

DP Coordinator Gina Renda
Languages English
T: +1 905 840 2802
W: www.dpcdsb.org/ndame

Oakridge Secondary School

1040 Oxford Street West, London ON N6H 1V4

DP Coordinator Jeff Kunder
Languages English
T: +1 519 452 2750
W: oakridge.tvdsb.ca

Parkdale Collegiate Institute

209 Jameson Avenue, Toronto ON M6K 2Y3

DP Coordinator Miro Bartnik
Languages English
T: +1 416 393 9000
W: schools.tdsb.on.ca/parkdale

Regiopolis-Notre Dame Catholic High School

130 Russell Street, Kingston ON K7K 2E9

DP Coordinator James David
Languages English
T: +1 613 545 1902
W: alcdsb.on.ca/school/regi

Richland Academy

11570 Yonge Street, Richmond Hill, ON L4E 3N7

PYP Coordinator Joanne Pace
Languages English, French
T: +1 905 224 5600
W: www.richlandacademy.ca

RIDLEY COLLEGE

PO Box 3013, 2 Ridley Road, St Catharines ON L2R 7C3

DP Coordinator Saralyn Covent
MYP Coordinator Paul O'Rourke
PYP Coordinator Marcie Lewis
Languages English
T: +1 905 684 1889
E: admissions@ridleycollege.com
W: www.ridleycollege.com

See full details on page 537

Riverside Secondary School

8465 Jerome Street, Windsor ON N8S 1W8

DP Coordinator Derek Tomkins
Languages English, French
T: +1 519 948 4116

Robert Bateman High School

5151 New Street, Burlington ON L7L 1V3

DP Coordinator Jennifer Bright
Languages English
T: +1 905 632 5151
W: www.rbh.hdsb.ca

Sacred Heart Catholic School

125 Huron Street, Guelph ON N1E 5L5

PYP Coordinator Natasha Finoro
Languages English, French
T: +1 519 824 2751

Sir Wilfrid Laurier Collegiate Institute

145 Guildwood Parkway, Scarborough ON M1E 1P5

DP Coordinator Charis Kelso
Languages English
T: +1 416 396 6820
W: www.sirwilfridlaurierci.ca

St Francis Xavier Secondary School

50 Bristol Road West, Mississauga ON L5R 3K3

DP Coordinator Eugene Ladna
Languages English
T: +1 905 507 6666
W: www.dpcdsb.org/STFXS

St John's - Kilmarnock School

2201 Shantz Station Road, Box 179, Breslau (Waterloo Region) ON N0B 1M0

DP Coordinator Jordan Grant
MYP Coordinator Rebecca Dufour
PYP Coordinator Jennifer Wilkinson
Languages English
T: +1 519 648 2183
W: www.sjkschool.org

St Jude's Academy

2150 Torquay Mews, Mississauga ON L5N 2M6

DP Coordinator Veronica Lopez
MYP Coordinator Melissa Chin
PYP Coordinator Marijana Haag
Languages English
T: +1 905 814 0202
W: www.stjudesacademy.com

St Robert Catholic High School

8101 Leslie Street, Thornhill ON L3T 7P4

DP Coordinator Andrea Steele
Languages English
T: +1 905 889 4982
W: www.strobertchs.com

St Thomas Aquinas Roman Catholic Secondary School

124 Dorval Drive, Oakville ON L6K 2W1

DP Coordinator Antonia Montanari
Languages English
T: +1 905 842 9494
W: secondary.hcdsb.org/sta

St. James Catholic Global Learning Centre

98 Wanita Rd, Mississauga ON L5G1B8

MYP Coordinator Steven Kelenc
PYP Coordinator Nicola Hughes
Languages English
T: +1 905 891 7619
W: dpcdsb.org/jamee

St. John Paul II Catholic Secondary School

685 Military Trail, Scarborough ON M1E 4P6

DP Coordinator Tracey Robertson
Languages English
T: +1 416 393 5531
W: www.tcdsb.org/schools/stjohnpaulii

St. Mary Catholic Academy

66 Dufferin Park Avenue, Toronto ON M6H 1J6

DP Coordinator Judi Calado Costa
Languages English
T: +1 416 393 5528
W: www.tcdsb.org/schools/stmarycatholicacademy

IB AMERICAS

St. Paul Secondary School
815 Atwater Avenue, Mississauga ON L5E 1L8
DP Coordinator Anne Marie Miki
Languages English, French
T: +1 905 278 3994
W: www3.dpcdsb.org/pauls

Sunnybrook School
469 Merton Street, Toronto ON M4S 1B4
PYP Coordinator Michael Rossiter
Languages English
T: +1 416 487 5308
W: www.sunnybrookschool.com

Superior Collegiate & Vocational Institute
333 N. High Street, Thunder Bay ON P7A 5S3
DP Coordinator Karen Watt
Languages English
T: +1 807 768 7284
W: superior.lakeheadschools.ca

TFS - CANADA'S INTERNATIONAL SCHOOL
306 Lawrence Avenue East, Toronto ON M4N 1T7
DP Coordinator Dr. Jennifer Elliott
MYP Coordinator Leslie Miller
PYP Coordinator Zein Odeh
Languages French, English
T: +1 416 484 6533
E: admissions@tfs.ca
W: www.tfs.ca
See full details on page 545

The Guelph Collegiate Vocational Institute
155 Paisley Street, Guelph ON N1H 2P3
DP Coordinator Angela Snell
Languages English
T: +1 519 824 9800
W: www.ugdsb.on.ca/gcvi

The Leo Baeck Day School
36 Atkinson Avenue, Thornhill ON L4J 8C9
MYP Coordinator Sheryl Faith
PYP Coordinator Sheryl Faith
Languages English
T: +1 905 709 3636
W: www.leobaeck.ca

The York School
1320 Yonge Street, Toronto ON M4T 1X2
DP Coordinator Marie Aragona
MYP Coordinator Fabio Biagiarelli
PYP Coordinator Kristy Purcell
Languages English
T: ADMISSIONS: +1 416 646 5275
SWITCHBOARD: +1 416 926 1325
W: www.yorkschool.com

TMS School
500 Elgin Mills Road East, Richmond Hill ON L4C 5G1
DP Coordinator Shane Small
MYP Coordinator Jessica Wong
Languages English
T: +1 905 889 6882
W: www.tmsschool.ca

Town Centre Montessori Private Schools
155 Clayton Drive, Markham ON L3R 7P3
DP Coordinator Kenneth Huber
MYP Coordinator Christine Lau
PYP Coordinator Magdalena Therrien
Languages English
T: +1 905 470 1200
W: tcmps.com

Turner Fenton Secondary School
7935 Kennedy Road South, Brampton ON L6V 3N2
DP Coordinator Angela De Jong
MYP Coordinator Michael Langford
Languages English
T: +1 905 453 9220
W: www.turnerfenton.com

Upper Canada College
200 Lonsdale Road, Toronto ON M4V 1W6
DP Coordinator Colleen Ferguson
MYP Coordinator Gillian Levene
PYP Coordinator Dianne Jojic
Languages English
T: +1 416 488 1125
W: www.ucc.on.ca

Victoria Park Collegiate Institute
15 Wallingford Road, North York ON M3A 2V1
DP Coordinator Anna Macinnis
Languages English
T: +1 416 395 3310
W: victoriaparkci.ca

Walden International School
1030 Queen Street West, Brampton ON L6X 0B2
PYP Coordinator Shelley Charanduk
Languages English, French
T: +1 905 338 6236
W: www.waldeninternationalschool.com

Westdale Secondary School
700 Main Street West, Hamilton ON L8S 1A5
DP Coordinator Kim Parkes-Hallmark
Languages English
T: +1 905 522 1387
W: www.hwdsb.on.ca/westdale

Weston Collegiate Institute
100 Pine Street, York, Toronto ON M9N 2Y9
DP Coordinator Anne Dale
Languages English
T: +1 416 394 3250
W: www.westonci.ca

Wheatley School
497 Scott Street, St Catharines ON L2M 3X3
MYP Coordinator Isabel N. Machinandiarena
Languages English
T: +1 905 641 3012
W: www.wheatleyschool.com

White Oaks Secondary School
1330 Montclair Drive, Oakville ON L6K 1Z5
DP Coordinator Erin Davidson
Languages English
T: +1 905 845 5200
W: www.wossweb.com

William Grenville Davis Senior Public School
491 Bartley Bull Parkway, Brampton ON L6W 2M7
MYP Coordinator Andre Laferriere
Languages English
T: +1 905 459 3661
W: www.wgdavis.com

Prince Edward Island

Charlottetown Rural High School
100 Raiders Road, Charlottetown PE C1E 1K6
DP Coordinator Philip Pierlot
Languages English
T: +1 902 368 6905
W: therural.ca

Colonel Gray High School
175 Spring Park Road, Charlottetown PE C1A 3Y8
DP Coordinator Angela MacCorquodale
Languages English
T: +1 902 368 6860

Quebec

Académie François-Labelle
1227 rue Notre Dame, Repentigny QC J5Y 3H2
PYP Coordinator Maryse Cadieux
Languages French
T: +1 450 582 2020
W: www.academiefrancoislabelle.qc.ca

Bishop's College School
80 Moulton Hill Road, PO Box 5001, Station Lennoxville, Sherbrooke QC J1M 1Z8
DP Coordinator Amber Rommens
Languages English
T: +1 819 566 0227
W: www.bishopscollegeschool.com

Carlyle Elementary School
109 Carlyle Avenue, Mount Royal QC H3R 1S8
PYP Coordinator Aspasia Tzovanis-Manolias
Languages English
T: +1 514 738 1256
W: www.emsb.qc.ca/carlyle

Cégep André-Laurendeau
1111 rue Lapierre, Lasalle QC H8N 2J4
DP Coordinator Marie-Pier Blanchard
Languages French
T: +1 514 364 3320
W: www.claurendeau.qc.ca

Cégep de Rivière-du-Loup
80, rue Frontenac, Rivière-du-Loup QC G5R 1R1
DP Coordinator Martine Riou
Languages English
T: +1 418 862 6903
W: www.cegeprdl.ca

Cégep Garneau
1660 boulevard de l'Entente, Québec QC G1S 4S3
DP Coordinator Annie Jacques
Languages French
T: +1 418 688 8310 EXT:2372
W: www.cegepgarneau.ca

Children's World Academy
2241 Ménard, LaSalle QC H8N 1J4
PYP Coordinator Guy Walker
Languages English, French
T: +1 514 595 2043
W: cwa.lbpsb.qc.ca

Clearpoint Elementary School
17 Cedar Avenue, Pointe-Claire QC H9S 4X9
PYP Coordinator Layla Barroca
Languages English, French
T: +1 514 798 0792
W: clearpoint.lbpsb.qc.ca

Collège Charlemagne
5000 rue Pilon, Pierrefonds, Montréal QC H9K 1G4
MYP Coordinator Luc Fortin
Languages French
T: +1 514 626 7060

Collège Charles-Lemoyne - Campus Longueuil

901, chemin Tiffin, Longueuil QC J4P 3G6
MYP Coordinator Caroline Jodoin-Malo
Languages English, French
T: +1 514 875 0505
W: www.monccl.com

Collège de l'Assomption

270 boulevard de l'Ange-Gardien, L'Assomption, Montréal QC J5Y 3R7
MYP Coordinator Hélène Pelland
Languages French
T: +1 450 589 5621
W: www.classomption.qc.ca

Collège Esther-Blondin

101 rue Sainte-Anne, Saint-Jacques QC J0K 2R0
MYP Coordinator Jessica Demers Lavigne
Languages French
T: +1 450 839 3672
W: collegeestherblondin.qc.ca

Collège Jean-de-Brebeuf

3200, chemin de la Côte-Sainte-Catherine, Montréal QC H3T 1C1
DP Coordinator Simon Fortin
MYP Coordinator Lyne Harvey
Languages French
T: +1 514 342 9342
W: www.brebeuf.qc.ca

Collège Jésus-Marie de Sillery

2047 chemin Saint-Louis, Québec City QC G1T 1P3
MYP Coordinator Christine Baillargeon
Languages French
T: +1 418 687 9250
W: www.collegejesusmarie.com

Collège Mont Notre-Dame de Sherbrooke

114 rue Cathédrale, Sherbrooke QC J1H 4MI
MYP Coordinator Nathalie Arès
Languages French
T: +1 819 563 4104
W: www.mont-notre-dame.qc.ca

Collège Notre-Dame-de-Lourdes

845 chemin Tiffin, Longueuil QC J4P 3G5
MYP Coordinator Marie-Josée Bellemare
Languages French
T: +1 450 670 4740
W: www.ndl.qc.ca

Collège Saint-Louis

275 36e Avenue, Lachine QC H8T 2A4
MYP Coordinator Denis Cadieux
Languages French
T: +1 514 855 4198
W: collegesaintlouis.ecolelachine.com

Collège Saint-Maurice

630 rue Girouard Ouest, Saint-Hyacinthe QC J2S 2Y3
MYP Coordinator Elsa Würtele
Languages French
T: +1 450 773 7478 Ext:222
W: www.csm.qc.ca

Collège Saint-Paul

235 rue Ste-Anne, Varennes QC J3X 1P9
MYP Coordinator Sophie Laflamme
Languages French
T: +1 450 652 2941
W: www.college-st-paul.qc.ca

Collège Ville-Marie

2850 rue Sherbrooke Est, Montréal QC H2K 1H3
MYP Coordinator Odie Miller-Maboungou
Languages French
T: +1 514 525 2516
W: www.cvmarie.qc.ca

Courtland Park International School

1075 Wolfe, St-Bruno QC J3V 3K6
PYP Coordinator Grace Palmieri
Languages English
T: +1 450 550 2514
W: www.rsb.qc.ca

École Bois-Joli Sacré-Coeur

775 Rue du Sacré-Coeur Ouest, Saint-Hyacinthe QC J2S 1V2
PYP Coordinator Julie Bessette
Languages French
T: +1 450 774 5130
W: www.cssh.qc.ca/ecole-bois-joli-sacre-coeur

École Centrale

682 Rue Principale, Saint-Joachim de Shefford QC J0E 2G0
PYP Coordinator Claude Boisseau
Languages French
T: +1 450 539 1816

École Chabot et du l'Oasis

1666 Avenue De Lozère, Charlesbourg QC G1G 3L4
PYP Coordinator Caroline Giguère
Languages French
T: +1 418 624 3752

Ecole de la Baie Saint Francois

70 rue Louis VI Major, Salaberry De Valleyfield QC J6T 3G2
MYP Coordinator Daniel Hébert
Languages French
T: +1 450 371 2004

École de la Magdeleine

1100 boulevard Taschereau, La Prairie QC J5R 1W8
MYP Coordinator Maude Lemieux
Languages French
T: +1 514 380 8899
W: www.lamag.qc.ca

École de l'Équinoxe

2949 boulevard de la Renaissance, Laval, QC H7L 0H3
PYP Coordinator Karine Bouffard
Languages English, French
T: +1 450 662 7000
W: delequinoxe.cslaval.qc.ca

École d'éducation internationale

720 rue Morin, McMasterville QC J3G 1H1
MYP Coordinator François Brophy
Languages French
T: +1 450 467 4222
W: eei.csp.qc.ca

École d'éducation internationale de Laval

5075 boul du souvenir, Laval QC H7W 1E1
MYP Coordinator Étienne Jacques
Languages French
T: +1 450 662 7000 4300
W: eeil.cslaval.qc.ca

École d'éducation internationale Filteau-St-Mathieu

830 rue de Saurel, Sainte Foy QC G1X 3P6
PYP Coordinator Susie Goulet
Languages French
T: +1 418 652 2152
W: www.csdecou.qc.ca/filteau

École d'éducation internationale Notre-Dame-des-Neiges

4140, boulevard Gastonguay, Québec QC G2B 1M7
PYP Coordinator Gabrielle Prévost
Languages French
T: +1 418 686 4040
W: cscapitale-ecole-notre-dame-des-neiges.ca

École du Petit-Collège

9343 Rue Jean-Milot, LaSalle QC H8R 1Y7
PYP Coordinator Christine Renaud
Languages English, French
T: +1 514 748 4661

École du Sentier

1225 rue Victorin, Drummondville, QC J2C 7Z9
PYP Coordinator Marylène Bienvenue
Languages French
T: +1 819 850 1632
W: www.dusentier.com

École Guy-Drummond

1475 avenue La Joie, Outremont QC H2V 1P9
PYP Coordinator Isabelle Gariépy
Languages French
T: +1 514 270 4866

École internationale de Montréal

11 chemin Côte St-Antoine, Westmount, Montréal QC H3Y 2H7
MYP Coordinator Tammy Salamé
PYP Coordinator Houda Bakas
Languages French
T: +1 514 596 7240
W: ecole-internationale.csdm.ca

École Internationale de Saint-Sacrement

1430 chemin Ste-Foy, Québec QC G1S 2N8
PYP Coordinator Sonya Fiset
Languages French
T: +1 418 686 4040
W: cscapitale-ecole-dest-sacrement.ca

École Internationale des Apprenants

4505 Boul Henri-Bourassa O, Saint-Laurent QC H4L 1A5
PYP Coordinator Adela Vintila
Languages French
T: +1 514 334 4153
W: ecoleia.ca

École internationale du Mont-Bleu

45 rue Boucher, Gatineau QC J8Y 6G2
PYP Coordinator Léticia Sanchez
Languages French
T: +1 819 777 5921
W: internationaledumontbleu.cspo.qc.ca

École internationale du Phare

405, rue Sara, Sherbrooke QC J1H 5S6
MYP Coordinator Stéphanie Dussault
Languages French
T: +1 819 822 5455
W: www.csrs.qc.ca/fr/internationale-du-phare

École internationale du Vieux-Longueuil

2301 boulevard Fernand-Lafontaine, Longueuil QC J4N 1N7
PYP Coordinator Claude Coupal
Languages English, French
T: +1 450 670 9494

École Internationale du Village

19, rue Symmes, Gatineau QC J9H 3J3
PYP Coordinator Mélanie Bazinet
Languages French
T: +1 819 685 2611
W: internationaleduvillage.cspo.qc.ca

École internationale Lucille-Teasdale

8350 boulevard Pelletier, Brossard QC J4X 1M8
MYP Coordinator Martin Laplante
Languages French
T: +1 450 465 6290

École internationale primaire de Greenfield Park

776 Cambell, Greenfield Park QC J4V 1YZ
PYP Coordinator Grace Palmieri
Languages French
T: +1 450 672 0042

École internationale Saint-François-Xavier

8-A, rue Pouliot, Rivière-du-Loup QC G5R 3R8
PYP Coordinator Nathalie Nolin
Languages French, English, Spanish
T: +1 418 862 6901
W: web.cskamloup.qc.ca/sfx

École Internationale Wilfrid-Pelletier

8301 boulevard Wilfrid-Pelletier, Montréal (Anjou) QC H1K 1M2
PYP Coordinator Nathalie Fortier
Languages French
T: +1 514 352 7300
W: www.wilfrid-pelletier.ca

École Jeanne-Mance

4240 rue de Bordeaux, Montréal QC H2H 1Z5
MYP Coordinator Adeline Roy
Languages English
T: +1 514 596 5815
W: jeanne-mance.csdm.ca

École Joseph François Perrault

7540 rue François Perrault, Montréal QC H2A 1L9
MYP Coordinator Cathy-Anne Boiteau
Languages French
T: +1 514 596 4620

École La Vérendrye

3055, rue Mousseau, Montréal QC H1L 4W1
PYP Coordinator Vicky Desaulniers
Languages French
T: +1 514 596 4845
W: la-verendrye.csdm.ca

École Le tandem

605 rue Notre-dame Ouest, Victoriaville QC G6P 6Y9
MYP Coordinator Caroline Bilodeau
Languages French
T: +1 819 758 1534

École l'Envolée

549 rue Fournier, Granby QC J2J 2K5
MYP Coordinator Martin Nadeau
Languages French
T: +1 450 777 7536
W: lenvolee.csvdc.qc.ca

École Les Mélèzes

393 de Lanaudière, Joliette QC J6E3L9
PYP Coordinator Caroline Beaulieu
Languages French
T: +1 450 752 4433
W: www.lesmelezes.qc.ca

École Marie-Clarac

3530 Boul Gouin Est, Montréal-Nord QC H1H 1B7
MYP Coordinator Annie Frenette
Languages French
T: +1 514 322 1160
W: www.ecolemarie-clarac.qc.ca

École Monseigneur Robert

769 rue de lEducation, Québec QC G1E 1J2
PYP Coordinator Julie Duplain
Languages French
T: +1 418 666 4490

École Paul-Hubert

250, boulevard Arthur-Buies Ouest, Rimouski QC G5L 7A7
MYP Coordinator Martin Cote
Languages French
T: +1 418 724 3439
W: paulhubert.csphares.qc.ca

École Père-Marquette

6030 rue Marquette, Montréal QC H2G 2Y2
MYP Coordinator Michel Clark
Languages French
T: +1 514 596 4128
W: pere-marquette.csdm.qc.ca

École Plein Soleil (Association Coopérative)

300, rue de Montréal, Sherbrooke QC J1H 1E5
PYP Coordinator François Normandeau
Languages French
T: +1 819 569 8359
W: www.pleinsoleil.qc.ca

École Pointe-Lévy

55 Rue des Commandeurs, Levis QC G6V 1P5
MYP Coordinator Manon Tessier
Languages French
T: +1 418 838 8402
W: www.pointe-levy.qc.ca

École Polyvalente Le Carrefour

125 Rue Self, Val d'Òr, Québec QC J9P 3N2
MYP Coordinator Lynn Couture
Languages French
T: +1 819 825 4670

École Polyvalente Saint-Jérôme

535 rue Filion, Saint-Jérôme QC J7Z 1J6
MYP Coordinator Chantal Dion
Languages French
T: +1 450 436 4330
W: epsjcsrdn.ca

École primaire d'éducation internationale

2750,boulevard des Forges, Trois-Rivières QC G8Z 1V2
PYP Coordinator Maryse Gélinas
Languages French
T: +1 819 379 6565
W: www.ecolepei.com

École primaire d'éducation internationale du secteur Est

175, rue Saint-Alphonse, Trois-Rivières QC G8T 7R8
PYP Coordinator Maryse Gélinas
Languages French
T: +1 819 840 4358
W: www.ecolepei.com

École primaire Terre des jeunes

128 25e Avenue, St-Eustache QC J7P 2V2
PYP Coordinator Suzanne Allard
Languages French
T: +1 450 473 9219
W: terre-des-jeunes.cssmi.qc.ca

École Saint-Barthélemy

7081 avenue des Érables, Montréal QC H2E 2R1
PYP Coordinator Isabelle Crête
Languages French
T: +1 514 596 4877
W: st-barthelemy.csdm.ca

École Saint-Jean

245, 2e Rue Ouest, Rimouski QC G5L 4Y1
MYP Coordinator Caroline Michaud
Languages French
T: +1 418 724 3381
W: stjean.csphares.qc.ca

École Saint-Pierre et des Sentiers

1090 chemin de Château-Bigot, Charlesbourg QC G2L 1G1
MYP Coordinator Melanie Tremblay
Languages French
T: +1 418 624 3757
W: www.sentiers.csdps.qc.ca

École Saint-Rémi

16 avenue Neveu, Beaconsfield QC H9W 5B4
PYP Coordinator Nancy Bourgeois
Languages English, French
T: +1 514 855 4206
W: saintremi.ecoleouest.com

École secondaire André-Laurendeau

7450 boulevard Cousineau, St-Hubert QC J3Y 3L4
MYP Coordinator Carole St-Amant
Languages French
T: +1 450 678 2080
W: andre-laurendeau.ecoles.csmv.qc.ca

Ecole Secondaire Armand-Corbeil

795 JF Kennedy Ouest, Terrebonne QC J6W 1X2
MYP Coordinator Julie Brideau
Languages French
T: +1 450 492 3619 Ext:1112

École secondaire Bernard-Gariépy

2800 boulevard des Érables, Sorel-Tracy QC J3R 2W4
MYP Coordinator Michel Coulombe
Languages French
T: +1 450 742 5601

École secondaire Camille-Lavoie

500 avenue des Métiers, Alma QC G8B 3C4
MYP Coordinator Dominique Fortin
Languages French
T: +1 418 669 6062
W: www.ecolecamillelavoie.com

École Secondaire Cavelier-De LaSalle

9199 rue Centrale, LaSalle QC H8R 2JG

MYP Coordinator Terez Kai Lawson

Languages French

T: +1 514 595 2044

École secondaire Charles-Gravel

350 rue Saint-Gérard, Chicoutimi QC G7G 1J2

MYP Coordinator Audrey Morin

Languages French

T: +1 418 541 4343

W: charlesgravel.csrsaguenay.qc.ca

École secondaire de l'Île

255 rue Saint-Rédempteur, Gatineau QC J8X 2T4

MYP Coordinator Jean-François Simard

Languages French

T: +1 819 771 6126

École secondaire De Mortagne

955 boulevard de Montarville, Boucherville QC J4B 1Z6

MYP Coordinator Amélie Charron

Languages French

T: +1 450 655 7311

W: demortagne.csp.qc.ca

École secondaire de Neufchâtel

3600 avenue Chauveau, Neufchâtel QC G2C 1A1

MYP Coordinator Guylaine Plante

Languages French

T: +1 418 847 7300

W: www.cscapitale.qc.ca/neufchatel

École secondaire de Rivière-du-Loup

464 rue Lafontaine, C.P. 910, Rivière du Loup QC G5R 3Z5

MYP Coordinator Caroline Lévesque

Languages French

T: +1 418 862 8201

W: www.cskamloup.qc.ca

École secondaire de Rochebelle

1095 de Rochebelle, Sainte Foy QC G1V 4P8

MYP Coordinator Karine Mercier

Languages French

T: +1 418 652 2167

W: www.derochebelle.qc.ca

École secondaire des Pionniers

1725, boulevard du Carmel, Trois-Rivières QC G8Z 3R8

MYP Coordinator Sylvie Gour

Languages French

T: +1 819 379 5822

W: despionniers.csduroy.qc.ca

École secondaire des Sources

2900 chemin Lake, Dollard-des-Ormeaux QC H9B 2P1

MYP Coordinator Inas Mourad

Languages French

T: +1 514 855 4208

W: www2.csmb.qc.ca/dessources/

École secondaire d'Oka

1700 Chemin Oka, Oka QC J0N 1E0

MYP Coordinator Mélanie Corneau

Languages French

T: +1 450 491 8410

École secondaire Dorval Jean XXIII

1301 avenue Dawson, Dorval QC H9S 1Y3

MYP Coordinator Bouchra Rhazi

Languages French

T: +1 514 855 4244

École secondaire Fernand-Lefebvre

265 rue de Ramezay, Sorel-Tracy QC J3P 4A5

MYP Coordinator Michel Coulombe

Languages French

T: +1 450 742 5901

W: esfl.cs-soreltracy.qc.ca

École secondaire Grande-Rivière

100 rue Broad, Gatineau QC J9H 6A9

MYP Coordinator Annie Lavigne

Languages French

T: +1 819 682 8222

W: esgr.cspo.qc.ca

École secondaire Guillaume-Couture

70 Rue Philippe-Boucher, Levis QC G6V 1M5

MYP Coordinator Marianne Rhéaume

Languages French

T: +1 418 838 8550

École secondaire Henri-Bourassa

6051 boul Maurice-Duplessis, Montréal-Nord QC H1G 1Y6

MYP Coordinator Francine Lalonde

Languages French

T: +1 514 328 3200 EXT:3210

École secondaire Hormisdas-Gamelin

580 rue Maclaren Est, Gatineau QC J8L 2W2

MYP Coordinator Marie-France Bastien

Languages French

T: +1 819 986 8511

W: eshg.csscv.gouv.qc.ca

École secondaire Hubert-Maisonneuve

364 Rue Académie, Rosemère QC J7A 1ZA

MYP Coordinator Isabelle Bois

Languages French

T: +1 450 621 2003

W: hubert-maisonneuve.cssmi.qc.ca

École secondaire Jacques-Rousseau

444 rue Gentilly est, Longueuil QC J4H 3X7

MYP Coordinator Nathalie Hosson

Languages French

T: +1 450 651 6800 EXT:467

École secondaire Jean-Baptiste-Meilleur

777 boul d`Iberville, Repentigny QC J5Y 1A2

MYP Coordinator Patricia Claude

Languages French

T: +1 450 492 3777

W: www.csaffluents.qc.ca/etablissements/secondaire/jean-baptiste-meilleur

École secondaire Jean-Jacques-Bertrand

255 rue Saint-André Sud, Farnham QC J2N 2B8

MYP Coordinator Julie Filion

Languages French

T: +1 450 293 3181 EXT:223

École secondaire Jeanne-Mance

45 avenue des Freres, Drummondville QC J2B 6A2

MYP Coordinator Mélanie Flamand

Languages French

T: +1 819 474 0753

École secondaire Joseph-François-Perrault

140 chemin Ste-Foy, Québec QC G1R 1T2

MYP Coordinator Audrey Cook

Languages French

T: +1 418 686 4040 EXT:6011

W: www.cscapitale.qc.ca/jfperrault

École secondaire Kénogami

1954 Boulevard des Etudiants, Jonquière, Québec QC G7X 4B1

MYP Coordinator Andrée Ménard

Languages French

T: +1 418 5423571

École secondaire La Courvilloise

2265 avenue Larue, Beauport QC G1C 1J9

MYP Coordinator François Couillard

Languages French

T: +1 418 821 4220

W: www.courvilloise.ca

École secondaire La Voie

6755 rue Lavoie, Montréal QC H3W 2K8

MYP Coordinator Karine Laroche

Languages French

T: +1 514 736 3500

W: la-voie.csdm.ca

École secondaire Le tandem boisé

605 rue Notre-dame Est, Victoriaville QC G6P 6Y9

MYP Coordinator Marie-Eve Jutras

Languages French

T: +1 819 758 1534

École secondaire Louis-Joseph-Papineau

378, rue Papineau, Papineauville QC J0V 1R0

MYP Coordinator Véronique Cloutier

Languages French

T: +1 819 427 6258

W: ljp.csscv.gouv.qc.ca

École secondaire Louis-Philippe-Paré

235 boulevard Brisebois, Châteauguay QC J6K 3X4

MYP Coordinator Mélanie Bissonnette

Languages French

T: +1 514 380 8899 EXT:5480

W: lpp.csdgs.qc.ca

École secondaire Louis-Riel

5850 avenue de Carignan, Montréal QC H1M 2V4

MYP Coordinator Nathalie Lacroix

Languages French

T: +1 514 596 4134

W: www.louis-riel.csdm.qc.ca

École secondaire Monseigneur Euclide-Théberge

677 rue Desjardins, Marieville QC J3M 1R1

MYP Coordinator Patrick Mullen

Languages French

T: +1 450 460 4491

École secondaire Mont Saint-Sacrement

200 boulevard Saint-Sacrement, Saint-Gabriel-de-Valcartier QC G0A 4S0

MYP Coordinator Jocelyne Boivin

Languages French

T: +1 418 844 3771 P35

W: www.mss.qc.ca

École secondaire Mont-Royal

50 avenue Montgomery, Ville Mont-Royal QC H3R 2B3
MYP Coordinator Élise Lalonde
Languages French
T: +1 514 731 2761
W: www.ecolesecondairemontroyal.ca

École secondaire Ozias-Leduc

525 rue Jolliet, Mont-Saint-Hilaire QC J3H 3N2
MYP Coordinator Anne-Marie Bellemare
Languages French
T: +1 450 467 0261

École secondaire Paul-Gérin-Lajoie-d'Outremont

475, avenue Bloomfield, Outremont, QC H2V 3R9
MYP Coordinator Christian Girouard
Languages French
T: +1 514 276 3746
W: www.paul-gerin-lajoie-doutremont.ca

École secondaire polyvalente de l'Ancienne-Lorette

1801 rue Notre-Dame, L'Ancienne-Lorette QC G2E 3C6
MYP Coordinator Mylène Bellavance
Languages French
T: +1 418 872 9836
W: pal.csdecou.qc.ca

École secondaire Rive-Nord

400 rue Joseph-Paquette, Bois des Filions QC J6Z 4P7
MYP Coordinator Pascale Gauthier
Languages French
T: +1 450 621 3686
W: rive-nord.cssmi.qc.ca

École secondaire Roger-Comtois

158 boulevard des Étudiants, Loretteville QC G2A 1N8
MYP Coordinator Jean-François Beaumont
Languages French
T: +1 418 847 7201

École secondaire Saint-Joseph de Saint-Hyacinthe

2875 avenue Bourdages Nord, Saint-Hyacinthe QC J2S 5S3
MYP Coordinator Michèle Lemelin
Languages French
T: +1 450 774 3775
W: www.essj.qc.ca

École secondaire Saint-Luc

6300, chemin de la Côte, Saint-Luc, Montréal QC H3X 2H4
MYP Coordinator Chantal Filion
Languages French
T: +1 514 596 5920
W: st-luc.csdm.ca

École secondaire Serge-Bouchard

640 boulevard Blanche, Baie-Comeau QC G5C 2B3
MYP Coordinator Chantal Bérubé
Languages French
T: +1 418 589 1301
W: www.csestuaire.qc.ca/ecoles-secondaires

École secondaire St-Gabriel

8 Rue Tassé, Ste Thérèse QC J7E 1V3
MYP Coordinator Isabelle Miron
Languages French
T: +1 450 433 5445
W: st-gabriel.cssmi.qc.ca

École Ste-Thérèse-de-l'Enfant-Jésus

700 9e rue, Saint-Jérôme QC J7Z 2Z5
PYP Coordinator Annie Beauchamp
Languages French
T: +1 450 438 8828
W: www2.csrdn.qc.ca/ecoles-et-centres/017-sainte-therese

École St-Noël

993 8e Avenue, Thetford Mines QC G6G 2E3
PYP Coordinator Lisa Vachon
Languages French
T: +1 418 335 9826
W: www.csappalaches.qc.ca/fr/ecoles-et-centres/ecoles-primaires/ecole-saint-noel

École Val-des-Ormes

199 chemin de la Grande-Côte, Rosemère QC J7A 1H6
PYP Coordinator Nancy Prézeau
Languages French
T: +1 450 437 5770
W: www6.cssmi.qc.ca/vdo

Heritage Regional High School

7445 Chambly Road, St Hubert QC J3Y 3S3
MYP Coordinator Angela Cavaliere
Languages English
T: +1 450 678 1070

Howard S Billings High School

210 McLeod, Chateauguay QC J6J 2H4
MYP Coordinator Paul Couture
Languages English
T: +1 450 691 3230
W: www.hsbillingsib.ca

JPPS-Bialik High School

6500 Kildare Road, Montreal QC H4W 3B8
MYP Coordinator Gayle Shulak
PYP Coordinator Elizabeth Doss
Languages English
T: +1 514 731 6456
W: www.jppsbialik.ca

Lakeside Academy

5050 Sherbrooke, Lachine QC H8T 1H8
MYP Coordinator Andrew Stepancic
Languages English
T: +1 514 637 2505
W: lakesideacademy.lbpsb.qc.ca

LaSalle Community Comprehensive High School

240-9th Avenue, LaSalle QC H8P 2N9
MYP Coordinator Julie Canty-Homier
Languages English
T: +1 514 595 2050
W: lcchs.lbpsb.qc.ca

Laurier Macdonald High School

7355 Boulevard Viau, St Leonard QC H1S 3C2
MYP Coordinator Valérie Barnabé
Languages English, French
T: +1 514 374 6000
W: www.lauriermacdonald.ca

Le Carrefour École Polyvalente

50 chemin de la Savane, Gatineau QC J8T 3N2
MYP Coordinator Sindy Poirier
Languages French
T: +1 819 568 9012
W: www.csdraveurs.qc.ca/carrefour

Le Collège Saint-Bernard

25 avenue des Frères, Drummondville QC J2B 6A2
MYP Coordinator Marie-Eve Poulin
Languages French
T: +1 819 478 3330

L'École des Ursulines de Québec

4 rue du Parloir, CP 820, Haute - Ville, Québec QC G1R 4S7
PYP Coordinator Veronique Dussault
Languages French
T: +1 418 692 2612

L'Externat Saint-Jean-Eudes

650 avenue du Bourg-Royal, Charlesbourg, Québec City QC G2L 1M8
MYP Coordinator Isabelle Therrien
Languages French
T: +1 418 627 1550
W: www.sje.qc.ca

Lower Canada College

4090, avenue Royal, Montréal QC H4A 2M5
DP Coordinator Lesa Currie
MYP Coordinator June Takacs
Languages English
T: +1 514 482 9916
W: www.lcc.ca

Marymount Academy

5100 Côte St-Luc Road, Montréal QC H3W 2G9
MYP Coordinator Maria Raskin
Languages English
T: +1 514 488 8144
W: www.emsb.qc.ca/marymount/

Michelangelo International Elementary School

9360 5e rue, Montréal QC H1E 1K1
PYP Coordinator Ida De Laurentiis
Languages English, French
T: +1 514 648 1218
W: www.michelangelo.emsb.qc.ca

Pensionnat du Saint-Nom-de-Marie

628 chemin de la Côte, St Catherine, Outremont QC H2V 2C5
MYP Coordinator Chantal Gobeil
Languages French
T: +1 514 735 5261
W: www.psnm.qc.ca

Pierrefonds Comprehensive High School

13800 Pierrefonds Boulevard, Pierrefonds QC H9A 1A7
MYP Coordinator Caroline Clarke
Languages English
T: +1 514 626 9610

Polyvalente Chanoine-Armand-Racicot

940 boulevard de Normandie, St Jean-Sur-Richelieu QC J3A 1A7
MYP Coordinator Valérie Gosselin
Languages French
T: +1 450 348 6134

Polyvalente de Charlesbourg

900, rue de la Sorbonne, Québec QC G1H 1H1
MYP Coordinator Cynthia Turcotte
Languages English, French
T: +1 418 622 7820
W: polyvalentedecharlesbourg.csdps.qc.ca

Polyvalente de Thetford Mines

561 rue St-Patrick, Thetford Mines QC G6G 5W1
MYP Coordinator Nathalie Houle
Languages French
T: +1 418 338 7832 EXT:1514

IB AMERICAS

Polyvalente des Quatre-Vents

1099 Boulevard Hamel, St-Félicien QC G8K 2R4

MYP Coordinator Marie-Andrée Plourde

Languages French

T: +1 418 275 4585

Polyvalente Deux-Montagnes

500 chemin des Anciens, Deux-Montagnes QC J7R 6A7

MYP Coordinator Marie-France Rochon

Languages French

T: +1 450 472 3070

Polyvalente Hyacinthe-Delorme

2700 Avenue T D Bouchard, Saint-Hyacinthe QC J2S 7G2

MYP Coordinator Isabelle Guertin

Languages French

T: +1 450 773 8401

Polyvalente Marcel-Landry

365 Avenue Landry, Saint-Jean-sur-Richelieu QC J2X 2P6

MYP Coordinator Jerome Bedard

Languages French

T: +1 450 347 1225

Polyvalente Saint Francois

228 Avenue Lambert, Beauceville QC G5X 3N9

MYP Coordinator Lina Carrier

Languages French

T: +1 418 228 5541

Saint Anthony Elementary School

17750 Rue Meloche, Pierrefonds QC H9J 3P9

PYP Coordinator Lucie Vinet

Languages English, French

T: +1 514 624 6614

W: stanthony.lbpsb.qc.ca

Saint Lambert International High School

675 Green Street, St Lambert QC J4P 1V9

MYP Coordinator Kristen Witczak

Languages English

T: +1 450 671 5534

W: www.saintlambertinternational.ca

St Thomas High School

120 Ambassador, Pointe-Claire QC H9R 1S8

MYP Coordinator Amber Carlon

Languages English

T: +1 514 694 3770

Saskatchewan

Aden Bowman Collegiate Institute

1904 Clarence Ave S, Saskatoon SK S7J 1L3

DP Coordinator Jeff Speir

Languages English

T: +1 306 683 7600

W: www.spsd.sk.ca

Bedford Road Collegiate

722 Bedford Road, Saskatoon SK S7L 0G2

DP Coordinator Kim Buglass

Languages English

T: +1 306 683 7650

W: www.spsd.sk.ca/school/bedfordroad

Luther College High School

1500 Royal Street, Regina SK S4T 5A5

DP Coordinator Derek Frostad

Languages English

T: +1 306 791 9150

W: www.luthercollege.edu

North Battleford Comprehensive High School

1791-110th Street, North Battleford SK S9A 2Y2

DP Coordinator Joshua Radchenko

Languages English

T: +1 306 445 6101

W: www.nbchs.north-battleford.sk.ca

CAYMAN ISLANDS

Cayman International School

P.O. Box 31364, 95 Minerva Drive, Camana Bay, Grand Cayman KY1-1206

DP Coordinator Sarah Dyer

Languages English

T: +1 345 945 4664

W: www.caymaninternationalschool.org

Prospect Primary School

169 Poindexter Road, P.O. Box 910, Grand Cayman KY1-1103

PYP Coordinator Charmaine Bravo

Languages English

T: +1 345 947 8889

W: schools.edu.ky/pps/Pages/Home.aspx

Savannah Primary School

1659 Shamrock Road, P.O. Box 435, Grand Cayman KY1-1500

PYP Coordinator Kiimia Hemmings

Languages English

T: +1 345 947 1344

W: schools.edu.ky/sav/Pages/Home.aspx

Sir John A. Cumber Primary School

44 Fountain Road, P.O. Box 405, Grand Cayman KY1-1302

PYP Coordinator Rachel Samaroo

Languages English

T: +1 345 949 3314

W: schools.edu.ky/jac/Pages/Home.aspx

CHILE

Bradford School

Avada Luis Pateur 6335, Vitacura, Santiago

DP Coordinator Ximena Long Arriagada

Languages English

T: +56 (2) 29 12 31 40

W: www.bradfordschool.cl

Colegio Alemán Chicureo

Av. Alemania 170, Piedra Roja, Chicureo, Santiago

MYP Coordinator María Soledad Amenábar

PYP Coordinator Maricarmen Rosenbaum

Languages Spanish

T: +56 223078962

W: www.dsch.cl

Colegio Alemán de Concepción

Camino El Venado 1075, Andalué, San Pedro de la Paz, Concepción, Biobío

DP Coordinator Cristian Muñoz

Languages Spanish

T: +56 41 2140000

W: www.dsc.cl

Colegio Alemán de San Felipe de Aconcagua

60 CH N° 501 Panquehue, San Felipe, Valparaíso

DP Coordinator Miriam Ramirez

Languages English, Spanish

T: +56 34 2 59 11 71

W: www.dssanfelipe.cl

Colegio Alemán de Temuco

Avenida Holandesa 0855, Temuco, Araucanía

DP Coordinator Leonardo Hernández Zapata

Languages Spanish

T: +56 45 963000

W: www.dstemuco.cl

Colegio Alemán de Valparaiso

Alvarez 2950, El Salto, Viña del Mar, Valparaíso

DP Coordinator Rafael Yanez

Languages Spanish

T: +56 32 216 1531

W: www.dsvalpo.cl

Colegio Alemán Los Angeles

Casilla 367, Av. Gabriela Mistral 1360 (ex 1751), Los Ángeles, Biobío

DP Coordinator Claudio Ibacache Soto

Languages Spanish

T: +56 43 2521111

W: www.dsla.cl

Colegio Alemán Puerto Varas

KM1, 4 Camino Ensenada, Puerto Varas, Los Lagos

PYP Coordinator Natalia Federici Maggi

Languages Spanish, German

T: +56 65 223 0450

W: www.dspuertovaras.com

Colegio Alemán St Thomas Morus

Avenida Pedro de Valdivia 320, Providencia, Santiago

DP Coordinator Matthias Waldow

Languages Spanish

T: +56 2 2729 1600

W: www.dsmorus.cl

Colegio Internacional SEK Chile

Avd Los Militares 6640, Las Condes, Santiago

DP Coordinator Marcela Gangas

Languages Spanish

T: +56 2 2127116

W: www.sekchile.com

Colegio Internacional SEK Pacifico

San Estanislao 50 Lomas de Montemar, Concón, Valparaíso

DP Coordinator Paola de la Fuente Estay

PYP Coordinator Wilma Lizana

Languages English, Spanish

T: +56 32 2275700

W: www.sekpacifico.com

Colegio 'La Maisonnette'

Avda Luis Pasteur 6076, Vitacura, Santiago

DP Coordinator Oriana Martínez

Languages Spanish

T: +56 2 228162945

W: www.lamaisonnette.cl

Craighouse School

Casilla 20 007, Correo 20., Santiago

DP Coordinator Fernanda Silva

MYP Coordinator Leonora Cardemil

PYP Coordinator Barbara Atkinson

Languages English, Spanish

T: +56 2 227560218

W: www.craighouseschool.cl

Instituto Alemán Carlos Anwandter

Los Laureles 050, Casilla 2-D, Valdivia, Los Ríos
DP Coordinator Sonia Videla
Languages Spanish
T: +56 63 2471100
W: www.dsv.cl

Instituto Alemán de Osorno

Los Carreras 818, Osorno, Los Lagos
DP Coordinator Carla Sommer
MYP Coordinator Jaime Serón
PYP Coordinator Leonardo Jara Adad
Languages Spanish
T: +56 64 233 1800/1805
W: www.dso.cl

Instituto Alemán Puerto Montt

Bernardo Phillipi #350, Sector Seminario, 5480000 Puerto Montt, Los Lagos
PYP Coordinator Jose Silva
Languages Spanish
T: +56 65 2 252560
W: www.ialeman.cl

INTERNATIONAL SCHOOL NIDO DE AGUILAS

Av. El Rodeo 14200, Lo Barnechea, Santiago
DP Coordinator Kurt Supplee
Languages English, Spanish
T: +56 2 2339 8100
E: admissions@nido.cl
W: www.nido.cl

See full details on page 508

Liceo A 43 'Liceo Siete'

Monseñor Sótero Sanz 060, Santiago
DP Coordinator Isabel Villarroel
Languages Spanish
T: +56 2 2235 7921
W: www.liceosiete.cl

Mackay School

Vicuña Mackenna 700, Viña del Mar, Valparaíso
DP Coordinator Silvio Bermudez Salas
MYP Coordinator Sebastián Díaz
PYP Coordinator Evangelina Di Girolamo
Languages English
T: +56 32 2386614
W: www.mackay.cl

Redland School

Camino El Alba 11357, Las Condes, 7600022 Santiago
DP Coordinator Ruth Guzmán
MYP Coordinator Cristian Barrera
PYP Coordinator Miguel Ramos
Languages Spanish
T: +56 2 29598500
W: www.redland.cl

Saint Gabriel's School

Avda Fco Bilbao 3070, Providencia, Santiago
DP Coordinator Laura Schiaffino
Languages Spanish
T: +56 22 462 5400
W: www.sangabriel.cl

SANTIAGO COLLEGE

Av. Camino Los Trapenses 4007, Lo Barnechea, Santiago
DP Coordinator Renato Hamel
MYP Coordinator Angel Girano
PYP Coordinator Mónika Naranjo
Languages Spanish, English
T: +56 2 27338800
E: master@scollege.cl
W: www.scollege.cl/index.php/es/

See full details on page 538

St John's School

Fundo el Venado, San Pedro de la Paz, Concepción, Biobío
DP Coordinator Gloria Soledad Guerrero Pastene
MYP Coordinator Patricia Uribe
PYP Coordinator Alexandra Krumm
Languages English, Spanish
T: +56 41 2466440
W: www.stjohns.cl

St Margaret's British School For Girls

Casilla 392, Viña del Mar, Valparaíso
DP Coordinator Andrea Villalobos Danessi
Languages Spanish
T: +56 32 245 1700
W: www.stmargarets.cl

St Paul's School

Merced Oriente 54, Viña del Mar, Valparaíso
PYP Coordinator Eliana Schmitt
Languages English, Spanish
T: (56 32) 314 2200
W: www.stpaul.cl

The Antofagasta British School

Pedro León Gallo 723, Antofagasta
DP Coordinator Cristian Daniel Retamales
MYP Coordinator Maria Fernanda Acevedo
PYP Coordinator Gonzalo Carrasco
Languages English, Spanish
T: +55 2 598931
W: abs.school

The British School - Punta Arenas

Waldo Seguel 454, Punta Arenas, Magallanes
DP Coordinator José Antonio Vergara Rodríguez
MYP Coordinator Ximena Morales Trabazo
PYP Coordinator Carolina Rees King
Languages Spanish, English
T: +56 61 2 22 33 81
W: www.britishschool.cl

The Mayflower School

Avda Las Condes 12 167, Las Condes, Santiago
DP Coordinator Andrea Edwards Neut
PYP Coordinator Constanza Postigo Gaete
Languages Spanish
T: +56 22 3523100
W: www.mayflower.cl

Wenlock School

Casilla 27169, Correo 27, Santiago
DP Coordinator Marta Poblete
Languages Spanish
T: +56 223631803
W: www.wenlock.cl

Aspaen Gimnasio Iragua

Av. Calle 170, No. 76-55, Barrio San José de Bavaria, Bogotá, D.C.
DP Coordinator Yamid Guerra Pedroza
Languages Spanish
T: +57 (1) 667 95 00
W: www.iragua.edu.co

British International School

Apartado Aéreo 4368, Barranquilla, Atlántico
DP Coordinator Jose Donado Coronell
MYP Coordinator Guisella Pilonieta
Languages English
T: +57 (5) 359 92 43
W: www.britishschool.edu.co

Buckingham School

Cra 52 No 214 - 55, Bogotá, D.C.
DP Coordinator Aramis Vega arias
MYP Coordinator Elena Rokhas
PYP Coordinator Julieta Galeano León
Languages English, Spanish
T: +57 (1) 676 08 12
W: cbk.edu.co

CAS Colombo American School

Carrera 73 No. 214-53, Bogotá, D.C.
PYP Coordinator Vanessa Buzeta
Languages English, Spanish
T: +57 31 668 50 77
W: www.colegiocolomboamericano.edu.co

CIEDI - Colegio Internacional de Educación Integral

Km 3 vía Suba-Cota, Bogotá, D.C.
DP Coordinator Ernesto Campos
MYP Coordinator Andrea Barrera Rico
PYP Coordinator Mark Gaylor
Languages Spanish, English
T: +57 (1) 683 06 04
W: www.ciedi.edu.co

Colegio Abraham Lincoln

Av. Calle 170 # 65 31, Bogotá, D.C.
DP Coordinator Glenda Liliana Buitrago Ramirez
Languages Spanish
T: +57 (1) 742 31 66
W: www.abrahamlincoln.edu.co

Colegio Albania

Calle 15 3-00, Campamento de Mushaisa, Cerrejón La Mina, La Guajira
DP Coordinator Juan Carlos Tarazona Bautista
MYP Coordinator Juan Carlos Tarazona Bautista
PYP Coordinator Rubys Chinchia
Languages English, Spanish
T: +57 (5) 350 56 48
W: www.colegioalbania.edu.co

Colegio Alemán

Autopista al Mar poste 89 Electricaribe, Baranquilla, Atlántico
DP Coordinator Heidys María Navarro Escorcia
Languages Spanish
T: +57 (5) 359 85 20
W: www.colegioaleman.edu.co

Colegio Anglo-Colombiano

Apartado Aéreo 253393, Avenida 19 N° 152A-48, Santa Fé, Bogotá, D.C.
DP Coordinator Camila Rueda
MYP Coordinator Rusbel Martinez Rodriguez
PYP Coordinator Christianne Cowie
Languages English, Spanish
T: +57 (1) 259 57 00
W: www.anglocolombiano.edu.co

Colegio Británico - The British School

Call 18 # 142-255 (Esquina), La Viga, Pance, Cali, Valle del Cauca
DP Coordinator Edilson Sánchez Buitrago
Languages Spanish
T: +57 (2) 555 75 45
W: www.thebritishschoolcali.edu.co

Colegio Británico de Cartagena

Anillo Vial Km. 12, Cartagena, Bolívar 130001
DP Coordinator Alexandra Martinez
Languages English, Spanish
T: +57 5 693 0982 83 84
W: www.colbritanico.edu.co/newcbc

Colegio Cambridge

Sede Cajicá, Kilómetro 2 Vía Cajicá, Chía Vereda El Canelón, Cajicá, Cundinamarca
DP Coordinator Juan Carlos Villamizar
Languages English, Spanish
T: +1 601 746 4737
W: colegiocambridge.edu.co

Colegio Colombo Británico

Avenida La Maria 69 Pance, Pance, Cali, Valle del Cauca
DP Coordinator Reynaldo Muñoz
MYP Coordinator Eleanor Alicia Cosh Lacouture
PYP Coordinator Claudia Fayad
Languages English, Spanish
T: +57 (2) 555 53 85
W: www.colombobritanico.edu.co

Colegio Colombo Gales

Avenida Guaymaral, Costado sur Aeropuerto, Bogotá, D.C.
DP Coordinator Nidia Elvira Gallego Vargas
PYP Coordinator Tilcia Ruth Melo Lugo
Languages Spanish
T: +57 (1) 668 49 10
W: www.colegiocolombogales.edu.co

Colegio de Cambridge (Cambridge International School)

Vereda La Aurora, Municipio La Calera, Bogotá, D.C.
DP Coordinator Claudia Patricia Torres Bojacá
Languages Spanish
T: +57 (1) 593 18 90
W: www.colegiocambridge.edu.co

Colegio de Inglaterra - The English School

Calle 170 #15-68, Bogotá, D.C.
DP Coordinator Álvaro Rodríguez Vásquez
MYP Coordinator Lizbeth Santana
PYP Coordinator Kristine Ertl
Languages English, Spanish
T: +57 (1) 676 77 00
W: www.englishschool.edu.co

Colegio Domingo Savio

Calle 24 Sur #24 f-16, Bogotá, D.C.
MYP Coordinator Andrea Guiovanna Sanchez Waltero
Languages English, Spanish
T: +57 366 61 63
W: www.domingosaviobilingualschool. edu.co

Colegio El Minuto de Dios Siglo XXI

Transversal 74 No 81 C - 05, Bogotá, D.C.
DP Coordinator Alba Orozco Bernal
Languages Spanish
T: +57 (1) 508 22 30
W: colegiosminutodedios.edu.co/sigloxxi

Colegio Gran Bretaña

Carrera 51 No 215-20, Bogotá, D.C.
DP Coordinator Monica Woodward
Languages English
T: +57 (1) 676 03 91
W: www.cgb.edu.co

Colegio Internacional Los Cañaverales

Carrera 29 No 10-500, Arroyohonfo, Vía Dapa Km 1 Yumbo, Yumbo, Valle del Cauca
DP Coordinator Carolina Avendaño Rodríguez
Languages English
T: +57 (2) 658 28 18
W: www.canaverales.edu.co

Colegio Los Ángeles Tunja

Calle 73A No. 2-02 E, Altos de la Arboleda, Tunja, Boyacá
DP Coordinator Derlly Rosmery Gomez Amarillo
Languages English, Spanish
T: +57 304 380 8353
W: colegiolosangelestunja.com

Colegio Los Tréboles

Vereda cerca de Piedra, Finca Santa Elena, Chía, Cundinamarca
DP Coordinator Clara Inés Díaz Rodríguez
Languages English, Spanish
T: +57 (1) 862 48 30
W: www.clt.edu.co

Colegio Mayor de los Andes

Kilómetro 3 vía Chía, Cajicá, Cundinamarca
DP Coordinator Adelina Nuñez Rojas
Languages Spanish
T: +57 (1) 866 29 56
W: www.colegiomayordelosandes.edu.co

Colegio Nueva Inglaterra (New England School)

Calle 218, No. 50-60, Bogotá, D.C.
DP Coordinator Adolfo De La Cruz Celis
Languages Spanish
T: +57 (1) 676 07 88
W: www.colegionuevainglaterra.edu.co

Colegio Nueva York

Calle 227 # 49-64 Urbanización el Jardín, Bogotá, D.C.
DP Coordinator Andrea Rueda Acosta
Languages English
T: +57 (1) 668 48 90
W: www.colegionuevayork.edu.co

Colegio San Viator - Sede Bogotá

Autopista Norte 209-51, Bogotá, D.C.
DP Coordinator Luis Fernando Peña Paladines
MYP Coordinator Erika Martínez Torres
PYP Coordinator Paola Cuesta
Languages English
T: +57 (1) 676 09 97
W: www.sanviator.edu.co

Colegio San Viator - Sede Tunja

Av Universitaria 62 - 100, Tunja, Boyacá
DP Coordinator Steffany Contreras Moreno
Languages English, Spanish
W: www.sanviatortunja.edu.co

Colegio Santa Francisca Romana

Calle 151 No. 16 - 40, Bogotá, D.C.
DP Coordinator Maria Consuelo Velasco
Languages English, Spanish
T: +57 1 580 44 44
W: www.csfr.edu.co

Colegio Tilatá

Kilómetro 9 vía La Calera, Bogotá, D.C.
DP Coordinator Paulo Lopez-Orellana
MYP Coordinator Diana Olivos Suarez
PYP Coordinator Marcela Castañeda
Languages English, Spanish
T: +57 (1) 592 14 14
W: www.colegiotilata.edu.co

Deutsche Schule - Cali / Kolumbien

Avenida Gualí Nº 31, Barrio Ciudad Jardín, Cali, Valle del Cauca
DP Coordinator Carlos Rojas Padilla
Languages German, Spanish
T: +57 (2) 685 89 00
W: www.dscali.edu.co

Deutsche Schule Medellín

Cra 61, No. 34-62, Itagüi, Antioquia
DP Coordinator Jaime Alonso López García
Languages Spanish
T: +57 (604) 2818811 (EXT:100)
W: www.dsmedellin.edu.co

Fundacion Gimnasio Ingles de Armenia (GI SCHOOL)

KM.3 Via Armenia-Circasia, Salento, Quindío 630007
DP Coordinator Milagros Zapata
Languages English, Spanish
T: +57 6 749 51 11
W: gi.edu.co

Fundación Gimnasio Los Portales

Calle 212 No. 77- 20, Bogotá, D.C.
DP Coordinator Juan Pulido
MYP Coordinator Alirio Sneider Saavedra
PYP Coordinator Caroll Marulanda Guzmán
Languages English, Spanish
T: +57 (1) 676 40 55
W: www.losportales.edu.co

Fundación Nuevo Marymount

Calle 169B, No 74A-02, Bogotá, D.C.
DP Coordinator Liliana Manzanera
Languages English
T: +57 (1) 669 90 77
W: www.marymountschool.edu.co

GCB - Bilingüe Internacional

Costado Sur - Occidental Aeropuerto Guaymaral, Bogotá, D.C.
DP Coordinator Jorge Eduardo Baquero Cañas
Languages English, Spanish
T: +57 1 668 39 99
W: www.gcb.edu.co

Gimnasio Británico

Calle 21 No 9A-58, Avenida Chilacos, Chía, Cundinamarca
DP Coordinator Gabriel Alfredo Piraquive García
Languages English, Spanish, French
T: +57 (1) 861 50 84
W: www.gimnasio-britanico.edu.co

Gimnasio Campestre la Fontana

Km 4 Vereda El Amor, Vía Multf. Centauros, Villavicencio, Meta
DP Coordinator Annamaria Gallo
Languages English, Spanish
T: +57 314 279 7928
W: www.lafontana.edu.co

Gimnasio Campestre Los Cerezos
Vereda Canelón, Cajicá, Cundinamarca
DP Coordinator Marcia Malpica Ortiz
PYP Coordinator Ingrid Mogollón
Languages Spanish
T: +57 866 26 79
W: www.gimnasioloscerezos.edu.co

Gimnasio Campestre San Rafael
Sede Campestre, Km 6 vía Siberia, Tenjo, Cundinamarca
DP Coordinator Juan Antonio Alonso de Juan
Languages Spanish
T: +57 593 30 40
W: colegiosminutodedios.edu.co/sanrafael

Gimnasio de Los Cerros
Calle 119 N° 0-68, Usaquén, Santa Fé, Bogotá, D.C.
DP Coordinator Jorge Arango
Languages Spanish
T: +57 (1) 657 60 00
W: www.loscerros.edu.co

Gimnasio del Norte
Calle 207 N° 70 - 50, Bogotá, D.C.
DP Coordinator Gloria Prada Ramírez
MYP Coordinator Adriana Rodríguez
PYP Coordinator Berta Gómez
Languages Spanish, English
T: +57 (1) 668 39 39
W: www.gimnasiodelnorte.edu.co

Gimnasio El Hontanar
Cra. 76 No. 150-26, Bogotá, D.C.
DP Coordinator Olga Lucía Illera Correal
Languages English, Spanish
T: +57 (1) 681 52 87
W: www.gimnasiohontanar.edu.co

Gimnasio Femenino
K7 #128-40, Bogotá, D.C.
DP Coordinator Fernando Rueda
MYP Coordinator Jimmy Pinilla Castillo
PYP Coordinator Gisela Toro López
Languages Spanish, English
T: +57 (1) 657 84 20
W: www.gimnasiofemenino.edu.co

Gimnasio Los Alcázares
Calle 63 Sur No 41-05 Sabaneta, Medellín, Antioquia
DP Coordinator Carlos Mejía
Languages Spanish
T: +57 (4) 305 40 00
W: www.alcazares.edu.co

Gimnasio Los Pinos
Calle 193 #38-20, Bogotá, D.C.
PYP Coordinator Tatiana Andrea Echeverry Rendón
Languages English, Spanish
T: +57 1 670 00 08
W: gimnasiolospinos.edu.co

Gimnasio Vermont
Cl 195 No 54-75, Bogotá, D.C.
DP Coordinator Claudia Aguirre
Languages Spanish
T: +57 (1) 674 80 70
W: www.gimnasiovermont.edu.co

Institución Educativa Liceo Departamental
Cra 37 A No. 8 -38 Barrio Eucarístico, 760001 Cali, Valle del Cauca
PYP Coordinator Gustavo Feijoo
Languages English, Spanish
W: ieliceodepartamental.edu.co

International Berckley School
Km 5 - Vía al Mar, Poste 115, Barranquilla, Atlántico
DP Coordinator Denys Coronell Vargas
Languages Spanish
T: +575 354 81 31
W: ibs.edu.co

Jardín Infantil Tía Nora y Liceo Los Alpes
Av 8 Norte, No. 66-05 Urbanización Menga, Cali, Valle del Cauca
DP Coordinator Luz Roldan
MYP Coordinator Ana Maria Palacios
PYP Coordinator Nini Johanna Ruiz Jaramillo
Languages Spanish, English
T: +57 (2) 665 41 20
W: www.jardintianorayliceolosalpes.edu.co

KSI Bogotá
Calle 221 No 115-51, Bogotá, D.C.
DP Coordinator Nelson Urrego
PYP Coordinator Andrea Roa
Languages English, Spanish
T: +57 (1) 676 29 02
W: www.ksi-bogota.com

Liceo Pino Verde
Vereda Los Planes kilometro, 5 Vía Cerritos Entrada 16, El Tigre, Pereira, Risaralda
DP Coordinator Rosa Damian Mesa
Languages English
T: +57 (6) 313 26 68
W: www.liceopinoverde.edu.co

Neil Armstrong School
Dir. Cr 44 Cl 14 El Buque, Villavicencio
DP Coordinator Saul Ernesto Soler Otalora
Languages English, Spanish
W: www.nas.edu.co

New Cambridge School Bucaramanga - Sede Cabecera
Cra. 39 No. 44-72, Bucaramanga, Santander
DP Coordinator Maria Alejandra Quinterro
Languages English, Spanish
T: +57 7 638 61 52
W: cambridge.edu.co

New Cambridge School Bucaramanga - Sede Cañaveral
Calle 32 No. 22-140, Floridablanca, Bucaramanga, Santander
DP Coordinator Maria Cristina Martin Ceballos
Languages English, Spanish
T: +57 7 638 61 52
W: cambridge.edu.co

Nuevo Gimnasio School
Kilometro 1 Autopista, Villavicencio, Meta
DP Coordinator Orlando Aguirre Urrutia
Languages English, Spanish
T: +57 310 801 52 83
W: www.nuevogimnasioschool.edu.co

The Victoria School
Calle 215 N° 50-60, Bogotá, D.C.
DP Coordinator María Bernal Baracaldo
MYP Coordinator Maria del Pilar Robles
PYP Coordinator Edna Esperanza Marin Steevens
Languages English, Spanish
T: +57 (1) 676 15 03
W: www.tvs.edu.co

Vermont School Medellín
Avenida Las Palmas Indiana Mall Km. 2 Vía La Fe, El Retiro, Antioquia
DP Coordinator Mauricio Ruíz Vahos
Languages English, Spanish
T: +57 (4) 520 60 60
W: vermontmedellin.edu.co

Academia Teocali
2.5 Km Norte de la Entrada Principal de Liberia, Carretera Interamericana Norte, Liberia, Guanacaste
DP Coordinator César Gabriel Lara Vanegas
Languages English
T: +506 2666 8780
W: www.academiateocali.ed.cr

Anglo American School
La Unión, 1 Km al norte de Sub Estación Electríca del ICE, Provincia de Cartago, Tres Rios, San Jose
DP Coordinator Bernal Villalobos Calvo
Languages Spanish
T: +506 2279 2626
W: anglo.ed.cr

Centro Educativo Futuro Verde
1 km este del Banco Nacional, Cóbano, Puntarenas 60111
DP Coordinator Khalida Lockheed
Languages English, Spanish
T: +506 2642 0291
W: www.futuro-verde.org

Centro Educativo Nueva Generacion
Sn Rafael de Heredia Del parqu 1 km al norte, Heredia 24-3015
DP Coordinator Nataly Campos
Languages English
T: +506 2237 8927
W: nuevageneracion.ed.cr/web

Colegio Bilingüe de Palmares
50 Metros sur Banco Popular, Palmares, Alajuela 215-4300
DP Coordinator Kendrich Vargas Vásquez
Languages Spanish
T: +506 2452 0157

Colegio de Bagaces
Contiguo al Gimnasio Municipal, Bagaces, Guanacaste
DP Coordinator Lelia Pineda Laguna
Languages Spanish
T: 506 2671 1116

Colegio de Santa Ana
300 oeste de la Cruz Roja, Uruca, Santa Ana, San José
DP Coordinator Francisco Javier Cortés González
Languages English, Spanish
T: +506 2282 2636

COLEGIO DEL VALLE S.A.(BLUE VALLEY SCHOOL)
From Multiplaza, 1.2 Km. northwest, right hand side of the road, Guachipelín, Escazú, San José
DP Coordinator Patricia Prats
Languages English, Spanish
T: +50 6 2215 2204
E: admissions@bluevalley.ed.cr
W: www.bluevalley.ed.cr

See full details on page 495

COSTA RICA

Colegio Internacional SEK Costa Rica

Cipreses de Curridabat, San José 963 2050

DP Coordinator Geovanny Cordero Gutiérrez

Languages English, Spanish

T: +506 2 272 5464

W: www.sekcostarica.com

Colegio Los Ángeles

Calle Luisa, San José

DP Coordinator Carlos Darío Quirós Morales

Languages English, Spanish

T: +506 2232 0122

W: www.colegiolosangeles.ed.cr

Colegio Miravalle

800m al sur de la esquina sureste de los Tribunales de Justicia, Cartago

DP Coordinator Susana Víquez Madrigal

Languages English, Spanish

T: +506 2552 7378

W: colegiomiravalle.com

Colegio Saint Francis

San Vicente, Moravia, San José

DP Coordinator María Laura Fernández Soto

Languages English, Spanish

T: +506 2430 7639

W: www.saintfranciscr.org

Del Mar Academy

P.O. Box: 130, Nosara, Nicoya, Guanacaste 5233

DP Coordinator Monica Marin

Languages English

T: +506 2682 1211

W: www.delmaracademy.com

European School

Heredia, San Pablo, P.O. Box: 177, Heredia

DP Coordinator Karen A Bye

Languages English

T: +506 2261 0717

W: www.europeanschool.com

Franz Liszt Schule

800 metros al sur de la gasolinera, Hermanos Montes a mano izq, Santa Ana, San José 10901

DP Coordinator Katelyn Tocci

Languages English, German

T: +506 2203 8128

W: www.fls.ed.cr

Golden Valley School

Del Lubricentro San Francisco 800 mts. Suroeste, Portones azules grandes a mano derecha, San Isidro, Heredia 40604

DP Coordinator Carlos Vega

Languages English, Spanish

T: +506 2268 9114

W: www.goldenvalleyschool.com

Instituto Dr. Jaim Weizman

100 norte, 100 oeste Compañía Nacional de Fuerza y Luz, Carretera Anonos, Mata Redonda, San José 4114-100

DP Coordinator María Alfaro Barrios

MYP Coordinator Helly Nuñez van Eyl

Languages English, Spanish

T: +506 2220 1050

Instituto de Educación Dr. Clodomiro Picado Twight

De la Universidad de Costa Rica, Sede del Atlántico 150 metros al oeste, Turrialba, Cartago

DP Coordinator Jesús Alonso Quirós Paniagua

Languages Spanish

T: +506 25560025

International Christian School

San Miguel de Santo Domingo, Heredia

DP Coordinator Chelsea McGill

Languages English, Spanish

T: +506 22411445

W: www.icscostarica.org

Iribó School

Del restaurante la casa de Doña, Lela 800 metros al sur, Curridabat, San José 662-2050 S

DP Coordinator Beatriz Vinueza

Languages Spanish

T: +506 4000 8989

W: iribo.org/site/

La Paz Community School

500 metros sur de la ferreteria, Buenaventura, Flamingo, Guanacaste 50309

DP Coordinator Martha Ortega

Languages English

T: +506 2654 4532

W: www.lapazschool.org

Liceo de Atenas Martha Mirambell Umaña

Atenas, Alajuela

DP Coordinator Ivannia María Campos Carranza

Languages English, Spanish

T: +506 2446 5124

W: liceoatenasbi.wixsite.com/info

Liceo de Cariari

1Km al Norte de la Agencia del Banco Nacional de Costa Rica, Mano izquierda, carretera a Semillero, Pococi, Limón 70205

DP Coordinator Edgar Ruiz Contreras

Languages Spanish

T: +506 27677180

Liceo de Costa Rica

Calle 9, Avenida 18 y 20, San José

DP Coordinator Lucas Peraza Orellana

Languages Spanish

T: +506 221 3792

Liceo de Cot

100 mts norte y 500 este de Palí de Cot, Cot, Oreamuno, Cartago 30702

DP Coordinator Sandra Córdoba Cortés

Languages Spanish

T: +506 2536 6509

W: www.liceodecot.com

Liceo de Miramar

Costado Oeste del Cementerio Municipal, Miramar de Montes de Oro, Puntarenas 6-01-04

DP Coordinator Dilana Ramirez

T: +506 26 39 90 69

W: liceomiramar.com

Liceo de Moravia

San Rafael de Moravia, San José

DP Coordinator Lesly Carolina Ramírez Peña

Languages English

T: +506 22351336

Liceo de Poás

500 m Norte del Templo Católico, de San Pedro de Poás, Alajuela 24059

DP Coordinator Jorge Araya Fonseca

Languages Spanish

T: +506 2448 50 27

W: www.liceodepoas.ed.cr

Liceo de Puriscal

Costado oeste del nuevo, Templo Católico, Santiago de Puriscal, San José 214-6000

DP Coordinator Sally Sánchez Jiménez

Languages Spanish

T: +506 2416 5424 /6163

W: www.liceodepuriscal.ed.cr

Liceo de Tarrazú

Carretera a San Pablo de León Cortés, Barrio Santa Cecilia,, 200 metros este de Coopesantos R. L., San Marcos de Tarrazú, San José 214

DP Coordinator Leonardo Vinicio Fonseca Hernández

Languages English

T: +506 25 46 60 12

W: tarrazu.edupage8.org

Liceo de Villarreal

200 metros Sur del centro de salud de Villarreal, Santa Cruz, Villarreal, Guanacaste 50309

DP Coordinator Siviany Piña Soto

Languages Spanish

T: +506 26530716

Liceo Gregorio José Ramirez Castro

200 m norte del plantel de MOPT, Montecillos de Alajuela, Alajuela

DP Coordinator Elenilzon Arroyo Bolaños

Languages Spanish

T: +506 2430 02 72

W: colegiogregoriojoseramirez.jimdo.com

Liceo Nuevo de Limón

Barrio La Colina, Contiguo a la Universidad de Costa Rica, Limón

DP Coordinator Andra Joyce Edwards Loban

Languages Spanish

T: +506 2758 09 80

Liceo Pacífico Sur

Principal hacia la Municipalidad de Osa, Cortés, Puntarenas

DP Coordinator Zaida Porras Santamaría

Languages Spanish

Liceo San Carlos

1 kilómetro al norte del parque de Ciudad Quesada, Quesada, Alajuela 21001

DP Coordinator Danny Gaitán Rodríguez

Languages English

T: +506 2460 0332

Liceo Santo Domingo

De la Clínica Dr. Hugo Fonseca, 150 Norte, San Vicente de Santo Domingo, Heredia 40302

DP Coordinator Osvaldo Molina Zamora

Languages Spanish

T: +506 2244 9549

W: www.liceosantodomingo.ed.cr

Liceo Sinaí

100 m E, de la Universidad Nacional, Sede Regional Brunca, San Isidro, Pérez Zeledón, San José

DP Coordinator Xédric Ureña Carvajal

Languages Spanish

T: +506 2770 66 69

W: www.liceosinai.com

Lighthouse International School

1 km north of the Guachipelin Tunnel, Escazú, San José 29028

DP Coordinator Amy Mishoe-Davenport

Languages English

T: +506 2215 2393

W: www.lis.ed.cr

Lincoln School

Barrio Socorro, Santo Domingo de Heredia
DP Coordinator Tucker Barrows
Languages English
T: +506 2247 6600
W: www.lincoln.ed.cr

Marian Baker School

PO Box 4269-1000, San José 1000
DP Coordinator Carolina Vargas
Languages English, Spanish
T: +506 2273 0024
W: www.mbs.ed.cr

Methodist School of Costa Rica

Sabanilla, Montes de Oca, San José 11502
DP Coordinator Guillermo Fernandez
Languages English, Spanish
T: +506 2280 1230
W: www.metodista.ed.cr

Pan-American School

632-4005 San Antonio de Belen, Heredia
DP Coordinator Henry Gutierrez
MYP Coordinator Jeff Lile
PYP Coordinator Nikki Merval
Languages English, Spanish
T: +506 2293 7393
W: www.panam.ed.cr

Saint Gregory School

San Juan de La Unión, Cartago
DP Coordinator Ivannia Brenes Flores
Languages English, Spanish
T: +1 506 2279 4444
W: www.saintgregory.cr

Saint Mary School

Apartado 1471, Escazu 1250, San José ESCAZÚ 1250
DP Coordinator Adriana Calvo Barrantes
Languages Spanish
T: +506 2215 2133
W: www.saintmary.ed.cr

Saint Paul College

San Rafael, Alajuela
DP Coordinator Catharine Whittaker
Languages English, Spanish
T: +506 2438 0824 (EXT:108)
W: www.saintpaul.ed.cr

St. Jude School

1.5 Kilometros al Oeste de Davivienda, Santa Ana, San José 488-6150
DP Coordinator Paula Forero
Languages Spanish
T: +506 2203 6474
W: www.stjude.ed.cr

The British School of Costa Rica

PO Box 8184, San José 1000
DP Coordinator Sundey Christensen
Languages English
T: +506 2220 0131
W: www.thebritishschoolofcostarica.com

UWC Costa Rica

De la esquina sureste de la Iglesia Católica, 400m al norte, Santa Ana, San José 10901
DP Coordinator Ben Fugill
Languages Spanish, English
T: +506 22825609
W: www.uwccostarica.org

Yorkín School

800 metros sur y 200 metros este de la casa de Doña Lela, Lomas de Ayarco Sur, Curridabat, San José 11801
DP Coordinator Harold Molina Venegas
Languages Spanish
T: +506 4000 8900
W: yorkin.org/site

CURAÇAO

International School of Curaçao

PO Box 3090, Koninginnelaan z/n, Emmastad
DP Coordinator Suhasini Iyengar
MYP Coordinator Daniel Cwik
Languages English
T: +599 9 737 3633
W: www.isc.cw

DOMINICAN REPUBLIC

Babeque Secundaria

Roberto Pastoriza #329, Ens. Naco, Distrito Nacional, Santo Domingo 10124
DP Coordinator Grace Baez
Languages Spanish
T: +1 809 567 9647
W: babequesecundaria.edu.do

Comunidad Educativa Conexus

Máximo Avilés Blonda 34, Evaristo, Santo Domingo
DP Coordinator Victor Hidalgo
Languages English, Spanish
T: +1 809 334 5634
W: www.conexus.edu.do

Instituto Iberia

José Giménez Miralles 12, Santiago De Los Caballeros 51054
DP Coordinator Jorge Hernández Valiente
Languages English, Spanish
T: +1 809 736 9111
W: www.iberia.edu.do

Saint George School

C/ Porfirio Herrera #6, Ens. Piantini, Santo Domingo
DP Coordinator Jose Montilla
Languages English, Spanish
T: +1 809 562 5262
W: www.stgeorge.do

DUTCH CARIBBEAN

St Dominic High School

LB Scot Road # 209, South Reward, St Maarten
DP Coordinator Marie Richardson
Languages English
T: +1 721 548 4277
W: www.stdominichigh.com

ECUADOR

Academia Cotopaxi American International School

PO Box 17-11-6510, Quito, Pichincha
DP Coordinator Harrison Shulman
PYP Coordinator Chanda Pinsent
Languages English
T: +593 (0)2 382 3270
W: www.cotopaxi.k12.ec

Academia Naval Almirante Illingworth

Ave José Gómez Gault KM 8 1/2, Vía Daule, Guayaquil, Guayas
DP Coordinator Betsy Medina
Languages Spanish
T: +593 (0)4 3703300
W: www.anai.edu.ec

APC Unidad Educativa

Imbabura 156-09 y Sucre, Loja
DP Coordinator Maria Angelina Orellana Aguilar
Languages Spanish
T: +593 7 257 3081
W: www.apc.edu.ec

Atenas Unidad Educativa

Calle Gabriel Roman y Av. Pedro Vasconez, Yacupamba, Izamba, Ambato, Tungurahua EC 180156
DP Coordinator Belén Quintana
Languages English, Spanish
T: +593 3 285 4297
W: www.atenas.edu.ec

Centro Educativo La Moderna

Km 2,5 Vía a Samborondón, Guayaquil, Guayas
DP Coordinator Harold Sojos
Languages English, Spanish
T: +593 42830581
W: www.lamoderna.edu.ec

Centro Educativo Naciones Unidas

Samborondón Km. 1 detrás del C.C. La Piazza, Samborondón, Guayas EC 092301
DP Coordinator Johanna Catalina Guachichullca Bohorquez
MYP Coordinator Carmen Cornejo Robelly
PYP Coordinator Heydy Lara Rodriguez
Languages English, Spanish
T: +593 (0)4 6018560
W: www.cenu.edu.ec

Colegio Alemán Humboldt - DS Samborondón

Av. Ing. León Febres-Cordero #4571, Ciudad Celeste, Samborondón, Guayas EC 090902
DP Coordinator Paola Gomez
Languages Spanish, German
T: +593 (4) 259 7800
W: www.alemanhumboldt.edu.ec

Colegio Alemán Humboldt de Guayaquil

Ciudadela Los Ceibos, Dr. Héctor Romero 216 y Av. Dr. José M. García Moreno, Guayaquil, Guayas EC 090904
DP Coordinator Nataniela Barreiro
Languages Spanish, German, English
T: +593 (0)4 2850260
W: www.cahgye.edu.ec

Colegio Alemán Stiehle Cuenca Ecuador

Autopista Cuenca - Azogues, Km 11,5, Sector Challuabamba, Cuenca, Azuay
DP Coordinator Susanna Wehner
Languages Spanish
T: +593 (0)7 4075646
W: www.casc.edu.ec

Colegio Americano De Guayaquil

Direccion General, Casilla 3304, Guayaquil, Guayas
DP Coordinator Whymper León Kuffó
Languages Spanish, English
T: +593 (0)4 3082 020
W: www.colegioamericano.edu.ec

Colegio Americano de Quito

Casilla 17-01-157, Quito, Pichincha
DP Coordinator David Weaver
MYP Coordinator Ana Maria Ricaurte
PYP Coordinator Estela Proaño
Languages English
T: +593 (0)2 3976 300
W: www.fcaq.k12.ec

ECUADOR

Colegio Balandra Cruz del Sur

Perimeter Road, The Prosperina, Guayaquil, Guayas
DP Coordinator Margarita Guillén Jiménez
Languages Spanish
T: +593 (0)4 285 0020
W: www.balandra.edu.ec

Colegio Becquerel

Tulipanes E12-50 y Los Rosales, Quito, Pichincha
DP Coordinator Ximena Del Pozo Espinosa
Languages Spanish
T: +593 (0)2 2257896
W: www.becquerel.edu.ec

Colegio Católico José Engling

Calle Juan Montalvo s/n, Barrio La Dolorosa, Tumbaco, Quito, Pichincha EC 17172010
DP Coordinator Ana Cristina Sevilla
Languages English, Spanish
T: +593 (0)2 237 4329
W: www.jengling.org

Colegio Experimental Británico Internacional

Amagasí del Inca, Calle de las Nueces E18-21, y Las Camelias, Quito, Pichincha
DP Coordinator Paola Morillo
MYP Coordinator Maria Brioso Augustin
PYP Coordinator Gabriela Gonzalez
Languages English, Spanish
T: +593 (0)2 3261254
W: www.colegiobritanico.edu.ec

Colegio Fiscomisional 'San José'

Calle Juan Montalvo y Misión Josefina, Tena, Napo
DP Coordinator Blanca Coello Guijarro
Languages Spanish
T: +593 06 288 6241

Colegio Internacional Rudolf Steiner

Calle Francisco Montalvo Nro 212, y Av Mariscal Sucre, (Av Occidental), Sector Cochabamba, Quito, Pichincha
DP Coordinator Fernando Rojas Aguilar
MYP Coordinator Clara Santillan
PYP Coordinator Martha Puga Cevallos
Languages Spanish
T: +593 2244 3315
W: www.colegiorudolfsteiner.edu.ec

Colegio Internacional SEK Ecuador

De los Guayacanes N51-69 y Carmen Olmo Mancebo, San Isidro de El Inca, Quito, Pichincha
DP Coordinator Marcelo Pérez
MYP Coordinator Carla Flores Dulce
PYP Coordinator Teresa Piedra
Languages English, Spanish
T: +593 2 2401 896
W: www.sekquito.com

Colegio Internacional SEK Guayaquil

Vía Salinas Km. 20.5, Guayaquil, Guayas EC 11373
DP Coordinator Hoover Mora
PYP Coordinator Marjorie Ladines
Languages Spanish, English
T: +593 4 3904794
W: www.sekguayaquil.com

Colegio Internacional SEK Los Valles

Eloy Alfaro S8-48 y De los Rosales, San Juan de Cumbayá, Quito, Pichincha EC 1717933
DP Coordinator Diana Bazurto Vergara
PYP Coordinator Mercedes Flores
Languages Spanish
T: +593 2 3566220
W: www.seklosvalles.ec

Colegio Intisana

Avenida Occidental 5329, y Marcos Joffre, Quito, Pichincha
DP Coordinator Diego Astudillo Cervantes
Languages Spanish
T: +593 2 2440 128
W: www.intisana.com

Colegio Letort

Los Guayabos Nro E 13-05 y Farsalias, San Isidro del Inca, Quito, Pichincha
DP Coordinator Lucía Carolina Pinzón Posada
MYP Coordinator Ana Maldonado
PYP Coordinator Cristina Gomez
Languages Spanish
T: +593 2 326 0202
W: www.colegioletort.edu.ec

Colegio Los Pinos

Calle Agustín Zambrano entre Vicente Pajuelo y Tomás Chariove, Quito, Pichincha EC 170104
DP Coordinator Idanelys Beltrán
Languages Spanish
T: +593 2 246 3189
W: www.colegiolospinos.ec

Colegio Municipal Experimental 'Sebastián de Benalcázar'

RECTORADO, Irlanda E10-77 y Av 6 de Diciembre, Apartado Postal 17-01-25-37, Quito, Pichincha
DP Coordinator Ramón Humberto Flores Pozo
Languages Spanish
T: +593 2 243 5313

Colegio Nacional Chordeleg

Juan Bautista Cobos y Gabriel Espinoza, Chordeleg, Azuay
DP Coordinator Maria Mercedes Lazo Carpio
Languages Spanish
T: +593 07222 3520

Colegio Nacional Primero de Abril

Calle Hnas Páez Oriente, Latacunga, Cotopaxi
DP Coordinator Teresa Jara
Languages Spanish
T: +593 3 2801610

Colegio Nacional Técnico Agropecuario '26 de Febrero'

Vía Interoceánica e India Pau, Paute, Azuay
DP Coordinator Efren Escandon
Languages English
T: +593 0722 50200

Colegio Séneca

Calle Juan Díaz y Paseo de la Universidad # 20, Urb. Iñaquito Alto, Quito, Pichincha EC 170523
DP Coordinator Paola Jaramillo
T: +593 22 922 544
W: www.seneca.edu.ec

Colegio Stella Maris

Avenida 6 y Calle 14, Manta, Manabí
DP Coordinator Valeria Sandoval Santacruz
Languages Spanish
T: +593 5 2611352
W: smaris.edu.ec

EducaMundo

Km 12 Av. León Febres-Cordero, Urb. Villa Club, entre las etapas Aura y Doral, Guayaquil, Guayas
DP Coordinator Alberto Ulises Ottati Baquero
Languages English, Spanish
T: +593 4372 5860
W: www.educamundo.edu.ec

EMDI School

EMDI sector B, Parroquia Alangasi, Valle de los Chilos, Quito, Pichincha
DP Coordinator Enrique Segovia
Languages English, Spanish
T: +593 2278 8652
W: www.emdischool.edu.ec/pags/inicio/inicio.html

Escuela Particular Liceo Panamericano - Sede Centenario

Dolores Sucre 302 y Nicolás Augusto González, Guayaquil
PYP Coordinator Eddna Peñafiel
Languages English, Spanish
T: +593 (0)4 3707888
W: liceopanamericano.edu.ec

Instituto Tecnologico Fiscomisional 'Nuestra Señora del Rosario'

9 DE Octubre y Eugenio Espejo, Catamayo, Loja EC 110301
DP Coordinator Narciza Quesada
Languages English
T: +593 0726 77024
W: www.tecnologicorosarista.edu.ec

ISM Academy Quito

San Miguel de Anagaes, Quito, Pichincha EC 170124
DP Coordinator Sandra Acosta
MYP Coordinator Lucia Guevara Espinosa
Languages Spanish
T: +593 2 2414 198
W: www.ism.edu.ec

ISM International Academy

Calle Unión 886 y Ave Geovanny Calle, Sector Calderon, Quito, Pichincha
DP Coordinator Julio Quinteros
MYP Coordinator Llania Castro
Languages English, Spanish
T: +593 2 282 0549
W: www.ism.edu.ec

Johannes Kepler

Av. Simón Bolívar s/n Vía a Nayón, Sector Bosque Protector Bellavista, Quito, Pichincha EC 170511
DP Coordinator Fernando Torres Usechi
Languages Spanish
T: +593 2 394 4180
W: www.jkepler.edu.ec

La Salle Conocoto

Av. Abdón Calderón S18 - 104, Conocoto, Quito, Pichincha EC 170156
DP Coordinator Adriana Carolina Ruiz Báez
Languages English, Spanish
T: +593 2 234 2115
W: www.lasalleconocoto.edu.ec

La Salle Latacunga

Calle Quijano y Ordoñez 532, Y Av. General Maldonado, Latacunga, Cotopaxi EC 050104
DP Coordinator Consuelo Acosta
Languages English
T: +593 32 807 884 / +593 32 801 333
W: www.lasallelatacunga.edu.ec

 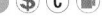

Liceo del Valle

km 1 vía a Pintag, Valle de los Chillos, Quito, Pichincha
DP Coordinator María de Lourdes Ochoa Delgado
MYP Coordinator Marta Salomé Moscoso Sánchez
PYP Coordinator Ma. Belén Arroyo
Languages Spanish
T: +593 2 2330703
W: www.liceodelvalle.edu.ec

Liceo José Ortega y Gasset

Calle de los Cipreses N64-332 y Manuel Ambrosi, Quito, Pichincha EC 170309
DP Coordinator Víctor Regalado Bolaños
Languages Spanish
T: +593 22482976
W: www.gasset.edu.ec

Liceo Panamericano Internacional

Km 3.5 vía Samborondón, Samborondon, Guayas
DP Coordinator Nadia Salmon
PYP Coordinator Erika Arguello
Languages English
T: +593 04 3707888
W: www.liceopanamericano.edu.ec

Logos Academy

Km 14.5 Via a la Costa, Guayaquil, Guayas
DP Coordinator Mariella Coral
Languages Spanish
T: +59 34 390 0125
W: www.logosacademy.edu.ec

Ludoteca Elementary & High School, Padre Victor Grados

Av Simón Bolívar y Camino de los Incas # 5-6, Nueva Vía Oriental, Quito, Pichincha
DP Coordinator Roberto Rojas
MYP Coordinator Amparo de Jesus Albán Grados
PYP Coordinator Gloria Rebeca Bedon Criollo
Languages English, Spanish
T: +593 2 268 8142
W: ludoteca.edu.ec

Martim Cererê Unidad Educativa Particular Bilingüe

De Los Guayacanes N51-01, y Los Álamos, Quito, Pichincha EC 170150
DP Coordinator Zoili Noboa
Languages English, Spanish
T: +593 2 380 2980
W: www.martimcerere.edu.ec

The British School Quito

Via Cununyacu, Km 2.5 Tumbaco, PO Box 17-21-52, Quito, Pichincha
DP Coordinator Paola Montenegro
Languages English
T: +593 2 2 374 649
W: www.britishschoolquito.edu.ec

Unidad Educativa Alberto Einstein

Av Diego Vásquez de Cepeda N77-157 y Alberto Einstein, Casilla Postal 17-11-5018, Quito, Pichincha
DP Coordinator Leonor Alvarez Herrera
MYP Coordinator Jorge Grijalva
PYP Coordinator Ana Maldonado
Languages Spanish, English
T: +593 2 393 2570
W: www.einstein.k12.ec

Unidad Educativa Atahualpa

Calle El Tejar y Avenida, 22 de Enero, Ambato, Tungurahua
DP Coordinator Narcisa Gardenia Rosero Núñez
Languages English
T: +593 03 2855812
W: www.colegioatahualpaambato.edu.ec

Unidad Educativa Bilingüe Delta

Kilómetro 12.5 Vía Puntilla-Samborondón, Guayaquil, Guayas
DP Coordinator Monica Macchiavello
Languages English, Spanish
T: +593 4 251 1266
W: www.uedelta.k12.ec

Unidad Educativa Bilingüe Hontanar

Calle El Canelo E17-121 y Las Nueces, Sector Amagasí del Inca., Quito
DP Coordinator Juan Francisco García Suárez
Languages English, Spanish
T: +593 2 3261 264
W: www.hontanar.edu.ec

Unidad Educativa Bilingüe Mixta Sagrados Corazones

El Oro 1219 y Avenida Quito, Guayaquil, Guayas
DP Coordinator Neyla Mora Rosales
Languages Spanish
T: +593 04 2440087
W: www.sscc.edu.ec

Unidad Educativa Bilingüe Nueva Semilla

Barrio Centenario Calle D and Argüelles, Guayaquil, Guayas
DP Coordinator Carolina Aldaz
Languages English
T: +593 4 2441174
W: www.nuevasemilla.com.ec

Unidad Educativa Bilingüe Nuevo Mundo

Calle Celeste Blacio de Rendón #112, y Km. 2,5 Vía Samborondón, Guayaquil, Guayas
DP Coordinator Fernando Castro
MYP Coordinator Mónica Aragundi
Languages English, Spanish
T: +593 4 2 830 095
W: www.nuevomundo.edu.ec

Unidad Educativa Bilingüe William Caxton College

Moises Luna Andrade y Calle 6, Quito, Pichincha EC 170144
DP Coordinator Paola Maldonado Sánchez
Languages English, Spanish
T: +593 2 340 6309
W: www.williamcaxton.edu.ec

Unidad Educativa Cristo Rey

Calle Cristo Rey entre Sucre y Baquerizo Moreno, Portoviejo, Manabí EC 13010014
DP Coordinator Carlos Orozco
Languages Spanish
T: +593 052632558
W: www.cristorey.edu.ec

Unidad Educativa 'Émile Jaques-Dalcroze'

Av. Ilaló y Río Pastaza No. 777, Valle de Los Chillos, Quito, Pichincha
DP Coordinator Sara Arroba Benítez
MYP Coordinator Andrea Torres Ramos
Languages Spanish
T: +593 2 2861 500
W: ejd.edu.ec

Unidad Educativa Internacional Pensionado Atahualpa

El Milagro, San Jose de Cananvalle S/N, Ibarra, Imbabura EC 100150
DP Coordinator Geovanna del Rocío Andrade Tapia
Languages Spanish
T: +593 6 2 542 115

Unidad Educativa Isaac Newton

Guayabos N50-120 y Los Álamos, Quito, Pichincha EC 170149
DP Coordinator Rosario Llerena
Languages Spanish
T: +593 22405001
W: www.isaacnewton.edu.ec

Unidad Educativa 'Isabel de Godín'

Juan de Velasco S/N y Alfonso Villagomez, Riobamba, Chimborazo
DP Coordinator Fernando Garcia
Languages Spanish
T: +593 3294 3843
W: subacadib.wixsite.com/website

Unidad Educativa 'Julio Verne'

De Los Nopales #58 Y De Los Helechos, Quito, Pichincha EC 170150
DP Coordinator Lucia del Carmen Aguinaga Cáceres
Languages English, Spanish
T: +593 2280 7117
W: www.julioverne.edu.ec

Unidad Educativa Maurice Ravel

Av. Cantabria OE2-18 y Av. Cacha (Sector San José de Morán), Quito, Pichincha EC 170155
DP Coordinator América Apolo
Languages Spanish
T: +593 2 202 3508
W: mauriceravel.edu.ec

Unidad Educativa Monte Tabor Nazaret

Km 13.5 Via Samborondón, Guayaquil, Guayas
DP Coordinator Lorena Arriaga
PYP Coordinator Virginia Lozada
Languages English, Spanish
T: +593 4 259 0370
W: www.montetabornazaret.edu.ec

Unidad Educativa Municipal del Milenio Bicentenario

Av. El Beaterio y Calle E2D, Quito, Pichincha EC 170150
DP Coordinator Maribel Jessenia Coello Almagro
Languages English
T: +593 2269 8620
W: www.educacion.quito.gob.ec/unidades/bicentenario

Unidad Educativa Naval Comandante César Endara Peñaherrera

Pasaje El Prado No. 1-192 y Av. González Suárez, Quito, Pichincha EC 170156
DP Coordinator Carmen Susana Miranda Coronel
Languages Spanish

ECUADOR

Unidad Educativa Particular Bilingüe Ecomundo

Av. Juan Tanca Marengo Km 2, Guayaquil, Guayas EC 90112
DP Coordinator Tannya Cardenas
MYP Coordinator Karrie Orellana
Languages English
T: +593 4 3703700 (Ext:115-118)
W: www.ecomundo.edu.ec

Unidad Educativa Particular Bilingüe Leonardo da Vinci

Vía a San Mateo Km. 2.4, a 100 metros de la Urbanización Ciudad del Mar, Manta, Manabí EC 130802
DP Coordinator Rubén Muñoz Pérez
Languages Spanish
T: +593 5 3 700 865
W: www.ueldv.edu.ec

Unidad Educativa Particular Bilingüe Principito y Marcel Laniado de Wind

Avenida Luis Ángel León Roman y 1era Avenida 5ta, Machala, El Oro EC 0701835
DP Coordinator Diego Ayala Anzoátegui
Languages English
T: +593 72981881
W: www.ueprim.edu.ec

Unidad Educativa Particular Bilingüe Santo Domingo de Guzmán

Calle 5ta # 608 y Las Monjas (URDESA), Guayaquil, Guayas
DP Coordinator Isaac Augusto Caicedo Vera
Languages Spanish
T: +593 2 882 561
W: www.stodomingo.edu.ec

Unidad Educativa Particular Hermano Miguel De La Salle

Av. Solano 7-01 y Luis Moreno Mora, Cuenca, Azuay
DP Coordinator Bernardita Vinueza
Languages English, Spanish
T: +593 7 281 0349
W: www.delasallecuenca.edu.ec

Unidad Educativa Particular Javier

Km 5.5 vía a la Costa, Guayaquil, Guayas
DP Coordinator Natalia Patino
Languages Spanish
T: +593 4 2001590/3520/0724
W: www.uejavier.com

Unidad Educativa Particular Politécnico

Campus Politécnico 'Gustavo Galindo Velasco', Km. 30.5 vía Perimetral, contiguo a Ceibos Norte, Guayaquil, Guayas
DP Coordinator Linda García Muñoz
MYP Coordinator Roxana Mariuxi Guamanquispe Intriago
PYP Coordinator Mónica Lasso Gallo
Languages Spanish
T: +593 4 226 9654
W: www.copol.edu.ec

Unidad Educativa Particular Redemptio

10 de Agosto 701 entre Colón y Juan Montalvo, Jipijapa, Manabí
DP Coordinator Gustavo Bykovsky Cañarte Gutiérrez
Languages English, Spanish
T: +593 5 2 600 475
W: www.redemptio.edu.ec

Unidad Educativa Particular 'Rosa de Jesús Cordero'

Parroquia Ricaurte, Sector el Tablón, Cuenca, Azuay EC 010162
DP Coordinator María José González
Languages Spanish
T: +593 7 2890503
W: www.catalinas.edu.ec

Unidad Educativa Paul Dirac

Av. Pedro Vicente Maldonado y la Cocha, Quito, Pichincha EC 170146
DP Coordinator Carmen Ramirez
Languages English, Spanish
T: +593 2 691 241 (Ext:1)
W: www.pauldirac.edu.ec

Unidad Educativa Sagrados Corazones de Rumipamba

Av. Atahualpa Oe1-20 y Av. 10 de Agosto, Quito, Pichincha EC 170521
DP Coordinator Cesar Patricio Montúfar Flores
Languages Spanish
T: +593 22 442 242
W: rumipamba.edu.ec

Unidad Educativa Saint Dominic School

César Davila N10-222 y Charles Darwin, Quito, Pichincha
DP Coordinator Francisco Flores Checa
Languages Spanish
T: +593 (0)2 3959960
W: www.saintdominic.edu.ec

Unidad Educativa Salesiana Cardenal Spellman

Mercadillo OE340 y Ulloa, Quito, Pichincha EC 1703125
DP Coordinator Alejandro Vinces
Languages Spanish
T: +593 2 3560 001/2/3
W: www.spellman.edu.ec

Unidad Educativa San Francisco de Sales

Av. Cristobal Colón E10-07 y Tamayo, Quito, Pichincha
DP Coordinator Andrea Sofía Narváez Ruano
Languages English, Spanish
T: +593 2903 861
W: frsales.edu.ec

Unidad Educativa San Jose La Salle

Tomás Martínez 501 y Baquerizo Moreno, Guayaquil, Guayas EC 090150
DP Coordinator Luiggi Saenz de Viteri
Languages Spanish
T: +593 4 25 631 37
W: lasalleguayaquil.edu.ec

Unidad Educativa San Martín

Calle Sigsipamba S-2159 y Picoazá, Quito, Pichincha EC 170613
DP Coordinator Miriam Zambrano Macías
Languages Spanish
T: +593 (0)2 3080979
W: www.sanmartin.edu.ec

Unidad Educativa Santana

Av. los Cerezos S/N y vía a Racar, Cuenca, Azuay
DP Coordinator Xavier Tenorio Sánchez
Languages Spanish
T: +593 7 4121879
W: www.santana.edu.ec

Unidad Educativa Terranova

Calle De Los Rieles 507, y Ave Simón Bolívar, San Juan Alto de Cumbayá, Quito, Pichincha
DP Coordinator Farah Jalile Mahauad Wittmer
MYP Coordinator Farah Jalile Mahauad Wittmer
PYP Coordinator Maria Tello Miño
Languages English, Spanish, French
T: +593 2 356 4000
W: www.colegioterranova.com.ec

Unidad Educativa Tomás Moro

Av De Las Orquideas E13-120, y De Los Guayacanes, Quito, Pichincha
DP Coordinator Jacqueline Rivadeneira Jaramillo
MYP Coordinator Ligia Rosales
PYP Coordinator Isabel Alcivar
Languages Spanish
T: +593 2 2405357
W: www.tomasmoro.ec

Unidad Educativo Bilingüe CEBI

Calle Modesto Chacón y Av. Pedro Vásconez Sevilla, Parroquia Izamba, Ambato, Tungurahua
DP Coordinator Rodrigo Naranjo
MYP Coordinator Maria Eugenia Fierro Echeverria
PYP Coordinator Cecilia Lopez
Languages Spanish, English
T: +593 3 373 0370
W: www.cebi.edu.ec

Victoria Bilingual Christian Academy

Melchor de Valdez Oe-9240, Pbx: 253-6116, Quito, Pichincha EC 170528
DP Coordinator Sarah Catalina Ingman Bastidas
Languages Spanish
T: +593 (0)2 2536116
W: victoriaacademy.edu.ec

Young Living Academy

Km. 24 vía a la Costa, Chongoncito, Guayaquil, Guayas
DP Coordinator Verónica Alexandra Piguave Ruiz
Languages English, Spanish
T: +593 9965 4897
W: www.younglivingacademy.edu.ec

EL SALVADOR

Academia Britanica Cuscatleca

Apartado Postal 121, Santa Tecla, La Libertad
DP Coordinator Sarah Diebelius
Languages English
T: +503 2201 6222/6252/6261
W: www.abc.edu.sv

Colegio La Floresta

Estamos en el Km. 13 1/2, Carretera al Puerto de La Libertad
DP Coordinator Laura Calderón
Languages English
T: +503 2534 8800
W: www.lafloresta.edu.sv

Colegio Lamatepec

Carretera al Puerto de La Libertad Km 12.5, Calle Nueva a Comasauga Santa Tecla, La Libertad, San Salvador
DP Coordinator Alfonso Humberto Castillo Mejía
Languages English, Spanish
T: +503 2534 8900
W: www.lamatepec.edu.sv

Deutsche Schule - Escuela Alemana San Salvador

Calle del Mediterráneo, Jardines de Guadalupe, Antiguo Cuscatlán, San Salvador CA
DP Coordinator Beatriz Dreyer
Languages Spanish
T: +503 2243 4898
W: www.ds.edu.sv

Centro Escolar Campoalegre

35 Calle and 12 Av Final, Zona 11, Código 01011
DP Coordinator Angela María Gabriela Martínez Orti
Languages English, Spanish
T: +502 2380 3900
W: www.campoalegre.edu.gt

Centro Escolar 'El Roble'

11 Avenida Sur Final Zona 11, Guatemala City 01011
DP Coordinator Luis Fernando Micheo Hernández
Languages Spanish
T: +502 2387 7000
W: www.ceroble.edu.gt

Centro Escolar Entrevalles

Km. 16.8 Antigua Carretera a El Salvador, Santa Catarina Pinula
DP Coordinator Aida Camacho
Languages Spanish, English
T: +502 6685 4700
W: www.entrevalles.edu.gt

Centro Escolar Solalto

Km. 22.5 Carretera a Fraijanes, Fraijanes
DP Coordinator Juan Carlos Velásquez Valladares
Languages English, Spanish
T: +502 6686 0500
W: www.solalto.edu.gt

The American School of Tegucigalpa

P.O. Box 2134, Tegucigalpa
DP Coordinator Daniel Dobbe
Languages English
T: +504 2276 8400
W: www.amschool.org

American International School of Kingston

2 College Green Avenue, Kingston
DP Coordinator Sophie Kropman
Languages English
T: +1 876 702 2070
W: www.aisk.com

Hillel Academy

PO Box 2687, 51 Upper Mark Way, Kingston 8
DP Coordinator Pauladene Steele
Languages English
T: +1 876 925 1980
W: hillelacademyjm.com/

Alexander Bain Colegio

Barranca de Pilares 29, Colonia Tlacopac, San Angel, México D.F. C.P. 01040
PYP Coordinator Loren Karam Karam
Languages Spanish
T: +52 55 5595 0493
W: www.colegioab.mx

American School Foundation of Chiapas

Blvd. Belisario Dominguez 5588-F, Fraccion Las Cinco Plumas, Terán, Tuxtla Gutierrez, Chiapas C.P. 29052
PYP Coordinator Aurora Topete
Languages English, Spanish
T: +52 961 346 4840
W: www.americanschool.edu.mx

Avalon International School

Av. San Jerónimo 1135, San Jerónimo de Lídice La Magdalena Contreras, Mexico D.F. C.P. 10200
PYP Coordinator Claudia Heimpel
Languages English, Spanish
T: +52 555 595 5582
W: avalon-school.mx

Bachillerato 5 de Mayo

Ave. del Trabajo # 6, Cuautlancingo, Puebla C.P. 72700
DP Coordinator María Del Rosario Ayala Rojas
Languages English
T: +52 222 2295500 EXT:2770
W: cmas.siu.buap.mx/portal_pprd/wb/b5mayo/inicio

Bachillerato Alexander Bain, SC

Las Flores 497, Tlacopac, San Ángel, Ciudad de México C.P. 01049
DP Coordinator Beatriz Marquez Navarro
MYP Coordinator Ana Elia Hernández
Languages Spanish, English, French
T: +52 (55) 5683 2911
W: www.bab.edu.mx

Bachillerato UPAEP Atlixco

Camino a la Uvera #2004, Ex-Hacienda La Blanca, 74365 Atlixco, Puebla
CP Coordinator Marco Emilio Domínguez Chánez
Languages English, Spanish
T: +52 244 445 1991
W: upaep.mx//prepa/atlixco

Bachillerato UPAEP San Martín

C/ Lardizabal s/n Col. La Purisima, San Martín Texmelucan, Puebla C.P. 74030
CP Coordinator Maria Del Rosario Rojas Rojas
Languages English, Spanish
W: upaep.mx/prepa/san-martin

Bachillerato UPAEP Santa Ana

Avenida Tecpanxochitl 52 A, San Pedro Tlalcuapan, Chiautempan, Tlaxcala C.P. 90845
CP Coordinator Elia Zempoaltecatl Ramírez
Languages English, Spanish
T: +52 246 46 496 33
W: upaep.mx/prepa/santa-ana

British American School S.C.

Fuente del Niño #16 Col. Tecamachalco, Naucalpan de Juárez, Estado de México C.P. 53950
PYP Coordinator María Guadalupe Antimo Rivera
Languages English
T: +55 52 94 37 21
W: www.british.edu.mx

Centro de Educación Media de la Universidad Autónoma de Aguascalientes

Av de la Convencion Esq, Con Av Independencia S/N Fraccionamiento Norte, Aguascalientes C.P. 20020
DP Coordinator Diana Cecilia Diaz Dena
Languages Spanish
T: +52 01 449 9 147708
W: www.uaa.mx/centros/cem/

Centro de Enseñanza Técnica y Superior - Campus Mexicali

Calzada del Cetys S/N, Colonia Rivera, Mexicali, Baja California C.P. 21259
DP Coordinator Gerardo Lopez Verdugo
Languages Spanish
T: +52 686 567 3704
W: www.cetys.mx

Centro de Ensenanza Tecnica y Superior - Campus Tijuana

Av. CETYS Universidad, No. 4 Fracc. El Lago, Tijuana, Baja California C.P. 22210
DP Coordinator Paulina Bueno
Languages Spanish
T: +52 664 903 1800
W: www.cetys.mx

Centro de Investigación y Desarrollo de Educación Bilingüe

Lázaro Cárdenas Al Ote, Sin Número, Unidad Mederos, Monterrey, Nuevo León C.P. 64930
DP Coordinator Jorge Jesús López Castro
Languages Spanish
T: +52 818 3294180
W: cideb.uanl.mx

Centro Educativo Alexander Bain Irapuato

Enrique del Moral Domínguez 335, Ejido Lo de Juárez, 36630, Irapuato, Guanajuato
DP Coordinator María Elena Victoria Jardón
PYP Coordinator Atala Gamboa Ruiz
Languages Spanish, English
T: +52 462 114 2246
W: www.alexbain.edu.mx

Centro Educativo CRECER AC

Calle del Vecino No 3, Atlihuetzia, Yahuquehmecan, Tlaxcala C.P. 90459
PYP Coordinator Lucero Getzany Rodríguez Ovando
Languages English, Spanish
T: +52 24 646 13 148
W: www.crecer.edu.mx

Centro Escolar Instituto La Paz, SC

Av Plan de San Luis 445, Col Nueva Santa María, Ciudad de México C.P. 02800
MYP Coordinator Maribel Sánchez
PYP Coordinator Maribel Sánchez
Languages Spanish, English
T: +52 55 55 56 66 46
W: www.institutolapaz.edu.mx

Churchill College

Moctezuma 125, Colonia San Pablo Tepetlapa, Ciudad de México C.P. 04620
DP Coordinator Isabel Rangel González
Languages English
T: +52 55 56 19 82 43
W: www.cc.edu.mx

MÉXICO

Colegio Álamos

Acceso al Aeropuerto 1000, Colonia Arboledas, Santiago de Querétaro, Querétaro C.P. 76940

DP Coordinator Kevin Coll
Languages English, Spanish
T: +52 442 182 0222
W: www.colegioalamos.edu.mx

Colegio Alemán de Guadalajara

Av Bosques de los Cedros No. 32, Las Cañadas, Zapopan, Jalisco C.P. 45132

DP Coordinator Patrick Weilandt
Languages Spanish
T: +52 33 3685 0136
W: alemangdl.edu.mx

Colegio Americano de San Carlos

Blvd. Luis Encinas S/N, esquina Faustino Félix, Colonia Miramar, Guaymas, Sonora C.P. 85450

PYP Coordinator Irene Velazquez Lastra
Languages English, Spanish
T: +52 622 221 2551
W: casc.edu.mx

Colegio Anglo de las Américas

Av. 5 de Febrero 1007, Valle del Tecnológico, Lázaro Cárdenas, Michoacán C.P. 60950

PYP Coordinator Perla Ríos Ramos
Languages English, Spanish
T: +52 753 537 7274
W: www.colegioanglo.mx

Colegio Arji

Avenida México # 2, esquina Periférico, Colonia del Bosque, Villahermosa, Tabasco C.P. 86160

DP Coordinator Andrea Tellaeche Merino
MYP Coordinator Yocelin Priego
PYP Coordinator Ligia Teresa Balcázar Avilés
Languages English, Spanish
T: +52 993 3 510 250
W: www.arji.edu.mx

Colegio Atid AC

Av. Carlos Echanove #224, Col. Vista Hermosa Cuajimalpa, Ciudad de México C.P. 05100

CP Coordinator Sandra Mejia
DP Coordinator Noemi Dos Santos Andrade
MYP Coordinator Susana Garcia Herrera
PYP Coordinator Gustavo Mejía
Languages English, Spanish
T: +52 55 5814 0800
W: www.atid.edu.mx

Colegio Bilingüe Carson de Ciudad Delicias

Ave 50 Aniversario 1709, Delicias, Chihuahua C.P. 33058

PYP Coordinator Sandra Rosales Escamilla
Languages Spanish
T: +52 (639) 472 9340
W: www.colegiocarson.com

Colegio Bosques

Prol. Zaragoza No. 701, Fracc. Valle de las Trojes, Aguascalientes C.P. 20115

MYP Coordinator Karla Marisol Valencia Quiroz
PYP Coordinator Manuel Macías Flores
Languages English, Spanish
T: +52 449 162 04 05
W: www.colegiobosques.edu.mx

Colegio Británico

Calle Pargo # 24, S.M. 3, Cancun, Quintana Roo C.P. 77500

DP Coordinator Silvia Ivette Luna Barra
PYP Coordinator Maria Del Carmen Zorrilla Velázquez
Languages English
T: +52 (998) 884 1295
W: www.cbritanico.edu.mx

Colegio Celta Internacional

Libramiento Sur-Poniente Km 4+200, Colonia Los Olvera, Villa Corregidora, Querétaro C.P. 76902

CP Coordinator Claudia Edith Molleda Ortega
MYP Coordinator Alicia Silva
PYP Coordinator Ma Flora del Piar Lavin Alvarez
Languages English, Spanish
T: +52 442 227 36 00
W: www.celta.edu.mx

Colegio Ciudad de México

Campos Elíseos # 139, Col Polanco, Ciudad de México C.P. 11560

DP Coordinator Sergio Morales
MYP Coordinator Sergio Morales
PYP Coordinator Maruja Esperante
Languages Spanish
T: +52 55 5254 4053
W: www.colegiociudad.edu.mx

Colegio Ciudad de Mexico - Plantel Contadero

Calle de la Bolsa 456, El Contadero, Cuajimalpa, Ciudad de México C.P. 05500

PYP Coordinator Ana Lilia Rueda Moreno
Languages Spanish
T: +52 58 12 06 10
W: www.colegiociudad.edu.mx/contadero.html

Colegio Discovery

Circuito Interior Norte Socorro Romero, Sánchez, No. 3525, Col. San Lorenzo, Tehuacán, Puebla

DP Coordinator Violeta Juárez
MYP Coordinator Violeta López Valerio
PYP Coordinator Beatriz Rodríguez
Languages Spanish
T: +52 238 3820005
W: colegiodiscovery.edu.mx

COLEGIO EL CAMINO

Callejon del Jornongo #210, Colonia El Pedregal, Cabo San Lucas, B.C.S. C.P. 23453

DP Coordinator Isaac Pérez
PYP Coordinator Ginger Fell
Languages English, Spanish
T: +52 624 143 2100 (EXT:112)
E: info@elcamino.edu.mx
W: www.elcamino.edu.mx

See full details on page 496

Colegio Fontanar

Camino al Fraccionamiento, Vista Real 119, Corregidora, Querétaro C.P. 76900

DP Coordinator Erika Duhne
Languages Spanish
T: +52 442 228 13 65
W: www.fontanar.edu.mx

Colegio Hebreo Maguen David

Antiguo Camino a Tecamachalco #370, Lomas de Vista Hermosa, Ciudad de México

DP Coordinator Shely Finkelbrand
MYP Coordinator Naomi Rojas
PYP Coordinator Graciela Silva Escobar
Languages Spanish, Hebrew, English
T: +52 (55) 52 46 26 00
W: www.chmd.edu.mx

Colegio Hebreo Monte Sinai AC

Av Loma de la Palma 133, Col Vista Hermosa, Cuajimalpa, Ciudad de México C.P. 05109

DP Coordinator Denisse Caram
MYP Coordinator Denisse Caram
PYP Coordinator Tania Navarro Elizalde
Languages Spanish, English
T: +52 55 52 53 01 68
W: www.chms.edu.mx

Colegio Internacional de México

Río Magdalena 263, Colonia Tizapan San Ángel, Álvaro Obregón, Ciudad de México D.P. 01090

MYP Coordinator Susana Valenzuela Esquivel
PYP Coordinator Andrea Pimentel Matute
Languages English, Spanish
T: +52 55 55 50 01 01
W: www.colegiointernacional.edu.mx

Colegio Internacional SEK Guadalajara

Daniel Comboni #850, Colonia Jardines de Guadalupe, Zapopan Jalisco C.P 45030

DP Coordinator Elvia Patricia Gallegos Teran
Languages English, Spanish
T: +52 33 36202423
W: www.sekmexico.com

Colegio Internacional Terranova

Av Palmira No. 705, Privadas del Pedregal, San Luis Potosí C.P. 78295

DP Coordinator Enriqueta Pérez
MYP Coordinator Enrique Freeman Rubio
PYP Coordinator María Covarrubias Gómez
Languages Spanish
T: +52 444 8 41 64 22
W: www.terranova.edu.mx

Colegio La Paz de Chiapas

Carretera Tuxtla, Villaflores N° 1170, Tuxtla Gutiérrez, Chiapas C.P. 29089

DP Coordinator Alejandra Fraguas Castañón
MYP Coordinator Ana Cecilia Toledo Palacio
Languages Spanish
T: +52 961 663 7000
W: www.colegio-lapaz.edu.mx

Colegio Laureles Chiapas

Blvd. Paso Limón No. 1581, Zona Sin Asignación de Nombre de Col 24, Tuxtla Gutiérrez, Chiapas C.P. 29049

DP Coordinator David Gomez
Languages English, Spanish
T: +52 55 5852 9002
W: colegiolaureleschiapas.mx

Colegio Laureles Chimalhuacan

Av. Ejido Colectivo, Tlatel Xochitenco, Chimalhuacan, Estado de México C.P. 56366

DP Coordinator Fernando Morales Reyes
Languages English, Spanish
T: +52 55 5852 9002
W: www.colegiolaureles.com

Colegio Linares AC

Marina Silva de Rodriguez 1301 Pte, Colonia centro Linares, Nuevo León C.P. 67700

DP Coordinator Norma Velasco
Languages Spanish
T: +52 821 212 0269
W: www.colegiolinares.edu.mx

Colegio Madison Chihuahua

Fuente Trevi #7001, Fracc. Puerta de Hierro, Chihuahua C.P. 31205
PYP Coordinator Rossana Ortegón Alvarez
Languages English, Spanish
T: +52 614 430 1464
W: www.colegiosmadison.edu.mx/colegios-madison-chihuahua.htm

Colegio Maria Montessori de Monclova

Blvd Harold R Pape Nro 2002, Col Jardines del Valle, Monclova, Coahuila C.P. 25730
DP Coordinator Sara Aimee Montes de Oca Nolla
Languages Spanish
T: +52 866 633 2993
W: www.montessorimonclova.com

Colegio Monteverde

Av Santa Lucia No 260, Col Prados de la Montaña, Cualjimalpa, Ciudad de México C.P. 05610
DP Coordinator Fernanda Sanemeterio
Languages Spanish
T: +52 55 50819700
W: www.colegiomonteverde.edu.mx

Colegio Nuevo Continente

Nicolás San Juan 1141, Colonia Del Valle, Ciudad de México C.P. 03100
DP Coordinator Elisa Aizpuru González
Languages English, Spanish
T: +52 55 5575 4066
W: www.nuevocontinente.edu.mx

Colegio Suizo de México - Campus Cuernavaca

Calle Amates s/n, Col. Lomas de Ahuatlán, Cuernavaca, Morelos C.P. 62130
DP Coordinator Dilip Verma
Languages English, Spanish
T: +52 777 323 5252
W: www.csm.edu.mx

Colegio Suizo de México - Campus México DF

Nicolás San Juan 917, Col del Valle, Ciudad de México C.P. 03100
DP Coordinator Aurelio Reyes
Languages English, Spanish
T: +52 55 55 43 78 62
W: www.csm.edu.mx

Colegio Suizo de México - Campus Querétaro

Circ. La Cima 901, Fracc. La Cima, Santiago de Querétaro, Querétaro C.P. 76146
DP Coordinator Pilar Eugenia Carrión Fajardo
Languages Spanish, German, English
T: +52 442 254 3390
W: www.csm.edu.mx

Colegio Vista Hermosa

Bachillerato, Av Loma de Vista Hermosa 221, Cuajimalpa, Ciudad de México C.P. 05100
DP Coordinator Ramón García Govea
MYP Coordinator Viviana Calleja
Languages Spanish
T: +52 55 50914630
W: www.cvh.edu.mx

Colegio Williams

Mixcoac Campus, Empresa 8, Col Mixcoac, Alcaldía Benito Juárez, Ciudad de México C.P. 03910
DP Coordinator Laura Silva Rico
MYP Coordinator Erika Daniela Mendoza Pineda
PYP Coordinator María del Pilar González Mata
Languages Spanish
T: +52 55 1087 9797
W: www.colegiowilliams.edu.mx

Colegio Williams de Cuernavaca

Luna #32, Jardines de Cuernavaca, Cuernavaca, Morelos C.P. 62360
DP Coordinator Martha Alicia Nocetti Vilchis
MYP Coordinator Alicia Martinez Lara
PYP Coordinator María López Covarrubias
Languages English, Spanish
T: +52 (777) 3223640
W: www.cwc.edu.mx

Colegio Williams Unidad San Jerónimo

Presa Reventada No 53, Col San Jerónimo Lídice, Del. Magdalena Contreras, Ciudad de México C.P. 10400
PYP Coordinator Alejandra Silva Bringas
Languages Spanish, English
T: +52 55 1087 9797
W: www.colegiowilliams.edu.mx

Colegio Xail

Calle Xail No 10, Col. Lázaro Cárdenas, San Francisco de Campeche, Campeche C.P. 24520
MYP Coordinator Balbina Guadalupe Sosa Bautista
PYP Coordinator Susana Gómez Rodríguez
Languages Spanish
T: +52 981 813 0322
W: www.xail.edu.mx

Discovery School

Chilpancingo No 102, Colonia Vista Hermosa, Cuernavaca, Morelos C.P. 62290
PYP Coordinator Luz Gabriela Briseño Tellez
Languages English, Spanish
T: +52 777 318 5721
W: www.discovery.edu.mx

Escuela Ameyalli SC

Calzada de las Águilas 1972, Axomiatla, Ciudad de México C.P. 01820
MYP Coordinator Analía Zarate
PYP Coordinator Paula Lara
Languages English, Spanish
T: +52 55 12 85 70 20
W: www.ameyalli.edu.mx

Escuela John F. Kennedy

Av Sabinos 272, Jurica, Querétaro C.P. 76100
DP Coordinator Maria Regina Velazquez
MYP Coordinator Laura Davis
PYP Coordinator Christine Scharf
Languages English, Spanish
T: +52 442 218 0075
W: www.jfk.edu.mx

Escuela Lomas Altas S.C.

Montañas Calizas #305, Lomas de Chapultepec, Ciudad de México C.P. 11000
PYP Coordinator Humberto Rodriguez Vega
Languages English
T: +52 55 55 20 53 75/20 37 25
W: www.lomasaltas.edu.mx

Escuela Mexicana Americana, A. C.

Gabriel Mancera 1611, Col. Del Valle, Ciudad de México C.P. 03100
DP Coordinator Eva Raquel López Jiménez
Languages English, Spanish
T: +52 55 240214
W: mexicanaamericana.edu.mx

Escuela Preparatoria Federal 'Lázaro Cárdenas'

Paseo de los Héroes #11161, Zona Rio, Tijuana, Baja California C.P. 22010
DP Coordinator Gustavo Enrique Camargo Negrete
Languages Spanish
T: +52 664 686 12 97
W: www.lazarocardenas.edu.mx

Eton, SC

Domingo García Ramos s/n, Col. Prados de la Montaña, Santa Fe, Cuajimalpa, Ciudad de México C.P. 05619
DP Coordinator Laura Alicia Salazar
MYP Coordinator Rosa María Olmos
Languages English, Spanish
T: +52 5 261 5800
W: www.eton.edu.mx

Formus

Cañón de la Mesa 6745, Monterrey, Nuevo León C.P. 64898
MYP Coordinator Aracely Garza Montes
Languages Spanish
T: +52 8317 8560
W: www.formus.edu.mx

Fundación Colegio Americano de Puebla

Av 9 Pte 2709, La Paz, Puebla C.P. 72160
CP Coordinator Enrique Cordero
DP Coordinator Emily Ueland
MYP Coordinator Christopher Collupy
PYP Coordinator Shannon Hickey
Languages English, Spanish
T: +52 22 2303 0400
W: www.cap.edu.mx

GREENGATES SCHOOL

Av. Circunvalación Pte. 102, Balcones de San Mateo, Naucalpan, Estado de México C.P. 53200
DP Coordinator David Grant
Languages English
T: +52 55 5373 0088
E: kuroda@greengates.edu.mx
W: www.greengates.edu.mx

See full details on page 506

Greenville International School

Prolongación Arco Noroeste s/n, Colonia González 1ra Sección, Villahermosa, Tabasco C.P. 86039
DP Coordinator Gerardo Ramírez
MYP Coordinator Alma Garcia
PYP Coordinator Silvia Gonzalez Cuevas
Languages English
T: +52 993 310 8060
W: www.greenville.edu.mx

Harmony School

Mariano Narváez 414, Col. Los Alpes Norte, Saltillo, Coahuila C.P 25253
PYP Coordinator Perla Patricia Rubio
Languages English, Spanish
T: +52 84 4485 5598
W: www.harmonyschool.mx

Humanitree

725 Sierra Madre, Lomas de Chapultepec, Miguel Hidalgo, Ciudad de México C.P. 11000
DP Coordinator Sue Ellingham
Languages English, Spanish
T: +52 55 8620 7301
W: www.humanitree.edu.mx

Instituto Alexander Bain SC

Cascada 320, Jardines del Pedregal, Ciudad de México
MYP Coordinator Beatriz Delia Marquez Navarro
PYP Coordinator Loxá Tamayo Márquez
Languages Spanish, English
T: +52 55 5595 6579
W: www.alexanderbain.edu.mx

MÉXICO

Instituto Anglo Británico Campus Cumbres

Paseo de los leones 7001, Avenida Bosque de las Lomas, Valle de Cumbres, García, Nuevo León C.P. 66035

PYP Coordinator Mrs Alejandra Tijerina Reyna

Languages English, Spanish

T: +52 81 8526 2222

W: www.colegiosmadison.edu.mx/instituto-anglo-britanico-campus-cumbres.htm

Instituto Anglo Británico Campus La Fe

Av. Isidoro Sepúlveda #555, Col. La Encarnación, Apodaca, Nuevo León C.P. 66633

MYP Coordinator Hiram Cisneros R

PYP Coordinator Brunhi Gebauer

Languages English, Spanish

T: +52 8183 21 5000

W: www.iab.edu.mx

Instituto Bilingüe Rudyard Kipling

Cruz de Valle Verde No 25, Santa Cruz del Monte, Naucalpan, Estado de México C.P. 53110

DP Coordinator Magali Guerrero Olvera

MYP Coordinator Sandra Lorena Padró Torres

PYP Coordinator Silvia Garcia

Languages Spanish, English

T: +52 55 5572 6282

W: www.kipling.edu.mx

Instituto Cervantes, A.C.

Prol. León García # 2355, Col. General I. Martínez, San Luis Potosí C.P. 78360

MYP Coordinator Marcela Robles Espinosa

PYP Coordinator inglise castillo martínez

Languages Spanish

T: +52 444 815 91 50

W: www.apostolica.mx

Instituto D'Amicis, AC

Camino a Morillotla s/n, Colonia Bello Horizonte, Puebla C.P. 72170

CP Coordinator Luis Jahir Mendoza

DP Coordinator Luis Jahir Mendoza

MYP Coordinator Adriana Cruz Hernández

PYP Coordinator Ma. Eugenia Tanus Diego

Languages English, Spanish

T: +52 222 303 2618

W: www.damicis.edu.mx

Instituto Educativo Olinca

Periférico Sur 5170, Col Pedregal de Carrasco, Delegación Coyoacán, Ciudad de México C.P. 04700

DP Coordinator Julieta López Olalde

MYP Coordinator Imelda Amaya Alcázar

PYP Coordinator Claudia Ghigliazza Lopez

Languages Spanish, English, French

T: +52 55 5606 3113/4197

W: www.olinca.edu.mx

Instituto Internacional Octavio Paz

Calle Internacional 63 Fracc. Las Brisas el Jaguey, Col. Las Redes, Chapala, Jalisco C.P. 45903

DP Coordinator Fátima Flores

Languages English

T: +52 376 766 0903

W: www.iiop.edu.mx

Instituto Jefferson Internacional

Boulevard Jefferson No 666, Morelia, Michoacán C.P. 58080

DP Coordinator Vanya Nohemí Soto Maldonado

MYP Coordinator Valeria López Morales

PYP Coordinator Valeria López Morales

Languages Spanish

T: +52 443 3237967

W: jefferson.edu.mx

Instituto Kipling de Irapuato

Villa Mirador 5724, Villas de Irapuato, Irapuato, Guanajuato C.P. 36670

MYP Coordinator Martha Sultane Caram Canavati

PYP Coordinator Diana Muttio Limas

Languages English, Spanish

T: +52 462 6230165

W: www.kiplingirapuato.edu.mx

Instituto Ovalle Monday - Plantel Secundaria

Guillermo Massieu Helguera 265, Col. Residencial La Escalera, Del. Gustavo A. Madero, Ciudad de México C.P. 07320

MYP Coordinator Maiella Martínez Jiménez

Languages Spanish

T: +52 5586 0316 (Ext:101)

W: www.ovallemonday.edu.mx

Instituto Piaget

Nubes 413, Col Jardines del Pedregal, Ciudad de México C.P. 01900

PYP Coordinator Mariana Mejía Fonseca

Languages English, Spanish

T: +52 555568 8881

W: www.institutopiaget.edu.mx

Instituto Sanmiguelense

Escuadrón 201, No. 10 Palmita de Landeta Km. 0.5, San Miguel de Allende, Guanajuato C.P. 37748

DP Coordinator Mayra Vianey Álvarez Soria

Languages Spanish

T: +52 415 154 8484

W: www.itses.edu.mx

Kipling Esmeralda

Av. Parque de los Ciervos No.1, Hacienda de Valle Escondido, Zona Esmeralda, Atizapan de Zaragoza, EEstado de México C.P. 52937

DP Coordinator Ariana Grimaldo Cardenas

MYP Coordinator Claudia García Ybarra

PYP Coordinator Irma Liliana Morales Lozano

Languages Spanish, English

T: +52 55 55726282

W: www.kiplingesmeralda.edu.mx

La Escuela de Lancaster A.C.

Av Insurgentes sur 3838, Tlalpan, Ciudad de México C.P. 14000

DP Coordinator Martha Susana García Ramírez

PYP Coordinator Caroline Horowitz

Languages English, Spanish

T: +52 5556 6697 96

W: www.lancaster.edu.mx

Liceo de Apodaca Centro Educativo

Ave. Virrey de Velazco No. 500, Apodaca, Nuevo León C.P. 66606

MYP Coordinator Julian Salinas

PYP Coordinator Monica Estrada

Languages English

T: +52 81 83862089

W: www.liceodeapodaca.edu.mx

Liceo de Monterrey

Humberto Junco Voigt #400, Col. Valle Oriente, San Pedro Garza García, Nuevo León C.P. 66269

DP Coordinator Fátima Montes Villegas

Languages English, Spanish

T: +52 (81) 8748 4146

W: www.liceodemonterrey.edu.mx

Liceo de Monterrey - Centro Educativo

Col Sendero San Jeronimo, Monterrey, Nuevo Leon C.P. 64659

DP Coordinator Mario Sanchez Monroy

Languages Spanish

T: +1 8122 8900

Liceo Federico Froebel de Oaxaca SC

Ajusco No 100, Colonia Volcanes, Oaxaca C.P. 68020

DP Coordinator Nancy Villanueva Castillo

Languages English, Spanish

T: +52 951 5200 675

W: www.federicofroebel.edu.mx

Lomas Hill

Av. Veracruz 158, Cuajimalpa, Ciudad de México C.P. 05000

PYP Coordinator Mariana Resa Romo

Languages English, Spanish

T: +52 55 5812 0818

W: lomashill.edu.mx

MADISON CAMPUS MONTERREY

Marsella #3055, Col. Alta Vista, Monterrey, Nuevo León C.P. 64840

MYP Coordinator Perla Priscila Vargas Andrade

PYP Coordinator Ricardo Domínguez Gámez

Languages English, Spanish

T: +52 81 8359 0627

E: contacto@colegiosmadison.edu.mx

W: madisonmonterrey.edu.mx

See full details on page 519

MADISON INTERNATIONAL SCHOOL

Camino Real #100, Col. El Uro, Monterrey, Nuevo León C.P. 64986

MYP Coordinator Eduardo Vargas

PYP Coordinator Rolando De La Torre

Languages English, Spanish

T: +52 81 8218 7909

E: admisiones@mis.edu.mx

W: www.mis.edu.mx

See full details on page 520

Madison International School Campus Country-Mérida

Calle 24776 s/n, Chablekal, Merida, Yucatán C.P. 97300

DP Coordinator Jhon Mariño Vargas

MYP Coordinator Fernando Ramírez

PYP Coordinator Kate Wade

Languages English, Spanish

T: +52 99 9611 9053

W: www.colegiosmadison.edu.mx/colegios-madison-merida.htm

Noordwijk International College

Blvd. del Mar #491, Fracc. Costa de Oro, Boca del Río, Veracruz C.P. 94299

MYP Coordinator Carolina Zuluaga Moreno

PYP Coordinator Sandra Gamboa

Languages English, Spanish

T: +52 229 130 0714

W: www.noordwijk.com.mx

Orbis International School

Km 3.5 Carretera Aeropuerto #551, Colonia Rivera, Mexicali, Baja California C.P. 21220
PYP Coordinator Gabriela Coutino
Languages English
T: +52 686 565 0877
W: orbis.edu.mx

Peterson School - Lomas

Monte Himalaya 615, Lomas de Chapultepec, Miguel Hidalgo, México D.F. C.P. 11000
DP Coordinator Bella Cherem Picciotto
Languages Spanish
T: +52 5520 2213
W: www.peterson.edu.mx/lomas

Prepa UNI

Carretera Panamerican Km 269, Celaya, Guanajuato C.P. 38080
DP Coordinator Alejandra Nuñez
Languages Spanish
T: +52 461 61 39099
W: www.udec.edu.mx

Prepa UPAEP Angelópolis

Av. del Sol No. 5, Col. Concepción La Cruz, San Andrés Cholula, Puebla C.P. 72160
CP Coordinator Laura Mariana Hernández De la Torre
DP Coordinator Laura Mariana Hernández de la Torre
Languages Spanish
T: +52 222 225 2291
W: upaep.mx/prepa/angelopolis

Prepa UPAEP Cholula

Av. Forjadores No. 1804, Col Barrio de Jesús, San Pedro Cholula, Puebla C.P. 72760
CP Coordinator Claudia Yamilet Lomas Mendoza
DP Coordinator Claudia Yamilet Lomas Mendoza
Languages Spanish
T: +52 222 403 7373
W: upaep.mx/prepa/cholula

Prepa UPAEP Huamantla

Carr. Lib. Carr. México-Veracruz Kilómetro 147.5, Santa Clara, Huamantla, Tlaxcala C.P. 90500
CP Coordinator Yolanda Sánchez Flores
Languages Spanish
T: +52 247 472 2550
W: upaep.mx/prepa/huamantla

Prepa UPAEP Lomas

Circuito Mario Molina No. 15, Lomas de Angelópolis, San Andrés Cholula, Puebla C.P. 72828
CP Coordinator Alejandra Paola Anaya Salas
DP Coordinator Alejandra Paola Anaya Salas
Languages English, Spanish
T: +52 (0)1 222 5822102
W: upaep.mx/prepa/lomas

Prepa UPAEP Santiago

Av 9 Pte 1508, Barrio de Santiago, Puebla C.P. 72160
CP Coordinator Gerardo Arroyo Barillas
DP Coordinator Gerardo Arroyo Barillas
Languages Spanish
T: +52 222 246 8264
W: upaep.mx/prepa/santiago

Prepa UPAEP Sur

Calle Independencia No. 6339, Col. Patrimonio, Puebla C.P. 72470
CP Coordinator Claudia Verenice Sotelo Duarte
DP Coordinator Claudia Verenice Sotelo Duarte
Languages Spanish
T: +52 222 233 1342
W: upaep.mx/prepa/sur

Prepa UPAEP Tehuacán

Boulevard Tehuacán San Marcos No. 1700, Col. El Humilladero, Tehuacán, Puebla
CP Coordinator Francisco Javier Martínez Orea
Languages English, Spanish
T: +52 238 383 7800
W: upaep.mx/prepa/tehuacan

Rootland School

Hortensia 6, Florida, Álvaro Obregón, Ciudad de México C.P. 01030
PYP Coordinator Ana Rocha Jove
Languages English, Spanish
T: +52 55 2096 3660
W: www.rootland.edu.mx

Tecnológico de Monterrey - PrepaTec Ciudad de México

Calle del Puente #222, Col. Ejidos de Huipulco, Tlalpan, Distrito Federal C.P. 14380
DP Coordinator Adolfo Grovas
Languages Spanish
T: +52 (55) 5483 2110
W: tec.mx/es/ciudad-de-mexico

Tecnológico de Monterrey - PrepaTec Cumbres

Linces #1000, Col. Cumbres Elite, Monterrey, Nuevo León C.P. 64639
DP Coordinator Ada Chavarría
Languages Spanish, English
T: +52 (81) 8158 4622
W: tec.mx/es/ubicacion/cumbres

Tecnológico de Monterrey - PrepaTec Esmeralda

Fracc. Conjunto Urbano, Col. Bosque Esmeralda, Manzana 7 Lote 1 y 2, Atizapán de Zaragoza, Estado de México C.P. 52930
DP Coordinator David Lee
Languages Spanish
T: +52 (55) 5864 5370 (Ext:2903)
W: tec.mx/wps/wcm/connect/campus/esm/esmeralda

Tecnológico de Monterrey - PrepaTec Estado de México

Carretera Lago de Guadalupe, Km 3.5, Col. Margarita Maza de Juárez, Atizapán de Zaragoza, Estado de México C.P. 52926
DP Coordinator Andrea Fabiola Rodríguez Iniesta
Languages Spanish, English
T: +52 (55) 5864 5714
W: tec.mx/en/estado-de-mexico-campus

Tecnológico de Monterrey - PrepaTec Eugenio Garza Lagüera

Topolobampo #4603, Valle de las Brisas, Monterrey, Nuevo León C.P. 64790
DP Coordinator Ana Isabel López
Languages Spanish
T: +52 (81) 8155 4490
W: tec.mx/en

Tecnológico de Monterrey - PrepaTec Eugenio Garza Sada

Dinamarca #451 Sur Col Del Carmen, Monterrey, Nuevo León C.P. 64710
DP Coordinator Mónica Otálora
Languages Spanish, English
T: +52 (81) 8151 4264
W: admisionprepatec.itesm.mx

Tecnológico de Monterrey - PrepaTec Metepec

Av. Las Torres 1957 Ote., San Salvador Tizatlali, Metepec C.P. 52172
DP Coordinator Ernesto Solís
Languages Spanish, English
T: +52 (722) 271 5977
W: tec.mx/en

Tecnológico de Monterrey - PrepaTec Querétaro

Av. Epigmenio González #500, Fracc. San Pablo, Santiago de Querétaro C.P. 76130
DP Coordinator Christina Norris
Languages Spanish
T: +52 (442) 238 3208
W: tec.mx/en/queretaro-campus

Tecnológico de Monterrey - PrepaTec Santa Catarina

Morones Prieto No 290 Pte., Col Jesús M. Garza, Santa Catarina, Nuevo León C.P. 66180
DP Coordinator Rosalba Serrano
Languages Spanish, English
T: +52 (81) 8153 4045
W: tec.mx/en

Tecnológico de Monterrey - PrepaTec Santa Fe

Av Carlos Lazo #100, Santa Fe, Delegación Alvaro Obregón C.P. 01389
DP Coordinator Karla Franceli Villagrán Guadarrama
Languages Spanish, English
T: +52 (55) 9177 8130
W: tec.mx/en/santa-fe-campus

Tecnológico de Monterrey - PrepaTec Valle Alto

Carretera Nacional #8002 Km. 267.7, Col. La Estanzuela, Monterrey, N.L C.P. 64986
DP Coordinator Marcela Valero
Languages English, Spanish
T: +52 (81)8228 5310
W: tec.mx/en

The American School Foundation, A.C.

Calle Sur 136-135, Colonia Las Americas, México D.F. C.P. 01120
DP Coordinator Lara Schupack
MYP Coordinator Kristen Leutheuser
PYP Coordinator Tara Munroe
Languages English, Spanish
T: +52 55 5227 4900
W: www.asf.edu.mx

The Churchill School

Felipe Villanueva No. 24, Col. Guadalupe Inn, Mexico City
MYP Coordinator Itzel Nava
PYP Coordinator Maria Garza Caligaris
Languages English
T: +52 55 50288800
W: www.churchill.edu.mx

The Edron Academy

Calz. Desierto de los Leones #5578, Col Olivar de Los Padres, Ciudad de México C.P. 1740
DP Coordinator Lorna Villasana
Languages English
T: +52 55 5585 1920
W: www.edron.edu.mx

Universidad de Monterrey Unidad Fundadores

Nova Scotia 109, between Av. Newfoundland and Av. General Mariano Escob+, Escobedo, Nuevo Leon C.P. 66054
CP Coordinator Homero Treviño
DP Coordinator Homero de Jesús Treviño Villagómez
Languages Spanish
T: +52 (81) 8215 4151
W: www.udem.edu.mx

IB AMERICAS

Universidad de Monterrey Unidad Valle Alto

Carretera Nacionala Salida Valle Alto
Km1, Colonia Valle Alto, Monterrey, NL
C.P. 64989
CP Coordinator Sara Esther Quiroga
Ramírez
DP Coordinator María Adriana
Rodríguez De la Garza
Languages English, Spanish
W: www.udem.edu.mx/Esp/Preparatoria/
Pages/Unidad-Valle-Alto.aspx

Universidad Regiomontana Preparatoria Campus Centro

Matamoros # 430 Pte., Col. Centro,
Monterrey, NL C.P. 64000
DP Coordinator Guillermo Acosta
Languages Spanish
T: +52 81 8220 4830
W: u-erre.mx

University of Monterrey

Av. Ignacio Morones Prieto 4500, Pte.,
66238, San Pedro Garza García, Nuevo
León C.P. 66238
CP Coordinator Nabor Rodríguez
Loera
DP Coordinator Patricia Menendez
Aguilar
Languages Spanish
T: +52 81 8215 1010
W: www.udem.edu.mx/prepaudem

Westhill Institute

Domingo Garcia Ramos No. 56, Col.
Prados de la Montaña, Santa Fe,
Cuajimalpa, Mexico City C.P. 05610
DP Coordinator Ana Isabel Almeida
Leñero
MYP Coordinator Ktyall Malik
PYP Coordinator Maricela Olguin
Languages English, Spanish, French
T: +52 55 8851 7000
W: www.westhillinstitute.edu.mx

Westhill Institute - Carpatos

Monte Carpatos 940, Lomas de
Chapultepec, México D.F. C.P. 11000
PYP Coordinator Rocío Alvarez
Languages English, Spanish
T: +52 55 88517067
W: www.westhillinstitute.edu.mx/
CampusCarpatos.html

Winpenny School

José María Castorena 318, Colonia
Cuajimalpa, México D. F. C.P. 05000
DP Coordinator Maria Paz Lindeman
Languages English, Spanish
T: +52 55 8000 6100
W: www.winpenny.edu.mx

Colegio Alemán Nicaragüense

Apartado 1636, Managua
DP Coordinator Hubert Luna
Palacios
Languages Spanish, English
T: +505 2265 8449
W: www.coalnic.edu.ni/index.php/en/

Notre Dame International School

Km 8.5 Carretera a Masaya, Managua
DP Coordinator Carlos Ordoñez
Mondragon
MYP Coordinator Alejandra Mendoza
PYP Coordinator Silvia Vallecillo
Languages English
T: +505 2276 0353 54
W: notredame.edu.ni

Boston School International

Ave. Arnulfo Arias Madrid Building.
#727, Balboa, Ancón, Panama City
DP Coordinator Ruth Mendoza
PYP Coordinator Nairobys Rojas
Languages English
T: +507 833 8888
W: www.bostonschool.edu.pa

Colegio Isaac Rabin

Edificio 130, Ciudad del Saber
DP Coordinator Reina Laura
Companioni
MYP Coordinator Sonia Martínez
Robles
PYP Coordinator Marissa Rocha De
Medina
Languages Spanish
T: +507 3170059
W: www.isaacrabin.com

International School of Panama

P.O. Box 0819-02588, Cerro Viento
Rural, Panama City
DP Coordinator Andrew Lin
Languages English
T: +507 293 3000
W: www.isp.edu.pa

KING'S COLLEGE, THE BRITISH SCHOOL OF PANAMA

Edificio 518, Calle al Hospital, Clayton
DP Coordinator Laura Guisasola
Languages English, Spanish
T: +507 282 3300
E: kcp.admissions@kingsgroup.org
W: www.panama.kingscollegeschools.org

See full details on page 513

METROPOLITAN SCHOOL OF PANAMA

Green Valley, Panama Norte, Panama
City
DP Coordinator Mr. Ryan Skinner
MYP Coordinator Mr. Ryan Manary
PYP Coordinator Ms. Shelley Love
Languages English
T: +507 317 1130
E: admissions@themetropolitanschool.
com
W: www.themetropolitanschool.com

See full details on page 524

Centro Educativo Arambé

Santísima Trinidad No 3.211, c/ Avda.
Ita Ybaté (Zona Brítez Cue), Luque,
Asunción
DP Coordinator Carolina Susana
Bianco Wehrli
Languages Spanish
T: +595 21 694 662
W: www.arambe.edu.py

Colegio Goethe Asunción

Cnl Silva esq Tte Rocholl, Asuncion
232
DP Coordinator Anna Gabel
Languages Spanish
T: +595 21 606860
W: www.goethe.edu.py

Faith Christian School

Del Maestro 3471 c/ Soriano
González, Barrio Herrera, Asunción
DP Coordinator Marisa Vaesken de
Ramos
Languages English, Spanish
T: +595 21 620 5024
W: www.faith.edu.py

St Anne's School

Tte. Manuel Pino Gonzalez y Eulalio
Facetti, Asunción
DP Coordinator Mirko Zayas
Languages English
T: +595 21 295649
W: www.sas.edu.py

American School

Av. Larco Nro 288, Urb. San Andrés,
Trujillo, La Libertad 13008
DP Coordinator Alana Lam Peña
Languages English, Spanish
T: +51 44 612370
W: www.americanschooltrujillo.com

Andino Cusco International School

Km 10.5 Carretera, Chinchero Distrito
de Cachimayo, Cusco
DP Coordinator Bruno Vázquez
Molinero
PYP Coordinator Emperatriz Yepez
Languages English, Spanish
T: +51 84 275135
W: www.andinoschool.edu.pe

Cambridge College Lima

Av. Alemeda de los Molinos 728-730,
La Encantada de Villa, Chorrillos, Lima
15067
DP Coordinator Adrian Everitt
Languages English, Spanish
T: +51 12 540107
W: cambridge.edu.pe

Casuarinas International College

Av Jacarandá 391, Valle Hermoso,
Monterrico, Santiago de Surco, Lima
15023
CP Coordinator Juan Carlos Ruiz
Malásquez
DP Coordinator Juan Carlos Ruiz
Malásquez
MYP Coordinator Luis Eduardo
Camelo Roa
PYP Coordinator Claudia Santana
Oliveros
Languages Spanish, English, French,
Portuguese, Mandarin
T: +51 13 444040
W: www.casuarinas.edu.pe

Clemente Althaus

Prolongación Jirón Cuzco 360, San
Miguel - Alt. Cdra. 12 Av. La Marina,
Lima 15086
DP Coordinator Katherine Fernandez
Alvarez
Languages Spanish
T: +51 14 194700
W: clementealthaus.edu.pe

Colegio Alpamayo

Calle Bucaramanga 145, Urb
Mayorazgo, Lima 15026
DP Coordinator Johan Fripp
Anicama
Languages Spanish
T: +51 13 490111
W: www.alpamayo.edu.pe

COLEGIO ALTAIR

Av. La Arboleda 385, Urb. Sirius, La
Molina, Lima 15024
DP Coordinator Yolanda Meneses
MYP Coordinator Paloma Krüger
PYP Coordinator Sandra Nicoli
Languages Spanish, English
T: +51 13 650298
E: admision@altair.pe
W: www.altair.edu.pe

See full details on page 494

Colegio Champagnat

Paseo de la República 7930, Santiago de Surco, Lima 15049

DP Coordinator Humberto Lara Ceroni

MYP Coordinator Karen Quinto Loa

PYP Coordinator Ana Elizabeth Gálvez Calderón

Languages Spanish

T: +51 15 1905000

W: www.champagnat.edu.pe

Colegio de Alto Rendimiento de Amazonas

Jirón Amazonas 120, Chachapoyas, Amazonas

DP Coordinator Ever Gustavo Marín Chávez

Languages Spanish

W: www.minedu.gob.pe/coar

Colegio de Alto Rendimiento de Ancash

Sector Llacshahuanca, Recuay, Ancash

DP Coordinator Rosana Malpaso Morales

Languages Spanish

W: www.minedu.gob.pe/coar

Colegio de Alto Rendimiento de Apurímac

Jiron Tupac Amaru S/N, Pairaca, Chalhuanca, Apurímac

DP Coordinator Alejandro Sanchez Pomalaza

Languages Spanish

W: www.minedu.gob.pe/coar

Colegio de Alto Rendimiento de Arequipa

Ca. Federico Barreto Nª 148, CEBA Nuestra Señora del Pilar, Arequipa

DP Coordinator Andres Quispe

Languages Spanish

W: www.minedu.gob.pe/coar

Colegio de Alto Rendimiento de Ayacucho

Jr. Mariano Ruiz de Castilla N° 150, Alameda Valdelirios, Ayacucho

DP Coordinator Cosme Gerardo Palomino Cárdenas

Languages Spanish

W: www.minedu.gob.pe/coar

Colegio de Alto Rendimiento de Cajamarca

Jirón José Pardo No 103, Distrito Jesús, Cajamarca

DP Coordinator Julio Trigoso Mori

Languages Spanish

W: www.minedu.gob.pe/coar

Colegio de Alto Rendimiento de Cusco

Sector Bellavista a 6 Km. del distrito de Anta, Pucyura, Cusco

DP Coordinator Gregory Enrique Hernández Borja

Languages Spanish

W: www.minedu.gob.pe/coar

Colegio de Alto Rendimiento de Huancavelica

Jr. José Gabriel Condorcanqui S/N, CP Santa Ana, Huancavelica

DP Coordinator Jaime Artica

Languages Spanish

W: www.minedu.gob.pe/coar

Colegio de Alto Rendimiento de Huánuco

Centro Poblado Canchán, a 12 km de Huánuco, Huánuco

DP Coordinator Saúl Mejía Ortíz

Languages Spanish

W: www.minedu.gob.pe/coar

Colegio de Alto Rendimiento de Ica

Calle José María Mejía S/N, Nazca, Ica

DP Coordinator Luisa Angélica Loredo Valdéz

Languages Spanish

W: www.minedu.gob.pe/coar

Colegio de Alto Rendimiento de Junín

Ca. Huayna Capac, Cdra. 4 IESTP Jaime Cerrón Palomino, Chongos Bajo, Chupaca, Junín

DP Coordinator Edith Alexandra Yalle Taboada

Languages Spanish

W: www.minedu.gob.pe/coar

Colegio de Alto Rendimiento de La Libertad

Campamento San José Carretera Trujillo, Chimbote, Virú, La Libertad

DP Coordinator Diana Rosales Murga

Languages Spanish

W: www.minedu.gob.pe/coar

Colegio de Alto Rendimiento de Lambayeque

Prolongación Bolognesi S/N, A media cuadra de la Av. José Leonardo Ortiz, Chiclayo, Lambayeque

DP Coordinator Javier Dueñas Ramírez

Languages Spanish

W: www.minedu.gob.pe/coar

Colegio de Alto Rendimiento de Lima-Provincias

Av. 5 de Diciembre s/n Santa María, Huaura, Lima

DP Coordinator Jose Wilder Tarrillo Vasquez

Languages Spanish

W: www.minedu.gob.pe/coar

Colegio de Alto Rendimiento de Loreto

Avenida Mariscal Cáceres con Pasaje Jorge Chávez S/N, Iquitos, Loreto

DP Coordinator Luis Alberto Tulumba Villacrez

Languages Spanish

W: www.minedu.gob.pe/coar

Colegio de Alto Rendimiento de Madre de Dios

Av. Madre de Dios cuadra 4 esquina con, Madre de Dios

DP Coordinator Marco Antonio Ruiz Onton

Languages Spanish

W: www.minedu.gob.pe/coar

Colegio de Alto Rendimiento de Moquegua

Prlg. Av. Mariano Lino Urquieta S/N, CP San Antonio, Moquegua

DP Coordinator Reynaldo Arteta Ávila

Languages Spanish

W: www.minedu.gob.pe/coar

Colegio de Alto Rendimiento de Pasco

Jr. Joseph Albert Walijewski Szydlo Nro 201, Oxapampa, Pasco

DP Coordinator Eduardo Verastegui Borja

Languages Spanish

W: www.minedu.gob.pe/coar

Colegio de Alto Rendimiento de Piura

Ca. Juan Velasco Alvarado S/N, AAHH Nueva Esperanza, CETPRO Bosconia, Piura

DP Coordinator Maritza Quintana Carlin

Languages Spanish

W: www.minedu.gob.pe/coar

Colegio de Alto Rendimiento de Puno

Av. Panamericana Nª943, a 17 km. de Puno- Carretera Chucuito, Seminario Ntra Señora de Guadalupe, Puno

DP Coordinator Denis Daniel Macedo Vilca

Languages Spanish

W: www.minedu.gob.pe/coar

Colegio de Alto Rendimiento de San Martin

Jr. Pedro Pascasio Noriega Nª 061, IESPP Generalísimo José de San Martín, San Martín

DP Coordinator Mario Campos

Languages Spanish

W: www.minedu.gob.pe/coar

Colegio de Alto Rendimiento de Tacna

Sector Irrigación Copare, por la carretera Panamericana Sur, IE Norah Flores Tor+, Tacna

DP Coordinator Freddy Edinson Jimenez Paredes

Languages Spanish

W: www.minedu.gob.pe/coar

Colegio de Alto Rendimiento de Tumbes

San Juan de la Vírgen s/n, Tumbes

DP Coordinator Efraín Villacorta Zárate

Languages Spanish

W: www.minedu.gob.pe/coar

Colegio de Alto Rendimiento de Ucayali

Psje. Huáscar S/N, PPJJ Micaela Bastidas, Calleria 61, Coronel Portillo, Ucayali

DP Coordinator Gianina Gil Rengifo

Languages Spanish

W: www.minedu.gob.pe/coar

Colegio Franklin Delano Roosevelt

Av. Las Palmeras 325, Camacho, Lima 15023

DP Coordinator Robert Allan

Languages English, Spanish

T: +51 14 350890

W: www.amersol.edu.pe

Colegio La Unión

Av. Cipriano Dulanto 1950, Pueblo Libre, Lima 15084

DP Coordinator Miriam Palacios Velasquez

Languages English

T: +51 12 610533

W: www.launion.edu.pe

Colegio León Pinelo

Calle Maimónides 610 (ex Los Manzanos), San Isidro, Lima 15076

DP Coordinator Yoana Kaliksztein Fihman

MYP Coordinator Diego Kierzner

PYP Coordinator Claudia Torres

Languages Spanish

T: +51 12 183040

W: www.lp.edu.pe

PERU

Colegio Los Álamos
Calle Estados Unidos 731, Jesús María, Lima 15701
DP Coordinator César Chora Chamochumbi
Languages Spanish
T: +51 14 631044
W: www.losalamos.edu.pe

Colegio Magister
Calle Francisco de Cuéllar 686, Monterrico, Santiago de Surco, Lima
DP Coordinator Edwin James Vargas Haro
Languages English, Spanish
T: +51 14 363063
W: www.magister.edu.pe

Colegio Mater Admirabilis
Av. Arica 898, San Miguel, Lima
MYP Coordinator Roxana Calderón
Languages Spanish
W: www.maternet.edu.pe

Colegio Max Uhle
Av. Fernandini s/n, Sachaca, Arequipa 04013
DP Coordinator Alejandro Gutiérrez Osorio
Languages Spanish
T: +51 54 232921
W: www.maxuhle.edu.pe

Colegio Mayor Secundario Presidente del Perú
Centro Vacacional de Huampaní, Carretera Central, Km 24.5, Chaclacayo, Lima
DP Coordinator Alcides Roman Rivas
Languages Spanish
T: +51 14 971278
W: www.colegiomayor.edu.pe

Colegio Montealto
Los Eucaliptos 491, San Isidro, Lima
DP Coordinator Tania Gonzales Sanez
Languages Spanish
T: +51 441 2685
W: montealto.edu.pe

Colegio Nuestra Señora del Pilar
Av. Virgen del Pilar 1711, Cercado, Arequipa
DP Coordinator Ricardo Enríquez Cáceres
Languages Spanish
T: +51 54 226262
W: www.cnspilar.edu.pe

Colegio Peruano - Alemán Reina del Mundo
Avenida Rinconada del Lago 675, La Molina, Lima
DP Coordinator Luis Ernesto Gutierrez
Languages Spanish
T: +51 14 792191
W: www.rdm.edu.pe

Colegio Peruano Alemán Beata Imelda
Carretera Central Km 29 s/n, Lurigancho-Chosica, Lima
DP Coordinator Martin Heinrich
Languages Spanish
T: +51 13 603119
W: www.cbi.edu.pe

Colegio Peruano Británico
Av. Vía Láctea 445, Monterrico, Santiago de Surco, Lima 15023
DP Coordinator María Del Pilar Vildoso
Languages English
T: +51 14 360151
W: www.britishschool.edu.pe

Colegio Peruano Norteamericano Abraham Lincoln
Av. José Antonio 475, Urb. Parque de Monterico, La Molina, Lima 15023
DP Coordinator Brenda Yohana Caycho Avalos
MYP Coordinator Eliana Alcalde
PYP Coordinator Karla Puente Garcia
Languages Spanish, English
T: +51 16 174500
W: www.abrahamlincoln.edu.pe

Colegio Pestalozzi (Colegio Suizo del Peru)
Casilla 18-1027, Aurora-Miraflores, Lima
DP Coordinator Karen Coral
Languages Spanish
T: +51 16 178600
W: www.pestalozzi.edu.pe

Colegio Sagrados Corazones 'Recoleta'
Av. Circunvalación del Golf 368, La Molina, Lima 15023
DP Coordinator Lourdes Olano Vargas De Cieza
Languages Spanish
T: +51 17 022500
W: www.recoleta.edu.pe

Colegio Salcantay
Av. Pío XII 261, Monterrico, Santiago de Surco, Lima 15023
DP Coordinator Rosa Elena Galagarza
Languages Spanish
T: +51 14 359224
W: www.salcantay.edu.pe

Colegio San Agustín
Av. Javier Prado Este 980, Urb. El Palomar, San Isidro, Lima
DP Coordinator Germán Ramos Ibias
PYP Coordinator Oscar Raúl Medina Ycaza
Languages Spanish
T: +51 16 164242
W: www.sanagustin.edu.pe

Colegio San Agustín de Chiclayo
Km. 8 Carretera Pimentel S/N, Pimentel, Chiclayo, Lambayeque
DP Coordinator José Rosell Rubio Monteza
Languages Spanish
T: +51 74 208173
W: www.sanagustinchiclayo.edu.pe

Colegio San Ignacio de Recalde
Calle Géminis 251, San Borja, Lima 15037
DP Coordinator Patricia Loo Salas
PYP Coordinator Glenis Blas Rojas
Languages English
T: +51 12 119430
W: www.sir.edu.pe

Colegio San Pedro
Calle Hurón 409, Rinconada del Lago, La Molina, Lima 15026
DP Coordinator Ella Tenorio
Languages English, Spanish
T: +51 16 149500
W: sanpedro.edu.pe

Colegio Santa Úrsula
Av. Nicolas de Rivera 132, San Isidro, Lima 15073
DP Coordinator Ana María Reyes Fajardo
Languages Spanish
T: +51 12 027430
W: www.santaursula.edu.pe

Colegio Santísimo Nombre de Jesús
Urbanización Chacarilla del Estanque Calle Mayorazgo 176, San Borja, Lima
DP Coordinator Edwin Borda Meza
Languages English, Spanish
T: +51 13 721655

Colegio Villa Caritas
Calle Hurón 409, Rinconada del Lago, La Molina, Lima 15026
DP Coordinator Fairuz Saba
Languages English, Spanish
T: +51 16 149500
W: villacaritas.edu.pe

Colegio Virgen Inmaculada de Monterrico
Av. Morro Solar No. 110, Santiago de Surco, Lima 15039
DP Coordinator Martin Ponce Guillen
Languages English, Spanish
T: +51 13 726499
W: virgeninmaculada.edu.pe

Collège André Malraux
Calle Batallón Concepción 245, Urb. Sta. Teresa, Santiago de Surco, Lima
DP Coordinator Ramiro Febres Tapia
Languages English
T: +51 12 754937
W: www.andremalraux.edu.pe

Davy College
Av. Hoyos Rubio 2684, Cajamarca 06001
DP Coordinator Cecilia Kanashiro
Languages English, Spanish, French
T: +51 76 367501
W: www.davycollege.edu.pe

Euroamerican College
Fundo Casablanca, Pachacamac, Lima
DP Coordinator Carla Gloria Piscoya Salinas
PYP Coordinator Karina Munoz
Languages Spanish, English
T: +51 12 311617
W: www.euroamericancollege.edu.pe

Fleming College
Av América Sur 3701, Trujillo, La Libertad 13008
DP Coordinator Angel Alarcon
PYP Coordinator Alba Morales
Languages English, Spanish
T: +51 44 284440
W: www.fleming.edu.pe

Hiram Bingham School
Av. Paseo la Castellana 919, Urbanización La Castellana, Santiago de Surco, Lima 15048
DP Coordinator Martha Marengo
MYP Coordinator Carrie Rabel
PYP Coordinator Cinthya Estremadoyro
Languages English, Spanish
T: +51 12 719880
W: www.hirambingham.edu.pe

IE Fuerza Aérea Peruana José Quiñones
Av. Evitamiento S/N-Urb, Camacho, La Molina, Lima
DP Coordinator Patricia Aparicio Vargas
Languages Spanish
W: www.cased.edu.pe/?cat=41

IE Pedro Ruiz Gallo

Av. Cdra 2 S/N Costado de la Clinica Maison de Sante Chorrillos, Chorrillos, Lima
DP Coordinator Luz Rosas
MYP Coordinator Paola Piña Yncio
Languages Spanish
T: +51 16 802673
W: prg.edu.pe

Institución Educativa Particular San Antonio de Padua

Av. Estados Unidos 569, Jesús Maria, Lima
DP Coordinator Jenny Polo Churrango
Languages Spanish
T: +51 16 143600
W: www.sanantoniodepadua.edu.pe

Institución Educativa Privada Lord Byron

Calle Grande 250, Sr. de la Caña, Cayma, Arequipa
DP Coordinator Jeffrey Dagmar Fernández Castillo
Languages Spanish
T: +51 54 255038
W: www.lordbyron.edu.pe

Liceo Naval 'Almirante Guise'

Calle Monti 350, San Borja, Lima 15037
DP Coordinator Carito Ayala Delgado
Languages Spanish
T: +51 14 758055
W: www.lnag.edu.pe

Lord Byron School

Jr. Viña del Mar 375 - 379, Sol de la Molina, Lima 15026
DP Coordinator Joselito Vallejos Avalos
MYP Coordinator Ysabel Martínez Lora
PYP Coordinator Roxana Ortega Tello
Languages English, Spanish
T: +51 14 791717
W: www.byron.edu.pe

Markham College

Calle Augusto Angulo 291, San Antonio, Miraflores, Lima 15048
DP Coordinator Guinevere Dyker
Languages English, Spanish
T: +51 13 156750
W: www.markham.edu.pe

Montessori International College

Maz. A Sub Lote 01A, Urb. Tecsup, Distrito Víctor Larco Herrera, Trujillo, La Libertad 13009
DP Coordinator Tatjana Merzyn
PYP Coordinator Inés Gabriela Velásquez Ramos
Languages Spanish, English
T: +51 44 340000
W: www.montessoricollege.edu.pe

Newton College

Av. Ricardo Elías Aparicio 240, Lima 15026
DP Coordinator Constanza Beck
MYP Coordinator Andrew Rothman
PYP Coordinator Daniel Kasnick
Languages English
T: +51 12 079900
W: www.newton.edu.pe

Prescott

Avenida Alfonso Ugarte No. 565, Arequipa 04000
DP Coordinator Patricio González Luna
MYP Coordinator Romina Ramos Solis
PYP Coordinator Katia Aita Fuentes
Languages English, Spanish
T: +51 54 232540
W: www.prescott.edu.pe

San Francisco College

Urb. El Oasis II, Calle Costa del Sol Mz 'D' Lote 14, (Pista Camino a Huacachina), Ica 11004
PYP Coordinator Guadalupe Khairel Márquez Larreátegui
Languages Spanish
T: +51 95 6298110
W: sanfranciscocollege.edu.pe

San Silvestre School

Av. Santa Cruz 1251, Miraflores, Lima 15074
DP Coordinator Rafaela Antezana
Languages English
T: +51 12 413334
W: www.sansilvestre.edu.pe

St George's College - Sede Miraflores

Av. General Ernesto Montagne No.360, Miraflores, Lima 15048
CP Coordinator Luis Sifuentes Maldonado
DP Coordinator Luis Sifuentes Maldonado
Languages English, Spanish
T: +51 14 458147
W: www.stgeorgescollege.edu.pe

Villa Alarife School

Jr. Alameda Don Augusto Mz. D Lt. 5, Urb. Los Huertos de Villa, Chorrillos, Lima 15067
DP Coordinator María Luz Rojas Bonilla
T: +51 12 346969
W: villaalarife.edu.pe

Robinson School

5 Nairn Street, San Juan 00907
DP Coordinator Yesenia Ramos
MYP Coordinator Carine Poinson Simon
PYP Coordinator María Turner
Languages English
T: +1 787 999 4600
W: www.robinsonschool.org

THE BALDWIN SCHOOL OF PUERTO RICO

PO Box 1827, Bayamón 00960-1827
DP Coordinator Mrs. Laura Maristany
MYP Coordinator Mrs. Cristina Castillo
PYP Coordinator Mrs. Sarah Loinaz
Languages English
T: +1 787 720 2421
E: admission@baldwin-school.org
W: www.baldwin-school.org

See full details on page 546

The International School of Port of Spain

1 International Drive, Westmoorings, Port of Spain
MYP Coordinator Angela Shahien
PYP Coordinator Angela Shahien
Languages English
T: +1 868 633 4777
W: www.isps.edu.tt

Colegio Stella Maris

Máximo Tajes 7357/7359, CP 11500 Montevideo 11500
DP Coordinator Maria Brossard Hitta
Languages English, Spanish
T: +598 2 600 0702
W: www.stellamaris.edu.uy

Escuela Integral Hebreo Uruguaya

Jose Benito Lamas 2835, Montevideo 11300
DP Coordinator Rosana Erosa
Languages Spanish
T: +598 2 708 1712
W: www.escuelaintegral.edu.uy

Escuela y Liceo Elbio Fernandez

Maldonado 1381, Montevideo 11200
DP Coordinator Rosanna Pereyra
MYP Coordinator Dora Sajevicius
Languages English, Spanish
T: +598 2901 1254
W: www.elbiofernandez.edu.uy

International College

Blvr Artigas y Avda del Mar, Punta del Este, Maldonado
DP Coordinator Claudia Gisela Jaukin
Languages English, Spanish
T: +598 42 228 888
W: www.ic.edu.uy

St Brendan's School

Av Rivera 2314, Montevideo CP 11200
CP Coordinator Maria del Rosario Rodríguez
DP Coordinator Maria del Rosario Rodríguez
MYP Coordinator Helena Sastre Abreu
PYP Coordinator Claudia Ourthe-Cabalè
Languages English, Spanish
T: +598 2409 4939
W: www.stbrendan.edu.uy

St Clare's College

California y los Médanos, Punta del Este, San Rafael 20000
DP Coordinator Josué Naranjo
Languages Spanish, English
T: +598 42 490200
W: www.scc.edu.uy

St Patrick's College

Camino Gigantes 2735, Montevideo 12100
MYP Coordinator José Antonio Padilla Agrafojo
Languages Spanish
T: +598 2 601 3474
W: www.stpatrick.edu.uy

The British Schools, Montevideo

Máximo Tajes 6400, esq Havre, Montevideo 11500
DP Coordinator Florencia Paullier
PYP Coordinator Maria Fernanda Sobral
Languages English, Spanish
T: +598 2 600 3421
W: www.british.edu.uy

Uruguayan American School

Saldún de Rodríguez 2375, Montevideo 11500
DP Coordinator Gabriel Amaral
Languages English
T: + (598) 2600 7681
W: www.uas.edu.uy

Woodlands School

San Carlos de Bolivar s/n entre Havre y Cooper, Montevideo 11500
MYP Coordinator Fanny Bozzo Aldecosea
Languages Spanish
T: +59 82 604 27 14
W: www.woodlands.edu.uy

Woodside School

Mercedes y Louvre. Barrio Cantegril, 20100 Punta del Este, Maldonado
DP Coordinator Ximena Indarte
Languages English, Spanish
T: +598 4225 2552

USA Alabama

Auburn High School

405 South Dean Road, Auburn AL 36830
DP Coordinator Davis Thompson
Languages English
T: +1 334 887 4970
W: www.auburnschools.org/ahs

Central High School, Tuscaloosa

905 15th Street, Tuscaloosa AL 35401
DP Coordinator Jennifer Hines
Languages English
T: +1 205 759 3720
W: www.tuscaloosacityschools.com/domain/10

Charles A. Brown Elementary School

4811 Court J, Birmingham AL 35208
PYP Coordinator Vieshell Tatum
Languages English
T: +1 205 231 6860
W: www.bhamcityschools.org/page/67

Columbia High School

300 Explorer Boulevard, Huntsville AL 35806
MYP Coordinator David Coker
Languages English
T: +1 256 428 7576
W: www.columbiahigh.org

Columbia High School

300 Explorer Boulevard, Huntsville AL 35806
CP Coordinator Karli LeCompte
DP Coordinator Karli LeCompte
Languages English
T: +1 256 428 7576
W: www.columbiahigh.org

Cornerstone Schools of Alabama

118 55th Street North, Birmingham AL 35212
PYP Coordinator Rebecca Stivender
Languages English
T: +1 205 591 7600
W: www.csalabama.org

Daphne High School

9300 Lawson Road, Daphne AL 36526
DP Coordinator Deborah Few
Languages English
T: +1 251 626 8787
W: www.daphnehs.com

Fairhope High School

One Pirate Drive, Fairhope AL 36532
DP Coordinator Darla Litaker
Languages English
T: +1 251 928 8309
W: www.fairhopehs.com

Hoover High School

1000 Buccaneer Drive, Hoover AL 35244
DP Coordinator Melissa Hamley
Languages English
T: +1 205 439 1200
W: www.hoovercityschools.net/hhs

Jefferson County IB School

6100 Old Leeds Road, Birmingham AL 35210
DP Coordinator April Miller
MYP Coordinator Lauren Brown
Languages English
T: +1 205 379 5356
W: jcib.jefcoed.com

John Herbert Phillips Academy

2316 7th Avenue North, Birmingham AL 35203
MYP Coordinator Jessica Jones Wedgeworth
PYP Coordinator Jessica Jones Wedgeworth
Languages English
T: +1 205 231 9500
W: www.bhamcityschools.org/Domain/31

MacMillan International Academy

4015 McInnis Road, Montgomery AL 36116
PYP Coordinator Theresa Smith
Languages English
T: +1 334 284 7137

Murphy High School

100 South Carlen Street, Mobile AL 36606
CP Coordinator Sarah Woltring
DP Coordinator Rebecca Mullins
Languages English
T: +1 251 221 3186
W: www.mhspanthers.com

Phillips Preparatory School

3255 Old Shell Road, Mobile AL 36607
MYP Coordinator Jennifer Morgan
Languages English
T: +1 251 221 2286
W: phillipsprep.com

Providence Elementary School

10 Chalkstone Street, Huntsville AL 35806
PYP Coordinator Michele Spray
T: +1 256 428 7125
W: www.huntsvillecityschools.org/schools/providence-elementary

Ramsay Alternative High School

1800 13th Avenue South AL 35205
DP Coordinator Jonathan Barr
MYP Coordinator Jessica Jones Wedgeworth
Languages English
T: +1 205 231 7000
W: www.bhamcityschools.org/ramsay

The Academy for Science and Foreign Language

3221 Mastin Lake Road, Huntsville AL 35810
MYP Coordinator Adam Landingham
PYP Coordinator Michele Spray
Languages English
T: +1 256 428 7000
W: www.huntsvillecityschools.org/schools/academies-science-foreign-language

Tuscaloosa Magnet Elementary School

315 McFarland Blvd. East, Tuscaloosa AL 35404
PYP Coordinator Kathryn Busby
Languages English
T: +1 205 759 3655
W: www.tuscaloosacityschools.com/tmse

Tuscaloosa Magnet Middle School

315 McFarland Blvd. East, Tuscaloosa AL 35404
MYP Coordinator Lavanda Wagenheim
Languages English
T: +1 205 759 3653
W: www.tuscaloosacityschools.com/Domain/25

W H Council Traditional School

751 Wilkinson Street, Mobile AL 36603-1397
PYP Coordinator Mrs. E Danae Bowman
Languages English
T: +1 251 221 1139

W P Davidson High School

3900 Pleasant Valley Road, Mobile AL 36609
DP Coordinator Ashley Cauley
Languages English
T: +1 251 221 3084
W: www.wpdavidson.org

Williams School

155 Barren Fork Blvd SW, Huntsville AL 35824
MYP Coordinator Jennifer Duncan
PYP Coordinator Michele Spray
Languages English
T: +1 256 428 7540/5
W: www.huntsvillecityschools.org/schools/williams-middle

Alaska

Inlet View Elementary School

1219 N Street, Anchorage AK 99501
PYP Coordinator Beth Daly-Gamble
Languages English, Spanish
T: +1 907 742 7630
W: www.asdk12.org/inletview

Palmer High School

1170 West Arctic Avenue, Ma -Su Borough School District, Palmer AK 99645
DP Coordinator Nichelle Henry
Languages English
T: +1 907 746 8408

West Anchorage High School

1700 Hillcrest Drive, Anchorage AK 99517
DP Coordinator John Ruhlin
Languages English
T: +1 907 742 2610
W: www.asdk12.org/domain/3104

Arizona

Barry Goldwater High School

2820 West Rose Garden Lane, Deer Valley United School Dist, Phoenix AZ 85027
DP Coordinator Bridget Romero
MYP Coordinator Bridget Romero
Languages English
T: +1 623 445 3000
W: www.dvusd.org/domain/39

Betty H Fairfax High School

8225 South 59th Avenue, Laveen AZ 85339
DP Coordinator Elana Payton
Languages English
T: +1 602 764 9020
W: www.bettyfairfaxhs.org

Buckeye Union High School

1000 E. Narramore, Buckeye AZ 85326
DP Coordinator Joshua Stringham
Languages English, Spanish
T: +1 623 386 4423
W: www.buhsd.org/buckeye

Cactus Shadows High School
PO Box 426, Cave Creek AZ 85327-0426
DP Coordinator Angela Thomas
Languages English
T: +1 480 575 2400
W: www.ccusd93.org/cshs

Canyon del Oro High School
25 West Calle Concordia, Oro Valley AZ 85704
DP Coordinator Amy Bomke
Languages English
T: +1 520 696 5560
W: www.amphi.com/cdo

Chandler High School
350 N. Arizona Ave., Chandler AZ 85225
CP Coordinator Courtney Kemp
DP Coordinator Jacqueline Hartrick
MYP Coordinator Laura Helt
Languages English
T: +1 480 812 7700
W: www.cusd80.com/chs

Cholla High Magnet School
2001 West Starr Pass Blvd, Tucson AZ 85713
DP Coordinator Ilse Billings
Languages English
T: +1 520 225 4000
W: www.tusd1.org/Cholla

Coconino High School
2801 N Izabel St, Flagstaff AZ 86004
DP Coordinator Chelsea Drey
Languages English, Spanish
T: +1 928 773 8200
W: www.fusd1.org/chs

Desert Garden Montessori
5130 E. Warner Rd., Phoenix AZ 85044
MYP Coordinator Krista John
Languages English
T: +1 480 496 9833
W: desertgardenmontessori.org

Desert Mountain High School
12575 E Via Linda, Scottsdale Unified, Scottsdale AZ 85259
DP Coordinator Laura Kamka
MYP Coordinator Kevin Sheh
Languages English
T: +1 480 484 7009
W: www.susd.org/Domain/19

EDUPRIZE Schools
580 W Melody Ave., Gilbert AZ 85233
DP Coordinator Amy Smith
Languages English
T: +1 480 888 1610
W: www.eduprizeschools.net

Estrella Mountain Elementary School
10301 S. San Miguel Road, Goodyear AZ 85338
MYP Coordinator Michele Bove
PYP Coordinator Zuzana Finn
Languages English
T: +1 623 386 3001

Florence High School
1000 S. Main St, Florence AZ 85232
DP Coordinator Edward Callahan
MYP Coordinator Edward Callahan
Languages English
T: +1 520 866 3560
W: fhs.fusdaz.com

Gilbert High School
1101 East Elliot Road, Gilbert AZ 85234
DP Coordinator Brendan Keyes
Languages English
T: +1 480 497 0177
W: www.gilbertschools.net/gilberthigh

Ironwood High School
6051 W. Sweetwater Ave, Glendale AZ 85304
DP Coordinator Ian Curtis
Languages English
T: +1 623 486 6400
W: www.peoriaunified.org/ironwood

Kyrene Middle School
1050 E Carver Rd, Tempe AZ 85284
MYP Coordinator Kathie Cigich
Languages English
T: +1 480 541 6600
W: www.kyrene.org/kyr

Madison Meadows Middle School
225 W. Ocotillo Rd, Phoenix AZ 85013
MYP Coordinator Claire Vacanti
Languages English
T: +1 602 664 7610
W: madisonaz.org/meadows-middle-school/home

Madison Simis Elementary School
7302 N. 10th Street, Phoenix AZ 85020
PYP Coordinator Melissa Powers
Languages English
T: +1 602 664 7300
W: madisonaz.org/simis-elementary-school/home

Marc T. Atkinson Middle School
4315 N. Maryvale Parkway, Phoenix AZ 85031
MYP Coordinator Suzi Brown
Languages English, Spanish
T: +1 623 691 1700
W: www.atkinson.csd83.org

Mesa Academy of Advanced Studies
6919 East Brown Road, Mesa AZ 85217
MYP Coordinator Michael Spencer
Languages English
T: +1 480 308 7400
W: www.mpsaz.org/academy

Millennium High School
14802 W Wigwam Blvd, Goodyear AZ 85395
DP Coordinator Monique Winfield
Languages English
T: +1 623 932 7200
W: www.aguafria.org/Domain/10

Mountain View Preparatory School
2939 Del Rio Drive, Cottonwood AZ 86326
PYP Coordinator Heather Langley
Languages English
T: +1 928 649 8144
W: mvp.cocsd.us

Mountainside Middle School
11256 N 128th Street, Scottsdale AZ 85259
MYP Coordinator Kate Hillman
Languages English
T: +1 480 484 5500
W: www.susd.org/mountainside

Nogales High School
1905 N. Apache Blvd., Nogales AZ 85621
DP Coordinator Jennifer Valenzuela
Languages English
T: +1 520 377 2021

Norterra Canyon School
2200 W Maya Way, Phoenix AZ 85085
MYP Coordinator Joseph Stempniewski
Languages English, French
T: +1 623 445 8200
W: www.dvusd.org/Domain/119

North Canyon High School
1700 East Union Hills Drive, Phoenix AZ 85024
DP Coordinator Matt Case
MYP Coordinator Ian Connell
Languages English
T: +1 623 780 4200
W: www.pvschools.net/schools/north-canyon-high/home

North High School
1101 E. Thomas Rd., Phoenix AZ 85014
DP Coordinator Estaban Flemons
Languages English
T: +1 602 826 4702
W: www.northhs.com

Quail Run Elementary School
3303 E. Utopia Rd., Phoenix AZ 85050
PYP Coordinator Dianna Rubey
Languages English
T: +1 602 449 4400
W: www.pvschools.net/qres

Rancho Solano Preparatory School
9180 E. Via de Ventura, Scottsdale AZ 85258
DP Coordinator Marco Garbarino
Languages English
T: +1 480 646 8200
W: www.ranchosolano.com

Summit Academy (7-8 Campus)
1550 Wets Summit Place, Chandler AZ 85224
MYP Coordinator Mary Roberts Winters
Languages English
T: +1 480 472 3430
W: www.mpsaz.org/summitacademy

Summit Academy (K-6 Campus)
1560 W Summit Place, Chandler AZ 85224
PYP Coordinator Camille Loudenbeck
Languages English
T: +1 480 472 3500
W: www.mpsaz.org/summitacademy

Tempe Academy of International Studies
3205 S. Rural Road, Tempe AZ 85282
MYP Coordinator Melissa Revel
Languages English
T: +1 480 730 7101
W: www.tempeschools.org

Tempe High School
1730 S Mill Avenue, Tempe AZ 85281
DP Coordinator James Michael Cooper
Languages English
T: +1 480 967 1661
W: www.tempeunion.org

The Odyssey Institute High School
1495 S Verrado Way, Buckeye AZ 85326
DP Coordinator Randy Hiatt
MYP Coordinator Randy Hiatt
Languages English
T: +1 623 327 1757
W: odyprep.com/oi

IB AMERICAS

Verde Valley School
3511 Verde Valley School Road, Sedona AZ 86351
DP Coordinator Andy Gill
Languages English
T: +1 928 284 2272
W: www.vvsaz.org
 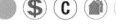

Vista Verde Middle School
2826 E. Grovers Ave., Phoenix AZ 85032
MYP Coordinator Ian Connell
Languages English
T: +1 602 449 5300
W: www.pvschools.net/domain/44

Westwood High School
945 West 8th Street, Mesa AZ 85201
CP Coordinator Jennifer Keller
DP Coordinator Jacob Davis
MYP Coordinator Brian Buck
Languages English
T: +1 480 472 4400
W: www.mpsaz.org/westwood

Willow Canyon High School
17901 West Lundberg St, Surprise AZ 85388
DP Coordinator Jason Ward
Languages English
T: +1 623 523 8000
W: www.dysart.org/schoolsite/?schoolid=210

Arkansas

Bentonville High School
1801 SE J Street, Bentonville AR 72712
DP Coordinator Derek Miller
Languages English
T: +1 479 254 5100
W: bhs.bentonvillek12.org/pages/bentonville_hs

Hot Springs High School
701 Emory Street, Hot Springs AR 71913
CP Coordinator Shannon Geoffrion
DP Coordinator Shannon Geoffrion
MYP Coordinator William Brazle
Languages English
T: +1 501 624 5286

Hot Springs Middle School
701 Main Street, Hot Springs AR 71913
MYP Coordinator William Brazle
Languages English
T: +1 501 624 5228

Park International Magnet School
617 Main Street, Hot Springs AR 71913
PYP Coordinator Kristal Brandon
Languages English
T: +1 501 623 5661

Springdale High School
1103 West Emma Avenue, Springdale AR 72764
DP Coordinator Megan Brazle
Languages English
T: +1 479 750 8832
W: www.sdale.org/o/springdale-high-school

Westwood Elementary School
1850 McRay Ave, Springdale AR 72762
PYP Coordinator Sharyn O'Hearn
Languages English
T: +1 479 750 8871
W: westwood.sdale.org

California

Academia Moderna Charter
2410 Broadway, Walnut Park CA 90255
PYP Coordinator Miram Choi
Languages English
T: +1 323 923 0383
W: www.academiamoderna.org

ACE Charter High School
570 Airport Way, Camarillo CA 93010
CP Coordinator Marina Morales
Languages English, Spanish
T: +1 805 437 1410
W: www.acecharterhigh.org

Agoura High School
28545 W Driver Avenue, Agoura Hills CA 91301
DP Coordinator Jennifer Correia
Languages English
T: +1 818 889 1262
W: www.agourahighschool.net

Al-Arqam Islamic School & College Preparatory
6990 65th Street, Sacramento CA 95823
DP Coordinator Leena Jamaleddin
Languages English
T: +1 916 391 3333
W: www.alarqamislamicschool.org

Albert Einstein Academy Charter School
3035 Ash Street, San Diego CA 92102
MYP Coordinator Corie Julius
PYP Coordinator Corie Julius
Languages English
T: +1 619 795 1190
W: www.aeacs.org

Alice Birney Elementary School
4345 Campus Ave., San Diego CA 92103
PYP Coordinator Jennifer Sims
Languages English
T: +1 619 497 3500
W: www.sandi.net/birney

Alto International School
475 Pope St, Menlo Park CA 94025
DP Coordinator Geneva Robinson
MYP Coordinator Veronique Merckling
PYP Coordinator Jacqueline Cody
Languages English, German
T: +1 650 324 8617
W: www.altoschool.org

Amelia Earhart Elementary School of International Studies
45-250 Dune Palms Road, Indio CA 92201
PYP Coordinator Jennifer Lindsay
Languages English
T: +1 760 200 3720
W: sites.google.com/desertsands.us/amelia-earhart-elementary

Anahuacalmecac International University Prep High School
4736 Huntington Drive South, Los Angeles CA 90032
MYP Coordinator Minnie Ferguson
PYP Coordinator Minnie Ferguson
Languages English
T: +1 323 225 4549 EXT:100
W: www.dignidad.org

Anahuacalmecac International University Preparatory
4736 Huntington Drive South, Los Angeles CA 90032
PYP Coordinator Minnie Ferguson
Languages English
T: +1 323 352 3148
W: www.dignidad.org

Andrew P Hill High School
3200 Senter Road, San Jose CA 95111-1399
DP Coordinator Michael Winsatt
MYP Coordinator John Estrela
Languages English
T: +1 408 347 4100
W: andrewphill.esuhsd.org

Armijo High School
824 Washington Street, Fairfield CA 94533
DP Coordinator Lori O'Connor
Languages English
T: +1 707 422 7500
W: www.fsusd.org/armijo

Arroyo Elementary School
1700 E. 7th Street, Ontario CA 91764
PYP Coordinator Silvia Bustamante
Languages English
T: +1 909 985 1012
W: www.omsd.net/Arroyo

Arroyo Valley High School
1881 W Base Line, San Bernardino CA 92411
DP Coordinator Erik Sanchez
MYP Coordinator Dimitrios Chronopoulos
Languages English
T: +1 909 381 4295

Azusa High School
240 North Cerritos Avenue, Azusa CA 91702
DP Coordinator Robert Colera
Languages English
T: +1 626 815 3400
W: www.ahs-ausd-ca.schoolloop.com

Beechwood School
780 Beechwood Avenue, Fullerton CA 92835
MYP Coordinator Jason Lee
Languages English
T: +1 714 447 2850
W: beechwood.fullertonsd.org

Bel Aire Park Magnet School
3580 Beckworth Drive, Napa CA 94558
PYP Coordinator Stacey Abeyta
Languages English
T: +1 707 253 3775
W: bape-nvusd-ca.schoolloop.com

Benjamin Franklin Elementary School
77-800 Calle Tampico, La Quinta CA 92253
PYP Coordinator Christina Winchester
Languages English
T: +1 760 238 9424
W: sites.google.com/a/desertsands.us/franklin-elem

Berkeley High School
1980 Allston Way, Berkeley CA 94704
DP Coordinator Keldon Clegg
Languages English
T: +1 510 644 6120
W: www.berkeleyschools.net/schools/high-schools/berkeley-high-school

Bishop Amat Memorial High School
14301 Fairgrove Avenue, La Puente CA 91746
DP Coordinator Jolene Joseph Pudvan
Languages English
T: +1 626 962 2495
W: www.bishopamat.org

IB AMERICAS

Blair High School

1135 S. Euclid Avenue, Pasadena CA 91106
CP Coordinator Karen Favor
DP Coordinator Karen Law
MYP Coordinator Christine McLaughlin
Languages English
T: +1 626 396 5820
W: blair.pasadenausd.org

Bob Holcomb Elementary School

1345 W 48th St, San Bernardino CA 92407
PYP Coordinator Krista Bjur
Languages English
T: +1 909 887 2505

Bon View Elementary School

2121 S. Bon View Avenue, Ontario CA 91761
PYP Coordinator Shawnna Viramontes
Languages English
T: +1 909 947 3932
W: www.omsd.net/bonview

Bonita Vista High School

751 Otay Lakes Road, Chula Vista CA 91913
DP Coordinator Jared Phelps
Languages English
T: +1 619 397 2000
W: bvh.sweetwaterschools.org

Cajon High School

1200 Hill Drive, San Bernardino CA 92407
DP Coordinator Matthew Reisenhofer
MYP Coordinator Matthew Reisenhofer
Languages English
T: +1 909 881 8120

Caleb Greenwood Elementary School

5457 Carlson Drive, Sacramento CA 95819
PYP Coordinator Kelly Cordero Cordero
Languages English
T: +1 916 277 6266
W: www.scusd.edu/calebgreenwood

Camerado Springs Middle School

2480 Merrychase Drive, Cameron Park CA 95682
MYP Coordinator Amy Gargani
Languages English, Spanish
T: +1 530 677 1658
W: www.buckeyeusd.org/csms

Canyon High School

220 S Imperial Highway, Anaheim Hills CA 92807
DP Coordinator Nancy Belinge
Languages English
T: +1 714 532 8000
W: www.canyonhighschool.org

Canyon Springs High School

23100 Cougar Canyon Rd., Moreno Valley CA 92557
DP Coordinator Amanda Tornero
T: +1 951 571 4760
W: canyonsprings.mvusd.net

Capistrano Valley High School

26301 Via Escolar, Mission Viejo CA 92692
DP Coordinator Dina Kubba
Languages English
T: +1 949 364 6100
W: www.cvhs.com/

Capuchino High School

1501 Magnolia Avenue, San Bruno CA 94066
DP Coordinator Martee Lopez-Schmitt
Languages English
T: +1 650 558 2700
W: www.smuhsd.org/capuchinohigh

Carl Hankey K-8 School

27252 Nubles, Mission Viejo CA 92692
MYP Coordinator Kathy Beitz
PYP Coordinator Stacy Rumpf
Languages English
T: +1 949 234 5315
W: chhawks.schoolloop.com

Casita Center for Technology, Science & Math

260 Cedar Rd., Vista CA 92083
PYP Coordinator Elizabeth Weiser
Languages English
T: +1 760 724 8442

Castle Park High School

1395 Hilltop Drive, Chula Vista CA 91911
DP Coordinator Robert Manroe
Languages English
T: +1 619 585 2000
W: cph.sweetwaterschools.org

Castle Rock Elementary School

2975 Castle Rock Road, Diamond Bar CA 91765
PYP Coordinator Kelly Howard
Languages English
T: +1 909 598 5006
W: www.castlerockknights.org

Cathedral City High School

69250 Dinah Shore Drive, Cathedral City CA 92234
DP Coordinator Ed Perry
Languages English
T: +1 760 770 0100
W: catcityhigh.com

Centennial High School

1820 Rimpau Avenue, Corona CA 92881
DP Coordinator Colleen Lum
MYP Coordinator Sheila Nguyen
Languages English
T: +1 951 739 5670

Cesar E Chavez Middle School

6650 N Magnolia Avenue, San Bernardino CA 92407
MYP Coordinator Zackary Peters
Languages English
T: +1 909 886 2050

Charter Oak High School

1430 E. Covina BLVD, Covina CA 91724
DP Coordinator Kathy Archer
Languages English
T: +1 626 915 5841
W: www.cousd.net/Domain/14

Citrus Hill High School

18150 Wood Rd., Perris CA 92570
DP Coordinator Andrea Williamson
Languages English
T: +1 951 460 0400
W: citrushill.valverde.edu

Claremont High School

1601 North Indian Hill Blvd, Claremont CA 91711
DP Coordinator Natalie Sieg
Languages English
T: +1 909 624 9053
W: chs-claremont-ca.schoolloop.com

Colfax High School

24995 Ben Taylor Rd, Colfax CA 95713
DP Coordinator Kara Diederichs
Languages English
T: +1 530 346 2284
W: sites.google.com/a/puhsd.k12.ca.us/colfax

Competitive Edge Charter Academy

34450 Stonewood Drive, Yucaipa CA 92399
MYP Coordinator Katherine Coutu
PYP Coordinator Jennifer Stahl
Languages English
T: +1 909 790 3207
W: ceca.yucaipaschools.com

Cook Elementary School

875 Cuyamaca Ave., Chula Vista CA 91911
PYP Coordinator Erika Gregg
Languages English
T: +1 619 422 8381
W: schools.cvesd.org/schools/cook

Cooper Academy

2277 W. Bellaire Way, Fresno CA 93705
MYP Coordinator Jayne Day
Languages English
T: +1 559 248 7050
W: www.fresnounified.org/schools/cooper

Cordova High School

2239 Chase Drive, Rancho Cordova CA 95670
CP Coordinator Chris Mahaffey
DP Coordinator Zandi Llanos
MYP Coordinator Grace Martinez
Languages English
T: +1 916 294 2450
W: www.fcusd.org/chs

Corona Fundamental Intermediate

1230 South Main Street, Corona CA 92882
MYP Coordinator Karen White
Languages English
T: +1 909 736 3321

Cyrus J Morris Elementary School

91785 E Calle Baja, Walnut CA 91789
PYP Coordinator Kelly Howard
Languages English
T: +1 909 594 0053
W: cjmorris.wvusd.k12.ca.us

Dailey Elementary Charter School

3135 N. Harrison Ave, Fresno CA 93704
PYP Coordinator Julia Cabrera
Languages English
T: +1 559 248 7060
W: fics.us/dailey

Damien High School

2280 Damien Avenue, La Verne CA 91750
CP Coordinator Melissa Pasillas
DP Coordinator Christopher Arbizu
Languages English
T: +1 909 596 1946
W: www.damien-hs.edu

David Starr Jordan High School

6500 Atlantic Avenue, Long Beach CA 90805
DP Coordinator Heather Banks
Languages English
T: +1 562 423 1471
W: www.lbjordan.schoolloop.com

IB AMERICAS

Del Mar High School

1224 Del Mar Avenue, San Jose CA 95128
DP Coordinator Jessica Olamit
Languages English
T: +1 408 626 3403
W: www.delmar.cuhsd.org

Diamond Bar High School

21400 East Pathfinder Rd, Diamond Bar CA 91765
DP Coordinator Margaret Ku
Languages English
T: +1 909 594 1405
W: dbhs.wvusd.k12.ca.us

Dos Pueblos High School

7266 Alameda Avenue, Goleta CA 93117
DP Coordinator Matt Moran
Languages English
T: +1 805 968 2541

Downtown Magnets High School

1081 W. Temple St, Los Angeles CA 90012
DP Coordinator Marilyn Watt
Languages English
T: +1 213 481 0371
W: www.downtownmagnets.org

Eagle Rock Junior/Senior High School

1750 Yosemite Drive, Los Angeles CA 90041
DP Coordinator Jonathan Malmed
MYP Coordinator Benjamin Elizondo
Languages English
T: +1 323 340 3500
W: www.erhs.la

EDGEWOOD HIGH SCHOOL

1625 W Durness, West Covina CA 91790
CP Coordinator Veronica Perez
DP Coordinator Veronica Perez
MYP Coordinator Manny Co
Languages English
T: +1 626 939 4600
E: vperez@wcusd.org
W: edgewoodib.wcusd.org

See full details on page 499

EDGEWOOD MIDDLE SCHOOL

1625 W. Durness St., West Covina CA 91790
MYP Coordinator Manny Co
Languages English
T: +1 626 939 4600
E: rmaddox@wcusd.org
W: edgewoodib.wcusd.org

See full details on page 500

El Rancho High School

6501 S. Passons Blvd., Pico Rivera CA 90660
DP Coordinator Parvin Qureshi
Languages English, Spanish
T: +1 562 801 7500
W: www.erusd.k12.ca.us/elrancho

El Segundo Middle School

332 Center St., El Segundo CA 90245
MYP Coordinator Crystal Winner
Languages English, Spanish
T: +1 310 615 2690 Ext:1102
W: www.elsegundomiddleschool.org

El Sereno Middle School

2839 North Eastern Avenue, Los Angeles CA 90032
MYP Coordinator George Lin
Languages English
T: +1 323 224 4700
W: www.elserenoms.org

Ellen Ochoa Prep Academy

8110 Paramount Boulevard, Pico Rivera CA 90660
DP Coordinator Esmeralda Montoya
Languages English, Spanish
T: +1 562 801 7560
W: ochoaprep.erusd.org

Empowering Possibilities International Charter School

2945 Ramco Street, Ste. 200, West Sacramento CA 95691
MYP Coordinator MJ Kiwan Gomez
PYP Coordinator Nina Semeryuk
Languages English, Russian
T: +1 916 286 1960
W: www.gcccharters.org/epics

Escuela Bilingüe Internacional

410 Alcatraz Avenue, Oakland CA 94609
MYP Coordinator Chloe Suberville
PYP Coordinator Ashley Black
Languages English
T: +1 510 653 3324
W: www.ebinternacional.org

Fairmont Private Schools - Historic Anaheim Campus

1557 W. Mable Street, Anaheim CA 92805
MYP Coordinator Karen O'Hanlon
PYP Coordinator Karen O'Hanlon
Languages English
T: +1 714 563 4050
W: www.fairmontschools.com/historic-anaheim-campus

Fairmont Private Schools - Preparatory Academy

2200 West Sequoia Avenue, Anaheim CA 92801
DP Coordinator Michael Wheeler
Languages English
T: +1 714 999 5055
W: www.fairmontprepacademy.com

Fallbrook High School

2400 S Stage Coach Lane, Fallbrook CA 92028
CP Coordinator George Herring
DP Coordinator George Herring
Languages English, Spanish
T: +1 760 723 6300
W: www.fallbrookhs.org

Farmdale Elementary School

2660 Ruth Swiggett Drive, Los Angeles CA 90032
PYP Coordinator Christina Dominguez
Languages English
T: +1 323 222 6659
W: farmdalees-lausd-ca.schoolloop.com

Foothill High School

19251 Dodge Avenue, Santa Ana CA 92705
DP Coordinator Josh Hermanson
Languages English
T: +1 714 730 7464
W: www.tustin.k12.ca.us/foothill

Frances E Willard Elementary Magnet School

301 South Madre Street, Pasadena CA 91107
PYP Coordinator Linda Wittry
Languages English
T: +1 626 793 6163
W: www.pusd.us/site/Default.aspx?PageID=41

Franklin High School

4600 E Fremont St, Stockton CA 95215
DP Coordinator Evelyn Reyes
MYP Coordinator Evelyn Reyes
Languages English
T: +1 209 933 7435
W: www.stocktonusd.net/franklin

French American International School & International High School

150 Oak Street, San Francisco CA 94102-5812
DP Coordinator Dina Srouji
Languages English
T: +1 415 558 2000
W: www.internationalsf.org

Fresno High School

1839 N Echo Avenue, Fresno CA 93704
CP Coordinator Kei Shabazz
DP Coordinator Kyra Orgill
MYP Coordinator Kyra Orgill
Languages English
T: +1 559 457 2793
W: go.fresnounified.org/fresno

Fullerton Union High School

201 E. Chapman Ave, Fullerton CA 92832
DP Coordinator Mark Henderson
Languages English
T: +1 714 626 3800
W: www.fullertonhigh.org

Gateway International School

900 Morse Avenue, Sacramento CA 95864
MYP Coordinator Deep Dhillon
PYP Coordinator Adrian Peer
Languages English
T: +1 916 286 1985
W: gischarter.org

George Sargeant Elementary

1200 Ridgecrest Way, Roseville CA 95661
PYP Coordinator Regina DeArcos
Languages English
T: +1 916 771 1800
W: sargeant.rcsdk8.org

Glen A Wilson High School

16455 East Wedgeworth Drive, Hacienda Heights CA 91745
DP Coordinator Christina Rouw
Languages English
T: +1 626 934 4401

Goethe International Charter School

12500 Braddock Dr, Los Angeles CA 90066
PYP Coordinator Angel Truong
Languages English, German
T: +1 310 306 3484
W: goethecharterschool.org

Granada High School

400 Wall Street, Livermore CA 94550
DP Coordinator Jon Cariveau
Languages English
T: +1 925 606 4800
W: www.granadahigh.com

IB AMERICAS

Granada Hills Charter High School

10535 Zelzah Avenue, Granada Hills CA 91344
DP Coordinator Sean Lewis
Languages English
T: +1 818 360 2361
W: www.ghchs.com

Granada Preparatory School

10400 Zelzah Avenue, Northridge CA 91326
MYP Coordinator Erica Berg Fonvergne
PYP Coordinator Paulette Collins
Languages English
T: +1 818 368 7254
W: www.gpsschool.org

Granite Bay High School

1 Grizzly Way, Granite Bay CA 95746
DP Coordinator Bernadette Cranmer
Languages English
T: +1 916 786 8676
W: granitebayhigh.org

Granite Hills High School

1719 East Madison Avenue, El Cajon CA 92021
DP Coordinator Matthew Davis
Languages English
T: +1 619 593 5500

Great Oak High School

32555 Deer Hollow Road, Temecula CA 92592
DP Coordinator January King
Languages English
T: +1 951 294 6450
W: gohs.tvusd.k12.ca.us

Grover Beach Elementary School

365 South Tenth Street, Grover Beach CA 93433
PYP Coordinator Petra Reynolds
Languages English
T: +1 805 474 3770
W: groverbeach.luciamarschools.org

Guajome Park Academy

2000 North Santa Fe Avenue, Vista Unified School District, Vista CA 92083
CP Coordinator Judd Thompson
DP Coordinator Judd Thompson
Languages English
T: +1 760 631 5000
W: www.guajome.net/gppa

H. Allen Hight Elementary School

3200 North Park Dr., Sacramento CA 95835
PYP Coordinator Cody Worrall
Languages English
T: +1 916 567 5700
W: www.natomasunified.org/hah

H. Clarke Powers Elementary School

3296 Humphrey Road, Loomis CA 95650
PYP Coordinator Samantha Mashinchi
Languages English
T: +1 916 652 2635
W: www.powers.loomis-usd.k12.ca.us

Harbor High School

300 La Fonda Ave., Santa Cruz CA 95062
DP Coordinator Katrina Wedding
Languages English
T: +1 831 429 3810

Harding University Partnership School

1625 Robbins Street, Santa Barbara CA 93101
PYP Coordinator Mikaela Burkett
Languages English
T: +1 805 965 8994
W: harding.sbunified.org

Harriet G. Eddy Middle School

9329 Soaring Oaks Drive, Elk Grove CA 95758
MYP Coordinator Carolynn Puccioni
Languages English
T: +1 916 683 1302

Hawthorne Elementary School

705 W. Hawthorne, Ontario CA 91762
PYP Coordinator Elizabeth Alapizco
Languages English
T: +1 909 986 6582
W: www.omsd.net/Hawthorne

Horace Mann School

55 North 7th Street, San Jose CA 95112
PYP Coordinator Sophia Rueda
Languages English
T: +1 408 535 6237
W: mann.sjusd.org

Hubert Howe Bancroft Middle School

323 N. Las Palmas Avenue, Los Angeles CA 90023
MYP Coordinator Terry Williamson
Languages English
T: +1 323 993 3400
W: bancroftmiddleschool.org

Inderkum High School

2500 New Market Drive, Sacramento CA 95835
DP Coordinator Jessica Downing
MYP Coordinator Theresa Quinby
Languages English
T: +1 916 567 5640
W: natomasunified.org/ihs

International Children's Academy

1046 South Robertson Blvd, Los Angeles CA 90035
PYP Coordinator Mike Hamberger
Languages English
T: +1 310 657 6798
W: www.icabh.org

INTERNATIONAL SCHOOL OF LOS ANGELES

1105 W. Riverside Drive, Burbank CA 91506
DP Coordinator Donald Buer
Languages English, French
T: +1 626 695 5159
E: admissions@lilaschool.com
W: www.internationalschool.la

See full details on page 510

International School of Monterey

1720 Yosemite Street, Seaside CA 93955
MYP Coordinator Rick Barlow
PYP Coordinator Rick Barlow
Languages English
T: +1 831 583 2165
W: ISMonterey.org

James A Foshay Learning Center

3751 S. Harvard Blvd., Los Angeles CA 90018
MYP Coordinator Michael Laska
PYP Coordinator Danielle Mabry
Languages English
T: +1 323 373 2700
W: www.foshaylc.org

Jefferson Elementary School

3743 Jefferson Street, Carlsbad CA 92009
PYP Coordinator Christy Haeberlein
Languages English
T: +1 760 331 5500
W: jefferson.schoolloop.com

Joe Michell K-8 School

1001 Elaine Ave, Livermore CA 94550
MYP Coordinator Ezgi Booth
PYP Coordinator Ezgi Booth
Languages English
T: +1 925 606 4738
W: www.livermoreschools.org/michell

John F Kennedy High School

8281 Walker Street, La Palma CA 90623
DP Coordinator Caylin Ledterman
Languages English
T: +1 714 220 4118

John Glenn Middle School

79-655 Miles Avenue, DSUSD, Indio CA 92201
MYP Coordinator James Harper
Languages English
T: +1 760 200 3700
W: www.dsusd.k12.ca.us/schools/JGMS

John W. North High School

1550 Third St., Riverside CA 92507
DP Coordinator Christine Schive
Languages English
T: +1 951 788 7311

Jurupa Hills High School

10700 Oleander Avenue, Fontana CA 92337
DP Coordinator David Camberos
MYP Coordinator Kelly Navas
Languages English
T: +1 909 357 6300
W: www.jhills.org

Kate Sessions Elementary School

2150 Beryl Street, San Diego CA 92109
PYP Coordinator Dianne Bermudez
Languages English
T: +1 858 273 3111
W: www.sandiegounified.org/sessions

Kavod Charter School

6991 Balboa Ave., San Diego CA 92111
MYP Coordinator Todd McKeown
Languages English, Hebrew
T: +1 858 386 0887
W: kavodelementary.org

Kit Carson Middle School

5301 N Street, Sacramento CA 95819
DP Coordinator Shawn D'Alesandro
MYP Coordinator Shawn D'Alesandro
Languages English
T: +1 916 277 6750
W: www.kitcarson.scusd.edu

La Costa Canyon High School

1 Maverick Way, Carlsbad CA 92009
DP Coordinator Cindi Schildhouse
Languages English
T: +1 760 436 6136
W: lc.sduhsd.net

La Mirada Academy
3697 La Mirada Drive, San Marcos CA 92078
MYP Coordinator Erin Myres
PYP Coordinator Erin Myres
Languages English
T: +1 760 290 2000

La Quinta High School
79-255 Westward Ho Drive, La Quinta CA 92253
DP Coordinator Elizabeth Van Dorn
Languages English
T: +1 760 772 4150
W: www.dsusd.k12.ca.us/schools/LQHS/

LA SCUOLA INTERNATIONAL SCHOOL
728 20th Street, San Francisco CA 94107
MYP Coordinator Douglas Lowney
PYP Coordinator Leticia Dias
Languages English, Italian And Spanish
T: +1 415 551 0000
E: admissions@lascuolasf.org
W: www.lascuolasf.org
See full details on page 515

Laguna Creek High School
9050 Vicino Drive, Elk Grove CA 95758
DP Coordinator Rod De Luca
MYP Coordinator Jose Oseguera
Languages English
T: +1 916 683 1339
W: www.egusd.net/schools/high-schools/laguna-creek-high-school

Laguna Hills High School
25401 Paseo de Valencia, Laguna Hills CA 92653
DP Coordinator Laurel Crossett
Languages English
T: +1 949 770 5447
W: www.svusd.org/schools/high-schools/laguna-hills

Las Positas Elementary School
1400 S. Schoolwood Drive, La Habra CA 90631
PYP Coordinator Dana Riggs
Languages English
T: +1 562 690 2356
W: www.lahabraschools.org/laspositas

Letha Raney Intermediate
1010 West Citron Street, Corona CA 92882
MYP Coordinator Bronya Martinez
Languages English
T: +1 951 736 3221

Lexington Elementary School
19700 Old Santa Cruz Highway, Los Gatos CA 95033
PYP Coordinator Kristin Johnson
Languages English
T: +1 408 335 2150
W: lex.lgusd.org

Linda Vista Magnet Elementary School
25222 Pericia Drive, Mission Viejo CA 92691
PYP Coordinator Barbara Poiriez
Languages English, Spanish
T: +1 949 830 0970
W: www.svusd.org/schools/elementary-a-l/linda-vista

Loomis Basin Charter School
5438 Laird Road, Loomis CA 95650
MYP Coordinator Justin VonSpreckelsen
PYP Coordinator Justin VonSpreckelsen
Languages English
T: +1 916 652 2642
W: www.loomischarter.org

Luther Burbank High School
3500 Florin Road, Sacramento CA 95823
DP Coordinator Katherine Bell
Languages English
W: lutherburbank.scusd.edu

Marco Antonio Firebaugh High School
5246 Martin Luther King Jr. Blvd, Lynwood CA 90262
DP Coordinator Omar Zúñiga
Languages English
T: +1 310 886 5200
W: fhs.lynwood.k12.ca.us

Maxwell Academy
733 Euclid Avenue, Duarte CA 91010
PYP Coordinator Johna Stienstra
Languages English
T: +1 626 599 5302
W: www.duarteusd.org/page/156

Mira Loma High School
4000 Edison Avenue, San Juan Unified, Sacramento CA 95821
DP Coordinator Rochelle Jacks
MYP Coordinator Rachel Volzer
Languages English
T: +1 916 971 7973
W: www.sanjuan.edu/Domain/64

Mission Bay High School
2475 Grand Ave., San Diego CA 92109
DP Coordinator Tracy Borg
Languages English
T: +1 858 273 1313
W: www.sandi.net/missionbay

Mission Viejo High School
25025 Chrisanta Drive, Mission Viejo CA 9269
DP Coordinator Sandra Hanneman
Languages English
T: +1 949 837 7722
W: www.svusd.org/schools/high-schools/mission-viejo

Modesto High School
First & H Street, Modesto City Schools, Modesto CA 95351
DP Coordinator Kerry Castellani
Languages English
T: +1 209 576 4404

Monte Vista Christian School
2 School Way, Watsonville CA 95076
DP Coordinator Josh Davis
Languages English
T: +1 831 722 8178
W: www.mvcs.org

Monterey High School
101 Herrmann Drive, Monterey CA 93940
DP Coordinator Nikki Ahrenstorff
MYP Coordinator Nikki Ahrenstorff
Languages English, Spanish
T: +1 831 392 3801
W: montereyhigh.mpusd.net

Montgomery High School
1250 Hahman Drive, Santa Rosa CA 95405
DP Coordinator Jim Rudesill
Languages English
T: +1 707 528 5512
W: www.montgomeryhighschool.com

Mount Vernon Elementary
8350 Mount Vernon Street, Lemon Grove CA 91945
PYP Coordinator Irisbelle Rodriguez-Mosler
Languages English
T: +1 619 825 5613
W: mve.lemongrovesd.net

Murrieta Valley High School
42200 Nighthawk Way, Murrieta CA 92562
DP Coordinator Alanna Fields
Languages English
T: +1 951 696 1408
W: www.murrieta.k12.ca.us/Domain/1416

Muwekma Ohlone Middle School
850 North Second Street, San Jose CA 95112
MYP Coordinator Jelani Canser
Languages English
T: +1 408 535 6267
W: ohlone.sjusd.org

Natomas Middle School
3200 North Park Drive, Sacramento CA 95835
MYP Coordinator Cody Worrall
Languages English
T: +1 916 567 5540
W: natomasunified.org/nms

New Covenant Academy
3119 W 6th Street, Los Angeles CA 90020
DP Coordinator Joseph Chai
Languages English
T: +1 213 487 5437
W: www.e-nca.org

Newbury Park High School
456 Reino Road, Newbury Park CA 91320
DP Coordinator Deborah Dogançay
Languages English
T: +1 805 498 3676
W: dev.nphs.org

Newport Harbor High School
600 Irvine Avenue, Newport Beach CA 92663
DP Coordinator Alma Di Giorgio
Languages English
T: +1 949 515 6300
W: nhhs.schoolloop.com

Nogales High School
401 Nogales Street, Rowland Unified School Distric, La Puente CA 91744
DP Coordinator Clay Woodside
Languages English
T: +1 626 965 3437

Norte Vista High School
6585 Crest Avenue, Riverside CA 92503
DP Coordinator Shawn Marshall
Languages English
T: +1 951 351 9316
W: www.alvord.k12.ca.us/nortevista

Northcoast Preparatory Academy
285 Bayside Rd, 1761 11th St., Arcata CA 95521
DP Coordinator Amy Bazemore
MYP Coordinator Amy Bazemore
Languages English
T: +1 707 822 0861

Oakmont High School

1710 Cirby Way, Roseville CA 95661
DP Coordinator Jolie Geluk
Languages English
T: +1 916 782 3781
W: ohs.rjuhsd.us

Ocean Knoll Elementary School

910 Melba Road, Encinitas CA 92024
PYP Coordinator Sanjana Bryant
Languages English
T: +1 760 944 4351
W: www.eusd.net/ok

Ocean View High School

17071 Gothard St., Huntington Beach CA 92647
DP Coordinator Brenda Mcdonough
Languages English
T: +1 714 848 0656
W: www.ovhs.info

ORANGEWOOD ELEMENTARY

1440 S. Orange Avenue, West Covina CA 91790
PYP Coordinator Mrs. Candice Hernandez
Languages English, Spanish, Mandarin
T: +1 626 939 4820
W: orangewood.wcusd.org

See full details on page 534

Pacific Beach Middle School

4676 Ingraham Street, San Diego CA 92109
MYP Coordinator Ashley Hensen
Languages English
T: +1 858 273 9070
W: www.sandiegounified.org/schools/pacific-beach-middle

Palmdale Learning Plaza

38043 Division Street, Palmdale CA 93551
MYP Coordinator Beverly Gonda
PYP Coordinator Beverly Gonda
Languages English
T: +1 661 538 9034
W: www.palmdalesd.org/Page/4471

Paso Verde School

3800 Del Paso Rd, Sacramento CA 95834
PYP Coordinator Kristen Martin
Languages English, Spanish
T: +1 916 567 5810
W: natomasunified.org/pvs

Pinole Valley High School

2900 Pinole Valley Rd, Pinole CA 94564
DP Coordinator Dayna Dibble
Languages English
T: +1 510 231 1442
W: www.wccusd.net/pinolevalley

Prepa Tec Middle School

6005 Stafford Ave., Huntington Park CA 90255
MYP Coordinator Vanessa Garcia
Languages English
T: +1 323 800 2738
W: altapublicschools.org

Primary Years Academy

1540 N.Lincoln St, Stockton CA 95204
PYP Coordinator Hina Lee
Languages English
T: +1 209 933 7355
W: www.stocktonusd.net/PYA

Quarry Lane School

6363 Tassajara Road, Dublin CA 94568
DP Coordinator Jyothi Kiran Hoskere
Languages English
T: +1 925 829 8000
W: www.quarrylane.org

Quartz Hill High School

6040 West Avenue L, Quartz Hill CA 93536
DP Coordinator Jeff Cassady
Languages English
T: +1 661 718 3100

Rancho Buena Vista High School

1601 Longhorn Drive, Vista CA 92081
DP Coordinator Melissa Neumann
Languages English
T: +1 760 727 7284

Ray Wiltsey Middle School

1450 E., Ontario CA 91764
MYP Coordinator Terri Bradley
Languages English
T: +1 909 986 5838
W: www.omsd.net/Wiltsey

Rio Mesa High School

545 Central Avenue, Oxnard CA 93030
CP Coordinator Ingrid Brennan
DP Coordinator Lori A Wrout
MYP Coordinator Lori A Wrout
Languages English
T: +1 805 278 5500
W: www.riomesahigh.us

Roosevelt Middle School

3366 Park Blvd., San Diego CA 92103
MYP Coordinator Deborah Christensen
Languages English
T: +1 619 293 4450
W: www.sandiegounified.org/roosevelt

Rowland High School

2000 S Otterbein Avenue, Rowland Heights CA 91748
DP Coordinator Stephen Ludlam
Languages English
T: +1 626 965 3448
W: www.rowlandhs.org

Royal High School

1402 Royal Avenue, Simi Valley CA 93065
DP Coordinator Kari Lev
Languages English
T: +1 805 306 4875 EXT:1
W: www.rhs.simi.k12.ca.us

Saddleback High School

2802 South Flower Street, Santa Ana CA 92707
DP Coordinator Dana Kassaei
Languages English
T: +1 714 569 6300
W: www.sausd.us/saddleback

San Clemente High School

700 Avenida Pico, San Clemente CA 92673
DP Coordinator Lisa Alizadeh
Languages English
T: +1 949 492 4165

San Diego High School of International Studies

1405 Park Boulevard, San Diego CA 92101
DP Coordinator Nirit Cohen-Vardi
Languages English
T: +1 619 525 7455
W: www.sandiegounified.org/sdhsis

San Jacinto Elementary

136 N. Ramona Blvd., San Jacinto CA 92583
PYP Coordinator Stacy Ward
Languages English
T: +1 951 654 7349
W: sjes.sanjacinto.k12.ca.us

San Jacinto High School

500 Idyllwild Drive, San Jacinto CA 92583
DP Coordinator Matthew Corum
Languages English
T: +1 951 654 7374
W: sjhs.sanjacinto.k12.ca.us

San Jacinto Valley Academy

480 N San Jacinto Avenue, San Jacinto CA 92583
DP Coordinator Jonathan Harrison
PYP Coordinator Kelly Perez
Languages English
T: +1 951 654 6113
W: www.sjva.net

San Jose High School

275 North 24th St., San Jose CA 95116-1109
CP Coordinator Gerson Sandoval
DP Coordinator Gerson Sandoval
MYP Coordinator Salvatore Martinico
Languages English
T: +1 408 535 6320
W: sjhs.sjusd.org

Santa Clarita Valley International School

28060 Hasley Canyon, Castaic CA 91384
DP Coordinator Cheryl Sena
Languages English
T: +1 661 705 4820
W: www.scvcharterschool.org

Santa Margarita Catholic High School

22062 Antonio Parkway, Rancho Santa Margarita CA 92688
DP Coordinator Maria D.S. Andrade Johnson
Languages English
T: +1 949 766 6000
W: www.smhs.org

Schools of the Sacred Heart

2222 Broadway, San Francisco CA 94115
DP Coordinator Devin DeMartini
Languages English
T: +1 415 563 2900
W: www.sacredsf.org

Scotts Valley High School

Principal, 555 Glenwood Drive, Scotts Valley CA 95066
DP Coordinator David Crawford
Languages English
T: +1 831 439 9555

Sequoia High School

1201 Brewster Avenue, Redwood City CA 94062
DP Coordinator Lisa McCahon
Languages English
T: +1 650 369 1411
W: www.sequoiahs.org

Short Avenue Elementary School

12814 Maxella Ave, Los Angeles CA 90066

PYP Coordinator Rachel Burris

Languages English, Spanish

T: +1 310 397 4234

W: www.shortavenue.org

Shu Ren International School

2125 Jefferson Avenue, Berkeley CA 94703

PYP Coordinator Alexandra Ditchey

Languages English, Mandarin

T: +1 510 841 8899

W: shurenschool.org

Sierra Elementary School

6811 Camborne Way, Rocklin CA 95677

PYP Coordinator Lisa Johnson

Languages English

T: +1 916 788 7141

W: ses.rocklinusd.org

Sonora High School

401 South Palm Street, Fullerton Joint Union, La Habra CA 90631

DP Coordinator Shannon Appenrodt

Languages English

T: +1 562 266 2013

South Hills High School

645 S. Barranca Street, West Covina CA 91791

DP Coordinator Marisol Marquez

Languages English

T: +1 626 974 6200

W: www.southhillshigh.com

Southwest High School

2001 Ocotillo Drive, El Centro CA 92243

DP Coordinator Marina Corral

Languages English

T: +1 760 336 4100

W: www.eaglesnet.net

St. Francis of Assisi Elementary School

2500 K Street, Sacramento CA 95816

PYP Coordinator Isabel Garcia

Languages English

T: +1 916 442 5494

W: www.stfranciselem.org

St. Mary's School

7 Pursuit, Aliso Viejo CA 92656

MYP Coordinator Jocelyn Williams

PYP Coordinator Lauren Sterner

Languages English

T: +1 949 448 9027

W: www.smaa.org

Stanley G Oswalt Academy

19501 Shadow Oak Drive, Walnut CA 91789

PYP Coordinator Raquel Bahena

Languages English

T: +1 626 810 4109

W: oswalt.rowlandschools.org

Stockton Collegiate International Elementary School

321 E. Weber Ave, Stockton CA 95202

PYP Coordinator John Piasecki

Languages English

T: +1 209 390 9861

W: www.stocktoncollegiate.org

Stockton Collegiate International Secondary School

PO Box 2286, Stockton CA 95201

DP Coordinator Manuel Aguilar

MYP Coordinator Hauna Zaich

Languages English

T: +1 209 464 7108

W: www.stocktoncollegiate.org

Stowers Magnet School of International Studies

13350 Beach Street, Cerritos CA 90703

PYP Coordinator Sharie Tom

Languages English

T: +1 562 229 7905

W: www.stowerses.us

Summit Charter Academy

1509 Lombardi Street, Porterville CA 93257

PYP Coordinator Shana Watson

Languages English

T: +1 559 788 6445

W: www.summitlombardi.org

Summit Charter Collegiate Academy

15550 Redwood Drive, Porterville CA 93257

MYP Coordinator Jenifer Sanders

Languages English, Spanish

T: +1 559 788 6440

W: www.summitcollegiate.org

Sunny Hills High School

1801 Warburton Way, Fullerton CA 92833

DP Coordinator Brian Wall

Languages English

T: +1 714 626 4213

W: www.sunnyhills.net

Sunnybrae Elementary School

1031 South Delaware Street, San Mateo CA 94402

PYP Coordinator Wynne Hegarty

Languages English

T: +1 650 312 7599

W: sunnybrae.smfcsd.net

Temescal Canyon High School

28755 El Toro Road, Lake Elsinore CA 92532

DP Coordinator Jason Garrison

Languages English

T: +1 951 253 7250

W: tch.leusd.k12.ca.us

The Healdsburg School

33H Healdsburg Avenue, Healdsburg CA 95448

PYP Coordinator Jami Trinidad

Languages English

T: +1 707 433 4847

W: www.thehealdsburgschool.org

Thomas Jefferson Elementary School

3770 Utah Street, San Diego CA 92104

PYP Coordinator Erin Knight

Languages English

T: +1 619 344 3300

W: www.sandiegounified.org/jefferson

Thomas Kelly Elementary School

6301 Moraga Drive, Carmichael CA 95608

PYP Coordinator Deb Olivarria-Matson

Languages English

T: +1 916 867 2401

W: www.sanjuan.edu/kelly

Trabuco Hills High School

27501 Mustang Run, Mission Viejo CA 92691

DP Coordinator Lindsay Casserly

Languages English

T: +1 949 768 1934

Tracy Joint Union High School

315 East 11th Street, Tracy Public Schools, Tracy CA 95376

DP Coordinator Jeff Alexandre

Languages English

T: +1 209 830 3360

W: tracyhigh.tracy.k12.ca.us

Troy High School

2200 East Dorothy Lane, Fullerton CA 92831

DP Coordinator Charlotte Kirkpatrick

Languages English

T: +1 714 626 4401

W: www.troyhigh.com

Valencia High School

500 N Bradford Avenue, Placentia CA 92870

DP Coordinator Fred Jenkins

Languages English

T: +1 714 996 4970

Valley Preparatory School

1605 Ford Street, Redlands CA 92373

PYP Coordinator Melanie Whitenack

Languages English, Spanish

T: +1 909 793 3063

W: www.valleypapredlands.org

Valley View Charter Montessori

1665 Blackstone Parkway, El Dorado Hills CA 95762

MYP Coordinator Amy Gargani

Languages English, Spanish

T: +1 916 939 9640

W: www.buckeyeusd.org/vvcm

Villanova Preparatory School

12096 N. Ventura Avenue, Ojai CA 93023

DP Coordinator Brian Roney

Languages English

T: +1 805 646 1464

W: www.villanovaprep.org

Vista Academy of Visual and Performing Arts

600 N. Santa Fe Avenue, Vista CA 92083

PYP Coordinator Sharon Scott-Gonzalez

Languages English

T: +1 760 941 0880

Vista Heights Middle School

23049 Old Lake Drive, Moreno Valley CA 92557

MYP Coordinator Susan Young

Languages English, Spanish

T: +1 951 571 4300

W: vistaheights.mvusd.net

Vista High School

1 Panther Way, Vista CA 92084

DP Coordinator Megan Ratliff

Languages English

T: +1 760 726 5611

W: vhs.vistausd.org

Vista Magnet Middle School

151 Civic Center Dr, Vista CA 92084

MYP Coordinator Jennifer Eckle

Languages English

T: +1 760 726 5766

W.E. Mitchell Middle School

2100 Zinfandel Drive, Rancho Cordova CA 95670
MYP Coordinator Suzanne Titchenal
Languages English
T: +1 916 635 8460
W: www.fcusd.org/mitchell

Walnut High School

400 N Pierre Rd, Walnut CA 91789
CP Coordinator Manette Idris
DP Coordinator Manette Idris
Languages English
T: +1 909 594 1333

Walter Colton Middle School

100 Toda Vista, Monterey CA 93940
MYP Coordinator Anne Davis
Languages English
T: +1 831 649 1951
W: wcms.mpusd.net

Warren T. Eich Middle School

1509 Sierra Gardens Drive, Roseville CA 95661-4804
MYP Coordinator Lisa Shrider
Languages English
T: +1 916 771 1770
W: eich.rcsdk8.org

West County Mandarin School

1575 Mann Drive, Pinole CA 94564
PYP Coordinator Jie Ni
Languages English, Chinese
T: +1 510 307 4523
W: wcmspta.org

West Valley High School

3401 Mustang Way, Hemet CA 92545
DP Coordinator Ahmed El-Sayad
Languages English, Spanish
T: +1 951 765 1600
W: www.wvhsmustangs.net

William F McKinley Elementary School

3045 Felton Street, San Diego CA 92104
PYP Coordinator Roni Greenwood
Languages English
T: +1 619 282 7694
W: www.sandiegounified.org/mckinley

Winston Churchill Middle School

4900 Whitney Avenue, Carmicheal CA 95608
MYP Coordinator Kristen Manchester
Languages English
T: +1 916 971 7324

Woodrow Wilson High School

4500 Multnomah Street, Los Angeles CA 90032
DP Coordinator Erica Welsh-Westfall
MYP Coordinator Erica Welsh-Westfall
Languages English
T: +1 323 276 1600
W: www.ibwilsonmules.com

Ybarra Academy of the Arts & Technology

1300 Brea Canyon Cut-off Road, Walnut CA 91789
PYP Coordinator Jacquie Robinson
Languages English, Spanish
T: +1 909 598 3744
W: ybarra.rowlandschools.org

Ygnacio Valley High School

755 Oak Grove Road, Concord CA 94518
DP Coordinator Carissa Weintraub
Languages English
T: +1 925 685 8414
W: yvhs.mdusd.org

Yosemite High School

50200 Road 427, Oakhurst CA 93644
DP Coordinator Arlene Aoki
Languages English
T: +1 559 683 4667
W: www.yosemiteusd.com/yosemite

Colorado

Academy International Elementary School

8550 Charity Drive, Colorado Springs CO 80920
PYP Coordinator Katherine Scott
Languages English
T: +1 719 234 4000
W: academyinternational.asd20.org/Pages/default.aspx

Alameda International High School

1255 S. Wadsworth Blvd., Lakewood CO 80232
CP Coordinator Steve Houwen
DP Coordinator Merinda Sautel
MYP Coordinator Erin Murphy
Languages English
T: +1 303 982 8160

Alpine Elementary School

2005 Alpine Street, Longmont CO 80504
PYP Coordinator Robert Roy
Languages English
T: +1 720 652 8140
W: aes.svvsd.org

Antelope Trails Elementary

15280 Jessie Drive, Colorado Springs CO 80921
PYP Coordinator Tia Guillan
Languages English
T: +1 719 234 4100
W: antelopetrails.asd20.org

Aspen High School

235 High School Road, Aspen CO 81611
DP Coordinator Eileen Knapp
Languages English
T: +1 970 925 3760
W: www.aspenk12.net/page/13

Aurora Hills Middle School

1009 S Uvalda, Aurora CO 80012
MYP Coordinator Sue Wagoner
Languages English
T: +1 303 341 7450
W: ahills.aurorak12.org

Bear Valley International School

3005 South Golden Way, Denver CO 80227
MYP Coordinator Alberto Martinez
Languages English
T: +1 720 423 9600

Bennett Elementary School

1125 Bennett Road, Fort Collins CO 80521
PYP Coordinator Kurt Woolner
Languages English
T: +1 970 488 4750
W: ben.psdschools.org

Boulder Country Day School

4820 Nautilus Court North, Boulder CO 80301
MYP Coordinator Gwynn Reback
Languages English
T: +1 303 527 4931
W: www.bouldercountryday.org

Bradley International School

3051 S. Elm St., Denver CO 80222
PYP Coordinator Jodie Leatherman
Languages English
T: +1 720 424 9468

Breckenridge Elementary School

312 S. Harris Street, PO Box 1213, Breckenridge CO 80424
PYP Coordinator Leigh Guevara
Languages English, Spanish
T: +1 970 368 1300
W: bre.summitk12.org

Brentwood Middle School

2600 24th Avenue Court, Greeley CO 80634
MYP Coordinator Andy Hartshorn
T: +1 970 348 3000
W: www.greeleyschools.org/domain/24

Brown International Academy

2550 Lowell Boulevard, Denver CO 80211
PYP Coordinator Melissa Capozza
Languages English
T: +1 720 424 9287

Cache La Poudre Elementary School

3511 W. County Rd., Laporte CO 80535
PYP Coordinator Mandy Parton
Languages English
T: +1 970 488 7600
W: cpe.psdschools.org

Cache La Poudre Middle School

3511 W. County Rd. 54 G, La Porte CO 80535
MYP Coordinator Delhia Mahaney
Languages English
T: +1 970 488 7400
W: clp.psdschools.org

Centaurus High School

10300 E South Boulder Road, Lafayette CO 80026
DP Coordinator Johanna Wintergerst
Languages English
T: +1 720 561 7500
W: www.centaurushs.org

Central Elementary School

1020 4th Avenue, Longmont CO 80501
PYP Coordinator Hillary Simonson
Languages English
T: +1 303 776 3236
W: centrales.svvsd.org

Century Middle School

13000 Lafayette Street, Thornton CO 80241
MYP Coordinator Holly Jones
Languages English
T: +1 720 972 5240
W: century.adams12.org

Charles Hay World School

3195 S Layfayette Street, Englewood CO 80113
PYP Coordinator Leah Meier
Languages English
T: +1 303 761 2433
W: www.englewoodschools.net/schools/charles-hay-world-school

Cherokee Trail High School

25901 E Arapahoe Road, Aurora CO 80016
DP Coordinator Karen Slusher
Languages English
T: +1 720 886 1900
W: www.cherrycreekschools.org/cherokeetrail

Corwin International Magnet School

1500 Lakeview Ave., Pueblo CO 81004
MYP Coordinator Cassie Pate
PYP Coordinator Jaime Quinn
Languages English
T: +1 719 549 7400
W: cims.pueblocityschools.us

Coyote Ridge Elementary School

7115 Avondale Road, Fort Collins CO 80525
PYP Coordinator Jennifer Bozic
Languages English
T: +1 970 679 9400
W: www.thompsonschools.org/coyoteridge

Dakota Ridge High School

13399 West Coal Mine Avenue, Littleton CO 80127
DP Coordinator Holly Davis
Languages English
T: +1 303 982 1970

Dillon Valley Elementary School

P.O. Box 4788, 0108 Deerpath, Dillon CO 80435
PYP Coordinator Jaime Levi
Languages English
T: +1 970 368 1400
W: dve.summitk12.org

Discovery Canyon Campus

1810 North Gate Blvd, Colorado Springs CO 80921
CP Coordinator Melissa Knight
DP Coordinator Melissa Knight
MYP Coordinator Alisa Schleder
PYP Coordinator Autumn Cave-Crosby
Languages English
T: +1 719 234 1800
W: dccelementary.asd20.org/Pages/default.aspx

Dos Rios Elementary School

2201 34th Street, Evans CO 80620
PYP Coordinator Christina Allem
Languages English
T: +1 970 348 1309
W: www.greeleyschools.org/dosrios

Douglas County High School

2842 Front Street, Castle Rock CO 80104
DP Coordinator Steven Fleet
MYP Coordinator Christine Veto
Languages English
T: +1 303 387 1004

Dunn Elementary School

501 South Washington, Fort Collins CO 80521
PYP Coordinator Esther Croak
Languages English
T: +1 970 482 0450

Eagle Valley Elementary School

PO Box 780, Eagle CO 81631
PYP Coordinator Anita ortiz
Languages English, Spanish
T: +1 970 328 6981
W: www.eagleschools.net/schools/eagle-valley-elementary

East Middle School

1275 Fraser Street, Aurora CO 80011
MYP Coordinator Tara Bakos
Languages English
T: +1 303 340 0660
W: east.aurorak12.org

Elkhart Elementary School

1020 Eagle Street, Aurora CO 80011
PYP Coordinator Michelle Karp
Languages English
T: +1 303 340 3050
W: elkhart.aurorak12.org

Fairview High School

1515 Greenbriar Blvd., Boulder CO 80305-7043
DP Coordinator Christopher Weber
Languages English
T: +1 720 561 3100
W: www.fairviewhs.org

Fountain International Magnet School

925 North Glendale Avenue, Pueblo CO 81001
PYP Coordinator Stephanie Burke
Languages English
T: +1 719 423 3050
W: fims.pueblocityschools.us

Frisco Elementary

PO Box 4820, Frisco CO 80443
PYP Coordinator Amy Hume
Languages English
T: +1 970 368 1500
W: fre.summitk12.org

Gateway High School

1300 S Sable Blvd, Aurora CO 80012
DP Coordinator Jason Dillon
MYP Coordinator Jason Dillon
Languages English
T: +1 303 755 7160
W: gateway.aurorak12.org

George Washington High School

655 S Monaco Pkwy, Denver CO 80224
DP Coordinator Richard Maez
Languages English
T: +1 303 394 8620

Global Intermediate Academy

7480 N. Broadway, Denver CO 80221
MYP Coordinator Rebeca Martinez
PYP Coordinator Emelina Pacheco
Languages English, Spanish
T: +1 303 853 1930
W: www.mapleton.us/Domain/1302

Global Leadership Academy

7480 North Broadway, Denver CO 80221
MYP Coordinator Rebeca Martinez
Languages English
T: +1 303 853 1930
W: www.mapleton.us/globalleadershipacademy

Global Primary Academy

7480 N. Broadway, Denver CO 80221
PYP Coordinator Brieanna Schwab
Languages English, Spanish
T: +1 303 853 1930
W: www.mapleton.us/Domain/14

Greeley West High School

2401 35th Avenue, Greeley CO 80634
DP Coordinator Bridget Koehler
MYP Coordinator Kaylyn Kingman
Languages English
T: +1 970 348 5400
W: www.west.greeleyschools.org

Hamilton Middle School

8600 East Dartmouth Avenue, Denver CO 80231
MYP Coordinator Rachel Langberg
Languages English, Spanish
T: +1 720 423 9500
W: hamilton.dpsk12.org

Harrison High School

2755 Janitell Road, Colorado Springs CO 80906
DP Coordinator Meredith McCann
MYP Coordinator Miranda Schaelling
Languages English
T: +1 719 579 2080
W: www.hsd2.org/hhs

Hinkley High School

1250 Chambers Road, Aurora CO 80011
CP Coordinator Matthew Brown
DP Coordinator Matthew Brown
MYP Coordinator David Nickoloff
Languages English
T: +1 303 340 1500
W: hinkley.aurorak12.org

International Academy of Denver at Harrington

2401 E. 37th Avenue, Denver CO 80205
PYP Coordinator Anne Witwer
Languages English, Spanish
T: +1 720 424 6420
W: www.internationalacademyofdenver.com

International School of Denver

7701 E. 1st Pl, Unit C, Denver CO 80230
MYP Coordinator Hope Forgey
Languages Chinese, English, French, Spanish
T: +1 303 340 3647
W: www.isdenver.org

John F. Kennedy High School

2855 S. Lamar St., Denver CO 80227
DP Coordinator Alissa Warren
Languages English
T: +1 720 423 4300

King-Murphy Elementary School

425 Circle K Ranch Road, Evergreen CO 80439
PYP Coordinator Anthony Pascoe
Languages English
T: +1 303 670 0005
W: king-murphy.ccsdre1.org

Lakewood High School

9700 W. 8th Ave., Lakewood CO 80215
DP Coordinator Joellen Kramer
Languages English
T: +1 303 982 7096

Leroy Drive Elementary School

1451 Leroy Drive CO 80233
PYP Coordinator Brianna Williams
Languages English
T: +1 720 972 5460

Lesher Middle School

1400 Stover Street, Fort Collins CO 80524
MYP Coordinator Beth Wilms
Languages English
T: +1 970 472 3800
W: les.psdschools.org

Liberty Point International School

484 S. Maher Dr., Pueblo West CO 81007
MYP Coordinator Kelly Jackson
Languages English
T: +1 719 547 3752
W: lpi.district70.org

Lincoln Middle School

1600 Lancer Drive, Fort Collins CO 80521
MYP Coordinator Julie Israelson
Languages English
T: +1 970 488 5700
W: lin.psdschools.org

Littleton High School

199 East Littleton Boulevard, Littleton CO 80121
DP Coordinator Claudia Anderson
Languages English
T: +1 303 347 7700
W: www.littleton.littletonpublicschools.net

Loveland High School

920 W 29th Street, Loveland CO 80538
DP Coordinator Michelle Ray
MYP Coordinator Tané Leach
Languages English
T: +1 970 613 5209
W: www.thompsonschools.org/loveland

Lucile Erwin Middle School

4700 Lucerne Ave., Loveland CO 80538
MYP Coordinator Tané Leach
Languages English
T: +1 970 613 7600
W: www.thompsonschools.org/erwin

Mackintosh Academy

7018 S Prince Street, Littleton CO 80120
MYP Coordinator Sharon Muench
PYP Coordinator Sharon Muench
Languages English
T: +1 303 794 6222
W: www.mackintoshacademy.com

McAuliffe International School

2540 Holly Street, Denver CO 80207
MYP Coordinator Becky Middleton
Languages English
T: +1 720 424 1540
W: mcauliffe.dpsk12.org

McGraw Elementary School

4800 Hinsdale drive, Fort Collins CO 80526
PYP Coordinator Paul Schkade
Languages English
T: +1 970 223 0137

Mesa Middle School

365 North Mitchell Street, Castle Rock CO 80104
MYP Coordinator Sandy Browning
Languages English
T: +1 303 387 4750

Mountain Ridge Middle School

9150 Lexington Drive, Colorado Springs CO 80920
MYP Coordinator Laura Clibor
Languages English
T: +1 719 234 3200
W: mountainridge.asd20.org

Niwot High School

8989 E Niwot Road, Niwot CO 80503
DP Coordinator Elzbieta Towlen
Languages English
T: +1 303 652 2550
W: nhs.svvsd.org

North Middle School

301 North Nevada Avenue, Colorado Springs CO 80903
MYP Coordinator Adam Millman
Languages English
T: +1 719 328 5078

Northfield High School

5500 Central Park Blvd, Denver CO 80238
DP Coordinator Brent Stickrath
Languages English
T: +1 720 423 8000

Overland Trail Middle School

455 North 19th Ave., Brighton CO 80601
MYP Coordinator Christy Meredith
Languages English, Spanish
T: +1 303 655 4000
W: www.sd27j.org/domain/21

Palisade High School

3679 G Road, Palisade CO 81526
DP Coordinator Laura Meinzen
MYP Coordinator Matthew Borgmann
Languages English
T: +1 970 254 4800

Patterson International School

1263 S Dudley St., Lakewood CO 80232
PYP Coordinator Ryan Livingston
Languages English
T: +1 303 982 8470

Poudre High School

201 Impala Drive, Fort Collins CO 80521
DP Coordinator Cori Hixon
MYP Coordinator Katy Sayers
Languages English
T: +1 970 488 6000
W: phs.psdschools.org

Pueblo East High School

9 MacNeil Road, Pueblo CO 81001
DP Coordinator Dora Davis
MYP Coordinator Dora Davis
Languages English
T: +1 719 549 7222
W: east.pueblocityschools.us

Pueblo West High School

661 Capistrano Drive, Pueblo West CO 81007
DP Coordinator Kati Wilson
MYP Coordinator Kati Wilson
Languages English
T: +1 719 547 8050
W: pwh.district70.org

Rampart High School

8250 Lexington Drive, Colorado Springs CO 80920
DP Coordinator Brian Herman
MYP Coordinator Brian Herman
Languages English
T: +1 719 234 2000
W: rampart.asd20.org

Ranch Creek Elementary School

9155 Tutt Blvd, Colorado Springs CO 80924
PYP Coordinator Teresa Mulholland
Languages English
T: +1 719 234 5500
W: ranchcreek.asd20.org/Pages/default.aspx

Ranch View Middle School

1731 Wildcat Reserve Parkway, Highlands Ranch CO 80129
MYP Coordinator Erin Isley
Languages English
T: +1 303 387 2300

Range View Elementary School

700 Ponderosa Drive, Severance CO 80550
PYP Coordinator Shauna Curtis
Languages English
T: +1 970 674 6000
W: rv.weldre4.k12.co.us

Riffenburgh Elementary School

1320 East Stuart Street, Fort Collins CO 80525
PYP Coordinator Jennifer McCoy
Languages English
T: +1 970 488 7935
W: rif.psdschools.org

Rifle High School

1350 Prefontaine Avenue, Rifle CO 81650
DP Coordinator Nathaniel Miller
Languages English
T: +1 970 665 7725

Rock Ridge Elementary School

400 N Heritage Road, Castle Rock CO 80104
PYP Coordinator Pam Gutierrez
Languages English
T: +1 303 387 5150

Rockrimmon Elementary School

194 W Mikado Drive, Colorado Springs CO 80919
PYP Coordinator Leigh Ann Lawrentz
Languages English
T: +1 719 234 5200
W: rockrimmon.asd20.org/Pages/default.aspx

Rose Stein Elementary School

80 S Teller Street, Lakewood CO 80226
PYP Coordinator Jon Turner
Languages English
T: +1 303 982 9144

Roxborough Primary and Intermediate School

8000 Village Circle West, Littleton CO 80125
PYP Coordinator Laura Maestas
Languages English
T: +1 303 387 6000

Sabin World Elementary School

3050 S Vrain Street, Denver CO 80236
PYP Coordinator Carrie Hartman
Languages English
T: +1 720 424 4520
W: sabin.dpsk12.org

Sand Creek Elementary School

550 Sand Creek Drive, Colorado Springs CO 80916
MYP Coordinator April Pratt
PYP Coordinator Marika Gillis
Languages English
T: +1 719 579 3760
W: www.hsd2.org/Domain/15

Semper Elementary School
7575 W 96th Ave., Westminster CO 80021
PYP Coordinator Stacy Heller
Languages English, Spanish
T: +1 303 982 6460

Silverthorne Elementary School
PO Box 1039, Silverthorne CO 80498
PYP Coordinator Madeline Johnson
Languages English
T: +1 970 368 1600
W: sve.summitk12.org

Smoky Hill High School
16100 E. Smoky Hill Rd., Aurora CO 80015
DP Coordinator Michael Ady
MYP Coordinator Kathleen Fitzgerald
Languages English
T: +1 720 886 5300
W: smokyhill.cherrycreekschools.org

South Ridge Elementary School
1100 South Street, Castle Rock CO 80104
PYP Coordinator Marne Katsanis
Languages English
T: +1 303 387 5075

Standley Lake High School
9300 W 104th Avenue, Westminster CO 80021
DP Coordinator Benjamin Thompson
MYP Coordinator Jeannine Mortell
Languages English
T: +1 303 982 3311

Summit Cove Elementary School
727 Cove Boulevard, Dillon CO 80435
PYP Coordinator Lesley Gregory
Languages English
T: +1 970 368 1700
W: sce.summitk12.org

Summit High School
PO Box 7, Frisco CO 80443
DP Coordinator Jotwan Daniels
MYP Coordinator Douglas Blake
Languages English
T: +1 970 368 1100
W: shs.summitk12.org

Summit Middle School
PO Box 7, Frisco CO 80443
MYP Coordinator Nelle Biggs
Languages English
T: +1 970 368 1100
W: sms.summitk12.org

Summit Ridge Middle School
11809 W Coal Mine Ave., Littleton CO 80127
MYP Coordinator Brittany Svaldi
Languages English
T: +1 303 982 9013

Sunset Middle School
1300 S. Sunset Street, Longmont CO 80501
MYP Coordinator Alex Armstrong
Languages English
T: +1 303 776 3963
W: sms.svvsd.org

Swigert International School
3480 Syracuse Street, Denver CO 80238
PYP Coordinator Caroline Dane
Languages English
T: +1 720 424 4800

Telluride Mountain School
Lawson Hill, 200 San Miguel River Dr., Telluride CO 81435
DP Coordinator Emily Durkin
Languages English
T: +1 970 728 1969
W: telluridemtnschool.org

Thornton High School
9351 North Washington Street, Thornton CO 80229
DP Coordinator Kristen McCloskey
MYP Coordinator Kelsey Barnes
Languages English
T: +1 720 972 4803

Thunder Ridge High School
1991 West Wildcat Reserve Pkwy, Highlands Ranch CO 80129
DP Coordinator Anne Morris
MYP Coordinator Cristina Berrett-Braun
Languages English
T: +1 303 387 2000

Upper Blue Elementary School
PO Box 1255, 1200 Airport Road, Breckenbridge CO 80424
PYP Coordinator Toni Napolitano
Languages English
T: +1 970 368 1800
W: ube.summitk12.org

Westminster High School
6933 Raleigh Street, Westminster CO 80030
CP Coordinator Jeff Dennis
DP Coordinator Jeff Dennis
Languages English
T: +1 720 542 5085
W: www.westminsterpublicschools.org/westminsterhs

Wheeling Elementary
472 S Wheeling Street, Aurora CO 80012
PYP Coordinator Tricia Dutton Morato
Languages English
T: +1 303 344 8670
W: wheeling.aurorak12.org

Whittier International Elementary School
2008 Pine Street, Boulder CO 80302
PYP Coordinator Alysia Hayas
Languages English
T: +1 303 442 2282
W: whittier.mpls.k12.mn.us

William J Palmer High School
301 N. Nevada Ave., Colorado Springs CO 80903
CP Coordinator Andrea Stemper
DP Coordinator Carolyn Moyer
MYP Coordinator Anton Schulzki
Languages English
T: +1 719 328 5000
W: www.d11.org/palmer

Woodmen-Roberts Elementary School
8365 Orchard Path Road, Colorado Springs CO 80919
PYP Coordinator Jordan Zettek
Languages English
T: +1 719 234 5300
W: woodmenroberts.asd20.org

York International School
9200 York Street, Thornton CO 80229
MYP Coordinator Loren Willson
PYP Coordinator Krystin Zwolinski
Languages English
T: +1 303 853 1600
W: www.mapleton.us/Domain/24

Connecticut

Brien McMahon High School
300 Highland Ave, Norwalk CT 06854
CP Coordinator Thomas Seuch
DP Coordinator Stephanie Peckham
Languages English
T: +1 203 852 9488
W: bmhs.norwalkps.org

Charter Oak International Academy
425 Oakwood Avenue, West Hartford CT 06110
PYP Coordinator Elizabete Nascimento
Languages English
T: +1 860 233 8506
W: charteroak.whps.org

Cheshire Academy
10 Main Street, Cheshire CT 06410
DP Coordinator Marc Aronson
Languages English
T: +1 203 272 5396
W: www.cheshireacademy.org

Connecticut IB Academy
857 Forbes Street, East Hartford CT 06118
DP Coordinator Travis Marciniak
MYP Coordinator Travis Marciniak
Languages English
T: +1 860 622 5590

Dr. Thomas S. O Connell Elementary School
301 May Rd, East Hartford CT 06118
PYP Coordinator Laurie Stock
Languages English
T: +1 860 622 5460

Global Communications Academy
85 Edwards Street, Hartford CT 06120
PYP Coordinator Ashley Lyman
Languages English
T: +1 860 695 6020
W: www.hartfordschools.org

Guilford High School
605 New England Road, Guilford CT 06437
DP Coordinator Kevin Buno
Languages English
T: +1 203 453 2741
W: ghs.guilfordps.org

International Magnet School for Global Citizenship
625 Chapel Road, South Windsor CT 06074
PYP Coordinator Katy Twyman
Languages English
T: +1 860 291 6001

King/Robinson Inter-District Magnet School
150 Fournier Street, New Haven CT 06511
MYP Coordinator Caterina Salamone
PYP Coordinator Caterina Salamone
Languages English
T: +1 203 691 2700

New Lebanon School
25 Mead Avenue, Greenwich CT 06830
PYP Coordinator Cheri Amster
Languages English
T: +1 203 531 9139
W: www.greenwichschools.org/NLS

IB AMERICAS

Notre Dame High School

One Notre Dame Way, West Haven CT 06516

DP Coordinator Kim Butz
Languages English, Spanish

T: +1 203 933 1673

W: www.notredamehs.com

Regional Multicultural Magnet School

1 Bulkeley Pl, New London CT 06320

PYP Coordinator Amy Rios
Languages English, Spanish

T: +1 860 437 7775

Robert E Fitch Senior High School

101 Groton Long Point Road, Groton CT 06340

CP Coordinator Anne Keefe-Forbotnick
DP Coordinator Kelley Donovan
Languages English

T: +1 860 449 7200 EXT. 4507

W: www.grotonschools.org/fitch

Rogers International School

202 Blachley Road, Stamford CT 06902

MYP Coordinator Virginia Maher
PYP Coordinator Virginia Maher
Languages English

T: +1 203 977 4562

W: www.stamfordpublicschools.org/rogers-international-school

Stamford High School

55 Strawberry Hill Avenue, Stamford CT 06902

DP Coordinator Tiffany Flynn
Languages English

T: +1 203 977 4223

W: www.stamfordhigh.org

Sunset Ridge Middle School

450 Forbes St, East Hartford CT 06118

MYP Coordinator Alexandra Turner
Languages English

T: +1 860 622 5800

The International School at Dundee

55 Florence Road, Riverside CT 06878

PYP Coordinator Rosanna Sangermano
Languages English

T: +1 203 637 3800

W: www.greenwichschools.org/isd

The Metropolitan Learning Center Interdistrict Magnet School

1551 Blue Hills Avenue, Bloomfield CT 06002

DP Coordinator Stacey Pagliaro
MYP Coordinator Emily Wright
Languages English

T: +1 860 242 7834

W: chooseml.com

Valley Regional High School

256 Kelsey Hill Rd, Deep River CT 06417

DP Coordinator Maria Ehrhardt
Languages English

T: +1 860 526 5328

Whitby School

969 Lake Avenue, Greenwich CT 06831

MYP Coordinator Shelley Castro
PYP Coordinator Diana Ljepoja
Languages English

T: +1 203 302 3900

W: www.whitbyschool.org

Delaware

John Dickinson High School

1801 Milltown Road, Wilmington DE 19808

DP Coordinator Geoffrey Ott
MYP Coordinator Valerie Morano
Languages English

T: +1 302 992 5500

W: www.redclayschools.com/dickinson

Mount Pleasant High School

5201 Washington St Extension, Wilmington DE 19809

DP Coordinator Leslie Carlson
MYP Coordinator Jeanne Beadle
Languages English

T: +1 302 762 7054

W: www.brandywineschools.org/mphs

Sussex Academy

21150 Airport Road, Georgetown DE 19947

DP Coordinator Janet Owens
Languages English

T: +1 302 856 3636

W: www.sussexacademy.org

Sussex Central High School

26026 Patriots Way, Georgetown DE 19947

DP Coordinator Kelly Deleon
Languages English

T: +1 302 934 3166

W: schs.irsd.net

Talley Middle School

1110 Cypress Road, Wilmington DE 19810

MYP Coordinator Stefanie Feder
Languages English

T: +1 302 475 3976

W: www.brandywineschools.org/talley

Wilmington Friends School

101 School Road, Wilmington DE 19803

DP Coordinator Michael Benner
Languages English

T: +1 302 576 2900

W: www.wilmingtonfriends.org

District of Columbia

Alexander R. Shepherd Elementary School

7800 14th Street NW, Washington DC 20012

PYP Coordinator Avani Mack
Languages English

T: +1 202 576 6140

W: www.shepherd-elementary.org

Alice Deal Middle School

3815 Fort Drive, NW, Washington DC 20016

MYP Coordinator Caitlin Daniels
Languages English

T: +1 202 939 2010

W: www.alicedealmiddleschool.org

Benjamin A Banneker Academic High School

800 Euclid Street NW, Washington DC 20001

DP Coordinator Tiffani Jones
Languages English

T: +1 202 673 7325

W: www.benjaminbanneker.org

British International School of Washington

2001 Wisconsin Avenue NW, Washington DC 20007

DP Coordinator Catherine Yates
Languages English

T: +1 202 829 3700

W: www.biswashington.org

DC International School

1400 Main Drive NW, Washington DC 20012

CP Coordinator Shane Donovan
DP Coordinator Jesse Nickelson
MYP Coordinator Dean Harris
Languages English, Spanish

T: +1 202 459 4790

W: www.dcinternationalschool.org

Eliot-Hine Middle School

1830 Constitution Ave NE, Washington DC 20002

MYP Coordinator Christopher Grenier
Languages English

T: +1 202 939 5380

Elsie Whitlow Stokes Community Freedom Public Charter School

Brookland Campus, 3700 Oakview Terrace NE, Washington DC 20017

PYP Coordinator Rebecca Courouble
Languages English

T: +1 202 265 7237

W: www.ewstokes.org

Friendship Public Charter School - Woodridge Campus

2959 Carlton Ave. NE, Washington DC 20018

PYP Coordinator Tiffany Arnold
Languages English

T: +1 202 635 6500

W: www.friendshipschools.org/schools/woodridge

Mary McLeod Bethune Day Academy PCS

1404 Jackson Street NE, Washington DC 20017

PYP Coordinator Sanjay Singh
Languages English

T: +1 202 459 4710

W: www.mmbethune.org

National Collegiate Preparatory Public Charter High School

4600 Livingston Road SE, Washington DC 20032

DP Coordinator Thmaine S. Morgan
Languages English

T: +1 202 832 7737

W: www.nationalprepdc.org

Strong John Thomson Elementary School

1200 L Street NW, Washington DC 20005

PYP Coordinator Crystal Overstreet
Languages English

T: +1 202 898 4660

W: www.thomsondcps.org

Turner at Green Elementary School

1500 Mississippi Avenue SE, Washington DC 20032

PYP Coordinator Marian Horton
Languages English

T: +1 202 645 3470

W: sites.google.com/a/dc.gov/turner-at-green-elementary-school

IB AMERICAS

Washington International School

3100 Macomb Street NW, Washington DC 20008
DP Coordinator James Bourke
PYP Coordinator Stephanie Sneed
Languages English
T: +1 202 243 1800
W: www.wis.edu

Washington Yu Ying Public Charter School

220 Taylor St. NE, Washington DC 20017
PYP Coordinator Rebecca J Rosenberg
Languages English, Mandarin
T: +1 202 635 1950; +1 202 635 1960
W: www.washingtonyuying.org

Whittle School & Studios - DC Campus

3007 Tilden St NW, Washington DC 20008
DP Coordinator Stephanie Tucker
Languages English
T: +1 202 417 3615
W: www.whittleschool.org

Florida

Ada Merritt K-8 Center

660 SW 3 Street, Miami FL 33130
MYP Coordinator Yosvany Hernandez
PYP Coordinator Jackeline Sanchez Jimenez
Languages English
T: +1 305 326 0791
W: adamerrittk-8center.org

Allen D Nease High School

10550 Ray Road, Ponte Vedra FL 32081
DP Coordinator Missy Kennedy
Languages English
T: +1 904 547 8300
W: www-nhs.stjohns.k12.fl.us

American Youth Academy

5905 E. 130th Ave, Tampa FL 33617
DP Coordinator Shabeah Usmanali
Languages English
T: +1 813 987 9282
W: www.ayatampa.org

Annabel C. Perry PK-8

6850 SW 34th Street, Miramar FL 33023
PYP Coordinator Jacqueline Foster
Languages English
T: +1 754 323 7050
W: www.browardschools.com/perryelem

Arthur I. Meyer Jewish Academy

5225 Hood Rd, Palm Beach Gardens FL 33418
MYP Coordinator Judy Edelman
Languages English
T: +1 561 686 6520
W: www.meyeracademy.org

Atlantic Community High School

2455 West Atlantic Ave, Palm Beach County, Delray Beach FL 33445
CP Coordinator Jill Meadow
DP Coordinator Corey Clawson
MYP Coordinator Holly Oran
Languages English
T: +1 561 243 1502
W: ahs.palmbeachschools.org

Bhaktivedanta Academy

17414 NW 112th Blvd, Alachua FL 32615
MYP Coordinator Jaya Kaseder
Languages English
T: +1 386 462 2886
W: www.bhaktischool.org

Biscayne Elementary Community School

800 77th Street, Miami Beach FL 33141
PYP Coordinator Iris Garcia
Languages English, Spanish
T: +1 305 868 7727
W: api.dadeschools.net/schoolwebsite/#!/?schoolId=0321

Boca Prep International School

10333 Diego Drive South, Boca Raton FL 33428
DP Coordinator Ivana Cvetkovic
MYP Coordinator Rachael Nassiri
PYP Coordinator Jodi-Kay Hylton-Senior
Languages English
T: +1 561 852 1410
W: www.bocaprep.net

Boyd H. Anderson High School

3050 NW 41st Street, Lauderdale Lakes FL 33309
DP Coordinator Clara Gonzalez
MYP Coordinator Clara Gonzalez
Languages English
T: +1 754 322 0200
W: www.browardschools1.com/boydanderson

Brigham Academy

601 Avenue C SE, Winter Haven FL 33880
PYP Coordinator Susie Kallan
Languages English, Spanish
T: +1 863 291 5300
W: brighamacademy.polk-fl.net

Brookside Middle School

3636 South Shade Avenue, Sarasota FL 34239
MYP Coordinator Holly Dewitt
Languages English
T: +1 941 361 6472
W: www.sarasotacountyschools.net/schools/brookside

C Leon King High School

6815 North 56th Street, Tampa FL 33610
DP Coordinator Joyce Hoehn-Parish
Languages English
T: +1 813 744 8333
W: king.mysdhc.org

Cape Coral High School

2300 Santa Barbara Blvd, Cape Coral FL 33991
DP Coordinator Katelyn Uhler
Languages English
T: +1 239 574 6766

Cardinal Newman High School

512 Spencer Drive, West Palm Beach FL 33409
DP Coordinator Scott Powell
Languages English
T: +1 561 683 6266
W: www.cardinalnewman.com

Carrollton School of the Sacred Heart

3747 Main Highway, Miami FL 33133
DP Coordinator Caroline Gillingham-Varela
Languages English
T: +1 305 446 5673
W: www.carrollton.org

Carrollwood Day School

1515 W. Bearss Avenue, Tampa FL 33613
DP Coordinator Nancy Hsu
MYP Coordinator Sabrina McCartney
PYP Coordinator Lisa Vicencio
Languages English
T: +1 813 920 2288
W: www.carrollwooddayschool.org

Carver Middle School

101 Barwick Road, Delray Beach FL 33445
MYP Coordinator Nadia Stewart
Languages English
T: +1 561 638 2100
W: crvm.palmbeachschools.org

Carver Middle School

4500 W Columbia Street, Orlando FL 32811
MYP Coordinator Debbie Villar
Languages English
T: +1 407 296 5110
W: www.carvermiddle.ocps.net

Celebration High School

1809 Celebration Boulevard, Celebration FL 34747
DP Coordinator Alissa Petersen
Languages English
T: +1 321 939 6600
W: www.osceolaschools.net/clhs

Choctawhatchee Senior High School

110 Racetrack Road NW, Fort Walton Beach FL 32547
DP Coordinator Katherine White
Languages English
T: +1 850 833 3614
W: www.okaloosaschools.com/choctaw

Clearwater Central Catholic High School

2750 Haines Bayshore Road, Clearwater FL 33760
DP Coordinator Alan Hamacher
Languages English
T: +1 727 531 1449
W: www.ccchs.org

Cocoa Beach Junior/Senior High School

1500 Minutemen Causeway, Cocoa Beach FL 32931
DP Coordinator Matt Kellam
MYP Coordinator Matt Kellam
Languages English
T: +1 321 783 1776
W: www.brevardschools.org/CocoaBeachJRSR

College Park Middle School

1201 Maury Road, Orlando FL 32804-3541
MYP Coordinator Debbie Villar
Languages English
T: +1 407 245 1800
W: collegeparkms.ocps.net

Conniston Community Middle School

673 Conniston Road, West Palm Beach FL 33405
MYP Coordinator Jeanette Machado
Languages English
T: +1 561 802 5477
W: cntm.palmbeachschools.org

Coral Gables Senior High School

450 Bird Road, Coral Gables FL 33146
DP Coordinator Diana Van Wyk
Languages English
T: +1 305 443 4871
W: www.coralgablescavaliers.org

Coral Reef High School
10101 SW 152 Street, Miami FL 33157
DP Coordinator Kelli Wise
Languages English
T: +1 305 232 2044
W: coralreef.dadeschools.net

Corbett Preparatory School of IDS
12015 Orange Grove Drive, Tampa FL 33618
MYP Coordinator Jennifer Jagdmann
PYP Coordinator Linda Wenzel
Languages English
T: +1 813 961 3087
W: www.corbettprep.com

Cornerstone Learning Community
2524 Hartsfield Road, Tallahassee FL 32303
MYP Coordinator Karen Metcalf
Languages English
T: +1 850 386 5550
W: www.cornerstonelc.com

Cypress Creek High School
1101 Bear Crossing Drive, Orange County, Orlando FL 32824
DP Coordinator Helen Philpot
Languages English
T: +1 407 852 3400

Deerfield Beach High School
910 Buck Pride Way, Deerfield Beach FL 33441
DP Coordinator Kelly Caputo
MYP Coordinator Kelly Caputo
Languages English
T: +1 754 322 0650
W: www.deerfieldbeachhigh.net

Deerfield Beach Middle School
701 SE 6th Avenue, Deerfield Beach FL 33441
MYP Coordinator MJ Caputo
Languages English
T: +1 754 322 3300
W: www.browardschools.com/deerfieldbeachmiddle

Deland High School
800 North Hill Avenue, Volusia, Deland FL 32724
DP Coordinator Lisa Nehrig
Languages English
T: +1 386 822 6909
W: www.delandhs.org

Dr Mary McLeod Bethune Elementary School
1501 Avenue 'U', Riviera Beach FL 33404
PYP Coordinator Sherrita Crummell
Languages English
T: +1 561 882 7600
W: mmbe.palmbeachschools.org

Dunbar High School
3800 E. Edison Avenue, Ft. Myers FL 33916
CP Coordinator Gayle Baisch
DP Coordinator Gayle Baisch
Languages English
T: +1 239 461 5322

Dundee Elementary Academy
415 E Frederick Ave, Dundee FL 33838
PYP Coordinator Phillip Daniels
Languages English
T: +1 863 421 3316

Dundee Ridge Academy
5555 Lake Trask Rd, Dundee FL 33838
MYP Coordinator Kerri Collins
Languages English
T: +1 863 419 3088

Earlington Heights Elementary School
4750 NW 22nd Avenue, Miami FL 33142
PYP Coordinator Star Grimm
Languages English
T: +1 305 635 7505
W: earlingtonheightselem.dadeschools.net

Eastside High School
1201 South East 43rd Street, Gainesville FL 32641-7698
DP Coordinator Anne Koon
Languages English
T: +1 352 955 6704
W: www.ehs.sbac.edu

Fienberg-Fisher K-8 Center
1420 Washington Ave, Miami Beach FL 33139
MYP Coordinator Pierrela JeanBaptiste
PYP Coordinator Pierrela JeanBaptiste
Languages English
T: +1 305 351 0419
W: www.fienbergfisherk8.com

Flagler Palm Coast High School
3265 Highway 100 East, Palm Coast FL 32164
DP Coordinator Roger M Tangney
Languages English
T: +1 386 437 7540
W: www.flagler.k12.fl.us

Forest Hill Community High School
3340 Forest Hill Boulevard, West Palm Beach FL 33405
CP Coordinator Marlaina Skowron
DP Coordinator Marlaina Skowron
MYP Coordinator Barbara Malone
Languages English
T: +1 561 540 2400

Forest Park Elementary School
1201 SW 3rd Street, Boynton Beach FL 33435
PYP Coordinator Simone Green
Languages English
T: +1 561 292 6900
W: www.edline.net/pages/forest_park_es

Fort Myers High School
2635 Cortez Boulevard, Fort Myers FL 33901
DP Coordinator Susan Postma
Languages English
T: +1 239 334 2167
W: www.lee.k12.fl.us/schools/fmh/home.asp

Frank C Martin Elementary School
14250 Boggs Drive, Miami FL 33176
MYP Coordinator Katheryn Capodiferro
PYP Coordinator Katheryn Capodiferro
Languages English
T: +1 305 238 3688
W: fcmartin.dadeschools.net

Franklin Academy - Boynton Beach
7882 S. Military Trail, Boynton Beach FL 33463
PYP Coordinator Yamile Francese
Languages English, Spanish
T: +1 561 767 4700
W: bb.franklin-academy.org

Franklin Academy - Cooper City Campus
6301 S. Flamingo Road, Cooper City FL 33330
MYP Coordinator Eileen Olmedo
Languages English
T: +1 954 780 5533
W: cc.franklin-academy.org

Franklin Academy - Palm Beach Gardens
5651 Hood Road, Palm Beach Gardens FL 33418
PYP Coordinator Leah Hanza
Languages English
T: +1 561 348 2525
W: pbg.franklin-academy.org

Franklin Academy - Pembroke Pines (K-12) Campus
5000 SW 207th Terrace, Pembroke Pines FL 33332
DP Coordinator Astrid Rivera-Ortiz
MYP Coordinator Eileen Olmedo
Languages English
T: +1 954 315 0770
W: pphs.franklin-academy.org

Franklin Academy - Pembroke Pines (K-8) Campus
18800 Pines Blvd, Pembroke Pines FL 33029
MYP Coordinator Kathy Ross
Languages English, Spanish
T: +1 954 703 2294
W: pp.franklin-academy.org

Franklin Academy - Sunrise Campus
4500 NW 103 Ave, Sunrise FL 33351
MYP Coordinator Alicia Glenn
Languages English, Spanish
T: +1 754 206 0850
W: sun.franklin-academy.org

Freedom 7 Elementary School of International Studies
400 4th Street South, Cocoa Beach FL 32931
PYP Coordinator Jennifer Noe
Languages English
T: +1 321 868 6610
W: www.brevardschools.org/Freedom7ES

Gateway High School
93 Panther Paws Trail, Osceola School District, Kissimmee FL 34744
DP Coordinator Heather Piper
Languages English
T: +1 407 935 3600

Glenridge Middle School
2900 Upper Park Road, Orlando FL 32814
MYP Coordinator Matthew Astone
Languages English
T: +1 407 623 1415
W: glenridgems.ocps.net

Grove Park Elementary School
8330 N. Military Trail, Palm Beach Gardens FL 33410
PYP Coordinator Tracy Chernow
Languages English
T: +1 561 904 7700
W: gpes.palmbeachschools.org

G-Star School of the Arts for Motion Pictures & Broadcasting
2065 Prairie Road, Building J, Palm Springs FL 33406
DP Coordinator Emily Snedeker
Languages English
T: +1 561 967 2023
W: www.gstarschool.org

Gulf High School
5355 School Road, New Port Richey FL 34652
DP Coordinator Cheryl Macri
Languages English
T: +1 727 774 3300
W: ghs.pasco.k12.fl.us

Gulliver Academy Middle School
12595 Red Road, Coral Gables FL 33156
MYP Coordinator Tiffany Medina
Languages English
T: +1 305 665 3593
W: www.gulliverschools.org

Gulliver Preparatory School
6575 North Kendall Drive, Miami FL 33156
DP Coordinator Jan Patterson
Languages English
T: +1 305 666 7937
W: www.gulliverschools.org

Haines City High School
2800 Hornet Drive, Haines City FL 33844
DP Coordinator Crystal Young
Languages English
T: +1 863 421 3281

Heights Elementary School
15200 Alexandria Court, Fort Myers FL 33908
PYP Coordinator Lacey Davis
Languages English
T: +1 239 481 1761

Herbert A Ammons Middle School
17990 SW 142 Avenue, Miami FL 33177
MYP Coordinator David Wilson
Languages English
T: +1 305 971 0158
W: www.ammonseagles.com

Hillsborough High School
5000 Central Avenue, Tampa FL 33603
DP Coordinator Lisa Sigmon
Languages English
T: +1 813 276 5620
W: hillsborough.mysdhc.org

Homestead Middle School
650 N.W. 2nd Avenue, Homestead FL 33030
MYP Coordinator Minelli Duclerc
Languages English
T: +1 305 247 4221
W: homesteadmiddle.org

Howard Middle School
1655 NW 10th Street, Ocala FL 34475
MYP Coordinator Angela Ponder
Languages English
T: +1 352 671 7225
W: www.marionschools.net/hms

Howell L. Watkins Middle School
9480 Mac Arthur Blvd, Palm Beach Gardens FL 33403
MYP Coordinator Shari Alexios
Languages English, Spanish
T: +1 561 776 3600
W: hlwm.palmbeachschools.org

Idyllwilde Elementary School
430 Vihlen Road, Sanford FL 32771
PYP Coordinator Julie Biggs
Languages English, Spanish
T: +1 407 320 3750
W: www.idyllwilde.scps.k12.fl.us

International Baccalaureate School at Bartow High School
1270 South Broadway Avenue, Bartow FL 33830
DP Coordinator Katherine Marsh
Languages English
T: +1 863 534 0194

J. Colin English Elementary School
120 Pine Island Rd., North Fort Myers FL 33903
PYP Coordinator Erica Littman
Languages English
T: +1 239 995 2258

J.H. Workman Middle School
6299 Lanier Avenue, Penacola FL 32504
MYP Coordinator Michael Burton
Languages English
T: +1 850 494 5665
W: jhwms-ecsd-fl.schoolloop.com

Jackson Middle School
6000 Stonewall Jackson Road, Orlando FL 32807
MYP Coordinator Lynne Newsom Newsom
Languages English
T: +1 407 249 6430
W: www.stonewalljackson.ocps.net

James B. Sanderlin PK-8
2350 22nd Avenue South, St Petersburg FL 33712
MYP Coordinator Katherine Gilson
PYP Coordinator Kristen Herman
Languages English
T: +1 727 552 1700
W: www.pcsb.org/sanderlinib

James S Rickards High School
3013 Jim Lee Road, Leon District Schools, Tallahassee FL 32301-7057
DP Coordinator Joe Williams
Languages English
T: +1 850 488 1783

Jewett Middle Academy
601 Ave T NE, Winter Haven FL 33881
MYP Coordinator Paulette Jacobs
Languages English
T: +1 863 291 5320

John A Ferguson Senior High School
15900 SW 56th Street, Miami FL 33185
DP Coordinator Denise Graham
Languages English
T: +1 305 408 2700
W: www.fergusonhs.org

John F Kennedy Middle School
1901 Avenue 'S', Riviera Beach FL 33404
MYP Coordinator Patreka Mckelton
Languages English
T: +1 561 845 4502
W: jfkm.palmbeachschools.org

Jones High School
801 South Rio Grande Avenue, Orlando FL 32805
DP Coordinator Nicole Blackmon
MYP Coordinator Nicole Blackmon
Languages English
T: +1 407 835 2300
W: www.jones.ocps.net

Kids Community College Southeast Campus
11519 McMullen Road, Riverview FL 33569
MYP Coordinator Stacey O'Neill
PYP Coordinator Diana Davila-Gonzalez
Languages English
T: +1 813 699 4600
W: www.kidscc.org

Lake Wales High School
1 Highlander Way, Lake Wales FL 33853
DP Coordinator Anuj Saran
Languages English
T: +1 863 678 4222
W: www.lakewaleshigh.com

Lake Weir High School
10351 SE Maricamp Road, Ocala FL 34472
DP Coordinator Colleen Wade
Languages English
T: +1 352 671 4820
W: www.marionschools.net/lwh

Lamar Louise Curry Middle School
15750 SW 47th Street, Miami FL 33185
MYP Coordinator Iran Miranda
Languages English
T: +1 305 222 2775

Land O'Lakes High School
20325 Gator Lane, Land O'Lakes FL 34639
DP Coordinator Marc Jarke
Languages English
T: +1 813 794 9400

Largo High School
410 Missouri Ave N, Largo FL 33770
DP Coordinator Nathan Lovelette
Languages English
T: +1 727 588 9158
W: www.largo-hs.pcsb.org

Largo Middle School
155 8th Avenue SE, Largo FL 33771
MYP Coordinator Stephanie Hornick
Languages English
T: +1 727 588 4600
W: www.pcsb.org/largo-ms

Lauderdale Lakes Middle School
3911 Northwest 30 th Avenue, Lauderdale Lakes FL 33309
MYP Coordinator Jeana Louis
Languages English
T: +1 (954) 497 3900

Lawton Chiles Middle Academy
400 North Florida Avenue, Lakeland FL 33801
MYP Coordinator Katelyn Gregory
Languages English
T: +1 863 499 2742

Lecanto High School
3810 W Educational Path, Lecanto FL 34461
DP Coordinator Jessica Price
Languages English
T: +1 352 746 2334

Lexington Middle School
16351 Summerlin Road, Fort Myers FL 33908
MYP Coordinator James Kroll
Languages English
T: +1 239 454 6130

Liberty Magnet Elementary School
6850 81st Street, Vero Beach FL 32967
PYP Coordinator Jamie Lunsford
Languages English
T: +1 772 564 5300

Lincoln Avenue Academy
1330 North Lincoln Avenue, Lakeland FL 33805
PYP Coordinator Diane Lokey
Languages English
T: +1 863 499 2955
W: lincolnavenuejaguars.weebly.com

Lincoln Elementary Magnet School
1207 E Renfro Street, Plant City FL 33563
PYP Coordinator Sarah Keel
Languages English
T: +1 813 757 9329
W: lincoln.mysdhc.org

Lincoln Park Academy
1806 Avenue I, St Lucie County, Fort Pierce FL 34950
DP Coordinator Carol Kuhn
MYP Coordinator Carol Kuhn
Languages English
T: +1 772 468 5474
W: schools.stlucie.k12.fl.us/lpa

Louise R Johnson Middle School
2121 26th Avenue East, Bradenton FL 34208
MYP Coordinator Christine Clem
Languages English
T: +1 941 741 3344
W: www.edline.net/pages/sdmcjohnsonms

Macfarlane Park Elementary Magnet School
1721 North MacDill Avenue, Tampa FL 33607
PYP Coordinator Angela Hartle
Languages English
T: +1 813 356 1760
W: macfarlanepark.mysdhc.org

Mariner Middle School
425 Chiquita Blvd N., Cape Coral FL 33993
MYP Coordinator Meghan Cassidy
Languages English
T: +1 239 772 1848

Maynard Evans High School
4949 Silver Star Road, Orlando FL 32808
DP Coordinator John Harrell
MYP Coordinator John Harrell
Languages English
T: +1 407 522 3400
W: www.evanshs.ocps.net

Melbourne High School
74 Bulldog Boulevard, Melbourne FL 32901
CP Coordinator Lesley Cosgrove
DP Coordinator Jennifer Mason
Languages English
T: +1 321 952 5880
W: www.brevardschools.org/MelbourneHS

Memorial Middle School
2220 W 29th Street, Orlando FL 32805
MYP Coordinator Alicia Morris
Languages English
T: +1 407 245 1810
W: www.memorial.ocps.net

Miami Beach Senior High School
2231 Prairie Avenue, Miami Beach FL 33139
DP Coordinator Melissa Balgobin
Languages English
T: +1 305 532 4515
W: miamibeachhigh.schoolwires.com

Mildred Helms Elementary School
561 S. Clearwater-Largo Rd., Largo FL 33770-3294
PYP Coordinator Jennifer Kelly
Languages English, Spanish
T: +1 727 588 3569
W: www.pcsb.org/mildred-es

Miramar High School
3601 SW 89th Avenue, Miramar FL 33025
DP Coordinator John Lamb
Languages English
T: +1 754 323 1350
W: www.browardschools.com/miramarhigh

Morikami Park Elementary School
6201 Morikami Park Road, Delray Beach FL 33484
PYP Coordinator Amy Mercier
Languages English
T: +1 561 865 3960

Nautilus Middle School
4301 N. Michigan Ave., Miami Beach FL 33140
MYP Coordinator Lissette Burns
Languages English
T: +1 305 532 3481
W: nautilus.dadeschools.net

New Gate School
5237 Ashton Road, Sarasota FL 34233
DP Coordinator Lydia Dumais
Languages English
T: +1 941 922 4949
W: www.newgate.edu

New Renaissance Middle School
10701 Miramar Blvd., Miramar FL 33025
MYP Coordinator Ermina Pierre
Languages English, Spanish
T: +1 754 323 3500
W: www.browardschools.com/newrenaissance

North Beach Elementary School
4100 Prairie Avenue, Miami Beach FL 33140
PYP Coordinator Lourdes West
Languages English
T: +1 305 531 7666
W: northbeachelementary.com

NORTH BROWARD PREPARATORY SCHOOL
7600 Lyons Road, Coconut Creek FL 33073
DP Coordinator Tamara Wolpowitz
Languages English
T: +1 954 247 0179
E: admissions@nbps.org
W: www.nbps.org
See full details on page 531

North Dade Middle School
1840 NW 157th Street, Miami Gardens FL 33054
MYP Coordinator Taneisha Webster
Languages English
T: +1 305 624 8415
W: northdademiddleschool.com

North Miami Middle School
700 NE 137th St, North Miami FL 33161
MYP Coordinator Chantil Brantley
Languages English
T: +1 305 891 3680
W: northmiamims.net

North Miami Senior High School
13110 NE 8 Avenue, North Miami FL 33161
DP Coordinator Rose Weintraub
Languages English
T: +1 305 891 6590
W: schoolsites.schoolworld.com/schools/NMSH

Oak Hammock Middle School
5321 Tice Street, Fort Myers FL 33905
MYP Coordinator Brandie Della-Luna
Languages English, Spanish
T: +1 239 693 0469

Oakcrest Elementary School
1112 NE 28th Street, Ocala FL 34470
PYP Coordinator Brittani Young
Languages English
T: +1 352 671 6350
W: www.marionschools.net/oce

Pahokee Elementary School
560 E Main Place, Pahokee FL 33476
PYP Coordinator Cassandra Moreland
Languages English
T: +1 561 924 9705
W: pes.palmbeachschools.org

Pahokee Middle Senior High School
900 Larrimore Road, Pahokee FL 33476
DP Coordinator Aya Hasegawa
MYP Coordinator Sonia SOTO
Languages English
T: +1 561 924 6400
W: pmsh.palmbeachschools.org

Palm Harbor University High School
1900 Omaha Street, Palm Harbor FL 34683
DP Coordinator Evette Striblen
Languages English
T: +1 727 669 1131

Palmer Trinity School
7900 SW 176th Street, Miami FL 33157
DP Coordinator Orlando Sarduy
Languages English
T: +1 305 251 2230
W: www.palmertrinity.org

Palmetto Elementary School
5801 Parker Ave., West Palm Beach FL 33405
PYP Coordinator Judith Ackerman
Languages English, Spanish
T: +1 561 202 0400
W: pmte.palmbeachschools.org

Parkway Middle School
857 Florida Parkway, Kissimmee FL 34743
MYP Coordinator Katalina Dasilva
Languages English
T: +1 407 344 7000
W: www.osceolaschools.net/pwms

Paxon School for Advanced Studies
3239 Norman E Thagard Blvd., Jacksonville FL 32254-1796
DP Coordinator Krystal Culpepper
Languages English
T: +1 904 693 7583
W: www.duvalschools.org/psas

IB AMERICAS

Pedro Menendez High School

600 State Road 206 West, St Augustine FL 32086
DP Coordinator Jonathan Higgins
Languages English
T: +1 904 547 8660
W: www-pmhs.stjohns.k12.fl.us

Pensacola High School

A and Maxwell Streets, Pensacola FL 32501
DP Coordinator Rebba Dickerson
Languages English
T: +1 850 595 1500
W: phs-ecsd-fl.schoolloop.com

Phillippi Shores Elementary School

4747 South Tamiami Trail, Sarasota FL 34231
PYP Coordinator Christina Slattery
Languages English
T: +1 941 361 6424
W: www.sarasotacountyschools.net/phillippi

Pine View Elementary School

5333 Parkway Boulevard, Land O'Lakes FL 34639
PYP Coordinator Erin Greco
Languages English, Spanish
T: +1 813 794 0600
W: pves.pasco.k12.fl.us

Pine View Middle School

5334 Parkway Boulevard, Land O'Lakes FL 34639
MYP Coordinator Rebecca Cardinale
Languages English
T: +1 813 794 4800
W: pvms.pasco.k12.fl.us

Plantation High School

6901 NW 16th Street, Plantation FL 33313
DP Coordinator Catherine Gonzalez
Languages English
T: +1 754 322 1850
W: www.browardschools.com/plantationhigh

Plantation Middle School

6600 West Sunrise Blvd, Plantation FL 33313
MYP Coordinator Pamela Van Horn
Languages English
T: +1 754 322 4100
W: browardschools.com/plantationmid

Ponce de Leon Middle School

5801 Augusto Street, Coral Gables FL 33146
MYP Coordinator Marlene Ramos
Languages English
T: +1 305 661 1611 EXT:2212
W: ponce.dadeschools.net

Port St Lucie High School

1201 S E Jaguar Lane, Port St Lucie FL 34952
DP Coordinator Caroline Whiddon-Miller
Languages English
T: +1 772 337 6770
W: www.stlucie.k12.fl.us/our-schools/profile/?sch=phs

Ridgeview High School Academy for Advanced Studies

466 Madison Avenue, Clay County, Orange Park FL 32065
DP Coordinator Angela Randall
Languages English
T: +1 904 213 5203
W: rhsibacademyofadvancedstudies.weebly.com

Riverdale High School

2600 Buckingham Road, Fort Myers FL 33905
DP Coordinator Traci Budmayr
Languages English
T: +1 239 694 4141

Riverhills Elementary Magnet

405 S. Riverhills Drive, Temple Terrace FL 33617
PYP Coordinator Diana Favata
Languages English
T: +1 813 987 6911
W: riverhills.mysdhc.org

Riverview High School

One Ram Way, Sarasota FL 34231
CP Coordinator Amy Earl
DP Coordinator James R Minor
Languages English
T: +1 941 923 1484
W: www.riverviewib.com

Robinson High School

6311 S Lois Avenue, Tampa FL 33616-1617
DP Coordinator Daniel Cribb
Languages English
T: +1 813 272 3006
W: robinsonhs.mysdhc.org

Robinswood Middle School

6305 Balboa Drive, Orlando FL 32818
MYP Coordinator Vernalee Bickerstaff
Languages English
T: +1 407 296 5140
W: robinswoodms.ocps.net

Roland Park K-8 Magnet School

1510 N. Manhattan Ave, Tampa FL 33607
MYP Coordinator Adrienne Rundle
PYP Coordinator Adrienne Rundle
Languages English
T: +1 813 872 5212
W: rolandpark.mysdhc.org

Royal Palm Beach High School

10600 Okeechobee Blvd., Royal Palm Beach FL 33411
DP Coordinator Daniel Dicurcio
Languages English
T: +1 561 753 4000

Rutherford High School

1000 School Avenue, Springfield FL 32401
DP Coordinator Catherine Rutland
Languages English
T: +1 850 767 4500
W: www.bayschools.com/rhs

Saint John Paul II Catholic School

4341 W Homosassa Trail, Lecanto FL 34461
MYP Coordinator Lee Sayago
Languages English
T: +1 352 746 2020
W: www.sjp2.us

Samuel W. Wolfson High School

7000 Powers Ave., Jacksonville FL 32217-3398
DP Coordinator Brandi Benga
Languages English
T: +1 904 739 5265
W: www.duvalschools.org/wolfson

Sarasota Military Academy

801 N. Orange Avenue, Sarasota FL 34236
DP Coordinator Hellen Harvey
Languages English
T: +1 941 926 1700
W: www.sarasotamilitaryacademy.org

Sebastian River High School

9001 Shark Blvd, Sebastian FL 32958
DP Coordinator Jaime Sturgeon
Languages English
T: +1 772 564 4170

Sebastian River Middle School

9400 Fellsmere Rd, Sebastian FL 32958
MYP Coordinator Christine Sturgeon
Languages English
T: +1 772 564 5111

Sebring High School

3514 Kenilworth Boulevard, Sebring FL 33870
DP Coordinator Jo Anna Cochlin
Languages English
T: +1 863 471 5500
W: www.highlands.k12.fl.us/~shs

Seminole High School

2701 Ridgewood Avenue, Seminole, Sanford FL 32773-4916
DP Coordinator Donna Noll
Languages English
T: +1 407 320 5100
W: www.seminolehs.scps.k12.fl.us

South Dade Senior High School

28401 SW 167 Ave., Homestead FL 33030
DP Coordinator Elena Delgado
Languages English
T: +1 305 247 4244
W: sdshs.net

South Fork High School

10000 SW Bulldog Way, Stuart FL 34997-2799
DP Coordinator Joseph Shewmaker
Languages English
T: +1 772 219 1840
W: sfhs.martinschools.org/pages/south_fork_high_school

South Pointe Elementary School

1050 4th Street, Miami Beach FL 33139
PYP Coordinator Roxanne Bressett
Languages English
T: +1 305 531 5437

Southeast High School

1200 37th Avenue East, Bradenton FL 34208
DP Coordinator Kathleen Grim
Languages English
T: +1 941 741 3366
W: www.manateeschools.net/southeast

Southside Middle School

2948 Knights Lane E, Jacksonville FL 32216-5697
MYP Coordinator Kassandra Kieffer
Languages English
T: +1 904 739 5238
W: www.duvalschools.org/southside

Spring Park Elementary School

2250 Spring Park Road, Jacksonville FL 32207

PYP Coordinator Charita Penny
Languages English

T: +1 904 346 5640

Springstead High School

3300 Mariner Boulevard, Spring Hill FL 34609

DP Coordinator John Imhof
Languages English

T: +1 352 797 7010

W: www.hernandoschools.org/Domain/29

Spruce Creek High School

801 Taylor Road, Port Orange FL 32127

DP Coordinator Karie Cappiello
Languages English

T: +1 386 322 6272

W: www.sprucecreekhigh.com

St Andrew's School

3900 Jog Road, Boca Raton FL 33434

DP Coordinator Charles Pawlik
MYP Coordinator Kimberly Yash
PYP Coordinator Sabah Rashid
Languages English

T: +1 561 210 2000

W: www.saintandrews.net

St Ann Catholic School

324 North Olive Avenue, West Palm Beach FL 33401

MYP Coordinator Philomena Smith
PYP Coordinator Susan Demes
Languages English

T: +1 561 832 3676

W: www.stannwpb.org

St John Vianney Catholic School

500 84th Avenue, St Pete Beach FL 33706

MYP Coordinator Sarah Fortier
Languages English

T: +1 727 360 1113

W: www.sjvcs.org

St Petersburg High School

2501 Fifth Avenue North, St Petersburg FL 33713

DP Coordinator Anthony Bryant
Languages English

T: +1 727 893 1842

W: www.pcsb.org/stpete-hs

St. Cecelia Interparochial Catholic School

1350 Court Street, Clearwater FL 33756

MYP Coordinator Leah Steele
PYP Coordinator Leah Steele
Languages English

T: +1 727 461 1200

W: www.st-cecelia.org

Stanton College Preparatory School

1149 West 13th Street, Jacksonville FL 32209

DP Coordinator Tamla Simmons
Languages English

T: +1 904 630 6760

W: www.duvalschools.org/stanton

Strawberry Crest High School

4691 Gallagher Road, Dover FL 33527

DP Coordinator Jamie Ferrario
Languages English

T: +1 813 707 7522

W: strawberrycrest.mysdhc.org

Suncoast Community High School

1717 Avenue S, Riviera Beach FL 33404

CP Coordinator Clarence Walker
DP Coordinator Maria Edgar
MYP Coordinator Brett Stubbs
Languages English

T: +1 561 882 3401

W: suh.palmbeachschools.org

Terry Parker High School

7301 Parker School Road, Jacksonville FL 32211

DP Coordinator MaryBeth Weaver
Languages English

T: +1 904 720 1650

W: www.duvalschools.org/tphs

Thacker Avenue Elementary School for International Studies

301 N. Thacker Avenue, Kissimmee FL 34741

PYP Coordinator Cathy Hesse
Languages English

T: +1 407 935 3540

W: www.osceolaschools.net/taes

THE BILTMORE SCHOOL

1600 S. Red Road, Miami FL 33155

PYP Coordinator Isbel Salgueiro
Languages English

T: +1 305 266 4666

E: info@biltmoreschool.com

W: www.biltmoreschool.com

See full details on page 547

The Discovery School

102 15th Street South, Jacksonville Beach FL 32250

PYP Coordinator Korri Zaharie
Languages English

T: +1 904 247 4577

W: thediscoveryschool.org

The Roig Academy

8000 SW 112 St, Miami FL 33156

PYP Coordinator Gustavo Roig
Languages English, Spanish

T: +1 305 235 1313

W: www.roigacademy.com

Treasure Island Elementary School

7540 East Treasure Drive, North Bay Village FL 33141

PYP Coordinator Tarese Joseph
Languages English

T: +1 305 865 3141

W: www.treasureislandschool.com

Union Academy Magnet School

1795 East Wabash Street, Bartow FL 33830

MYP Coordinator Deborah Draper
Languages English

T: +1 863 534 7435

University High School

11501 Eastwood Drive, Orange County, Orlando FL 32817

DP Coordinator Wanda Alvarado
Languages English

T: +1 407 482 8700

Vanguard High School

7 NW 28th Street, Ocala FL 34475

DP Coordinator Stephanie DeVilling
Languages English

T: +1 352 671 4900

W: www.marionschools.net/vhs

Venice High School

1 Indian Ave., Venice FL 34285

CP Coordinator Gretchen Myers
DP Coordinator Kathleen Jones
Languages English

T: +1 941 488 6726

W: sarasotacountyschools.net/schools/venicehigh

Walker Middle Magnet School

8282 North Mobley Road, Odessa FL 33556

MYP Coordinator Josephine Corder
Languages English

T: +1 813 631 4726

W: walker.mysdhc.org

Westward Elementary School

1101 Golf Avenue, Palm Beach, West Palm Beach FL 33401

PYP Coordinator Bernadette Beneby-Coleman
Languages English

T: +1 561 802 2130

W: wses.palmbeachschools.org

Wicklow Elementary School

100 Placid Lake Drive, Sanford FL 32773

PYP Coordinator Ann Glass
Languages English, Spanish

T: +1 407 320 1250

W: www.wicklow.scps.k12.fl.us

William T Dwyer High School

13601 N Military Trail, Palm Beach Gardens FL 33418

DP Coordinator Susan Mulligan
Languages English

T: +1 561 625 7858

W: wtdh.palmbeachschools.org

Williams Middle Magnet School for International Studies

5020 N 47th Street, Tampa FL 33610

MYP Coordinator Cory Puppa
Languages English

T: +1 813 744 8600

W: www.williams.mysdhc.org/

Wilton Manors Elementary School

2401 NE 3rd Avenue, Wilton Manors FL 33305

PYP Coordinator Gina Pineda
Languages English

T: +1 754 322 8950

W: www.browardschools.com/wiltonmanors

Windermere Preparatory School

6189 Winter Garden Vineland Road, Windermere FL 34786

DP Coordinator Anne Lyng
Languages English

T: +1 407 905 7737

W: www.windermereprep.com

Winter Park High School

2100 Summerfield Road, Winter Park FL 32792

CP Coordinator Donald Blackmon
DP Coordinator Donald Blackmon
Languages English

T: +1 407 622 3212

Winter Springs High School

130 Tuskawilla Road, Winter Park FL 32708

DP Coordinator Courtney Doherty
Languages English

T: +1 407 320 8750

W: www.winterspringshs.scps.k12.fl.us

Georgia

Jackson County Comprehensive High School

1668 Winder Highway, Jefferson GA 30549

DP Coordinator Michelle Golden
Languages English
T: +1 706 367 5003
W: jcchs.jacksonschoolsga.org

4/5 Academy at Fifth Avenue

101 5th Avenue, Decatur GA 30030
PYP Coordinator Shannon Stewart
Languages English
T: +1 404 371 6680
W: fifthavenue.csdecatur.net

A.L. Burruss School

325 Manning Road, Marietta GA 30064
PYP Coordinator Kristen Green
Languages English
T: +1 770 429 3144
W: alburruss.marietta-city.org

Academy of Richmond County

910 Russell Street, Augusta GA 30904
CP Coordinator Chequita Stephens
DP Coordinator Chequita Stephens
Languages English
T: +1 706 737 7152
W: www.rcboe.org/arc

Alpharetta High School

3595 Webb Bridge Road, Alpharetta GA 30005
DP Coordinator Frank Fortunato
Languages English
T: +1 470 254 7640
W: school.fultonschools.org/hs/alpharetta

ATLANTA INTERNATIONAL SCHOOL

2890 North Fulton Drive, Atlanta GA 30305
DP Coordinator Adam Lapish
MYP Coordinator Carmen Samanes
PYP Coordinator Leonie Ley-Mitchell
Languages English, Chinese, French, German, Spanish
T: +1 404 841 3840
E: admission@aischool.org
W: www.aischool.org

See full details on page 493

Atlanta Neighborhood Charter School

820 Essie Ave, Atlanta GA 30316
MYP Coordinator Somer Hobby
Languages English
T: +1 678 904 0051
W: atlncs.org

Avondale Elementary School

10 Lakeshore Drive, Avondale Estates GA 30052
PYP Coordinator Lisa Bonner
Languages English
T: +1 678 676 5202
W: www.avondalees.dekalb.k12.ga.us

Beecher Hills Elementary School

2257 Bollingbrook Drive, SW, Atlanta GA 30311
PYP Coordinator Tiffany Harvey
Languages English
T: +1 404 802 8300
W: www.atlanta.k12.ga.us/Domain/316

Benjamin H Hardaway High School

2901 College Drive, Columbus GA 31906
CP Coordinator Ashley Snow
DP Coordinator Ashley Snow
Languages English
T: +1 706 649 0748

Benteen Elementary School

200 Cassanova Street SE, Atlanta GA 30315
PYP Coordinator Samuel Jones
Languages English, Spanish
T: +1 404 802 7300
W: www.atlantapublicschools.us/Domain/942

Bolton Academy Elementary School

2268 Adams Dr., Atlanta GA 30318
PYP Coordinator Felica Topper
Languages English
T: +1 404 802 8350
W: www.atlanta.k12.ga.us/domain/1979

Brandon Hall School

1701 Brandon Hall Drive, Atlanta GA 30350
DP Coordinator Nicole Chapman
Languages English
T: +1 770 394 8177
W: www.brandonhall.org

Burgess-Peterson Academy

480 Clifton Street, Atlanta GA 30316
PYP Coordinator Melanie Searcy
Languages English
T: +1 404 802 3400
W: www.atlantapublicschools.us/Domain/1407

Burke County High School

1057 Burke Veterans Parkway, Waynesboro GA 30830
CP Coordinator LaChonna Avery
Languages English
T: +1 706 554 6691
W: bchs.burke.k12.ga.us

Campbell High School

5265 Ward Street, Cobb County, Smyrna GA 30080
DP Coordinator Lisha Wood
Languages English
T: +1 678 842 6850
W: www.cobbk12.org/campbellhs

Campbell Middle School

3295 South Atlanta Road, Smyrna GA 30080
MYP Coordinator Tanika Parrish
Languages English
T: +1 678 842 6873
W: www.cobbk12.org/campbellms/

Carrollton High School

202 Trojan Drive, Carrollton GA 30117
DP Coordinator Noah Brewer
Languages English
T: +1 770 834 7726
W: chs.carrolltoncityschools.net

Centennial High School

9310 Scott Road, Roswell GA 30076
DP Coordinator T Lee
Languages English
T: +1 470 254 4230
W: school.fultonschools.org/hs/centennial

Central High School, Macon

2155 Napier Avenue, Macon GA 31204
DP Coordinator Joshua Mccorkle
Languages English
T: +1 478 779 2300

Clubview Elementary School

2836 Edgewood Road, Columbus GA 31906
PYP Coordinator Kimberly Schorr
Languages English
T: +1 706 565 3017
W: sites.muscogee.k12.ga.us/clubview

Coastal Middle School

4595 US Highway 80 East, Savannah GA 31410
MYP Coordinator Deborah Looye
Languages English
T: +1 912 395 3950

Continental Colony Elementary School

3181 Hogan Rd SW, Atlanta GA 30331
PYP Coordinator Annette Mitchell
Languages English, Spanish
T: +1 404 802 8000
W: www.atlantapublicschools.us/domain/457

D. M. Therrell High School

3099 Panther Trail SW, Atlanta GA 30311
CP Coordinator Sarah Talluri
MYP Coordinator Vincent Tolbert
Languages English
T: +1 404 802 5300
W: www.atlantapublicschools.us/domain/1327

Dalton High School

1500 Manly Street, Dalton GA 30720
DP Coordinator Marybeth Meadows
Languages English
T: +1 706 278 8757
W: dhs.daltonpublicschools.com

Decatur High School

310 N. McDonough St., Decatur GA 30030
CP Coordinator Duane Sprull
DP Coordinator Debbie Woolard
MYP Coordinator Debra LeDoux
Languages English
T: +1 404 370 4170
W: dhs.csdecatur.net

Deerwood Academy

3070 Fairburn Road, Atlanta GA 30331
PYP Coordinator Demiris Gates
Languages English
T: +1 404 802 3300
W: www.atlantapublicschools.us/deerwood

Douglas County High School

8705 Campbellton Street, Douglasville GA 30134
DP Coordinator Grant Fossum
Languages English
T: +1 770 651 6500

Druid Hills High School

1798 Haygood Drive NE, Atlanta GA 30307
DP Coordinator Anne Bracewell
Languages English
T: +1 678 874 6300
W: www.druidhillshs.dekalb.k12.ga.us

Druid Hills Middle School

3100 Mount Olive Drive, Decatur GA 30033
MYP Coordinator Kim Colossale
Languages English
T: +1 678 874 7602
W: www.druidhillsms.dekalb.k12.ga.us

Dublin High School

1127 Hillcrest Parkway, Dublin GA 31021
DP Coordinator Amber Donnell
Languages English
T: +1 478 277 4107
W: www.dublinschools.net/dublinscioto_home.aspx

IB AMERICAS

E Rivers Elementary School

8 Peachtree Battle Avenue, Atlanta GA 30305
PYP Coordinator Paul Hulsing
Languages English
T: +1 404 802 7050
W: www.atlantapublicschools.us/rivers

Fernbank Elementary School

157 Heaton Park Dr, Atlanta GA 30307
PYP Coordinator Jessica Elgin
Languages English
T: +1 678 874 9302
W: www.fernbankes.dekalb.k12.ga.us

Garden Hills Elementary School

285 Sheridan Drive, Atlanta GA 30305
PYP Coordinator Melissa Gilbert
Languages English
T: +1 404 842 3103
W: www.gardenhillselementary.com

Heards Ferry Elementary School

6151 Powers Ferry Road, Sandy Springs GA 30339
PYP Coordinator Allie Yancey
Languages English
T: +1 470 254 6190
W: school.fultonschools.org/es/heardsferry

Hephzibah Elementary School

2542 Hwy 88, Hephzibah GA 30815
PYP Coordinator Jennifer Williams
Languages English, Spanish
T: +1 706 592 4561
W: www.rcboe.org/hes

Hephzibah High School

4558 Brothersville Road, Hephzibah GA 30815
MYP Coordinator Tabatha Tucker
Languages English, Spanish
T: +1 706 592 2089
W: www.rcboe.org/hhs

Hephzibah Middle School

2427 Mims Road, Hephzibah GA 30815
MYP Coordinator Cassandra Rogers
Languages English, Spanish
T: +1 706 592 4534
W: www.rcboe.org/HMS

High Meadows School

1055 Willeo Road, Roswell GA 30188
PYP Coordinator Danielle Wright
Languages English
T: +1 770 993 2940
W: www.highmeadows.org

High Point Elementary School

520 Greenland Rd NE, Sandy Springs GA 30342
PYP Coordinator Riana Kidder
Languages English
T: +1 470 254 7716
W: school.fultonschools.org/es/highpoint

International Charter School of Atlanta

1335 Northmeadow Parkway, Suite 100, Roswell GA 30076
PYP Coordinator Severine Plesnarski
Languages English, French
T: +1 470 222 7420
W: www.icsatlanta.org

International Community School

2418 Wood Trail Lane, Decatur GA 30033
PYP Coordinator Diamond Jefferies
Languages English
T: +1 404 499 8969
W: www.intcomschool.org

International Studies Elementary Charter School

2237 Cutts Drive, Albany GA 31705
PYP Coordinator Amber Davis
Languages English
T: +1 229 431 3384

Johnson High School

3305 Poplar Springs Road, Gainesville GA 30507
DP Coordinator Holly Wilson
Languages English
T: +1 770 536 2394
W: jhs.hallco.org/web

Lake Forest Elementary School

5920 Sandy Springs Circle, Sandy Springs GA 30328
PYP Coordinator Stephanie Soldo
Languages English
T: +1 470 254 8740
W: school.fultonschools.org/es/lakeforest

Lake Forest Hills Elementary School

3140 Lake Forest Drive, Augusta GA 30909
PYP Coordinator Crystal Coleman
Languages English
T: +1 706 737 7317
W: www.rcboe.org/lakeforesthills

Lakeside High School

533 Blue Ridge Drive, Evans GA 30809
DP Coordinator Stacey Brown
Languages English
T: +1 706 863 0027
W: lakesidehs.ccboe.net

Langford Middle School

3019 Walton Way, Augusta GA 30909
MYP Coordinator Thaddeaus Mohler
Languages English
T: +1 706 737 7301
W: www.rcboe.org/langford

Marietta High School

1171 Whitlock Avenue, Marietta GA 30064
CP Coordinator Barbara Manwell
DP Coordinator Barbara Manwell
MYP Coordinator Pamela Holman
Languages English
T: +1 770 428 2631
W: www.marietta-city.k12.ga.us/mhs

Marietta Middle School

121 Winn Street, Marietta GA 30064
MYP Coordinator Jill Sims
Languages English
T: +1 770 422 0311
W: www.marietta-city.k12.ga.us/mms

Marietta Sixth Grade Academy

340 Aviation Road, Marietta GA 30060
MYP Coordinator Tamara Edwards
Languages English
T: +1 770 429 3115
W: www.marietta-city.k12.ga.us

Marshpoint Elementary School

135 Whitemarsh Island Road, Savannah GA 31410
PYP Coordinator Deborah Looye
Languages English
T: +1 912 898 4000
W: internet.savannah.chatham.k12.ga.us/schools/mes/default.aspx

Martin Luther King Jr High School

3991 Snapfinger Road, Lithonia GA 30038
DP Coordinator Hanifah Ali
Languages English
T: +1 678 874 5402
W: www.mlkinghs.dekalb.k12.ga.us

Martin Luther King, Jr. Middle School (GA)

545 Hill Street SE, Atlanta GA 30312
MYP Coordinator Shekela Edwards
Languages English
T: +1 404 802 5400
W: www.atlantapublicschools.us/page/8440

Maynard Holbrook Jackson High School

801 Glenwood Ave SE, Atlanta GA 30316
CP Coordinator Yusef King
DP Coordinator Yusef King
MYP Coordinator Debra Ross
Languages English
T: +1 404 802 5200
W: www.atlanta.k12.ga.us/domain/3508

Midvale Elementary School

3836 Midvale Road, Tucker GA 30084
PYP Coordinator Ashley Little
Languages English
T: +1 678 874 3402
W: midvalees.dekalb.k12.ga.us

Montessori Academy Sharon Springs

2830 Old Atlanta Road, Cumming GA 30041
DP Coordinator Carmen Serghi
Languages English, Spanish
T: +1 770 205 6277
W: montessoriacademysharonsprings.com

Morgan County High School

1231 College Drive, Madison GA 30650
DP Coordinator Lisa Hamilton
Languages English
T: +1 706 342 2336
W: www.morgan.k12.ga.us/mchs

Morris Brandon Elementary School

2741 Howell Mill Road, Atlanta GA 30327
PYP Coordinator Samuel De Carlo
Languages English
T: +1 770 350 2153
W: www.morrisbrandon.com

Norcross High School

5041 Staverly Lane, Norcross GA 30092
DP Coordinator Dan Byrne
MYP Coordinator Elizabeth O'Halloran
Languages English
T: +1 770 448 3674
W: www.gcpsk12.org/norcrosshs

North Atlanta High School

4111 Northside Parkway, Atlanta GA 30327
CP Coordinator Danielle Costarides
DP Coordinator Danielle Costarides
MYP Coordinator Nikia Showers
Languages English
T: +1 404 802 4700
W: www.atlanta.k12.ga.us/domain/3377

North Hall High School
4885 Mt Vernon Road, Gainesville GA 30506
DP Coordinator Lori Barrett
Languages English
T: +1 770 534 1080
W: nhhs.hallco.org

Notre Dame Academy, GA
4635 River Green Parkway, Duluth GA 30096
DP Coordinator Daniel Jewitt
MYP Coordinator Rose Downs
PYP Coordinator Patricia Miletello
Languages English
T: +1 678 387 9385
W: www.ndacademy.org

Peachtree Elementary School
5995 Crooked Creek Road, Peachtree Corners GA 30092
PYP Coordinator Brian Ginley
Languages English
T: +1 770 448 8710
W: www.peachtreees.org

Pinckneyville Middle School
5440 West Jones Bridge Road, Norcross GA 30092
MYP Coordinator Varonica Donham
Languages English
T: +1 770 263 0860
W: www.pinckneyvillemiddle.org

Ralph J. Bunche Middle School
1925 Niskey Lake Rd SW, Atlanta GA 30331
MYP Coordinator Kennette Blackman
Languages English
T: +1 404 802 6700
W: www.atlantapublicschools.us/bunche

Renfroe Middle School
220 W. College Ave., Decatur GA 30030
MYP Coordinator Kristen Karably
Languages English
T: +1 404 370 4440
W: renfroe.csdecatur.net

Richards Middle School
2892 Edgewood Road, Columbus GA 31906
MYP Coordinator Kimberly M. Casleton
Languages English
T: +1 706 569 3697
W: sites.muscogee.k12.ga.us/richards

Ridgeview Middle School
5340 S Trimble Road, Atlanta GA 30342
MYP Coordinator Andrea von Biberstein
Languages English
T: +1 404 843 7710
W: www.fultonschools.org/ridgeviewms

Riverwood International Charter School
5900 Heards Drive NW, Atlanta GA 30328
DP Coordinator Diane Kopkas
MYP Coordinator Andrea von Biberstein
Languages English
T: +1 404 847 1980
W: www.riverwoodics.org

Salem Middle School
5333 Salem Road, Lithonia GA 30058
MYP Coordinator Anne Marion
Languages English
T: +1 678 676 9402
W: www.salemms.dekalb.k12.ga.us

Sandy Creek High School
360 Jenkins Road, Tyrone GA 30290
DP Coordinator Karina Grewe
Languages English
T: +1 770 969 2840
W: www.fcboe.org/Page/45

Sarah Smith Elementary School
4141 Wieuca Road, NE, Atlanta GA 30342
PYP Coordinator Karla Lamar
Languages English
T: +1 404 802 3880
W: www.sarahsmithelementary.com

Sawyer Road Elementary School
840 Sawyer Road, Marietta GA 30062
PYP Coordinator Summer Davis
Languages English
T: +1 770 429 9923
W: www.marietta-city.org/sawyerroad

Shiloh High School
4210 Shiloh Road, Snellville GA 30039
DP Coordinator Kirsten Menosky
Languages English
T: +1 770 972 8471
W: www.shilohhighschool.org

Shiloh Middle School
4285 Shiloh Road, Snellville GA 30039-6146
MYP Coordinator Stacee Brown
Languages English
T: +1 770 972 3224
W: shilohms.com

Sol C Johnson High School
3012 Sunset Blvd, Savannah GA 31404
CP Coordinator Amanda Fanelli
DP Coordinator Jason Buelterman
MYP Coordinator Amanda Fanelli
Languages English
T: +1 912 395 6400
W: internet.savannah.chatham.k12.ga.us/schools/jhs

South Forsyth High School
585 Peachtree Parkway, Forsyth County, Cumming GA 30041
CP Coordinator Tera Graham
DP Coordinator Kevin Denney
Languages English
T: +1 770 781 2264
W: www.forsyth.k12.ga.us/site/Default.aspx?PageID=22248

Southwest Middle School
6030 Ogeechee Road, Savannah GA 31419
MYP Coordinator Lakisha Gilford
Languages English
T: +1 912 395 3540
W: swms.sccpss.com

St Andrew's School
601 Penn Waller Road, Savannah GA 31410
DP Coordinator Tiffany Phillips
Languages English
T: +1 912 897 4941
W: www.saintschool.com

Summerour Middle School
585 Mitchell Road, Norcross GA 30071
MYP Coordinator Sunny Thompson
Languages English
T: +1 770 448 3045
W: www.gwinnett.k12.ga.us/summerourms

Sutton Middle School
2875 Northside Drive NW, Atlanta GA 30305
MYP Coordinator Colette Minnifield
Languages English
T: +1 404 802 5600
W: www.suttonmiddleschool.org

Teasley Elementary School
3640 Spring Hill Parkway, Smyrna GA 30080
PYP Coordinator Alice Maclellan
Languages English, Spanish
T: +1 770 437 5945
W: www.cobbk12.org/teasley

Tucker High School
5036 Lavista Road, Tucker GA 30084
CP Coordinator Melissa Edwards
DP Coordinator Stephanie Willocks
Languages English
T: +1 678 874 3702
W: www.tuckerhs.dekalb.k12.ga.us

Tucker Middle School
2160 Idlewood Road, Tucker GA 30084
MYP Coordinator Deborah Mau
Languages English
T: +1 678 875 0902
W: www.tuckerms.dekalb.k12.ga.us

South Forsyth High School
Valdosta High School
3101 N Forrest Street, Valdosta GA 31601
DP Coordinator Betsy McTier
Languages English
T: +1 229 333 8540
W: vhs.gocats.org

Warren T Jackson Elementary School
1325 Mt Paran Road, Atlanta GA 30327
PYP Coordinator Bria Pete
Languages English
T: +1 404 802 8800
W: www.wtjackson.org

Wesley International Academy
211 Memorial Drive, Atlanta GA 30312
MYP Coordinator Jatoyia Armour
PYP Coordinator Teri Swain
Languages English
T: +1 678 904 9137
W: www.wesleyacademy.org

West Hall High School
5500 McEver Road, Oakwood GA 30566
CP Coordinator Julie Pritchard
DP Coordinator Julie Pritchard
Languages English
T: +1 770 967 9826
W: whhs.hallco.org/web

West Manor Elementary School
570 Lynhurst Dr SW, Atlanta GA 3031
PYP Coordinator Azuree Walker
Languages English, Spanish
T: +1 404 802 3350
W: www.atlantapublicschools.us/westmanor

Westlake High School, Atlanta
2400 Union Road, Atlanta GA 30331
DP Coordinator Alanna Johnson
Languages English
T: +1 470 254 6400
W: www.westlakehs.org

Windsor Forest High School
12419 Largo Drive, Savannah GA 31419
CP Coordinator Jody Ranous
DP Coordinator Jody Ranous
MYP Coordinator Jennifer Dobbins
Languages English
T: +1 912 395 3400
W: internet.savannah.chatham.k12.ga.us/schools/wfhs

Hawaii

Aina Haina Elementary School

801 W. Hind Drive, Honolulu HI 96821
PYP Coordinator Trisha Shipman-Lameier
Languages English
T: +1 808 377 2419
W: www.ainahaina.k12.hi.us

Haha`ione Elementary School

595 Pepeekeo Street, Honolulu HI 96825
PYP Coordinator Denise Kealoha
Languages English
T: +1 808 397 5822
W: www.hahaionees.org

Henry J Kaiser High School

511 Lunalilo Home Road, Honolulu HI 96825
CP Coordinator Shareen Murayama
DP Coordinator Bradley Bogard
MYP Coordinator Kristie Yamamoto
Languages English
T: +1 808 394 1200
W: www.kaiserhighschoolhawaii.org

Island Pacific Academy

909 Haumea Street, Kapolei HI 96707
DP Coordinator Susan Goya
Languages English
T: +1 808 674 3523
W: www.ipahawaii.org

James Campbell High School

91-980 North Road, Ewa Beach HI 96706
DP Coordinator Jo-Hannah Liz Valdez
Languages English
T: +1 808 689 1200
W: www.campbellhigh.org

Kamiloiki Elementary School

7788 Hawaii Kai Drive, Honolulu HI 96825
PYP Coordinator Amber Stanley
Languages English
T: +1 808 397 5800
W: www.kamiloikielementary.org

Koko Head Elementary School

189 Lunalilo Home Road, Honolulu HI 96825
PYP Coordinator Jared Kagihara
Languages English
T: +1 808 397 5811
W: kokoheadschool.org

Le Jardin Academy

917 Kalanianaole Highway, Kailua HI 96734
DP Coordinator Lindsey Schiffler
MYP Coordinator Rachel Domenic
PYP Coordinator Lori Shigehara
Languages English
T: +1 808 261 0707
W: www.lejardinacademy.org

Mid-Pacific Institute

2445 Kaala Street, Honolulu HI 96822
DP Coordinator Kymbal Roley
Languages English
T: +1 808 973 5020
W: www.midpac.edu

Niu Valley Middle School

310 Halemaumau Street, Honolulu HI 96821
MYP Coordinator Gwen Lee
Languages English
T: +1 808 377 2440
W: niuvalleymiddle.org

Idaho

Alturas International Academy

151 N Ridge Avenue, Idaho Falls ID 83402
MYP Coordinator Jennifer Radford
PYP Coordinator Dayna Crose
Languages English, Spanish
T: +1 208 522 5145
W: www.alturasacademy.org

North Star Charter School

1400 N Park Lane, Eagle ID 83616
DP Coordinator Danica Holladay
Languages English
T: +1 208 939 9600
W: www.northstarcharter.org

Renaissance High School

1307 East Central Drive, Meredian ID 83642
CP Coordinator Michelle Farrell
DP Coordinator Michelle Farrell
Languages English
T: +1 208 350 4380
W: www.westada.org/domain/58

Riverstone International School

5521 Warm Springs Avenue, Boise ID 83716
DP Coordinator Brittany Roper
MYP Coordinator Jennifer Bistritz
PYP Coordinator Jessica Waugh
Languages English
T: +1 208 424 5000
W: www.riverstoneschool.org

Sage International School of Boise

457 E Parkcenter Blvd, Boise ID 83706
CP Coordinator Guy Falconer
DP Coordinator Andrea Reak
MYP Coordinator Bryce Mercer
PYP Coordinator Kadie Johnson
Languages English
T: +1 208 343 7243

Illinois

Academy for Global Citizenship

4647 West 47th Street, Chicago IL 60632
MYP Coordinator Massiel Zaragoza
PYP Coordinator Meredith McNamara
Languages English
T: +1 312 316 7373
W: www.agcchicago.org

Agassiz Elementary School

2851 N. Seminary Ave., Chicago IL 60657
MYP Coordinator Bernadette Moore
PYP Coordinator Freeda Pirillis
Languages English
T: +1 773 534 5725
W: agassizschool.org

Andrew Carnegie Elementary School

1414 East 61st Place, Chicago IL 60637
MYP Coordinator Franci Boateng
Languages English
T: +1 773 535 0882
W: www.carnegie.cps.edu

Back of the Yards College Preparatory High School

2111 West 47th Street, Chicago IL 60609
CP Coordinator Dawn Cox
DP Coordinator Dawn Cox
MYP Coordinator Katherine Smith
Languages English
T: +1 773 520 1774
W: www.boycp.org

Barnard Elementary School

10354 S. Charles Street, Chicago IL 60643
MYP Coordinator Madeline Lee
Languages English
T: +1 773 535 2625

Beacon Academy

622 Davis St., Evanston IL 60201
DP Coordinator Hayley Ropiequet
Languages English
T: +1 224 999 1177
W: www.beaconacademyil.org

Belding Elementary School

4257 North Tripp Ave., Chicago IL 60641
MYP Coordinator Michele Stefl
Languages English, Spanish
T: +1 773 534 3590
W: beldingelementary.com

Benito Juarez Community Academy

1450 - 1510 W Cermak Rd, Chicago IL 60608
DP Coordinator Fadwa Fino Rantisi
MYP Coordinator Fadwa Fino Rantisi
Languages English
T: +1 773 534 7030
W: www.benitojuarez.net

Bogan Computer Technical High School

3939 West 79th Street, Chicago IL 60652
DP Coordinator Nora Dandurand
MYP Coordinator Nora Dandurand
Languages English
T: +1 773535 8138
W: www.boganhs.org

British International School of Chicago, South Loop

161 W. 9th Street, Chicago IL 60605
DP Coordinator Jennifer Taylor
Languages English
T: +1 773 599 2472
W: www.bischicagosl.org

Bronzeville Scholastic Institute

4934 South Wabash Avenue, Chicago IL 60615
DP Coordinator Sarah Collins
MYP Coordinator Sarah Collins
Languages English
T: +1 773 535 1101
W: www.bronzevillescholastic.org

Carl Schurz High School

3601 N. Milwaukee Ave, Chicago IL 60641
DP Coordinator Lori Kingen-Gardner
MYP Coordinator Lori Kingen-Gardner
Languages English
T: +1 773 534 3420
W: www.schurzhs.org

Christian Ebinger Elementary School

7350 West Pratt Avenue, Chicago IL 60631
MYP Coordinator Gregory Joseph Spadoni
Languages English
T: +1 773 534 1070
W: ebingerschool.org

Coretta Scott King Magnet School

1009 Blackhawk Drive, University Park IL 60484
PYP Coordinator Shannon Bruns
Languages English
T: +1 708 672 2651

Crete-Monee Middle School

635 Olmstead Ln, University Park IL 60484
MYP Coordinator Christina Flores Colbert
Languages English, Spanish
T: +1 708 367 2400

David G. Farragut Career Academy High School

2345 S. Christiana Avenue, Chicago IL 60623
DP Coordinator Emily Brightwell
MYP Coordinator Emily Brightwell
Languages English
T: +1 773 534 1300
W: www.farragutcareeracademy.org

Daystar Academy

1550 S. State St., Chicago IL 60605
DP Coordinator Alison Good
MYP Coordinator Alison Good
PYP Coordinator Vanessa Espinosa
Languages English, Spanish
T: +1 312 791 0001
W: www.daystaracademy.org

DePaul College Prep

3633 North California Avenue, Chicago IL 60618
DP Coordinator Heidi Bojorges
Languages English
T: +1 773 539 3600
W: www.depaulprep.org

Dr. Edward Alexander Bouchet International Academy

7355 S. Jeffery Boulevard, Chicago IL 60649
MYP Coordinator Franchesca Little
PYP Coordinator Tina Franklin-Bertrand
Languages English, Spanish
T: +1 773 535 0501
W: www.bouchet-brynmawr.cps.edu

Edward K. Duke Ellington Elementary School

243 N Parkside Ave, Chicago IL 60644
MYP Coordinator Anna Baskin-Tines
Languages English
T: +1 773 534 6361
W: www.ellingtoncps.weebly.com

Elizabeth Sutherland Elementary School

10015 South Leavitt Avenue, Chicago IL 60643
MYP Coordinator Meredith Parker
Languages English
T: +1 773 535 2580

Esmond Elementary School

1865 W Montvale Avenue, Chicago IL 60643
MYP Coordinator Bernika Green
Languages English
T: +1 773 535 2650

Francisco I Madero Middle School

3202 West 28th Street, Chicago IL 60623
MYP Coordinator Wendy Preciado
Languages English
T: +1 773 535 4466

Frazier International Magnet School

4027 West Grenshaw Street, Chicago IL 60624
MYP Coordinator Laurie Bryant
PYP Coordinator Laurie Bryant
Languages English
T: +1 773 534 6880
W: fraziermagnet.cps.edu

GEMS World Academy Chicago

350 E. South Water St., Chicago IL 60601
DP Coordinator Emma Habgood
MYP Coordinator Rachel Robinson
PYP Coordinator Taneal Sanders
Languages English
T: +1 312 809 8900
W: www.gemschicago.org

George Washington High School

3535 East 114th Street, Chicago IL 60617
DP Coordinator Mike Pestich
MYP Coordinator Karolina Walkosz
Languages English
T: +1 773 535 6430

German International School Chicago

1447 West Montrose Ave, Chicago IL 60613
PYP Coordinator Katharina Koch
Languages English
T: +1 773 880 8812
W: www.germanschoolchicago.com

Gwendolyn Brooks Middle School

325 S Kenilworth Ave, Oak Park IL 60302
MYP Coordinator Veena Rajashekar
Languages English
T: +1 708 524 3050
W: www.op97.org/brooks

Hansberry College Prep

8748 S. Aberdeen St., Chicago IL 60620
DP Coordinator Matthew Wienclawski
Languages English
T: +1 773 729 3400
W: nobleschools.org/hansberry

Helen C. Peirce School of International Studies

1423 W. Bryn Mawr, Chicago IL 60660
MYP Coordinator Samuel Lee
PYP Coordinator Kimberly Lebovitz
Languages English
T: +1 773 534 2440
W: peirce.cps.edu

Henry R Clissold School

2350 West 110th Place, Chicago IL 60643
MYP Coordinator Teena Van Dyke
Languages English
T: +1 773 535 2560
W: www.clissold-school.org

Holy Family Catholic Academy

2515 Palatine Road, Inverness IL 60067
PYP Coordinator Laura Clark
Languages English
T: +1 847 907 3452
W: holyfamilycatholicacademy.net

Homewood-Flossmoor High School District 233

999 Kedzie Avenue, Flossmoor IL 60422
DP Coordinator Krystal Davis
Languages English
T: +1 708 799 3000
W: www.hfhighschool.org

Hubbard High School

6200 South Hamlin Avenue, Chicago IL 60629
DP Coordinator Jean Brown
Languages English
T: +1 773 535 2403

Hyde Park Academy

6220 South Stoney Island Ave, Chicago IL 60637
CP Coordinator Meghan Hoff
DP Coordinator Katharine Braggs
MYP Coordinator Rosette Edinburg
Languages English
T: +1 773 535 0882

Ida B Wells Preparatory Elementary Academy

249 E 37TH St, Chicago IL 60653
MYP Coordinator Rozetta Toney
Languages English
T: +1 773 535 1204
W: wellsprepelementary.com

Iles School

1700 South 15th Street, Springfield IL 62703
PYP Coordinator Carolyn Korza
Languages English
T: +1 217 525 3226
W: www.springfield.k12.il.us/schools/iles

Irvin C. Mollison Elementary

4415 South King Drive, Chicago IL 60653
MYP Coordinator Adele Wright
Languages English
T: +1 773 535 1804

James B McPherson Elementary School

4728 N Wolcott, Chicago IL 60640
MYP Coordinator Marianne Turk
Languages English
T: +1 773 534 2625

John F. Kennedy High School

6325 West 56th Street, Chicago IL 60638
CP Coordinator James Clarke
DP Coordinator James Clarke
MYP Coordinator Allison Wika
Languages English
T: +1 773 535 2325
W: www.kennedyhschicago.org

John Fiske Elementary

6020 S Langley Avenue, Chicago IL 60637
MYP Coordinator Joi Tillman
Languages English
T: +1 773 535 0990
W: fiskeelementary.org

John H. Kinzie Elementary School

5625 S. Mobile Ave., Chicago IL 60638
MYP Coordinator Lorraine O'Malley
Languages English, Spanish
T: +1 773 535 2425
W: kinzie.cps.edu

John L Marsh Elementary School

9810 South Exchange Avenue, Chicago IL 60617
MYP Coordinator Armando Avila
Languages English
T: +1 773 535 6430

John M Smyth Magnet School

1059 West 13th Street, Chicago IL 60608
MYP Coordinator Kiyana Grayer
PYP Coordinator Debra Ellis
Languages English
T: +1 773 534 7180

Jones-Farrar Magnet School

1386 South Kiwanis Drive, Freeport IL 61032
PYP Coordinator Laura Stocker
Languages English
T: +1 815 232 0610
W: www.fsd145.org/Domain/11

Jose de Diego Community Academy

1313 N Claremont, Chicago IL 60622
MYP Coordinator Lyndsay Whitfield
Languages English
T: +1 773 534 4451
W: josedediego.org

Josephinum Academy

1501 North Oakley Boulevard, Chicago IL 60622
DP Coordinator Renee Vai
Languages English
T: +1 773 276 1261
W: www.josephinum.org

Joshua D Kershaw Elementary

6450 S Lowe Avenue, Chicago IL 60621
MYP Coordinator Aileen Lopez
PYP Coordinator Aileen Lopez
Languages English
T: +1 773 535 3050
W: www.kershawmagnet.org

Kate Starr Kellogg Elementary School

9241 S Leavitt Street, Chicago IL 60643
MYP Coordinator Diane Pajkos
Languages English
T: +1 773 535 2590
W: kellogg.cps.edu

Legacy Academy of Excellence Charter School

4029 Prairie Road, Rockford IL 61102
MYP Coordinator Lynn Victorov
Languages English
T: +1 815 961 1100
W: www.legacy-academy.com

LINCOLN PARK HIGH SCHOOL

2001 North Orchard Street, Chicago IL 60614
CP Coordinator James Conzen
DP Coordinator Mary Enda Tookey
MYP Coordinator Theresa McCormick
Languages English
T: +1 773 534 8149
E: lpibprogram@aol.com
W: www.lincolnparkhs.org

See full details on page 516

Locke Elementary School

2828 North Oak Park Avenue, Chicago IL 60634
MYP Coordinator Edgar Valentin
Languages English
T: +1 773 534 3300
W: www.lockeschool.org

Lycée Français de Chicago

1929 W Wilson Ave, Chicago IL 60640
DP Coordinator Sebastien Tourlouse
MYP Coordinator Sebastien Tourlouse
Languages English, French
T: +1 773 665 0066
W: www.lyceechicago.org

Mansueto High School

2911 W. 47th Street, Chicago IL 60632
DP Coordinator Thomas Evans
Languages English
T: +1 773 349 8200
W: nobleschools.org/mansueto

Marie Sklodowska Curie Metropolitan High School

4959 South Archer Avenue, Chicago IL 60632
CP Coordinator Alexandra Rake
DP Coordinator Sharyl Barnes
MYP Coordinator Maria Chavez
Languages English
T: +1 773 535 2100
W: www.curiehs.org

Marquette Elementary School

3939 West 79th Street, Chicago IL 60652
MYP Coordinator Michael Marzano
Languages English
T: +1 773 535 2174

Michael M. Byrne Elementary School

5329 S. Oak Park Avenue, Chicago IL 60638
MYP Coordinator Anyine Galvan-Rodriguez
Languages English, Spanish
T: +1 773 535 2170
W: www.byrnecps.org

Mildred I. Lavizzo Elementary School

138 West 109th Street, Chicago IL 60628
MYP Coordinator Kathleen Vaulman
Languages English, Spanish
T: +1 773 535 5300
W: lavizzo.cps.edu

Moos Elementary School

1711 N. California Ave, Chicago IL 60647
MYP Coordinator Tiffany Frayer
Languages English
T: +1 773 534 4340
W: www.mooselementary.org

Morgan Park High School

1744 West Pryor, Chicago IL 60643
CP Coordinator Bethany Kaufmann
DP Coordinator Morgan Mudron
MYP Coordinator Bethany Kaufmann
Languages English
T: +1 773 535 2550
W: www.morganparkcps.org

Nicholas Senn High School

5900 Glenwood Avenue, Chicago IL 60660
CP Coordinator David Gregg
DP Coordinator Claire Saura
MYP Coordinator Lauren Lucchesi
Languages English
T: +1 773 534 2365

Oscar DePriest Elementary School

139 South Parkside Avenue, Chicago IL 60644
MYP Coordinator Tanya Bateson
Languages English
T: +1 773 534 6800
W: depriestschool.org

Oscar F Mayer Elementary School

2250 N Clifton Avenue, Chicago IL 60614
MYP Coordinator Jill Kittinger
Languages English
T: +1 773 534 5535
W: mayermagnet.org

Percy Julian Middle School

416 S Ridgeland Ave, Oak Park IL 60302
MYP Coordinator Kenya Walker
Languages French, Spanish
T: +1 708 524 3040
W: www.op97.org/julian

Prosser Career Academy

2148 N Long Avenue, Chicago IL 60639
CP Coordinator Jessica Stephenson
DP Coordinator Jessica Stephenson
Languages English
T: +1 773 534 3200
W: www.prosseracademy.org

Proviso Mathematics & Science Academy

8601 W. Roosevelt Rd, Forest Park IL 60130
DP Coordinator Rebecca Tanaka
Languages English
T: +1 708 338 4100
W: www.pths209.org/pmsa

Proviso West High School

4701 West Harrison, Hillside IL 60162
CP Coordinator Rebecca Tanaka
Languages English, Spanish
T: +1 708 449 6400
W: www.pths209.org/west

Pulaski International School of Chicago

2230 W McLean Ave, Chicago IL 60647
MYP Coordinator Rosabel Sanchez
PYP Coordinator Rosabel Sanchez
Languages English
T: +1 773 534 4390
W: www.pulaskischool.org

Richard Edwards School

4815 S Karlov Avenue, Chicago IL 60632
MYP Coordinator Elpidio Pintor
Languages English
T: +1 773 535 4878
W: edwardsib.org

Richwoods High School

6301 N. University Street, Peoria IL 61614
DP Coordinator Thomas Hayes
Languages English
T: +1 309 693 4400
W: www.peoriapublicschools.org/richwoods

Roald Amundsen High School

5110 N Damen Avenue, Chicago IL 60625
CP Coordinator Colleen Murray
DP Coordinator Colleen Murray
MYP Coordinator Irwin Lim
Languages English
T: +1 773 534 2320

Roberto Clemente Community Academy

1147 N. Western Avenue, Chicago IL 60622
CP Coordinator Ashten Cales
DP Coordinator Ashten Cales
MYP Coordinator Gillian Dryjanski
Languages English
T: +1 773 534 4000
W: www.rccachicago.org

South Shore International College Prep

1955 E. 75th Street, Chicago IL 60649
CP Coordinator Donna Delmonico
DP Coordinator Donna Delmonico
MYP Coordinator Maureen Waters
Languages English
T: +1 773 535 8350
W: www.southshoreinternational.org

St. Laurence High School

5556 West 77th Street, Burbank IL 60459
DP Coordinator Pete Lotus
Languages English, Spanish
T: +1 708 458 6900
W: www.stlaurence.com

St. Matthias School

4910 N. Claremont Ave, Chicago IL 60625
MYP Coordinator Jennifer Reckamp
PYP Coordinator Nicole Pacholski
Languages English
T: +1 773 784 0999
W: www.stmatthiasschool.org

Steinmetz College Prep High School

3030 North Mobile Avenue, Chicago IL 60634
DP Coordinator Amy Hank
MYP Coordinator Rachel Rezny
Languages English
T: +1 773 534 3030
W: steinmetzcollegeprep.org

The Ogden International School of Chicago

1250 W Erie, Chicago IL 60642
DP Coordinator John McGinnis
MYP Coordinator Sara Fliehman Levinstein
PYP Coordinator Sara Schneeberg
Languages English
T: +1 773 534 0866
W: ogden.cps.edu

Thomas Kelly College Preparatory

4136 South California Avenue, Chicago IL 60632
DP Coordinator Carolyn Brown
Languages English
T: +1 773 535 4915
W: www.kellycollegeprep.org

Thornridge High School

15000 Cottage Grove, Dolton IL 60419
DP Coordinator Jason Curl
Languages English
T: +1 708 271 4403
W: www.district205.net/thornridge

Thornton Township High School

15001 S. Broadway, Harvey IL 60426
DP Coordinator Bradley Ablin
Languages English
T: +1 708 225 4102
W: www.district205.net/thornton

Thornwood High School

17101 South Park Avenue, South Holland IL 60473
DP Coordinator Jennifer Merwald
Languages English
T: +1 708 225 4700
W: www.district205.net/thornwood

Trinity College Preparatory High School

7574 West Division Street, River Forest IL 60305
DP Coordinator Rose Crnkovich
Languages English
T: +1 708 771 8383
W: www.trinityhs.org

Wildwood IB World Magnet School

6950 N Hiawatha, Chicago IL 60646
MYP Coordinator Tammy Kreydick
PYP Coordinator Tammy Kreydick
Languages English
T: +1 773 534 1187
W: www.wildwoodworldmagnet.org

William H. Seward Communication Arts Academy

4600 S. Hermitage, Chicago IL 60609
MYP Coordinator Lorel Madden
Languages English
T: +1 773 535 4890
W: seward.cps.edu

William Howard Taft High School

6530 West Bryn Mawr Avenue, Region 1 Area 19, Chicago IL 60631
CP Coordinator Lauren Zucchero
DP Coordinator Irene Kondos
MYP Coordinator Sarah Gomez
Languages English
T: +1 773 534 1000

Indiana

Allisonville Elementary School

4900 E 79th Street, Indianapolis IN 46228
PYP Coordinator Pamela Weiger
Languages English
T: +1 317 845 9441
W: av.msdwt.k12.in.us

Carmel High School

520 East Main Street, Carmel IN 46032
DP Coordinator Kathleen Overbeck
Languages English
T: +1 317 846 7721
W: www.ccs.k12.in.us/chs

Cathedral High School

5225 East 56th Street, Indianapolis IN 46226
DP Coordinator Lizabeth Bradshaw
Languages English
T: +1 317 542 1481
W: www.gocathedral.com

Center for Inquiry School 2

725 N. New Jersey Street, Indianapolis IN 46202
MYP Coordinator Christine Snow
PYP Coordinator Christine Snow
Languages English
T: +1 317 226 4202
W: myips.org/cfischools/cfi-school-2

Center for Inquiry School 27

545 E. 19th Street, Indianapolis IN 46202
MYP Coordinator Karen Sullivan
PYP Coordinator Karen Sullivan
Languages English
T: +1 317 226 4227
W: myips.org/cfischools/cfi-school-27

Center for Inquiry School 70

510 46th Street, Indianapolis IN 46205
MYP Coordinator Karla Reilly
PYP Coordinator Karla Reilly
Languages English, Spanish
T: +1 317 226 4270
W: myips.org/cfischools/cfi-school-70

Center for Inquiry School 84

440 E. 57th Street, Indianapolis IN 46220
MYP Coordinator Rachel Green Sharpe
PYP Coordinator Rachel Green Sharpe
Languages English
T: +1 317 226 4284
W: myips.org/cfischools/cfi-school-84

Central Middle School

303 E. Superior St, Kokomo IN 46901
MYP Coordinator Chantel Sullivan
Languages English
T: +1 765 454 7000
W: www.kokomoschools.com

Chesterton High School

2125 S 11th Street, Chesterton IN 46304
DP Coordinator Rebecca Uehling
Languages English
T: +1 219 983 3730
W: www.duneland.k12.in.us/chs

Childs Elementary School

2211 S. High Street, Bloomington IN 47401
PYP Coordinator Kris Stewart
Languages English
T: +1 812 330 7756
W: www.mccsc.edu/childs

Clearwater Elementary School

3575 E 79th St., Indianapolis IN 46240
PYP Coordinator Anat Pinsky
Languages English
T: +1 317 259 5465
W: cw.msdwt.k12.in.us

Crooked Creek Elementary School

2150 Kessler Blvd W Drive, Indianapolis IN 46228
PYP Coordinator Kelly Ouattara
Languages English
T: +1 317 259 5478
W: cc.msdwt.k12.in.us

Eastwood Middle School

4401 East 62nd St., Indianapolis IN 46220
MYP Coordinator Chad Hyatt
Languages English
T: +1 317 259 5401
W: ew.msdwt.k12.in.us

Fishers High School

13000 Promise Road, Fishers IN 46038
DP Coordinator Jennifer Gabbard
Languages English
T: +1 317 915 4290
W: hse.k12.in.us/fhs

Floyd Central High School

6575 Old Vincennes Road, Floyd Knobs IN 47119
DP Coordinator Karen Mayer-Sebastian
Languages English
T: +1 812 542 3005
W: fchs.nafcs.k12.in.us

Fox Hill Elementary School

802 Fox Hill Drive, Indianapolis IN 46228
PYP Coordinator Emily Dickerson
Languages English
T: +1 317 259 5371
W: fh.msdwt.k12.in.us

Goshen High School

401 Lincolnway East, Goshen IN 46526
DP Coordinator Theresa Collins
Languages English
T: +1 574 533 8651

Goshen Middle School

1216 S Indiana Ave., Goshen IN 46526
MYP Coordinator Lisa Carpenter
Languages English, Spanish
T: +1 574 533 0391

Greenbriar Elementary School

8201 Ditch Road, Indianapolis IN 46260
PYP Coordinator Katherine Sorrell
Languages English
T: +1 317 259 5445
W: gb.msdwt.k12.in.us

Guerin Catholic High School

15300 Gray Road, Noblesville IN 46062
DP Coordinator Meaghan Neman
Languages English
T: +1 317 582 0120
W: www.guerincatholic.org

International School of Indiana

4330 N. Michigan Road, Indianapolis IN 46208
DP Coordinator Jane Bramhill
MYP Coordinator Marithe Benavente-Llamas
PYP Coordinator Stacy Gruen
Languages English
T: +1 317 923 1951
W: www.isind.org

James R. Watson Elementary

901 Eckhart Avenue, Auburn IN 46706
PYP Coordinator Michelle Wagner
Languages English
T: +1 260 920 1014
W: jrw.dekalbcentral.net

John Adams High School

808 South Twyckenham Blvd, South Bend IN 46615
DP Coordinator Rebecca Hernandez
Languages English
T: +1 574 283 7700

Kokomo High School

2501 S. Berkley Road, Kokomo IN 46902
CP Coordinator Christa Jordan
DP Coordinator Leslie G. Fatum
MYP Coordinator Lori Magnuson
Languages English
T: +1 765 455 8040
W: www.kokomoschools.com

Lafayette Park Elementary School

919 N. Korby, Kokomo IN 46901
PYP Coordinator Nicole Geary
Languages English
T: +1 765 454 7060
W: www.kokomoschools.com

Lawrence Central High School

7300 East 56th Street, Indianapolis IN 46226
DP Coordinator Kathleen Legge
Languages English
T: +1 317 454 5301

Lawrence North High School

7802 Hague Road, Indianapolis IN 46256
DP Coordinator Jason Floyd
Languages English
T: +1 317 964 7700
W: lawrencenorth.ltschools.org

Nora Elementary School

1000 East 91st Street, Indianapolis IN 46240
PYP Coordinator Kelli Glassley
Languages English
T: +1 317 844 5436
W: no.msdwt.k12.in.us

North Central High School

1801 E 86th St., Indianapolis IN 46240
DP Coordinator Andrew Hodson
MYP Coordinator Jocelyn Sisson
Languages English
T: +1 317 259 5301
W: www.nchs.cc

Northridge High School

57697-1 Northridge Drive, Middlebury IN 46540
DP Coordinator Tracy Wogoman
Languages English
T: +1 574 825 2142
W: www.mcsin-k12.org/nhs

Northview Middle School

8401 Westfield Boulevard, Indianapolis IN 46240
MYP Coordinator Glenda Ritz
Languages English
T: +1 317 259 5421
W: nv.msdwt.k12.in.us

Pike High School

5401 West 71th street, Indianapolis IN 46268
DP Coordinator Danielle D. Vohland
Languages English
T: +1 317 387 2600
W: www.pike.k12.in.us/4/home

Prairie View Elementary

30 Regent Street, Goshen IN 46526
PYP Coordinator AnnDee Reiff
Languages English, Spanish
T: +1 574 534 4710

Shortridge High School

3401 N. Meridian Street, Indianapolis IN 46208
CP Coordinator Jessica Carlson
DP Coordinator Mel Coryell
MYP Coordinator Garret Merle
Languages English
T: +1 317 226 2810
W: www.myips.org/shs

Signature School

610 Main Street, Evansville IN 47708
DP Coordinator Shannon Hughes
Languages English
T: +1 812 421 1820
W: www.signature.edu

South Side High School, Fort Wayne

3601 S Calhoun St., Fort Wayne IN 46807
DP Coordinator Kara Fultz
Languages English
T: +1 260 467 2600
W: www.fortwayneschools.org/SouthSide

Spring Mill Elementary School

8250 Spring Mill Road, Indianapolis IN 46260
PYP Coordinator Julie Lowe
Languages English
T: +1 317 259 5462
W: sm.msdwt.k12.in.us

Sycamore Elementary School

1600 E. Sycamore St., Kokomo IN 46901
PYP Coordinator Laura Yates
Languages English
T: +1 765 454 7090
W: www.kokomoschools.com

Templeton Elementary

1400 S. Brenda Lane, Bloomington IN 47401
PYP Coordinator Amie Easton
Languages English
T: +1 812 330 7735
W: www.mccsc.edu/templeton

University Elementary School

1111 N. Russell Road, Bloomington IN 47408
PYP Coordinator Mary D'Eliso
Languages English
T: +1 812 330 7753
W: www.mccsc.edu/domain/21

Valparaiso High School

2727 North Campbell Street, Valparaiso IN 46383
DP Coordinator Lauren Pickett
Languages English
T: +1 219 531 3070

West Goshen Elementary

215 Dewey Ave, Goshen IN 46526
PYP Coordinator Ruth Metcalfe
Languages English
T: +1 574 533 7855

Westlane Middle School

1301 W. 73rd Street, Indianapolis IN 46260
MYP Coordinator Leigh Muller
Languages English
T: +1 317 259 5412
W: wl.msdwt.k12.in.us

Iowa

Brody Middle School

2501 Park Avenue, Des Moines IA 50321
MYP Coordinator Timm Pilcher
Languages English
T: +1 515 242 8443
W: brody.dmschools.org

Carter Lake Elementary

1000 Willow Dr, Carter Lake IA 51510
PYP Coordinator Erin Schoening
Languages English
T: +1 712 347 5876
W: www.cb-schools.org/Domain/110

College View Elementary School

1225 College Road, Council Bluffs IA 51503
PYP Coordinator Erin Schoening
Languages English
T: +1 712 328 6452
W: www.cb-schools.org/domain/111

East High School

214 High Street, Waterloo IA 50703
DP Coordinator Ellen Shay
Languages English
T: +1 319 433 1800
W: www.waterlooschools.org/schoolsites/easthigh

Goodrell Middle School

3300 East 29th Street, Des Moines IA 50317
MYP Coordinator Lori Bonnstetter
Languages English
T: +1 515 242 8444

Hoover High School
4800 Aurora Ave., Des Moines IA 50310
MYP Coordinator Megan Austin
Languages English
T: +1 515 242 7300
w: hoover.dmschools.org

Hubbell Elementary School
800 42nd Street, Des Moines IA 50312
PYP Coordinator Kati Medick
Languages English
T: +1 515 242 8414
w: hubbell.dmschools.org

Kirn Middle School
1751 Madison Avenue, Council Bluffs IA 51503
MYP Coordinator Debora Masker
Languages English, Spanish
T: +1 712 328 6454
w: www.cb-schools.org/Domain/116

Meredith Middle School
4827 Madison Ave., Des Moines IA 50310
MYP Coordinator Holly Meagher
Languages English
T: +1 515 242 7250
w: meredith.dmschools.org

Merrill Middle School
5301 Grand Avenue, Des Moines IA 50312
MYP Coordinator Danielle Taylor
Languages English
T: +1 515 242 8448
w: merrill.dmschools.org

Moore Elementary School
3716 50th Street, Des Moines IA 50310
PYP Coordinator Laura Manroe
Languages English
T: +1 515 242 8426
w: moore.dmschools.org

Park Avenue Elementary School
3141 SW 9th Street, Des Moines IA 50315
PYP Coordinator Debora Belden
Languages English
T: +1 515 242 8429
w: parkavenue.dmschools.org

Stowe Elementary School
1411 East 33rd Street, Des Moines IA 50317
PYP Coordinator Tricia McCarty
Languages English
T: +1 515 242 8435
w: stowe.dmschools.org

Walnut Street School
901 Walnut Street, Des Moines IA 50309
PYP Coordinator Leslie Barnhizer
Languages English
T: +1 515 242 8438
w: walnutstreet.dmschools.org

West High School
425 E. Ridgeway Avenue, Waterloo IA 50702
DP Coordinator Ellen Shay
Languages English
T: +1 319 433 1800
w: www.waterlooschools.org/schoolsites/westhigh

Wilson Middle School
715 N 21st Street, Council Bluffs IA 51501
MYP Coordinator Erin Eckholt
Languages English, Spanish
T: +1 712 328 6476
w: www.cb-schools.org/Domain/123

Kansas

Campus High School
2100 W. 55th St. South, Wichita KS 67217
DP Coordinator Casey Meier
Languages English
T: +1 316 554 2236
w: usd261.com/Campus

Hutchinson High School
810 East 13th St, Hutchinson KS 67501
CP Coordinator Todd Ray
DP Coordinator Todd Ray
Languages English
T: +1 620 615 4100
w: www.usd308.com/node/14

Shawnee Mission East High School
7500 Mission Road, Shawnee Mission KS 66208-4298
DP Coordinator Meredith Sternberg Sternberg
Languages English
T: +1 913 993 6600
w: smeast.smsd.org

Shawnee Mission North High School
7401 Johnson Drive, Overland Park KS 66202
DP Coordinator Jonathan Durham
Languages English
T: +1 913 993 6900
w: smnorth.smsd.org

Shawnee Mission Northwest High School
12701 West 67th Street, Shawnee KS 66216
DP Coordinator Amy Walker
Languages English
T: +1 913 993 7200
w: smnorthwest.smsd.org

Sumner Academy of Arts and Science
1610 N 8th Street, Kansas City KS 66101
CP Coordinator Edward Gunter
DP Coordinator Paula Biggar
Languages English
T: +1 913 627 7200
w: sumner.schools.kckps.org

Washburn Rural High School
5900 SW 61st Street, Topeka KS 66619
DP Coordinator Nick Bowling
Languages English
T: +1 785 339 4100
w: www.wrhs.net

Wichita High School East
2301 East Douglas, Wichita KS 67211
DP Coordinator Michael Boykins
Languages English
T: +1 316 973 7289
w: www.usd259.org/East

Kentucky

Atherton High School
3000 Dundee Road, Louisville KY 40205
DP Coordinator Theresa Beckley
Languages English
T: +1 502 485 8202
w: schools.jefferson.kyschools.us/high/atherton

Highland Middle School
1700 Norris Place, Louisville KY 40205
MYP Coordinator Todd Stanis
Languages English
T: +1 502 485 8266
w: highlandmiddle.com

Holmes High School
2500 Madison Ave., Covington KY 41014
DP Coordinator Renata Kennison
Languages English
T: +1 859 655 9545
w: www.covington.kyschools.us/1/home

Sacred Heart Academy
3175 Lexington Road, Louisville KY 40206
DP Coordinator Candace Kresse
MYP Coordinator Tricia Forde
Languages English
T: +1 502 897 6097
w: sha.shslou.org

Sacred Heart Model School
3107 Lexington Road, Louisville KY 40206
MYP Coordinator Tricia Forde
PYP Coordinator Kris Grimm
Languages English
T: +1 502 896 3931
w: shms.shslou.org

Tates Creek Elementary School
1113 Centre Parkway, Lexington KY 40517
PYP Coordinator Lisa Johnson
Languages English
T: +1 859 381 3606
w: tces.fcps.net

Tates Creek High School
1111 Centre Parkway, Lexington KY 40517
DP Coordinator John Hatfield
Languages English
T: +1 859 381 3620
w: www.tchs.fcps.net

Tates Creek Middle School
1105 Centre Parkway, Lexington KY 40517
MYP Coordinator Kelly Sirginnis
Languages English
T: +1 859 381 3052
w: www.tcms.fcps.net

Whitney M Young Elementary School
3526 West Muhammad Ali Boulevard, Louisville KY 40212
PYP Coordinator Mary Jo Wimsatt
Languages English
T: +1 502 485 8354
w: www.jefferson.kyschools.us/schools/profiles/young-elementary

Louisiana

Baton Rouge International School
5015 Auto Plex Drive, Baton Rouge LA 70809
DP Coordinator Ms. Xiaoping Liu
MYP Coordinator Ms. Aareena Dhillon
Languages English, French, Spanish, Chinese, Portuguese
T: +1 225 293 4338
w: www.brintl.com

Hammond Eastside Elementary Magnet School
45050 River Road, Hammond LA 70401
MYP Coordinator Stephanie Ciresi
PYP Coordinator Katherine Johnson
Languages English
T: +1 985 474 8660
w: www.tangischools.org/heems

Hammond High Magnet School

45168 River Road, Hammond LA 70401
CP Coordinator Deirdra Disher
DP Coordinator Deirdra Disher
Languages English
T: +1 985 345 7235
W: www.tangischools.org/hhms

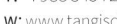

International High School of New Orleans

727 Carondelet Street, New Orleans LA 70130
DP Coordinator Cody Bourque
Languages English
T: +1 504 613 5703
W: www.ihsnola.org

John Ehret High School

4300 Patriot Street, Marrero LA 70072
DP Coordinator Milena Cajina-Axinn
Languages English
T: +1 504 340 7651
W: www.jpschools.org/Domain/29

KEHOE-FRANCE NORTHSHORE

25 Patricia Drive, Covington LA 70433
PYP Coordinator Brandy Calato
Languages English
T: +1 985 892 4415
E: kfninfo@kf-ns.com
W: www.kf-ns.com
See full details on page 512

Kehoe-France School

720 Elise Avenue, Metairie LA 70003
PYP Coordinator Samantha Gammon
Languages English, Spanish
T: +1 504 733 0472
W: www.kehoe-france.com

Louisiana State University Laboratory School

45 Dalrymple Drive, Baton Rouge LA 70803-0501
DP Coordinator Candence Robillard
Languages English
T: +1 225 578 9147
W: www.uhigh.lsu.edu

Morris Jeff Community School

3368 Esplanade Ave, New Orleans LA 70119
DP Coordinator Carmen Mack
MYP Coordinator Jestin Moorehead
PYP Coordinator Laura Krebs
Languages English
T: +1 504 373 6200
W: www.morrisjeffschool.org

Riverdale High School

240 Riverdale Drive, Jefferson LA 70121
DP Coordinator Monique Pontiff
Languages English
T: +1 504 833 7288
W: www.jpschools.org/Domain/67

Maine

FOXCROFT ACADEMY

975 West Main Street, Dover-Foxcroft ME 04426
DP Coordinator Donna Newhouse
Languages English
T: +1 207 564 8351
E: admissions@foxcroftacademy.org
W: www.foxcroftacademy.org
See full details on page 503

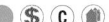

Gray-New Gloucester High School

10 Libby Hill Road, Gray ME 04039
DP Coordinator Bobbie-Jo Thibodeau
Languages English
T: +1 207 657 9306
W: msad15.org/gray-new-gloucester-high-school

Greely High School

303 Main Street, Cumberland ME 04021
DP Coordinator Vanessa Gribbin
Languages English
T: +1 207 829 4805
W: sites.google.com/a/msad51.org/greely_high_school

Kennebunk High School

89 Fletcher Street, Kennebunk ME 04043
DP Coordinator William Putnam
Languages English
T: +1 207 985 1110
W: www.rsu21.net/khs

Ocean Avenue Elementary School

150 Ocean Avenue, Portland ME 04103
PYP Coordinator Patricia Sprague
Languages English
T: +1 207 874 8180

Maryland

Albert Einstein High School

11135 Newport Mill Road, Kensington MD 20895
DP Coordinator John Howard
Languages English
T: +1 301 929 2200

Annapolis High School

2700 Riva Road, Annapolis MD 21401
CP Coordinator Nicholas Coldiron
DP Coordinator Nicholas Coldiron
MYP Coordinator Jay Koller
Languages English
T: +1 410 266 5240
W: www.annapolishighschool.org

Annapolis Middle School

1399 Forest Drive, Annapolis MD 21403
MYP Coordinator Molly Courtien
Languages English
T: +1 410 267 8658
W: www.aacps.org/Page/3949

Archbishop Spalding High School

8080 New Cut Road, Severn MD 21144
DP Coordinator Angela Bentzley
Languages English
T: +1 410 969 9105
W: www.archbishopspalding.org

Baltimore City College

3220 The Alameda, Baltimore MD 21218
DP Coordinator Ndaneh Smart-Smith
MYP Coordinator Sarah Jeanblanc
Languages English
T: +1 410 396 6557
W: www.baltimorecitycollege.us

Baltimore International Academy

4410 Frankford Avenue, Baltimore MD 21206
MYP Coordinator Henriette Sindjui
PYP Coordinator Henriette Sindjui
Languages Spanish, Mandarin, Arabic, Russian, French
T: +1 410 426 3650
W: www.baltimoreinternationalacademy.org

Bethesda Chevy Chase High School

4301 East West Highway, Bethesda MD 20814
DP Coordinator Christine Smithson
MYP Coordinator Tony Louis
Languages English
T: +1 240 497 6300
W: www2.montgomeryschoolsmd.org/schools/bcchs

Central High School

200 Cabin Branch Road, Capitol Heights MD 20743
DP Coordinator Shaun Devlin Shepard
Languages English
T: +1 301 499 7080
W: www.pgcps.org/central

College Gardens Elementary School

1700 Yale Place, Rockville MD 20850
PYP Coordinator Michael Dushel
Languages English
T: +1 301 279 8470
W: www.mcps.k12.md.us/schools/collegegardenses

Crossland High School

6901 Temple Hill Road, Temple Hills MD 20748
DP Coordinator Melissa Boyd
Languages English
T: +1 301 449 4800
W: www.pgcps.org/crossland

Dwight D Eisenhower Middle School

13725 Briarwood Drive, Laurel MD 20708
MYP Coordinator Steve Mellen
Languages English
T: +1 301 497 3620
W: www.pgcps.org/dwightdeisenhower

Eastport Elementary School

420 Fifth Street, Annapolis MD 21403
PYP Coordinator Corinne Codjoe
T: +1 410 222 1605
W: www.aacps.org/Page/4283

Edgewood High School

2415 Willoughby Beach Road, Edgewood MD 21040
DP Coordinator Jamie Childs
Languages English
T: +1 410 612 1500
W: www.hcps.org

Francis Scott Key Middle School

910 Schindler Drive, Silver Spring MD 20903
MYP Coordinator Beth Hester
Languages English
T: +1 301 422 5600
W: www.mcps.k12.md.us/schools/fskms

Frank Hebron-Harman Elementary School

7660 Ridge Chapel Road, Hanover MD 21076
PYP Coordinator Lacey Gandy
Languages English
T: +1 410 859 4510
W: www.aacps.org/Page/4463

Frederick Douglass High School

8000 Croom Road, Upper Marlboro MD 20772
DP Coordinator Kim Watson
MYP Coordinator Letty Maxwell
Languages English
T: +1 301 952 2400
W: www.pgcps.org/douglass

Germantown Elementary School

1411 Cedar Park Road, Annapolis MD 21401
PYP Coordinator Erika Boltz
Languages English
T: +1 410 222 1615
W: www.aacps.org/Page/4448

Jacobsville Elementary

3801 Mountain Road, Pasadena MD 21122
PYP Coordinator Chelsea Wenzel
Languages English, Spanish
T: +1 410 222 6460
W: www.aacps.org/page/4523

James Madison Middle School

7300 Woodyard Road, Upper Marlboro MD 20772
MYP Coordinator Dana Blair
Languages English
T: +1 301 599 2422
W: www.pgcps.org/jamesmadison

John F Kennedy High School

1901 Randolph Road, Silver Spring MD 20902
DP Coordinator Kia Patrice Davis
Languages English
T: +1 301 929 2100
W: www.mcps.k12.md.us/schools/kennedyhs

Julius West Middle School

651 Great Falls Road, Rockville MD 20850
MYP Coordinator Krista Fiabane
Languages English
T: +1 301 279 3979
W: www.montgomeryschoolsmd.org/schools/westms

Kenwood High School

501 Stemmers Run Road, Essex MD 21221
DP Coordinator Lacey Forman
MYP Coordinator Angela Single
Languages English
T: +1 410 887 0153

Laurel High School

8000 Cherry Lane, Laurel MD 20707
DP Coordinator Allen Diewald
Languages English
T: +1 301 497 2050
W: www.pgcps.org/laurelhs

MacArthur Middle School

3500 Rockenbach Road, Fort Meade MD 20755
MYP Coordinator Vanessa Facer
Languages English
T: +1 410 679 0032
W: www.aacps.org/Page/6091

Manor View Elementary School

2900 Macarthur Road, Fort Meade MD 20755
PYP Coordinator Marcia Ross
Languages English
T: +1 410 518 6473
W: www.aacps.org/Page/4613

Martin Luther King, Jr. Middle School (MD)

13737 Wisteria Dr., Germantown MD 20874
MYP Coordinator Jennifer Scavullo
Languages English
T: +1 301 353 8080
W: www.montgomeryschoolsmd.org/schools/mlkms

MARYLAND INTERNATIONAL SCHOOL

6135 Old Washington Road, Elkridge MD 21075
DP Coordinator Nikki Tanner
MYP Coordinator Nikki Tanner
PYP Coordinator Rebekah Ghosh
Languages English
T: +1 410 220 3792
E: info@marylandinternationalschool.org
W: www.marylandinternationalschool.org

See full details on page 521

Maya Angelou French Immersion School

2000 Callaway Street, Temple Hills MD 20748
PYP Coordinator Alphonse Talon
Languages English
T: +1 301 702 3950
W: www.pgcps.org/mayaangelou

Meade Senior High School

1100 Clark Road, Ft Meade MD 20755
CP Coordinator Jennifer Quinn
DP Coordinator Jennifer Quinn
MYP Coordinator Jenna Lerro
Languages English
T: +1 410 674 7710
W: www.aacps.org/Page/7917

Melwood Elementary School

7100 Woodyard Road, Upper Marlboro MD 20772
PYP Coordinator Stephanie Major
Languages English
T: +1 301 599 2500
W: www.pgcps.org/melwood

Mercy High School Baltimore

1300 E. Northern Parkway, Baltimore MD 21239
MYP Coordinator Samantha Pomplon
Languages English, Spanish
T: +1 410 433 8880
W: mercyhighschool.com

Middle River Middle School

800 Middle River Road, Middle River MD 21220
MYP Coordinator Carey Schuler
Languages English
T: +1 443 809 0165

Monarch Global Academy

430 Brock Bridge Road, Laurel MD 20724
PYP Coordinator Beth Ann Matthews
Languages English
T: 301-886-8648
W: www.monarcacademy.org/global

Montgomery Village Middle School

19300 Watkins Mill Road, Germantown MD 20886
MYP Coordinator Wendy Farmer
Languages English
T: +1 301 840 4660
W: montgomeryschoolsmd.org/schools/mvms

Mount Washington School

1801 Sulgrave Avenue, Baltimore MD 21209
MYP Coordinator Sarah Martin
Languages English
T: +1 410 396 6354
W: mountwashingtonschool.org

Neelsville Middle School

11700 Neelsville Church Road, Germantown MD 20876
MYP Coordinator Daisy Peay
Languages English
T: +1 301 353 8064
W: montgomeryschoolsmd.org/schools/neelsvillems

New Town High School

4931 New Town Blvd, Owings Mills MD 21117
CP Coordinator Chanell Johnson
DP Coordinator Chanell Johnson
MYP Coordinator Weston Rafe Park
Languages English
T: +1 443 809 1614

Newport Mill Middle School

11311 Newport Mill Road, Kensington MD 20895
MYP Coordinator Benjamin Legarreta
Languages English
T: +1 301 929 2244
W: www.montgomeryschoolsmd.org/schools/newportmillms

North Hagerstown High School

1200 Pennsylvania Ave, Hagerstown MD 21742
CP Coordinator Chris Downs
DP Coordinator Kevin G Jackson
MYP Coordinator Chris Downs
Languages English
T: +1 301 766 8238
W: www.wcpsmd.com/schools/high-schools/north-hagerstown-high

Northern Middle School

701 Northern Avenue, Hagerstown MD 21742
MYP Coordinator James Rossi
Languages English
T: +1 301 766 8258
W: wcpsmd.com/schools/middle-schools/northern-middle

Old Mill High School

600 Patriot Lane, Millersville MD 21108
CP Coordinator Virginia Sutherin
DP Coordinator Virginia Sutherin
MYP Coordinator Monica Batterden
Languages English
T: +1 410 969 9010
W: www.oldmillhs.org

Old Mill Middle School North

610 Patriot Lane, Millersville MD 21108
MYP Coordinator Diana Christadore
Languages English
T: +1 410 969 5950
W: www.aacps.org/Page/5264

Our Lady of Good Counsel High School

17301 Old Vic Boulevard, Olney MD 20832
DP Coordinator Megan Dean
Languages English
T: +1 240 283 3200
W: www.olgchs.org

Overlook Elementary
401 Hampton Road, Linthicum MD 21090
PYP Coordinator Marcia Ross
Languages English
T: +1 410 222 6585
W: www.aacps.org/Page/4793

Parkdale High School
6001 Good Luck Road, Riverdale MD 20737
DP Coordinator Erycka Constant
Languages English
T: +1 301 513 5700

Richard Montgomery High School
250 Richard Montgomery Drive, Rockville MD 20852
DP Coordinator Amanda Trivers
MYP Coordinator Molly Clarkson
Languages English
T: +1 301 279 8400
W: montgomeryschoolsmd.org/schools/rmhs

Roberto Clemente Middle School
18808 Waring Station Road, Germantown MD 20874
MYP Coordinator Liz Gall
Languages English
T: +1 301 284 4750
W: montgomeryschoolsmd.org/schools/clementems

Rochambeau, The French International School
9600 Forest Rd, Bethesda MD 20814
DP Coordinator Sandra Percy
Languages English, French
T: +1 301 530 8260
W: www.rochambeau.org

Rockville High School
2100 Baltimore Road, Rockville MD 21805
CP Coordinator Laurie Ainsworth
DP Coordinator Laurie Ainsworth
Languages English
T: +1 301 517 8105
W: www.montgomeryschoolsmd.org/schools/rockvillehs

Seneca Academy
15601 Germantown Road, Darnestown MD 20874
PYP Coordinator Melissa Karasek
Languages English
T: +1 301 869 3728
W: www.senecaacademy.org

Seneca Valley High School
19401 Crystal Rock Drive, Germantown MD 20874
CP Coordinator Natasha Ezerski
DP Coordinator Natasha Ezerski
Languages English
T: +1 301 353 8000
W: www.senecavalleyhighschool.com

Silver Creek Middle School
3701 Saul Road, Kensington MD 20895
MYP Coordinator Renee Hill
Languages English
T: +1 240 740 2200
W: www.montgomeryschoolsmd.org/schools/silvercreekms

Silver Spring International Middle School
313 Wayne Avenue, Silver Spring MD 20910
MYP Coordinator Molly Kuhn
Languages English
T: +1 301 650 6544
W: www.mcps.k12.md.us/schools/ssims

South Shore Elementary School
1376 Fairfield Loop Rd, Crownsville MD 21032
PYP Coordinator Erika Boltz
Languages English
T: +1 410 222 3865
W: www.aacps.org/Page/5063

Southgate Elementary School
290 Shetlands Ln, Glen Burnie MD 21061
PYP Coordinator Heather Giustiniani
Languages English
T: +1 410 222 6445
W: www.aacps.org/Page/5078

Springbrook High School
201 Valley Brook Drive, Silver Spring MD 20904
DP Coordinator John Weinshel
MYP Coordinator Lindsey Lipinski
Languages English
T: +1 301 989 5700
W: www.mcps.k12.md.us/schools/springbrookhs

Springdale Preparatory School
1000 Green Valley Rd, New Windsor MD 21776
DP Coordinator Dalin Chen
Languages English
T: +1 443 671 0072
W: springdaleprep.org

St. Francis of Assisi
3617 Harford Rd, Baltimore MD 21218
MYP Coordinator Clare Banks
Languages English
T: +1 410 467 1683
W: www.sfa-school.org

St. Timothy's School
8400 Greenspring Ave, Stevenson MD 21153
DP Coordinator Ghada Jaber
MYP Coordinator Ghada Jaber
Languages English
T: +1 410 486 7400
W: www.stt.org

Stemmers Run Middle School
201 Stemmers Run Rd, Essex MD 21221
MYP Coordinator Nicole Boyd
Languages English
T: +1 443 809 0177

Suitland High School
5200 Silver Hill Road, Forestville MD 20747
DP Coordinator Kamilah Williams
Languages English
T: +1 301 817 0500
W: www1.pgcps.org/suitlandhs

Sunset Elementary School
8572 Ft. Smallwood Road, Pasadena MD 21122
PYP Coordinator Heather Giustiniani
Languages English
T: +1 410 222 6478
W: www.aacps.org/Page/5093

Tarbiyah Academy
6785 Business Pky, Elkridge MD 21075
PYP Coordinator Hagar Aboubakr
Languages English
T: +1 844 827 2492
W: www.tarbiyahacademy.com

The Boys' School of St Paul's Parish
PO Box 8100, Brooklandville MD 21022-8100
DP Coordinator Andrew Mezeske
Languages English
T: +1 410 825 4400
W: www.stpaulsschool.org

The Calverton School
300 Calverton School Rd, Huntingtown MD 20639
DP Coordinator Susan Dice
Languages English
T: +1 410 535 0216
W: www.calvertonschool.org

Thomas Jefferson Elementary
605 Dryden Drive, Baltimore MD 21229
PYP Coordinator Tracy Taylor
Languages English
T: +1 410 396 0534

Tracey's Elementary School
20 Deale Road, Tracys Landing MD 20779
PYP Coordinator Corinne Codjoe
Languages English
T: +1 410 222 1633
W: www.aacps.org/Page/5108

Urbana High School
3471 Campus Drive, Ijamsville MD 21754
DP Coordinator Jessica McBroom
Languages English
T: +1 240 236 7600

Watkins Mill High School
10301 Apple Ridge Road, Gaithersburg MD 20879
CP Coordinator Lisa Ingram
DP Coordinator Lisa Ingram
MYP Coordinator Richard Courtot Iii
Languages English
T: +1 301 840 3959

Waugh Chapel
840 Sunflower Drive, Odenton MD 21113
PYP Coordinator Lacey Gandy
Languages English
T: +1 410 222 6542
W: www.aacps.org/page/5153

Wellwood International School
2901 Smith Ave, Baltimore MD 21208
PYP Coordinator Katherine Lugli
Languages English, French
T: +1 410 887 1212

Westland Middle School
5511 Massachusetts Avenue, Bethesda MD 20816
MYP Coordinator Rachel Johns
Languages English
T: +1 301 320 6515

Windsor Mill Middle School
8300 Windsor Mill Rd, Milford Mill MD 21244
MYP Coordinator Rebecca Macri
Languages English
T: +1 443 809 0618

Woodmoor Elementary School
3200 Elba Drive, Baltimore MD 21207
PYP Coordinator Cecelia Saunders
Languages English, Spanish
T: +1 410 887 1318

Massachusetts

Abby Kelley Foster Charter Public School
10 New Bond Street, Worcester MA 01606
DP Coordinator Kelly Davila
Languages English
T: +1 508 854 8400
W: www.akfcs.org

British International School of Boston
416 Pond Street, Boston MA 02130
DP Coordinator Karen McWilliam
Languages English
T: +1 617 522 2261
W: www.bisboston.org

Brockton High School
470 Forest Ave, Brockton MA 02301
DP Coordinator Todd Erickson
Languages English
T: +1 508 580 7633
W: www.bpsma.org/schools/brockton-high-school

Eagle Hill School
242 Old Petersham Road, P.O. Box 116, Hardwick MA 01037
DP Coordinator Jason Przypek
Languages English
T: +1 413 477 6000
W: www.eaglehill.school

INTERNATIONAL SCHOOL OF BOSTON
45 Matignon Road, Cambridge MA 02140
DP Coordinator Mr. John Bray
Languages English, French, Spanish
T: +1 617 499 1451
E: admissions@isbos.org
W: www.isbos.org

See full details on page 509

Joseph F Plouffe Academy
150 Clinton Street, Brockton MA 02302
MYP Coordinator Bonnie Brady
Languages English
T: +1 508 894 4301
W: www.bpsma.org/schools/middle-schools/plouffe-academy

Josiah Quincy Upper School
152 Arlington Street, Boston MA 02116
DP Coordinator Kristina Danahy
MYP Coordinator Jessica Tsai
Languages English
T: +1 617 635 8940
W: bostonpublicschools.org/jqus

Kensington International School
31 Kensington Avenue, Springfield MA 01108
PYP Coordinator Sheree Nolley
Languages English
T: +1 413 787 7522
W: kensington.springfieldpublicschools.com

Marthas Vineyard Public Charter School
P.O. Box 1150, 424 State Road, West Tisbury MA 02575
CP Coordinator Scott Goldin
DP Coordinator Hillary Smith
Languages English
T: +1 508 693 9900
W: mvpcs.org

Mystic Valley Regional Charter School
770 Salem Street, Malden MA 02148
DP Coordinator Jonathan Keating
Languages English
T: +1 781 388 0222
W: www.mvrcs.org

Nauset Regional High School
100 Cable Road, Eastham MA 02642
DP Coordinator Amy Roberts
Languages English
T: +1 508 255 1505
W: www.nausetschools.org/page/537

Notre Dame Academy, MA
1073 Main Street, Hingham MA 02043-3996
DP Coordinator Meaghan Roach
Languages English, French
T: +1 781 749 5930
W: www.ndahingham.com

Pioneer Valley Chinese Immersion Charter School
317 Russell Street, Hadley MA 01035
DP Coordinator Mary MacPherson
Languages English
T: +1 413 582 7040
W: www.pvcics.org

Provincetown Schools
12 Winslow Street, Provincetown MA 2657
MYP Coordinator Richard Gifford
PYP Coordinator Elizabeth Francis
Languages English
T: +1 508 487 5000
W: www.provincetownschools.com

Quabbin Regional High School
800 South Street, Barre MA 01005
DP Coordinator Janet Hicks
Languages English
T: +1 978 355 4651

Snowden International School
150 Newbury Street, Boston MA 02116
DP Coordinator Denise Bylaska
Languages English
T: +1 617 635 9989
W: www.snowdeninternational.net

Stoneleigh-Burnham School
574 Bernardston Road, Greenfield MA 01301
DP Coordinator Miriam Przybyla-Baum
Languages English
T: +1 413 774 2711
W: www.sbschool.org

Sturgis Charter School
Administration, 427 Main Street, Hyannis MA 02601
DP Coordinator Cynthia Gallo
Languages English
T: +1 508 778 1782
W: www.sturgischarterschool.com

THE NEWMAN SCHOOL
247 Marlborough Street, Boston MA 02116
DP Coordinator Andrew Nagy
MYP Coordinator Elizabeth Esposito
Languages English
T: +1 617 267 4530
E: admissions@newmanboston.org
W: www.newmanboston.org

See full details on page 550

Wareham High School
7 Viking Drive, Wareham MA 02571
DP Coordinator Ashlie Yates-Paquin
Languages English
T: +1 508 291 3510
W: www.warehamps.org/domain/34

Woodrow Wilson Elementary School
169 Leland St, Framingham MA 01702
PYP Coordinator Heather Flugrad
Languages English, Portuguese
T: +1 508 626 9164
W: www.framingham.k12.ma.us/wilson

Michigan

Adams Elementary School
1005 Adams Drive, Midland MI 48642
PYP Coordinator Melissa Ahearn
Languages English
T: +1 989 923 6037
W: ade.midlandps.org

Adrian High School
785 Riverside Avenue, Adrian MI 49221
DP Coordinator Marie Lucius
Languages English
T: +1 517 263 2115
W: www.adrianmaples.org/schools/adrian-high-school.php

Algonac High School
5200 Taft Road, Clay Township MI 48001
DP Coordinator Miechelle Landrum
Languages English
T: +1 810 794 4911 Ext:1202
W: www.acsk12.us/schools/algonac_jr_sr_high/index.php

Bloomfield Hills High School
3456 Lahser Road, Bloomfield Hills MI 48302
DP Coordinator Amy Merchant
MYP Coordinator Cathy McDonald
Languages English
T: +1 248 341 5700
W: www.bloomfield.org/schools/bloomfield-hills-high-school

Bloomfield Hills Middle School
4200 W Quarton Road, Bloomfield Hills MI 48304
MYP Coordinator Kathy Janelle
Languages English
T: +1 248 341 6000
W: www.bloomfield.org/schools/bloomfield-hills-middle-school

Cass Technical High School
2501 Second Ave., Detroit MI 48201
DP Coordinator Sherise Hedgespeth
Languages English
T: +1 313 263 2079
W: www.detroitk12.org/casstech

Central Academy
2459 South Industrial Hwy, Ann Arbor MI 48104
PYP Coordinator Mandy Kaufman
Languages English
T: +1 734 822 1100
W: centralacademy.net

Central Park Elementary School
1400 Rodd Street, Midland MI 48640
PYP Coordinator Whitney Jacobs
Languages English, Spanish
T: +1 989 923 6836
W: www.cpe.midlandps.org

Charyl Stockwell Preparatory Academy
1032 Karl Greimel Drive, Brighton MI 48116
DP Coordinator Elizabeth Holland
T: +1 810 225 9940
W: www.csaschool.org/schools/csa-elementary

Chestnut Hill Elementary School

3900 Chestnut Hill Drive, Midland MI 48642
PYP Coordinator Sarah Westervelt
Languages English
T: +1 989 923 6634
W: che.midlandps.org

City High Middle School

1400 Fuller Avenue NE, Grand Rapids MI 49505
DP Coordinator Jesse Antuma
MYP Coordinator Jesse Antuma
Languages English
T: +1 616 819 2380
W: www.grpublicschools.org/city/

Clarkston High School

6093 Flemings Lake Road, Clarkston MI 48346
DP Coordinator Rebecca Kroll
Languages English
T: +1 248 623 3600
W: chs.clarkston.k12.mi.us

Clear Lake Elementary School

2085 W Drahner Rd, Oxford MI 48371
PYP Coordinator Stephanie Niemi
Languages English
T: +1 248 969 5200

Coit Creative Arts Academy

617 Coit Ave NE, Grand Rapids MI 49503
PYP Coordinator Anne E. Crylen
Languages English
T: +1 616 819 2390
W: www.grps.org/coit

Conant Elementary School

4100 West Quarton Road, Bloomfield Hills MI 48302
PYP Coordinator Stephanie Olson
Languages English
T: +1 248 341 7000
W: www.bloomfield.org/schools/conant-elementary-school

Daniel Axford Elementary School

74 Mechanic Street, Oxford MI 48371
PYP Coordinator Courtney Morin
Languages English
T: +1 248 969 5050

Detroit Country Day School

22305 West 13 Mile Road, Beverly Hills MI 48025
DP Coordinator Ryan Parrish
Languages English
T: +1 248 646 7717
W: www.dcds.edu

Detroit Edison Public School Academy

1903 Wilkins Street, Detroit MI 48207
DP Coordinator Kimberly Bland
MYP Coordinator Kimberly Bland
Languages English
T: +1 313 833 1100

Dexter High School

2200 North Parker Road, Dexter MI 48130
DP Coordinator Debora Marsh
Languages English
T: +1 734 424 4240
W: dexterschools.org

East Grand Rapids High School

2211 Lake Drive SE, Grand Rapids MI 49506
DP Coordinator Jeff Webb
Languages English
T: +1 616 235 7555
W: egrhs.egrps.org

East Hills Middle School

2800 Kensington Road, Bloomfield Hills MI 48304
MYP Coordinator Julia Beattie
Languages English
T: +1 248 341 6200
W: www.bloomfield.org/schools/east-hills-middle-school

Farmington High School

32000 Shiawassee St., Farmington MI 48336
CP Coordinator Janet Cadeau
DP Coordinator Kevin Miesner
Languages English
T: +1 248 489 3455
W: www.farmington.k12.mi.us/fhs

Fenton High School

3200 W Shiawassee Avenue, Fenton MI 48430
DP Coordinator Mark Suchowski
Languages English
T: +1 810 591 2600
W: www.fentonschools.org

Franklin High School

31000 Joy Road, Livonia MI 48150
DP Coordinator Sunshine Weber
Languages English
T: +1 734 744 2655
W: franklin.livoniapublicschools.org

Genesee Academy

9447 Corunna Road, Swartz Creek MI 48473
MYP Coordinator Hana Sankari
Languages English
T: +1 810 250 7557
W: www.gaflint.org

Handley Elementary School

224 N Elm Street, Saginaw MI 48602
PYP Coordinator Shannon Main-Petelka
Languages English
T: +1 989 399 4250
W: www.spsd.net/handley

Helen Keller Elementary School

1505 N Campbell Road, Royal Oak MI 48067
PYP Coordinator Kara Daunt
Languages English
T: +1 248 542 6500
W: www.royaloakschools.org/elementary/keller

Herbert Henry Dow High School

3901 North Saginaw Road, Midland MI 48640
DP Coordinator Sarah Pancost
Languages English
T: +1 989 923 5382
W: www.dhs.midlandps.org

Heritage High School

3465 N Center Road, Saginaw MI 48603
DP Coordinator Brian Blaine
Languages English
T: +1 989 799 5790
W: www.stcs.org/HHS

Hillside Middle School

774 N. Center St., Northville MI 48167
MYP Coordinator William Lambdin
Languages English
T: +1 248 344 8493
W: hillside.northvilleschools.org

Huda School and Montessori

32220 Franklin Road, Franklin MI 48025
MYP Coordinator Aamna Saleem
Languages English
T: +1 248 626 0900
W: www.hudaschool.org

Huron High School

2727 Fuller Road, Ann Arbor MI 48105
CP Coordinator Carrie James
DP Coordinator Carrie James
MYP Coordinator Todd Newell
Languages English
T: +1 734 994 2040
W: www.a2schools.org/huron

International Academy

1020 East Square Lake Road, Bloomfield Hills MI 48304
DP Coordinator Joanne Juco
MYP Coordinator Joanne Juco
Languages English
T: +1 248 341 5900
W: www.iatoday.org

International Academy of Macomb

42755 Romeo Plank Road, Clinton Township MI 48038
DP Coordinator Joyce Arbaugh
MYP Coordinator Rene Ribant-Amthor
Languages English
T: +1 586 723 7200
W: www.iamacomb.org

Lakeville Elementary School

1400 E Lakeville Rd, Oxford MI 48371
PYP Coordinator Rita Flynn
Languages English
T: +1 248 969 1850

Lansing Eastern High School

220 North Pennsylvania Ave, Lansing MI 48912
DP Coordinator Symantha Outwater
Languages English
T: +1 517 325 6500

Leland Public School

200 N. Grand Ave, Leland MI 49654
MYP Coordinator Jeanne Gross
PYP Coordinator Ellen Keen
Languages English
T: +1 231 256 9857

Leonard Elementary School

335 East Elmwood, Leonard MI 48367
PYP Coordinator Rita Flynn
Languages English
T: +1 248 969 5300

Lone Pine Elementary

3100 Lone Pine Road, Orchard Lake MI 48323
PYP Coordinator Stephanie Olson
Languages English
T: +1 248 341 7300
W: www.bloomfield.org/schools/lone-pine-elementary-school

Meads Mill Middle School

16700 Franklin Rd., Northville MI 48168
MYP Coordinator Sandra Brock
Languages English
T: +1 248 344 8435
W: meadsmill.northvilleschools.org

Midland High School

1301 Eastlawn Drive, Midland MI 48642
DP Coordinator Amy Rankin
Languages English
T: +1 989 923 5181
W: mhs.midlandps.org

USA: MICHIGAN

Mitchell Elementary School

3550 Pittsview Dr., Ann Arbor MI 48108
PYP Coordinator Wendy Rothman
Languages English
T: +1 734 997 1216
W: www.a2schools.org/mitchell

Northville High School

45700 Six Mile Road, Northville MI 48168
DP Coordinator James Davis
MYP Coordinator Sandra Brock
Languages English
T: +1 248 344 3800
W: nhs.northvilleschools.org

Norup International School

14450 Manhattan, Oak Park MI 48237
MYP Coordinator Jennifer Wilcox
PYP Coordinator Jennifer Wilcox
Languages English
T: +1 248 837 8300
W: www.berkleyschools.org/schools/norup-international

Notre Dame Preparatory School & Marist Academy

1300 Giddings Road, Pontiac MI 48340
DP Coordinator Katrina Sagert
MYP Coordinator Katherine Thomas
PYP Coordinator Paul Frank
Languages English
T: +1 248 373 5300
W: www.ndpma.org

Novi High School

24062 Taft Road, Novi MI 48375
DP Coordinator Alaina Brown
Languages English
T: +1 248 449 1500
W: hs.novi.k12.mi.us

Owosso High School

765 East North Street, Owosso MI 48867
MYP Coordinator Lance Little
Languages English
T: +1 989 723 8231
W: www.owosso.k12.mi.us

Owosso Middle School

219 North Water Street, Owosso MI 48867
MYP Coordinator Lance Little
Languages English
T: +1 989 723 3460
W: owossomiddle.mi.opm.schoolsites.com

Oxford Elementary School

109 Pontiac Street, Oxford MI 48371
PYP Coordinator Courtney Morin
Languages English
T: +1 248 969 1850

Oxford High School

745 North Oxford Road, Oxford MI 48371
DP Coordinator Nicole Barnett
MYP Coordinator Molly Darnell
Languages English
T: +1 248 969 5101

Oxford Middle School

1420 Lakeville Road, Oxford MI 48371
MYP Coordinator Molly Darnell
Languages English
T: +1 248 969 1800

Plymouth Elementary School

1105 East Sugnet Rd, Midland MI 48642
PYP Coordinator Whitney Jacobs
Languages English
T: +1 989 923 7616
W: pme.midlandps.org

Plymouth High School

8400 Beck Road, Canton MI 48187
DP Coordinator Casey Swanson
Languages English
T: +1 734 582 6936
W: www.pccsk12.com/our-schools/plymouth-canton-educational-park

Portage Central High School

8135 South Westnedge Avenue, Portage MI 49002
DP Coordinator Eric Lancaster
Languages English
T: +1 269 323 5255
W: portageps.org/chs

Portage Northern High School

1000 Idaho Avenue, Portage MI 49024-1233
DP Coordinator Rick Searing
Languages English
T: +1 269 323 5455
W: portageps.org/nhs

Post Oak Magnet School

2320 Post Oak Lane, Lansing MI 48912
PYP Coordinator Ann Jones
Languages English
T: +1 517 755 1610

Raisinville Elementary School

2300 North Raisinville Road, Monroe MI 48162
PYP Coordinator Kelly Davis
Languages English
T: +1 734 265 4800
W: www.monroe.k12.mi.us/res

Renaissance High School

6565 W. Outer Drive, Detroit MI 48235
DP Coordinator Melissa Jones
Languages English
T: +1 313 416 4600
W: www.detroitk12.org/renaissance

Royal Oak High School

1500 Lexington Blvd., Royal Oak MI 48073
DP Coordinator Leah Barnett
MYP Coordinator Deniescha Malone
Languages English
T: +1 248 435 8500
W: www.royaloakschools.org/high-school

Royal Oak Middle School

709 N. Washington Ave, Royal Oak MI 48067
MYP Coordinator Lindsey Belzyt
Languages English
T: +1 248 541 7100
W: www.royaloakschools.org/middle-school

Scarlett Middle School

3300 Lorraine St, Ann Arbor MI 48108
MYP Coordinator Ryan Soupal
Languages English
T: +1 734 997 1220
W: www.a2schools.org/scarlett

Sherwood Park Global Studies Academy

3859 Chamberlain Ave. SE, Grand Rapids MI 49508
PYP Coordinator Susan Lee
Languages English, Spanish
T: +1 616 819 3095
W: www.grps.org/sherwood

Siebert Elementary School

5700 Siebert Street, Midland MI 48640
PYP Coordinator Melissa Ahearn
Languages English
T: +1 989 923 7835
W: sbe.midlandps.org

Southfield High School for the Arts and Technology

24675 Lahser Road, Southfield MI 48033
DP Coordinator Angela Mallory
Languages English
T: +1 248 746 8600
W: www.southfieldk12.org/schools/hs/southfield-high-school

Spring Lake High School

16140 148th Avenue, Spring Lake MI 49456
DP Coordinator Ann Henke
Languages English
T: +1 616 846 5500
W: springlakeschools.org/high

Thompson K-8 International Academy

16300 Lincoln Drive, Southfield MI 48076
MYP Coordinator Angela Mallory
PYP Coordinator Angela Mallory
Languages English
T: +1 248 746 7400
W: www.southfieldk12.org/schools/elem/thompson-k-8-international-academy

Utica Academy for International Studies

37400 Dodge Park Road, Sterling Heights MI 48312
DP Coordinator Christopher Layson
Languages English
T: +1 586 797 3100
W: uais.uticak12.org

Walled Lake Western High School

600 Beck Road, Walled Lake MI 48390
DP Coordinator Ami Friedman
Languages English
T: +1 248 956 4400
W: www.wlcsd.org/Western.cfm

Washtenaw International High School

510 Emerick, Ypsilanti MI 48198
DP Coordinator Daniel Giddings
MYP Coordinator Jessica Garcia
Languages English
T: +1 734 994 8100 EXT:1263
W: www.wihi.org

West Hills Middle School

2601 Lone Pine Road, West Bloomfield MI 28323
MYP Coordinator Jennifer Teal
PYP Coordinator Kristen Vigier
Languages English
T: +1 248 341 6100
W: www.bloomfield.org/schools/west-hills-middle-school

West Ottawa High School

3685 Butternut Drive, Holland MI 49424
DP Coordinator Corban Van Dam
Languages English
T: +1 616 994 5001
W: www.westottawa.net

Wood Creek Elementary

28400 Harwich Drive, Farmington Hills MI 48334
PYP Coordinator Melissa Wiercinski
Languages English, Spanish
T: +1 248 785 2077
W: www.farmington.k12.mi.us/wck

Woodcrest Elementary School

5500 Drake Street, Midland MI 48640
PYP Coordinator Robin Harshman-Rogers
Languages English
T: +1 989 923 7940
W: wce.midlandps.org

Ypsilanti International Elementary School

503 Oak Street, Ypsilanti MI 48198
PYP Coordinator Chelsea Chambers
Languages English, Spanish
T: +1 734 221 2400
W: www.ycschools.us

Minnesota

Annunciation Catholic School

525 W 54th St, Minneapolis MN 55419
PYP Coordinator Sheila Loschy
Languages English
T: +1 612 823 4394
W: annunciationmsp.org/school

Anwatin Middle School

256 Upton Ave. S., Minneapolis MN 55405-1997
MYP Coordinator Sarah Wernimont
Languages English, Spanish
T: +1 612 668 2450
W: anwatin.mpls.k12.mn.us

Aquila Elementary School

8500 W 31st Street, St Louis Park MN 55426
PYP Coordinator Olivia Tolzin
Languages English
T: +1 952 928 6500
W: www.slpschools.org/aq

Bancroft Elementary School

3829 13th Ave So, Minneapolis MN 55407
PYP Coordinator Susan Francis
Languages English
T: +1 612 668 3550
W: bancroft.mpls.k12.mn.us

Benjamin E. Mays Magnet School

560 Concordia Ave., St Paul MN 55103
PYP Coordinator Andrea George
Languages English
T: +1 651 325 2400
W: benmays.spps.org

Central High School, St Paul

275 Lexington Pkwy N, St Paul MN 55105
DP Coordinator Ethan Cherin
MYP Coordinator Sarah Arneson
Languages English
T: +1 651 744 4900
W: central.spps.org

Champlin Park High School

6025 109th Avenue North, Champlin MN 55316
CP Coordinator Chris Baker-Raivo
DP Coordinator Ashley Brown
Languages English
T: +1 763 506 6800
W: www.anoka.k12.mn.us/cphs

Fridley High School

6000 West Moore Lake Drive, Fridley MN 55432
CP Coordinator Jessica Baker
DP Coordinator Jessica Baker
MYP Coordinator Kari Reiter
Languages English
T: +1 763 502 5600
W: fhs.fridleyschools.org

Fridley Middle School

6100 West Moore Lake Drive, Fridley MN 55432
MYP Coordinator Kari Reiter
Languages English
T: +1 763 502 5400
W: fms.fridleyschools.org

Fridley Preschool

6085 7th St NE, Fridley MN 55432
PYP Coordinator Karin Beckstrand
Languages English
T: +1 763 502 5117
W: www.fridleyschools.org/our-schools/fridley-preschool

Global Academy

4065 Central Ave NE, Columbia Heights MN 55421
PYP Coordinator Melissa Storbakken
Languages English
T: +1 763 404 8200
W: www.globalacademy.us

Grand Rapids Senior High School

800 Conifer Drive, Grand Rapids MN 55744
DP Coordinator Dale Christy
Languages English
T: +1 218 327 5760
W: www.isd318.org

Great River School

1326 Energy Park Drive, St Paul MN 55108
DP Coordinator Lindsey Weaver
Languages English
T: +1 651 305 2780
W: www.greatriverschool.org

Harding High School

1540 E. Sixth Street, St Paul MN 55106
CP Coordinator Daniel Weyandt
DP Coordinator Daniel Weyandt
MYP Coordinator Jake Lindeman
Languages English
T: +1 651 793 4700
W: harding.spps.org

Hayes Elementary School

615 Mississippi Street NE, Fridley MN 55432
PYP Coordinator Cara Claggett
Languages English
T: +1 763 502 5200
W: www.fridley.k12.mn.us

Hazel Park Preparatory Academy

1140 White Bear Avenue, St. Paul MN 55106
MYP Coordinator April Hayes
PYP Coordinator Lynette Scott
Languages English
T: +1 651 293 8970
W: hppa.spps.org

Highland Park Elementary School

1700 Saunders Ave., St Paul MN 55116
PYP Coordinator Michelle Strecker
Languages English
T: +1 651 293 8770
W: highlandel.spps.org

Highland Park Middle School

975 S Snelling Ave., St Paul MN 55116
MYP Coordinator Linda Jones
Languages English
T: +1 651 293 8950
W: highlandms.spps.org

Highland Park Senior High School

1015 Snelling Ave S, Saint Paul MN 55116
DP Coordinator Randolph Stagg
MYP Coordinator Marissa Bonk
Languages English
T: +1 651 293 8940
W: highlandsr.spps.org

Hopkins North Junior High School

10700 Cedar Lake Rd., Minnetonka MN 55305
MYP Coordinator Angela Wilcox
Languages English, French, German, Spanish
T: +1 952 988 4800
W: www.hopkinsschools.org/schools/hopkins-north-junior-high

Hopkins West Junior High School

3830 Baker Road, Hopkins MN 55305
MYP Coordinator Jennifer Poncelet
Languages English
T: +1 952 988 4401
W: www.hopkinsschools.org/schools/hopkins-west-junior-high

International Spanish Language Academy

5959 Shady Oak Road, Minnetonka MN 55343
PYP Coordinator Karen Speich
Languages English, Spanish
T: +1 952 746 6020
W: isla-academy.org

Kaposia Education Center

1225 First Avenue South, South St Paul MN 55075
PYP Coordinator Chris Bretz
Languages English
T: +1 651 451 9260
W: kaposia.sspps.schoolfusion.us

Lakes International Language Academy

246 11th Avenue SE, Forest Lake MN 55025
DP Coordinator Gina Graham
MYP Coordinator Natalie Kainz
PYP Coordinator Amy Mueller
Languages Spanish, Mandarin
T: +1 651 464 0771
W: www.mylila.org

Lakeview Elementary School

4110 Lake Drive North, Robbinsdale MN 55422
PYP Coordinator Molly James
Languages English
T: +1 763 504 4100
W: lve.rdale.org

Lincoln Center Elementary School

357 9th Avenue North, South St Paul MN 55075
PYP Coordinator Diane Tiffany
Languages English
T: +1 651 457 9426
W: lincoln.sspps.schoolfusion.us

Matoska International

2530 Spruce Place, White Bear Lake MN 55110
PYP Coordinator Julie Stonehouse
Languages English
T: +1 651 653 2847
W: www.whitebear.k12.mn.us/mis/index.html

Minnetonka High School

18301 Highway 7, Minnetonka MN 55345

DP Coordinator Laura Herbst
Languages English
T: +1 952 401 5703
W: www.minnetonka.k12.mn.us/mhs

Northeast College Prep

300 Industrial Blvd. NE, Minneapolis MN 55413

PYP Coordinator Joanna Waggoner-Norquest
Languages English
T: +1 612 248 8240
W: www.northeastcollegeprep.org

Northeast Middle School

2955 Hayes Street North East, Minneapolis MN 55418

MYP Coordinator Angela Evenson
Languages English
T: +1 612 668 1500
W: northeast.mpls.k12.mn.us

Olson Middle School

1607 51st Ave. N., Minneapolis MN 55430

MYP Coordinator Kate Andrews Van-Horne
Languages English
T: +1 612 668 1640
W: olson.mpls.k12.mn.us

Park Center Senior High School

7300 Brooklyn Boulevard, Brooklyn Park MN 55443

DP Coordinator Michael Cassidy
MYP Coordinator Jon Eversoll
Languages English
T: +1 763 569 7600
W: schools.district279.org/pcsh

Park High School

8040 80th Street South, Cottage Grove MN 55016

DP Coordinator Lisa Martineau
Languages English
T: +1 651 768 3701
W: phs.sowashco.org

Patrick Henry Senior High School

4320 Newton Ave N, Minneapolis MN 55412

CP Coordinator Kazuko Shiba
DP Coordinator Chad Owen
MYP Coordinator Natalie Tourtelotte
Languages English
T: +1 612 668 2000
W: henry.mpls.k12.mn.us

Peter Hobart Elementary School

6500 West 26th Street, St Louis Park MN 55416

PYP Coordinator Anne LaLonde-Laux
Languages English
T: +1 952 928 6600
W: www.slpschools.org

Ramsey Middle School

1700 Summit Ave., St Paul MN 55105

MYP Coordinator Elisabeth Fontana
Languages English
T: +1 651 293 8860
W: ramsey.spps.org

Rice Elementary

200 NE Third Avenue, Rice MN 56367

PYP Coordinator Nancy Davis
Languages English
T: +1 320 393 2177
W: www.isd47.org/rice

Robbinsdale Cooper High School

8230-47th Avenue North, New Hope MN 55428

DP Coordinator Kari Christensen
MYP Coordinator Kari Christensen
Languages English
T: +1 763 504 8501
W: chs.rdale.org

Robbinsdale Middle School

3730 Toledo Ave. N., Robbinsdale MN 55422

MYP Coordinator Jennifer Holtgrewe
Languages English
T: +1 763 504 4801
W: rms.rdale.org

Robert Louis Stevenson Elementary School

6080 East River Road, Fridley MN 55432

PYP Coordinator Katherine Talafous
Languages English
T: +1 763 502 5300
W: www.fridley.k12.mn.us/page.cfm?p=2558

Rochester Arts and Sciences Academy

400 5th Avenue SW, Rochester MN 55902

PYP Coordinator Brianna Zabel
Languages English
T: +1 507 206 4646
W: www.rasamn.org

Rochester Montessori School

5099 7th Street NW, Rochester MN 55901

MYP Coordinator Bre Scheer
Languages English
T: +1 507 288 8725
W: www.rmschool.org

Rockford High School

7600 County Road 50, Rockford MN 55373

CP Coordinator Jill Gordee
DP Coordinator Jill Gordee
Languages English
T: +1 763 477 5846
W: www.rockford.k12.mn.us/Domain/158

Roosevelt High School

4029 28th Avenue South, Minneapolis MN 55406

CP Coordinator Nicole Lamb
DP Coordinator Lisa Purcell
MYP Coordinator Nicole Lamb
Languages English
T: +1 612 668 4800
W: roosevelt.mpls.k12.mn.us

Saint John's Preparatory School

1857 Watertower Road, Collegeville MN 56321

DP Coordinator Martina Talic
Languages English
T: +1 320 363 3315
W: www.sjprep.net

Sanford Middle School

3524 42nd Avenue S., Minneapolis MN 55406

MYP Coordinator Elizabeth O'Connell
Languages English
T: +1 612 668 4900
W: sanford.mpls.k12.mn.us

Scandia Elementary School

14351 Scandia Trail North, Scandia MN 55073

PYP Coordinator Anthony Hansen
Languages English
T: +1 651 982 3301
W: sc.forestlake.k12.mn.us

South St. Paul Secondary

700 North Second Street, South St Paul MN 55075

DP Coordinator Conrad Anderson
MYP Coordinator Melissa Miller
Languages English
T: +1 651 457 9408
W: southp.schoolwires.net/domain/8

Southwest High School

3414 West 47th Street, Minneapolis MN 55410

CP Coordinator Maria Kimmes
DP Coordinator James Lipps
MYP Coordinator Margaret Berg
Languages English
T: +1 612 668 3036
W: southwest.mpls.k12.mn.us

St Louis Park Middle School

2025 Texas Avenue North, St. Louis Park MN 55426

MYP Coordinator Mia Waldera
Languages English
T: +1 952 928 6300
W: www.slpschools.org/domain/12

St Louis Park Senior High School

6425 W 33rd Street, St Louis Park MN 55426

DP Coordinator Alissa Case
Languages English
T: +1 952 928 6107
W: www.slpschools.org

Susan B Anthony Middle School

5757 Irving Avenue South, Minneapolis MN 55419

MYP Coordinator Joy Misselt
Languages English
T: +1 612 668 3240
W: anthony.mpls.k12.mn.us

Susan Lindgren Elementary School

4801 West 41st Street, St Louis Park MN 55416

PYP Coordinator Maurna Rome
Languages English
T: +1 952 928 6700
W: www.slpschools.org/sl

Thomas Edison High School

700 22nd Ave. NE, Minneapolis MN 55418

DP Coordinator Sarah Gregg
MYP Coordinator Sharon Cormany
Languages English
T: +1 612 668 1300
W: edison.mpls.k12.mn.us

Washburn High School

201 West 49th St., Minneapolis MN 55419

DP Coordinator Aaron Percy
Languages English
T: +1 612 668 3400
W: washburn.mpls.k12.mn.us

Whittier International Elementary School

315 West 26th Street, Minneapolis MN 55404
PYP Coordinator Libby Dominguez
Languages English
T: +1 612 668 4170
W: whittier.mpls.k12.mn.us

Mississippi

Barack H. Obama Magnet

750 N. Congress Street, Jackson MS 39202
PYP Coordinator Beth West Roach
Languages English
T: +1 601 960 5333
W: www.jackson.k12.ms.us/obama

Jim Hill High School

2185 Coach Fred Harris Drive, Jackson MS 39204
DP Coordinator Felicia Jennings-Wolfe
MYP Coordinator Tracee Thompson
Languages English
T: +1 601 960 5354
W: jimhill.jpsms.org

Northwest Magnet Middle School

7020 Highway 49N, Jackson MS 39213
MYP Coordinator Lakeisha Holmes
Languages English
T: +1 601 960 8700

Ocean Springs High School

PO Box 7002, Ocean Springs MS 39566
DP Coordinator Nell Driggers
Languages English
T: +1 228 875 0333
W: oshs.ossdms.org

Missouri

Academie Lafayette

6903 Oak Street, Kansas City MO 64113
MYP Coordinator Katy Wilson
Languages French
T: +1 816 361 7735
W: www.academielafayette.org

ATI St. Louis

3840 Washington Blvd., St. Louis MO 63108
DP Coordinator Jennifer Fu
Languages English
T: +1 314 884 1637
W: thoughtandindustry.com/st-louis

Boyd Elementary School

1409 N. Washington Ave., Springfield MO 65802
PYP Coordinator Jamie Quirk
Languages English
T: +1 417 523 1500
W: boyd.spsk12.org

Camdenton High School

662 Laker Pride Road, Camdenton MO 65020
DP Coordinator Jody Welsh
Languages English
T: +1 573 346 9232
W: camdentonschools.schoolwires.net/chs

Central High School, Springfield

423 E. Central St., Springfield MO 65802
CP Coordinator Donita Cox
DP Coordinator Molly Gray
MYP Coordinator Gretchen Teague
Languages English
T: +1 417 523 9600
W: central.spsk12.org

Eugene Field Elementary School

2120 E. Barataria, Springfield MO 65804
PYP Coordinator Jamie Quirk
Languages English
T: +1 417 523 4800
W: field.spsk12.org

Foreign Language Academy

3450 Warwick Blvd., Kansas City MO 64111
PYP Coordinator Debra Lainez
Languages English, Spanish
T: +1 816 418 6000
W: www.kcpublicschools.org/foreignlanguage

Lee's Summit High School

400 Blue Parkway, Lee's Summit MO 64063
CP Coordinator Michelle Edwards
DP Coordinator Michelle Edwards
Languages English
T: +1 816 986 2000
W: lshs.lsr7.org

Lee's Summit North High School

901 NE Douglas, Lee's Summit MO 64086
CP Coordinator Robert Rossiter
DP Coordinator Robert Rossiter
Languages English
T: +1 816 986 3005
W: lsnhs.lsr7.org

Lee's Summit West High School

2600 SW Ward Road, Lee's Summit MO 64082
CP Coordinator Christy Dabalos
DP Coordinator Christy Dabalos
Languages English
T: +1 816 986 4000

Lincoln College Preparatory Academy

2111 Woodland Ave., Kansas City MO 64108
DP Coordinator Christopher Jennens
Languages English
T: +1 816 418 3000
W: www.kcpublicschools.org/domain/10

Lindbergh High School

5000 S. Lindbergh Blvd., St Louis MO 63126
DP Coordinator Miranda Gelven
Languages English
T: +1 314 729 2410
W: go.lindberghschools.ws/domain/8

Metro Academic & Classical High School

4015 McPherson Avenue, St Louis MO 63108
DP Coordinator Zachary Oreto
Languages English
T: +1 314 534 3894

North Kansas City High School

620 East 23rd Avenue, North Kansas City School Distr, North Kansas City MO 64116
CP Coordinator Chad Lower
DP Coordinator Mitsi Nessa
Languages English
T: +1 816 413 5900
W: www.nkcschools.org/Domain/35

Ozark High School

1350 West Bluff Drive, Ozark MO 65721
DP Coordinator Stacie Wood
Languages English
T: +1 417 582 5701
W: www.ozarktigers.org/Domain/14

Pipkin Middle School

1215 N. Boonville, Springfield MO 65802
MYP Coordinator Elizabeth Troutman
Languages English
T: +1 417 523 6000
W: www.sps.org/pipkin

Raymore-Peculiar High School

PO Box 789, Peculiar MO 64078
DP Coordinator Steve Meek
Languages English
T: +1 816 892 1400
W: www.raypec.k12.mo.us/102/Raymore-Peculiar-High-School

Rountree Elementary School

333 E. Grand St., Springfield MO 65804
PYP Coordinator Nicki Foltz
Languages English
T: +1 417 523 4900
W: www.sps.org/rountree

Montana

Big Sky High School

3100 South Ave. West, Missoula MT 59804
DP Coordinator Cameron Johnson
Languages English
T: +1 406 728 2401
W: www.mcpsmt.org/bigsky

Flathead High School

644 4th Avenue West, Kalispell Public Schools, Kalispell MT 59901
DP Coordinator Kelli Higgins
Languages English
T: +1 406 751 3462
W: www.sd5.k12.mt.us

Hellgate High School

900 South Higgins Avenue, Missoula MT 59801
DP Coordinator Hallie Koppang
Languages English
T: +1 406 728 2402
W: www.mcpsmt.org/hellgate

Lewis and Clark Elementary School

2901 Park Street, Missoula MT 59801
PYP Coordinator Kari Henderson
Languages English
T: +1 406 542 4035
W: www.mcpsmt.org/lewisclark

Lone Peak High School

45465 Gallatin Road, Gallatin Gateway MT 59730
DP Coordinator Tim Sullivan
Languages English
T: +1 406 995 4281
W: www.bssd72.org/lone-peak-high-school

McCluer North High School

705 Waterford Drive, Florissant MO 63033
DP Coordinator Byron Crawford
Languages English
T: +1 314 506 9200
W: www.fergflor.org/mccluer-north-high

Missoula International School

1100 Harrison Street, Missoula MT 59802
MYP Coordinator Jeffrey Kessler
PYP Coordinator Julie Lennox
Languages Spanish, English
T: +1 406 542 9924
W: www.mismt.org

Ophir Elementary School

45465 Gallatin Road, Gallatin Gateway MT 59730
PYP Coordinator Brittany Shirley
Languages English
T: +1 406 995 4281
W: www.bssd72.org/ophir-elementary

Nebraska

Bess Streeter Aldrich Elementary

506 N 162nd Avenue, Omaha NE 68118
PYP Coordinator Jodi Fidone
Languages English
T: +1 402 715 2020
W: aldrich.mpsomaha.org

Black Elk Elementary

6708 S 161st Ave, Omaha NE 68135
PYP Coordinator Nicole Beins
Languages English, Spanish
T: +1 402 715 6200
W: blackelk.mpsomaha.org

Central High School

124 North 20th Street, Omaha NE 68102
DP Coordinator Cathy Andrus
MYP Coordinator Paul Nielson
Languages English
T: +1 531 299 2660

Lewis and Clark Middle School

6901 Burt Street, Omaha NE 68132
MYP Coordinator Lisa Tingelhoff
Languages English
T: +1 402 557 4300

Lincoln High School

2229 J Street, Lincoln NE 68510
DP Coordinator J.P. Caruso
Languages English
T: +1 402 436 1301
W: lhs.lps.org

Millard North High School

1010 S 144th Street, Millard Public Schools, Omaha NE 68154
DP Coordinator Rhonda Betzold
MYP Coordinator Elizabeth Swedlund
Languages English
T: +1 402 715 1411
W: mnhs.mpsomaha.org

Millard North Middle School

2828 South 139th Plaza, Omaha NE 68144
MYP Coordinator Melissa Betts
Languages English
T: +1 402 715 1280
W: nms.mpsomaha.org

Nevada

Basic Academy of International Studies

400 N. Palo Verde Dr., Henderson NV 89015
CP Coordinator James Mitchell
DP Coordinator Cylia Lagunas
MYP Coordinator James Mitchell
Languages English
T: +1 702 799 8000
W: www.basicacademy.org

Brown Junior High School

307 N. Cannes St, Henderson NV 89015
MYP Coordinator Erika Benedict
Languages English
T: +1 702 799 8900
W: www.brownjhs.org

Clarence A. Piggott Academy of International Studies

9601 Red Hills Drive, Las Vegas NV 89117
PYP Coordinator Tara Albidrez
Languages English
T: +1 702 799 4450
W: www.clarencepiggott.org

Earl Wooster High School

1331 East Plumb Lane, Reno NV 89502
CP Coordinator Dustin Coli
DP Coordinator Jennifer Lienau
MYP Coordinator Zeynep Evenson
Languages English
T: +1 775 333 5100
W: www.woostercolts.com

Green Valley High School

460 Arroyo Grande Blvd., Henderson NV 89014
DP Coordinator Angelique Callicoat
Languages English
T: +1 702 799 0950
W: greenvalleyhs.org

Kit Carson International Academy

1735 North D. Street, Las Vegas NV 89106
PYP Coordinator Robert Mitchell
Languages English
T: +1 702 799 7113
W: www.kitcarsoncougars.org

Palo Verde High School

333 Pavilion Center Drive, Las Vegas NV 89144
DP Coordinator Amy Reed
Languages English
T: +1 702 799 1450
W: www.paloverde.org

Roy W. Martin Middle School

200 N. 28th St., Las Vegas NV 89101
MYP Coordinator Jennifer Cain
Languages English
T: +1 702 799 7922
W: roymartinms.org

Sandy Searles Miller Academy for International Studies

4851 East Lake Mead Blvd, Las Vegas NV 89115
PYP Coordinator Lynn Tyrell
Languages English
T: +1 702 799 8830
W: www.sandymilleracademy.com

Sheila Tarr Academy of International Studies

9400 W. Gilmore Ave., Las Vegas NV 89129
PYP Coordinator Tracy Baldwin
Languages English, Spanish
T: +1 702 799 6710
W: tarracademy.weebly.com

Spring Valley High School

3750 Buffalo Drive, Las Vegas NV 89147
CP Coordinator Anthony Gebbia
DP Coordinator Anthony Gebbia
MYP Coordinator Tiffany Hemberger
Languages English
T: +1 702 799 2580
W: www.springvalleyhs.com

Valley High School

2839 S Burnham Ave., Las Vegas NV 89169
DP Coordinator Andrew Magness
MYP Coordinator Andrew Magness
Languages English
T: +1 702 799 5450
W: www.valleyhs.vegas

Vaughn Middle School

1200 Bresson Avenue, Reno NV 89502
MYP Coordinator Leilani Konyshev
Languages English
T: +1 775 333 5160
W: www.washoeschools.net/vaughn

Walter Johnson Academy of International Studies

7701 Ducharme Ave, Las Vegas NV 89145-4937
MYP Coordinator Kirsten Lewis
Languages English
T: +1 702 799 4480

New Hampshire

Bedford High School

47 Nashua Road, Bedford NH 03110
DP Coordinator Stephanie Nichols
Languages English
T: +1 603 310 9000
W: www.sau25.net/highschool/BHShome.htm

NEW HAMPTON SCHOOL

70 Main Street, New Hampton NH 03256
DP Coordinator Jennifer McMahon
Languages English
T: +1 603 677 3401
E: admission@newhampton.org
W: www.newhampton.org

See full details on page 530

New Jersey

All Saints Episcopal Day School

707 Washington Street, Hoboken NJ 07030
MYP Coordinator Elizabeth Vino
Languages English
T: +1 201 792 0736
W: www.allsaintsdayschool.org

Bergen County Academies

200 Hackensack Avenue, Hackensack NJ 07601
DP Coordinator Michelle Pinke
Languages English
T: +1 201 343 6000 EXT:3385
W: www.bergen.org

Biotechnology High School

5000 Kozloski Road, Freehold NJ 07728
DP Coordinator Linda Rogers
Languages English
T: +1 732 431 7208
W: www.bths.mcvsd.org

Donovan Catholic

711 Hooper Ave, Toms River NJ 08753
DP Coordinator Jillian Kelly
Languages English
T: +1 732 349 8801
W: donovancatholic.org

Dr. Orlando Edreira Academy, School 26

631-657 Westminster Avenue, Elizabeth NJ 07208
MYP Coordinator William Clark
PYP Coordinator Diane Bliss
Languages English
T: +1 908 436 5970
W: edreira.epsnj.org/pages/dr__orlando_edreira_academy_no

East Side High School

238 Van Buren St, Newark NJ 07105
DP Coordinator Matthew Ramsay
Languages English
T: +1 973 465 4900
W: www.nps.k12.nj.us/EAS

Fort Lee High School

3000 Lemoine Ave, Fort Lee NJ 07024
DP Coordinator Brandon Barron
Languages English
T: +1 201 585 4675

Freehold Township High School

281 Elton Adelphia Rd, Freehold NJ 07728
DP Coordinator Michael Dillon
Languages English
T: 732-431-8460
W: www.frhsd.com/freeholdtwp

Hatikvah International Academy Charter School

7 Lexington Avenue, East Brunswick NJ 08816
MYP Coordinator Amanda Rosenberg
Languages English
T: +1 732 254 8300
W: hatikvahcharterschool.com

Howell High School

405 Squankum-Yellowbrook Road, Farmingdale NJ 07727
DP Coordinator Kristine Jenner
Languages English
T: +1 732 919 2131
W: www.frhsd.com/Domain/13

International High School

200 Grand Street, Paterson NJ 07501
DP Coordinator Catherine Forfia-Dion
Languages English
T: +1 973 321 2280
W: ihs-pps-nj.schoolloop.com

Learning Ladders

35 Hudson Street, Jersey City NJ 07302
PYP Coordinator Cherry Estrada
Languages English
T: +1 201 885 2960
W: www.learningladdersnj.com

Linden High School

121 W St Georges Avenue, Georges Avenue, Linden NJ 07036
DP Coordinator Anthony Fischetti
Languages English
T: +1 908 486 5432

Morris Knolls High School

50 Knoll Drive, Rockaway NJ 07866
DP Coordinator Scott Gambale
Languages English
T: +1 973 664 2200
W: www.mhrd.org/mkhs

Newark Academy

91 South Orange Avenue, Livingston NJ 07039
DP Coordinator Neil Stourton
Languages English
T: +1 973 992 7000
W: www.newarka.edu

Princeton Junior School

90 Fackler Road, Princeton NJ 08540
PYP Coordinator Catherine Blas
Languages English
T: +1 609 924 8126
W: www.princetonjuniorschool.org

Princeton Montessori School

487 Cherry Valley Road, Princeton NJ 08540
MYP Coordinator Michelle Morrison
Languages English
T: +1 609 924 4594
W: www.princetonmontessori.org

Red Bank Regional High School

101 Ridge Road, Little Silver NJ 07739
DP Coordinator Lisa Boyle
Languages English
T: +1 732 842 8000
W: www.rbrhs.org

Rosa International Middle School

485 Browning Lane, Cherry Hill NJ 08003
MYP Coordinator Al Morales
Languages English
T: +1 856 616 8787
W: rosa.chclc.org

Salem High School

219 Walnut St, Salem NJ 08079
DP Coordinator Jordan Pla
Languages English
T: +1 856 935 3900

Science Park High School

260 Norfolk Street, Newark NJ 10703
DP Coordinator Thomas Ammazzalorso
Languages English
T: +1 973 733 8787
W: www.nps.k12.nj.us/SCI

Shore Regional High School

132 Monmouth Park Highway, West Long Branch NJ 07764
DP Coordinator Vanessa Miano
Languages English
T: +1 732 222 9300 EXT 210
W: www.shoreregional.org

Solomon Schechter Day School of Bergen County

275 McKinley Ave, New Milford NJ 07646
MYP Coordinator Jennifer Coxe
Languages English
T: +1 201 262 9898
W: www.ssdsbergen.org

The Red Oaks School

340 Speedwell Ave., Morristown NJ 07960
MYP Coordinator Benjamin Wagor
Languages English
T: +1 973 998 9424
W: www.redoaksschool.org

Waterfront Montessori

150 Warren St., Suite 108, Jersey City NJ 7302
MYP Coordinator Sarah Woodruff
Languages English
T: +1 201 333 5600
W: www.waterfrontmontessori.com

West Morris Central High School

259 Bartley Road, Chester NJ 07930
CP Coordinator Erin Feltmann
DP Coordinator Debbie Gonzalez
Languages English
T: +1 908 879 5212

West Morris Mendham High School

65 East Main Street, Mendham NJ 07945
CP Coordinator Lindsay Schartner
DP Coordinator Laura Pereira
Languages English
T: +1 973 543 2501
W: www.wmmhs.org

World of ABC

159 2nd St, Jersey City NJ 07302
PYP Coordinator Courtney Bode
Languages English
T: +1 201 963 5555
W: www.worldofabc.com

YINGHUA INTERNATIONAL SCHOOL

25 Laurel Avenue, Kingston NJ 08528-0088
PYP Coordinator WenLin Su
Languages English, Chinese
T: +1 609 375 8015
E: admissions@yhis.org
W: yhis.org

See full details on page 556

New Mexico

Corrales International School

5500 Wilshire Ave NE, Albuquerque NM 87113
MYP Coordinator Ana Perea
PYP Coordinator Ana Perea
Languages English
T: +1 505 344 9733
W: corralesis.org

Cottonwood Classical Preparatory School

1776 Montano Road NW, Building 3, Los Ranchos de Albuquerque NM 87107
DP Coordinator Meghan Lowe
Languages English
T: +1 505 998 1021
W: www.cottonwoodclassical.org

Mandela International Magnet School

1720 Llano St, Santa Fe NM 87505
DP Coordinator Jessie Gac
MYP Coordinator Holly Call
Languages English
T: +1 505 467 3370

NAVAJO PREPARATORY SCHOOL

1220 West Apache Street, Farmington NM 87401
DP Coordinator Donna Fernandez
Languages English
T: +1 505 326 6571
E: sbecenti@navajoprep.com
W: www.navajoprep.com

See full details on page 529

New Mexico International School

8650 Alameda Blvd NE, Albuquerque NM 87122
PYP Coordinator Cynthia Pedrotty
Languages English
T: +1 505 503 7670
W: nmis.org

Sandia High School

7801 Candelaria NE, Albuquerque NM 87110
DP Coordinator Derek Maestas
Languages English
T: +1 505 294 1511
W: sandia.aps.edu

Taos International School

Diamond Plaza, 118 Este Es Road, Taos NM 87571
MYP Coordinator Nadine Vigil
PYP Coordinator Yvett Driskell
Languages English, Spanish
T: +1 575 751 7115
W: taosinternationalschool.weebly.com

The International School at Mesa del Sol

2660 Eastman Crossing SE, Albuquerque NM 87106
MYP Coordinator Bonnie Jackson
PYP Coordinator Rebecca Mattingly
Languages English
T: +1 505 508 3295
W: www.tisnm.org

IB AMERICAS

UWC-USA

State Rte 65, Montezuma NM 87731
DP Coordinator Alexis Mamaux
Languages English
T: +1 505 454 4252
W: www.uwc-usa.org

New York

Albany High School

700 Washington Avenue, Albany NY 12203
DP Coordinator Leah Evans
Languages English
T: +1 518 475 6200
W: ahs.albany.k12.ny.us

Archbishop Walsh Academy

208 North 24th Street, Olean NY 14760
DP Coordinator Maryanne Cole
Languages English
T: +1 716 372 8122
W: www.stcswalsh.org

Baccalaureate School for Global Education

34-12 36th Avenue, Astoria NY 11106
DP Coordinator Jaime Meisler
Languages English
T: +1 718 361 5275
W: www.bsge.org

Ballston Spa High School

220 Ballston Avenue, Ballston Spa NY 12020
DP Coordinator Nicole Stehle
Languages English
T: +1 518 884 7150
W: www.bscsd.org/domain/87

Barack Obama Elementary School

176 William Street, Hempstead NY 11550
PYP Coordinator Vicki McMillan
Languages English, Spanish
T: +1 516 434 4400
W: www.hempsteadschools.org/domain/12

Bay Shore High School

155 Third Avenue, Bay Shore NY 11706
DP Coordinator Jonathan Nelson
Languages English
T: +1 631 968 1157
W: www.bayshore.k12.ny.us/SeniorHigh.cfm

BELA Charter School

125 Stuyvesant Ave., Brooklyn NY 11221
DP Coordinator Esteban Madrigal
Languages English
T: +1 347 473 8830
W: www.belahs.org

Binghamton High School

31 Main Street, Binghamton NY 13905
CP Coordinator Steve McGovern
DP Coordinator James Gill
MYP Coordinator Mark Ward
Languages English
T: +1 607 762 8200

Bishop Ludden Junior Senior High School

815 Fay Road, Syracuse NY 13219
DP Coordinator Heidi Busa
Languages English
T: +1 315 468 2591
W: www.bishopludden.org

Bloomfield Elementary School

45 Maple Avenue, Suite B, Bloomfield NY 14469
PYP Coordinator Kathryn Taylor
Languages English
T: +1 585 657 6121
W: bloomfieldcsd.org

Bloomfield High School

PO Box 250, Oakmount Avenue, East Bloomfield NY 14469
DP Coordinator Melissa Arber
Languages English
T: +1 585 657 6121
W: www.bloomfieldcsd.org

Boerum Hill School for International Studies

284 Baltic Street, Brooklyn NY 11201
DP Coordinator Lindsay Zackman
MYP Coordinator Emily Brandt
Languages English
T: +1 718 330 9390
W: www.K497.org

Bronx Early College Academy

250 East 164th Street, Bronx NY 10456
CP Coordinator Kathy Briceno-Paul
DP Coordinator Kathy Briceno-Paul
Languages English
T: +1 718 681 8287
W: www.beca324.org

Brooklyn Arts and Science Elementary School

443 St. Marks Ave., Brooklyn NY 11238
PYP Coordinator Christina Soriano
Languages English
T: +1 718 230 0851
W: www.brooklynartselementary.org

Brooklyn Friends School

375 Pearl Street, Brooklyn, New York NY 11201
DP Coordinator Daniel Paccione
Languages English
T: +1 718 852 1029
W: www.brooklynfriends.org

Brooklyn Prospect Charter School

80 Willoughby Street, Brooklyn NY 11201
DP Coordinator Jamie Vaughan
Languages English
T: +1 718 722 7634
W: www.brooklynprospect.org

Buffalo Academy of the Sacred Heart

3860 Main Street, Buffalo NY 14226
DP Coordinator Meghan D'Andrea
Languages English
T: +1 716 834 2101
W: www.sacredheartacademy.org

Canandaigua Academy

1 Academy Circle, Canandaigua NY 14424
DP Coordinator Keith Pedzich
Languages English
T: +1 585 396 3802

Center Moriches High School

311 Frowein Road, Center Moriches NY 11934
DP Coordinator Richard Roberts
Languages English
T: +1 631 878 0540

Center Moriches Middle School

311 Frowein Road, Center Moriches NY 11934
MYP Coordinator Teresa Horoszewski
Languages English, French
T: +1 631 878 2519

Chestnut Ridge Middle School

892 Chestnut Ridge Road, Chestnut Ridge NY 10977
MYP Coordinator Dr. Monifa Tippitt
Languages English
T: +1 845 577 6300
W: www.ercsd.org/chestnutridge

Churchville-Chili Senior High School

5786 Buffalo Road, Churchville NY 14428
DP Coordinator Kelley Fahy
Languages English
T: +1 585 293 4540
W: www.cccsd.org/seniorhighschool_home.aspx

City Honors School

186 E North Street, Buffalo NY 14204
DP Coordinator Elissa Morganti Banas
MYP Coordinator James Moses
Languages English
T: +1 716 816 4230
W: www.cityhonors.org

Clarkstown High School North

151 Congers Road, New City NY 10956-6272
DP Coordinator Andrea Miranda
Languages English
T: +1 845 639 6500
W: www.ccsd.edu/Domain/19

Clarkstown Senior High School South

31 Demarest Mill Road, West Nyack NY 10994
DP Coordinator Melina Balducci-Flugger
Languages English
T: +1 845 624 3400
W: www.ccsd.edu/south

Commack High School

1 Scholar Lane, Commack NY 11725-1297
DP Coordinator Eric Biagi
Languages English
T: +1 631 912 2106
W: www.commack.k12.ny.us/commackhighschool_home.aspx

Commack Middle School

700 Vanderbilt Parkway, Commack NY 11725
MYP Coordinator Kristen Kornweiss
Languages English
T: +1 631 858 3500
W: www.commack.k12.ny.us/commackmiddleschool_home.aspx

Corning-Painted Post High School

201 Cantigney St., Corning NY 14830
DP Coordinator Kristie Radford
MYP Coordinator Tammie Edinger
Languages English
T: +1 607 654 2988
W: www.corningareaschools.com/1/home

Corning-Painted Post Middle School

35 Victory Highway, Painted Post NY 14870
MYP Coordinator Cathy Honness
Languages English
T: +1 607 654 2966
W: www.corningareaschools.com/2/home

CULTURAL ARTS ACADEMY CHARTER SCHOOL AT SPRING CREEK

1400 Linden Blvd, Brooklyn NY 11212
PYP Coordinator Sara Pena
Languages English, Spanish
T: +1 718 683 3300
E: caacs@caa-ny.org
W: www.culturalartsacademy.org

See full details on page 497

Curtis High School

105 Hamilton Avenue, Staten Island NY 10301
CP Coordinator Alicia Isasi-Endress
DP Coordinator Kathleen Francis
Languages English
T: +1 718 390 1800
W: www.curtishs.org

Cypress Hills Collegiate Prep

999 Jamaica Avenue, Brooklyn NY 11208
DP Coordinator Amy Yager
Languages English, Spanish
T: +1 718 647 1672
W: chcpschool.org

David Paterson Elementary School

40 Fulton Street, Hempstead NY 11550
PYP Coordinator Elyse Amos
Languages English, Spanish
T: +1 516 434 4450
W: www.hempsteadschools.org/domain/11

Dobbs Ferry High School

505 Broadway, Dobbs Ferry NY 10522
DP Coordinator Marion Halberg
MYP Coordinator Jennifer Hickey
Languages English
T: +1 914 693 7645
W: www.dfsd.org/hs

Dobbs Ferry Middle School

505 Broadway, Dobbs Ferry NY 10522
MYP Coordinator Jennifer Hickey
Languages English
T: +1 914 693 7640
W: www.dfsd.org/ms

DWIGHT SCHOOL

291 Central Park West, New York NY 10024
DP Coordinator Liz Hutton
MYP Coordinator Beth Billard
PYP Coordinator Brittany Dallal
Languages English
T: +1 212 724 6360
E: admissions@dwight.edu
W: www.dwight.edu

See full details on page 498

East Middle School

167 E Frederick Street, Binghamton NY 13904
MYP Coordinator Mark Ward
Languages English
T: +1 607 762 8300

Eastridge High School

2350 East Ridge Road, Rochester NY 14622
CP Coordinator Andrew Walter
DP Coordinator Terry Reynolds
Languages English
T: +1 585 339 1450
W: www.eastiron.org/Domain/9

EF ACADEMY NEW YORK

582 Columbus Avenue, Thornwood NY 10594
DP Coordinator Amy Park
Languages English
T: +1 914 495 6056
E: academy.admissions@ef.com
W: www.efacademy.org

See full details on page 501

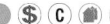

FRENCH-AMERICAN SCHOOL OF NEW YORK

320 East Boston Post Road, Mamaroneck NY 10543
DP Coordinator Jaimeson Lynch
Languages English, French
T: +1 914 250 0000
E: admissions@fasny.org
W: www.fasny.org

See full details on page 504

Global Community Charter School

2350 Fifth Avenue, New York NY 10037
PYP Coordinator Jasmin Candelario
Languages English
T: +1 646 360 2363
W: www.globalcommunitycs.org

Greenville Central School District

Route 81, PO Box 129, Greenville NY 12083
DP Coordinator Kendall Fritze
Languages English
T: +1 518 966 5190
W: www.greenville.k12.ny.us

Harlem Village Academies High

35 West 124th Street, New York NY 10027
DP Coordinator David Quinn
Languages English
T: +1 646 812 9200
W: www.harlemvillageacademies.org/high-school

Harrison High School

255 Union Avenue, Harrison NY 10528
DP Coordinator Christopher Tyler
MYP Coordinator Shari Heyen
Languages English
T: +1 914 630 3095
W: www.harrisoncsd.org

Hauppauge High School

PO Box 6006, Hauppauge NY 11788
DP Coordinator Kelly Barry
Languages English
T: +1 631 761 8302
W: www.hauppauge.k12.ny.us/site/Default.aspx?PageID=9

Highview School

200 North Central Avenue, Hartsdale NY 10530
PYP Coordinator Sharon Harris
Languages English
T: +1 914 946 6946
W: www.greenburghcsd.org/domain/154

Hilton High School

400 East Avenue, Hilton NY 14468
DP Coordinator Tim Ackroyd
MYP Coordinator Steve Cudzilo
Languages English
T: +1 585 392 1000

Horizons-on-the-Hudson Magnet School

137 Montgomery Street, Newburgh NY 12550
PYP Coordinator Robert Glowacki
Languages English
T: +1 845 563 3725
W: www.newburghschools.org/horizons.php

International School of Brooklyn

477 Court Street, Brooklyn, New York NY 11231
MYP Coordinator Katie Rogers
PYP Coordinator Selena Lynn
Languages English, French, Spanish
T: +1 718 369 3023
W: www.isbrooklyn.org

Jackson Main School

451 Jackson Street, Hempstead NY 11550
PYP Coordinator Saritha Perez
Languages English, Spanish
T: +1 516 434 4650
W: www.hempsteadschools.org/site/Default.aspx?PageID=21

James A Beneway High School

6200 Ontario Center Road, Ontario Center NY 14520
DP Coordinator Ryan VanAllen
Languages English
T: +1 315 524 1050
W: wh.waynecsd.org

John Adams High School

101-01 Rockaway Blvd, Ozone Park NY 11417
DP Coordinator Jagroop Singh
Languages English
T: +1 718 322 0500
W: www.johnadamsnyc.org

Jordan-Elbridge Middle School

19 N. Chappell Street, Jordan NY 13080
MYP Coordinator Alexis Farnsworth
Languages English
T: +1 315 689 8520

Joseph A. McNeil Elementary School

335 South Franklin Street, Hempstead NY 11550
PYP Coordinator Juanita Winfield
Languages English, Spanish
T: +1 516 434 4500
W: www.hempsteadschools.org/domain/10

Joseph C Wilson Foundation Academy

200 Genesee Street NY 14611
MYP Coordinator Lori Locker
PYP Coordinator Katherine Chinappi
Languages English
T: +1 585 463 4100
W: www.rcsdk12.org/wilsonfoundation

Joseph C Wilson Magnet High School

501 Genesee Street, Rochester NY 14611
DP Coordinator Amy McLaughlin
MYP Coordinator Nickole Lobdell
Languages English
T: +1 585 328 3440
W: www.rcsdk12.org/wilsoncommencement

Kenmore East High School

350 Fries Road, Tonawanda NY 14150
DP Coordinator Paul Lasch
Languages English
T: +1 716 874 8402
W: www.kenton.k12.ny.us/kentonkehs

Kenmore West High School

33 Highland Parkway, Buffalo NY 14223
DP Coordinator Laura Howse Howse
Languages English
T: +1 716 874 8401
W: www.kenton.k12.ny.us/kentonkwhs

Khalil Gibran International Academy

362 Schermerhorn Street, Brooklyn NY 11217

DP Coordinator Jennifer DeFilippo
Languages English
T: +1 718 237 2502
W: www.khalilgibranhs.org

Knowledge & Power Preparatory Academy (KAPPA) International

500 East Fordham Road, Bronx, New York NY 10458

DP Coordinator Elizabeth Calvert-Kilbane
Languages English
T: +1 718 933 1247

LA SCUOLA D'ITALIA GUGLIELMO MARCONI

12 East 96th Street, New York NY 10128
DP Coordinator Dr. Beatrice Paladini
Languages English, Italian
T: +1 212 369 3290
E: admissions@lascuoladitalia.org
W: www.lascuoladitalia.org
See full details on page 514

Lee F Jackson Elementary School

2 Saratoga Road, White Plains NY 10607

PYP Coordinator Valarie Williams
Languages English
T: +1 914 948 2992
W: www.greenburghcsd.org/domain/153

Léman Manhattan Preparatory School

41 Broad Street, New York NY 10004
DP Coordinator Luz Garcelon
Languages English
T: +1 212 232 0266
W: www.lemanmanhattan.org

Link IB World School

51 Red Hill Road, New City NY 10956
PYP Coordinator Lauren Haugh
Languages English
T: +1 845 6243494
W: www.ccsd.edu/Domain/11

Locust Valley High School

99 Horse Hollow Road, Locust Valley NY 11560

DP Coordinator Angela Manzo
Languages English
T: +1 516 277 5105
W: www.lvcsd.k12.ny.us/our_schools/high_school

Long Beach High School

322 Lagoon Drive West, Lido Beach NY 11561
DP Coordinator Christine Graham
Languages English
T: +1 516 897 2013
W: www.lbeach.org/schools/long_beach_high_school

Long Beach Middle School

239 Lido Boulevard, Lido Beach NY 11561
MYP Coordinator Eliot Lewin
Languages English
T: +1 516 897 2162
W: www.lbeach.org/schools/long_beach_middle_school

Louis M. Klein Middle School

50 Union Ave., Harrison NY 10528
MYP Coordinator Michael Greenfield
Languages English
T: +1 914 630 3033
W: lmk.harrisoncsd.org

LYCEUM KENNEDY FRENCH AMERICAN SCHOOL

225 East 43rd Street, New York NY 10017
DP Coordinator Dr. Vera Pohland
Languages French, English
T: +1 212 681 1877
E: lkadmissions@LyceumKennedy.org
W: www.LyceumKennedy.org
See full details on page 518

Massena Central High School

84 Nightengale Avenue, Massena NY 13662
DP Coordinator Jan Normile
Languages English
T: +1 315 764 3710
W: mhs.mcs.k12.ny.us

Merton Williams Middle School

200 School Lane, Hilton NY 14468
MYP Coordinator Steve Cudzilo
Languages English
T: +1 585 392 1000 (EXT: 30)
W: www.hilton.k12.ny.us/MertonMiddle.cfm

Millbrook High School

70 Church Street, Millbrook NY 12545
DP Coordinator Georgia Herring
Languages English
T: +1 845 677 2510
W: www.millbrookcsd.org/domain/91

Mott Hall Bronx High School

1595 Bathgate Avenue, Bronx, New York NY 10457
DP Coordinator Catherine Friesen
Languages English
T: +1 718 466 6800

MOTT HALL SCIENCE AND TECHNOLOGY ACADEMY

250 East 164th Street, Bronx, New York NY 10456
MYP Coordinator Mr. Thomas Moore
Languages English, Spanish
T: +1 718 293 4017
E: MHSTAIB@motthallsta.org
W: www.motthallsta.org
See full details on page 527

Mount Vernon High School

100 California Road, Mount Vernon NY 10552
DP Coordinator Daphne Platt
Languages English, Spanish
T: +1 914 665 5300
W: ny01913181.schoolwires.net/Domain/21

North Shore High School

450 Glen Cove Avenue, Glen Head NY 11545
DP Coordinator Kerri Titone
Languages English
T: +1 516 277 7801

Northport High School

154 Laurel Hill Road, Northport NY 11768
DP Coordinator Anna Kessler
Languages English
T: +1 631 262 6654
W: northport.k12.ny.us/schools/northport_high_school

Northwood Elementary School

433 North Greece Road, Hilton NY 14468
MYP Coordinator Steve Cudzilo
Languages English
T: +1 585 392 1000 EXT:45
W: www.hilton.k12.ny.us/NorthwoodElementary.cfm

Odyssey Academy

750 Maiden Lane, Rochester NY 14615
DP Coordinator Jonathan Ivers
Languages English
T: +1 585 966 5200
W: www.greececsd.org/Domain/13

P.S. 316 Elijah G. Stroud Elementary School

750 Classon Avenue, Brooklyn NY 11238
PYP Coordinator Alissa Porto
Languages English
T: +1 718 638 4043
W: www.ps316brooklyn.org

Palmyra-Macedon High School

151 Hyde Parkway, Palmyra NY 14522
DP Coordinator Pamela Wagner
MYP Coordinator Pamela Wagner
Languages English
T: +1 315 597 3420
W: www.palmaccsd.org/1/home

Palmyra-Macedon Middle School

163 Hyde Parkway, Palmyra NY 14522
MYP Coordinator Pamela Wagner
Languages English
T: +1 315 597 3450
W: www.palmaccsd.org/2/home

Palmyra-Macedon Primary School

120 Canandaigua Street, Palmyra NY 14522
PYP Coordinator Katie HerrGesell
Languages English, Spanish
T: +1 315 597 3475
W: www.palmaccsd.org/4/home

Pelham Middle School

28 Franklin Place, Pelham NY 10803
MYP Coordinator Sean Llewellyn
Languages English
T: +1 914 738 8190
W: pms.pelhamschools.org

Pierson High School

200 Jermain Avenue, Sag Harbor NY 11963
DP Coordinator Michael Edward Guinan
Languages English
T: +1 631 725 5302
W: www.sagharborschools.org/o/pierson-high-school

Pine Street School

25 Pine Street, New York NY 10005
PYP Coordinator Eileen Freely Baker
Languages English, Spanish, Mandarin
T: +1 212 235 2325
W: www.pinestreetschool.com

Port Chester High School

One Tamarack Road, Port Chester NY 10573
DP Coordinator Rich Laconi
Languages English
T: +1 914 934 7950
W: shs.portchesterschools.org

Portledge School

355 Duck Pond Road, Locust Valley NY 11560-2499
DP Coordinator Trish Rigg
Languages English
T: +1 516 750 3100
W: www.portledge.org

Prospect School

185 Peninsula Boulevard, Hempstead NY 11550
PYP Coordinator Rhonda Chung
Languages English, Spanish
T: +1 516 434 4000
W: www.hempsteadschools.org

Putnam Valley High School

146 Peekskill Hollow Road, Putnam Valley NY 10579
DP Coordinator Vincent DeGregorio
Languages English
T: +1 845 526 7847
W: pvcsd.org/index.php/hs

Queensbury High School

409 Aviation Rd, Queensbury NY 12804
DP Coordinator Marnie DeJohn
Languages English
T: +1 518 824 4601
W: www.queensburyschool.org

Quest Elementary School

225 West Ave, Hilton NY 14468
PYP Coordinator Andrea Geglia
Languages English
T: +1 585 392 1000 (6100)
W: www.hilton.k12.ny.us/QuestElementary.cfm

Red Hook Central High School

103 West Market Street, Red Hook NY 12571
DP Coordinator Michael McCrudden
Languages English
T: +1 845 758 2241 EXT3247
W: www.redhookcentralschools.org

Richard J Bailey Elementary School

33 West Hillside Avenue, White Plains NY 10607
PYP Coordinator Lenore Rotanelli
Languages English
T: +1 914 948 2992
W: www.greenburghcsd.org/domain/155

Saint Edmund Preparatory High School

2474 Ocean Avenue, Brooklyn, New York NY 11229
DP Coordinator Crissa Kostadaras
Languages English
T: +1 718 743 6100
W: www.stedmundprep.org

Schenectady High School

1445 The Plaza, Schenectady NY 12308
DP Coordinator Patricia Embree
Languages English
T: +1 518 370 8190

Somers High School

PO Box 620, 120 Primrose Street, Lincolndale NY 10540
DP Coordinator Alison Scanlon
Languages English
T: +1 914 248 8585
W: www.somersschools.org/domain/8

South Side High School

140 Shepherd Street, Rockville Centre NY 11570
DP Coordinator Elizabeth Nisler
Languages English
T: +1 516 255 8834
W: sshs.rvcschools.org

South Side Middle School

67 Hillside Avenue, Rockville Centre NY 11570
MYP Coordinator Kristen Aksionoff
Languages English
T: +1 516 255 8978

Stanley Makowski Early Childhood Center

1095 Jefferson Avenue, Buffalo NY 14208
PYP Coordinator Natasha Marciano
Languages English
T: +1 716 816 4180

The British International School of New York

20 Waterside Plaza, New York NY 10010
MYP Coordinator Ann Marie Hourigan
PYP Coordinator Alicia Gibson
Languages English
T: +1 212 481 2700
W: www.bis-ny.org

The Brooklyn Latin School

325 Bushwick Ave, 4th floor, Brooklyn, New York NY 11206
DP Coordinator Daniel Lao
Languages English
T: +1 718 366 0154
W: www.brooklynlatin.org

The Clinton School

10 East 15th Street, New York NY 10003
DP Coordinator Lauren Pournaras
Languages English
T: +1 212 524 4360
W: theclintonschool.net

The High School for Enterprise, Business, and Technology

850 Grand St, Brooklyn NY 11211
DP Coordinator Erwin Lara
Languages English, Spanish
T: +1 718 387 2800
W: www.ebtbrooklyn.com

Thomas J Corcoran High School

919 Glenwood Avenue, Syracuse NY 13207
CP Coordinator Ryan Terpening
DP Coordinator Carrianne Kirby
MYP Coordinator Cassandra Malley-Donovan
Languages English
T: +1 315 435 4321

United Nations International School

24-50 Franklin D Roosevelt Drive, New York NY 10010
DP Coordinator Anthony Staccone
Languages English
T: +1 212 684 7400
W: www.unis.org

Vestal High School

205 Woodlawn Drive, Vestal NY 13850
DP Coordinator Jeffrey Dunham
Languages English
T: +1 607 757 2281
W: www.vestal.stier.org/highschool_home.aspx/

Victor Central High School

953 High Street, Victor NY 14564
DP Coordinator Karl Dubash
Languages English
T: +1 585 924 3252
W: www.victorschools.org

Village Elementary School

100 School Lane, Hilton NY 14468
MYP Coordinator Steve Cudzilo
Languages English
T: +1 585 392 1000 (EXT: 51)
W: www.hilton.k12.ny.us

Walton Avenue School

1425 Walton Avenue, Bronx NY 10452
PYP Coordinator Taisha Rodriguez
Languages English, Spanish
T: +1 718 293 5970
W: www.ps294.org

West Islip High School

1 Lions Path, West Islip NY 11795
DP Coordinator James Gilmartin
Languages English
T: +1 631 893 3250
W: www.wi.k12.ny.us

West Middle School

West Middle Avenue, Binghamton NY 13905
MYP Coordinator Mark Ward
Languages English
T: +1 607 763 8400

WESTLAKE MIDDLE SCHOOL

825 West Lake Drive, Thornwood NY 10594
MYP Coordinator TBD
Languages English
T: +1 914 769 8540
E: amungioli@mtplcsd.org
W: wms.mtplcsd.org
See full details on page 553

Woodlands Middle/High School

475 West Hartsdale Avenue, Hartsdale NY 10570
DP Coordinator Steven Rounds
MYP Coordinator Katherine Tovar
Languages English
T: +1 914 761 6052
W: www.greenburghcsd.org/domain/157

Yonkers Middle/High School

150 Rockland Avenue, Yonkers NY 10705
DP Coordinator Marcella Lentine
Languages English
T: +1 914 376 8191
W: www.yonkerspublicschools.org/ymhs

Young Diplomats Magnet Academy

134 West 122nd Street, New York NY 10473
PYP Coordinator Iffat Hossain
Languages English, French
T: +1 212 678 2908
W: www.ps242.com

North Carolina

Albemarle Road Middle School

6900 Democracy Drive, Charlotte NC 28212
MYP Coordinator Kimberly Lynch
Languages English
T: +1 980 343 6420

Ben L Smith High School

2407 South Holden Road, Greensboro NC 27407
DP Coordinator Margaret Powers
Languages English
T: +1 336 294 7300
W: www.gcsnc.com/Smith_High

Billingsville Elementary School

124 Skyland Avenue, Charlotte NC 28205
PYP Coordinator Debra Grimm
Languages English
T: +1 980 343 5520
W: schools.cms.k12.nc.us/billingsvillees

Broughton Magnet High School

723 St Mary's Street, Raleigh NC 27605
DP Coordinator David Brooks
Languages English
T: +1 919 856 7810
W: www.wcpss.net/broughtonhs

Burton Magnet Elementary School

1500 Mathison Street, Durham NC 27701
PYP Coordinator Amy Sanchez
Languages English
T: +1 919 560 3908
W: burton.dpsnc.net

Cedar Ridge High School

1125 New Grady Brown School Rd, Hillsborough NC 27278
DP Coordinator Tabitha Campbell
Languages English
T: +1 919 245 4000
W: www.orangecountyfirst.com/crhs

Charlotte Country Day School

1440 Carmel Road, Charlotte NC 28226
DP Coordinator Stewart Peery
Languages English
T: 0017049434500
W: www.charlottecountryday.org

Cloverleaf Elementary School

300 James Farm Road, Statesville NC 28625
PYP Coordinator Alison Whitaker
Languages English
T: +1 704 978 2111
W: cloverleaf.issnc.org

Coddle Creek Elementary School

141 Frank's Crossing Loop, Mooresville NC 28115
PYP Coordinator Lindsey Mehall
Languages English
T: +1 704 439 4077
W: coddlecreek.issnc.org

Concord High School

481 Burrage Road NE, Concord NC 28025
DP Coordinator Marie Deal
MYP Coordinator Megan Wingfield
Languages English
T: +1 704 786 4161
W: www.cabarrus.k12.nc.us/concordhs

Cotswold Elementary School

300 Greenwich Road, Charlotte NC 28211
PYP Coordinator Debra Grimm
Languages English
T: +1 980 343 6720
W: schools.cms.k12.nc.us/cotswoldes

East Garner Magnet Middle School

6301 Jones Sausage Road, Garner NC 27529
MYP Coordinator Joanne Edwards
Languages English
T: +1 919 662 2339
W: www.wcpss.net/eastgarnerms

East Mecklenburg High School

6800 Monroe Road, Charlotte NC 28212
CP Coordinator Heather Hays
DP Coordinator Heather Hays
MYP Coordinator Heather Hays
Languages English
T: +1 980 343 6430
W: schools.cms.k12.nc.us/eastmecklenburghs

Enloe Magnet High School

128 Clarendon Crescent, Raleigh NC 27610
DP Coordinator April Ellis
Languages English
T: +1 919 856 7918
W: www.wcpss.net/enloehs

Farmington Woods Elementary School

1413 Hampton Valley Road, Cary NC 27511
PYP Coordinator Anna Norris Goodrum
Languages English
T: +1 919 460 3469
W: www.wcpss.net/farmingtonwoodses

Ferndale Middle School

701 Ferndale Blvd, High Point NC 27262
MYP Coordinator Tammy Taylor Patterson
Languages English
T: +1 336 819 2855
W: www.gcsnc.com/Ferndale_Middle

Fox Road Magnet Elementary School

7101 Fox Road, Raleigh NC 27616
PYP Coordinator Martha Hayes
Languages English
T: +1 919 850 8845
W: www.wcpss.net/foxroades

Garner Magnet High School

2101 Spring Drive, Garner NC 27529
CP Coordinator Gerald Siemering
DP Coordinator Jon Sherwin
MYP Coordinator Amy Bennett
Languages English
T: +1 919 662 2379
W: www.wcpss.net/garnerhs

Grimsley High School

801 Westover Terrace, Greensboro NC 27408
DP Coordinator Ben Barnard
Languages English
T: +1 336 370 8184

Hairston Middle School

3911 Naco Road, Greensboro NC 27401
MYP Coordinator Karen Martin-Jones
Languages English
T: +1 336 378 8280
W: www.gcsnc.com/Hairston_Middle

Harding University High School

2001 Alleghany Street, Charlotte NC 28208
DP Coordinator Falisa Hankins
MYP Coordinator Falisa Hankins
Languages English
T: +1 980 343 6007
W: schools.cms.k12.nc.us/hardinguniversityHS

Harold E. Winkler Middle School

4501 Weddington Road, Concord NC 28027
MYP Coordinator Andrea Kiser
Languages English
T: +1 704 260 6450
W: www.cabarrus.k12.nc.us/winkler

Hickory Day School

2535 21st Ave NE, Hickory NC 28601
PYP Coordinator Alison Tompkins
Languages English
T: +1 828 256 9492
W: www.hickoryday.org

High Point Central High School

801 Ferndale Blvd., High Point NC 27262
DP Coordinator David Williams
Languages English
T: +1 336 819 2825
W: www.gcsnc.com/high_point_central_high

Hillside High School

3727 Fayetteville Street, Durham NC 27707
DP Coordinator Angelia Euba McKoy
MYP Coordinator Keshetta Henderson
Languages English
T: +1 919 560 3925
W: www.hillside.dpsnc.net

Huntingtowne Farms Elementary School

2520 Huntingtowne Farms Lane, Charlotte NC 28210
PYP Coordinator Nancy Bullard
Languages English
T: +1 980 343 3625
W: schools.cms.k12.nc.us/huntingtownefarmsES

J. N. Fries Magnet Middle School

133 Stonecrest Circle, Concord NC 28027
MYP Coordinator Shanna Turner-Meehan
Languages English
T: +1 704 788 4140
W: www.cabarrus.k12.nc.us/fries

J.Y. Joyner Magnet Elementary School

2300 Lowden Street, Raleigh NC 27608
PYP Coordinator Sheryl Davis
Languages English, Spanish
T: +1 919 856 7650
W: www.wcpss.net/joyneres

Jacksonville High School

1021 Henderson Drive, Jackonsville NC 28540
CP Coordinator Amber Lumley
DP Coordinator Amber Lumley
Languages English
T: +1 910 989 2048
W: www.onslow.k12.nc.us/jacksonvillehs

James E. Shepard Magnet Middle

2401 Dakota Street, Durham NC 27707
MYP Coordinator Patrice Fletcher
Languages English
T: +1 919 560 3938
W: www.dpsnc.net/shepard

JM Alexander Middle School

12010 Hambright Road, Huntersville NC 28078
MYP Coordinator Mary Kendrick
Languages English
T: +1 980 343 3830
W: schools.cms.k12.nc.us/jmalexanderms

John T. Hoggard High School

4305 Shipyard Boulevard, Wilmington NC 28403
DP Coordinator Mary Lillge
Languages English
T: +1 910 350 2072
W: www.nhcs.net/hoggard

Kinston High School

2601 North Queen Street, Kinston NC 28501
DP Coordinator Joshua Bridges
Languages English
T: +1 252 527 8067

Lansdowne Elementary School

6400 Prett Court, Charlotte NC 28270
PYP Coordinator Sylvia Moras
Languages English
T: +1 980 343 6733
W: schools.cms.k12.nc.us/lansdownees

Lee County High School

1708 Nash Street, Sanford NC 27330
DP Coordinator Katherine Brown
Languages English
T: +1 919 776 7541
W: www.lee.k12.nc.us/Domain/17

Legette Blythe Elementary School

12202 Hambright Rd, Huntersville NC 28078
PYP Coordinator Erik Hoover
Languages English
T: +1 980 343 5770
W: schools.cms.k12.nc.us/blythees

Marie G. Davis K-8 School

3351 W Griffith St., Charlotte NC 28203
MYP Coordinator Kirsten Rodgers
PYP Coordinator Kirsten Rodgers
Languages English
T: +1 980 343 0006
W: schools.cms.k12.nc.us/mariegdavisES

Marvin Ridge High School

2825 Crane Road, Waxhaw NC 28173
DP Coordinator Lindsey Arant
Languages English
T: +1 704 290 1520
W: mrhs.ucps.k12.nc.us

Millbrook High School

2201 Spring Forest Road, Raleigh NC 27615
DP Coordinator Loren Baron
MYP Coordinator Lashonda Haddock
Languages English
T: +1 919 850 8787
W: mhs.wcpss.net

Morganton Day School

305 West Concord Street, Morganton NC 28655
PYP Coordinator Teresa Cape
Languages English
T: +1 828 437 6782
W: www.morgantondayschool.com

Mount Mourne School

1431 Mecklenburg Highway, Mooresville NC 28115
MYP Coordinator Elisabeth White
Languages English
T: +1 704 892 4711
W: www.iss.k12.nc.us/domain/1964

Myers Park High School

2400 Colony Road, Charlotte NC 28209
DP Coordinator Katie Willett
MYP Coordinator Katie Willett
Languages English
T: +1 704 343 5800
W: schools.cms.k12.nc.us/myersparkHS

North Mecklenburg High School

11201 Old Statesville Road, Huntersville NC 28078
DP Coordinator Amy Pasko
MYP Coordinator Amy Pasko
Languages English
T: +1 980 343 3840

Northview School

625 Carolina Avenue, Statesville NC 28677
MYP Coordinator Elisabeth White
Languages English
T: +1 704 873 7354
W: www.iss.k12.nc.us/domain/1227

Northwood Elementary School

818 W Lexington Avenue, High Point NC 27262
PYP Coordinator Sara Carter
Languages English
T: +1 336 819 2920
W: www.gcsnc.com/Domain/80

Paisley Magnet School

1400 Grant Street, Winston-Salem NC 27105
MYP Coordinator Erin Knapp
Languages English
T: +1 336 727 2775
W: www.wsfcs.k12.nc.us/paisley

Parkland High School

1600 Brewer Road, Winston-Salem NC 27127
CP Coordinator Laurel Lokant
DP Coordinator Laurel Lokant
Languages English
T: +1 336 771 4700
W: www.wsfcs.k12.nc.us/Domain/1012

Piedmont Open Middle School

1241 East 10th Street, Charlotte NC 28204
MYP Coordinator Maranda Thornburg
Languages English
T: +1 980 343 5435
W: schools.cms.k12.nc.us/piedmontMS

Ralph L Fike High School

500 Harrison Drive, Wilson NC 27893
DP Coordinator Jill Wheeler
Languages English
T: +1 252 399 7905
W: fike.wilsonschoolsnc.net

Randolph Middle School

4400 Water Oak Road, Charlotte NC 28211
MYP Coordinator Dayanara Noboa
Languages English
T: +1 980 343 6700
W: schools.cms.k12.nc.us/randolphMS

Ranson Middle School

5850 Statesville Road, Charlotte NC 28269
MYP Coordinator Shanniska Howard
Languages English
T: +1 980 343 6800
W: schools.cms.k12.nc.us/ransonMS

Reidsville High School

1901 South Park Drive, Reidsville NC 27320
DP Coordinator Wayne Knight
Languages English
T: +1 336 349 6361
W: www.rock.k12.nc.us

Rocky Mount High School

1400 Bethlehem Road, Rocky Mount NC 27803
DP Coordinator Jeffrey Pageau
Languages English
T: +1 252 977 3085
W: www.nrms.k12.nc.us/Domain/32

Smith Magnet Elementary School

1101 Maxwell Drive, Raleigh NC 27603
PYP Coordinator Megan Flynn
Languages English
T: +1 919 662 2458
W: smithes.wcpss.net

Smithfield-Selma High School

700 Booker Dairy Rd., Smithfield NC 27577
CP Coordinator Carlos Sousa
DP Coordinator Cynthia Hutchings
Languages English
T: +1 919 934 5191
W: johnston.k12.nc.us/sss

South Iredell High School

299 Old Mountain Road, Statesville NC 28677
CP Coordinator Latonia Bostic
DP Coordinator Latonia Bostic
MYP Coordinator Latonia Bostic
Languages English
T: +1 704 528 4536
W: southhigh.issnc.org

South View High School

4184 Elk Road, Cumberland County, Hope Mills NC 28348
CP Coordinator W Oxendine
DP Coordinator Dawn Curle
Languages English
T: +1 910 425 8181

Southeast Raleigh Magnet High School

2600 Rock Quarry Road, Raleigh NC 27610
DP Coordinator Shanora Kingsberry
Languages English
T: +1 919 856 2800
W: www.wcpss.net/southeastraleighhs

Speas Global Elementary School

2000 W. Polo Road, Winston-Salem NC 27106
PYP Coordinator Katryna Jacober
Languages English, Spanish
T: +1 336 703 4135
W: www.wsfcs.k12.nc.us/domain/5628

Statesville Road Elementary

5833 Milhaven Road, Charlotte NC 28213
PYP Coordinator Susan Patterson
Languages English
T: +1 980 343 6815
W: schools.cms.k12.nc.us/statesvilleroadES

The British International School of Charlotte

7000 Endhaven Lane, Charlotte NC 28277
DP Coordinator Julie Tombs
Languages English
T: +1 704 341 3236
W: www.britishschoolofcharlotte.org

The Montessori School of Raleigh

408 Andrews Chapel Road, Durham NC 27703
DP Coordinator Alyssa Brinkley
Languages English, Spanish
T: +1 919 848 1545
W: msr.org

W. M. Irvin Elementary School

1400 Gold Rush Drrive, Concord NC 28025
PYP Coordinator Debra Bralley
Languages English, Spanish
T: +1 704 260 6330
W: www.cabarrus.k12.nc.us/Domain/24

Waldo C Falkener IB Elementary School

3931 Naco Road, Greensboro NC 27401
PYP Coordinator Keaira Price
Languages English
T: +1 336 370 8150
W: www.gcsnc.com/Domain/29

Walter Hines Page High School

201 Alma Pinnix Drive, Greensboro NC 27405
DP Coordinator Elizabeth Hackney
Languages English
T: +1 336 370 8200
W: www.gcsnc.com/Domain/84

Walter M. Williams High School

1307 South Church Street, Burlington NC 27215-4919
DP Coordinator Denise Wall
Languages English, Spanish
T: +1 336 570 6161
W: www.abss.k12.nc.us/wwh

Weddington Hills Elementary School

4401 Weddington Rd, Concord NC 28027
PYP Coordinator Mary Hooks
Languages English
T: +1 704 795 9385
W: www.cabarrus.k12.nc.us/Domain/22

West Cabarrus High School

4100 Weddington Road, Concord NC 28027
DP Coordinator Jennifer Ward
Languages English
T: +1 704 260 5970
W: www.cabarrus.k12.nc.us/wchs

West Charlotte High School

2219 Senior Drive, Charlotte NC 28216
DP Coordinator LaDawna Robinson
MYP Coordinator LaDawna Robinson
Languages English
T: +1 980 343 6060
W: schools.cms.k12.nc.us/westcharlotteHS

West Millbrook Middle School

8115 Strickland Road, Raleigh NC 27615
MYP Coordinator Jessica Collins
Languages English
T: +1 919 870 4050
W: www.wcpss.net/westmillbrookms

Ohio

Alliance Middle School

3205 S. Union Ave., Alliance OH 44601
MYP Coordinator Andy Toth
Languages English
T: +1 330 829 2254
W: www.alliancecityschools.org/o/middle-school

Beaumont School

3301 North Park Boulevard, Cleveland Heights OH 44118
DP Coordinator Ann Hoelzel
Languages English
T: +1 216 321 2954
W: www.beaumontschool.org

Boulevard Elementary School

14900 Drexmore Road, Shaker Heights OH 44120
PYP Coordinator Jennifer Goulden
Languages English
T: +1 216 295 4020
W: www.shaker.org/boulevardschool_home.aspx

Campus International High School

3100 Chester Ave, Cleveland OH 44114
DP Coordinator Sarah Schneider
MYP Coordinator Maria Vazquez-Listenbee
Languages English
T: +1 216 838 8100
W: www.clevelandmetroschools.org/cihs

Campus International School

3000 Euclid Ave, Cleveland OH 44115
MYP Coordinator Sheila Orourke
PYP Coordinator Sheila Orourke
Languages English
T: +1 216 431 2225
W: www.clevelandmetroschools.org/CIS

Canterbury Elementary School

2530 Canterbury Road, Cleveland Heights OH 44118
PYP Coordinator Melissa Garcar Garcar
T: +1 216 371 7470
W: www.chuh.org/canterburyelementary_home.aspx

Case Elementary School

400 W. Market St., Akron OH 44303
PYP Coordinator Jennifer Victor
Languages English
T: +1 330 873 3350

Central Academy of Ohio

2727 Kenwood Blvd, Toledo OH 43606
PYP Coordinator Jen Pierce
Languages English
T: +1 419 205 9800
W: www.ohiocentralacademy.net

Columbus Alternative High School

2632 McGuffey Road, Columbus OH 43211
DP Coordinator Alice Webb
Languages English
T: +1 614 365 6006
W: www.ccsoh.us/CAHS

Discovery School

855 Millsboro Rd, Mansfield OH 44903
PYP Coordinator Simon Clark
Languages English
T: +1 419 756 8880
W: www.discovery-school.net

Dublin Coffman High School

6780 Coffman Road, Dublin OH 43107-1099
DP Coordinator Eric Bringardner
Languages English
T: +1 614 764 5900
W: www.dublinschools.net/dublincoffman_home.aspx

Dublin Jerome High School

8300 Hyland-Croy Road, Dublin OH 43016
DP Coordinator Ann Tiefenthaler
Languages English
T: +1 614 873 7377
W: www.dublinschools.net/dublinjerome_home.aspx

Dublin Scioto High School

400 Hard Road, Dublin OH 43016-8349
DP Coordinator Eric Bringardner
Languages English
T: +1 614 718 8300
W: www.dublinschools.net/dublinscioto_home.aspx

Eastwood Elementary School

198 East College Street, Oberlin OH 44074
PYP Coordinator Maureen Freda
Languages English
T: +1 440 775 3473
W: eastwood.oberlinschools.net

Fairfax Elementary School

3150 Fairfax Road, Cleveland Heights OH 44118
PYP Coordinator Leslie Garrett
Languages English
T: +1 216 371 7480
W: www.chuh.org/fairfaxelementary_home.aspx

Fairmont High School

3301 Shroyer Road, Kettering OH 45429
DP Coordinator Darren McGarvey
Languages English
T: +1 937 499 1601
W: www.ketteringschools.org/1/Home

Fernway Elementary School

17420 Fernway Road, Shaker Heights OH 44120
PYP Coordinator Jean Reinhold
Languages English
T: +1 216 295 4040
W: www.shaker.org/fernwayschool_home.aspx

Firestone High School

333 Rampart Avenue, Akron OH 44313
DP Coordinator Judith Harrison
Languages English
T: +1 330 873 3315

GlenOak High School

1801 Schneider Street NE, Canton OH 44721
DP Coordinator Emily Palmer
Languages English
T: +1 330 491 3800
W: www.plainlocal.org/17/home

Kent State University Child Development Center

775 Loop Rd., Kent OH 44242
PYP Coordinator Adonia Porto
Languages English
T: +1 330 672 2559
W: www.kent.edu/ehhs/centers/cdc

King Community Learning Center

805 Memorial Parkway, Akron OH 44303
PYP Coordinator Janet Lippincott
Languages English
T: +1 330 761 7962

Lakewood Catholic Academy

14808 Lake Avenue, Lakewood OH 44107
MYP Coordinator Eileen Murphy
Languages English
T: +1 216 521 0559
W: www.lakewoodcatholicacademy.com

Langston Middle School
150 North Pleasant Street, Oberlin OH 44074
MYP Coordinator Kristin Miller
Languages English, Spanish, Mandarin
T: +1 440 775 7961
W: langston.oberlinschools.net

Litchfield Middle School
470 Castle Blvd, Akron OH 44313
MYP Coordinator Sandra Cline
Languages English
T: +1 330 761 2775
W: www.akronschools.com

Lomond Elementary School
17917 Lomond Boulevard, Shaker Heights OH 44122
PYP Coordinator Shifa Isaacs
Languages English
T: +1 216 295 4050
W: www.shaker.org/lomondschool_home.aspx

McKinley Elementary School
602 Plum Street, Fairport Harbor OH 44077
PYP Coordinator Candace Vahcic
Languages English
T: +1 440 354 5400
W: www.fhevs.org/mckinley

Mercer Elementary School
23325 Wimbledon Road, Shaker Heights OH 44122
PYP Coordinator Maria Baker
Languages English
T: +1 216 295 4070
W: www.shaker.org/mercerschool_home.aspx

Monticello Middle School
3665 Monticello Blvd., Cleveland Heights OH 44121
MYP Coordinator Leslie Garrett
Languages English
T: +1 216 371 6520
W: www.chuh.org/monticellomiddle_home.aspx

Notre Dame Academy, OH
3535 W Sylvania Avenue, Toledo OH 43623
DP Coordinator Angela Joseph
Languages English
T: +1 419 475 9359
W: www.nda.org

Oberlin High School
281 North Pleasant Street, Oberlin OH 44074
DP Coordinator Rebecca Lahetta
MYP Coordinator Kristin Miller
Languages English
T: +1 440 774 1295
W: ohs.oberlinschools.net

Onaway Elementary School
15600 Parkland Boulevard, Shaker Heights OH 44120
PYP Coordinator Denise Brown
Languages English
T: +1 216 295 4080
W: www.shaker.org/onawayschool_home.aspx

Portage Path Community Learning Center
55 S Portage Path, Akron OH 44303
PYP Coordinator Jill Holcomb
Languages English
T: +1 330 761 2795

Princeton High School
11080 Chester Road, Princeton City Schools, Cincinnati OH 45246
DP Coordinator Michele Ritzie
Languages English
T: +1 513 864 1500
W: www.princetonschools.net/Domain/8

Purcell Marian High School
2935 Hackberry Street, Cincinnati OH 45206
DP Coordinator Bob Herring
Languages English
T: +1 513 751 1230
W: www.purcellmarian.org

Resnik Community Learning Center
65 N. Meadowcroft Dr., Akron OH 44313
PYP Coordinator Lori Wammes
Languages English, French
T: +1 330 873 3370

Roxboro Elementary School
2405 Roxboro Road, Cleveland Heights OH 44106
PYP Coordinator Melissa Garcar Garcar
Languages English
T: +1 216 371 7115
W: www.chuh.org/roxboroelementary_home.aspx

Roxboro Middle School
2400 Roxboro Road, Cleveland Heights OH 44106
MYP Coordinator Melissa Garcar Garcar
Languages English
T: +1 216 320 3500
W: www.chuh.org/heightsmiddle.aspx

Shaker Heights High School
15911 Aldersyde Drive, Shaker Heights OH 44120
DP Coordinator Amy Brodsky
MYP Coordinator Molly Miles
Languages English
T: +1 216 295 4200
W: www.shaker.org/highschool_home.aspx

Shaker Heights Middle School
20600 Shaker Blvd, Shaker Heights OH 44122
MYP Coordinator Addie Tobey
Languages English
T: +1 216 295 4100
W: www.shaker.org/middleschool_home.aspx

Springfield High School
701 East Home Road, Springfield OH 45504
DP Coordinator Beth Biester
Languages English
T: +1 937 342 4100
W: www.scsdoh.org/Domain/2242

St Edward High School
13500 Detroit Avenue, Lakewood OH 44107
DP Coordinator Nicholas Kuhar
MYP Coordinator Nicholas Kuhar
Languages English
T: +1 216 221 3776
W: sehs.net

Tri-County International Academy
c/o Wooster H.S., 515 Oldman Road, Wooster OH 44691
DP Coordinator Victoria Birk
Languages English
T: +1 330 345 4000 EXT:3004

Upper Arlington High School
1650 Ridgeview Road, Upper Arlington OH 43221
CP Coordinator Cynthia Ballheim
DP Coordinator Cynthia Ballheim
Languages English
T: +1 614 487 5200
W: www.uaschools.org/upperarlingtonhighschool_home.aspx

Westerville South High School
303 South Otterbein Avenue, Westerville OH 43081
DP Coordinator Bill Heinmiller
Languages English
T: +1 614 797 6000
W: www.westerville.k12.oh.us/31/Home

Westlake Elementary School
27555 Center Ridge Road, Westlake OH 44145
PYP Coordinator Deb Wadden
Languages English
T: +1 440 250 1200
W: www.wlake.org/our-schools/westlake-elementary-school

Westlake High School
27200 Hilliard Blvd., Westlake OH 44145
DP Coordinator Matthew Planisek
Languages English
T: +1 440 250 1260
W: www.wlake.org/our-schools/westlake-high

Woodbury Elementary School
15400 South Woodland Road, Shaker Heights OH 44120
MYP Coordinator Addie Tobey
Languages English
T: +1 216 295 4150
W: www.shaker.org/woodburyschool_home.aspx

Worthington Kilbourne High School
1499 Hard Road, Columbus OH 43235
DP Coordinator Jeannie Goodwin
Languages English
T: +1 614 883 2550
W: www.worthington.k12.oh.us/Domain/9

Oklahoma

Booker T Washington High School
1514 E. Zion St., Tulsa OK 74106
DP Coordinator Sharon Lazdins
MYP Coordinator Joyelle Payne
Languages English
T: +1 918 925 1000
W: btw.tulsaschools.org

Classen School of Advanced Studies
1901 North Elison Street, Oklahoma City OK 73106
DP Coordinator Mitch McIntosh
Languages English
T: +1 405 587 5400
W: www.okcps.org/domain/80

George Washington Carver Magnet Middle School
624 E Oklahoma Place, Tulsa OK 74106
MYP Coordinator Emily Baker
Languages English
T: +1 918 595 2939

Jenks West Elementary School

205 East B. Street, Jenks OK 74037
PYP Coordinator Cathryn McCarthy
Languages English
T: +1 918 299 4415
W: www.jenksps.org

Oregon

Bend Senior High School

230 NE 6th Street, Bend OR 97701
DP Coordinator Paul Hutter
Languages English
T: +1 541 383 6293
W: www.bend.k12.or.us/bendhigh

Cedar Park Middle School

11100 SW Park Way, Portland OR 97225
MYP Coordinator Amy Hattendorf
Languages English
T: +1 503 672 3620
W: cedarpark.beaverton.k12.or.us

Cleveland High School

3400 SE 26 Ave, Portland OR 97202
DP Coordinator Jennifer Wiandt Owens
Languages English
T: +1 503 916 5120

Dr Martin Luther King Jr Elementary School

4906 NE 6th Avenue, Portland OR 97211
PYP Coordinator Paige Thomas
Languages English
T: +1 503 916 6155
W: www.pps.net/Domain/130

Eugene International High School

400 East 19th Avenue, Eugene OR 97401
DP Coordinator Steven Smith
Languages English
T: +1 541 687 3196
W: www.schools.4j.lane.edu/ihs/

French American International School

8500 NW Johnson Street, Portland OR 97229-6780
MYP Coordinator Anne Prouty
PYP Coordinator Kathlin Gabaldon
Languages English, French
T: +1 503 292 7776
W: www.faispdx.org

German International School of Portland

3900 SW Murray Blvd, Beaverton OR 97005
PYP Coordinator Michelle Bahr
Languages German, English
T: +1 503 626 9089
W: www.gspdx.org

Gresham High School

1200 North Main Street, Gresham OR 97030-3899
DP Coordinator Alan Simpson
Languages English
T: +1 503 674 5500
W: www.gresham.k12.or.us/ghs

Hillsboro High School

3285 SE Rood Bridge Road, Hillsboro OR 97123
DP Coordinator Ashley Clemens
Languages English
T: +1 503 844 1980
W: schools.hsd.k12.or.us/hilhi

International School of Beaverton

17770 SW Blanton Street, Beaverton OR 97007
DP Coordinator Amy Schuff
MYP Coordinator Gina Velasco
Languages English
T: +1 503 259 3800
W: isb.beaverton.k12.or.us

Lincoln High School

1600 SW Salmon St., Portland OR 97205
DP Coordinator Kim Bliss
Languages English
T: +1 503 916 5200
W: www.pps.net/domain/136

Meadow Park Middle School

14100 SW Downing Street, Beaverton OR 97006
MYP Coordinator Megan Poole
Languages English, Spanish
T: +1 503 672 3660
W: meadowpark.beaverton.k12.or.us

Mountainside High School

12500 SW 175th Avenue, Beaverton OR 97007
DP Coordinator Brooke Mayo
MYP Coordinator Jeremiah Hubbard
Languages English
T: +1 503 356 3500
W: mountainside.beaverton.k12.or.us

Nellie Muir Elementary School

1800 W Hayes St, Woodburn OR 97071
PYP Coordinator Mary Parra
Languages English, Spanish
T: +1 503 981 2670
W: www.woodburnsd.org/nellie-muir-elementary-school

Newport High School

322 NE Eads Street, Newport OR 97365
DP Coordinator Jody Hanna
Languages English
T: +1 541 265 9281

North Eugene High School

200 Silver Lane, Eugene OR 97404
CP Coordinator Taylor Madden
DP Coordinator Kendall Lawless
Languages English
T: +1 541 790 4500
W: nehs.4j.lane.edu

North Salem High School

765 14th Street NE, Salem OR 97301
CP Coordinator Amy Green
DP Coordinator Amy Green
Languages English
T: +1 503 399 3241
W: north.salkeiz.k12.or.us

Oregon Trail Academy

36520 SE Proctor Rd, Boring OR 97009
DP Coordinator Kasshawna Knoll
MYP Coordinator Emily Hafer
PYP Coordinator Emily Hafer
Languages English
T: +1 503 668 4133
W: oregontrailschools.com/ota

Pilot Butte Middle School

1501 N.E. Neff Road, Bend OR 97701
MYP Coordinator Lyndsey Hendrix
Languages English
T: +1 541 355 7520
W: www.bend.k12.or.us/pilotbutte

Rex Putnam High School

4950 SE Roethe Road, Milwaukie OR 97267
DP Coordinator Traci Clarke
Languages English
T: +1 503 353 5860
W: www.nclack.k12.or.us/phs

Sabin School

4013 NE 18 Avenue, Portland OR 97212
PYP Coordinator Sacha Luria
Languages English
T: +1 503 916 6181
W: www.pps.k12.or.us/schools/sabin

Seven Peaks School

19660 SW Mountaineer Way, Bend OR 97702
MYP Coordinator Hope Royes
Languages English
T: +1 541 382 7755
W: www.sevenpeaksschool.org

Skyline School

11536 NW Skyline Blvd, Portland OR 97231
MYP Coordinator Melissa Dunn
PYP Coordinator Bradley Manker
Languages English
T: +1 503 916 5412
W: www.pps.k12.or.us/schools/skyline

South Salem High School

1910 Church Street SE, Salem OR 97302
DP Coordinator Jennifer Harris-Clippinger
Languages English
T: +1 503 399 3252
W: www.southsaxons.com

Southridge High School

9625 SW 125th Street, Beaverton OR 97008
CP Coordinator Wayne Grimm
DP Coordinator Natalie Ballard Strauhal
Languages English
T: +1 503 259 5400
W: southridge.beaverton.k12.or.us

Sunset High School

13840 NW Cornell Road, Portland OR 97229
DP Coordinator Jill Boeschenstein
Languages English
T: +1 503 259 5050

The International School

025 SW Sherman Street, Portland OR 97210
PYP Coordinator Kelly Rogers
Languages Chinese, Japanese, Spanish
T: +1 503 226 2496
W: www.intlschool.org

Tigard High School

9000 SW Durham Rd., Tigard OR 97224
DP Coordinator Michael Savage
Languages English
T: +1 503 431 5400
W: www.ttsdschools.org/ths

Tualatin High School

22300 SW Boones Ferry Rd, Tualatin OR 97062
DP Coordinator Lisa Lacy
Languages English
T: +1 503 431 5600
W: www.ttsdschools.org/tuhs

Valley Inquiry Charter School

5774 Hazel Green Road, Salem OR 97305
PYP Coordinator Taylor Tuepker
Languages English
T: +1 503 399 3150

Vernon School

2044 N.E. Killingsworth Street, Portland OR 97211
MYP Coordinator Lyndsey Mackenzie
PYP Coordinator Lyndsey Mackenzie
Languages English
T: +1 503 916 6415
W: www.pps.net/Domain/158

Willamette High School

1801 Echo Hollow Road, Eugene OR 97402
DP Coordinator Jade Starr
Languages English
T: +1 541 689 0731

Woodburn High School

1785 N Front Street, Woodburn OR 97071
DP Coordinator Doug Peterson
Languages English
T: +1 503 981 2600

Pennsylvania

Barack Obama Academy of International Studies

515 N. Highland Avenue, Pittsburg PA 15206
DP Coordinator Joseph Ehman
MYP Coordinator Michael Chapman
Languages English
T: +1 412 622 5980
W: www.pghschools.org/ibworld2

Boyce Middle School

1500 Boyce Road, Upper St Clair PA 15241
MYP Coordinator Christina Caragein
Languages English
T: +1 412 833 1600

Central High School

1700 W Olney Avenue, Philadelphia PA 19141
DP Coordinator Aviva Hockfield
Languages English
T: +1 215 276 5262
W: centralhs.philasd.org

Chambersburg Area Senior High School

511 South Sixth Street, Chambersburg PA 17201
DP Coordinator Kristofer Cole
Languages English
T: +1 717 261 3324
W: www.casdonline.org/Domain/224

Cumberland Valley High School

6746 Carlisle Pike, Mechanicsburg PA 17050
DP Coordinator Amy Miller
Languages English
T: +1 717 506 3454

Downingtown STEM Academy

335 Manor Avenue, Downingtown PA 19335
DP Coordinator Michael Sheehan
Languages English
T: +1 610 269 8460
W: www.dasd.org

Fort Couch Middle School

515 Ft Couch Road, Upper St Clair PA 15241
MYP Coordinator Andrew Bowers
Languages English
T: +1 412 833 1600

GEORGE SCHOOL

1690 Newtown Langhorne Rd, Newtown PA 18940-2414
DP Coordinator Kim McGlynn
Languages English
T: +1 215 579 6500
E: admission@georgeschool.org
W: www.georgeschool.org

See full details on page 505

George Washington High School

10175 Bustleton Avenue, Philadelphia PA 19116
DP Coordinator Maria Pacheco
Languages English
T: +1 215 961 2001
W: gwhs.philasd.org

Harrisburg Academy

10 Erford Road, Wormleysburg PA 17043
DP Coordinator Maureen Smith
Languages English
T: +1 717 763 7811
W: www.harrisburgacademy.org

Harriton High School

600 North Ithan Avenue, Rosemont PA 19010
DP Coordinator Thomas O'Brien
Languages English
T: +1 610 658 3970
W: www.lmsd.org

Hill-Freedman World Academy

6200 Crittenden Street, Philadelphia PA 19138
DP Coordinator Thomas Emerson
MYP Coordinator Katherine Lauher
Languages English
T: +1 215 276 5260
W: hfwa.philasd.org

J P McCaskey High School

445 North Reservoir St, Lancaster PA 17602
CP Coordinator Kelly White
DP Coordinator Benjamin Deardorff
Languages English
T: +1 717 291 6211
W: www.lancaster.k12.pa.us

Lehigh Valley Academy Regional Charter School

1560 Valley Center Parkway, Suite 200, Bethlehem PA 18017
CP Coordinator Andrew Hall
DP Coordinator Andrew Hall
MYP Coordinator Jacob March
PYP Coordinator Kelly Eddinger
Languages English
T: +1 610 866 9660

Manheim Township High School

PO Box 5134, School Road, Lancaster PA 17606
DP Coordinator Larry Penner
Languages English
T: +1 717 560 3097

Mayfair Elementary School

3001 Princeton Avenue, Philadelphia PA 19149
MYP Coordinator Jenna Fell
PYP Coordinator Jessica O'Neill
Languages English
T: +1 215 400 3280
W: mayfair.philasd.org

MERCYHURST PREPARATORY SCHOOL

538 East Grandview Boulevard, Erie PA 16504
DP Coordinator Paul Cancilla
Languages English
T: +1 814 824 2323
E: aorlando@mpslakers.com
W: www.mpslakers.com

See full details on page 522

Northeast High School

Cottman & Algon Avenues, Philadelphia PA 19111
DP Coordinator Bonnie Taylor
Languages English
T: +1 215 728 5018
W: nehs.philasd.org

Owen J. Roberts High School

901 Ridge Road, Pottstown PA 19465
CP Coordinator William Richardson
Languages English, Spanish
T: +1 610 469 5100
W: www.ojrsd.com/Domain/14

Pan American Academy Charter School

2830 North American Street, Philadelphia PA 19133
MYP Coordinator David Shemaria
PYP Coordinator Mercedes Mason
Languages English, Spanish
T: +1 215 425 1212
W: www.panamcs.org

Philadelphia High School for Girls

1400 West Olney Avenue, Philadelphia PA 19141-2398
DP Coordinator Megan McNamara
Languages English
T: +1 215 276 5258
W: girlshs.philasd.org

Plymouth Whitemarsh High School

201 East Germantown Pike, Plymouth Meeting PA 19462
CP Coordinator Rebecca Duffy
Languages English
T: +1 610 825 1500
W: www.colonialsd.org/our-schools/plymouth-whitemarsh-high

School Lane Charter School

2400 Bristol Pike, Bensalem PA 19020
DP Coordinator Katherine Hewitt
MYP Coordinator Karen Schade
Languages English
T: +1 215 245 6055
W: www.schoollane.org

State College Area High School, Pennsylvania

650 Westerly Parkway, State College PA 16801
CP Coordinator Jennifer Schreiber
DP Coordinator Jennifer Schreiber
Languages English
T: +1 814 231 1111
W: www.scasd.org/schighschool

Streams Elementary School

1560 Ashlawn Avenue, Upper St Clair PA 15241
PYP Coordinator Katie Hendrickson
Languages English
T: +1 412 833 1600
W: www.uscsd.k12.pa.us/Domain/542

Upper St. Clair High School

1825 McLaughlin Run Road, Upper St. Clair PA 15241
DP Coordinator Tanya Chothani
MYP Coordinator Gordon Mathews
Languages English
T: +1 412 833 1600
W: uscsd.k12.pa.us/Domain/59

William W Bodine High School for International Affairs

1101 North 4th Street, Philadelphia PA 19123
DP Coordinator Kelli Mackay
Languages English
T: +1 215 351 7332
W: bodine.philasd.org

Woodrow Wilson Middle School

1800 Cottman Ave., Philadelphia PA 19111
MYP Coordinator Rosalinda Echevarria
Languages English
T: +1 215 728 5015
W: wwilson.philasd.org

York Academy Regional Charter School

32 West North Street, PO Box 1787, York PA 17401
MYP Coordinator Carol Alvarnaz
PYP Coordinator Kristin Sipe
Languages English
T: +1 717 801 3900

York County School of Technology

2179 S. Queen St., York PA 17402
CP Coordinator Brandon May
Languages English
T: +1 717 741 0820

Young Scholars of Central PA Charter School

1530 Westerly Parkway, State College PA 16801
MYP Coordinator Baris Yilmaz
Languages English
T: +1 814 237 9727
W: www.yscp.org

Rhode Island

International Charter School

334 Pleasant St., Pawtucket RI 02860
PYP Coordinator Michelle Johnson
Languages English
T: +1 401 721 0824
W: internationalcharterschool.org

Prout School

4640 Tower Hill Road, Wakefield RI 02879
DP Coordinator Christopher Bromley
Languages English
T: +1 401 789 9262
W: www.theproutschool.org

St. Andrew's School (RI)

63 Federal Road, Barrington RI 02806
DP Coordinator Ryan Alescio
Languages English
T: +1 401 246 1230
W: www.standrews-ri.org

South Carolina

A C Flora High School

1 Falcon Drive, Columbia SC 29204
DP Coordinator Stephen Keller
Languages English
T: +1 803 738 7300
W: flora.richlandone.org

Aynor High School

201 Jordanville Road, Aynor SC 29511
DP Coordinator Renee Atkinson
Languages English
T: +1 843 488 7100
W: www.horrycountyschools.net/aynor_high_school

Buist Academy for Advanced Studies

103 Calhoun Street, Charleston SC 29401
MYP Coordinator Sara Lyle
PYP Coordinator Sara Lyle
Languages English
T: +1 843 724 7750
W: buist.ccsdschools.com

Christ Church Episcopal School

245 Cavalier Drive, Greenville SC 29607
DP Coordinator Amanda Beckrich
PYP Coordinator Stephanie Morgan
Languages English
T: +1 864 299 1522
W: www.cces.org

Concord Elementary School

2701 Calrossie Road, Anderson SC 29621
PYP Coordinator Monica Loftis
Languages English
T: +1 864 260 5105
W: www.anderson5.net/concord

E. L. Wright Middle School

2740 Alpine Road, Columbia SC 29223
MYP Coordinator Latoya Young
Languages English
T: +1 803 736 8740
W: www.richland2.org/elwm

Fork Shoals Elementary School

916 McKelvey Road, Pelzer SC 29669
PYP Coordinator Amy Giles
Languages English
T: +1 864 243 5680
W: www.greenville.k12.sc.us/forksh

Fort Dorchester High School

8500 Patriot Boulevard, North Charleston SC 29420
DP Coordinator Janel Raquet
Languages English
T: +1 843 760 4450

Greer High School

3032 East Gap Creek Road, Greer SC 29651
DP Coordinator Mary Smith
Languages English
T: +1 864 355 5819
W: www.greenville.k12.sc.us/greerhs

Hartsville High School

701 Lewellyn Avenue, Hartsville SC 29550
DP Coordinator Paula Alvarez
Languages English
T: +1 843 857 3700

Hendrix Elementary School

1084 Springfield Road, Boiling Springs SC 29316
PYP Coordinator Allison Watson
Languages English
T: +1 864 216 4000
W: hes.spart2.org

Hilton Head Elementary School

30 School Road, Hilton Head Island SC 29926
PYP Coordinator Karen Perdue
Languages English
T: +1 843 342 4100

Hilton Head High School

70 Wilborn Road, Beaufort, Hilton Head Island SC 29926
CP Coordinator Mary Beth White
DP Coordinator Mary Beth White
MYP Coordinator Curtis Ewing
Languages English
T: +1 843 689 4801

Hilton Head Island Middle School

55 Wilborn Road, Hilton Head Island SC 29926
MYP Coordinator Kathleen Harper
Languages English
T: +1 843 689 4500

Hopkins Middle School

1601 Clarkson Road, Hopkins SC 29061
MYP Coordinator Sharon Newton
Languages English
T: +1 803 695 3331
W: www.richlandone.org/Domain/40

Irmo High School

6671 St Andrews Road, Columbia SC 29212
CP Coordinator Sarah Ostergaard
DP Coordinator Sarah Ostergaard
Languages English
T: +1 803 732 8100
W: www.lexrich5.org/ihs

James Island High School

1000 Fort Johnson Road, Charleston SC 29412
DP Coordinator Jennifer Smillie
Languages English
T: +1 843 762 2754
W: jichs.ccsdschools.com

Jesse Boyd Elementary School

1505 Fernwood Glendale Road, Spartanburg SC 29307
PYP Coordinator Jennifer Squires
Languages English
T: +1 864 594 4430
W: boyd.spartanburg7.org

Latta High School

618 N. Richardson St., Latta SC 29565
DP Coordinator Christy Berry
Languages English
T: +1 843 752 5751
W: www.dillon3.k12.sc.us/lhs

Lexington Elementary School

116 Azalea Drive, Lexington SC 29072
PYP Coordinator Lynn Dempsey
Languages English, Spanish
T: +1 803 821 4000
W: les.lexington1.net

Lexington High School

2463 Augusta Highway, Lexington SC 29072
DP Coordinator Derek Allison
Languages English
T: +1 803 821 3400
W: sites.google.com/lexington1.net/lhswebsite/home

Lower Richland High School

2615 Lower Richland Blvd, Hopkins SC 29061
CP Coordinator Elvionna White
DP Coordinator Atonce Joseph
MYP Coordinator Constantina Green
Languages English
T: +1 803 695 3000
W: www.richlandone.org/Domain/52

Memminger Elementary School

20 Beaufain Street, Charleston SC 29401
PYP Coordinator Maggie McClary
Languages English
T: +1 843 724 7778
W: memminger.ccsdschools.com

Northwestern High School

2503 West Main Street, Rock Hill SC 29732
DP Coordinator Patti Tate
Languages English
T: +1 803 981 1200
W: www.rock-hill.k12.sc.us/domain/31

Richland Northeast High School

7500 Brookfield Road, Columbia SC 29223
CP Coordinator Andrea Dickey
DP Coordinator Sonja Merriwether-Hawki
MYP Coordinator Deb Cooper
Languages English
T: +1 803 699 2800
W: www.richland2.org/rnh

Rock Hill High School

320 West Springdale Road, Rock Hill SC 29730
DP Coordinator Patricia Sanford
Languages English
T: +1 803 981 1300
W: www.rock-hill.k12.sc.us/Domain/32

Rosewood Elementary

2240 Rosewood Drive, Rock Hill SC 29730
PYP Coordinator Kallie Cromer
Languages English
T: +1 803 981 1540
W: www.rock-hill.k12.sc.us/Domain/22

Sara Collins Elementary School

1200 Parkins Mill Road, Greenville SC 29607
PYP Coordinator Carrie Johnson
Languages English
T: +1 864 355 3200

Socastee High School

4900 Socastee Boulevard, Myrtle Beach SC 29588
DP Coordinator Danny Wilson
Languages English
T: +1 843 293 2513
W: www.horrycountyschools.net/Socastee_High_School

South Pointe High School

806 Neely Road, Rock Hill SC 29730
DP Coordinator Laura Hall
Languages English
T: +1 803 984 3558
W: www.rock-hill.k12.sc.us/Domain/33

Southeast Middle School

731 Horrell Hill Road, Hopkins SC 29061
MYP Coordinator Yolanda Daniels
Languages English
T: +1 803 695 5700
W: www.richlandone.org/Domain/43

Southside High School

6630 Frontage Rd, Greenville SC 29605
DP Coordinator Julie McGaha
Languages English
T: +1 864 355 8700
W: www.greenville.k12.sc.us/shs

Spartanburg Day School

1701 Skylyn Drive, Spartanburg SC 29307
PYP Coordinator Katie Clayton
Languages English
T: +1 864 582 8380
W: www.spartanburgdayschool.org

Sullivan Middle School

1825 Eden Terrace, Rock Hill SC 29730
MYP Coordinator Kallie Cromer
Languages English
T: +1 803 981 1450
W: www.rock-hill.k12.sc.us/Domain/29

Sumter High School

2580 McCray's Mill Road, School District 17, Sumter SC 29154-6098
DP Coordinator Marie Broadway
Languages English
T: +1 803 481 4480

Travelers Rest High School

301 North Main Street, Travelers Rest SC 29690
DP Coordinator Wendy Barnes
Languages English
T: +1 864 355 0000
W: www.greenville.k12.sc.us/trest

Williams Middle School

1119 North Irby Street, Florence SC 29501
MYP Coordinator Joe Anderson
Languages English
T: +1 843 664 8162
W: f1s.org/Domain/26

Wilson High School

1411 Old Marion Highway, Florence SC 29506
DP Coordinator Brian Howell
MYP Coordinator Brian Howell
Languages English
T: +1 843 664 8440
W: www.f1s.org/Wilson

Windsor Elementary School

9800 Dunbarton Dr, Columbia SC 29223
PYP Coordinator Jennifer Boone
Languages English
T: +1 803 736 8723
W: www.richland2.org/we

Woodmont High School

2831 West Georgia Road, Piedmont SC 29673
DP Coordinator Emily Styer
Languages English
T: +1 864 355 8600

Tennessee

Antioch High School

1900 Hobson Pike, Antioch TN 37013
CP Coordinator Andrew Price
DP Coordinator Tosha Mannings
Languages English
T: +1 615 641 5400
W: schools.mnps.org/antioch-high-school

Avery Trace Middle School

230 Raider Drive, Cookeville TN 38501
MYP Coordinator Jessica Etheredge
Languages English
T: +1 931 520 2200

Balmoral Ridgeway Elementary

5905 Grosvenor Avenue, Memphis TN 38119
PYP Coordinator Lanna Byrd
Languages English
T: +1 901 416 2128
W: schools.scsk12.org/balmoralridgeway-es

Bearden Middle School

1000 Francis Road, Knoxville TN 37909
MYP Coordinator Shannon Siebe
Languages English
T: +1 865 539 7839
W: www.knoxschools.org/beardenms

Bellevue Middle School

655 Colice Jeanne Road, Nashville TN 37221
MYP Coordinator Catie Dougherty
Languages English
T: +1 615 662 3000
W: schools.mnps.org/bellevue-middle-prep

Bolton High School

7323 Brunswick Road, Arlington TN 38002
DP Coordinator Ebony Johnson
Languages English
T: +1 901 873 8150
W: www.boltonhigh.org

Cookeville High School

1 Cavalier Drive, Cookeville TN 38506
DP Coordinator Emily Chambers
Languages English
T: +1 931 520 2287
W: www.cookevillecavaliers.com

Eakin Elementary School

2500 Fairfax Avenue, Nashville TN 37212
PYP Coordinator Kirsten Clark
Languages English
T: +1 615 298 8076
W: schools.mnps.org/eakin-elementary-school

East Nashville Magnet High School

110 Gallatin Ave., Nashville TN 37206
DP Coordinator Scott Wofford
MYP Coordinator Scott Wofford
Languages English

East Nashville Magnet Middle School

110 Gallatin Ave., Nashville TN 37206
MYP Coordinator Scott Wofford
Languages English, Spanish
T: +1 615 262 6670

Franklin High School

810 Hillsboro Road, Franklin TN 37064
DP Coordinator Ray Scheetz
MYP Coordinator Ray Scheetz
Languages English
T: +1 615 472 4468

Germantown High School

7653 Old Poplar Pike, Germantown TN 38138
DP Coordinator Melinda Keller
Languages English
T: +1 901 756 2350
W: www.germantownreddevils.org

Goodlettsville Middle School

1460 McGavock Pike, Nashville TN 37216
MYP Coordinator Ronald Wooding
Languages English
T: +1 615 227 1042
W: schools.mnps.org/goodlettsville-middle-prep

Hillsboro Comprehensive High School

3812 Hillsboro Road, Nashville TN 37215
CP Coordinator Sharon Humphrey
DP Coordinator Sharon Humphrey
MYP Coordinator Matthew King
Languages English
T: +1 615 298 8400

Hunters Lane High School

1150 Hunters Lane, Nashville TN 37207
DP Coordinator Sara Hoyal
MYP Coordinator Olivia Roller
Languages English
T: +1 615 860 1401
W: schools.mnps.org/hunters-lane-high-school

J T Moore Middle School

4425 Granny White Pike, Nashville TN 37204
MYP Coordinator Colin Hunt
Languages English
T: +1 615 298 8095
W: www.jtmoore.org

Julia Green Elementary School

3500 Hobbs Road, Nashville TN 37215
PYP Coordinator Sarah Parnell
Languages English
T: +1 615 298 8082
W: www.juliagreen.org

Lausanne Collegiate School

1381 West Massey Road, Memphis TN 38120
DP Coordinator Rocio Rodriguez del Rio
MYP Coordinator Michelle Spain
PYP Coordinator Erica McBride
Languages English
T: +1 901 474 1001
W: www.lausanneschool.com

Oak Forest Elementary

7440 Nonconnah View Cove, Memphis TN 38119
PYP Coordinator Timkia Bryant
Languages English
T: +1 901 416 2257
W: schools.scsk12.org/oakforest-es

Oakland High School

2225 Patriot Drive, Murfreesboro TN 37130
DP Coordinator Ann Borombozin
Languages English
T: +1 615 904 3780
W: ohs.rcschools.net

Ooltewah High School

6123 Mountain View Road, Ooltewah TN 37363
DP Coordinator Erica Hitchcox
Languages English
T: +1 423 498 6920
W: ohs.hcde.org

Ridgeway High School

2009 Ridgeway Road, Memphis TN 38119
DP Coordinator Amy Dorsey
Languages English
T: +1 901 416 8820
W: www.ridgewayhigh.org

Ridgeway Middle School

6333 Quince Road, Memphis TN 38119
MYP Coordinator Patrice Carter
Languages English
T: +1 901 416 1588
W: schools.scsk12.org/ridgeway-ms

Signal Mountain Middle/ High School

2650 Sam Powell Trail, Signal Mountain TN 37377
DP Coordinator Tara Tharp
MYP Coordinator Melissa Bouldin
Languages English
T: +1 423 886 0880
W: smmhs.hcde.org

West End Middle School

3529 West End Avenue, Nashville TN 37205
MYP Coordinator Elizabeth Seamon
Languages English
T: +1 615 298 8425
W: westendptso.org

West High School

3300 Sutherland Avenue, Knoxville TN 37919
CP Coordinator Valerie Schmidt-Gardner
DP Coordinator Valerie Schmidt-Gardner
MYP Coordinator Shannon Siebe
Languages English
T: +1 865 594 4477
W: www.knoxschools.org/wesths

Texas

Alcuin School

6144 Churchill Way, Dallas TX 75230
DP Coordinator Margaret Davis
MYP Coordinator Joanne Chatlos
Languages English
T: +1 972 239 1745
W: www.alcuinschool.org

Allen High School

300 Rivercrest Boulevard, Allen TX 75002
DP Coordinator Lauren Cammack
Languages English
T: +1 972 727 0400
W: www.allenisd.org/allenhs

Alonzo De Leon Middle School

4201 North 29th St, McAllen TX 78504
MYP Coordinator Kimberly Alaniz
Languages English
T: +1 956 632 8800
W: deleon.mcallenisd.org

Amarillo High School/AISD

4225 Danbury Drive, Amarillo TX 79109
DP Coordinator Phillip Miller
Languages English
T: +1 806 326 2000

Anderson Mill Elementary School

10610 Salt Mill Hollow, Austin TX 78750
PYP Coordinator Jennifer Foster
Languages English
T: +1 512 428 3700
W: andersonmill.roundrockisd.org

Andress High School

5400 Sun Valley Dr., El Paso TX 79924
DP Coordinator Frances Morales
Languages English
T: +1 915 236 4000
W: www.episd.org/andress

Arlington High School

818 W Park Row, Arlington TX 76013
DP Coordinator Christine B. Fougerousse
Languages English
T: +1 682 867 8100

Arthur Kramer Elementary IB World School

7131 Midbury Drive, Dallas TX 75230
PYP Coordinator Kim West
Languages English
T: +1 972 794 8300
W: www.dallasisd.org/domain/540

Austin Eco Bilingual School (Austin EBS) USA

8707 Mountain Crest Dr, Austin TX 78735
PYP Coordinator Adriana Rodriguez
Languages English
T: +1 512 299 5731
W: www.austinbilingualschool.com

Austin Elementary

700 E Austin Ave, Harlingen TX 78550
PYP Coordinator Hortencia Juarez
Languages English, Spanish
T: +1 956 427 3060
W: hcisd-austin.edlioschool.com

Baker Middle School

3445 Pecan Street, Corpus Christi TX 78411
MYP Coordinator Marlo Bazan
Languages English
T: +1 361 878 4600
W: baker.ccisd.us

Barbara Bush Middle School

515 Cowboys Parkway, Irving TX 75063
MYP Coordinator Christina Flatt
Languages English
T: +1 972 968 3700
W: bush.cfbisd.edu

Bellaire High School

5100 Maple Street, Houston ISD, Bellaire TX 77401
DP Coordinator Ann Linsley
Languages English
T: +1 713 295 3704
W: www.houstonisd.org/bellairehigh

Benjamin Franklin International Exploratory Academy

6920 Meadow Road, Dallas TX 75230
MYP Coordinator Calli Davis
Languages English
T: +1 972 502 7100
W: www.dallasisd.org/franklin

Berta Palacios Elementary

801 E. Thomas Road, Pharr TX 78577
PYP Coordinator Ashely Clark
Languages English, Spanish
T: +1 956 354 2930
W: www.psjaisd.us/palacios

Bluebonnet Trail Elementary

11316 Farmhaven Road, Austin TX 78754
PYP Coordinator Callista Janosky
Languages English, Spanish
T: +1 512 278 4125
W: www.manorisd.net/domain/9

Borman Elementary School

1201 Parvin St., Denton TX 76205
PYP Coordinator Heather Thornburg
Languages English
T: +1 940 369 2500
W: www.dentonisd.org/bormanes

Briargrove Elementary School

6145 San Felipe, Houston TX 77057
PYP Coordinator Quinetta Sampy
Languages English, Spanish
T: +1 713 917 3600
W: www.houstonisd.org/briargrovees

Briarmeadow Charter School

3601 Dunvale Rd, Houston TX 77063-5707
PYP Coordinator Saundra Mouton
Languages English
T: +1 713 458 5500
W: www.houstonisd.org/briarmeadow

Bright Academy

7600 Woodstream Drive, Frisco TX 75034
PYP Coordinator Christina McLain
Languages English, Spanish
T: +1 469 633 2700

Brighter Horizons Academy

3145 Medical Plaza Dr., Garland TX 75044
PYP Coordinator Nadia Elatrash
Languages English
T: +1 972 675 2062
W: www.bhaprep.org

Briscoe Elementary School

2015 S. Flores St., San Antonio TX 78204
PYP Coordinator Cari Richter
Languages English, Spanish
T: +1 210 228 3305
W: schools.saisd.net/page/112.homepage

British International School of Houston

2203 North Westgreen Boulevard, Katy TX 77449
CP Coordinator D Lifton
DP Coordinator Ashley Thorpe
Languages English
T: +1 713 290 9025
W: www.bishouston.org

Bryan High School

3450 Campus Drive, Bryan TX 77802
DP Coordinator Sarah Patterson
Languages English
T: +1 979 209 2400
W: bryanhs.bryanisd.org

Caldwell Heights Elementary

4010 Eagles Nest, Round Rock TX 78665
PYP Coordinator Macy Lane
Languages English
T: +1 512 428 7300
W: caldwellheights.roundrockisd.org

Calhoun Middle School

709 Congress Street, Denton TX 76201
MYP Coordinator Chris Slocum
Languages English
T: +1 940 369 2400
W: www.dentonisd.org/calhounms

CC Mason Elementary

1501 N. Lakeline Blvd, Cedar Park TX 78613
PYP Coordinator Geeta Erickson
Languages English
T: +1 512 570 5500
W: mason.leanderisd.org

Cesar E. Chavez High School

8501 Howard Dr., Houston TX 77017
CP Coordinator Jason Busby
DP Coordinator Christina Coleman
Languages English
T: +1 713 495 6950
W: www.houstonisd.org/chavez

Chandler Oaks Elementary

3800 Stone Oak Drive, Round Rock TX 78681
PYP Coordinator Elizabeth Hall
Languages English
T: +1 512 704 0400
W: chandleroaks.roundrockisd.org

Coppell High School

185 West Parkway Blvd, Coppell TX 75019
DP Coordinator Michael Brock
Languages English
T: +1 214 496 6100
W: www.coppellisd.com/chs

Coronado High School, El Paso

100 Champions Place, El Paso TX 79912
DP Coordinator Leslie Harris
Languages English
T: +1 915 236 2000
W: www.episd.org/coronado

Coronado High School, Lubbock

4910 29th Drive, Lubbock TX 79410
CP Coordinator Dana Gustafson
Languages English
T: +1 806 219 1100
W: www.lubbockisd.org/chs

Cunae International School LLC

5655 Creekside Forest Drive, Spring TX 77389
DP Coordinator Maria Jose Ferrer Garay
PYP Coordinator Maria Jose Ferrer Garay
Languages English
T: +1 281 516 3770
W: www.doortomyschool.com

Dallas International School

17811 Waterview Pkwy, Dallas TX 75252
DP Coordinator Zahra Boudaoui
Languages English
T: +1 469 250 0001
W: www.dallasinternationalschool.org

Daniel Ortiz Middle School

6767 Telephone Road, Houston TX 77061-2056
MYP Coordinator Tina Garcia
Languages English
T: +1 713 845 5650
W: www.houstonisd.org/page/79424

Denton High School

1007 Fulton Street, Denton TX 76201
DP Coordinator Beth Hughes
MYP Coordinator Crystal Sullivan
Languages English
T: +1 940 369 2000
W: www.dentonisd.org/dentonhs

Dr. Pablo Perez Elementary School

7801 N. Main Street, Mc Allen TX 78504
PYP Coordinator Marla Skretta
Languages English
T: +1 956 971 1125
W: perez.mcallenisd.org

Durham Elementary School

4803 Brinkman Street, Houston TX 77018
PYP Coordinator Anne Baumgarten
Languages English, Spanish
T: +1 713 613 2527
W: www.houstonisd.org/Domain/12141

Dwight D Eisenhower High School

7922 Antoine Drive, Houston TX 77088
DP Coordinator Mary Williams
MYP Coordinator Mary Williams
Languages English
T: +1 281 878 0900

E A Murchison Middle School

3700 North Hills Drive, Austin TX 78731
MYP Coordinator Jana Tucker
Languages English
T: +1 512 414 3254

Edgar Allan Poe Elementary School

5100 Hazard Street, Houston TX 77098
PYP Coordinator Shara Tsai
Languages English
T: +1 713 535 3780
W: www.houstonisd.org/poees

Eisenhower Ninth Grade School

3550 W Gulf Bank Road, Houston TX 77088
MYP Coordinator Shameka Garner
Languages English
T: +1 281 878 7700
W: eisenhower9.aldineisd.org

El Dorado High School

12401 Edgemere, El Paso TX 79938
DP Coordinator Rosa Harding
Languages English
T: +1 915 937 3200
W: www.sisd.net/eldoradohs

Esprit International School

4890 W Panther Creek Dr, The Woodlands TX 77381
PYP Coordinator Rosemary Brumbelow
Languages English
T: +1 281 298 9200
W: www.espritinternationalschool.com

Fondren Middle School

6333 South Braeswood Blvd, Houston TX 77096
MYP Coordinator Melodye Montgomery
Languages English
T: +1 713 778 3360
W: www.houstonisd.org/fondrenms

Durham Elementary School

Forest Park Middle School

1644 North Eastman Road, Longview TX 75601
MYP Coordinator Sonya Taylor
Languages English
T: +1 903 446 2510
W: www.lisd.org/forestpark/fpjump.htm

Francisca Alvarez Elementary School

2606 Gumwood Avenue, McAllen TX 78501
PYP Coordinator Marisela Chapa
Languages English
T: +1 956 971 4471
W: alvarez.mcallenisd.org

Frisco High School

6401 Parkwood Blvd, Frisco TX 75034
DP Coordinator Jenna Gates
Languages English

Garland High School

310 S. Garland Ave., Garland TX 75040
DP Coordinator Timothy Schmidt
Languages English
T: +1 972 494 8492
W: www.garlandisdschools.net/ghs

Geneva Heights Elementary School

2911 Delmar Avenue, Dallas TX 75206
PYP Coordinator Rhonda Barnwell
Languages English
T: +1 972 749 7400
W: www.dallasisd.org/relee

Graciela Garcia Elementary School

1002 W. Juan Balli Road, Pharr TX 78577
PYP Coordinator Fernanda Sanchez
Languages English, Spanish
T: +1 956 354 2790
W: www.psjaisd.us/garcia

Grandview Hills Elementary

12024 Vista Parke Drive, Austin TX 78726
PYP Coordinator Erin Carroll
Languages English
T: +1 512 434 7266

Grisham Middle School

10805 School House Lane, Austin TX 78750
MYP Coordinator Lei Lani De Santiago
Languages English
T: +1 512 428 2650
W: grisham.roundrockisd.org

Harry Stone Montessori Academy

4747 Veterans Dr., Dallas TX 75216
MYP Coordinator Reneice Reed
Languages English
T: +1 972 794 3400
W: www.dallasisd.org/stone

Harvard Elementary School

810 Harvard Street, Houston TX 77007-1607
PYP Coordinator Jessica Berry
Languages English
T: +1 713 867 5210
W: www.houstonisd.org/harvardes

Headwaters School

801 Rio Grande, Austin TX 78701
DP Coordinator Paul Cronin
Languages English
T: +1 512 480 8142
W: headwaters.org

Heights High School

413 East 13th Street, Houston TX 77008-7021
CP Coordinator Cristina Bagos
DP Coordinator Anne Nelson
MYP Coordinator Natalie Martinez
Languages English
T: +1 713 865 4400
W: www.houstonisd.org/heights

Hernandez Middle School

1901 Sunrise Road, Round Rock TX 78664
MYP Coordinator Emilee Hinegardner
Languages English
T: +1 512 424 8800
W: hernandez.roundrockisd.org

Herrera Elementary School

525 Bennington, Houston 77511
PYP Coordinator Melody Vizi
Languages English, Spanish
T: +1 713 696 2800
W: www.houstonisd.org/herreraelem

Hillcrest High School

9924 Hillcrest Road, Dallas TX 75230
DP Coordinator Jeri Smith
Languages English
T: +1 972 502 6800
W: www.dallasisd.org/hillcrest

Hirschi High School

3106 Borton Lane, Wichita Falls TX 76306-6952
DP Coordinator Linda Fain
Languages English
T: +1 940 716 2800
W: www.wfisd.net/hirschi

Huffman Elementary School

5510 Channel Isle Drive, Plano TX 75093
PYP Coordinator Callie Anthony
Languages English, Spanish
T: +1 469 752 1900
W: www.pisd.edu/huffman

Humble High School

1700 Wilson Road, Humble TX 77338
DP Coordinator Sherrill Rene Lane
Languages English
T: +1 281 641 8129
W: www.humbleisd.net/hhs

Hutchinson Middle School

3102 Canton Ave, Lubbock TX 79410
MYP Coordinator Toby Klameth
Languages English
T: +1 806 219 3800
W: www.lubbockisd.org/hutchinson

IDEA College Prep Brownsville

4395 Paredes Line Road, Brownsville TX 78526
DP Coordinator Norma Jimenez Cerda
T: +1 956 832 5150
W: ideapublicschools.org/our-schools/idea-brownsville

IDEA College Preparatory McAllen

201 N. Bentsen Rd., McAllen TX 78501
DP Coordinator Leticia Silva
Languages English
T: +1 956 429 4100
W: ideapublicschools.org/our-schools/idea-mcallen

IDEA College Preparatory South Flores

6919 South Flores Street, San Antonio TX 78221
DP Coordinator Caitlin McCloskey
Languages English, Spanish
T: +1 210 239 4150
W: www.ideapublicschools.org/our-schools/idea-south-flores

IDEA Donna

401 S. 1st St., Donna TX 78537
DP Coordinator Dikla Medina
Languages English
T: +1 956 464 0203
W: www.ideapublicschools.org/our-schools/idea-donna

IDEA Frontier

2800 S. Dakota Ave, Brownsville TX 78521
DP Coordinator Hermelinda Kaney
Languages English
T: +1 956 541 2002
W: ideapublicschools.org/our-schools/idea-frontier

Imagine International Academy of North Texas

2860 Virginia Parkway, McKinney TX 75071
DP Coordinator Hannah Nayakanti
MYP Coordinator Pamela Hinterscher
PYP Coordinator Kim Wood
Languages English
T: +1 214 491 1500
W: www.imaginenorthtexas.org

International School of Texas

4402 Hudson Bend, Austin TX 78734
PYP Coordinator Ashley Swindle
Languages English
T: +1 512 351 3403
W: www.internationalschooloftexas.com

J. L. Everhart Elementary

2919 Tryon Rd, Longview TX 75602
PYP Coordinator Samantha Chastain
Languages English
T: +1 903 758 5622
W: w3.lisd.org/our-schools/everhart-elementary

J.L. Long Middle School

6116 Reiger Avenue, Dallas TX 75214
MYP Coordinator Kymberle Allen
Languages English
T: +1 972 502 4700
W: www.dallasisd.org/Long

Jack Yates High School

3650 Alabama St., Houston TX 77004
DP Coordinator April LaSalle
Languages English
T: +1 713 748 5400
W: www.houstonisd.org/yates

James Bowie High School

2101 Highbank Drive, Arlington TX 76018
DP Coordinator Amy Hayes
Languages English
T: +1 682 867 4500

James S Hogg Middle School

1100 Merrill Street, Houston TX 77009
MYP Coordinator Lynn Graham
Languages English
T: +1 713 802 4700
W: www.houstonisd.org/hogg

Joel C. Harris Middle School

325 Pruitt Ave., San Antonio TX 78204
MYP Coordinator Amanda McKay
Languages English, Spanish
T: +1 210 228 1220
W: schools.saisd.net/page/047.homepage

Judson High School

9142 FM Road 78, Converse TX 78109
DP Coordinator Alexis Mcjilton
Languages English
T: +1 210 945 1100
W: www.judsonisd.org/Domain/36

Killeen High School

500 N. 38th Street, Killeen TX 76543-4161
DP Coordinator Keina Cook
Languages English
T: +1 254 336 7208
W: tx02205734.schoolwires.net/Page/99

KIPP University Prep

4343 W. Commerce Street, San Antonio TX 78237
DP Coordinator Jonathan Villegas-Caine
Languages English
T: +1 210 290 8720
W: kipptexas.org/school/kipp-university-prep

Klein Oak High School

22603 Northcrest Drive, Spring TX 77389
DP Coordinator Elizabeth Bowling
Languages English, Spanish
T: +1 834 484 5000

Kujawa EC/PK/K School

7111 Fallbrook Dr., Houston TX 77086
PYP Coordinator Jodi Angen
Languages English
T: +1 281 878 1514
W: kujawaec.aldineisd.org

L C Anderson High School

8403 Mesa Drive, Austin TX 78759
DP Coordinator Jill Spencer
Languages English
T: +1 512 414 2538
W: www.andersononline.org

L.D. Bell High School

1601 Brown Trail, Hurst TX 76054
DP Coordinator Nancy Shane
Languages English
T: +1 817 282 2551
W: www.hebisd.edu/Domain/33

Lamar Academy

1009 N 10th Street, McAllen TX 78501
DP Coordinator Rachelle Downey
MYP Coordinator Rachelle Downey
Languages English
T: +1 956 632 3222
W: lamar.mcallenisd.org

Lamar High School

3325 Westheimer Road, Houston TX 77098-1003
CP Coordinator David Munoz
DP Coordinator Suzanne Acord
MYP Coordinator Dennis Gillespie
Languages English
T: +1 713 522 5960
W: www.houstonisd.org/lamarhs

Lamar High School

1400 Lamar Blvd West, Arlington TX 76012
DP Coordinator Kathy Hitt
Languages English
T: +1 682 867 8300

Lanier Middle School

2600 Woodhead, Houston TX 77098-1534
MYP Coordinator Kathleen Rhymes
Languages English
T: +1 713 942 1900
W: www.houstonisd.org/domain/3518

Las Colinas Elementary

2200 Kinwest Parkway, Irving TX 75063
PYP Coordinator Kristen Schroder
Languages English
T: +1 972 968 2200
W: lascolinas.cfbisd.edu

Leander High School

3301 South Bagdad Road, Leander TX 78641
DP Coordinator Shawn Doctor
Languages English
T: +1 512 435 8000

Liberty Middle School

1212 S Fir Street, Pharr TX 78577
MYP Coordinator Emma Saenz
Languages English
T: +1 956 354 2610
W: liberty.psjaisd.us

Lincoln Middle School

500 Mulberry Ave., El Paso TX 79932
MYP Coordinator Karen Reid
Languages English, Spanish
T: +1 915 236 3400
W: www.episd.org/lincoln

Longfellow Middle School

1130 E Sunshine Dr, San Antonio TX 78228
MYP Coordinator Jacqueline Carter
Languages English, Spanish
T: +1 210 438 6520
W: schools.saisd.net/page/050.homepage

Longview High School

PO Box 3268, Longview TX 75606
DP Coordinator Beverly Coker
Languages English
T: +1 903 663 1301
W: www.lisd.org/lhs

Lubbock High School

2004 19th Street, Lubbock TX 79401
DP Coordinator Erin Castle
Languages English
T: +1 806 766 1444
W: www.lubbockisd.org/lhs

Luther Burbank High School

1002 Edwards Street, San Antonio TX 78204
DP Coordinator Angela Meyer
MYP Coordinator Tate Jaeger
Languages English
T: +1 210 532 4241 EXT:103

Lycée International de Houston

15950 Park Row, Houston TX 77084
DP Coordinator Bruce Kirsch
Languages English, French
T: +1 832 474 1013
W: www.lihouston.org

Magellan International School

7938 Great Northern Boulevard, Austin TX 78757
MYP Coordinator Nicolas Puga
PYP Coordinator Julieta Carrillo
Languages English, Spanish
T: +1 512 782 2327
W: www.magellanschool.org

Magnolia High School

14350 FM 1488, Magnolia TX 77354
DP Coordinator Derek Parsons
Languages English
T: +1 281 356 3572
W: mhs.magnoliaisd.org

Magnolia West High School

42202 FM 1774, Magnolia TX 77354-0426
DP Coordinator Jeremy Day
Languages English
T: +1 281 252 2550
W: mwhs.magnoliaisd.org

Manara Leadership Academy

8001 Jetstar Dr #100, Irving TX 75063
DP Coordinator Laura Bectarte
Languages English
T: +1 972 304 1155

Marcellus Elliot Foster Elementary

3919 Ward Street, Houston TX 77021
PYP Coordinator D'Arnisha Allen
Languages English
T: +1 713 746 8260
W: www.houstonisd.org/page/6956

Marin B. Fenwick Academy

1930 Waverly Ave., San Antonio TX 78228
PYP Coordinator Christina Sims
Languages English, Spanish
T: +1 210 438 6540
W: schools.saisd.net/page/123.homepage

Mark Twain Elementary School

7500 Braes Blvd, Houston TX 77025
PYP Coordinator Kathleen Blakeslee
Languages English
T: +1 713 295 5230

Mary Huppertz Elementary School

247 Bangor Drive, San Antonio TX 78228
PYP Coordinator Veronika Gutierrez
Languages English, Spanish
T: +1 210 438 6580
W: schools.saisd.net/page/139.homepage

Massey Ranch Elementary School

3900 Manvel Road, Pearland TX 77584
PYP Coordinator Jennifer Hoot
Languages English
T: +1 281 727 1700
W: www.pearlandisd.org/masseyranch

Meridian School

2555 North IH-35, Round Rock TX 78664
DP Coordinator Stela Holcombe
MYP Coordinator Kristen Machczynski
PYP Coordinator Leah Lieurance
Languages English
T: +1 512 660 5232
W: www.mwschool.org

Morehead Middle School

5625 Confetti Dr., El Paso TX 79912
MYP Coordinator Francisco Vasquez
Languages English, Spanish
T: +1 915 236 3500
W: morehead.episd.org

Mountainview Elementary School

5901 Bishop Drive, Waco TX 76710
PYP Coordinator Ashlee Brewster
Languages English
T: +1 254 772 2520
W: www.wacoisd.org/mountainview

Newton Rayzor Elementary School

1400 Malone Street, Denton TX 76201
PYP Coordinator Linda Marquez-Gavilanes
Languages English
T: +1 940 369 3700
W: www.dentonisd.org/Domain/4079

Nolan Richardson Middle School

11350 Loma Franklin Dr., El Paso TX 79934
MYP Coordinator Deena Roberts
Languages English, Spanish
T: +1 915 236 6650
W: www.episd.org/richardson

Northline Elementary

821 E Witcher Ln, Houston TX 77076-4818
PYP Coordinator Jenn Martinez
Languages English
T: +1 713 696 2890
W: www.houstonisd.org/northline

Odessa High School

1301 Dotsy Ave., Odessa TX 79763
DP Coordinator Melissa Roth
Languages English
T: +1 432 456 0029
W: www.ectorcountyisd.org/Domain/40

Patterson Dual Language Literature Magnet School

5302 Allendale Road, Houston TX 77017-6214
PYP Coordinator Luis Saenz
Languages English, Spanish
T: +1 713 943 5750
W: www.houstonisd.org/pattersones

Pinkerton Elementary

260 Southwestern Blvd., Coppell TX 75019
PYP Coordinator Marnie Ward
Languages English
T: +1 214 496 6800
W: www.coppellisd.com/pinkerton

Plano East Senior High School

3000 Los Rios Boulevard, Plano TX 75074
DP Coordinator Karen Stanton
Languages English
T: +1 469 752 9000
W: www.pisd.edu/pesh

Presidential Meadows Elementary

13252 George Bush Street, Manor TX 78653
PYP Coordinator Rebecca Garcia
Languages English, Spanish
T: +1 512 278 4225
W: pme.manorisd.net

Preston Hollow Elementary School

6423 Walnut Hill Lane, Dallas TX 75230
PYP Coordinator Araceli Hernandez
Languages English
T: +1 972 794 8500
W: www.dallasisd.org/prestonhollow

R E Good Elementary School

1012 Study Lane, Carrollton TX 75006
PYP Coordinator Kristen Schroder
Languages English
T: +1 972 968 1900
W: cfbisd.edu/schools/elementary-schools/good-elementary

Ramirez Elementary School

702 Ave. T, Lubbock TX 79401
PYP Coordinator Amber Faske
Languages English
T: +1 806 219 6500
W: ramirez.lubbockisd.org

Ranchview High School

8401 E Valley Ranch Parkway, Irving TX 75063
DP Coordinator Leslie Yager
MYP Coordinator Leslie Yager
Languages English
T: +1 972 968 5000
W: ranchview.cfbisd.edu

River Oaks Elementary School

2008 Kirby Drive, Houston TX 77019
PYP Coordinator Bryant Johnson
Languages English
T: +1 713 942 1460
W: www.houstonisd.org/riveroakseib

Roberts Elementary School

6000 Greenbriar Drive, Houston TX 77030
PYP Coordinator Kristina Tran
Languages English
T: +1 713 295 5272
W: www.houstonisd.org/robertselem

Rockwall High School

901 Yellowjacket Lane, Rockwall TX 75087
DP Coordinator Michelle Ghormley
Languages English
T: +1 972 771 7339
W: www.rockwallisd.com/Domain/8

Rockwall-Heath High School

801 Laurence Drive, Heath TX 75032
DP Coordinator Gretchen Kimpel
Languages English
T: +1 972 772 2474
W: www.rockwallisd.com/Domain/9

Roscoe Wilson Elementary School

2807 25th Street, Lubbock TX 79410
PYP Coordinator Amber Faske
Languages English
T: +1 806 766 0922
W: rwilson.lubbockisd.org

Sam Houston Elementary Dual Language Academy

301 E Taft Street, Harlingen TX 78550
PYP Coordinator Hortencia Juarez
Languages English, Spanish
T: +1 956 427 3110
W: hcisd-houston.edlioschool.com

Sam Houston High School

2000 Sam Houston Drive, Arlington TX 76014
DP Coordinator Poppy Moore
Languages English
T: +1 682 867 8200

Samuel Clemens High School

1001 Elbel Road, Schertz TX 78154
DP Coordinator Lauren Rollins
Languages English
T: +1 210 945 6100
W: www.scuc.txed.net/Domain/2065

Sci-Tech High School

10704 Bradshaw Road, Austin TX 78747
DP Coordinator Derrick Stewart
Languages English
T: +1 512 220 9104
W: waysideschools.org/stp

Scott Elementary School

2301 West Ave. P, Temple TX 76504
PYP Coordinator Chelsea Molton
Languages English
T: +1 254 215 6222
W: scott.tisd.org

Sharpstown International School

8330 Triola Lane, Houston TX 77036-6310
DP Coordinator Alexander Brahm
MYP Coordinator Robin Bissell
Languages English, Spanish
T: +1 713 778 3440
W: www.houstonisd.org/sis

Shotwell Middle School

6515 Trail Valley Way, Houston TX 77086
MYP Coordinator Peggy Tomme
Languages English
T: +1 281 878 0960
W: shotwellms.aldineisd.org

South Texas Business Education & Technology Academy

510 S. Sugar Road, Edinburg TX 78539
DP Coordinator Erika Sarabia
Languages English
T: +1 956 383 1684

Spicewood Elementary School

11601 Olson Drive, Austin TX 78750
PYP Coordinator Jessica Oates
Languages English
T: +1 512 428 3600
W: spicewood.roundrockisd.org

Springwoods Village Middle School

1120 Crossgate Blvd., Spring TX 77373
MYP Coordinator Melissa Lynch
Languages English, Spanish
T: +1 281 891 8100
W: www.springisd.org/springwoods

St Anthony Academy

3732 Myrtle Street, Dallas TX 75215
PYP Coordinator Kimberly Stephens
Languages English
T: +1 214 421 3645
W: www.stanthonydallas.org

Stony Point High School

1801 Tiger Trail, Round Rock TX 78664
DP Coordinator Andi Brosché
Languages English
T: +1 512 428 7000
W: stonypoint.roundrockisd.org

Sylvan Rodriguez Elementary

5858 Chimney Rock, Houston TX 77081
PYP Coordinator Minerva Gonzalez
Languages English
T: +1 713 295 3870
W: www.houstonisd.org/rodriguezes

Tanglewood Middle School

5215 San Felipe, Houston TX 77056-3605
MYP Coordinator Tal Gribbins
Languages English
T: +1 713 625 1411
W: www.houstonisd.org/grady

Temple High School

415 North 31st Street, Temple TX 76504
DP Coordinator Kaleigh Verett
Languages English
T: +1 254 215 7000
W: ths.tisd.org

The Awty International School

7455 Awty School Lane, Houston TX 77055-7222
DP Coordinator Isabel Van Dyck
Languages English
T: +1 713 686 4850
W: www.awty.org

The Post Oak School

4600 Bissonnet Street, Bellaire TX 77401
DP Coordinator James Quillin
Languages English
T: +1 713 661 6688
W: www.postoakschool.org

The School at St. George Place

5430 Hidalgo St., Houston TX 77056
PYP Coordinator Megan King
Languages English
T: +1 713 625 1499
W: www.houstonisd.org/stgeorge

THE VILLAGE SCHOOL

13051 Whittington Drive, Houston TX 77077
DP Coordinator Kerri Peters
Languages English
T: +1 281 496 7900
E: admissions@thevillageschool.com
W: www.thevillageschool.com

See full details on page 551

The Westwood School

14340 Proton Road, Dallas TX 75244
DP Coordinator Gail Macalik
Languages English
T: +1 972 239 8598
W: www.westwoodschool.org

The Woodlands Preparatory School

27440 Kuykendahl Road, Tomball TX 77375
DP Coordinator Dalba Castello
MYP Coordinator Dalba Castello
PYP Coordinator Oscar Lopez
Languages English
T: +1 281 516 0600
W: www.woodlandsprep.org

Theodore Roosevelt Elementary School

4801 S 26th St, McAllen TX 78503
PYP Coordinator Christian A. Trevino
Languages English, Spanish
T: +1 956 971 4424
W: roosevelt.mcallenisd.org

Thomas Jefferson High School

723 Donaldson Ave., San Antonio TX 78201
DP Coordinator Yareli Melendez
MYP Coordinator Jennifer Love
Languages English, Spanish
T: +1 210 438 6570
W: schools.saisd.net/page/007.homepage

Travis Science Academy

1551 S. 25th Street, Temple TX 76504
MYP Coordinator Kathy Cook
Languages English
T: +1 254 215 6300
W: travis.tisd.org

Trinity High School

500 North Industrial, Euless TX 76039
DP Coordinator William Wells
Languages English
T: +1 817 571 0271
W: www.hebisd.edu/Domain/34

Uplift Atlas Preparatory

4600 Bryan Street, Dallas TX 75204
DP Coordinator Highland Turby
MYP Coordinator Sarah Boykins
PYP Coordinator Markie Leftwich
Languages English
T: +1 214 276 0879
W: www.uplifteducation.org/domain/322

Uplift Grand Preparatory

300 E Church Street, Grand Prairie TX 75050
DP Coordinator Grace Kirkland
MYP Coordinator Elizabeth Coughenour
PYP Coordinator Maria del Carmen Maciel
Languages English, Spanish
T: +1 972 854 0600
W: www.uplifteducation.org/domain/1994

Uplift Hampton Preparatory

8915 S. Hampton Road, Dallas TX 75232
DP Coordinator Shaun Thompson
MYP Coordinator Anita Scott
PYP Coordinator Brittany Murrell
Languages English
T: +1 972 421 1982
W: www.uplifteducation.org/domain/47

Uplift Heights Preparatory

2650 Canada Drive, Dallas TX 75212
DP Coordinator Chelsea Rink
MYP Coordinator Naima Blakes
PYP Coordinator Rachel McCann
Languages English
T: +1 214 442 7094
W: www.uplifteducation.org/domain/729

Uplift Infinity Preparatory

1401 S. MacArthur Street, Irving TX 75060
DP Coordinator Jesus Sesma
MYP Coordinator Christine Massieh
PYP Coordinator Chataqua Mangum
Languages English
T: +1 469 621 9200
W: www.uplifteducation.org/domain/884

Uplift Luna Preparatory

2020 N. Lamar Street, Dallas TX 75202
DP Coordinator Benjamin Higgins
MYP Coordinator Emily Simmons
PYP Coordinator Lucy Gutierrez
Languages English
T: +1 214 442 7882
W: www.uplifteducation.org/domain/787

Uplift Meridian Preparatory

1801 South Beach Street, Fort Worth TX 76105
PYP Coordinator Ann Wilson
Languages English
T: +1 817 288 1700
W: www.uplifteducation.org/domain/932

Uplift Mighty Preparatory

3700 Mighty Mite Drive, Fort Worth TX 76105
DP Coordinator Sellesse Booth
MYP Coordinator Yvonne Moore
PYP Coordinator Emily Deaso
Languages English
T: +1 817 288 3800
W: www.uplifteducation.org/domain/930

Uplift North Hills Preparatory

606 East Royal Lane, Irving TX 75039
DP Coordinator Katherine Biela
MYP Coordinator Nicolau Pereira
PYP Coordinator Julie Hills
Languages English
T: +1 972 501 0645
W: www.uplifteducation.org/domain/147

Uplift Pinnacle Preparatory

2510 South Vernon Ave, Dallas TX 75224
PYP Coordinator Octavia Silas
Languages English
T: +1 21 444 26100
W: www.uplifteducation.org/domain/841

Uplift Summit International Preparatory

1305 North Center Street, Arlington TX 76011
DP Coordinator Tobias Rather
MYP Coordinator Tamara Phillips
PYP Coordinator Danielle Erbert
Languages English
T: +1 817 287 5121
W: www.uplifteducation.org/domain/449

Uplift Triumph Preparatory

9411 Hargrove Drive, Dallas TX 75220
PYP Coordinator Sarah Santoyo
Languages English, Spanish
T: +1 972 590 5100
W: www.uplifteducation.org/domain/1427

Uplift Williams Preparatory

1750 Viceroy Drive, Dallas TX 75235
DP Coordinator Jessica Staggs
MYP Coordinator Joshua Hamlin
PYP Coordinator Yamid Barraza
Languages English
T: +1 214 276 0352
W: www.uplifteducation.org/domain/606

Uplift Wisdom High School

301 W Camp Wisdom Road, Dallas TX 75232
DP Coordinator Colin Davis
Languages English, Spanish
T: +1 214 453 6900
W: www.uplifteducation.org/domain/3380

Vandegrift High School

9500 McNeil Dr., Austin TX 78750
DP Coordinator Sherilyn Green
Languages English
T: +1 512 570 2300
W: vhs.leanderisd.org

W B Ray High School

1002 Texan Trail, Corpus Christi TX 78411
DP Coordinator Lorinda Hamilton
MYP Coordinator Lorinda Hamilton
Languages English
T: +1 361 878 7300
W: ray.ccisd.us

Westchester Academy for International Studies

901 Yorkchester, Houston TX 77079
CP Coordinator Sara Sebesta-Camano
DP Coordinator Jesse Tachiquin
MYP Coordinator Cheryl Wegscheid
Languages English
T: +1 713 251 1800
W: wais.springbranchisd.com

Western Hills High School

3600 Boston Avenue, Fort Worth TX 76133
DP Coordinator Jane Card
Languages English
T: +1 817 871 2000
W: www.fwisd.org/WesternHills

WESTLAKE ACADEMY

2600 J.T. Ottinger Road, Westlake TX 76262
DP Coordinator Dr. James Owen
MYP Coordinator Terri Watson
PYP Coordinator Alison Schneider
Languages English
T: +1 817 4905757
E: info@westlakeacademy.org
W: www.westlakeacademy.org
See full details on page 554

Westwood High School

12400 Mellow Meadow, Austin TX 78750
DP Coordinator Christin Key
Languages English
T: +1 512 464 4000
W: westwood.roundrockisd.org

William B. Lipscomb Elementary School

5801 Worth Street, Dallas TX 75214
PYP Coordinator Torrian Timms
Languages English
T: +1 972 794 7300
W: www.dallasisd.org/lipscomb

William Wharton K-8 Dual Language Academy

900 West Gray Street, Houston TX 77019
PYP Coordinator Patricia Selin
Languages English, Spanish
T: +1 713 535 3771
W: www.houstonisd.org/whartondla

Windsor Park Elementary School

4525 South Alameda Street, Corpus Christi TX 78412
PYP Coordinator Duvesa Sanchez
Languages English
T: +1 361 994 3664
W: windsorpark.ccisd.us

Woodlawn Academy

1717 W. Magnolia Ave, San Antonio TX 78201
MYP Coordinator Xochitl Gonzalez
PYP Coordinator Ana Femath
Languages English
T: +1 210 438 6560
W: schools.saisd.net/page/175.homepage

Woodlawn Hills Elementary School

110 W. Quill Drive, San Antonio TX 78228
PYP Coordinator Sharon Franco
Languages English, Spanish
T: +1 210 438 6565
W: schools.saisd.net/page/176.homepage

Woodrow Wilson High School

100 S Glasgow, Dallas TX 75214
DP Coordinator Kelly Renea Ritchie
Languages English
T: +1 972 502 4400
W: www.woodrowwildcats.org

Worthing Early College High School

9215 Scott Street, Houston TX 77051-3302
CP Coordinator Sheena Blain
Languages English
T: +1 713 733 3433
W: www.houstonisd.org/worthing

Utah

Bountiful High School

695 South Orchard Drive, Bountiful UT 84010
DP Coordinator Luisa (Vickie) Ludwig
Languages English
T: +1 801 402 3900
W: www.davis.k12.ut.us/Domain/7221

Channing Hall

13515 South 150 East, Draper UT 84020
MYP Coordinator Jane Kilby
PYP Coordinator Jane Kilby
Languages English
T: +1 801 572 2709
W: www.channinghall.org

Clearfield High School

931 South 1000 East, Clearfield UT 84015
DP Coordinator Connie Kearl
Languages English
T: +1 801 408 8200
W: www.davis.k12.ut.us/domain/7356

Hawthorn Academy

9062 S 2200 W, West Jordan UT 84088
PYP Coordinator Candalyn Mettmann
Languages English
T: +1 801 282 9066
W: www.hawthornacademy.org

Highland High School

2166 South 1700 East, Salt Lake City UT 84106
DP Coordinator Kyle Bracken
Languages English
T: +1 801 484 4343
W: highland.slcschools.org

Hillcrest High School

7350 South 900 East, Midvale UT 84047
CP Coordinator Lisa Veenstra
DP Coordinator John Olsen
Languages English
T: +1 801 256 5484

Midvale Middle School

7852 S Pioneer St, Midvale UT 84047
MYP Coordinator Shelley Allen
Languages English
T: +1 801 826 7300
W: www.canyonsdistrict.org/midvale-middle

Ogden High School

2828 Harrison Blvd, Ogden UT 84403
CP Coordinator Alexi Flint
DP Coordinator Alexi Flint
Languages English
T: +1 801 737 8700
W: ogdenhigh.ogdensd.org

Providence Hall Charter School

4557 West Patriot Ridge Drive, Herriman UT 84096
DP Coordinator Hannah Thompson
MYP Coordinator Ally Turley
PYP Coordinator Kimberly Andersen
Languages English
T: +1 801 727 8260
W: www.providencehall.com

Skyline High School

3251 East 3760 South, Salt Lake City UT 84109
DP Coordinator Kirsten Rector
Languages English
T: +1 385 646 5420
W: schools.graniteschools.org/skylinehigh

Walden School of Liberal Arts

4266 N University Avenue, Provo UT 84604
DP Coordinator Lara Candland
Languages English
T: +1 801 623 1388
W: www.waldenschool.us

Weber High School

430 West Weber High Drive, Pleasant View UT 84414
DP Coordinator Marcia Kloempken
Languages English
T: +1 801 476 3700
W: whs.wsd.net

West High School

241 North 300 West, Salt Lake City UT 84103
CP Coordinator Kelly Boren
DP Coordinator Kelly Boren
Languages English
T: +1 801 578 8500
W: west.slcschools.org

West Jordan High School

8136 South 2700 West, West Jordan UT 84088
DP Coordinator Chandler Bishop
Languages English
T: +1 801 256 5600
W: www.westjordanhigh.org

Vermont

Bridport Central School

3442 Vt Route 22a, Bridport VT 05734
PYP Coordinator C.Joy Dobson
Languages English
T: +1 802 758 2331
W: www.acsdvt.org/bridport

Cornwall School

112 School Road, Cornwall VT 05753
PYP Coordinator C.Joy Dobson
Languages English
T: +1 802 462 2463
W: www.acsdvt.org/cornwall

Long Trail School

1045 Kirby Hollow Road, Dorset VT 05251
DP Coordinator Kelley Swarthout
Languages English
T: +1 802 867 5717
W: www.longtrailschool.org

Mary Hogan Elementary School

201 Mary Hogan Drive, Middlebury VT 05753
PYP Coordinator C. Joy Dobson
Languages English
T: +1 802 388 4421
W: www.acsdvt.org/maryhogan

Middlebury Union High School

73 Charles Avenue, Middlebury VT 05753
DP Coordinator Cindy Atkins
MYP Coordinator Courtney Krahn
Languages English
T: +1 802 382 1500
W: www.acsdvt.org/muhs

Middlebury Union Middle School

48 Deerfield Lane, Middlebury VT 05753
MYP Coordinator Courtney Krahn
Languages English
T: +1 802 382 1600
W: www.acsdvt.org/mums

Ripton Elementary School

753 Lincoln Rd, Ripton VT 05766
PYP Coordinator C.Joy Dobson
Languages English
T: +1 802 388 2208
W: www.acsdvt.org/ripton

Salisbury Community School

286 Kelly Cross Road, Salisbury VT 05769
PYP Coordinator C. Joy Dobson
Languages English
T: +1 802 352 4291
W: www.acsdvt.org/salisbur

Sam Houston Math, Science, and Technology Center

9400 Irvington Blvd., Houston TX
MYP Coordinator Bryan White
Languages English, Spanish
T: +1 713 696 0200
W: www.houstonisd.org/Domain/648

Shoreham Elementary School

130 School Road, Shoreham VT 05770
PYP Coordinator C.Joy Dobson
Languages English
T: +1 802 897 7181
W: www.acsdvt.org/shoreham

The Dover School

9 Schoolhouse Road, East Dover VT 05341
PYP Coordinator Susan Neuman
Languages English
T: +1 802 464 5386
W: www.doverschool.net

Weybridge Elementary School

210 Quaker Village Road, Weybridge VT 05753
PYP Coordinator C.Joy Dobson
Languages English
T: +1 802 545 2113
W: www.acsdvt.org/weybridge

Virginia

Academy for Discovery at Lakewood

1701 Alsace Avenue, Norfolk VA 23509
MYP Coordinator Judy Gulledge
Languages English
T: +1 757 628 2477
W: www.npsk12.com/afdl

Annandale High School

4700 Medford Drive, Annandale VA 22003
DP Coordinator Linda Bradshaw
MYP Coordinator Jeniva Miller
Languages English
T: +1 703 642 4100
W: annandalehs.fcps.edu

Antietam Elementary School

12000 Antietam Rd, Woodbridge VA 22192
PYP Coordinator Melissa Bloomrose
Languages English
T: +1 703 497 7619

IB AMERICAS

Atlee High School

9414 Atlee Station Road, Mechanicsville VA 23116
DP Coordinator Wendy Edelman
Languages English
T: +1 804 723 2100

Belvedere Elementary School

6540 Columbia Pike, Falls Church VA 22101
PYP Coordinator Ellen Rogers
Languages English
T: +1 703 916 6800
W: belvederees.fcps.edu

Brooke Point High School

1700 Courthouse Road, Stafford VA 22554
DP Coordinator Meghan Stone
Languages English
T: +1 540 658 6080
W: www.staffordschools.net/BP

Buckland Mills Elementary School

10511 Wharfdale Place, Gainesville VA 20155
PYP Coordinator Amy Hardt
Languages English
T: +1 703 530 1560
W: bucklandmillses.pwcs.edu

Chimborazo Elementary School

3000 East Marshall Street, Richmond VA 23223
PYP Coordinator Andrea Stewart
Languages English
T: +1 804 780 8392
W: web.richmond.k12.va.us/ces/Home.aspx

Clarke County High School

627 Mosby Blvd, Berryville VA 22611
DP Coordinator Thom Potts
Languages English
T: +1 540 955 6130
W: cchs.clarke.k12.va.us

Dogwood Elementary School

12300 Glade Drive, Reston VA 20191
PYP Coordinator Adrienne Schumer
Languages English, Spanish
T: +1 703 262 3100
W: dogwoodes.fcps.edu

Edgar Allen Poe Middle School

7000 Cindy Lane, Annandale VA 2203
MYP Coordinator Darcy Hood
Languages English
T: +1 703 813 3800
W: poems.fcps.edu

Ellen Glasgow Middle School

4101 Fairfax Parkway, Alexandria VA 22312
MYP Coordinator Chinoyerem (Nonye) Oladimeji
Languages English
T: +1 703 813 8700
W: glasgowms.fcps.edu

Ellis Elementary School

10400 Kim Graham Lane, Manassas VA 20109
PYP Coordinator Alicia Strahan
Languages English
T: +1 703 365 0287
W: ellises.pwcs.edu

Fairfield Middle School

5121 Nine Mile Road, Henrico VA 23223
MYP Coordinator Cara Sederbaum
Languages English
T: +1 804 328 4020
W: fairfield.henricoschools.us

Fred M. Lynn Middle School

1650 Prince William Parkway, Woodbridge VA 22191
MYP Coordinator Greg Patterson
Languages English
T: +1 703 494 5157
W: lynnms.pwcs.edu

Galileo Magnet High School

230 South Ridge Road, Danville VA 24541
DP Coordinator Tim Saddler
Languages English
T: +1 434 773 8186

Gar-Field High School

14000 Smoketown Road, Woodbridge VA 22192
CP Coordinator Michelle Schneider
DP Coordinator Brian Bassett
MYP Coordinator Della Gordon
Languages English
T: +1 703 730 7000
W: gar-fieldhs.pwcs.edu

George C Marshall High School

7731 Leesburg Pike, Falls Church VA 22043
DP Coordinator Matthew Axelrod
Languages English
T: +1 703 714 5402
W: marshallhs.fcps.edu

George H Moody Middle School

7800 Woodman Road, Richmond VA 23228
MYP Coordinator April Craver
Languages English
T: +1 804 261 5015
W: schools.henrico.k12.va.us/moody

George M. Hampton Middle School

14800 Darbydale Avenue, Woodbridge VA 22193
MYP Coordinator Rhonda Parker
Languages English
T: +1 703 670 6166
W: hamptonms.pwcs.edu

George Mason High School

7124 Leesburg Pike, Falls Church VA 22043
DP Coordinator Daniel Coast
MYP Coordinator Rory Dippold
Languages English
T: +1 703 248 5500
W: www.fccps.org/o/gmhs

Granby High School

7101 Granby Street, Norfolk VA 23505
DP Coordinator Rebecca Gardner
Languages English
T: +1 757 451 4110
W: www.npsk12.com/ghs

Green Run Collegiate

1700 Dahlia Drive, Virginia Beach VA 23456
CP Coordinator Rianne Patricio
DP Coordinator Rianne Patricio
MYP Coordinator Tonia Waters
Languages English
T: +1 757 648 5350
W: greenruncollegiate.vbschools.com

Hampton High School

1491 W Queen Street, Hampton City Schools, Hampton VA 23669
DP Coordinator Haneef Majied
Languages English
T: +1 757 825 4430
W: www.sbo.hampton.k12.va.us

Hanover High School

10307 Chamberlayne Road, Mechanicsville VA 23116
DP Coordinator Jessica Orth
Languages English
T: +1 804 723 3700

Henrico High School

302 Azalea Avenue, Richmond VA 23227
CP Coordinator Priscilla Biddle
DP Coordinator Priscilla Biddle
MYP Coordinator Priscilla Biddle
Languages English
T: +1 804 228 2700
W: henrico.henricoschools.us

Holmes Middle School

6525 Montrose Street, Alexandria VA 22312
MYP Coordinator Donna Starace
Languages English
T: +1 703 658 5900
W: holmesms.fcps.edu

Hugh Mercer Elementary School

2100 Cowan Blvd, Fredericksburg VA 22401
PYP Coordinator Stephanie Teri
Languages English
T: +1 540 372 1115

James Monroe High School

2300 Washington Ave, Fredericksburg VA 22401
DP Coordinator Jason Pope
MYP Coordinator Shamus Gordon
Languages English
T: +1 540 372 1100
W: www.cityschools.com/jamesmonroehighschool

James W Robinson, Jr Secondary School

5035 Sideburn Road, Fairfax County Public Schools, Fairfax VA 22032
DP Coordinator Wendy Vu
MYP Coordinator Debbie Scott
Languages English
T: +1 703 426 2100
W: www.fcps.edu/RobinsonSS

Jefferson Houston Prek-8 School

1501 Cameron Street, Alexandria VA 22314
MYP Coordinator Anthony Washington
PYP Coordinator Anthony Washington
Languages English, Spanish
T: +1 703 706 4400
W: www.acps.k12.va.us/Domain/15

John Randolph Tucker High School

2910 North Parham Road, Henrico VA 23294
DP Coordinator Ellie Harper
MYP Coordinator Ellie Harper
Languages English
T: +1 804 527 4600
W: tucker.henricoschools.us

Justice High School

3301 Peace Valley Lane, Falls Church VA 22044
DP Coordinator Jennifer Kresse-Rodríguez
MYP Coordinator Katherine Naughton
Languages English
T: +1 703 824 3900
W: justicehs.fcps.edu

Key Middle School

6402 Franconia Road, Springfield VA 22150
MYP Coordinator Danielle Danz
Languages English
T: +1 703 313 3900
W: keyms.fcps.edu

King Abdullah Academy
2949 Education Dr, Herndon VA 20171
DP Coordinator Jalaika Hasan
MYP Coordinator Deborah Mohammed
Languages Arabic, English
T: +1 571 351 5520
W: www.kaa-herndon.com

King's Fork High School
351 King's Fork Road, Suffolk VA 23434
DP Coordinator Shawn Barnard
Languages English
T: +1 757 923 5240
W: kfhs.spsk12.net

Lafayette Upper Elementary School
3 Learning Lane, Fredericksburg VA 22401
PYP Coordinator Katya Zablotney
Languages English
T: +1 540 310 0029
W: www.cityschools.com/lafayetteupperelementaryschool

Langston Hughes Middle School
11401 Ridge Heights Road, Reston VA 20191
MYP Coordinator Chris Delgrosso
Languages English
T: +1 703 715 3600

Lee High School
6540 Franconia Road, Fairfax county, Springfield VA 22150
CP Coordinator Stephanie Dawley
DP Coordinator Mariano Acevedo
MYP Coordinator Stephanie Bilimoria
Languages English
T: +1 703 924 8300
W: www.fcps.edu/LeeHS

Lee-Davis High School
7052 Mechanicsville Pike, Hanover County, Mechanicsville VA 23111-3629
DP Coordinator Lesa Berlinghoff
Languages English
T: +1 804 723 2200

Lucille Brown Middle School
6300 Jahnke Road, Richmond VA 23225
MYP Coordinator Tracy S. Cady
Languages English
T: +1 804 319 3013
W: www.rvaschools.net/Domain/27

Mark Twain Middle School
4700 Franconia Road, Alexandria VA 22310
MYP Coordinator Jodi Cohen
Languages English
T: +1 703 313 3700
W: twainms.fcps.edu

Mary Ellen Henderson Middle School
7130 Leesburg Pike, Falls Church VA 22043
MYP Coordinator Rory Dippold
Languages English
T: +1 703 720 5702
W: www.fccps.org/o/meh

Massanutten Military Academy
614 South Main Street, Woodstock VA 22664
CP Coordinator Hannah Watterson
Languages English
T: +1 540 459 2167
W: www.militaryschool.com

Meadowbrook High School
4901 Cogbill Road, North Chesterfield VA 23234
DP Coordinator Jelani Lynch
Languages English
T: +1 804 743 3675
W: sites.google.com/a/ccpsnet.net/mbkhs

Midlothian High School
401 Charter Colony Parkway, Chesterfield County, Midlothian VA 23114
DP Coordinator Stuart Jones
Languages English
T: +1 804 378 2440
W: sites.google.com/a/ccpsnet.net/mdhs

Mount Vernon High School
8515 Old Mount Vernon Road, Alexandria VA 22309
CP Coordinator Berkeley McHugh
DP Coordinator Berkeley McHugh
MYP Coordinator Nikolas Short
Languages English
T: +1 703 619 3103
W: www.fcps.edu/MtVernonHS

Mountain View High School
2135 Mountain View Road, Stafford VA 22556
DP Coordinator Theresa Gaddy
Languages English
T: +1 540 658 6840
W: www.staffordschools.net/MVHS

Mullen Elementary School
8000 Rodes Drive, Manassas VA 20109
PYP Coordinator Elizabeth Hooker
Languages English
T: +1 703 330 0427

Murray High School
1200 Forest Street, Charlottesville VA 22903
DP Coordinator Joshua Flaherty
Languages English
T: +1 434 296 3090
W: mcs.k12albemarle.org

Oscar F Smith High School
1994 Tiger Drive, Chesapeake VA 23320
DP Coordinator Kerri Lancaster
Languages English
T: +1 757 548 0696
W: cpschools.com/osh

Patrick Henry High School
12449 West Patrick Henry Road, Ashland VA 23005
DP Coordinator Luke Kupscznk
Languages English
T: +1 804 365 8011

Plaza Middle School
3080 South Lynnhaven Road, Virginia Beach VA 23452
MYP Coordinator Catherine Susewind
Languages English
T: +1 757 431 4060
W: www.plazams.vbschools.com

Prince George High School
7801 Laurel Spring Road, Prince George VA 23875
MYP Coordinator Michelle Bowen
Languages English
T: +1 804 733 2720
W: prince-george-high-school.echalksites.com

Princess Anne High School
4400 Virginia Beach Boulevard, Virginia Beach VA 23462-3198
DP Coordinator Jamie LaCava-Owen
MYP Coordinator Jamie LaCava-Owen
Languages English
T: +1 757 473 5000
W: www.princessannehs.vbschools.com

Randolph Elementary School
1306 S Quincy Street, Arlington VA 22204
PYP Coordinator Shannon Quinn
Languages English
T: +1 703 228 5830

Rosa Parks Elementary School
13446 Princedale Drive, Woodbridge VA 22193
PYP Coordinator Alicia Strahan
Languages English
T: +1 703 580 9665

Saint Mary's Catholic School
9501 Gayton Road, Richmond VA 23229
MYP Coordinator Carole Forkey
Languages English
T: +1 804 740 1048
W: www.saintmary.org

Salem High School
400 Spartan Drive, Salem VA 24153
DP Coordinator Sara Epperly
Languages English
T: +1 540 387 2437
W: shs.salem.k12.va.us

South Lakes High School
11400 South Lakes Drive, Reston VA 20191
CP Coordinator Susan Brownsword
DP Coordinator Marie Turner
MYP Coordinator Desiree Satterfield
Languages English
T: +1 703 715 4500

Spotsylvania High School
6975 Courthouse Road, Spotsylvania VA 22551
DP Coordinator Catherine Larocco
Languages English
T: +1 540 582 3882
W: www.spotsyschools.us/shs

Stonewall Jackson High School
8820 Rixlew Lane, Manassas VA 20109
CP Coordinator Herman Hruska
DP Coordinator Katie Hodgson
MYP Coordinator Alaina Lynard
Languages English
T: +1 703 365 2900

Stonewall Middle School
10100 Lomond Drive, Manassas VA 20109
MYP Coordinator Jeanine Fox
Languages English
T: +1 703 361 3185
W: stonewallms.pwcs.edu

Strelitz International Academy
5000 Corporate Woods Driv, Suite 180, Virginia Beach VA 23462
PYP Coordinator Alicia Pahl-Cornelius
Languages English, Hebrew
T: +1 757 424 4327
W: strelitzinternationalacademy.org

Stuart M Beville Middle School
4901 Dale Boulevard, Woodbridge VA 22193-4700
MYP Coordinator Patricia Kramolisch
Languages English
T: +1 703 878 2593

The Hague School
739 Yarmouth St., Norfolk VA 23510
DP Coordinator Bonnie Schneider
Languages English, French
T: +1 757 317 3033
W: www.thehagueschool.org

Thomas Alva Edison High School

5801 Franconia Road, Alexandria VA 22310
DP Coordinator Sabra Devers
MYP Coordinator Corinne Nuttall
Languages English
T: +1 703 924 8007
W: edisonhs.fcps.edu

Thomas Jefferson Elementary

601 South Oak Street, Falls Church VA 22046
PYP Coordinator Carrie Checca
Languages English
T: +1 703 248 5661
W: www.fccps.org/o/tje

Thomas Jefferson High School

4100 West Grace Street, Richmond VA 23230
DP Coordinator Melissa Johnston
MYP Coordinator Tracy S. Cady
Languages English
T: +1 804 780 6028
W: www.rvaschools.net/Domain/14

Thomas Jefferson Middle School

125 S Old Glebe Road, Arlington VA 22204
MYP Coordinator Christopher "Kip" Malinosky
Languages English
T: +1 703 228 5900
W: www.apsva.us/jefferson

Trinity Episcopal School

3850 Pittaway Road, Richmond VA 23235
DP Coordinator Marti Truman
Languages English
T: +1 804 272 5864
W: www.trinityes.org

Tuckahoe Middle School

9000 Three Chopt Road, Henrico VA 23229
MYP Coordinator Marie Wilcox
Languages English
T: +1 804 673 3720
W: tuckahoems.henricoschools.us

Walker-Grant Middle School

One Learning Lane, Fredericksburg VA 22401
MYP Coordinator Stephen Ventura
Languages English
T: +1 540 372 1145
W: www.cityschools.com/walkergrantmiddleschool

Walt Whitman Middle School

2500 Parkers Lane, Alexandria VA 22306
MYP Coordinator Dana Bayer
Languages English
T: +1 703 660 2400

Warwick High School

51 Copeland Lane, Newport News VA 23601
DP Coordinator Maranda Hall
Languages English
T: +1 757 591 4700
W: warwick.nn.k12.va.us

Washington-Liberty High School

1301 N Stafford St, Arlington VA 22201
DP Coordinator Julie Cantor
Languages English
T: +1 703 228 6200
W: washingtonlee.apsva.us

Williamsburg Christian Academy

101 School House Lane, Williamsburg VA 23188
DP Coordinator Johnny Graham
Languages English, Spanish
T: +1 757 220 1978
W: private-christian-school.williamsburgchristian.org

York High School

9300 George Washington, Memorial Highway, Yorktown VA 23692
DP Coordinator Kevin Valliant
Languages English
T: +1 757 898 0354
W: ycsd.yorkcountyschools.org/YHS

Washington

A C Davis High School

212 South 6th Avenue, Yakima WA 98902
DP Coordinator Diane Main
Languages English
T: +1 509 573 2501
W: www.yakimaschools.org/davis

Alderwood Elementary School

3400 Hollywood Avenue, Bellingham WA 98225
PYP Coordinator Gretchen Stiteler
Languages English
T: +1 360 676 6404
W: alderwood.bellinghamschools.org

Annie Wright Schools

827 N Tacoma Avenue, Tacoma WA 98403
DP Coordinator Emily Lynn
MYP Coordinator Briana Samuelson
PYP Coordinator Jennifer Bills
Languages English
T: +1 253 272 2216
W: www.aw.org

Beach Elementary School

3786 Centerview Rd, Lummi Island WA 98262
PYP Coordinator Kathy Buford
Languages English
T: +1 360 383 9440
W: www.ferndalesd.org/beach

Bellevue Children's Academy

14600 NE 24th St., Bellevue WA 98007
PYP Coordinator Kristen Blum
Languages English
T: +1 425 649 0791
W: www.bcacademy.com

Birchwood Elementary School

3200 Pinewood Avenue, Bellingham WA 98225
PYP Coordinator Cori Stothart
Languages English
T: +1 360 676 6466
W: birchwood.bellinghamschools.org

Capital High School

2707 Conger Avenue, Olympia WA 98502
DP Coordinator Ken Joling
Languages English
T: +1 360 753 8880
W: capital.osd.wednet.edu

Carl Cozier Elementary School

1330 Lincoln St., Bellingham WA 98229
PYP Coordinator Monica Savory
Languages English
T: +1 360 676 6410
W: carlcozier.bellinghamschools.org

Cedar Heights Middle School

2220 Pottery Ave, Port Orchard WA 98366
MYP Coordinator Jennifer Knowles
Languages English
T: +1 360 874 6020
W: www.kent.k12.wa.us/Domain/9

Chief Sealth International High School

2600 SW Thistle, Seattle WA 98126
CP Coordinator Allison Hays
DP Coordinator Allison Hays
Languages English
T: +1 206 252 8550
W: chiefsealthhs.seattleschools.org

Columbia River High School

800 North West 99th Street, Vancouver WA 98665
CP Coordinator Morgan Parker
DP Coordinator Julie A Nygaard
Languages English
T: +1 360 313 3900
W: river.vansd.org

Discovery Middle School

800 E. 40th Street, Vancouver WA 98663
MYP Coordinator Mark Phelan
Languages English
T: +1 360 313 3300
W: disco.vansd.org

Eastern Senior High School

1700 East Capitol Street NE, Washington DC 20003
DP Coordinator Elizabeth Braganza
Languages English
T: +1 202 698 4500
W: www.easternhighschooldc.org

Edmonds-Woodway High School

7600 212th St South West, Edmonds WA 98026
DP Coordinator Nick Wellington
Languages English
T: +1 425 431 7900

Giaudrone Middle School

4902 S Alaska Street, Tacoma WA 98408
MYP Coordinator Ulrike Puryear
Languages English
T: +1 253 571 5810
W: www.tacomaschools.org/giaudrone

Harrison Preparatory School

9103 Lakewood DR SW, Lakewood WA 98499
DP Coordinator Erika Cox
MYP Coordinator Erika Cox
Languages English
T: +1 253 583 5419
W: www.cloverpark.k12.wa.us

IB AMERICAS

Henry Foss High School

2112 South Tyler Street, Tacoma WA 98405
DP Coordinator T.J. Purdy
MYP Coordinator T.J. Purdy
Languages English
T: +1 253 571 7300
W: www.tacoma.k12.wa.us/foss

Idlewild Elementary School

10806 Idlewild Rd. SW, Lakewood WA 98499
PYP Coordinator Dori Zukowski
Languages English
T: +1 253 583 5290
W: www.cloverpark.k12.wa.us

Inglemoor High School

15500 Simonds Rd NE, Kenmore WA 98028
DP Coordinator Christopher McQueen
Languages English
T: +1 425 408 7200
W: www.nsd.org/inglemoor

Ingraham High School

1819 North 135th Street, Seattle WA 98133-7709
DP Coordinator Guy Thomas
Languages English
T: +1 206 252 3923

Interlake High School

16245 NE 24th St., Bellevue WA 98008
DP Coordinator Teresa Cairns
Languages English
T: +1 425 456 7200
W: bsd405.org/interlake

Kennewick High School

500 S. Dayton Street, Kennewick WA 99336
DP Coordinator Ashley Williams
Languages English
T: +1 509) 222-7100
W: kennewick.ksd.org

Kent-Meridian High School

10020 SE 256th Street, Kent WA 98031
DP Coordinator Beth Shoemaker
Languages English
T: +1 253 373 7405

Kilo Middle School

4400 S. 308th St, Auburn WA 98001
MYP Coordinator Theresa Lee
Languages English
T: +1 253 945 4700
W: www.fwps.org/Domain/32

Liberty Bell Junior-Senior High School

24 Twin Lakes Rd, Winthrop WA 98862
MYP Coordinator Matt Hinckley
Languages English
T: +1 509 996 2215
W: methow.org/schools/liberty-bell-jr-sr-high

McCarver Elementary

2111 S. J St, Tacoma WA 98405
PYP Coordinator Ryan Prosser
Languages English
T: +1 253 571 4900
W: www.tacomaschools.org/mccarver/Pages

Methow Valley Elementary

18 Twin Lakes Rd, Winthrop WA 98862
PYP Coordinator Kelly Wiest
Languages English
T: +1 509 996 2186
W: methow.org/methow-valley-elementary-school

Mount Rainier High School

22450 19th Avenue S, Des Moines WA 98198
DP Coordinator Veronica Fairchild
MYP Coordinator Jim Dyer
Languages English
T: +1 206 631 7000
W: mrhs.highlineschools.org

Northern Heights Elementary

4000 Magrath Road, Bellingham WA 98226
PYP Coordinator Kacey EMerson
Languages English
T: +1 360 647 6820
W: northernheights.bellinghamschools.org

PRIDE SCHOOLS

811 E Sprague Ave, Spokane WA 99202
DP Coordinator Nicky Jones
MYP Coordinator Nicky Jones
Languages English, Spanish
T: +1 509 309 7680
E: info@prideschools.org
W: www.prideschools.org

See full details on page 536

Rainier Beach High School

8815 Seward Park Avenue S WA 98118
DP Coordinator Steven Miller
Languages English
T: +1 206 252 6350
W: rainierbeachhs.seattleschools.org

Renton High School

400 S Second Street, Renton WA 98057
DP Coordinator Malcolm Robert Montgomery Collie
Languages English
T: +1 425 204 3400
W: rentonhs.rentonschools.us

Saint George's School

2929 W. Waikiki Road, Spokane WA 99208
DP Coordinator Elizabeth Tender
Languages English
T: +1 509 466 1636 EXT:331
W: www.sgs.org

Skyline High School

1122 228th Avenue SE, Issaquah School District, Sammamish WA 98075-6914
CP Coordinator Stephania Gullikson
DP Coordinator Chris Wilder
Languages English
T: +1 425 837 7700
W: www.issaquah.wednet.edu/skylinehs

Soundview School

6515 196th Street SW, Lynnwood WA 98036
MYP Coordinator Chrissy Sinclair
Languages English
T: +1 425 778 8572
W: www.soundview.org

South Charleston High School

One Eagle Way, South Charleston WA 25309
DP Coordinator Sarah Carroll
Languages English
T: +1 304 766 0352

South Kitsap High School

425 Mitchell Ave, Port Orchard WA 98366
CP Coordinator Michelle Duchene
DP Coordinator Michelle Duchene
Languages English
T: +1 360 874 5600
W: www.skitsap.wednet.edu/domain/31

St. Luke School

17533 St Luke Place N, Shoreline WA 98133
MYP Coordinator Anne Taylor
PYP Coordinator Meaghan Roach
Languages English
T: +1 206 542 1133
W: www.stlukeshoreline.net

Sumner High School

1707 Main Street, Sumner WA 98390
DP Coordinator Monica Swigart
Languages English
T: +1 253 891 5500
W: www.sumner.wednet.edu

Thomas Jefferson High School

4248 S. 288th Street, Auburn WA 98001
CP Coordinator Jennifer McKay
DP Coordinator Kailey Harem
MYP Coordinator Shari Winslow
Languages English
T: +1 253 945 5600
W: www.fwps.org/tjhs

Totem Middle School

26630 40th Avenue S., Kent WA 98032
MYP Coordinator Liz Andrade
Languages English
T: +1 253 945 5100
W: www.fwps.org/Domain/37

Wade King Elementary School

2155 Yew Street Road, Bellingham WA 98229
PYP Coordinator Hana Anderson
Languages English
T: +1 360 647 6840
W: wadeking.bellinghamschools.org

Wainwright Intermediate School

130 Alameda Avenue, Fircrest WA 98466
PYP Coordinator Cheryl Steighner
Languages English, Spanish
T: +1 253 571 2100
W: wainwright.tacomaschools.org

Washington Preparatory School

18323 Bothell-Everett Highway, Suite 220, Bothell WA 98012
DP Coordinator Joe Kennedy
Languages English
T: +1 425 892 8669
W: waprep.org

West Sound Academy

16571 Creative Drive NE, Poulsbo WA 98370
DP Coordinator Catherine Freeman
Languages English
T: +1 360 598 5954
W: www.westsoundacademy.org

Whittier Elementary School

777 Elmtree Lane, Fircrest WA 98466
PYP Coordinator Traci Frank
Languages English, Spanish
T: +1 253 571 7500
W: whittier.tacomaschools.org

Willows Preparatory School

12280 NE Woodinville-Redmond Rd, Redmond WA 98052
DP Coordinator Clarissa Toupin
MYP Coordinator Clarissa Toupin
Languages English
T: +1 425 649 0791
W: www.willowsprep.com

Wisconsin

Academy of Accelerated Learning

3727 South 78th Street, Milwaukee WI 53220
PYP Coordinator Renee Bast
Languages English
T: +1 414 604 7300
W: www2.milwaukee.k12.wi.us/aal

Bay Port High School

2710 Lineville Road, Green Bay WI 54313
DP Coordinator Chad McAllister
Languages English
T: +1 920 662 7000
W: bayporthssd.weebly.com

Casimir Pulaski High School

2500 W Oklahoma Ave, Milwaukee WI 53215
CP Coordinator Robin Harris
DP Coordinator Christine Lemon
MYP Coordinator Christine Lemon
Languages English, Spanish
T: +1 414 902 8900
W: www5.milwaukee.k12.wi.us/school/pulaski

Catholic Memorial High School

601 East College Avenue, Waukesha WI 53186
CP Coordinator Nicholas Doyle
DP Coordinator Nicholas Doyle
Languages English
T: +1 262 542 7101
W: www.catholicmemorial.net

Chappell Elementary School

205 N Fisk Street, Green Bay WI 54303
PYP Coordinator Jackie Brosteau
Languages English
T: +1 920 492 2630
W: chappell.gbaps.org

Darrell Lynn Hines College Preparatory Academy of Excellence

7151 North 86th Street, Milwaukee WI 53224
PYP Coordinator Monica Carrington
Languages English
T: +1 414 358 3542

Franklin Middle School

1233 Lore Lane, Green Bay WI 54303
MYP Coordinator Jennifer Burgraff
Languages English
T: +1 920 492 2670
W: franklin.gbaps.org

Green Bay West High School

966 Shawano Avenue, Green Bay WI 54303
DP Coordinator Stephane Bielen
MYP Coordinator Andrew Evenson
Languages English
T: +1 920 492 2730
W: west.gbaps.org

Green Lake School

612 Mill Street, PO Box 369, Green Lake WI 54941
DP Coordinator Joshua LeGreve
MYP Coordinator Mary Hunter
PYP Coordinator Katie James
Languages English
T: +1 920 294 6411
W: www.glsd.k12.wi.us

Holy Family School

1204 S. Fisk Street, Green Bay WI 54304
MYP Coordinator Taylor Lepak
Languages English
T: +1 920 494 1931
W: holyfamilygreenbay.com

Isthmus Montessori Academy

1802 Pankratz Street, Madison WI 53704
DP Coordinator Caleb Wilson
Languages English, Spanish
T: +1 608 661 8200
W: isthmusmontessoriacademy.org

Jefferson Lighthouse Elementary

1722 West Sixth Street, Racine WI 53404
PYP Coordinator Colleen Strain
Languages English
T: +1 262 664 6900
W: www.rusd.org/jefferson

Jerome I Case High School

7345 Washington Avenue, Racine WI 53406
CP Coordinator Rebecca Madsen
DP Coordinator Nicola Malacara
Languages English
T: +1 262 619 4200
W: www.rusd.org/case

Lincoln High School

1433 South Eighth Street, Manitowoc WI 54220
DP Coordinator Lee Thennes
Languages English
T: +1 920 663 9602
W: www.manitowocpublicschools.org

Lowell Elementary School

4360 S. 20th Street, Milwaukee WI 53221
PYP Coordinator Janet Key
Languages English
T: +1 414 304 6600
W: www5.milwaukee.k12.wi.us/school/lowell.html

MacDowell Montessori School

6415 W Mount Vernon Avenue, Milwaukee WI 53216
DP Coordinator Nicholas Beermann
Languages English
T: +1 414 256 8300
W: www5.milwaukee.k12.wi.us/school/macdowell/

Madison Country Day School

5606 River Road, Waunakee WI 53597
DP Coordinator Mark Childs
Languages English
T: +1 608 850 6000
W: www.madisoncountryday.org

McKinley Middle School

2340 Mohr Avenue, Racine WI 53405
MYP Coordinator Stephanie Skaarnes
Languages English
T: +1 262 664 6150
W: www.rusd.org/mckinley/welcome

North Woods International School

2541 Sablewood Road, La Crosse WI 54601
PYP Coordinator Sara DePaolo
Languages English, Spanish
T: +1 608 789 7000
W: www.lacrosseschools.org/northwoods-international

Notre Dame de la Baie Academy

610 Maryhill Drive, Green Bay WI 54303
DP Coordinator Matthew Schultz
Languages English
T: +1 920 429 6100
W: www.NotreDameAcademy.com

Oconomowoc High School

641 East Forest Street, Oconomowoc WI 53066-3888
CP Coordinator Carrie Schultz
DP Coordinator Carrie Schultz
Languages English
T: +1 262 560 3100
W: www.oasd.k12.wi.us/page.cfm?p=6767

Ronald Reagan High School

4965 South 20 Street, Milwaukee WI 53221
CP Coordinator Jamie Gonzalez
DP Coordinator David Walker
MYP Coordinator Teri Knight
Languages English
T: +1 414 304 6100
W: www.milwaukee.k12.wi.us/pages/mps/school/highs/reagan

Roosevelt Elementary

3322 Roosevelt Road, Kenosha WI 53142
PYP Coordinator Leah Ebener
Languages English
T: +1 262 359 6097
W: www.kusd.edu/roosevelt

Rufus King International School - High School Campus

1801 West Olive Street, Milwaukee WI 53209
DP Coordinator Daniel Gatewood
MYP Coordinator Laura Lewandowski
Languages English
T: +1 414 267 0705
W: www.rkhs.org

Rufus King International School - Middle School Campus

121 E Hadley St, Milwaukee WI 53212
MYP Coordinator Vernita Phillips
Languages English
T: +1 414 616 5200
W: www5.milwaukee.k12.wi.us/school/rkims

St. Joan Antida High School

1341 N. Cass Street, Milwaukee WI 53202
CP Coordinator Cynthia McLinn
Languages English
T: +1 414 272 8423
W: www.saintjoanantida.org

Wausau East High School

2607 N 18th Street, Wausau WI 54403
DP Coordinator Darlene Beattie
Languages English
T: +1 715 261 0650
W: www.wausau.k12.wi.us/east/

Wauwatosa Catholic

1500 Wauwatosa Avenue, Wauwatosa WI 53213
MYP Coordinator Karen Scharrer-Erickson
PYP Coordinator Karen Scharrer-Erickson
Languages English
T: +1 414 258 9977
W: www.wauwatosacatholic.org

Wedgewood Park International School

6506 W Warnimont Avenue, Milwaukee WI 53220
MYP Coordinator Jeannette Bahr
Languages English
T: +1 414 604 7800

West Ridge Elementary School

1347 S. Emmertsen Road, Racine WI 53406
PYP Coordinator Michael Maxwell
T: +1 262 664 6200
W: www.rusd.org/westridge

Wyoming

Cheyenne East High School

2800 E Pershing Blvd, Cheyenne WY 82001
DP Coordinator Jonathon Lever
Languages English
T: +1 307 771 2663 EXT 108
W: www.east.laramie1.org/

Journeys School

700 Coyote Canyon Road, Jackson WY 83001
DP Coordinator David Porter
Languages English
T: +1 307 733 3729
W: www.journeysschool.org

Natrona County High School

930 Elm Street, Casper WY 82601
DP Coordinator Brandi Ramage
Languages English
T: +1 307 253 1700

Colegio Guayamuri

Av. Luisa Cáceres de Arismendi, Atamo Norte, La Asunción
DP Coordinator Alexandra De Fina
Languages English, Spanish
T: +58 295 2423048
W: www.guayamuri.com

Colegio Integral El Avila

Centro de Artes Integradas, Urb. Terrazas del Avila, La Urbina Norte, Caracas 1073
DP Coordinator Carmen Winkler
Languages Spanish
T: +58 243.58.20
W: www.elavila.org

Colegio Integral El Manglar

Carrera N°41 S/N Sector Nueva Barcelona, Barcelona 6001, Anzoategui
DP Coordinator Ma Eugenia Behrens
Languages English, Spanish
T: +58 0281 317 21 70
W: elmanglar.org.ve

Colegio Internacional de Caracas

Calle Colegio, entre Los Samanes y Las Minas de Baruta, Caracas 1080
DP Coordinator Mike East
MYP Coordinator Mike East
Languages English, Spanish
T: +58 212 945 0444
W: cic-caracas.org

Colegio Los Campitos

Ruta C, Urbanización Los Campitos, Prados del Este, Miranda
DP Coordinator Margot Peña
Languages Spanish
T: +58 212 977 1768
W: colegioloscampitosweb.com

Colegio Moral y Luces 'Herzl-Bialik'

Final Ave. Los Chorros, SEDE CLUB HEBRAICA (Frente al INAM), Los Chorros CARACAS 1071
DP Coordinator Naily Gamboa
Languages English
T: +58 212 273 6894/6807
W: www.secmyl.edu.ve

Escuela Bella Vista

67th Street between Av. 3D and 3E "La Lago" sector, Macaracaibo, Zulia 4001
DP Coordinator Greg Sipp
Languages English
T: +58 261 794 0000
W: www.ebv.org.ve

Escuela Campo Alegre

Final Calle La Cinta, Las Mercedes, Caracas
DP Coordinator Matthew Sheets
Languages English
T: +58 212 993 3922
W: www.ecak12.com

Instituto Educacional Juan XXIII

Calle San Enrique No 85-70, Trigal Centro, Valencia, Estado Carabobo 2002
CP Coordinator Jorge Bolivar Manzano
DP Coordinator Elkys Sequera
Languages English, Spanish
T: +58 241 8425732
W: www.juanxxiii.e12.ve

Liceo Los Robles

Urbanización el Doral Norte, Calle 34 esquina con Avenida, Fuerzas Armadas, Mar, Estado Zulia 4002
DP Coordinator Jesús Antonio Vilchez Chávez
Languages Spanish
T: +58 0261 7421833
W: losroblesenlinea.com.ve

The British School Caracas

PO Box 668708, c/o Jet International 489, Miami FL 33166, USA
DP Coordinator Stephanie Mitchell
Languages English
T: +58 212 265 58 70
W: www.tbscaracas.com

WASHINGTON ACADEMY

Calle C, Urb. Colinas de Valle Arriba, Caracas 1080
DP Coordinator Prof. Yajaira Graterol
MYP Coordinator Prof. Gianna De Sena
Languages Spanish, English
T: +58 212 9757077
E: academiawashington@aw.edu.ve
W: www.washington.academy

See full details on page 552

Virgin Islands Montessori School & Peter Gruber International Academy

6936 Vessup Lane, St Thomas VI 00802
DP Coordinator Matthew Stocking
MYP Coordinator Bennett Ott
Languages English
T: +1 340 775 6360
W: www.vimsia.org

Appendices

1. Addresses of all IB Offices
2. Location of IB World Schools
3. Diploma Programme Subjects Offered in 2022
    (May and November sessions)
4. Associations of IB World Schools
5. University Recognition

1. Addresses of all IB Offices

IB FOUNDATION OFFICE

International Baccalaureate
Route des Morillons 15
Grand–Saconnex, Genève
CH – 1218
SWITZERLAND

IB GLOBAL CENTRES

Africa, Europe, Middle East

IB Global Centre, The Hague
Churchillplein 6
2517 JW
The Hague
The Netherlands

IB Global Centre, Cardiff
Peterson House, Malthouse Avenue
Cardiff Gate
Cardiff, Wales
CF23 8GL
United Kingdom

Americas

IB Global Centre, Washington DC
7501 Wisconsin Avenue, Suite 200 West
Bethesda, Maryland 20814
USA

Asia – Pacific

IB Global Centre, Singapore
600 North Bridge Road,
#21 – 01 Parkview Square,
Singapore 188778
Republic of Singapore

2. Location of IB World Schools

Location (as of 14 October 2021)	IB World Schools	Number of Programmes				Total number of Programmes
		PYP	MYP	CP	DP	
ALBANIA	3	2	2		3	7
ANDORRA	3			1	2	3
ANGOLA	1	1	1		1	3
ANGUILLA	1	1				1
ANTIGUA AND BARBUDA	1				1	1
ARGENTINA	59	7	2		58	67
ARMENIA	3	1	1		3	5
AUSTRALIA	208	147	44	3	83	277
AUSTRIA	18	5	5	1	17	28
AZERBAIJAN	6	4	3		6	13
BAHAMAS	3	3	1	1	3	8
BAHRAIN	13	2	1	1	13	17
BANGLADESH	7	7	3	1	5	16
BARBADOS	1	1	1		1	3
BELGIUM	12	5	6	1	10	22
BERMUDA	3		1	1	3	5
BOLIVIA	3	1			3	4
BOSNIA AND HERZEGOVINA	4		1		4	5
BOTSWANA	2	2	1		1	4
BRAZIL	49	22	9		37	68
BRITISH VIRGIN ISLANDS	1	1	1		1	3
BRUNEI DARUSSALAM	2				2	2
BULGARIA	9	1	2	1	8	12
BURKINA FASO	2				2	2
CAMBODIA	6	4	3	1	5	13
CAMEROON	4	1	1		4	6
CANADA	376	96	160	6	186	448
CAYMAN ISLANDS	4	3			1	4
CHILE	29	14	9		25	48
CHINA	243	142	58	2	149	351
COLOMBIA	55	18	15		52	85
COSTA RICA	48	1	3		48	52
CROATIA	5	1	2		4	7
CUBA	1				1	1
CURACAO	1		1		1	2
CYPRUS	4				4	4

CZECH REPUBLIC	16	2	1	1	16	20
DENMARK	20	5	5		17	27
DOMINICAN REPUBLIC	5				5	5
ECUADOR	77	19	18		76	113
EGYPT	34	13	11	1	30	55
EL SALVADOR	4				4	4
ERITREA	1				1	1
ESTONIA	6	5	4		4	13
ETHIOPIA	3	1			3	4
FIJI	2	2	2		2	6
FINLAND	20	3	4	1	16	24
FRANCE	23	7	3	1	20	31
GABON	3	2	1		2	5
GEORGIA	3	2	2		3	7
GERMANY	83	27	14	6	78	125
GHANA	9	5	4	1	7	17
GREECE	19	5	6		15	26
GUAM	1				1	1
GUATEMALA	4				4	4
GUERNSEY	1			1	1	2
HONDURAS	1				1	1
HONG KONG	69	40	16	6	37	99
HUNGARY	9		1		8	9
ICELAND	1				1	1
INDIA	197	121	49	1	148	319
INDONESIA	62	35	20	4	46	105
IRAQ	6	5	3		2	10
IRELAND	5	2	2		4	8
ISLAMIC REPUBLIC OF IRAN	6	3	3		3	9
ISLE OF MAN	1				1	1
ISRAEL	3		1		3	4
ITALY	37	18	16		33	67
IVORY COAST	2		1		2	3
JAMAICA	2				2	2
JAPAN	91	48	27		58	133
JERSEY	1			1	1	2
JORDAN	21	11	14	2	20	47
KAZAKHSTAN	10	7	9		6	22
KENYA	8	3	3	2	7	15
KOSOVO	1	1	1			2
KUWAIT	5	4	2		2	8
KYRGYZSTAN	2	1	1		2	4
LATVIA	7	3	3	1	5	12

LEBANON	21	8	4		17	29
LESOTHO	1				1	1
LITHUANIA	14	2	3		12	17
LUXEMBOURG	5		1		4	5
MACAU	3	1	1		3	5
MADAGASCAR	1	1			1	2
MALAWI	1	1	1		1	3
MALAYSIA	35	10	21	2	19	52
MALI	1				1	1
MALTA	2			1	2	3
MAURITIUS	5	2	2	1	3	8
MEXICO	122	59	39	17	80	195
MONACO	1			1	1	2
MONGOLIA	3	1	1		3	5
MONTENEGRO	2	1	1		2	4
MOROCCO	15	2	8		5	15
MOZAMBIQUE	4	3	2		3	8
MYANMAR	4	1			3	4
NAMIBIA	1	1			1	2
NEPAL	3	2	1		1	4
NEW ZEALAND	27	17	4		13	34
NICARAGUA	3	1	1		2	4
NIGER	1				1	1
NIGERIA	5	2			3	5
NORWAY	42	20	18	1	24	63
OMAN	7	6	4		5	15
PAKISTAN	31	23	10		15	48
PALESTINIAN TERRITORY	2	1	1		1	3
PANAMA	5	3	2		5	10
PAPUA NEW GUINEA	1				1	1
PARAGUAY	4				4	4
PEOPLE'S DEMOCRATIC REPUBLIC LAO	1	1	1		1	3
PERU	75	16	10	2	73	101
PHILIPPINES	22	6	2	1	20	29
POLAND	63	13	13		55	81
PORTUGAL	13	4	4		12	20
PUERTO RICO	2	2	2		2	6
QATAR	15	10	9	1	14	34
REPUBLIC OF KOREA	20	12	8	1	16	37
REPUBLIC OF NORTH MACEDONIA	4	2	1		2	5
ROMANIA	9	4	3		7	14
RUSSIAN FEDERATION	51	27	23		29	79
RWANDA	1				1	1

SAUDI ARABIA	24	18	7		13	38
SENEGAL	6	1	2		6	9
SERBIA	7 .	2	2		6	11
SINGAPORE	40	23	8	2	29	62
SINT MAARTEN	1				1	1
SLOVAKIA	5	2	2		4	8
SLOVENIA	6	1	2		5	8
SOLOMON ISLANDS	1	1				1
SOUTH AFRICA	12	10	2		3	15
SPAIN	171	43	34	1	155	233
SRI LANKA	1	1	1		1	3
SUDAN	2	2	1		2	5
SWAZILAND	1				1	1
SWEDEN	36	10	13	3	28	54
SWITZERLAND	56	14	12	6	52	84
TAIWAN	13	5	5		10	20
THAILAND	29	15	8	1	23	47
THE DEMOCRATIC REPUBLIC OF THE CONGO	3	2	1		2	5
THE NETHERLANDS	27	9	15	3	21	48
TIMOR-LESTE	1	1	1			2
TOGO	2	1	1		2	4
TRINIDAD AND TOBAGO	1	1	1			2
TUNISIA	3	2	1		2	5
TURKEY	97	49	12		60	121
UGANDA	4	2	2		4	8
UKRAINE	4	1	1		4	6
UNITED ARAB EMIRATES	53	32	23	16	48	119
UNITED KINGDOM	129	9	24	46	91	170
UNITED REPUBLIC OF TANZANIA	6	6	4		5	15
UNITED STATES	1894	608	563	147	952	2270
UNITED STATES VIRGIN ISLANDS	1		1		1	2
URUGUAY	11	2	4	1	8	15
UZBEKISTAN	2	2	1		1	4
VENEZUELA	12		2	1	12	15
VIETNAM	17	7	5		17	29
ZAMBIA	3	2	1		3	6
ZIMBABWE	1	1	1		1	3
Grand Total	**5401**	**2043**	**1548**	**304**	**3487**	**7382**

*Programme count does not include European Platform or MYP Partners
**School count does not include European Platform, includes MYP Partner Schools

3. Diploma Programme Subjects offered in 2022 (May and November sessions)

Language and literature
Language A: literature HL
Language A: literature SL
Language A: language and literature HL
Language A: language and literature SL

Language acquisition
Language B HL
Language B SL
Language *ab initio* SL
Classical languages HL
Classical languages SL

Individuals and societies
Business management HL
Business management SL
Digital Society HL (First exam session 2024)
Digital Society SL (First exam session 2024)
Economics HL
Economics SL
Geography HL
Geography SL
Global politics HL
Global politics SL
History HL
History SL
Information technology in a global society HL
Information technology in a global society SL
Philosophy HL
Philosophy SL
Psychology HL
Psychology SL
Social and cultural anthropology HL
Social and cultural anthropology SL
World religions SL

Sciences
Biology HL
Biology SL
Chemistry HL
Chemistry SL
Computer science HL
Computer science SL
Design technology HL
Design technology SL
Nature of Science (Pilot) SL

Physics HL
Physics SL
Sports, exercise and health science HL
Sports, exercise and health science SL

Mathematics
Mathematics: analysis and approaches HL
Mathematics: analysis and approaches SL
Mathematics: applications and interpretation HL
Mathematics: applications and interpretation SL

The arts
Dance HL
Dance SL
Film HL
Film SL
Music HL
Music SL
Theatre HL
Theatre SL
Visual arts HL
Visual arts SL

Core requirements
Creativity, activity, service
Extended essay
Theory of knowledge

Interdisciplinary subjects
Environmental systems and societies SL
Literature and performance SL

School based syllabuses

Art history
Astronomy
Brazilian social studies
   (also examined in November session)
Classical Greek & Roman studies

Food science and technology
Marine science
Modern history of Kazakhstan
Political thought
Turkey in the 20th century
World arts and cultures

Languages offered in studies in language and literature

Language A: literature

Afrikaans A (Nov only)	French A	Norwegian A (May only)
Albanian A (May only)	Georgian A (May only)	Persian A (May only)
Amharic A (May only)	German A	Polish A (May only)
Arabic A (May only)	Hebrew A (May only)	Portuguese A
Armenian A (May only)	Hindi A (May only)	Romanian A (May only)
Azerbaijani A (May only)	Hungarian A (May only)	Russian A (May only)
Bengali A (May only)	Icelandic A (May only)	Serbian A (May only)
Bosnian A (May only)	Indonesian A	Sesotho A (May only)
Bulgarian A (May only)	Italian A (May only)	Siswati A (November only)
Catalan A (May only)	Japanese A	Slovak A (May only)
Chinese A	Khmer (May only)	Slovene A (May only)
Croatian A (May only)	Korean A	Spanish A
Czech A (May only)	Latvian A (May only)	Swahili A (May only)
Danish A (May only)	Lithuanian A (May only)	Swedish A (May only)
Dutch A (May only)	Macedonian A (May only)	Thai A (May only)
English A	Malay A (May only)	Turkish A
Estonian A (May only)	Modern Greek A (May only)	Ukrainian A (May only)
Filipino A (May only)	Mongolian (May only)	Urdu A (May only)
Finnish A (May only)	Nepali A (May only)	Vietnamese A (May only)

Language A: language and literature

Arabic A (May only)	Indonesian A (May only)	Portuguese A
Chinese A	Italian A (May only)	Russian A (May only)
Dutch A (May only)	Japanese A	Spanish A
English A	Korean A (May only)	Swedish A (May only)
French A	Modern Greek A (May only)	Thai A (May only)
German A	Norwegian A (May only)	

Literature and performance

English
Spanish

Language B

Arabic B (May only)	German B	Norwegian B (May only)
Chinese B – Cantonese (May only)	Hebrew B (SL only, May only)	Portuguese B (May only)
Chinese B – Mandarin	Hindi B (May only)	Russian B (May only)
Danish B (May only)	Indonesian B	Spanish B
Dutch B (May only)	Italian B (May only)	Swahili B (May only)
English B	Japanese B	Swedish B (May only)
Finnish B (May only)	Korean B (May only)	Tamil B (Nov only, SL only)
French B	Malay B (SL only, Nov only)	

Language ab initio

Arabic (May only)	German (May only)	Russian (May only)
Danish (May only)	Indonesian (Nov only)	Spanish
Dutch (May only)	Italian (May only)	Swahili (May only)
English	Japanese	Swedish (May only)
French	Mandarin	

Classical languages

Classical Greek (English) May only
Latin (English and Spanish)

Language B Notes:
Malay SL and Tamil SL are available only in the November session. Therefore, any candidate registered for a May session wishing to take Malay SL or Tamil SL must be additionally registered for a November session C1.6 Availability of subjects for 2022 and 2023 examination sessions Diploma Programme Assessment procedures 2021 51 (usually, but not necessarily, in the preceding year). They must take all Malay SL or Tamil SL assessment components (IA, paper 1 and paper 2) in that November session. Note: Italian B and Portuguese B were withdrawn from the November session after the November 2019 session. Note: The Chinese B – Cantonese (May session only) and Chinese B – Mandarin (both May and November sessions) examination papers will continue to be produced in both traditional and simplified characters.

Language ab initio Notes:
Indonesian is not available in the May session. Therefore, any candidate registered for a May session wishing to take Indonesian must be additionally registered for a November session (usually, but not necessarily, in the preceding year). They must take all Indonesian assessment components (IA, paper 1 and paper 2) in that November session. There is no special request service for language ab initio.

4. Associations of IB World Schools

Associations of IB World Schools (AIBWS) are groups of IB World Schools, who come together in order to provide mutual support to the community of IB World Schools. AIBWS are organized in various ways, sizes and constituencies, depending on their local circumstances and provide a forum for school collaboration, hold periodic meetings, deliver professional development and share best practice among members.

Each AIBWS is an independent entity that is not run or managed by the IB, but in order to formalize its relationship with the IB, they must meet certain criteria, by means of a recognition agreement and licence. They have their own constitution that describes their structure, membership and financial responsibilities. The IB works closely with all the recognized AIBWS.

Associations are often an indispensable resource for schools discovering the IB for the first time, offer a wealth of IB experience and support, and are often active at district, state or government level raising awareness of all IB programmes within their area of representation. They may also, working closely with their regional IB office, assist in negotiations with governments for acceptance of all IB programmes and with universities for recognition for the Diploma Programme.

Association of IB World Schools benefits

The IB raises the profile of the AIBWS by featuring them on its website, IBWS yearbook, inviting their representatives to regional meetings, as well to dedicated IB Associations' events at IB Conferences. AIBWS have access to IB materials the same way as IBWS, permitting their use of a specially created logo for use under licence on their websites and in publicity to denote their status, and have multiple communication channels with IB.

Establishing an Association of IB World Schools

Groups of schools who wish to be recognized by the IB as an AIBWS should ensure that they can meet IB criteria for recognition. Full overview of the criteria, as well as detailed guideline on how to form an AIBWS is available on the IB website.

More information is available on AIBWS website: www.ibo.org/contact-the-ib/associations-of-ib-schools

List of recognized Associations of IB World Schools

AIBWS family is growing and there are 64 recognized AIBWS globally, that cover 61 countries, 55 states and provinces on six continents.

Associations of IB World Schools in Africa

Country/region	Name	Contact	Website
Morocco	Association des Ecoles du BI du Maroc	cherrouk@madina.ma +212 6 61 30 88 96	www.aebim-ma.org

Associations of IB World Schools in Europe

Country/region	Name	Contact	Website
Andorra, Portugal and Spain (Iberian peninsula)	Asociacion Ibérica de Colegios de BI	comunicacion@asibi.org +34 645 851 604	asibi.org
Andorra, Spain	Asociación de Centros del BI de España	jvarela@colegioobradoiro.es +34 667 534 647	
Austria, Croatia, Czech Republic, Hungary, Poland, Romania, Serbia, Slovakia, Slovenia	Association of Central European IB Schools	coordinator@aces-ib.org +420 739 021 601	www.aces-ib.org
Finland	The Association of Finnish IB Schools	jyrki.rosti@lahti.fi +358 505 597 840	sites.google.com/eduespoo.fi/afib/home
Germany	Association of German International Schools	julia@agis-schools.org +49 17610224981	agis-schools.org
Greece	IB Schools in Greece Association	zgeitona@cgs.edu.gr +30 210 6663930	ibsiga.wordpress.com
Italy	AIBWS in Italy	info@aibwsi.it	www.aibwsi.it
Norway	Norwegian IB Schools	miksjo@hedmark.org +47 404 495 77	norwegianibschoolsnibs.org
Sweden	Association of Swedish IB Schools	asibboard@gmail.com +46 8 5925721	www.swedishibschools.se
The Netherlands	The Dutch International Secondary Schools	secondary@dutchinternationalschools.nl	www.dutchinternationalschools.nl
Turkey	Turkish IB Schools Association	merim@aci.k12.tr +90 532 6532 575	
United Kingdom and Ireland, Channel Islands and Isle of Man	IB Schools and Colleges Association	ibsca@oxfordcoursemanagers.org +44 1865 636 400	www.ibsca.org.uk

Associations of IB World Schools in Middle East

Country/region	Name	Contact	Website
Egypt	International Baccalaureate Schools in Egypt Association	slubani@mescairo.com +202 26170020	www.ibsea.org
Jordan	Jordan Chapter	sjouaneh@jubilee.edu.jo + 962 79 599 8044	
Kingdom of Saudi Arabia	Saudi IB Association	dpmc@jks.edu.sa; natashaawada@gmail.com; +966 557 658 510	
Lebanon	The Association of IB World Schools in Lebanon	mona.majzoub@mak-hhhs.edu.lb +961 7739 898	
Qatar	The Association of IB World Schools in Qatar	inassoura@qf.org.qa +97 433 626 610	sites.google.com/qaw.qfschools.qa/qiba/home

United Arab Emirates	UAE Association of IB Schools	klekanides@jess.sch.ae +971 04 361 9019	

Associations of IB World Schools in Canada

Province	Name	Contact	Website
Alberta	Alberta Association of IBWS	abibspresident@gmail.com 403-938-4431, ext. 271	www.abibs.ca
Bermuda, New Brunswick, Newfoundland & Labrador, Nova Scotia and Prince Edward Island	Atlantic Canadian AIBWS	acaibws@gmail.com +1 902 957 1314	sites.google.com/view/acaibws
British Columbia	British Columbia AIBWS	rohly@aspengroveschool.com +1 250 933 8029	bcaibws.ca/
Manitoba, Saskatchewan	Prairie AIBWS	jpeter@sjsd.net +1 204 888 0684	www.paibws.org
Ontario	IB Schools of Ontario	ibschoolsont@ibso.ca	www.ibschoolsofontario.ca
Quebec	Société des Écoles du Monde du BI du Québec et de la Francophonie	sec@sebiq.ca +1 450 593 33 93	www.sebiq.ca

Associations of IB World Schools in Latin America

Country	Name	Contact	Website
Argentina	Asociación de Colegios del Bachillerato Internacional del Rio de la Plata	pmanzitti@scms.edu.ar +549 114 078 4222	
Brazil	Brazil AIBWS	shirley.hazell@stfrancis.com.br +55 11 3728 8052	www.baibs.org.br
Chile	Asociación Chilena del Bachillerato Internacional	karla@achbi.cl +569 9331 5395	www.achbi.cl
Colombia	Asociación Andina de Colegios de Bachillerato Internacional	presidenciaaacbi@gmail.com +573124578603	www.aacbi.org.co
Costa Rica	Asociación de Colegios del BI de Costa Rica	info@asobitico.org +506 2220-0131 ext.157	asobitico.org
Ecuador	Asociación Ecuatoriana de Colegios con Bachillerato Internacional	coordinacion@aseccbi.edu.ec +593 987673197	www.aseccbi.edu.ec
Mexico	Asociación de colegios IB de México	enlace@ibamex.mx +52 55 43 23 10 11	www.ibamex.com
Peru	Asociación de Colegios IB Perú	ascibp@gmail.com +511 957 222 090	ascibp.pe
Uruguay	Uruguay AIBWS	aucbiuruguay@gmail.com +59 898 123 510	www.aucbi.edu.uy
Venezuela	Asociación de Colegios Del Mundo BI de Venezuela	juan@juanxxiii.e12.ve +58 4124 883 254	

Associations of IB World Schools in the United States of America

State(s)	Name	Contact	Website
Alaska, Idaho, Montana, Oregon, Washington	Northwest AIBWS	gathomas1@seattleschools.org	www.northwestibassociation.com
Arizona	Arizona AIBWS	jadavis@mpsaz.org +1 480 472 4419	www.azibs.org
Arkansas, Iowa, Kansas, Missouri, Nebraska, Oklahoma	Midwest IB Schools	christy.dabalos@lsr7.net 1 816-986-4061	sites.google.com/view/midwestibschools/home
California	California AIBWS	cawsedir@gmail.com +1 909 896 9557	cawsib.org
Colorado, Wyoming	Rocky Mountain AIBWS	director@ibarms.org +1 720 878 7430	www.ibarms.org/ib
Connecticut, Maine, Massachusetts, New Hampshire, New Jersey, New York, Pennsylvania (east), Rhode Island, Vermont	Guild of IB Schools of the Northeast	gibsnortheast@gmail.com +1 212-724-6360 x318	gibs.wildapricot.org
Delaware, DC, Maryland, Pennsylvania, Virginia	Mid-Atlantic AIBWS	johnLday@mac.com +1 608 238 1284	www.ibmidatlantic.org
Florida	Florida League of IB Schools	info@flibs.org +1 850 597 0671	flibs.org
Georgia	AIBWS of Georgia		www.ibgeorgia.com
Illinois	Illinois Association of IB Schools	ilibschools@gmail.com +1 312 945 8240	ilibschools.org
Indiana	Hoosier AIBWS		hoosieribschools.weebly.com
Louisiana	Louisiana IB Schools		sites.google.com/a/selu.edu/libs
Michigan	IB Schools of Michigan	ibsom@icloud.com	www.ibsom.org
Minnesota	Minnesota AIBWS	director@mnibschools.org +1 612 483 3749	www.mnibschools.org
Nevada	Nevada Association of IBWS	feinsbc@nv.ccsd.net +1 702 799 2580	www.naibws.org
North Carolina	IB Schools of North Carolina	ibschoolsofnc@gmail.com +1 980 239 7547	ibsnc.org
Ohio	Ohio AIBWS	OhioIBWorldSchools@gmail.com + 1 937 475 5177	www.ohioib.org/index.html
South Carolina	South Carolina IB Schools	SCIBS.President@gmail.com	www.facebook.com/SouthCarolinaIB
Tennessee	Tennessee IB Association of World Schools	Emily.munn.seibert@gmail.com 615-333-5175 ext. 858009	sites.google.com/site/tennesseeibschools
Texas	Texas IB Schools	karen@texasibschools.org 972-834-8934	www.texasibschools.org
Utah	AIBWS of Utah	kelly.boren@slcschools.org 801-578-8500	www.ibschoolsofutah.org

| Wisconsin | Wisconsin AIBWS | gatewodr@milwaukee.k12.wi.us
+1 414 688 5889 | ibwisconsin.org |

Associations of IB World Schools in Asia – Pacific region

Country	Name	Contact	Website
Australia, Fiji, New Zealand and Papua New Guinea and the South-West Pacific	IB Schools Australasia	office@ibaustralasia.org +61404440298	ibaustralasia.org
Commonwealth of Independent States (CIS): Armenia, Azarbaijan, Belarus, Kazakhstan, Kyrgystan, Moldova, Russian Federation, Tajikistan, Uzbekisatan	The IB Schools Association of Commonwealth of Independent States (CIS)	natalyab@mes.ru +7 499 255 0070	ibsa.su
India	The Association of International Schools of India	info@taisi-india.org +91 997118852	www.taisi-india.org
Japan	IB Association of Japan		ibaj.or.jp
Mainland China, Hong Kong, Macau, Taiwan	Chong Wa International Baccalaureate Schools Association	CISA-2020@163.com +86 1371 152 0841	
Pakistan	Association of IB World Schools in Pakistan	info@ibpak.pk +92 21 3583 5805-6	ibpak.pk

Cooperation with other groups of schools

In addition to the work with the AIBWS and in order to support IB World Schools, the IB communicates and collaborates with other groups of schools and international school associations on an informal basis.

5. University Recognition

IB Diploma Programme

The IB Diploma Programme is an excellent passport to higher education. Universities around the world welcome the unique characteristics of IB Diploma Programme students and recognize the way in which the programme helps to prepare students for higher education.

Each year the IB is asked by students and their schools to send transcripts to over 4,500 different universities and colleges, in over 100 different countries. The most popular destinations include the United States (40%), United Kingdom (17%), Australia (10%), Canada (10%) and Netherlands (4%).

IB students routinely gain admission to some of the best universities and colleges in the world. Every year the IB sends significant numbers of transcripts to the university members of:

- the Ivy League in the United States
- the Russell Group in the United Kingdom
- the U15 group in Canada
- the Group of Eight in Australia
- the RU11 group in Japan
- the U15 group in Germany

As well as other academically elite universities across the globe.

The IB has established strong relationships with universities who have granted recognition of the IB Diploma programme in a number of different ways. It is recommended that schools, students and parents visit the individual university websites in order to gain the most up to date information regarding recognition.

Admission

The IBDP is widely accepted as a valid qualification for entry into higher education, without the need for other tests or qualifications. Note that this does not guarantee admission to a particular university, rather provides the opportunity to compete for a place at the institution.

Students wishing to be admitted for certain degree programmes may be required to study certain subjects, which may be specified at either standard or higher level. Students may also be required to achieve a particular number of points for the Diploma and may be required to gain a certain number of points in individual subjects.

The IBDP also acts of proof of English Language proficiency for admission into university in a number of countries.

A number of universities also accept students who are not completing the full IBDP, but are instead studying for one or more IB DP Courses.

Credit and Advanced Placement

Many universities, particularly in the United States, will offer students Credit and/or Advanced Placement on their chosen university degree programme. This may reduce the overall tuition cost, or the time required to complete their degree.

Scholarship

A number of universities have established scholarships specifically for IB graduates. The value and nature of these awards will vary from university to university and are aimed to support the student during their time in higher education.

IB Career-Related Programme

Since its launch in 2014, the IBCP has grown its reputation with universities as a valid route for students to progress to higher education, as well as the world of employment.

CP students have requested that their transcripts be sent to universities and colleges in 35 countries, across North America, Africa, Europe, the Middle East, Asia and Australasia. They have requested that their transcripts be sent to over 1,000 universities around the world, including more than 750 institutions in the United States and more than 130 in the United Kingdom.

The IB continues to work with universities to improve the knowledge and understanding of the CP, as well as its recognition.

For more information regarding recognition or both the DP and CP, please see the University Admissions section of the IB website www.ibo.org/university-admission/

Index

An index of all IB World Schools listed alphabetically.